INTERNATIONAL
Vital Records
Handbook

INTERNATIONAL
Vital Records Handbook

Thomas Jay Kemp

6th Edition

Published by Genealogical Publishing Co., Inc.
3600 Clipper Mill Road, Suite 260
Baltimore, Maryland 21211-1953

Library of Congress Catalogue Card Number 2013949105
International Standard Book Number 978-0-8063-1981-0
Made in the United States of America

Dedication

To my wife, Vi, and children, Andrew and Sarah

A family without a genealogy
is like a country without a history

A traditional Chinese saying

CONTENTS

About the Author

Thomas Jay Kemp, a well-known genealogist and librarian, has spent more than four decades in the field. He is the author of over 35 genealogy books and hundreds of articles about genealogy and family history. He is currently the Director of Genealogy Products at GenealogyBank.

Kemp has served on many national and regional library and genealogy boards, including the Board of Directors of the Federation of Genealogical Societies and the American Library Association's (ALA) Local History Committee, and has served as Chair of the Council of National Library and Information Associations (CNLIA); President of the American Society of Indexers (ASI); Chair of the ALA History Section; Chair of the ALA Genealogy Committee; Chair of the ALA Genealogy and Local History Discussion Group; and VP of the Association of Professional Genealogists. He also previously served as Library Director of the Historical Society of Pennsylvania and the New England Historic Genealogical Society.

He is a life member of the Association for the Bibliography of History, the New England Archivists, the New Hampshire Library Association, and the New York Genealogical & Biographical Society.

INTRODUCTION

At one time or another all of us need copies of birth, marriage, death, divorce, or pre-adoption certificates for driver's licenses, passports, jobs, social security, family history research, or for simple proof of identity. But the fact is that the requirements and fees needed to obtain copies of vital records vary from state to state and from country to country, often requiring tedious research and wading through confusing websites of large agencies before the appropriate forms can be obtained and the correct procedures followed. The *International Vital Records Handbook* is designed to put an end to all that, as it offers complete, up-to-date information on where and how to request vital records. It also includes copies of the application forms, where available, thus simplifying and speeding up the process by which vital records are obtained, regardless of the number or type of application forms required.

This new 6th edition of the *International Vital Records Handbook* contains the latest forms and information for each of the fifty states and also furnishes details about records that were created prior to statewide vital records registration, as well as vital records collections, online databases, and institutions of interest to genealogy researchers. Then, in alphabetical sequence, it covers the other countries of the world, giving instructions and—in cases where neither a centralized vital records registration system nor a vital records application form is available—providing key addresses of repositories or embassies that might help you obtain copies of vital records.

How to Order Records

The *International Vital Records Handbook* provides the application forms issued by every state vital records office. Simply photocopy—or scan and print—the form you need, follow the instructions, and send the fee and the completed form, with the identity documentation specified, to the appropriate record office. This book also includes addresses and forms, where available, to help you locate vital records all around the world. (The phone numbers listed in the International section include the codes needed to dial the country in question from the U.S.)

Vital records can also be ordered in person at the state vital records offices (except in California, where requests must be made by mail) and online, usually for an extra fee through the online service www.vitalchek.com, though a few states and countries provide their own online ordering service at no additional cost. Some vital records offices accept fax and/or phone orders as well.

Note: The URLs, fees, and contact information listed in this book were accurate at the time of publication, but they are subject to change so you should check the website of the state vital records office for the most up-to-date information on ordering methods and fees.

The fee for certificates listed in this book include the cost of one certified copy or certificate of failure to find, and cover one search period—generally a 5-year span. There are often additional postage charges, and expedited service is generally available from the record offices for an additional fee.

Restrictions on Records

A word of caution: For privacy reasons vital records are restricted in most states, usually for a period of 50 to 100 years, depending on the type of record. To obtain a copy of a restricted record, you must be the person named on the record (if you are over 18) or immediate family member, or demonstrate a legal right to the record. Immediate family is usually defined as spouse, parent or legal guardian, child, or sibling and sometimes grandparent or grandchild. This list varies by state; in Indiana, for example, aunts and uncles are eligible to obtain restricted vital records, and in California a domestic partner is eligible. Genealogists representing immediate family members may also be eligible. Check with the state in question to find out if its records are restricted and who is allowed to access them.

Proof of Identity

In an attempt to stop the illegal use of vital records and reduce identity theft, states have set tougher requirements for obtaining certified copies of vital records. Requestors must now attach a copy of a government-issued photo ID (driver's license, state ID, passport, or military ID) and verification of relationship to the person named on the record. Some states require that your application be completed by a notary public. If you do not have a government-issued photo ID, many states will accept two of the following instead: social security number, bank statement with current address, car registration or title with current address, utility bill with current address, pay stub with your name and social security number, voter registration card, income tax return, etc.

Genealogy Research

If you are doing genealogy research and are not eligible to access a restricted record, you may be able to obtain an "informational copy" of the record, which will contain all of the information found on the certified copy but will have a statement stamped on it saying that the document is for informational purposes only and cannot be used to establish identity. When a state does provide an informational copy for genealogy research, it is noted in this book. A number of searchable, free databases containing historical vital records are now available online, and many of these too have been noted in this book, as have specific repositories containing vital records collections that are accessible by genealogists.

The Family History Library of The Church of Jesus Christ of Latter-day Saints (LDS) has microfilmed millions of vital records from church registers and government record offices all over the United States and the world. This ongoing and extraordinary program has made the Family History Library the world's largest repository of vital records. To find out which vital records are available, contact the Family History Library, 35 North West Temple Street, Salt Lake City, UT 84150, (866) 234-2067 for research help; visit one of the LDS branch FamilySearch Centers; or visit https://familysearch.org.

Some Caveats

Because of the large volume of requests processed at the state level, it can sometimes take weeks or months to get your certificates. You can often obtain your certificate(s) more quickly from the recorder's office, clerk's office, or health department in the county or town where the event took place. If you are using a state application form but are submitting your request to a county office for processing, you should check first with the county office to confirm its fees, as they may be different from the state fees. The websites of many state vital records offices include a link to a directory of county offices that issue vital records.

In obtaining copies of vital records, you should also keep in mind that copies of the original certificate might be on file in several different jurisdictions, depending on the state or country. For example, if a vital record is not available from the state or national office of vital records, you should check with the appropriate provincial or city office to see if they have a copy.

Locating vital records in countries other than the United States can be a difficult, or even impossible, task, since many countries do not have an established central civil registration authority or a history of compulsory registration. Some have had long periods of civil war or natural disasters resulting in the destruction of records storage facilities. Records in some countries were destroyed during World War II, and for political reasons you will sometimes not be able to obtain a record. Parish priests, local civil offices and authorities, and the country's embassy in the United States might all be able to help in your search.

ACKNOWLEDGMENTS

I am grateful for the guidance and assistance of registrars, archivists, keepers of public records, librarians, and scholars from around the world who have helped me compile the *International Vital Records Handbook*. We owe the modern-day custodians of the world's vital records our gratitude for preserving the records of the past four centuries and providing the records and documentation of the individual lives of the majority of the 7 billion people alive on the earth today. I would especially like to thank Marian Hoffman of Genealogical Publishing for her dedicated work in reviewing and revising this manuscript. Her skill was essential in making this edition even stronger for researchers around the world. I am grateful for her attention to detail and work ethic. I would also like to thank:

Bettina Kann, Österreichische Nationalbibliothek; Mrs. Suzanne M. Ducille, Deputy Registrar General, Bahamas; M. Thompson, Registration Office, Barbados; Miss. L.A. Danies, Assistant Registrar and Raymond A. Usher, Deputy Registrar, Registrar General's Office, Belize; Anita Lisbey, Belize Archives Department; M. Nestor Houeto, Director General, Institut National de la Statistique et de l'Analyse Economique, Contonou, Benin; Esterley M. Patterson, Administrative Assistant to the Registry General, Bermuda; S.G. Otladisa, Registrar, Civil Registration and Vital Events, Botswana; Codru Rasvan Vrabie, Blagoevgrad, Bulgaria; Berta Belmar Ruiz, Director General, Servicio de Registro Civil e Identificacion, Chile; Roné Béyom Ncakoutou, Director of Statistics, Economic & Demographic Studies, Chad; Mrs. M.Y. Li, Office of the Director of Immigration, Hong Kong; Leonardo Luis de Matos, Director, Direcão de Servicços de Justiça, China/Macau; Lic. María Isabel Acebedo Isasi, Directora de Registros y Notaria, Ministerio de Justicia, Cuba; Jindriska Pospisilova and Zdenek Matusik, Czech National Library; Henrik Stissing Jensen, Statens Arkiver Rigsarkivet, Denmark; Hanne Willumsen, Indenrigs Ministeriet, Denmark; Jan Tuxen, Kerteminde, Denmark; Ruth Hedegaard, Vendsyssel Historiske Museum, Aalborg, Denmark; Margit Tammur, National Library of Estonia; Eeva K. Murtomaa, Helsinki, Finland; Anna Mantakou, Hellenic Institute of International & Foreign Law, Athens, Greece; Carolyn R. Garrido, Registrar, Guam.

Dr. Márta Dóczi, Budapest, Hungary; R.G. Mitra, Deputy Registrar General of India; Anup K. Pujari, Office of the Minister for Law and Justice, India; G.B. Hanumantharayappa, Deputy Registrar, High Court of Karnataka, India; Mr. M. Halder, Special Officer, Office of the Registrar General West Bengal, India; G. Prakasam, Joint Chief Registrar of Births & Deaths, Bangalore, Karnataka, India. Raj Gautam Mitra, Deputy Registrar General, India, New Delhi, India; Andrea Capaccioni, Biblioteca dell'Universitá per Stranieri, Perugia, Italy; Shotaro Hamura, Okayama University of Science, Okayama, Japan; Yoshiaki Omura, Japan; Judy Rao, University of the West Indies, Jamaica; J.G. Kinyua, Department of the Registrar General, Kenya; Mr. Uriam Reiti, Registrar General of Kiribati; Jichang Ryo, Seoul, Korea; Dr. Abdus Sattar, Secretariat of Planning, Libya; A Šolitūnas, Director, Lietuvos Archyv Departamentas, Lithuania; T. Gustiene, Director of Information Centre, Lithuanian National Library; Flossie Matenje, Malawi Library Association; Mrs. Yatimah Rimun, Malaysia National Archives.

Lic. Susana E. Natali Abella, Coordinadora de Estudios Poblacionales, Dirección General del Registro Nacional de Población e Identificación Personal, Mexico City, Mexico; Snyder H. Simon, Clerk of Courts, Pohnpei Supreme Court, Federated States of Micronesia; Prof. Paul Vlaardingerbroek, Tilburg University, Tilburg, Netherlands; Thomas van Ek, Wageningen, Netherlands; E.J. Rowland, Deputy Registrar General, New Zealand; J.G. Moore, Commonwealth Recorder, Commonwealth of the Northern Mariana Islands; Orana S. Castro, Vital Statistics Division, Northern Mariana Islands; Gunnar Thorvaldsen, Registreringssentral for Historiske Data, Tromsø, Norway; Torbjørn Låg, Riksarkivet, Oslo, Norway; Felix Murillo Alfaro, Jefe Instituto Nacional De Estadística e Informatica (INEI); Carlito B. Lalicon, Chief, Civil Registry Division, National Statistics Office, Philippines.

Munvazese Paustin, Minister de l'intérieur et du Developpement Communal, Kigali, Rwanda; Georgina Strickland, Deputy Registrar General of Births, Deaths & Marriages, Apia, Western Samoa; Alymana, Panos Institut, Dakar, Senegal; V. Labiche, Director General, Ministry of Administration and Manpower, Victoria, Seychelles; Joeanne Lee, NHB, Singapore; Chua Ser Ching, Assistant Registrar, Supreme Court, Singapore; Mrs. Tan Yeow Liang, Office of Registrar of Marriages, Singapore; Lee Fook Wah, Registrar of Births & Deaths, Singapore; PhDr. Peter Kartous, CSc., DirectorMinisterstvo Vnútra Slovenskej Republiky, Bratislava, Slovenia; L. Coetzee, Head National Archives Repository, Pretoria, South Africa; Elisabeth Thorsell, Järfälla, Sweden; D.M. Mwita, Registrar General, Tanzania; Mrs. Fatai L. Vaihu and Frederick E. L. Tuita, Office of the Registrar, Supreme Court, Tonga; K.S. Harripersad, Registrar General, Trinidad and Tobago; Barney Tyrwhitt-Drake, United Kingdom; Dale Westerterp, Petaluma, CA; Richard C. Fipphen, Stamford, CT; S. Mususa, Acting Registrar, Department of National Registration, Passport and Citizenship, Zambia.

The U.S. Department of State's website at http://travel.state.gov/ provided a great deal of information on the availability of country documents.

1. United States

UNITED STATES—Citizens Abroad

Send your requests to:

U.S. Department of State
Passport Services
Vital Records Section
1111 19th Street, NW, Suite 510
Washington, DC 20036

Tel. (202) 955-0521

Cost for all Consular Reports	$50.00

The Passport Services Vital Records Section of the Department of State (DOS) provides documentation of births, deaths, and marriages of U.S. citizens abroad. A Consular Report of a Birth Abroad, also known as Form FS-240, is primary proof of American citizenship for a child born abroad to a U.S. citizen; copies can be obtained from the above address. The DOS no longer issues Form DS-1350 (Certificate of Report of Birth). However, all DS-1350s that DOS previously issued are still valid as proof of identity and citizenship, and for other legal purposes. The Consular Report of the Death of an American Citizen Abroad (Form OF-180) is required in U.S. legal proceedings instead of the foreign death certificate. You may request up to 20 certified copies of this document at no additional charge.

To obtain a copy of a Certificate of Witness to Marriage (FS-87), write to the address above. Since November 9, 1989, a Consular Officer has no longer served as a witness to marriages performed abroad. Persons married abroad after 1989 should contact the embassy or consulate of the country where the marriage was performed for a certified copy. Foreign marriage documents are not maintained by the U.S. Department of State.

Reports of Death filed before 1975 are maintained by the National Archives and Records Service, Diplomatic Records Branch, Washington, DC 20408. Requests for such records should be sent directly to that office.

Reports of Deaths of persons serving in the Armed Forces of the United States (Army, Navy, Marines, Air Force, or Coast Guard) or civilian employees of the Department of Defense are not maintained by the U.S. Department of State. In these cases requests for copies of records should be sent to the National Personnel Records Center (Military Personnel Records), 9700 Page Avenue, St. Louis, MO 63132-5100.

When a birth or death occurs on the high seas, whether in an aircraft or on a vessel, the record is usually filed at the next port of call. If the vessel or aircraft docked or landed at a foreign port, requests for copies of the record may be made to the U.S. Department of State. If the first port of entry was in the U.S., write to the registration authority in the city where the vessel or aircraft docked or landed in the U.S. If the vessel was of U.S. registry, contact the local authorities at the port of entry and/or search the vessel logs at the U.S. Coast Guard Facility at the vessel's final port of call for that voyage.

CONSULAR VITAL RECORD SEARCH REQUEST FORM

Date: ____________________

Purpose of Request: ____________________

Name at (circle one) Birth/Death/Marriage ____________________

Name after adoption (IF APPLICABLE) ____________________

Date of (CIRCLE ONE) Birth/Death/Marriage ____________________

Country of (CIRCLE ONE) Birth/Death/Marriage ____________________

Father's Name: ____________________

Father's Date and Place (STATE/COUNTRY) of Birth: ____________________

Mother's Name: ____________________

Mother's Date and Place (STATE/COUNTRY) of Birth: ____________________

If you have a Report of Birth/Death or a Certificate of Witness to Marriage, please enclose a copy to aid in our file search.

Passport - First Entry into the United States ____________________

Name of Bearer: ____________________

Date of Issuance ____________________

Passport Number: ____________________

Date of Inclusion (if passport was not issued to the subject): ____________________

Current Passport Information ____________________

Name of Bearer ____________________

Date of Issuance: ____________________

Passport Number: ____________________

Signature: ____________________

(Signed by [please circle one] Subject, Parent, or Guardian)

Address: ____________________

Telephone (Daytime) ____________________

Send your requests to:

Alabama Department of Public Health
Center for Health Statistics
Alabama Vital Records
(Location: 201 Monroe Street, Suite 1150)
P.O. Box 5625
Montgomery, AL 36103-5625

Tel. (334) 206-5418
Fax (334) 206-2659
www.adph.org/vitalrecords/

Birth and death records are on file at the Office of Vital Records from January 1, 1908. Births are filed under the father's name by the date of the event and the place where it occurred. Birth records are confidential with restricted access for 125 years; death records are restricted for 25 years. Marriage records are on file from August 1, 1936, and divorce records from January 1, 1950. Marriage and divorce certificates are not confidential and may be obtained by anyone. An automated vital records system called ViSION allows vital records to be issued through all 67 county health departments.

The Center for Health Statistics sells microfilm copies of the following vital records indexes: Marriages (1936-1969), Divorces (1950–1959), and Deaths (1908–1959).

Cost for a certified Birth Certificate	$15.00
Cost for a certified Marriage or Divorce Certificate	$15.00
Cost for a certified Death Certificate	$15.00
Cost for a duplicate copy, when ordered at the same time	$6.00
Cost for a Keepsake Birth Certificate	$45.00

For Marriage Records before August 1936, contact:

Probate Judge
County Court House
(County Seat), Alabama

For Divorce Records before 1950, contact:

Circuit Court
(County Seat), Alabama

For Genealogy Research:

The Birmingham Public Library's Southern History Department (2100 Park Place, Birmingham, AL 35203; www.bplonline.org/resources/genealogy/) has a large collection of genealogy resources.

The Alabama Department of Archives and History (624 Washington Avenue, Montgomery, AL 36130-0100; tel. 334-242-4435; www.archives.state.al.us/) has copies of early county vital records as well as indexes to the birth, death, marriage, and divorce records held at the Center for Health Statistics/Vital Records Office.

For Adoption Record information, contact:

Alabama Vital Records—Adoption Section
P.O. Box 5625
Montgomery, AL 36103-5625

Tel. (334) 206-5426

In 2000 the Alabama legislature amended the vital records law to allow an adult adoptee or other person whose original birth certificate was placed in a "sealed file" to obtain a non-certified copy of that record and any other documents in the "sealed file." The fee for a non-certified copy of a birth certificate from a sealed file is $25.00.

USE ONLY FOR A VITAL EVENT WHICH OCCURRED IN ALABAMA

The fee for a birth, death, marriage or divorce record search is $15.00, which includes the cost of one certified copy OR Certificate of Failure to Find. For additional copies of the same record ordered at the same time, the fee is $6.00 each. For information on how to expedite a document, call 334-206-5418. Amendments, adoptions, legitimations, and delayed certificates must be processed through the Center for Health Statistics. The fee is $20.00 to amend a record or file a delayed certificate which also covers the cost of one certified copy of the record. The fee is $25.00 to prepare a new certificate of birth after adoption or legitimation which also covers the cost of one certified copy of the record. Make check or money order payable to the "State Board of Health." **Fees are non-refundable.** Do not request two different types of certificates on the same form. **PRINT ALL INFORMATION LEGIBLY**. You must **complete & sign the applicant section** or your request cannot be processed.

TAKE THIS FORM TO YOUR LOCAL ALABAMA COUNTY HEALTH DEPARTMENT OR **MAIL THIS FORM TO:**
Alabama Department of Public Health, Center for Health Statistics, P.O. Box 5625, Montgomery, Alabama 36103-5625
For information on ordering a vital record via the Internet, visit our web site at: http: //www.adph.org

APPLICANT SECTION (THIS SECTION MUST BE COMPLETED) Birth certificates less than 125 years old and death certificates less than 25 years old are restricted records. You must be an immediate family member OR demonstrate a legal right to the record in order to obtain a copy of the record (§ 22-9A-21). Anyone falsely applying for a record is subject to a penalty upon conviction of up to three months in the county jail or a fine of up to $500. Code of Ala. 1975, § 13A-10-109. By signing, you are certifying you have a legal right to the record requested.

Your Signature__________ Date__________

Print Your Name __________ Address __________

City __________ State_____ Zip______ Daytime Phone (_____)__________

Your Relationship to Person Whose Record is Being Requested __________

Reason for Request (if not immediate family)__________

I allow the following individual to pick up the certificate(s)__________

BIRTH:

NUMBER OF COPIES ________ AMOUNT PAID $________

FULL NAME AS ON BIRTH CERTIFICATE__________
FIRST MIDDLE LAST

DATE OF BIRTH __________ SEX__________

COUNTY OF BIRTH __________ HOSPITAL__________

FULL MAIDEN NAME OF MOTHER__________
FIRST MIDDLE LAST

FULL NAME OF FATHER__________
FIRST MIDDLE LAST

DEATH:

NUMBER OF COPIES ________ AMOUNT PAID $________

LEGAL NAME OF DECEASED__________
FIRST MIDDLE LAST

DATE OF DEATH __________ COUNTY OF DEATH __________ SEX__________

SSN __________ DATE OF BIRTH OR AGE __________ RACE__________

NAME OF SPOUSE__________
FIRST MIDDLE LAST

NAME OF PARENTS__________

STARTING WITH 1991 DEATHS, CERTIFICATES MAY BE ISSUED WITHOUT A CAUSE OF DEATH. Indicate the number of copies of each type of certificate you want:______WITH CAUSE OF DEATH ______WITHOUT CAUSE OF DEATH

☐ MARRIAGE OR ☐ DIVORCE:

NUMBER OF COPIES ________ AMOUNT PAID $________

FULL NAME OF HUSBAND__________
FIRST MIDDLE LAST

FULL MAIDEN NAME OF WIFE__________
FIRST MIDDLE LAST

DATE OF MARRIAGE__________ (OR) DATE OF DIVORCE__________

IF MARRIAGE, COUNTY WHERE LICENSE WAS ISSUED__________

IF DIVORCE, COUNTY OF DIVORCE__________

COUNTY REGISTRAR USE: This application has been reviewed for the individual's right to receive the requested document(s).

__________ __________ __________
County Registrar's Signature Date County Health Department Receipt Number

Informational materials in alternative formats will be made available upon request. **ADPH-HS14/Rev. 10-01-2009**

ALABAMA
REQUEST FOR KEEPSAKE BIRTH CERTIFICATE

The Center for Health Statistics may issue a Keepsake Birth Certificate for anyone born in Alabama for whom there is a record on file in our office. Even though the Center began collecting birth certificates in 1908, most Keepsake Birth Certificates are requested for younger children, especially since **the Keepsake Birth Certificate is not a record that can be used for legal purposes**.

By Alabama law, birth certificates are confidential records with restricted access for 125 years from the date of birth. They may be obtained by the following persons, upon payment of the proper fee:

Person Named on the Certificate, Mother/Father of Person Named on Certificate
Husband/Wife of Person Named on Certificate, Son/Daughter of Person Named on Certificate
Sister/Brother of Person Named on Certificate

If you are not one of the authorized individuals above, such as a grandparent, one of the above individuals MUST give you written and signed permission to obtain a Keepsake Birth Certificate. The permission MUST accompany this request form and the required fee.

The fee to search for and provide one copy of a Keepsake Birth Certificate is **$45.00**. Make check or money order payable to "State Board of Health." **FEES ARE NON-REFUNDABLE.** If the record is not located, you will receive a Certificate of Failure to Find but will still be responsible for the $15.00 fee to search for the record. Each Keepsake Birth Certificate requested is $45.00 even if it is for the same child.

YOU MUST PROVIDE ALL INFORMATION BELOW AND SIGN THE APPLICANT SECTION OR YOUR REQUEST CANNOT BE PROCESSED. **DO NOT USE THIS FORM to order legal certified copies of birth certificates.**

For additional information/questions call 334.206.5418 or visit our website at: www.adph.org/vitalrecords

MAIL COMPLETED FORM AND FEE TO:
ALABAMA CENTER FOR HEALTH STATISTICS
P.O. BOX 5625
MONTGOMERY, ALABAMA 36103-5625

BIRTH:

Number of Copies Requested ________ Amount Enclosed **$**__________

Please indicate the design you would like: _____Kites _____ Bunnies _____Nature

FULL NAME AS ON BIRTH CERTIFICATE ______________________________
FIRST MIDDLE LAST

DATE OF BIRTH ______________________________ SEX__________

COUNTY OF BIRTH ______________________________ HOSPITAL__________

FULL MAIDEN NAME OF MOTHER ______________________________
FIRST MIDDLE LAST

FULL NAME OF FATHER ______________________________
FIRST MIDDLE LAST

APPLICANT SECTION (THIS SECTION MUST BE COMPLETED)

Anyone falsely applying for a record that is restricted by law is subject to a penalty upon conviction of up to three months in the county jail or a fine of up to $500. Code of Ala. 1975, § 13A-10-109. By signing, you are certifying you have a legal right to the record requested.

YOUR SIGNATURE ______________________________ **DATE** __________

PRINT YOUR NAME ______________________________ **DAY TIME PHONE (________)** __________

ADDRESS______________________________

CITY__________________ **STATE**__________________ **ZIP**__________

Your Relationship to Person Whose Record is Being Requested ______________________________

I allow the following individual to order the Keepsake Birth certificate(s): ______________________________

ADPH-HS-14H/12-15-2009

Order Form for Old Vital Record Indexes Available on Microfilm
Alabama Center for Health Statistics

You may order old **death, marriage, and divorce** indexes available on rolls of **16mm microfilm** from the Center for Health Statistics. This film contains copies of old paper indexes as they were originally created to use to search for or locate vital records in the Center for Health Statistics. Rolls available are listed below.

Cost: The cost for each roll is $50. The cost for all 18 rolls is $900.
To Order: Please enter the number of rolls you wish to purchase. If you want copies of all rolls, please mark that box.
Questions: If you have any questions, please call **334.206.5426.**

- **Death Indexes -** Indexes contain Name of Deceased, Code for County of Death, Date of Death, and State Certificate Number (Volume and Page) **1908-1922 Sorted Alphabetically; 1923-1959 Sorted by Soundex Code**

_____ ROLL 1 1908-1916 (all); 1917-1919 (A-K)
_____ ROLL 2 1917-1919 (L - Z); 1920-1922 (all); 1923-1924 (all); 1925-1927 (all); 1928-1932 (A - G)
_____ ROLL 3 1928-1932 (H - Z); 1933 (all); 1934-1936 (all); 1937-1939 (all)
_____ ROLL 4 1940 (all); 1941 (all); 1942 (all); 1943 (all); 1944 (all); 1945 (all); 1946 (all)
_____ ROLL 5 1947 (all); 1948 (all); 1949-1951 (all); 1952-1959 (A - G)
_____ ROLL 6 1952-1959 (H - Z)

- **Marriage Indexes -** Indexes contain Name of Bride or Groom, Code for County Where Marriage License Was Issued, Date of Marriage, and State Certificate Number (Volume and Page) **All Sorted by Soundex Code**

_____ ROLL 1 1936-1939 (all)
_____ ROLL 2 1940 (all); 1941 (all); 1942 (A - K)
_____ ROLL 3 1942 (L - Z); 1943 (all); 1944 (all)
_____ ROLL 4 1945 (all); 1946 (all)
_____ ROLL 5 1947 (all); 1948 (all); 1949 (all); 1950-1953 (A - D)
_____ ROLL 6 1950-1953 (E - Z); 1954-1959 (A - F)
_____ ROLL 7 1954-1959 (G - Z)
_____ ROLL 8 1960-1969 (A - D)
_____ ROLL 9 1960-1969 (E - L Soundex Code 521)
_____ ROLL 10 1960-1969 (L Soundex Code 522 - S Soundex Code 510)
_____ ROLL 11 1960-1969 (S Soundex Code 512 - Z)

- **Divorce Indexes -** Indexes contain Name of Husband, First Name of Wife, Code for County of Divorce, Date of Divorce, and State Certificate Number (Volume and Page) **Sorted by Soundex Code**

_____ ROLL 1 1950-1959 (all)

- **All Rolls -** All 18 rolls include: Death Indexes, Rolls 1-6; Marriage Indexes, Rolls 1-11; Divorce Indexes Roll 1

_____ ALL 18 ROLLS COST $900.

Complete the mailing information below and include a check or money order for the correct amount. Make check or money order payable to "State Board of Health." Please do not send cash.
Mail To: Center for Health Statistics, P. O. Box 5625, Montgomery, AL 36103-5625

Name_____________________ Amount Enclosed_____________

Street Address_____________________ Daytime Telephone_____________

City_____________ State_____________ Zip Code_____________

ADPH-HS-71/July 2012

REQUEST FOR PRE-ADOPTION OR OTHER BIRTH CERTIFICATE FROM AN ALABAMA SEALED FILE

WHO MAY REQUEST A COPY:
- The person named on the birth certificate -- no other family member.
- Person must be 19 years of age or older.
- Person must have been born in Alabama.
- Person must have had an original birth certificate removed from the files due to an adoption, legitimation or paternity determination.

WHAT THE APPLICANT WILL RECEIVE:
- The applicant will receive a copy of the original birth certificate clearly marked that it is not a certified copy and it may not be used for legal purposes. Note that the information on the birth certificate in the file is shown as it was provided by the birth parent (s) at the time of birth. The information may or may not be accurate.
- The applicant will receive copies of all other documents in the "sealed file" which often include the legal documents from the court where the adoption or paternity determination took place or other legal documents for a legitimation. These files do not contain medical or other information about the birth parents.
- In the case of persons who were adopted, the revision of the law in 2000 allows birth parents to submit a Contact Preference Form which will be placed in the sealed file upon receipt. If a Contact Preference Form is in the file at the time the original birth record is requested, it will be sent to the applicant.

HOW TO ORDER:
- The fee to search for and provide one non-certified copy of a birth certificate from a sealed file is $25.00. This fee includes copies of the legal documents in the sealed file with the original birth certificate. **Fees are non-refundable.** Make check or money order payable to "Alabama Vital Records."
- Provide as much of the following information as possible for us to locate your current birth certificate, which is necessary to locate the sealed file. You must complete & sign the Applicant Section or your request cannot be processed. For additional information or questions call **334.206.5426.**

MAIL THIS FORM TO:
CENTER FOR HEALTH STATISTICS
P.O. BOX 5625
MONTGOMERY, ALABAMA 36103-5625

BIRTH:

FULL NAME AS IT CURRENTLY APPEARS ON BIRTH CERTIFICATE ______________________
FIRST MIDDLE LAST

DATE OF BIRTH ______________________ SEX ______________________

COUNTY OF BIRTH ______________________ HOSPITAL ______________________

FULL MAIDEN NAME OF MOTHER AS IT CURRENTLY APPEARS ON BIRTH CERTIFICATE ______________________
FIRST MIDDLE LAST

FULL NAME OF FATHER AS IT CURRENTLY APPEARS ON BIRTH CERTIFICATE ______________________
FIRST MIDDLE LAST

APPLICANT SECTION (THIS SECTION MUST BE COMPLETED) **Amount Enclosed $ ____________**

Anyone falsely applying for a record is subject to a penalty upon conviction of up to three months in the county jail or a fine of up to $500. Code of Ala. 1975, § 13A-10-109. By signing, you are certifying you have a legal right to the record requested.

YOUR SIGNATURE ______________________ DATE ______________________

PRINT YOUR NAME ______________________ DAY TIME PHONE (__________) ______________________

ADDRESS ______________________

CITY ______________________ STATE ______________________ ZIP ______________________

ADPH-HS 95/REV. 10/2009

ALASKA

Send your requests to:

Bureau of Vital Statistics
Alaska Department of Health & Social Services
(Location: 5441 Commercial Boulevard)
P.O. Box 110675
Juneau, AK 99801-0675

Tel. (907) 465-3391
Fax (907) 465-3618
E-mail: BVSOFFICE@health.state.ak.us
http://dhss.alaska.gov/dph/VitalStats/Pages/default.aspx

The Bureau of Vital Statistics also has offices in Anchorage and Fairbanks; check the website for contact information for those locations. There are birth, marriage, and death records available from January 1, 1913, and divorce records from January 1, 1950. If the requested record cannot be found, the fee will be used for a three-year search and a statement of search will be issued. Access to records is restricted for 100 years for birth records and 50 years for death, marriage, and divorce records. Divorce records can also be obtained from the clerk of the Superior Court in the judicial district where the divorce decree was issued. Contact the Superior Court, (County Seat), Alaska.

Cost for a certified Birth Certificate	$30.00
Cost for a certified Marriage Certificate	$30.00
Cost for a certified Divorce Record	$30.00
Cost for a certified Death Certificate	$30.00
Cost for a duplicate copy, when ordered at the same time	$25.00
Cost for an Heirloom Birth Certificate	$55.00
Cost for additional Heirloom Birth Certificate	$50.00
Cost for an Heirloom Marriage Certificate	$65.00
Cost for additional Heirloom Marriage Certificate	$60.00

For Genealogy Research:

The Alaska State Archives (141 Willoughby Avenue, Juneau, AK 99811; tel. 907-465-2270; www.archives.state.ak.us/genealogy/genealogy.html) holds many records of genealogical interest, including vital statistics 1816–1998, naturalization records 1888–1972, and probate indexes 1883–1960.

For Adoption Record information, contact:

Department of Health & Social Services
Special Services Unit
P.O. Box 110675
Juneau, AK 99801-0675

Tel. (907) 465-3618
E-mail: BVSSpecialServices@health.state.ak.us

Adoptees may receive copies of their original birth certificate at age 18.

STATE OF ALASKA
BIRTH CERTIFICATE REQUEST FORM

- You may type directly on this form and print it or you may print the form first and then complete it by hand. If you enter the ordering information on this form the fees and shipping charges will automatically be calculated.
- If completed by hand, be sure that all information is printed neatly and is legible.
- **Expedited (Rush) requests must be faxed to 907.465.3618 for processing**. Do not mail expedited requests. Please call 907.465.3391 Monday-Friday, 8 a.m. to 4 p.m. Alaska time, to confirm the receipt of your fax.
- Please read the instructions on the previous page. **Incomplete or inaccurate requests or requests that do not include a copy of a government-issued ID with a signature below the ID will be returned unprocessed.**

FULL First, Middle, and Last Name on the Birth Certificate: __________

Date of Birth: __________ City or Village of Birth: __________

Mother's **FULL** name before she was first married: __________

Father's **FULL** name: __________

Purpose of the request: __________
(Personal Records, Legal Purposes, Inheritance/Estate Settlement, Govt. Assistance/Benefits, Insurance/Pension, Retirement, etc.)

Your Relationship to the Child Named on the Record: __________
(Self, mother, father, legal representative, etc.)

Signature of the Person Requesting the Record: __________ Contact Phone Number: __________

Mail this form with a money order, a check, or credit card information. Checks must be preprinted with your name and address. Please note there is a $30.00 NSF fee for returned checks. Expedited (Rush) requests must be faxed to 907.465.3618 for processing (Add $11.00).

Make Checks Payable to:
Bureau of Vital Statistics
P.O. Box 110675
Juneau, AK 99811-0675

Phone: (907) 465-3391
Fax: (907) 465-3618

 # Copies — You may enter the ordering information in this form and the fees and shipping charges will automatically be calculated. — **Amount**

____ **Birth Certificates: $30 first copy; $25 each additional copy of the same record ordered at the same time.** ____

____ **Apostille fee (please see instructions for fees)** ____

Country needed for: __________

____ **Heirloom Certificates: $55 first copy; $50 each additional copy** ____

Heirloom Certificate Selected:
- ○ **Rie Muñoz, "The Embrace"**
- ○ **Jon Van Zyle, "Polar Bears"**

○ **Expedited (Rush) Service* (Add $11.00)** ____
***Does not include shipping fees.**

Ship by:
(Call our office for shipping rates outside the U.S)

- ○ **Regular Mail (no additional fee)**
- ○ **Priority Mail (Add $5.60)** ____
- ○ **Registered Mail (Add $11.20)** ____
- ○ **Express Mail (Add $19.95)** ____
- ○ **FedEx (No PO Box / Add $18.50)** ____

Total ____

PLEASE ENTER YOUR MAILING ADDRESS BELOW

Name: __________

Street: __________

City, State, Zip __________

Credit Card Information (When paying by credit card)

Name on credit card: __________

Billing address: __________

Number: __________ **Expiration date:** __________

Visa ○ **MasterCard** ○ **Discover** ○

Cardholder signature (required): __________

(Rev. 04/13)

STATE OF ALASKA
HEIRLOOM BIRTH CERTIFICATE REQUEST FORM

- You may type directly on this form and print it or you may print the form first and then complete it by hand. If you enter the ordering information in this form the fees and shipping charges will automatically be calculated.
- If completed by hand, be sure that all information is printed neatly and is legible.
- If you are purchasing an heirloom certificate please complete sections A and B.
- If you are ordering a gift certificate you only need to complete section B. The gift certificate will be sent to the purchaser. You do not need to include a photocopy of your ID when ordering a gift certificate.
- Please read the instructions on the previous page. The information you provide must be complete and accurate. **Incomplete or inaccurate requests or requests that do not include a copy of a government-issued ID with a signature below the ID will be returned unprocessed.**

A

FULL Name of the Child: ______
(First, Middle, and Last Name on the Birth Certificate)

Mother's Maiden Name: ______
(First, Middle, and Last Name before first married)

Father's Name: ______

Date of Birth: ______ Place of Birth: ______

Signature of the Person Requesting the Record: ______

B

Purchaser's Name: ______

Purchaser's Street Address: ______

Purchaser's City, State, Zip: ______

Purchaser's Contact Phone #: ______ Relationship to the Child: ______
(Mother, father, friend, relative, etc.)

Certificate of Birth

Polar Bears

Birth Certificate

The Embrace

Mail this form with a money order, a check, or credit card information. Checks must be preprinted with your name and address. Please note there is a $30.00 NSF fee for returned checks.

Make Checks Payable to:
Bureau of Vital Statistics
P.O. Box 110675
Juneau, AK 99801-0675

Phone: (907) 465-3391
Fax: (907) 465-3618

 # Copies — You may enter the ordering information in this form and the fees and shipping charges will automatically be calculated. — **Amount**

____ **Heirloom Certificates: $55 first copy; $50 each additional copy** ____

Heirloom Certificate Selected:
- ○ **Rie Muñoz, "The Embrace"**
- ○ **Jon Van Zyle, "Polar Bears"**

Ship by:
(Call our office for shipping rates outside the U.S)

- ○ **Regular Mail (no additional fee)**
- ○ **Priority Mail (Add $5.15)** ____
- ○ **Express Mail (Add $18.95)** ____
- ○ **FedEx (No PO Box / Add $18.50)** ____

Total ____

Credit Card Information (When paying by credit card)

Name on credit card: ______

Billing address: ______

Number: ______ **Expiration date:** ______

Visa ○ **MasterCard** ○ **Discover** ○

Cardholder signature (required): ______

(Rev. 01/13)

STATE OF ALASKA
MARRIAGE CERTIFICATE REQUEST FORM

- You may type directly on this form and print it or you may print the form first and then complete it by hand. If you enter the ordering information on this form the fees and shipping charges will automatically be calculated.
- If completed by hand, be sure that all information is printed neatly and is legible.
- **Expedited (Rush) requests must be faxed to 907.465.3618 for processing.** Do not mail expedited requests. Please call 907.465.3391 Monday-Friday, 8 a.m. to 4 p.m. Alaska time, to confirm the receipt of your fax.
- Please read the instructions on the previous page. The information you provide must be complete and accurate. **Incomplete or inaccurate requests or requests that do not include a copy of a government-issued ID with a signature below the ID will be returned unprocessed.**

FULL Name of the Husband: ______
(First, Middle, and Last Name on the Marriage Certificate)

FULL Name of the Wife: ______
(First, Middle, and Last Name on the Marriage Certificate)

Date of Marriage: ______ City, Village, or Place of Marriage: ______

Purpose of the request: ______
(Personal Records, Legal Purposes, Inheritance/Estate Settlement, Govt. Assistance/Benefits, Insurance/Pension, Retirement, etc.)

Your Relationship to the Persons Named on the Record: ______
(Husband, wife, legal representative, etc.)

Signature of the Person Requesting the Record: ______ Contact Phone Number: ______

Mail this form with a money order, a check, or credit card information. Checks must be preprinted with your name and address. Please note there is a $30.00 NSF fee for returned checks. Expedited (Rush) requests must be faxed to 907.465.3618 for processing.

Make Checks Payable to:
Bureau of Vital Statistics
P.O. Box 110675
Juneau, AK 99811-0675

Phone: (907) 465-3391
Fax: (907) 465-3618

Marriage Certificates: $30 first copy; $25 each additional copy of the same record ordered at the same time. ______

Apostille fee (please see instructions for fees) ______

Country needed for: ______

Heirloom Certificates: $65 first copy; $60 each additional copy ______

Heirloom Certificate Selected:
- ○ **Rie Muñoz, "Tenakee Wedding"**
- ○ **Dale DeArmond, "Raven in Love"**
- ○ **Byron Birdsall, "McKinley Moonlight"**

○ **Expedited (Rush) Service* (Add $11.00)** ______
***Faxed requests must include the $11 expedite fee. Does not include shipping fees.**

Ship by:
(Call our office for shipping rates outside the U.S)
- ○ **Regular Mail (no additional fee)**
- ○ **Priority Mail (Add $5.60)** ______
- ○ **Registered Mail (Add $11.20)** ______
- ○ **Express Mail (Add $19.95)** ______
- ○ **FedEx (No PO Box / Add $18.50)** ______

Total ______

PLEASE ENTER YOUR MAILING ADDRESS BELOW

Name: ______

Street: ______

City, State, Zip ______

Credit Card Information (When paying by credit card)

Name on credit card: ______

Billing address: ______

Number: ______ **Expiration date:** ______

Visa ○ **MasterCard** ○ **Discover** ○

Cardholder signature (required): ______

(Rev. 04/13)

STATE OF ALASKA
HEIRLOOM MARRIAGE CERTIFICATE REQUEST FORM

- You may type directly on this form and print it or you may print the form first and then complete it by hand. If you enter the ordering information in this form the fees and shipping charges will automatically be calculated.
- If completed by hand, be sure that all information is printed neatly and is legible.
- If you are purchasing an heirloom certificate please complete sections A and B.
- If you are ordering a gift certificate you only need to complete section B. The gift certificate will be sent to the purchaser. You do not need to include a photocopy of your ID when ordering a gift certificate.
- Please read the instructions on the previous page. The information you provide must be complete and accurate. **Incomplete or inaccurate requests or requests that do not include a copy of a government-issued ID with a signature below the ID will be returned unprocessed.**

A

FULL Name of the Husband: ____________________
(First, Middle, and Last Name on the Marriage Certificate)

FULL Name of the Wife: ____________________
(First, Middle, and Last Name on the Marriage Certificate)

Date of Marriage: __________ City, Village, or Place of Marriage: __________

Signature of the Person Requesting the Record: ____________________

B

Purchaser's Name: ____________________

Purchaser's Street Address: ____________________

Purchaser's City, State, Zip: ____________________

Purchaser's Contact Phone #: __________ Relationship to the Couple: __________
(Husband, wife, friend, relative, etc.)

Tenakee Wedding

Raven in Love

McKinley Moonlight

Mail this form with a money order, a check, or credit card information. Checks must be preprinted with your name and address. Please note there is a $30.00 NSF fee for returned checks.

Make Checks Payable to:
Bureau of Vital Statistics
P.O. Box 110675
Juneau, AK 99801-0675

Phone: (907) 465-3391
Fax: (907) 465-3618

 # Copies — You may enter the ordering information in this form and the fees and shipping charges will automatically be calculated. — **Amount**

____ **Heirloom Certificates: $65 first copy; $60 each additional copy** ____

Heirloom Certificate Selected:
- ○ **Rie Muñoz, "Tenakee Wedding"**
- ○ **Dale DeArmond, "Raven in Love"**
- ○ **Byron Birdsall, "McKinley Moonlight"**

Ship by:
(Call our office for shipping rates outside the U.S)
- ○ **Regular Mail (no additional fee)**
- ○ **Priority Mail (Add $5.15)** ____
- ○ **Express Mail (Add $18.95)** ____
- ○ **FedEx (No PO Box / Add $18.50)** ____

Total ____

Credit Card Information (When paying by credit card)

Name on credit card: ____________________

Billing address: ____________________

Number: __________ **Expiration date:** __________

Visa ○ **MasterCard** ○ **Discover** ○

Cardholder signature (required): ____________________

(Rev. 01/13)

STATE OF ALASKA
DIVORCE CERTIFICATE REQUEST FORM

- You may type directly on this form and print it or you may print the form first and then complete it by hand. If you enter the ordering information on this form the fees and shipping charges will automatically be calculated.
- If completed by hand, be sure that all information is printed neatly and is legible.
- **Expedited (Rush) requests must be faxed to 907.465.3618 for processing**. Do not mail expedited requests. Please call 907.465.3391 Monday-Friday, 8 a.m. to 4 p.m. Alaska time, to confirm the receipt of your fax.
- Please read the instructions on the previous page. **Incomplete or inaccurate requests or requests that do not include a copy of a government-issued ID with a signature below the ID will be returned unprocessed.**

FULL Name of the Husband: ____________________
(First, Middle, and Last Name on the Divorce Certificate)

FULL Name of the Wife: ____________________
(First, Middle, and Last Name on the Divorce Certificate)

Date of Divorce: __________ Date of Marriage (for this divorce): __________

City or Village of Divorce: ____________________

Purpose of the request: ____________________
(Personal Records, Legal Purposes, Inheritance/Estate Settlement, Govt. Assistance/Benefits, Insurance/Pension, Retirement, etc.)

Your Relationship to the Persons Named on the Record: ____________________
(Husband, wife, legal representative, etc.)

Signature of the Person Requesting the Record: ____________________ Contact Phone Number: __________

Mail this form with a money order, a check, or credit card information. Checks must be preprinted with your name and address. Please note there is a $30.00 NSF fee for returned checks. Expedited (Rush) requests must be faxed to 907.465.3618 for processing.

Make Checks Payable to:
Bureau of Vital Statistics
P.O. Box 110675
Juneau, AK 99811-0675

Phone: (907) 465-3391
Fax: (907) 465-3618

 # Copies You may enter the ordering information in this form and the fees and shipping charges will automatically be calculated. **Amount**

______ **Divorce Certificates: $30 first copy; $25 each additional copy of the same record ordered at the same time.** ______

______ **Apostille fee (please see instructions for fees)** ______

Country needed for: ____________________

◯ **Expedited (Rush) Service* (Add $11.00)** ______
***Does not include shipping fees.**

Ship by:

(Call our office for shipping rates outside the U.S)

◯ **Regular Mail (no additional fee)**
◯ **Priority Mail (Add $5.60)** ______
◯ **Registered Mail (Add $11.20)** ______
◯ **Express Mail (Add $19.95)** ______
◯ **FedEx (No PO Box / Add $18.50)** ______

Total ______

PLEASE ENTER YOUR MAILING ADDRESS BELOW

Name: ____________________

Street: ____________________

City, State, Zip ____________________

Credit Card Information (When paying by credit card)

Name on credit card: ____________________

Billing address: ____________________

Number: ____________________ **Expiration date:** __________

Visa ◯ **MasterCard** ◯ **Discover** ◯

Cardholder signature (required): ____________________

(Rev. 04/13)

STATE OF ALASKA
DEATH CERTIFICATE REQUEST FORM

- You may type directly on this form and print it or you may print the form first and then complete it by hand. If you enter the ordering information on this form the fees and shipping charges will automatically be calculated.
- If completed by hand, be sure that all information is printed neatly and is legible.
- **Expedited (Rush) requests must be faxed to 907.465.3618 for processing.** Do not mail expedited requests. Please call 907.465.3391 Monday-Friday, 8 a.m. to 4 p.m. Alaska time, to confirm the receipt of your fax.
- Please read the instructions on the previous page. **Incomplete or inaccurate requests or requests that do not include a copy of a government-issued ID with a signature below the ID will be returned unprocessed.**

FULL Name of the Deceased: ____

Date of Death: ____ City or Village of Death: ____

Purpose of the request: ____
(Personal Records, Legal Purposes, Inheritance/Estate Settlement, Govt. Assistance/Benefits, Insurance/Pension, Retirement, etc.)

Your Relationship to the Deceased: ____
(Spouse, parent, child, sibling, legal representative, etc.)

Signature of the Person Requesting the Record: ____ Contact Phone Number: ____

ADDITIONAL HELPFUL SEARCH CRITERIA BUT NOT REQUIRED

FULL Name of the Deceased's Mother before she was first married: ____

FULL Name of the Deceased's Father: ____

Date of Birth of the Deceased: ____

Mail this form with a money order, a check, or credit card information. Checks must be preprinted with your name and address. Please note there is a $30.00 NSF fee for returned checks. Expedited (Rush) requests must be faxed to 907.465.3618 for processing (Add $11.00).

Make Checks Payable to:
Bureau of Vital Statistics
P.O. Box 110675
Juneau, AK 99811-0675

Phone: (907) 465-3391
Fax: (907) 465-3618

 # Copies You may enter the ordering information in this form and the fees and shipping charges will automatically be calculated. **Amount**

____ **Death Certificates: $30 first copy; $25 each additional copy of the same record ordered at the same time.** ____

____ **Apostille fee (please see instructions for fees)** ____

Country needed for: ____

○ **Expedited (Rush) Service* (Add $11.00)** ____
***Does not include shipping fees.**

Ship by:
(Call our office for shipping rates outside the U.S)

○ **Regular Mail (no additional fee)**
○ **Priority Mail (Add $5.60)** ____
○ **Registered Mail (Add $11.20)** ____
○ **Express Mail (Add $19.95)** ____
○ **FedEx (No PO Box / Add $18.50)** ____

Total ____

PLEASE ENTER YOUR MAILING ADDRESS BELOW

Name: ____

Street: ____

City, State, Zip ____

Credit Card Information (When paying by credit card)

Name on credit card: ____

Billing address: ____

Number: ____ **Expiration date:** ____

Visa ○ **MasterCard** ○ **Discover** ○

Cardholder signature (required): ____

(Rev. 04/13)

Send your requests to:

Office of Vital Records
(Location: 1818 West Adams Street)
P.O. Box 3887
Phoenix, AZ 85030

Tel. (602) 255-3260; (888) 816-5907
E-mail: webovr@azdhs.gov
www.azdhs.gov/vital-records/

The Office of Vital Records officially began recording birth and death events in July 1909 but maintains a sampling of delayed birth records from 1855 and death records from 1877. Births that occurred more than 75 years ago and deaths that occurred more than 50 years ago are public records. When ordering certificates by mail, you must include a self-addressed, stamped envelope.

Marriage and divorce records are maintained by the clerk of the Superior Court in the county where the event occurred and are not available from the Office of Vital Records. Go to the website at www.azcourts.gov/AZCourts/AZCourtsLocator.aspx for the addresses of the Superior Courts where you should send your requests.

Cost for a certified Birth Certificate	$20.00
Cost for a certified Death Certificate	$20.00

For Genealogy Research:

The Arizona Department of Health Services maintains a free genealogy website at http://genealogy.az.gov that contains microfilmed images of original birth certificates at least 75 years old and death certificates at least 50 years old.

The History and Archives Division of the Arizona State Library, Archives and Public Records (1901 West Madison, Phoenix, AZ 85009; tel. 602-926-3720; www.lib.az.us/archives/) contains many types of public records that may be useful to family historians, including birth records from the 1890s through 1930 and death records from the 1890s through 1955, as well as Superior Court records containing pre-WWII marriage licenses.

For Adoption Record information, contact:

Arizona Confidential Intermediary Program
Arizona Supreme Court
1501 West Washington Street, Suite 104
Phoenix, AZ 85007

Tel. (602) 452-3378

Arizona's adoption records are confidential. If you were adopted and are looking for your birth parents, or if you are the birth parent of an adoptee and are looking for your child, you will need to engage the services of a Confidential Intermediary.

REQUEST FOR COPY OF BIRTH CERTIFICATE

WARNING: False application for a birth certificate is a felony offence. Signature of applicant must be NOTARIZED or this form must be accompanied by a copy of a VALID GOVERNMENT ISSUED PICTURE I.D. which contains the applicant signature.

Date

Enclosed $ ________ (amount) in ________ (form of payment) for ________ (number of copies)

I. Registrant (Person on Certificate or new name if amended)

State File Number

Full Name at Birth or new name on certificate if name changed | Date of Birth | Sex

Notary Stamp Here

Place of Birth (City, County, State) | Mother's Maiden Name (First, Middle, Last) | Mother's Place of Birth

Hospital or Facility | Father's Name (First, Middle, Last) | Father's Place of Birth

II. Applicant (Person Making Request)

Print Plainly - Return Address

Credit/Debit Card **MC** ☐ **Visa** ☐

☐☐☐☐☐☐☐☐☐☐☐☐☐☐☐☐

Exp. Date MM/YY

Your Signature ⇨

Your Name

Your Mailing Address (Number & Street)

(Town, State, Zip Code) | e-Mail Address

Relationship to Registrant (e.g. parent, attorney, etc.) | Reason for Request | Phone Number (Required)

State of

County of

On this ____ day of ________, 20____

before me personally appeared ________ (name of signer),

whose identity was proved to me on the basis of satisfactory evidence to be the person whose name is subscribed to this document, and who acknowledged that he/she signed the above/attached document.

Notary Signature

My Commission Expires

PLEASE INCLUDE A SELF ADDRESSED STAMPED ENVELOPE WITH YOUR REQUEST

PARTICIPATING OFFICE LOCATIONS

For Arizona births that occurred from 1990 to the present, you can request certified copies by mail or in person from the county office locations or from the state office. **Please note payment types accepted at office locations: Cash (C) - in person only, Money Order (MO), Personal Checks (PC), Credit Cards (CC), Debit Cards (DC). For all births that occurred before 1990, you MUST file your application with the state office.**

NOTE: THE STATE OFFICE DOES NOT ACCEPT PERSONAL CHECKS (PC)

Apache County Health Department 75 W. Cleveland St. Johns, AZ 85936 (928) 337-7525 **(C) (MO)** ***Mail to:*** PO Box 697 St. Johns, AZ 85936	**Cochise Health & Social Services** 4115 E. Foothills Dr. Sierra Vista, AZ. 85635 (520) 803-3900 **(C) (MO) (DC/CC)** **(Amex, Discover, MC only)**	**Cochise Health & Social Services** 1415 W. Melody Ln., Bldg. A Bisbee, AZ 85603 (520) 432-9400 **(C) (MO) (DC/CC)** **(Amex, Discover, MC only)**	**Coconino County Public Health Svcs. Dist** 2625 N. King St. Flagstaff, AZ 86004 (928) 679-7272 **(C) (MO) (DC) (CC) (Visa/MC/Discover)** **In-person only**
Graham County Health Department 826 W. Main Safford, AZ 85546 (928) 428-4441 **(C) (MO) (PC)**	**Greenlee County** Health Department Office of Vital Registration 253 5th Street Clifton, AZ 85533 (928) 865-2601 **(C), (MO)** ***Mail to:*** PO Box 936 Clifton, AZ 85533	**Maricopa County** Office of Vital Registration 3003 W. Thomas Rd., Suite 200B Phoenix, AZ 85017 (602) 506-6805 **(C) (MO) (CC)** ***Mail to:*** PO Box 2111 Phoenix, AZ 85001	**Maricopa County** Office of Vital Registration 3221 N. 16th St., Suite 100 Phoenix, AZ 85016 (602) 506-6805 **(C) (MO) (CC)** ***Mail to:*** PO Box 2111 Phoenix, AZ 85001
Maricopa County Office of Vital Registration 4419 E. Main St., Suite 105 Mesa, AZ 85205 (602) 506-6805 **(C) (MO) (CC)** ***Mail to:*** PO Box 2111 Phoenix, AZ 85001	**Mohave County Public Health** County Administration Building Drop Box in lobby: 700 W. Beale Street Kingman, AZ 86401 Mail to: PO Box 7000 Kingman, AZ 86402 (928) 753-0748 **(C) (MO)**	**Navajo County** Health Department 117 E. Buffalo St. Holbrook, AZ 86025 (928) 524-4750 **(MO)**	**Pima County** Health Department Vital Records Office 3950 S. Country Club Road Ste. 100 Tucson, AZ 85714 (520) 243-7930 **(C) (MO) (PC) (CC) (DC)**
Pinal County Health Department 41600 W. Smith-Enke Rd., Bldg. 15 Maricopa, AZ 85138 (520) 866-4621 / (800) 231-8499 **(C) (MO) (PC)** ***Mail to:*** PO Box 2945 Florence, AZ 85132	**Pinal County** Health Department 36235 N. Gantzel Rd. San Tan Valley, AZ 85142 (520) 866-4670 / (800) 231-8499 **(C) (MO) (PC)** Mail to: PO Box 2945 Florence, AZ 85132	**Yavapai County** Health Department 1090 Commerce Prescott, AZ 86305 (928) 771-3125 **(C) (MO) (PC) (CC) (DC)** Certified Copies of Birth Certificates are Available by Mail Only	**Yuma County Health Services** Vital Records Department 2200 W. 28th Street Yuma, AZ 85364 **(928) 317-4530** **(C) (MO)**
	Several other county offices are preparing to make this service available. If your county is not listed, call the (602) 364-1300, or see www.azdhs.gov/vitalrcd for information on where to file your request. The state office has all Arizona birth records back to the 1800's available. For all **births that occurred before 1990**, you MUST file your application with the state office.		**State Office of Vital Records** 1818 W. Adams St. Phoenix, AZ 85007 (602) 364-1300 **(C) (MO) (CC) (DC)** ***Mail to:*** PO Box 3887 Phoenix, AZ 85030

VS-11 (4/17/13)

REQUEST FOR COPY OF ☐ DEATH ☐ FETAL DEATH ☐ BIRTH RESULTING IN STILLBIRTH

WARNING: False application for a death certificate is a felony offence. If applying by mail signature of applicant must be NOTARIZED or this form must be accompanied by a copy of a VALID GOVERNMENT ISSUED PICTURE I.D. which contains the applicant signature.

Date

Enclosed $ __________ (amount) in __________ (form of payment) for __________ (number of copies)

I. Decedent (Person on Certificate or new name if amended)

Name of Deceased (First, Middle, Last) | Date of Death | Sex | State File Number

Notary Stamp Here

Social Security Number | Are Copies to be Used for US Gov't Claims? ☐ Yes ☐ No | If Yes, List Each Type of Claim

Place of Death - Hospital or Residence (City, County, State)

II. Applicant (Person Making Request)

Credit/Debit Card **MC** ☐ **Visa** ☐

☐☐☐☐☐☐☐☐☐☐☐☐☐☐☐☐

Exp. Date MM/YY

Print Plainly - Return Address

Your Signature ⇨

Your Name

Your Mailing Address (Number & Street)

(Town, State, Zip Code) | e-Mail Address

Relationship to Registrant (e.g. parent, attorney, etc.) | Reason for Request | Phone Number (Required)

State of __________

County of __________

On this ______ day of __________, 20____

before me personally appeared __________ (name of signer), whose identity was proved to me on the basis of satisfactory evidence to be the person whose name is subscribed to this document, and who acknowledged that he/she signed the above/ attached document.

__________ Notary Signature

__________ My Commission Expires

PLEASE INCLUDE A SELF ADDRESSED STAMPED ENVELOPE WITH YOUR REQUEST

PARTICIPATING OFFICE LOCATIONS

Requests for certified copies of death events that occurred prior to 2008 must be requested from the State Office of Vital Records, requests for certified copies beginning 2008 to present can be obtained from a County Office or the State Office. Please note payment types accepted at office locations: Cash (C) - in person only, Money Order (MO), Personal Checks (PC), Credit Cards (CC), Debit Cards (DC).

NOTE: THE STATE OFFICE OF VITAL RECORDS DOES NOT ACCEPT PERSONAL CHECKS (PC)

Apache County Health Department 75 W. Cleveland St. Johns, AZ 85936 (928) 337-7668 **(C) (MO)** ***Mail to:*** PO Box 697 St. Johns, AZ 85936	**Cochise County** Health Department 1415 W. Melody Ln., Bldg. A Bisbee, AZ 85603 (520) 432-9400 **(C) (MO) (DC)** **(CC - Amex, Discover, MC only)**	**Cochise County** Health Department 4115 E. Foothills Drive Sierra Vista, AZ 85635 (520) 803-3900 **(C) (MO) (DC)** **(CC - Amex, Discover, MC only)**	**Coconino County** Health Department 2500 N. Fort Valley Rd., Bldg. 3 Flagstaff, AZ 86001 (928) 679-8775 **(C) (MO) (PC) (CC)**
Gila County Health Department 5515 S. Apache Ave. Suite 300 Globe, Arizona 85501 (928) 425-8811 **(C) (MO) (PC)**	**Graham County** Health Department 826 W. Main Safford, AZ 85546 (928) 428-0110 **(C) (MO) (PC)**	**Greenlee County** Health Department Office of Vital Registration 253 5th Street Clifton, AZ 85533 (928) 865-2601 **(C), (MO)** ***Mail to:*** PO Box 936 Clifton, AZ 85533	**La Paz County** Health Department 1112 Joshua Ave., #206 Parker, AZ 85344 (928) 669-1100 **(C) (MO)**
Maricopa County Office of Vital Registration 3221 N. 16th St., Suite 100 Phoenix, AZ 85016 (602) 506-6805 **(C) (MO) (CC)** ***Mail to:*** PO Box 2111 Phoenix, AZ 85001	**Maricopa County** Office of Vital Registration Department of Public Health 3003 W. Thomas Rd., Suite 200B Phoenix, AZ 85017 (602) 506-6805 **(C) (MO) (CC)** ***Mail to:*** PO Box 2111 Phoenix, AZ 85001	**Maricopa County** Office of Vital Registration Department of Public Health 4419 E. Main St., Suite 105 Mesa, AZ 85205 **(C) (MO) (CC)** ***Mail to:*** PO Box 2111 Phoenix, AZ 85001	**Mohave County** Health Department 700 West Beale Street Kingman, AZ 86401 **(C) (MO) (PC)** ***Mail to:*** PO Box 7000 Kingman, AZ 86401
Navajo County Health Department 117 E. Buffalo St. Holbrook, AZ 86025 (928) 524-4750 **(MO)**	**Pima County** Health Department Vital Records Office 3950 S. Country Club Road Ste. 100 Tucson, AZ 85714 (520) 243-7930 **(C) (MO) (PC) (CC) (DC)**	**Pinal County** Health Department 41600 W. Smith-Enke Rd., Bldg. 15 Maricopa, AZ 85138 (520) 866-4621 / (800) 231-8499 **(C) (MO) (PC)** ***Mail to:*** PO Box 2945 Florence, AZ 85232	**Pinal County Health Department** (Mortuaries Only) 971 N. Jason Lopez Cir., Bldg. G Florence, AZ 85132 (520) 866-7318 / (800) 231-8499 **(C) (MO) (PC)** ***Mail to:*** PO Box 2945 Florence, AZ 85132
Pinal County Health Department 36235 N. Gantzel Rd. San Tan Valley, AZ 85142 (520) 866-4670 / (800) 231-8499 **(C) (MO) (PC)** ***Mail to:*** PO Box 2945 Florence, AZ 85132	**Santa Cruz County** Health Services 2150 N. Congress Dr. Suite 115 Nogales, Arizona 85621 (520) 375-7900 **(C) (MO) (CC)**	**State Office of Vital Records** 1818 W. Adams St. Phoenix, AZ 85007 (602) 364-1300 **(C) (MO) (CC) (DC)** ***Mail to:*** PO Box 3887 Phoenix, AZ 85030	**Yavapai County** Health Department 1090 Commerce Prescott, AZ 86305 (928) 771-3125 **(C) (MO) (PC) (CC) (DC)** ***Requests by mail only***
Yuma County Health Services Vital Records Department 2200 W. 28th Street Yuma, AZ 85364 (928) 317-4530 **(C) (MO)**			

ARKANSAS

Send your requests to:

Arkansas Department of Health
Vital Records, Slot 44
4815 West Markham Street
Little Rock, AR 72205

Tel. (501) 661-2336; (800) 637-9314
Fax (501) 661-2717
www.healthy.arkansas.gov/programsServices/certificatesVitalRecords/Pages/default.aspx

The Division of Vital Records has birth and death records on file from February 1, 1914. There are also a limited number of birth records available prior to 1914 and original copies of some Little Rock and Fort Smith births dating from 1881, as well as a limited number of records available for deaths occurring between 1881 and 1914 in Little Rock and Fort Smith. Births that occurred more than 100 years ago and deaths that occurred more than 50 years ago are public records.

Marriage records have been kept since January 1, 1917, and divorce records since January 1, 1923. If you want a copy of the actual license or decree, you must contact the county clerk or circuit clerk where the marriage or divorce was recorded. Arkansas Vital Records issues a certified copy of the coupon of marriage or divorce. You may search and order death certificates from 1935 to 1961 via the Online Death Certificate Search and Order Service (https://www.ark.org/doh_dcs/).

Cost for a certified Birth Certificate	$12.00
Cost for each additional certified Birth Certificate	$10.00
Cost for a certified Marriage Coupon	$10.00
Cost for a certified Divorce Coupon	$10.00
Cost for a certified Death Certificate	$10.00
Cost for each additional certified Death Certificate	$8.00

For Genealogy Research:

Family members who are conducting genealogical research and genealogists representing relevant family members may obtain copies of vital records.

The Arkansas History Commission (1 Capitol Mall, Little Rock, AR 72201; www.ark-ives.com) holds a wealth of records from each of Arkansas' 75 counties, including county court records; birth, marriage, and death records; wills; deeds; and tax records, among many others.

For Adoption Record information, contact:

Arkansas Department of Human Services
Division of Children and Family Services
Adoption Registry
P.O. Box 1437, Slot S565
Little Rock, AR 72203-1437

https://dhs.arkansas.gov/dcfs/heartgallery/mcvar.htm

Date ____________________

ARKANSAS DEPARTMENT OF HEALTH
VITAL RECORDS, Slot 44
4815 West Markham Street
Little Rock, AR 72205

BIRTH CERTIFICATE APPLICATION

Only Arkansas births are recorded in this office. There are a limited number of birth records filed in this office prior to February 1, 1914. The fee is $12.00 for the first copy ordered and $10.00 for each additional copy of the same record. The fee must accompany the application. Send check or money order payable to the Arkansas Department of Health. **DO NOT SEND CASH.** Of the total fee you send, $12.00 will be kept to cover search charges if no record of the birth is found. Only the names and dates listed will be searched for the $12.00 fee. Names and other dates submitted later will require an additional $12.00 non-refundable fee. Mail this application, a copy of your photo id and the money to the address above. **Please allow 4-6 weeks for delivery.**

List Below All Possible Birth Dates and Names Under Which the Certificate May be Registered. (Type or Print)

1 Full Name at Birth	First Name	Middle Name	Last Name		
2 Date of Birth	Month	Day	Year	Sex	Age Last Birthday
3. Place of Birth	City or Town	County	State		
	Name of Hospital or Street Address				
4. Full Name of Father	First Name	Middle Name	Last Name		
5. Full Maiden Name of Mother (Name Before Marriage)	First Name	Middle Name	Last Name		

If this child has been adopted, please give original name if known.

If this is a delayed certificate, when was it filed?

What is your relationship to the person whose certificate is being requested?

What is your reason for requesting this certificate?

Is the person whose certificate is being requested still living? ☐ Yes ☐ No

Signature and telephone number of person requesting this certificate.
X

All requests for certificates require photo identification.

Certificates may also be ordered by the following methods:
Internet: www.vitalchek.com. All internet orders are expedited. The service fee and the certificate fee are charged to your debit or credit card (Visa, Master Card, Discover or American Express). Overnight shipping is available for an additional fee.

OR

Telephone: Toll free (866) 209-9482. All telephone orders are expedited. The service fee and the certificate fee are charged to your debit or credit card (Visa, Master Card, Discover or American Express). Overnight shipping is available for an additional fee.

OR

Walk-in: You may order a certified copy of the birth record by coming into this office. Orders are accepted for same day issuance from 8:00 A.M. until 4:00 P.M. Monday through Friday. The office is located at 4815 West Markham St. Little Rock, AR 72205. Please order family history and genealogy by mail or internet.

HOW MANY ☐

1st copy costs $12.00
Each additional copy costs $10.00

AMOUNT OF MONEY ENCLOSED $ ____

Please PRINT the name and address of the person who is to receive this request on the line below.

____
____
____

Any person who willfully and knowingly makes any false statement in an application for a certified copy of a vital record filed in this state is subject to a fine of not more than ten thousand dollars ($10,000) or imprisoned not more than five (5) years, or both (Arkansas Statutes 20-18-105).

VR-7 (R 8/11)

DATE ____________

ARKANSAS DEPARTMENT OF HEALTH
VITAL RECORDS, Slot 44
4815 West Markham
Little Rock, AR 72205

MARRIAGE COUPON APPLICATION

Only Arkansas events of marriage are filed in this office. Marriage records start with 1917. The fee is $10.00 for each copy requested. This fee must accompany the application. Send check or money order payable to the Arkansas Department of Health. **DO NOT SEND CASH**. Of the total fee sent, $10.00 will be kept to cover the search charge if the record is not located in our files. Mail this application, a copy of your photo id and the money to the address above. **Please allow 4-6 weeks for processing and delivery.**

NAME OF GROOM ____________

MAIDEN NAME OF BRIDE ____________

DATE OF MARRIAGE ____________
Month Day Year

COUNTY IN WHICH LICENSE WAS ISSUED ____________

PLEASE ANSWER ALL QUESTIONS

What is your relationship to the parties named on the requested record?

____

What is your reason for requesting a copy of this record?

____

Signature and Telephone Number of Person Requesting this Certificate

X ____________

All requests for certificates require photo identification.

Certificates may be ordered by the following methods:

Internet: www.vitalchek.com. The service fee and the certificate fee are charged to your credit card (Visa, Master Card, Discover and American Express). Certificates may be returned over night for the additional shipment fee.

OR

Telephone: (866) 209-9482. The service fee and the certificate fee are charged to your credit card (Visa, Master Card, Discover or American Express). Certificates may be returned over night for the additional shipment fee.

OR

Walk in: The certificate may be ordered by coming into this office. If you want the copy the same day, our hours for same day service are 8:00 A.M. until 4:00 P.M. Monday – Friday. The office is located at 4815 West Markham St, Little Rock, AR 72205. **Please order family history and genealogy by mail or Internet.**

CERTIFIED COPIES

Each copy is $10.00.

HOW MANY ______

AMOUNT OF MONEY ENCLOSED

$________

Please PRINT the name and address of the person who is to receive the request on the line below.

NAME ____________

ADDRESS ____________

CITY ____________ STATE ________ ZIP ________

Any person who willfully and knowingly makes any false statement in an application for a certified copy of a vital record filed in this state is subject to a fine of not more than ten thousand dollars ($10,000) or imprisoned not more than five (5) years, or both (Arkansas Statutes 20-18-105).

VR-9 (R 8/11)

DATE ____________________

ARKANSAS DEPARTMENT OF HEALTH
Vital Records, Slot 44
4815 West Markham
Little Rock, AR 72205

DIVORCE COUPON APPLICATION

Only Arkansas events of divorce are filed in this office. Divorce records start with 1923. The fee is $10.00 for each copy requested. This fee must accompany the application. Send the completed application, a copy of your photo id and a check or money order payable to the Arkansas Department of Health . **DO NOT SEND CASH**. $10.00 will be kept to cover the search charge if the record is not located in our files. Mail this application, a copy of your photo id and the money to the address above. **Please allow 4-6 weeks for processing and delivery.**

NAME OF HUSBAND ____

NAME OF WIFE ____

DATE OF DIVORCE OR DISMISSAL ____
Month Day Year

COUNTY IN WHICH DIVORCE WAS GRANTED/DISMISSED

____

PLEASE ANSWER ALL QUESTIONS

What is your relationship to the parties named on the requested record?

____

What is your reason for requesting a copy of this record?

____

Signature and Telephone Number of Person Requesting this Certificate
X
____

All requests for certificates require photo identification.

Certificates may also be ordered by the following methods:

Internet: www.vitalchek.com . The service fee and the certificate fee are charged to your credit card (Visa, Master Card, Discover and American Express). Certificates may be returned over night for the additional shipment fee.

OR

Telephone: Toll free (866) 209-9482. The service fee and the certificate fee are charged to your credit card (Visa, Master Card, Discover or American Express). Certificates may be returned over night for the additional shipment fee.

OR

Walk in: The certificate may be ordered by coming into this office. If you want the copy the same day, our hours for same day service are 8:00 A.M. until 4:00 P.M. Monday – Friday. The office is located at 4815 West Markham St, Little Rock, AR 72205. **Please order family history and genealogy by mail or Internet.**

CERTIFIED COPIES

Each copy is $10.00.

HOW MANY ______

AMOUNT OF MONEY ENCLOSED
$__________

Please PRINT the name and address of the person who is to receive the request on the lines below.

NAME ____

ADDRESS ____

CITY ______________ STATE ______ ZIP ______

Any person who willfully and knowingly makes any false statement in an application for a certified copy of a vital record filed in this state is subject to a fine of not more than ten thousand dollars ($10,000) or imprisoned not more than five (5) years, or both (Arkansas Statutes 20-18-105).

VR-10 (R 8/11)

ARKANSAS DEPARTMENT OF HEALTH
VITAL RECORDS, Slot 44
4815 West Markham
Little Rock, AR 72205

Date ____________________

DEATH CERTIFICATE APPLICATION

Only Arkansas deaths are recorded in this office. There are only a limited number of death records filed in this office for deaths prior to February 1, 1914. The fee is $10.00 for the first certified copy requested and $8.00 for each additional certified copy of the record. The fee must accompany the application. Send check or money order payable to the Arkansas Department of Health. **DO NOT SEND CASH**. Of the total fee you send, $10.00 will be kept to cover search charges if no record of the death is found. Only the names and dates listed will be searched for the $10.00 fee. Names and other dates submitted later will require an additional $10.00 non-refundable fee. Mail this application, a copy of your photo id and the money to the address above. **Please allow 4-6 weeks for processing.**

List Below All Possible Dates of Death and Names Under Which the Certificate May be Registered. (Type or Print)

1 Full Name of Deceased	First Name	Middle Name	Last Name		
2 Date of Death	Month	Day	Year	Age of Deceased	Sex
3. Place Where Death Occurred	City or Town	County	State		
If unknown, give last place of residence.	City or Town	County	State		
4. Name of Funeral Home					
5. Address of Funeral Home					
6. Name and Address of Attending Certifier					

If deceased was an infant, was it stillborn? ☐ Yes ☐ No

What is your relationship to the person whose certificate is being requested?

What is your reason for requesting a copy of this certificate?

Signature and telephone number of person requesting this certificate:
X

HOW MANY ☐

1st Copy costs $10.00
Each additional copy costs $8.00

AMOUNT OF MONEY ENCLOSED
$ _____

All requests for certificates require photo identification.

Certificates may also be ordered by the following methods:

Internet: www.vitalchek.com. The service fee and the certificate fee are charged to your credit card (Visa, Master Card, Discover or American Express). Certificates may be returned over night for the additional shipment fee.

OR

Telephone: (866) 209-9482. The service fee and the certificate fee are charged to your credit card (Visa, Master Card, Discover or American Express). Certificates may be returned over night for the additional shipment fee.

OR

Walk-in: You may order a certified copy of the death record by coming into this office. Orders are accepted for same day issuance from 8:00 A.M. until 4:00 P.M. Monday through Friday. The office is located at 4815 West Markham St. Little Rock, AR 72205.

Please PRINT the name and address of the person who is to receive this request on the lines below.

____

____

____

Any person who willfully and knowingly makes any false statement in an application for a certified copy of a vital record filed in this state is subject to a fine of not more than ten thousand dollars ($10,000) or imprisoned not more than five (5) years, or both (Arkansas Statutes 20-18-105.)

VR-8 (R 8/11)

CALIFORNIA

Send your requests to:

California Department of Public Health
Vital Records—M.S. 5103
P.O. Box 997410
Sacramento, CA 95899

Tel. (916) 445-2684
Fax (800) 858-5553
Email: VRmail@cdph.ca.gov
www.cdph.ca.gov/certlic/birthdeathmar/Pages/default.aspx

The Office of Vital Records does not currently have a public counter; requests should be submitted by mail. Vital Records has births and deaths on file from July 1, 1905. In the State of California, authorized copies of vital records can only be obtained by the individual named on the record, parents of the individual named on the record, and certain other individuals or entities specified in law. See the website for more information. The State makes available a microfiche index to deaths from 1905 to 1995.

The Office of Vital Records has kept marriage records dating back to 1905; however, they will only provide certified copies of marriage records 1949–1986 and 1998–1999, and it may take them more than six months to process requests. Therefore, it's best to get marriage certificates from the County Recorder's Office in the county where the marriage license was issued; see www.cdph.ca.gov/certlic/birthdeathmar/Pages/CountyRecorderOffice.aspx for contact information.

Vital Records can only issue a Certificate of Divorce Record—and only for divorces that occurred between 1962 and June 1984. Certified copies of the actual divorce decrees are available only from the Superior Court in the county where the decree was filed; go to www.courts.ca.gov/superiorcourts.htm for a list of Superior Courts.

Cost for a certified Birth Certificate	$20.00
Cost for a public Marriage Certificate	$14.00
Cost for a Dissolution of Marriage Certificate	$13.00
Cost for a certified Death Certificate	$16.00

For Genealogy Research:

If you cannot obtain an authorized copy of a vital record under California law, you may be able to obtain an informational copy. An informational copy contains the same information as an authorized copy but will have a legend across the face with the statement "Informational, not a valid document to establish identity."

The California State Archives (1020 O Street, Sacramento, CA 95814; tel. 916-653-7715; www.sos.ca.gov/archives/archives.htm) has vital records from some counties, as well as a variety of other records of interest to genealogists.

For Adoption Record information, contact:

California Department of Social Services
Adoption Support Unit
774 P Street, MS 8-12-31
Sacramento, CA 95814

Tel. (916) 651-8088
www.childsworld.ca.gov/PG1301.htm

APPLICATION FOR CERTIFIED COPY OF BIRTH RECORD

PLEASE READ THE INSTRUCTIONS ON PAGE 2 BEFORE COMPLETING THIS APPLICATION

As part of statewide efforts to prevent identity theft, California law (Health and Safety Code Section 103526) permits only authorized individuals as listed on the application to receive certified copies of birth records. All others will be issued **Certified Informational Copies** marked with the legend, **"Informational, Not A Valid Document to Establish Identity."**

Please indicate the type of certified copy you are requesting:

☐ I would like a **Certified Copy.** This copy will establish the identity of the registrant. (To receive a Certified Copy you **MUST INDICATE YOUR RELATIONSHIP TO THE REGISTRANT** by selecting from the list below **AND COMPLETE THE ATTACHED SWORN STATEMENT** declaring that you are eligible to receive the Certified Copy. The Sworn Statement **MUST BE NOTARIZED** if the application is submitted by mail **unless you are a law enforcement or local or state governmental agency**.)

☐ I would like a **Certified Informational Copy.** This document will be printed with a legend on the face of the document that states, **"INFORMATIONAL, NOT A VALID DOCUMENT TO ESTABLISH IDENTITY."**

(A Sworn Statement does not need to be provided.)

NOTE: Both documents are certified copies of the original document on file with our office. With the exception of the legend and redaction of signatures and Social Security Number, the documents contain the same information.

Fee: **$20 per copy** (payable to CDPH Vital Records). **PLEASE SUBMIT CHECK OR MONEY ORDER – DO NOT SEND CASH** (CDPH cannot be held responsible for fees paid in cash that are lost, misdirected, or undelivered).

PLEASE ATTACH CHECK HERE

To receive a **Certified Copy** I am:

☐ The registrant (person listed on the certificate) or a parent or legal guardian of the registrant. **(Legal guardian must provide documentation.)**

☐ A party entitled to receive the record as a result of a court order or an attorney or a licensed adoption agency seeking the birth record in order to comply with the requirements of Section 3140 or 7603 of the Family Code. **(Please include a copy of the court order.)**

☐ A member of a law enforcement agency or a representative of another governmental agency, as provided by law, who is conducting official business. **(Companies representing a government agency must provide authorization from the government agency.)**

☐ A child, grandparent, grandchild, brother or sister, spouse, or domestic partner of the registrant.

☐ An attorney representing the registrant or the registrant's estate, or any person or agency empowered by statute or appointed by a court to act on behalf of the registrant or the registrant's estate.

☐ Appointed rights in a power of attorney, or an executor of the registrant's estate. **(Please include a copy of the power of attorney, or supporting documentation identifying you as executor.)**

APPLICANT INFORMATION (PLEASE PRINT OR TYPE) Today's Date:

Agency Name (if applicable)		Agency Case Number	Inmate ID Number
Print Name of Applicant		Signature of Applicant	Purpose of Request
Mailing Address – Number, Street		Amount Enclosed – **DO NOT SEND CASH** $ ______ Check $ _____ Money Order	Number of Copies
City		Name of Person Receiving Copies, if Different from Applicant	
State/Province	ZIP Code	Mailing Address for Copies, if Different from Applicant	
Daytime Telephone (include area code) ( )	Country	City	State / ZIP Code

BIRTH RECORD INFORMATION (PLEASE PRINT OR TYPE) Adopted: ☐ No ☐ Yes (If Yes, see #4 on Page 2)

Complete the information below as shown on the birth record, to the best of your knowledge.

FIRST Name	**MIDDLE** Name	**LAST** Name
City of Birth (must be in California)		County of Birth
Date of Birth – MM/DD/CCYY (If unknown, enter approximate date of birth)		Sex ☐ Female ☐ Male
Father/Parent FIRST Name	**MIDDLE** Name	**LAST** Name (Before Marriage/Domestic Partnership)
Mother/Parent FIRST Name	**MIDDLE** Name	**LAST** Name (Before Marriage/Domestic Partnership)

SWORN STATEMENT

I, ________________________________, declare under penalty of perjury under the laws of the State of California,
(Applicant's Printed Name)

that I am an authorized person, as defined in California Health and Safety Code Section 103526 (c), and am eligible to receive a certified copy of the birth, death, or marriage certificate of the following individual(s):

Name of Person Listed on Certificate	**Applicant's Relationship to Person Listed on Certificate** **(Must Be a Relationship Listed on Page 1 of Application)**

(The remaining information must be completed in the presence of a Notary Public or CDPH Vital Records staff.)

Subscribed to this _______ day of ______________, 20___, at _________________________, ________________.
(Day) (Month) (City) (State)

____
(**Applicant's** Signature)

Note: If submitting your order by mail, you must have your Sworn Statement notarized using the Certificate of Acknowledgment below. The Certificate of Acknowledgment must be completed by a Notary Public. (Law enforcement and local and state governmental agencies are exempt from the notary requirement.)

CERTIFICATE OF ACKNOWLEDGMENT

State of ____________________)

County of ___________________)

On _______________ before me, _________________________________, personally appeared ____________________________,
(insert name and title of the officer)

who proved to me on the basis of satisfactory evidence to be the person(s) whose name(s) is/are subscribed to the within instrument and acknowledged to me that he/she/they executed the same in his/her/their authorized capacity(ies), and that by his/her/their signature(s) on the instrument the person(s), or the entity upon behalf of which the person(s) acted, executed the instrument. I certify under PENALTY OF PERJURY under the laws of the State of California that the foregoing paragraph is true and correct.

WITNESS my hand and official seal.
(SEAL)

____
SIGNATURE OF NOTARY PUBLIC

APPLICATION FOR CERTIFIED COPY OF MARRIAGE RECORD

PLEASE READ THE INSTRUCTIONS ON PAGE 2 BEFORE COMPLETING THIS APPLICATION

☐ I would like a **Certified Copy.** This copy will establish the identity of the registrant. (To receive a Certified Copy you **MUST INDICATE YOUR RELATIONSHIP TO THE REGISTRANT** (select from the list below) **AND COMPLETE THE ATTACHED SWORN STATEMENT** declaring that you are eligible to receive the Certified Copy. The Sworn Statement **MUST BE NOTARIZED** if the application is submitted by mail **unless you are a law enforcement or local or state governmental agency.)**	☐ I would like a **Certified Informational Copy**. This document will be printed with a legend on the face of the document that states, **"INFORMATIONAL, NOT A VALID DOCUMENT TO ESTABLISH IDENTITY."** **(A Sworn Statement does not need to be provided.)**

NOTE: Both documents are certified copies of the original document on file with our office. With the exception of the legend, the documents contain the same information.

Fee: **$14 per copy** (payable to CDPH Vital Records). **PLEASE SUBMIT CHECK OR MONEY ORDER – DO NOT SEND CASH**
(CDPH cannot be held responsible for fees paid in cash that are lost, misdirected, or undelivered).

PLEASE ATTACH CHECK HERE

To receive a **Certified Copy** I am:

- ☐ The registrant (person listed on the certificate) or a parent or legal guardian of the registrant. **(Legal guardian must provide documentation.)**
- ☐ A party entitled to receive the record as a result of a court order. **(Please include a copy of the court order.)**
- ☐ A member of a law enforcement agency or a representative of another governmental agency, as provided by law, who is conducting official business. **(Companies representing a government agency must provide authorization from the government agency.)**
- ☐ A child, grandparent, grandchild, brother or sister, spouse, or domestic partner of the registrant.
- ☐ An attorney representing the registrant or the registrant's estate, or any person or agency empowered by statute or appointed by a court to act on behalf of the registrant or the registrant's estate.
- ☐ Appointed rights in a power of attorney, or an executor of the registrant's estate. **(Please include a copy of the power of attorney, or supporting documentation identifying you as executor.)**

APPLICANT INFORMATION (PLEASE PRINT OR TYPE) Today's Date:

Agency Name (if applicable)	Agency Case Number	Inmate ID Number
Name of Applicant	Signature of Applicant	Purpose of Request
Mailing Address – Number, Street	Amount Enclosed – **DO NOT SEND CASH** $________ Check $_______ Money Order	Number of Copies

City		Mailing Address of Person Receiving Copies, if Different from Applicant		
State/Province	ZIP Code	Mailing Address for Copies, if Different from Applicant		
Daytime Telephone (include area code) ( )	Country	City	State	ZIP Code

MARRIAGE RECORD INFORMATION (PLEASE PRINT OR TYPE)

Complete** First Person and Second Person **information below as shown on the marriage record, to the best of your knowledge.

Name of First Person – **FIRST** Name	**MIDDLE** Name	**CURRENT LAST** Name	**LAST** Name (Before Marriage/Domestic Partnership)
Date of Birth (MM/DD/CCYY)	County of Birth (CA **ONLY**)	**Father/Parent** of First Person (First, Middle, Last)	
Name of Second Person – **FIRST** Name	**MIDDLE** Name	**CURRENT LAST** Name	**LAST** Name (Before Marriage/Domestic Partnership)
Date of Birth (MM/DD/CCYY)	County of Birth (CA **ONLY**)	**Father/Parent** of Second Person (First, Middle, Last)	
Date of Marriage – Month, Day, Year	If Date Unknown, Enter Year(s)	County That Issued License	County Where Marriage Took Place

SWORN STATEMENT

I, ______________________________, declare under penalty of perjury under the laws of the State of California,
(**Applicant's** Printed Name)

that I am an authorized person, as defined in California Health and Safety Code Section 103526 (c), and am eligible to receive a certified copy of the birth, death, or marriage certificate of the following individual(s):

Name of Person Listed on Certificate	**Applicant's Relationship to Person Listed on Certificate** **(Must Be a Relationship Listed on Page 1 of Application)**

(The remaining information must be completed in the presence of a Notary Public or CDPH Vital Records staff.)

Subscribed to this ______ day of ______________, 20___, at ______________________________, ____________.
(Day) (Month) (City) (State)

____
(**Applicant's** Signature)

Note: If submitting your order by mail, you must have your Sworn Statement notarized using the Certificate of Acknowledgment below. The Certificate of Acknowledgment must be completed by a Notary Public. (Law enforcement and local and state governmental agencies are exempt from the notary requirement.)

CERTIFICATE OF ACKNOWLEDGMENT

State of ______________________)

County of _____________________)

On ___________before me, ______________________________, personally appeared ______________________________,
(insert name and title of the officer)

who proved to me on the basis of satisfactory evidence to be the person(s) whose name(s) is/are subscribed to the within instrument and acknowledged to me that he/she/they executed the same in his/her/their authorized capacity(ies), and that by his/her/their signature(s) on the instrument the person(s), or the entity upon behalf of which the person(s) acted, executed the instrument. I certify under PENALTY OF PERJURY under the laws of the State of California that the foregoing paragraph is true and correct

WITNESS my hand and official seal.
(SEAL)

____
SIGNATURE OF NOTARY PUBLIC

APPLICATION FOR CERTIFIED COPY OF DIVORCE RECORD

INFORMATION:

Divorce records have been maintained in the California Department of Public Health Vital Records only from **1962 to June 1984**. For these years, we are only able to provide you with a Certificate of Record, which identifies the names of the parties, filing date, county, and case number of the divorce. Copies of the **actual divorce decree** can only be obtained from the Superior Court in the county where the divorce took place. ***Our processing time for divorce records can be quite lengthy and may exceed six months.***

INSTRUCTIONS:

1. Complete a separate application for each divorce record requested.
2. Complete the **Applicant Information** section and provide your signature where indicated. Provide both **First Person and Second Person** information to identify the divorce record. If the information you furnish is incomplete or inaccurate, we may not be able to locate the record.
3. Submit $13 for **each** copy requested. If no divorce record is found, the fee will be retained for searching the record (as required by law) and a "Certificate of No Public Record" will be issued to the applicant. Indicate the number of copies you want and include the correct fee(s) in the form of a personal check or postal or bank money order (International Money Order for out-of-country requests) made payable to **CDPH Vital Records**. **PLEASE SUBMIT CHECK OR MONEY ORDER – DO NOT SEND CASH** (CDPH cannot be held responsible for fees paid in cash that are lost, misdirected, or undelivered).
4. Mail completed applications with the fee(s) to:

California Department of Public Heath
Vital Records – MS 5103
P.O. Box 997410
Sacramento, CA 95899-7410
(916) 445-2684

PLEASE ATTACH CHECK HERE

Fee: **$13 per copy** (payable to CDPH Vital Records). **PLEASE SUBMIT CHECK OR MONEY ORDER – DO NOT SEND CASH**
(CDPH cannot be held responsible for fees paid in cash that are lost, misdirected, or undelivered).

APPLICANT INFORMATION (PLEASE PRINT OR TYPE)		**Today's Date:**		
Agency Name (if applicable)		Agency Case Number	Inmate ID Number	
Print Name of Applicant		Signature of Applicant	Purpose of Request	
Mailing Address – Number, Street		Amount Enclosed – **DO NOT SEND CASH** $ ________Check $ ________Money Order	Number of Copies	
City		Mailing Address of Person Receiving Copies, if Different from Applicant		
State/Province	ZIP Code	Mailing Address for Copies, if Different from Applicant		
Daytime Telephone (include area code) ( )	Country	City	State	ZIP Code

DIVORCE RECORD INFORMATION (PLEASE PRINT OR TYPE) ***Complete** First Person **and** Second Person **information below as shown on the divorce record, to the best of your knowledge.***			
Name of First Person – **FIRST** Name	**MIDDLE** Name	**CURRENT LAST** Name	**LAST** Name (Before Marriage/Domestic Partnership)
Name of Second Person – **FIRST** Name	**MIDDLE** Name	**CURRENT LAST** Name	**LAST** Name (Before Marriage/Domestic Partnership)
Date of Divorce – Month, Day, Year (If Date Unknown, Enter Year(s))	County of Divorce		

DIVORCE

APPLICATION FOR CERTIFIED COPY OF DEATH RECORD

PLEASE READ THE INSTRUCTIONS ON PAGE 2 BEFORE COMPLETING THIS APPLICATION

As part of statewide efforts to prevent identity theft, California law (Health and Safety Code Section 103526) permits only authorized individuals as listed on the application to receive certified copies of death records. All others will be issued **Certified Informational Copies** marked with the legend, **"Informational, Not A Valid Document to Establish Identity."**
Please indicate the type of certified copy you are requesting:

☐ I would like a **Certified Copy.** This copy will establish the identity of the registrant. (To receive a Certified Copy you **MUST INDICATE YOUR RELATIONSHIP TO THE REGISTRANT** by selecting from the list below **AND COMPLETE THE ATTACHED SWORN STATEMENT** declaring that you are eligible to receive the Certified Copy. The Sworn Statement **MUST BE NOTARIZED** if the application is submitted by mail **unless you are a law enforcement or local or state governmental agency**.)

☐ I would like a **Certified Informational Copy.** This document will be printed with a legend on the face of the document that states, **"INFORMATIONAL, NOT A VALID DOCUMENT TO ESTABLISH IDENTITY."**

(A Sworn Statement does not need to be provided.)

NOTE: Both documents are certified copies of the original document on file with our office. With the exception of the legend and redaction of signatures, the documents contain the same information.

Fee: **$16 per copy** (payable to CDPH Vital Records). **PLEASE SUBMIT CHECK OR MONEY ORDER – DO NOT SEND CASH**
(CDPH cannot be held responsible for fees paid in cash that are lost, misdirected, or undelivered).

PLEASE ATTACH CHECK HERE

To receive a **Certified Copy** I am:

- ☐ A parent or legal guardian of the registrant (person listed on the certificate). **(Legal guardian must provide documentation.)**
- ☐ A party entitled to receive the record as a result of a court order. **(Please include a copy of the court order.)**
- ☐ A member of a law enforcement agency or a representative of another governmental agency, as provided by law, who is conducting official business. **(Companies representing a government agency must provide authorization from the government agency.)**
- ☐ A child, grandparent, grandchild, brother or sister, spouse, or domestic partner of the registrant.
- ☐ An attorney representing the registrant or the registrant's estate, or any person or agency empowered by statute or appointed by a court to act on behalf of the registrant or the registrant's estate.
- ☐ Any agent or employee of a funeral establishment who acts within the course and scope of his or her employment and who orders certified copies of a death certificate on behalf of an individual specified in paragraphs (1) to (5), inclusive, of subdivision (a) of Section 7100 of the Health and Safety Code.
- ☐ Appointed rights in a power of attorney, or an executor of the registrant's estate. **(Please include a copy of the power of attorney, or supporting documentation identifying you as executor.)**

APPLICANT INFORMATION (PLEASE PRINT OR TYPE) Today's Date:

Agency Name (if applicable)		Agency Case Number	Inmate ID Number
Print Name of Applicant		Signature of Applicant	Purpose of Request
Mailing Address – Number, Street		Amount Enclosed – **DO NOT SEND CASH** $______Check $______Money Order	Number of Copies
City		Name of Person Receiving Copies, if Different from Applicant	
State/Province	ZIP Code	Mailing Address for Copies, if Different from Applicant	
Daytime Telephone (include area code) ( )	Country	City / State / ZIP Code	

DEATH RECORD INFORMATION (PLEASE PRINT OR TYPE)

Complete the information below as shown on the death record, to the best of your knowledge.

DECEDENT FIRST Name	**MIDDLE** Name	**LAST** Name	Sex ☐ Female ☐ Male
City of Death (must be in California)	County of Death	Date of Birth – MM/DD/CCYY	State of Birth
Date of Death – MM/DD/CCYY (Or Period of Years to be Searched)		Social Security Number	
Mother/Parent Name (First, Middle, Last)		Name of Spouse/Domestic Partner of Decedent (First, Middle, Last)	

SWORN STATEMENT

I, ______________________________, declare under penalty of perjury under the laws of the State of California,
(**Applicant's** Printed Name)

that I am an authorized person, as defined in California Health and Safety Code Section 103526 (c), and am eligible to receive a certified copy of the birth, death, or marriage certificate of the following individual(s):

Name of Person Listed on Certificate	Applicant's Relationship to Person Listed on Certificate (Must Be a Relationship Listed on Page 1 of Application)

(The remaining information must be completed in the presence of a Notary Public or CDPH Vital Records staff.)

Subscribed to this _______ day of _____________, 20___, at ________________________, _______________.
(Day) (Month) (City) (State)

____
(**Applicant's** Signature)

Note: If submitting your order by mail, you must have your Sworn Statement notarized using the Certificate of Acknowledgment below. The Certificate of Acknowledgment must be completed by a Notary Public. (Law enforcement and local and state governmental agencies are exempt from the notary requirement.)

CERTIFICATE OF ACKNOWLEDGMENT

State of ___________________)

County of __________________)

On _______________ before me, ______________________________, personally appeared ____________________________,
(insert name and title of the officer)

who proved to me on the basis of satisfactory evidence to be the person(s) whose name(s) is/are subscribed to the within instrument and acknowledged to me that he/she/they executed the same in his/her/their authorized capacity(ies), and that by his/her/their signature(s) on the instrument the person(s), or the entity upon behalf of which the person(s) acted, executed the instrument. I certify under PENALTY OF PERJURY under the laws of the State of California that the foregoing paragraph is true and correct.

WITNESS my hand and official seal.
(SEAL)

____
SIGNATURE OF NOTARY PUBLIC

COLORADO

Send your requests to:

Colorado Department of Public Health and Environment
Vital Records Section
4300 Cherry Creek Drive South
HSVRD-VR-A1
Denver, CO 80246-1530

Tel. (303) 692-2200
Fax (800) 423-1108
E-mail: vital.records@state.co.us
www.colorado.gov/cs/Satellite/CDPHE-CHEIS/CBON/1251593016787

The Vital Records Section has birth records from 1910 and death records from 1900. Births that occurred more than 100 years ago (unless that person is still alive) and deaths that occurred more than 50 years ago are public records. Certified copies of certificates are also available from county offices.

Marriage records for the entire state are available for the following years: 1900 to 1939, and 1975 to present. Verifications for the years 1940 to 1974 must be obtained from the county where the license was obtained. Dissolution (divorce, separation, and annulment) records for the entire state are available for the following years: 1851 to 1939 and 1968 to present, but verifications for the years 1940 to 1967 must be obtained from the county where the dissolution was decreed. The verifications for the years 1851 to 1939 also contain date of marriage and children of marriage.

Cost for a certified Birth Certificate	$17.75
Cost for a certified verification of a Marriage Record	$17.00
Cost for Heirloom Birth and Marriage Certificates	$35.00
Cost for a certified verification of a Divorce Record	$17.00
Cost for a certified Death Certificate	$20.00
Cost for an Heirloom Death Certificate	$50.00
Cost for a duplicate Birth, Marriage, or Divorce Record, when ordered at the same time	$10.00
Cost for a duplicate Death Record, when ordered at the same time	$13.00

For Genealogy Research:

The Colorado State Archives (1313 Sherman Street, Denver, CO 80203; www.colorado.gov/dpa/doit/archives/geneal.htm) has numerous indexes to vital records, many searchable online at www.colorado.gov/dpa/doit/archives/hrd/HRD.htm.

The Vital Records Section maintains a web page with information on locating early vital records and other helpful links; look for the "genealogy" tab on their website.

For Adoption Record information, contact:

Colorado Voluntary Adoption Registry
Health Statistics and Vital Records
4300 Cherry Creek Drive South (HSVR-VR-A1)
Denver, CO 80246-1530

Tel. (303) 692-2188

Cost for registration with the Adoption Registry	$20.00

Colorado Department of Public Health and Environment

Colorado Birth Certificate Request

Apply in person for same-day services
Walk-in Hours: Monday-Friday 8:30 – 4:30
Correction Hours: Monday-Friday 8:30 – 3:30

Vital Records Section HSVR-VR-A1
4300 Cherry Creek Drive South
Denver, CO 80246-1530
www.colorado.gov/cdphe/vitalrecords
Email: vital.records@state.co.us
Phone: (303) 692-2200

Phone Orders: 1-866-300-8540
Online Orders: www.vitalchek.com
Phone/Online Follow-Up:
1-866-632-2604
Fax Orders: 1-800-423-1108

Colorado has birth records for the entire state since 1910. Birth certificates are also available from the county office(s); for all county locations visit http://www.colorado.gov/cdphe/vitalrecords

✓ **Requirements:**
- ❑ This request must be completed in full.
- ❑ Enclose a copy of a current driver's license, passport or State identification. (See reverse side for complete list for primary and secondary ID's)
- ❑ Enclose appropriate fees
- ❑ Person requesting to receive a birth certificate must sign below.
- ❑ Proof of Relationship is required (Parents and Registrant excluded)
- ❑ Enclose a copy of the death certificate if the person is deceased.

Requestor Information

Print name of person making request	First	Middle	Last		Email:
Mailing Address	Apt# City		State	Zip	Daytime Phone ( )
Physical Address	Apt# City		State	Zip	Alt Phone Number ( )

Relationship to Registrant (person named on certificate)*see reverse side: ❑ Self ❑ Parent ❑ Grandparent ❑ Step-parent ❑ Sibling ❑ Spouse ❑ Child ❑ Stepchild ❑ Legal guardian ❑ Legal representative ❑ Other:

Reason for Request: ❑ Newborn ❑ Travel/Passport ❑ Records ❑ School ❑ Insurance ❑ Other:

Registrant Information

Information about person whose birth certificate is being requested – Please type or print
If **adopted**, provide adoptive information and see special service on other side.

Full Name at Birth	First	Middle	Last
Date of Birth	Month Day Year	Is this Person Deceased?	❑ Yes ❑ No *If yes, must provide a copy of the death certificate*
Place of Birth	City	County	State **Colorado ONLY**
Full Name of Father	First	Middle	Last
Full Name of Mother	First	Middle	**Maiden Last Name** (name prior to first marriage)

Pursuant to Colorado Revised Statutes, 1982, 25-2-118 and as defined by Colorado Board of Health Rules and Regulations, applicant must have a direct and tangible interest in the record requested. The penalties for obtaining a record under false pretenses include a fine of not more than $1,000.00, or imprisonment in the county jail for not more than one year or both such fine and imprisonment (CRS 25-2-118).

By signing below, I have read and understand that there are penalties for obtaining a record under false pretenses. Today's date

SIGN HERE

Ways to Order:

****Order certificates online** at www.colorado.gov/cdphe/vitalrecords Certificate(s) mailed 3-5 days after receipt of all required documentation.
****Fax your application** with credit card information: within continental U.S. fax 1-800-423-1108; outside continental U.S. fax 1-303-691-9307. Certificate(s) mailed at the end of five business days upon receipt of all required documentation.
Mail in application with check, money order, or credit card information. Make check or money order payable to Vital Records. Please do not send cash. Certificate(s) mailed within three weeks upon receipt of all required documentation

****Credit card orders:**

Card Type: ❑ VISA ❑ MasterCard ❑ Discover ❑ American Express

Cardholder name: ______

Card Number: ______

Expiration Date: ___/___
** $10.00 convenience charge to be added

Charges: (FEES NON-REFUNDABLE)
Cost of certificates:
$17.75 for one (or search when no record found)........ ______
$10.00 for each additional certificate of same record ordered at same time........ ______
$10.00 credit card convenience charge (walk-ins excluded)........ ______
$35 for each heirloom certificate........ ______

Please check your shipping method:
❑ Regular mail ($0.00)
❑ FedEx* (check, money order, cash orders ONLY) ($20.00)
❑ Express Mail* ($19.95)
❑ UPS* (credit card orders ONLY)($19.00)

Total Charges........ ______
*Within continental U.S.

***Certified birth certificates may be issued to:**

Please note that proof of relationship is required if your name is not listed on the birth certificate: (e.g. marriage certificates, birth certificates, court orders)

The registrant (person named on the certificate)
Parents
Grandparents
Great grandparents
Grandchild
Stepparents
Siblings
Spouse
Adult children
Legal guardian
Legal representatives of any of the above must present proof of client relationship
For complete list visit: http://www.colorado.gov/cdphe/vitalrecords

The Office of the State Registrar ov Vital Statistics requires the following documentation:

At least 1 of the following:
(No expired documents accepted)

'Primary' List:

- Alien Registration Receipt/Permanent
- Resident Card
- Certificate of U.S. Citizenship
- City of Denver County Jail Inmate ID
- Colorado Department of Corrections ID card
- CO Temporary Driver's License (with hole-punched Driver's License)
- Department of Human Services Youth Corrections ID
- Employment Authorization Card (I-766)
- Foreign Passport
- Government Work ID
- Job Corps ID
- Photo Driver's License
- Photo ID Card (DMV)
- School, University or College ID Card (must be current)
- Temporary Resident Card
- U.S. B1/B2 Visa card with I-94
- U.S. Certificate of Naturalization
- U.S. Citizenship ID Card (I-197)
- U.S. Military ID Card
- U.S. Passport

Or at least 2 of the following:
(Any document expired more than six months will not be accepted)

'Secondary' List:

- Acknowledgment of Paternity document (Colorado only)
- Birth Certificate of Applicant (U.S. only)
- Court order of adoption or name change
- Craft or trade license (Colorado only)
- DD-214
- Divorce Decree (U.S. only)
- Hospital birth worksheet (ID for mothers- within 6 months of event)
- Hunting or Fishing License (must be current-Colorado only)
- IRS-TIN card
- Marriage license (U.S. only)
- Medicare Card
- Merchant mariner card
- Mexican voter registration card
- Motor vehicle registration or title (must be current -U.S. only)
- Pilot license
- Selective Service Card (U.S. only)
- Social Security Card
- Social Services Card (Medicaid, WIC)
- State or Federal Prison or Corrections Card
- Tribal ID Card
- Weapon or gun permit (U.S. only)
- Work ID, Paycheck Stub (within 3 months), or W-2 (last tax year)
- Any Expired document from the "Primary" List (cannot be expired more than 6 months)

We are sorry, but we cannot accept:

- Matricula Consular Card
- Novelty ID Card
- Non-expiring Identification Cards
- City or County Prison/Jail ID
- Souvenir Birth Certificates
- Temporary Driver's Licenses or Temporary State ID Card

If you cannot provide acceptable identification, it is suggested that you ask a spouse, parent, grandparent, sibling, or adult child, who can provide appropriate identification, to request the certificate. Proof of relationship is required, such as a birth certificate or marriage certificate.

*****OPTION AVAILABLE FOR ADOPTIONS*****

Only an adoptive parent or adopted person is eligible for this special service. ONLY sign below if you wish the statement "ISSUED PURSUANT TO ADOPTION" to appear on the birth certificate which indicates this person is adopted.

SIGN HERE

Signature of: ❑ adopted person ❑ adoptive parent
Relationship to registrant (chek one ✔)

Number of copies to be issued with "Issued pursuant to adoption" requested: _____

COLORADO DEPARTMENT OF PUBLIC HEALTH AND ENVIRONMENT
VITAL RECORDS SECTION/HSVRD-VR-A1
4300 Cherry Creek Drive South
Denver, Colorado 80246-1530

303-692-2200 www.colorado.gov/cdphe/vitalrecords vital.records@state.co.us

For Office Use Only			
ID	____	Cash	____
ISS	____	CK	____
		CC	____
		Other	____
SF#	____-________		

Application for Certified Verification of a Marriage Record

INFORMATION ABOUT PERSONS WHOSE MARRIAGE RECORD IS REQUESTED -- please type or print

This office has indices for 1900 to 1939 and 1975 to present.

Name of Husband	First	Middle	Last
Name of Wife	First	Middle	Last
County Where License Was Issued		Date of Marriage*	Today's Date
Purpose for copy		Relationship **see reverse side (Please submit proof of relationship)	
Signature of Person Making Request		e-mail address ^	Daytime Phone ( )
Street Address	City	State	Zip

^ I consent for communications via e-mail

All requests must be accompanied by a photocopy of the requestor's identification before processing. PLEASE RETURN YOUR REQUEST WITH A PHOTOCOPY OF YOUR DRIVER'S LICENSE, STATE ID OR PASSPORT.

This office will not have a record of the marriage if the county did not forward the information for the State Index. Verifications for the years 1940-1974 are not available from this office and must be obtained from the county where the license was obtained. You may need to contact each of the counties if you do not know where the license was obtained. County clerk offices are located in the county seat. A list of counties, county seats, and ZIP codes is provided on the reverse side of this form.

Ways to order:

Apply in person for same day service. Office hours are from 8:30 a.m. to 4:30 p.m., Monday-Friday.

Order verifications online** at http://www.cdphe.state.co.us/certs. Verification(s) mailed mailed 2-3 days after receipt of all required documentation.

Fax your application with credit card information**: within continental USA fax 1-800-423-1108; outside continental USA fax:1-303-691-9307. Verification(s) mailed in five business days upon receipt of all required documentation.

Mail in application with check, money order, or credit card information**. Verification(s) mailed within three weeks upon receipt of all required documentation.

**Convenience charge to be added. See fees below.

Make check or money order payable to to Vital Records. Please do not send cash.

Credit card orders:

Card Type: ☐ VISA ☐ MasterCard ☐ Discover ☐ American Express

Cardholder name: ____________________

Card Number: ____________________ Exp. Date: ____/____

*NOTE: If date is unknown, an additional fee of $1.00 per year can be submitted.

Charges: (FEES NON-REFUNDABLE)

Search fee where date of marriage is unknown....................................	$________
$17 for 1st standard copy (or search when no record found).................	$________
$10 for each additional copy of same record ordered at same time...........	$________
$10 credit card convenience charge (walk-ins excluded).......................	$________
$35 for each heirloom copy............	$________
a) Regular mail ($0.00) b) FedEx* (check, money order, cash orders ONLY) ($20.00) c) Express Mail* ($19.95) d) UPS* (credit card orders ONLY)($19.00) (circle one)...	$________
Total Charges..................................	$________

*Within continental U.S.

PLEASE COMPLETE THIS AREA

PRINT name and address of person to whom the verification is to be mailed to or issued to over the counter:

____
Name

____
Address

____
City/State/Zip

marigver.pdf (08/13)

COLORADO DEPARTMENT OF PUBLIC HEALTH AND ENVIRONMENT
VITAL RECORDS SECTION/HSVRD-VR-A1
4300 Cherry Creek Drive South
Denver, Colorado 80246-1530
303-692-2200 vital.records@state.co.us
www.colorado.gov/cdphe/vitalrecords

For Office Use Only			
ID	____	Cash	____
ISS	____	CK	____
		CC	____
		Other	____
SF#	____-________		

Application for Certified Verification of a Dissolution of Marriage

INFORMATION ABOUT PERSONS WHOSE MARRIAGE DISSOLUTION IS REQUESTED -- *please type or print*
This office has indices for 1851 to 1939 and 1968 to present.

* The verifications for the years **(1851-1939)** also contain date of marriage and children of marriage

Name of Husband	First	Middle	Last
Name of Wife	First	Middle	Last
County Where Decree Was Issued		Date of Decree*	Today's Date
Purpose for copy	Relationship **see reverse side (Please submit proof of relationship)		
Signature of Person Making Request	e-mail address ^	Daytime Phone ( )	
Street Address	City	State	Zip

^ I consent for communications via e-mail

All requests must be accompanied by a photocopy of the requestor's identification before processing. PLEASE RETURN YOUR REQUEST WITH A PHOTOCOPY OF YOUR DRIVER'S LICENSE, STATE ID OR PASSPORT.

This office will not have a record of the divorce, separation, or annulment if the county did not forward the information for the State Index. Verifications for the years 1940-1967 are not available from this office and must be obtained from the county where the dissolution was decreed. You may need to contact each of the counties if you do not know where the decree was granted. District courts are located in the county seat. A list of counties, county seats, and ZIP codes is provided for your convenience on the reverse side of this form.

Ways to order:

- Apply in person for same day service. Office hours are from 8:30 a.m. to 4:30 p.m., Monday-Friday.
- Order verifications online** at www.state.co.gov/cdphe/vitalrecords. Verification(s) mailed mailed 2-3 days after receipt of all required documentation.
- Fax your application with credit card information:** within continental USA fax 1-800-423-1108; outside continental USA fax:1-303-691-9307. Verification(s) mailed in five business days upon receipt of all required documentation.
- Mail in application with check, money order, or credit card information**. Verification(s) mailed within three weeks upon receipt of all required documentation.

**Convenience charge to be added. See fees below.

**NOTE: If date is unknown, an additional fee of $1.00 per year can be submitted.*

Make check or money order payable to to Vital Records Section. Please do not send cash.

Credit card orders:

Card Type: ☐ VISA ☐ MasterCard ☐ Discover ☐ American Express

Cardholder name: ________________________

Card Number: ________________ Exp. Date: ____/____

Charges: (FEES NON-REFUNDABLE)

Search fee where date of dissolution is unknown....................................	$________
$17 for 1st standard copy (or search when no record found)..................	$________
$10 for each additional copy of same record ordered at same time...........	$________
$10 credit card convenience charge (walk-ins excluded)........................	$________
a) Regular mail ($0.00) b) FedEx* (check, money order, cash orders ONLY) ($20.00) c) Express Mail* ($19.95) d) UPS* (credit card orders ONLY)($19.00) (circle one)...	$________
Total Charges..................................	$________

*Within continental U.S.

PLEASE COMPLETE THIS AREA

PRINT name and address of person to whom the verification is to be mailed to or issued to over the counter:

____
Name

____
Address

____
City/State/Zip

FOR OFFICE USE ONLY:
____pick up ____call
____mail ____email

Colorado Department of Public Health and Environment

Colorado Death Certificate Request

Apply in person for same-day services
Walk-in Hours: Monday-Friday 8:30 – 4:30
Correction Hours: Monday-Friday 8:30 – 3:30

Vital Records Section HSVR-VR-A1
4300 Cherry Creek Drive South
Denver, CO 80246-1530
www.colorado.gov/cdphe/vitalrecords
Email: vital.records@state.co.us
Phone: (303) 692-2200

Phone Orders: 1-866-300-8540
Online Orders: www.vitalchek.com
Phone/Online Follow-Up:
1-866-632-2604
Fax Orders: 1-800-423-1108

This office has death certificates for the entire state since 1900. Death certificates are also available in the county Vital Records office where the death occurred. Death certificates are considered public record after 75 years

✓ **Requirements:**
- ☐ This request must be completed in full.
- ☐ Enclose a copy of a current driver's license, passport or State identification. (The complete list of primary and secondary ID's are available online at www.colorado.gov/cdphe/vitalrecords)
- ☐ Enclose appropriate fees.
- ☐ Person requesting to receive death certificate must sign below.
- ☐ Proof of relationship or legal interested is required (see reverse side).

Requestor Information

Print name of person making request	First	Middle	Last		Email:
Mailing Address	City	State	Zip		Daytime Phone ( )
Physical Address	City	State	Zip		Alt Phone Number ( )

Relationship to deceased **(must sibmit proof of relationship)** ***see reverse side**
☐ Parent ☐ Spouse ☐ Grandparent ☐ Sibling ☐ Child ☐ Funeral Director
☐ Legal Representative ☐ Other:

Reason for Request: ☐ Insurance ☐ Social Security ☐ Property ☐ Genealogy ☐ Other:

Deceased Information

☐ Check here if you are requesting a certificate of stillbirth

Full Name of deceased	First			Middle	Last	
Date of death* (or range of dates)	Month	Day	Year __ __ __ __	Date of birth or age at death (optional)		State of birth (optional)
Place of death	City			County	State **Colorado ONLY**	

Pursuant to Colorado Revised Statutes, 1982, 25-2-118 and as defined by Colorado Board of Health Rules and Regulations, applicant must have a direct and tangible interest in the record requested. The penalties for obtaining a record under false pretenses include a fine of not more than $1,000.00, or imprisonment in the county jail for not more than one year or both such fine and imprisonment (CRS 25-2-118).

By signing below, I have read and understand that there are penalties for obtaining a record under false pretenses. Today's date

SIGN HERE

Ways to Order:
- ****Order certificates online** at www.vitalchek.com Certificate(s) mailed 3-5 days after receipt of all required documentation.
- ****Fax your application** with credit card information: within continental U.S. fax 1-800-423-1108; outside continental U.S. fax 1-303-691-9307 Certificate(s) mailed at the end of five business days upon receipt of all required documentation
- **Mail in application** with check, money order, or credit card information. Make check or money order payable to Vital Records. Please do not send cash. Certificate(s) mailed within three weeks upon receipt of all required documentation.
- Apply in person for same-day service. Office hours are from 8:30 a.m. to 4:30 p.m., Monday-Friday.

****Credit card orders:** ($10.00 convenience charge to be added)

Card Type: ☐ VISA ☐ MasterCard ☐ Discover ☐ American Express

Cardholder name: ______________________

Cardholder signature: ______________________

Card Number: ______________________

Expiration Date: ____/____

Charges: (FEES NON-REFUNDABLE)

***Search fee where date of death is unknown**
($1.00 per year)........ ______

Cost of standard death certificate:
$20.00 for one (or search when no record found)........ ______
$13.00 for each additional certificate of same record ordered at same time........ ______
$10.00 credit card convenience charge (walk-ins excluded)........ ______

Cost of verification of death:
$20.00 for one (or search when no record is found)........ ______
$13.00 for additional verifications of same record ordered at the same time........ ______

Please check your shipping method:
☐ Regular mail ($0.00)
☐ FedEx* (check, money order, cash orders ONLY) ($20.00)
☐ Express Mail* ($19.95)
☐ UPS* (credit card orders ONLY)($19.00)
.... ______

Total Charges........ ______

CONNECTICUT

Send your requests to:

Connecticut State Department of Public Health
State Office of Vital Records
410 Capitol Avenue, MS#11VRS
P.O. Box 340308
Hartford, CT 06134-0308

Tel. (860) 509-7700
Fax (860) 509-7964
www.ct.gov/dph/site/default.asp

The State Office of Vital Records has birth, marriage, and death records from January 1, 1897. It also has death indexes 1949–present and marriage indexes 1959–present. For vital records prior to that date, contact the town where the vital event occurred. Connecticut restricts access to birth records for the past 100 years; however, all marriage and death certificates are open to the public. Certificate requests for events that occurred in Hartford should be directed to the Hartford Vital Records Registrar (550 Main Street, Hartford, CT 06103), unless a *state* certified copy of the vital record is needed.

For faster processing, you can obtain an official, certified copy of a birth, death, or marriage certificate from the town where the event occurred. Vital records offices are located in each of the 169 towns in Connecticut; each maintains a registry of all births, marriages, civil unions, deaths, and fetal deaths that occur within that town. A list of town and city clerks/registrars is available at www.ct.gov/dph/lib/dph/hisr/PDF/CT_TownCityClerks.pdf. There are separate forms to use if you apply from the town/city rather than from the state.

Cost for a certified Birth Certificate from the state office	$30.00
Cost for a certified Birth Certificate from the town	$20.00
Cost for a wallet-size Birth Certificate from the town	$15.00
Cost for a certified Marriage Certificate	$20.00
Cost for a copy of Civil Union Certificate	$20.00
Cost for a certified Death Certificate	$20.00

For Divorce Records, contact:

Clerk of Superior Court
(Town), CT

See www.jud.state.ct.us/external/super/default.htm for a list of Superior Courts.

For Genealogy Research:

If you are a current member of a genealogical society that is incorporated or authorized to do business or conduct affairs in Connecticut (see the current list at www.cslib.org/genesoc.htm), you are entitled to access all vital records except confidential files on adoption, paternity, gender re-assignment, and gestational agreements. You may call for an appointment to search the vital records at a local town or at the State Office of Vital Records. For pre-1897 records, contact the local vital records office or the History and Genealogy Unit of the Connecticut State Library (231 Capitol Avenue, Hartford, CT 06106; tel. 860-757-6580; www.cslib.org/handg.htm). The Library's Barbour Collection of Connecticut Town Vital Records is the chief resource in Connecticut genealogy.

Most vital records to about 1900 have been microfilmed by the Genealogical Society of Utah and are available for use at the Connecticut State Library or through LDS FamilySearch Centers.

For Adoption Record information, contact:

Office of Foster and Adoption Services
Department of Children and Families
Search Unit
505 Hudson Street
Hartford, CT 06106-7107

Tel. (888) 550-6582
www.ct.gov/dcf/site/default.asp

The Department of Children and Families has a master database that lists all adoptions, both public and private, that have occurred in Connecticut since 1944. For adoptions prior to 1944, the adoptee should contact the Probate Court that handled the adoption.

REQUEST FOR A CERTIFIED COPY OF A BIRTH RECORD FROM THE TOWN

Mail this request to the Town Vital Records office. For the address and phone number of Town Vital Records offices in Connecticut, please refer to the Town website or the DPH website at www.ct.gov/dph.

PLEASE PRINT

FULL NAME ON CERTIFICATE*: ______________________
FIRST MIDDLE LAST NAME

DATE OF BIRTH: ____/____/____ **PLACE OF BIRTH:** ______________________
MONTH DAY YEAR TOWN/CITY

FATHER'S FULL NAME: ______________________
FIRST MIDDLE LAST NAME

MOTHER'S MAIDEN NAME: ______________________
FIRST MIDDLE LAST NAME

PERSON MAKING THIS REQUEST:

NAME: ______________________
FIRST MIDDLE LAST NAME

ADDRESS: ______________________
NUMBER/STREET/UNIT #

TOWN/CITY: ____________ **STATE:** ________ **ZIP CODE:** ________

TELEPHONE NO: ____________ **E-MAIL ADDRESS:** ____________

SIGNATURE: X______________________

RELATION TO PERSON NAMED ON CERTIFICATE: ______________________

REASON FOR MAKING REQUEST: ______________________

CERTIFICATE SIZE:

FULL SIZE	WALLET SIZE	TOTAL NUMBER OF COPIES:
$20.00 EACH NUMBER OF COPIES: ________	The wallet size birth certificate contains less information than the full size certificate. It does not satisfy the proof of identification requirements needed for a passport or a driver's license. **$15.00 EACH** NUMBER OF COPIES: ________	______ X $20.00 = $ ______ ______ X $15.00 = $ ______ TOTAL: $ ______ **Send Postal Money Order Only. Do Not Mail Cash or Personal Checks.**

Attach a copy of the requester's valid government issued photo ID or passport below:

Or two (2) forms of the following:

- Social security (SS) card
- Paycheck Stub or a W-2 form that contains the SS #
- Current school or college photo ID
- Automobile registration
- Copy of utility bill or bank statement showing name and address
- See website ct.gov\dph for other forms of ID accepted

Please mail the completed request with the following required documents:

Money order made payable to City/Town (refer to the Town or DPH website cited above)

Current government issued photo ID

(If applicable) verification of relationship to the registrant (for example, an individual requesting his/her parent's birth certificate must provide a certified copy of his/her own birth certificate).

*If adopted, please provide your adoptive name and adoptive parents' information.
*If the requester had a legal name change, please provide a copy of the court documents authorizing the name change.

STATE OF CONNECTICUT DEPARTMENT OF PUBLIC HEALTH
VITAL RECORDS SECTION, CUSTOMER SERVICES
410 CAPITOL AVENUE, MS #11VRS
P.O. BOX 340308
HARTFORD, CT 06134-0308

REQUEST FOR A CERTIFIED COPY OF A BIRTH RECORD FROM THE STATE

FEE: $30.00 PER COPY. REMIT MONEY ORDER MADE PAYABLE TO: 'TREASURER, STATE OF CT'

PLEASE PRINT

FULL NAME ON CERTIFICATE*: ______________________________
FIRST MIDDLE LAST NAME

DATE OF BIRTH: _____/_____/_____ **PLACE OF BIRTH:** ______________________
MONTH DAY YEAR TOWN/CITY

FATHER'S FULL NAME: ______________________________
FIRST MIDDLE LAST NAME

MOTHER'S MAIDEN NAME: ______________________________
FIRST MIDDLE LAST NAME

PERSON MAKING THIS REQUEST:

NAME: ______________________________
FIRST MIDDLE LAST NAME

ADDRESS: ______________________________
NUMBER/STREET/UNIT #

TOWN/CITY: ____________ **STATE:** ______ **ZIP CODE:** ______

TELEPHONE NO: ____________ **E-MAIL ADDRESS:** ____________

SIGNATURE: X______________________________

RELATION TO PERSON NAMED ON CERTIFICATE: ______________________

REASON FOR MAKING REQUEST: ______________________

CERTIFICATE SIZE:

FULL SIZE	WALLET SIZE	TOTAL NUMBER OF COPIES:
NUMBER OF COPIES: ________	The wallet size birth certificate contains less information than the full size certificate. It does not satisfy the proof of identification requirements needed for a passport or driver's license. NUMBER OF COPIES: ________	______ X $30.00 = $ ______ SEND POSTAL MONEY ORDER ONLY **DO NOT MAIL CASH OR PERSONAL CHECKS - THEY WILL NOT BE ACCEPTED.**

Attach a copy of the requester's valid government issued photo ID or passport below:	Please mail the completed request with the following requirements:
Or two (2) forms of the following: - Social security (SS) card - Paycheck Stub or a W-2 form showing SS # - Current school or college photo ID - Automobile registration - Copy of utility bill or bank statement showing name and address - See our website ct.gov\dph for other forms of ID accepted	Money order made payable to 'Treasurer, State of CT' Current government issued photo ID (If applicable) verification of relationship to the registrant (for example, an individual requesting his/her parent's birth certificate must provide a certified copy of his/her own birth certificate).

***If adopted, please provide your adoptive name and adoptive parents' information.**

Birth Request REV 5-12

***If the requester had a legal name change, please provide a copy of the court documents authorizing the name change.**

Request for a Certified Copy of **Marriage** Record from the **Town/City** Vital Records

VS-39M Revised: 9/10/2009

Mail this request to the Town Vital Records office. For the address and phone number of Town Vital Record offices in Connecticut, please refer to our website at www.ct.gov/dph.com.

PLEASE PRINT **DO NOT MAIL CASH**

Groom/Spouse	**Full Legal Name Before Marriage** First Middle Last
Bride/Spouse	**Full Legal Name Before Marriage** First Middle Last
Date of Marriage * (Month/Day/Year))	**Town of Marriage**

PLEASE NOTE: In accordance with C.G.S. §7-51A, only the bride, groom or spouse listed on the marriage certificate or other persons authorized by the Department of Public Health, shall be issued a certified copy of a marriage certificate containing the Social Security numbers of the bride, groom or spouse. All other requesters will receive a certified copy of the marriage certificate without the social security numbers.

PERSON MAKING THIS REQUEST:

Name: ______________________________

First Middle Last Name

Address: ______________________________

Number Street

Town/City: ______________ **State:** ______________ **Zip Code:** __________

Telephone No.: ______________ E-Mail Address: (optional): ______________

Relation to Person Named in Certificate: ______________________________

Signature: ______________________________

The fee for a copy of Marriage Certificate at the State or Town is $20.00 per copy.

Number of Copies Requested: __________ **Amount Enclosed: $**______________

FEE: $20.00 PER COPY. Remit a *Postal Money Order* made payable to the *City/Town*
(Personal Checks are not accepted)

Mail this request to the *City/Town* (for town contact information, refer to our website at www.ct.gov/dph**).**

* **Note**: Copies of death or marriage certificates for events that occurred less than 4 months prior to the date of the request should be sent to the Vital Records office in the town of the event. Refer to our website at www.ct.gov/dph for town contact information.

Request for a Certified Copy of <u>Marriage</u> Record from the <u>State</u> Vital Records Office

VS-39MST Revised: 9/10/09

PLEASE PRINT **DO NOT MAIL CASH**

Groom/Spouse	**Full Legal Name Before Marriage** First Middle Last
Bride/Spouse	**Full Legal Name Before Marriage** First Middle Last
Date of Marriage * (Month/Day/Year))	**Town of Marriage**

PLEASE NOTE: In accordance with C.G.S. §7-51A, only the bride, groom or spouse listed on the marriage certificate or other persons authorized by the Department of Public Health, shall be issued a certified copy of a marriage certificate containing the Social Security numbers of the bride, groom or spouse. All other requesters will receive a certified copy of the marriage certificate without the social security numbers.

PERSON MAKING THIS REQUEST:

Name: ______________________________

First Middle Last Name

Address: ______________________________

Number Street

Town/City: ______________ **State:** ______________ **Zip Code:** ________

Telephone No.: ______________ E-Mail Address: (optional): ______________

Relation to Person Named in Certificate: ______________________________

Signature: ______________________________

The fee for a copy of Marriage Certificate at the State or Town is $20.00 per copy.

Number of Copies Requested: ________ **Amount Enclosed: $**____________

FEE: $20.00 PER COPY. Remit a *<u>Postal Money Order</u>* made payable to: '*Treasurer, State of CT*'
(Personal Checks are not accepted)

Mail This Request To:

Connecticut Department of Public Health
Vital Records Section
Customer Services, MS # 11 VRS
P.O. Box 340308
Hartford, CT 06134-0308

* **Note:** Copies of death or marriage certificates for events that occurred less than 4 months prior to the date of the request should be sent to the Vital Records office in the town of the event. Refer to our website at www.ct.gov/dph for town contact information.

REQUEST FOR COPY OF CIVIL UNION CERTIFICATE
VS-39CU Revised: 9-10-2009

PLEASE PRINT **DO NOT MAIL CASH**

PARTY 1	FULL NAME	FIRST	MIDDLE	LAST
PARTY 2	FULL NAME	FIRST	MIDDLE	LAST
DATE OF CIVIL UNION (MONTH/DAY/YEAR)		PLACE OF CIVIL UNION	TOWN	

PLEASE NOTE: IN ACCORDANCE WITH C.G.S. §7-51A, ONLY THE PARTIES TO THE CIVIL UNION, OFFICIATOR OF THE UNION, TOWN CLERK OR REGISTRAR LISTED ON THE CIVIL UNION CERTIFICATE, OR OTHER PERSONS AUTHORIZED BY THE DEPARTMENT OF PUBLIC HEALTH, SHALL BE ISSUED A CERTIFIED COPY OF A CIVIL UNION CERTIFICATE THAT CONTAINS THE SOCIAL SECURITY NUMBERS OF THE PARTIES. ALL OTHER REQUESTERS WILL RECEIVE A CERTIFIED COPY OF THE CIVIL UNION CERTIFICATE WITHOUT THE SOCIAL SECURITY NUMBERS.

PERSON MAKING THIS REQUEST:

NAME: ______________________________
FIRST MIDDLE LAST NAME

ADDRESS: ______________________________
NUMBER STREET

TOWN/CITY: ____________________ STATE: __________ ZIP CODE: __________

TELEPHONE NO.: ____________________ E-MAIL ADDRESS (optional): ____________________

RELATIONSHIP TO PERSON NAMED IN CERTIFICATE____________________

SIGNATURE: **X**______________________________

THE LEGAL FEE IS $20.00 PER COPY.
NUMBER OF COPIES WANTED: __________ AMOUNT ATTACHED: $__________

FEE: $20.00 PER COPY MONEY ORDER MADE PAYABLE TO THE TOWN/CITY OF CIVIL UNION
MAIL THIS REQUEST WITH PAYMENT TO THE TOWN CLERK AT THE TOWN/CITY OF CIVIL UNION
FOR TOWN CLERK ADDRESSES PLEASE SEE ALPHABETICAL LISTING BY TOWN
at the Department of Public Health website: http://www.dph.state.ct.us/oppe/townclerks.htm

REQUEST FOR COPY OF CIVIL UNION CERTIFICATE
VS-39CU ST Revised: 9/10/2009

PLEASE PRINT **DO NOT MAIL CASH**

PARTY 1	FULL NAME FIRST MIDDLE LAST
PARTY 2	FULL NAME FIRST MIDDLE LAST
DATE OF CIVIL UNION (MONTH/DAY/YEAR)	PLACE OF CIVIL UNION TOWN

PLEASE NOTE: IN ACCORDANCE WITH C.G.S. §7-51A, ONLY THE PARTIES TO THE CIVIL UNION, OFFICIATOR OF THE UNION, TOWN CLERK OR REGISTRAR LISTED ON THE CIVIL UNION CERTIFICATE, OR OTHER PERSONS AUTHORIZED BY THE DEPARTMENT OF PUBLIC HEALTH, SHALL BE ISSUED A CERTIFIED COPY OF A CIVIL UNION CERTIFICATE THAT CONTAINS THE SOCIAL SECURITY NUMBERS OF THE PARTIES. ALL OTHER REQUESTERS WILL RECEIVE A CERTIFIED COPY OF THE CIVIL UNION CERTIFICATE WITH THE SOCIAL SECURITY NUMBERS REMOVED.

PERSON MAKING THIS REQUEST:

NAME: ______________________________
FIRST MIDDLE LAST NAME

ADDRESS: ______________________________
NUMBER STREET

TOWN/CITY: ____________ STATE: ____________ ZIP CODE: ____________

TELEPHONE NO.: ____________ E-MAIL ADDRESS (optional): ____________

RELATIONSHIP TO PERSON NAMED IN CERTIFICATE____________

SIGNATURE:
X______________________________

THE LEGAL FEE IS $20.00 PER COPY.
NUMBER OF COPIES WANTED: ____________ AMOUNT ATTACHED: $____________

FEE: $20.00 PER COPY. REMIT *MONEY ORDER* MADE PAYABLE TO: 'TREASURER, STATE OF CT'
(Personal Checks are not accepted)
MAIL THIS REQUEST TO:

STATE OF CONNECTICUT
DEPARTMENT OF PUBLIC HEALTH
VITAL RECORDS SECTION
CUSTOMER SERVICES, MS 11VRS
P.O. BOX 340308
HARTFORD, CT 06134-0308

STATE OF CONNECTICUT
DEPARTMENT OF PUBLIC HEALTH (DPH)

Request for a Certified Copy of a Death Certificate from the Town of Death Vital Records Office

VS-39DTW Revised: 9/6/2011

PLEASE PRINT **DO NOT MAIL CASH OR PERSONAL CHECKS**

Full Name of Deceased: (First, Middle, Last):		SEX ☐ M ☐ F	**Date of Death:** (Month/Day/Yr): *
Town of Death:	**Date of Birth** (Month/Day/Yr):	**Place of Birth** (Town, State or Country):	
Father's Name:	**Mother's Name:**	**If Married, Spouse's Name:**	

Person Requesting the Death Certificate:

Name: _ ______________________________
First Middle Last Name

Address: ______________________________
Number Street Town/City State Zip Code

(______)______________ ______________________ **Relationship To Deceased: **** ______________________
Telephone No. E-Mail Address (optional)

______________________________ **Signature**: X______________________________
Intended Use of Certified Copy (e.g. Benefits, Genealogy, etc.)

** **Note:** Per CT law (C.G.S. §7-51A), for deaths occurring on or after July 1, 1997, only the Funeral Director and the surviving spouse or next of kin may obtain a copy of the death certificate with the decedent's Social Security number listed on the death certificate. All other requesters will receive a certified copy without the decedent's Social Security number.
If eligible, do you want the decedent's Social Security number on the copy of the certificate? No: _____ Yes: _______
If "Yes," there is no need for the spouse or next of kin to submit a copy of their ID or proof of relationship to the deceased.

One Time Fee Waiver for A Copy of a Veteran's Death Certificate:

Effective 10/1/2011, CT law (C.G.S. §7-74 (c)) allows the **spouse, child or parent** of a deceased veteran to obtain one (1) free copy of the deceased's death certificate **provided the requester presents a copy of their valid Government issued photo I.D. and proof of their relationship to the deceased.** Examples of proof of relationship include a marriage certificate for a spouse, one's own birth certificate, if a child of the deceased, or the deceased's birth certificate, if a parent of the deceased.
Are you requesting the one time waiver of the $20.00 fee and enclosing required documentation? No: ____ Yes ____
The fee will be waived only if the request includes the required valid ID, proof of relationship to the veteran, **and if the veteran status** is indicated on the death certificate.

The fee for a copy of a Death Certificate from the State or Town is $ 20.00 per copy. Personal checks are not accepted.

# of Copies Requested: ______ Amount Enclosed: $ _______ Fee Waiver Request: ________

Please mail this request with a *Postal Money Order* made payable to the *City or Town of death.*

For town contact information, refer to the Town Vital Records Directory on the Department of Public Health's Vital Records website at www.ct.gov/dph.com.

* **Note**: Copies of death or marriage certificates for events that occurred less than 4 months prior to the date of the request should be sent to the Vital Records office in the town of the event. Refer to our website at www.ct.gov/dph for town contact information.

STATE OF CONNECTICUT
DEPARTMENT OF PUBLIC HEALTH (DPH)

Request for a Certified Copy of a Death Certificate from the State Vital Records Office

VS-39DST Revised: 9/6/2011

PLEASE PRINT **DO NOT MAIL CASH OR PERSONAL CHECKS**

Full Name of Deceased: (First, Middle, Last):		SEX ☐ M ☐ F	**Date of Death:** (Month/Day/Yr): *
Town of Death:	**Date of Birth** (Month/Day/Yr):	**Place of Birth** (Town, State or Country):	
Father's Name:	**Mother's Name:**	**If Married, Spouse's Name:**	

Person Requesting the Death Certificate:

Name: ____
First Middle Last Name

Address: ____
Number Street Town/City State Zip Code

(_____)_____________ ____________________ **Relationship To Deceased: **** ____________________
Telephone No. E-Mail Address (optional)

______________________________ **Signature**: X______________________________
Intended Use of Certified Copy (e.g. Benefits, Genealogy, etc.)

** **Note:** Per CT law (C.G.S. §7-51A), for deaths occurring on or after July 1, 1997, only the Funeral Director and the surviving spouse or next of kin may obtain a copy of the death certificate with the decedent's Social Security number listed on the death certificate. All other requesters will receive a certified copy without the decedent's Social Security number.
If eligible, do you want the decedent's Social Security number on the copy of the certificate? No: _____ Yes: ______
If "Yes," there is no need for the spouse or next of kin to submit a copy of their ID or proof of relationship to the deceased.

One Time Fee Waiver for A Copy of a Veteran's Death Certificate:

Effective **10/1/2011**, CT law (C.G.S. §7-74 (c)) allows the **spouse, child or parent** of a deceased veteran to obtain one (1) free copy of the deceased's death certificate **provided the requester presents a copy of their valid Government issued photo I.D. and proof of their relationship to the deceased.** Examples of proof of relationship include a marriage certificate for a spouse, one's own birth certificate, if a child of the deceased, or the deceased's birth certificate, if a parent of the deceased.
Are you requesting the one time waiver of the $20.00 fee and enclosing required documentation? No: ____ Yes ____
The fee will be waived only if the request includes the required valid ID, proof of relationship to the veteran, **and if the veteran status** is indicated on the death certificate.

The fee for a copy of a Death Certificate from the State or Town is $ 20.00 per copy. Personal checks are not accepted.

# of Copies Requested: ______ Amount Enclosed: $ ______ Fee Waiver Request: ________

Please send this request with a *Postal Money Order* made payable to the: *'Treasurer, State of CT,'* to:

Connecticut Department of Public Health
Vital Records Section
Customer Services, MS # 11 VRS
Hartford, CT 06134-0308

* **Note**: Copies of death or marriage certificates for events that occurred less than 4 months prior to the date of the request should be sent to the Vital Records office in the town of the event. Refer to our website at www.ct.gov/dph for town contact information.

DELAWARE

Send your requests to:

Office of Vital Statistics
Division of Public Health
417 Federal Street
Dover, DE 19901

Tel. (302) 744-4700; phone orders (877) 888-0248
www.dhss.delaware.gov/dhss/dph/ss/vitalstats.html

Delaware law has required the recording of births, deaths, and marriages since 1913. Prior to 1913 it was the duty of each county's Recorder of Deeds to record events. Certified copies of birth, death, and marriage records can be ordered in person at three locations around the state—at the above address in Dover; in New Castle County (258 Chapman Road, Newark, DE 19702); and in Sussex County (546 S. Bedford Street, Georgetown, DE 19947).

The Office of Vital Statistics handles requests for birth records less than 72 years old, and marriage and death records less than 40 years old. It also holds divorce records from 1935 to the present but does not provide certified copies of those records; certified copies of divorce records may be obtained from the county where divorce was granted. For divorce records 1976 to the present, contact the Family Court in the county where the divorce was granted; prior to 1976, go to the Prothonotary at the county level. Once a birth record reaches 72 years of age and marriage and death records reach 40 years of age, they then become open to the public and are available on microfilm at the Delaware Public Archives (121 Duke of York Street, Dover, DE 19901; 302-744-5000; http://archives.delaware.gov/collections/vital.shtml).

Cost for a certified Birth Certificate	$25.00
Cost for an Adoptees Copy of Original Birth Certificate	$25.00
Cost for a certified Marriage Certificate	$25.00
Cost for a certified Civil Union Certificate	$25.00
Cost for a certified Death Certificate	$25.00

For Genealogy Research:

Family members doing genealogical research and genealogists representing a family member may obtain copies of records needed for their research. Unless the registrant is deceased, appropriate authorization is required from the registrant or relevant family members as defined in Section 3110(b) for the release of the records. If family members, or genealogists representing them, are unable to establish the death of a registrant or identify those closer family members authorized by Section 3110(b), they may obtain copies of marriage and death records only upon presentation of evidence satisfactory to the State Registrar that they are directly descended from a parent or grandparent of the registrant.

For Adoption Record Information, contact:

Delaware allows all adoptees who have reached the age of 21 to request information from their adoption records. Adopted persons can request a copy of their original birth certificate from the Office of Vital Records by completing the Adoptee's Application for Copy of Original Birth Certificate.

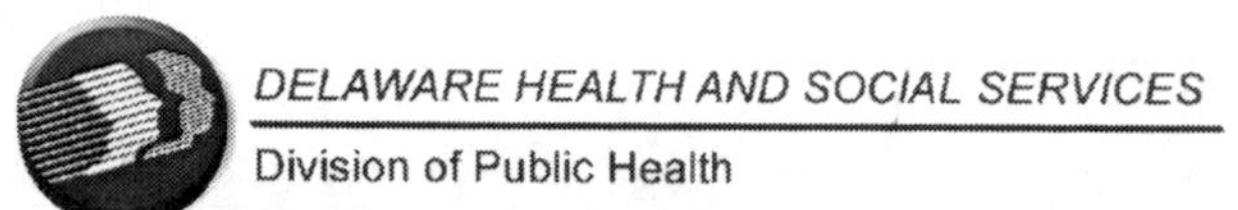

OFFICE OF VITAL STATISTICS

JESSE S. COOPER BLDG.	CHOPIN BUILDING	THURMAN ADAMS STATE SERV CTR.
417 FEDERAL STREET	258 CHAPMAN RD.	546 S. BEDFORD ST.
DOVER , DE 19901	NEWARK, DE 19702	GEORGETOWN, DE 19947
☏ (302) 744-4549	☏ (302) 283-7130	☏ (302) 856-5495

CREDIT CARD ORDERS VIA THE INTERNET: www.vitalchek.com

APPLICATION FOR A CERTIFIED COPY OF A DELAWARE BIRTH CERTIFICATE

PLEASE PRINT AND COMPLETE ALL ITEMS REQUESTED BELOW AS ACCURATELY AS POSSIBLE.

Name on Birth Certificate ______________________________
First Name Middle Name Last Name at Birth

Sex ☐ Male ☐ Female Date of Birth (mm/dd/yyyy) ______________

Place of Birth ______________________________
City State Hospital if Known

Name of Mother or Name of Parent A ______________________________
First Name Middle Name Last Name at Birth

Name of Father or Name of Parent B ______________________________
First Name Middle Name Last Name at Birth

RELATIONSHIP TO THE PERSON WHOSE BIRTH CERTIFICATE YOU ARE REQUESTING (PLEASE CHECK ONE BOX)

- ☐ Myself
- ☐ My current husband or wife
- ☐ My current civil union spouse
- ☐ My Child
- ☐ My Parent
- ☐ I am the Legal Guardian (court order required)
- ☐ I am the Authorized agent, attorney or legal representative of the person listed in 1-6 (proof required)
- ☐ Genealogy (proof required)

Number of copies requested:

REQUIRED UPON FILING OF APPLICATION

1. Cost: $25.00 per copy (If record is not located, fee will be retained for search). Make checks or money orders payable to the "**Office of Vital Statistics**".
2. Copy of your official valid photo identification (Drivers license, State ID or Work ID)
3. Parents Identification needed for children

PERSON APPLYING FOR CERTIFICATE

I hereby certify that all the above information is true to the best of my knowledge. It is a felony violation of Delaware Law (16 Del. C.§3111) to make a false statement on this application or to unlawfully obtain a certified copy of a birth certificate.

Print name of person applying for certificate ______________

Signature of person applying for certificate ______________ Date ______

Street Address ______________

City/Town ______________ State ______

Zipcode ______________ Daytime Phone ______

FOR OFFICE OF VITAL STATISTICS USE ONLY

Identification:

Doc. No. 35-05-20/09/08/02

DELAWARE HEALTH AND SOCIAL SERVICES

Division of Public Health

OFFICE OF VITAL STATISTICS

JESSE S. COOPER BLDG.	CHOPIN BUILDING	THURMAN ADAMS STATE SERV CTR.
417 FEDERAL STREET	258 CHAPMAN RD.	546 S. BEDFORD ST.
DOVER , DE 19901	NEWARK, DE 19702	GEORGETOWN, DE 19947
☏ (302) 744-4549	☏ (302) 283-7130	☏ (302) 856-5495

CREDIT CARD ORDERS VIA THE INTERNET: www.vitalchek.com

ADOPTEES APPLICATION FOR A CERTIFIED COPY OF ORIGINAL BIRTH CERTIFICATE

PLEASE PRINT AND COMPLETE ALL ITEMS REQUESTED BELOW AS ACCURATELY AS POSSIBLE.

Today's Date (mm/dd/yyyy)	Number of copies requested
First, Middle & Last Name at Birth (If known)	First, Middle & Last Name Given You Upon Adoption
Date of Birth (mm/dd/yyyy)	Place of Birth (Hospital, if known)
Birth Mother's Full Maiden Name (If known)	Birth Father's Full Name (If known)
Full Name of Adopted Mother or Parent A	Full Name of Adopted Father or Parent B

REQUIRED UPON FILING OF APPLICATION

1. **PHOTO IDENTIFICATION MUST BE PRESENTED** to vital statistics verifying that you are indeed the adoptee who is named above.
2. Cost: $25.00 per copy (If record is not located, fee will be retained for search). Make checks or money orders payable to the "**Office of Vital Statistics**".

PLEASE COMPLETE YOUR NAME AND MAILING ADDRESS

Name

Street/Development/Rural Delivery/Box Number

City/Town

State	Zip	Daytime Telephone Number

*****PLEASE BE AWARE THAT THIS PROCESS CAN TAKE UP TO THREE MONTHS*****

FOR OFFICE OF VITAL STATISTICS USE ONLY

Identification:

Doc. No. 35-05-20/09/08/01

DELAWARE HEALTH AND SOCIAL SERVICES
Division of Public Health

OFFICE OF VITAL STATISTICS

JESSE S. COOPER BLDG.
417 FEDERAL STREET
DOVER , DE 19901
☏ (302) 744-4549

CHOPIN BUILDING
258 CHAPMAN RD.
NEWARK, DE 19702
☏ (302) 283-7130

THURMAN ADAMS STATE SERV CTR.
546 S. BEDFORD ST.
GEORGETOWN, DE 19947
☏ (302) 856-5495

CREDIT CARD ORDERS VIA THE INTERNET: www.vitalchek.com

APPLICATION FOR A CERTIFIED COPY OF A DELAWARE MARRIAGE CERTIFICATE

PLEASE PRINT AND COMPLETE ALL ITEMS REQUESTED BELOW AS ACCURATELY AS POSSIBLE.

Wife's Name on Marriage Certificate First Name Middle Name Maiden Name

Date of Birth of Wife (mm/dd/yyyy)

Husband's Name on Marriage Certificate First Name Middle Name Last Name

Date of Birth of Husband (mm/dd/yyyy)

Date of Marriage (mm/dd/yyyy) Place of Marriage

RELATIONSHIP TO THE PERSON WHOSE MARRIAGE CERTIFICATE YOU ARE REQUESTING (PLEASE CHECK ONE BOX)

- ☐ Myself
- ☐ My Child
- ☐ My Parent
- ☐ I am the Legal Guardian
- ☐ I am the Authorized agent, attorney or legal representative
- ☐ Genealogy (proof required)

Number of copies requested:

REQUIRED UPON FILING OF APPLICATION

1. Cost: $25.00 per copy - A portion of the fee is donated to domestic violence programs. (If record is not located, fee will be retained for search). Make checks or money orders payable to the "**Office of Vital Statistics**".
2. Copy of your official valid photo identification (Drivers license, State ID or Work ID)
3. Parents Identification needed for children

PERSON APPLYING FOR CERTIFICATE

I hereby certify that all the above information is true to the best of my knowledge. It is a felony violation of Delaware Law (16 Del. C.§3111) to make a false statement on this application or to unlawfully obtain a certified copy of a marriage certificate.

Print name of person applying for certificate

Signature of person applying for certificate Date

Street Address

City/Town State

Zipcode Daytime Phone

FOR OFFICE OF VITAL STATISTICS USE ONLY

Identification

Doc. No. 35-05-20/09/08/04

DELAWARE HEALTH AND SOCIAL SERVICES
Division of Public Health

OFFICE OF VITAL STATISTICS

JESSE S. COOPER BLDG.	CHOPIN BUILDING	THURMAN ADAMS STATE SERV CTR.
417 FEDERAL STREET	258 CHAPMAN RD.	546 S. BEDFORD ST.
DOVER , DE 19901	NEWARK, DE 19702	GEORGETOWN, DE 19947
☏ (302) 744-4549	☏ (302) 283-7130	☏ (302) 856-5495

CREDIT CARD ORDERS VIA THE INTERNET: www.vitalchek.com

APPLICATION FOR A CERTIFIED COPY OF A DELAWARE CIVIL UNION CERTIFICATE

PLEASE PRINT AND COMPLETE ALL ITEMS REQUESTED BELOW AS ACCURATELY AS POSSIBLE.

Name of Party A on Civil Union Certificate First Name Middle Name Last Name at Birth

Date of Birth of Party A (mm/dd/yyyy)

Name of Party B on Civil Union Certificate First Name Middle Name Last Name at Birth

Date of Birth of Party B (mm/dd/yyyy)

Date of Civil Union (mm/dd/yyyy) Place of Civil Union

RELATIONSHIP TO THE PERSON WHOSE CIVIL UNION CERTIFICATE YOU ARE REQUESTING (PLEASE CHECK ONE BOX)

- ☐ Myself
- ☐ My Child
- ☐ My Parent
- ☐ I am the Legal Guardian
- ☐ I am the Authorized agent, attorney or legal representative
- ☐ Genealogy (proof required)

Number of copies requested:

REQUIRED UPON FILING OF APPLICATION

1. Cost: $25.00 per copy - A portion of the fee is donated to domestic violence programs. (If record is not located, fee will be retained for search). Make checks or money orders payable to the "**Office of Vital Statistics**".
2. Copy of your official valid photo identification (Drivers license, State ID or Work ID)
3. Parents Identification needed for children

PERSON APPLYING FOR CERTIFICATE

I hereby certify that all the above information is true to the best of my knowledge. It is a felony violation of Delaware Law (16 Del. C.§3111) to make a false statement on this application or to unlawfully obtain a certified copy of a civil union certificate.

Print name of person applying for certificate

Signature of person applying for certificate Date

Street Address

City/Town State

Zipcode Daytime Phone

FOR OFFICE OF VITAL STATISTICS USE ONLY

Identification

Doc. No. 35-05-20/09/08/04

DELAWARE HEALTH AND SOCIAL SERVICES

Division of Public Health

OFFICE OF VITAL STATISTICS

JESSE S. COOPER BLDG.	CHOPIN BUILDING	THURMAN ADAMS STATE SERVICE CTR.
417 FEDERAL STREET	258 CHAPMAN RD.	546 S. BEDFORD ST.
DOVER , DE 19901	NEWARK, DE 19702	GEORGETOWN, DE 19947
☎ (302) 744-4549	☎ (302) 283-7130	☎ (302) 856-5495

CREDIT CARD ORDERS VIA THE INTERNET: www.vitalchek.com

APPLICATION FOR A CERTIFIED COPY OF A DELAWARE DEATH CERTIFICATE

PLEASE PRINT AND COMPLETE ALL ITEMS REQUESTED BELOW AS ACCURATELY AS POSSIBLE.

Name on Death Certificate ______________________________

First Name Middle Name Last Name

Sex ☐ Male ☐ Female Date of Death (mm/dd/yyyy) ______________

Place of Death ______________________________

Name of Mother or
Name of Parent A First Name Middle Name Last Name at Birth

Name of Father or
Name of Parent B First Name Middle Name Last Name at Birth

RELATIONSHIP TO THE PERSON WHOSE DEATH CERTIFICATE YOU ARE REQUESTING (PLEASE CHECK ONE BOX)

- ☐ My current husband or wife
- ☐ My current civil union spouse
- ☐ My child
- ☐ My parent
- ☐ I am the Legal Guardian
- ☐ I am the authorized agent, attorney or legal representative of the registrant
- ☐ Genealogy (proof required)

Number of copies requested:

REQUIRED UPON FILING OF APPLICATION

1. Cost: $25.00 per certificate - A portion of the fee is donated to the distressed cemetery fund (If record is not located, fee will be retained for search). Make checks or money orders payable to the "**Office of Vital Statistics**".
2. Copy of your official valid photo identification (Drivers license, State ID or Work ID)
3. Parents Identification needed for children

PERSON APPLYING FOR CERTIFICATE

I hereby certify that all the above information is true to the best of my knowledge. It is a felony violation of Delaware Law (16 Del. C.§3111) to make a false statement on this application or to unlawfully obtain a certified copy of a death certificate.

Print name of person applying for certificate ______________________________

Signature of person applying for certificate ______________________ Date ____________

Street Address ______________________________

City/Town ______________________ State ____________

Zipcode ______________________ Daytime Phone ____________

FOR OFFICE OF VITAL STATISTICS USE ONLY

Identification:

DISTRICT OF COLUMBIA

Send your requests for Birth and Death Certificates to:

Department of Health
Vital Records Division
899 North Capitol Street, NE, First Floor
Washington, DC 20002

Tel. (202) 442-9303
http://doh.dc.gov/service/vital-records

Birth certificates are available from August 1874 and death certificates from 1855, though no death records were filed during the Civil War. Access to records is restricted for 100 years for birth records and 50 years for death records. Aunts, uncles, grandparents, and other relatives not part of the immediate family cannot obtain a birth or death certificate from Vital Records prior to the record becoming open to the public unless the approval guidelines spelled out on the Vital Records website are met. All mail-in requests must include a stamped, self-addressed No. 10 (4⅛" x 9½") return envelope.

Cost for a certified Birth Certificate	$23.00
Cost for an Adoptee Birth Certificate	$33.00
Cost for a certified Death Certificate	$18.00

Send your requests for Marriage Records and Divorce Records to:

DC Superior Court
500 Indiana Avenue, NW
(Room 4335 for Divorce Decree or
Room 4485 for Marriage License)
Washington, DC 20001

Tel. (202) 879-4840 (marriage information);
(202) 879-1261 (divorce information)
www.dcappeals.gov/internet/public/aud_marriage/marriage.jsf

Marriage records from 1811 and divorce records after September 16, 1956, are available. The fee for a marriage certificate is $10.00.

Send your requests for Divorce Certificates (before September 16, 1956) to:

U.S. District Court for the District of Columbia
333 Constitution Avenue, NW
Washington DC 20001-2802

Tel. (202) 273-0555

For Genealogy Research:

The DC Genweb Project has some vital records online at www.theusgenweb.org/dcgenweb/.

Birth Certificate Request*
Vital Records Division

For District of Columbia Occurrences Only
RESTRICTION: Family or legal representatives only. See page two for details

Mail-In Form (See below for Instructions)

1. Certificate Holder's Name: (First) (Middle) (Last)

2. Birth Date: / / (mm/dd/yyyy)

3. Sex: ○ Male ○ Female

4. Hospital:

5. City: Washington, DC

6. Father's Name: (First) (Middle) (Last)

7. Mother's Maiden Name: (First) (Middle) (Maiden)

8a. Number of Original Certificate Forms Requested:

$23.00 each Total Cost: $

8b. Total Amount Enclosed:* * $

9. Relationship to Certificate Holder: ○ Self ○ Mother ○ Father ○ Other

10. Signature of Requester: ______________________

11. Date: ________/________/________ (mm/dd/yy)

Mail Certificate(s) to:

12. Name:

13. Address:

14. City/State/Zip Code::

15. Day Phone: (Required)

*** Copy of Requester's Photo ID Required.**
If record is not located a "Certificate of Search" will be issued.

****Beginning January 1, 2009, all mail-in requests must include a stamped self addressed No. 10 (4 1/8" x 9 1/2") business size return envelope.**

****The DC Treasurer requires that all checks have an address imprinted on them to be accepted for deposit. Starter checks are not accepted.**

Instructions to be completed:
1. Print, sign, enclose requestor's photo ID and date the form
2. Enclose check or money order payable to DC Treasurer
3. Mail to: **Department of Health**
Vital Records Division
899 North Capitol Street, NE, 1st Floor
Washington, DC 20002
(202) 442-9303

Birth Application Instructions

The birth certificate request form contains 12 questions. A separate copy of the request form should be completed for each person whose birth record is being requested. However, multiple copies of a single birth record may be requested on the same form.

Items 1-7: Personal information about the certificate holder.

Item 8a: Please indicate the total number of original form certificates that you are requesting. To calculate the total cost, multiply the number of requested certificates by $23.

The DC Vital Records Division **does not process online orders**. For your convenience, you can process online requests through VitalChek Network, Inc., an independent company that Vital Records has partnered with to provide you this service. VitalChek can be reached either through its website www.vitalchek.com or by phone at 1 (877) 572 6332. An additional fee is charged by VitalChek for using this service, and all major credit cards are accepted including American Express, Discover, MasterCard or Visa.

Item 8b: Please indicate the total amount of money that you are enclosing. **If you send your request by mail, please enclose a check or money order payable to the DC Treasurer. The DC Treasurer requires that all checks have an address imprinted on them to be accepted for deposit.**

Item 9: The relationship of the requester to the certificate holder.

Items 10-11: The person who is requesting the certificate(s) must sign and date the request and enclose a photocopy of his or her official picture identification card.

Items 12-15: Information about the designated recipient of the certificate(s).

After you have printed out and signed your request, mail it with your payment to:

Department of Health
Vital Records Division
899 North Capitol Street, NE, First Floor
Washington, DC 20002
(202) 442-9303

If record is not located a "Certificate of Search" will be issued.

Vital Records Division

Death Certificate Request*
For District of Columbia Occurrences Only

RESTRICTION: Family or legal representative only. For details, see page 2

Mail-In Form

1. Name of Deceased:

2. Social Security Number of Deceased: - -

3. Sex: ○ Male ○ Female

4. Date of Death: (mm/dd/yyyy)

5. Death Certificate No: (if known)

6a. Total number of copies of certificate requested: @ $18.00 each:

6b.(a) Number with cause of death included:

(b) Number with cause of death omitted:

6c. Total Amount Enclosed: $

7. Relationship to Deceased: ○ Mother ○ Father ○ Spouse ○ Other

8. Signature of Requester: ______________________

9. Date: ____/_____/________

Make Check/Money Order Payable to: DC Treasurer**

Mail Certificate(s) to:

10. Name:

11. Address:

12. City/State/Zip Code

13. Day Phone: (required)

***Copy of Requester's Photo ID is Required!**

Beginning January 1, 2009, all Mail-In requests must include a stamped self addressed return No. 10 (4 1/8" x 9 1/2 ") business size envelope.

The DC Treasurer requires that all checks have an address imprinted on them to be

accepted for deposit.

Instructions to be completed:

1. Print, sign, date form and a copy of requester's photo ID
2. Enclose check / money order payable to: DC Treasurer
3. Mail to: **Government of the District of Columbia**

Department of Health
Vital Records Division
899 North Capitol Street, NE, First Floor
Washington, DC 20002/ Phone: (202) 442-9303

Death Application Instructions
If record is not located a "Certificate of Search" will be issued and the payment for the search is non-refundable.

The death transcript request form contains 13 questions. A separate copy of the request form should be completed for each person whose death record is being requested. However, multiple copies of a single death record may be requested on the same form.

Items 1-4: Information about the deceased.

Items 5: Information about the record being requested.
Note: Persons entitled to purchase a vital record birth or death certificate included:

- The registrant
- An immediate nuclear family member
- A legal guardian
- A legal representative

Item 6a: Please indicate the total number of certificates that you are requesting.

Item 6b/a: Please indicate the number of requested copies of certificates on which you wish to have the cause of death included.

Item 6b/b: Please indicate the number of requested copies of certificates on which you wish to have the cause of death omitted.

Item 6c: Please indicate the total amount of money that you are enclosing. This amount should equal the requested number of transcripts multiplied by $18.
If you send your request by mail, please enclose a check or money order payable to the DC Treasurer. The DC Treasurer requires that all checks must have an address imprinted on them to be accepted for deposit. The cost of either type of transcript is $18.

Item 7: The requester's relationship to the deceased.

Item 8: Please sign your signature once the mail-in form has been completed.

Item 9: Please date the form.

Item 10:-13 Information about the designated recipient of the certificate(s).

After you print and sign your request, click the clear button to erase the data you have entered, mail the form and a copy of your picture ID with your payment to:

Department of Health
Vital Records Division
899 North Capitol Street, NE, First Floor
Washington, DC 20002
(202) 442-9303
If record is not located a "Certificate of Search" will be issued and the payment for the search is non-refundable.

<u>**RESTRICTION**</u> on Access to Death Certificates: Pursuant to D.C. Official Code Sec. 7-220, the Vital Records Division may issue a certified copy of a death certificate ONLY to an applicant having a direct and tangible interest in the requested death certificate.

NOTE: This form should be used ONLY by a member of the registrant's immediate family, his/her guardian or legal representative.

FLORIDA

Send your requests to:

Office of Vital Statistics
(Location: 1217 Pearl Street)
P.O. Box 210
Jacksonville, FL 32231-0042

Tel. (904) 359-6900
Fax (904) 359-6931
E-mail: VitalStats@doh.state.fl.us
www.doh.state.fl.us/planning_eval/vital_statistics/index.html

Vital record registration was not required by state law until 1917, but some earlier records are on file. The Office of Vital Statistics has birth records from April 1865 (though records are limited for the years 1865–1916); death records from August 1877; and marriage and divorce records from June 6, 1927. For earlier marriage and divorce records, contact the clerk of court in the county where the event took place (see www.myfloridaclerks.com/ for contact information). Birth records are restricted for 100 years, death records for 50 years.

Cost for a computer-generated certified Birth Certificate	$9.00
Cost for a photocopy certification of registered Birth	$14.00
Cost for a commemorative Birth or Marriage Certificate	$34.00
Cost for a certified Marriage Certificate or Divorce Report	$5.00
Cost for a commemorative Marriage Certificate	$30.00
Cost for a certified Death Certificate	$5.00
Cost for a duplicate copy, when ordered at the same time	$4.00

For Genealogy Research:

Certified copies of vital records are issued to qualified applicants for identification, genealogical, and legal purposes. Consult the website of the Office of Vital Statistics to see the requirements for applicants.

The State Archives of Florida (500 South Bronough Street, Talahassee, FL 32399-0250; tel. 850-245-6700; http://dlis.dos.state.fl.us/archives/genealogy.cfm) holds microfilm copies of county marriage records and a few original registers of birth and death records, as well as many other records of interest to genealogists.

For Adoption Record information, contact:

Florida's Adoption Reunion Registry
1317 Winewood Boulevard
Tallahassee, FL 32399-0700

Tel. (800) 96-ADOPT (in Florida); (904) 353-0679 (outside of Florida)
www.adoptflorida.com/Reunion-Registry.htm

Cost for initial filing with Adoption Reunion Registry	$35.00
Cost for updating information with Adoption Reunion Registry	$10.00

AFFIDAVIT TO RELEASE BIRTH CERTIFICATION

(If you are eligible to receive the birth certificate requested below, you may use ***this form*** to name another person to receive the birth certificate for you.)

State of:________________________ County of:________________________

My Name is: *(print name)*______________________________________ .

I am eligible, by law, to receive the birth certificate requested below, because I am the: *(check one)*

__ Child named on the birth certificate, and of legal age (18).

__ Parent listed on the child's birth certificate.

__ Legal Guardian of the child named on the birth certificate (Documentation required).

__ Legal Representative of the child or parent named on the birth certificate (Documentation required).

I authorize the Department of Health, Office of Vital Statistics to issue the birth certificate of:

________________________________ **to** ________________________________.
(child named on birth certificate) **(print name of person to receive birth certificate)**

(Required) I have attached a photocopy of my valid photo ID:

______________________________ .
type of Identification attached ***(If attorney, only bar number required)***

NOTE: Pursuant to s. 382.026, Florida Statutes, it is a 3rd degree felony to obtain and use a Florida birth record fraudulently, punishable as set forth in s. 775.082, s. 775.083, or s. 775.084, Florida Statutes.

I hereby swear or affirm the above statements are true and correct.

____
signature of person checked above

Subscribed and sworn before me this _______ day of __________________, 20____ by

______________________________, who is: __ personally known to me, or, __ who has
(print name of person checked above)

produced _______________________ as Identification. My Commission Expires: _________.
(type of identification produced)

____________________________ ____________________________
(signature of notary) ***(print, type or stamp name of notary)*** (SEAL)

Even if personally known to the notary, the rules of the Department of Health require the person completing this form to provide a photocopy of valid photo identification.

DH Form 1958, August 2010 (Obsoletes previous editions)
64V-1.0131, Florida Administrative Code

State of Florida
Department of Health
Office of Vital Statistics
APPLICATION FOR FLORIDA BIRTH RECORD

Requirement for ordering: If applicant is self, parent, guardian, or legal representative, then the applicant must complete this application and provide a copy of a **valid photo identification**. If applicant is not one of the above, the Affidavit to Release a Birth Certificate must be completed by an authorized person and submitted in addition to this application form. Acceptable forms of identification are the following: **Driver's License, State Identification Card, Passport, and/or Military Identification Card**.

CHILD'S FULL NAME AS SHOWN ON BIRTH RECORD	**FIRST**		**MIDDLE**	**LAST**	**SUFFIX**
IF NAME WAS CHANGED SINCE BIRTH, INDICATE NEW NAME	**FIRST**		**MIDDLE**	**LAST**	**SUFFIX**
DATE OF BIRTH	**MONTH**	**DAY**	**YEAR (4-DIGIT)**	**STATE FILE NUMBER (If known)**	**SEX**
PLACE OF BIRTH	**HOSPITAL**		**CITY OR TOWN**	**COUNTY**	
MOTHER'S MAIDEN NAME (Name before marriage)	**FIRST**		**MIDDLE**	**LAST**	**SUFFIX**
FATHER'S NAME	**FIRST**		**MIDDLE**	**LAST**	**SUFFIX**

A BIRTH RECORD SEARCH REQUIRES ADVANCE PAYMENT OF A NON-REFUNDABLE SEARCH FEE OF $9.00 AND VALID PHOTO IDENTIFICATION.

A Computer Certification requires the $9.00 fee which entitles the applicant to one registered birth (1917 to present) or **if a record is not found, a certified "No Record Found" statement will be issued.** • The Computer Certification is recognized and accepted by **ALL** State and Federal Agencies. • If birth occurred prior to 1917 select Computer Certification for $9.00. • **Normal processing time is 3-4 business days,** provided the record and application are complete and in order.	$9.00	X		=	$0.00
A Photocopy Certification (***In place of a Computer Certification***) requires an additional charge of $5.00 and includes the $9.00 search fee. Normal processing time is approximately 10 business days. **Definitions of the two types of Certifications are on the reverse side.**	$14.00	X		=	$0.00
Additional Computer Certifications: $4.00 for each subsequent Computer Certification	$4.00	X		=	$0.00
Additional Photocopy Certifications: $4.00 for each subsequent Photocopy Certification	$4.00	X		=	$0.00
Additional Years to be Searched: $2.00 for each additional year. The maximum additional year search fee is $ 50.00 regardless of the total number of years to be searched. **(Indicate the range of years to be searched in the 2nd Box.)**	$2.00	X		=	$0.00
RUSH ORDERS (Optional): RUSH Fees are an additional $10.00. If you desire RUSH service, mark the outside of your envelope **"RUSH"** *(Processing time is 1-2 business days)*	Check here for rush order ☐			=	$0.00
TOTAL AMOUNT ENCLOSED: Check or Money Order Payable to: Vital Statistics. **(DO NOT SEND CASH)** International payments should be made by Cashiers Check or Money Order in U. S. Dollars. ***Florida Law imposes an additional service charge of $15.00 for dishonored checks.***	**ENCLOSE COPY OF VALID PHOTO IDENTIFICATION OR YOUR ORDER WILL NOT BE COMPLETED**				$0.00

APPLICANT INFORMATION

Any person who willfully and knowingly provides any false information on a certificate, record or report required by Chapter 382, Florida Statutes, or on any application or affidavit, or who obtains confidential information from any Vital Record under false or fraudulent purposes, commits a felony of the third degree, punishable as provided in Chapter 775, Florida Statutes.

Applicant's Name **TYPE OR PRINT**	FIRST	MIDDLE	LAST (INCLUDING ANY SUFFIX)	
ADDRESS (INCLUDE APT. NO., IF APPLICABLE)		CITY STATE		ZIP CODE
HOME PHONE NUMBER WORK PHONE NUMBER		RELATIONSHIP TO REGISTRANT	SIGNATURE OF APPLICANT	
IF ATTORNEY, PROVIDE BAR/PROFESSIONAL LICENSE NO.		IF ATTORNEY , PROVIDE NAME OF PERSON YOU REPRESENT AND THEIR RELATIONSHIP TO REGISTRANT		

IF THE CERTIFICATION IS TO BE MAILED TO ANOTHER PERSON OR ADDRESS USE THE SPACES BELOW TO SPECIFY SHIP TO NAME AND ADDRESS.

SHIP TO NAME **TYPE OR PRINT**	FIRST	MIDDLE	LAST (INCLUDING ANY SUFFIX)	
HOME PHONE NUMBER	SHIP TO STREET ADDRESS (AND APT. NO. IF APPLICABLE)			
WORK PHONE NUMBER	CITY STATE			ZIP CODE

INFORMATION AND INSTRUCTIONS FOR BIRTH RECORD APPLICATION

COMPUTER CERTIFICATION: The Computer Certifications are accepted by all State and Federal Agencies and used for any type of travel.
3-4 business days is the Normal Response time, provided the record and application are complete and in order.
A Computer Certification has two different formats which are:

- A certification of a registered birth (2004 to Present), supplies the following facts of birth: Childs Name, Date of Birth, Sex, Time, Weight, Place of Birth (City, County and Location) and Parents Information.
- A certification of a registered birth (1917 to 2003), supplies the following facts of birth: Childs Name, Date of Birth, Sex, County of Birth and Parents Name.
- If the birth occurred prior to 1917, only photocopies are available. When ordering, select Computer Copy for $9.00. Records are available from 1865 to present but are limited from years 1865-1916.

PHOTOCOPY: A photocopy is a certificate of the registered birth on file. Photocopies of birth certificates are certified documents. Normal response time for photocopies is approximately 10 business days.

AVAILABILITY: Birth registration was not required by state law until 1917, but there are some records on file dating back to 1865. Birth records under seal by reason of adoption, paternity determination or court order cannot be ordered in this manner. For a record under seal, write to ATTN: Records Amendment Section at the address below.

ELIGIBILITY: Birth certificates can be issued only to:

1. Registrant (the child named on the record) if of legal age (18)
2. Parent(s) listed on the Birth Record
3. Legal Guardian (must provide guardianship papers)
4. Legal representative of one of the above persons
5. Other person(s) by court order (must provide recorded or certified copy of court order)

In the case of a deceased registrant, upon receipt of the death certificate of the decedent, a certification of the birth certificate can be issued to the spouse, child, grandchild, sibling, if of legal age, or to the legal representative of any of these persons as well as to the parent.
Any person of legal age may be issued a certified copy of a birth record (except for those birth records under seal) for a birth event that occurred over 100 years ago.

REQUIREMENT FOR ORDERING: If applicant is self, parent, legal guardian or legal representative, then the applicant must provide a completed application along with a copy of a valid photo identification. If legal guardian, a copy of the appointment orders must be included with your request. If legal representative, your attorney bar number, and a notation of whom you represent and their relationship to the registrant must be included with your request. If you are an agent of local, state or federal agency requesting a record, indicate in the space provided for "relationship" the name of the agency. Acceptable forms of identification are the following: **Driver's License**, **State Identification Card**, **Passport** and/or **Military Identification Card**

RELATIONSHIP TO REGISTRANT: A person ordering his or her own certificate should enter "SELF" in this space. Also, explain if name has been changed; married name, name changed legally (when and where), etc. Others must identify themselves clearly as eligible (see ELIGIBILITY above).

NONREFUNDABLE: Vital record fees are nonrefundable, with one exception. Fees paid for additional copies when no record is found will be refunded upon written request.

APPLICANT'S SIGNATURE: Is required, as well as his/her printed name, residence address and telephone number.

OPTIONS FOR RUSH SERVICE:

- **CREDIT CARDS:** The state office currently does not accept credit cards but there is a private firm that accepts such charges and transfers the order to Vital Statistics for a fee of $7.00 plus a $10.00 Rush Fee charged by the State Office. You may telephone 1-877-550-7330 or you may fax your request to the private firm at 1-877-550-7428. In any event, you may dial (904) 359-6900 and follow the prompts on the telephone system to be transferred free of charge to the contracted vendor. If you have any questions please call the Office of Vital Statistics at (904) 359-6900.

- **MAIL IN:** An order with an envelope marked RUSH with a $10 rush fee enclosed, provided the record and application are complete and in order, will be processed before the normal processing time. This does not include birth records requiring an amendment action. If an amendment action is necessary, additional processing time will be required.
- **WALK-IN SERVICE:** Is available at 1217 Pearl Street, Jacksonville, Florida, between 8:00 am – 4:30 pm. Orders prepaid by Noon may be picked up after 3:30 p.m. Orders prepaid after Noon may be picked up after 10:00 a.m. the next workday. Each request must be accompanied by picture identification Certifications for photocopies rush service requires an additional fee of $10.

TIME OF BIRTH: This item was not collected on the birth events between 1949 – 1969.

MAIL THIS APPLICATION WITH PAYMENT TO

STATE OFFICE OF VITAL STATISTICS

ATTN: CLIENT SERVICES

P.O. BOX 210

Jacksonville, FL 32231-0042

PLEASE VISIT OUR WEBSITE

http://www.doh.state.fl.us/planning_eval/vital_statistics/index.html

State of Florida - Department of Health
Vital Statistics
APPLICATION FOR FLORIDA COMMEMORATIVE BIRTH CERTIFICATE
(Available only from the State Office of Vital Statistics)

Requirement for ordering: Application to be used ONL Y if requesting a Commemorative Birth Certificate (also includes issuance of one computer certification). If only computer certification or photocopy desired, use DH 726 Application for Certificate of Birth. If event is less than 100 years old and if applicant is the registrant (child named on record) of legal age; parent listed on record; legal guardian; or legal representative of any of these, then the applicant must complete this application and provide a **copy of valid unexpired photo identification**. If ordering as a gift: In accordance with Florida Law, if you are not an authorized person, you must provide an Affidavit to Release a Birth Certificate, DH Form 1958 completed by an authorized person, authorizing you as the named individual, to obtain the commemorative certificate and you must present a copy of a valid unexpired photo identification:. A photocopy of the required ID will be accepted verifying that you are, in fact, that named individual shown on the affidavit to obtain the birth certificate submitted in addition to this application form. Acceptable forms of identification are the following: **Driver's License, State Identification Card, Passport, and/or Military Identification Card**. The affidavit is available on our w ebsite at www.doh.state.fl.us . Once you access, click on A-Z topics, then Birth and Death Certificates and lastly Forms and Applications. If event is over 100 years old, no photo ID required as birth records over 100 years old are public record and available to anyone.

CHILD'S FULL NAME AS SHOWN ON BIRTH RECORD	FIRST			MIDDLE	LAST	SUFFIX
DATE OF BIRTH	MONTH	DAY	YEAR (4-DIGIT)	STATE FILE NUMBER (If known)	SEX	
PLACE OF BIRTH (MUST HAVE OCCURRED IN FLORIDA)	HOSPITAL			CITY OR TOWN	COUNTY	
MOTHER'S MAIDEN NAME (Name before marriage)	FIRST			MIDDLE	MAIDEN LAST	SUFFIX
FATHER'S NAME	FIRST			MIDDLE	LAST	SUFFIX

Commemorative birth certificates are signed by the current Governor and State Registrar of Vital Statistics. The certificates contain calligraphy style printing, gold state seal, and are suitable for framing and preserving as family heirlooms. Commemorative certificates are mailed encased in cardboard shields to ensure protection. Information on the application is requested to assist us in our search for the record. Information that is shown on a commemorative certificate is taken from the actual birth certificate not the information provided on this application.

➢ **Include a check or money order in U.S. dollars for $34.00 made payable to the "Office of Vital Statistics".** The fee covers the search, one computer certification, one commemorative certificate, and mailing 1ST class mail. The computer certification will be mailed within 3-5 business days and the commemorative will follow within 4 -6 weeks. ➢ **If the birth record is not located,** a No Record Found Statement of that fact is issued along with a form to request a refund for $25.00 and any additional copy fee. The $9.00 search fee is non refundable. If for any reason we are unable to provide a commemorative certificate due to the type of record filed, the $25.00 fee will be refunded.	$34	x	1	$34
➢ Additional Computer Certification, when ordered at the same time is $4.00 each.	$4	x	0	$0
➢ Additional Commemorative Certification, when ordered at the same time is $25.00 each	$25	x	0	$0
➢ TOTAL AMOUNT ENCLOSED: *Florida Law imposes an additional service charge of $15.00 for dishonored checks*			TOTAL	$34

***Be Sure** To Check Appropriate Box For Your Special Commemorative Design Selection*
(Larger images of the commemorative options can be viewed at our website)

☐ 

PALM

☐ 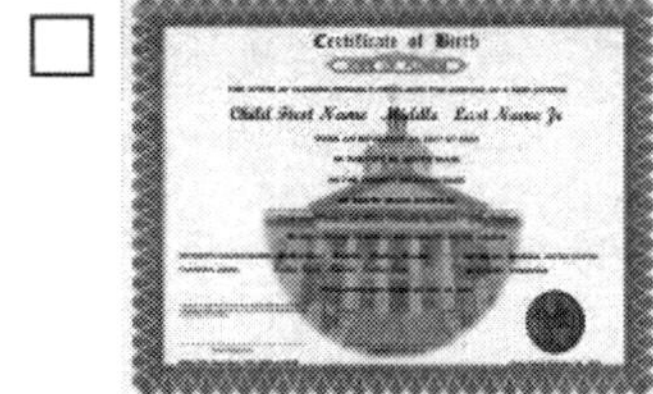

TRADITIONAL (Florida Capitol background)

☐ 

BEACH (Small Footprints/Ball/Bucket)

APPLICANT NAME/DELIVERY INFORMATION
Any person who willfully and knowingly provides any false information on a certificate, record or report required by Chapter 382, Florida Statutes, or on any application or affidavit, or who obtains confidential information from any Vital Record under false or fraudulent purposes, commits a felony of the third degree, punishable as provided in Chapter 775, Florida Statutes.

Applicant's Name **TYPE OR PRINT**	FIRST	MIDDLE	LAST (INCLUDING ANY SUFFIX)	
DELIVERY ADDRESS (INCLUDE APT. NO., IF APPLICABLE)		CITY STATE		ZIP CODE
HOME PHONE NUMBER	WORK PHONE NUMBER	RELATIONSHIP TO REGISTRANT	**SIGNATURE OF APPLICANT**	
IF ATTORNEY, PROVIDE BAR/PROFESSIONAL LICENSE NO.		IF ATTORNEY . PROVIDE NAME OF PERSON YOU REPRESENT AND THEIR RELATIONSHIP TO REGISTRANT		

IF THE CERTIFICATION IS TO BE MAILED TO ANOTHER PERSON OR ADDRESS USE THE SPACES BELOW TO SPECIFY SHIP TO NAME AND ADDRESS.

SHIP TO NAME **TYPE OR PRINT**	FIRST	MIDDLE	LAST (INCLUDING ANY SUFFIX)	
HOME PHONE NUMBER	SHIP TO STREET ADDRESS (AND APT. NO. IF APPLICABLE)			
WORK PHONE NUMBER		CITY STATE		ZIP CODE

DH 726C, 5/09 **MAIL TO: OFFICE OF VITAL STATISTICS, P.O.BOX 210, JACKSONVILLE, FL 32231-0042**

State of Florida
Department of Health
Office of Vital Statistics

APPLICATION FOR A MARRIAGE RECORD FOR LICENSES ISSUED IN FLORIDA

NAME OF GROOM	FIRST			MIDDLE	LAST	SUFFIX
NAME OF BRIDE	FIRST			MIDDLE	LAST	
DATE OF MARRIAGE	MONTH	DAY	YEAR (4-DIGIT)	INDICATE ADDITIONAL YEARS TO BE SEARCHED	STATE FILE NUMBER (If known)	
PLACE OF MARRIAGE	CITY OR TOWN				COUNTY	
PLACE LICENSE WAS ISSUED	CITY OR TOWN				COUNTY	

CORRECTED or AMENDED Has the Clerk of Court corrected/amended an item on this Marriage Record and forwarded the newly corrected Record to the Office of Vital Statistics? ☐ Yes ☐ No

A MARRIAGE RECORD SEARCH REQUIRES ADVANCE PAYMENT OF A NON-REFUNDABLE SEARCH FEE OF $5.00

The $5.00 fee entitles the applicant to one Certification of Marriage **(June 1927 to present)** or **if a record is not found, a certified "No Record Found" statement will be issued.**

- The Certification of Marriage is recognized and accepted by **ALL** State and Federal Agencies.
- **Normal processing time is 5-7 business days,** provided the record and application are complete and in order.

$5.00 X ☐ = ☐

Additional Certifications:
$4.00 for each subsequent Certification

$4.00 X ☐ = ☐

Additional Years to be Searched:
$2.00 for each additional year. The maximum additional year search fee is $ 50.00 regardless of the total number of years to be searched. **(Indicate the range of years to be searched in the 2nd Box.)**

$2.00 X ☐ = ☐

RUSH ORDERS (Optional): RUSH Fees are an additional $10.00.
If you desire RUSH service, mark the outside of your envelope **"RUSH"** (*Processing time is 3-4 business days*) Check here for rush order ☐ = ☐

TOTAL AMOUNT ENCLOSED: Check or Money Order Payable to: Vital Statistics. **(DO NOT SEND CASH)** ☐
International payments should be made by Cashiers Check or Money Order in U. S. Dollars.
Florida Law imposes an additional service charge of $15.00 for dishonored checks.

APPLICANT INFORMATION

Any person who willfully and knowingly provides any false information on a certificate, record or report required by Chapter 382, Florida Statutes, or on any application or affidavit, or who obtains confidential information from any Vital Record under false or fraudulent purposes, commits a felony of the third degree, punishable as provided in Chapter 775, Florida Statutes.

Applicant's Name TYPE OR PRINT	FIRST	MIDDLE	LAST (INCLUDING ANY SUFFIX)	
ADDRESS (INCLUDE APT. NO.. IF APPLICABLE)		CITY	STATE	ZIP CODE
HOME PHONE NUMBER WORK PHONE NUMBER		RELATIONSHIP TO REGISTRANT	SIGNATURE OF APPLICANT APPLICANT'S SIGNATURE	
IF ATTORNEY, PROVIDE BAR/PROFESSIONAL LICENSE NO.		IF ATTORNEY , PROVIDE NAME OF PERSON YOU REPRESENT AND THEIR RELATIONSHIP TO REGISTRANT		

IF THE CERTIFICATION IS TO BE MAILED TO ANOTHER PERSON OR ADDRESS USE THE SPACES BELOW TO SPECIFY SHIP TO NAME AND ADDRESS.

SHIP TO NAME TYPE OR PRINT	FIRST	MIDDLE	LAST (INCLUDING ANY SUFFIX)	
HOME PHONE NUMBER	SHIP TO STREET ADDRESS (AND APT. NO. IF APPLICABLE)			
WORK PHONE NUMBER	CITY		STATE	ZIP CODE

INFORMATION AND INSTRUCTIONS FOR A MARRIAGE RECORD FOR LICENSES ISSUED IN FLORIDA

CERTIFICATION: A Certification of *Marriage (***June 1927 to present)** that has been recorded by the Clerk of Court. This certification is accepted by all State and Federal Agencies and used as evidence of the marriage. Normal Response time is 5-7 business days, provided the record and application are complete and in order.

AVAILABILITY: After the ceremony, the Marriage License is returned to the Clerk of the Court to be filed and recorded. The Clerk will forward the original license to this office for permanent filing. If the date of Marriage is current, it generally takes up to 60 days to be received by this office from the Clerk of the Court. If the current marriage ceremony is less than sixty days from the date of this application and you need evidence of the marriage for legal purposes, you may wish to contact the county Clerk of the Court where the Marriage License was issued.

Marriage Licenses from June 6, 1927 to the present are available at this office. Any Marriage Record prior to June 6, 1927 is obtainable from the county Clerk of the Court where the Marriage License was issued. Beginning with 1972, the application to marry section was incorporated to the front of the Marriage Record. The application to marry may be available from the Clerk of the Court for events prior to 1972.

ELIGIBILITY: Marriage Records are Public Record. No identification is required unless the bride or groom is requesting their own Social Security Number. If this personal information is requested, one of the following forms of identification must be included: **Driver's License**, **State Identification Card**, **Passport** and/or **Military Identification Card**.

PROCESSING TIME: If the Marriage Record is on file, with the Office of Vital Statistics the normal processing time will be 5-7 business days. However, the response time may vary due to the availability of current events as described above. The processing time may occasionally reach four to six weeks, depending whether or not the Marriage Record has been received by this office from the Clerk of Court

RELATIONSHIP TO REGISTRANT: A person ordering his or her own certificate should enter "SELF" in this space. Also, explain if name has been changed; married name, name changed legally (when and where), etc.

NONREFUNDABLE: Vital record fees are nonrefundable, with one exception. Fees paid for additional copies when no record is found will be refunded upon written request.

APPLICANT'S SIGNATURE: Is required, as well as his/her printed name, residence address and telephone number.

OPTIONS FOR RUSH SERVICE:

- **CREDIT CARDS:** The state office currently does not accept credit cards but there is a private firm that accepts such charges and transfers the order to Vital Statistics for a fee of $7.00 plus a $10.00 Rush Fee charged by the State Office. You may telephone 1-877-550-7330 or you may fax your request to the private firm at 1-877-550-7428. In any event, you may dial (904) 359-6900 and follow the prompts on the telephone system to be transferred free of charge to the contracted vendor. If you have any questions please call the Office of Vital Statistics at (904) 359-6900, Ext. 9000 and our Client Services personnel will be able to assist you.
- **MAIL IN:** An order with an envelope marked RUSH and with a $10.00 rush fee enclosed, (provided the record and application are complete and in order) will be processed before the normal processing time. This does not include marriage records requiring an amendment action. If an amendment action is necessary, additional processing time will be required.
- **WALK-IN SERVICE:** Is available at 1217 Pearl Street, Jacksonville, Florida, between 8:00 am – 4:30 pm. Orders prepaid by Noon may be picked up after 3:30 p.m. Orders prepaid after Noon may be picked up after 10:00 a.m. the next workday. Each request must be accompanied by picture identification Certifications for photocopies rush service requires a rush fee of $10.00.

MAIL THIS APPLICATION WITH PAYMENT TO

STATE OFFICE OF VITAL STATISTICS,

ATTN: CLIENT SERVICES

P.O. BOX 210,

Jacksonville, FL 32231-0042

PLEASE VISIT OUR WEBSITE

http://www.doh.state.fl.us/planning_eval/vital_statistics/index.html

State of Florida - Department of Health
Vital Statistics
APPLICATION FOR FLORIDA COMMEMORATIVE MARRIAGE CERTIFICATE
(Available only from the State Office of Vital Statistics)

Requirement/Availability for ordering: This application is to be used for requesting a Commemorative Marriage Certificate (also includes issuance of a computer certification). If requesting only computer certification or photocopy and no commemorative, do not use this form. Use Application for Marriage Record For Licenses Issued in Florida, DH 261. Marriage records are public record and may be issued to anyone; these, therefore, make excellent gifts. Marriage records from June 6, 1927 are available at this office and beginning with 1972, the marriage application is an integral part of the record issued here. Marriage records prior to June 6, 1927 and Application to Marry prior to 1972 are obtainable only from the clerk of court (www.doh.flclerks.com) in the county where the marriage license was issued.

GROOM	FIRST NAME		MIDDLE NAME	LAST NAME INCLUDING SUFFIX		DATE OF BIRTH	RACE
BRIDE	FIRST NAME		MIDDLE NAME	LAST NAME	MAIDEN, IF DIFFERENT	DATE OF BIRTH	RACE
DATE OF MARRIAGE	MONTH	DAY	YEAR (4-DIGIT)	CITY OR COUNTY WHERE MARRIAGE LICENSED WAS ISSUED		STATE FILE NO.*(If known)*	
ADDITIONAL YEARS TO BE SEARCHED	LIST THE SPAN OF YEARS TO BE SEARCHED (ONLY if you do no know the exact year of the event)						

A Commemorative Marriage Certificate is signed by the current Governor and State Registrar of Vital Statistics. The certificates contain calligraphy style printing, gold state seal, and are suitable for framing and preserving as family heirlooms. The commemorative certificates are mailed encased in cardboard shields to ensure protection. Information on the application is requested to assist us in our search for the record. Information that is shown on a commemorative certificate is taken from the actual marriage certificate not the information provided on this application.

➢ **Include a check or money order in US Dollars for $30.00 made payable to the "Office of Vital Statistics".** The fee covers the search for the record, one computer certification, one commemorative certificate, and mailing. The computer certification will be mailed promptly, if event occurred prior to 1970 a certified copy will be mailed ahead of routine orders and the commemorative will follow within 4 -6 weeks.	$30	X	1	$30
➢ **If the marriage record is not located,** a No Record Found Statement of that fact is issued along with a form to request a refund for $25.00 and any additional copy fee. The $5.00 search fee is non refundable.				
➢ Additional Computer Certification, when ordered at the same time is $4.00 each.	$4	X		$0
➢ Additional Years Search is $2.00 per year and is required ONLY when the exact year of the marriage is not known and you wish more than one year searched. The maximum additional year search fee is $ 50.00 regardless of the total number of years to be searched. *(Be sure to Indicate the range of years to be searched in Information Section above)*	$2	X		$0
➢ Additional Commemorative Certification, when ordered at the same time is $25.00 each.	$25			$0
TOTAL AMOUNT ENCOLSED: ***Florida Law imposes an additional service charge of $15.00 for dishonored checks***			TOTAL	$30

Be Sure To Check Box Below For Your Special Commemorative Design Selection
(Larger images of the commemorative options can be viewed at our website at www.doh.state.fl.us)

☐ 

TRADITIONAL

☐ PALM

APPLICANT NAME/DELIVERY INFORMATION
Any person who willfully and knowingly provides any false information on a certificate, record or report required by Chapter 382, Florida Statutes, or on any application or affidavit, or who obtains confidential information from any Vital Record under false or fraudulent purposes, commits a felony of the third degree, punishable as provided in Chapter 775, Florida Statutes.

Applicant's Name TYPE OR PRINT	FIRST	MIDDLE	LAST (INCLUDING ANY SUFFIX)
DELIVERY ADDRESS (INCLUDE APT. NO., IF APPLICABLE)	CITY STATE		ZIP CODE
HOME PHONE NUMBER WORK PHONE NUMBER	RELATIONSHIP TO REGISTRANT	SIGNATURE OF APPLICANT	
IF ATTORNEY, PROVIDE BAR/PROFESSIONAL LICENSE NO.	IF ATTORNEY, PROVIDE NAME OF PERSON YOU REPRESENT AND THEIR RELATIONSHIP TO REGISTRANT		

IF THE CERTIFICATION IS TO BE MAILED TO ANOTHER PERSON OR ADDRESS USE THE SPACES BELOW TO SPECIFY SHIP TO NAME AND ADDRESS.

SHIP TO NAME TYPE OR PRINT	FIRST	MIDDLE	LAST (INCLUDING ANY SUFFIX)
HOME PHONE NUMBER	SHIP TO STREET ADDRESS (AND APT. NO. IF APPLICABLE)		
WORK PHONE NUMBER	CITY STATE		ZIP CODE

DH 261C, 5/09

MAIL TO: OFFICE OF VITAL STATISTICS, P.O.BOX 210, JACKSONVILLE, FL 32231-0042

State of Florida
Department of Health
Office of Vital Statistics
APPLICATION FOR DISSOLUTION OF MARRIAGE REPORT (DIVORCE OR ANNULMENT) GRANTED IN FLORIDA

NAME OF HUSBAND	FIRST			MIDDLE	LAST		SUFFIX
NAME OF WIFE	FIRST			MIDDLE	LAST	MAIDEN SURNAME	
DATE OF DISSOLUTION	MONTH	DAY	YEAR (4-DIGIT)	INDICATE ADDITIONAL YEARS TO BE SEARCHED		STATE FILE NUMBER (If known)	
PLACE WHERE DISSOLUTION GRANTED	CITY OR TOWN					COUNTY	

CORRECTED or AMENDED *Has the Clerk of Court corrected/amended an item on this Dissolution of Marriage Report (Divorce or Annulment) and forwarded the newly corrected Record to the Office of Vital Statistics?* ☐ Yes ☐ No

A DISSOLUTION OF MARRIAGE RECORD SEARCH REQUIRES ADVANCE PAYMENT OF A NON-REFUNDABLE SEARCH FEE OF $5.00.

The $5.00 fee entitles the applicant to one Certification of *Dissolution of Marriage Report (Divorce or Annulment)* **from June 1927 to present or if a record is not found, a certified "No Record Found" statement will be issued.** $5.00 X ___ = ___

- The Certification of *Dissolution of Marriage Report* is recognized and accepted by **ALL** State and Federal Agencies.
- **Normal processing time is 5-7 business days,** provided the record and application are complete and in order.

Additional Certifications:
$4.00 for each subsequent Computer Certification $4.00 X ___ = ___

Additional Years to be Searched:
$2.00 for each additional year. The maximum additional year search fee is $ 50.00 regardless of the total number of years to be searched. **(Indicate the range of years to be searched in the 2nd Box.)** $2.00 X ___ = ___

RUSH ORDERS (Optional): RUSH Fees are an additional $10.00.
If you desire RUSH service, mark the outside of your envelope **"RUSH"** (*Processing time is 3-4 business days*) Check here for rush order ☐ = ___

TOTAL AMOUNT ENCLOSED: Check or Money Order Payable to: Vital Statistics. **(DO NOT SEND CASH)** ___
International payments should be made by Cashiers Check or Money Order in U. S. Dollars.
Florida Law imposes an additional service charge of $15.00 for dishonored checks.

APPLICANT NAME/DELIVERY INFORMATION

Any person who willfully and knowingly provides any false information on a certificate, record or report required by Chapter 382, Florida Statutes, or on any application or affidavit, or who obtains confidential information from any Vital Record under false or fraudulent purposes, commits a felony of the third degree, punishable as provided in Chapter 775, Florida Statutes.

Applicant's Name TYPE OR PRINT	FIRST	MIDDLE	LAST (INCLUDING ANY SUFFIX)	
DELIVERY ADDRESS (INCLUDE APT. NO., IF APPLICABLE)		CITY	STATE	ZIP CODE
HOME PHONE NUMBER WORK PHONE NUMBER		RELATIONSHIP TO REGISTRANT	SIGNATURE OF APPLICANT Applicant's Signature	
IF ATTORNEY, PROVIDE BAR/PROFESSIONAL LICENSE NO.		IF ATTORNEY, PROVIDE NAME OF PERSON YOU REPRESENT AND THEIR RELATIONSHIP TO REGISTRANT		

IF THE CERTIFICATION IS TO BE MAILED TO ANOTHER PERSON OR ADDRESS USE THE SPACES BELOW TO SPECIFY SHIP TO NAME AND ADDRESS.

SHIP TO NAME TYPE OR PRINT	FIRST	MIDDLE	LAST (INCLUDING ANY SUFFIX)	
HOME PHONE NUMBER	SHIP TO STREET ADDRESS (AND APT. NO. IF APPLICABLE)			
WORK PHONE NUMBER	CITY		STATE	ZIP CODE

INFORMATION AND INSTRUCTIONS FOR A DISSOLUTION OF MARRIAGE REPORT GRANTED IN FLORIDA

CERTIFICATION: A certification of a *Dissolution of Marriage Report (Divorce or Annulment) from* **June 1927 to present** that has been recorded by the Clerk of Court. This certification is accepted by all State and Federal Agencies and used as evidence that a divorce was finalized and recorded. Normal Response time is 5-7 business days, provided the record and application are complete and in order.

AVAILABILITY: After a divorce has been recorded, the Clerk of the Court sends a Report of Dissolution of Marriage to this office. If the divorce was recently granted, it generally takes up to 60 days to be received by this office from the Clerk of the Court. The divorce decree and other court papers remain on file at the Clerk's office. If the current dissolution of marriage is less than 60 days from the date of this application and you need evidence of the divorce for legal purposes, you may wish to contact the county where the Dissolution of Marriage was granted.

We have reports dating from June 6, 1927 to the present. Any divorces prior to June 6, 1927 are obtainable from the Clerk of the Court in the County where the divorce was granted.

ELIGIBILITY: No restriction applies because Dissolution of Marriage Reports (Divorce or Annulment) are public records.

PROCESSING TIME: If the Dissolution of Marriage is on file, the normal processing time will be 5-7 days. However, the response time may vary due to the availability of current events as described above. The processing time may occasionally reach four to six weeks, depending whether or not the Dissolution of Marriage was granted and has been received by this office from the Clerk of Court.

NONREFUNDABLE: Vital record fees are nonrefundable, with one exception. Fees paid for additional copies when no record is found will be refunded upon written request.

APPLICANT'S SIGNATURE: Is required, as well as his/her printed name, residence address and telephone number.

OPTIONS FOR RUSH SERVICE:

- **CREDIT CARDS:** The state office currently does not accept credit cards but there is a private firm that accepts such charges and transfers the order to Vital Statistics for a fee of $7.00 plus a $10.00 Rush Fee charged by the State Office. You may telephone 1-877-550-7330 or you may fax your request to the private firm at 1-877-550-7428. In any event, you may dial (904) 359-6900 and follow the prompts on the telephone system to be transferred free of charge to the contracted vendor. If you have any questions, please call the Office of Vital Statistics at (904) 359-6900, Ext. 9000 and our Client Services personnel will be able to assist you.
- **MAIL IN:** An order with an envelope marked RUSH and with a $10.00 rush fee enclosed, (provided the record and application are complete and in order) will be processed before the normal processing time. This does not include marriage records requiring an amendment action. If an amendment action is necessary, additional processing time will be required.
- **WALK-IN SERVICE:** Is available at 1217 Pearl Street, Jacksonville, Florida, between 8:00 am – 4:30 pm. Orders prepaid by Noon may be picked up after 3:30 p.m. Orders prepaid after Noon may be picked up after 10:00 a.m. the next workday. Each request must be accompanied by picture identification Certifications for photocopies rush service requires a rush fee of $10.00.

MAIL THIS APPLICATION WITH PAYMENT TO

STATE OFFICE OF VITAL STATISTICS,
ATTN: CLIENT SERVICES
P.O. BOX 210,
Jacksonville, FL 32231-0042

PLEASE VISIT OUR WEBSITE

http://www.doh.state.fl.us/planning_eval/vital_statistics/index.html

State of Florida
Department of Health
Bureau of Vital Statistics
APPLICATION FOR FLORIDA DEATH OR FETAL DEATH RECORD

Read the FRONT AND BACK OF this application: **Anyone may apply for a death certification. When cause of death information is also requested and the death occurred less than 50 years ago, a copy of valid photo ID must accompany this application AND the applicant OR person being represented must be an eligible person as outlined in statute (see Eligibility on the reverse of this form). Relationship to the decedent must be entered in the space provided at the bottom of this form when requesting cause of death. Acceptable forms of valid ID are: driver's license, state identification card, passport, and/or military ID card. When requesting a death certification without cause of death OR if the death occurred over 50 years prior to the request, photo identification is not required. If a funeral home or an attorney, see additional information under Eligibility on reverse side of this form to ensure proper completion of this application.**

SECTION A INFORMATION ON TYPE OF RECORD AND DECEDENT PLEASE CHECK APPROPRIATE BOX: ☐ DEATH ☐ FETAL DEATH

NAME OF DECEDENT	FIRST	MIDDLE	LAST	SUFFIX
ALIAS NAME(IF APPLICABLE)			IF MARRIED FEMALE, MAIDEN SURNAME (if known)	
DATE OF DEATH	MONTH / DAY / YEAR (4-DIGIT)	STATE FILE NUMBER (If known)	SEX	
ADDITIONAL YEARS TO BE SEARCHED (Required *only* when exact year is *not* known)	Below indicate the range of years to be searched	PLACE OF DEATH CITY OR TOWN	PLACE OF DEATH COUNTY	
NAME OF SURVIVING SPOUSE AS RECORDED ON DEATH RECORD (if applicable and if known))	FIRST	MIDDLE	LAST	SUFFIX
SOCIAL SECURITY NUMBER		FUNERAL HOME NAME		

IMPORTANT INFORMATION

Any person who willfully and knowingly provides any false information on a certificate, record or report required by Chapter 382, Florida Statutes, or on any application or affidavit, or who obtains confidential information from any Vital Record under false or fraudulent purposes, commits a felony of the third degree, punishable as provided in Chapter 775, Florida Statutes.

SECTION B – FEES: A *RECORD SEARCH REQUIRES ADVANCE PAYMENT OF A* <u>*NON-REFUNDABLE*</u> *SEARCH FEE OF $5.00*

	Fee		Quantity		Total
1st CERTIFICATION - Fee of $5.00 entitles applicant to ONE certification. Check appropriate box: ☐ Without Cause of Death ☐ With Cause of Death (See Eligibility on the reverse side of this form)	$5.00	X		=	
Additional Certifications WITHOUT Cause of Death: $4.00 for each subsequent certification	$4.00	X		=	
Additional Certifications WITH Cause of Death (See Eligibility on the reverse side of this form): $4.00 for each subsequent certification	$4.00	X		=	
Additional Years to be Searched: Required *only* when exact year is *not* known. $2.00 for each additional year. The maximum additional year search fee is $ 50.00 regardless of the total number of years to be searched.	$2.00	X	Total additional years	=	
RUSH ORDERS (Optional): RUSH Fees are an additional $10.00. See reverse side "Options for Rush Service" for **ALL** RUSH options and response times. This section applies ONLY to mail in rush orders. Your Envelope must be marked "RUSH"	Check here for rush order ☐			=	

TOTAL AMOUNT ENCLOSED: Check or Money Order Payable to: Vital Statistics. **(DO NOT SEND CASH)** International payments should be made by Cashiers Check or Money Order in U. S. Dollars. ***Florida Law imposes an additional service charge of $15.00 for dishonored checks.***

ENCLOSE COPY OF VALID PHOTO IDENTIFICATION IF CAUSE OF DEATH CERTIFICATIONS ARE ORDERED OR YOUR ORDER WILL NOT BE COMPLETED

SECTION C – MAILING INFORMATION:

Applicant's Name **TYPE OR PRINT**	FIRST, MIDDLE, LAST (INCLUDING ANY SUFFIX)	Applicant Signature
If Funeral Director or Attorney listed as Applicant and requesting Cause of Death Information	LICENSE/BAR NUMBER	NAME OF PERSON YOU ARE REPRESENTING
If requesting cause of death, state your relationship (OR if a funeral director or an attorney, the relationship of the person you are representing) to the decedent.	RELATIONSHIP TO DECEDENT	
HOME PHONE NUMBER	ADDRESS FOR MAILING *(BE SURE TO INCLUDE ANY BUILDING OR APARTMENT NUMBER.)*	
ALTERNATE PHONE NUMBER	CITY	STATE / ZIP CODE

IF THE CERTIFICATION IS TO BE MAILED TO ANOTHER PERSON OR ADDRESS USE THE SPACES BELOW TO SPECIFY SHIP TO NAME AND ADDRESS.

SHIP TO NAME **TYPE OR PRINT**	FIRST	MIDDLE	LAST (INCLUDING ANY SUFFIX)
HOME PHONE NUMBER	SHIP TO STREET ADDRESS (AND APT. NO. IF APPLICABLE)		
WORK PHONE NUMBER	CITY	STATE	ZIP CODE

DH 727, 9/08 64V-1.0131, Florida Administrative Code

INFORMATION / INSTRUCTIONS

This application is not to be used for requesting an amendment to a death record. If an amendment is required, use DH Form 433(non medical amendment) or DH 434 (medical amendment).

AVAILABILITY: Death registration was not required by state law until 1917; however, it was many years before we had consistent registration. While there are some records on file dating back to 1877, not all events were registered.

ELIGIBILITY:

WITHOUT CAUSE OF DEATH: Any person of legal age (18) may be issued a certified copy of a death record without the cause of death.

CAUSE OF DEATH INFORMATION: Cause of Death for any record over 50 years old may be issued to any applicant. Death records less than 50 years old with the cause of death information included may only be issued to the following individuals: the decedent's spouse or parent; to the decedent's child, grandchild or sibling, if of legal age; to any person who provides a will, insurance policy or other document that demonstrates his or her interest in the estate of the decedent, or to any person who provides documentation that he or she is acting on behalf of any of the above named persons. All requests for certification of a death certificate that includes the cause of death information must state the qualifying eligibility, or a notarized Affidavit to Release Cause of Death Information (DH Form 1959), which is available upon request. If after reading the above information you are still uncertain regarding your eligibility for cause of death information, call our office (904) 359-6900 extension 9000 for assistance.

A funeral director or attorney representing an eligible person as defined above must include their professional license number, and the name and relationship of the person they are representing, if requesting cause of death. If not representing someone identified above as eligible to receive cause of death information, then a completed Affidavit to Release Cause of Death Information (DH Form 1959) must accompany this request. **SPECIAL NOTE:** Florida clerks of court will not accept a death record with "cause of death information included" when filing probate.

DATE OF DEATH NOT KNOWN: If date of death is unknown, the entire year specified will be searched. If you do not know the year of the event and you wish to have more than one year searched, you must specify the span of years you wish searched (Example: 1970 to present) and pay the $2.00 per year for each additional year to be searched.

INFORMATION NEEDED: A search **cannot be made without the decedent's name and year of death**. If any of the other items requested in Section A on the front of this form are available, this information may be helpful to us in our search particularly when multiple records are found for common names. Please provide as much information as possible.

PROCESSING TIME Normal response time is 10 – 14 business days; however, the processing time can exceed this timeframe dependent upon the volume of work received and the resources available at the time your request is received.

OPTIONS FOR RUSH SERVICE:

- **CREDIT CARDS:** The state office currently does not accept credit cards but there is a private firm that accepts such charges and transfers the requests to Vital Statistics for a fee of $7.00 plus a $10.00 Rush Fee charged by the State Office. Telephone number is (877) 550-7330 or fax (877) 550-7428. All requests taken by this firm will be expedited in our office with a processing time exceeding that of routine processing, (usually 5-7 business days for regular mail). Certification(s) will be mailed 1st class mail UNLESS special mailing is requested and paid for at the time of your order. If special mailing (UPS) is requested at the time you place your order with this contracted firm, the request will be processed in our office within 1-2 days.
- **MAIL IN:** Orders marked RUSH and with $10 rush fee included with the search fee, will be searched priority over routine processing (usually 5-7 days response time for RUSH service). Include a self addressed stamped envelope with your request. Certification(s) will be mailed 1st class mail UNLESS a prepaid special mailing envelope is included with your request.
- **WALK-IN SERVICE:** Requests may be made at the state office in Jacksonville, located at **1217 Pearl Street.** Orders prepaid before noon may be picked up after 3:30 p.m. Orders prepaid after noon may be picked up after 10:00 a.m. the next workday.

RECORD NOT FOUND: If a death record is not found, you will be issued a "not found" statement in lieu of the certification. Fees are nonrefundable, with one exception. Fees paid for additional copies when no record is found will be refunded upon written request.

MAIL THIS APPLICATION WITH PAYMENT TO

STATE OFFICE OF VITAL STATISTICS
ATTN: CLIENT SERVICES
P.O. BOX 210
Jacksonville, FL 32231-0042

PLEASE VISIT OUR WEBSITE

http://www.doh.state.fl.us/planning_eval/vital_statistics/index.html

AFFIDAVIT TO RELEASE CAUSE OF DEATH INFORMATION

(If you are eligible to receive the death certificate requested below, you may use ***this form*** to name another person to receive the death certificate for you.)

State of:________________________ County of:________________________

My Name is: *(print name)*____ .

I am eligible, by law, to receive the death certificate requested below, because I am the: *(check one)*

__ Surviving spouse listed on the death certificate.

__ Parent listed on the death certificate.

__ Child (or grandchild) of the decedent and of legal age (18).

__ Sibling of the decedent and of legal age (18).

__ Representative of one of the above (Documentation required).

__ Other: beneficiary or other interest in the estate (Documentation required).

I authorize the Department of Health, Office of Vital Statistics to issue the death certificate with cause of death of:

__________________________________ **to** __________________________________.
(person named on death certificate) **(print name of person to receive death certificate)**

(Required) I have attached a photocopy of my valid photo ID:

______________________________ .
type of Identification attached **(If attorney or funeral director, only bar or license number required)**

NOTE: Pursuant to s. 382.026, Florida Statutes, it is a 3rd degree felony to obtain and use a Florida death record fraudulently, punishable as set forth in s. 775.082, s. 775.083, or s. 775.084, Florida Statutes.

I hereby swear or affirm the above statements are true and correct.

____
(signature of person checked above)

Subscribed and sworn before me this _______ day of ___________________, 20____ by

______________________________, who is: __ personally known to me, or, __ who has
(print name of person checked above)

produced _________________________ as Identification. My Commission Expires: _________.
(type of Identification produced)

______________________________ ______________________________
(signature of notary) ***(print, type or stamp name of notary)*** (SEAL)

Even if personally known by the notary, the rules of the Department of Health require the person completing this form to provide a photocopy of valid photo identification.

DH Form 1959, August 2010 (Obsoletes previous editions)
64V-1.0131, Florida Administrative Code

GEORGIA

Send your requests to:

Vital Records
2600 Skyland Drive, NE
Atlanta, GA 30319-3640

Tel. (404) 679-4702
Fax (404) 679-4730
E-mail: phvitalrecords@gdph.state.ga.us
http://health.state.ga.us/programs/vitalrecords/

The State Office of Vital Records maintains birth and death records from 1919 to the present (though there are some birth records on file before 1919). Marriage applications and licenses from 1952 to 1996 are also available. No divorce records are kept by Vital Records, but an index of divorce events from 1952 to the present is available. Certified copies may also be obtained from the county where the event occurred; some older records may be available at the county level.

You can also order certified copies of birth and death certificates online for an additional processing fee (http://gta.georgia.gov/rover).

Cost for a certified Birth Certificate	$25.00
Cost for a certified Marriage Certificate	$10.00
Cost for verification of Divorce Decree	$10.00
Cost for a certified Death Certificate	$25.00
Cost for a duplicate copy, when ordered at the same time	$5.00

For Marriage Records before 1952, contact:

County Probate Court
(County Seat), GA

For Divorce Records, contact:

Clerk of Superior Court
(County Seat), GA

For Genealogy Research

The Georgia Archives (5800 Jonesboro Road, Morrow, Georgia 30260-1101; tel. 404-364-3710; www.georgiaarchives.org/) has some early birth, death, and marriage records, as well as numerous other records of interest to genealogists. The images of some vital records are available online, including scanned images of Georgia death certificates from 1919 through 1927.

For Adoption Record information, contact:

Georgia Adoption Reunion Registry
2 Peachtree Street, NW, Suite 8-407
Atlanta, GA 30303-3142

Tel. (888) 328-0055 toll free
Fax (404) 656-2463 fax
www.ga-adoptionreunion.com

PLEASE RETURN THIS FORM TO: VITAL RECORDS, 2600 SKYLAND DRIVE, NE, ATLANTA, GA 30319

Please indicate below the type and number of copies requested and forward this form with either a money order or certified check for the correct amount, made payable to Vital Records.

[ ] Full size copy $25.00 Additional copies $5.00 each at this time

[ ] Total number of copies Requested

[ ] Amount Received $____________

[ ] Photocopy of valid photo ID

BIRTH CERTIFICATE REQUESTS

FILL IN INFORMATON BELOW CONCERNING PERSON WHOSE BIRTH CERTIFICATE IS REQUESTED

Name at birth: ____
(first) (middle) (last)

Date of birth: ______________ Age: ______________ Race: ______________ Sex: ______________

Place of birth: ____
(hospital) (city) (county) (state)

Full name of father: ____

Full name of mother before marriage: ____

DEATH CERTIFICATE REQUESTS

FILL IN INFORMATION BELOW CONCERNING DECEDENT

Name: ____

Date of death: ______________ Age: ______________ Race: ______________ Sex: ______________

Place of death: ____
(hospital) (city) (county) (state)

If married, name of husband or wife: ____

Occupation of deceased: ____

Funeral director's name: ____

Name of doctor: ____

Place of burial: ____
(city) (county) (state)

MAILING ADDRESS

List below the name and address of the person to whom the certificate is to be mailed and indicate their relationship to the person whose name is on the certificate:

Name: ______________________________ Relationship: ______________________________

Address: ____
(No. & Street or RFD and Box No.) (Apt. No.)

____
(city) (state) (zip code)

Phone: ______________________________

Georgia Department of Community Health
Vital Record
2600 Skyland Drive, NE
Atlanta, GA 30319

REQUEST FOR SEARCH OF DEATH RECORDS

The fee for searches of vital records has been established by the State Board of Human Resorces as twenty-five dollars ($ 25.00), in accordance with Section 31-10-27 of the Georgia Code. The $25 fee includes a certified copy if the record is found. Each additional copy paid for at the same time is five dollars ($5.00). Three years are searched.

PLEASE INDICATE BELOW THE NUMBERS OF COPIES NEEDED AND FORWARD THIS FORM WITH EITHER A MONEY ORDER OR CHECK FOR THE CORRECT AMOUNT MADE PAYABLE TO VITAL RECORDS.

☐ Total Number of Copies

Amount Received $ ____________

FILL IN INFORMATION BELOW CONCERNING PERSON WHOSE CERTIFICATE IS REQUESTED

Name ______________________________ Date of Death ____________
(First) (Middle) (Last)

Age ____________ Race ____________ Sex ____________

Place of Death ______________________________
(Hospital) (City) (County) (State)

If Married, Name of Husband or Wife ______________________________

Occupation of Deceased ______________________________

Funeral DirectorÕs Name ______________________________

Name of Doctor ______________________________

Place of Burial ______________________________

- -

ADDRESS CORRESPONDENCE TO:
Vital Records
2600 Skyland Drive, NE
Atlanta, GA 30319

(MAILING LABEL)

PRINT YOUR NAME AND ADDRESS BELOW (legibly and correctly)

____
Name

____
Street Name/Number Apt. No.

____
City State Zip

____
Phone

PLEASE RETURN THIS FORM TO: VITAL RECORDS, 2600 SKYLAND DRIVE, NE, ATLANTA, GA 30319

MARRIAGE CERTIFICATE REQUESTS

Please indicate below the type and number of copies requested and forward this form with either a money order or certified check for the correct amount, made payable to Vital Records.

[ ] Full size copy $10.00; additional copies are $5.00 each at this time [ ] Total Number of Copies Requested

NOTE: Records prior to June 9, 1952 must be requested at the Office of the Probate Judge in the county where the license was issued If you are requesting a marriage certificate prior to this date, complete this application and mail it to the county's Probate Court's office in which the marriage was granted. Contact their office concerning their fee requirements, as their prices may differ from our prices.

COMPLETE ALL INFORMATION FOR THE MARRIAGE RECORD BEING REQUESTED:

Groom's Name:____

(First) (Middle) (Last)

Bride's Name:____

(First) (Middle) (Last)

Date of Marriage: ____

(Month) (Day) (Year)

Place of Marriage:____

(City) (County) (State)

Signature of Requestor:____

Relationship (if other than Bride or Groom):____

DIVORCE VERIFICATION REQUESTS ONLY

Please indicate below the type and number of verifications requested and forward this form with either a money order or certified check for the correct amount, made payable to Vital Records. Divorce records are kept for statistical purposes only; therefore, copies are never issued by the State Office.

[ ] One Certified Statement $10.00; Additional statements are $5.00 at this time [ ] Total Number of Statements Requested

NOTE: Records prior to June 9, 1952 must be requested at the Clerk of the Superior Court in the county where the divorce was granted. If you are requesting a divorce record prior to this date, complete this application and mail it to the Clerk of the Superior Court in the county where the divorce was granted. Contact their office concerning their fee requirements, as their prices may differ from our prices.

COMPLETE ALL INFORMATION FOR THE DIVORCE VERIFICATION BEING REQUESTED:

Groom's Name:____

(First) (Middle) (Last)

Bride's Name:____

(First) (Middle) (Last)

Date of Divorce:____

(Month) (Day) (Year)

Place of Divorce:____

(City) (County) (State)

Signature of Requestor:____

Relationship (if other than Bride or Groom):____

MAILING ADDRESS

List below the name and address of the person to whom the certificate is to be mailed and indicate their relationship to the person whose name is on the certificate:

Name:____ Relationship: ____________________

Address: ____

(No. & Street or RFD and Box No.) (Apt. No.)

____

(city) (state) (zip code)

HAWAII

Send your requests to:

Hawaii Department of Health
Office of Health Status Monitoring
Issuance/Vital Statistics Section
(Location: 1250 Punchbowl Street, Room 103)
P.O. Box 3378
Honolulu, HI 96801-3378

Tel. (808) 586-4533
E-mail: vr-info@doh.hawaii.gov
http://health.hawaii.gov/vitalrecords/

The Issuance/Vital Statistics Section has birth, marriage, and death records from 1853, and divorce records from July 1951. Divorce records are also available from the Circuit Court in the county where the divorce was granted. Fees vary. Hawaiian vital records are restricted for 75 years.

All applications requesting certified copies of birth, death, marriage, and divorce certificates must generally be made by mail or in person; telephone, fax, or e-mail requests are not accepted. However, you may order certified copies of birth and marriage/civil union certificates from July 1909 to the present online (www.ehawaiigov.org/ohsm) for a small additional fee. When applying by mail, the applicant must include a photocopy of his/her government-issued photo ID, such as a State ID, driver's license, etc. Personal checks are not accepted.

Cost for a certified Birth Certificate	$10.00
Cost for a certified Marriage Certificate	$10.00
Cost for a certified Civil Union Certificate	$10.00
Cost for a certified Divorce Record	$10.00
Cost for a certified Death Certificate	$10.00
Cost for a duplicate copy, when ordered at the same time	$4.00

For Genealogy Research:

Records of events that occurred more than 75 years prior to the current year can be ordered by persons working on genealogy projects. For vital records that occurred less than 75 years prior to the current year, the applicant must establish a direct and tangible interest in the records. Since genealogy requests are not considered urgent, they are not processed as priority requests. For more information on how to apply for a genealogy request, check the "genealogy request" link on the Vital Records website.

Microfilm copies of selected vital records indexes are available at the Hawaii State Library's Main Library (Hawaii and Pacific Collection, 478 South King Street, Honolulu; tel. 808-586-3535). Indexes to birth records for the years 1896–1909 are also at the Hawaii State Library (Main Library, Hilo, Kahului, Kaneohe, Lihue, and Kailua-Kona) and the University of Hawaii Library, Hawaiian Collection. Microfilm copies of selected vital records are available at the LDS FamilySearch Centers in Hawaii.

For Adoption Record information, contact:

Hawaii's Family Courts deal with legal matters regarding adoptions. For contact information, visit www.courts.state.hi.us/courts/family/family_courts.html.

STATE OF HAWAII, DEPARTMENT OF HEALTH
OFFICE OF HEALTH STATUS MONITORING

REQUEST FOR CERTIFIED COPY OF **BIRTH** RECORD

1	FIRST CERTIFIED COPY	= $	10.00
0	ADDITIONAL COPIES AT $4.00 EACH	= $	0.00
0	OTHER:____________________	= $	0.00
1	TOTAL COPIES	**TOTAL AMOUNT DUE**	**$ 10.00**

NAME ON CERTIFICATE: FIRST | MIDDLE | LAST | MALE/FEMALE ☐ M ☐ F

DATE OF BIRTH: MONTH | DAY | YEAR

PLACE OF BIRTH: CITY OR TOWN | ISLAND

FATHER'S NAME: FIRST | MIDDLE | LAST

MOTHER'S NAME: FIRST | MIDDLE | MAIDEN NAME

RELATIONSHIP OF REQUESTOR TO PERSON NAMED ON CERTIFICATE

REASON FOR THIS REQUEST

SIGNATURE OF REQUESTOR:

TELEPHONE NUMBERS

RES:

BUS:

PRINT NAME OF REQUESTOR:

ADDRESS OF REQUESTOR: NO. AND STREET OR P.O. BOX

CITY | STATE | ZIP

IF MAILING TO A LOCATION OTHER THAN ABOVE, PLEASE FILL THIS SECTION.
IF THE INFORMATION GIVEN IS INCORRECT, THE CERTIFICATE WILL FAIL TO REACH THE DESTINATION.

NAME OF PERSON TO RECEIVE CERTIFICATE

AGENCY OR ORGANIZATION

NUMBER AND STREET OR P.O. BOX

CITY | STATE | ZIP

FOR OFFICE USE ONLY

_______ _______ HBC

_______ DBC

_______ UNREC. BC

_______ NR FILE

_______ PENDING:

INDEX SEARCHED FROM TO		VOLUMES SEARCHED FROM TO	DATE COPY PREPARED
YEAR	VOLUME	CERTIFICATE	RECEIPT NUMBER

OHSM 135 (Rev. 9/13/05)

* **Be sure to sign the "Signature of Requestor" Box before submitting this form.**

ONCE A REQUEST IS SUBMITTED:

1. **All fees are non-refundable.**
2. If a vital record is not found, all fees will be retained to cover the cost of the search.
3. Only one name is allowed on the request form.
4. After a request is submitted, additional copies require a new request.

SUBMIT THE COMPLETED REQUEST FORM:

1. **By postal mail to:** State Department of Health
   Office of Health Status Monitoring
   Vital Records Issuance Section
   PO Box 3378
   Honolulu, Hawaii 96801

All fees must be prepaid. Enclose a money order or cashier's check for the exact amount of fees made payable to: Hawaii State Department of Health. Do not send payment in cash. **PERSONAL CHECKS NOT ACCEPTED.**

2. **In-person at:** Room 103, 1250 Punchbowl Street, Honolulu
   7:45 AM to 2:30 PM, Monday through Friday (Except Holidays)

Payment of fees must be made by cash, money order, or cashier's check.

Personal checks will not be accepted

STATE OF HAWAII, DEPARTMENT OF HEALTH
OFFICE OF HEALTH STATUS MONITORING

REQUEST FOR CERTIFIED COPY OF **MARRIAGE** RECORD

1	FIRST CERTIFIED COPY	= $	10.00
0	ADDITIONAL COPIES AT $4.00 EACH	= $	0.00
0	OTHER:____________________	= $	0.00
1	TOTAL COPIES	**TOTAL AMOUNT DUE**	**$ 10.00**

GROOM'S NAME:	FIRST	MIDDLE	LAST
BRIDE'S NAME:	FIRST	MIDDLE	LAST
DATE OF MARRIAGE:	MONTH	DAY	YEAR
PLACE OF MARRIAGE:	CITY OR TOWN	ISLAND	

RELATIONSHIP OF REQUESTOR TO PERSON NAMED ON CERTIFICATE	REASON FOR THIS REQUEST
SIGNATURE OF REQUESTOR:	TELEPHONE NUMBERS RES:
PRINT NAME OF REQUESTOR:	BUS:

ADDRESS OF REQUESTOR:	NO. AND STREET OR P.O. BOX	
CITY	STATE	ZIP

IF MAILING TO A LOCATION OTHER THAN ABOVE, PLEASE FILL THIS SECTION. IF THE INFORMATION GIVEN IS INCORRECT, THE CERTIFICATE WILL FAIL TO REACH THE DESTINATION.	NAME OF PERSON TO RECEIVE CERTIFICATE AGENCY OR ORGANIZATION NUMBER AND STREET OR P.O. BOX CITY STATE ZIP

FOR OFFICE USE ONLY

______ NR FILE

______ PENDING:

INDEX SEARCHED FROM TO	VOLUMES SEARCHED FROM TO	DATE COPY PREPARED

YEAR	VOLUME	CERTIFICATE	RECEIPT NUMBER

OHSM 137 (Rev. 9/13/05)

*** Be sure to sign the "Signature of Requestor" Box before submitting this form.**

ONCE A REQUEST IS SUBMITTED:

1. **All fees are non-refundable.**

2. If a vital record is not found, all fees will be retained to cover the cost of the search.

3. Only one name is allowed on the request form.

4. After a request is submitted, additional copies require a new request.

SUBMIT THE COMPLETED REQUEST FORM:

1. **By postal mail to:** State Department of Health
Office of Health Status Monitoring
Vital Records Issuance Section
PO Box 3378
Honolulu, Hawaii 96801

All fees must be prepaid. Enclose a money order or cashier's check for the exact amount of fees made payable to: Hawaii State Department of Health. Do not send payment in cash. **PERSONAL CHECKS NOT ACCEPTED.**

2. **In-person at:** Room 103, 1250 Punchbowl Street, Honolulu
7:45 AM to 2:30 PM, Monday through Friday (Except Holidays)

Payment of fees must be made by cash, money order, or cashier's check.

Personal checks will not be accepted

STATE OF HAWAII, DEPARTMENT OF HEALTH
OFFICE OF HEALTH STATUS MONITORING

REQUEST FOR CERTIFIED COPY OF CIVIL UNION RECORD

___1___ FIRST CERTIFIED COPY		= $ 10.00
________ ADDITIONAL COPIES AT $4.00 EACH		= $________
________ OTHER:________________		= $________
________ TOTAL COPIES	TOTAL AMOUNT DUE	= $________

PARTNER A'S NAME:	FIRST	MIDDLE	LAST
PARTNER B'S NAME:	FIRST	MIDDLE	LAST
DATE OF CIVIL UNION:	MONTH	DAY	YEAR
PLACE OF CIVIL UNION:	CITY OR TOWN	ISLAND	

RELATIONSHIP OF REQUESTOR TO PERSON NAMED ON CERTIFICATE	REASON FOR THIS REQUEST
SIGNATURE OF REQUESTOR:	TELEPHONE NUMBERS RES: BUS:
PRINT NAME OF REQUESTOR:	

ADDRESS OF REQUESTOR:	NO. AND STREET OR P.O. BOX	
CITY	STATE	ZIP

IF MAILING TO A LOCATION OTHER THAN ABOVE, PLEASE FILL THIS SECTION.

IF THE INFORMATION GIVEN IS INCORRECT, THE CERTIFICATE WILL FAIL TO REACH THE DESTINATION.

NAME OF PERSON TO RECEIVE CERTIFICATE

AGENCY OR ORGANIZATION

NUMBER AND STREET OR P.O. BOX

CITY | STATE | ZIP

FOR OFFICE USE ONLY

_____ NR FILE
_____ PENDING:

INDEX SEARCHED FROM TO	VOLUMES SEARCHED FROM TO	DATE COPY PREPARED	
YEAR	VOLUME	CERTIFICATE	RECEIPT NUMBER

OHSM 139 (Rev. 1/11/12) STATE OF HAWAII, DEPARTMENT OF HEALTH

***Be sure to sign the "Signature of Requestor" Box before submitting this form**

ONCE A REQUEST IS SUBMITTED:

1. **All fees are non-refundable.**
2. If a vital record is not found, all fees will be retained to cover the cost of the search.
3. Only one name is allowed on the request form.
4. After a request is submitted, additional copies require a new request.

SUBMIT THE COMPLETED REQUEST FORM:

1. **By postal mail to:** State Department of Health
Office of Health Status Monitoring
Vital Records Issuance Section
PO Box 3378
Honolulu, Hawaii 96801

All fees must be prepaid. Enclose a money order or cashier's check for the exact amount of fees made payable to: Hawaii State Department of Health. Do not send payment in cash. **PERSONAL CHECKS NOT ACCEPTED.**

2. **In-person at:** Room 103, 1250 Punchbowl Street, Honolulu
7:45 AM to 2:30 PM, Monday through Friday (Except Holidays)

Payment of fees must be made by cash, money order, or cashier's check.

Personal checks will not be accepted

STATE OF HAWAII, DEPARTMENT OF HEALTH
OFFICE OF HEALTH STATUS MONITORING

REQUEST FOR CERTIFIED COPY OF **DIVORCE** RECORD

IMPORTANT! THIS OFFICE ONLY HAS DIVORCE RECORDS FROM July 1951 TO December 2002
ALL OTHER DIVORCE RECORDS ARE KEPT IN THE COURT WHERE THE DIVORCE TOOK PLACE.

1	FIRST CERTIFIED COPY	= $	10.00
0	ADDITIONAL COPIES AT $4.00 EACH	= $	0.00
0	OTHER:____________________	= $	0.00
1	TOTAL COPIES	**TOTAL AMOUNT DUE**	**$ 10.00**

HUSBAND'S NAME:	FIRST	MIDDLE	LAST
WIFE'S NAME:	FIRST	MIDDLE	MAIDEN
DATE OF DIVORCE:	MONTH	DAY	YEAR
PLACE OF DIVORCE:	CITY OR TOWN		ISLAND

RELATIONSHIP OF REQUESTOR TO PERSON NAMED ON CERTIFICATE	REASON FOR THIS REQUEST
SIGNATURE OF REQUESTOR:	TELEPHONE NUMBERS RES: BUS:
PRINT NAME OF REQUESTOR:	

ADDRESS OF REQUESTOR:	NO. AND STREET OR P.O. BOX	
CITY	STATE	ZIP

IF MAILING TO A LOCATION OTHER THAN ABOVE, PLEASE FILL THIS SECTION. IF THE INFORMATION GIVEN IS INCORRECT, THE CERTIFICATE WILL FAIL TO REACH THE DESTINATION.	NAME OF PERSON TO RECEIVE CERTIFICATE AGENCY OR ORGANIZATION NUMBER AND STREET OR P.O. BOX CITY STATE ZIP

FOR OFFICE USE ONLY

_______ NR FILE

_______ PENDING:

INDEX SEARCHED FROM TO	VOLUMES SEARCHED FROM TO	DATE COPY PREPARED

YEAR	VOLUME	CERTIFICATE	RECEIPT NUMBER

OHSM 138 (Rev. 9/13/05)

*** Be sure to sign the "Signature of Requestor" Box before submitting this form.**

ONCE A REQUEST IS SUBMITTED:

1. **All fees are non-refundable.**
2. If a vital record is not found, all fees will be retained to cover the cost of the search.
3. Only one name is allowed on the request form.
4. After a request is submitted, additional copies require a new request.

SUBMIT THE COMPLETED REQUEST FORM:

1. **By postal mail to:** State Department of Health
Office of Health Status Monitoring
Vital Records Issuance Section
PO Box 3378
Honolulu, Hawaii 96801

All fees must be prepaid. Enclose a money order or cashier's check for the exact amount of fees made payable to: Hawaii State Department of Health. Do not send payment in cash. **PERSONAL CHECKS NOT ACCEPTED.**

2. **In-person at:** Room 103, 1250 Punchbowl Street, Honolulu
7:45 AM to 2:30 PM, Monday through Friday (Except Holidays)

Payment of fees must be made by cash, money order, or cashier's check.

Personal checks will not be accepted

STATE OF HAWAII, DEPARTMENT OF HEALTH
OFFICE OF HEALTH STATUS MONITORING

REQUEST FOR CERTIFIED COPY OF **DEATH** RECORD

1	FIRST CERTIFIED COPY	= $	10.00
0	ADDITIONAL COPIES AT $4.00 EACH	= $	0.00
0	OTHER:____________________	= $	0.00
1	TOTAL COPIES	**TOTAL AMOUNT DUE**	**$ 10.00**

NAME OF DECEASED: FIRST | MIDDLE | LAST | MALE /FEMALE ☐ MALE ☐ FEMALE

DATE OF DEATH: MONTH | DAY | YEAR

PLACE OF DEATH: CITY OR TOWN | ISLAND

SOCIAL SECURITY NUMBER:

RELATIONSHIP OF REQUESTOR TO PERSON NAMED ON CERTIFICATE | REASON FOR THIS REQUEST

SIGNATURE OF REQUESTOR:

PRINT NAME OF REQUESTOR:

TELEPHONE NUMBERS
RES:
BUS:

ADDRESS OF REQUESTOR: NO. AND STREET OR P.O. BOX

CITY | STATE | ZIP

IF MAILING TO A LOCATION OTHER THAN ABOVE, PLEASE FILL THIS SECTION

IF THE INFORMATION GIVEN IS INCORRECT, THE CERTIFICATE WILL FAIL TO REACH THE DESTINATION.

NAME OF PERSON TO RECEIVE CERTIFICATE

AGENCY OR ORGANIZATION

NUMBER AND STREET OR P.O. BOX

CITY | STATE | ZIP

FOR OFFICE USE ONLY

_______ NR FILE
_______ PENDING:

INDEX SEARCHED FROM TO	VOLUMES SEARCHED FROM TO	DATE COPY PREPARED

YEAR	VOLUME	CERTIFICATE	RECEIPT NUMBER

OHSM 136 (Rev. 9/13/05)

*** Be sure to sign the "Signature of Requestor" Box before submitting this form.**

ONCE A REQUEST IS SUBMITTED:

1. **All fees are non-refundable.**

2. If a vital record is not found, all fees will be retained to cover the cost of the search.

3. Only one name is allowed on the request form.

4. After a request is submitted, additional copies require a new request.

SUBMIT THE COMPLETED REQUEST FORM:

1. **By postal mail to:** State Department of Health
Office of Health Status Monitoring
Vital Records Issuance Section
PO Box 3378
Honolulu, Hawaii 96801

All fees must be prepaid. Enclose a money order or cashier's check for the exact amount of fees made payable to: Hawaii State Department of Health. Do not send payment in cash. **PERSONAL CHECKS NOT ACCEPTED.**

2. **In-person at:** Room 103, 1250 Punchbowl Street, Honolulu
7:45 AM to 2:30 PM, Monday through Friday (Except Holidays)

Payment of fees must be made by cash, money order, or cashier's check.

Personal checks will not be accepted

IDAHO

Send your requests to:

Idaho Bureau of Vital Records and Health Statistics
(Location: 450 West State Street)
P.O. Box 83720
Boise, ID 83720-0036

Tel. (208) 334-5988
Fax (208) 332-7260
E-mail: IVR@dhw.idaho.gov
www.healthandwelfare.idaho.gov

The Vital Records Bureau has birth and death records from July 1, 1911, and marriage and divorce records from May 1, 1947. Some counties may have older birth, death, marriage, or divorce records in their files. Birth certificates are restricted for 100 years. Death, stillbirth, marriage, and divorce certificates are restricted for 50 years. Requests must include a copy of a government-issued picture ID of the person requesting the certificate. Only immediate family members, their legal representative, or those who provide documentation showing it is needed for their property right may order legally confidential certificates.

Cost for a computer-generated certified Birth Certificate	$13.00
Cost for a computer-generated certified Marriage or Divorce Certificate	$13.00
Cost for a computer-generated certified Death Certificate	$14.00
Cost for a Birth, Marriage, or Divorce certified photocopy	$18.00
Cost for a Death certified photocopy	$19.00

For earlier records, contact:

County Clerk
County Court House
(County Seat), ID

For Genealogy Research:

BYU-Idaho Special Collections has marriage and death indexes available online at http://abish.byui.edu/specialCollections/index.cfm.

The Idaho State Historical Society/Idaho State Archives (2205 Old Penitentiary Road, Boise, ID 83712; tel. 208-334-2620; http://history.idaho.gov) has selected county vital records from 1864 to 1920 on microfilm.

For Adoption Record information, contact:

Voluntary Adoption Registry
Bureau of Vital Records and Health Statistics
P.O. Box 83720
Boise, ID 83720-0036

Tel. (208) 334-5990

Cost for registering with the Voluntary Adoption Registry	$10.00

IDAHO VITAL STATISTICS CERTIFICATE REQUEST

IDAHO VITAL RECORDS • P.O. Box 83720 • Boise, ID 83720-0036 • (208) 334-5988 • www.vitalrecords.dhw.idaho.gov

Instructions for completing this form are located on the back of this document. Please read these instructions carefully. Failure to do so may cause a significant delay in processing your request.

YOUR MAILING ADDRESS INFORMATION (PERSON REQUESTING THE CERTIFICATE)

FULL FIRST NAME	FULL MIDDLE NAME	FULL LAST NAME

STREET AND NUMBER (P.O. BOX)	CITY	STATE, ZIP CODE

CONTACT PHONE NUMBER (DAY TIME)	YOUR RELATIONSHIP TO PERSON NAMED ON CERTIFICATE (SELF, MOTHER, ETC.)

PURPOSE FOR THE CERTIFICATE

SIGNATURE OF THE PERSON REQUESTING THE CERTIFICATE:

▶

REQUESTS MUST INCLUDE A COPY (FRONT AND BACK) OF A CURRENT GOVERNMENT-ISSUED SIGNED PICTURE ID OF THE PERSON REQUESTING THE CERTIFICATE. ***(SEE INSTRUCTIONS ON THE BACK OF THIS DOCUMENT)***

IMPORTANT: BIRTH, DEATH, STILLBIRTH, MARRIAGE OR DIVORCE MUST HAVE OCCURRED IN IDAHO.

☑ **INDICATE CERTIFICATE REQUESTED: BIRTH ☐ STILLBIRTH ☐** Available from July 1911

NAME ON CERTIFICATE:

FULL FIRST NAME	FULL MIDDLE NAME	FULL LAST NAME
DATE OF BIRTH	CITY OF BIRTH	NUMBER OF COPIES YOU ARE REQUESTING

FATHER'S NAME:

FULL FIRST NAME	FULL MIDDLE NAME	FULL LAST NAME

MOTHER'S MAIDEN NAME:

FULL FIRST NAME	FULL MIDDLE NAME	FULL LAST MAIDEN NAME

DEATH Available from July 1911

NAME ON CERTIFICATE:

FULL FIRST NAME	FULL MIDDLE NAME	FULL LAST NAME
DATE OF DEATH	CITY OF DEATH	NUMBER OF COPIES YOU ARE REQUESTING

☑ **INDICATE CERTIFCATE REQUESTED: MARRIAGE ☐ DIVORCE ☐** Available from May 1947

HUSBAND'S NAME:

FULL FIRST NAME	FULL MIDDLE NAME	FULL LAST NAME

WIFE'S NAME:

FULL FIRST NAME	FULL MIDDLE NAME	FULL LAST NAME (at time of event)
DATE OF EVENT	CITY OF EVENT	NUMBER OF COPIES YOU ARE REQUESTING

# of copies	FEES*	$ cost
____	BIRTH-STILLBIRTH-MARRIAGE-DIVORCE CERTIFIED COPY @ $13.00 EACH	= ____
____	DEATH CERTIFIED COPY @ $14.00 EACH	= ____
____	BIRTH-STILLBIRTH-MARRIAGE-DIVORCE CERTIFIED PHOTOCOPY @ $13.00 EACH + $5.00 PROCESSING FEE	= ____
____	DEATH CERTIFIED PHOTOCOPY @ $14.00 EACH + $5.00 PROCESSING FEE	= ____
____	SPECIAL HANDLING @ $5.00 (RUSH ORDERS ONLY)♦	= ____
____	PROCESSING FEE FOR LEGAL ACTIONS @ $13.00 EACH	= ____
TOTAL ENCLOSED		=

* See the back of this document for further instructions, information, and explanation of fees.

♦ If you would like to RUSH your order, please include a one-time charge of $5.00 (per order) and write **RUSH** on the outside of your envelope. There is no shipping charge for regular mail. If express mail is desired, you may express mail your request to us and include a prepaid express mail envelope back to yourself. We cannot send your order C.O.D.

PLEASE READ THESE INSTRUCTIONS CAREFULLY

WHO CAN ORDER

Only immediate family members, their legal representative, or those who provide documentation showing it is needed for their property right may order legally confidential certificates. Immediate family includes: spouse, sibling, parent, child, grandparent, and grandchild.

Proof of relation/legal representation may be required. Step-relatives, in-laws, great-grandparents, aunts, uncles, cousins, etc. are not immediate family as defined by Idaho Statute.

IDENTIFICATION IS REQUIRED

The applicant (person signing this request) must provide a photocopy of their driver's license or other current signed government [state, federal or tribal] issued picture identification. If this is not available, copies of two other forms of identification are required; one of which **MUST** include the applicant's signature. (Refer to the following list) **ID is accepted upon validity verification by our office**.

IMPORTANT: If acceptable identification is NOT enclosed, and/or your application is incomplete, your request will be returned and significant delays in processing your order may occur.

APPROVED IDENTIFICATION LIST

Current Government Issued Picture Identification with a signature	OR Two Forms of CURRENT ID – One MUST have a Signature		OR
• Driver's License • State ID Card • Passport • Tribal ID Card • Concealed Weapons Permit • Prison ID Card	• Social Security Card with signature • Work ID Card with picture or signature • Auto registration with signature • Traffic Ticket with signature • Court Record with signature • College/School ID with picture • Matricula Card with signature.	• Insurance Record • Auto Insurance • Driver Permit • Pay stub • Doctor/Medical Record • Hunting/Fishing License • Passport Card	• Notarized Signature on the Request • Have an immediate family member (that has current ID from the approved list) request it for you (Please Note: Proof of relation may be required.) • Court Order

FEES

Each certified copy or record search of a Birth, Stillbirth, Marriage or Divorce Certificate is $13.00. Each certified copy or record search of a Death Certificate is $14.00. Certified copies are computer-generated and are valid for most legal purposes. If the requested certificate cannot be found a statement of search will be issued. A certified *photocopy* (not computer-generated) of a Birth, Stillbirth, Marriage or Divorce certificate can be ordered for $18.00; each additional certified photocopy of that record, ordered at the same time, is $13.00. A certified photocopy (not computer-generated) of a Death Certificate can be ordered for $19.00; each additional certified photocopy of that record, ordered at the same time, is $14.00. Pursuant to 2010 legislation, a fee of $1.00 has been added to each death certificate to pay for county coroner education.

The Processing fee to complete an adoption, paternity, delayed registration or court order name change is $13.00. (Does not include a copy of the certificate)

Make checks or money orders payable to Idaho Vital Records.

If you would like to RUSH your order, please include a one-time charge of $5.00 (per order) and write **RUSH** on the outside of your envelope. There is no shipping charge for regular mail. If express mail is desired, you may express mail your request to us and include a prepaid express mail envelope back to yourself. We cannot send your order C.O.D.

To order by fax or on-line, through VitalChek, please see our website at http://www.vitalrecords.dhw.idaho.gov. or fax your request to (866) 559-9629. *Additional charges will apply.* All credit card orders are processed through Vitalchek.

SUBMITTING THE REQUEST

Complete the request form and mail it to the address on the front of the form. Remember to sign your request and enclose the correct fees and a copy of *both sides* of your signed picture ID.

WARNING: False application for a certified copy of a vital record is a felony punishable by a fine up to $5,000, five years in prison, or both (*Title 39, Chapter 2,* ***Idaho Code***).

ILLINOIS

Send your requests for Birth and Death Certificates to:

Illinois Department of Public Health
Division of Vital Records
925 East Ridgely Avenue
Springfield, IL 62702-2737

Tel. (217) 782-6553; TTY (800) 547-0466
Fax (217) 785-3209
E-mail: vitalrecords@idph.state.il.us
www.idph.state.il.us/vitalrecords/index.htm

The Division of Vital Records has birth and death records from January 1, 1916. Birth and death records are not public records; consult the website for information on requirements for obtaining records. Be sure to include a legible/readable copy of your valid photo identification when ordering certificates.

Vital Records does not issue certified copies of marriage, civil union, and divorce records. However, it can verify the facts of a marriage or divorce that has taken place from 1962 to the present.

Cost for a certified Birth Certificate	$15.00
Cost for a certified short-form, computerized Birth Certificate	$10.00
Cost for a duplicate Birth Certificate, when ordered at the same time	$2.00
Cost for a commemorative Birth Certificate	$40.00
Cost for duplicate copy of commemorative Birth Certificate, when ordered at the same time	$5.00
Cost for a verified Marriage or Divorce Record	$5.00
Cost for a certified Death Certificate	$19.00
Cost for a duplicate Death Certificate when ordered at the same time	$4.00

For earlier records and Marriage or Divorce Certificates, contact:

County Clerk
County Court House
(County Seat), IL

For Genealogy Research:

Uncertified copies may be available for genealogical researchers and others on a restricted basis; see www.idph.state.il.us/vitalrecords/genealogicalinfo.htm for more information.

Births and deaths before January 1, 1916, and marriages before January 1, 1962, are recorded only in the county clerk's office where the event occurred. Most county clerks have indexes to these records; see www.idph.state.il.us/vitalrecords/countylisting.htm for a list of county vital records websites and contact information. The Illinois State Archives has searchable vital record databases available online at www.cyberdriveillinois.com/departments/archives/databases/home.html, including the Statewide Death Index (1916–1950); Statewide Death Index, pre-1916; and Statewide Marriage Index, 1763–1900. The Illinois Regional Area Depository (IRAD) has birth, death, and marriage records for many counties; see www.cyberdriveillinois.com/departments/archives/IRAD/home.html.

For Adoption Record information, contact:

Illinois Adoption Registry
Illinois Department of Public Health
Division of Vital Records
925 East Ridgely Avenue
Springfield, IL 62702-2737

Tel. (217) 557-5160
www.idph.state.il.us/vitalrecords/adoptioninfo.htm

Cost for registration in Illinois Adoption Registry	$40.00

Illinois Department of Public Health
APPLICATION FOR SEARCH OF BIRTH RECORD FILES

The state began recording birth records on January 1, 1916.

The Division of Vital Records offers the choice between a certified copy or a certification copy of a birth record.

Please indicate your choice below and return this form with the proper fee and a legible copy of your non-expired, government issued photo ID.

Illinois Law (ILCS410/535/25(1)) requires advanced payment for the search of birth record files. This $10.00 search fee, included in the price of the copy(ies) you are requesting, is non-refundable.

DO NOT SEND CASH – Make check or money order payable to: **ILLINOIS DEPARTMENT OF PUBLIC HEALTH**

CERTIFIED (8.5 x 11 in size) **$15.00 first copy $2.00 each additional copy** **Amount enclosed $__________ for** **_____ total copies**	**CERTIFICATION (6 x 8.5 in size - may not list parents' names)** **$10.00 first copy $2.00 each additional copy** **Amount enclosed $__________ for** **_____ total copies**

FOREIGN BIRTH (births of adopted persons born outside of the U.S. who were re-adopted in Illinois) OR ADMINISTRATIVE FOREIGN BIRTH RECORD (both 8.5 x 11 in size) $5.00 each copy

Amount enclosed $______ for _____ total copies

FULL NAME	**First**	**Middle**	**Last name prior to first marriage/civil union**	
PLACE OF BIRTH	**Hospital**	**City or Town**	**County**	**State**
DATE OF BIRTH	**Month Day Year**	**SEX**	**BIRTH FILE NUMBER, IF KNOWN**	
FATHER/CO-PARENT'S NAME First	Middle	Last name prior to first marriage/civil union	Current legal last name	
MOTHER/CO-PARENT'S NAME First	Middle	Last name prior to first marriage/civil union	Current legal last name	

INDIVIDUAL REQUESTING COPIES

PRINT NAME ______________________

STREET ADDRESS ______________________

CITY __________ STATE _____ ZIP _____

YOUR RELATIONSHIP TO PERSON ______________________

INTENDED USE ______________________

SIGNATURE ______________________

MAIL RECORD(S) TO: (If other than applicant)

NAME ______________________

AGENCY ______________________

STREET ADDRESS ______________________

CITY ______________________

STATE _____ ZIP _____

NOTE: Birth Certificates are confidential records and copies can ***only*** be issued to persons entitled to receive them (for a complete list, see other side). The application must indicate the requestor's relationship to the person and the intended use of the document. (SEE OTHER SIDE)

MAIL TO: Illinois Department of Public Health, Division of Vital Records, 925 E. Ridgely Ave., Springfield, IL 62702-2737
For more information - www.idph.state.il.us/vitalrecords/index.htm

VR 180 (Rev. 2/12) Printed by Authority of the State of Illinois P.O.#1412127 10M 12/11 IOCI 12-385

State of Illinois
Illinois Department of Public Health

ELIGIBILTY TO OBTAIN AN ILLINOIS BIRTH RECORD

Before a request for a certification copy, a certified copy or a copy of a Record of Foreign Birth can be considered (all are certified by the State of Illinois), you must specify your eligibility to obtain it. ILCS410/535/25(4) states that a certification or certified copy of birth records may only be issued upon:

- The order of a court of competent jurisdiction
- The specific written request for a certification or certified copy by the person, if of legal age (18 or older), or by a parent or other legal representative* of the person to whom the record of birth relates; or
- The specific written request for a certification or certified copy by a department of the state, a municipal corporation, or the federal government

**77 Illinois AdmCode 500.10 refers to "Legal representative" as*

- *An attorney acting on behalf of a person(s) named on a birth certificate;*
- *An agent authorized by power of attorney;*
- *A court-appointed personal representative;*
- *An agent with written, notarized authorization from a person(s) named on a birth certificate for the purpose of obtaining a certified copy or certification for that person; or*
- *Any other agent, approved by the State Registrar as a legal representative of the person to whom the birth certificate relates.*

NOTE: Any person who, willfully and knowingly uses or attempts to use, or furnishes to another for use, for any purpose of deception, any certificate, record, report, certification or certified copy thereof so made, altered, amended, or mutilated; or,

Any person who with the intention to deceive, willfully uses or attempts to use any certification or certified copy of a record of birth knowing that such certification or certified copy was issued upon a record that is false in whole or in part or that relates to the birth of another person, is guilty of a Class 4 felony in the state of Illinois (ILCS 410/535/27(f)).

ACCEPTABLE PROOF OF ID

A NON-EXPIRED, GOVERNMENT ISSUED PHOTO ID, such as a driver's license. If you have an extension sticker on your license, submit a **copy of both sides** of the license. If you do not have a driver's license, a photo ID Card issued by the Department of Motor Vehicles can be provided.

If your driver's license or ID Card is **expired or not available**, you must submit TWO (2) pieces of documentation with your name on them. In addition to your name, one piece must also have your current address on it to prove your identity.

ONE piece of documentation can be a bill or other USPS mail; the SECOND must be one of the items listed below:

- **Medical/car insurance card**
- **Credit card statement**
- **Paycheck stub with imprinted information**
- **Voter's registration card**
- **Car registration paperwork**
- **Bank statement**
- **Public assistance card**
- **Active duty military ID w/ issued and expiration dates**

SOCIAL SECURITY CARDS ARE NOT ACCEPTABLE

Matrícula Consular card issued after October 2006 is acceptable on its own. However, if issued prior to October 2006, we need ONE additional type of documentation showing current address as noted above. If you do not have any of the items listed above, please submit a copy of a current utility bill (electricity, cellular phone, water, etc.) showing your name and current address.

If you are currently incarcerated, you can submit a dated copy of your prison intake/offender summary sheet containing your photo. If you have been released from prison within the last six months, a copy of the release papers along with the prison photo ID will be accepted.

If you are writing from a state or federal agency, you can submit a copy of your photo work badge.

State of Illinois
Department of Public Health

Commemorative Birth Certificate
Application Form

Send Certificate to:

____
Name

____
Address

______________________________ IL ______________ ______________
City State ZIP Code

Please complete the information below:

____
Name on Record (first, middle, last)

______________________________ ______________
Date of Birth (month, day, year) Sex

Place of Birth: ______________________________ ______________
City of Birth County of Birth

____
Father's Full Name

____
Mother's Full and **Maiden Name**

____
Name of Person Ordering the Certificate and Relationship

____
Signature of Person Ordering Certificate

Submit a Copy of Your Current Photo ID

Illinois Department of Public Health
Division of Vital Records
925 East Ridgely Ave.
Springfield, IL 62702-2737

217-782-6553 or
TTY (hearing impaired use only) 800-547-0466

Rev. May 2010

Illinois Department of Public Health
APPLICATION FOR VERIFICATION OF MARRIAGE RECORD FILES

Certified copies can only be obtained by writing to the county clerk where the marriage occurred. The Department began recording marriage information on January 1, 1962.

FURNISH ALL POSSIBLE INFORMATION

Name of GROOM	First	Middle	Last	Date of Birth
Name of BRIDE	First	Middle	Last/Maiden	Date of Birth
Place of MARRIAGE	City	County	State	
Date of MARRIAGE	Month	Day	Year	

For a non-refundable $5 fee (410 ILCS 530/3), facts of a *marriage* that took place between 1962 and current index year may be available. Additional copies of the same verification requested at the same time are $5 each. For a non-refundable fee of $10 received from any federal or public agency of another state (410 ILCS 535/25 (13)), facts of a *marriage* that took place between the same years may be available.

Amount enclosed $ _________ for _________ total copies

APPLICATION MADE BY

Name		
Street Address		
City	State	ZIP
Signature		

Make check or money order payable to Illinois Department of Public Health. **DO NOT SEND CASH.**

Return this form with the proper fee and a legible copy of your non-expired, government issued photo I.D.

Mail To:

Illinois Department of Public Health
Division of Vital Records
925 E. Ridgely Ave.
Springfield, IL 62702-2737

IOCI 12-814

State of Illinois
Illinois Department of Public Health

Illinois Department of Public Health
APPLICATION FOR VERIFICATION OF DISSOLUTION OF MARRIAGE RECORD FILES

Certified copies can only be obtained by writing to the circuit clerk where the dissolution of marriage was granted. The Department began recording dissolution of marriage information on January 1, 1962.

FURNISH ALL POSSIBLE INFORMATION

Name of HUSBAND	First	Middle	Last	Date of Birth
Name of WIFE	First	Middle	Last/Maiden	Date of Birth
Place of DISSOLUTION OF MARRIAGE	City	County	State	
Date of DISSOLUTION OF MARRIAGE	Month	Day	Year	

For a non-refundable $5 fee (410 ILCS 530/3), facts of a *dissolution of marriage* that took place between 1962 and current index year may be available. Additional copies of the same verification requested at the same time are $5 each. For a non-refundable fee of $10 received from any federal or public agency of another state (410 ILCS 535/25 (13)), facts of a *dissolution of marriage* that took place between the same years may be available.

Amount enclosed $ _________ for _________ total copies

APPLICATION MADE BY

Name		
Street Address		
City	State	ZIP
Signature		

Make check or money order payable to Illinois Department of Public Health. **DO NOT SEND CASH.**

Return this form with the proper fee and a legible copy of your non-expired, government issued photo I.D.

Mail To:

Illinois Department of Public Health
Division of Vital Records
925 E. Ridgely Ave.
Springfield, IL 62702-2737

IOCI 12-814

Illinois Department of Public Health
APPLICATION FOR SEARCH OF DEATH RECORD FILES

The state began recording death records on January 1, 1916

PLEASE NOTE: The state of Illinois, Division of Vital Records, in Springfield, issues certified death certificates from its electronic *Illinois Vital Registration System* (IVRS), if the death occurred from 2008 forward. Any death record, from 2007 or before, is issued from the original paper record or from microfilm. As a result, these certificates may look slightly different, according to the year of the event, but they are all certified copies and suitable for all legal purposes.

______________________________ ______________________________

YOUR RELATIONSHIP TO DECEASED **INTENDED USE OF DOCUMENT**

(SEE OTHER SIDE FOR ACCEPTABLE PROOF OF RELATIONSHIP AND INTENDED USE)

Please indicate below the type and number of copies requested and return this form with the proper fee and a legible copy of your non-expired government issued photo ID. If an extension sticker is affixed to the back of the ID, both sides of the photo ID must be submitted.

(SEE OTHER SIDE FOR ACCEPTABLE PROOF OF ID)

DO NOT SEND CASH – Make check or money order payable to: **ILLINOIS DEPARTMENT OF PUBLIC HEALTH**

CERTIFIED	**GENEALOGICAL (uncertified) (records older than 20 years)**
$19 first copy $4 each additional copy	**$10 first copy $2 each additional copy**
Amount enclosed $__________ for _____ total copies	**Amount enclosed $__________ for _____ total copies**

FULL NAME OF DECEASED	**First**	**Middle**	**Last (legal name at time of death)**
PLACE OF DEATH	**Hospital**	**City or Town**	**County**	**State**

DATE OF DEATH Month Day Year	**SEX**	**RACE**	**OCCUPATION**	**SOCIAL SECURITY NUMBER**

DATE LAST KNOWN TO BE ALIVE Month Day Year	**LAST KNOWN ADDRESS**	**STATUS (married, divorced, civil union)**

DATE OF BIRTH Month Day Year	**BIRTH PLACE (City and State)**	**NAME OF SPOUSE OR CIVIL UNION PARTNER**

NAME OF FATHER/CO-PARENT OF DECEASED PRIOR TO FIRST MARRIAGE/CIVIL UNION	**NAME OF MOTHER/CO-PARENT OF DECEASED PRIOR TO FIRST MARRIAGE/CIVIL UNION**

INDIVIDUAL REQUESTING COPIES

PRINT NAME____________________

STREET ADDRESS ____________________

CITY__________ STATE ___ ZIP ______

SIGNATURE ____________________

MAIL RECORD(S) TO: (If other than applicant)

NAME ____________________

AGENCY ____________________

STREET ADDRESS ____________________

CITY__________ STATE ___ ZIP ______

NOTE: Death Certificates are confidential records and copies can ***only*** be issued to persons entitled to receive them. The application must indicate the requestor's relationship to the person and the intended use of the document. (SEE OTHER SIDE)

MAIL TO: Illinois Department of Public Health, Division of Vital Records, 925 E. Ridgely Ave., Springfield, IL 62702-2737
For more information - www.idph.state.il.us/vitalrecords/index.htm

VR 280 (Rev. 10/12) Printed by Authority of the State of Illinois P.O.#1413133 2M 10/12 IOCI 13-292

State of Illinois
Illinois Department of Public Health

ELIGIBILITY TO OBTAIN AN ILLINOIS DEATH RECORD

Before a request for an uncertified or certified copy can be considered, you must specify your eligibility to obtain it. IICS410/535/25/4(d) states that copies of death or fetal death records may be issued upon:

- The specific written request for an uncertified or certified copy by a person, or his duly authorized agent, having a genealogical, (record must be more than 20 years old), personal or property right interest in the record.

If you are requesting a death certificate as the **duly authorized agent** or **legal representative**, please know that you must provide proof.

- We will review the request if you have a written document naming you as one of the following: a licensed attorney acting on behalf of a decedent or his/her estate; an agent authorized by power of attorney; a court-appointed personal representative, executor/administrator; or an agent with expressed, notarized authorization.

If you are requesting a death certificate as someone claiming a **legal, personal or property interest**, please know that you must provide proof.

- We will review the request if you have a written document demonstrating that you have a personal or property interest at stake, such as a will naming you, a letter on a firm's letterhead or a file-stamped copy of a complaint at law.

If you are eligible, please indicate on the front of this application your relationship to the deceased person, whose record you are requesting, the intended use of the copy and proof.

ACCEPTABLE PROOF OF ID

A valid government issued photo identification (ID) includes a driver's license, a state issued photo identification (ID) or a passport. (If your driver's license has an extension sticker on the back, submit copies of both sides).

If you do not have a valid, government issued photo ID, you will need to submit two pieces of documentation with your name, one of which must show your current address, to prove your identity. One piece of documentation can be a bill or other mail. The other piece of documentation must be one of the following items listed below:

- **Medical/car insurance card**
- **Credit card statement**
- **Paycheck stub with imprinted information**
- **Voter's registration card**
- **Car registration paperwork**
- **Bank statement**
- **Public assistance card**
- **Active duty military ID w/ issued and expiration dates**

SOCIAL SECURITY CARDS ARE NOT ACCEPTABLE

A Matrícula Consular card issued after October 2006 is acceptable on its own. However, if issued prior to October 2006, you will need to submit ONE additional type of documentation showing current address as noted above. If you do not have any of the items listed above, please submit a copy of a current utility bill (electricity, cellular phone, water) showing your name and current address.

If you are currently incarcerated, you can submit a dated copy of your prison intake/offender summary sheet containing your photo. If you have been released from prison within the last six months, a copy of the release papers along with the prison photo ID will be accepted.

If you are writing from a state or federal agency, you can submit a copy of your photo work badge.

Illinois Department of Public Health
ILLINOIS ADOPTION REGISTRY
AND MEDICAL INFORMATION EXCHANGE APPLICATION

This application is ❑ a new registration ❑ an update to a prior registration (please note any updates must be accompanied by ID).

I am registering/registered as (check one) ❑ an adult adopted or surrendered person; ❑ a birth parent; ❑ adoptive parent or legal guardian of an adopted or surrendered person; ❑ surviving relative of a deceased birth parent; ❑ surviving relative of a deceased adopted or surrendered person as stated on the registration identification.

Section A. REGISTRANT INFORMATION

Name: ____ Today's date: __________
(first) (middle) (maiden if applicable) (last)

Mailing address: ____
(street) (city) (state) (ZIP code)

Sex: __________ SSN______-_____-__________ Phone: (____) ______________
(male or female) (OPTIONAL)

Section B. COMPLETE WHEN OPTIONAL PHOTOGRAPH(S) ARE BEING FILED

The enclosed photograph(s) is (are) to be released to the person(s) specified on my Information Exchange Authorization form. The photograph(s) does (do) not include identifying information pertaining to any person other than myself, and do not include anyone else.

(NOTE: Photograph(s) are to be no larger than 8 fi" x 11") ______________________________
Applicant Signature/Date

Section C. COMPLETE WHEN OPTIONAL WRITTEN STATEMENT IS BEING FILED

An optional written statement (on the prescribed form) is enclosed and is to be released to the person(s) specified on my Information Exchange Authorization form. This statement does not include any identifying information pertaining to any person other than myself and does not include any specific names, dates or places.

____
Applicant Signature/Date

Section D. SIGN WHEN REQUESTING NON-IDENTIFYING INFORMATION BE RELEASED

I, the undersigned, request that any non-identifying information, as detailed in 750 ILCS 50/18.4(a)(c), be released to me. I understand that non-identifying information can only be provided to an adopted person, adoptive parent or legal guardian who is a registrant of the Illinois Adoption Registry.

Adopted/Surrendered name______________________________

Date of birth ____________________ ______________________________
Applicant Signature/Date

Section E. SIGN WHEN REQUESTING ACTUAL DATE AND PLACE OF BIRTH BE RELEASED TO BIRTH PARENT

I, the undersigned, request that I be provided with the actual date and place of birth of the child I placed for adoption per 750 ILCS 50/18.4(d).

____
Applicant Signature/Date

See other side for a list of required documentation.

REQUIRED DOCUMENTATION

Adopted/Surrendered Person or Adoptive Parent or Legal Guardian of an adopted/surrendered person

- ❑ Appropriate Registration Identification form
- ❑ Adoption Registry Application form
- ❑ Photocopy of photo identification
- ❑ Information Exchange Authorization form ***OR***
  With *one* of the following:
  a. Completed Medical Questionnaire form
  b. $40.00 registration fee made payable to IDPH
- ❑ Denial of Information Exchange Authorization form
  With $40.00 registration fee made payable to IDPH
- ❑ If born *outside of ILLINOIS*, certified copy of birth certificate
- ❑ If a legal guardian, certified copy of court ordered guardianship

Birth Mother/Father

- ❑ Appropriate Registration Identification form
- ❑ Adoption Registry Application form
- ❑ Photocopy of photo identification
- ❑ Information Exchange Authorization form ***OR***
  With *one* of the following:
  a. Completed Medical Questionnaire form
  b. $40.00 registration fee made payable to IDPH
- ❑ Denial of Information Exchange Authorization form
  With $40.00 registration fee made payable to IDPH

Surviving Relative of a Deceased Birth Parent (birth parent's non-surrendered child, sister or brother)

- ❑ Appropriate Registration Identification form
- ❑ Adoption Registry Application form
- ❑ Photocopy of photo identification
- ❑ Information Exchange Authorization form ***OR***
  With *one* of the following:
  a. Completed Medical Questionnaire form
  b. $40.00 registration fee made payable to IDPH
- ❑ Denial of Information Exchange Authorization form
  With $40.00 registration fee made payable to IDPH
- ❑ Certified copy of birth and death certificate of birth parent
- ❑ Certified copy of your birth certificate

Surviving Relative of a Deceased Adopted/Surrendered Person (adult child or spouse with a minor child)

- ❑ Appropriate Registration Identification form
- ❑ Adoption Registry Application form
- ❑ Photocopy of photo identification
- ❑ Information Exchange Authorization form ***OR***
  With *one* of the following:
  a. Completed Medical Questionnaire form
  b. $40.00 registration fee made payable to IDPH
- ❑ Denial of Information Exchange Authorization form
  With $40.00 registration fee made payable to IDPH
- ❑ Certified copy of birth and death certificate of adopted/surrendered person
- ❑ Certified copy of the adopted/surrendered persons child's birth certificate
- ❑ If spouse with minor child, certified copy of marriage certificate

State of Illinois
Illinois Department of Public Health

Illinois Adoption Registry and Medical Information Exchange (IARMIE)
REQUEST FOR A NON-CERTIFIED COPY OF AN ORIGINAL BIRTH CERTIFICATE

I, ____, hereby request a non-certified copy of

(check the appropriate option):

☐ 1. My original birth certificate. Notary **NOT** required.

☐ 2. The original birth certificate of my deceased adopted or surrendered parent. **Notary required/below.**

☐ 3. The original birth certificate of my deceased adopted or surrendered spouse. **Notary required/below.**

The adopted or surrendered person was born in the city of__________________________________,

county of__________________________ on ________________ (Date), _________ (Year) and the adopted name is:

First name ________________________________ Middle name ________________________________

Last name ____

In the event that one or both of the birth parents have requested their identity not be released:

☐ a. I wish to receive a non-certified copy of the original birth certificate from which identifying information pertaining to my birth parents, who requested anonymity, has been redacted; or

☐ b. I do not wish to receive a redacted copy of the original birth certificate.

PLEASE NOTE:
Regardless of your selection above, all options require that you submit a copy of a non-expired, government issued photo ID and a check or money order made to IDPH for $15.

If you selected option 2 or 3, you must be registered with the IARMIE as a surviving relative of the deceased adopted or surrendered person. If you need to register, please contact the IARMIE at 877-323-5299.

____ ____________________
Signature Date

Mailing address ____ City ______________________________

State ______________________ ZIP code ________________

Notary required if you checked option 2 or 3 above.

(Notary Public use only)

State of ____________________ County of __________________________

I, a Notary Public, in and for the said county, in the state aforesaid, do hereby certify that

_________________________________ personally known to me to be the same person whose name is subscribed to the foregoing request, appeared before me in person and acknowledged that (he or she) signed such request as (his or her) free and voluntary act and that the statements in such request are true.

Given under my hand and notarial seal on ______________________________, ________

____

Mail to: Illinois Department of Public Health, Division of Vital Records, 925 E. Ridgely Ave., Springfield, IL 62702-2737

IOCI 13-608

INDIANA

Send your requests for Birth and Death Certificates to:

Vital Records Department
Indiana State Department of Health
P.O. Box 7125
Indianapolis, IN 46206-7125

Tel. (317) 233-2700
www.in.gov/isdh/20444.htm

The Vital Records Department has birth records from October 1907 and death records from 1900. Certificates are available from the Department by mail, or from the local health department in the county where the event occurred on a walk-in basis. Earlier records are filed only with the local health department in the county where the event occurred. For deaths occurring from 1900 to 1917, the city and/or county of death is required in order to locate the record. Local health department contact information and fees are available at www.in.gov/isdh/20422.htm.

Indiana law (IC16-37-1-10) specifically requires a purchaser of a birth or death certificate to have a direct interest. A direct interest is defined as a documented personal financial or legal interest in the record, or immediate kinship (parent, grandparent, or adult sibling) to the person named on the record.

Cost for a certified Birth Certificate	$10.00
Cost for a certified Death Certificate	$8.00
Cost for a duplicate copy, when ordered at the same time	$4.00

For Marriage and Divorce Certificates, contact:

Clerk of the Court
County Court House
(County Seat), IN

For Genealogy Research:

The Indiana State Library's Genealogy Collection (140 North Senate Avenue, Indianapolis, IN 46202; tel. 317-232-3689; www.in.gov/library) is one of the largest in the Midwest and includes indexed and abstracted vital records. The Index to Indiana Marriages Through 1850 is online at http://web.isl.lib.in.us/INMarriages1850/marriages_search.asp.

The Allen County Public Library (900 Library Plaza, Fort Wayne, IN 46802; tel. 260-421-1225; www.genealogycenter.org/Home.aspx) has the second largest genealogy collection in the United States, with many valuable resources, including indexes to some Indiana marriages and deaths.

For Adoption Record information, contact:

Indiana Adoption History Registry
Indiana State Department of Health
Vital Records Division, Section B-4
2 North Meridian Street
Indianapolis, IN 46204

Tel. (317) 233-7279

There is no charge for adoption registration and information.

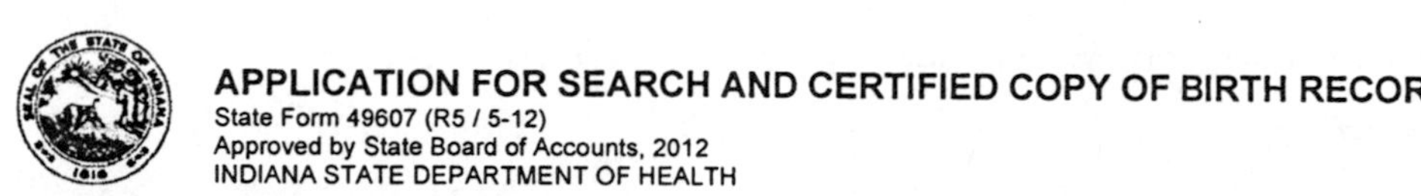

APPLICATION FOR SEARCH AND CERTIFIED COPY OF BIRTH RECORD

State Form 49607 (R5 / 5-12)
Approved by State Board of Accounts, 2012
INDIANA STATE DEPARTMENT OF HEALTH

BIRTH RECORDS IN THE STATE VITAL RECORDS OFFICE BEGIN WITH OCTOBER 1907. Prior to October 1907, records of birth are filed ONLY with the local health department in the county where the birth actually occurred.

FEES ARE ESTABLISHED BY LAW (IC 16-37-1-11 and IC 16-37-1-11.5). Each search for a record costs $10.00. The fee is non-refundable. Included in one search is a 5-year period: the reported year of birth and, if the record is not found in that year, the 2 years before and after. A certified copy of the record, if found, is included in the search fee. Additional copies of the same record purchased at the same time are $4.00 each. Amendments made to the record are an additional $8.00.

WARNING: FALSE APPLICATION, ALTERING, MUTILATING, OR COUNTERFEITING INDIANA BIRTH CERTIFICATES IS A CRIMINAL OFFENSE UNDER IC 16-37-1-12.

IDENTIFICATION IS REQUIRED according to IC 16-37-1-7 (SEE REQUIREMENTS AND ACCEPTABLE DOCUMENTATION LIST). Requests for birth certificates sent without proper identification will be returned to the requester without processing. Please complete all items below as required pursuant to IC 16-37-1-10 (a):

Full Name at Birth

Could this birth be recorded under any other name? If Yes, Please Give Name.

Has the person ever been adopted? If Yes, Please Give Name AFTER Adoption.

Place of Birth: City	Place of Birth: County

Name of Hospital

Date of Birth (*Month, Day, Year*)	Is this Person Deceased? (*Please Check One*) ☐ YES ☐ NO ☐ UNKNOWN If YES which state, if known ______________

Full Name of Father (*If adopted, Give Name of Adopted Father.*)

Full Name of Mother including Maiden Name (*If adopted, Give Name of Adopted Mother.*)

Purpose for which record is to be used

Your Relationship to the Individual Named on the requested certificate

Total Certificates
Standard Size ______________ (*Passport Acceptable*) **Long Form** ______________ (*Statistical Version*)
(Please note: if a long form is unavailable, standard size will be sent.)

Is this certificate for an Apostille? (*Please Check One*) ☐ Yes ☐ No	Delivery Preference (*Please call agency for current express delivery rate.*) ☐ Regular Mail ☐ Express Courier, Signature upon delivery required	Total Fee

Print Name of Applicant	Signature of Applicant

Mailing Address (*Number, Street, City, State, ZIP Code*) ***ADDRESS MUST MATCH THE IDENTIFICATION PROVIDED.***

Daytime Telephone Number (*including Area Code*)	Today's Date (*Month, Day, Year*)

Send this application(s) with a check or money order payable to the Indiana State Department of Health, along with copy of Government State, or Military valid identification and,/or required documentation to: Vital Records, Indiana State Department of Health, P O Box 7125, Indianapolis, IN 46206-7125. Web address www.in.gov/ISDH. Please note: Average processing time is 3-4 weeks. If identification does not match the address provided, your request will not be processed.

FOR OFFICE USE ONLY

Date received (*Month, Day, Year*)	Receipt Number	Volume Number
Certificate Number	Application Number	Initials of Verifier

APPLICATION FOR SEARCH FOR CERTIFIED RECORD OF MARRIAGE

State Form 54764 (R / 2-12)
Approved by State Board of Accounts, 2012
INDIANA STATE DEPARTMENT OF HEALTH

Beginning in 1958, the State Vital Records Office became the central repository for all marriage records. Copies are also maintained by the Clerk of Courts in the county where the marriage was filed. For information prior to 1958, and for ALL divorce information, contact the Clerk of Courts where the marriage or divorce was filed. THE INDIANA STATE VITAL RECORDS OFFICE DOES NOT STORE DIVORCE RECORDS.

FEES ARE ESTABLISHED BY LAW (IC 16-37-1-11-5). Each Record of Marriage search costs $8.00 per date provided. This fee is non-refundable and includes a certified copy of the record, if found. A certified copy of the Record of Marriage will be provided within 10-15 business days after the request is received.

IDENTIFICATION IS REQUIRED. Requests for information sent without proper identification will be returned to the requestor without processing. Please complete as much of the information requested below *to ensure the greatest chance of our office finding the record you are requesting*. If no record is found a letter will be sent indicating no record found.

Groom's Name:	First	Middle	Last
Bride's Name:	First	Middle	Maiden

Date of Marriage *(month, day, year)* At this time, ISDH is only able to provide certified records for marriages **from 1958 through 2005**. Those outside this range, can be requested from the Clerk of Courts where the marriage was filed. Please contact the Clerk of Courts for more information.

County of Marriage	City of Marriage if known

Signature of applicant

Mailing address *(number and street, city, state, and ZIP code)* ***MAILING ADDRESS MUST MATCH IDENTIFICATION ADDRESS***

Daytime telephone number *(including area code)*	Today's date *(month, day, year)*

Send this application, check or money order payable to the Indiana State Department of Health, and a copy of your identification to: Vital Records, Indiana State Department of Health, PO Box 7125, Indianapolis, IN 46206-7125

The following individuals are eligible to receive marriage information under IC 16-37-1-10:

1. Bride
2. Groom
3. Individual with direct interest in the record **(must provide documentation to confirm they meet the criteria)**.
4. Individual demonstrating the information is necessary for the determination of personal or property rights **(must provide documentation to confirm they meet the criteria).**
5. Individual demonstrating the information is necessary for compliance with state or federal law **(must provide state of federal documentation to confirm they meet the criteria).**

FOR OFFICE USE ONLY

Period Checked	Marriage Date *(month, day, year)*	County Occurred	Initials of verifier

APPLICATION FOR SEARCH AND CERTIFIED COPY OF DEATH RECORD

State Form 49606 (R4 / 9-11)
Approved by State Board of Accounts, 2011
INDIANA STATE DEPARTMENT OF HEALTH

DEATH RECORDS IN THE STATE VITAL RECORDS OFFICE BEGIN WITH 1900. Prior to 1900, records of death are filed ONLY with the local health department in the county where the death actually occurred. For deaths occurring from 1900 to 1917, the city and/or county of death is required in order to locate the record.

FEES ARE ESTABLISHED BY LAW (IC 16-37-1-11). Each search for a record costs $8.00. The fee is non-refundable. Included in one search is a 5-year period: the reported year of death and, if the record is not found in that year, the 2 years before and after. For records prior to 1917, the search covers a 5-year period and only one county. A certified copy of the record, if found, is included in the search fee. Additional copies of the same record purchased at the same time are $4.00 each.

IDENTIFICATION IS REQUIRED according to IC 16-37-1-7 (SEE REQUIREMENTS AND ACCEPTABLE DOCUMENTATION LIST). Request for death certificates sent without proper identification will be returned to the requester without processing. Please complete all items below as required pursuant to IC 16-37-1-10 (a):

Name of Deceased *	Stillborn? ☐ Yes ☐ No
**If decedent was a married, divorced, or widowed woman, ISDH must have her legal name at the time of death. Please do not give the maiden name of woman who changed her name by marriage during her lifetime).*	
Date of Death (*Month, Day, Year*)	
City of Death	County of Death
Total Certificates With Cause of Death ________ Without Cause of Death ________	Total Fee (s)
Delivery Preference ☐ Regular Standard Mail ☐ Express Courier, Signature upon delivery required (*Additional fee, please call agency for current rate.)*	
Date of Birth of Deceased (*if known*)	
Name of Father	Maiden Name of Mother
Your Relationship to the Individual Named on the Requested Certificate	
Purpose for which the record is to be used	
Printed Name of Applicant	Signature of Applicant
Mailing Address (*Number, Street, City, State and ZIP Code*) ***ADDRESS MUST MATCH THE IDENTIFICATION PROVIDED.***	
Daytime Telephone Number (*including area code*)	Today's date (*Month, Day, Year*)

Send this application(s) with a check or money order payable to the Indiana State Department of Health, along with copy of a Government, State, or Military valid identification, and/or required documentation to: Vital Records, Indiana State Department of Health, P O Box 7125, Indianapolis, IN 46206-7125. (IF IDENTIFICATION DOES NOT MATCH THE ADDRESS PROVIDED YOUR REQUEST WILL NOT BE PROCESSED). Web address www.in.gov/ISDH

FOR OFFICE USE

Date Received (*Month, Day, Year*)	Receipt Number	Volume Number
Certificate Number	Application Number	Initials of Verifier

INDIANA ADOPTION MATCHING REGISTRY
IDENTIFYING INFORMATION CONSENT

State Form 47896 (R4 / 2-13)
INDIANA STATE DEPARTMENT OF HEALTH
IC 31-19-19-1

FOR OFFICE USE ONLY	
Date *(month, day, year)*	State File Number
Locator Number	

INSTRUCTIONS: Participant (s) must be eighteen (18) years of age or older to register for the Indiana Adoption Matching Registry. Participant must be twenty-one (21) years of age or older to obtain Adoption Information. A valid state or government issued identification with photo is required. All Information, except the written signature(s), must be typed or clearly printed in ***Black*** *ink.*
All parts must be completed before this consent form can be filed.

Part I – Your Filing Status *(Please check only ONE box in this section.)*

I am the: ☐ Adult Adoptee ☐ Adoptive Parent ☐ Birth Parent ☐ Birth Sibling

☐ Spouse of Deceased Adoptee *(If the relationship existed at the time of the adoptee's death, a marriage license must be provided.)*

☐ Relative of Deceased Adoptee *(If the relationship existed at the time of the adoptee's death, proof of relationship must be provided, i.e. birth certificate, court documents, etc.)*

☐ Spouse of a Deceased Birth Parent *(If the relationship existed at the time of birth parent's death, a marriage license must be provided.)*

☐ Relative of a Deceased Birth Parent *(If the relationship existed at the time of birth parent's death, proof of relationship must be provided, i.e. birth certificate, court documents, etc.)*

Part II – Contact Information of the person selected in Part I

Name ______________________________

Date of Birth *(month, day, year)* ______________________________

Mailing Address ______________________________
Number, Street, City, State, ZIP Code

Daytime Telephone Number *(please include area code)* ______________________________

Please Note: Your government or state issued identification with photo must accompany this form.

Part III – Adoptee's Birth Information

Birth Name ______________________________

Date of Birth *(month, day, year)* ______________________________ Gender ______________

Place of Birth ______________________________

*Full Name of Birth Father ______________________________

*Full Name of Birth Mother *(including maiden name)* ______________________________

(Please submit death certificate for all deceased persons listed in Part III.)

Part IV – Adoptee's Information

Name After Adoption ______________________________

Date of Birth *(month, day, year)* ______________________________

Place of Birth ______________________________

Full Name of Adoptive Father ______________________________

Full Name of Adoptive Mother ______________________________

Part V – Identifying Information Consent

My Information may be released to all parties selected below: *(Please note: you are giving your consent to release your Indentifying Information. **Select All** parties you consent to having your information, including yourself.)*

☐ Adult Adoptee ☐ Adoptive Parent ☐ Birth Parent ☐ Birth Sibling

☐ Spouse of Deceased Adoptee *(If the relationship existed at the time of the adoptee's death, a marriage license must be provided.)*

☐ Relative of Deceased Adoptee *(If the relationship existed at the time of the adoptee's death, proof of relationship must be provided, i.e. birth certificate, court documents, etc.)*

☐ Spouse of a Deceased Birth Parent *(If the relationship existed at the time of birth parent's death, a marriage license must be provided.)*

☐ Relative of a Deceased Birth Parent *(If the relationship existed at the time of birth parent's death, proof of relationship must be provided, i.e. birth certificate, court documents, etc.)*

Part VI – Affirmation

I affirm, under the penalties for perjury, that these representations are true to the best of my knowledge and beliefs, and that I am qualified to receive adoption matching information under IC 31-19-18-2.

______________________________ ______________________________

Signature Date *(month, day, year)*

Please send this form to:

Indiana State Department of Health
Attn: Indiana Matching Registry – Vital Records
2 North Meridian Street
Indianapolis, Indiana 46204

IOWA

Send your requests to:

Iowa Department of Public Health
Bureau of Health Statistics
Lucas State Office Building, 1st Floor
321 East 12th Street
Des Moines, IA 50319-0075

Tel. (515) 281-4944
E-mail: fdhs@dhs.state.ia.us
www.idph.state.ia.us/apl/health_statistics.asp

The Bureau of Health Statistics has records of births, marriages, and deaths from July 1, 1880. To search marriage records 1880–1915 or death records 1880–1895, the county of occurrence and the year must be furnished. Records from this office are not open to the public; all applicants must satisfactorily establish entitlement to the record being requested. See the website for more information. Written requests must include a clear photocopy of a current government-issued photo ID, as well as the applicant's signature signed in front of a notary public or in the presence of an Iowa Registrar of Vital Records.

Local registrars are located in county recorders offices and maintain records of birth, death, and marriages that have occurred in that county, except for those records from 1921 to 1941.

Cost for a certified Birth Certificate	$15.00
Cost for a commemorative Birth Certificate	$35.00
Cost for a certified Marriage Certificate	$15.00
Cost for a commemorative Marriage Certificate	$35.00
Cost for a certified Death Certificate	$15.00
Cost for a duplicate copy, when ordered at the same time	$15.00

For earlier records, contact:

Clerk
District Court
(County Seat), IA

For Genealogy Research:

Although vital records maintained at the state level are not open to public inspection, at the county level all vital records occurring in that county (excluding fetal death, adoptive records, and out-of-wedlock births prior to July 1, 1995) are open to the public. There may be a fee to inspect the records.

Iowa census enumerations began in 1850, with the final census taken in 1925. These records are open to the public. For more information, visit or write to the Iowa Department of Cultural Affairs, Library Archives Bureau (State Historical Museum, 600 E. Locust Street, Des Moines, IA 50319). Genealogical information and assistance may also be obtained by writing to the Iowa Genealogical Society (628 E. Grand Avenue, Des Moines, IA 50309-1924).

Many counties have transcribed vital records and made them available online; see http://iagenweb.org/state/research/bmdguide.htm for more information.

For Adoption Record information, contact:

Bureau of Vital Records
Iowa Department of Public Health
Lucas Office Building, 1st Floor
Des Moines, IA 50319

Tel. (515) 281-4944; (515) 281-4174
www.dhs.state.ia.us/Consumers/Child_Welfare/Adoption/AdoptionRecords.html

Cost for Mutual Consent Voluntary Adoption Registry	$25.00

BIRTH

APPLICATION FOR A SEARCH FOR AN IOWA RECORD

Requests require the applicant's **current government- issued photo identification (i.e., driver's license) and signature signed in front of a notary public** or in the presence of an Iowa Registrar of Vital Records.

1. **PERSON'S NAME AS IT APPEARS ON THE RECORD** ______________________
FIRST MIDDLE, if any SURNAME (Last)

2. **DATE OF BIRTH** – BE SPECIFIC – Month/Day/Year ______________________

3. **PLACE OF BIRTH** (City and/or County) ______________________

4. **MOTHER'S NAME PRIOR TO MARRIAGE** – FIRST/MIDDLE, if any/LAST ______________________

5. **FATHER'S FULL NAME** – FIRST/MIDDLE, if any/SURNAME (Last) ______________________

---

6. WAS THE MOTHER MARRIED AT THE TIME OF CONCEPTION OR BIRTH? ☐ Yes ☐ No ☐ Unknown

7. **LEGAL ACTIONS PREVIOUSLY RECORDED (if any)** ☐ None ☐ Adoption ☐ Paternity Establishment ☐ Legal Change of Name on Birth Certificate

   7a. IF A LEGAL ACTION OCCURRED, LIST PREVIOUS NAME (on birth certificate) ______________________
   Marriage does NOT change the birth certificate.

---

8. **PURPOSE FOR COPY** ______________ 9. **BIRTHDATE of APPLICANT/RECIPIENT** ______________

10. **HOW ARE YOU RELATED TO THE PERSON NAMED ON THE RECORD?** ______________________

11. **NAME AND ADDRESS OF PERSON TO RECEIVE THIS COPY:** (MUST BE AGE 18 OR OLDER & ENTITLED TO THE RECORD)

    12a. Name of Applicant/Recipient ______________________

    12b. Street address and P.O. Box (if any) ______________________

    12c. City, State and Zip Code ______________________

12. **THE SEARCH RESULT IS TO BE** (Check one) ☐ Mailed ☐ Picked up (for in-person requests only)

13. **THE <u>NON-REFUNDABLE</u> FEE TO SEARCH IS $15.00** and one certified copy is issued if the record is located.
    Each additional copy of the same record is $15.00. Indicate the number of copies of this record you need. ______________

14. **THIS SEARCH PAID BY** (Check one) ☐ Check ☐ Money Order ☐ Cash (In-person only) **15. AMOUNT ENCLOSED** ______________

Checks must be drawn from the applicants' account; money orders must be in the name of the applicant. Fee payment must accompany this form. Checks should be payable to 'Iowa Dept. of Public Health' (IDPH).

16. **APPLICANT'S NAME** (Print clearly) ______________________ **17. DAYTIME PHONE #** ______________
(Include area code)

I certify that the information provided on this application is accurate and complete to the best of my knowledge and that I have legal entitlement to a certified copy of this record. I have signed below in front of a notary public or an Iowa registrar of vital records.

18. **APPLICANT'S SIGNATURE** ______________________ **19. DATE** ______________

APPLICANT'S NAME AS APPEARS ON PHOTO I.D. *(Print clearly)* ______________________ State of ______________ County of ______________ ss (SEAL) Signed and affirmed in my presence on this _____ day of ____________, ________. ______________________, My commission expires: ____________ (Notary Public Signature)	**Administrative Use Only** I.D. __________ Initials _______

PRIOR TO MAILING:

- **INCLUDE A CLEAR PHOTO COPY OF YOUR IDENTIFICATION (i.e., driver's license)**
- **SIGN THIS APPLICATION IN FRONT OF A NOTARY PUBLIC**
- **INCLUDE PAYMENT AS DESCRIBED IN ITEM 13, 14 AND 15 ABOVE**

SEE OTHER SIDE FOR ADDITIONAL INSTRUCTIONS

To Request a Search for an Iowa Birth Record for the Purpose of Obtaining a Certified Copy

In Iowa, official registration of births began July 1, 1880. Original records that were registered are on file with the Iowa Department of Public Health, Bureau of Health Statistics. Statewide record searches are available from the state registrar. Local vital records registrars are located in county recorders' offices, where records of births that have occurred in that county are maintained. ***County registrars are not authorized by law to have records of single-parent births prior to July 1, 1995; adoptions; delayed registrations; legal changes of name; any record ordered sealed by a court of law; a birth between the years 1921 to 1941.*** Per Iowa law, information about a specific record is not available over the telephone or by prepared lists. Iowa law provides for public viewing in the county where the record is maintained, or certified copies issued to entitled persons.

Applications to search for a vital record event for the purpose of obtaining a certified copy must be in writing, completely identify the record, and establish entitlement to the record being requested. Entitled persons include the person named on the record or that person's spouse, children, legal parents, grandparents, grandchildren, siblings, or legal representative or guardian. Legal guardians and representatives must also provide additional proof of guardianship or representation. Applicants must be 18 or older. Requests must include the applicant's current government-issued photo identification (i.e., driver's license), except if by mail, a clear photocopy of the I.D., and the applicant's signature signed in front of a notary public or in the presence of an Iowa Registrar of Vital Records.

PAYMENT: A non-refundable $15 fee is required to search for a record and includes one certified copy if the record is located. Each additional copy of the same record is $15. Fees are payable in U.S. funds by check or money order to the issuing registrar's office. Checks must be drawn from the applicants' account; money orders must be in the name of the applicant. Fees must be paid at the time of the application (Iowa Constitution, Article VII, Section 1).

STATE CERTIFIED COPIES.

Certified copies of birth certificates may be obtained from the state Bureau of Health Statistics by telephone, in-person, or through a postal service. Fees are payable in U.S. funds by check or money order to the Iowa Department of Public Health. In-person requests may also be paid in cash. Genealogy requests take at least 60 days.

Telephone: Customers can call a **toll-free** number **866-809-0290** from 6:00 am CST through 7:00 pm CST, Monday through Friday, except for holidays. A fee of $15.00 is required for the record search and includes one copy if a record is on file in our office. Each additional copy of the record is also $15.00. A VitalChek operator will take your information, screen your credit card, authenticate your identity and complete your order. The fee to screen your credit card and authenticate the caller is an additional $13.00. If you request a group order which consists of more than one Vital Event (i.e. Birth, Death or Marriage) within one order there is an additional $3.00 fee. Turnaround time is usually 10 to 14 days, depending on seasonal demands and mail service. ***Genealogy requests are not available through the credit card line.***

In-person: Applications may be made in-person at the state Bureau of Health Statistics 7:00 a.m. to 5:00 p.m., Monday through Friday, except for state-observed holidays, at the address below, just inside the north lobby entrance and to the right. The Lucas building is just east of the state Capitol and south of Grand Avenue. Applicants must provide current government-issued photo identification and sign their request in the presence of registrar staff. Copies may either be picked up after two working days or mailed to an entitled person. Genealogy requests take at least 60 days.

Postal service: Written requests and fees are mailed to the address below. Requests must state the relationship to the person named on the record and the purpose for the copy. Filled requests take 30-45 days, depending on seasonal demands and mail service. Genealogy requests take at least 60 days. ***The request must be signed in front of a notary public and include a clear photocopy of the applicant's current government-issued photo identification.***

Iowa Department of Public Health
Bureau of Health Statistics
Lucas State Office Building, 1st Floor
321 E. 12th Street
Des Moines, Iowa 50319-0075

SEE OTHER SIDE FOR AN APPLICATION FORM.
FORM MAY BE USED FOR EITHER A COUNTY-CERTIFIED OR A STATE-CERTIFIED COPY OF AN IOWA VITAL RECORD

State of Iowa Commemorative Certificate of Birth

The Iowa Department of Public Health is pleased to offer commemorative certificates of birth, which makes a memorable keepsake or gift.

This parchment certificate features a gold foil border, image of the state capital of Iowa, and calligraphy print of the individuals' personal information. Gold embossed State and Iowa Department of Public Health seals make it a valid certified copy and legal document. Each certificate is signed by both the Governor of Iowa and the State Registrar. Its 8-1/2" x 11" size is suitable for framing.

Certificates are delivered in protective envelopes within 30 days of application. All applicants must meet the same qualifying direct-and-tangible interest standards (i.e., immediate family) as for any certified birth certificate request. Submit each fully completed application form with $35 (check or money order) to:

Iowa Department of Public Health
Office of Vital Records
321 E. 12th Street
Lucas State Office Building, 1st Floor
Des Moines IA 50319-0075.

The information on the other side must be completed in order to make application for the Iowa commemorative birth certificate. Registration of births in Iowa officially began July 1, 1880. The original records of all births registered in Iowa are maintained in the Office of Vital Records, Iowa Department of Public Health.

The $35 fee for the commemorative birth certificate includes the search for the record and one commemorative certificate. If the record is not located, the applicant will receive a notification of the record search results and a $20 refund, with $15 retained in this office to cover the cost of the search as required by statute.

Each additional commemorative certificate for the same record is $35 and can be ordered on the same application form.

Application for regular certified birth certificates requires a fee of $15 for a state record search and includes one certified copy. Each additional copy of the same record is also $15. If the record is not located, the applicant receives a notification to that affect. The $15 fee is retained in this office for the search.

Applications to search for a vital record event for the purpose of obtaining a commemorative copy must be in writing, completely identify the record, and establish entitlement to the record being requested. Entitled persons include the person named on the record or that person's spouse, children, legal parents, grandparents, grandchildren, siblings, or legal representative or guardian. Legal guardians and representatives must also provide additional proof of guardianship or representation. Applicants must be 18 or older. Requests must include the applicant's current government-issued photo identification (e.g., driver's license), except if by mail, a clear photocopy of the I.D., and the applicant's signature signed in front of a notary public or in the presence of an Iowa Registrar of Vital Records.

SEE OTHER SIDE FOR AN APPLICATION FORM.

COMMEMORATIVE BIRTH

APPLICATION FOR IOWA COMMEMORATIVE BIRTH CERTIFICATE

Requests require the applicant's **current government- issued photo identification (e.g., driver's license) and signature signed in front of a notary public** or in the presence of an Iowa Registrar of Vital Records.

1. **PERSON'S NAME AS IT APPEARS ON THE RECORD** ______________________
   FIRST MIDDLE, if any SURNAME (Last)
2. **DATE OF BIRTH** – BE SPECIFIC – Month/Day/Year ______________________
3. **PLACE OF BIRTH** (City and/or County) ______________________
4. **MOTHER'S NAME PRIOR TO MARRIAGE** – FIRST/MIDDLE, if any/LAST ______________________
5. **FATHER'S FULL NAME** – FIRST/MIDDLE, if any/SURNAME (Last) ______________________

6. WAS THE MOTHER MARRIED AT THE TIME OF CONCEPTION OR BIRTH? ☐ Yes ☐ No ☐ Unknown
7. **LEGAL ACTIONS PREVIOUSLY RECORDED (if any)** ☐ None ☐ Adoption ☐ Paternity Establishment ☐ Legal Change of Name on Birth Certificate

   7a. IF A LEGAL ACTION OCCURRED, LIST PREVIOUS NAME (on birth certificate) ______________________
   Marriage does NOT change the birth certificate.

8. **PURPOSE FOR COPY** ______________________ 9. **BIRTHDATE of APPLICANT/RECIPIENT** ______________________
10. **HOW ARE YOU RELATED TO THE PERSON NAMED ON THE RECORD?** ______________________
11. **NAME AND ADDRESS OF PERSON TO RECEIVE THIS COPY:** (MUST BE AGE 18 OR OLDER & ENTITLED TO THE RECORD)

    12a. Name of Applicant/Recipient ______________________

    12b. Street address and P.O. Box (if any) ______________________

    12c. City, State and Zip Code ______________________

12. **THE SEARCH RESULT IS TO BE** (Check one) ☐ Mailed ☐ Picked up (for in-person requests only)
13. **THE NON-REFUNDABLE FEE TO SEARCH IS $15.00**, total cost for one commemorative copy is $35.00 if the record is located. Each additional copy is $35.00. Indicate the number of copies of this record you need. ______________________
14. **THIS SEARCH PAID BY** (Check one) ☐ Check ☐ Money Order ☐ Cash (in-person only) **15. AMOUNT ENCLOSED** ______________________

Checks must be written from the applicant's account; money orders must be in the name of the applicant. Fee payment must accompany this form. Make check or money order payable to 'Iowa Dept. of Public Health' (IDPH).

16. **APPLICANT'S NAME** (Print clearly) ______________________ **17. DAYTIME PHONE #** ______________________
    (Include area code)

I certify that the information provided on this application is accurate and complete to the best of my knowledge and that I have legal entitlement to a certified copy of this record. I have signed below in front of a notary public or an Iowa registrar of vital records.

18. **APPLICANT'S SIGNATURE** ______________________ **19. DATE** ______________________

APPLICANT'S NAME AS APPEARS ON PHOTO I.D. *(Print clearly)* ______________________ State of ____________ County of ____________ ss (SEAL) Signed and affirmed in my presence on this _____ day of ____________, ________. ______________________, My commission expires: ____________ (Notary Public Signature)	**Administrative Use Only** I.D. ________ Initials ________

BEFORE MAILING:

☐ **INCLUDE A CLEAR PHOTOCOPY OF YOUR IDENTIFICATION (e.g., driver's license)**

☐ **SIGN THIS APPLICATION IN FRONT OF A NOTARY PUBLIC**

☐ **INCLUDE FEE PAYMENT AS DESCRIBED IN ITEM 13, 14 AND 15 ABOVE**

SEE OTHER SIDE FOR ADDITIONAL INSTRUCTIONS

MARRIAGE

APPLICATION FOR A SEARCH FOR AN IOWA RECORD

Requests require the applicant's **current government- issued photo identification (i.e., driver's license) and signature signed in front of a notary public** or in the presence of an Iowa Registrar of Vital Records.

---

1. **PARTY A NAME AS IT APPEARS ON THE RECORD** ______________________
   Bride Groom Spouse (select one) FIRST MIDDLE, if any LAST BEFORE AFTER

2. **PARTY B NAME AS IT APPEARS ON THE RECORD** ______________________
   Bride Groom Spouse (select one) FIRST MIDDLE, if any LAST BEFORE AFTER

3. **DATE OF MARRIAGE** – BE SPECIFIC – Month/Day/Year ______________________

4. **PLACE OF MARRIAGE** (City and/or County where license obtained) ______________________

---

5. **PURPOSE FOR COPY** ______________ 6. **BIRTHDATE of APPLICANT/RECIPIENT** ______________

7. **HOW ARE YOU RELATED TO THE PERSON NAMED ON THE RECORD?** ______________

8. **NAME AND ADDRESS OF PERSON TO RECEIVE THIS COPY:** (MUST BE AGE 18 OR OLDER & ENTITLED TO THE RECORD)

   8a. Name of Applicant/Recipient ______________________

   8b. Street address and P.O. Box (if any) ______________________

   8c. City, State and Zip Code ______________________

9. **THE SEARCH RESULT IS TO BE** (Check one) ☐ Mailed ☐ Picked up (for in-person requests only)

10. **THE NON-REFUNDABLE FEE TO SEARCH IS $15.00** and one certified copy is issued if the record is located. Each additional copy of the same record is $15.00. Indicate the number of copies of this record you need. ______________

11. **THIS SEARCH PAID BY** (Check one) ☐ Check ☐ Money Order ☐ Cash (In-person only) **12. AMOUNT ENCLOSED** ______________
    Checks must be drawn from the applicants' account; money orders must be in the name of the applicant. Fee payment must accompany this form. Checks should be payable to 'Iowa Dept. of Public Health' (IDPH).

13. **APPLICANT'S NAME** (Print clearly) ______________ **14. DAYTIME PHONE #** ______________ (Include area code)

I certify that the information provided on this application is accurate and complete to the best of my knowledge and that I have legal entitlement to a certified copy of this record. I have signed below in front of a notary public or an Iowa registrar of vital records.

15. **APPLICANT'S SIGNATURE** ______________________ **16. DATE** ______________

APPLICANT'S NAME AS APPEARS ON PHOTO I.D. *(Print clearly)* ______________________ State of ______________ County of ______________ ss (SEAL) Signed and affirmed in my presence on this _____ day of ____________, _______. ______________________, My commission expires: ____________ (Notary Public Signature)	**Administrative Use Only** I.D. _________ Initials _______

PRIOR TO MAILING:

- **INCLUDE A CLEAR PHOTO COPY OF YOUR IDENTIFICATION (i.e., driver's license)**
- **NOTARIZE YOUR SIGNATURE ON THIS APPLICATION**
- **INCLUDE PAYMENT AS DESCRIBED IN ITEM 13, 14 AND 15 ABOVE**

SEE OTHER SIDE FOR ADDITIONAL INSTRUCTIONS

To Request a Search for an Iowa Marriage Record for the Purpose of Obtaining a Certified Copy

In Iowa, official registration of marriages began July 1, 1880. Original records that were registered are on file with the Iowa Department of Public Health, Bureau of Health Statistics. Statewide record searches are available from the state registrar. Local vital records registrars are located in county recorders' offices, where records of births and deaths that have occurred in that county are maintained. Marriage records are maintained in the county where the license to marry was obtained. ***County registrars are not authorized by law to have records for marriages between the years 1921 to 1941.*** Per Iowa law, information about a specific record is not available over the telephone or by prepared lists. Iowa law provides for public viewing in the county where the record is maintained, or certified copies issued to entitled persons.

Applications to search for a vital record event for the purpose of obtaining a certified copy must be in writing, completely identify the record, and establish entitlement to the record being requested. Entitled persons include the person named on the record or that person's spouse, children, legal parents, grandparents, grandchildren, siblings, or legal representative or guardian. Legal guardians and representatives must also provide additional proof of guardianship or representation. Applicants must be 18 or older. Requests must include the applicant's current government-issued photo identification (i.e., driver's license), except if by mail, a clear photocopy of the I.D., and the applicant's signature signed in front of a notary public or in the presence of an Iowa Registrar of Vital Records.

PAYMENT: A non-refundable $15 fee is required to search for a record and includes one certified copy if the record is located. Each additional copy of the same record is $15. Fees are payable in U.S. funds by check or money order to the issuing registrar's office. Checks must be drawn from the applicants' account; money orders must be in the name of the applicant. Fees must be paid at the time of the application (Iowa Constitution, Article VII, Section 1).

STATE CERTIFIED COPIES.

Certified copies of marriage certificates may be obtained from the state Bureau of Health Statistics by telephone, in-person, or through a postal service. Fees are payable in U.S. funds by check or money order to the Iowa Department of Public Health. In-person requests may also be paid in cash. Genealogy requests take at least 60 days.

Telephone: Customers can call a **toll-free** number **866-809-0290** from 6:00 am CST through 7:00 pm CST, Monday through Friday, except for holidays. A fee of $15.00 is required for the record search and includes one copy if a record is on file in our office. Each additional copy of the record is also $15.00. A VitalChek operator will take your information, screen your credit card, authenticate your identity and complete your order. The fee to screen your credit card and authenticate the caller is an additional $13.00. If you request a group order which consists of more than one Vital Event (i.e. Birth, Death or Marriage) within one order there is an additional $3.00 fee. Turnaround time is usually 10 to 14 days, depending on seasonal demands and mail service. ***Genealogy requests are not available through the credit card line.***

In-person: Applications may be made in-person at the state Bureau of Health Statistics 7:00 a.m. to 5:00 p.m., Monday through Friday, except for state-observed holidays, at the address below, just inside the north lobby entrance and to the right. The Lucas building is just east of the state Capitol and south of Grand Avenue. Applicants must provide current government-issued photo identification and sign their request in the presence of registrar staff. Copies may either be picked up after two working days or mailed to an entitled person. Genealogy requests take at least 60 days.

Postal service: Written requests and fees are mailed to the address below. Requests must state the relationship to the person named on the record and the purpose for the copy. Filled requests take 30-45 days, depending on seasonal demands and mail service. Genealogy requests take at least 60 days. ***The request must be signed in front of a notary public and include a clear photocopy of the applicant's current government-issued photo identification.***

Iowa Department of Public Health
Bureau of Health Statistics
Lucas State Office Building, 1st Floor
321 E. 12th Street
Des Moines, Iowa 50319-0075

SEE OTHER SIDE FOR AN APPLICATION FORM.
FORM MAY BE USED FOR EITHER A COUNTY-CERTIFIED OR A STATE-CERTIFIED COPY OF AN IOWA VITAL RECORD

State of Iowa
Commemorative
Certificate of Marriage

The Iowa Department of Public Health is pleased to offer commemorative certificates of marriage, which makes a memorable keepsake or gift.

This parchment certificate features a gold foil border, image of the state capital of Iowa, and calligraphy print of the individuals' personal information. Gold embossed State and Iowa Department of Public Health seals make it a valid certified copy and legal document. Each certificate is signed by both the Governor of Iowa and the State Registrar. Its 8-1/2" x 11" size is suitable for framing.

Certificates are delivered in protective envelopes within 30 days of application. All applicants must meet the same qualifying direct-and-tangible interest standards (i.e., immediate family) as for any certified marriage certificate request. Submit each fully completed application form with $35 (check or money order) to:

Iowa Department of Public Health
Office of Vital Records
321 E. 12th Street
Lucas State Office Building, 1st Floor
Des Moines IA 50319-0075.

The information on the other side must be completed in order to make application for the Iowa commemorative marriage certificate. Registration of marriages in Iowa officially began July 1, 1880. The original records of all marriages registered in Iowa are maintained in the Office of Vital Records, Iowa Department of Public Health.

The $35 fee for the commemorative marriage certificate includes the search for the record and one commemorative certificate. If the record is not located, the applicant will receive a notification of the record search results and a $20 refund, with $15 retained in this office to cover the cost of the search as required by statute.

Each additional commemorative certificate for the same record is $35 and can be ordered on the same application form.

Application for regular certified marriage certificates requires a fee of $15 for a state record search and includes one certified copy. Each additional copy of the same record is also $15. If the record is not located, the applicant receives a notification to that affect. The $15 fee is retained in this office for the search.

Applications to search for a vital record event for the purpose of obtaining a commemorative copy must be in writing, completely identify the record, and establish entitlement to the record being requested. Entitled persons include the person named on the record or that person's spouse, children, legal parents, grandparents, grandchildren, siblings, or legal representative or guardian. Legal guardians and representatives must also provide additional proof of guardianship or representation. Applicants must be 18 or older. Requests must include the applicant's current government-issued photo identification (e.g., driver's license), except if by mail, a clear photocopy of the I.D., and the applicant's signature signed in front of a notary public or in the presence of an Iowa Registrar of Vital Records.

SEE OTHER SIDE FOR AN APPLICATION FORM.

COMMEMORATIVE MARRIAGE

APPLICATION FOR IOWA COMMEMORATIVE MARRIAGE CERTIFICATE

Requests require the applicant's **current government- issued photo identification (e.g., driver's license) and signature signed in front of a notary public** or in the presence of an Iowa Registrar of Vital Records.

---

1. **PARTY A NAME AS IT APPEARS ON THE RECORD** ______________________________
   Bride Groom Spouse (select one) FIRST MIDDLE, if any LAST BEFORE AFTER
2. **PARTY B NAME AS IT APPEARS ON THE RECORD** ______________________________
   Bride Groom Spouse (select one) FIRST MIDDLE, if any LAST BEFORE AFTER
3. **DATE OF MARRIAGE** – BE SPECIFIC – Month/Day/Year ______________________________
4. **PLACE OF MARRIAGE** (City and/or County where license obtained) ______________________________

---

5. **Officiate who performed the marriage ceremony** (if known) ______________________________
6. **Witnesses who signed the marriage certificate** (if known) 1. ______________________________
   2. ______________________________
7. **HOW ARE YOU RELATED TO THE PERSON NAMED ON THE RECORD?** ______________________________
8. **NAME AND ADDRESS OF PERSON TO RECEIVE THIS COPY:** (MUST BE AGE 18 OR OLDER & ENTITLED TO THE RECORD)
   8a. Name of Applicant/Recipient ______________________________
   8b. Street address and P.O. Box (if any) ______________________________
   8c. City, State and Zip Code ______________________________
9. **THE SEARCH RESULT IS TO BE** (Check one) ☐ Mailed ☐ Picked up (for in-person requests only)
10. **THE NON-REFUNDABLE FEE TO SEARCH IS $15.00**, total cost for one commemorative copy is $35.00 if the record is located. Each additional copy is $35.00. Indicate the number of copies of this record you need. ______________
11. **PAID BY** (Check one) ☐ Check ☐ Money Order ☐ Cash (In-person only) **12. AMOUNT ENCLOSED** ______________

Checks must be written from the applicant's account; money orders must be in the name of the applicant. Fee payment must accompany this form. Make check or money order payable to 'Iowa Dept. of Public Health' (IDPH).

13. **APPLICANT'S NAME** (Print clearly) ______________________ **14. DAYTIME PHONE #** ______________ (Include area code)

I certify that the information provided on this application is accurate and complete to the best of my knowledge and that I have legal entitlement to a certified copy of this record. I have signed below in front of a notary public or an Iowa registrar of vital records.

15. **APPLICANT'S SIGNATURE** ______________________ **16. DATE** ______________

APPLICANT'S NAME AS APPEARS ON PHOTO I.D. *(Print clearly)* ______________________ State of ____________ County of ______________ ss (SEAL) Signed and affirmed in my presence on this _____ day of ___________, _______. ______________________, My commission expires: __________ (Notary Public Signature)	**Administrative Use Only** I.D. ________ Initials _______

PRIOR TO MAILING:

☐ **INCLUDE A CLEAR PHOTOCOPY OF YOUR IDENTIFICATION (e.g., driver's license)**

☐ **SIGN THIS APPLICATION IN FRONT OF A NOTARY PUBLIC**

☐ **INCLUDE FEE PAYMENT AS DESCRIBED IN ITEM 10, 11 AND 12 ABOVE**

SEE OTHER SIDE FOR ADDITIONAL INSTRUCTIONS

DEATH

APPLICATION FOR A SEARCH FOR AN IOWA RECORD

Check One ☐ DEATH ☐ FETAL DEATH ☐ BIRTH RESULTING IN STILLBIRTH (Fetal Death must be on file)

Requests require the applicant's **current government - issued photo identification (e.g., driver's license) and signature signed in front of a notary public** or in the presence of an Iowa Registrar of Vital Records.

---

1. **PERSON'S NAME AS IT APPEARS ON THE RECORD** ______________________________
   FIRST MIDDLE, if any SURNAME (Last)
2. **DATE OF DEATH** – BE SPECIFIC – Month/Day/Year ______________________________
3. **PLACE OF DEATH** (City and/or County) ______________________________
4. **MOTHER'S FULL MAIDEN NAME** – FIRST/MIDDLE, if any/LAST ______________________________
5. **FATHER'S FULL NAME** – FIRST/MIDDLE, if any/SURNAME (Last) ______________________________

---

6. **PURPOSE FOR COPY** ____________________ 5. **BIRTHDATE of APPLICANT/RECIPIENT** ____________
7. **HOW ARE YOU RELATED TO THE PERSON NAMED ON THE RECORD?** ______________________________
8. **NAME AND ADDRESS OF PERSON TO RECEIVE THIS COPY:** (MUST BE AGE 18 OR OLDER & ENTITLED TO THE RECORD)
   - **7a. Name of Applicant/Recipient** ______________________________
   - **7b. Street address and P.O. Box** (if any) ______________________________
   - **7c. City, State and Zip Code** ______________________________
9. **THE SEARCH RESULT IS TO BE** (Check one) ☐ Mailed ☐ Picked up (for in-person requests only)
10. **THE NON-REFUNDABLE FEE TO SEARCH IS $15.00** and one certified copy is issued if the record is located. Each additional copy of the same record is $15.00. Indicate the number of copies of this record you need. ____________
11. **THIS SEARCH PAID BY** (Check one) ☐ Check ☐ Money Order ☐ Cash (In-person only) **12. AMOUNT ENCLOSED** ____________

Checks must be written from the applicant's account; money orders must be in the name of the applicant. Fee payment must be in U.S. funds and be included with this application. Make checks and money orders payable to the 'Iowa Dept. of Public Health' (state copy) or the appropriate county registrar of vital records in the county of the event.

13. **APPLICANT'S NAME** (Print clearly) ____________________ **14. DAYTIME PHONE #** ____________
    (Include area code)

I certify that the information that I provided on this application is accurate and complete to the best of my knowledge and that I have legal entitlement to a certified copy of this record. I have signed below in front of a Notary Public or an Iowa registrar of vital records.

15. **APPLICANT'S SIGNATURE** ______________________________ **16. DATE** ____________

	Administrative Use Only
APPLICANT'S NAME AS APPEARS ON PHOTO I.D. *(Print clearly)* ______________________________	I.D. ________
State of ____________ County of ____________ ss (SEAL)	Initials ________
Signed and affirmed in my presence on this _____ day of ____________, ________.	
______________________, My commission expires: ____________ (Notary Public Signature)	

BEFORE MAILING:

- **INCLUDE A CLEAR PHOTOCOPY OF YOUR IDENTIFICATION (e.g., driver's license)**
- **SIGN THIS APPLICATION IN FRONT OF A NOTARY PUBLIC**
- **INCLUDE FEE PAYMENT AS DESCRIBED IN ITEM 10, 11 AND 12 ABOVE**

SEE OTHER SIDE FOR ADDITIONAL INSTRUCTIONS

To Request a Search for an Iowa Death Record for the Purpose of Obtaining a Certified Copy

In Iowa, official registration of deaths began July 1, 1880. Original records that were registered are on file with the Iowa Department of Public Health, Bureau of Health Statistics. Statewide record searches are available from the state registrar. Local vital records registrars are located in county recorders' offices, where records of deaths that have occurred in that county are maintained. ***County registrars are not authorized by law to have records sealed by a court of law; death between the years 1921 to 1941.*** Per Iowa law, information about a specific record is not available over the telephone or by prepared lists. Iowa law provides for public viewing in the county where the record is maintained, or certified copies issued to entitled persons.

Applications to search for a vital record event for the purpose of obtaining a certified copy must be in writing, completely identify the record, and establish entitlement to the record being requested. Entitled persons include the person named on the record or that person's spouse, children, legal parents, grandparents, grandchildren, or siblings. Legal representatives must also provide additional proof of representation. Applicants must be 18 or older. Requests must include the applicant's current government-issued photo identification (i.e., driver's license), except if by mail, a clear photocopy of the I.D., and the applicant's signature signed in front of a notary public or in the presence of an Iowa Registrar of Vital Records.

PAYMENT: A non-refundable $15 fee is required to search for a record and includes one certified copy if the record is located. Each additional copy of the same record is $15. Fees are payable in U.S. funds by check or money order to the issuing registrar's office. Checks must be drawn from the applicants' account; money orders must be in the name of the applicant. Fees must be paid at the time of the application (Iowa Constitution, Article VII, Section 1).

STATE CERTIFIED COPIES.

Certified copies of death certificates may be obtained from the state Bureau of Health Statistics by telephone, in-person, or through a postal service. Fees are payable in U.S. funds by check or money order to the Iowa Department of Public Health. In-person requests may also be paid in cash. Genealogy requests take at least 60 days.

Telephone: Customers can call a **toll-free** number **866-809-0290** from 6:00 am CST through 7:00 pm CST, Monday through Friday, except for holidays. A fee of $15.00 is required for the record search and includes one copy if a record is on file in our office. Each additional copy of the record is also $15.00. A VitalChek operator will take your information, screen your credit card, authenticate your identity and complete your order. The fee to screen your credit card and authenticate the caller is an additional $13.00. If you request a group order which consists of more than one Vital Event (i.e. Birth, Death or Marriage) within one order there is an additional $3.00 fee. Turnaround time is usually 10 to 14 days, depending on seasonal demands and mail service. ***Genealogy requests are not available through the credit card line.***

In-person: Applications may be made in-person at the state Bureau of Health Statistics 7:00 a.m. to 5:00 p.m., Monday through Friday, except for state-observed holidays, at the address below, just inside the north lobby entrance and to the right. The Lucas building is just east of the state Capitol and south of Grand Avenue. Applicants must provide current government-issued photo identification and sign their request in the presence of registrar staff. Copies may either be picked up after two working days or mailed to an entitled person. Genealogy requests take at least 60 days.

Postal service: Written requests and fees are mailed to the address below. Requests must state the relationship to the person named on the record and the purpose for the copy. Filled requests take 30-45 days, depending on seasonal demands and mail service. Genealogy requests take at least 60 days. ***The request must be signed in front of a notary public and include a clear photocopy of the applicant's current government-issued photo identification.***

Iowa Department of Public Health
Bureau of Health Statistics
Lucas State Office Building, 1st Floor
321 E. 12th Street
Des Moines, Iowa 50319-0075

SEE OTHER SIDE FOR AN APPLICATION FORM.
FORM MAY BE USED FOR EITHER A COUNTY-CERTIFIED OR A STATE-CERTIFIED COPY OF AN IOWA VITAL RECORD

KANSAS

Send your requests to:

Office of Vital Statistics
1000 SW Jackson, Suite 120
Topeka, KS 66612-2221

Tel. (785) 296-1400
E-mail: Vital.Records@kdheks.gov
www.kdheks.gov/vital

Birth certificates are on file at the Office of Vital Statistics from July 1, 1911, with a few delayed birth certificates dating back to the 1860s. Marriage records from May 1, 1913, divorce records from July 1, 1951, and death records from July 1, 1911, are also available. Birth, death, marriage, and divorce records (vital records) in Kansas are not public records. Certified copies of vital records are released only to the person named on the record, immediate family, a legal representative, or anyone who can prove a direct interest.

Cost for a certified Birth Certificate	$15.00
Cost for a certified Marriage or Divorce Certificate	$15.00
Cost for a certified Death Certificate	$15.00
Cost for a duplicate copy, when ordered at the same time	$15.00

For earlier records, contact:

County Clerk
County Court House
(County Seat), KS

www.kssos.org/forms/communication/county.pdf (for a list of county clerks)

For Genealogy Research:

Currently, the Office of Vital Statistics does allow requests for genealogical research. Pre-1940 records may be requested by an individual related as at least a cousin; post-1940 records must be requested by an immediate family member. Genealogy requests are not considered urgent and must be requested through regular mail.

Kansas State Historical Society (6425 SW Sixth Avenue, Topeka, KS 66615-1099; tel. 785-272-8681; www.kshs.org/p/genealogy-vital-records-in-kansas/11313) has copies on microfilm of some county and city vital records between 1885 and 1911. They also have a large collection of Kansas newspapers on microfilm, which can be searched for death, birth, and marriage announcements.

For Adoption Record information, contact:

Adoption Clerk
Office of Vital Statistics
1000 SW Jackson, Suite 120
Topeka, KS 66612-2221

Tel. (785) 296-1436

Adult adoptees may receive copies of their records at age 18.

APPLICATION FOR CERTIFIED COPY OF KANSAS BIRTH CERTIFICATE

BIRTH CERTIFICATES ARE ON FILE FROM JULY 1, 1911 TO PRESENT

(PLEASE PRINT)

REQUESTOR INFORMATION:

YOUR NAME (PLEASE PRINT) ______

YOUR MAILING ADDRESS ______

______

CITY STATE ZIP CODE

REASON FOR REQUEST (PLEASE BE SPECIFIC) ______

(We ask this so that we can provide appropriate service for your needs)

YOUR **DAYTIME** TELEPHONE NUMBER ______

YOUR RELATIONSHIP TO PERSON NAMED ON CERTIFICATE (REQUIRED) ______

(SEE REVERSE SIDE FOR ELIGIBILITY REQUIREMENTS)

YOUR SIGNATURE (REQUIRED) ______ TODAY'S DATE ______

CERTIFICATE INFORMATION:

$15.00 FOR ONE CERTIFIED COPY AND **$15.00** FOR EACH ADDITIONAL CERTIFIED COPY OF THE SAME RECORD

NUMBER OF CERTIFICATES REQUESTED **FEE INFORMATION ON REVERSE SIDE**

______ CERTIFIED COPIES 0 ______ TOTAL FEE

NAME ON CERTIFICATE ______

FIRST MIDDLE LAST NAME AT BIRTH

DATE OF BIRTH ______ PRESENT AGE OF THIS PERSON ______ RACE ______

MONTH DAY YEAR

DATE OF DEATH, IF APPLICABLE ______ SEX: M ☐ F ☐

PLACE OF BIRTH ______

CITY COUNTY STATE **(MUST BE KANSAS)** HOSPITAL

MOTHER'S NAME ______ BIRTHPLACE ______

FIRST MIDDLE MAIDEN

FATHER'S NAME ______ BIRTHPLACE ______

FIRST MIDDLE LAST

ADOPTION INFORMATION: **IF PERSON NAMED ON CERTIFICATE HAS BEEN ADOPTED (SEE REVERSE SIDE)**

ADOPTED? YES ☐ NO ☐ Is request for record before adoption? YES ☐ NO ☐

ORIGINAL NAME, IF KNOWN ______

YOU MUST INCLUDE A COPY OF PHOTO ID WITH THIS FORM
OR TWO ALTERNATIVE DOCUMENTS (SEE REVERSE SIDE FOR LIST)

MAILING ADDRESS:
KANSAS DEPARTMENT OF HEALTH AND ENVIRONMENT
OFFICE OF VITAL STATISTICS
1000 SW JACKSON, SUITE 120
TOPEKA, KS 66612-2221
WALK-IN CUSTOMER SERVICE HOURS: 9:00 - 4:00, MONDAY - FRIDAY
OFFICE HOURS: 8:00 - 5:00, MONDAY – FRIDAY, **PHONE (785) 296-1400**
www.kdheks.gov/vital

PLEASE ENCLOSE A BUSINESS SIZE SELF-ADDRESSED STAMPED ENVELOPE.

FORM VS 235 05/12

IDENTIFICATION

ID IS REQUIRED OF PERSON COMPLETING FORM

Due to identity theft and other fraudulent use of vital records, acceptable ID is limited.
DO NOT send original ID with application

YOU MUST PROVIDE A PHOTOCOPY OF A GOVERNMENT (STATE OR FEDERAL) ISSUED PHOTO ID. THIS CAN BE ISSUED BY THE U.S. OR OTHER COUNTRY OF RESIDENCE.

ACCEPTABLE IDENTIFICATIONS INCLUDES: (Please include photocopy of front and back)

- Photocopy of CURRENT Driver's License
- Photocopy of CURRENT State ID Card
- Photocopy of CURRENT Passport or Visa
- Photocopy of CURRENT Military ID

Temporary drivers' license must have one additional ID submitted with request.

IF YOU DO NOT HAVE A GOVERNMENT ISSUED PHOTO ID, YOU MUST SEND PHOTOCOPIES OF ANY *TWO* OF THE FOLLOWING (MUST BE TWO DIFFERENT FORMS OF ID):

- Social Security Card (must be signed)
- Bank Statement With Current Address
- Car Registration or Title With Current address
- Current Utility Bill With Current Address
- Current Pay Stub (must include your name, social security number plus name and address of business)

FEE INFORMATION

K.A.R. 28-17-6 requires the following fee(s).

The correct fee must be submitted with the request. The fee for certified copies of birth certificates is $15.00 for one certified copy and $15.00 for each additional certified copy of the same record ordered at the same time. This fee allows a 5-year search of the records, including the year indicated plus two years before and two years after, or you may indicate the consecutive 5-year period you want searched. You may specify more than one 5-year span, but each search cost $15.00

IF THE CERTIFICATE IS NOT LOCATED, A $15.00 FEE MUST BE RETAINED FOR THE RECORD SEARCH.

Make checks or money orders payable to KANSAS VITAL STATISTICS. For your protection, **do not send cash.**

Fees expire 12 months from the date of the request.

MULTIPLE REQUESTS FOR DIFFERENT RECORDS MAY BE HANDLED AND MAILED SEPARATELY.

ELIGIBILITY

By state law, vital records filed with this office are not open for public inspection and the requestor must meet eligibility requirements -- must be named on the record, an immediate family member, or someone who can provide legal proof the record is necessary for the determination of personal or property rights. [K.S.A. 65-2422d]

If legal guardianship has been established through the courts, please provide copy of guardianship papers.

ADOPTION

When an adoption has occurred, the biological family may not have a legal right to the adoptee's record nor may the adoptee have a legal right to the biological family's records.

WARNING: COPYING, ALTERING, or FRAUDULENT ACTIVITY PROHIBITED

Except as authorized by the Uniform Vital Statistics Act, no person shall prepare or issue any certificate (vital record) which purports to be an original, certified copy or abstract or copy of a certificate [K.S.A. 65-2422d.(g)]. Vital records identity theft related to obtaining certificates or making, counterfeiting, altering, amending any certified copy of a vital record with the intent to sell or obtain for any purpose of deception a certified copy of a vital record is a severity level 8, nonperson felony. [K.S.A. 21-3830a (d) and K.S.A 21-3830a (e)].

APPLICATION FOR CERTIFIED COPY OF <u>KANSAS MARRIAGE</u> CERTIFICATE

MARRIAGE CERTIFICATES ARE ON FILE FROM MAY 1, 1913 TO PRESENT

(PLEASE PRINT)

$15.00 FOR ONE CERTIFIED COPY AND **$15.00** FOR EACH ADDITIONAL CERTIFIED COPY OF THE SAME RECORD

NUMBER OF CERTIFICATES REQUESTED **FEE INFORMATION ON REVERSE SIDE**

______ CERTIFIED COPIES 0______ TOTAL FEE

GROOM__________________________________ DATE OF BIRTH ____________
FIRST MIDDLE LAST MO DAY YR

BRIDE __________________________________ DATE OF BIRTH ____________
FIRST MIDDLE LAST MO DAY YR
(MAIDEN OR PREVIOUS MARRIED SURNAME)

DATE OF MARRIAGE______________________
MONTH DAY YEAR

PLACE IN WHICH MARRIAGE LICENSE WAS ISSUED______________________
COUNTY STATE **(MUST BE KANSAS)**

CITY IN WHICH MARRIAGE TOOK PLACE ______________________

YOU MUST INCLUDE A COPY OF PHOTO ID WITH THIS FORM
OR *TWO* ALTERNATIVE DOCUMENTS (SEE REVERSE SIDE FOR LIST)

YOUR NAME (PLEASE PRINT)______________________

YOUR MAILING ADDRESS______________________

____
CITY STATE ZIP CODE

REASON FOR REQUEST (PLEASE BE SPECIFIC) ______________________
(We ask this so that we can provide appropriate service for your needs)

YOUR **DAYTIME** TELEPHONE NUMBER ______________________

YOUR RELATIONSHIP TO PERSON NAMED ON CERTIFICATE (REQUIRED)______________________
(See reverse side for eligibility requirements)

YOUR SIGNATURE (REQUIRED) ______________________ TODAY'S DATE ____________

MAILING ADDRESS:

KANSAS DEPARTMENT OF HEALTH AND ENVIRONMENT
OFFICE OF VITAL STATISTICS
1000 SW JACKSON, SUITE 120
TOPEKA, KS 66612-2221
WALK-IN CUSTOMER SERVICE HOURS: 9:00 - 4:00, MONDAY - FRIDAY
OFFICE HOURS: 8:00 - 5:00, MONDAY – FRIDAY, **PHONE (785) 296-1400**
<u>www.kdheks.gov/vital</u>

PLEASE ENCLOSE A BUSINESS SIZE SELF-ADDRESSED STAMPED ENVELOPE.

Form VS-237 rev 10/09

IDENTIFICATION
ID IS REQUIRED OF PERSON COMPLETING FORM

Due to identity theft and other fraudulent use of vital records, acceptable ID is limited.
DO NOT send original ID with application

YOU MUST PROVIDE A PHOTOCOPY OF A GOVERNMENT (STATE OR FEDERAL) ISSUED PHOTO ID. THIS CAN BE ISSUED BY THE U.S. OR OTHER COUNTRY OF RESIDENCE.

ACCEPTABLE IDENTIFICATIONS INCLUDES: (Please include photocopy of front and back)

Photocopy of CURRENT Driver's License
Photocopy of CURRENT State ID Card
Photocopy of CURRENT Passport or Visa
Photocopy of CURRENT Military ID

Temporary drivers' license must have one additional ID submitted with request.

IF YOU DO NOT HAVE A GOVERNMENT ISSUED PHOTO ID, YOU MUST SEND PHOTOCOPIES OF ANY *TWO* OF THE FOLLOWING (MUST BE TWO DIFFERENT FORMS OF ID):

Social Security Card (must be signed)
Bank Statement With Current Address
Car Registration or Title With Current address
Current Utility Bill With Current Address
Current Pay Stub (must include your name, social security number plus name and address of business)

FEE INFORMATION

K.A.R. 28-17-6 requires the following fee(s).

The correct fee must be submitted with the request. The fee for certified copies of marriage licenses is $15.00 for one certified copy and $15.00 for each additional certified copy of the same record ordered at the same time. This fee allows a 5-year search of the records, including the year indicated plus two years before and two years after, or you may indicate the consecutive 5-year period you want searched. You may specify more than one 5-year span, but each search costs $15.00.

IF THE CERTIFICATE IS NOT LOCATED, A $15.00 FEE MUST BE RETAINED FOR THE RECORD SEARCH.

Make checks or money orders payable to **KANSAS VITAL STATISTICS**. For your protection, **do not send cash**.

Fees expire 12 months from date of the request.

MULTIPLE REQUESTS FOR DIFFERENT RECORDS MAY BE HANDLED AND MAILED SEPARATELY.

ELIGIBILITY

By state law, vital records filed with this office are not open for public inspection and the requestor must meet eligibility requirements -- must be named on the record, an immediate family member, or someone who can provide legal proof the record is necessary for the determination of personal or property rights. [K.S.A. 65-2422d]

WEBSITE

For additional information, please access the web site at: **www.kdheks.gov/vital**

WARNING: COPYING OR ALTERING PROHIBITED

Except as authorized by the Uniform Vital Statistics Act, no person shall prepare or issue any certificate (vital record) which purports to be an original, certified copy or copy of a certificate [K.S.A. 65-2422d.(g)]. Any person who willfully makes or alters any certificate or certified copy, except as authorized by the Uniform Vital Statistics Act, shall be fined or imprisoned, or both. [K.S.A. 65-2434.(1)].

APPLICATION FOR CERTIFIED COPY OF KANSAS DIVORCE CERTIFICATE

DIVORCE CERTIFICATES ARE ON FILE FROM JULY 1, 1951 TO PRESENT

(PLEASE PRINT)

$15.00 FOR ONE CERTIFIED COPY AND **$15.00** FOR EACH ADDITIONAL CERTIFIED COPY OF THE SAME RECORD

NUMBER OF CERTIFICATES REQUESTED **FEE INFORMATION ON REVERSE SIDE**

_____ CERTIFIED COPIES 0_____ TOTAL FEE

HUSBAND____
FIRST MIDDLE LAST

BRIDE ____
FIRST MIDDLE LAST MAIDEN

DATE OF DIVORCE _____________________________
MONTH DAY YEAR

PLACE IN WHICH DIVORCE WAS GRANTED_______________________________
COUNTY CITY STATE **(MUST BE KANSAS)**

YOU MUST INCLUDE A COPY OF PHOTO ID WITH THIS FORM
OR *TWO* ALTERNATIVE DOCUMENTS (SEE REVERSE SIDE FOR LIST)

YOUR NAME (PLEASE PRINT) _______________________________________

YOUR MAILING ADDRESS_______________________________________

____
CITY STATE ZIP CODE

REASON FOR REQUEST (PLEASE BE SPECIFIC)_______________________________
(We ask this so that we can provide appropriate service for your needs)

YOUR **DAYTIME** TELEPHONE NUMBER _______________________________

YOUR RELATIONSHIP TO PERSON NAMED ON CERTIFICATE (REQUIRED)_______________
(See reverse side for eligibility requirements)

YOUR SIGNATURE (REQUIRED) ______________________ TODAY'S DATE ____________

MAILING ADDRESS: KANSAS DEPARTMENT OF HEALTH AND ENVIRONMENT
OFFICE OF VITAL STATISTICS
1000 SW JACKSON, SUITE 120
TOPEKA, KS 66612-2221
WALK-IN CUSTOMER SERVICE HOURS: 9:00 - 4:00, MONDAY - FRIDAY
OFFICE HOURS: 8:00 - 5:00, MONDAY – FRIDAY, **PHONE (785) 296-1400**
www.kdheks.gov/vital

PLEASE ENCLOSE A BUSINESS SIZE SELF-ADDRESSED STAMPED ENVELOPE.

Form VS-238 rev 10/09

IDENTIFICATION

ID IS REQUIRED OF PERSON COMPLETING FORM

Due to identity theft and other fraudulent use of vital records, acceptable ID is limited.
DO NOT send original ID with application

YOU MUST PROVIDE A PHOTOCOPY OF A GOVERNMENT (STATE OR FEDERAL) ISSUED PHOTO ID. THIS CAN BE ISSUED BY THE U.S. OR OTHER COUNTRY OF RESIDENCE.

ACCEPTABLE IDENTIFICATIONS INCLUDES: (Please include photocopy of front and back)

Photocopy of CURRENT Driver's License
Photocopy of CURRENT State ID Card
Photocopy of CURRENT Passport or Visa
Photocopy of CURRENT Military ID

Temporary drivers' license must have one additional ID submitted with request.

IF YOU DO NOT HAVE A GOVERNMENT ISSUED PHOTO ID, YOU MUST SEND PHOTOCOPIES OF ANY *TWO* OF THE FOLLOWING (MUST BE TWO DIFFERENT FORMS OF ID):

Social Security Card (must be signed)
Bank Statement With Current Address
Car Registration or Title With Current address
Current Utility Bill With Current Address
Current Pay Stub (must include your name, social security number plus name and address of business)

FEE INFORMATION

K.A.R. 28-17-6 requires the following fee(s).

The correct fee must be submitted with the request. The fee for certified copies of marriage licenses is $15.00 for one certified copy and $15.00 for each additional certified copy of the same record ordered at the same time. This fee allows a 5-year search of the records, including the year indicated plus two years before and two years after, or you may indicate the consecutive 5-year period you want searched. You may specify more than one 5-year span, but each search costs $15.00.

IF THE CERTIFICATE IS NOT LOCATED, A $15.00 FEE MUST BE RETAINED FOR THE RECORD SEARCH.

Make checks or money orders payable to **KANSAS VITAL STATISTICS**. For your protection, **do not send cash**.

Fees expire 12 months from date of the request.

MULTIPLE REQUESTS FOR DIFFERENT RECORDS MAY BE HANDLED AND MAILED SEPARATELY.

ELIGIBILITY

By state law, vital records filed with this office are not open for public inspection and the requestor must meet eligibility requirements -- must be named on the record, an immediate family member, or someone who can provide legal proof the record is necessary for the determination of personal or property rights. [K.S.A. 65-2422d]

WEBSITE

For additional information, please access the web site at: **www.kdheks.gov/vital**

WARNING: COPYING OR ALTERING PROHIBITED

Except as authorized by the Uniform Vital Statistics Act, no person shall prepare or issue any certificate (vital record) which purports to be an original, certified copy or copy of a certificate [K.S.A. 65-2422d.(g)]. Any person who willfully makes or alters any certificate or certified copy, except as authorized by the Uniform Vital Statistics Act, shall be fined or imprisoned, or both. [K.S.A. 65-2434.(1)].

APPLICATION FOR CERTIFIED COPY OF KANSAS DEATH CERTIFICATE

DEATH CERTIFICATES ARE ON FILE FROM JULY 1, 1911 TO PRESENT

(PLEASE PRINT)

$15.00 FOR ONE CERTIFIED COPY AND **$15.00** FOR EACH ADDITIONAL CERTIFIED COPY OF THE SAME RECORD

NUMBER OF CERTIFICATES REQUESTED **FEE INFORMATION ON REVERSE SIDE**

_______ CERTIFIED COPIES 0_______ TOTAL FEE

NAME ON CERTIFICATE ______________________________

FIRST MIDDLE LAST

DATE OF DEATH ______________________ CHECK IF STILLBIRTH ☐ RACE __________

MONTH DAY YEAR

SEX: M☐ F☐

PLACE OF DEATH ______________________________

CITY COUNTY STATE **(MUST BE KANSAS)**

MARITAL STATUS AT DEATH __________ NAME OF SPOUSE __________

FATHER'S NAME/MOTHER MAIDEN NAME __________

DATE OF BIRTH (OR AGE AT DEATH) __________ PLACE OF BIRTH __________

RESIDENCE OF DEATH __________ FUNERAL HOME __________

CITY/COUNTY WHERE BURIED __________

YOU MUST INCLUDE A COPY OF PHOTO ID WITH THIS FORM OR TWO ALTERNATIVE DOCUMENTS (SEE REVERSE SIDE FOR LIST)

YOUR NAME (PLEASE PRINT) __________

YOUR MAILING ADDRESS __________

____

CITY STATE ZIP CODE

REASON FOR REQUEST (PLEASE BE SPECIFIC) __________

(We ask this so that we can provide appropriate service for your needs)

YOUR **DAYTIME** TELEPHONE NUMBER __________

YOUR RELATIONSHIP TO PERSON NAMED ON CERTIFICATE (REQUIRED) __________

(See reverse side for eligibility requirements)

YOUR SIGNATURE (REQUIRED) __________ TODAY'S DATE __________

MAILING ADDRESS: KANSAS DEPARTMENT OF HEALTH AND ENVIRONMENT
OFFICE OF VITAL STATISTICS
1000 SW JACKSON, SUITE 120
TOPEKA, KS 66612-2221
WALK-IN CUSTOMER SERVICE HOURS: 9:00 - 4:00, MONDAY - FRIDAY
OFFICE HOURS: 8:00 - 5:00, MONDAY – FRIDAY, **PHONE (785) 296-1400**
www.kdheks.gov/vital

PLEASE ENCLOSE A BUSINESS SIZE SELF-ADDRESSED STAMPED ENVELOPE.

FORM VS-236 10/09

IDENTIFICATION
ID IS REQUIRED OF PERSON COMPLETING FORM

Due to identity theft and other fraudulent use of vital records, acceptable ID is limited.
DO NOT send original ID with application

YOU MUST PROVIDE A PHOTOCOPY OF A GOVERNMENT (STATE OR FEDERAL) ISSUED PHOTO ID. THIS CAN BE ISSUED BY THE U.S. OR OTHER COUNTRY OF RESIDENCE.

ACCEPTABLE IDENTIFICATIONS INCLUDES: (Please include photocopy of front and back)

- Photocopy of CURRENT Driver's License
- Photocopy of CURRENT State ID Card
- Photocopy of CURRENT Passport or Visa
- Photocopy of CURRENT Military ID

Temporary drivers' license must have one additional ID submitted with request.

IF YOU DO NOT HAVE A GOVERNMENT ISSUED PHOTO ID, YOU MUST SEND PHOTOCOPIES OF ANY *TWO* OF THE FOLLOWING (MUST BE TWO DIFFERENT FORMS OF ID):

- Social Security Card (must be signed)
- Bank Statement With Current Address
- Car Registration or Title With Current address
- Current Utility Bill With Current Address
- Current Pay Stub (must include your name, social security number plus name and address of business)

FEE INFORMATION

K.A.R. 28-17-6 requires the following fee(s).

The correct fee must be submitted with the request. The fee for certified copies of death certificates is $15. 00 for one certified copy and $15.00 for each additional certified copy of the same record ordered at the same time. This fee allows a 5-year search of the records, including the year indicated plus two years before and two years after, or you may indicate the consecutive 5-year period you want searched. You may specify more than one 5-year span, but each search costs $15.00.

IF THE CERTIFICATE IS NOT LOCATED, A $15.00 FEE MUST BE RETAINED FOR THE RECORD SEARCH.

Make checks or money orders payable to **KANSAS VITAL STATISTICS**. For your protection, do not send cash.

Fees expire 12 months from date of the request.

MULTIPLE REQUESTS FOR DIFFERENT RECORDS MAY BE HANDLED AND MAILED SEPARATELY.

ELIGIBILITY

By state law, vital records filed with this office are not open for public inspection and the requestor must meet eligibility requirements -- must be named on the record, an immediate family member, or someone who can provide legal proof the record is necessary for the determination of personal or property rights. [K.S.A 65-2422d]

WEBSITE

For additional information, please access the web site at: **www.kdheks.gov/vital**

WARNING: COPYING OR ALTERING PROHIBITED

Except as authorized by the Uniform Vital Statistics Act, no person shall prepare or issue any certificate (vital record) which purports to be an original, certified copy or copy of a certificate [K.S.A. 65-2422d.(g)]. Any person who willfully makes or alters any certificate or certified copy, except as authorized by the Uniform Vital Statistics Act, shall be fined or imprisoned, or both. [K.S.A. 65-2434.(1)].

KENTUCKY

Send your requests to:

Office of Vital Statistics
275 East Main Street, 1E-A
Frankfort, KY 40621

Tel. (502) 564-4212
http://chfs.ky.gov/dph/vital/

The Office of Vital Statistics has birth and death records from January 1, 1911, and marriage and divorce records from June 1, 1958. Copies of marriage certificates prior to June 1958 may be obtained from the county clerk in the county where the license was issued. Records of divorce proceedings are available from the clerk of the Circuit Court that granted the decree.

Cost for a certified Birth Certificate	$10.00
Cost for a certified Marriage Certificate	$6.00
Cost for a certified Divorce Record	$6.00
Cost for a certified Death Certificate	$6.00

For Genealogy Research:

The Online Kentucky Vital Records Index (http://ukcc.uky.edu/vitalrec/) lists deaths from 1911 to 1992, and marriages and divorces from 1973 to 1993.

The Kentucky Department for Libraries and Archives (300 Coffee Tree Road, P.O. Box 537, Frankfort, KY 40602-0537; tel. 502-564-8300; http://kdla.ky.gov/researchers) has birth, marriage, and death records 1852–1862, 1874–1879, and 1891–1910; birth and death registers before 1911 for the cities Covington, Lexington, Louisville, and Newport; and death certificates 1911–1960.

The Martin F. Schmidt Research Library of the Kentucky Historical Society (100 West Broadway, Frankfort, KY 40601; tel. 502-564-1792; http://history.ky.gov/) has a great many resources for genealogists, including Kentucky vital records 1852–1910 on microfilm.

On the KYGenWeb site (www.kygenweb.net/vitals/index.html), you can search the Kentucky Death Index 1911–2000, the Kentucky Birth Index 1911–1912, and Kentucky Marriages 1973–2000.

For Adoption Record information, contact:

Adult Adoption Division
Kentucky Cabinet for Health and Family Services
275 East Main Street, 3rd Floor
Frankfort, KY 40601

Tel. (502) 564-2147
http://chfs.ky.gov/dcbs/dpp/ADOPTION+SEARCH.htm

Non-identifying information is available to adoptees 21 and older from the state and adoption agencies without a court order. Visit www.kyadoptions.com/ for information about the Kentucky Adoption Reunion Registry.

VS-37
(Rev 1/30/2012)

BIRTH

COMMONWEALTH OF KENTUCKY
STATE REGISTRAR OF VITAL STATISTICS

APPLICATION FOR A CERTIFIED COPY OF BIRTH CERTIFICATE
Certificates of Birth that occurred in Kentucky since 1911 are on file in this office

Please Print or Type All Information Required On This Form

BIRTH CERTIFICATE INFORMATION					
1. Full Name at Birth	*First*	*Middle*	*Last*		
2. Date of Birth	*Month*	*Day*	*Year*	*Sex*	*Age Last Birthday*
3. Place of Birth	*Kentucky City or Town*	*Kentucky County*	*Name of Hospital*		
4. Mother's Maiden Name	*First*	*Middle*	*Last*		
5. Father's Name	*First*	*Middle*	*Last*		

If this child has been adopted, please give original name if known:

____

What is your relationship to the person whose certificate is being requested?

____

Signature and telephone number of the person requesting this certificate:

______________________ ______________
Signature Telephone

DO NOT WRITE IN THIS SPACE	
Volume	
Certificate	
Year	
Date	
Searched by	

Certificates may also be ordered by the following methods:

Internet: Certificates may be ordered on the internet using a credit card (Visa, MasterCard, Discover or American Express) or check. An additional charge card fee will apply. This is in addition to the fee for each certified copy requested. Certificates requested via internet, www.vitalchek.com/kentucky-express-birth-certificates.aspx, may be returned by overnight courier for the cost of the additional shipment fee if that record is available.

Telephone: Orders may be placed by telephone using a credit card (Visa, MasterCard, Discover or American Express) or check. An additional charge card fee will apply. This is in addition to the fee for each certified copy requested. Certificates requested via telephone may be returned by overnight courier for the cost of the additional shipment fee. The telephone number to place your order is (800) 241-8322. choose option 1.

Mail: Orders are accepted by mail, using a check or money order in U.S. dollars drawn on a U.S. bank for payment. It can take up to 30 working days to process your request from the date payment is posted. Mail to Vital Statistics, 275 East Main Street 1E-A, Frankfort, KY 40621. The Office of Vital Statistics telephone number is (502) 564-4212.

Walk-in: You may order a certified copy of the birth record by coming to this office. The office is located at the address above. Orders are accepted for same day issuance from 8:00 AM until 3:30 PM Monday through Friday.

FEES

A fee is to be paid for certified copies or records, **or** for a search of the files or records when no copy is available. The fee for a certified copy of a birth certificate is $10.00 U.S. Additional copies are $10.00 U.S. each. Make check or money order payable to "Kentucky State Treasurer." **This fee is non refundable.**

________ Certified Copies @ $10.00 each
How many

Total Amount Enclosed ________

THIS SECTION MUST BE COMPLETE FOR ALL ORDERS

REQUESTORS INFORMATION:

______________________ NAME

______________________ MAILING ADDRESS

____

______________________ CITY, STATE, ZIP CODE

VS-230
(Rev 1/30/2012

MARRIAGE/DIVORCE

COMMONWEALTH OF KENTUCKY
STATE REGISTRAR OF VITAL STATISTICS

APPLICATION FOR A CERTIFIED COPY OF MARRIAGE/DIVORCE CERTIFICATE

Please Print or Type All Information Required On This Form

MARRIAGE/DIVORCE CERTIFICATE INFORMATION						
1. Full Name of Husband	*First*		*Middle*		*Last*	
2. Maiden Name of Wife	*First*		*Middle*		*Last*	
3. County in Which Marriage License Issued	*Kentucky County*	**4. Date of Marriage**	*Month*	*Day*	*Year*	
5. County in Which Divorce Decree Granted	*Kentucky County*	**6. Date of Divorce**	*Month*	*Day*	*Year*	

Signature and telephone number of the person requesting this certificate:

_________________________ _______________
Signature Telephone

DO NOT WRITE IN THIS SPACE	
Volume	
Certificate	
Year	
Date	
Searched by	

Certificates may also be ordered by the following methods:

Internet: Certificates may be ordered on the internet using a credit card (Visa, MasterCard, Discover or American Express) or check. An additional charge card fee will apply. This is in addition to the fee for each certified copy requested. Certificates requested via internet, www.vitalchek.com/kentucky-express-birth-certificates.aspx, may be returned by overnight courier for the cost of the additional shipment fee if that record is available.

Telephone: Orders may be placed by telephone using a credit card (Visa, MasterCard, Discover or American Express) or check. An additional charge card fee will apply. This is in addition to the fee for each certified copy requested. Certificates requested via telephone may be returned by overnight courier for the cost of the additional shipment fee. The telephone number to place your order is (800) 241-8322, choose option 1.

Mail: Orders are accepted by mail, using a check or money order in U.S. dollars drawn on a U.S. bank for payment. It can take up to 30 working days to process your request from the date payment is posted. Mail to Vital Statistics, 275 East Main Street 1E-A, Frankfort, KY 40621. The Office of Vital Statistics telephone number is (502) 564-4212.

Walk-in: You may order a certified copy of the marriage/divorce record by coming to this office. The office is located at the address above. Orders are accepted for same day issuance from 8:00 AM until 3:30 PM Monday through Friday.

FEES

A fee is to be paid for certified copies or records, **or** for a search of the files or records when no copy is available. The fee for a certified copy of a Marriage/Divorce certificate is $6.00 U.S. Additional copies are $6.00 U.S. each. Make check or money order payable to "Kentucky State Treasurer." **This fee is non refundable.**

________ Marriage Certificates @ $6.00 each
How many

________ Divorce Certificates @ $6.00 each
How many

Total Amount Enclosed __________

THIS SECTION MUST BE COMPLETE FOR ALL ORDERS

REQUESTORS INFORMATION:

_______________________________ NAME

_______________________________ MAILING ADDRESS

____

_______________________________ CITY, STATE, ZIP CODE

VS-31
(Rev 1/30/2012)

COMMONWEALTH OF KENTUCKY
STATE REGISTRAR OF VITAL STATISTICS

DEATH APPLICATION FOR A CERTIFIED COPY OF DEATH CERTIFICATE

Certificates of Death that occurred in Kentucky since 1911 are on file in this office

Please Print or Type All Information Required On This Form

DEATH CERTIFICATE INFORMATION				
1. Full Name at Death	*First*	*Middle*	*Last*	
2. Date of Death	*Month*	*Day*	*Year*	*Age Last Birthday*
3. Place of Death	*Kentucky City or Town*	*Kentucky County*	*Name of Hospital (if any)*	
4. Attending Physicians Name	*First*	*Middle*	*Last*	
5. Funeral Service Provider	*Name of Establishment*	*Address*	*Telephone Number*	

What is your relationship to the person whose certificate is being requested?

____

Signature and telephone number of the person requesting this certificate:

______________________ ______________
Signature Telephone

DO NOT WRITE IN THIS SPACE	
Volume	
Certificate	
Year	
Date	
Searched by	

Certificates may also be ordered by the following methods:

Internet: Certificates may be ordered on the internet using a credit card (Visa, MasterCard, Discover or American Express) or check. An additional charge card fee will apply. This is in addition to the fee for each certified copy requested. Certificates requested via internet, www.vitalchek.com/kentucky-express-birth-certificates.aspx, may be returned by overnight courier for the cost of the additional shipment fee if that record is available.

Telephone: Orders may be placed by telephone using a credit card (Visa, MasterCard, Discover or American Express) or check. An additional charge card fee will apply. This is in addition to the fee for each certified copy requested. Certificates requested via telephone may be returned by overnight courier for the cost of the additional shipment fee. The telephone number to place your order is (800) 241-8322, choose option 1.

Mail: Orders are accepted by mail, using a check or money order in U.S. dollars drawn on a U.S. bank for payment. It can take up to 30 working days to process your request from the date payment is posted. Mail to Vital Statistics, 275 East Main Street 1E-A, Frankfort, KY 40621. The Office of Vital Statistics telephone number is (502) 564-4212.

Walk-in: You may order a certified copy of the death record by coming to this office. The office is located at the address above. Orders are accepted for same day issuance from 8:00 AM until 3:30 PM Monday through Friday.

FEES

A fee is to be paid for certified copies or records, **or** for a search of the files or records when no copy is available. The fee for a certified copy of a death certificate is $6.00 U.S. Additional copies are $6.00 U.S. each. Make check or money order payable to "Kentucky State Treasurer." **This fee is non refundable.**

________ Certified Copies @ $6.00 each
How many

Total Amount Enclosed __________

THIS SECTION MUST BE COMPLETE FOR ALL ORDERS

REQUESTORS INFORMATION:

______________________________ NAME

______________________________ MAILING ADDRESS

____

______________________________ CITY, STATE, ZIP CODE

LOUISIANA

Send your requests to:

Center for Records and Statistics
Vital Records Registry
(Location: 1450 Poydras Street, Suite 400)
P.O Box 60630
New Orleans, LA 70160

Tel. (504) 593-5100
Fax (504) 568-8716
E-mail: _dhh-vitalweb@la.gov
http://new.dhh.louisiana.gov/index.cfm/subhome/21

The Louisiana Vital Records Registry maintains birth records for the past 100 years and death records for the past 50 years. Birth and death records archived by the Vital Records Registry are confidential and are not public record. The Registry also holds marriage records for the past 50 years from Orleans Parish.

Cost for a certified long-form Birth Certificate	$15.00
Cost for a short-form Birth Certification Card	$9.00
Cost for a certified Orleans Parish Marriage Certificate	$5.00
Cost for a certified Death Certificate	$7.00
Fee for each mail-in order	$0.50

For Divorce Records and Marriage Records outside of Orleans Parish, contact:

Clerk of Court
(Parish Seat), LA

http://laclerksofcourt.org/clerksofcourt.htm (for a list of clerks)

For Orleans Parish Birth Records over 100 years old and Marriage and Death records over 50 years old; and statewide Death Records over 50 years old, contact:

Louisiana State Archives
(Location: 3851 Essen Lane)
P.O. Box 94125
Baton Rouge, LA 70809-9125

Tel. (225) 922-1000
E-mail: archives@sos.la.gov
www.sos.la.gov/HistoricalResources/LearnAbout
TheArchives

For Genealogy Research:

The Erbon and Marie Wise Genealogical Library, located on the first floor of the State Archives (see contact information above) provides access to selected marriage, death, and birth records for Orleans Parish and death records for the remainder of the state, as well as many other records of interest to genealogical researchers, including colonial documents, passenger manifests for the port of New Orleans, military service records, Confederate pension applications, and records from the State Land Office.

The Archives' online Vital Records Index (www.sos.la.gov/HistoricalResources/ResearchHistoricalRecords/Pages/Online PublicVitalRecordsIndex.aspx) contains searchable databases of deaths that occurred in Louisiana over 50 years ago, Orleans Parish birth records over 100 years old, and Orleans Parish marriage records over 50 years old. Certified copies of these records can be ordered by mail for $5.00.

The Louisiana Division of the New Orleans Public Library (219 Loyola Avenue, New Orleans, LA 70112-2044; tel. 504-596-2610; www.nutrias.org/spec/speclist.htm) has an extensive genealogy collection containing microfilms, periodicals, and books. It also maintains online indexes, including New Orleans Justices of the Peace Marriage Records 1846–1880 and the New Orleans Marriage Index from the *Daily Picayune* 1837–1857.

For Adoption Record information, contact:

Louisiana Voluntary Adoption Registry
P.O. Box 3318
Baton Rouge, LA 70821

Tel. (888) 524-3578
www.dss.louisiana.gov/index.cfm?md=pagebuilder&
tmp=home&pid=116

Cost for registering with the Voluntary Registry	$25.00

Center for Records and Statistics

Mail completed application to:
Center for Records and Statistics
P.O. Box 60630
New Orleans, LA 70160

APPLICATION FOR CERTIFIED COPY OF BIRTH/DEATH CERTIFICATE

☐ **Short-Form Birth Certification Card**	Number of Copies Requested: ______	**$9.00** each	______
☐ **Long-Form Birth Certificate**	Number of Copies Requested: ______	**$15.00** each	______
☐ **Death Certificate**	Number of Copies Requested: ______	**$7.00** each	______
If no record is found, you will be notified and fees will be retained for the search per R.S. 40:40		SUBTOTAL	______
	Mail orders add **$0.50** state charge per transaction (no coins)		______
		TOTAL FEES DUE	______

ALL MAIL ORDER PAYMENTS MUST BE **CHECK** OR **MONEY ORDER** ONLY - Payable to **LOUISIANA VITAL RECORDS**

Record Information

NOTE: Birth records over **100 years old** and Death records over **50 years old** can be obtained by writing the Secretary of State. Address: Louisiana State Archives, P.O. Box 94125, Baton Rouge, LA 70804-9125.

Name at Birth/Death

First ______ Middle ______ Last ______

Date of Birth/Death ______ Sex ______

City of Birth/Death ______ Parish of Birth/Death ______

Father's Name

First ______ Middle ______ Last ______

Mother's Full Maiden Name before Marriage

First ______ Middle ______ Maiden ______

Relationship to Person Named on the Certificate *(must submit photo ID)*

☐ Self ☐ Father ☐ Grandparent ☐ Sister ☐ Legal Guardian (with judgement of custody)

☐ Mother ☐ Child ☐ Grandchild ☐ Brother ☐ Current Spouse ☐ Other (specify): ______

Applicant Information

First Name ______ Last Name ______ Day Phone ______

Residence Address ______ City ______ State ______

Email ______ ZIP Code ______

Mailing Address for Certificates

Name ______

Address ______

City ______ State ______

ZIP ______

Office Use Only

I am aware that any person who willfully and knowingly makes any false statement on an application for a certified copy of a vital record is subject upon conviction to a fine of not more than $10,000 or imprisonment of not more than five years, or both.

Signature ______

Rev 5/12

Order will be returned if items not completed and included: ☐ Signed application ☐ Copy of Federal or State photo ID ☐ Correct fees

Center for Records and Statistics

APPLICATION FOR CERTIFIED COPY OF ORLEANS PARISH MARRIAGE CERTIFICATE

A marriage record is available from Vital Records only if the marriage license was issued in **Orleans Parish within 50 years.** Otherwise you must contact the **Clerk of Court** in the parish where the marriage occurred, or the **State Archives** if the Orleans Parish marriage is older than 50 years

☐ **Orleans Parish Marriage Certificate** Number of Copies Requested: ________ **$5.00** each ________

Mail orders add **.50** state charge per transaction ________

TOTAL FEES DUE ________

If no record is found, you will be notified and fees will be retained for the search per R.S. 40:40

Marriage Information:

Groom's Information

First ________ Middle ________ Last ________

Bride's Information

First ________ Middle ________ Last ________

Date of Marriage ☐

Mailing Address for Certificates:

First Name ________ Last Name ________ Day Phone ________

Residence Address ________ City ________ State ________

Email ________ ZIP Code ________

Mail completed application to:
Center for Records and Statistics
P.O. Box 60630
New Orleans, LA 70160

Office Use Only

Rev 11/11

Public Vital Records Available at the Louisiana State Archives

Researchers may obtain any of the following vital records by visiting the Louisiana State Archives Research Library or may request the records by ***postal mail only*** The Louisiana State Archives maintains the following

- **Orleans Parish birth records for 1819–1912 (births over 100 years ago)***
- **(Index for 1790–1818, but no records)**
- **Statewide birth records for 1911-1912 (births over 100 years ago)***
- **Orleans Parish marriage records for 1870–1962 (marriages over 50 years ago)****
- **(Index for 1831–1869, but no records)**
- **Orleans Parish death records for 1819–1962 (deaths over 50 years ago)***
- **(Index for 1804–1818, but no records)**
- **Statewide death records for 1911–1962 (deaths over 50 years ago)***

Please visit our online Vital Records Index on our website, www.sos.la.gov. This index is not comprehensive and contains only the following indexes at this time

- **Orleans Parish birth index: 1895–1912**
- **Statewide birth index: 1911-1912**
- **Orleans Parish marriage index: 1831–1919, 1925–1962**
- **Orleans Parish death index: 1911–1962**
- **Statewide death index: 1911–1962**

*The only birth records that are currently available at the Archives prior to 1911 are from Orleans Parish Statewide birth records (other than Orleans Parish) begin in 1911, but are not comprehensive for all parishes The only death records currently available prior to 1911 are from Jefferson and Orleans Parishes Records from Orleans are filed separately from the combined statewide listing of all the other parishes in the state Records prior to the dates listed above are probably nonexistent unless the parish where the birth or death occurred kept such a record. If the person being researched was Catholic, birth and death information would probably be shown in the sacramental records of the church or diocese where that person lived

** **All marriage records**, other than Orleans Parish, are maintained by the office of the Clerk of Court in the parish where the marriage licenses are purchased

The Archives charges $5.00 for each certified copy (postal mail only), which includes a *three year search per surname*. Fees must be retained for both successful and unsuccessful searches. Searches are processed by a given year, therefore, a name, place, and date, or a span of three years is required to research a request. Patrons can also obtain a non-certified copy for 50 cents if they conduct their own research at the Louisiana State Archives Research Library

(Please see following page for application form)

For current records, such as births less than 100 years, deaths less than 50 years and Orleans marriages less than 50 years, please contact

Department of Health and Hospitals
Vital Records Registry
P.O. Box 60630
New Orleans, LA 70160
Email: _dhh-vitalweb@la.gov
Phone 504.593.5100 or visit their website at new.dhh.louisiana.gov

LFP 3 & LH 8 (Rev 06/13)

Application For Certified Copy of Public Vital Records

Check only one of the two following categories. Please print information clearly.

1. ___ Orleans Parish/Statewide birth record (birth over 100 years ago)*

or

2. ___ Orleans Parish/Statewide death record (death over 50 years ago)*

____

Name (First, Middle, Last)

______________________ ________ ____________

Date (If unknown, indicate three year span to be researched) Volume (if known) Page (if known)

__________ ______________________

City Parish

3. ___Orleans Parish marriage record (marriage over 50 years ago)**

____

Groom's Name (First, Middle, Last)

____

Bride's Name (First, Middle, Maiden Name)

______________________ ________ ____________

Date (If unknown, indicate three year span to be researched) Volume (if known) Page (if known)

Submit check or money order to:	Secretary of State Vital Records P.O. Box 94125 Baton Rouge, LA 70804-9125	Please do not send cash! Phone 225.922.2012 for assistance NOTE: Limit Ten (10) Requests Per Mailing

Name: ______________________________________

Address: ______________________________________

City / State / Zip Code: ______________________________

Telephone number (day) including area code: ________________

Number of copies requested ______ Total fees due ($5 each) ________

For current records, such as births less than 100 years, deaths less than 50 years and Orleans marriages less than 50 years, please contact:

Department of Health and Hospitals
Vital Records Registry
P.O. Box 60630
New Orleans, LA 70160
Email: dhh-vitalweb@la.gov
Phone 504.593.5100 or visit their website at www.dhh.louisiana.gov

LFP 3 & LH 8 (Rev 06/13)

MAINE

Send your requests from 1923 to the present to:

Maine Department of Health and Human Services
Office of Vital Records
244 Water Street, Station 11
Augusta, ME 04333-0011

Tel. (207) 287-3181
www.maine.gov/dhhs/mecdc/public-health-systems/data-research/vital-records/order/index.shtml

The Office of Vital Records has birth, death, and marriage records from 1923 to the present, and divorce records from 1892 to the present. You must include a long, self-addressed, stamped envelope with your mail-in application form.

Cost for a certified Birth Certificate	$15.00
Cost for a certified Marriage or Divorce Certificate	$15.00
Cost for a certified Death Certificate	$15.00
Cost for an uncertified Vital Record	$10.00
Cost for a duplicate copy, when ordered at the same time	$6.00

For Birth, Death, and Marriage Records from 1892–1922, contact:

Maine State Archives
(Location—230 State Street)
State House Complex, Station 84
Augusta, ME 04333-0084
Tel. (207) 287-5795
www.maine.gov/sos/arc/

The Archives will provide certified and uncertified copies of vital records.

For Genealogy Research:

The Maine State Archives has many records of interest to those pursuing family history. These records—including microfilm copies of birth, marriage, and death records from 1922 to 1955—can be viewed by the public in the State Archives' Search Room. Before 1892 records of births, marriages, and deaths were kept by the towns and cities of Maine. Some of these early town records are available at the State Archives on their Delayed Vital Records Microfilm.

The State Archives has several online databases with Maine vital record information, including Marriage History Search Form 1892–2009 (https://portal.maine.gov/marriage/archdev.marriage_archive.search_form) and Death History Search Form 1960–2009 (https://portal.maine.gov/death/archdev.death_archive.search_form).

For Adoption Record information, contact:

Department of Health and Human Services
Maine Adoption Reunion Registry
244 Water Street, Station 11
Augusta, ME 04333-0011

Tel. (207) 287-3771
www.maine.gov/dhhs/ocfs/cw/adoption/reunionregistry.htm

Cost for Adoption Reunion Registry	$50.00

Maine Center for Disease Control and Prevention (Maine CDC)
244 Water Street
11 State House Station
Augusta, Maine 04333-0011
(207) 287-3771
Fax: (207) 287-1093 TTY Users: Dial 711 (Maine Relay)

Application for a Search and Certified Copy of a Vital Record

Non-Refundable Fees: $15.00 for certified copy, $6.00 for additional copies of same record, $10.00 for non-certified (not a legal copy)

Applicant: Please fill in the information in the appropriate box for the record you are requesting, the reason for requesting the record, and the name and address for mailing the certified copy. Enclose a check or money order payable to Treasurer, State of Maine and mail application to the address above:

Birth Record	Full Name of Child
	Date of Birth
	Place of Birth
	Father's Full Name
	Mother's Full Name
Death Record	Full Name of Decedent
	Date of Death
	Place of Death
Marriage Record	Full Name of Groom/Spouse
	Full Maiden Name of Bride/Spouse
	Date of Marriage
	Place of Marriage
Divorce Record	Full Name of Husband/Spouse
	Full Maiden Name of Wife/Spouse
	Date of Divorce or Annulment
	Place [Superior Court, County or District (Division)]

You must include a copy of your government issued ID and proof of your relationship to the record requested or a direct and legitimate interest in the record. Please see our pamphlet regarding Direct and Legitimate Interest – Accessing Closed Records in Maine.

Phone and online orders for Vital Records may also be placed through VITALCHEK, using a credit card, at the toll free number 1-877-523-2659 or over the Internet at www.vitalchek.com.

Applicant's signature: ______________________________

Applicant's address: ______________________________

Phone number: (___)______________________ Email:______________________

S:\vradminf\AMaster forms\vrform2 R 2/2013

Department of Health and Human Services
Maine People Living Safe, Healthy and Productive Lives

Maine Center for Disease Control and Prevention (Maine CDC)
244 Water Street
11 State House Station
Augusta, Maine 04333-0011
(207) 287-3771
Fax : (207) 287-1093 TTY: 1-800-606-0215

Department of Health and Human Services

Instructions for Adoption Reunion Registry Application

WHO MAY REGISTER:

- Adopted persons 18 years of age or older, born or adopted in Maine.
- Adopted persons 18 years of age or older, whose adoptions were subsequently annulled or whose adoptive parents no longer have parental rights.
- Persons 18 years of age or older who were freed for adoption but were never subsequently adopted.
- Biological parent of an adopted person or of a person freed for adoption but not subsequently adopted.
- Adoptive parent or legal custodian or guardian of an adopted person who is under 18 years old or has been determined to be incapacitated.
- Adoptive parent of an adopted person who has died.
- Legal custodian or guardian of a person whose adoption was annulled, whose adoptive parents no longer have custody, who was freed for adoption but not subsequently adopted, or who has been determined by a court to be incapacitated.
- Full or half-sibling (age 18 or older) of an adopted person or person freed for adoption.
- Legal custodian or guardian of a person under 18 who is a full or half-sibling of an adopted person or person freed for adoption.
- Certain relatives of the biological parent of an adopted person, if that biological parent is deceased: mother, father, grandparent, full sibling, half sibling, aunt, uncle, cousin.

HOW TO APPLY:

1. Fill in all items in order to ensure accurate identification of registrants. Complete the application form that applies to you:
   VS210A-Biological Parents and Other Relatives or Persons Acting on their Behalf
   VS210B-Adopted Person or Person Acting on His or Her Behalf
   VS210C-Person Freed for Adoption but Not Subsequently Adopted or Person Acting on His or Her Behalf.
2. Sign and date the certification statement.
3. Attach a certified copy of your own birth certificate as verification of your identity.
4. If you are a full or half-sibling of an adopted person, you must provide a certified copy of your own birth certificate as documentation of your relationship to the adopted person.
5. If you are registering on behalf of a minor child who is a full or half-sibling of the adopted person, you must provide a certified copy of the minor's birth certificate as documentation of the relationship and a copy of the court order giving you guardianship of custody.
6. If you are registering as a relative of a deceased biological parent, you must also provide: a certified copy of his or her death certificate and documentation of your relationship to the deceased.
7. Mail the application and supporting documents, together with the $50.00 registration fee, to address listed above.
8. All supporting documents will be returned to you after your application has been processed.

PLEASE REMEMBER TO KEEP US INFORMED OF ANY CHANGES IN ADDRESS

You may withdraw from the registry at any time by writing to the Maine CDC vital records office.

Department of Health and Human Services

Maine People Living Safe, Healthy and Productive Lives

Maine Center for Disease Control and Prevention (Maine CDC)
244 Water Street
11 State House Station
Augusta, Maine 04333-0011
(207) 287-3771
Fax : (207) 287-1093 TTY: 1-800-606-0215

Department of Health and Human Services

Adoption Reunion Registry Application - Biological Parents and Other Relatives or Persons Acting on Their Behalf – VS210A

Certificate Number____________________

ADOPTED PERSON	1. Name of adopted person at birth		
	2. Birthdate	3. Sex	4. Birthplace

"Adopted Person" includes those whose adoption was annulled or whose adoptive parents no longer have parental rights.

BIOLOGICAL PARENTS	5. Biological mother's maiden name	6. Father's name on birth certificate

APPLICANT

7. Name

8. Mailing address

9. Status (Check only one.)

☐ Biological parent of the adopted person.
☐ Full or half-sibling (age 18 or older) of the adopted person.
☐ Legal custodian/guardian of person under 18 who is a full or half-sibling of adopted person.

☐ Relative of the **deceased biological parent** of the adopted person:

☐ Mother	☐ Father	☐ Grandparent
☐ Full Sibling	☐ Half Sibling	
☐ Aunt	☐ Uncle	☐ Cousin

(Death certificate of biological parent and proof of relationship required)

CONTACT

10. I wish contact with adopted person if he or she is 18 years of age or older.	☐ Yes	☐ No
11. If the adopted person is under age 18 or is incapacitated, I wish contact with his or her adoptive parent or legal guardian.	☐ Yes	☐ No
12. If the adopted person has died, I wish contact with his/her adoptive parents.	☐ Yes	☐ No

SPECIAL INSTRUCTIONS

CERTIFICATION I hereby certify that I am the biological parent or specified other relative of the adopted person named above, or the legal custodian or guardian of a minor sibling of that adopted person, and that I wish contact with him or her or with the other individuals indicated above.

Signed: ____________________________ Date: ________________

Check No. ________ **Amount Paid** ________

Department of Health and Human Services

Maine People Living
Safe, Healthy and Productive Lives

Maine Center for Disease Control and Prevention (Maine CDC)
244 Water Street
11 State House Station
Augusta, Maine 04333-0011
(207) 287-3771
Fax : (207) 287-1093 TTY: 1-800-606-0215

Department of Health and Human Services

Adoption Reunion Registry Application – Adopted Persons or Person Acting on His or Her Behalf – VS210B

Certificate Number____________________

ADOPTED PERSON	1. Name after adoption		
	2. Birthdate	3. Sex	4. Birthplace
"**Adopted Person**" includes those whose adoption was annulled or whose adoptive parents no longer have parental rights.			
ADOPTIVE PARENTS	5a. Adoptive mother's maiden name		5b. Adoptive father's name
ADOPTION DATA	6a. Date of Adoption		6b. Court
APPLICANT	7. Name		
	8. Mailing address		
	9. Status (Check only one.) ☐ Adopted person 18 years of age or older. ☐ Adopted person 18 years of age or older whose adoption was annulled. ☐ Adopted person 18 years of age or older whose adoptive parents no longer have parental rights. ☐ Adoptive parent or legal custodian/guardian of an adopted person who is under age 18 or who is incapacitated. ☐ Legal custodian/guardian of a person under age 18 whose adoption was annulled or whose adoptive parents no longer have custody. ☐ Adoptive parent(s) of an adopted person who has died.		
CONTACT DESIRED	10. I wish contact with my biological parents. ☐ Yes ☐ No 11. I wish contact with my biological full siblings who are 18 years of age or older. ☐ Yes ☐ No 12. I wish contact with my biological half-siblings who are 18 years of age or older. ☐ Yes ☐ No 13. If my biological mother or father has died, I wish contact with these relatives of that parent. ☐ Mother ☐ Father ☐ Grandparent ☐ Full Sibling ☐ Half Sibling ☐ Aunt ☐ Uncle ☐ Cousin		
SPECIAL INSTRUCTIONS			
CERTIFICATION	I hereby certify that I am the adopted person named above, or the adoptive parent or legal custodian or guardian of that person, and that I wish contact with the biological parents and/or other relatives as indicated above. Signed: ____________________ Date: ________________		

S:\vradmin\AMaster forms\VS-210B R 12/2011

Check No.__________ **Amount Paid** __________

MARYLAND

Send your requests to:

Maryland Department of Health & Mental Hygiene
Division of Vital Records
(Location—6550 Reisterstown Road)
P.O. Box 68760
Baltimore, MD 21215-0036

Tel. (410) 764-3038; (800) 832-3277
Fax (410) 358-0738
www.vsa.state.md.us/

The Division of Vital Records has birth records from January 1875 to present for Baltimore City and from August 1898 to present for Maryland counties; death records from 1969 to present; marriage records from January 1990 to present; divorce verifications from January 1992 to present. Certified copies of certificates for earlier marriages and divorces can be obtained from the clerk of the Circuit Court in the county where the event took place.

Cost for a certified Birth Certificate	$24.00
Cost for a commemorative Birth Certificate	$50.00
Cost for a certified Marriage Certificate	$12.00
Cost for verification of a Divorce	$12.00
Cost for a certified Death Certificate	$24.00
Cost for a duplicate Death Certificate, when ordered at the same time	$12.00

For earlier records contact:

Maryland State Archives
350 Rowe Boulevard
Annapolis, MD 21401

Tel. (410) 260-6400
www.msa.md.gov

For Genealogy Research:

To obtain records for genealogical purposes, contact the Maryland State Archives (see above for contact information). Birth records are restricted for 100 years or until the death of the named individual; state law allows researchers to obtain death certificates over 10 years old. The Archives has many records of interest to genealogists, including early birth, marriage, death, divorce, and adoption records. Modern birth and death registration began only in 1875 in Baltimore City and in 1898 for the rest of the state. However, incomplete records, taken from church and civil sources, exist from the colonial period to 1884. The Archives can search for and provide copies from early records, provided that a specific church or county circuit court and year are given.

The Archives' Vital Records Indexing Project (http://mdvitalrec.net/cfm/index.cfm) currently has indexes online to death records 1898–1944 for all 23 counties and 1875–1972 for Baltimore City.

For Adoption Record information, contact:

Maryland Department of Human Resources
Social Services Administration
Adoption Search, Contact and Reunion Services
311 West Saratoga Street
Baltimore, MD 21201

Tel. (800) 392-3678
www.dhr.state.md.us/blog/?page_id=3220

Cost for Voluntary Adoption Registry	$25.00

BIRTH **Application for Certified Copy of Maryland Birth Record** **BIRTH**

Maryland Department of Health and Mental Hygiene • Division of Vital Records

By my signature below, I state that I am the person I represent myself to be herein, and I affirm that the information submitted on this form is complete and accurate and submitted subject to the criminal penalties set forth at Maryland Code Annotated, Health-General Section 4-227.

Signature of person making request: ______________________

Date of Application: ______________________

For Issuing Office Only
❑ Photo ID ❑ Mailed

NOTE: A copy of a birth record may only be issued to the person named on the Certificate; a parent or court-appointed guardian; a representative with a notarized letter signed by the person named on the Certificate or a parent or guardian granting permission to obtain a Certificate; a surviving spouse, an individual with a court order directing that the Certificate be issued; or an individual permitted to obtain a certificate under Md. Code Ann., Family Law Title 5, Subtitles 3A or 4B relating to adoptions.

PRINT or TYPE your name & CURRENT address.

Name: ______________________ Your relationship to the person named on the Certificate: ______________

Address: ______________________

City: ______________________ **State:** __________ **Zip:** __________

Daytime phone number: (_____) _______ - _________ **E-mail Address:** ______________________

PHOTO ID REQUIRED: The individual requesting the record should submit a legible copy of his/her VALID GOVERNMENT-ISSUED PHOTO ID with completed application. (Examples: State issued driver's license or non-driver photo ID with requestor's current address; passport). If you do not have a Government-issued photo ID, read and sign the following statement: I declare that I do not have a government-issued photo ID and that I am presenting the attached two documents that include my name and current address as proof of identification. (*Note: These documents must include two of the following: Utility bill, car registration form, pay stub, bank statement, copy of income tax return/W-2 form, letter from a government agency requesting a vital record, or lease/rental agreement. Please submit photocopies since these documents will not be returned to you. If you do not have a Government-issued photo ID, the certificate(s) will be mailed to the address listed on the documents that you present.*)

Signature: ______________________

PRINT or **TYPE** information below with regard to the individual named on the requested certificate:

Name at Birth: ______________________

If name has changed since birth due to adoption, court order, or any reason other than marriage, please list new name here: ______________________

Date of Birth: ______________ (Month/Day/Year) **Current age:** ________ **Sex:** □ Male □ Female

Place of Birth: ______________ (County or Baltimore City) **Hospital:** ______________ **Certificate No.** (if known) __________

Full Maiden Name of Mother: ______________________

Full Name of Father: ______________________

ORDER INFORMATION

Number of certificates requested	
Fee per copy*	x $24.00
Amount enclosed	

A non–refundable $24 fee is required for each copy of a certificate*. Send check or money order. **Do not send cash when applying by mail.** When paying by check, you must include a copy of your driver's license or other government-issued photo ID that lists your current address, or other acceptable ID as noted above.

When ordering by mail, send completed application, legible copy of ID, a self-addressed, stamped envelope, and check or money order payable to the DIVISION OF VITAL RECORDS to the Division of Vital Records, P.O. Box 68760, Baltimore, Maryland 21215-0036.

You may also apply for a birth record in person, on line, by telephone or by fax. For further information, visit the Vital Statistics Administration website at http://www.vsa.state.md.us/vsa/html/apps.html.

*There is no fee for: (a) A copy of a certificate of a current or former armed forces member that is requested by the member; or (b) A copy of a certificate of a current or former armed forces member or of a surviving spouse or child of the member, if the copy will be used in connection with a claim for a dependent or beneficiary of the member. Proof of service in the armed forces must be provided.

Birth records filed over 100 years ago are available through the Maryland State Archives in Annapolis (telephone number 410-260-6400).

Rev. 01/12

COMMEMORATIVE Application for Commemorative Certificate COMMEMORATIVE

Maryland Department of Health and Mental Hygiene • Division of Vital Records

By my signature below, I state that I am the person I represent myself to be herein, and I affirm that the information submitted on this form is complete and accurate and submitted subject to the criminal penalties set forth at Maryland Code Annotated, Health-General Section 4-227.

For Issuing Office Only
❑ Photo ID ❑ Mailed

Signature of person making request: ______________________________

Date of Application: ______________________________

<u>**NOTE**</u>: A copy of a birth record may only be issued to the person named on the Certificate; a parent or court-appointed guardian; a representative with a notarized letter signed by the person named on the Certificate, a parent or guardian granting permission to obtain a Certificate; an individual with a court order directing that the Certificate be issued; or an individual permitted to obtain a certificate under Md. Code Ann., Family Law Title 5, Subtitles 3A or 4B relating to adoptions.

PRINT or TYPE your name & CURRENT address.

Name: ______________________ Your relationship to the person named on the Certificate: ______________

Address: ______________________________

City: ______________________ **State**: ______________ **Zip**: __________

Daytime phone number: (_____) _______- _________ **E-mail Address**: ______________________

PHOTO ID REQUIRED: The individual requesting the record should submit a legible copy of his/her <u>VALID</u> GOVERNMENT-ISSUED PHOTO ID with completed application. (Examples: State issued driver's license or non-driver photo ID with requestor's <u>current address;</u> passport). <u>If you do not have a Government-issued photo ID, read and sign the following statement:</u> I declare that I do not have a government-issued photo ID and that I am presenting the attached two documents that include my name and current address as proof of identification. (*Note: These documents must include two of the following: Utility bill, car registration form, pay stub, bank statement, copy of income tax return/W-2 form, letter from a government agency requesting a vital record, or lease/rental agreement. Please submit photocopies since these documents will <u>not</u> be returned to you. If you do not have a Government-issued photo ID, the certificate(s) will be mailed to the address listed on the documents that you present.*)

Signature: ______________________________

PRINT or **TYPE** information below with regard to the individual named on the requested certificate:

Name at Birth: ______________________________

If name has changed since birth due to adoption, court order, or any reason <u>other than marriage</u>, please list new name here: ______________________

Date of Birth: ______________________ **Current age**: ________ **Sex**: ▫ Male ▫ Female
(Month/Day/Year)

Place of Birth: ______________________ **Hospital**: ______________ **Certificate No.** (if known) ________
(County or Baltimore City)

Full Maiden Name of Mother: ______________________________

Full Name of Father: ______________________________

ORDER INFORMATION

Number of certificates requested	
Fee per copy*	x $50.00
Amount enclosed	

A fee of $50 is required for each certificate. Send check or money order. **Do not send cash when applying by mail.** When paying by check, you must include a copy of your driver's license or other government-issued photo ID that lists your current address, or other acceptable ID as noted above.

When ordering by mail, send completed application, <u>legible copy of ID,</u> and check or money order payable to the DIVISION OF VITAL RECORDS to the Division of Vital Records, P.O. Box 68760, Baltimore, Maryland 21215-0036.

You may also apply for a birth record in person, on line, by telephone or by fax. For further information, visit the website of the Vital Statistics Administration at http://www.vsa.state.md.us/vsa/html/apps.html.

*If a search provides no record, $26 will be refunded and a Certificate of No Record Found will be issued. A $24 search fee must be retained as required by Maryland law.

Rev. 04/13

MARRIAGE Application for Certified Copy of Maryland Marriage Record MARRIAGE

Maryland Department of Health and Mental Hygiene • Division of Vital Records

By my signature below, I state that I am the person I represent myself to be herein, and I affirm that the information submitted on this form is complete and accurate and submitted subject to the criminal penalties set forth at Maryland Code Annotated, Health-General Section 4-227.

Signature of person making request: ____________________

Date of Application: ____________________

For Issuing Office Only
❑ Photo ID ❑ Mailed

NOTE: A Copy of a Certificate of Marriage can be released to the married parties, a representative of the married parties (provided the representative shows a notarized letter stating he or she has permission to obtain a copy of the marriage certificate), an attorney representing the married parties, or a court of law. **Certified copies of certificates for marriages performed PRIOR TO JANUARY 1, 1990 are available only at the circuit court in the county where the marriage took place.**

Applicant's name: ____________________ Applicant's relationship to persons named on the Certificate: ____________________

Applicant's address: ____________________

City: ____________________ **State:** __________ **Zip:** ________

Daytime phone number: (_____) _______- _________ **E-mail Address:** ____________________

**PHOTO ID REQUIRED: The individual requesting the record should submit a legible copy of his/her VALID GOVERNMENT-ISSUED PHOTO ID with completed application. (Examples: State issued driver's license or non-driver photo ID with requestor's current address; passport). If you do not have a Government-issued photo ID, read and sign the following statement: I declare that I do not have a government-issued photo ID and that I am presenting the attached two documents that include my name and current address as proof of identification. (*Note: These documents must include two of the following: Utility bill, car registration form, pay stub, bank statement, copy of income tax return/W-2 form, letter from a government agency requesting a vital record, or lease/rental agreement. Please submit photocopies since these documents will not be returned to you. If you do not have a Government-issued photo ID, the certificate(s) will be mailed to the address listed on the documents that you present.)*

Signature: ____________________

PRINT or **TYPE** information below:

Names of Spouses: ____________________
(First/middle/last) Birth Name (if different)

____
(First/middle/last) Birth Name (if different)

Date of Marriage: ____________________ (Month/Day/Year) **Place of Marriage:** ____________________ (County or Baltimore City)

Person you represent (if applicable): ____________________

Reason for requesting certificate: ____________________

ORDER INFORMATION

Number of certificates requested	
Fee per copy*	x $12.00
Amount enclosed	

A non–refundable $12 fee is required for each copy of a certificate.* Send check or money order. **Do not send cash when applying by mail.** When paying by check, you must include a photocopy of your driver's license or other government-issued photo ID that lists your current address, or other acceptable ID as noted above.

When ordering by mail, send completed application, legible copy of ID, a self-addressed, stamped envelope, and check or money order payable to the DIVISION OF VITAL RECORDS to the Division of Vital Records, P.O. Box 68760, Baltimore, Maryland 21215-0036.

You may also apply for a marriage record in person, on line, by telephone or by fax. For further information, visit the website of the Vital Statistics Administration at http://www.vsa.state.md.us/vsa/html/apps.html.

*There is no fee for: (a) A copy of a certificate of a current or former armed forces member that is requested by the member; or (b) A copy of a certificate of a current or former armed forces member or of a surviving spouse or child of the member, if the copy will be used in connection with a claim for a dependent or beneficiary of the member. Proof of service in the armed forces must be provided. .

STATE OF MARYLAND
DEPARTMENT OF HEALTH AND MENTAL HYGIENE
DIVISION OF VITAL RECORDS
P.O. BOX 68760
BALTIMORE, MD 21215

APPLICATION FOR VERIFICATION OF DIVORCE RECORD

PLEASE PRINT. Date________________________________

Names of Spouses ____
(first/middle/last) birth name (if different)

____
(first/middle/last) birth name (if different)

Date of divorce____
(month/day/year)

Place of divorce____
(city/county)

Reason for divorce____

Person you represent____

NOTE: A non-refundable fee of $12.00 is required for each verification requested. The Division of Vital Records verifies divorces that occurred on or after January 1, 1990. Divorces that occurred during the years 1983 and 1984 cannot be searched. If the record is found, only the information on record concerning the place, date, and type of divorce can be given. You may apply in person or by mail. You must present a valid, unexpired, government-issued photo ID displaying a date issued *and* an expiration date. Applicants unable to supply valid photo ID must present two (2) different pieces of alternative documentation. Acceptable documents are social security card, pay stub, current car registration, bank statement, letter from a government agency, lease/rental agreement, utility bill with current address, or a copy of your income tax return or W-2 form. **At least one of these documents must contain your current mailing address.** Applicants unable to provide valid photo ID will **not** be able to receive their requests the same day. Their requests will be mailed to the address displayed on the documents provided. When applying by mail, please enclose the requested information, copies of required identification, fee, and a self-addressed, stamped envelope. The circuit court where the divorce took place must be contacted for a copy of the decree.

APPLICANT'S NAME (Print) ____

APPLICANT'S SIGNATURE____

MAILING ADDRESS____

CITY/STATE/ZIP CODE____

FOR OFFICE USE ONLY:

TYPE OF DIVORCE: **AV – Absolute**________________________________

AB – Annulment________________________________

DATE OF DIVORCE VERIFIED: ________________________________

VERIFICATION COMPLETED BY: ________________________________

DATE VERIFIED: ________________________________

VRC-81
DHMH
Rev. 1/13

DEATH Application for Certified Copy of Maryland Death Record DEATH

Maryland Department of Health and Mental Hygiene • Division of Vital Records

By my signature below, I state that I am the person I represent myself to be herein, and I affirm that the information submitted on this form is complete and accurate and submitted subject to the criminal penalties set forth at Maryland Code Annotated, Health-General Section 4-227.

Signature of person making request: ______________________________

Date of Application: ______________________________

For Issuing Office Only
❑ Photo ID ❑ Mailed

NOTE: A copy of a death certificate may only be issued to applicants who have a direct and tangible interest in the content of the record as described in Code of Maryland Regulations (COMAR) 10.03.08.

PRINT or TYPE your name & CURRENT address.

Name: ______________________ Your relationship to the person named on the Certificate: ______________

Address: ______________________________

City: ______________________ State: __________ Zip: __________

Daytime phone number: (______) _______ - __________ E-mail Address: ______________________

PHOTO ID REQUIRED: The individual requesting the record should submit a legible copy of his/her VALID GOVERNMENT-ISSUED PHOTO ID with completed application. (Examples: State issued driver's license or non-driver photo ID with requestor's current address; passport). If you do not have a Government-issued photo ID, read and sign the following statement: I declare that I do not have a government-issued photo ID and that I am presenting the attached two documents that include my name and current address as proof of identification. (*Note: These documents must include two of the following: Utility bill, car registration form, pay stub, bank statement, copy of income tax return/W-2 form, letter from a government agency requesting a vital record, or lease/rental agreement. Please submit photocopies since these documents will not be returned to you. If you do not have a Government-issued photo ID, the certificate(s) will be mailed to the address listed on the documents that you present.*)

Signature: ______________________________

PRINT or **TYPE** information below with regard to the individual named on the requested certificate:

Name of Decedent: ______________________________

Date of Death: ______________ (Month/Day/Year) **Age at death:** ________ **Sex:** □ Male □ Female

Place of Death: ______________ (County or Baltimore City)

Name of funeral home: ______________________________

Reason for requesting certificate: ______________________________

ORDER INFORMATION

Number of certificates requested	
Fee for first paid copy*	$24
Fee for each additional copy	$12
Amount enclosed	

There is a non–refundable fee of $24 for the first copy of a death certificate purchased in a single transaction.* There is a fee of $12 for each additional copy of the same certificate purchased in the same transaction. Send check or money order. **Do not send cash when applying by mail.** When paying by check, you must include a copy of your driver's license or other government-issued photo ID that lists your current address, or other acceptable ID as noted above.

When ordering by mail, send completed application, legible copy of ID, a self-addressed, stamped envelope, and check or money order payable to the DIVISION OF VITAL RECORDS to the Division of Vital Records, P.O. Box 68760, Baltimore, Maryland 21215-0036.

You may also apply for a death record in person, on line, by telephone or by fax. For further information, visit the Vital Statistics Administration website at http://www.vsa.state.md.us/vsa/html/apps.html.

*There is no fee for: (a) A copy of a certificate of a current or former armed forces member that is requested by the member; or (b) A copy of a certificate of a current or former armed forces member or of a surviving spouse or child of the member, if the copy will be used in connection with a claim for a dependent or beneficiary of the member. Proof of service in the armed forces must be provided.

To obtain death records for genealogical purposes, contact the Maryland State Archives in Annapolis (telephone number 410-260-6400).

Rev. 06/12

MASSACHUSETTS

Send your requests to:

Massachusetts Department of Public Health
Registry of Vital Records and Statistics
150 Mt. Vernon Street, 1st floor
Dorchester, MA 02125-3105

Tel. (617) 740-2600
E-mail: vital.recordsrequest@state.ma.us
www.mass.gov/dph/rvrs

The Registry of Vital Records and Statistics maintains birth, death, and marriage records from 1921 to the present. Vital records have been registered in Massachusetts since 1635; statewide collection began in 1841. Enclose a business-size, self-addressed envelope when ordering certified copies by mail.

Copies of divorce records are available from the probate court where the divorce was obtained. The Registry maintains an index of divorces from 1952 to the present.

Cost for a certified Birth, Death, or Marriage Certificate, in person	$20.00
Cost for a certified Birth, Death, or Marriage Certificate, by mail	$32.00
Cost for a certified Birth, Death, or Marriage Certificate, by expedited mail	$42.00

For records from 1841 to 1920, contact:

Massachusetts Archives
220 Morrissey Boulevard
Boston, MA 02125

Tel. (617) 727-2816
E-mail: archives@sec.state.mas.us
www.sec.state.ma.us/arc/arcidx.htm

For earlier records, contact the city or town where the event occurred (www.mass.gov/portal/government-taxes/local/cities-towns/).

For Genealogy Research:

The Massachusetts Registry of Vital Records office is open to the public for research purposes. The cost for research is $9.00/hour. Researchers can use the public indexes to birth, death, marriage, and divorce records, and can also examine birth, death, and marriage records and extract information from public records. Certain Massachusetts records are restricted to the public.

The Massachusetts Archives (see contact information above) holds birth, marriage, and death records for all Massachusetts cities and towns, 1841 through 1920. Indexes to these records are available in a searchable database on the Archives' website (www.sec.state.ma.us/arc/arcsrch/VitalRecordsSearchContents.html).

The Archives also has many other records and databases of interest to genealogical researchers. Holdings date from the beginning of the Massachusetts Bay Colony in 1628.

The New England Historic Genealogical Society's website (www.americanancestors.org/home.html) has several online databases containing vital record information, including Massachusetts Vital Records, 1841–1910, Massachusetts Vital Records to 1850, and Massachusetts Vital Records 1911–1915.

For Adoption Record information, contact:

Massachusetts Department of Public Health
Registry of Vital Records and Statistics
150 Mt. Vernon Street, 1st Floor
Dorchester, MA 02125-3105

Tel. (617) 740-2600

In 2007 a law passed in Massachusetts allowing an adopted person born on or before July 17, 1974, to access his or her original birth certificate.

MASSACHUSETTS DEPARTMENT OF PUBLIC HEALTH
REGISTRY OF VITAL RECORDS AND STATISTICS
150 MT. VERNON STREET, 1st Floor
DORCHESTER, MA 02125-3105

APPLICATION FOR VITAL RECORD

(Please print legibly.)

Please fill out and return this form to the address above, along with a stamped, self-addressed, business-letter-sized envelope and a check or money order for $32.00 for each record. Make checks payable to the Commonwealth of Massachusetts. Do not submit more than 5 requests per letter. DO NOT SEND CASH THROUGH THE MAIL. If the date of event is unknown provide us with a ten-year period that you would like us to search.

BIRTH RECORD Number of copies:____________

Name of Subject:______________________ (first) (middle) (last)	
Date of Birth:	City or Town of Birth:
Mother's Name:______________________ (first) (middle) (maiden) (last)	
Father's Name:______________________ (first) (middle) (last)	

MARRIAGE RECORD Number of copies:____________

PARTY A:______________________ (first) (middle) (last)	
PARTY B:______________________ (first) (middle) (maiden)	
Date of Marriage:	City or Town of Marriage:

DEATH RECORD Number of copies:____________

Name of Deceased:______________________ (first) (middle) (last) (maiden, if applicable)	
Spouse's Name:______________________ (first) (middle) (last) (maiden, if applicable)	
Social Security Number (if known):	
Date of Death:	City or Town of Death:
Father's Name:______________________ (first) (middle) (last)	
Mother's Name:______________________ (first) (middle) (maiden) (last)	

Relationship of requestor to subject(s) named on record:______________________

Mail record to:
Address:
City/State/ZIP Code:
Your signature:
Date of request:______________________ month/day/year

PLEASE NOTE: The earliest records available from this office are for calendar year 1921.

MASSACHUSETTS DEPARTMENT OF PUBLIC HEALTH
REGISTRY OF VITAL RECORDS AND STATISTICS
150 MT. VERNON STREET, 1st Floor
DORCHESTER, MA 02125-3105

RVRS USE ONLY
Rec'd________
#________
Cert #________
Completed________
Initials________

APPLICATION FOR A NON-CERTIFIED RECORD OF BIRTH PRIOR TO ADOPTION
(Please print legibly.)

Please fill out and return this form to the address above. If you are requesting a record by mail, make your check or money order payable to the Commonwealth of Massachusetts and include $32.00 for each copy requested. DO NOT SEND CASH THROUGH THE MAIL. Records requested in-person at the Registry counter are $20.00 per copy. Checks, money orders, and cash are accepted at the counter. Credit/debit cards are not accepted. See additional instructions on the reverse of this form.

SUBJECT OF THE RECORD (ADOPTEE)	**Number of Copies:**
Full Name on Current Birth Record (name at adoption) (First, Middle, Last)	**Date of Birth*** (Month, Day, Year)
Full Name of Adoptive Mother/Parent (First, Middle, Last)	**Maiden surname of Adoptive Mother**
Full Name of Adoptive Father/Parent (First, Middle, Last)	**City/Town of Birth**
Name on Pre-Adoption Birth Record (name at birth), if known	

PERSON MAKING REQUEST

Full Legal Name (Current Name) (First, Middle, Last)	**Relationship to Adoptee** ☐Self ☐Adoptive parent ☐Adult child of deceased adoptee ☐Legal guardian of child (under 18 years) of a deceased adoptee
Mailing Address (Street/PO Box/Apt. #) (City/Town, State, Zip)	Telephone number(s)

AFFIDAVIT OF APPLICANT (If you are applying by mail, you must sign and date this section in the presence of a notary.)
WARNING: Providing false information under this oath or affirmation is punishable by fine and imprisonment under M.G.L. c.268 §6.

I hereby swear or affirm under the penalties of perjury that the information on this application is true to the best of my knowledge and belief.

______________________________ Signature ______________ Date

On this ____________ day of ______________________, __________ before me, the undersigned notary public, personally appeared ______________________________ who proved to me through satisfactory evidence of identification, which were ______________________________, to be the person whose name is signed on this document and who swore or affirmed to me that the contents of the document were truthful and accurate to the best of their knowledge and belief and that they signed this form voluntarily for its stated purpose.

Notary Public ______________________________

My Commission Expires: ______________________________

IDENTIFICATION AND SUPPLEMENTAL DOCUMENTATION (see additional information on the reverse of this form)

IDENTIFICATION If you are applying in-person you will need to show **one** of the following identification documents. If you are applying by mail, you must enclose a clear, legible, photocopy of the identification document. Alternative identification documents require prior approval by RVRS.

☐Valid, non-expired, driver's license **☐ Valid, non-expired, identification card issued by a department of motor vehicles** **☐Valid, non-expired, passport**

DOCUMENTATION If you are applying in-person and additional documentation is required (see reverse of form), you must provide an original certified copy for inspection. If you are applying by mail and additional documentation is required, you must send an original certified copy that will be returned to you with completion of your order.

Proof of name change:	**Proof of death:**	**Proof of relationship:**
☐Certified copy of a marriage certificate	☐Certified copy of death certificate	☐Certified copy of your birth certificate
☐Certified copy of a legal change of name decree		☐ **Certified copy of legal guardianship**
☐Other (specify):		

*Records on file at the Registry of Vital Records and Statistics date back to 1921. Earlier records are housed at the State Archives.

Form R-109 (11/2007)

APPLICATION FOR RECORD OF BIRTH PRIOR TO ADOPTION
Application Instructions

Who May Apply?
Beginning December 5, 2007, certain individuals specified by state law may apply for a copy of an initial birth record established prior to an adoption (without first obtaining a judicial court order):

- Adoptees who were born in Massachusetts on or before July 14, 1974.
- An adult child (18 years or older) of a deceased parent who was an adoptee born in Massachusetts on or before July 14, 1974.
- The parent or guardian of a child (under 18 years of age) whose deceased parent was an adoptee born in Massachusetts on or before July 14, 1974.

Beginning January 1, 2008, the following additional individuals specified by state law may also apply:

- The adoptive parent of a child (under 18 years of age) born in Massachusetts on or after January 1, 2008.

Beginning January 1, 2026, the following additional individuals specified by state law may also apply:

- An adult adoptee (18 years or older) who was born in Massachusetts on or after January 1, 2008.

Submit your application by mail or in person

If you are applying by mail, you must include copies of all identification and documentation listed below, and your signature must be notarized. The fee for applying by mail is $32.00. Please do not send cash by mail. Checks and money orders should be made payable to the "Commonwealth of Massachusetts." Credit and debit cards are not accepted. RVRS will also accept applications by walk-in customers. If you are applying in person, your application will be reviewed for completeness, your identification and documentation will be checked, payment will be taken, and the application will be processed in the order it was received. The fee for applying in person is $20.00.

What you will receive if, after processing of your application, RVRS locates your birth record prior to adoption

You will receive a copy of the birth record that was registered with RVRS prior to adoption that lists among other items, the legal parent or parents listed on the record at the time of birth. In a very few cases, there may have been an amendment prior to the adoption, for which you will receive the initial record and any relevant amendments (e.g., paternity establishment).

The copy will be made on security paper to deter potential fraudulent use, and will contain, the following statement mandated by state law: "The contents of this birth record are being released under section 2B of chapter 46 of the Massachusetts General Laws or under a court order. This record was amended by adoption. This is not a certified copy of a birth record."

Refunds
If the application can not be processed for any reason, it will be returned to you with a refund.

If you do not sign for the record that is sent to you by certified mail, and the record is returned to RVRS, you will NOT be issued a refund, as the cost has already been incurred.

Identification Requirements

1. *If you are applying for your OWN record:*

A current government-issued photo ID. (For applications by mail, attach a photocopy of the ID):

- Current, not expired, driver's license, or
- Current, not expired, other ID issued by your state's department of motor vehicles, or
- Current, not expired, passport
- If you cannot provide one of the identification items listed above, please call RVRS to be certain the ID you plan to provide is adequate.

Documentation of a change of name. If the name on your ID is different from your name at the time of your adoption, you must provide documentation that will prove you are the person listed on the birth record. (For applications by mail, attach an original certified copy of the requested documentation. Your original documents will be returned to you with the completed order). For example:

- If your ID shows a *married name*, provide a certified copy of your marriage certificate that shows your name as it appears on your current (adoptive) birth certificate and your name after marriage as it appears on your ID.
- If your ID reflects a *legal change of name*, provide a certified copy of your legal change of name decree that shows your name as it appears on your current (adoptive) birth certificate and your legal name as decreed by a court and as appears on your ID.

2. *If you are applying for YOUR PARENT'S record:*

You must provide the identification listed above in numbered section 1, AND also show or provide:

- A certified copy of your parent's death record. If you are applying by mail, attach an original certified copy of your parent's death record.
- A certified copy of your birth record that shows you are the decedent's child. If you are applying by mail, attach an original certified copy of your parent's death record.
- Documentation of any change of name not reflected on the death certificate. If your parent's death certificate does not contain in some format a reference to his or her name at the time of adoption (e.g, maiden name, or name at birth or adoption), then you will need to provide evidence of the change of name as described above in numbered section 1.

3. *If you are applying for YOUR ADOPTED CHILD'S record (beginning January 1, 2008):*
   - You must provide the identification listed above in numbered section 1.

For all requests submitted by mail, notarization is required:
For requests by mail only, sign and date your application in the presence of a notary who will certify that your signature is authentic.

Questions
Contact the Registry of Vital Records and Statistics at (617) 740-2600 or by email at vital.recordsrequest@state.ma.us.

MICHIGAN

Send your requests to:

Michigan Department of Community Health
Vital Records Requests
(Location: 201 Townsend Street, Capitol
View Building, 3rd Floor)
P.O. Box 30721
Lansing, MI 48909

Tel. (517) 335-8656; (517) 335-8666
Fax (517) 321-5884
E-mail: VRCustomerService@michigan.gov
www.michigan.gov/mdch/

The Vital Records Office has records of births, marriages, and deaths from 1867 (though the initial registration year varies by the county where the birth occurred) and divorces from 1897. Birth records are restricted for 100 years and a photo ID is required, but anyone can order a death or marriage record.

Cost for a certified Birth Certificate	$26.00
Cost for an Heirloom Birth Certificate	$40.00
Cost for a certified Senior Citizen Birth Certificate	$7.00
Cost for a certified Marriage Certificate	$26.00
Cost for a certified Divorce Certificate	$26.00
Cost for a certified Death Certificate	$26.00
Cost for a duplicate certified copy, when ordered at the same time	$12.00

For earlier records, contact:

County Clerk
County Court House
(County Seat), MI

For Genealogy Research:

Michigan death records from 1867 to 1897 can be searched online at www.mdch.state.mi.us/gendisx/search.htm (more records are being added regularly). In addition, death records from 1897 to 1920 and other digital collections can be viewed on the Seeking Michigan website at http://seekingmichigan.org/.

The Archives of Michigan (7023 W. Kalamazoo Street, Lansing, MI 48913; tel. 517-373-3559, option 3; www.michigan.gov/archivesofmi) offers a wide range of family history research materials, including microfilm copies of the indexes to many vital records.

For Adoption Record information, contact:

Michigan Department of Human Services
Adoption Division
P.O. Box 30037
Lansing, MI 48909

APPLICATION FOR A **CERTIFIED** COPY **MICHIGAN BIRTH RECORD**

PART 1: APPLICANT'S INFORMATION — PHOTO IDENTIFICATION REQUIRED

Applicant's Name: ______________________ State Driver's License or Identification # ______________

Mailing Address: ______________________ City: ____________ State: _____ Zip: ________
(Cannot Send to General Delivery)

Daytime Phone - Required: (   ) ______________ Other Phone: (   ) ______________

PHOTO IDENTIFICATION REQUIRED (See back for details)

PART 2: CERTIFICATION OF INFORMATION PROVIDED

By signing this application, I understand that I am agreeing to pay for a search of the State of Michigan Vital Records. This does not guarantee that a record will be found.

Statement of Entitlement: Misstating an identity or assuming the identity of another person is subject to criminal penalties, e.g., Michigan Compiled Laws 333.2894(b) and 333.2898 and federal laws relating to falsification in obtaining a birth record. By signing this application, I state that I am eligible to receive this birth record as indicated in the Eligibility Section of this application.

► **Applicant's Signature:** ______________________ **Date:** __________

IDENTITY THEFT PROTECTION ACT 445.65(1) and 445.69(1) prohibits anyone from obtaining a vital record by misrepresenting a person's identity or attempting to use another person's identifying information. A person who violates this law is guilty of a felony punishable by imprisonment for up to 5 years or a fine of up to $25,000 or both.

PART 3: PURPOSE FOR REQUESTING THE RECORD ______________________

PART 4: ELIGIBILITY - Select the category that qualifies YOU to request and receive the requested Michigan birth record per MCL 333.2882

- ☐ Person named on the record
- ☐ Parent named on the record
  Note: If adopted, only adoptive parents are eligible
- ☐ Legal guardian of the person named on the record
  (Copy of court documented guardianship papers required)
- ☐ Legally licensed attorney of subject of the record
  (Letter on official letterhead required: Must provide state bar number and the name of the person you represent)
- ☐ Heir of the deceased person named on the record, and
  - Relationship to decedent: ______________
  - Decedent's name at time of death: ______________
  - State where death occurred: ______________
  - Date of death (Year): ______________

  If not a Michigan death, must provide death certificate
- ☐ Court of competent jurisdiction (Court order & fee required)
- ☐ Birth record is at least 100 years old (no photo ID required)

PART 5: INFORMATION NEEDED TO FIND BIRTH RECORD BEING REQUESTED

Date of Birth (mm, dd, year)	Sex ☐ Male ☐ Female	Place of Birth (hospital, city, county)

Please include first, middle, and last names below:

Full Name at Birth: ______________________

Mother's Birth Name: ______________________

Father's Birth Name: ______________________

Is the person named on the record **adopted**? ☐ Yes ☐ No

Full Name **After** Adoption: ______________________

Adopted Mother's Birth Name: ______________________

Adopted Father's Name: ______________________

If the applicant's current name is different than the way their birth name appears on the record, provide info below (required):

☐ Marriage: Place of Marriage (state) ______________ Date of Marriage ______________

☐ Court Ordered New Legal Name (court order must be provided): First __________ Middle __________ Last __________

PART 6: FEES - *Includes one certified copy or no-find letter*

Base Fee: Includes One Year Search Age 64 and Under	$26.00	$
Or Senior Citizen (Age 65+) *Reduced Fee* *(Must Be Requesting Own Record)*	$ 7.00	$
Additional Certified Copies (Each)	____ x $12.00	$
Additional Years Search (when exact year unknown) Indicate years you want searched:	____ x $12.00	$
EXPEDITED "**RUSH**" SERVICE (Additional)	$10.00	$
PAYMENT TOTAL:		**$**

For Accounting Use Only

Is your request complete? Don't forget photo ID!

HAVE YOU ??

- **Listed your name/mailing address in Part 1**
  Cannot send to General Delivery addresses
  Included a telephone number to reach you
  Enclosed proper ID
- **Signed your name in Part 2**
  Do not print, must be signature
- ***Indicated purpose for requesting the record in Part 3***
- **Indicated your eligibility in Part 4**
  Provide all necessary documentation
- **Completed all items in Part 5**
  "Unknown" if information unavailable
  "N/A" if not applicable
  Filled out purpose for requesting the record
- **Completed Part 6 for fees**
  Total all fees that apply
- **Enclosed payment**
  Checks payable to "State of Michigan"

APPLYING IN PERSON

If you wish to apply in person to order a Michigan vital record, you may do so at the office located at 201 Townsend St, Capitol View Building, 3rd Floor, Lansing MI 48913 (across from the State Capitol). Lobby hours are 8:00 am - 5:00 pm. Directions are available by logging onto our website at: www.michigan.gov/mdch or by calling **517-335-8666**.

Orders at our counter must be placed by 3:00 pm in order to receive same-day service. An additional "rush" fee of $10.00 is required for same-day service and you must allow up to a 2 hour waiting period for the order to be processed. Genealogy requests may take somewhat longer.

A money order, credit card or cash can be used at our front counter if same-day service is requested. A personal check can also be used if the request is NOT same-day service.

PAYMENT INFORMATION

SEARCH FEES ARE NON-REFUNDABLE: Fees are established by state statute. A basic one year search fee includes either one certified copy of the record or an official statement that the record is not filed with the state. A basic statewide search includes the files for the year specified as the birth year.

REFUNDABLE FEES: Payment for additional copies will be refunded if the search indicated that the record is not filed with the state. A refund check would be mailed to you by the Michigan Department of Treasury, usually within 3-4 weeks.

MAIL APPLICATION TO

REGULAR MAIL TO:	**RUSH MAIL TO:**
Vital Records Requests	**Vital Records RUSH**
PO Box 30721	**PO Box 30721**
Lansing MI 48909	**Lansing MI 48909**

www.michigan.gov/mdch ***517-335-8666***

PROCESSING TIMES FOR MAIL REQUESTS

REGULAR SEARCH – The processing time for a regular request will be approximately 5 weeks, depending on the volume of requests received in our office.

EXPEDITED (RUSH) SEARCH – The processing time for a "rush" request will be approximately 2 weeks, depending on the volume of requests received in our office.

ADDITIONAL INFORMATION - If you find that the processing times listed do not meet your needs, we suggest that you call our Eligibility Unit at 517-335-8666 and speak with a customer service representative. They may be able to offer additional help to meet your individual situation.

IDENTIFICATION REQUIREMENTS

FOR APPLYING IN PERSON OR BY MAIL
FOR A MICHIGAN BIRTH RECORD
**** Please Send Photocopies - Not Original Documents ****

Under Michigan law, birth records are restricted documents. To request a birth record, a current valid, government issued identification is required in order to establish eligibility (except for an unrestricted birth record that is at least 100 years old). To protect you and the community from identity theft, we require a copy of the applicant's government issued identification to be presented along with the application. Individuals **under the age of 15** cannot request a copy of their own birth record.

At least one of the following ID's is required:

- Current driver's license with photo if unexpired, or expired less than one year and issued within the last five years
- Current state issued photo identification card unexpired, or expired less than one year and issued within the last five years
- Unexpired U.S. or foreign passport
- U.S. military photo identification or military dependent photo identification with current expiration date
- Employment identification with photo, accompanied by a current pay stub or W-2 form
- Department of Corrections photo identification card, accompanied by probation or discharge papers dated within last year
- If a currently incarcerated prisoner, a Department of Corrections photo identification card, accompanied by a verification of incarceration by the facility on letterhead
- For persons age 15-20, current student photo ID with either a report card or transcript

Alternative documents can be submitted to be reviewed by a supervisor if a current, valid government issued ID is not available. If you do not have one of the above, you will need to submit at least three of the following, and one MUST be dated within the last year. Please note we cannot use a Social Security Card or junk mail.

Examples might be: expired state or federal photo ID, marriage or divorce certificate, child's birth record, W-2, paycheck stub, bank statement, voter or car registration, health insurance/Medicaid card, state benefit card, utility bill, doctor/dentist/hospital bill, baptismal certificate, letter from a government agency such as Social Security or the IRS, numident letter or benefit statement from Social Security, school records, tax records, incarceration records or land/rental agreement.

If you are still unable to provide any of the above-mentioned forms of identification, please contact the Michigan Vital Records Office at 517-335-8666 and speak with a customer service representative.

APPLICATION FOR A **NON–CERTIFIED** COPY **MICHIGAN HEIRLOOM BIRTH RECORD**

PART 1: APPLICANT'S INFORMATION **PHOTO IDENTIFICATION REQUIRED** **(See back for details)**

Applicant's Name: ______________________ State Driver's License or Identification # ______________

Mailing Address: ______________________ City: ____________ State: _____ Zip: ________
(Cannot Send to General Delivery)

Daytime Phone - Required: ( ) ______________ Other Phone: ( ) ______________

PART 2: CERTIFICATION OF INFORMATION PROVIDED

By signing this application, I understand that I am agreeing to pay for a search of the State of Michigan Vital Records. This does not guarantee that a record will be found.

Statement of Entitlement: Misstating an identity or assuming the identity of another person is subject to criminal penalties, e.g., Michigan Compiled Laws 333.2894(b) and 333.2898 and federal laws relating to falsification in obtaining a birth record. By signing this application, I state that I am eligible to receive this birth record as indicated in the Eligibility Section of this application.

► **Applicant's Signature:** ______________________ **Date:** __________

IDENTITY THEFT PROTECTION ACT 445.65(1) and 445.69(1) prohibits anyone from obtaining a vital record by misrepresenting a person's identity or attempting to use another person's identifying information. A person who violates this law is guilty of a felony punishable by imprisonment for up to 5 years or a fine of up to $25,000 or both.

PART 3: Select the Heirloom Certificate Format **(Separate application required for each request)**

☐ Option 1	☐ Option 2	☐ Option 3	☐ Option 4	☐ Option 5
Quantity _____	Quantity _____	Quantity _____	Quantity _____	Quantity _____

☐ Option 6 I would like to purchase ______ (Quantity) gift certificate(s). Please indicate below the recipient's name(s) If more than two, please attach an additional page with the additional recipients' names. (Please skip to Part 6)

Recipient Name (First and Last): ______________________ Total Number of Copies: ________

Recipient Name (First and Last): ______________________

PART 4: ELIGIBILITY - Select the category that qualifies **YOU** to request and receive the requested Michigan birth record per MCL 333.2882

- ☐ Child or Parent named on the record
  Note: Only adoptive parents are eligible (if applicable)
- ☐ Legally licensed attorney of subject of the record
- ☐ Heir of the deceased person named on the record
  - Relationship to decedent: ______________ Decedent's name at time of death: ______________
  - State where death occurred: ______ (If not MI, you must provide a death certificate) • Date of death (Year): ______________
- ☐ Legal guardian of the person named on the record
  Note: Copy of court documented guardianship papers required.
- ☐ Record at least 100 years old (no photo ID required)

PART 5: INFORMATION NEEDED TO FIND BIRTH RECORD BEING REQUESTED

Date of Birth (MM / DD / YR)	Sex: ☐ Male ☐ Female	Place of Birth (hospital, city, county)

Please include first, middle, and last names AT BIRTH below:	Is the person named on the record **adopted**? ☐ Yes ☐ No
Full Name: ______________	Full Name **After** adoption: ______________
Mother's Maiden Name: ______________	Adopted Mother's Name: ______________
Father's Name:	Adopted Father's Name:

If the applicant's current name is different than the way their birth name appears on the record, provide info below (required):

☐ Marriage: Place of Marriage (state) ______________ Date of Marriage ______________

☐ Court Ordered New Legal Name (court order must be provided): First __________ Middle __________ Last __________

PART 6: FEES

Total copies or certificates from Part 3 ________ Times $40.00 Per Copy X $40.00 Total Fee ⇨	
Redeeming Gift Certificate Number ________	Enclosed

For Accounting Use Only

HEIRLOOM BIRTH RECORDS: The State of Michigan issues non-certified heirloom birth certificates with your choice of five designs, signed by the current Governor. The five certificates are suitable for framing and are mailed encased in cardboard shields to ensure protection. The certificates can be preserved as a family heirloom, but they are not intended as proof of birth.

By purchasing an heirloom certificate, or a gift certificate, you are also contributing to the Michigan Children's Trust Fund which was established in 1982. The Fund serves as a voice for Michigan's children and families, and promotes their health, safety and welfare by providing financial support for local programs and services that prevent child abuse and neglect. For more information on the Children's Trust Fund, please visit their website at http://www.michigan.gov/ctf

HAVE YOU ??

- **Listed your name/mailing address in Part 1**
- **Signed your name in Part 2**
  Do not print, must be signature
- **Indicated which format you would like to receive in Part 3**
- **Indicated your eligibility in Part 4**
  Provide all necessary documentation
- **Completed all items in Part 5**
  "Unknown" if information unavailable
- **Completed Part 6 for fees**
  Total all fees that apply
- **Enclosed payment**
  Checks payable to "State of Michigan"
- **Enclose legible copy of ID**
  Must agree with Part 1 information

APPLYING IN PERSON

Heirloom birth records cannot be processed same-day. The application should be mailed to the address listed below. Or, if you wish, you may come in to our Lansing office and drop off an application, and it will be processed and mailed to you within 4-5 weeks.

Our office is located at 201 Townsend St, Capitol View Building, 3rd Floor, Lansing MI 48913 (across from the State Capitol). Lobby hours are 8:00 am - 5:00 pm. Directions are available by logging onto our website at: www.michigan.gov/mdch or by calling **517-335-8666**.

A money order, personal check, credit card or cash can be used at our front counter for requests.

PAYMENT INFORMATION

SEARCH FEES ARE NON-REFUNDABLE: Fees are established by state statute. A basic one year search fee includes either one non-certified copy of the heirloom record or an official statement that the record is not filed with the state. A basic statewide search includes the files for the year specified as the birth year.

MAIL APPLICATION TO

MAIL TO:
Vital Records Requests
PO Box 30721
Lansing MI 48909

www.michigan.gov/mdch 517-335-8666

DCH-0569-BX HEIRLOOM 3-2013
By Authority of MCL 333.2882(1)(a)(b) and MCL 333.2891(1-4)(8)

PROCESSING TIME FOR HEIRLOOM BIRTH RECORDS

The processing time for an heirloom birth record request will be approximately 4-5 weeks, depending on the volume of requests received. Same day service is not available.

IDENTIFICATION REQUIREMENTS

FOR APPLYING IN PERSON OR BY MAIL
FOR A NON-CERTIFIED MICHIGAN HEIRLOOM BIRTH RECORD
**** Please Send Photocopies - Not Original Documents ****

Under Michigan law, birth records are restricted documents. To request an heirloom birth record, a current valid, government issued identification is required in order to establish eligibility (except for an unrestricted birth record that is at least 100 years old). To protect you and the community from identity theft, we require a copy of the applicant's government issued identification to be presented along with the application. Individuals **under the age of 15** cannot request a copy of their own birth record.

At least one of the following ID's is required:

- Current driver's license with photo if unexpired, or expired less than one year and issued within the last five years
- Current state issued photo identification card unexpired, or expired less than one year and issued within the last five years
- Unexpired U.S. or foreign passport
- U.S. military photo identification or military dependent photo identification with current expiration date
- Employment identification with photo, accompanied by a current pay stub or W-2 form
- Department of Corrections photo identification card, accompanied by probation or discharge papers dated within last year
- If a currently incarcerated prisoner, a Department of Corrections photo identification card, accompanied by a verification of incarceration by the facility on letterhead
- For persons age 15-20, current student photo ID with either a report card or transcript

Alternative documents can be submitted to be reviewed by a supervisor if a current, valid government issued ID is not available. If you do not have one of the above, you will need to submit at least three of the following, and one MUST be dated within the last year. Please note we cannot use a Social Security Card or junk mail.

Examples might be: expired state or federal photo ID, marriage or divorce certificate, child's birth record, W-2, paycheck stub, bank statement, voter or car registration, health insurance/Medicaid card, state benefit card, utility bill, doctor/dentist/hospital bill, baptismal certificate, letter from a government agency such as Social Security or the IRS, numident letter or benefit statement from Social Security, school records, tax records, incarceration records or land/rental agreement.

If you are still unable to provide any of the above-mentioned forms of identification, please contact the Michigan Vital Records Office at 517-335-8666 and speak with a customer service representative.

REQUEST FOR VERIFICATION OF A MICHIGAN BIRTH RECORD

For Additional Information: (517) 335-8666 **www.michigan.gov/mdch**

Please type or print clearly and legibly

APPLICANT (PERSON REQUESTING VERIFICATION)	DATE: / /
Agency Name	
Applicant's Name	
Mailing Address	
City/State/Zip	

APPLICANT'S SIGNATURE: (Sign Here) ______________________________

Must be signed in order to process. By signing this application, I understand that I am agreeing to pay for a search of the State of Michigan vital records. This does not guarantee that a record will be found.

VERIFICATION INFORMATION - A request for a verification of a Michigan birth record will be returned to you stamped with an indication that a record was identified which matched the supplied facts, or that no record could be identified which matched the supplied facts. State law (MCL 333.2881(2)) allows for verification of **ONLY name of the subject of the birth record, date of birth, place of birth and filing date.** This information must match exactly what is on the record. No copy of the record or additional information can be verified or supplied by the Vital Records Office. State law requires a $10.00 fee for each search of the facts for verification.

FACTS TO BE VERIFIED
Must match exactly what is on the record

Child's Name

____
First Middle Last

Child's Date of Birth

____
Month Day Year

Child's Place of Birth

____
County

Date of Filing - (Date the record was filed – Enter ONLY if you have a copy of the record)

____
Month Day Year

TURN-AROUND TIME

REGULAR SEARCH - Processing time for mail-in requests will be approximately 3 weeks, depending on volume of requests received.

EXPEDITED SEARCH – Processing time for a mail-in request will be approximately 2 weeks, depending on volume of requests received. A counter request will be processed in 1-2 hours.

PAYMENT – For mail-in requests, payment can be made in U.S. funds by check or money order payable to the "State of Michigan". In addition, cash or a credit card can be used for counter requests. No checks if same-day service is requested.

Each Verification Search (Non-Refundable)	$ 10.00
* **EXPEDITED SEARCH** (Non-Refundable) (In addition to the regular search fee)	$ 10.00
TOTAL ENCLOSED	**$**

We cannot process your request without payment. When mailing, please remember to include check or money order.

IF REGULAR SEARCH:
VITAL RECORDS REQUESTS
P.O. Box 30721
Lansing MI 48909

IF EXPEDITED SEARCH:
VITAL RECORDS RUSH
PO Box 30721
Lansing MI 48909

If you wish to have the results of the verification faxed to you, please indicate the fax number here:

( ) ____________________

VERIFICATION STAMP (for Vital Records Official Stamp)

DCH-0569-VERAOP Rev 10/2010 By Authority of MCL 333.2881(2) and 333.2891(4)(f)

APPLICATION FOR A **CERTIFIED** COPY

MICHIGAN MARRIAGE RECORD

REQUESTING A MICHIGAN MARRIAGE RECORD: The Michigan Vital Records office has records of marriages that occurred in Michigan and were **filed** with the state since **1867**. Some records were not filed with the state. Anyone is eligible to request a copy of a Michigan marriage record if the application is completed and signed and the required fee is paid.

PART 1: APPLICANT'S INFORMATION (Person Requesting Record)

Applicant's Name: ____________________

Mailing Address: ____________________ City: ____________ State: _____ Zip: ________

Daytime Phone (   ) ____________________ Other Phone: (   ) ____________________

PART 2: CERTIFICATION OF INFORMATION PROVIDED

By signing this application, I understand that I am agreeing to pay for a search of the State of Michigan Vital Records with the information that I provided. This does not guarantee that a record will be found.

▶ **Applicant's Signature:** ____________________ **Date:** ____________

PART 3: PURPOSE FOR REQUESTING THE RECORD ____________________

PART 4: MARRIAGE INFORMATION NEEDED TO FIND RECORD

If the exact date of marriage is unknown, please indicate the year you want searched.
If you need additional years searched, please see the payment box for fee information.

DATE OF MARRIAGE

(mm/dd/yyyy) ____________________

GROOM'S NAME — First / Middle / Last	(At time of application for marriage license) BRIDE'S NAME — First / Middle / Last
	(Before first married, if different from above) BRIDE'S NAME — First / Middle / Last
GROOM'S FATHER'S NAME — First / Middle / Last	BRIDE'S FATHER'S NAME — First / Middle / Last
GROOM'S MOTHER'S NAME — First / Middle / Last	BRIDE'S MOTHER'S NAME — First / Middle / Last
LOCATION OF MARRIAGE: City / County / State	LOCATION WHERE LICENSE WAS OBTAINED: County

PART 5: FEES - Includes one certified copy *or* no-find letter

Base Fee: Includes One Year Search	$26.00	$ 26.00
Additional Certified Copies (Each)	____ x $12.00	$
Additional Years Search (when exact year unknown) Indicate years you want searched:	____ x $12.00	$
EXPEDITED "**RUSH**" SERVICE (Additional)	$10.00	$
PAYMENT TOTAL:		**$**

For Accounting Use Only

Is your request complete? See checklist on back!

HAVE YOU ??

- **Listed your name/mailing address in Part 1**
  Did you remember to list a phone number?
- **Signed your name in Part 2**
  Do not print, must be signature
- **Indicated purpose for requesting the record in Part 3**
- **Completed all items in Part 4**
  "Unknown" if information unavailable
  "N/A" if not applicable
- **Completed Part 5 for fees**
  Total all fees that apply
- **Enclosed payment**
  Checks payable to "State of Michigan"

APPLYING IN PERSON

If you wish to apply in person to order a Michigan vital record, you may do so at the office located at 201 Townsend St, Capitol View Building, 3rd Floor, Lansing MI 48913 (across from the State Capitol). Lobby hours are 8:00 am - 5:00 pm. Directions are available by logging onto our website at: www.michigan.gov/mdch or by calling **517-335-8666**.

A money order, credit card or cash can be used at our front counter if same-day service is requested. A personal check can also be used if the request is NOT same-day service.

Orders at our counter must be placed by 3:00 pm in order to receive same-day service. An additional "rush" fee of $10.00 is required for same-day service and you must allow up to a 2 hour waiting period for the order to be processed.

PAYMENT INFORMATION

SEARCH FEES ARE NON-REFUNDABLE: Fees are established by state statute. A basic one year search fee includes either one certified copy of the record or an official statement that the record is not filed with the state. A basic statewide search includes the files for the year specified as the marriage year.

REFUNDABLE FEES**:** Payment for additional copies will be refunded if the search indicated that the record is not filed with the state. A refund check would be mailed to you by the Michigan Department of Treasury, usually within 3-4 weeks.

PROCESSING TIMES FOR MAIL REQUESTS

REGULAR SEARCH – The processing time for a regular request will be approximately 5 weeks, depending on the volume of requests received.

EXPEDITED (RUSH) SEARCH – The processing time for a "rush" request will be approximately 2 weeks, depending on the volume of requests received.

ADDITIONAL INFORMATION - If you find that the processing times listed do not meet your needs, we suggest that you call our Eligibility Unit at 517-335-8666 and speak with a customer service representative. They may be able to offer additional help to meet your individual situation.

MAIL APPLICATION TO

REGULAR MAIL TO:
Vital Records Requests
PO Box 30721
Lansing MI 48909

RUSH MAIL TO:
Vital Records RUSH
PO Box 30721
Lansing MI 48909

DCH-0569-MX Rev 7-2012
By Authority of MCL 333.2882(1)©, MCL 333.2883(2) and MCL 333.2891(1-4)

REQUEST FOR VERIFICATION OF A MICHIGAN MARRIAGE RECORD

For Additional Information: (517) 335-8666 **www.michigan.gov/mdch**

Please type or print clearly and legibly

APPLICANT (PERSON REQUESTING VERIFICATION)	DATE: / /
Agency Name	
Applicant's Name	
Mailing Address	
City/State/Zip	

APPLICANT'S SIGNATURE: **(Sign Here)** ______________________________

Must be signed in order to process. By signing this application, I understand that I am agreeing to pay for a search of the State of Michigan vital records. This does not guarantee that a record will be found.

VERIFICATION INFORMATION - A request for a verification of a Michigan marriage record will be returned to you stamped with an indication that a record was identified which matched the supplied facts, or that no record could be identified which matched the supplied facts. State law (MCL 333.2881(2)) allows for verification of **ONLY name of the subjects of the marriage record, date of marriage, place of marriage and filing date.** This information must match exactly what is on the record. No copy of the record or additional information can be verified or supplied by the Vital Records Office. State law requires a $10.00 fee for each search of the facts for verification.

FACTS TO BE VERIFIED
Must match exactly what is on the record

Names on the Marriage Record

____
First Middle Last

____
First Middle Last

Date of Marriage

____
Month Day Year

Place of Marriage

____
County

Date of Filing - (Date the record was filed – Enter ONLY if you have a copy of the record)

____
Month Day Year

TURN-AROUND TIME

REGULAR SEARCH - Processing time for mail-in requests will be approximately 3 weeks, depending on volume of requests received.

EXPEDITED SEARCH – Processing time for a mail-in request will be approximately 2 weeks, depending on volume of requests received. A counter request will be processed in 1-2 hours.

PAYMENT – For mail-in requests, payment can be made in U.S. funds by check or money order payable to the "State of Michigan". In addition, cash or a credit card can be used for counter requests. No checks if same-day service is requested.

Each Verification Search (Non-Refundable)	$ 10.00
*** EXPEDITED SEARCH** (Non-Refundable) (In addition to the regular search fee)	$ 10.00
TOTAL ENCLOSED	$

We cannot process your request without payment. When mailing, please remember to include check or money order.

IF REGULAR SEARCH:
VITAL RECORDS REQUESTS
P.O. Box 30721
Lansing MI 48909

IF EXPEDITED SEARCH:
VITAL RECORDS RUSH
PO Box 30721
Lansing MI 48909

If you wish to have the results of the verification faxed to you, please indicate the fax number here:

( ) ______________________

VERIFICATION STAMP (for Vital Records Official Stamp)

DCH-0569-VERMX Rev 10/2010 By Authority of MCL 333.2881(2) and 333.2891(4)(f)

APPLICATION FOR A **CERTIFIED** COPY

MICHIGAN DIVORCE RECORD

REQUESTING A MICHIGAN DIVORCE RECORD: The Michigan Vital Records office has records of divorces that occurred in Michigan and were **filed** with the state since **1897**. Some records were not filed with the state. Anyone is eligible to request a copy of a Michigan divorce or annulment record if the application is completed and signed and the required fee is paid.

PART 1: APPLICANT'S INFORMATION *(Person Requesting Record)*

Applicant's Name: ______________________________

Mailing Address: ____________________ City: ____________ State: _____ Zip: ________

Daytime Phone ( ) ____________________ Other Phone: ( ) ____________________

PART 2: CERTIFICATION OF INFORMATION PROVIDED

By signing this application, I understand that I am agreeing to pay for a search of the State of Michigan Vital Records with the information that I provided. This does not guarantee that a record will be found.

► **Applicant's Signature:** ______________________ **Date:** __________

PART 3: PURPOSE FOR REQUESTING THE RECORD ______________________

PART 4: INFORMATION NEEDED TO SEARCH FOR RECORD

If the exact date of divorce is unknown, please indicate the year you want searched. If you need additional years searched, please see the payment box for fee information. The State of Michigan will only have the record of divorce. If you need the actual divorce decree, you will need to contact the court that finalized the divorce.

Date of Divorce or Annulment

(mm/dd/yyyy) __________________

HUSBAND'S NAME:	First	Middle	Last
WIFE'S NAME AT TIME OF DIVORCE OR ANNULMENT:	First	Middle	Last
COUNTY WHERE DIVORCE OR ANNULMENT WAS GRANTED:			

PART 5: FEES - *Includes one certified copy or no-find letter*

Base Fee: ***Includes One Year Search***	$26.00	$ 26.00
Additional Certified Copies (Each)	____ x $12.00	$
Additional Years Search (when exact year unknown) Indicate years you want searched:	____ x $12.00	$
EXPEDITED "**RUSH**" SERVICE (Additional)	$10.00	$
PAYMENT TOTAL:		**$**

For Accounting Use Only

Is your request complete? See checklist on back!

HAVE YOU ??

- **Listed your name/mailing address in Part 1**
  Did you remember to list a phone number?
- **Signed your name in Part 2**
  Do not print, must be signature
- **Indicated purpose for requesting the record in Part 3**
- **Completed all items in Part 4**
  "Unknown" if information unavailable
  "N/A" if not applicable
- **Completed Part 5 for fees**
  Total all fees that apply
- **Enclosed payment**
  Checks payable to "State of Michigan"

PROCESSING TIMES FOR MAIL REQUESTS

REGULAR SEARCH – The processing time for a regular request will be approximately 5 weeks, depending on the volume of requests received.

EXPEDITED (RUSH) SEARCH – The processing time for a "rush" request will be approximately 2 weeks, depending on the volume of requests received.

ADDITIONAL INFORMATION - If you find that the processing times listed do not meet your needs, we suggest that you call our Eligibility Unit at 517-335-8666 and speak with a customer service representative. They may be able to offer additional help to meet your individual situation.

APPLYING IN PERSON

If you wish to apply in person to order a Michigan vital record, you may do so at the office located at 201 Townsend St, Capitol View Building, 3rd Floor, Lansing MI 48913 (across from the State Capitol). Lobby hours are 8:00 am - 5:00 pm. Directions are available by logging onto our website at: www.michigan.gov/mdch or by calling **517-335-8666**.

A money order, credit card or cash can be used at our front counter if same-day service is requested. A personal check can also be used if the request is NOT same-day service.

Orders at our counter must be placed by 3:00 pm in order to receive same-day service. An additional "rush" fee of $10.00 is required for same-day service and you must allow up to a 2 hour waiting period for the order to be processed.

PAYMENT INFORMATION

SEARCH FEES ARE NON-REFUNDABLE: Fees are established by state statute. A basic one year search fee includes either one certified copy of the record or an official statement that the record is not filed with the state. A basic statewide search includes the files for the year specified as the divorce year.

REFUNDABLE FEES: Payment for additional copies will be refunded if the search indicated that the record is not filed with the state. A refund check would be mailed to you by the Michigan Department of Treasury, usually within 3-4 weeks.

MAIL APPLICATION TO

REGULAR MAIL TO:	RUSH MAIL TO:
Vital Records Requests	**Vital Records RUSH**
PO Box 30721	**PO Box 30721**
Lansing MI 48909	**Lansing MI 48909**

REQUEST FOR VERIFICATION OF A MICHIGAN DIVORCE RECORD

For Additional Information: (517) 335-8666 **www.michigan.gov/mdch**

Please type or print clearly and legibly

APPLICANT (PERSON REQUESTING VERIFICATION)	**DATE: / /**
Agency Name	
Applicant's Name	
Mailing Address	
City/State/Zip	

APPLICANT'S SIGNATURE: (Sign Here) ______________________

Must be signed in order to process. By signing this application, I understand that I am agreeing to pay for a search of the State of Michigan vital records. This does not guarantee that a record will be found.

VERIFICATION INFORMATION - A request for a verification of a Michigan divorce record will be returned to you stamped with an indication that a record was identified which matched the supplied facts, or that no record could be identified which matched the supplied facts. State law (MCL 333.2881(2)) allows for verification of **ONLY name of the subjects of the divorce record, date of divorce, place of divorce and filing date.** This information must match exactly what is on the record. No copy of the record or additional information can be verified or supplied by the Vital Records Office. State law requires a $10.00 fee for each search of the facts for verification.

FACTS TO BE VERIFIED
Must match exactly what is on the record

Names on the Divorce Record

____
First Middle Last

____
First Middle Last

Date of Divorce

____
Month Day Year

Place of Divorce

____
County

Date of Filing - (Date the record was filed – Enter ONLY if you have a copy of the record)

____
Month Day Year

TURN-AROUND TIME

REGULAR SEARCH - Processing time for mail-in requests will be approximately 3 weeks, depending on volume of requests received.

EXPEDITED SEARCH – Processing time for a mail-in request will be approximately 2 weeks, depending on volume of requests received. A counter request will be processed in 1-2 hours.

PAYMENT – For mail-in requests, payment can be made in U.S. funds by check or money order payable to the "State of Michigan". In addition, cash or a credit card can be used for counter requests. No checks if same-day service is requested.

Each Verification Search (Non-Refundable)	$ 10.00
*** EXPEDITED SEARCH** (Non-Refundable) (In addition to the regular search fee)	$ 10.00
TOTAL ENCLOSED	**$**

We cannot process your request without payment. When mailing, please remember to include check or money order.

IF REGULAR SEARCH:
VITAL RECORDS REQUESTS
P.O. Box 30721
Lansing MI 48909

IF EXPEDITED SEARCH:
VITAL RECORDS RUSH
PO Box 30721
Lansing MI 48909

If you wish to have the results of the verification faxed to you, please indicate the fax number here:

( ) ______________________

VERIFICATION STAMP (for Vital Records Official Stamp)

APPLICATION FOR A **CERTIFIED** COPY

MICHIGAN DEATH RECORD

REQUESTING A MICHIGAN DEATH RECORD: The Michigan Vital Records office has records of deaths that occurred in Michigan and were **filed** with the state since **1867**. Some of the records were not filed with the state; more records are missing from the pre-1906 files. Death records are not restricted documents in Michigan. Anyone can request that a search be conducted if the application is completed and signed, and submitted with the required fee paid.

PART 1: APPLICANT'S INFORMATION *(Person Requesting Record)*

Applicant's Name: ____________________

Mailing Address: ____________________ City: ____________ State: _____ Zip: _______

Daytime Phone (   ) ____________________ Other Phone: (   ) ____________________

PART 2: CERTIFICATION OF INFORMATION PROVIDED

By signing this application, I understand that I am agreeing to pay for a search of the State of Michigan Vital Records with the information that I provided. This does not guarantee that a record will be found.

▶ **Applicant's Signature:** ____________________ **Date:** __________

PART 3: PURPOSE FOR REQUESTING THE RECORD ____________________

PART 4: DEATH INFORMATION NEEDED TO FIND THE RECORD

If the exact date of death is unknown, please indicate the year you want searched. If you need additional years searched, please see the payment box for fee information. We can do a search without the "county" of death, but it will not be a thorough search.

NAME OF DECEASED (Name at time of death) First / Middle / Last		DATE OF BIRTH (If Known) (mm/dd/yyyy)	DATE OF DEATH mm/dd/yyyy)
GENDER ☐ Male ☐ Female	DECEDENT'S PLACE OF DEATH City / County / State	Other variations of same name or locations:	
Please provide any of the following additional information (if known) that would help us locate the death record:			
DECEDENT'S PLACE OF BIRTH State / Country		DECEDENT'S SOCIAL SECURITY NUMBER ___ __ ____	
DECEDENT'S MOTHER'S NAME First / Middle / Last		DECEDENT'S FATHER'S NAME First / Middle / Last	

PART 5: FEES - Includes one certified copy or no-find letter

Base Fee: ***Includes One Year Search***	$26.00	$ 26.00
Additional Certified Copies (Each)	____ x $12.00	$
Additional Years Search (when exact year unknown) Indicate years you want searched:	____ x $12.00	$
EXPEDITED "**RUSH**" SERVICE (Additional)	$10.00	$
PAYMENT TOTAL:		**$**

For Accounting Use Only

Is your request complete? See checklist on back!

HAVE YOU ??

- **Listed your name/mailing address in Part 1**
  Did you remember to list a phone number?
- **Signed your name in Part 2**
  Do not print, must be signature
- **Indicated purpose for requesting the record in Part 3**
- **Completed all items in Part 4**
  "Unknown" if information unavailable
  "N/A" if not applicable
  Provided additional information, if possible
- **Completed Part 5 for fees**
  Total all fees that apply
- **Enclosed payment**
  Checks payable to "State of Michigan"

PROCESSING TIMES FOR MAIL REQUESTS

REGULAR SEARCH – The processing time for a regular request will be approximately 5 weeks, depending on the volume of requests received.

EXPEDITED (RUSH) SEARCH – The processing time for a "rush" request will be approximately 2 weeks, depending on the volume of requests received.

ADDITIONAL INFORMATION - If you find that the processing times listed do not meet your needs, we suggest that you call our Eligibility Unit at 517-335-8666 and speak with a customer service representative. They may be able to offer additional help to meet your individual situation.

APPLYING IN PERSON

If you wish to apply in person to order a Michigan vital record, you may do so at the office located at 201 Townsend St, Capitol View Building, 3rd Floor, Lansing MI 48913 (across from the State Capitol). Lobby hours are 8:00 am - 5:00 pm. Directions are available by logging onto our website at: www.michigan.gov/mdch or by calling **517-335-8666**.

A money order, credit card or cash can be used at our front counter if same-day service is requested. A personal check can also be used if the request is NOT same-day service.

Orders at our counter must be placed by 3:00 pm in order to receive same-day service. An additional "rush" fee of $10.00 is required for same-day service and you must allow up to a 2 hour waiting period for the order to be processed.

PAYMENT INFORMATION

SEARCH FEES ARE NON-REFUNDABLE: Fees are established by state statute. A basic one year search fee includes either one certified copy of the record or an official statement that the record is not filed with the state. A basic statewide search includes the files for the year specified as the death year.

REFUNDABLE FEES: Payment for additional copies will be refunded if the search indicated that the record is not filed with the state. A refund check would be mailed to you by the Michigan Department of Treasury, usually within 3-4 weeks.

MAIL APPLICATION TO

REGULAR MAIL TO:
Vital Records Requests
PO Box 30721
Lansing MI 48909

RUSH MAIL TO:
Vital Records RUSH
PO Box 30721
Lansing MI 48909

REQUEST FOR VERIFICATION OF A MICHIGAN DEATH RECORD

For Additional Information: (517) 335-8666 **www.michigan.gov/mdch**

Please type or print clearly and legibly

APPLICANT (PERSON REQUESTING VERIFICATION)	**DATE: / /**
Agency Name	
Applicant's Name	
Mailing Address	
City/State/Zip	

APPLICANT'S SIGNATURE: **(Sign Here)** ______________________________

Must be signed in order to process. By signing this application, I understand that I am agreeing to pay for a search of the State of Michigan vital records. This does not guarantee that a record will be found.

VERIFICATION INFORMATION - A request for a verification of a Michigan death record will be returned to you stamped with an indication that a record was identified which matched the supplied facts, or that no record could be identified which matched the supplied facts. State law (MCL 333.2881(2)) allows for verification of **ONLY name of the subject of the death record, date of death, place of death and filing date.** This information must match exactly what is on the record. No copy of the record or additional information can be verified or supplied by the Vital Records Office. State law requires a $10.00 fee for each search of the facts for verification.

FACTS TO BE VERIFIED
Must match exactly what is on the record

Decedent's Name

____
First Middle Last

Decedent's Date of Death

____
Month Day Year

Decedent's Place of Death

____
County

Date of Filing - (Date the record was filed – Enter ONLY if you have a copy of the record)

____
Month Day Year

TURN-AROUND TIME

REGULAR SEARCH - Processing time for mail-in requests will be approximately 3 weeks, depending on volume of requests received.

EXPEDITED SEARCH – Processing time for a mail-in request will be approximately 2 weeks, depending on volume of requests received. A counter request will be processed in 1-2 hours.

PAYMENT – For mail-in requests, payment can be made in U.S. funds by check or money order payable to the "State of Michigan". In addition, cash or a credit card can be used for counter requests. No checks if same-day service is requested.

Each Verification Search (Non-Refundable)	$ 10.00
*** EXPEDITED SEARCH** (Non-Refundable) (In addition to the regular search fee)	$ 10.00
TOTAL ENCLOSED	**$**

We cannot process your request without payment. When mailing, please remember to include check or money order.

IF REGULAR SEARCH:
VITAL RECORDS REQUESTS
P.O. Box 30721
Lansing MI 48909

IF EXPEDITED SEARCH:
VITAL RECORDS RUSH
PO Box 30721
Lansing MI 48909

If you wish to have the results of the verification faxed to you, please indicate the fax number here:

( ) ______________________

VERIFICATION STAMP (for Vital Records Official Stamp)

REQUEST BY ADULT ADOPTEE FOR IDENTIFYING INFORMATION

State of Michigan
Department of Human Services

I hereby request. from my adoption records. my name before placement in adoption. the names of my biological parents. including their current names. if available. most recent address or addresses of biological parents. and names of biological siblings at the time of termination.

CURRENT INFORMATION

Current Name (Last, First, Middle)	Birth Date Month Day Year
Current Address (Street Number and Name)	Apartment Number
City State Zip Code	Telephone Number A/C ( )

ADOPTION INFORMATION

Adoptive Name (Last, First, Middle)	Name Before Adoption (If Known)
Adoptive Mother's Name	Adoptive Father's Name
Birth Mother's Name	Birth Father's Name
Name of Probate Court	Name of Placing Agency

☐ Also, please send me non-identifying information from my file.

Additional Comments

DISTRIBUTION: Original - Adoption Agency or Court that Finalized the Adoption Copy - Keep for Your Records	Adult Adoptee's Signature Date
AUTHORITY: MCLA 710.68. COMPLETION: Voluntary. PENALTY: None.	Department of Human Services (DHS) will not discriminate against any individual or group because of race, sex, religion, age, national origin, color, height, weight, marital status, political beliefs or disability. If you need help with reading, writing, hearing, etc., under the Americans with Disabilities Act, you are invited to make your needs known to a DHS office in your area.

DHS-1925 (Rev. 8-05) Previous edition may be used. MS Word

MINNESOTA

Send your requests to:

Minnesota Department of Health
Central Cashiering—Vital Records
P.O. Box 64499
St. Paul, MN 55164-0499

Tel. (651) 201-5980
Fax (651) 201-5750
E-mail: health.issuance@state.mn.us
www.health.state.mn.us/macros/topics/certificates.html

A certified or non-certified (for information purposes only) birth or death certificate may be obtained by mail, e-mail, or fax from the Minnesota Department of Health (MDH) or in person from a local issuance office (see www.health.state.mn.us/divs/chs/osr/registrars.html for addresses). The Department of Health has birth records from January 1, 1900, and death records from January 1, 1908. For earlier birth or death records, contact the local issuance office in the county where the event occurred.

Cost for a certified Birth Certificate	$26.00
Cost for a duplicate certified Birth Certificate, when ordered at the same time	$19.00
Cost for a certified Death Certificate	$13.00
Cost for a non-certified Birth or Death Certificate	$13.00
Cost for a duplicate Death Certificate or non-certified Birth or Death Certificate, when ordered at the same time	$6.00

Send your requests for Marriage and Divorce Certificates to:

County Recorder
(Town), MN

www.health.state.mn.us/divs/chs/osr/registrars.html

Copies of certificates of marriage are available from the county that issued the marriage license, and divorce decrees are available from the county that granted the divorce.

For Genealogy Research:

The Minnesota Birth Certificates Index 1900–1934, with selected pre-1900 records (http://people.mnhs.org/bci/), and Death Certificates Index 1908–2001 (http://people.mnhs.org/dci/) are available online; non-certified copies of certificates are available from these websites. More births and deaths will be added to the indexes over time.

The Minnesota Historical Society (345 W. Kellogg Boulevard, St. Paul, MN 55102-1906; tel. 651-259-3000; www.mnhs.org) has many other records of interest to family researchers, including microfilms of original county marriage applications, licenses, certificates, and District Court divorce records.

For Adoption Record information, contact:

Minnesota Department of Health
P.O. Box 64499
St. Paul, MN 55164-0499

An adopted child age 19 or older may request a non-certified copy of the original birth record.

Birth Certificate Application

The information requested on this application is required by Minnesota Statutes, section 144.225, subdivision 7 and Minnesota Rules, part 4601.2600. If you do not complete all fields, the application may be returned.

Birth Record Information		
First Name	Middle Name	Last Name
Date of Birth	☐Male ☐Female	City and County of Birth
Mother's First Name	Middle Name	Maiden Name
Father's First Name	Middle Name	Last Name

Requester Information				
Name				Date of Birth
Mailing Address – Street	Apt/Unit #	City	State	ZIP
Daytime Phone	Email			

What is your relationship to the subject of the record (tangible interest)? You must check one.

☐I am the subject of the record ☐I am the child of the subject ☐I am the spouse of the subject

☐I am the parent ☐I am the grandparent of the subject ☐I am the grandchild of the subject

☐I am the party responsible for filing the birth record

☐I am the legal custodian, guardian or conservator of the subject **(you must include a certified copy of a court order showing this relationship)**

☐I am the health care agent of the subject **(you must include the health care agent power of attorney)**

☐I am a personal representative and the certified copy is required for the administration of the estate

☐I am a successor of the subject as defined my MN statutes, section 524.1-201, and the subject is deceased

☐I have documentation that the record is necessary for the determination or protection of personal or property rights **(you must submit documentation showing this relationship)**

☐I represent an adoption agency and the record is needed to complete a confidential post-adoption search **(you must include a copy of your employee ID)**

☐I am an attorney and I have attached proof of my licensure

☐I am presenting your office with a court order issued by a court of competent jurisdiction **(this must be a certified copy)**

☐I represent a local, state or federal governmental agency and the record is necessary for the governmental agency to perform its authorized duties **(you must include a copy of your employee ID)**

☐I am a representative authorized by a person listed above **(you must include a notarized statement from a person listed above)**

Signature and Notary (application must be signed in front of a notary if applying by mail, fax, or email)

I certify that the information provided on this application is accurate and complete to the best of my knowledge.

Requester Signature	
Signed or attested before me on: _______ day of ___________________, 20_______	Notary Stamp/Seal
Notary Public Signature	
My Commission Expires:	

PENALTIES: Any person who willfully and knowingly provides false information for a certified vital record may be sentenced up to 1 year in jail or a fine of up to $3000 or both (Minnesota Statutes, section 144.227 and section 609.02, subdivision 3 and 4).

B102 REV 03/2013

Birth Certificate Application

Requester Name:

Fee and Payment Information

Item	Number requested	Fee per item	Total
One birth certificate	1	$26	**$26**
Additional certificate(s) for the same birth record **(optional)**		$19 each	
Federal Express delivery **(optional)** – This is an additional fee that applies only to the method of delivery. ☐ Please check here if you want Federal Express to require a signature for receipt. If you do not check this box, no signature will be required. **Federal Express will not deliver to P.O. boxes or A.P.O. addresses.**		$16	
Total amount submitted or to be charged to credit card: (This amount must be at least $26.)			

Type of payment: ☐ Credit Card ☐ Money order ☐ Check

If paying by credit card (MasterCard/VISA/Discover):

Name on card	Card number	Expiration date	3-digit security code

If paying by check or money order (make payable to Minnesota Department of Health):

Check/money order number

Due to high administrative costs, we are unable to issue refunds for overpayment.
Checks returned for non-payment will be charged a $30 fee according to Minnesota Statutes, section 604.113, subdivision 2 and civil penalties may be imposed.

Send application and payment:

By FAX to 651-201-5740

By EMAIL to health.issuance@state.mn.us

By MAIL to:
Minnesota Department of Health
Central Cashiering – Vital Records
PO Box 64499
St. Paul, MN 55164-0499

If you have questions, please contact us at health.issuance@state.mn.us.

If you submit this application to a local issuance office, Federal Express delivery may not be an option. All payment types may not be accepted. Call the local issuance office before sending your application to confirm payment types and return mail options.

Noncertified Birth Record Transcript Application

The noncertified transcript is for informational use only.
It will not show an issuance office or issue date.

Birth Record Information		
First Name	Middle Name	Last Name
Date of Birth	☐Male ☐Female	City and County of Birth
Mother's First Name	Middle Name	Maiden Name
Father's First Name	Middle Name	Last Name

Please check one of the following:

☐I would like a copy of the civil registration information on the birth record **(available for all births 1900 to present)**

☐I would like a copy of the civil registration and health information on the birth record **(available only to the mother named on the record and for births 2001 to present)**

Requester Information				
Name				
Mailing Address – Street	Apt/Unit #	City	State	ZIP
Daytime Phone	Email			

Data Classification of Birth Records
(If you are requesting only the civil registration information on a public birth record, you may skip this part.)

A record may be confidential if the subject of the record was born to unmarried parents and the mother did not designate the record as public at the time of birth. A confidential record is available only to the individuals listed below.

- If you are requesting a copy of a confidential record, you must check one of the relationships below and your signature must be notarized.
- If you are the mother requesting health information on a public or confidential record, you must check your relationship below and your signature must be notarized.

☐I am the subject of the record age 16 or older

☐I am the parent

☐I am the legal custodian, guardian or conservator of the subject **(include a certified copy of a court order showing this relationship)**

☐I am a representative of the Minnesota Department of Human Services **(you must include a copy of your employee ID)**

☐I am presenting your office with a court order issued by a court of competent jurisdiction **(this must be a certified copy)**

☐I am a representative authorized by a person listed above **(you must submit a notarized statement from a person listed above)**

Signature and Notary
(Complete if you are requesting a confidential record or are the mother requesting a record with health information.)

I certify that the information provided on this application is accurate and complete to the best of my knowledge.

Requester Signature	
Signed or attested before me on: ______ day of ________________, 20_____	Notary Stamp/Seal
Notary Public Signature	
My Commission Expires:	

PENALTIES: Any person who willingly and knowingly without authority and with intent to deceive obtains a vital record is guilty of a gross misdemeanor (Minnesota Statutes, section 144.227).

Noncertified Birth Record Transcript Application

Requester Name:

Fee and Payment Information

Item	Number requested	Fee per item	Total
One noncertified birth transcript	1	$13	**$13**
Additional noncertified transcript(s) for the same birth record **(optional)**		$6 each	
Federal Express delivery **(optional)** – This is an additional fee that applies only to the method of delivery. ☐Please check here if you want Federal Express to require a signature for receipt. If you do not check this box, no signature will be required. **Federal Express will not deliver to P.O. boxes or A.P.O. addresses.**		$16	
Total amount submitted or to be charged to credit card: (This amount must be at least $13.)			

Type of payment: ☐Credit Card ☐Money order ☐Check

If paying by credit card (MasterCard/VISA/Discover):

Name on card	Card number	Expiration date	3 digit security code

If paying by check or money order (make payable to Minnesota Department of Health):

Check/money order number

Due to high administrative costs, we are unable to issue refunds for overpayment.
Checks returned for non-payment will be charged a $30 fee according to Minnesota Statutes, section 604.113, subdivision 2 and civil penalties may be imposed.

Send application and payment:

By FAX to 651-201-5740

By EMAIL to health.issuance@state.mn.us

By MAIL to:
Minnesota Department of Health
Central Cashiering – Vital Records
PO Box 64499
St. Paul, MN 55164-0499

If you have questions, please contact us at health.issuance@state.mn.us.

If you submit this application to a local issuance office, Federal Express delivery may not be an option. All payment types may not be accepted. Call the local issuance office before sending your application to confirm payment types and return mail options.

Death Certificate Application

The information requested on this application is required by Minnesota Statutes, section 144.225, subdivision 7 and Minnesota Rules, part 4601.2600. If you do not complete all fields, the application may be returned.

Death Record Information		
First Name	Middle Name	Last Name
Date of Death	Date of Birth or Age	City and County of Death
Mother's Name	Father's Name	Spouse on Record (if any)

Please check one of the following:

☐I would like a death certificate with cause of death information

☐I would like a death certificate **without** cause of death information (only available for records 1997 to present)

Requester Information				
Name			Date of Birth	
Mailing Address - Street	Apt/Unit #	City	State	ZIP
Daytime Phone	Email			

What is your relationship to the subject of the record (tangible interest)? You must check one.

☐I am the child of the subject ☐I am the parent of the subject ☐I am the sibling of the subject

☐I am the spouse on the record ☐I am the grandparent of the subject ☐I am the grandchild of the subject

☐I am the party responsible for filing the death record

☐I am a personal representative and the certified copy is required for the administration of the estate

☐I am a successor of the subject as defined in Minnesota Statutes, section 524.1-201 and the certified copy is required for the administration of the estate

☐I am a trustee of a trust and the certified copy is required for the proper administration of the trust

☐I have documentation that the record is necessary for the determination or protection of personal or property rights **(you must submit documentation showing this relationship)**

☐I represent an adoption agency and the record is needed to complete a confidential post-adoption search **(you must include a copy of your employee ID)**

☐I am an attorney and I have attached proof of my licensure

☐I am presenting your office with a court order issued by a court of competent jurisdiction **(this must be a certified copy)**

☐I represent a local, state or federal governmental agency and the record is necessary for the governmental agency to perform its authorized duties **(you must include a copy of your employee ID)**

☐I am a representative authorized by a person listed above **(you must include a notarized statement from a person listed above)**

Signature and Notary (application must be signed in front of a notary if applying by mail, fax, or email)

I certify that the information provided on this application is accurate and complete to the best of my knowledge.

Requester Signature	
Signed or attested before me on: _______ day of ___________________, 20_______	Notary Stamp/Seal
Notary Public Signature	
My Commission Expires:	

PENALTIES: Any person who willfully and knowingly provides false information for a certified vital record may be sentenced up to 1 year in jail or a fine of up to $3000 or both (Minnesota- Statutes, section 144.227 and section 609.02, subdivision 3 and 4).

Death Certificate Application

Requester Name:

Fee and Payment Information

Item	Number requested	Fee per item	Total
One death certificate	1	$13	**$13**
Additional certificate(s) for the same death record **(optional)**		$6 each	
Federal Express delivery **(optional)** – This is an <u>additional</u> fee that applies only to the method of delivery. ☐Please check here if you want Federal Express to require a signature for receipt. If you do not check this box, no signature will be required. **Federal Express will not deliver to P.O. boxes or A.P.O addresses.**		$16	
Total amount submitted or to be charged to credit card: (This amount must be at least $13.)			

Type of payment:	☐Credit Card	☐Money order	☐Check

If paying by credit card (MasterCard/VISA/Discover):

Name on card:	Card number	Expiration date	3 digit security code

If paying by check or money order (make payable to Minnesota Department of Health):

Check/money order number

Due to high administrative costs, we are unable to issue refunds for overpayment.
Checks returned for non-payment will be charged a $30 fee according to Minnesota Statutes, section 604.113, subdivision 2 and civil penalties may be imposed.

Send application and payment:

By FAX to 651-201-5740

By EMAIL to health.issuance@state.mn.us

By MAIL to:
Minnesota Department of Health
Central Cashiering – Vital Records
PO Box 64499
St. Paul, MN 55164-0499

If you have questions, please contact us at health.issuance@state.mn.us.

If you submit this application to a local issuance office, Federal Express delivery may not be an option. All payment types may not be accepted. Call the local issuance office before sending your application to confirm payment types and services available.

Noncertified Death Record Transcript Application

The noncertified transcript is for informational use only.
It will not show an issuance office or issue date.

Death Record Information		
First Name	Middle Name	Last Name
Date of Death	Date of Birth or Age	City and County of Death
Mother's Name	Father's Name	Spouse on Record (if any)

Requester Information				
Name				
Mailing Address – Street	Apt/Unit #	City	State	ZIP
Daytime Phone	Email			

PENALTIES: Any person who willingly and knowingly without authority and with intent to deceive obtains a vital record is guilty of a gross misdemeanor (Minnesota Statutes, section 144.227).

Fee and Payment Information

Item	Number requested	Fee per item	Total
One noncertified death transcript		$13	**$13**
Additional noncertified transcript(s) for the same death record **(optional)**		$6 each	
Federal Express delivery **(optional)** – This is an additional fee that applies only to the method of delivery. ☐Please check here if you want Federal Express to require a signature for receipt. If you do not check this box, no signature will be required. **Federal Express will not deliver to P.O. boxes or A.P.O addresses.**		$16	
Total amount submitted or to be charged to credit card: (This amount must be at least $13.)			

Type of payment: ☐Credit Card ☐Money order ☐Check

If paying by credit card (MasterCard/VISA/Discover):

Name on card	Card number	Expiration date	3 digit security code

If paying by check or money order (make payable to Minnesota Department of Health):

Check/money order number

Due to high administrative costs, we are unable to issue refunds for overpayment.
Checks returned for non-payment will be charged a $30 fee according to Minnesota Statutes, section 604.113, subdivision 2 and civil penalties may be imposed.

Send application and payment:

By FAX to 651-201-5740

By MAIL to:
Minnesota Department of Health
Central Cashiering – Vital Records
PO Box 64499
St. Paul, MN 55164-0499

By EMAIL to health.issuance@state.mn.us

If you have questions, please contact us at health.issuance@state.mn.us.

If you submit this application to a local issuance office, Federal Express delivery may not be an option. All payment types may not be accepted. Call the local issuance office before sending your application to confirm payment types and return mail services.

D103 REV 03/2013

ADOPTEE'S REQUEST FOR ORIGINAL BIRTH RECORD INFORMATION AND SEARCH FOR AFFIDAVIT OF DISCLOSURE/NON-DISCLOSURE

To be completed by the adopted person age 19 or older, original signature notarized and submitted to the Minnesota Department of Health including a $13 fee.

CURRENT INFORMATION				
FIRST NAME	MIDDLE NAME		LAST NAME
DATE OF BIRTH	SEX	RACE	CITY & COUNTY OF BIRTH
MOTHER'S FIRST NAME	MIDDLE NAME		MAIDEN NAME
FATHER'S FIRST NAME	MIDDLE NAME		LAST NAME

BIRTH INFORMATION (IF KNOWN)			
FIRST NAME	MIDDLE NAME		LAST NAME
DATE OF BIRTH	SEX	RACE	CITY & COUNTY OF BIRTH
MOTHER'S FIRST NAME	MIDDLE NAME		MAIDEN NAME
FATHER'S FIRST NAME	MIDDLE NAME		LAST NAME

ADOPTION (IF KNOWN)		
ADOPTION TYPE	COUNTY OR ADOPTION AGENCY	
☐ Customary/Tribal ☐ International ☐ State Guardianship ☐ Private Domestic ☐ Step-Parent		
	DATE ADOPTION FINALIZED	COURT WHERE ADOPTION OCCURED

Applicant Name (please print)			
Address			
Daytime Phone		Email	

Your signature must be notarized.

Applicant Signature		Date	

Signed or attested before me on: ____________________ Notary Public Signature: ____________________

My commission expires: ____________________

Please mail request form and $13 fee to:
Minnesota Department of Health
Vital Records Office
PO Box 64882
St. Paul, MN 55164-0882

Send your requests to:

Mississippi State Department of Health
Vital Records
(Location: 571 Stadium Drive)
P.O. Box 1700
Jackson, MS 39215-1700

Tel. (601) 576-7450; (601) 576-7981
E-mail: VRInfo@msdh.state.ms.us
www.msdh.state.ms.us/

The Vital Records Office has birth and death records from November 1, 1912, and marriage records from January 1, 1926, to June 30, 1938, and from January 1, 1942, to present. For marriage records July 1, 1938, to December 31, 1941, contact the Circuit Court clerk in the county where the marriage license was issued.

Vital Records does not maintain divorce records, but a five-year search of the divorce indexes is available for January 1, 1926, to June 30, 1938, and for January 1, 1942, to present, for a fee of $15.00. For a certified copy of the divorce decree, contact the Chancery clerk in the county in which the divorce was granted.

Cost for a certified Birth Certificate	$15.00
Cost for a certified Marriage Certificate	$15.00
Cost for a certified Death Certificate	$15.00
Cost for a duplicate copy, when ordered at the same time	$5.00

For Genealogy Research:

The Mississippi Department of Archives & History Library (200 North Street, P.O. Box 571, Jackson, MS 39205-0571; tel. 601-576-6876; http://mdah.state.ms.us/arrec/gen_research.php) has copies on microfiche of the Department of Health's death certificates November 1912–1943; microfilm copies of most of the original marriage books held by the county courthouses; and an index to Session Acts 1817–1865 that lists divorces. A portion of the 50 microfilm rolls pertaining to the operation of the Mississippi Freedmen's Bureau includes marriage records of some of the newly freed slaves.

For Adoption Record information, contact:

Mississippi Department of Human Services
Post Adoption Unit
P.O. Box 352
Jackson, MS 39205

Tel. (800) 345-6626
www.mdhs.state.ms.us/fcs_adoptall.html

APPLICATION FOR CERTIFIED MISSISSIPPI BIRTH CERTIFICATE
Mississippi State Department of Health
Vital Records
Post Office Box 1700, Jackson, Mississippi 39215-1700

FULL NAME ON BIRTH RECORD	FIRST	MIDDLE	LAST
HAS NAME CHANGED SINCE BIRTH? □ Yes □ No	If so, what was original name?		
DATE OF BIRTH	MONTH	DAY	YEAR
STATE FILE NUMBER IF KNOWN			
PLACE OF BIRTH	COUNTY	CITY	STATE
SEX □ MALE □ FEMALE	**RACE**		
FULL MAIDEN NAME OF MOTHER	FIRST	MIDDLE	LAST
FULL NAME OF FATHER	FIRST	MIDDLE	LAST
PERSON REQUESTING CERTIFIED COPY			
RELATIONSHIP TO APPLICANT	**PURPOSE FOR WHICH NEEDED**		
SIGNATURE OF APPLICANT	**DATE**		

A BIRTH RECORD SEARCH REQUIRES ADVANCE PAYMENT OF A ***NON REFUNDABLE*** SEARCH FEE OF $15.00 AND VALID PHOTO IDENTIFICATION.

The $15.00 fee entitles the applicant to one Certified copy of the birth record on file of if the record is not found a "Not on File" statement will be issued. Surrounding counties and five years centered on year of birth are searched if record is not located within county or year specified.

$ 15.00 X 1 = $15.00

Additional Certified copies of the same record ordered at the same. $5.00 for each additional certified copy.

$ 5.00 X ___ = ___

TOTAL AMOUNT ENCLOSED. Check or Money Order payable to Mississippi Vital Records. Mississippi law allows an additional Service charge for dishonored checks. **(DO NOT SEND CASH)**

TOTALS No. of copies ___ Amt. Enclosed ___

PHOTO IDENTIFICATION REQUIRED

Failure to provide the proper identification will result in the application being returned to you without processing. Acceptable forms of identification are: **Valid Driver's License, State Issued Identification Card, Passport, and/or Military Identification Card, Valid School, College or University Identifications.** (See back for other acceptable forms).

APPLICANT NAME/DELIVERY INFORMATION

Pursuant to Section 41-57-2 of the Mississippi Code of 1972, Annotated and as defined by Mississippi State Board of Health Rules and Regulations only person having legitimate and tangible interest in a birth certificate is entitled to obtain a copy. Anyone obtaining a copy of a birth certificate under false pretenses is subject to the penalties as described in Section 41-57-27 of the Mississippi Code.

PRINT YOUR MAILING ADDRESS HERE

Applicant Name (Type or Print)			
Delivery Address (include apt number)			
City	**State**	**ZIP Code**	**Phone Number, including area code**

DO NOT WRITE IN THE SPACES BELOW – FOR OFFICE USE ONLY

12 –36	S.C.	SUP.
37 – 66	S.C.	P.
S.C.	C.D.	CWA.

INFORMATION AND INSTRUCTIONS FOR BIRTH RECORD APPLICATION

Eligibility: A certified copy of a birth certificate can be issued only to a person with legitimate and tangible interest as defined by the Rules Governing the Registration and Certification of Vital Events. Primarily this is:

1) Registrant (the child named on the record), if of legal age.
2) Parent(s) listed on the birth record, if VR office has not been notified of termination of parental rights.
3) Spouse, sibling(s), or grandparent(s)/child(ren) of registrant, proof of relationship required.
4) Legal Guardian, guardianship papers must be provided.
5) Legal representative of one of the above persons, proof of representation must be provided.
6) Licensed adoption agencies working within the statutory authority of §93-17-205.
7) Other person(s) by court order, certified copy of court order must be provided.

Birth records are available for genealogy purposes for birth events occurring over 100 years ago. Genealogy must be provided as purpose for certificate and family relationship to the registrant must be specified. Plain paper copies rather than certified copies are provided for genealogy purposes.

Requirements for Ordering: If applicant is self, spouse, parent, grandparent, sibling, child, grandchild, guardian, or legal representative, then the applicant must provide a completed application and a copy of a valid photo identification of the applicant. Acceptable forms of identification are the following:

■ Photo Driver's License	■ Photo State Issued ID	■ Employment ID
■ School, College or University ID	■ US Military ID	■ Tribal ID
■ Alien Registration/Permanent Resident Card	■ Temporary Resident Card	■ US Passport

OR two forms of identification from the following list:

■ Social Security Card	■ Utility Bill (showing address)	■ Medicaid Card
■ Snap/EBT card (showing address)	■ Work Identification	■ Veteran Universal Access ID Card

Guardian or legal representative must submit proof of guardianship/legal representation with this application. Legal representatives must provide attorney bar number, name of person represented, and their relationship to the registrant. If you are an agent of local, state or federal agency requesting a record, indicate in the space provided for "relationship" the name of the agency. If you do not have one of the above referenced documents, please contact Vital Records at 601-576-7981.

Relationship to Applicant: A person ordering his or her own certificate should enter "SELF" in this space. Also, explain if name has been changed by marriage, legal name change (when and where), etc. Others must identify their relationship to the registrant clearly.

Nonrefundable: Vital record fees are nonrefundable, with the exception of fees paid for additional copies when no record is found.

Failure to Receive: Complaints of failure to receive certified records will be honored within 6 months of the original request. If the copy was to be returned to you by U.S. Postal Service, please allow 3 weeks after mailing the request before inquiring. Inquiry about copies ordered with payment for special courier delivery should be made within 7 days of the request. Mail returned because of insufficient address or address changes will be re-mailed if this office is notified of correct address within 6 months of request.

Options for Service: Certified copies of birth records may be ordered in person, by mail, or, if paying by credit card, online or by telephone. Processing time is generally 7 – 10 working days after receipt of request. If amendment action is necessary, additional processing time will be required. **Payment of fees is required at the time of ordering.**

- **WALK-IN SERVICE** is available at 571 Stadium Drive, Jackson, Mississippi between the hours of 8:00 am and 5:00 pm. Most records will be available while you wait, some require special processing and will be mailed within 7 - 10 days of the request.
- **MAIL-IN** requests, either on the form provided or as a free form request will be processed in the order received and will be returned by regular U.S. Postal Service, unless accompanied by a prepaid special courier self-addressed envelope.
- **PAYMENT BY CREDIT CARD** can be done using an online service or by telephone. The private company approved to handle credit card transactions for Mississippi birth records can be accessed by calling 601-576-7988 or by visiting www.msdh.state.ms.us/phs and clicking on link for online ordering. If you have questions or need additional assistance call 601-576-7981. A recorded message outlining ordering requirements and options can be accessed by dialing 601-576-7450.

MAIL THIS APPLICATION WITH PAYMENT AND COPY OF IDENTIFICATION TO:
MISSISSIPPI VITAL RECORDS
P.O. BOX 1700
JACKSON, MS 39215-1700

APPLICATION FOR CERTIFIED MISSISSIPPI STATISTICAL RECORD OF MARRIAGE

Mississippi State Department of Health
Vital Records
P. O. Box 1700, Jackson, Mississippi 39215-1700

INFORMATION ABOUT BRIDE AND GROOM WHOSE STATISTICAL RECORD OF MARRIAGE IS REQUESTED (Please Print)			
NAME OF GROOM	FIRST NAME	MIDDLE NAME	LAST NAME
NAME OF BRIDE	FIRST NAME	MIDDLE NAME	LAST NAME
DATE OF MARRIAGE	MONTH	DAY	YEAR (FOUR DIGIT)
PLACE OF MARRIAGE	COUNTY	CITY OR TOWN	STATE
PLACE LICENSE WAS ISSUED	COUNTY	CITY OR TOWN	STATE

PERSON REQUESTING CERTIFIED COPY	
RELATIONSHIP OR INTEREST OF PERSON REQUESTING CERTIFICATE	**PURPOSE FOR WHICH COPY IS TO BE USED**
SIGNATURE OF APPLICANT	**DATE**

A MARRIAGE RECORD SEARCH REQUIRES ADVANCE PAYMENT OF A *NON-REFUNDABLE* SEARCH FEE OF $15.00 AND VALID PHOTO IDENTIFICATION

The $15.00 fee entitles the applicant to on Certified copy of the marriage record on file (Records have been kept since January 1, 1926. From July 1, 1938 to December 31, 1941, records were kept only by the Circuit Court Clerk in the county in which the marriage license was issued.) If the record is not found, a "Not on File" statement will be issued. Surrounding counties and five years centered on year of marriage are searched if record is not located within county or year specified.

$15.00 X 1 = $15.00

Additional Certified copies of the same certificate ordered at the same time. $5.00 for each additional copy.

$ 5.00 X ____ = ____

TOTAL AMOUNT ENCLOSED. Check or Money Order payable to Mississippi Vital Records. Mississippi law allows an additional Service charge for dishonored checks. **(DO NOT SEND CASH)**

	No. of copies	Amt. Enclosed
TOTALS		

PHOTO IDENTIFICATION REQUIRED

Failure to provide the proper identification will result in the application being returned to you without processing. Acceptable forms of identification are: **Valid Driver's License, State Issued Identification Card, Passport, and/or Military Identification Card, Valid School, College or University Identifications.** (See back for other acceptable forms).

APPLICANT NAME/DELIVERY INFORMATION

Pursuant to Section 41-57-2 of the Mississippi Code of 1975, Annotated, and as defined by Mississippi State Board of Health Rules and Regulations, I hereby certify that I have a legitimate and tangible interest in the death record requested. I understand that obtaining a record under false pretenses may subject me to the penalty as described in Section 41-57-27 of the Mississippi Code of 1972, Annotated.

PRINT YOUR MAILING ADDRESS HERE

Applicant Name (Type or Print)			
Delivery Address, including APT. number if applicable			**Home phone number, including area code**
City	**State**	**ZIP code**	**Work phone number, including area code**

DO NOT WRITE IN THE SPACES BELOW – FOR OFFICE USE ONLY

12 – 36	S.C.	SUP.
37 – 66	S.C.	P.
S.C.	C.D.	CWA.

INFORMATION AND INSTRUCTIONS FOR MARRIAGE RECORD APPLICATION

Eligibility: A certified copy of a marriage certificate can be issued only to a person with legitimate and tangible interest as defined by the Rules Governing the Registration and Certification of Vital Events. Primarily this is:

1) Registrant(s), persons listed on the record.
2) Parent(s) of the registrant listed on the marriage record, proof of relationship required.
3) Spouse, sibling(s), or grandparent(s)/child(ren) of registrant, proof of relationship required.
4) Legal representative of one of the above persons, proof of representation must be provided.
5) Other person(s) by court order, certified copy of court order must be provided.

Marriage records are available for genealogy purposes for marriage events occurring over 100 years ago. Genealogy must be provided as purpose for certificate and family relationship to the registrant must be specified. Plain paper copies rather than certified copies are provided for genealogy purposes.

Requirements for Ordering: If applicant is self, spouse, parent, grandparent, sibling, child, grandchild, or legal representative, then the applicant must provide a completed application and a copy of a valid photo identification of the applicant. Acceptable forms of identification are the following:

■ Photo Driver's License	■ Photo State Issued ID	■ Employment ID
■ School, College or University ID	■ US Military ID	■ Tribal ID
■ Alien Registration/Permanent Resident Card	■ Temporary Resident Card	■ US Passport

OR two forms of identification from the following list:

■ Social Security Card	■ Utility Bill (showing address)	■ Medicaid Card
■ Snap/EBT card (showing address)	■ Work Identification	■ Veteran Universal Access ID Card

Legal representative must submit proof of legal representation with this application. Legal representatives must provide attorney bar number, name of person represented, and their relationship to the registrant. If you are an agent of local, state or federal agency requesting a record, indicate in the space provided for "relationship" the name of the agency.

Relationship to Registrant:: A person ordering his or her own certificate should enter "SELF" in this space. Also, explain if name has been changed by marriage, legal name change (when and where), etc. Others must identify their relationship to the registrant clearly.

Nonrefundable: Vital record fees are nonrefundable, with the exception of fees paid for additional copies when no record is found.

Failure to Receive: Complaints of failure to receive certified records will be honored within 6 months of the original request. If the copy was to be returned to you by U.S. Postal Service, please allow 3 weeks after mailing the request before inquiring. Inquiry about copies ordered with payment for special courier delivery should be made within 7 days of the request. Mail returned because of insufficient address or address changes will be re-mailed if this office is notified of correct address within 6 months of request.

Options for Service: Certified copies of birth records may be ordered in person, by mail, or, if paying by credit card, online or by telephone. Processing time is generally 7 – 10 working days after receipt of request. If amendment action is necessary, additional processing time will be required. **Payment of fees is required at the time of ordering.**

- **WALK-IN SERVICE** is available at 571 Stadium Drive, Jackson, Mississippi between the hours of 8:00 am and 5:00 pm. Marriage records are not available same day, all records will be mailed 7 – 10 business days after receipt of request.
- **MAIL-IN** requests, either on the form provided or as a free form request will be processed in the order received and will be returned by regular U.S. Postal Service, unless accompanied by a prepaid special courier self-addressed envelope.
- **PAYMENT BY CREDIT CARD** can be done using an online service or by telephone. The private company approved to handle credit card transactions for Mississippi birth records can be accessed by calling 601-576-7988 or by visiting www.msdh.state.ms/phs and clicking on link for online ordering. If you have questions or need additional assistance call 601-576-7981. A recorded message outlining ordering requirements and options can be accessed by dialing 601-576-7450.

MAIL THIS APPLICATION WITH PAYMENT TO

MISSISSIPPI VITAL RECORDS
P.O. BOX 1700
JACKSON, MS 39215-1700

APPLICATION FOR CERTIFIED MISSISSIPPI DEATH CERTIFICATE

Mississippi State Department of Health
Vital Records
P. O. Box 1700, Jackson, Mississippi 39215-1700

FULL NAME OF DECEASED	FIRST		MIDDLE	LAST
DATE OF DEATH	MONTH		DAY	YEAR(4 DIGITS)
PLACE OF DEATH	COUNTY		CITY OR TOWN	STATE
SEX	**RACE**	**SOCIAL SECURITY NUMBER**	**AGE AT DEATH**	**STATE FILE NUMBER**
NAME OF FATHER			**NAME OF MOTHER**	
FUNERAL DIRECTOR	NAME		ADDRESS	

PERSON OR FACILITY REQUESTING COPY		
RELATIONSHIP OR INTEREST OF PERSON REQUESTING CERTIFICATE	**PURPOSE FOR WHICH CERTIFIED COPY IS TO BE USED**	
SIGNATURE OF APPLICANT		**DATE**

A DEATH RECORD SEARCH REQUIRES ADVANCE PAYMENT OF A ***NON REFUNDABLE*** SEARCH FEE OF $15.00 AND VALID PHOTO IDENTIFICATION.

The $15.00 fee entitles the applicant to one Certified copy of the death record on file (November 1, 1912 to present) or if the record is not found, a "Not on File" statement will be issued. Surrounding counties and five years centered on year of death are searched if record is not located within county or year specified.	$15.00	X	1	=	$15.00
Additional Certified copies of the same certificate ordered at the same time. $5.00 for each additional certified copy.	$ 5.00	X		=	
			No. of Copies		**Amt. Enclosed**
TOTAL AMOUNT ENCLOSED. Check or Money Order payable to Mississippi Vital Records. Mississippi law allows an additional Service charge for dishonored checks. **(DO NOT SEND CASH)**	**TOTALS**				

PHOTO IDENTIFICATION REQUIRED

Failure to provide the proper identification will result in the application being returned to you without processing. Acceptable forms of identification are: **Valid Driver's License, State Issued Identification Card, Passport, and/or Military Identification Card, Valid School, College or University Identifications.** (See back for other acceptable forms).

APPLICANT NAME/DELIVERY INFORMATION

Pursuant to Section 41-57-2 of the Mississippi Code of 1975, Annotated, and as defined by Mississippi State Board of Health Rules and Regulations, I hereby certify that I have a legitimate and tangible interest in the death record requested. I understand that obtaining a record under false pretenses may subject me to the penalty as described in Section 41-57-27 of the Mississippi Code of 1972, Annotated.

PRINT YOUR MAILING ADDRESS HERE

Applicant Name (Type or Print)			
Delivery Address, including APT number if applicable			**Home phone number, including area code**
City	**State**	**ZIP Code**	**Work phone number, including area code**

DO NOT WRITE IN THE SPACES BELOW – FOR OFFICE USE ONLY

12 – 36	S.C.	SUP.
37 – 66	S.C.	P.
S.C.	C.D.	CWA.

INFORMATION AND INSTRUCTIONS FOR DEATH RECORD APPLICATION

Eligibility: A certified copy of a death certificate can be issued only to a person with legitimate and tangible interest as defined by the Rules Governing the Registration and Certification of Vital Events. Primarily this is:

1) Parent(s) listed on the death record.
2) Spouse, sibling(s), or grandparent(s)/child(ren) of registrant, proof of relationship required.
3) Informant, must be listed on death record.
4) Legal Guardian, guardianship papers much be provided.
5) Legal representative of one of the above persons, proof of representation must be provided.
6) Other person(s) by court order, certified copy of court order must be provided.
7) Funeral Home, must be the funeral home on record that took possession of the body.

Death records are available for genealogy purposes for death events occurring over 50 years ago. Genealogy must be provided as purpose for certificate and family relationship to the registrant must be specified. Plain paper copies rather than certified copies are provided for genealogy purposes.

Requirements for Ordering: If applicant is spouse, parent, grandparent, sibling, child, grandchild, or informant, guardian, legal representative, then the applicant must provide a completed application and a copy of a valid photo identification of the applicant. Acceptable forms of identification are the following:

■ Photo Driver's License	■ Photo State Issued ID	■ Employment ID
■ School, College or University ID	■ US Military ID	■ Tribal ID
■ Alien Registration/Permanent Resident Card	■ Temporary Resident Card	■ US Passport

OR two forms of identification from the following list:

■ Social Security Card	■ Utility Bill (showing address)	■ Medicaid Card
■ Snap/EBT card (showing address)	■ Work Identification	■ Veteran Universal Access ID Card

Guardian or legal representative must submit proof of guardianship/legal representation with this application. Legal representatives must provide attorney bar number, name of person represented, and their relationship to the registrant. If you are an agent of local, state or federal agency requesting a record, indicate in the space provided for "relationship" the name of the agency. If you do not have one of the above referenced documents, please contact Vital Records at 601-576-7981

Relationship or interest to Applicant: A person ordering a death certificate should enter the relationship or interest in this space. Others must identify their relationship to the registrant clearly.

Nonrefundable: Vital record fees are nonrefundable, with the exception of fees paid for additional copies when no record is found.

Failure to Receive: Complaints of failure to receive certified records will be honored within 6 months of the original request. If the copy was to be returned to you by U.S. Postal Service, please allow 3 weeks after mailing the request before inquiring. Inquiry about copies ordered with payment for special courier delivery should be made within 7 days of the request. Mail returned because of insufficient address or address changes will be re-mailed if this office is notified of correct address within 6 months of request.

Options for Service: Certified copies of death records may be ordered in person, by mail, or, if paying by credit card, online or by telephone. Processing time is generally 7 – 10 working days after receipt of request. If amendment action is necessary, additional processing time will be required. **Payment of fees is required at the time of ordering.**

- **WALK-IN SERVICE** is available at 571 Stadium Drive, Jackson, Mississippi between the hours of 8:00 am and 5:00 pm. Death records are not available same day, all records will be mailed 7 – 10 business days after receipt of request.
- **MAIL-IN** requests, either on the form provided or as a free form request will be processed in the order received and will be returned by regular U.S. Postal Service, unless accompanied by a prepaid special courier self-addressed envelope.
- **PAYMENT BY CREDIT CARD** can be done using an online service or by telephone. The private company approved to handle credit card transactions for Mississippi death records can be accessed by calling 601-576-7988 or by visiting www.msdh.state.ms.us/phs and clicking on link for online ordering. If you have questions or need additional assistance call 601-576-7981. A recorded message outlining ordering requirements and options can be accessed by dialing 601-576-7450.

MAIL THIS APPLICATION WITH PAYMENT TO
MISSISSIPPI VITAL RECORDS
P.O. BOX 1700
JACKSON, MS 39215-1700

MISSOURI

Send your requests to:

Missouri Department of Health and Senior Services
Bureau of Vital Records
(Location: 912 Wildwood)
P.O. Box 570
Jefferson City, MO 65102-0570

Tel. (573) 751-6387
E-mail: VitalRecordsInfo@health.mo.gov
http://health.mo.gov/data/vitalrecords/index.php

The Bureau of Vital Records has birth and death records from January 1, 1910, and marriage and divorce indexes from July 1, 1948. Missouri vital records are not open to the general public and can only be obtained by the individual, guardian, or other legal party.

People born in Missouri can also obtain a copy of their birth certificate from any local public health department. (Note: Vital records are not available at the St. Louis City Health Department; Missouri-born citizens can obtain records in the St. Louis City area at the Recorder of Deeds office at City Hall, 1200 Market Street, Room 127, St. Louis, MO 63103.)

Certified copies of marriage licenses are available from the Recorder of Deeds in the county where the license was obtained. Certified copies of divorce decrees are available from the Circuit Court clerk in the county where the decree was granted.

Cost for a certified Birth Certificate	$15.00
Cost for certified statement of Marriage	$15.00
Cost for certified statement of Divorce	$15.00
Cost for a certified Death Certificate	$13.00
Cost for a duplicate Death Certificate, when ordered at the same time	$10.00

For Genealogy Research:

The Missouri State Archives (600 W. Main Street, P.O. Box 1747, Jefferson City, MO 65102; tel. 573-751-3280; www.sos.mo.gov/archives/contact.asp) has microfilm copies of county records that include marriages, deeds, and circuit and probate court materials. It also makes available an online database of pre-1910 birth and death records and an online database containing death records created after 1910 and over 50 years old (www.sos.mo.gov/archives/resources/birthdeath/).

For Adoption Record information, contact:

Missouri Department of Social Services
Children's Division
Adoption Information Registry
P.O. Box 88
Jefferson City, MO 65103-0088

Tel. (573) 751-2981
www.dss.mo.gov/cd/adopt/adoir.htm

MISSOURI DEPARTMENT OF HEALTH AND SENIOR SERVICES
BUREAU OF VITAL RECORDS

P.O. Box 570
Jefferson City, Missouri 65102-0570

APPLICATION FOR A VITAL RECORD

Applicants must show identification when requesting certified copies of a vital record at the state health department. **Mail-in requests must be notarized by an acceptable notary public.**

Missouri law requires a non-refundable search fee for each five-year search of the files. If eligibility requirements are met and a record is found, applicant is entitled to certified copies. A statement will be issued if no record is found. **FEE MUST ACCOMPANY APPLICATION**. FEES ARE VALID FOR ONE YEAR. Check or money order payable to: **Missouri Department of Health and Senior Services.**

State recording of birth and death records began January 1, 1910.

☐ **BIRTH** ☐ **FETAL DEATH REPORT** ☐ **STILLBIRTH** NUMBER OF COPIES ______ (FIRST COPY ISSUED $15; EACH ADDITIONAL COPY $15)

FULL NAME ON CERTIFICATE ______________________

ALSO KNOWN AS (INDICATE IF BIRTH COULD BE RECORDED UNDER ANOTHER NAME) ______________________

DATE OF BIRTH __________ PLACE OF BIRTH (CITY, COUNTY, STATE) ______________________

HOSPITAL ______________________ SEX FEMALE ☐ MALE ☐ RACE __________

FULL NAME OF FATHER ______________________

FULL MAIDEN NAME OF MOTHER ______________________

DEATH NUMBER OF COPIES ______ (FIRST COPY ISSUED $13; EACH ADDITIONAL COPY OF THE SAME RECORD ORDERED AT THE SAME TIME $10)

FULL NAME ON CERTIFICATE ______________________

DATE OF BIRTH ______________________ SEX FEMALE ☐ MALE ☐ RACE __________

DATE OF DEATH __________ PLACE OF DEATH (CITY, COUNTY, STATE) ______________________

FULL NAME OF SPOUSE ______________________

FULL NAME OF FATHER ______________________

FULL MAIDEN NAME OF MOTHER ______________________

PLEASE ENCLOSE A SELF ADDRESSED STAMPED ENVELOPE WITH YOUR REQUEST (PRINT THE FOLLOWING INFORMATION)

APPLICANT'S NAME ______________________ PHONE NUMBER __________

APPLICANT'S STREET ADDRESS ______________________

APPLICANT'S CITY/TOWN ______________________ STATE __________ ZIP __________

PURPOSE FOR CERTIFICATE REQUEST ______________________

YOUR RELATIONSHIP TO PERSON NAMED ON RECORD (IF LEGAL GUARDIAN, MUST PROVIDE GUARDIANSHIP PAPERS). IF LEGAL REPRESENTATIVE, INDICATE LEGAL RELATIONSHIP. ______________________

➢ **MAIL-IN REQUESTS MUST BE NOTARIZED. ALL APPLICATIONS MUST BE SIGNED.**

I ______________________, SUBJECT TO THE PENALTY OF PERJURY, DO SOLEMNLY DECLARE AND AFFIRM THAT I AM ELIGIBLE TO RECEIVE A CERTIFIED COPY OF THE VITAL RECORD(S) REQUESTED ABOVE AND THAT THE INFORMATION CONTAINED IN THIS APPLICATION IS TRUE AND CORRECT TO THE BEST OF MY KNOWLEDGE.

➢ **APPLICANT'S SIGNATURE** ______________________ **DATE** __________

NOTARY PUBLIC EMBOSSER SEAL	STATE		COUNTY
	SUBSCRIBED, DECLARED AND AFFIRMED BEFORE ME, THIS ______ DAY OF __________, 20 ___		USE RUBBER STAMP IN CLEAR AREA BELOW
	NOTARY PUBLIC SIGNATURE	MY COMMISSION EXPIRES	
	NOTARY PUBLIC NAME (TYPED OR PRINTED)		

WARNING: False application for a certified copy of a vital record is a crime.

MISSOURI DEPARTMENT OF HEALTH AND SENIOR SERVICES
BUREAU OF VITAL RECORDS
APPLICATION FOR A VITAL RECORD

P.O. Box 570
Jefferson City, Missouri 65102-0570

Applicants must show identification when requesting certified copies of a vital record at the state health department. **Mail-in requests must be notarized by an acceptable notary public.**

Missouri law requires a non-refundable search fee for each five-year search of the files. If eligibility requirements are met and a record is found, applicant is entitled to certified copies. A statement will be issued if no record is found. **FEE MUST ACCOMPANY APPLICATION.** FEES ARE VALID FOR ONE YEAR. Check or money order payable to: **Missouri Department of Health and Senior Services.**

State recording of marriage and divorce reports began July 1, 1948.

MARRIAGE STATEMENT NUMBER OF COPIES ________ (FIRST COPY ISSUED $15; EACH ADDITIONAL COPY $15)

FOR A COPY OF A MARRIAGE LICENSE CONTACT THE RECORDER OF DEEDS IN THE COUNTY WHERE THE LICENSE WAS ISSUED.

FULL NAME OF GROOM ____________________

FULL MAIDEN NAME OF BRIDE ____________________

DATE OF MARRIAGE ____________________ PREVIOUS **MARRIED** NAME ____________________

LICENSE ISSUED (CITY, COUNTY) ____________________

DIVORCE STATEMENT NUMBER OF COPIES ________ (FIRST COPY ISSUED $15; EACH ADDITIONAL COPY $15)

FOR DIVORCE DECREE OF MARRIAGE CONTACT THE CIRCUIT CLERK'S OFFICE IN THE COUNTY WHERE THE DECREE WAS GRANTED.

FULL NAME OF HUSBAND ____________________

FULL MAIDEN NAME OF WIFE ____________________

DATE DECREE ISSUED ____________________ PREVIOUS **MARRIED** NAME ____________________

DECREE ISSUED (CITY, COUNTY) ____________________

PLEASE ENCLOSE A SELF ADDRESSED STAMPED ENVELOPE WITH YOUR REQUEST (PRINT THE FOLLOWING INFORMATION)

APPLICANT'S NAME ____________________ PHONE NUMBER ____________________

APPLICANT'S STREET ADDRESS ____________________

APPLICANT'S CITY/TOWN ____________________ STATE ____________ ZIP ____________

PURPOSE FOR CERTIFICATE REQUEST ____________________

YOUR RELATIONSHIP TO PERSON NAMED ON RECORD (IF LEGAL GUARDIAN, MUST PROVIDE GUARDIANSHIP PAPERS). IF LEGAL REPRESENTATIVE, INDICATE LEGAL RELATIONSHIP. ____________________

- **MAIL-IN REQUESTS MUST BE NOTARIZED. ALL APPLICATIONS MUST BE SIGNED.**

I ____________________, SUBJECT TO THE PENALTY OF PERJURY, DO SOLEMNLY DECLARE AND AFFIRM THAT I AM ELIGIBLE TO RECEIVE A CERTIFIED COPY OF THE VITAL RECORD(S) REQUESTED ABOVE AND THAT THE INFORMATION CONTAINED IN THIS APPLICATION IS TRUE AND CORRECT TO THE BEST OF MY KNOWLEDGE.

- **APPLICANT'S SIGNATURE** ____________________ **DATE** ____________________

NOTARY PUBLIC EMBOSSER SEAL	STATE		COUNTY
	SUBSCRIBED, DECLARED AND AFFIRMED BEFORE ME, THIS ________ DAY OF ____________, 20 ____		USE RUBBER STAMP IN CLEAR AREA BELOW
	NOTARY PUBLIC SIGNATURE	MY COMMISSION EXPIRES	
	NOTARY PUBLIC NAME (TYPED OR PRINTED)		

WARNING: False application for a certified copy of a vital record is a crime.

MO 580-2995 (3-11)

VS-151MD

MISSOURI DEPARTMENT OF SOCIAL SERVICES
CHILDREN'S DIVISION
ADOPTION INFORMATION REGISTRY

RETURN TO: MISSOURI CHILDREN'S DIVISION
ADOPTION INFORMATION REGISTRY
P.O. BOX 88
JEFFERSON CITY, MISSOURI 65103

TO BE COMPLETED BY ADULT ADOPTEE WHO DESIRES CONTACT WITH BIOLOGICAL PARENTS OR SIBLINGS

ADOPTED ADULT REGISTRATION

NOTE: THE REGISTRATION BY AN ADOPTED ADULT CAN BE ACCEPTED ONLY IF THE ADOPTEE IS 18 YEARS OF AGE OR OLDER.

SECTION A – REQUEST

PURSUANT TO THE AUTHORITY GRANTED IN 453.121 RSMo I AM REQUESTING REGISTRATION OF MY DESIRE FOR FUTURE CONTACT WITH MY BIOLOGICAL PARENT/S OR BIOLOGICAL SIBLING/S. I UNDERSTAND THAT I MAY CHANGE THIS INFORMATION AT A LATER DATE SHOULD MY LOCATION OR CIRCUMSTANCES CHANGE.

PLEASE CHECK AND PROVIDE A COPY OF ONE OF THE FOLLOWING TO CONFIRM YOUR IDENTITY:

☐ BIRTH CERTIFICATE ☐ ADOPTION DECREE ☐ DRIVER'S LICENSE OR PHOTO ID

FULL BIRTH NAME	LAST	FIRST	MIDDLE	RACE ☐ White ☐ Black ☐ Indian/Alaskan ☐ Asian/Pacific Islander	SEX ☐ M ☐ F
FULL ADOPTED NAME	LAST	FIRST	MIDDLE		
CURRENT NAME	LAST	FIRST	MIDDLE	SOCIAL SECURITY NUMBER	
CURRENT ADDRESS				PHONE NUMBER	
DATE OF BIRTH	PLACE OF BIRTH	CITY	STATE	COUNTY	
AGENCY/INDIVIDUAL THAT MADE PLACEMENT			COUNTY WHERE ADOPTION FINALIZED	DATE OF ADOPTION	
ADDRES	STREET	CITY	STATE	ZIP	

SECTION B- ADOPTIVE PARENTS

ADOPTIVE FATHER'S FULL NAME	LAST	FIRST	MIDDLE	SOCIAL SECURITY NUMBER
CURRENT OR LAST KNOWN ADDRESS				PHONE NUMBER
ADOPTIVE MOTHER'S FULL NAME	LAST	FIRST	MIDDLE	SOCIAL SECURITY NUMBER
CURRENT OR LAST KNOWN ADDRESS				PHONE NUMBER

SECTION C – BIOLOGICAL PARENTS and SIBLING INFORMATION (COMPLETE ALL KNOWN INFORMATION)				
BIOLOGICAL FATHER'S FULL NAME	LAST	FIRST	MIDDLE	SOCIAL SECURITY NUMBER
BIOLOGICAL MOTHER'S FULL NAME	LAST	FIRST	MIDDLE	SOCIAL SECURITY NUMBER
OTHER KNOWN LAST NAMES USED BY MOTHER				
BIOLOGICAL SIBLING NAMES				DATES OF BIRTH
PLEASE INDICATE HOW YOU ARE AWARE OF YOUR SIBLINGS				

SECTION D – CERTIFICATION		
I SOLEMNLY CERTIFY THAT ALL OF THE INFORMATION PROVIDED ON THIS REGISTRATION IS TRUE AND ACCURATE TO THE BEST OF MY KNOWLEDGE	SIGNATURE OF REGISTRANT	DATE

TO BE COMPLETED BY CHILDREN'S DIVISION STAFF

REGISTRATION REQUEST FILED BY:	BIOLOGICAL PARENT	DATE
	ADOPTED CHILD	DATE
	BIOLOGICAL SIBLING	DATE
POSSIBLE MATCH LOCATED		DATE

NOTICE SENT TO LOCAL OFFICE FOR CONFIRMATION OF IDENTITY AND/OR NOTIFICATION OF OTHER PARTY TO MATCH IF IDENTITY CONFIRMED

☐ YES ☐ NO DATE

SECTION G – *TO BE COMPLETED BY LOCAL OFFICE STAFF/PRIVATE AGENCY*

DETERMINE STATUS OF BIOLOGICAL PARENT NOT REGISTERED WITH ADOPTION REGISTRY

☐ UNKNOWN
☐ DECEASED
☐ CANNOT BE LOCATED
☐ HAS NOW COMPLETED ADOPTION REGISTRY FORM (ATTACHED)
☐ REFUSED TO REGISTER
☐ HAS FILED AFFIDAVIT WITH COURT
CONFIRMED DATE

WORKER	DATE	ADDRESS
PRIVATE/COUNTY AGENCY		

MONTANA

Send your requests to:

Office of Vital Statistics
Montana Department of Public Health
and Human Services
Vital Records Office
(Location: 111 North Sanders, Room 6)
P.O. Box 4210
Helena, MT 59604-4210

Tel. (406) 444-2685
E-mail: HHSVitalRecords@mt.gov
https://dphhs.mt.gov/certificates/ordercertificates.shtml

The Vital Records Office has birth and death records from 1907 to the present. Informational copies of a birth certificate are available from the Vital Records Office to anyone as long as the event occurred more than 30 years prior to the date of application. Certified death certificates will be issued to anyone who submits a completed application, establishes his or her identity, and lists the reason for needing the copy.

Certified copies of marriage and divorce records are not available from the Vital Records Office.

Cost for a certified Birth Certificate	$12.00
Cost for a certified Death Certificate	$12.00
Cost for a duplicate copy, when ordered at the same time	$ 5.00
Cost for an informational copy of Birth Certificate	$10.00
Cost for an informational copy of Death Certificate	$10.00

Send your requests for Marriage and Divorce Certificates and early vital records to:

Clerk
County District Court
(County Seat), MT

For Genealogy Research:

The Montana Historical Society (225 N. Roberts, P.O. Box 201201, Helena, MT 59620-1201; tel. 406-444-2694; http://mhs.mt.gov/research/library/collections.asp) has been the unofficial archives of the Montana state government since 1865 and the official state archives since 1969. Their holdings include marriage records and naturalization records from the District Court clerk's office. The Research Center of the Montana Historical Society maintains a large collection of library, archival, and photographic materials that may be useful in compiling family histories.

For Adoption Record information, contact:

Montana Department of Public Health and Human Services
Child & Family Services
P.O. Box 8005
Helena, MT 59604-8005

Tel. (406) 841-2400

MONTANA VITAL STATISTICS
111 N SANDERS RM 6 / PO BOX 4210
HELENA, MONTANA 59604-4210
Phone: 406-444-2685

PLEASE READ THESE INSTRUCTIONS CAREFULLY

WHO CAN ORDER A BIRTH CERTIFICATE?

Only those authorized by 50-15-121 MCA and 37.8.126 ARM, which includes the registrant (14 years old or older), the registrant's spouse, children (with proof of relationship), parents, grandparents (with proof of relationship), a caretaker relative, guardian, an authorized representative, or those who provide documentation showing it is needed for determination or protection of the individuals personal or property rights. Proof of relationship, guardianship, caretaker relative, or authorization is required to obtain a certify copy of a birth record.

Step-relatives, in-laws, aunts, uncles, cousins, ex-spouses, and a natural parent of an adoptive child are not eligible to receive a certified copy of a birth certificate.

IDENTIFICATION IS REQUIRED

The person signing the request must provide an enlarged legible photocopy of both sides of their valid driver's license or other legal picture identification with a signature or the requestor must have this application notarized.

Suggested Identification

Picture ID with a Signature	OR Two Forms of ID – One MUST have a Signature		OR
• Driver's License • State ID Card • Passport • Military ID Card • Tribal	• Social Security Card • Work ID Card • Car registration/Insurance • Doctor/Medical record • Fishing License • US Military DD214 • Utility Bill with a current address • Voter Registration Card	• Credit/Debit/ATM Card • School ID Card • Library Card • Insurance Record • Pay Stub • Traffic/ Pawn ticket • Court record • Year Book	• Notarized Montana Office of Vital Statistics Statement to Identify certified Birth or Death Certificate Applicant form (you must provide the original letter, not a photocopy or faxed copy) • Have an authorized family member that has an ID order the certificate

If a picture ID with a signature is not available, two other forms of identification are required; one **MUST** have a signature. Please include photocopies **of both sides** of the ID when mailing your request

IMPORTANT: If the identification requirement is NOT met or if the application is incomplete, your request will be returned and significant delays in processing your order may occur.

FEE (All fees must be U.S. funds)

- CERTIFIED COPIES OF A BIRTH CERTIFICATE cost $12.00 for the first copy, $5.00 for each additional copy of the same record. **(non-refundable)**
- INFORMATIONAL COPIES OF A BIRTH CERTIFICATE may be issued to anyone as long as the birth occurred 30 years prior to the date of application, **the cost is $10.00. (non-refundable)**
- CERTIFIED COPIES OF DOCUMENTS on file with the state (i.e. Acknowledgment of Paternity, correction affidavits), **the cost is $12.00 (non-refundable)**
- SEARCHES: $10.00 for the first 5 years searched, then $1.00 per year over the first five years per name requested. (An informational copy will be issued if record is found) **(non-refundable)**

PLEASE MAKE CHECKS PAYABLE TO: MONTANA VITAL RECORDS

Please complete the following information.

FULL First, Middle and Last Name on Birth Certificate: ____________________

Has name ever been changed other than marriage _____ No _____ Yes if so original name ____________________

Date of Birth: ____________________ Place of Birth (City or County): ____________________

Mother's **Full Maiden** Name: ____________________

Father's Full Name: ____________________ ____________# of copies needed

Your relationship to the certificate holder : ______________(self, mother, father etc) Reason the Birth Certificate is needed: ______________

Mailing or Delivery Address:

Name: ____________________ Applicant's Signature ____________________

Address: ____________________

City, State, Zip: ____________________ Daytime Telephone Number: ______________

Notary (For use if needed)

____________________ personally appeared before me and whose identity I proved on the basis of satisfactory evidence to be the signer of the above instrument.

Subscribed and sworn to before me this________ day of ______________ 20___

SEAL

Signature: ____________________
Printed Name: ____________________
Notary Public in and for the State of ____________________
Residing at ___________My commission Expires___________

Official Use Only

Date ____________________
Rec# ____________________
Amount ____________________
Cert # ____________________
Ser # ____________________
Comment ____________________
____

NOTICE: STATE LAW PROVIDES PENALTIES FOR PERSONS WHO WILLFULLY AND KNOWINGLY USE OR ATTEMPT TO USE THIS CERTIFICATE FOR ANY PURPOSE OF DECEPTION. (50-15-114, MCA)

MONTANA OFFICE OF VITAL STATISTICS
111 N SANDERS RM 6 / PO BOX 4210
HELENA, MONTANA 59604-4210
Phone: 406-444-2685

PLEASE READ THESE INSTRUCTIONS CAREFULLY

WHO CAN ORDER A DEATH CERTIFICATE?

Complete copies of a certified death certificate will be issued to anyone who submits a completed application, establishes their identity, and lists the reason for needing the copy. If a death certificate lists the cause of death as "pending autopsy" or "pending investigation", a certified copy which has the cause of death information removed will be issued.

IDENTIFICATION IS REQUIRED

The person signing the request must provide an enlarged legible photocopy of both sides of their valid driver's license or other legal picture identification with a signature or the requestor must have this application notarized.

Suggested Identification

Picture ID with a Signature	OR Two Forms of ID – One MUST have a Signature		OR
• Driver's License • State ID Card • Passport • Military ID Card • Tribal	• Social Security Card • Work ID Card • Car registration/Insurance • Doctor/Medical record • Fishing License • US Military DD 214 • Utility Bill with a current address • Voter Registration Card	• Credit/Debit/ATM Card • School ID Card • Library Card • Insurance Record • Pay Stub • Traffic/ Pawn ticket • Court record • Year Book	• Notarized Montana Office of Vital Statistics Statement to Identify certified Birth or Death Certificate Applicant form (you must provide the original letter, not a photocopy or faxed copy) • Have an authorized family member that has an ID order the certificate

If a picture ID with a signature is not available, two other forms of identification are required; one **MUST** have a signature. Please include photocopies **of both sides** of the ID when mailing your request

IMPORTANT: If the identification requirement is NOT met or if the application is incomplete, your request will be returned and significant delays in processing your order may occur.

FEE (All fees must be U.S. funds)

- **CERTIFIED COPIES OF A DEATH CERTIFICATE** cost $12.00 for the first copy, $5.00 for each additional copy of the same record. **(non-refundable)**
- **INFORMATIONAL COPIES OF A DEATH CERTIFICATE** the cost is $10.00. **(non-refundable)**
- **CERTIFIED COPIES OF DOCUMENTS** on file with the state (i.e., correction affidavits). **the cost is $12.00 (non-refundable)**
- **SEARCHES**: $10.00 for the first 5 years searched, then $1.00 per year over the first five years per name requested. (An informational copy will be issued if record is found) **(non-refundable)**

Please complete the following information.

Decedent's Name: ______________________

Date of Death (We need a date to begin searching if date is unknown): ______________ Date of Birth: ______________

Place of Death: ______________ Place of Birth: ______________

Parents Names: ______________________

Occupation: ______________ Spouse's Name: ______________

Number of Copies ________ Type of record needed? Certified ________ Not Certified ________

Reason record is needed ______________________

Mailing or Delivery Address:

Name: ______________________

Address: ______________________

City, State, Zip: ______________ Daytime Telephone Number: ______________

Signature of Applicant: ______________ **Relationship:** ______________

Notary (For use if needed)

______________ personally appeared before me and whose identity I proved on the basis of satisfactory evidence to be the signer of the above instrument.

Subscribed and sworn to before me this______________ day of ______________ 20___

Signature: ______________
Printed Name: ______________
SEAL Notary Public in and for the State of ______________
Residing at ______________My commission expires______________

Official Use Only

Date ______________
Rec # ______________
Amount ______________
Cert # ______________
Ser # ______________
Comment ______________

NOTICE: STATE LAW PROVIDES PENALTIES FOR PERSONS WHO WILLFULLY AND KNOWINGLY USE OR ATTEMPT TO USE THIS CERTIFICATE FOR ANY PURPOSE OF DECEPTION. (50-15-114, MCA)

NEBRASKA

Send your requests to:

Nebraska Department of Health & Human Services
Vital Records
(Location: 1333 O Street, Suite 130)
P.O. Box 95065
Lincoln, NE 68509-5065

Tel. (402) 471-2871
E-mail: DHHS.VitalRecords@nebraska.gov
http://dhhs.ne.gov/publichealth/pages/vitalrecords.aspx

The Vital Records Office has birth and death records from 1904, and marriage and divorce records from January 1, 1909. Birth certificates can be ordered over the Internet at the same price as mail or walk-in requests; go to https://www.nebraska.gov/hhs/birthcert/birthapp.php for more information.

For marriage records occurring prior to 1909, contact either the county clerk of the county in which the marriage license was issued or the State Historical Society (P.O. Box 82554, Lincoln, NE 68501; www.nebraskahistory.org).

For divorce records occurring prior to 1909, contact the clerk of the District Court in the county where the divorce was granted.

Cost for a certified Birth Certificate	$12.00
Cost for a certified Marriage Certificate	$11.00
Cost for a certified Divorce Record	$11.00
Cost for a certified Death Certificate	$11.00

For Genealogy Research:

Genealogy requests to the Vital Records Office must be made by mail and not through the Internet process. Only records that are 50 years old or older may be requested for family history. For more information about genealogy requests, go to http://dhhs.ne.gov/publichealth/Pages/ced_genealog.aspx.

The Nebraska State Historical Society (P.O. Box 82554, 1500 R Street, Lincoln, NE 68501; tel. 402-471-3270; www.nebraskahistory.org/) has the Omaha Birth Registry 1869–1907; Omaha Death Registry 1873–1915; a few vital records for early eastern Nebraska; records from some District Courts that may include divorces; and many other collections of interest to genealogical researchers.

For Adoption Record information, contact:

Adoption Search
Nebraska Department of Health & Human Services
Division of Children & Family Services
P.O. Box 95026
Lincoln, NE 68509-5044

Tel. (402) 471-9254
http://dhhs.ne.gov/children_family_services/Pages/adoption_searches.aspx

APPLICATION FOR CERTIFIED COPY OF BIRTH CERTIFICATE

This office has been registering births for persons born in Nebraska since **1904**.

PLEASE TYPE OR PRINT LEGIBLY

Full name at birth____
(If adopted, list adoptive name)

Month, day, and year of birth ____

City or town of birth ____________________ County of birth ____________________

Father's full name ____
(If adopted, list adoptive father's name)

Mother's full maiden name____
(If adopted, list adoptive mother's name)

Is this the record of an adopted person? ❑ Yes ❑ No

For what purpose is this record to be used? ____

If this is not your record, how are you related to the person named on the record? ____________________

Delayed Birth Certificate - Legislation passed in 1941 provides for the filing of delayed birth certificates for persons who were born prior to 1904 OR for persons whose births were not recorded at the time of birth.

Is this a delayed birth certificate? ❑ Yes ❑ No

WARNING: Section 71-649, Nebraska Revised Statutes: It is a felony to obtain, possess, use, sell, furnish, or attempt to obtain any vital record for purposes of deception.

SIGNATURE OF REQUESTOR ____________________

Type or print name____________________

Street Address____________________

City, State, Zip ____________________

Telephone Number: ____________________

Today's Date ____________________

(Please enclose a photocopy of your photo ID [i.e. current driver's license] when mailing in this request).

FOR OFFICE USE ONLY

❑ Check ❑ MO ❑ Cash

Amount Received____________________

Date Received ____________________

By Whom Received ____________________

PROOF OF IDENTIFICATION;

DL STATE ID OTHER

____

Fees are subject to change without notice. Please call our 24-hour recorded message at (402) 471-2871 to verify fees.

Number of certified copies________ x $12.00 each = $________ Total
(Please make checks payable to Vital Records)

Mail to:
Vital Records
PO Box 95065
Lincoln, NE 68509-5065
(Please enclose a stamped, self-addressed business size envelope.)

Bring to:
Vital Records
1033 O Street, Suite 130
Lincoln, NE 68508-3621

APPLICATION FOR CERTIFIED COPY OF MARRIAGE CERTIFICATE

This office has been registering marriages occuring in Nebraska since 1909. (For records prior to 1909, contact the County Clerk of the county where the marriage license was issued or the State Historical Society, P.O. Box 82554, Lincoln, NE 68501. They both will require a file search fee.)

PLEASE TYPE OR PRINT LEGIBLY

Full name of groom ____________________

Full maiden name of bride ____________________
(Please list any other name(s) bride may have used)

County in which license was issued ____________________

Month, day, and year of marriage ____________________

For what purpose is this record to be used? ____________________

If this is not your marriage record, how are you related to the person listed on the record? ____________________

WARNING: Section 71-649, Nebraska Revised Statutes: It is a felony to obtain, possess, use, sell, furnish, or attempt to obtain any vital record for purposes of deception.

SIGNATURE OF REQUESTOR ____________________

Type or print name ____________________

Street Address ____________________

City, State, Zip ____________________

Daytime Telephone Number: ____________________

Today's Date ____________________

(Please enclose a photocopy of your photo ID [i.e. current driver's license] when mailing in this request).

IMPORTANT INFORMATION REQUIRED. If not specified you will receive abstract of the marriage certificate, please select which form you want to receive:

______ Long Form Marriage Certificate

(THIS OPTION IS AVAILABLE FOR EVENTS DATED AFTER JANUARY 1, 2007)
______ Abstract of Marriage Certificate

Fees are subject to change without notice. Please call our 24-hour recorded message at (402) 471-2871 to verify fees.

Number of certified copies______ x $11.00 each = $______ Total
(Please make checks payable to Vital Records)

Mail to:
Vital Records
PO Box 95065
Lincoln, NE 68509-5065
(Please enclose a stamped, self-addressed business size envelope.)

Bring to:
Vital Records
1033 O Street, Suite 130
Lincoln, NE 68508-3621

FOR OFFICE USE ONLY

❑ Check ❑ MO ❑ Cash

Amount Received ____________________

Date Received ____________________

By Whom Received ____________________

PROOF OF IDENTIFICATION;

DL STATE ID OTHER

____

APPLICATION FOR CERTIFIED COPY OF DISSOLUTION OF MARRIAGE (DIVORCE) CERTIFICATE

This office has been registering dissolution of marriages (divorces) occurring in Nebraska since 1909. (For records occurring prior to 1909, or if you wish to obtain the divorce decree, contact the District Court in the county where the divorce was granted).

PLEASE TYPE OR PRINT LEGIBLY

Full name of husband ______________________________

Full name of wife ______________________________

City or county where granted______________________________

Month, day, and year granted ______________________________

For what purpose is this record to be used? ______________________________

If this is not your divorce certificate, how are you related to the persons listed on the record?______________________________

WARNING: Section 71-649, Nebraska Revised Statutes: It is a felony to obtain, possess, use, sell, furnish, or attempt to obtain any vital record for purposes of deception.

SIGNATURE OF REQUESTOR ______________________________

Type or print name______________________________

Street Address______________________________

City, State, Zip ______________________________

Daytime Telephone Number ______________________________

Today's Date ______________________________

(Please enclose a photocopy of your photo ID [i.e. current driver's license] when mailing in this request).

Fees are subject to change without notice. Please call our 24-hour recorded message at (402) 471-2871 to verify fees.

Number of certified copies________ x $11.00 each = $________ Total
(Please make checks payable to Vital Records)

Mail to:
Vital Records
PO Box 95065
Lincoln, NE 68509-5065
(Please enclose a stamped, self-addressed business size envelope.)

Bring to:
Vital Records
1033 O Street, Suite 130
Lincoln, NE 68508-3621

FOR OFFICE USE ONLY

❑ Check ❑ MO ❑ Cash

Amount Received______________________________

Date Received ______________________________

By Whom Received ______________________________

PROOF OF IDENTIFICATION;

DL STATE ID OTHER

____

HHS-83 (55083) 7/09

APPLICATION FOR CERTIFIED COPY OF DEATH CERTIFICATE

This office has been registering deaths occurring in Nebraska since **1904**.

PLEASE TYPE OR PRINT LEGIBLY

Full name of deceased ______________________________
(If female, list married name or any other name(s) decedent may have used)

City or town of death ____________________ County of death ____________________
(If exact place of death is not known, list last known address)

Month, day and year of death ______________________________
(If exact date of death is unknown, list date decedent was last known to be alive or indicate a span of years to search)

How are you related to decedent? ______________________________

For what purpose is this record to be used? ______________________________

****

The information in this section is helpful in assisting our office in locating and identifying the requested record:

Year of birth ____________________ Birthplace ____________________

Spouse's full name ____________________ Home address ____________________

Father's full name ______________________________

Mother's full name ______________________________

Funeral Director ____________________ City ____________________

WARNING: Section 71-649, Nebraska Revised Statutes: It is a felony to obtain, possess, use, sell, furnish, or attempt to obtain any vital record for purposes of deception.

IF OTHER THAN FUNERAL DIRECTOR, PLEASE ENCLOSE A PHOTOCOPY OF YOUR PHOTO ID (i.e., CURRENT DRIVER'S LICENSE) WHEN MAILING IN THIS REQUEST.

SIGNATURE OF REQUESTOR ____________________

Type or print name ____________________

If funeral director -

Type or print name of firm ____________________

Mailing Address ____________________

City, State, Zip ____________________

Telephone Number: ____________________

Today's Date ____________________

If copies are to be sent to another address, enter that mailing address below:

Name ____________________

Street Address ____________________

City, State, Zip ____________________

Fees are subject to change without notice. Please call our 24-hour recorded message at (402) 471-2871 to verify fees.

Number of certified copies________ x $11.00 each = $________ Total
(Please make checks payable to Vital Records)

Mail to:
Vital Records
PO Box 95065
Lincoln, NE 68509-5065
(Please enclose a stamped, self-addressed business size envelope.)

Bring to:
Vital Records
1033 O Street, Suite 130
Lincoln, NE 68508-3621

FOR OFFICE USE ONLY

❑ Check ❑ MO ❑ Cash

Amount Received ____________________

Date Received ____________________

By Whom Received ____________________

PROOF OF IDENTIFICATION;

DL STATE ID OTHER

____

HHS-92 (55092) 7/09

NEVADA

Send your requests to:

Office of Vital Records
4150 Technology Way, Suite 104
Carson City, NV 89706

Tel. (775) 684-4242
Fax (775) 684-4156
E-mail: vitalrecords@health.nv.gov
http://health.nv.gov/VS.htm

The Office of Vital Records has birth and death records from July 1, 1911, and marriage and divorce indexes from 1968. Birth and death records are confidential in the State of Nevada and may only be released to those applicants who can prove a relationship or a need to facilitate a legal process. Birth and death records from 1887 to the present are also recorded in each county, either in the office of the county recorder or the County Health Office.

Marriage and divorce records are held at the county level and are not available from the state. For certified copies of marriage certificates, you must write to the county recorder in the county where the license was purchased. For divorce records you must write to the county clerk in the county where the divorce was granted. For more information about obtaining marriage and divorce records, go to http://health.nv.gov/PDFs/FP_Forms/2010-12/countyaddressess_marri.pdf.

Cost for a certified Birth Certificate	$20.00
Cost for a search/verification of a record	$10.00
Cost for a certified Death Certificate	$20.00

For Genealogy Research:

The Nevada State Library and Archives (100 N. Stewart Street, Carson City, NV 89701-4285; tel. 775-684-3360; http://nsla.nevadaculture.org) has a number of records of genealogical interest for the various Nevada counties and Carson City. Carson City birth and death records can be searched online at http://www.carson.org/Index.aspx?page=2193.

Some early Nevada marriages can be searched online at http://abish.byui.edu/specialCollections/westernStates/search.cfm.

For Adoption Record information, contact:

Nevada Adoption Registry
Nevada Division of Child and Family Services
4126 Technology Way, Third Floor
Carson City, NV 89706

Tel. (775) 684-4415
www.dcfs.state.nv.us/DCFS_Guide_ReunionRegistry.htm

State of Nevada Health Division
Bureau of Health Statistics Planning, Epidemiology and Response
Office of Vital Records and Statistics
4150 Technology Way, Suite 104
Carson City, Nevada 89706
Telephone (775) 684-4242
www.health.nv.gov/vs.htm

BIRTH CERTIFICATE APPLICATION

☐ **$20.00 for one certified copy** **Number of copies**___________

Or

☐ **$10.00 Search/Verification of a record (search/verifications do not include a certified copy. Choose this option if you are only wanting verification that the record is on file with Nevada Office of Vital Records)**

Check, or Money Order, made payable to Vital Records

★PHOTOCOPY OF APPLICANT'S ID /DRIVERS LICENSEAND PAYMENT IN FULL IS REQUIRED TO OBTAIN CERTIFICATE★

Full name at birth:

First	Middle	Last

Date of birth: ______________________________

Place of birth: ______________________________

Father's name: ______________________________

Mother's maiden name: ______________________________

NRS 440.650 and NAC 440.070 require that a relationship or a need to facilitate a legal process be established in order to receive a certified copy of a record.

Please state your relationship and your legal need for this record:______________________________

____

Signature of applicant: ______________________________

Phone number: ______________________________

Your name and address (please print):______________________________

____

FOR OFFICE USE ONLY	
Amount received: ______________	**Receipt number:** ______________
No. of copies issued: ______________	**Date:** ______________

(Rev.01/31/2013)

State of Nevada Health Division
Bureau of Health Statistics Planning, Epidemiology and Response
Office of Vital Records and Statistics
4150 Technology Way, Suite 104
Carson City, Nevada 89706
Telephone (775) 684-4242

REQUEST FOR SEARCH RECORDS

Cash, Check, or Money Order, made payable to Vital Records

Non-Refundable Search Fee of $10.00 per Event

Please circle one: **Marriage** **Divorce**

Name of Groom: ______________________________

Name of Bride: ______________________________

Date of Event: ______________________________

Any other information or comment: ______________________________

____

____

____

Your name and address (please print): ______________________________

____

City, State, Zip Code: ______________________________

____

Phone number: ______________________________

FOR OFFICE USE ONLY	
Amount received: ____________	**Receipt number:** ____________
No. of copies issued: ____________	**Date:** ____________

(Rev.2/16/12)

State of Nevada
Health Division
Bureau of Health Planning and Statistics
Office of Vital Records and Statistics
4150 Technology Way, Suite 104
Carson City, Nevada 89706
Telephone (775)684-4242
www.health.nv.gov/vs.htm

DEATH CERTIFICATE APPLICATION

☐ **$20.00 per certified copy** **Number of copies**____________________

☐ **$10.00 Search/Verification of a record**

Check or Money Order only

PHOTOCOPY OF APPLICANT'S ID /DRIVERS LICENSE AND PAYMENT IN FULL IS REQUIRED TO OBTAIN CERTIFICATE

Full name of decedent:

First	Middle	Last

Date of death: ______________________________ **Social Security No:** ______________________________

Place of death: ____

Decedent's father's name: ____

Decedent's mother's *maiden* name: ____

Mortuary/Funeral Home in charge of arrangements: ____

NRS 440.650 and NAC 440.070 require that a **relationship** or a need to facilitate a **legal process** be established in order to receive a certified copy of a record.

Please state your relationship and your legal need for this record: ______________________________

____

Signature of applicant: ____

Phone number: ____

Name and mailing address (please print): ____

____

____

FOR OFFICE USE ONLY

Amount received: ______________________ **Receipt number:** ______________________

No. of copies issued: ______________________ **Date:** ______________________

(Rev.01/31/2013)

NEW HAMPSHIRE

Send your requests to:

New Hampshire Department of State
Division of Vital Records Administration
Registration/Certification
71 South Fruit Street
Concord, NH 03301-2410

Tel. (603) 271-4650
E-mail: vitalrecords@sos.state.nh.us
http://sos.nh.gov/vital_records.aspx

The Division of Vital Records has birth, marriage, and death records from 1640, and divorce records from 1880. To obtain a certified copy of a record, you must prove a "direct and tangible" interest in obtaining a record. The Heirloom Birth Certificate is available to all New Hampshire-born citizens who were born between 1948 and the present.

Cost for a certified Birth Certificate	$15.00
Cost for an Heirloom Birth Certificate	$25.00
Cost for a certified Marriage or Civil Union Certificate	$15.00
Cost for a certified Divorce or Civil Union Dissolution Record	$15.00
Cost for a certified Death Certificate	$15.00
Cost for a duplicate certified copy, when ordered at the same time	$10.00

Vital records are also available from:

Town Clerk
Town Hall
(Town), NH

See www.sos.nh.gov/vitalrecords/Publications/clerks_list_12-2005.pdf for town clerk contact information.

For Genealogy Research:

Birth records prior to 1911 and death, marriage, and divorce records prior to 1961 are available with unrestricted access. Individuals wishing to research these genealogical records may do so by visiting the Genealogical Research Center located at the Division of Vital Records office. Alternatively, a completed application (with proper identification and fee) may be mailed to the Division of Vital Records Administration and the staff will perform research for you.

Town and county reports are good sources of birth, marriage, and death records in New Hampshire. Many of the towns published annual reports, especially during the mid-1800s, and these reports included all births, marriages, and deaths, with great detail on those events. The counties often published similar reports. For more information contact the library, historical society, or town clerk of the specific town involved, or consult the New Hampshire State Archives (71 South Fruit Street, Concord, NH 03301; tel. 603-271-2236; www.sos.nh.gov/archives/genealogy.html). The Genealogy Section of the New Hampshire State Library (20 Park Street, Concord, NH 03301; tel. 603-271-2144; www.nh.gov/nhsl/services/public/genealogy.html) also has a great deal of information of interest to genealogical researchers.

For Adoption Record information, contact the Division of Vital Records Administration at the above address, consult the website www.sos.nh.gov/vitalrecords/Preadoption_birth_records.html, or contact:

Division for Children, Youth & Families
New Hampshire Department of Health and Human Services
Post-Adoption Services
129 Pleasant Street
Concord, NH 03301

APPLICATION FOR A CERTIFIED COPY OF A VITAL RECORD

New Hampshire Department of State
Division of Vital Records Administration
71 South Fruit Street
Concord, NH 03301-2410

REGISTRANT EVENT(S) Please complete online prior to signing!

Birth Number of copies ____ (**first** copy issued at $15.00; each **additional** copy, $10.00)

Name of Child ______________________ Child's Sex ____________

Father's/Parent's Full (Maiden) Name ______________________ Child's Birthdate ____________

Mother's/Parent's Full (Maiden) Name ______________________ Child's Birthplace ____________

Death Number of copies ____ (**first** copy issued at $15.00; each **additional** copy, $10.00)

Full Name of Deceased ______________________ Sex ____________

Date of Death ____________ Place of Death ____________ Issued ☐ **With** / ☐ **Without** Cause of Death

---

Marriage / Civil Union Number of copies ____ (**first** copy issued at $15.00; each **additional** copy, $10.00)

Prior Full Name of Groom/Person A ______________________ Date of Marriage/Civil Union ____________

Prior Full Name of Bride/Person B ______________________ Place of Marriage/Civil Union ____________

Divorce / Civil Union Dissolution Number of copies ____ (**first** copy issued at $15.00; each **additional** copy, $10.00)

Full Name of Husband/Person A ______________________ Date of Decree ____________

Full Name of Wife/Person B ______________________ Place of Decree (County) ____________

New Hampshire law (RSA 5-C:10) requires that a **nonrefundable** search fee be collected for each record requested. If the record is located and you meet eligibility requirements, you will be issued the requested number of certified copies of that record.

Applicant's Name: ______________________
(FIRST) (MIDDLE) (LAST)

Applicant's Address: ______________________
(ATTENTION INFORMATION/BUSINESS NAME) (STREET) (APT)

____
(CITY/TOWN) (STATE) (COUNTRY) (ZIP CODE)

Applicant's Phone No.: ______________________ Email: ______________________
(AREA CODE & NUMBER)

Reason for Certificate Request: ______________________
IF the Certificate is for a Foreign Consulate, you should *CLICK HERE*.

Applicant's Signature: ______________________ *Your* relationship as applicant *to* the Registrant: ______________________
(Original signature is required.)

NOTICE: Any person shall be guilty of a CLASS B Felony if he/she willfully and knowingly makes any false statement in an application for a certified copy of a vital record. (RSA 5-C:14)

PLEASE NOTE: **A LEGIBLE PHOTOCOPY OF THE APPLICANT'S GOVERNMENT ISSUED PHOTO ID MUST BE INCLUDED WITH THIS REQUEST (i.e. driver's license, non-driver's ID, passport). IF THE APPLICANT DOES NOT POSSESS A PHOTO ID, THEY SHOULD** *CLICK HERE*. ***YOU MUST PROVIDE EVIDENCE THAT THE ADDRESS TO WHICH THE VITAL RECORD IS TO BE SENT IS INDEED YOUR ADDRESS (eg. personal check, driver's license, utility bill), OTHERWISE*** *CLICK HERE* ***AND FILL OUT THE BOTTOM HALF.***

DO NOT SEND CASH. PLEASE MAKE CHECKS PAYABLE TO: Treasurer-State of New Hampshire

I have enclosed a stamped, self-addressed, business-letter-sized envelope.

DID YOU...

- Sign the Application?
- Incl. a photocopy of Gov Issued ID?
- Enclose Payment?

If not, application must be returned!

OFFICIAL USE ONLY:
NBR
TYPE(S)/AMT(S)
ISSUED

Rev. 02/13 VR201

NON-CERTIFIED DOCUMENT APPLICATION FORM

New Hampshire Department of State
Division of Vital Records Administration
71 South Fruit Street
Concord, NH 03301-2410

REGISTRANT EVENT(S) Please complete online prior to signing.
The following documents are available as Non-Certified ***ONLY.***

Stillborn/Fetal Death Certificate Number of copies ____ (**first** copy issued at $15.00; each **additional** copy, $10.00)
Name of Child ______________________ Child's Sex __________
Father's/Parent's Full (Maiden) Name ______________________ Child's Birthdate __________
Mother's/Parent's Full (Maiden) Name ______________________ Child's Birthplace __________

Affidavit of Paternity Number of copies ____ (**first** copy issued at $15.00; each **additional** copy, $10.00)
Name of Child ______________________ Child's Sex __________
Father's/Parent's Full (Maiden) Name ______________________ Child's Birthdate __________
Mother's/Parent's Full (Maiden) Name ______________________ Child's Birthplace __________

Pre-adoption Birth Record Number of copies ____ (**first** copy issued at $15.00; each **additional** copy, $10.00)
Name of Applicant after Adoption ______________________ Child's Sex __________
Adoptive Father's/Parent's Full (Maiden) Name ______________________ Child's Birthdate __________
Adoptive Mother's/Parent's Full (Maiden) Name ______________________ Child's Birthplace __________

Decorative Heirloom Birth Certificate: *for immediate family members **only**.*
Decorative Heirloom Birth Certificate Gift Card: *for cousins, in-laws, friends and immediate family.*
Please specify type and quantity: Heirloom Birth Certificate(s) ____ and/or Gift Card(s) ____ at $25.00 ***each***.
Name of Child ______________________ Child's Sex __________
Father's/Parent's Full (Maiden) Name ______________________ Child's Birthdate __________
Mother's/Parent's Full (Maiden) Name ______________________ Child's Birthplace __________

New Hampshire law (**RSA 5-C:10**) requires that a **nonrefundable** search fee be collected for each record requested. If the record is located and you meet eligibility requirements, you will be issued the requested number of certified copies of that record.

Applicant's Name: ____
(FIRST) (MIDDLE) (LAST)

Applicant's Address: ____
(ATTENTION INFORMATION/BUSINESS NAME) (STREET) (APT)

____
(CITY/TOWN) (STATE) (COUNTRY) (ZIP CODE)

Phone No.: ______________________ Email: ______________________
(AREA CODE & NUMBER)

Reason for Certificate Request: ____

Applicant's Signature: ______________________ *Your* relationship as applicant *to* the Registrant: ______________________
(Signature is required.)

NOTICE: Any person shall be guilty of a CLASS B Felony if he/she willfully and knowingly makes any false statement in an application for a certified copy of a vital record. (**RSA 5-C:14**)

PLEASE NOTE: **A LEGIBLE PHOTOCOPY OF THE APPLICANT'S GOVERNMENT ISSUED PHOTO ID MUST BE INCLUDED WITH THIS REQUEST (i.e. driver's license, non-driver's ID, passport). IF THE APPLICANT DOES NOT POSSESS A PHOTO ID, THEY SHOULD** *CLICK HERE.*

DO NOT SEND CASH. PLEASE MAKE CHECKS PAYABLE TO: Treasurer-State of New Hampshire

DID YOU...
* Sign the application?
* Incl. a **photocopy** of Gov. Issued ID?
* Enclose payment?

If not, application must be returned.

OFFICIAL USE ONLY:
NBR
TYPE(S)/AMT(S)
ISSUED

New Hampshire Department of State
Division of Vital Records Administration
71 South Fruit Street
Concord, New Hampshire 03301-2410

CONTACT PREFERENCE FORM FOR BIRTH PARENTS OF ADOPTED CHILDREN

The New Hampshire Division of Vital Records Administration needs the following information to find and match your request with your records.

Please print

Name of Child
on Original Birth Record: ____
first *middle* *last*

Date of Birth ______________________________ Sex: ☐ Male ☐ Female
mm/dd/yyyy

Hospital Name: ______________________ City: ______________________

Mother's Name
on Original Birth Record: ____
first *middle* *last*

Adoption agency involved with adoption (if known): ______________________

IF THE ORIGINAL BIRTH CERTIFICATE IS RELEASED, WHAT IS YOUR PREFERENCE REGARDING CONTACT WITH THE ADOPTEE?

The Division of Vital Records Administration cannot accept the Contact Preference Form unless it is fully completed.

I am the: ☐ Birth Mother ☐ Birth Father Date: ______________________

Please check one of the three boxes below and provide the required information.

☐ **I would like to be contacted**

Current Name: ______________________

Address: ______________________

Telephone: ______________________

☐ **I would prefer to be contacted through an intermediary only**

☐ **I prefer not to be contacted at this time**

If I decide later that I would like to be contacted, I will register with the Division of Vital Records Administration. I have completed a Birth Parent Updated Medical History form and have filed it with the Division of Vital Records Administration.

IF NO CONTACT IS YOUR PREFERENCE YOU MUST REQUEST AND COMPLETE A BIRTH PARENT UPDATED MEDICAL HISTORY FORM.

For additional information or forms, please contact the adoption agency involved with the adoption or the following office:

Division of Vital Records Administration
Attn: Adoption Coordinator
71 South Fruit Street
Concord, NH 03301-2410 (603) 271-4650

NEW JERSEY

Send your requests to:

New Jersey Office of Vital Statistics and Registry
(Location: 140 East Front Street)
P.O. Box 370
Trenton, NJ 08625-0370

Tel. (609) 292-4087; (866) 649-8726
www.state.nj.us/health/vital/index.shtml

The Office of Vital Statistics has birth, marriage, and death records from 1901 to the present; civil union records back to 2007, and domestic partnership records back to 2004. Vital records are also available from the local vital records office in the municipality where the event occurred (see www.state.nj.us/health/vital/regbycnty.shtml for contact information).

Cost for a certified Birth Certificate	$25.00
Cost for a certified Marriage/Civil Union/Domestic Partnership Certificate	$25.00
Cost for a certified Death Certificate	$25.00
Cost for a duplicate certificate, when ordered at the same time	$2.00

For Birth, Marriage, and Death Records from May 1848 to 1900, contact:

New Jersey State Archives
(Location: 225 West State Street)
P.O. Box 307
Trenton, NJ 08625-0307

Tel. (609) 292-6260
www.nj.gov/state/archives/index.html

For Divorce Records, contact:

Superior Court of New Jersey Records Center
P.O. Box 971
Trenton, NJ 08625-0971

Tel. (609) 421-6100

For Genealogy Research:

The Office of Vital Statistics issues genealogical copies of vital records, which are not valid for legal purposes. Genealogical records are defined as birth, death, and marriage records for people who are deceased and where the birth occurred more than 80 years ago, the marriage more than 50 years ago, and the death more than 40 years ago. For these "certification copies," you do not need to provide proof of relationship. For more information on obtaining birth, death, and marriage records for genealogical purposes, go to www.state.nj.us/health/vital/genealogical.shtml.

The State Archives (see above for contact information) holds original birth, marriage, and death records for the period May 1848–1900, as well as microfilm copies of births 1902–1923, marriages 1901–1940, and deaths 1901–1940. These materials are available for in-person use only. Searchable databases available on the Archives' website include marriage records 1666–1799, an index to marriages May 1848–May 1878, and death records June 1878–June 1888.

For Adoption Record information, contact:

New Jersey Department of Children and Families
Division of Youth and Family Services
Adoption Registry Coordinator
(Location: 50 East State Street)
P.O. Box 717
Trenton, NJ 08625-7474

Tel. (609) 888-8816
E-mail: dcfadoptionregistry@dcf.state.nj.us
www.state.nj.us/njfosteradopt/adoption/registry/

There is no charge for registration with the Adoption Registry.

New Jersey Department of Health
Vital Statistics and Registry
P.O. Box 370
Trenton, NJ 08625-0370

APPLICATION FOR A *NON-GENEALOGICAL* CERTIFICATION OR CERTIFIED COPY OF A VITAL RECORD
APLICACIÓN PARA COPIAS CERTIFICADAS Ó CERTIFICACIONES DE REGISTROS CIVILES NO-ANCESTRO

☐ I would like a ***Certified Copy***. *(Quiero una copia certificada.)*
☐ I will be forwarding the **Certified Copy** for an **Apostille Seal**. *(Enviaré esta copia certificada para ser Apostillada.)*
☐ I would like a ***Certification***. *(Quiero una certificación.)*

If available, I prefer the format of the certified copy to be: *(Prefiero:)*
☐ Computer Generated copy of original. *(Copia del Original-Generado por Computadora)*
☐ Digital Image/Photocopy of original. *(Imagen Digital/Fotocopia del Original)*

Name of Applicant *(Nombre de Aplicante)*	Relationship to person on record (Proof is required if certified copy requested.) *[Relación al individuo (Prueba es requerida para copia certificada.)]*	Reasons for Request: *(Motivo de solicitud)*
Current Mailing Address ***(Must Match address on ID)*** *[Dirección Postal (Debe coelncedir con identificación)]*		☐ Passport *(Pasaporte)* ☐ Driver's License *(Licensia de Conducir)* ☐ School/Sports *(Escuela/Deportes)* ☐ Veterans' Benefits *(Beneficios veteranos)* ☐ Social Security Card *(Tarjeta Seguro Social)* ☐ Social Security Disability *(SSI / Incapacidad)* ☐ Other SS Benefits *(Otros beneficios de seguro social)* ☐ Medicare *(Medicare)* ☐ Welfare *(Asistencia Pública)* ☐ Other *(Otro)* ________
City *(Ciudad)* State *(Estado)* Zip Code *(Codigo Postal)*	Daytime Telephone Number *(Número Telefónico)*	
Applicant's Signature *(Firma del Aplicante)*	Date of Application *(Fecha)*	

☐ **BIRTH** *(NACIMIENTO)*	Full Name of Child at Time of Birth *(Nombre Completo al Nacer)*		No. Requested Copies *(No. de Copias)*
	Place of Birth (City, Town) *[Lugar de Nacimiento (Ciudad. Pueblo)]*	County *(Condado)*	Exact Date of Birth *(Fecha de Nacimiento)*
	Child's Mother's Full Maiden Name *(Nombre completo de soltera de la Madre)*	Child's Father's Name (if on record) *[Nombre del Padre (si esta registrado)]*	
	If the Child's Name was Changed, Indicate New Name and How it was Changed: *(Si el nombre del niño fue cambiado, indique el nuevo nombre y como fue cambiado):*		
☐ **MARRIAGE** *(MATRIMONIO)* ☐ **CIVIL UNION** *(UNIÓN CIVIL)* ☐ **DOMESTIC PARTNERSHIP** *(SOCIEDAD DOMÉSTICA)*	Name of Husband/ Partner *(Nombre de Esposo/Pareja)*		No. Requested Copies *(No. de Copias)*
	Maiden Name of Wife/ Partner *(Nombre Soltera de Esposa/Pareja)*		Exact Date of Event *(Fecha Exacta del Evento)*
	Place of Event (City, Town) *[Lugar del Evento (Ciudad, Pueblo)]*		County *(Condado)*
☐ **DEATH** *(DEFUNCIÓN)*	Name of Deceased *(Nombre del Fallecido)*	Social Security Number *(See Note)* *[Numero de Seguro Social (Ver Indice)]*	No. Requested Copies *(No. de Copias)*
	Exact Date of Death *(Fecha Exacta ded Evento)*	Place of Event (City/Town) *[Lugar del Evento (Ciudad, pueblo)]*	County *(Condado)*
	Maiden Name of Deceased Individual's Mother *(Nombre Soltera de la Madre)*	Name of Deceased Individual's Father *(Nombre del Padre)*	

Application Check List: Have you enclosed and completed all required information?
(Lista Comprobada: ¿A Usted Incluido y Completado Toda la Información Requerida en la Aplicación?)
☐ All Items on Application *(Todo Articulos en la Aplicación)* ☐ Payment *(Pago)* ☐ Acceptable Forms of ID *(Identificación Aceptable)* ☐ Proof of Relationship *(Prueba de Parentesco)* ☐ Mailing Address Matches ID *(Dirección Postal Coincidente con ID)*

FOR STATE USE ONLY			
Payment Type: ☐ Cash ☐ M/O ☐ Check ☐ Waived	Payment Amount: $	ID Viewed:	Processed By

REG-27
JUL 12

New Jersey Department of Health
Vital Statistics and Registry
P.O. BOX 370
Trenton, NJ 08625-0370

APPLICATION FOR A *GENEALOGICAL* CERTIFICATION OR CERTIFIED COPY OF A VITAL RECORD
APLICACIÓN POR UNA COPIA CERTIFICADA Ó CERTIFICACIONES DE UN REGISTRO CIVIL ANCESTRO

☐ I would like a ***Certified Copy***.
(Quiero una copia certificada.)
☐ I will be forwarding the **Certified Copy** for an **Apostille Seal**.
(Enviaré esta copia certificada para ser Apostillada.)
☐ I would like a ***Certification***.
(Quiero una certificación.)

If available, I prefer the format of the certified copy to be:
(Prefiero:)
☐ Computer Generated copy of original.
(Copia del Original- Generado por Computadora)
☐ Digital Image/Photocopy of original.
(Imagen Digital/Fotocopia del Original)

Name of Applicant *(Nombre de Aplicante)*			Relationship to person on record (Proof is required if certified copy requested.) *[Relación al individuo (Prueba es requerida para copia certificada.)]*	Reasons for Request: *(Motivo de solicitud)* ☐ Genealogy *(Ancestral)* ☐ Dual Citizenship *(Doble Ciudadania)* ☐ Estate Matters *(Cuestiones de Herencia)* ☐ Other *(Otro)* ________
Current Mailing Address ***(Must Match address on ID)*** *[Dirección Postal (Debe coencedir con identificación)]*				
City *(Ciudad)*	State *(Estado)*	Zip Code *(Codigo Postal)*	Daytime Telephone Number *(Número Telefónico)*	
Applicant's Signature *(Firma del Aplicante)*			Date of Application *(Fecha)*	

☐ **BIRTH** *(NACIMIENTO)* **(over 80 years ago)** ***(más de 80 años)***	Full Name of Child at Time of Birth *(Nombre Completo al Nacer)*		No. Requested Copies *(No. de Copias)*
	Place of Birth (City, Town) **(Optional)** *[Lugar de Nacimiento (Ciudad, Pueblo)]*	County *(Condado)*	Date of Birth or Year(s) to be searched *(Fecha de Nacimiento ó años de busqueda)*
	Child's Mother's Full Maiden Name **(Optional)** *(Nombre completo de soltera de la Madre)*	Child's Father's Name **(Optional)** *(Nombre del Padre)*	
	If the Child's Name was Changed, Indicate New Name and How it was Changed: *(Si el nombre del niño fue cambiado, indique el nuevo nombre y como fue cambiado):*		
☐ **MARRIAGE** *(MATRIMONIO)* **(over 50 years ago)** ***(más de 50 años)***	Name of Husband *(Nombre de Esposo)*		No. Requested Copies *(No. de Copias)*
	Maiden Name of Wife *(Nombre Soltera de Esposa)*		Date of Event or Year(s) to be searched *(Fecha del Evento ó años de busqueda)*
	Place of Event (City, Town) **(Optional)** *[Lugar del Evento (Ciudad, Pueblo)]*		County *(Condado)*
☐ **DEATH** *(DEFUNCIÓN)* **(over 40 years ago)** ***(más de 40 años)***	Name of Deceased *(Nombre del Fallecido)*		No. Requested Copies *(No. de Copias)*
	Place of Event (City/Town) **(Optional)** *[Lugar del Evento (Ciudad, pueblo)]*	County *(Condado)*	Date of Death or Year(s) to be searched *(Fecha de muerte ó años de busqueda)*
	Maiden Name of Deceased Individual's Mother **(Optional)** *(Nombre Soltera de la Madre)*	Name of Deceased Individual's Father **(Optional)** *(Nombre del Padre)*	

Application Check List: Have you enclosed and completed all required information?
(Lista Comprobada: ¿A Usted Incluido y Completado Toda la Información Requerida en la Aplicación?)

☐ All Items on Application *(Todo Articulos en la Aplicación)* ☐ Payment *(Pago)* ☐ Acceptable Forms of ID *(Identificación Aceptable)* ☐ Proof of Relationship *(Prueba de Parentesco)* ☐ Mailing Address Matches ID *(Dirección Postal Coincidente con ID)*

FOR STATE USE ONLY			
Payment Type: ☐ Cash ☐ M/O ☐ Check ☐ Waived	Payment Amount: $	ID Viewed:	Processed By

REG-28
AUG 12

NEW MEXICO

Send your requests to:

New Mexico Department of Health
Bureau of Vital Records and Health Statistics
(Location: 1105 South St. Francis Drive)
P.O. Box 225767
Albuquerque, NM 87125

Tel. (505) 827-0121; (866) 534-0051
http://vitalrecordsnm.org/

The Bureau of Vital Records and Health Statistics was created in 1919 to register births and deaths that occurred in New Mexico. New Mexico birth records are restricted for 100 years, death records for 50 years.

Copies of marriage licenses are available from the county clerk of the county where the marriage license was issued. Copies of divorce decrees are available from the District Court where the court order was filed.

Cost for a certified Birth Certificate	$10.00
Cost for a certified Death Certificate	$5.00

For Genealogy Research:

Locating Catholic Church Records in New Mexico (www.nmgs.org/Chrchs-intro.htm) is an ongoing online project to help researchers find the church records that recorded their ancestors' birth, marriage, and death. You can search death records 1899–1949 online at the New Mexico Death Index Project's website (www.usgwarchives.net/nm/nmdi.htm).

Many marriage records have been abstracted and published by the New Mexico Genealogical Society and other groups and individuals. Additionally, many marriage records can be found in the microfilmed and archival collections of county records located at the New Mexico State Records Center and Archives (1205 Camino Carlos Rey, Santa Fe, NM 87507; tel. 505-476-7948; www.nmcpr.state.nm.us/archives/archives_hm.htm).

The Genealogy Center at the Albuquerque Main Library (501 Copper Avenue NW, Albuquerque, NM 87102; tel. 505-768-5131; http://library.cabq.gov/genealogy) has a number of resources for genealogists, including microfilm of Catholic Church records, New Mexico county records, and death certificates. In addition, the Genealogy Center is a depository for the LDS Family History Library—any microfilm ordered from www.familysearch.org can be delivered to the Center.

For Adoption Record information, contact:

Adoption Unit
New Mexico Children, Youth & Families Department
P.O. Drawer 5160
Santa Fe, NM 87502-5160

www.cyfd.org/child_all

BIRTH RECORD

SEARCH APPLICATION

Identification Type:	
State Identification Issued:	
Identification Number:	
ID Expiration Date:	
This section for Vital Records Use Only	
Order No:	
SP#:	Clerk: Date:

Mail Application to:
New Mexico Department of Health
Bureau of Vital Records and Health Statistics
PO Box 25767 Albuquerque, NM 87125

Average application processing time is 6-12 weeks.
Processing time is subject to change, dependent on volume of incoming applications.

Warning: False application for a vital record is a criminal offense and punishable by fine and/or imprisonment. New Mexico Vital Records requires a photocopy of your government issued picture identification.

1. APPLICANT: Complete each item on application legibly. An incomplete application will be rejected.

Name of Applicant	Name of Agency (If Applicant is Organization)
Mailing Address (include City, State and Zip code)	
Provide physical address, If mailing address is PO box.	
Daytime Telephone Number ( )	Alternate Daytime Telephone Number ( )

Only immediate family is eligible to obtain a vital record. Immediate family is defined as registrant's mother, father, sibling, child, grandchild, current spouse, maternal-grandparent and paternal-grandparent. Father and paternal grandparent are only eligible if father is listed on birth record. Non-immediate family must provide tangible proof of legal interest for requested record.

2. Applicant's Relationship: Indicate your relationship to the person on the certificate

☐ Self ☐ Mother ☐ Father ☐ Sibling ☐ Child
☐ Grandchild ☐ Current Spouse ☐ Maternal Grandparent ☐ Paternal Grandparent
☐ Other (Specify)

3. Registrant's Full Name at Birth: Print the First, Middle and Last name of the person on certificate (mandatory for search). Gender

Date of Birth: Month/Day/Year (mandatory for search)

Place of Birth: City/County — New Mexico

Mother's Full Maiden Name (mandatory for search)

Father's Name

Make payment payable to: New Mexico Vital Records. The fee is for the search of the record and will include one certified copy of record, if available. Search fee is non-refundable if record is not filed.

4. Payment & Quantity

Quantity Birth Certificate @ $ 10.00:	
Quantity Chargeable Amendment @ $ 10.00:	
TOTAL Fees Enclosed:	**$**

☐ Check ☐ Money Order
Check or Money Order Number:

5. Purpose of Request: *Check the reason(s) for use*

☐ Amendment to Vital Record ☐ Estate/ Probate ☐ Employment
☐ Genealogy ☐ Identification ☐ Insurance ☐ Medical
☐ Passport/Visa ☐ Sports ☐ Tax Purpose ☐ Retirement
☐ School ☐ Social Security ☐ Other (state other reason):

Signature of Applicant	Date of Application

DEATH RECORD

SEARCH APPLICATION

Mail Application to:
New Mexico Department of Health
Bureau of Vital Records and Health Statistics
PO Box 25767 Albuquerque, NM 87125

Identification Type:	
State Identification Issued:	
Identification Number:	
ID Expiration Date:	
This section for Vital Records Use Only	
Order No:	
SP#:	Clerk: Date:

Average application processing time is 6-12 weeks.
Processing time is subject to change, dependent on volume of incoming applications.

Warning: False application for a vital record is a criminal offense and punishable by fine and/or imprisonment. New Mexico Vital Records requires a photocopy of your government issued picture identification.

1. APPLICANT: Complete each item on application legibly. An incomplete application will be rejected.

Name of Applicant	Name of Agency (If Applicant is Organization)
Mailing Address (include City, State and Zip code)	
Provide physical address, If mailing address is PO box.	
Daytime Telephone Number ( )	Alternate Daytime Telephone Number ( )

Only immediate family is eligible to obtain a vital record. Immediate family is defined as registrant's mother, father, sibling, child, grandchild, current spouse, maternal-grandparent and paternal-grandparent. Father and paternal grandparent are only eligible if father is listed on birth record. **Non-immediate family must provide tangible proof of legal interest for requested record.**

2. Applicant's Relationship: What is your relationship to the person on the certificate

☐ Daughter ☐ Son ☐ Mother ☐ Father ☐ Brother ☐ Sister
☐ Grandchild ☐ Current Spouse ☐ Maternal Grandparent ☐ Paternal Grandparent ☐ Other (Specify)

3. Decedent's Full Name at death: Print First, Middle and Last name of person named on certificate (mandatory)

		Gender
Date of death: Month/Day/Year (mandatory)	**Place of Death: City/County** New Mexico	
Social Security Number (if known)	**Date of Birth: Month/Day/Year (If known)**	**Spouse's Maiden Name (if married at time of death):**

Make payment payable to: New Mexico Vital Records. The fee is for the search of the record and will include one certified copy of record, if available. Search fee is non-refundable if record is not filed.

4. Payment & Quantity

Quantity Death Certificate @ $ 5.00:	
Quantity Chargeable Amendment @ $ 10.00:	
TOTAL Fees Enclosed:	$

☐ Check ☐ Money Order
Check or Money Order Number:

5. Purpose of Request: *Check the reason(s) for use*

☐ Amendment to Vital Record ☐ Estate/ Probate ☐ Discharge Loan
☐ Genealogy ☐ Legal ☐ Insurance ☐ Medical
☐ Passport/Visa ☐ Social Security ☐ Tax Purpose
☐ Other (state other reason):

Signature of Applicant	Date of Application

NEW YORK—NEW YORK CITY

Send your requests for Birth and Death Records to:

NYC Department of Health and Mental Hygiene
Office of Vital Records
125 Worth Street, CN-4, Room 133
New York, NY 10013-4090

Tel. 311 (within NYC); (212) 639-9675 (outside of NYC)
www.nyc.gov/html/doh/html/services/vr.shtml

The Office of Vital Records has birth certificates from 1910 for people who were born in one of the five boroughs of New York City (Manhattan, Brooklyn, Queens, the Bronx, or Staten Island), and death certificates from 1949 for people who died in one of the five boroughs.

For earlier records, contact:

Municipal Archives
NYC Department of Records
31 Chambers Street
New York, NY 10007

www.nyc.gov/html/records/html/home/home.shtml

The Municipal Archives maintains records of births reported in the five Boroughs of New York City (Manhattan, Brooklyn, the Bronx, Queens, and Staten Island) prior to 1910; deaths reported prior to 1949; and marriages reported prior to 1930.

For Marriage Records 1930-present, contact:

City Clerk of New York
141 Worth Street
Attn: Record Room
New York, NY 10013

www.cityclerk.nyc.gov/html/home/home.shtml

The city clerk has copies of marriage licenses from 1930 to the present. Marriage records are restricted for 50 years. You may obtain a marriage record from 1996 to the present in person at any of the city clerk's office locations (see www.cityclerk.nyc.gov/html/about/office.shtml for locations). Marriage records from 1930 through 1995 can be obtained in person only from the Record Room Division located at the Manhattan office (141 Worth Street, New York, NY 10013).

Using City Clerk Online, you can fill out an application for a marriage record request and submit it online directly to the city clerk's office (https://www.nyc.gov/portal/site/cityclerkformsonline).

Divorce records are available from the court clerk in the county where the decree was granted.

Fees for the Office of Vital Records:

Cost for a certified Birth Certificate	$15.00
Cost for a certified Marriage Certificate	$15.00
Cost for a certified Death Certificate	$15.00
Cost for a duplicate copy, when ordered at the same time	$15.00
Cost for extra year searched	$3.00

Fees for City Clerk:

Cost for a copy of a Marriage License	$15.00
Cost for a duplicate copy, when ordered at the same time	$10.00

Fees for the Municipal Archives:

Cost for a certified Birth Certificate	$15.00
Cost for an Heirloom Birth Certificate	$25.00/1st page, $10.00/reverse page
Cost for a certified Death Certificate	$15.00
Cost for a duplicate certified copy, when ordered at the same time	$10.00

For Genealogy Research:

In addition to the public records available at the Municipal Archives (see above), there are a number of online databases with early vital records information. See www.italiangen.org/VRECLIST.stm.

Health

Office of Vital Records
125 Worth Street, CN-4, Room 133
New York, N.Y. 10013-4090

SEE INSTRUCTIONS AND APPLICABLE FEES BELOW AND ON BACK

OFFICE USE ONLY

DO NOT WRITE IN THIS SPACE

BIRTH CERTIFICATE APPLICATION

(Please Print Clearly)

1. LAST NAME ON BIRTH CERTIFICATE	2. FIRST NAME	3. ☐ FEMALE ☐ MALE
4a. IF YOU KNOW THE EXACT DATE OF BIRTH MM DD YYYY	4b. IF YOU DON'T KNOW THE EXACT DATE OF BIRTH BEGIN SEARCH MM DD YYYY END SEARCH MM DD YYYY	***SEE BELOW FOR FEE INFORMATION***
5. NAME OF HOSPITAL OR ADDRESS WHERE BORN		6. BOROUGH WHERE BORN
7. MOTHER/PARENT'S NAME BEFORE MARRIAGE (MAIDEN NAME): FIRST LAST		8. BIRTH CERTIFICATE NUMBER *(if known)*
9. FATHER/PARENT'S NAME FIRST LAST		10. WHY DO YOU NEED THIS BIRTH CERTIFICATE
11. DO YOU NEED A LETTER OF EXEMPLIFICATION? ☐ YES ☐ NO	12. HOW MANY COPIES DO YOU NEED? 1☐ 2☐ 3☐	13. HOW ARE YOU RELATED TO THE PERSON ON THIS BIRTH CERTIFICATE? SELF/PARENT/OTHER *(please explain)*

PLEASE PRINT YOUR MAILING AND CONTACT INFORMATION CLEARLY BELOW

NAME			DAYTIME PHONE NUMBER Area Code – Telephone Number
STREET ADDRESS		APT. NO.	
CITY	STATE	ZIP CODE	E-MAIL ADDRESS

NOTE: Copy of a birth record can be issued only to persons to whom the record of birth relates, if of age, or to a parent or human service organizations. It is a violation of law to make a false, untrue or misleading statement or forge the signature of another on this application. Violations are a misdemeanor punishable by a fine of up to $2,000.

14. CUSTOMER SIGNATURE AND DATE	15. CUSTOMER COMMENTS/ADDITIONAL INFORMATION
SIGNATURE: ________ **DATE:** ________	

FEES

$15 per copy x ________ copies $ ________

Cost of certified copy includes a two consecutive year search

$3 for each extra year searched x ________ years $ ________

Total Amount Enclosed: $ ________

IF RECORD IS NOT ON FILE, A CERTIFIED "NOT FOUND STATEMENT" WILL BE ISSUED. CASH IS NOT ACCEPTED BY MAIL OR IN PERSON.

APPLICATIONS SUBMITTED BY MAIL MUST BE NOTARIZED

STATE OF ________

COUNTY OF ________

SUBSCRIBED AND SWORN BEFORE ME:

THIS ____ DAY OF ________ , 20 ____

____
NOTARY PUBLIC SIGNATURE

NOTARY PUBLIC SEAL

ORDER BIRTH CERTIFICATES QUICKLY AND SECURELY AT WWW.NYC.GOV/VITALRECORDS

VR 67 (Rev. 7/11)

IMPORTANT BIRTH CERTIFICATE INFORMATION

- ➢ You can obtain a birth certificate for yourself if you are at least 18 years old, or for your child, with current identification. Detailed instructions for attorneys submitting requests on behalf of their clients are available online at www.nyc.gov/vitalrecords.
- ➢ Falsifying information, including forging a signature, to obtain a birth certificate is a misdemeanor and violators may also be subject to a fine of up to $2,000 per violation.
- ➢ Submitting fraudulent identification is a crime and violators are subject to prosecution.
- ➢ Credit cards are not accepted for mail-in orders. If from a foreign country, send an international money order.
- ➢ Please allow 10–15 days processing time for all long form/vault certificate orders submitted in-person.
- ➢ Processing of mailed applications takes approximately 30 days.

3 WAYS TO ORDER A NEW YORK CITY BIRTH CERTIFICATE

- **Online:** Visit www.nyc.gov/vitalrecords to order using a credit card, debit card, or electronic check. Online orders are processed within 24 hours on weekdays, and UPS express mail delivery is available.
- **Walk-In:** Go to 125 Worth Street in Lower Manhattan and use the Lafayette Street (handicapped accessible) or Centre Street entrances. We are open Monday through Friday 9:00AM – 3:30PM. Lines are shortest in the morning.
- **By Mail:** All mailed applications must be notarized. Mail your application to 125 Worth Street, CN-4, New York, NY 10013. Be sure to include a self-addressed, stamped, envelope with your check or money order payable to the NYC Department of Health and Mental Hygiene. You must provide a photocopy of Category 1 identification or original copies of identification from either Category 2 or Category 3 (*see below*).

Identification (ID) Requirements to get a Birth Certificate for you or your child.

Category 1: We accept any of the following, **IF** it includes your photo, your signature and is unexpired:

- Driver's License
- Passport
- Government ID
- Employment ID with pay stub

Category 2: If you don't have any of the above, we also accept the following:
(certificate will be mailed to address on documents provided)

- Inmate photo ID with release papers
- Two different documents as indicated below IF they show your name and address and are dated within the past 60 days:
  - Utility or telephone bills
  - Letter from a government agency

Category 3: If you can't provide the above, please get:

- An original letter (we do not accept photocopies) on letterhead from a recognized organization such as the police department or a social services agency explaining why you are unable to provide photo ID from either category above

Department of Records
Municipal Archives

31 Chambers Street
New York, N.Y. 10007
Phone: 311 or (212) NEW-YORK (outside NYC)
nyc.gov/records

BIRTH

APPLICATION FOR A SEARCH AND/OR CERTIFIED COPY OF A BIRTH RECORD PRIOR TO 1910:

FEES:

$15.00 Issuance of certified copy, when certificate number is provided, or search of birth records in one year and one City/Borough for one name and issuance of one certified copy or "not found" statement.

$ 2.00 Per additional year to be searched in one City/Borough for the same name.

$ 2.00 Per additional City/Borough to be searched in one year for same name.

$10.00 Per additional copy of record.

$ 5.00 Per letter of exemplification. Enclose payment for a letter of exemplification in a separate check or money order. If the record is "not found" the payment for the letter will be returned.

- Enclose stamped, self-addressed envelope.
- Make check or money order payable to: NYC Department of Records.
- To expedite processing, please send each request separately.

PLEASE PRINT OR TYPE

Last name on birth record	First name	Female/Male

Date of birth

Month Day Year (s)

Place of birth – if at home, house number and street	City/Borough

Father's name, if known	Mother's name, if known

Your relationship to person named above	Certificate no., if known

Purpose for which this record will be used	Number of copies requested

Your Name, please print	Signature

Address

City	State	Zip Code

MA-22(02-09)

Check form desired:
☐ **Short form**
☐ **Extended form**
☐ **Other**

THE CITY OF NEW YORK
OFFICE OF THE CITY CLERK
MARRIAGE LICENSE BUREAU

MAIL REQUEST FOR MARRIAGE RECORDS

(From 1930 to present)*

NOTE: Marriage records less than fifty (50) years old will be released **only:**

(a) to parties to the marriage;
(b) to persons presenting written authorization from one of the parties to the marriage; or
(c) to attorneys in cases where such records are required as evidence *(When making a request, attorneys, on their official stationery, must indicate the party or parties that they represent, the nature of any pending action, and make an affirmative statement that such records are required as evidence in such proceedings.)*

(PRINT CLEARLY IN BLACK INK)

Date of marriage ceremony:	Month:	Day:	Year:	Borough where the license was issued:
If uncertain, specify other years you want searched:				License number:
Spouse 1 Full legal name before marriage:				Birth date:
Spouse 2 Full legal name before marriage:				Birth date:
Reason search & copy are needed:			Number of copies requested:	
Name of person requesting search:	Your relationship to either spouse:		Your telephone no:	
Your address:	Street	City	State	Zip Code

I solemnly swear, under penalty of perjury, that the foregoing information is true and correct and *(CHECK ONE BOX ONLY)*

(_) **I am a party to the marriage.** (EITHER SPOUSE)

(_) **The written authorization from a party to the marriage is a genuine request from such party and such party has authorized me to request and receive such records.** (THIRD PARTY WITH WRITTEN AUTHORIZATION ONLY)

(_) **I am an attorney in good standing or a representative thereof and such records are required as evidence in a legal proceeding.** (ATTORNEYS OR THEIR REPRESENTATIVES ONLY)

(_) **I am the spouse or prospective spouse of the above-named person and I am not divorced from such person.** (SPOUSE OR PROSPECTIVE SPOUSE ONLY)

(_) **I am the ________ (relation) of the above-named person and the marriage record will be used for a proper purpose.** (RELATIVE OF EITHER SPOUSE)

(_) **I am a law enforcement officer or ________ and the marriage record will be used for a proper purpose.** (LAW ENFORCEMENT PERSONNEL ONLY)

X ____________________ **Date:** __________
Signature (DO NOT PRINT)

*Records from 1866 to 1929 can be obtained from the Municipal Archives, 31 Chambers Street, Rm. 103, New York, NY 10007.
Call 311 or (212) NEW YORK if outside New York

FORM CC2002B 7/12/11

INSTRUCTIONS

Complete this form. **Be sure to check off the appropriate sworn statement and sign in the signature block. No request will be processed without a signed sworn statement. Enclose a photocopy of your identification. Acceptable forms of identification are: driver's license issued by any state of the USA or its territories (including learner's permit); Non-driver's identification card issued by any state of the USA or its territories; active U. S. military ID; passport; permanent resident card (green card); employment authorization card issued by the Bureau of Immigration and Customs of the Department of Homeland Security and Certificate of Naturalization issued less than ten years ago. You should copy the pages in the passport with your picture and personal information. Enclose the appropriate fee and mail to:**

City Clerk of New York
141 Worth Street
New York, NY 10013
Att: Record Room

Fee Schedule: **All fees are payable in advance by United States postal money order or money order/certified check drawn on a United States bank or other financial institution and payable in U.S. currency to "The City Clerk of New York." Each certified copy of a marriage certificate costs $10.00. The first one-year seach costs $5.00. A search for a second year costs an additional $1.00 and searches for any additional year after the second year cost an additional 50 cents each. For example a four year search and one certified copy would cost $17.00. Please note that the average request costs $15.00.**

PLEASE NOTE THERE ARE DIFFERENT TYPES OF MARRIAGE CERTIFICATES. For instance, if you require a marriage certificate for use in a foreign jurisdiction (including obtaining a passport from a US-based foreign consulate) you need an extended form which costs $35 for the initial copy and $30 for any additional copies. For most domestic purposes, you will need a short form which costs $15 for the initial copy and $10 for any additional copies. If you are unsure of the form of marriage certificate you need, please call 311 or (212) NEW YORK if outside of New York. If you do not specify the form you desire you will be sent a short form.

********DO NOT WRITE BELOW---THIS SPACE FOR OFFICE USE ONLY********

License number:		Microfilm cart number:	
Searched by:		Type of cert:	
Receipt no:	Amount: $	Typist:	
Date completed:		Cert no.(s):	

Prior marriage of (__) spouse 1 (__) spouse 2 ( ) Yes ( ) No

Identification presented:

Driver's license (USA & its territories only) (including learner's permit)	State	Exp. date
Non-driver's identification card (USA & its territories only)	State	Exp. date
U.S. military ID		Number
Passport	Country	Exp. date
Permanent resident card (Green card)		Number
Certificate of naturalization		Number
Other:		

FORM CC2002B 6/20/11

Health
Office of Vital Records
125 Worth Street, CN-4, Room 133
New York, N.Y. 10013-4090

SEE INSTRUCTIONS AND APPLICABLE FEES BELOW

OFFICE USE ONLY

DO NOT WRITE IN THIS SPACE

DEATH CERTIFICATE APPLICATION

(Please Print Clearly)

1. LAST NAME AT TIME OF DEATH	2. FIRST NAME	3. ☐ FEMALE ☐ MALE
4. DATE OF DEATH MM DD YYYY	5. IF YOU DON'T KNOW THE EXACT DATE OF DEATH BEGIN SEARCH MM DD YYYY END SEARCH MM DD YYYY	
6. PLACE OF DEATH	7. BOROUGH	8. AGE
9. HOW MANY COPIES DO YOU NEED?	10. DO YOU NEED A LETTER OF EXEMPLIFICATION ☐ YES ☐ NO	
11. SPOUSE OR DOMESTIC PARTNER'S NAME	12. LAST KNOWN ADDRESS	13. OCCUPATION OF DECEASED
14. FATHER/PARENT'S NAME	15. MOTHER/PARENT'S NAME BEFORE MARRIAGE	
16. SOCIAL SECURITY NUMBER	17. CERTIFICATE NUMBER *(if known)*	
18. WHY DO YOU NEED THIS CERTIFICATE?	19. WHAT IS YOUR RELATIONSHIP TO DECEASED?	

PLEASE PRINT YOUR MAILING AND CONTACT INFORMATION CLEARLY BELOW

NAME		DAYTIME PHONE NUMBER Area Code Telephone Number
STREET ADDRESS	APT. NO.	
CITY STATE	ZIP CODE	E-MAIL ADDRESS

NOTE: The confidential medical report of death, including the cause of death, can only be issued for deaths occurring on or after January 1, 2010.

20. DO YOU NEED THE CAUSE OF DEATH? ☐ YES ☐ NO
Cause of Death is only available for deaths occurring on or after January 1, 2010. You are only entitled to the cause of death if your relationship to the decedent is listed below:
Please check the appropriate box
☐ Spouse or Domestic Partner ☐ Child ☐ Parent/Legal Guardian
☐ Person in control of disposition as written on death certificate
☐ The legal representative of one of the above;
please specify ____________

By my signature below, I state I am the person whom I represent myself to be herein. I affirm the information within this form is complete and accurate including the need for and the entitlement to cause of death information. In addition, I acknowledge that misstating my identity or assuming the identity of another person including forging a signature may subject me to a misdemeanor and violators may also be subject to a fine of up to $2,000 per violation.

22. CUSTOMER SIGNATURE. IF BY MAIL MUST BE NOTARIZED

Signature (required) ____________ **Date** ____________

21. **FEES**
$15 per copy x ______ copies $ ______
Cost of certified copy includes a two consecutive year search
$3 for each extra year searched x ______ years $ ______
Total Amount Enclosed: $ ______

IF RECORD IS NOT ON FILE, A CERTIFIED "NOT FOUND STATEMENT" WILL BE ISSUED.

APPLICATIONS SUBMITTED BY MAIL MUST BE NOTARIZED

STATE OF ____________
COUNTY OF ____________
SUBSCRIBED AND SWORN BEFORE ME:
THIS ____ DAY OF ____________, 20 ____

NOTARY PUBLIC SIGNATURE

NOTARY PUBLIC SEAL

Credit cards are not accepted for mail-in orders. Please make your check or money order payable to the NYC Department of Health and Mental Hygiene. If from a foreign country, send an international money order or check drawn on a U.S. bank. Cash is not accepted by mail or in person.

ORDER DEATH CERTIFICATES QUICKLY AND SECURELY AT WWW.NYC.GOV/VITALRECORDS

VR 66 (Rev. 12/11)

IMPORTANT DEATH CERTIFICATE INFORMATION

- You can obtain a death certificate if you are the spouse or other blood relative of the deceased, or if you establish your right to obtain this document *(see documentation requirements below)*.
- All death certificates are mailed, usually within 2-4 weeks. Certificates can be picked-up upon request if you can document the urgent situation. You will be contacted for pick-up.
- Falsifying information, including forging a signature, to obtain a death certificate is a misdemeanor and violators may also be subject to a fine of up to $2,000 per violation.
- Submitting fraudulent identification is a crime and violators are subject to prosecution.
- Please see below for identification requirements, fees and other important information.
- ID requirements are subject to change.

3 WAYS TO ORDER A NEW YORK CITY DEATH CERTIFICATE

- **Online:** Visit www.nyc.gov/vitalrecords to order using a credit card, debit card or electronic check. Only spouses, domestic partners, or other blood relatives of the deceased may submit orders online.
- **Walk-In:** Go to 125 Worth Street in Lower Manhattan and use the Lafayette Street (handicapped accessible) or Centre Street entrances. We are open Monday through Friday 9:00AM – 3:30PM. Lines are shortest in the morning.
- **By Mail: Applications submitted by mail must be signed in the presence of a Notary Public.** Mail your application to 125 Worth Street, CN-4, New York, NY 10013. Be sure to include a self-addressed, stamped, envelope with your check or money order. You also will need to provide a photocopy of the required identification and any necessary documentation (*see below*).

Identification (ID) Requirements if you are a blood relative (including the deceased's spouse or domestic partner) of the deceased

We accept any of the following, **IF** it includes your photo, your signature and is unexpired:

- Driver's License
- Passport
- Government ID
- Employment ID with pay stub

If you don't have any of the above, we also accept:

- Inmate photo ID with release papers
- Two different documents as indicated below IF they show your name and address and are dated within the past 60 days:
  - Utility or telephone bills
  - Letter from a government agency

Documentation Requirements for applicants NOT related to the deceased

In addition to the above identification requirements, you will need to establish your right to obtain a death certificate by providing any of the following original or certified documents which include **both** your name and the name of the deceased:

- Insurance Policy
- Will
- Bank Book or statement
- Property Deed
- Other document showing entitlement

If you are unable to provide the required documents, ask us for help by calling 311.

New York City Department of Records and Information Services
Municipal Archives
31 Chambers Street, New York, NY 10007
Tel: (212) 788-8580
www.nyc.gov/html/doris

FULL-COLOR HEIRLOOM CERTIFICATE ORDER FORM

- Heirloom Certificate copies are computer-scanned from the *original records*. These full-color laser copies are printed on acid-free, heavy weight paper stock.
- Certificates are shipped flat in cardboard mailers.
- The heirloom certificate copies are NOT certified, unless requested (the certification process, which involves imprinting a raised seal, may deface the document). There is no additional charge for certification.
- Certificates are provided for personal use only and may not be sold to another individual or institution. Permission must be obtained before any certificate may be published or re-duplicated in any way (Form MA-45).
- Payment must be submitted with order. Make check payable to *NYC DEPARTMENT OF RECORDS*. Allow 3 weeks for completion of order.

PRICES:

- ***$25.00*** for the first page of a certificate, and ***$10.00*** for the reverse or additional copies of the same certificate. (Please indicate below whether the reverse side of a certificate is requested.)

PLEASE PRINT OR TYPE

Name on Certificate:		
❑ Birth	❑ Death	❑ Marriage

Borough:	Year:	Certificate number: (Required. Please submit copy of certificate if possible.)
Reverse? ❑ Yes ❑ No		Certified? ❑ Yes ❑ No

Your Name:	Phone #:
Mailing Address:	
City, State:	Zip Code:

Certificate:	$25.00
Reverse side @ $10.00:	
Additional copies @ $10.00:	
Postage and handling:	$3.00
Total:	

For office use only:

PAID: CASH	CHECK	DATE:

MA-95 (8-02)

NEW YORK—NEW YORK STATE

Send your requests to:

New York State Department of Health
Vital Records Section
Certification Unit
P.O. Box 2602
Albany, NY 12220-2602

Tel. (518) 474-3077
E-mail: vr@health.state.ny.us
www.health.state.ny.us/vital_records/

The Vital Records Section provides eligible applicants with copies of certificates for births and deaths 1881–present in New York State outside of New York City; marriage licenses 1880–present obtained in New York State outside of New York City; and dissolution of marriage certificates 1963–present for all of New York State. Birth records are restricted for 75 years, while marriage and death records are restricted for 50 years. Birth and death records are also available from the local registrar of the municipality where the event occurred. Marriage records are also available from the town or city clerk of the municipality where the marriage license was issued.

The New York State Department of Health does not have records of birth, death, and marriage from the cities of Albany, Buffalo, and Yonkers prior to January 1, 1914. To obtain records from these municipalities, contact the local registrar for birth and death record requests or the city clerk for marriage record requests (see www.health.ny.gov/vital_records/genealogy.htm for addresses of these offices). The Vital Records Section also does not have any New York City records except for births occurring in Queens and Richmond counties for the years 1881–1897. (See New York—New York City for record information.)

Cost for a certified Birth Certificate	$30.00
Cost for a genealogical Birth Certificate	$22.00
Cost for a certified Marriage Certificate	$30.00
Cost for a Dissolution of Marriage Record	$30.00
Cost for a certified Death Certificate	$30.00
Cost for a genealogical Death Certificate	$22.00

For Genealogy Research:

Vital records registration started in New York State outside of New York City in 1881. The New York State Vital Records Section provides uncertified copies of the following types of records for genealogy research purposes: birth certificates, if on file for at least 75 years and the person whose name is on the birth certificate is known to be deceased; death certificates, if on file for at least 50 years; and marriage certificates, if on file for at least 50 years and the bride and groom are both known to be deceased. For more information about genealogical resources in New York State, go to www.health.ny.gov/vital_records/genealogy.htm.

The New York State Archives (Cultural Education Center, New York State Education Department, Albany, NY 12230; tel. 518-474-8955) has microfilm indexes to vital records held by the New York State Vital Records Section.

For Adoption Record information, contact:

New York State Department of Health
Adoption Information Registry
P.O. Box 2602
Albany, NY 12220-2602

Tel. (518) 474-9600
www.health.state.ny.us/vital_records/adoption.htm

NEW YORK STATE DEPARTMENT OF HEALTH
Vital Records Section

Mail-in Application for Copy of Birth Certificate

Information Page — Mail-in Application for Copy of Birth Certificate

General Instructions

- **Do not** use this application to submit your request *by fax*.
- Use this application only if you are the person named on the birth certificate or that person's parents.
- Use this application only if the birth occurred in New York State *outside* of New York City. **Do not** use this application if the birth occurred in any of the five (5) boroughs of New York City.
- **Do not** use this application for *genealogy requests*.
- Print a copy of this application, complete and sign.
- **Mail** application along with check or money order and a copy of the required documentation (see below).

For regular handling send by first class mail, registered mail, certified mail or U.S. Priority Mail to:

Certification Unit
Vital Records Section
New York State Department of Health
P.O. Box 2602
Albany, NY 12220-2602

For priority handling (add $15.00 per copy ordered), submission by overnight carrier is recommended. Send to:

Certification Unit
Vital Records Section / 2nd Floor
New York State Department of Health
800 North Pearl Street
Menands, NY 12204

Identification Requirements: Application *must* be submitted with copies of either A *or* B:

Note: Copy of Passport required if request is made from a foreign country that requires a U.S. Passport for travel.

A. One (1) of the following forms of valid photo-ID:
   - Driver license
   - Non-driver license
   - Passport
   - Other government issued photo-ID

B. Two (2) of the following showing the applicant's name and address:
   - Utility bill or telephone bill
   - Letter from a government agency dated within the last six (6) months

Fees: If no record is on file, a **No Record Certification** is issued and the fee is **not** refunded.

- **For regular handling:** The fee is $30.00 per copy. — Total for one (1) copy is $30.00. Total for two (2) copies is $60.00, etc.
- **For priority handling:** The fee is $30.00 + $15.00 per copy. — Total for one (1) copy is $45.00. Total for two (2) copies is $90.00, etc. Submitting the application by overnight carrier is recommended. Completed requests will be returned by first class mail unless a **pre-paid** return mailer for overnight delivery is provided with the request.
- Send check or money order payable to the New York State Department of Health. **Do not send cash.**

Note: Payment submitted from foreign countries must be made by a check drawn on a United States bank or by international money order. **Do not send cash.**

Processing Time

- For the latest information on processing times, please visit our web page at *www.nyhealth.gov/vital_records/processingtime.htm*
- For faster processing, you may wish to use your credit card and submit your request by e-mail, fax, or telephone.

Completing the Form

- If you are using Adobe Reader® 5.0 or newer (available as a free download from *www.adobe.com*) you can fill in the form directly in Adobe Reader by clicking on the appropriate space and entering the information (use the TAB key to move to the next field, shift-TAB to move backwards). Print the completed form, sign and mail to the above address.
- You can print out a blank copy of the form and then type or print the required information.
- Be sure to sign the form before mailing and include a check or money order made payable to the New York State Department of Health along with copies of the required identification.

NEW YORK STATE DEPARTMENT OF HEALTH
Vital Records Section

Mail-in Application for Copy of Birth Certificate

Required ID must be included with application. Make check or money order payable to New York State Department of Health.

For regular handling: Enclose $30 per copy or No Record Certification. Send to:

New York State Department of Health
Vital Records Section / Certification Unit
P.O. Box 2602
Albany, NY 12220-2602

For priority handling: Enclose $45 per copy or No Record Certification. Submission by overnight carrier is recommended. Send to:

New York State Department of Health
Vital Records Section / Certification Unit
800 North Pearl Street - 2nd Floor
Menands, NY 12204

Name: (as listed on birth certificate)

First *Middle* *Last*

Date of Birth: *(mm / dd / yyyy)*

Town, city or village where birth occurred:

Name of hospital where birth occurred: (If known)

Maiden Name of Mother: (as listed on birth certificate)

First *Middle* *Maiden Last*

Birth Certificate No.: *(If known)*

Local Registration No.: *(If known)*

Father: (as listed on birth certificate)

First *Middle* *Last*

Number of Copies Requested:

Standard Size: Wallet Size:

Purpose for which Record is Required: *(Check one)*

- ☐ Passport
- ☐ Social Security
- ☐ Retirement
- ☐ Other *(specify)*
- ☐ Employment
- ☐ Working Papers
- ☐ School entrance
- ☐ Drivers license
- ☐ Marriage license
- ☐ Welfare assistance
- ☐ Veteran's benefits
- ☐ Court proceeding
- ☐ Entrance into Armed Forces

What is your relationship to person whose record is required? (If self, state "SELF".)

If attorney, give name and relationship of your client to person whose record is required:

This office requires written authorization of the person/parents whose record is requested.

Signature of Applicant:

Date Signed: Month Day Year

▶

Regular Handling ☐ $30.00 x
(Check Only One) OR
Priority Handling ☐ $45.00 x Copies = $

Address of Applicant:

(Applicant's Name)

(Street)

(City) *(State)* *(Zip)*

Telephone No.: ( )

Please print or type the name and address where record should be sent: *(If delivery is to a P.O. Box or third party, you must submit with this application a* ***notarized*** *statement signed by the applicant and a copy of the applicant's drivers license.)*

(Name)

(Street)

(City) *(State)* *(Zip)*

Mail-in Application for Copy of Marriage Certificate

Information Page — Mail-in Application for Copy of Marriage Certificate

General Instructions

- Use this application if you are the bride, groom or spouse named on the marriage certificate.
- If you are **not** the bride, groom or spouse named on the marriage certificate, then you must submit with this application a copy of documentation establishing a judicial or other proper purpose (see below).
- Use this application only if the marriage license was obtained in New York State *outside* of New York City. **Do not** use this application if the marriage license was obtained in any of the five (5) boroughs of New York City.
- **Do not** use this application for genealogy requests.
- If delivery is to a P.O. Box or to a third party you must submit, with this application, a **notarized** statement signed by the bride, groom or spouse **and** a copy of the bride, groom or spouse's driver license.
- Print a copy of this application, complete and sign.
- **Mail** application with check or money order and a copy of any required documentation (see below).

For regular handling send by first class mail, registered mail, certified mail or U.S. Priority Mail to:

New York State Department of Health
Vital Records Certification Unit
P.O. Box 2602
Albany, NY 12220-2602

For priority handling (add $15.00 per copy ordered), submission by overnight carrier is recommended. Send to:

New York State Department of Health
Vital Records Certification Unit
800 North Pearl Street - 2nd Floor
Menands, NY 12204

What is a judicial or other proper purpose?

- If the applicant is not the bride, groom or spouse, a judicial or other proper purpose must be documented. An example of a judicial or other proper purpose would be a marriage record needed by the applicant to claim a benefit.
- Documentation would consist of a copy of a court order or an official letter verifying that a copy of the requested marriage record is required from the applicant in order to process a claim.

Identification Requirements -- Application *must* be submitted with copies of either A or B:

Note: Copy of Passport required if request is made from a foreign country that requires a U.S. Passport for travel.

A. One (1) of the following forms of valid photo-ID:
   - Driver license
   - State Issued Non-Driver Photo-ID Card
   - Passport
   - U.S. Military Issued Photo-ID

   – OR –

B. Two (2) of the following showing the applicant's current name and address:
   - Utility or telephone bills
   - Letter from a government agency dated within the last six (6) months

Fees: If no record is on file, a **No Record Certification** is issued and the fee is **not** refunded.

- **For regular handling:** The fee is $30.00 per copy. — Total for one (1) copy is $30.00. Total for two (2) copies is $60.00, etc.
- **For priority handling:** The fee is $30.00 + $15.00 per copy — Total for one (1) copy is $45.00. Total for two (2) copies is $90.00, etc. Submitting the application by overnight carrier is recommended. Completed requests will be returned by first class mail unless a **pre-paid return** mailer for overnight delivery is provided with the request.
- Send check or money order payable to the New York State Department of Health. Do not send cash.

Note: Payment submitted from foreign countries must be made by a check drawn on a United States bank or by international money order. **Do not send cash.**

Processing Time

- For the latest information on processing times, please visit our web page at *www.health.ny.gov/vital_records/processingtime.htm*
- For faster processing, you may wish to use your credit card and submit your request on-line or by telephone. For credit card fees and ordering information visit our web page at *www.health.ny.gov/vital_records/vitalchek.htm*

Completing the Form

- If you are using Adobe Reader® 7.0 or newer (available as a free download from *www.adobe.com*) you can fill in the form directly in Adobe Reader by clicking on the appropriate space and entering the information (use the TAB key to move to the next field, shift-TAB to move backwards). Print the completed form, sign and mail to the above address.
- You can print out a blank copy of the form and then **type or print** the required information.
- Be sure to sign the form before mailing and include a check or money order made payable to the New York State Department of Health along with any required documentation.

NEW YORK STATE DEPARTMENT OF HEALTH
Vital Records Section

Mail-in Application for Copy of Marriage Certificate

Required ID must be included with application. Make check or money order payable to New York State Department of Health.

For regular handling: Enclose $30 per copy or No Record Certification. Send to:

New York State Department of Health
Vital Records Certification Unit
P.O. Box 2602
Albany, NY 12220-2602

For priority handling: Enclose $45 per copy or No Record Certification. Submission by overnight carrier is recommended. Send to:

New York State Department of Health
Vital Records Certification Unit
800 North Pearl Street - 2nd Floor
Menands, NY 12204

Bride/Groom/Spouse

Name (as recorded on marriage license):

First *Middle* *Last* *Birth Name (if different)*

Date of Birth: *(or age at time of marriage)*

If Previously Married, State Name Used at that Time:

First *Middle* *Last*

Residence (at time of marriage):

County *State*

Bride/Groom/Spouse

Name (as recorded on marriage license):

First *Middle* *Last* *Birth Name (if different)*

Date of Birth: *(or age at time of marriage)*

If Previously Married, State Name Used at that Time:

First *Middle* *Last*

Residence (at time of marriage):

County *State*

Marriage Information

Place Where Marriage License Was Issued:

Town or City *County*

Place Where Marriage Was Performed:

Town or City *County*

Marriage Certificate No.: *(if known)*

Local Registration No.: *(if known)*

Purpose for which record is required:

Date of Marriage or Period Covered by Search:

Married on or Search from: ________ *(mm / dd / yyyy)*

Search to: (if searching period) ________ *(mm / dd / yyyy)*

In what capacity are you acting?:

What is your relationship to person whose record is required? (If self, state "SELF".)

If attorney, give name and relationship of your client to person whose record is required:

If you are not the bride, groom or spouse on the record, you must submit documentation of a judicial or other proper purpose.

Signature of Applicant:

Date Signed: Month Day Year

▶

Regular Handling ☐ $30.00 x
(Check Only One) OR
Priority Handling ☐ $45.00 x ______ Copies = $ ______

Address of Applicant:

(Applicant's Name)

(Street)

(City) *(State)* *(Zip)*

Telephone No.: (   )

Please print or type the name and address where record should be sent: *(If delivery is to a P.O. Box or third party, you must submit with this application a **notarized** statement signed by the applicant and a copy of the applicant's driver license.)*

(Name)

(Street)

(City) *(State)* *(Zip)*

Mail-in Application for Copy of Divorce Certificate

Information Page — Mail-in Application for Copy of Divorce Certificate

General Instructions

- Use this application if you are the wife, husband or spouse named on the divorce certificate.
- If you are **not** the wife, husband or spouse named on the certificate, then you must submit with this application a copy of a New York State Court Order requiring the divorce certificate.
- Use this application only if the divorce was granted in New York State (*including* New York City) on or after January 1, 1963. Contact the county clerk of the county where the divorce was granted if prior to January 1, 1963.
- **Do not** use this application for genealogy requests.
- If delivery is to a P.O. Box or to a third party you must submit, with this application, a **notarized** statement signed by the wife, husband or spouse **and** a copy of the wife, husband or spouse's driver license.
- Print a copy of this application, complete and sign.
- **Mail** the application along with a check or money order and a copy of any required documentation (see below).

For regular handling send by first class mail, registered mail, certified mail or U.S. Priority Mail to:

New York State Department of Health
Vital Records Certification Unit
P.O. Box 2602
Albany, NY 12220-2602

For priority handling (add $15.00 per copy ordered), submission by overnight carrier is recommended. Send to:

New York State Department of Health
Vital Records Certification Unit
800 North Pearl Street - 2nd Floor
Menands, NY 12204

Who is eligible to obtain a divorce certificate copy?

- If the applicant is not the wife, husband or spouse, a New York State Court Order is required to obtain a copy of the divorce certificate.
- A copy of the New York State Court Order must be submitted along with the application if the request is being made by someone other than the wife, husband or spouse on the record.

Identification Requirements -- Application *must* be submitted with copies of either A or B:

Note: Copy of Passport required if request is made from a foreign country that requires a U.S. Passport for travel.

A. One (1) of the following forms of valid photo-ID:
  - Driver license
  - State Issued Non-Driver Photo-ID Card
  - Passport
  - U.S. Military Issued Photo-ID

  – OR –

B. Two (2) of the following showing the applicant's current name and address:
  - Utility or telephone bills
  - Letter from a government agency dated within the last six (6) months

Fees: If no record is on file, a **No Record Certification** is issued and the fee is **not** refunded.

- **For regular handling:** The fee is $30.00 per copy. — Total for one (1) copy is $30.00. Total for two (2) copies is $60.00, etc.
- **For priority handling:** The fee is $30.00 + $15.00 per copy — Total for one (1) copy is $45.00. Total for two (2) copies is $90.00, etc. Submitting the application by overnight carrier is recommended. Completed requests will be returned by first class mail unless a **pre-paid return** mailer for overnight delivery is provided with the request.
- Send check or money order payable to the New York State Department of Health. Do not send cash.

Note: Payment submitted from foreign countries must be made by a check drawn on a United States bank or by international money order. **Do not send cash.**

Processing Time

- For the latest information on processing times, please visit our web page at *www.health.ny.gov/vital_records/processingtime.htm*
- For faster processing, you may wish to use your credit card and submit your request on-line or by telephone. For credit card fees and ordering information visit our web page at *www.health.ny.gov/vital_records/vitalchek.htm*

Completing the Form

- If you are using Adobe Reader® 7.0 or newer (available as a free download from *www.adobe.com*) you can fill in the form directly in Adobe Reader by clicking on the appropriate space and entering the information (use the TAB key to move to the next field, shift-TAB to move backwards). Print the completed form, sign and mail to the above address.
- You can print out a blank copy of the form and then **type or print** the required information.
- Be sure to sign the form before mailing and include a check or money order made payable to the New York State Department of Health along with any required documentation.

NEW YORK STATE DEPARTMENT OF HEALTH
Vital Records Section

Mail-in Application for Copy of Divorce Certificate

Required ID must be included with application. Make check or money order payable to New York State Department of Health.

For regular handling: Enclose $30 per copy or No Record Certification. Send to:

New York State Department of Health
Vital Records Certification Unit
P.O. Box 2602
Albany, NY 12220-2602

For priority handling: Enclose $45 per copy or No Record Certification. Submission by overnight carrier is recommended. Send to:

New York State Department of Health
Vital Records Certification Unit
800 North Pearl Street - 2nd Floor
Menands, NY 12204

Wife/Husband/Spouse

Name:

First *Middle* *Last* *Birth Name (if different)*

Address at Time of Decree:

Town or City *County*

Wife/Husband/Spouse

Name:

First *Middle* *Last* *Birth Name (if different)*

Address at Time of Decree:

Town or City *County*

Marriage and Divorce Information

Place Where Marriage License Was Issued:

Town or City *County*

Date of Marriage:

(mm / dd / yyyy)

Local Registration No.: *(if known)*

Date of Final Decree or Period Covered by Search:

Decree Issued on or Search from: *(mm / dd / yyyy)*

Search to: (if searching period) *(mm / dd / yyyy)*

Purpose for which record is required?

Divorce Certificate No.: *(if known)*

County in Which Divorce Decree Was Filed:

In what capacity are you acting?:

What is your relationship to person whose record is required? (If self, write "SELF".)

If attorney, give name and relationship of your client to person whose record is required:

If you are not the wife, husband or spouse named in the Decree, you must submit copy of New York State Court Order.

Signature of Applicant:

Date Signed: Month Day Year

Regular Handling ☐ $30.00 x
(Check Only One) OR
Priority Handling ☐ $45.00 x ______ Copies = $ ______

Address of Applicant:

(Applicant's Name)

(Street)

(City) *(State)* *(Zip)*

Telephone No.: ( )

Please print or type the name and address where record should be sent: *(If delivery is to a P.O. Box or third party, you must submit with this application a* ***notarized*** *statement signed by the applicant and a copy of the applicant's driver license.)*

(Name)

(Street)

(City) *(State)* *(Zip)*

Mail-in Application for Copy of Death Certificate

Information Page — Mail-in Application for Copy of Death Certificate

General Instructions

- **Do not** use this application for *fax requests*.
- Use this application if you are the spouse, parent or child of the deceased.
- If you are **not** the spouse, parent or child of the deceased, then you must submit with this application a copy of documentation establishing a lawful right or claim (see below).
- Use this application only if the death occurred in New York State outside of New York City. **Do not** use this application if the death occurred in any of the five (5) boroughs of New York City.
- **Do not** use this application for *genealogy requests*.
- Print a copy of this application, complete and sign.
- **Mail** application with check or money order and a copy of any required documentation (see below).

For regular handling send by first class mail, registered mail, certified mail or U.S. Priority Mail to:

New York State Department of Health
Vital Records Section
Certification Unit
P.O. Box 2602
Albany, NY 12220-2602

For priority handling (add $15.00 per copy ordered), submission by overnight carrier is recommended. Send to:

New York State Department of Health
Vital Records Section / 2nd Floor
Certification Unit
800 North Pearl Street
Menands, NY 12204

What is a lawful right or claim?

- If the applicant is not the spouse, parent or child of the decedent, a lawful right or claim must be documented. An example of a lawful right or claim would be a death record needed by the applicant to claim a benefit.
- Documentation would consist of a copy of a court order or an official letter verifying that a copy of the requested death record is required from the applicant in order to process a claim.

Identification Requirements -- Application *must* be submitted with copies of either A *or* B:

Note: Copy of Passport required if request is made from a foreign country that requires a U.S. Passport for travel.

A. One (1) of the following forms of valid photo-ID:
- Driver license
- Non-Driver Photo-ID Card
- Passport
- Other government issued photo-ID

B. Two (2) of the following showing the applicant's name and address:
- Utility or telephone bills
- Letter from a government agency dated within the last six months

Fees: If no record is on file, a **No Record Certification** is issued and the fee is **not** refunded.

- **For regular handling:** The fee is $30.00 per copy. — Total for one (1) copy is $30.00. Total for two (2) copies is $60.00, etc.
- **For priority handling:** The fee is $30.00 + $15.00 per copy — Total for one (1) copy is $45.00. Total for two (2) copies is $90.00, etc. Submitting the application by overnight carrier is recommended. Completed requests will be returned by first class mail unless a **pre-paid** return mailer for overnight delivery is provided with the request.
- Send check or money order payable to the New York State Department of Health. Do not send cash.

Note: Payment submitted from foreign countries must be made by a check drawn on a United States bank or by international money order. **Do not send cash.**

Processing Time

- For the latest information on processing times, please visit our web page at *www.nyhealth.gov/vital_records/processingtime.htm*
- For faster processing, you may wish to use your credit card and submit your request by e-mail, fax, or telephone.

Completing the Form

- If you are using Adobe Reader® 5.0 or newer (available as a free download from *www.adobe.com*) you can fill in the form directly in Adobe Reader by clicking on the appropriate space and entering the information (use the TAB key to move to the next field, shift-TAB to move backwards). Print the completed form, sign and mail to above address.
- You can print out a blank copy of the form and then type or print the required information.
- Be sure to sign the form before mailing and include a check or money order made payable to the New York State Department of Health along with copies of any required documentation.

Mail-in Application for Copy of Death Certificate

Required ID must be included with application. Make check or money order payable to New York State Department of Health.

For regular handling: Enclose $30 per copy or No Record Certification. Send to:

New York State Department of Health
Vital Records Section / Certification Unit
P.O. Box 2602
Albany, NY 12220-2602

For priority handling: Enclose $45 per copy or No Record Certification. Submission by overnight carrier is recommended. Send to:

New York State Department of Health
Vital Records Section / Certification Unit
800 North Pearl Street - 2nd Floor
Menands, NY 12204

Name of Deceased:

First *Middle* *Last*

Social Security No. of Deceased:

Date of Death or Period to be Covered by Search: (*mm/dd/yyyy)*

From *To*

Date of Birth of Deceased:

mm / dd / yyyy

Age at Death:

Maiden Name of Mother of Deceased:

First *Middle* *Maiden Last*

Death Certificate No.: *(If known)*

Name of Father of Deceased:

First *Middle* *Last*

Local Registration No.: *(If known)*

Place of Death:

Name of Hospital or Street Address *Village, town or city* *County*

Purpose for which Record is Required:

What is your relationship to person whose record is required?

In what capacity are you acting?

If attorney, give name and relationship of your client to person whose record is required:

Submit documentation of a lawful right or claim if you are not the spouse, parent or child of the deceased.

Signature of Applicant:

▶

Date Signed:

Month	Day	Year

Regular Handling ☐ $30.00 x
(Check Only One) OR
Priority Handling ☐ $45.00 x ____ Copies = $ ____

Address of Applicant:

(Applicant's Name)

(Street)

(City) *(State)* *(Zip)*

Telephone No.: ( )

Please print or type the name and address where record should be sent: *(If delivery is to a P.O. Box or third party, you must submit with this application a* ***notarized*** *statement signed by the applicant and a copy of the applicant's drivers license.)*

(Name)

(Street)

(City) *(State)* *(Zip)*

General Information and Application for Genealogical Services

Information Page — Mail-in Application for Genealogical Services

General Instructions

- Use this application only for *genealogy requests.*
- Print a copy of this application, complete and sign.
- **Mail** application with check or money order and a copy of any required documentation (see below) to:

New York State Department of Health
Vital Records Section
Certification Unit
P.O. Box 2602
Albany, NY 12220-2602

Fees: If no record is on file, a **No Record Report** will be issued and the fee is **not** refunded.

- **For standard search:** This includes a three (3) year search. The fee is $22.00 per copy. The fee is for **each** name or type of record requested.
- **For long search:** When more than a three-year search is requested, the fee for each record in need of a longer search is higher according to the following schedule:

1 - 3 years	$22.00	31 - 40 years	$102.00
4 - 10 years	$42.00	41 - 50 years	$122.00
11 - 20 years	$62.00	51 - 60 years	$142.00
21 - 30 years	$82.00	61 - 70 years	$162.00

The fee applies separately to each record requested. For example, the fee for a request consisting of one birth record (1-year search), plus one death record (24-year search), plus one marriage record (11-year search) is a total of $166.00 ($22 + $82 + $62 = $166)

- Send check or money order payable to the New York State Department of Health. Do not send cash.

Note: Payment submitted from foreign countries must be made by a check drawn on a United States bank or by international money order. **Do not send cash.**

Processing Time

For the latest information on processing times, please visit our web page at:
www.nyhealth.gov/vital_records/processingtime.htm

Available Records

- No information shall be released from a record unless the person to whom the record relates is known to the applicant to be deceased.
- No information shall be released unless the record has been on file for a minimum required period: birth records must have been on file for at least 75 years, death records for 50 years, marriage records for 50 years (both parties to the marriage must be deceased).
- The time periods above are waived if the applicant is a descendant and provides documentation of direct line descent. A party acting on behalf of a descendant shall further provide documentation that the descendant authorized the party to make such application.

Completing the Form

- If you are using Adobe Reader® 5.0 or newer (available as a free download from *www.adobe.com*) you can fill in the form directly in Adobe Reader by clicking on the appropriate space and entering the information (use the TAB key to move to the next field, shift-TAB to move backwards). Print the completed form, sign and mail to the address shown above.
- You can print out a blank copy of the form and then type or print the required information.
- Be sure to sign the form before mailing and include a check or money order made payable to the New York State Department of Health along with copies of any required documentation.

General Information and Application for Genealogical Services

VITAL RECORDS COPIES CANNOT BE PROVIDED FOR COMMERCIAL PURPOSES.

Return to: New York State Department of Health, Vital Records Section, P.O. Box 2602, Albany, NY 12220-2602

1. FEE - $22.00 includes search and uncertified copy or notification of no record.
2. Original records of births and marriages for the entire state begin with 1881, deaths begin with 1880, EXCEPT for records filed in Albany, Buffalo and Yonkers prior to 1914. Applications for these cities should be made directly to the local office.
3. The New York State Department of Health does not have New York City records except for births occurring in Queens and Richmond counties for the years 1881 through 1897.
4. Please read the Administrative Rule Summary on the reverse side of this sheet which specifies years available for genealogical research.

To insure a complete search, provide as much information as possible.
Please complete the applicable section for each type of record requested: birth, death or marriage.

Birth	Name at Birth Date of Birth ______ State File Number ______ Place of Birth Father's Name Mother's Maiden Name	**Birth**	Name at Birth Date of Birth ______ State File Number ______ Place of Birth Father's Name Mother's Maiden Name
Marriage	Name of Bride Name of Groom Date of Marriage ______ State File Number ______ Place of Marriage and/or License	**Marriage**	Name of Bride Name of Groom Date of Marriage ______ State File Number ______ Place of Marriage and/or License
Death	Name at Death Date of Death ______ Age at Death ______ Place of Death Names of Parents Name of Spouse State File Number	**Death**	Name at Death Date of Death ______ Age at Death ______ Place of Death Names of Parents Name of Spouse State File Number

For what purpose is information required? ______

What is your relationship to person whose record is requested? ______

In what capacity are you acting? ______

SIGNATURE OF APPLICANT ______ DATE ______

Address ______ Phone ______

Send record to: (please print) Name ______ Address ______ City ______ State ______ Zip Code ______	If requesting birth and marriage records, please sign the following statement: To the best of my knowledge, the person(s) named in the application are deceased. ______ SIGNATURE OF APPLICANT

New York State
Department of Health

Adoption Information Registry
Adoptee Registration Form

COMPLETE THIS APPLICATION AND RETURN TO:

New York State Department of Health
Adoption Information Registry
P.O. Box 2602
Albany, New York 12220-2602
(518) 474-9600

REGISTRY NUMBER ____________________
DATE ____________________

OFFICIAL USE ONLY

NOTE: This registration can be accepted only if the adoptee was born and **adopted** in New York State. **Complete as much information as possible and include a copy of adoptee's birth certificate and adoption order, if available.**

Please indicate if this registration is for: (check all that apply)

☐ **Non-identifying information** (*) -- Available general and medical information about biological parents at time of adoption.

☐ **Non-identifying Medical Information** (**) -- Updated medical information, if/when submitted by biological parents after the adoption.

☐ **Identifying information** (***) - About biological parents, if/when registered.

☐ **Identifying Information** (***) - About biological siblings, if/when registered.

(*) Adoptee must be 18 years of age or older.
(**) No age restriction, but adoptive parent must sign this registration, if adoptee is under 18 years of age.
(***) Adoptee must be 18 years of age or older. Unless this box is checked, you will not be notified of a match even if your birth parents or biological siblings are registered.

Note: If the Adoption Registry determines that an agency was involved in your adoption, non-identifying and identifying information will be released to you by the agency .

☐ **Check box, if you do not want the information released by the agency that handled your adoption. If the box is checked, the New York State Department of Health will obtain the information from the agency and share it with you.**

PLEASE COMPLETE ALL INFORMATION. MISSING INFORMATION MAY DELAY PROCESSING.

1. Name and address of adoptee

LAST FIRST MIDDLE MAIDEN

MAILING ADDRESS STREET CITY/TOWN

STATE ZIP CODE ( ) TELEPHONE NUMBER

2. Date of birth of adoptee

MONTH DAY YEAR

3. Adoptive parents

A. MOTHER: LAST FIRST MIDDLE MAIDEN

B. FATHER: LAST FIRST MIDDLE

C. ADDRESS AT TIME OF ADOPTION, if known STREET CITY/TOWN

STATE ZIP CODE

4. Place of birth of adoptee

HOSPITAL, if known

CITY, TOWN OR VILLAGE COUNTY/BOROUGH

5. Indicate the name of the agency and court of adoption, if known

A. NAME OF AGENCY

CITY, TOWN OR VILLAGE — COUNTY/BOROUGH

☐ Check box if you have already received non-identifying information from adoption agency.

Date received: MONTH | DAY | YEAR

B. NAME OF COURT

C. DATE OF ADOPTION: MONTH | DAY | YEAR

6. Is the adoptee in contact with birth brother(s) and/or sister(s)?

☐ YES ☐ NO If yes, please provide the following information for each sibling with whom adoptee is in contact.

NAME	DATE OF BIRTH	ADDRESS (include zip code)
1.		
2.		
3.		
4.		
5.		
6.		
7.		

7. Signature and Notarization.

State of ____________ }
County of ____________ } SS.

I solemnly attest that all of the information provided on this application is true and accurate to the best of my knowledge under the penalty of perjury.

SIGNATURE OF REGISTRANT
Signature must be notarized

NOTE: Adoptive Parent must sign if the adoptee is under 18 years of age. Notarization must include Notary's stamp or raised seal.

Sworn to before me this ____________ Day

Of ____________ , ____________ .

Notary Public

New York State
Department of Health

Adoption Information Registry
Birth Parent Registration Form

COMPLETE THIS APPLICATION AND RETURN TO:

New York State Department of Health
Adoption Information Registry
P.O. Box 2602
Albany, NY 12220-2602
(518) 474-9600

REGISTRY NUMBER ____________________
DATE ____________________

OFFICIAL USE ONLY

Please indicate if this registration is to: (check all that apply)

- ☐ Register for identifying information (Adoptee must be 18 years of age or older)
- ☐ Submit medical information diagnosed after the adoption (No age restriction)

Medical information must be submitted on medical care provider's letterhead and include: medical care provider's name, address, telephone number, and signature.

---

1. Name and address of birth mother

LAST ______ FIRST ______ MIDDLE ______ MAIDEN ______

CURRENT MAILING ADDRESS ______ STREET ______ CITY/TOWN ______

STATE ______ ZIP CODE ______ ( ) CURRENT TELEPHONE NUMBER ______

BIRTH MOTHER'S DATE OF BIRTH

MONTH	DAY	YEAR

2. Were you married at the time of the child's birth? ☐ YES ☐ NO

IF YES, NAME OF HUSBAND ______

3. List any other name you may have been using at the time of the child's birth, (i.e., former married name, assumed name, alias, etc.)

______

4. Name and address of birth father

LAST ______ FIRST ______ MIDDLE ______

MONTH	DAY	YEAR

BIRTH FATHER'S DATE OF BIRTH

CURRENT MAILING ADDRESS ______ STREET ______ CITY/TOWN ______

STATE ______ ZIP CODE ______ ( ) CURRENT TELEPHONE NUMBER ______

5. Name given to child at birth

____
LAST FIRST MIDDLE

6. Date of birth of child MONTH DAY YEAR **Time of birth** ___:___ ☐ **AM** ☐ **PM**

7. Sex of child ☐ **Female** ☐ **Male**

8. Place of birth of child

HOSPITAL (if not hospital, give street address) NAME OF PHYSICIAN

CITY, TOWN OR VILLAGE COUNTY/BOROUGH

9. Name of agency where child was placed for adoption ☐ **Check, if private placement**

NAME OF AGENCY NAME OF CASE WORKER

CITY, TOWN OR VILLAGE COUNTY/BOROUGH

10. Indicate name of Court, if known

A. NAME OF COURT

MONTH DAY YEAR
B. DATE OF ADOPTION

11. Signature and notarization

State of ______________________)
SS
County of ______________________)

I solemnly attest that all of the information provided on this application is true and accurate to the best of my knowledge under the penalty of perjury.

SWORN TO BEFORE ME THIS

________ day of ________ ________

____
Notary Public

SIGNATURE OF BIRTH PARENT
Signature must be notarized

NOTE: Notorization must include Notary's stamp or raised seal.

NORTH CAROLINA

Send your requests to:

North Carolina Department of Health and Human Services
Vital Records Unit
(Location: 225 North McDowell Street)
1903 Mail Service Center
Raleigh, NC 27699-1903

Tel. (919) 733-3000
http://vitalrecords.nc.gov/

The Vital Records Unit has birth records from 1913, death records from 1930, marriage records from 1962, and divorce records from 1958. Births and deaths have been registered in North Carolina only since 1913; prior to that, the state did not use birth records or certificates of any kind.

The register of deeds in each county (see www.ncard.us/Directory/CountyMap.htm for locations) maintains copies of the birth, marriage, and death certificates for events that occurred in that county. An exception is Mecklenburg County, where the local health department maintains birth and death certificates. Divorce decrees are maintained by the clerk of court's office in the county of the divorce.

Cost for a certified Birth Certificate	$24.00
Cost for a certified Marriage Certificate	$24.00
Cost for a certified Divorce Record	$24.00
Cost for a certified Death Certificate	$24.00
Cost for a duplicate copy, when ordered at the same time	$15.00

For pre-1913 Birth Records & pre-1962 Marriage Certificates, contact:

County Register of Deeds
(County Seat), NC

For pre-1930 Death Records, contact:

North Carolina State Archives
(Location: 109 East Jones Street)
4610 Mail Service Center
Raleigh, NC 27699-4610

Tel. (919) 807-7310
www.archives.ncdcr.gov/

A few delayed death records may exist back to 1909.

For Genealogy Research:

The North Carolina Vital Records Office will provide uncertified copies of certificates to anyone who requests them, unless legal restrictions apply (with the exception of birth certificates for adopted persons).

The North Carolina State Archives (see above for contact information) has a number of county records.

For Adoption Record information, contact:

Adoption Services
North Carolina State Division of Social Services
(Location: 325 North Salisbury Street)
2425 Mail Service Center
Raleigh, NC 27699-2425

Tel. (919) 733-9464
www.ncdhhs.gov/dss/adoption/searchinfo.htm

North Carolina Department of Health and Human Services
Division of Public Health • Vital Records Unit
http://vitalrecords.nc.gov
Telephone: 919-733-3000

Mail: 1903 Mail Service Center
Raleigh, NC 27699-1903

Location: 225 North McDowell St.
Raleigh, NC 27603-1382

PLEASE PRINT

Application for a Copy of a North Carolina Birth Certificate

Certificate Information

Full Name on Certificate (If adopted, provide new information) ______ First Name / Middle Name / Last Name

Date of Birth ____ | ____ | ______ Month / Day / Year

Sex ☐ Male ☐ Female

Were parents married at time of birth? ☐ Yes ☐ No

Place of Birth ______ City / County

Is this person deceased? ☐ Yes ☐ No

Full Maiden Name of Mother (Adoptive mother, if applies) ______ First Name / Middle Name / Last Name (before any marriage)

Full Name of Father (Adoptive father, if applies) ______ First Name / Middle Name / Last Name

CUSTOMER MUST COMPLETE

Check all boxes that apply; add the fees in 1–3 and place the total amount in #4. See further instructions on Page 2.

1. Order Certificate
Processing times vary.
Check website for current information.
(Non-refundable fee)

- ☐ Certificate Search and First Copy ($24) $______
- ☐ #___ additional copies x $15 $______
- ☐ Certified (Legally suitable for any purpose)
- ☐ Uncertified (Suitable for research purposes)

2. Record Changes (Only if applies)
Appointment required for in-person services.
($15 non-refundable processing fee)

- ☐ Adoption $______
- ☐ Amendment $______
- ☐ Name Change $______
- ☐ Legitimation Court Order $______
- ☐ Legitimation (mother married father after child's birth) $______
- ☐ Paternity (no fee) $ 00.00
- ☐ Other ______ $______

3. Faster Service (Choose only one)
Optional for mail-in requests
($15 non-refundable expedite fee)

- ☐ Walk-in Service ($15) $______
- ☐ Expedited Processing ($15) $______ (Shipped by regular mail)
- ☐ Expedited Processing and Expedited Shipping ($35) $______ (Call for expedited shipping fees outside the continental United States)

4. Total Fees
(Add 1+2+3 above for total) $______

Your Relationship to the Person Whose Certificate is Requested: (Check one)

- ☐ Self
- ☐ Spouse (Current)
- ☐ Brother/Sister
- ☐ Child
- ☐ Parent/Step-Parent
- ☐ Grandparent
- ☐ Authorized agent, attorney or legal representative of the person listed ***(Proof REQUIRED)***
- ☐ Other *(may not be entitled to a certified copy)* Specify

How do you plan to use this record?

(Please Print)
Requestor: ______ *Print Name of Person Requesting a Certificate*

Address: ______ *Street Address (P.O. Box cannot be used for expedited shipping)*

______ *P.O. Box (If mailing to a P.O. Box, street address must also be listed above)*

______ *City, State, Zip Code*

______ *(Area Code) Telephone Number (During business hours)*

Email Address: ______

Payment: Please pay with a cashier's check or money order made payable to N.C. Vital Records. Personal checks are not accepted. Requests that are submitted with no payment, ***or*** incomplete payment ***or*** incomplete information will be returned. Credit card payment is available for walk-in customers.

ID OF THE PERSON REQUESTING A CERTIFICATE IS REQUIRED: See Page 2 for a list of acceptable IDs. Requests that do not include proper identification will be returned.

I hereby certify that all the above information is true to the best of my knowledge. **Note: It is a felony violation of N.C. Law (G.S. 130A-26A) to make a false statement on this application or to unlawfully obtain a copy or a certified copy of a birth certificate.**

______ *Signature of Person Requesting a Certificate* ______ *Date*

Office Use Only: SFN ______ DCN ______ Cartridge/Frame ______
Amount received: $______ Identification presented ______
Request number ______ Request date ______

DHHS-VR-B (Revised 07/13)
N.C. Vital Records (Review 07/16)

Order Certificate

A certificate search costs $24 and includes one copy if the certificate is located. The search covers a three year period. Requests are processed in the order received and can take up to five weeks plus the mail delivery time. The search fee is required to process a request and is non-refundable even if a record cannot be located.

Record Changes

Complete this section only if you are making a request to change information on the birth certificate. The $15 processing fee to review your request is non-refundable. In-person assistance for this service is by appointment only. Please call (919) 792-5986 to schedule an appointment. If your request involves more than one birth record, the $15 processing fee applies to each individual's birth record that requires change(s).

Faster Service

To receive expedited service you **MUST write "Expedite"** on the outside of the envelope. Expedited requests will be processed within 10 business days. This does not include the additional day(s) for shipping. This is a non-refundable fee.

Identification Requirement

Due to identity theft and other fraudulent use of vital records, **ID of the person requesting a certificate is REQUIRED. Requests that do not include ID will be returned. You MUST include a legible photocopy of one of the photo IDs listed below with your request:**

- Current state-issued driver's license (address must match requestor's address on application)
- Current state-issued non-driver photo ID card (address must match requestor's address on application)
- Current Passport or Visa (must include photo)
- Current U.S. military ID
- Current Department of Corrections photo ID card dated within the last year
- Current state or U.S. government agency photo ID card (for persons requesting certificates as part of that agency's business)
- Current student ID card with copy of transcript

If you do not have one of the IDs listed above, you must provide legible photocopies of TWO of the following (must be two DIFFERENT forms of ID):

- Temporary driver's license
- Current utility bill with current address
- Car registration or title with current address
- Bank statement with current address
- Pay stub with current address
- Income tax return/W-2 form showing current address
- Letter from government agency dated within the last six months and showing current address
- State-issued concealed weapon permit showing current address

If you are unable to meet our ID requirements, a family member or other person who is entitled to obtain the certificate, and who can meet the ID requirements, may request it. A list of persons entitled to obtain certificates is located on our website at http://vitalrecords.nc.gov/faqs.htm.

North Carolina Department of Health and Human Services
Division of Public Health • Vital Records Unit
http://vitalrecords.nc.gov

Mail: 1903 Mail Service Center
Raleigh, NC 27699-1903

Location: 225 North McDowell St.
Raleigh, NC 27603-1382

Application for North Carolina Death, Marriage or Divorce Record

A Death, Marriage or Divorce Certificate search costs $24 and includes one copy if a certificate is located. The search covers a three-year period. **This search fee is non-refundable.** There is a fee of $15 for each additional certificate copy requested from the same search. If you want same-day walk-in service, an additional $15 expedited processing fee is required. Mail-in applicants may also receive expedited service. Include the $15 expedite fee and write "Expedite" on the envelope. For expedited processing and expedited shipping add $35. (Call for expedited shipping fees outside the continental United States.) Make your certified check or money order payable to "N.C. Vital Records." Please do not send cash in the mail. **Personal checks are not accepted.** If you have questions, our telephone number is 919-733-3000.

Please Print **Identification of the person requesting a certificate is required. See page 2 for a list of acceptable IDs. Requests that do not include proper identification will be returned.**

Death Certificate **Number of Copies Requested** **Certified** _____ **Uncertified** _____

Full Name of Deceased ______________________________

Date of Death *(Month/Day/Year)* ______________ Age at Time of Death ___ Race ______________

Location of Death *(City or County)* ______________________

Date of Birth *(Month/Day/Year)* ______________________

Office Use Only
Book ____ Page ____

Marriage Certificate **Number of Copies Requested** **Certified** _____ **Uncertified** _____

Full Name of Groom ______________________________

Full Maiden Name of Bride ______________________________

Date of Marriage *(Month/Day/Year)* ______________________

Location of Marriage *(City or County)* ______________________

Office Use Only
Book ____ Page ____

Divorce Certificate **Number of Copies Requested** **Certified** _____ **Uncertified** _____

Full Name of Husband ______________________________

Full Maiden Name of Wife ______________________________

Date of Divorce *(Month/Day/Year)* ______________________

Location of Divorce *(City or County)* ______________________

Office Use Only
Book ____ Page ____

Required for All Certificates Requested

Your Relationship to the Person Whose Certificate is Requested: ***(Check one)***

- ☐ Self
- ☐ Spouse (current)
- ☐ Brother/Sister
- ☐ Child
- ☐ Parent/Step-Parent
- ☐ Grandparent
- ☐ Authorized agent, attorney or legal representative of the person listed ***(Proof Required)***
- ☐ Other *(may not be entitled to a certified copy)*
  Specify ______________________

How do you plan to use this record?

I hereby certify that all the above information is true to the best of my knowledge. **Note: It is a FELONY VIOLATION of North Carolina Law (G.S. 130A-26A) to make a false statement on this application or to unlawfully obtain a certified copy of a vital record.**

____
Signature of Person Applying for Certificate

____
Street Address or P.O. Box (P.O. Box cannot be used for expedited shipping.)

____
City, State and Zip Code

______________________ ______________________
Date *(Area Code) Telephone Number*

Office Use Only
Identification furnished
____
____
____
Amount Received $__________

DHHS-VR-DMD (Revised 07/13)
N.C. Vital Records (Review 07/16)

Order Certificate

A certificate search costs $24 and includes one copy if the certificate is located. The search covers a three-year period. Requests are processed in the order received and can take up to five weeks plus the mail delivery time. The search fee is required to process a request and is non-refundable even if a record cannot be located.

Faster Service

To receive expedited service you **MUST write "Expedite"** on the outside of the envelope. Expedited requests will be processed within 10 business days. This does not include the additional day(s) for shipping. This is a non-refundable fee.

Identification Requirement

Due to identity theft and other fraudulent use of vital records, **ID of the person requesting a certificate is REQUIRED. Requests that do not include ID will be returned. You MUST include a legible photocopy of one of the photo IDs listed below with your request:**

- Current state-issued driver's license (address must match requestor's address on application)
- Current state-issued non-driver photo ID card (address must match requestor's address on application)
- Current Passport or Visa (must include photo)
- Current U.S. military ID
- Current Department of Corrections photo ID card dated within the last year
- Current state or U.S. government agency photo ID card (for persons requesting certificates as part of that agency's business)
- Current student ID card with copy of transcript

If you do not have one of the IDs listed above, you must provide legible photocopies of TWO of the following (must be two DIFFERENT forms of ID):

- Temporary driver's license
- Current utility bill with current address
- Car registration or title with current address
- Bank statement with current address
- Pay stub with current address
- Income tax return/W-2 form showing current address
- Letter from government agency dated within the last six months and showing current address
- State-issued concealed weapon permit showing current address

If you are unable to meet our ID requirements, a family member or other person who is entitled to obtain the certificate, and who can meet the ID requirements, may request it. A list of persons entitled to obtain certificates is located on our website at http://vitalrecords.nc.gov/faqs.htm.

NORTH DAKOTA

Send your requests to:

North Dakota Department of Health
Division of Vital Records
600 East Boulevard Avenue, Department 301
Bismarck, ND 58505-0200

Tel. (701) 328-2360
Fax (701) 328-1850
E-mail: vitalrec@nd.gov
www.ndhealth.gov/vital/

The Division of Vital Records has birth records from 1870; marriage records from July 1, 1925; an index of divorce decrees from July 1, 1949; and death records from 1881. Certificates can be ordered through the Division of Vital Records on the Internet or by fax, as well as by mail and in person. Proof of identity is needed for all individuals ordering a birth or death certificate; see the website of the Division of Vital Records for more information.

Cost for a certified Birth Certificate	$7.00
Duplicate copy of Birth Certificate, when ordered at the same time	$4.00
Cost for a certified Death Certificate	$5.00
Duplicate copy of Death Certificate, when ordered at the same time	$2.00

For Marriage Certificates and Divorce Records, contact:

County Clerk of Court or Recorder
District County Court
(County Seat), ND

Certified copies of marriage and divorce records must be obtained through the county where the marriage license was issued or the divorce was decreed. See www.ndhealth.gov/vital/marriage.htm for contact information for marriage certificates, and www.ndhealth.gov/vital/divorce.htm for divorce contact information.

For Genealogy Research:

The North Dakota Division of Vital Records will issue an informational copy of a death record for genealogical purposes. This copy is similar to a full death record and could be issued to anyone for any reason; however, it would not include the cause of death or social security number.

The Public Death Index is available online at https://secure.apps.state.nd.us/doh/certificates/deathCertSearch.htm. An index to deaths in the state is also available for use in the reading room of the State Historical Society of North Dakota (612 East Boulevard Avenue, Bismarck, ND 58505-0830; tel. 701-328-2666; www.nd.gov/hist/index.html).

For Adoption Record information, contact:

North Dakota Department of Human Services
Children and Family Services
600 East Boulevard Avenue, Department 325
Bismarck, ND 58505-0250

Tel. (701) 328-2316
E-mail: dhscfs@nd.gov
www.nd.gov/dhs/services/childfamily/adoption/disclosure.html

INSTRUCTIONS FOR OBTAINING A CERTIFIED COPY OF A BIRTH RECORD

The Division of Vital Records can issue copies of birth certificates only for births that occurred in North Dakota. We have records on file starting with 1870 to the present.

Effective January 1, 2008:

> **NDCC 23-02.1-27 (1)** – A certified copy of a birth record may be issued to the individual named on the record if that individual is at least 16 years old, to a parent named on the record, to an authorized representative, or by the order of a court of competent jurisdiction. If the individual named on the birth record is deceased, a certified copy of that record may also be issued to a relative. A relative means a person's current or surviving spouse, a parent or legal guardian, a child, a grandparent, or a grandchild.

Because of these new restrictions, we must require proof of identification before we can release a certified copy of a birth record. **Proof of identification can be established by submitting a legible photocopy of one of the following forms of identification**:

1. State Government issued Photo ID or Driver's License
2. Bureau of Indian Affairs issued tribal ID card
3. US Government issued Military ID card
4. US Government issued Passport or Visa
5. US Government issued Permanent Resident Card

The fee for a search of the files is $7; one search fee pays for one certified copy. Additional copies of the same record issued at the same time are $4 each. Please make your check or money order payable to North Dakota Department of Health. We will issue a certified raised-seal paper copy for each copy requested.

Once received in our office, copies are usually mailed in 5 to 7 business days **(this does not include the mailing time).** Copies to be sent by Federal Express or UPS are processed the same day, provided the request is in our office by 10:00 a.m. Central Time.

Certified copies **CANNOT** be faxed. The certified copies will be sent by first class mail unless you specify and include the funds for special shipping through **Federal Express** for an **additional $16.00** (add $6 for delivery to Alaska or Hawaii) or **UPS** for an **additional $16.**

This form may be completed and mailed with fees to:

Vital Records
600 East Boulevard Ave. Dept. 301
Bismarck, ND 58505-0200

If you prefer, you may complete this form and fax it with your **Visa, Master Card,** or **Discover** credit card number and expiration date to (701) 328-1850. Remember to fax a copy of your ID!!

Our web page is at: www.ndhealth.gov/vital

Our email address is: vitalrec@nd.gov

REQUEST FOR CERTIFIED COPY OF A BIRTH RECORD

NORTH DAKOTA DEPARTMENT OF HEALTH
DIVISION OF VITAL RECORDS
SFN 8140 (Rev. 6-2009)

PLEASE PRINT - ALL ITEMS MUST BE COMPLETED AND LEGIBLE TO LOCATE AND IDENTIFY THE RECORD

1. Full Name at Birth		2. Gender ☐ Male ☐ Female
3. Date of Birth (Month, Day, Year)	4. Place of Birth (City, Township or County)	
5. Full Name of Father (First, Middle, Last)		
6. Full Name of Mother (First, Middle, Maiden)		

7. Number of Certified Copies Requested **($7.00 - 1st Copy; $4.00 for each additional)**

________ Certified (For all official purposes, including U.S. Passport, Driver's License, Social Security, etc.)

________ Genealogy (For researching family history - not available for births occurring after 2005)

8. Your Relationship to Person on Line 1*

☐ Self (must be 16 or older) ☐ Mother/Father ☐ Public (Only if record is over 100 years old) ☐ Authorized Representative (Needs to include court order)

☐ Legal Guardian (must include guardianship papers-Social Services must also include employment photo ID)

If individual on line #1 is deceased and you are the ☐ spouse, ☐ parent, ☐ child, ☐ grandparent, or ☐ grandchild, you may request birth record. **You must include a certified copy of the death record.**

**INDIVIDUAL SIGNING HERE MUST SUPPLY THEIR PHOTO ID OR NOTARIZED SIGNATURE BELOW

Signature			Date	
Printed Name			Daytime Telephone Number	
Mailing Address	Apartment No.	City	State	ZIP Code

If Copy is to be Mailed Elsewhere, please provide mailing address below

Mailing Name				
Mailing Address	Apartment No.	City	State	ZIP Code

Shipping Instructions: (First Class Mail is the default)	***Credit Card Information:***	Card Number
☐ First Class Mail – (No Charge)	☐ Visa	Expiration (Month/Year)
☐ FedEx - $16 (Add $6 for AK or HI; add $50 for International)	☐ Mastercard	3-Digit Security Code
☐ UPS - $16 (Add $50 for International)	☐ Discover	
☐ Waive Signature for FedEx or UPS Delivery		

***IDENTIFICATION** – All applicants must submit **EITHER** a clear copy of a government issued photo ID that contains the applicant's signature **OR** submit a notarized application.*

Subscribed to and sworn before me this (date):	SEAL
Signature of Notary Public	
My Commission Expires	

***Warning** – NDCC 23-02.1-32(c) Penalties. Any person who willfully or knowingly uses or attempts to use or to furnish to another for use, for any purpose of deception, any certificate, record, report, or certified copy thereof so made, altered, amended or mutilated shall be guilty of a class C felony.*

PLEASE DO NOT ENTER ANYTHING BELOW THE LINE - THIS PORTION FOR OFFICIAL VITAL RECORDS OFFICE USE ONLY

Identification Verified	Fee Received

INSTRUCTIONS FOR OBTAINING A CERTIFIED COPY OF A DEATH RECORD

The Division of Vital Records can issue copies of death certificates only for deaths that occurred in North Dakota. We have records on file starting with 1881 to the present.

Effective January 1, 2008:

NDCC 23-02.1-27 (2) – A certified copy of a death record may be issued to a relative, an authorized representative, the child fatality review board, or a funeral director reporting the facts of death, or by the order of a court of competent jurisdiction and may include the cause of death and the social security number. A certified copy of a death record that includes the facts of death and the social security number may be issued to any person that may obtain a certified copy of a death record or to any licensed attorney who requires the copy for a bona fide legal determination. A certified informational copy of a death record may be issued to the general public, but the copy may not contain the cause of death or the social security number. A relative means a person's current or surviving spouse, a parent or legal guardian, a child, a grandparent, or a grandchild.

Because of these new restrictions, we must require proof of identification before we can release a certified copy of a birth record. **Proof of identification can be established by submitting a legible photocopy of one of the following forms of identification**:

1. State Government issued Photo ID or Driver's License
2. Bureau of Indian Affairs issued tribal ID card
3. US Government issued Military ID card
4. US Government issued Passport or Visa
5. US Government issued Permanent Resident Card

The fee for a search of the files is $5; one search fee pays for one certified copy. Additional copies of the same record issued at the same time are $2 each. Please make your check or money order payable to North Dakota Department of Health. We will issue a certified raised-seal paper copy for each copy requested.

Once received in our office, copies are usually mailed in 5 to 7 business days **(this does not include the mailing time).** Copies to be sent by Federal Express or UPS are processed the same day, provided the request is in our office by 10:00 a.m. Central Time.

Certified copies **CANNOT** be faxed. The certified copies will be sent by first class mail unless you specify and include the funds for special shipping through **Federal Express** for an **additional $16.00** (add $6 for delivery to Alaska or Hawaii) or **UPS** for an **additional $16.**

This form may be completed and mailed with fees to:

Vital Records
600 East Boulevard Ave. Dept. 301
Bismarck, ND 58505-0200

If you prefer, you may complete this form and fax it with your **Visa, Master Card,** or **Discover** credit card number and expiration date to (701) 328-1850. Remember to fax a copy of your ID!!

Our web page is at: www.ndhealth.gov/vital

Our email address is: vitalrec@nd.gov

REQUEST FOR CERTIFIED COPY OF A DEATH RECORD

NORTH DAKOTA DEPARTMENT OF HEALTH
DIVISION OF VITAL RECORDS
SFN 5531 (Rev. 3-2009)

PLEASE PRINT - ALL ITEMS MUST BE COMPLETED AND LEGIBLE TO LOCATE AN D IDENTIFY THE RECORD

1. Full Name of Deceased	2. Gender ☐ Male ☐ Female

3. Date of Death (Month, Day, Year)	4. Place of Death (City, Township or County)

5. Number of Certified Copies Requested **($5.00 - 1st Copy; $2.00 for each additional)**

_________ Full (Contains both Cause of Death and SSN – For Life Insurance and Veteran's Administration)

_________ Facts of Death (Contains SSN, no Cause of Death - For financial institutions)

_________ Informational (Contains no Cause of Death or SSN – issued to requestors not qualified to have full or facts of death)

6. Is this for genealogy/family history? ☐ Yes ☐ No

7. Your Relationship to Person on Line 1*

☐ Spouse ☐ Parent ☐ Child ☐ Grandparent ☐ Grandchild ☐ Funeral Director ☐ General Public (Informational only)

☐ Licensed Attorney (Facts of Death only) ☐ Authorized Representative (include court order) ☐ Other ____________

** NDCC 23-02.1-27 (2) – A certified copy of a death record may be issued to a relative, an authorized representative, the child fatality review board, or a funeral director reporting the facts of death, or by the order of a court of competent jurisdiction and may include the cause of death and the social security number. A certified copy of a death record that includes the facts of death and a social security number may be issued to any person that may obtain a certified copy of a death record or to any licensed attorney who requires the copy for a bona fide legal determination. A certified informational copy of a death record may be issued to the general public, but the copy may not contain the cause of death or the social security number.*

Signature			Date	
Printed Name			Daytime Telephone Number	
Mailing Address	Apartment No.	City	State	ZIP Code

If Copy is to be Mailed Elsewhere, please provide mailing address below

Mailing Name				
Mailing Address	Apartment No.	City	State	ZIP Code

Shipping Instructions: (First Class Mail is the default)

☐ First Class Mail – (No Charge)
☐ FedEx - $16 (Add $6 for AK or HI; add $50 for International)
☐ UPS - $16 (Add $50 for International)
☐ Waive Signature for FedEx or UPS Delivery

Credit Card Information:

☐ Visa
☐ Mastercard
☐ Discover

Card Number
Expiration (Month/Year)
3-Digit Security Code

***IDENTIFICATION** – All applicants must submit **EITHER** a clear copy of a government issued photo ID that contains the applicant's signature **OR** submit a notarized application.*

Subscribed to and sworn before me this (date):	SEAL
Signature of Notary Public	
My Commission Expires	

***Warning** – NDCC 23-02.1-32(c) Penalties. Any person who willfully or knowingly uses or attempts to use or to furnish to another for use, for any purpose of deception, any certificate, record, report, or certified copy thereof so made, altered, amended or mutilated shall be guilty of a class C felony.*

PLEASE DO NOT ENTER ANYTHING BELOW THE LINE - THIS PORTION FOR OFFICIAL VITAL RECORDS OFFICE USE ONLY

Identification Verified	Fee Received

OHIO

Send your requests to:

Ohio Department of Health
Office of Vital Statistics
(Location: 225 Neilston Street)
P.O. Box 15098
Columbus, OH 43215-0098

Tel. (614) 466-2531
E-mail: vitalstat@odh.ohio.gov
www.odh.ohio.gov/vitalstatistics/vitalmisc/vitalstats.aspx

The Vital Statistics Office has birth records from December 20, 1908, and death records from January 1, 1954. Birth records are also available from any city or county health department, and death records are also available from the city or county health department where the event occurred.

The Vital Statistics Office does not have marriage licenses or divorce decrees on file but does maintain an index of marriages and divorces that occurred in Ohio from January 1, 1954, to the present. You can obtain a marriage license from the county Probate Court where the original marriage license is on file (for a directory visit www.franklincountyohio.gov/probate/ohio_judges.cfm). For divorce decrees, contact the clerk of courts in the county where the original divorce decree is on file (for a directory visit www.occaohio.com/).

Cost for a certified Birth Certificate	$21.50
Cost for an Heirloom Birth Certificate	$25.00
Cost for a certified Death Certificate	$21.50

For Genealogy Research:

The Ohio Historical Society (800 E. 17th Avenue, Columbus, OH 43211; tel. 614-297-2300; e-mail: reference@ohiohiostory.org; www.ohiohistory.org) has birth and death records from several Ohio counties from 1867 through December 19, 1908; microfilm copies of death certificates for the entire state from December 20, 1908, through December 31, 1953; and marriage and divorce records from some counties and varying time periods. An online, digitized version of the Ohio Death Certificate Index, 1913–1944, is available at http://ohsweb.ohiohistory.org/death/. From this website, you can request copies of death certificates for the years 1909–1912 and 1945–1953.

For Adoption Record information, contact:

Ohio Department of Health
Office of Vital Statistics
P.O. Box 15098
Columbus, OH 43215

Tel. (614) 466-2531

Pre-January 1, 1964, adoption records are open to people who were adopted in Ohio.

Cost for copy of an Adoption File	$20.00

Ohio Department of Health • Office of Vital Statistics
Application For Certified Copies

Reason for order

Driver's License	☐	Passport	☐
Insurance	☐	Genealogy	☐
School	☐	International Use	☐
Marriage License	☐	Other	☐

Mail-in order

Send completed application with required fee to:
Ohio Department of Health,
Vital Statistics
P.O. Box 15098
Columbus, Ohio 43215-0098
(614) 466-2531

This space for office use only
Order Number (AFS)
Service
Certificate Number

Certificate Requested: *(What type of certificate is being ordered)*

Birth Certificate $21.50 per certificate	☐	**Heirloom Birth Certificate** $25.00 per commemorative certificate	☐	**Paternity Affidavit** $7.00 per certified copy	☐
Death Certificate $21.50 per certified copy	☐	**Fetal Death Certificate** $21.50 per certified copy	☐	**Stillbirth Commemorative Abstract** Free to birth parents for stillbirth events taking place after September 26, 2003	☐

Registrant Information: *(Information about the person on the requested record)*

Full name *(for birth, indicate child's full name as shown on original birth record):*		**Date of birth:**
Place of birth/death *(City/County in Ohio):*	**Date of death:**	**CPR stamp number** *(Paternity only):*
Full name of father:	**Full name of mother** *(maiden name prior to first marriage):*	
Have there been any corrections or legal changes made to the information on this certificate? ☐ **Yes** ☐ **No**	**If name was changed since birth, indicate new name:**	**Did the stillbirth event occur after 20 weeks or less gestation?** *(Fetal Death/Stillbirth only)* ☐ **Yes** ☐ **No**

Charges: *Please include check or money order* **(do not send cash)** *made payable to "TREASURER, STATE OF OHIO"*

Total number of standard copies or abstracts (birth, death, fetal death):	**X $21.50 =**	**$**
Total number of heirloom commemorative birth certificates:	**X $25.00 =**	**$**
Total number of paternity affidavits:	**X $7.00 =**	**$**
Refunds will be issued only for orders where a certified document cannot be issued, and may be subject to search fees. Overpayment of $2.00 or less will not be refunded.	**TOTAL AMOUNT DUE:**	**$**

Applicant Information: *(Information about the person requesting the record)*

Please print clearly as this will be used for your receipt, mailing address, and/or for future contact to complete your record request.

Applicant Name:	Email:
Street Address:	Phone Number:
City, State, & ZIP:	Signature of Applicant:

For only $25 you will have a legal document that can be passed from generation to generation as a cherished keepsake. The proceeds go to further a good cause: **Ohio's Family and Children First Initiative.**

The Family and Children First Initiative is a unique partnership between state and local government, communities, and Ohio's families. Their purpose is to help families by streamlining and coordinating services, resources and systems.

The Ohio Family and Children First Cabinet Council's vision is to ensure all children thrive and succeed within healthy communities. To accomplish this vision, focus remains on:

- Increased coordination of support for children who are at risk of developmental delays, and/or have special needs.
- Decreasing the number of children in out of home placements, including institutionalizations.
- Improving quality of life for families.
- Increasing graduation rates.
- Increasing post-secondary education attainment.
- Increasing successful employment of students transitioning out of education.

For more information about Ohio Family and Children First, visit www.fcf.ohio.gov

Ohio Department of Health

John Kasich
Governor

Theodore E. Wymyslo, M.D.
Director of Health

An Equal Opportunity Employer/Provider

HEA 2740 Rev. 1/13

State of Ohio

Heirloom Birth Certificates

Honor your special date in history

Celebrate the birth of your baby or a special birthday of a friend or loved one by purchasing one of Ohio's new, certified heirloom birth certificates.

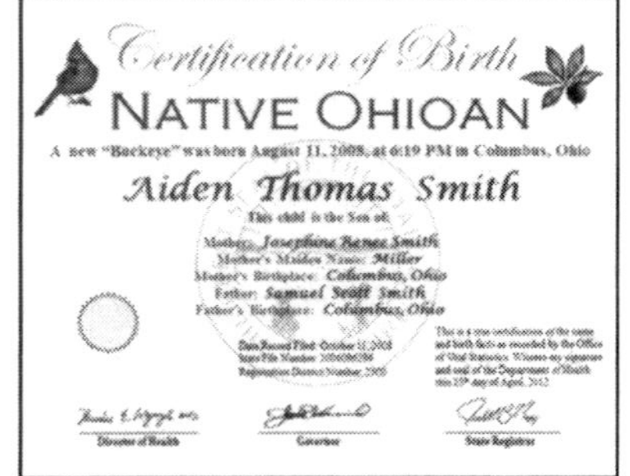

Native Ohioan

There are four styles to choose from, such as the Native Ohioan design, which honors the birth of a Buckeye with traditional scarlet colors. The Commemorative design features Ohio achievements including Neil Armstrong's walk on the moon. You can also request a Newborn Footprints certificate, which offers space for you to capture a precious stamp of your child's feet. For a more traditional design, choose the Statehouse Lawn scenic format.

All certificates are printed on 8.5 by 11 inch high quality paper **with a raised seal**, which allows them to be used for official business in addition to display.

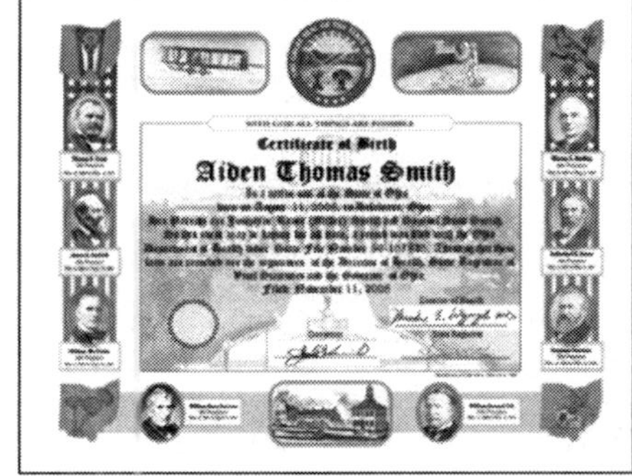

Commemorative

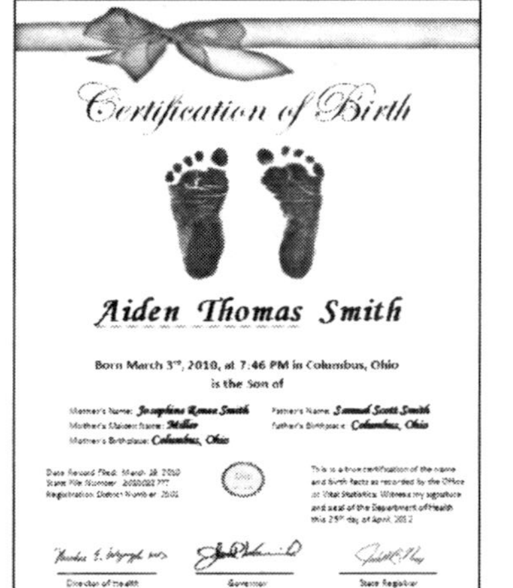

Newborn Footprints

Statehouse Lawn

ORDER FORM:

Full name on record:
Place of birth (city/county):
Date of birth:
Mother's full name:
Mother's maiden name:
Father's full name:
Choose design: ☐ Native Ohioan ☐ Newborn Footprints ☐ Commemorative ☐ Statehouse Lawn
Applicant name:
Complete mailing address:
Phone number:
Applicant signature:

All information must be completed. The fee for each heirloom birth certificate is $25. Allow 4-6 weeks for delivery. Please be advised that due to registration requirements, requests for newborn birth certificates may take up to three months to process. Make check or money order payable to: Treasurer, State of Ohio. Mail to:

Ohio Department of Health, Vital Statistics
P.O Box 15098
Columbus, OH 43215-0098

OKLAHOMA

Send your requests to:

Vital Records Service
Oklahoma State Department of Health
(Location: 1000 N.E. 10th Street)
P.O. Box 53551
Oklahoma City, OK 73152-3551

Tel. (405) 271-4040
E-mail: AskVR@health.ok.gov
www.ok.gov/health/Birth_and_Death_Certificates/index.html

The Vital Records Service has birth and death records from October 1908, though they are sketchy prior to 1940. Records are restricted—see the Vital Records Service website for applicant requirements. Certificates can also be picked up in person at the James O. Goodwin Health Center (5051 S. 129th East Avenue, Tulsa) and the Pittsburg County Health Department (1400 East College Avenue, McAlester).

Cost for a certified Birth Certificate	$15.00
Cost for an Heirloom Birth Certificate	$35.00
Cost for a certified Death Certificate	$15.00

For Marriage Certificates and Divorce Records, contact:

County Clerk
County Court House
(County Seat), OK

For contact information for each county, visit www.naco.org/Counties/Pages/FindACounty.aspx.

For Genealogy Research:

The Oklahoma Historical Society (OHS) (2401 N. Laird Avenue, Oklahoma City, OK 73105; tel. 405-521-2491; www.okhistory.org/) has records on microfilm of marriages occurring in the Indian Territory for Muskogee (July 1890–Nov. 1906), McAlester (June 1890–Nov. 1907), and Ardmore (Apr. 1895–Feb 2, 1934), plus an extensive collection of records related to the Five Civilized Tribes, Dawes Commission, and other tribal entities. An index to the Dawes Rolls is now online at www.okhistory.org/research/dawes.

Oklahoma County marriage records 1889–1951 and marriage licenses from the Federal Court, Western District, Indian Territory 1903–1907 are searchable online at www.okhistory.org/research/marriagerec, and copies from these databases can be ordered from the OHS by using the form available online at the above URL. Oklahoma divorce records 1923–1944 are searchable online at www.okhistory.org/research/divorce, and deaths listed in the 1918 and 1920–1923 Oklahoma City directories are searchable at www.okhistory.org/research/okcdeaths.

Also online is the Choctaw Nation Marriage Index 1890–1907 (www.okgenweb.org/~okgarvin/kinard/chocmarriageindex.htm) and the Chickasaw Nation Marriage Index 1895–1907 (www.okgenweb.org/~okgarvin/kinard/chicmarriageindex.htm).

The Oklahoma State Archives (200 N.E. 18th Street, Oklahoma City, OK; tel. 405-522-3579; www.odl.state.ok.us/oar/resources/genealogy.htm) also has many records of interest to genealogists.

For Adoption Record information, contact:

Child Welfare Services
Oklahoma Mutual Consent Voluntary Registry
P.O. Box 25352
Oklahoma City, OK 73125

Tel. (405) 521-2475
www.okdhs.org/programsandservices/postadopt/docs/adoptreg.htm

Cost for Mutual Consent Voluntary Registry	$20.00

Birth Certificate Request

Phone:
(405) 271-4040

Division of Vital Records
1000 NE 10th Street
Oklahoma City, OK 73117

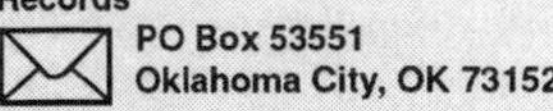
PO Box 53551
Oklahoma City, OK 73152

Walk-in Hours:
Mon-Fri 8:30-4:00

Full Name AT BIRTH: (If a change to the name has occurred, please see instruction on back) ☐ Male ☐ Female

First ______ Middle ______ Last ______

If Child less than 2 yrs: ______ Name of Hospital or Midwife

Date of Birth: ____ / ____ / ____ (Month Day Year) **Place of Birth:** ______ (City and/or County), **OKLAHOMA**

Full Name of Father: ______ First ______ Middle ______ Last

Full MAIDEN Name of Mother: ______ First ______ Middle ______ Last Name prior to first marriage

This request is being made by:
☐ Person Himself/Herself ☐ Parent ☐ Legal Guardian or Custodian ☐ Authorized Agent, must specify: ______

Current Address (REQUIRED):

Name ______ Daytime Telephone Number: (____) ____ - ____

Mailing Address ______ Apt ____ City, State and Zip ______

E-mail Address ______ ☐ No email

Purpose for which the birth certificate is needed:
☐ Drivers License ☐ Social Security ☐ Passport ☐ School ☐ State Assistance Pgm ☐ Other, specify: ______

By signing below, I declare that all information provided on this request is true and correct.

Signature: ______ **Date Signed:** ______
(Request will not be processed without the signature of the requestor and established eligibility.)

Fees

A fee is to be paid for a search of the files or records, even when no copy is available. Search fees are non-transferable and non-refundable.

☐ Number of certified copies requested ($15 each and includes search fee)

☐ Delayed registration, amendment, paternity, adoption, or legitimation fee ($40 - Includes one certified copy)

☐ Number of Heirloom certificates requested: ($35 each and includes one certified copy)

☐ Total Amount enclosed — Make checks payable to OSDH. Do not send cash by mail.

FEES: A record search is $15 and includes the issuance of one certified copy if the record is found; additional copies are $15 each. If no record is found: the fee will not be refunded. The fee to amend a record is $40 ($25 processing fee + $15 for one certified copy). Should you receive a request for more information, please respond promptly as all fees and files will expire one year after the date paid.

STOP

Requirements:
1) This request must be completed in full.
2) Enclose a copy of a current legal photo ID (See back for list of acceptable IDs)
3) Enclose appropriate fees
4) Person requesting to receive a birth certificate must sign above
5) If submitting by mail, enclose a self-addressed stamped envelope

OFFICE USE ONLY

Mail
Reviewed by: ______ Date: ____ / ____ / ____
Fees Enclosed: $ ______ Fees Due: $ ______
ID Enclosed: ______

Front Desk
Clerk: ______ Date: ____ / ____ / ____
Fees Paid: $ ______ ☐ Check ☐ Cash ☐ MO ☐ CC

Birth Certificate Request Instruction Sheet

ELIGIBILITY

By state law, birth records filed with this office are not open for public inspection. The person requesting the certificate must meet one of the following eligibility standards:

- Be the subject of the record
- Acting in such person's best interest (and authorized by the subject of the record)
- Court order

By signing the request, you are indicating that you are the person who is the subject of the records, a court appointed legal guardian, a custodial guardian, or an authorized agent working in the best interest of the subject of record. *Additional documentation may be required demonstrating the requestor's authorization to obtain the birth record requested.* When an adoption has occurred, the biological family and the adoptee no longer have the same legal right to each other's birth record that they had prior to the adoption. Additional documentation may be required to show the requestor's authorization to obtain an adoptee's birth record.
For more information, go to http://www.ok.gov/health/Birth_and_Death_Certificates/Birth_Certificate_Eligibility/index.html

ACCEPTABLE PHOTO IDENTIFICATION

A photocopy of a valid government issued photo ID by either the applicant or an individual attesting for the applicant is required for issuance of certificates. **Note: Send a photocopy.** Do not send your original ID. Photocopies must be legible and cannot be expired.

- U.S. Issued Driver's license or Identification card
- U.S. Passport
- Foreign Issued Passport with Visa (I-94)
- Government issued Military photo ID
- Tribal Photo ID Card containing the bearer's signature
- Ok Self-Defense Act (SDA) License or Concealed Carry permit
- Resident Alien Card (Form I-551)
- Employment Authorization Card (Form I-766)
- Employment Authorization Card (Form I-688A)
- Temporary Resident Card (Form I-688)
- Oklahoma Dept of Corrections Consolidated Record Card (CRC)

For more information, go to http://www.ok.gov/health/Birth_and_Death_Certificates/Acceptable_Identification/index.html

HEIRLOOM BIRTH CERTIFICATES **$ 35.00 and includes one certified copy of the original certificate.**

The Heirloom Birth Certificate is 8 1/2 x 11" with a chocolate brown and mint green color palette bearing a depiction of a redbud - the state tree redbud. The certificate will reflect the child's name, date of birth, gender, place of birth and the names of the parents. Proceeds from the issuance of Heirloom Birth Certificates are used by the Child Abuse Training and Coordination Program to provide training and technical assistance to judges, prosecutors and members of the multidisciplinary child abuse teams who intervene in circumstances of child abuse.

FEES: A record search is $15 and includes the issuance of one certified copy if the record is found; additional copies are $15 each. If no record is found; the fee will not be refunded. The fee to amend a record is $40 ($25 processing fee + $15 for one certified copy). Should you receive a request for more information, please respond promptly as all fees and files will expire one year after the date paid.

IF BOTH PARENTS DO NOT APPEAR ON THE BIRTH CERTIFICATE

If both parents' names are not indicated on the original Certificate of Birth a complete copy of the birth record can be obtained only if requested by the named parent, the subject of the birth record if of legal age, or a person having legal custody or guardianship of the subject of the birth record. If the certificate is required for "adoption purposes," the signature of the attorney of record and a statement from him/her to that effect is required.

NAME CHANGES

If a change to the name of the subject of the birth record has occurred as a result of **legal** action the person requesting the birth record must identify in the place marked "full name at birth" the current legally altered name of the subject of the birth record, and that name must agree with the information that now appears on the certificate. If a change needs to be made to the record, complete the request with the information that currently appears on the certificate and attach a letter specifying the changes. *(Additional Instructions will be mailed once the request has been reviewed.)*

SUBJECT OF THE BIRTH RECORD IS DECEASED

If the subject of the original Certificate of Birth is deceased, the birth record will be marked with a notation indicating that the subject of the record is deceased.

NOT BORN IN OKLAHOMA?

If you were not born in Oklahoma, please visit http://www.cdc.gov/nchs/howto/w2w/w2welcom.htm for a complete listing of national vital statistics offices.

QUESTIONS

If you have any questions visit our official website http://www.health.ok.gov/program/vital or call our office at (405) 271-4040.

Death Certificate Application

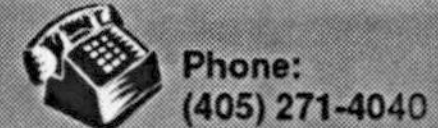
Phone:
(405) 271-4040

Division of Vital Records
1000 NE 10th Street
Oklahoma City, OK 73117

PO Box 53551
Oklahoma City, OK 73152

Walk-in Hours:
Mon-Fri 8:30-4:00

Section 1: REQUIRED INFORMATION: Complete in full ☐ **Check box if death was stillbirth or fetal death**

Full Name of Deceased: ______ First ______ Middle ______ Last

Date of Death: ___ Month / ___ Day / ___ Year **Place of Death** ______ City and/or County, **OKLAHOMA**

Applicant Information: Name ______ Daytime Telephone Number: ( ) -

Mailing Address ______ Apt ___ City, State and Zip ______

E-mail Address ______ ☐ No email

Relationship to the Decedent ☐ Family: specific ______ ☐ Legal Rep of the Estate ☐ Funeral Director ☐ Court Order ☐ Other ______

Purpose for which the death certificate is needed: ☐ Estate Settlement ☐ Genealogy ☐ Other, specify: ______

By signing below, I declare that all information provided on this application is true and correct.

Signature: ______ **Date Signed:** ______

(Application will not be processed without the signature of the requestor and established eligibility)

Section 2: OPTIONAL INFORMATION: May assist in locating a record

Social Security Number: ___-___-___ **Gender:** ☐ Female ☐ Male **Spouse Name:** ______

Funeral Home Name and Address: ______

Date of Birth: ___ Month / ___ Day / ___ Year **Place of Birth:** ______ City and/or County, ______ State

Father's Name and Birthplace: ______

Mother's Name and Birthplace: ______

Fees

A fee is to be paid for a search of the files or records, even when no copy is available. Search fees are non-transferable and non-refundable.

☐ Number of certified copies requested (**$15 per copy** which includes a search fee)

☐ Amendment Fee ($35 Required to amend non-medical certification items. Includes 1 certified copy.)

☐ Total Amount enclosed — Make checks payable to OSDH. Do not send cash by mail.

FEES: A record search is $15 and includes the issuance of one certified copy if the record is found; additional copies are $15 each. If no record is found; the fee will not be refunded. The fee to amend a record is $35 ($20 processing fee + $15 for one certified copy). Should you receive a request for more information, please respond promptly as all fees and files will expire one year after the date paid.

STOP

Requirements:

1) Section 1 must be completed in full.
2) Section 2 is optional but may provide additional information to locate the record
3) Enclose a copy of a current legal photo ID (See back for list of acceptable IDs)
4) Enclose appropriate fees
5) Person applying to receive a death certificate must sign above
6) If submitting by mail, enclose a self-addressed stamped envelope

OFFICE USE ONLY

Mail		Front Desk	
Reviewed by: ______	Date: __/__/__	Clerk: ______	Date: __/__/__
Fees Enclosed: $______	Fees Due: $______	Fees Paid: $______	☐ Check ☐ Cash ☐ MO ☐ CC
ID Enclosed: ______			

Death Application Instruction Sheet

ELIGIBILTY

By state law, death records filed with this office are not open for public inspection. The person requesting the certificate must be acting in the decedent's best interest:

(1) A surviving spouse, parent, child, grandparent, sibling, ex-spouse or legal guardian;
(2) Legal representative of the estate of the deceased as documented by an order from a court of competent jurisdiction;
(3) An individual who can establish a familial relationship with the deceased demonstrated through certified copies of birth, death and/or marriage certificates;
(4) Law enforcement or government officials in the capacity of official governmental business;
(5) Funeral director of record or agent thereto, working in the capacity of their official business;
(6) Person with a court order from a court of competent jurisdiction;
(7) A person who was a co-owner or a joint tenant on real or personal property of the decedent; or
(8) A person listed in a will of the decedent, provided the will is in probate;

By signing the request, you are indicating that you are working in the best interest of the subject of record. *Additional documentation may be required demonstrating the requestor's authorization to obtain the death record requested.*
For more information, go to http://www.ok.gov/health/Birth_and_Death_Certificates/Birth_Certificate_Eligibility/index.html

ACCEPTABLE PHOTO IDs

Note: Send a photocopy. Do not send your original ID. Photocopies must be legible and cannot be expired.

- U.S. Issued Driver's license or Identification card
- U.S. Passport
- Foreign Issued Passport with Visa (I-94)
- Government issued Military photo ID
- Tribal Photo ID Card containing the bearer's signature
- Ok Self-Defense Act (SDA) License or Concealed Carry permit
- Resident Alien Card (Form I-551)
- Employment Authorization Card (Form I-766)
- Employment Authorization Card (Form I-688A)
- Temporary Resident Card (Form I-688)
- Oklahoma Dept of Corrections Consolidated Record Card (CRC)

FEES: A record search is $15 and includes the issuance of one certified copy if the record is found; additional copies are $15 each. If no record is found; the fee will not be refunded. The fee to amend a record is $35 ($20 processing fee + $15 for one certified copy). Should you receive a request for more information, please respond promptly as all fees and files will expire one year after the date paid.

RECORD SEARCHES

REQUIRED INFORMATION

Certain information is required in order for to us to be able to process your request in an expedient manner and to prevent unnecessary delays. Incorrect information will delay the search and may result in your document not being located. You can be assured that every attempt will be made to locate the record you have requested. The minimum facts required include: 1) the full name of the decedent at the time of death, 2) the date of death, and 3) the place of death.

OPTIONAL INFORMATION

Any additional information you may have can assist us in our search such as nicknames, a husband's name of a married female, whether the deceased was an infant, or the name of the funeral director in charge of the decedent. You can be assured that every attempt is made to locate the record you have requested.

HOW RECORDS ARE SEARCHED

When an application is submitted (Example: William Thomas Public-March 25, 1932-Tulsa County), we will search for the proper name, as well as other variations of the name (Example: Will, W.T. Bill, Billy, Willy). We also conduct a generalized search over a span of years (Example: 1930-1940) as well as in surrounding counties (Example: Washington, Muskogee, Wagoner etc.) Please be aware that these generalized searches may not result in a record being found if the name is common. In that case, more specific information will be required.

AVAILABLE RECORDS

Oklahoma began filing death records in October of 1908; however filing did not become mandatory until 1917. Prior to 1940 filing continued to be somewhat sporadic, which may prove problematic for families who may need proof of death for the settlement of death claims or to obtain entitled benefits.

RESPONSIBILITY FOR FILING DEATH CERTIFICATES

It is the responsibility of the funeral director in charge of the decedent at the time of death to properly obtain the information needed from an immediate family member, obtain the physician's signature and cause of death information, and then file the certificate in a timely manner.

QUESTIONS

If you have any questions, visit our official website http://www.health.ok.gov or call our office at (405) 271-4040.

OREGON

Send your requests to:

Oregon Department of Human Resources
State Health Division
Vital Statistics Office
(Location: 800 N.E. Oregon Street, Suite 205)
P.O. Box 14050
Portland, OR 97293-0050

Tel. (971) 673-1190; (971) 673-1180
Fax (971) 673-1203
E-mail: dhs.info@state.or.us
http://public.health.oregon.gov/BirthDeathCertificates/GetVitalRecords/Pages/index.aspx

The Vital Statistics Office has birth and death records from July 1903, marriage records from 1906, and divorce certificates (not decrees) from 1925. The Vital Statistics Office also provides pre-adoption birth records to adoptees 21 years or older (born in Oregon), or their legal representatives, for cases where the Office received an adoption report that sealed the original record and created a new record. All birth records (including indexes) are restricted for 100 years; death, marriage, divorce, and domestic partnership records are restricted for 50 years.

Marriage records, including some records prior to 1906, may also be requested from the county marriage office that issued the license. Divorce decrees (judgments), both certified and uncertified, are also available from the Oregon county court that granted the divorce.

Cost for a certified Birth Certificate	$20.00
Cost for an Heirloom Birth Certificate	$45.00
Cost for a pre-Adoption Birth Record	$20.00
Cost for a certified Marriage or Divorce Certificate	$20.00
Cost for a certified Domestic Partnership Declaration	$20.00
Cost for a certified Death Certificate	$20.00
Cost for a duplicate copy, when ordered at the same time	$15.00

For Genealogy Research:

The Oregon State Archives (800 Summer Street N.E., Salem, OR 97310; tel. 503-373-0701; e-mail: reference.archives@state.or.us; http://arcweb.sos.state.or.us/index.html) has birth records filed before 1903; death records filed after 1903 that are over 50 years old; state marriage records 1906–1910 and after 1945 if they are over 50 years old; and state divorce certificates filed after 1945 if they are over 50 years old. For a small fee, the Archives will provide uncertified copies of vital records that have become public records. A number of their vital records are searchable online in the Oregon Historical Records Index (http://genealogy.state.or.us/).

For Adoption Record information, contact:

Department of Human Services
Adoption Registry, 2nd Floor South
500 Summer Street NE, E71
Salem, OR 97301-1068

Tel. (503) 945-6643
www.oregon.gov/DHS/children/adoption/adopt_registry/registry.shtml

Cost for registering for identifying Adoption information	$25.00
Cost for registering for non-identifying Adoption information	$45.00
Cost for an assisted search for Adoption information	$400.00

ARE YOU ORDERING
A VITAL RECORD BY MAIL?

YOU MUST:

- ❑ Sign the form
- ❑ Include a photocopy of your ID

See form for details.

Thank you!

Oregon Vital Records

Center for Health Statistics

Oregon Birth Record
ORDER FORM

______ Number of certified records requested.
QUANTITY $20 first record/$15 each additional copy of the same record ordered at the same time.

1. Full name on record: ______ (First) (Full middle) (Full last)

2. Date of birth: ______ (MM/DD/YYYY) 3. Sex: ______ (M or F) 4. Place of birth: ______ (City) (County) **OREGON**

5. Mother's full maiden name: ______ (First) (Full middle) (Full maiden)

6. Father's full name: ______ (First) (Full middle) (Full last)

7. Your relationship to person named in line 1: ______

8. Reason for needing record: ______

9. Daytime telephone number: ______ 10. Email: ______

11. Name of person ordering: ______

12. Your address: ______

13. City/State/ZIP: ______

14. Required: Signature of person ordering: ______

15. ID Required: Person ordering must attach legible photocopy of current, valid ID or legal representative document. See back of form for alternative ID options.

OFFICE USE ONLY

DO NOT WRITE IN THIS SPACE

Certificate number:

	1	2
Film		
Film (P)		
Computer		
Indexes		
Index (P)		
DF/CO		

Refund: $

❑ Excess fee ❑ Out/state
❑ No record ❑ Uncompleted

Check #:

File date:	Amendment fee:
NRL/ref issued:	Full issued:
Follow-up:	Computer copy:

Send to:	**Make checks/money orders payable to:**
OREGON VITAL RECORDS	**OHA/Vital Records**
PO BOX 14050	**PLEASE DO NOT SEND CASH**
PORTLAND OR 97293-0050	**Checks/money orders in U. S. Dollars**

In accordance with law – ORS 432.121, only the person named on the record, immediate family members, legal representatives, government agencies and persons licensed or registered under ORS 703.430 are eligible to access birth records. For all others, access to birth records is restricted for 100 years. Legal guardians must enclose a copy of the legal document. If you are not eligible, enclose a written permission note with a notarized signature of an eligible person.

Providing false information is a felony under ORS 432.900.

$20.00 FOR THE FIRST RECORD; $15.00 FOR EACH ADDITIONAL COPY OF THE SAME RECORD ORDERED AT THE SAME TIME. The $20.00 fee is non-refundable once the search for the record has been completed. Administrative Rule 333-011-0106 (2)

This form available in alternative formats. See back for details.

ENTER YOUR MAILING ADDRESS
THIS SECTION WILL BE DETACHED AND USED AS A MAILING LABEL

Name		
Street		
City	State	ZIP

Non-Sufficient Funds (NSF) check processing policy: In the event that your check is returned unpaid for insufficient or uncollected funds, we may present your check electronically. In the ordinary course of business, your check will not be provided to you with your bank statement, but a copy can be retrieved by other means. A $25.00 penalty may be assessed for NSF checks per ORS 30.701(5).

See back of form for ordering options and processing times. Information is also available on our Web page at: www.healthoregon.org/chs or by calling 971-673-1190.

45-13A (01/12)

Center for Health Statistics

HEIRLOOM BIRTH RECORD ORDER
$45 each -- $15 Tax deductible for each

_____ Number of Heirloom Records Requested

1. Full Name On Record ____________________ (First) (Full Middle) (Full Last)
2. Date of Birth ______________ 3. Sex ________ 4. Place of Birth ______________ OR
5. Mother's Full Maiden Name ____________________
6. Father's Full Name ____________________
7. Your Relationship to the Person Name on Record ____________________
8. Daytime Telephone Number ______________ 9. Email ______________
10. Your Name ____________________
11. Your Address ____________________
12. City/State/Zip ____________________
13. *Ship to Name ____________________
    If you are not an immediate family member
14. *Ship to Address ____________________
    If you are not an immediate family member
15. **Required: Signature of Person Ordering** ____________________
16. **ID Required: Person ordering must attach a legible photocopy of current, valid ID or legal representative document. If you do not have current, valid ID see second page of this form for alternate ID suggestions.**

DO NOT WRITE IN THIS SPACE
CERTIFICATE #:

FILM ______
FILM (P) ______
COMPUTER ______
INDEXES ______
INDEX (P) ______
DF/CO ______

REFUND$ ______
Excess Fee: Out/State:
No Record: Uncompleted:
CHECK # ______

***Note: State law requires that a birth certificate must be mailed directly to the person named on the record or an immediate family member, if the applicant is anyone except the registrant or an immediate family member.**

Send to:
OREGON VITAL RECORDS
PO BOX 14050
PORTLAND OR 97293-0050

Make checks/money orders to:
OHA Vital Records
PLEASE DO NOT SEND CASH
Checks/money orders in U.S. Dollars

FOR OFFICE USE ONLY

File Date	Amendment Fee
NRL/Ref Issued	Full Issued
Follow Up	Computer copy

RECORDS ARE $45 EACH. AN $18 SEARCH FEE WILL BE RETAINED FOR THE SEARCH OF THE FILES

For current ordering information call (971) 673-1190 or find Vital Records on our web page: www.healthoregon.org/chs

Warning: Providing false information is a felony under ORS 432.900

$15 from each order for an Heirloom Birth Certificate goes to support the Children's Trust Fund. This independent fund was created in 1985 by the Oregon Legislature to fund programs to prevent child abuse and neglect before it starts.

_____ I would like to make an additional tax-deductible contribution to support the Children's Trust Fund.

Enclosed is my check for $ ______________

Non-Sufficient Funds (NSF) Check Processing Policy: In the event that your check is returned unpaid for insufficient or uncollected funds, we may present your check electronically. In the ordinary course of business, your check will not be provided to you with your bank statement, but a copy can be retrieved by other means. A $25 penalty may be assessed for NSF checks per ORS 30.701 (5)

Center for Health Statistics

PREADOPTION BIRTH RECORD ORDER

$20 for first record / $15 each additional copy of the same record ordered at the same time

______ Number of Certified Copies Requested

1. Full Name on Record After Adoption ______________________ (First) (Full middle) (Full Last)
2. Date of Birth ____________ 3. Sex ______ 4. Place of Birth ______________ OREGON
5. Adoptive Mother's Full Maiden Name ______________________
6. Adoptive Father's Full Name ______________________
7. Your Relationship to Person Named on Record ______________________
8. Your Reason for Ordering Record ______________________
9. Daytime Telephone Number ____________ 10. Email ____________
11. Name of Person Ordering ______________________
12. Your Address ______________________
13. City/State/Zip ______________________
14. **Required: Signature of Person Ordering** ______________________
15. **ID Required: Attach legible photocopy of current, valid ID. If you do not have current, valid ID see second page of this form for alternative ID suggestions. Legal representatives should provide a notarized permission note from the person named on the record.**

DO NOT WRITE IN THIS SPACE

Certificate #

FILM ______

FILM (P) ______

COMPUTER ______

INDEXES ______

INDEX (P) ______

DF/CO ______

REFUND: $ ______

Excess Fee: Out/State:

No Record: Uncompleted:

CHECK # ______

In accordance with law - ORS 432.240 only a registrant age 21 or over may order a pre-adoption birth record. Under ORS 432.420, all other persons may order only with a court order from an Oregon Court. If you are not the registrant, enclose a written permission note with a notarized signature of the registrant.

FOR OFFICE USE ONLY

File Date	Amendment Fee
NRL/Ref Issued	Full Issued
Follow Up	Computer Copy

Send to:
OREGON VITAL RECORDS
PO BOX 14050
PORTLAND OR 97293-0050

Make checks/money orders to:
OHA/Vital Records
Payment in U.S dollars only
PLEASE DO NOT SEND CASH

$20 FOR THE FIRST RECORD; $15 FOR EACH ADDITIONAL COPY OF THE SAME RECORD ORDERED AT THE SAME TIME

Processing time for pre-adoption birth record orders is six to eight weeks.

If the requested record cannot be found, the $20 fee must be retained as a search fee as prescribed by Administrative Rule 333-011-0106 (2)

For current ordering information call 971-673-1190 or find Vital Records on our web page: www.healthoregon.org/chs

Warning: Providing false information is a felony under ORS 432.900

Please see second page of form for additional information about ordering.

Non-Sufficient Funds (NSF) check processing policy: In the event that your check is returned unpaid for insufficient or uncollected funds, we may present your check electronically. In the ordinary course of business, your check will not be provided to you with your bank statement, but a copy can be retrieved by other means. A $25 penalty may be assessed for NSF checks per ORS 30.701 (5)

Name ______________________

Street ______________________

City/State/Zip ______________________

THIS IS YOUR MAILING LABEL - PRINT CLEARLY

Center for Health Statistics

Marriage Record Order Form

$20 for first record / $15 each additional copy of the same record ordered at the same time

________ Number of Certified Copies Requested

1. Name of Groom ______________________________
   (First) (Full Middle) (Full Last) (Other Surname at Birth)
2. Name of Bride ______________________________
   (First) (Full Middle) (Full Last) (Other Surname at Birth)
3. Date of Marriage ______________________________
4. Place License Issued ______________________ OREGON
5. Place Marriage Occurred ______________________ OREGON
6. Your Relation to the Person Named on Line 1 or Line 2 Or Reason You Need Record ______________________
7. Daytime Telephone Number ______________ 8. Email ______________
9. Name of Person Ordering ______________________
10. Your Address ______________________
11. City/State/Zip ______________________
12. **Required: Signature of Person Ordering:** ______________________
13. **ID Required: Person ordering must attach legible photocopy of current, valid ID. If you do not have current, valid ID see second page of this form for alternative ID suggestions.**

DO NOT WRITE IN THIS SPACE

Certificate #

FILM ______

FILM (P) ______

COMPUTER ______

INDEXES ______

INDEX (P) ______

DF/CO ______

REFUND: $ ______

Excess Fee: Out/State

No Record: Uncompleted:

CHECK # ______

In accordance with law - ORS 432.121, access to marriage records is restricted for 50 years to family members, legal representatives, government agencies, persons licensed or registered under ORS 703.430 and persons with a personal or property right. Legal guardians must enclose a copy of the legal document. If you are not eligible, enclose a notarized permission note signed by an eligible person.

Send to:
OREGON VITAL RECORDS
PO BOX 14050
PORTLAND OR 97293-0050

Make checks/money orders to:
OHA/Vital Records
Payment in U.S dollars only
PLEASE DO NOT SEND CASH

FOR OFFICE USE ONLY

File Date	Amendment Fee
NRL/Ref Issued	Full Issued
Follow Up	Computer Copy

$20 FOR THE FIRST RECORD; $15 FOR EACH ADDITIONAL COPY OF THE SAME RECORD ORDERED AT THE SAME TIME

If the requested record cannot be found, the $20 fee must be retained as a search fee as prescribed by Administrative Rule 333-011-0106 (2)

For current ordering information call 971-673-1190 or find Vital Records on our web page: www.healthoregon.org/chs

Warning: Providing false information is a felony under ORS 432.900

Please see second page of form for additional information about ordering.

Non-Sufficient Funds (NSF) check processing policy: In the event that your check is returned unpaid for insufficient or uncollected funds, we may present your check electronically. In the ordinary course of business, your check will not be provided to you with your bank statement, but a copy can be retrieved by other means. A $25 penalty may be assessed for NSF checks per ORS 30.701 (5)

Name ______________________

Street ______________________

City/State/Zip ______________________

THIS IS YOUR MAILING LABEL - PRINT CLEARLY

45/13c/Marriage(06/12)

Center for Health Statistics

Declaration of Domestic Partnership Order Form

$20 for first record / $15 each additional copy of the same record ordered at the same time

______ Number of Certified Copies Requested

1. Name of Partner 1 ______________________
   (First) (Full Middle) (Full Last) (Other Surname at Birth)
2. Name of Partner 2 ______________________
   (First) (Full Middle) (Full Last) (Other Surname at Birth)
3. Date Declaration of Domestic Partnership was Registered at County ______________________
4. County of Filing ______________________ OREGON
5. Your Relationship to Person Named In Line 1 or Line 2 ______________________
6. Your Reason for Ordering the Record ______________________
7. Daytime Telephone Number ____________ 8. Email ______________________
9. Name of Person Ordering ______________________
10. Your Address ______________________
11. City/State/Zip ______________________
12. **Required: Signature of Person Ordering** ______________________
13. **ID Required: Person ordering must attach legible photocopy of current, valid ID. If you do not have current, valid ID, see second page of this form for alternative ID suggestions.**

DO NOT WRITE IN THIS SPACE
Certificate #

FILM ____
FILM (P) ____
COMPUTER ____
INDEXES ____
INDEX (P) ____
DF/CO ____
REFUND: $ ____
Excess Fee: Out/State:
No Record: Uncompleted:
CHECK #: ____
DATE: ____

In accordance with law - ORS 432.121, access to Oregon registered declaration of domestic partnership records is restricted for 50 years to family members, legal representatives, government agencies, persons licensed or registered under ORS 703.430, and persons with a personal or property right. Legal guardians must enclose a copy of the legal document. If you are not eligible, enclose a notarized permission note signed by an eligible person.

Send to:
OREGON VITAL RECORDS
PO BOX 14050
PORTLAND OR 97293-0050

Make checks/money orders to:
OHA/Vital Records
Payment in U.S dollars only
PLEASE DO NOT SEND CASH

FOR OFFICE USE ONLY

File Date	Amendment Fee
NRL/Ref Issued	Full Issued
Follow Up	Computer Copy

$20 FOR THE FIRST RECORD; $15 FOR EACH ADDITIONAL COPY OF THE SAME RECORD ORDERED AT THE SAME TIME

If the requested record cannot be found, the $20 fee must be retained as a search fee as prescribed by Administrative Rule 333-011-0106 (2)

For current ordering information call 971-673-1190 or find Vital Records on our web page: www.healthoregon.org/chs

Warning: Providing false information is a felony under ORS 432.900

Please see second page of form for additional information about ordering.

Non-Sufficient Funds (NSF) check processing policy: In the event that your check is returned unpaid for insufficient or uncollected funds, we may present your check electronically. In the ordinary course of business, your check will not be provided to you with your bank statement, but a copy can be retrieved by other means. A $25 penalty may be assessed for NSF checks per ORS 30.701 (5)

Name ______________________

Street ______________________

City/State/Zip ______________________

THIS IS YOUR MAILING LABEL - PRINT CLEARLY

45/16 DP (06/12)

Center for Health Statistics

Divorce Record Order Form

$20 for first record / $15 every additional record ordered and paid for at the same time

______ Number of Certified Copies Requested

1. Full Name of Husband ______________________
   (First) (Full Middle) (Last) (Other Surname at Birth)
2. Full Name of Wife ______________________
   (First) (Full Middle) (Last) (Other Surname at Birth)
3. Date of Divorce or Time Period to Search ______________________
4. County Where Divorce Was Granted ______________ OREGON
5. Your Relationship to Person Named on Line 1 or Line 2 Above ______________________
6. Your Reason for Ordering the Record ______________________
7. Daytime Telephone Number ______________ 8. Email ______________
9. Name of Person Ordering ______________________
10. Your Address ______________________
11. City/State/Zip ______________________
12. **Required: Signature of Person Ordering** ______________________
13. **ID Required: Person ordering must attach legible photocopy of current, valid ID. If you do not have current, valid ID, see second page of this form for alternative ID suggestions.**

DO NOT WRITE IN THIS SPACE
Certificate #

FILM ______
FILM (P) ______
COMPUTER ______
INDEXES ______
INDEX (P) ______
DF/CO ______

REFUND: $ ______
Excess Fee: Out/State:
No Record: Uncompleted:
CHECK #: ______
DATE: ______

In accordance with law - ORS 432.121, access to divorce records is restricted for 50 years to family members, legal representatives, government agencies, persons licensed or registered under ORS 703.430, and persons with a personal or property right. Legal guardians must enclose a copy of the legal document. If you are not eligible, enclose a notarized permission note signed by an eligible person.

Send to:
OREGON VITAL RECORDS
PO BOX 14050
PORTLAND OR 97293-0050

Make checks/money orders to:
OHA/Vital Records
Payment in U.S dollars only
PLEASE DO NOT SEND CASH

$20 FOR THE FIRST RECORD; $15 FOR EACH ADDITIONAL COPY OF THE SAME RECORD ORDERED AT THE SAME TIME

If the requested record cannot be found, the $20 fee must be retained as a search fee as prescribed by Administrative Rule 333-011-0106 (2)

For current ordering information call 971-673-1190 or find Vital Records on our web page: www.healthoregon.org/chs

Warning: Providing false information is a felony under ORS 432.900

Please see second page of form for additional information about ordering.

Name ______________________

Street ______________________

City/State/Zip ______________________

FOR OFFICE USE ONLY

File Date	Amendment Fee
NRL/Ref Issued	Full Issued
Follow Up	Computer Copy

Non-Sufficient Funds (NSF) check processing policy: In the event that your check is returned unpaid for insufficient or uncollected funds, we may present your check electronically. In the ordinary course of business, your check will not be provided to you with your bank statement, but a copy can be retrieved by other means. A $25 penalty may be assessed for NSF checks per ORS 30.701 (5)

THIS IS YOUR MAILING LABEL - PRINT CLEARLY

45/13d/Divorce (06/12)

Center for Health Statistics

Oregon Death Record ORDER FORM

_____ QUANTITY Certified, long form with cause of death

_____ QUANTITY Certified, fact of death

(Available 1978 through the present.)

$20 first record/$15 each additional copy of the same record ordered at the same time.

1. Name of deceased: ______________ (First) ______________ (Full middle) ______________ (Full last)

2. Date of death: ______________ (MM/DD/YYYY) 3. Place of death: ______________ (City) ______________ (County) **OREGON**

4. Spouse of decedent: ______________ (First) ______________ (Full middle) ______________ (Full maiden)

5. Your relationship to person on request: ______________

6. Reason for needing record: ______________

7. Daytime telephone number: ______________ 8. E-mail: ______________

9. Name of person ordering: ______________

10. Your address: ______________

11. City/State/ZIP: ______________

12. Signature of person ordering: ______________

13. **Person ordering: Attach legible photocopy of current, valid ID or legal representative document. See back of form for alternative ID options.**

Send to:	**Make checks/money orders payable to:**
OREGON VITAL RECORDS	**OHA/Vital Records**
PO BOX 14050	**PLEASE DO NOT SEND CASH**
PORTLAND OR 97293-0050	**Checks/money orders in U. S. Dollars**

In accordance with law – ORS 432.121, access to death records is restricted for 50 years except for family members, legal representatives, government agencies, persons licensed or registered under ORS 703.430 and persons with a personal or property right. Legal guardians must enclose a copy of the legal document. If you are not eligible, enclose a written permission note with a notarized signature of an eligible person.

OFFICE USE ONLY

DO NOT WRITE IN THIS SPACE

Certificate number:

	1	2
Film		
Film (P)		
Computer		
Indexes		
Index (P)		
DF/CO		

Refund: $

❑ Excess fee ❑ Out/state
❑ No record ❑ Uncompleted

Check #:

File date:	Amendment fee:
NRL/ref. issued:	Full issued:
Follow-up:	Computer copy:

Providing false information is a felony under ORS 432.900

$20.00 FOR THE FIRST RECORD; $15.00 FOR EACH ADDITIONAL COPY OF THE SAME RECORD ORDERED AT THE SAME TIME. The $20.00 fee is non-refundable once the search for the record has been completed. Administrative Rule 333-011-0106 (2)

This form available in alternative formats. See second page for details.

ENTER YOUR MAILING ADDRESS
THIS SECTION WILL BE DETACHED AND USED AS A MAILING LABEL

Name		
Street		
City	State	ZIP

Non-Sufficient Funds (NSF) check processing policy: In the event that your check is returned unpaid for insufficient or uncollected funds, we may present your check electronically. In the ordinary course of business, your check will not be provided to you with your bank statement, but a copy can be retrieved by other means. A $25.00 penalty may be assessed for NSF checks per ORS 30.701(5).

See second page of form for ordering options and processing times. Information is also available on our Web page at: www.healthoregon.org/chs or by calling 971-673-1190.

45-13B (05/11)

PENNSYLVANIA

Send your requests to:

Pennsylvania Department of Health
Division of Vital Records
(Location: 101 South Mercer Street, Room 401)
P.O. Box 1528
New Castle, PA 16103

Tel. (724) 656-3100
Fax (724) 652-8951
www.dsf.health.state.pa.us/health/

The Division of Vital Records has birth and death records from January 1906 to the present. Birth records are restricted for 105 years, and death records are restricted for 50 years.

Requests for vital records may be made in person at the Vital Records offices in Erie, Harrisburg, Philadelphia, Pittsburgh, and Scranton, as well as at the New Castle office. The addresses of these other offices are as follows—Erie: 1910 West 26th Street; Harrisburg: Forum Place, 555 Walnut Street, 1st Floor; Philadelphia: 110 North 8th Street, Suite 108; Pittsburgh: 411 7th Avenue, Suite 360; Scranton: 100 Lackawanna Avenue, Room 112.

Birth and death records can also be ordered online from the Vital Records office. Check their website for information.

Cost for a certified Birth Certificate	$10.00
Cost for a certified Death Certificate	$9.00
Records of veterans, veterans' spouses and their minor children	No Charge

For Marriage or Divorce Certificates, contact:

County Clerk
County Court House
(County Seat), PA

For county contact information, visit www.portal.state.pa.us/portal/server.pt/community/marriage_and_divorce_certificates/14126.

For Genealogy Research:

The original birth records for 1906–1907 and death records for 1906–1962 are housed at the Pennsylvania State Archives (350 North Street, Harrisburg, PA 17120; tel. 717-783-3281; www.phmc.state.pa.us). You can search indexes of these records at www.portal.state.pa.us/portal/server.pt/community/public_records/20686. Non-certified copies of birth and death records are available. The Archives also has many original colonial and state government records, county government records, and municipal vital records on microfilm. For the years 1885 through 1891, the state's Department of Internal Affairs kept a Record of Marriages, with sections of alphabetically arranged entries for both brides and grooms. Images of these registers 1885–1889 are available online at www.phmc.state.pa.us/bah/dam/rg/di/r14-25RecordMarriages/r14-25MainInterface.htm; the records from 1889–1891 have not yet been digitized but are available in paper copy.

For Adoption Record information, contact:

Pennsylvania Adoption Information Registry
P.O. Box 4379
Harrisburg, PA 17111-0379

www.adoptpakids.org/SearchReunion.aspx

H105.102 REV 07/2012

Application for Certified Copy of Birth Record

BIRTH **Pennsylvania Department of Health ♦ Division of Vital Records** **BIRTH**

PART 1: **By my signature below, I state I am the person whom I represent myself to be herein, and I affirm the information within this form is complete and accurate and made subject to the penalties of 18 Pa.C.S. §4904 relating to unsworn falsification to authorities. In addition, I acknowledge that misstating my identity or assuming the identity of another person may subject me to misdemeanor or felony criminal penalties for identity theft pursuant to 18 Pa.C.S. §4120 or other sections of the Pennsylvania Crimes Code. (Note: Signature must agree with name listed in Parts 2 and 5 of this form.)**

Signature of person making request *(Do not print)*: ______________________________

Signature required on ALL requests. Must be 18 years of age or older to apply. If under 18, immediate family member must request record.

PART 2: **PRINT** or **TYPE** name of individual requesting record and his/her **current mailing address.**

Name: ______________________ Relationship to Person Named on Record: ______________________

Address: ______________________________

City: ______________________ State: __________ Zip: __________

Daytime phone number: (_____) ______ - ________ E-mail Address: ______________________

Intended Use of Certified Copy: ☐ Travel/Passport ☐ Social Security/Benefits ☐ School ☐ Employment

☐ Driver's License ☐ Voter ID* ☐ Other (List reason: ______________________)

**In conjunction with Act 18 of 2012, Pennsylvania citizens may request a birth certificate for Voter ID. The certificate will be issued free of charge to those individuals without proper ID that will allow them to vote. The free birth certificate will include a stamp indicating that it is only to be used to obtain identification relevant to voter ID and is not valid for any other purpose.*

PART 3: **PRINT** or **TYPE** information below regarding person named on requested record: **Number of copies:** _______

Name at Birth: ______________________________

If name has changed since birth due to adoption, court order, or any reason other than marriage, *please list that name here:* ______________________

Date of Birth: ______________________ Age Now: _________ Sex: ☐ Male ☐ Female

(Month/Day/Year - Records available from 1906 to the present)

Place of Birth: ______________________ Hospital: ______________________

(County) (City/Boro/Twp. In Pennsylvania)

Full Maiden Name of Mother: ______________________________

Full Name of Father: ______________________________

PART 4: **BIRTH: $10.00 each.** *If fee is required, make check/money order payable to:* VITAL RECORDS.

Fees may be waived for individuals and their dependents who served or are currently serving in the Armed Forces *(complete the following)*:

Armed Forces Member's Name: ______________________ Service Number: ______________________

Relationship to Armed Forces Member: ______________________ Rank and Branch of Service: ______________________

PART 5: VALID GOVERNMENT ISSUED PHOTO ID REQUIRED

- **Individual requesting record must send a legible copy of his/her valid government issued photo ID that verifies name and mailing address as listed in Part 2 above.**
- Examples: State issued driver's license or non-driver photo ID *(if address has been changed, include copy of update card).*
- If possible, enlarge photo ID on copier by at least 150% (copies of ID will be shredded upon review).
- If acceptable ID not available, visit our website at www.health.state.pa.us/vitalrecords for further information.

Mail with self-addressed, stamped envelope to:

Division of Vital Records
ATTN: Birth Unit
PO BOX 1528
NEW CASTLE, PA 16103

Print or type name and address in the space provided below (Must agree with name and current address in Part 2 and ID documentation):

Name
Street
City, State, Zip Code

Have you?

- ✓ **Signed your name in Part 1** *(do not print)*
- ✓ **Listed your name and current mailing address in Parts 2 and 5**
- ✓ **Completed all items in Part 3** *(enter unknown if information unavailable)*
- ✓ **Enclosed payment** *(or completed Part 4 for waiver of fee)*
- ✓ **Enclosed legible copy of ID** *(must agree with your name and address in Parts 2 and 5)*

You are welcome to visit one of our public offices listed on the reverse side of this form.

For EXPEDITED ON-LINE ORDERING or additional information, visit our website: www.health.state.pa.us/vitalrecords

H105.102 REV 07/2012

DEATH Application for Certified Copy of Death Record DEATH

Pennsylvania Department of Health ♦ Division of Vital Records

PART 1: **By my signature below, I state I am the person whom I represent myself to be herein, and I affirm the information within this form is complete and accurate and made subject to the penalties of 18 Pa.C.S. §4904 relating to unsworn falsification to authorities. In addition, I acknowledge that misstating my identity or assuming the identity of another person may subject me to misdemeanor or felony criminal penalties for identity theft pursuant to 18 Pa.C.S. §4120 or other sections of the Pennsylvania Crimes Code. (Note: Signature must agree with name listed in Parts 2 and 5 of this form.)**

Signature of person making request *(Do not print)*: ______________________

Signature required on ALL requests. Must be 18 years of age or older to apply. If under 18, immediate family member must request record.

PART 2: **PRINT** or **TYPE** name of individual requesting record and his/her **current mailing address**.

Name: ______________________ Relationship to Person Named on Record: ______________________ *(If attorney, please indicate representation)*

Address: ______________________

City: ______________________ State: __________ Zip: __________

Daytime phone number: (____) ______ - ______ E-mail Address: ______________________

Intended Use of Certified Copy: *(Documentation required verifying your direct interest if you are not related to the decedent or are not the attorney for the estate)* ☐ Social Security/Benefits ☐ Insurance ☐ Financial Institution ☐ Genealogy ☐ Estate Settlement

☐ Other (List reason: ______________________)

PART 3: **PRINT** or **TYPE** information below regarding person who died: **Number of copies:** ______

Name at Death: ______________________ Sex: ☐ Male ☐ Female

Date of Death: ______________________ **Place of Death:** ______________________
(Month/Day/Year - Records available from 1906 to the present) (County) (City/Boro/Twp. in Pennsylvania)

Social Security #: ______________ Age at Time of Death: ______ Date of Birth: ______________

Full Maiden Name of Mother: ______________________

Full Name of Father: ______________________

Funeral Director: ______________________

PART 4: **DEATH: $9.00 each.** *If fee is required, make check/money order payable to:* VITAL RECORDS.

Fees may be waived for individuals and their dependents who served or are currently serving in the Armed Forces *(complete the following)*:

Armed Forces Member's Name: ______________________ Service Number: ______________________

Relationship to Armed Forces Member: ______________ Rank and Branch of Service: ______________

PART 5: VALID GOVERNMENT ISSUED PHOTO ID REQUIRED

- **Individual requesting record must include a legible copy of his/her valid government issued photo ID that verifies name and mailing address as listed in Part 2 above.**
- Examples: State issued driver's license or non-driver photo ID *(if address has been changed, include copy of update card)*.
- If possible, enlarge photo ID on copier by at least 150% (copies of ID will be shredded upon review).
- If acceptable ID not available, visit our website at www.health.state.pa.us/vitalrecords for further information.

Mail with self-addressed, stamped envelope to:

Division of Vital Records
ATTN: Death Unit
PO Box 1528
New Castle, PA 16103

Print or type name and address in the space provided below
(Must agree with name and current address in Part 2 and ID documentation):

Name
Street
City, State, Zip Code

You are welcome to visit one of our offices in the following cities in Pennsylvania

- **Erie:** 1910 West 26th Street
- **Harrisburg:** Forum Place 555 Walnut St., 1st Floor
- **New Castle:** Central Bldg. (Room 401) 101 South Mercer Street
- **Philadelphia:** 110 North 8th Street (Suite 108)
- **Pittsburgh:** 411 7th Avenue (Suite 360)
- **Scranton:** Scranton State Office Bldg. (Room 112), 100 Lackawanna Avenue

For EXPEDITED ON-LINE ORDERING **or additional information, visit our website:** www.health.state.pa.us/vitalrecords

Rev. 8/07

Application for Multi-Year Search of Birth Record

BIRTH

Pennsylvania Department of Health ◆ Division of Vital Records

(Records available from 1906 to the present)

By my signature below, I state I am the person whom I represent myself to be herein, and I affirm the information within this form is complete and accurate and made subject to the penalties of 18 Pa.C.S. §4904 relating to unsworn falsification to authorities. In addition, I acknowledge that misstating my identity or assuming the identity of another person may subject me to misdemeanor or felony criminal penalties for identity theft pursuant to 18 Pa.C.S. §4120 or other sections of the Pennsylvania Crimes Code.

Signature of person making request:______________________________________

Signature required on ALL requests. Must be 18 years of age or older to apply. If under 18, eligible requestor must sign above.

PRINT or **TYPE** your name & CURRENT address.

Name: ________________________ Relationship to Person Named on Certificate: ________________

Address: ____

City: ____________________State: ____________Zip:____________

Daytime phone number: (_______) ________- _________ E-mail Address: ____________________

Reason for Request____

PHOTO ID REQUIRED: The individual requesting the record must send a legible copy of his/her VALID GOVERNMENT ISSUED PHOTO ID which will be shredded after review. (Examples: State issued driver's license or non-driver photo ID with requestor's current address. If possible, enlarge photo ID on copier by at least 150%.)

The Division of Vital Records offers a multi-year **BIRTH** search procedure to those who do not know the exact date of birth. An eligible applicant can request a "search" to have two to ten birth years alphabetically indexed for a fee of $35.00 (fee includes one certification). Additional spans of two to ten years are indexed at a rate of $25.00. The Division has birth records that were registered in Pennsylvania from 1906 to the present.

I request Vital Records to index the years ________________ through ________________ for the birth record of:
(Beginning year) **(Ending year)**

Name at Birth:____

List changed name (if name has changed since birth due to adoption, court order or any reason other than marriage) ________________________

Age Now:________________________ Sex: Male Female

Place of Birth:________________________ ____________________
(County) (City/Township/Borough in Pennsylvania) (Name of Hospital)

Full Maiden Name of Mother: ________________________________

Full Name of Father:____________________________________

If the subject is deceased, please provide the following statistical information:

________________ ____________ ____________________
Name at Death Date of Death Place of Death

Provide the following additional information, if known, to assist our office in locating this record:

Mother: ______ ____________ ____________ __________________
(at time of this birth) Age Birthplace Occupation Residence

Father: ______ ____________ ____________ __________________
(at time of this birth) Age Birthplace Occupation Residence

____________________ Other: ____________________________
Attending physician

Make check or money order payable to: VITAL RECORDS. Mail this completed application and <u>a legible copy of ID</u> to: Division of Vital Records, 101 South Mercer St., PO Box 1528, New Castle, PA 16103.

Webste address: www.health.state.pa.us/vitalrecords

RHODE ISLAND

Send your requests to:

Division of Vital Records
Rhode Island Department of Health
3 Capitol Hill, Room 101
Providence, RI 02908-5097

Tel. (401) 222-2812
www.health.ri.gov/

The Division of Vital Records keeps birth and marriage records for 100 years and death records for 50 years. City and town clerk offices have records for all the births, deaths, marriages, and civil unions that occur in those cities and towns (including earlier records)—visit www.health.ri.gov/records/about/clerkoffices/index.php for contact information. In most cases you will receive your records more quickly from the city and town locations than from the Division of Vital Records.

Cost for a certified Birth Certificate	$20.00
Cost for a certified Marriage Certificate	$20.00
Cost for a certified Death Certificate	$20.00
Cost for a duplicate copy, when ordered at the same time	$15.00

For Divorce Records, contact:

Clerk of Family Court
Garrahy Judicial Complex
1 Dorrance Plaza
Providence, RI 02903

For Divorce Records 1749–1900, contact:

Rhode Island Judicial Records Center
5 Hill Street
Pawtucket, RI 02860

Tel. (401) 721-2641
E-mail: judicialrecordscenter@courts.ri.gov

For Genealogy Research:

The Rhode Island State Archives (337 Westminster Street, Providence, RI 02903; tel. 401-222-2353; e-mail: statearchives@sos.ri.gov; http://sos.ri.gov/archives) maintains the original statewide manuscript filings for birth and marriage records over 100 years old (since 1853) and death records over 50 years old (since 1853). Alphabetical indexes for these records include 1852–1900 (birth and marriage) and 1853–1945 (deaths). Aside from these original manuscripts, the State Archives also maintains an extensive collection on microfilm of pre-1852 municipal vital records, dating from the earliest recordings in Providence, Westerly, Portsmouth, etc.

The library of the Rhode Island Historical Society (121 Hope Street, Providence, RI 02906; tel. 401-331-8575; www.rihs.org/) has birth records 1636–1898, marriage records 1636–1900, and death records 1636–1920. State vital record indexes are available for births and marriages 1853–1900 and for deaths 1853–1920. The Rhode Island Historical Cemeteries database is searchable online at www.rihistoriccemeteries.org/webdatabase.aspx.

For Adoption Record information, contact:

Voluntary Adoption Reunion Registry
Juvenile Department
Garrahy Judicial Complex
1 Dorrance Plaza
Providence, RI 02903

The Office of Vital Records provides non-certified copies of pre-adoption birth records for a fee of $20.00.

PLEASE TYPE OR PRINT CLEARLY

Mail to RI Department of Health, Office of Vital Records, 3 Capitol Hill, Rm. 101, Providence, RI 02908

Application for a Certified Copy of a Birth Record

Please complete ALL items 1-5 below. If you type your information, use the tab key on your keyboard to move to each gray-shaded field.

1. Please fill in the information below for the person whose birth record you are requesting.

Full name at birth: Age now:

New name if changed in court **(excluding marriage)**:

Date of birth: City/town of birth: Hospital:

Mother's/parent's full name at birth:

Father's/parent's full name at birth:

2. I am applying for the birth record of (complete one of the following):

☐ myself ☐ my child ☐ my mother/father

☐ my spouse/civil union partner/registered domestic partner ☐ my brother/sister

☐ my grandchild (parent of mother) ☐ my grandchild (parent of father)

☐ my client—I'm an attorney representing: The name of the law firm is:

☐ another person (specify your relationship):

3. Why do you need this record? (We ask this question so that we can supply you with a certified copy that will be suitable for your needs.)

☐ school ☐ license ☐ vets benefits ☐ social security ☐ passport/travel ☐ foreign gov't

☐ work ☐ WIC ☐ welfare ☐ other use (specify):

4. Copies cost $20.00. Any additional copies of this record purchased this same day cost $15.00 each.

How many copies do you want? (Make check payable to: General Treasurer of RI)

5. I hereby state that the information supplied in item #2 above is true and that I am not in violation of Section 23-3-28 of the General Laws of RI (printed below).

Please sign ____ ____________________

signature of person completing this form date signed

Type or print your name: Type or print your phone #: ( )

Type or print your address:

(include street or mailing address, city/town, state, and zip code.)

ATTACH PHOTOCOPY OF VALID GOVERNMENT ISSUED PICTURE ID

From Section 23-3-28 of the General Laws of Rhode Island:

"§23-3-28 Penalties. — (a) Any person who willfully and knowingly makes any false statement in a report, record, or certificate required to be filed under this chapter, or in an application for an amendment of those, or who willfully and knowingly supplies false information intending that this false information be used in the preparation of any report, record, or certificate, or amendment [...] shall be punished (if convicted) by a fine of not more than one thousand dollars ($1,000) or imprisoned not more than one (1) year or both."

PLEASE TYPE OR PRINT CLEARLY

Mail to RI Department of Health, Office of Vital Records, 3 Capitol Hill, Rm. 101, Providence, RI 02908

Application for a Non-Certified Pre-Adoption Birth Record

You must be 25 years of age or older to receive a non-certified copy of a pre-adoption birth record. To apply, please complete the items below. If you type your information, use the tab key on your keyboard to move to each gray-shaded field.

Name of applicant after adoption: First: ______ Middle: ______ Last: ______

Date of birth: ______

Sex: ☐ Male ☐ Female

Place of birth: City: ______ State: ______

Adoptive father/parent's name at birth: First: ______ Middle: ______ Last: ______

Adoptive mother/parent's name at birth: First: ______ Middle: ______ Maiden Last: ______

Copies cost $20.00. Any additional copies of this record purchased this same day cost $15.00 each.

How many copies do you want? _____ (Make check or money order payable to: General Treasurer of RI. Note that your check/money order will be deposited when it is received.)

Fill in your mailing address below. The record will be mailed to this address to the adult adoptee only. (You may also request your record in person at the State Office of Vital Records. Office hours are Monday-Friday, 12:30 to 4:00 p.m.)

Name: ______

Street address: ______

City, State, Zip Code: ______

Telephone number (optional) (   )   -

I understand that Section 23-3-28 of the General Laws of Rhode Island provides penalties for either of the following violations: Any person who willfully and knowingly makes any false statement in a report, record, certificate or application for an amendment thereof, or who willfully and knowingly supplies false information intending that such information be used in the preparation of any of the such report, record, or certificate, or amendment thereof . . . shall be punished (if convicted) by a fine of not more than one thousand dollars ($1,000) or imprisoned not more than one (1) year or both.

Please sign ______________________________ ______________

signature of person completing this form — date signed

ATTACH PHOTOCOPY OF VALID GOVERNMENT ISSUED PICTURE ID
(Please note that if you pick up your record in person, you must bring valid government-issued picture ID.)

PLEASE TYPE OR PRINT CLEARLY

Mail to RI Department of Health, Office of Vital Records, 3 Capitol Hill, Rm. 101, Providence, RI 02908

Application for a Certified Copy of a Marriage or Civil Union Record

Please complete ALL items 1-5 below. If you type your information, use the tab key on your keyboard to move to each gray-shaded field.

1. Please fill in the information below for the person whose marriage or civil union record you are requesting.

Full name of Groom/Party A:

Full name of Bride/Party B:

Full name at birth of Groom/Party A (if different):

Full name at birth of Bride/Party B (if different):

Date of marriage: civil union: City/Town of marriage/civil union:

2. I am applying for the marriage or civil union record of (complete one of the following):

☐ myself ☐ my parent ☐ my child
☐ my grandparents ☐ my brother or sister

☐ my client. I'm an attorney representing: . The name of the law firm is:

☐ another person (please specify):

3. Why do you need this record? (We ask this question so that we can supply you with a certified copy that will be suitable for your needs.)

☐ update records ☐ health insurance ☐ foreign government ☐ vets benefits
☐ legal purposes ☐ other use (specify):

4. Copies cost $20.00. Any additional copies of this record purchased this same day cost $15.00 each.

How many copies do you want? (Make check payable to: General Treasurer of RI)

5. I hereby state that the information supplied in item #2 above is true and that I am not in violation of Section 23-3-28 of the General Laws of RI (printed below).

Please sign ______________________________ ______________
signature of person completing this form date signed

Type or print your name: Type or print your phone number: ( ) -

Type or print your address:

(include street or mailing address, city/town, state, and zip code.)

ATTACH PHOTOCOPY OF VALID GOVERNMENT ISSUED PICTURE ID

From Section 23-3-28 of the General Laws of Rhode Island:
"§23-3-28 Penalties. — (a) Any person who willfully and knowingly makes any false statement in a report, record, or certificate required to be filed under this chapter, or in an application for an amendment of those, or who willfully and knowingly supplies false information intending that this false information be used in the preparation of any report, record, or certificate, or amendment [...] shall be punished (if convicted) by a fine of not more than one thousand dollars ($1,000) or imprisoned not more than one (1) year or both."

PLEASE TYPE OR PRINT CLEARLY

Mail to RI Department of Health, Office of Vital Records, 3 Capitol Hill, Rm. 101, Providence, RI 02908

Application for a Certified Copy of a Death Record

Please complete ALL items 1-5 below. If you type your information, use the tab key on your keyboard to move to each gray-shaded field.

1. Please fill in the information below for the person whose death record you are requesting.

Full name:

Date of death: Place of death (city/town/hospital name):

Name of spouse/civil union partner/domestic registered partner (if applicable):

Mother's/parent's full name at birth:

Father's/parent's full name at birth:

2. I am applying for the death record of (complete one of the following):

☐ my parent ☐ my spouse/civil union partner/registered domestic partner

☐ my child ☐ my grandparent ☐ other relative (specify):

☐ my client. I am an attorney representing: . The name of the law firm is:

☐ my client. The name of the insurance company is:

☐ another person (specify):

3. Why do you need this record? (We ask this question so that we can supply you with a certified copy that will be suitable for your needs.)

☐ probate ☐ social security ☐ vets benefits ☐ property title

☐ foreign government ☐ other use (specify):

4. Copies cost $20.00. Any additional copies of this record purchased this same day cost $15.00 each.

How many copies do you want? (Make check payable to: General Treasurer of RI)

5. I hereby state that the information supplied in item #2 above is true and that I am not in violation of Section 23-3-28 of the General Laws of RI (printed below).

Please sign ______________________________ ____________

signature of person completing this form date signed

Type or print your name: Type or print your phone number: ( )

Type or print your address:

(include street or mailing address, city/town, state, and zip code.)

ATTACH PHOTOCOPY OF VALID GOVERNMENT ISSUED PICTURE ID

From Section 23-3-28 of the General Laws of Rhode Island:

"§23-3-28 Penalties. — (a) Any person who willfully and knowingly makes any false statement in a report, record, or certificate required to be filed under this chapter, or in an application for an amendment of those, or who willfully and knowingly supplies false information intending that this false information be used in the preparation of any report, record, or certificate, or amendment [...] shall be punished (if convicted) by a fine of not more than one thousand dollars ($1,000) or imprisoned not more than one (1) year or both."

SOUTH CAROLINA

Send your requests to:

South Carolina Department of Health and Environmental Control
Division of Vital Records
2600 Bull Street
Columbia, SC 29201-1797

Tel. (803) 898-3630
Fax (803) 898-3761
www.scdhec.net/administration/vr/

The Office of Vital Records has birth and death records from January 1, 1915; marriage records from July 1, 1950; and divorce records from January 1, 1962. Death certificates become public records after 50 years and then any person may obtain an uncertified copy of the death certificate. The Office of Vital Records does not have a copy of the divorce decree; the actual divorce decree must be obtained from the clerk of court's office in the county where the final divorce hearing was held.

There are seven regional vital records offices, which issue birth and death certificates from 2005 forward. In addition, each South Carolina county has a vital records office. These branch offices have limited services; contact the county office for details. Visit www.scdhec.net/administration/vr/locations.htm for locations of regional and county offices.

Cost for a certified Birth Certificate	$12.00
Cost for a wallet-size Birth Certificate (available only from the county)	$12.00
Cost for a certified Marriage or Divorce Certificate	$12.00
Cost for a certified Death Certificate	$12.00
Cost for a duplicate copy, when ordered at the same time	$3.00

For pre-July 1, 1950 Marriage Certificates, contact:

Probate Judge
Probate Court
(County Seat), SC

For Divorce Decrees since 1911, contact:

Clerk of the Court
County Court
(County Seat), SC

For Genealogy Research:

On the South Carolina Death Indexes 1915–1957 website (www.scdhec.net/administration/vr/vrdi.htm), you will find links to all of the Division of Vital Records Death Index log files.

Death records are available for public viewing at the South Carolina Department of Archives and History (8301 Parklane Road, Columbia, SC 29223; tel. 803-896-6104; http://archives.sc.gov/) 50 years after the date of death. The Archives also has a number of colonial and state records of interest to genealogical researchers.

For Adoption Record information, contact:

Adoption Services
South Carolina Department of Social Services
P.O. Box 1520
Columbia, SC 29202-1520

Tel. (803) 898-7318
www.state.sc.us/dss/adoption/

Vital Records Birth/Death Application

A photocopy of a government, school or employer photo identification of the **applicant** must be submitted with all requests. Applications without proper identification will be returned unprocessed.

Name of applicant:______________________________ **Day phone number:**______________

Address: ______________________________

City:______________________ State:______________ Zip code:______________

E-mail address: ______________________________

Address certificate to be mailed to if different than applicant's address:

Name: ______________________________

Address: ______________________________

City: ______________________ State: ______________ Zip code: ______________

Your relationship to person named on the certificate. (Check one)

____Self ____ Adult child ____ Family member (specify) ______________

____Parent ____ Guardian ____ Legal representative (for whom?)______________

For what purpose are you requesting this certificate? ______________________________

By signing this application, I understand that making a false application for a vital record is a felony under state law.

Signature of applicant: ______________________________

Printed name of applicant: ______________________________

BIRTH CERTIFICATES

Full name: ______________________________
First Middle Last Suffix

Date of birth:______________Sex: ________City of birth:______________ County of birth: ______________

Name of mother prior to any marriage:______________________________
First Middle Last

Name of father:______________________________
First Middle Last

Were parents married at time of birth: ___ Yes ___ No Number of children born in SC to this mother?__________

Name at birth if ever changed for any reason other than marriage: ______________________________

Specify the number and type of certification(s) requested:

____ Birth long ($12) ____ Additional long ($3 each) ____ Birth short ($12) ____ Additional short ($3 each)

Total fees submitted:______________ ____ Expedite Additional $5

DEATH CERTIFICATES

Name of deceased: ______________________________
First Middle Last Suffix

Date of death: ______________Age at death:__________Social security number ______________

Sex:__________City of death:______________County of death: ______________

Specify the number and type of certification(s) requested:

____ Death long ($12) ____ Additional long ($3 each) ____ Death short ($12) ____ Additional short ($3 each)

____ Death statement ($12) ____ Additional statement ($3 each)

Total fees submitted:______________ ____ Expedite Additional $5

Send completed application/photocopy of identification to: **SC DHEC – Vital Records**
2600 Bull Street, Columbia, SC 29201

OFFICE USE ONLY

Date received: __________ BC SFN__________R/F__________ DC SFN__________ R/F__________

BC 1st Search __________ BC Issue Date__________ Ist Search __________ DC Issue Date__________

BC 2nd Search__________ DCN__________ 2nd Search __________ DCN__________

LOC __________ __________ DNL __________ __________

NFL/DNL __________ __________ __________

DHEC 0640 (10/2009) **SOUTH CAROLINA DEPARTMENT OF HEALTH AND ENVIRONMENTAL CONTROL**

Vital Records Application for Birth and Death Certificates
Instructions and Information

1) **One form may be used to request a certified copy of a birth certificate only, or a certified copy of a death certificate only, or a certified copy of a birth and death certificate if for the same individual.**
2) **Complete all of the information in the top section of the form and all information in the birth and/or death sections based upon whether a birth, death or both certificate(s) are being requested.**

Information

BIRTHS AND DEATHS – SC Law did not require the filing of birth and death records until January 01, 1915. No birth or death records on file at SCDHEC (county or state) are available for public viewing.

A death record becomes public record fifty (50) years after the date of death. Non-certified copies of public death records are issued unless a certified copy is specifically requested. The $12 "search fee" is required for each request of a public death record.

Death records are avaliable for public viewing fifty (50) years after the date of death ONLY at the SC Department of Archives and History, 8301 Parklane Road, Columbia, 29223, website: http://archives.sc.gov.

TURNAROUND TIME – The usual turnaround time for 'waiting' on-site customers is approximately thirty (30) minutes during non-peak hours (8:30 am - 11:00 am and 2:00 pm - 4:00 pm). The usual turnaround time for 'mail' requests is approximately three (3) weeks from the date of receipt. Expedited requests are processed and a response provided within 3 business days of receipt. The expedite fee is an additional $5.00 for a birth and/or death request.

If it has been more than four (4) weeks since you submitted your request, call (803) 898 3630 to determine the status.

IDENTIFICATION – A valid/current government, school or employer issued photo identification document of the **applicant** is required before a search of the records will be conducted. Requests that do not contain proper identification will be returned unprocessed. Acceptable documents are:

1. Any United States' DMV Office issued picture identification i.e. Driver's License, ID card, Learner's Permit (unexpired)
2. Current school or employer picture identification card
3. Military card (unexpired – active duty or retired member)
4. United States Passport (unexpired)
5 Foreign Passport with Visa (I-94 or I-94W – unexpired)
6. Re-Entry Permit (I-327 – unexpired)
7. Refuge Travel Document (form I-571 – unexpired)
8. United States Citizen Identification Card (form I-197)
9. Temporary Resident Card (form I-688 – unexpired)
10. Permanent Resident Card (form I-551 – unexpired)
11. Weapon or gun permit issued by federal, state or municipal government (unexpired)

Website – www.scdhec.gov/vr/ provides additional information on SC Vital Records.

PAYMENT – Acceptable methods of payment for mail requests are a money order or cashier's check made payable to SC DHEC. Onsite customer service also accepts credit and debit cards and cash.

SEARCH FEE – A $12 "search fee" is required by law. **If the record is not found, the $12 search fee is non-refundable.** The required search fee includes one (1) certification, if record is located. If additional copies of the same type certification are ordered at the same time, additional copies are $3 each.

TYPE OF CERTIFICATIONS

Birth Long contains parentage
Birth Short/Wallet does not include parentage

Death Long includes cause of death
Death Short does not include cause of death
Death Statement only includes fact of death

Vital Records Marriage/Divorce Application

A photocopy of a government, school or employer photo identification must be submitted with all requests. Applications without proper identification will be returned unprocessed.

Name of applicant:__________ **Day phone number:**__________
Address: __________
City:__________ State:__________ Zip code:__________
E-mail address: __________

Address certificate to be mailed to if different than applicant's address:
Name: __________
Address: __________
City: __________ State: __________ Zip code: __________

Your relationship to person named on the certificate? (Check One)
____Self ____ Adult child ____ Present or former spouse
____ Legal representative (for whom?)__________

For what purpose are you requesting this certificate? __________

By signing this application, I understand that making a false application for a vital record is a felony under state law.

Signature of applicant: __________

Printed name of applicant: __________

MARRIAGE

Name of bride:__________
First Middle Last Suffix

Other married surnames used by bride: __________

Name of groom: __________
First Middle Last Suffix

Date of marriage: __________

County where marriage license obtained: __________
South Carolina

Specify the number and type of certification(s) requested:
_____ Marriage long form ($12)
_____ Additional marriage long forms ($3 each)
_____ Statement of marriage (names, date and county only - $12)
_____ Additional statements ($3 each)

Total fees submitted: __________

DIVORCE/ANNULMENT

Name of wife: __________
First Middle Last Suffix

Other married surnames used by wife: __________

Name of husband: __________
First Middle Last Suffix

Date of divorce or annulment: __________

County where divorce obtained: __________
South Carolina

Specify the number and type of certification(s) requested:
_____ Divorce long form ($12)
_____ Additional divorce long forms ($3 each)
_____ Statement of divorce (names, date and county only - $12)
_____ Additional statements ($3 each)

Total fees submitted: __________

Send completed application/photocopy of identification to: **SC DHEC – Vital Records**
2600 Bull Street, Columbia, SC 29201

OFFICE USE ONLY

Date Received __________
ML 1st Search __________
ML 2nd Search__________
DNL __________

ML SFN__________
BC Issue Date__________
DCN__________

RD SFN__________
Ist Search __________ RD Issue Date__________
2nd Search __________ DCN__________
DNL__________

DHEC 0639 (12/2007) **SOUTH CAROLINA DEPARTMENT OF HEALTH AND ENVIRONMENTAL CONTROL**

Vital Records Application for Marriage and Divorce
Instructions and Information

1) **One form may be used to request a certified copy of a marriage license only, or a report of divorce/annulment only, or for both a marriage license and report of divorce if for the same couple.**
2) **Complete all of the information in the top section of the form and all information in the marriage and/or divorce sections based upon whether a marriage, divorce or both certificate(s) are being requested.**

Information

MARRIAGES/DIVORCES – The central filing of marriages was not required until July 01, 1950. Marriages prior to that date must be obtained from the Office of the Probate Judge in the county where the license was obtained. Reports of divorce are available from July 01, 1962 forward. SCDHEC does not have a copy of the divorce decree. The actual divorce decree must be obtained from the Office of the Clerk of Court in the county where the final divorce hearing was held.

TURNAROUND TIME – The usual turnaround time for 'Mail' requests is approximately three (3) weeks from the date of receipt. The usual turnaround time for 'waiting' on-site customers is approximately thirty (30) minutes during non-peak hours (8:30 am – 11:00 am and 2:00 pm – 4:00 pm). Expedited requests are processed and a response provided within 3 business days of receipt.

If it has been more than four (4) weeks since you submitted your request, call (803) 898 3630 to determine the status.

IDENTIFICATION – A valid/current government, school or employer issued photo identification document of applicant is required before a search of the records will be conducted. Requests that do not contain proper identification will be returned unprocessed. Acceptable documents are:

1. Any United States' DMV Office issued picture identification ie Driver's License, ID card, Learner's Permit (unexpired)
2. Current school or employer picture identification card
3. Military card (unexpired – active duty or retired member)
4. United States Passport (unexpired)
5 Foreign Passport with Visa (I-94 or I-94W – unexpired)
6. Re-Entry Permit (I-327 – unexpired)
7. Refuge Travel Document (form I-571 – unexpired)
8. United States Citizen Identification Card (form I-197)
9. Temporary Resident Card (form I-688 – unexpired)
10. Permanent Resident Card (form I-551 – unexpired)
11. Weapon or gun permit issued by federal, state or municipal government (unexpired)

WEBSITE – www.scdhec.gov/vr/ provides additional information on SC Vital Records.

PAYMENT – Acceptable methods of payment for mail requests are a money order or cashier's check made payable to SC DHEC. Onsite customer service also accepts credit and debit cards and cash.

SEARCH FEE – A $12 "search fee" is required by law. **If the record is not found, the $12 search fee is non-refundable.** The required search fee includes one (1) certification, if record is located. If additional copies of the same type certification are ordered at the same time, additional copies are $3 each.

SOUTH DAKOTA

Send your requests to:

South Dakota Department of Health
Vital Records
207 East Missouri, Suite 1-S
Pierre, SD 57501-2536

Tel. (605) 773-4961
E-mail: mariah.pokorny@state.sd.us
http://doh.sd.gov/records/

The Vital Records Office has birth, death, marriage, and divorce records from July 1905. Some birth records from the 1800s and early 1900s are also available, but the records before 1905 are not complete. Births more than 100 years old are searchable online at http://apps.sd.gov/applications/PH14Over100BirthRec/index.aspx.

The Register of Deeds in each county also holds copies of birth, death, and marriage records. In some instances the county offices have records filed prior to 1905. You will find a list of each county's holdings at http://doh.sd.gov/records/county/.

Cost for a certified or informational Birth Certificate	$15.00
Cost for a certified or informational Marriage Certificate	$15.00
Cost for a certified or informational Divorce Record	$15.00
Cost for a certified or informational Death Certificate	$15.00

For Genealogy Research:

Although certified copies of South Dakota vital records are restricted, any person who submits an application and the applicable fee to the Office of Vital Records can obtain an informational copy of a vital record. If you are ordering a record for genealogy purposes, your order should be placed through the mail.

Counties are allowed to make available an index of death certificates and marriage records to conduct genealogical research provided that you are a member of the South Dakota Genealogical Society (P.O. Box 1101, Pierre, SD 57501-1101; e-mail: sdgensoc@midco.net).

The Archives of the South Dakota State Historical Society (900 Governors Drive, Pierre, SD 57501; tel. 605-773-3804; http://history.sd.gov/Archives/) has a number of resources of interest to genealogists, including cemetery records, naturalization records, and a searchable database of South Dakota newspapers.

For Adoption Record information, contact:

South Dakota Department of Social Services
Adoption Unit
700 Governors Drive
Pierre, SD 57501

Tel. (605) 773-3227
http://dss.sd.gov/adoption/adoptionregistry/

There is no charge for registration in the Voluntary Adoption Registry.

South Dakota Application for a Birth Record

VITAL RECORDS
207 E MISSOURI AVE, STE 1A
PIERRE SD 57501
605-773-4961

To receive a birth record you must:

- Choose an ordering method (see **Ordering Methods** in the instructions).
- Choose the type of identification that you need (see **Identification** in the instructions).
- Determine what fees apply to your request (see **Fees** in the instructions).
- Determine if you meet the eligibility requirements (see **Eligibility** in the instructions).

NOTE: If you want to order more than one type of Vital Record (e.g., a birth and marriage record) you need to complete Sections 1 and 2 (and Sections 3 or 4 if applicable) on this form and the **Application for Vital Records Addendum.**

Section 1

CUSTOMER				
	CUSTOMER'S FULL NAME			
	STREET ADDRESS (if your mailing address is a PO Box, please include your street address of residence)			
	CITY	STATE	ZIP	PHONE NUMBER ( )

I understand that by signing this application, the information that I provide is accurate to the best of my knowledge.

Customer's Signature: **Today's Date:**

Section 2

BIRTH RECORD			
FIRST NAME		MIDDLE NAME	LAST NAME
# OF COPIES ($15 per copy)	GENDER ☐ Male ☐ Female	DATE OF BIRTH	CITY AND/OR COUNTY OF BIRTH
MOTHER'S FIRST NAME		MIDDLE NAME	MAIDEN NAME/NAME PRIOR TO FIRST MARRIAGE
FATHER'S FIRST NAME		MIDDLE NAME	LAST NAME

TYPE OF COPY	RELATIONSHIP - This area must be completed to receive a certified copy
☐ Certified ☐ Certified Photostatic ☐ Informational ☐ Informational Photostatic -See **Eligibility** in the instructions	☐ Self ☐ Child ☐ Grandparent, grandchild over 18 or sibling only ☐ Current Spouse ☐ Guardian ☐ Designated Agent (Please complete section 4) ☐ Parent ☐ Funeral Director, Attorney or Physician ☐ Personal or Property Right ☐ Record over 100 years

Section 3

MAIL APPLICANTS ONLY - Applicants who are applying by mail must submit **EITHER** a clear copy of a government issued photo ID that contains the applicant's signature **OR** submit a notarized application.

Subscribed to and sworn before me this (date): ______

Signature of Notary Public: ______

My commission expires:

SEAL

Section 4

DESIGNATED AGENTS ONLY - The individual who is designating an agent to collect their record must complete this section and have their signature notarized.

I, ________________________________ after being duly sworn upon oath,

do here by authorize ________________________________ to act as my designated agent to obtain certified copies of vital records.

Signature of person designating an agent:

SEAL

Subscribed to and sworn before me this (date):

Signature of Notary Public:

My commission expires:

FOR OFFICE USE ONLY

VITAL RECORD APPLICATION INSTRUCTIONS

To receive a birth record you must:

1. Choose an ordering method (see **Ordering Methods**).
2. Choose the type of identification that you need (see **Identification**).
3. Determine what fees apply to your request (see **Fees**).
4. Determine if you meet the eligibility requirements (see **Eligibility**).

NOTE: If you are ordering multiple types of vital record (e.g., a birth and marriage record) you need to complete Sections 1 and 2 (and Sections 3 or 4 if applicable) on this form and the **Application for Vital Records Addendum.**

ORDERING METHODS

Vital Records Requests can be made using the following methods:

- **Internet** orders at www.vitalchek.com with a credit card. An additional fee of $11.50 for expedited processing applies if you choose this method.
- **Telephone** orders at (605) 773-4961. An additional fee of $11.50 for expedited processing applies if you choose this method.
- **Mail** orders may be sent to VITAL RECORDS
  Requests made via mail **must submit**: a completed application form, the appropriate fees and proof of identity as described below. Please mail requests to the address listed in the upper right portion of the South Dakota Application for a Birth Record.
- **In-Person** requests can be processed at any South Dakota county Register of Deeds office or at the State Vital Records Office. Please be ready to provide proof of your identity as outlined below in the Identification section, pay the appropriate fees and complete this application form.

IDENTIFICATION

Applicants who are applying by mail must **EITHER** submit a clear copy of a CURRENT government issued photo ID that contains the applicant's signature **OR** have a notary public notarize their signature on Section 3 of the application. **No government issued ID**? You must send a clear photocopy of any **two** of the following:

Social Security Card
Utility bill with current address
Bank statement with current address
Pay stub (must include your name, social security number and the name and address of the business)
Car registration or title with current address

FEES - Payment should be made in the form of a check or money order to : VITAL RECORDS

Certified or informational copy of a Birth Record or a certified or informational notification of a record searched....................$15 per record
Expedited processing fee (phone or internet requests only)....................$11.50 in addition to $15 per record

ELIGIBILITY

By state law, vital records are not open for public inspection. Vital records may be issued in the form of a certified or an informational copy. **Only certain individuals are eligible to obtain a certified copy of a vital record** (see below to determine if you qualify). **Not qualified to receive a certified copy of a vital record?** Any person who submits an application and the applicable fee can obtain an informational copy of a vital record.

Certified Copies
The record will be computer generated, issued on security paper with a raised seal and have the signature of the issuing agent. Individuals eligible for a certified copy are the following:

Self
Current Spouse, Child
Parent, Guardian - If guardian, please submit documentation of your legal guardianship.
Next of Kin - Grandparents, grandchildren over 18 and siblings only
Attorneys, Physicians or Funeral Directors acting on behalf of the family
Designated Agent - Someone given the authority by another individual to obtain a vital record on his or her behalf must complete Section 4.
Personal or Property Right - A right to the record not included in the categories above. Please submit documentation of the right with your application.

Informational Copies

These copies will be issued on plain paper and contain the statement "For Informational Purposes Only. Not for Legal Proof of Identification." An informational copy will not contain a raised seal or the signature of the issuing agent.

Photostatic Copies (Certified or Informational)
This record is a photo copy of the original. These records may be requested if the computer generated copy does not contain the information needed. Generally, these copies are intended for genealogy purposes. They can be issued certified for legal purposes or informational.

South Dakota Application for a Marriage Record

VITAL RECORDS
207 E MISSOURI AVE, STE 1A
PIERRE SD 57501
605-773-4961

- Choose an ordering method (see **Ordering Methods** in the instructions).
- Choose the type of identification that you need (see **Identification** in the instructions).
- Determine what fees apply to your request (see **Fees** in the instructions).
- Determine if you meet the eligibility requirements (see **Eligibility** in the instructions).

NOTE: If you want to order more than one type of Vital Record (e.g., a birth and marriage record) you need to complete Sections 1 and 2 (and Sections 3 or 4 if applicable) on this form and the **Application for Vital Records Addendum.**

Section 1

CUSTOMER				
	CUSTOMER'S FULL NAME			
	STREET ADDRESS (if your mailing address is a PO Box, please include your street address of residence)			
	CITY	STATE	ZIP	PHONE NUMBER ( )

I understand that by signing this application, the information that I provide is accurate to the best of my knowledge.

Customer's Signature: **Today's Date:**

Section 2

MARRIAGE RECORD			
	GROOM'S FIRST NAME	MIDDLE NAME	LAST NAME
	BRIDE'S FIRST NAME	MIDDLE NAME	LAST NAME PRIOR TO MARRIAGE
	# OF COPIES ($15 per copy)	DATE OF MARRIAGE	CITY AND/OR COUNTY OF

TYPE OF COPY

☐ Certified ☐ Informational
☐ Certified Photostatic ☐ Informational Photostatic

-See **Eligibility** in the instructions

RELATIONSHIP - This area must be completed to receive a certified copy

☐ Self ☐ Child ☐ Grandparent, grandchild over 18 or sibling only
☐ Current Spouse ☐ Guardian ☐ Designated Agent (Please complete section 4)
☐ Parent ☐ Funeral Director, Attorney or Physician
☐ Personal or Property Right

Section 3

MAIL APPLICANTS ONLY - Applicants who are applying by mail must submit **EITHER** a clear copy of a government issued photo ID that contains the applicant's signature **OR** submit a notarized application.

Subscribed to and sworn before me this (date): ______________________

Signature of Notary Public: ______________________ SEAL

My commission expires:

Section 4

DESIGNATED AGENTS ONLY - The individual who is designating an agent to collect their record must complete this section and have their signature notarized.

I, ______________________ after being duly sworn upon oath,

do here by authorize ______________________ to act as my designated agent to obtain certified copies of vital records. SEAL

Signature of person designating an agent:

Subscribed to and sworn before me this (date):

Signature of Notary Public:

My commission expires:

FOR OFFICE USE ONLY

VITAL RECORD APPLICATION INSTRUCTIONS

To receive a marriage record you must:

1. Choose an ordering method (see **Ordering Methods**).
2. Choose the type of identification that you need (see **Identification**).
3. Determine what fees apply to your request (see **Fees**).
4. Determine if you meet the eligibility requirements (see **Eligibility**).

***NOTE*:** If you are ordering multiple types of vital record (e.g., a birth and marriage record) you need to complete Sections 1 and 2 (and Sections 3 or 4 if applicable) on this form and the **Application for Vital Records Addendum.**

ORDERING METHODS

Vital Records Requests can be made using the following methods:

- **Internet** orders at www.vitalchek.com with a credit card. An additional fee of $11.50 for expedited processing applies if you choose this method.
- **Telephone** orders at (605) 773-4961. An additional fee of $11.50 for expedited processing applies if you choose this method.
- **Mail** orders may be sent to VITAL RECORDS
  Requests made via mail **must submit**: a completed application form, the appropriate fees and proof of identity as described below. Please mail requests to the address listed in the upper right portion of the South Dakota Application for a Marriage Record.
- **In-Person** requests can be processed at any South Dakota county Register of Deeds office or at the State Vital Records Office. Please be ready to provide proof of your identity as outlined below in the Identification section, pay the appropriate fees and complete this application form.

IDENTIFICATION

Applicants who are applying by mail must **EITHER** submit a clear copy of a CURRENT government issued photo ID that contains the applicant's signature **OR** have a notary public notarize their signature on Section 3 of the application. **No government issued ID?** You must send a clear photocopy of any **two** of the following:

Social Security Card
Utility bill with current address
Bank statement with current address
Pay stub (must include your name, social security number and the name and address of the business)
Car registration or title with current address

FEES - **Payment should be made in the form of a check or money order to** VITAL RECORDS

Certified or informational copy of a Marriage Record or a certified or informational notification of a record searched..$15 per record
Expedited processing fee (phone or internet requests only)..........................$11.50 in addition to $15 per record

ELIGIBILITY

By state law, vital records are not open for public inspection. Vital records may be issued in the form of a certified or an informational copy. **Only certain individuals are eligible to obtain a certified copy of a vital record** (see below to determine if you qualify). **Not qualified to receive a certified copy of a vital record?** Any person who submits an application and the applicable fee can obtain an informational copy of a vital record.

Certified Copies

The record will be computer generated, issued on security paper with a raised seal and have the signature of the issuing agent. Individuals eligible for a certified copy are the following:

Self
Current Spouse, Child
Parent, Guardian - If guardian, please submit documentation of your legal guardianship.
Next of Kin - Grandparents, grandchildren over 18 and siblings only
Attorneys, Physicians or Funeral Directors acting on behalf of the family
Designated Agent - Someone given the authority by another individual to obtain a vital record on his or her behalf must complete Section 4.
Personal or Property Right - A right to the record not included in the categories above. Please submit documentation of the right with your application.

Informational Copies

These copies will be issued on plain paper and contain the statement "For Informational Purposes Only. Not for Legal Proof of Identification." An informational copy will not contain a raised seal or the signature of the issuing agent.

Photostatic Copies (Certified or Informational)

This record is a photo copy of the original. These records may be requested if the computer generated copy does not contain the information needed. Generally, these copies are intended for genealogy purposes. They can be issued certified for legal purposes or informational.

South Dakota Application for a Divorce Record

VITAL RECORDS
207 E MISSOURI AVE, STE #1A
PIERRE SD 57501
605-773-4961

To receive a divorce record you must:

- Choose an ordering method (see **Ordering Methods** in the instructions).
- Choose the type of identification that you need (see **Identification** in the instructions).
- Determine what fees apply to your request (see **Fees** in the instructions).
- Determine if you meet the eligibility requirements (see **Eligibility** in the instructions).

NOTE: If you want to order more than one type of Vital Record (e.g., a birth and marriage record) you need to complete Sections 1 and 2 (and Sections 3 or 4 if applicable) on this form and the **Application for Vital Records Addendum.**

Section 1

CUSTOMER			
CUSTOMER'S FULL NAME			
STREET ADDRESS (if your mailing address is a PO Box, please include your street address of residence)			
CITY	STATE	ZIP	PHONE NUMBER ( )

I understand that by signing this application, the information that I provide is accurate to the best of my knowledge.

Customer's Signature: **Today's Date:**

Section 2

DIVORCE RECORD		
HUSBAND'S FIRST NAME	MIDDLE NAME	LAST NAME
WIFE'S FIRST NAME	MIDDLE NAME	MAIDEN NAME/NAME PRIOR TO FIRST MARRIAGE
# OF COPIES ($15 per copy)	DATE OF DIVORCE	FILING CITY AND/OR COUNTY OF DIVORCE

TYPE OF COPY

- ☐ Certified
- ☐ Certified Photostatic
- ☐ Informational
- ☐ Informational Photostatic

- See Eligibility in the instructions

RELATIONSHIP - This area must be completed to receive a certified

- ☐ Self
- ☐ Child
- ☐ Grandparent, grandchild over 18 or sibling only
- ☐ Current Spouse
- ☐ Guardian
- ☐ Designated Agent (Please complete section 4)
- ☐ Parent
- ☐ Funeral Director, Attorney or Physician
- ☐ Personal or Property Right

Section 3

MAIL APPLICANTS ONLY - Applicants who are applying by mail must submit **EITHER** a clear copy of a government issued photo ID that contains the applicant's signature **OR** submit a notarized application.

Subscribed to and sworn before me this (date): ______________________

SEAL

Signature of Notary Public: ______________________

My commission expires:

Section 4

DESIGNATED AGENTS ONLY - The individual who is designating an agent to collect their record must complete this section and have their signature notarized.

I, ______________________ after being duly sworn upon oath,

do here by authorize ______________________ to act as my designated agent to obtain certified copies of vital records.

SEAL

Signature of person designating an agent:

Subscribed to and sworn before me this (date):

Signature of Notary Public:

My commission expires:

FOR OFFICE USE ONLY

VITAL RECORD APPLICATION INSTRUCTIONS

To receive a divorce record you must:

1. Choose an ordering method (see **Ordering Methods**).
2. Choose the type of identification that you need (see **Identification**).
3. Determine what fees apply to your request (see **Fees**).
4. Determine if you meet the eligibility requirements (see **Eligibility**).

***NOTE*:** If you are ordering multiple types of vital record (e.g., a birth and marriage record) you need to complete Sections 1 and 2 (and Sections 3 or 4 if applicable) on this form and the **Application for Vital Records Addendum.**

ORDERING METHODS

Vital Records Requests can be made using the following methods:

- **Internet** orders at www.vitalchek.com with a credit card. An additional fee of $11.50 for expedited processing applies if you choose this method.
- **Telephone** orders at (605) 773-4961. An additional fee of $11.50 for expedited processing applies if you choose this method.
- **Mail** orders may be sent to VITAL RECORDS
  Requests made via mail **must submit:** a completed application form, the appropriate fees and proof of identity as described below. Please mail requests to the address listed in the upper right portion of the South Dakota Application for a Divorce Record.
- **In-Person** requests can be processed at the State Vital Records Office. Please be ready to provide proof of your identity as outlined belowin the Identification section, pay the appropriate fees and complete this application form.

IDENTIFICATION

Applicants who are applying by mail must **EITHER** submit a clear copy of a CURRENT government issued photo ID that contains the applicant's signature **OR** have a notary public notarize their signature on Section 3 of the application. **No government issued ID**? You must send a clear photocopy of any **two** of the following:

Social Security Card
Utility bill with current address
Bank statement with current address
Pay stub (must include your name, social security number and the name and address of the business)
Car registration or title with current address

FEES – Payment should be made in the form of a check or money order to VITAL RECORDS

Certified or informational copy of a Divorce Record or a certified or informational notification of a record searched........$15 per record
Expedited processing fee (phone or internet requests only)........$11.50 in addition to $15 per record

ELIGIBILITY

By state law, vital records are not open for public inspection. Vital records may be issued in the form of a certified or an informational copy. **Only certain individuals are eligible to obtain a certified copy of a vital record** (see below to determine if you qualify). **Not qualified to receive a certified copy of a vital record?** Any person who submits an application and the applicable fee can obtain an informational copy of a vital record.

Certified Copies

The record will be computer generated, issued on security paper with a raised seal and have the signature of the issuing agent. Individuals eligible for a certified copy are the following:

Self
Current Spouse, Child
Parent, Guardian - If guardian, please submit documentation of your legal guardianship.
Next of Kin - Grandparents, grandchildren over 18 and siblings only
Attorneys, Physicians or Funeral Directors acting on behalf of the family
Designated Agent - Someone given the authority by another individual to obtain a vital record on his or her behalf must complete Section 4.
Personal or Property Right - A right to the record not included in the categories above. Please submit documentation of the right with your application.

Informational Copies

These copies will be issued on plain paper and contain the statement "For Informational Purposes Only. Not for Legal Proof of Identification." An informational copy will not contain a raised seal or the signature of the issuing agent.

Photostatic Copies (Certified or Informational)

This record is a photo copy of the original. These records may be requested if the computer generated copy does not contain the information needed. Generally, these copies are intended for genealogy purposes. They can be issued certified for legal purposes or informational.

South Dakota Application for a Death Record

VITAL RECORDS
207 E MISSOURI AVE, STE 1A
PIERRE SD 57501
605-773-4961

To receive a death record you must:

- Choose an ordering method (see **Ordering Methods** in the instructions).
- Choose the type of identification that you need (see **Identification** in the instructions).
- Determine what fees apply to your request (see **Fees** in the instructions).
- Determine if you meet the eligibility requirements (see **Eligibility** in the instructions).

***NOTE*:** If you want to order more than one type of Vital Record (e.g., a birth and marriage record) you need to complete Sections 1 and 2 (and Sections 3 or 4 if applicable) on this form and the **Application for Vital Records Addendum.**

Section 1

CUSTOMER	CUSTOMER'S FULL NAME			
	STREET ADDRESS (if your mailing address is a PO Box, please include your street address of residence)			
	CITY	STATE	ZIP	PHONE NUMBER ( )

I understand that by signing this application, the information that I provide is accurate to the best of my knowledge.

Customer's Signature: **Today's Date:**

Section 2

DEATH RECORD	FIRST NAME		MIDDLE NAME	LAST NAME	STATE FILE NUMBER
	# OF COPIES ($15 per copy)	GENDER ☐ Male ☐ Female	DATE OF DEATH	CITY AND/OR COUNTY OF DEATH	

TYPE OF COPY	RELATIONSHIP - This area must be completed to receive a certified copy
☐ Certified ☐ Informational ☐ Certified Photostatic ☐ Informational Photostatic -See **Eligibility** in the instructions	☐ Current Spouse ☐ Child ☐ Grandparent, grandchild over 18 or sibling only ☐ Parent ☐ Guardian ☐ Designated Agent (Please complete section 4) ☐ Funeral Director, Attorney or Physician ☐ Personal or Property Right

Section 3

MAIL APPLICANTS ONLY - Applicants who are applying by mail must submit **EITHER** a clear copy of a government issued photo ID that contains the applicant's signature **OR** submit a notarized application.

Subscribed to and sworn before me this (date): ____________________

Signature of Notary Public: ____________________

My commission expires:

SEAL

Section 4

DESIGNATED AGENTS ONLY - The individual who is designating an agent to collect their record must complete this section and have their signature notarized.

I, ____________________ after being duly sworn upon oath,

do here by authorize ____________________ to act as my designated agent to obtain certified copies of vital records.

Signature of person designating an agent:

SEAL

	FOR OFFICE USE ONLY
Subscribed to and sworn before me this (date):	
Signature of Notary Public:	
My commission expires:	

VITAL RECORD APPLICATION INSTRUCTIONS

To receive a death record you must:

1. Choose an ordering method **(see Ordering Methods)**.
2. Choose the type of identification that you need **(see Identification)**.
3. Determine what fees apply to your request **(see Fees)**.
4. Determine if you meet the eligibility requirements **(see Eligibility)**.

NOTE: If you are ordering multiple types of vital record (e.g., a death and marriage record) you need to complete Sections 1 and 2 (and Sections 3 or 4 if applicable) on this form and the **Application for Vital Records Addendum.**

ORDERING METHODS

Vital Records Requests can be made using the following methods:

- **Internet** orders at www.vitalchek.com with a credit card. An additional fee of $11.50 for expedited processing applies if you choose this method.
- **Telephone** orders at (605) 773-4961. An additional fee of $11.50 for expedited processing applies if you choose this method.
- **Mail** orders may be sent to VITAL RECORDS
  Requests made via mail **must submit**: a completed application form, the appropriate fees and proof of identity as described below. Please mail requests to the address listed in the upper right portion of the South Dakota Application for a Death Record.
- **In-Person** requests can be processed at any South Dakota county Register of Deeds office or at the State Vital Records Office. Please be ready to provide proof of your identity as outlined below in the Identification section, pay the appropriate fees and complete this application form.

IDENTIFICATION

Applicants who are applying be mail must **EITHER** submit a clear copy of a CURRENT government issued photo ID that contains the applicant's signature **OR** have a notary public notarize their signature on Section 3 of the application. **No government issued ID**? You must send a clear photocopy of any **two** of the following:

Social Security Card
Utility bill with current address
Bank statement with current address
Pay stub (must include your name, social security number and the name and address of the business)
Car registration or title with current address

FEES - Payment should be made in the form of a check or money order to VITAL RECORDS

Certified or informational copy of a Death Record or a certified or informational notification of a record searched.......$15 per record
Expedited processing fee (phone or internet requests only).......$11.50 in addition to $15 per record

ELIGIBILITY

By state law, vital records are not open for public inspection. Vital records may be issued in the form of a certified or an informational copy. **Only certain individuals are eligible to obtain a certified copy of a vital record** (see below to determine if you qualify). **Not qualified to receive a certified copy of a vital record**? Any person who submits an application and the applicable fee can obtain an informational copy of a vital record.

Certified Copies

The record will be computer generated, issued on security paper with a raised seal and have the signature of the issuing agent. Individuals eligible for a certified copy are the following:

Current Spouse, Child
Parent, Guardian - If guardian, please submit documentation of your legal guardianship.
Next of Kin - Grandparents, grandchildren over 18 and siblings only
Attorneys, Physicians or Funeral Directors acting on behalf of the family
Designated Agent - Someone given the authority by another individual to obtain a vital record on his or her behalf must complete Section 4.
Personal or Property Right - A right to the record not included in the categories above. Please submit documentation of the right with your application.

Informational Copies

These copies will be issued on plain paper and contain the statement "For Informational Purposes Only. Not for Legal Proof of Identification." An informational copy will not contain a raised seal or the signature of the issuing agent.

Photostatic Copies (Certified or Informational)

This record is a photo copy of the original. These records may be requested if the computer generated copy does not contain the information needed. Generally, these copies are intended for genealogy purposes. They can be issued certified for legal purposes or informational.

TENNESSEE

Send your requests to:

Tennessee State Department of Health and Environment
Vital Records Office
Central Services Building, First Floor
421 5th Avenue North
Nashville, TN 37243

Tel. (615) 741-1763
Fax (615) 741-9860
http://health.state.tn.us/vr/index.htm

The Vital Records Office keeps birth records for 100 years and death, marriage, and divorce records for 50 years. All in-person routine orders for certified copies must be submitted using the self-service kiosks located in the lobby of the Vital Records Office.

Many county health departments can issue short-form birth certificates for births that occurred anywhere in Tennessee since 1949, and most can issue death certificates for deaths that occurred in that county within the past few years; visit http://health.state.tn.us/localdepartments.htm for contact information.

Cost for a certified Birth Certificate	$15.00
Cost for a short-form Birth Certificate (1949–present only)	$8.00
Cost for verification of Birth Facts	$15.00
Cost for a certified Marriage Certificate	$15.00
Cost for verification of Marriage Facts	$15.00
Cost for a certified Divorce Record	$15.00
Cost for verification of Divorce Facts	$15.00
Cost for a duplicate copy of a Birth, Marriage, or Divorce Record, when ordered at the same time	$5.00
Cost for a certified Death Certificate	$7.00
Cost for verification of Death Facts	$15.00
Identity Authentication Fee	$4.00

For Genealogy Research:

Certified copies of Tennessee vital records can only be provided to the person named on the certificate or certain family members. However, verification of information from the records of the Vital Records Office (excluding cause of death) is available to any requester.

Birth records older than 100 years and death, marriage, and divorce records older than 50 years are available at the Tennessee State Library and Archives (403 7th Avenue North, Nashville, TN 37243-0312; tel. 615-741-2764; www.tennessee.gov/tsla/) for public access and family research. There was no official statewide registration of births and deaths in Tennessee before 1908. However, four cities—Chattanooga, Knoxville, Memphis, and Nashville—did keep some earlier birth and death records, which are available at the State Library & Archives. The Index to Tennessee Death Records 1908–1912 is available online at www.tennessee.gov/tsla/history/vital/death2.htm. Also online is the Index to Davidson County Death Records 1900–1913; see www.tennessee.gov/tsla/history/vital/davidson1.htm.

An Index to Nashville Birth Records 1881–1913 (http://www.nashvillearchives.org/births.htm) and an Index to Davidson County Birth Records 1908–1912 (http://www.nashvillearchives.org/births-co.htm) have been posted online by the Friends of the Metropolitan Archives of Nashville and Davidson County.

The website for the Shelby County Register of Deeds (http://register.shelby.tn.us/) has online indexes and images for many Shelby County vital records.

The Statewide Index to Tennessee Death Records 1914–1933 (www.tennessee.gov/tsla/history/vital/tndeath.htm) is a long-term project to index Tennessee death records for the years 1914 on.

For Adoption Record information, contact:

Department of Children's Services
Cordell Hull Building, 7th floor
436 Sixth Avenue, North
Nashville, TN 37243

Tel. (615) 741-9701
www.state.tn.us/youth/

TENNESSEE DEPARTMENT OF HEALTH
OFFICE OF VITAL RECORDS

APPLICATION FOR CERTIFIED COPY OF CERTIFICATE OF BIRTH
(La versión en español al reverso de la página)

Date: ______________________________

Full name on birth certificate: ______________________________
First **Middle** **Last Name**

Has the name ever been changed other than by marriage? ☐ Yes ☐ No

If yes, what was original name? ______________________________

Date of birth: ______________________________ **Sex:** Male or Female
Month **Day** **Year**

Place of birth: ______________________________
City **County** **State**

Hospital where birth occurred: ______________________________

Full name of father: ______________________________

Full maiden name of mother: ______________________________

Last name of mother at time of birth: ______________________________

Next older brother or sister: ______________ **Younger:** ______________

Signature of person making request: ______________________________

Relationship: ______________________________

Purpose of copy: ______________________________

Indicate number of each type of certificate desired and enclose appropriate fee:

For years 1949-Current:

___ **Short form**- $8.00 first copy. Additional copies of same record purchased at same time-$5.00 each.

___ **Long form**- $15.00 first copy. Additional Copies of same record purchased at the same time-$5.00 each.

For births **before 1949**:
No short form available

___ $15.00 first copy. Additional copies of same record purchased at the same time -$5.00 each.

The above fees are charged for the search of records and will not be refunded even if no record is on file in this office. A 3-year search is provided for the initial fee.

Telephone number where you may be reached for additional information: ( ) ______________

IT IS UNLAWFUL TO WILLFULLY AND KNOWINGLY MAKE ANY FALSE STATEMENT ON THIS APPLICATION.

All items must be completed and appropriate fees attached to process this request. Do not send cash. Send check or money order payable to: Tennessee Vital Records. **In addition, unless this application is notarized, you must send a photocopy of a government issued ID showing your signature.** If you have not received a response within 45 days, please write or call Tennessee Vital Records at (615) 741-1763.

PH-1654 (rev 11/2008) RDA N/A

FILL OUT BELOW/ DO NOT DETACH

PRINT name and address of person to whom the certified copy is to be mailed.

____
Name

____
Address or Route

____
City and State **Zip Code**

SEND TO:

Tennessee Vital Records
421 5th Avenue North
1st floor, Central Services Building
Nashville, TN 37243

TENNESSEE DEPARTMENT OF HEALTH
OFFICE OF VITAL RECORDS

APPLICATION FOR VERIFICATION OF BIRTH FACTS

THIS APPLICATION MUST BE ACCOMPANIED BY A CHECK OR MONEY ORDER MADE PAYABLE TO TENNESSEE VITAL RECORDS FOR $15.00.

Name and mailing address where verification is to be sent:

______________________________ **Name of Individual or Requesting Agency** ______________ **Date**

______________________________ **Street Address** ( ) ______________ **Telephone No.**

____

City **State** **Zip**

In order for the Office of Vital Records' staff to search the files of birth records, please provide the following information from the record you are requesting:

____
Year of Birth

______________ **or** ______________ **or** ______________
Name of Child at Birth **or** Name of Father (if named) **or** Name of Mother (if no father named)

Also complete items 1-6 below if you have that information. This allows the Office of Vital Records to perform a more accurate search.

A fee of $15.00 is charged for the search of the year and the name entered above. This fee is charged even if no record is found. If you want to search more than one year of records, please enclose $15.00 for each additional year.

1. Full name at Birth: ______________________________
First Middle Last
2. Date of Birth: ______________________________
Month Day Year
3. Gender: (Circle One) **Male** **Female**
4. City or County of Birth: ______________________________
5. Mother's Full Maiden Name: ______________________________
First Middle Last
6. Father's Full Name: ______________________________
First Middle Last

MAIL THIS APPLICATION TO:

TENNESSEE DEPARTMENT OF HEALTH
OFFICE OF VITAL RECORDS
421 5th Avenue North
1st Floor Central Services Building
Nashville, TN 37243

PH-3061 (rev. 11/2008) RDA N/A

TENNESSEE DEPARTMENT OF HEALTH
OFFICE OF VITAL RECORDS

APPLICATION FOR CERTIFIED COPY OF CERTIFICATE OF MARRIAGE

Date: ______________________ **Number of copies:** ______________
First Copy $15.00 each additional copy $5.00

Name of Groom: ____
First Middle Last Name

Name of Bride at Birth: ____
First Middle Last Name

Place Where License was Issued: ____
City County State

Date of Marriage: ____
Month Day Year

Place of Marriage: ____
City County State

Signature of Person Making Request: ____

Relationship of Requestor: ____

Purpose of copy: ____

Telephone number where you may be reached for additional information: ( ) ______________

IT IS UNLAWFUL TO WILLFULLY AND KNOWINGLY MAKE ANY FALSE STATEMENT ON THIS APPLICATION.

Records are filed in this office for the past fifty (50) years. Records prior to this date are available in the county where the license was obtained.

A fee of $15.00 is charged for the search of the records even if no record is found and includes one copy if the record is filed in this office. If the certificate is not found with the date of marriage you have provided, a search will be made in the records for the year before and the year after that date; this search is routine and is included in the $15.00 fee. Do not send cash. Send a check or money order made payable to Tennessee Vital Records. In addition, unless this application is notarized, you must send a photocopy of a government issued ID showing your signature. If you have not received a response within 45 days, please write or call Tennessee Vital Records at 615-741-1763.

PH-1670 (rev. 11/2008) RDA N/A

FILL OUT BELOW/ DO NOT DETACH

PRINT name and address of person to whom the certified copy is to be mailed.

____
Name

____
Address or Route

____
City **State** **Zip Code**

SEND TO:

Tennessee Vital Records
421 5th Avenue North
1st floor, Central Services Building
Nashville, TN 37243

TENNESSEE DEPARTMENT OF HEALTH
OFFICE OF VITAL RECORDS

APPLICATION FOR VERIFICATION OF MARRIAGE FACTS

THIS APPLICATION MUST BE ACCOMPANIED BY A CHECK OR MONEY ORDER MADE PAYABLE TO TENNESSEE VITAL RECORDS FOR $15.00.

Name and mailing address where verification is to be sent:

______________________________ ______________
Name of Individual or Requesting Agency **Date**

______________________________ ( )
Address **Telephone No.**

____
City **State** **Zip**

In order for the Office of Vital Records' staff to search the files of marriage records, please provide the following information from the record you are requesting:

__________ ______________________ **or** ______________________
Year of Marriage Name of Groom (Required for 1993 and earlier) Maiden Name of Bride

For marriages prior to 1994, the groom's name is required for the search of the records.
For marriages from 1994 to present, a search can be done using either the bride's maiden name or the groom's name.

A fee of $15.00 is charged for the search of the year and the name entered above. This fee is charged even if no record is found. If you want to search more than one year of records, please enclose $15.00 for each additional year. The Office of Vital Records maintains marriage records for the past fifty (50) years only. Earlier records may be obtained from the State of Tennessee Library & Archives or from the clerk of the county where the marriage license was issued.

Also complete items 1-3 below if you have that information. This allows the Office of Vital Records to perform a more accurate search.

1. Date of Marriage: ______________________________
   Month Day Year

2. Place of Marriage: ______________________________
   City County

3. County Where License was obtained: ______________________

MAIL THIS APPLICATION TO:

TENNESSEE DEPARTMENT OF HEALTH
OFFICE OF VITAL RECORDS
421 5th Avenue North
1st Floor Central Services Building
Nashville, TN 37243

PH-3331 (rev. 11/2008) RDA N/A

TENNESSEE DEPARTMENT OF HEALTH
OFFICE OF VITAL RECORDS

APPLICATION FOR CERTIFIED COPY OF CERTIFICATE OF DIVORCE OR ANNULMENT

Today's Date: ______________________ **Number of copies** __________
First Copy $15.00, each additional copy $5.00

Name of Husband: ____
First Middle Last Name

Name of Wife: ____
First Middle Maiden Name

Date of Divorce: ____
Month Day Year

Place of Divorce: ____
City County State

Signature of Person Making Request: ______________________________

Relationship of Requestor: ______________________________

Purpose of Copy: ______________________________

Telephone number where you may be reached for additional information: ( ) __________

IT IS UNLAWFUL TO WILLFULLY AND KNOWINGLY MAKE ANY FALSE STATEMENT ON THIS APPLICATION.

Records are filed in this office for the past fifty (50) years. Records prior to this date are available from the clerk of the court where the divorce was granted and may be available from the State Library and Archives.

A fee of $15.00 is charged for the search of the records even if no record is found and includes one copy if the record is filed in this office. If the certificate is not found with the date of divorce that you provide, a search will be made in the records for the year before and the year after the date indicated; this search is routine and is included in the fee. Do not send cash. Send a check or money order made payable to Tennessee Vital Records. In addition, unless this application is notarized, you must send a photocopy of a government issued ID showing your signature. If you have not received a response within 45 days, please write or call Tennessee Vital Records at 615-741-1763.

PH-1671 (rev. 11/2008) RDA N/A

FILL OUT BELOW/ DO NOT DETACH

Name and address of person to whom the certified copy is to be mailed. (Please Print)

____
Name

____
Address or Route, Include Apartment Number

____
City State Zip Code

SEND TO:

Tennessee Vital Records
421 5th Avenue North
1st floor, Central Services Building
Nashville, TN 37243

TENNESSEE DEPARTMENT OF HEALTH
OFFICE OF VITAL RECORDS

APPLICATION FOR VERIFICATION OF DIVORCE OR ANNULMENT FACTS

THIS APPLICATION MUST BE ACCOMPANIED BY A CHECK OR MONEY ORDER MADE PAYABLE TO TENNESSEE VITAL RECORDS FOR $15.00.

Name and mailing address where verification is to be sent:

Name of Individual or Requesting Agency ______________________ **Today's Date** ______________________

Address ______________________ ( ) **Telephone No.** ______________________

City ______________________ **State** ______________________ **Zip** ______________________

In order for the Office of Vital Records to search the files of divorce records, please provide the following information from the record you are requesting:

Year of Divorce ______________ **Name of Husband (Required for 1993 and earlier)** ______________ or **Maiden Name of Wife** ______________

For divorces prior to 1994, the husband's name is required for the search of the records.
For divorces from 1994 to present, a search can be done using either the wife's maiden name or the husband's name.

A fee of $15.00 is charged for the search of the year and the name entered above. The fee is charged even if no record is found. If you want to search more than one year of records, please enclose $15.00 for each additional year. The Office of Vital Records maintains divorce records for the past fifty (50) years only. Earlier records may be obtained from the State of Tennessee Library and Archives or from the clerk of the court where the divorce was granted.

Also complete items 1-2 below if you have that information. This allows the Office of Vital Records to perform a more accurate search.

1. Date of Divorce: ______________ Month ______________ Day ______________ Year
2. City or County of Divorce: ______________ City ______________ County

MAIL THIS APPLICATION TO:

TENNESSEE DEPARTMENT OF HEALTH
Office of Vital Records
421 5th Avenue North
1st Floor Central Services Building
Nashville, TN 37243

TENNESSEE DEPARTMENT OF HEALTH
OFFICE OF VITAL RECORDS

APPLICATION FOR CERTIFIED COPY OF CERTIFICATE OF DEATH

Date: ______________________ **Number of Copies** ______________
Enclose $7.00 for each copy.

Full Name of Deceased: ____
First Middle Last Name

Date of Death: ______________________ **Sex:** Male or Female **Age at Death:** __________
Month Day Year

Place of Death: ____
City County State

Name of Funeral Home: ____

Location of Funeral Home: ____
City County State

Signature of Person Making Request: ____

Relationship to the Deceased: ____

Purpose of Copy: ____

Cause of Death is available only to the decedent's parent, child, spouse, or a documented authorized representative or agency acting on behalf of the decedent's estate or qualifying family member. ALL requests require a photocopy of a government issued form of identification which includes the requester's signature. Copies of any documents supporting the requester's entitlement to the record or information requested should also be submitted.

Do You Want the Certificate to Show Cause of Death? ☐ YES ☐ NO

Telephone Number Where You may be Reached for Additional Information: ( ) ______________

IT IS UNLAWFUL TO WILLFULLY AND KNOWINGLY MAKE ANY FALSE STATEMENT ON THIS APPLICATION.

A fee of $7.00 is charged for the search of the records even if no record is found and includes one copy if the record is filed in this office. If the certificate is not found with the date of death you provide, a search will be made in the records for the year before and the year after the date indicated; this search is routine and is included in the $7.00 fee. Do not send cash. Send a check or money order made payable to Tennessee Vital Records. If you have not received a response within 45 days, please write or call Tennessee Vital Records at 615-741-1763.

PH-1663 (Rev. 08/12) RDA S836.1

FILL OUT BELOW/ DO NOT DETACH

PRINT name and address of person to whom the certified copy is to be mailed. **SEND TO:**

Name ______________________________

Address or Route ______________________________

____
City **State** **Zip Code**

Tennessee Vital Records
421 5th Avenue North
1st floor, Central Services Building
Nashville, TN 37243

TENNESSEE DEPARTMENT OF HEALTH
OFFICE OF VITAL RECORDS

APPLICATION FOR VERIFICATION OF DEATH FACTS

THIS APPLICATION MUST BE ACCOMPANIED BY A CHECK OR MONEY ORDER MADE PAYABLE TO TENNESSEE VITAL RECORDS FOR $15.00.

Name and mailing address where verification is to be sent:

_______________________________ _______________
Name of Individual or Requesting Agency **Date**

_______________________________ (   ) _______________
Street Address **Telephone No.**

____
City **State** **Zip**

In order for the Office of Vital Records' staff to search the files of death records, please provide the following information from the record you are requesting:

__________ _______________________________
Year of Death **Name of Deceased Person**

Also complete items 1-5 below if you have that information. This allows the Office of Vital Records to perform a more accurate search.

A fee of $15.00 is charged for the search of the year and the name entered above. This fee is charged even if no record is found. If you want to search more than one year of records, please enclose $15.00 for each additional year. The Office of Vital Records maintains death records for the past fifty (50) years. Earlier years may be obtained at the State Library & Archives.

1. Full name of Deceased: _______________________________
   First Middle Last
2. Date of Death: _______________________________
   Month Day Year
3. Place of Death: _______________________________
   City County State
4. Residence at Time of Death: _______________________________
   City County State
5. Decedent's parents:

   Mother's: __________ __________ __________
   First Middle Maiden Name

   Father's: __________ __________ __________
   First Middle Last

MAIL THIS APPLICATION TO:

TENNESSEE DEPARTMENT OF HEALTH
Office of Vital Records
421 5th Avenue North
1st Floor Central Services Building
Nashville, TN 37243

PH 3055 (rov. 11/2008) RDA N/A

TEXAS

Send your requests to:

Texas Vital Statistics
Department of State Health Services
(Location: 1100 West 49th Street)
P.O. Box 12040
Austin, TX 78711-2040

Tel. (888) 963-7111
Fax (512) 458-7711 (for expedited service)
E-mail: registrar@dshs.state.tx.us
www.dshs.state.tx.us/vs/

The Bureau of Vital Statistics has birth and death records from January 1, 1903. Birth records are restricted for 75 years, death records for 25 years. The Bureau of Vital Statistics can verify marriages from January 1, 1966, and divorces from January 1, 1968. However, certified copies of marriage licenses are only available from the county clerk in the county where the event occurred; certified copies of divorce decrees are only available from the county's district clerk (see www.dshs.state.tx.us/vs/field/localremotedistrict.shtm for contact information for county clerks, district clerks, and local registrars). Indexes (lists) of marriage or divorce records by year may be purchased or downloaded for free from the Bureau of Vital Statistics website (www.dshs.state.tx.us/vs/marriagedivorce/default.shtm).

Birth and death certificates, as well as birth, death, marriage, and divorce verification letters, can be ordered at no extra charge through TexasOnline (www.texasonline.state.tx.us/tolapp/ovra/), the official eGovernment website for the State of Texas.

Cost for a certified Birth Certificate or Birth Verification	$22.00
Cost for an heirloom Birth Certificate	$60.00
Cost for the verification of a Marriage Certificate	$20.00
Cost for the verification of a Divorce Record	$20.00
Cost for a certified Death Certificate or Death Verification	$20.00
Cost for a duplicate copy of Death Certificate, when ordered at the same time	$3.00

For Genealogy Research:

When you order a birth verification or death verification letter for an event that was filed with the State of Texas, you will receive a letter that includes the person's name, date of event, county in which the event occurred, and state file number. Verification letters are available for births or deaths that have occurred since 1903.

The Genealogy Collection of the Texas State Library and Archives Commission (P.O. Box 12927, Austin, TX 78711-2927; tel. 512-463-5463; www.tsl.state.tx.us/arc/genfirst.html) has indexes to Texas births and deaths from 1903 (with some delayed birth indexes as early as 1880); marriage indexes from 1966 through the most recent year available; and divorce indexes from 1968 through the most recent year available.

An index of County Records Available on Microfilm can be viewed online at www.tsl.state.tx.us/arc/local/index.html.

For Adoption Record information, contact:

Central Adoption Registry
Department of State Health Services
P.O. Box 149347
Austin, TX 78714-9347

Tel. (888) 963-7111, ext. 6279
www.dshs.state.tx.us/vs/reqproc/adoptionregistry.shtm

Cost to register with the Central Adoption Registry	$30.00

For faster service at no extra charge, order online at www.Texas.gov

OFFICE USE ONLY
Cert #
DOCUMENT CONTROL #
By__________

TEXAS Department of State Health Services

MAIL APPLICATION FOR BIRTH OR DEATH RECORD

OFFICE USE ONLY
Remit No.
By__________ ZZ 708-153

PLEASE PRINT. INCLUDE A PHOTOCOPY OF YOUR VALID PHOTO ID WHEN SENDING THE REQUEST.

☐Birth Certificates			
Type	Cost X	# of copies=	Total
Certified Copy	$22		
Heirloom-Flag	$60		
Heirloom-Bassinet	$60		
(optional) $8.00 Lone Star OR $19.95 USPS Express return delivery			
Total			

☐Death Certificates			
Type	Cost X	# of copies=	Total
Certified Copy (1 copy)	$20		
Additional copies	$3		
(optional) $8.00 Lone Star OR $19.95 USPS Express return delivery			
Total			

Make check or money order payable to: DSHS

All funds are deposited directly to the Texas Comptroller of Public Accounts. Refunds available only on written request. For any search of the files where a record is not found, the searching fee is not refundable or transferable.

1. Full Name of Person on Record	First Name	Middle Name		Last Name
2. Date of Birth or Death	Month	Day	Year	3. Sex
4. Place of Birth or Death	City or Town	County		State
5. Full Name of Father	First Name	Middle Name		Last Name
6. Full Maiden Name of Mother	First Name	Middle Name		Maiden Name

7. YOUR NAME

8. TELEPHONE # ( ) -
(MON-FRI 8:00-5:00)

EMAIL ADDRESS ______________________

9. MAILING ADDRESS: ______________________
STREET ADDRESS CITY STATE ZIP

10. RELATIONSHIP TO PERSON NAMED IN ITEM 1: __________ 11. PURPOSE FOR OBTAINING THIS RECORD: __________

12. WILL THIS RECORD BE USED TO OBTAIN A PASSPORT, FOR IMMIGRATION OR FOR THE INDIAN REGISTRY? ☐ YES ☐ NO

13. ADDITIONAL INFORMATION FOR DEATH CERTIFICATE: BIRTHDATE __________ BIRTH PLACE __________

☐ I authorize mailing to the address below instead of my mailing address. I have verified that the address below will receive my order.

NAME ______________________ STREET ADDRESS ______________________

CITY ______________________ STATE __________ ZIP __________

WARNING: IT IS A FELONY TO FALSIFY INFORMATION ON THIS DOCUMENT. THE PENALTY FOR KNOWINGLY MAKING A FALSE STATEMENT ON THIS FORM OR FOR SIGNING A FORM WHICH CONTAINS A FALSE STATEMENT IS 2 TO 10 YEARS IMPRISONMENT AND A FINE OF UP TO $10,000. (HEALTH AND SAFETY CODE, CHAPTER 195, SEC. 195.003)

Your Signature ______________________ Date of Application __________

APPLICATIONS WITHOUT SIGNATURE OF APPLICANT WILL NOT BE PROCESSED.

MAIL THIS APPLICATION, PAYMENT AND A PHOTOCOPY OF YOUR VALID PHOTO ID (APPLICATIONS WITHOUT PHOTO ID WILL NOT BE PROCESSED) **TO:**

Texas Vital Records
Department of State Health Services
P.O. Box 12040
Austin, TX 78711-2040

VS-142.3 Rev. 02/2013

OFFICE USE ONLY
Cert #
DOCUMENT CONTROL #
By_____________

EXPEDITED APPLICATION FOR BIRTH OR DEATH RECORD

OFFICE USE ONLY
Remit No.
By_____________

PLEASE PRINT. INCLUDE A PHOTOCOPY OF VALID PHOTO ID OR ORDER WILL NOT BE PROCESSED.

Birth Certificates			
Type	Cost X	# of copies=	Total
Certified Copy	$22		
Heirloom-Flag	$60		
Heirloom-Bassinet	$60		
(optional) $8 Lone Star **OR** $19.95 USPS Express mail ($4.95 Priority mail for overseas military address ONLY)			
Expedite fee (required)			$5.00
Total			

Death Certificates			
Type	Cost X	# of copies=	Total
1st Copy	$20	1	$20
Additional copies	$3		
(optional) $8 Lone Star **OR** $19.95 USPS Express Mail ($4.95 Priority mail for overseas military address ONLY)			
Expedite fee (required)			$5.00
Total			

Make check or money order payable to: DSHS
Refunds available only on written request. For any search of the files where a record is not found, the searching fee is not refundable or transferable.

1. Full Name of Person on Record	First Name	Middle Name		Last Name
2. Date of Birth or Death	Month	Day	Year	3. Sex
4. Place of Birth or Death	City or Town	County		State
5. Full Name of Father	First Name	Middle Name		Last Name
6. Full Maiden Name of Mother	First Name	Middle Name		Maiden Name

7. YOUR NAME ______________________ 8. TELEPHONE # ( ) - AM or PM (circle)
(MON-FRI 8:00-5:00)

9. MAILING ADDRESS: ______________________
STREET ADDRESS CITY STATE ZIP

10. RELATIONSHIP TO PERSON NAMED IN ITEM 1: ____________ 11. PURPOSE FOR OBTAINING THIS RECORD: ____________

11. WILL THIS RECORD BE USED TO OBTAIN A PASSPORT, FOR IMMIGRATION OR FOR THE INDIAN REGISTRY? ☐ YES ☐ NO

☐ I authorize mailing to the address below instead of my mailing address. I have verified that the address below will receive my order.

NAME ______________________ STREET ADDRESS ______________________

CITY ______________________ STATE __________ ZIP ______________

WARNING: IT IS A FELONY TO FALSIFY INFORMATION ON THIS DOCUMENT. THE PENALTY FOR KNOWINGLY MAKING A FALSE STATEMENT ON THIS FORM OR FOR SIGNING A FORM WHICH CONTAINS A FALSE STATEMENT IS 2 TO 10 YEARS IMPRISONMENT AND A FINE OF UP TO $10,000. (HEALTH AND SAFETY CODE, CHAPTER 195, SEC. 195.003)

Your Signature ______________________ Date of Application ______________

APPLICATIONS WITHOUT SIGNATURE OF APPLICANT WILL NOT BE PROCESSED

SEND THIS APPLICATION VIA AN OVERNIGHT MAIL SERVICE (SUCH AS FEDEX, LONE STAR, UPS, ETC. DO NOT SEND VIA USPS PRIORITY MAIL) WITH PHOTOCOPY OF VALID PHOTO ID (APPLICATIONS WITHOUT A COPY OF VALID PHOTO ID AND SIGNATURE OF APPLICANT WILL NOT BE PROCESSED) **AND PAYMENT TO:**

Texas Vital Records MC 2096
Department of State Health Services
1100 West 49th Street
Austin, TX 78756

OVERNIGHT MAIL ORDERS ARE PROCESSED IN 10-15 BUSINESS DAYS

VS-142.21 Rev. 02/2013

OFFICE USE ONLY
Cert # ____
DOCUMENT CONTROL # ____
____
____
By____

TEXAS Department of State Health Services

MAIL APPLICATION FOR BIRTH OR DEATH VERIFICATION LETTER

OFFICE USE ONLY
Remit No. ____
Amount $____
Payment Method ____
Date____
By____

A verification letter is a letter than verifies whether or not a birth or death was filed with the State of Texas. It is not a certified copy of a birth or death certificate.

PLEASE PRINT

Type	Number X	Cost =	Total
Birth verification letter		$22.00	
Death verification letter		$20.00	
Total (Check or Money Order enclosed)			

1. Full Name of Person on Record	First Name	Middle Name		Last Name
2. Date of Birth or Death	Month	Day	Year	3. Sex
4. Place of Birth or Death	City or Town	County		State
5. Full Name of Father	First Name	Middle Name		Last Name
6. Full Maiden Name of Mother	First Name	Middle Name		Maiden Name

7. YOUR NAME:____ 8. TELEPHONE # (____)____-____ (MON-FRI 8:00-5:00)

9. MAILING ADDRESS:____
STREET ADDRESS CITY STATE ZIP

10. If certified copy is to be mailed to some other person, please complete:

Name____ Street Address____

City____ State____ Zip Code____

For any search of the files where a record is not found, the searching fee is not refundable or transferable.

WARNING: THE PENALTY FOR KNOWINGLY MAKING A FALSE STATEMENT IN THIS FORM CAN BE 2-10 YEARS IN PRISON AND A FINE OF UP TO $10,000. (HEALTH AND SAFETY CODE, CHAPTER 195, SEC. 195.003)

APPLICATIONS WITHOUT SIGNATURE OF APPLICANT WILL NOT BE PROCESSED.

Your Signature ____ Date of Application ____

MAIL THIS APPLICATION, PAYMENT AND A PHOTOCOPY OF YOUR VALID PHOTO ID (APPLICATIONS WITHOUT PHOTO ID WILL NOT BE PROCESSED) **TO:**
Texas Vital Records
Department of State Health Services
P.O. Box 12040
Austin, TX 78711-2040

VS-142.6 7/2012

OFFICE USE ONLY
Cert # ______
DOCUMENT CONTROL # ______
______
______
By______

TEXAS Department of State Health Services

MAIL APPLICATION FOR MARRIAGE OR DIVORCE VERIFICATION

OFFICE USE ONLY
Remit No. ______
Amount $______
Payment Method ______
Date______
By______

PLEASE PRINT

Type	Cost	Total
Marriage verification	$20.00	
Divorce verification	$20.00	
Return by ☐ Lonestar Overnight ($8) or ☐ Express Mail ($19.95)	$8.00 or $19.95	$8.00 or $19.95
Total (Check or Money Order enclosed)		

Processing time for most request is 6 to 8 weeks from the date received.

1. Full Name of Husband	First Name	Middle Name	Last Name
2. Date of Marriage or Divorce	Month	Day	Year
4. Place of Marriage or Divorce	City or Town	County	State Texas
5. Full Name of Wife	First Name	Middle Name	Maiden Name
6. Ages or Dates of Birth at time of Marriage or Divorce	Age or Date of Birth of Husband	Age or Date of Birth of Wife	

7. YOUR NAME: ______ 8. TELEPHONE # (______) ______ - ______
(MON-FRI 8:00-5:00)

9. MAILING ADDRESS: ______
STREET ADDRESS CITY STATE ZIP

10. If verification is to be mailed to some other person, please complete:

Name______ Street Address______

City ______ State ______ Zip Code ______

For any search of the files where a record is not found, the searching fee is not refundable or transferable.

A verification is a letter verifying whether or not a marriage or divorce was recorded with the State of Texas. To order a certified copy of the marriage license, you must contact the County Clerk's Office in the county in which the marriage license was obtained. To order a copy of a divorce decree, you must contact the District Clerk's Office in the District in which the divorce was filed.

> WARNING: THE PENALTY FOR KNOWINGLY MAKING A FALSE STATEMENT IN THIS FORM CAN BE 2-10 YEARS IN PRISON AND A FINE OF UP TO $10,000. (HEALTH AND SAFETY CODE, CHAPTER 195, SEC. 195.003)

APPLICATIONS WITHOUT PHOTOCOPY OF VALID PHOTO ID AND SIGNATURE OF APPLICANT WILL NOT BE PROCESSED.

Your Signature ______ Date of Application ______

MAIL THIS APPLICATION AND PAYMENT TO:
Texas Vital Records
Department of State Health Services
P.O. Box 12040
Austin, TX 78711-2040

VS 142.9 02/2013

Department of State Health Services

Texas Voluntary Adoption Registry
REGISTRATION APPLICATION

Part I: REGISTRANT INFORMATION (all applicants complete this section) VSU Form 2271 (7/09)

NAME — First	Middle	Last	Maiden Name	Suffix

OTHER NAMES USED (including married, aliases, nicknames)	Sex ☐ Male ☐ Female

Birth Date	Age	Social Security Number (optional)	E-mail address (optional)

Mailing Address for registry correspondence	City	State	Zip

Telephone (include Area Code)	Birth City	Birth County	Birth State/Country

I am: *(check all that apply)*
☐ Adoptee ☐ Birth Mother ☐ Birth Father ☐ Sibling

Part II: INFORMATION TO BE COMPLETED BY ADOPTEE (complete as many items as possible)

How old were you when you were placed in your adoptive home?	County of Adoption	Date of adoption or approximate year

Adoptive Mother's name (including maiden name)	Date of Birth	Her religious affiliation	What city and/or county were your adoptive parents living in when you were placed with them?
Adoptive Father's name	Date of Birth	His religious affiliation	

Was an adoption agency used? ☐ Yes ☐ No ☐ Unknown If yes, state name of agency, address & phone no.	Attorney's Name, address & phone no.

Was child welfare or child protective services involved? ☐ Yes ☐ No ☐ Unknown	If yes, where was the child living when removed from care (city and/or county)?	Year of removal

Name of Birth Mother ☐ Unknown	Her date of birth and her age at time of your birth	Delivering Doctor's name
Name of Birth Father ☐ Unknown	His date of birth and his age at time of your birth	Are you aware of any siblings? ☐ Yes ☐ No If yes, please complete Part IV. ☐ Unknown

Part III: INFORMATION TO BE COMPLETED BY BIRTH PARENT (complete as much as possible)
If you are looking for more than one child, please complete a separate application for each child.

Birth name of child (First, Middle, Last, Maiden) ☐ Unknown	Adoptive name of child (First, Middle, Last, Maiden) ☐ Unknown

Date of birth of child (If unknown, give year and approximate time of year)	Sex ☐ Male ☐ Female ☐ Unknown

Hospital or maternity home	City and/or County of Birth & State	Delivering Doctor's Name

Did the birth mother use an alias at the hospital or maternity home? ☐ Yes ☐ No ☐ Unknown	If yes, state name used.	Birth mother's religious affiliation

Birth mother's name at birth of child (include maiden name)	Date of birth and age at child's birth	State/city of birth
Birth father's name and last known address	Date of birth and age at child's birth	State/city of birth

Was the birth mother married at the time of this child's birth? ☐ Yes ☐ No ☐ Unknown	If yes, please provide husband's name

Was the child placed with an adoption agency? ☐ Yes ☐ No ☐ Unknown	If yes, name of agency	If no, name of attorney or law firm

Was child welfare or child protective services involved? ☐ Yes ☐ No ☐ Unknown	If yes, where was the child living when removed from care (city and/or county)?	Year of removal

Your other birth children:

Name of child (and any aliases or nicknames)	Maiden Name	Date of Birth	Place of Birth City/State	Name of Other Birth Parent and Date of Birth

Part IV: INFORMATION TO BE COMPLETED BY BIRTH-SIBLING (complete as many items as possible) If there is more than one sibling you are searching for, please duplicate this page, as needed.

Is the sibling you are looking for a: ☐ Full-sibling OR ☐ Half-sibling	If half-sibling, are you related by: ☐ Mother ☐ Father	What order in the biological mother's family is this child? (Example, first of five)	☐ Male ☐ Female ☐ Unknown

Adoptive name of child (First, Middle, Last, Maiden) ☐ Unknown	Birth Name of Child ☐ Unknown

Date of birth of child	City of Birth	County of Birth	Hospital

Birth mother's name at birth of child, including maiden name	Her date of birth and age at time of child's birth	Her city/state of birth	Her religious affiliation

Was an alias used by the birth mother at the hospital or maternity home? ☐ Yes ☐ No ☐ Unknown	If yes, state named used

Birth father's name	Birth father's date of birth and age	His city/state of birth

Was the birth mother married at the time of this child's birth? ☐ Yes ☐ No ☐ Unknown	If yes, please provide her husband's name, his date of birth.

Was an adoption agency used? ☐ Yes ☐ No ☐ Unknown	If yes, name of agency	Name of attorney or law firm

Was child welfare or child protective services involved? ☐ Yes ☐ No ☐ Unknown	If yes, where was the child living when removed from care (city and/or county)? and with whom?

If you are a sibling, please provide: ☐ Unknown Your birth mother's full name including maiden and all married names.	Your birth father's full name ☐ Unknown

If you are adopted, your adopted or legal mother's full name, including (maiden) and date of birth.	If you are adopted, your adopted or legal father's full name, including date of birth

Why do you believe you have a biological sibling(s)?

Names of other birth siblings	Maiden Name	Date of Birth	Place of Birth	Half-Sibling or Full-Sibling	Name of Birth Parents
				☐ Full ☐ Half	Mother Father
				☐ Full ☐ Half	Mother Father
				☐ Full ☐ Half	Mother Father

Part V: COMMENTS SECTION *(story of placement, additional information not listed above)* **Use separate page, if needed.**

Part VI: ALL APPLICANTS COMPLETE THIS SECTION

I am willing to allow my identity to be disclosed to those registrants **eligible** to learn my identity.................................... ☐ yes ☐ no

I authorize the administrator of the registry to inspect all vital statistics records, court records, hospital records and agency records including confidential records.. ☐ yes ☐ no

I consent to the disclosure of my identity after my death to those registrants eligible to learn my identity......................... ☐ yes ☐ no

For adoptees only: I want to be informed if registry records indicate that a biological sibling has also registered........... ☐ yes ☐ no

Your application is good for 99 years unless you state a shorter period of time here .... ____________

I certify that the information contained in this form is true and correct to the best of my knowledge.

X Signature ______________________________ Date ________________

Mail application, proof of ID and $30, payable to DSHS:
VSU – CAR (MC 2096), PO Box 149347, Austin TX 78714-9347

ZZ 708-153

APPLICATION FOR IDENTITY OF COURT OF ADOPTION

PLEASE PRINT AND INCLUDE A PHOTOCOPY OF A VALID PHOTO ID WITH YOUR REQUEST

1. Full Adoptive Name of Person on Record	First Name	Middle Name		Last Name
2. Date of Birth	Month	Day	Year	3. Sex
4. Place of Birth	City or Town	County		State
5. Full Name of Adoptive Father	First Name	Middle Name		Last Name
6. Full Name of Adoptive Mother	First Name	Middle Name		Maiden Name

7. YOUR NAME: ____________________ 8. TELEPHONE # (______) ____-________
(MON-FRI 8:00-5:00)

9. MAILING ADDRESS: ____
STREET ADDRESS CITY STATE ZIP

Your Signature ______________________ Date of Application ____________

INSTRUCTIONS:
Please mail
- **this application**
- **$10 payment by check or money order**
- a photocopy of valid photo ID

TO:
Texas Vital Records
Department of State Health Services
P.O. Box 12040
Austin, TX 78711-2040

VS-143 12/2005

CENTRAL ADOPTION REGISTRY

REQUEST FOR OPEN RECORDS

In 1984, we started collecting and maintaining social and medical information on private non-related adoptions. We also have records from many out-of-business child-placing agencies. To review the list of available records that we maintain, please visit us online at: http://www.dshs.state.tx.us/vs/reqproc/adoptagencies.shtm

As required by law, we will redact the confidential portion of the record. Specifically, Texas Family Code §162.018 - Access to Information, requires us to edit the record to protect the identity of the biological parents and any other person whose identity is confidential.

TO REQUEST A COPY OF YOUR RECORD, PLEASE COMPLETE THE FOLLOWING:

The more information you are able to provide us with will help us locate and process your request promptly.

Today's Date	I am the: ☐ Adoptee ☐ Adoptive Parent ☐ Other ______	
Full Adopted Name (Including Maiden)		
The Adopted Person is a: ☐ Male ☐ Female	Adoptee's Date of Birth	Adoptee's Place of Birth
Child Placing Agency: ☐ Unknown		
State and County of Adoption: ☐ Unknown	Adoptee's Age at adoption: ☐ Newborn ☐ Toddler ☐ Child ☐ Teenager	
Adoptive Father's Name:	Adoptive Mother's Name (including her maiden name):	
Your Name Today:		
Your Mailing Address:		
City	State	Zip
Phone: ( )	Email Address:	
Reason(s) for requesting records: ☐ Medical ☐ Heritage ☐ Proof of adoption ☐ Other (please explain)		

☐ Informed of updated medical by the adoption registry.

Signature ______________________ Date ______________

Your request **must** be accompanied with a **copy of a valid photo ID** in order to be processed. We will respond to your request within 10 business days after the date it is received by our department. Once you have completed this form, please send it along with a **copy of a valid government-issued photo ID** to:

Central Adoption Registry (MC 1966)
PO Box 149347
Austin, Texas 78714-9347
Or via email at: warren.magjarevich@dshs.state.tx.us

PLEASE NOTE: If your record is 50 pages or less, there will not be a charge assessed to receive a copy. If the record is 50 pages or more, we will contact you with an estimate before proceeding with processing the record.

VS-210 Rev. 12/2012

UTAH

Send your requests to:

Office of Vital Records and Statistics
Utah Department of Health
(Location: 288 North 1460 West)
P.O. Box 141012
Salt Lake City, UT 84114-1012

Tel. (801) 538-6105
http://health.utah.gov/vitalrecords/

The Office of Vital Records has birth and death records from January 1, 1905, and can provide verifications of marriage and divorce records from 1978 to present. Birth records are restricted for 100 years, and death certificates for 50 years. You can order certified copies of birth certificates online, directly through Vital Records, for no additional fee.

Certified copies of marriage certificates less than 75 years old are available from the county clerk in the county where the marriage took place; certified copies of divorce certificates less than 75 years old are obtainable from the District Court in the county where the divorce was finalized (www.utcourts.gov/directory).

Cost for a certified Birth Certificate	$18.00
Cost for a Marriage Certification	$16.00
Cost for a Divorce Certification	$16.00
Cost for a certified Death Certificate	$16.00
Cost for a duplicate copy, when ordered at the same time	$8.00

For Marriage Certificates and Divorce Certificates 75 years old or more, contact:

The Research Center of the Utah State Archives
300 South Rio Grande Street, Salt Lake City, UT 84101

Tel. (801) 533-3535
http://historyresearch.utah.gov/

For Genealogy Research:

Death certificates more than 50 years old and birth certificates more than 100 years old are sent to the Research Center of the Utah State Archives (see above for contact information). The Archives has microfilm copies of most birth and death registers for Utah counties 1898–1905. Indexes to birth records for many counties are available online (see http://archives.utah.gov/research/guides/birth.htm for a list), as are indexes to the death registers 1898–1905 for Beaver and Sanpete counties. The Archives also has adoption records more than 100 years old and divorce decrees 1852–1895, as well as divorce records more than 50 years old that have been transferred there from some District Courts. The Utah Death Certificate Index 1904–1956 is available online at http://archives.utah.gov/research/indexes/20842.htm.

UTGenWeb (www.rootsweb.ancestry.com/~utgenweb/) hosts several online databases, including Index to Marriage and Death Notices in the *Deseret News Weekly* (1852–1888) and Index to Marriage and Death Notices Unique to the *Deseret News Semi-Weekly* (1865–1900). BYU-Idaho Family History Center has the online index Western States Marriages (http://abish.byui.edu/specialCollections/westernStates/search.cfm).

For Adoption Records, contact:

Mutual Consent Voluntary Adoption Reunion Registry
Bureau of Vital Records
288 North 1460 West
P.O. Box 141012
Salt Lake City, UT 84114-1012

Tel. (801) 538-6363

Cost for registering with the Adoption Registry	$25.00

BIRTH CERTIFICATE REQUEST

Office of Vital Records and Statistics, 288 North 1460 West, Salt Lake City, Utah 84114-1012.
Website: silver.health.utah.gov

Vital Records validation only

WARNING: It is a criminal violation to make false statements on vital records application forms or to fraudulently obtain a birth certificate

INSTRUCTIONS

1. This request must be completed in full.
2. Identification is required of the person signing this request. (See acceptable identification list on back.
3. If ordering by mail, enclose the application, an enlarged, easily identifiable photo copy of the front and back of your ID, and appropriate fees.
4. Please check your certificate for accuracy. Your copy can only be replaced within 90 days from issuance date. After 90 days you must repay applicable fees.
5. If requestor does not respond to a written request for information within 90 days, Vital Records may retain all monies paid.

IDENTIFYING INFORMATION

FULL NAME AS IT SHOULD APPEAR ON CERTIFICATE____________________

DATE/PLACE OF BIRTH__________ (Date) __________ (City) __________ (County) __________ (Hospital)

FULL NAME OF FATHER __________________ __________ (Birth Date) __________ (State or Country)

FULL MAIDEN NAME OF MOTHER__________________ __________ (Birth Date) __________ (State or Country)

REQUESTOR

RELATIONSHIP: **I am:** ☐ Self ☐ Mother ☐ Father ☐ Sibling ☐ Spouse ☐ Child ☐ Grandparent ☐ Grandchild

☐ Other (Specify)____________________

Your Signature____________________ Date__________

Printed Name____________________ Telephone Number__________

Your Address ____________________ (City, State & Zip)

Purpose for which the birth certificate is needed:
☐ Drivers License ☐ Social Security ☐ Passport ☐ School ☐ State Assistance Pgm. ☐ Other (Specify)__________

NUMBER OF CERTIFIED COPIES REQUESTED		(If this order is to be mailed, please **PRINT** the name and mailing address below)
_1_ **Certified Copy**	$ 18.00 +	____________________
____ **Additional** Certified Copies ($8.00 each)	$______	____________________
TOTAL FEE	$______	____________________

Mailing Address: Office of Vital Records and Statistics, P O Box 141012, Salt Lake City, Utah 84114-1012.

For OFFICE USE ONLY (do not write below)

PAID: Check Cash Money Order Credit Card

Clerk's Initials__________

UDOH-OVRS-11 Revised 04/09

MARRIAGE OR DIVORCE REQUEST

Office of Vital Records and Statistics, 288 North 1460 West, Salt Lake City, Utah 84114-1012.

WARNING: It is a criminal violation to make false statements on vital records application forms or to fraudulently obtain a Marriage or Divorce certificate.

Vital records validation only

INFORMATION

1. State Vital Records can only verify marriages or divorces (1978-2005) taking place in Utah.
2. There is a fee of $16.00 for each search of our files. Records provided are certification summaries. They are not copies of the original records.
3. If ordering by mail, enclose the application, an enlarged, easily identifiable photo copy of the front and back of your ID, and appropriate fees.
4. Please check your certificate for accuracy. Your copy can only be replaced within 90 days from issuance date. After 90 days you must repay applicable fees.
5. If requestor does not respond to a written request for information within 90 days, Vital Records may retain all monies paid.

MARRIAGE CERTIFICATION IDENTIFYING INFORMATION

GROOM'S NAME :____

BRIDE'S MAIDEN NAME: ____________________________________

MARRIAGE DATE: __________________ PLACE OF MARRIAGE: __________________

DIVORCE CERTIFICATION IDENTIFYING INFORMATION

HUSBAND'S NAME :____

WIFE'S NAME: ____

DATE OF DIVORCE: __________________ PLACE OF DIVORCE: __________________

DATE OF MARRIAGE: __________________ PLACE OF MARRIAGE: __________________

APPLICANT

RELATIONSHIP: **I am:** ☐Husband ☐Wife ☐Mother ☐Father ☐Sibling ☐Child ☐Grandparent ☐Grandchild

☐Other (If other, reason for requesting certificate:)____________________

Your Signature______________________________ Date____________

Printed Name__________________________ Telephone Number____________

Your Address ____
(City, State & Zip)

NUMBER OF CERTIFIED COPIES REQUESTED			(If this order is to be mailed, please **PRINT** the name and mailing address below)
____	1st Certified Abstract	$ 16.00 +	____________________
____	Additional Certified Abstract ($8.00 each)	$______	____________________
	TOTAL FEE	$______	____________________

Mailing Address: Office of Vital Records and Statistics, P O Box 141012, Salt Lake City, Utah 84114-1012.

For OFFICE USE ONLY

PAID: Check Cash Money Order Credit Card

Clerks Initials______

UDOH-OVRS-11 Revised 06\09

DEATH CERTIFICATE REQUEST

Office of Vital Records and Statistics, 288 North 1460 West, Salt Lake City, Utah 84114-1012.

WARNING: It is a criminal violation to make false statements on vital records application forms or to fraudulently obtain a certificate.

Vital Records validation only

INSTRUCTIONS

1. This request must be completed in full.
2. Identification is required of the person signing this request. (See acceptable identification list on back.
3. If ordering by mail, enclose the application, an enlarged, easily identifiable photo copy of the front and back of your ID, and appropriate fees.
4. Please check your certificate for accuracy. Your copy can only be replaced within 90 days from issuance date. After 90 days you must repay applicable fees.
5. If requestor does not respond to a written request for information within 90 days, Vital Records may retain all monies paid.

IDENTIFYING INFORMATION

FULL NAME OF DECEASED________________________ SOCIAL SECURITY NO________________

DATE OF DEATH________________ (If not known, specify years to be searched)________________

PLACE OF DEATH (City)________________________ (County)________________

BIRTHPLACE OF DECEDENT (State or County)________________ DATE OF BIRTH OF DECEDENT________________

USUAL RESIDENCE OF DECEDENT (City & State)________________________________

FULL NAME OF FATHER________________________________

FULL MAIDEN NAME OF MOTHER________________________________

IF DECEASED WAS MARRIED, NAME OF SPOUSE________________________________

APPLICANT

RELATIONSHIP: **I am:** ☐ Mother ☐ Father ☐ Sibling ☐ Spouse ☐ Child ☐ Grandparent ☐ Grandchild
☐ Other (Specify) ________________________________

If other, reason for requesting certificate:________________________________

Your Signature________________________________ Date________________

Printed Name________________________________ Telephone Number________________

Your Address ________________________________
(City, State & Zip)

NUMBER OF CERTIFIED COPIES REQUESTED			(If this order is to be mailed, please **PRINT** the name and mailing address below)
1	**Certified Copy**	$ 16.00 +	________________
____	**Additional** Certified Copies ($8.00 each)	$______	________________
	TOTAL FEE	$______	________________

Mailing Address: Office of Vital Records and Statistics, P O Box 141012, Salt Lake City, Utah 84114-1012.

For OFFICE USE ONLY (do not write below)

PAID: Check Cash Money Order Credit Card

Clerk's Initials________

UDOH-OVRS - Revised 06/09

VERMONT

Send your requests for records from the past five years to:

Vermont Department of Health
Vital Records Office
(Location: 108 Cherry Street)
P.O. Box 70
Burlington, VT 05402-0070

Tel. (802) 863-7200; in Vermont (800) 439-5008
E-mail: vitalrecords@state.vt.us
http://healthvermont.gov/research/records/vital_records.aspx

Send your requests for records older than five years to:

Vermont State Archives and Records Administration (VSARA)
Public Records Division
Reference/Research Section
1078 U.S. Route 2, Middlesex
Montpelier, VT 05633-7701

Tel. (802) 828-3700
Fax (802) 828-3710
E-mail: vitals@sec.state.vt.us
www.vermont-archives.org

Vital records are maintained by two state agencies. For certified copies of births, deaths, and other vital events that occurred within the past five years, contact the Vermont Department of Health. Records older than the past five years are transferred to the Vermont State Archives and Records Administration (VSARA), which can provide certified copies of vital records going back to 1909.

Vital records for all years are also available from the town clerk of the town where the vital event took place. Holdings at the town level will date back to 1857, when the registry system for vital records started. Recordings of vital events that occurred prior to 1857 will vary by town. Contact information for all Vermont town clerks can be found online at http://vermont-elections.org/elections1/town_clerks_guide.html.

Cost for a certified Birth Certificate	$10.00
Cost for a certified Marriage Certificate	$10.00
Cost for a certified Divorce Record	$10.00
Cost for a certified Death Certificate	$10.00

You can also order birth, death, marriage, civil union, divorce, or civil union dissolution records more than five years old from VSARA online (https://secure.vermont.gov/VSARA/vitalrecords/) for a fee of $12.00.

For Genealogy Research:

Non-certified informational copies of vital records are available free of charge from VSARA (see above for contact information).

Records that comprise the State's register of vital events were compiled from various sources dating from 1760. Some Vermont birth, marriage, and death records in the state registry from 1760 to 1954 are searchable online at www.familysearch.org.

Ancestry.com, a subscription site, has Vermont birth, marriage, and death records from 1909 to 2008. Vermont residents can research these records for free with an account on MyVermont.gov (https://secure.vermont.gov/myvermont/).

The Vermont Historical Society's Leahy Library (60 Washington Street, Barre, VT 05641-4209; tel. 802-479-8500; e-mail: vhs-info@state.vt.us; http://vermonthistory.org/) has a microfilmed index to Vermont vital records to 1870, as well as a strong collection of family and town histories, published vital records, and transcriptions of Vermont cemeteries. Some transcriptions from published vital records are available online, including Marriages in Montpelier, Burlington and Berlin, Vermont 1789–1876 and Early Marriages 1789–1876.

The Nye Index at the Vermont State Archives is a name and subject index to 18th- and 19th-century (mostly pre-1840) Vermont State records; see http://vermont-archives.org/research/database/nye.asp.

For Adoption Record information, contact:

Vermont Adoption Registry
103 South Main Street
Waterbury, VT 05671-2401

Tel. (802) 241-2122
http://dcf.vermont.gov/fsd/vermont_adoption_registry

VSARA-08
10/2012

Vermont State Archives and Records Administration
Office of the Secretary of State
1078 US RTE 2, Middlesex • Montpelier, VT 05633-7701 • Tel: (802) 828-3700 • Fax: (802) 828-3710 • www.vermont-archives.org

CERTIFIED COPY OF A BIRTH OR DEATH CERTIFICATE

VSARA holds certificates for births and deaths that occurred between 1909 and 2007.

Individual Requesting the Certificate

Name: ______________________________

Address: ______________________________

City: ______________________ **State:** ________ **Zip:** ________

Daytime Phone: ____________ **Email Address:** ______________________

Certificate Information

Event: (check one) ☐ Birth ☐ Death **Sex:** ☐ Male ☐ Female

Name on Certificate: ______________________________

Date of Event: ____________ **Town/City of Event:** ______________________

Maiden Name of Mother: ______________________________

Name of Father: ______________________________

Name of Spouse: ______________________________

Other Useful Information: ______________________________

Copies and Payment

Number of Copies Desired:

Certified Copy with Seal ($10 each).

Amount Enclosed: __________

☐ Cash
☐ Check
☐ Money Order
☐ Agency Invoice
Customer #

$3.00 of the fee is applied to the search and is nonrefundable. Vital records fees are defined in 32 V.S.A. § 1715.

Make checks or money orders (U.S. funds) payable to the Vermont Secretary of State. Mail your payment with this form and a self-addressed stamped envelope to the address shown above.

Department of Health
Agency of Human Services

- **Complete** and **print** the application below.
- **Sign** and **date** the application.
- Make check or money order payable to "**Vermont Department of Health**".
- The fee for certified copies is **$10.00 per copy**.
- **Return** the application with your check or money order to the address below. **Do NOT mail cash**.

VERMONT DEPARTMENT OF HEALTH	**Application for a Certified Copy of a Birth Certificate**	**For office use only** ID# CPA# REC#

Number of Copies:
Amount Enclosed $
Name on Birth Certificate:
Sex
F **M** **Date of Birth:**
Town or City of Birth:
Name of Father:
Maiden Name of Mother:
Your Name:
Address:
Town: **State:**
Zip: **Phone Number:**
Your relationship to the person on birth certificate:

Intended use of certificate

☐ **Social Security** ☐ **School Enrollment** ☐ **Passport** ☐ **Driver's License** ☐ **Family History** ☐ **Other (specify)**

Date: ______________________________

Signature: ____

Vermont Department of Health | 108 Cherry Street | Burlington, VT 05402
Voice: 802-863-7200 | In Vermont 800-464-4343 | Fax: 802-865-7754 | TTY/TDD: Dial 711 first

VSARA-09
10/2012

Vermont State Archives and Records Administration

Office of the Secretary of State

1078 US RTE 2, Middlesex • Montpelier, VT 05633-7701 • Tel: (802) 828-3700 • Fax: (802) 828-3710 • www.vermont-archives.org

CERTIFIED COPY OF A MARRIAGE/CIVIL UNION OR DIVORCE/DISSOLUTION RECORD

VSARA holds certificates for marriages and divorces that occurred between 1909 and 2007. Civil Unions were not authorized prior to July 1, 2000; therefore no civil union records exist prior to this date. Only civil union records from July 1, 2000 to 2007 are available from VSARA. More recent certificates must be requested from the Vermont Department of Health.

Your Name and Contact Information:

Name: ______________________________

Address: ______________________________

City: ______________________ **State:** ______ **Zip:** ________

Daytime Phone: ______________ **Email Address:** ______________________

Certificate Information

Event: (check one) ☐ Marriage/Civil Union ☐ Divorce/Dissolution

Names on Certificate:

PERSON A:	**PERSON B:**
Birthplace:	**Birthplace:**
Father:	**Father:**
Mother's Maiden Name:	**Mother's Maiden Name:**
Date of Marriage / Civil Union:	**Town/City of Marriage / Civil Union:**
Date of Divorce / Dissolution:	**Town/City of Divorce / Dissolution:**

Other Useful Information:

____

Copies and Payment

Number Desired: **Certified Copy w/ Seal - $10.00 ea.** **Amount Enclosed:**

☐ **Marriage / Civil Union**
☐ **Divorce**
☐ **Both**

☐ Cash
☐ Check
☐ Money Order

$3.00 of the fee is applied to the search and is nonrefundable. Vital records fees are defined in 32 V.S.A. § 1715.

Make checks or money orders (U.S. funds) payable to the Vermont Secretary of State. Mail your payment with this form and a self-addressed stamped envelope to the address shown above.

- Contact the Vermont State Archives and Records Administration (VSARA)
- Order the marriage certificate from the Department of Health

Department of Health Vital Records Order

- **Complete** and **print** the application below.
- **Sign** and **date** the application.
- Make check or money order payable to "**Vermont Department of Health**".
- The fee for certified copies is **$10.00 per copy**.
- **Return** the application with your check or money order to the address below. **Do NOT mail cash**.

VERMONT DEPARTMENT OF HEALTH	**Application for a Certified Copy of a Marriage Certificate**	**For office use only** ID# CPA# REC#

Number of Copies:
Amount Enclosed $
Date of Marriage:
Town where license was purchased :

☐ **Bride** ☐ **Groom** ☐ **Spouse** (Please check one)

Name:
Date of Birth:
Name of Father/Parent:
Name of Mother/Parent:

☐ **Bride** ☐ **Groom** ☐ **Spouse** (Please check one)

Name:
Date of Birth:
Name of Father/Parent:
Name of Mother/Parent:

Your Name :
Address:
Town:

State:
Zip:
Phone Number:
Your relationship to couple on marriage certificate

Intended use of certificate

☐ **Proof of Marriage** ☐ **Family History** ☐ **Other: (specify)**

Date: ____________________________

Signature: ____

Send to: Vermont Department of Health, Vital Records, PO Box 70, Burlington, VT 05402-0070 with check or money order payable to Vermont Department of Health.

Vermont Department of Health | 108 Cherry Street | Burlington, VT 05402
Voice: 802-863-7200 | In Vermont 800-464-4343 | Fax: 802-865-7754 | TTY/TDD: Dial 711 first
| | |

Department of Health
Agency of Human Services

- **Complete** and **print** the application below.
- **Sign** and **date** the application.
- Make check or money order payable to "**Vermont Department of Health**"
- The fee for certified copies is **$10.00 per copy**..
- **Return** the application with your check or money order to the address below. **Do NOT mail cash**.

VERMONT
DEPARTMENT OF HEALTH

Application for a Certified Copy of a Certificate of Civil Union

For office use only

ID#
CPA#
REC#

Number of Copies:
Amount Enclosed $
Date of Civil Union:
Town where license was purchased:

PARTY A Name :
Date of Birth:
Name of Father:
Name of Mother:

PARTY B Name:
Date of Birth:
Name of Father:
Name of Mother:

Your Name :
Address:
Town:
State:
Zip:
Phone Number:
Your Relationship to couple on civil union certificate:

Intended use of certificate

☐ Proof of Civil Union ☐ Family History ☐ Other: (specify)

Date: ______________________

Signature: ____

Send to: Vermont Department of Health, Vital Records, PO Box 70, Burlington, VT 05402-0070

- **Complete** and **print** the application below.
- **Sign** and **date** the application.
- Make check or money order payable to "**Vermont Department of Health**".
- The fee for certified copies is **$10.00 per copy**.
- **Return** the application with your check or money order to the address below. **Do NOT mail cash**.

VERMONT DEPARTMENT OF HEALTH	**Application for a Certified Copy of a Divorce Certificate**	For office use only ID# CPA# REC#

Number of Copies:
Amount Enclosed $
☐ **Husband** ☐ **Wife** ☐ **Spouse** (Please check one)
Name:
☐ **Husband** ☐ **Wife** ☐ **Spouse (Please check one)**
Name:

Date Divorce Became Final:
County of Divorce:
Date of Marriage:

Your Name:
Address:
Town:
State:
Zip:
Phone Number:
Your Relationship to people named on certificate

Intended use of certificate

☐ Proof of Divorce ☐ Personal Use ☐ Other: (specify)

Date: ______________________________

Signature: ____

Send to: Vermont Department of Health, Vital Records, PO Box 70, Burlington, VT 05402-0070

Application for a Certified Copy of a Death Certificate

For office use only

ID#
CPA#
REC#

Number of Copies:
Amount Enclosed $
Name on Death Certificate:
Sex: M F

Date of Death:
Town or City of Death:
Date of Birth:
State of Birth:
Age at Death:
Name of Spouse:

Your Name:
Address:
Town:
State:
Zip:
Phone Number:
Your Relationship to person on death certificate

Intended use of certificate

- Benefits
- Settlement of Estate
- Family History
- Other: (specify)

Date: ______________________________

Signature: ____

Send to: Vermont Department of Health, Vital Records, PO Box 70, Burlington, VT 05402-0070

Death certificates are available from the Department of Health only for deaths which occurred within the past five years. After five years, the records are transferred to the Vermont State Archives and Records Administration (VSARA).

- **Complete** and **print** the application below.
- **Sign** and **date** the application.
- Make check or money order payable to "**Vermont Department of Health**".
- The fee for certified copies is **$10.00 per copy**.
- **Return** the application with your check or money order to the address below. **Do NOT mail cash**.

VSARA-13
Revised: 10/2012

Vermont State Archives and Records Administration
Office of the Secretary of State
1078 US RTE 2, Middlesex • Montpelier, VT 05633-7701 • Tel: (802) 828-3700 • Fax: (802) 828-3710 • www.vermont-archives.org

VITAL RECORDS REQUEST FORM

INFORMATIONAL COPIES ONLY! DO NOT USE FOR REQUESTING CERTIFIED COPIES!

The Vermont State Archives and Records Administration welcomes your records requests. ***We will search up to two requests submitted at a time.*** Due to the volume of requests received and limited resources, please wait to hear back from us before submitting another request. Your cooperation will allow us to continue waiving the $3.00 statutory fee for informational copies.

Did you know? Most vital records in the Vermont State Archives can now be researched online. Please visit us at http://vermont-archives.org/research/genealogy/vitals/ to find out more information.

YOUR NAME AND CONTACT INFORMATION

Name: ______________________

Address: ______________________

City: ______________________ State: __________ Zip: __________

Daytime Phone: __________ Email Address: ______________________

Please note that we will e-mail copies of any records that we find provided that an e-mail address is listed above.

YOUR RECORD REQUEST:

Event: (check all that apply) ☐ Birth ☐ Death ☐ Marriage/Civil Union ☐ Divorce/Dissolution

Name at time of Birth: ______________________

Gender: ☐ Male ☐ Female

Name at time of Marriage or Civil Union: ______________________

Name at time of Divorce or Dissolution: ______________________

Name at time of Death: ______________________

Date of Birth: __________ **Town/City:** __________

Date of Marriage: __________ **Town/City:** __________

Date of Divorce or Dissolution: __________ **Town/City:** __________

Date of Death: __________ **Town/City:** __________

Name of Mother: ______________________

Name of Father: ______________________

Name of Spouse/Partner: ______________________

Other Useful Information:

VSARA USE ONLY: ☐ **Found /** ☐ **Not Found /** ☐ **Second Check /**

Please mail this completed form to the address above or e-mail to vitals@sec.state.vt.us

VIRGINIA

Send your requests to:

Virginia Department of Health
Division of Vital Records
(Location: 2001 Maywill Street)
P.O. Box 1000
Richmond, VA 23218-1000

Tel. (804) 662-6200
www.vdh.virginia.gov/vital_records/

The Division of Vital Records has birth and death records from 1853 to 1896 and from June 1912 to present (there was no law for the registration of births and deaths between 1896 and June 14, 1912); marriage records from 1853; and divorce records from 1918. Birth records are restricted for 100 years; death, marriage, and divorce records are restricted for 50 years.

Only immediate family members are entitled to full certified copies of death certificates; however, non-immediate family members can receive a verification of death, which will show the name of the decedent, date of death, place of death, date of birth, and the last four digits of the Social Security Number.

Cost for a certified Birth Certificate	$12.00
Cost for a certified Marriage Certificate	$12.00
Cost for a certified Divorce Record	$12.00
Cost for a certified Death Certificate	$12.00

Vital records are also kept by:

County Clerk
County Court House
(County Seat), VA

For Genealogy Research:

The Library of Virginia (800 East Broad Street, Richmond, VA 23219-1905; tel. 804-692-3888; www.lva.virginia.gov/) has copies of surviving Virginia birth and death records for the period 1853–1896 and marriage records 1853–1935, with some extant marriage bonds prior to 1853. These records are public information and are available on microfilm. A list of the Library's microfilm holdings is available at www.lva.virginia.gov/public/guides/BMDregisters/index.htm.

A fully searchable index to Virginia city and county death registers compiled 1853–1896 is available online; it's an on-going project sponsored by the Virginia Genealogical Society. Visit www.lva.virginia.gov/public/guides/opac/dripabout.htm#project for more information. Also online is a searchable database of marriage information from a variety of sources, primarily covering the 1700s and 1800s (www.lva.virginia.gov/public/guides/marriage-records/search.asp).

For Adoption Record information, contact:

Adoption Program
Virginia Department of Social Services
7 North Eighth Street
Richmond, VA 23219-3301

Tel. (800) 362-3678
www.dss.virginia.gov/family/ap/index.cgi

The Virginia Department of Social Services keeps a permanent record of all adoptions finalized in Virginia since July 1, 1942.

VS6-2/06

COMMONWEALTH OF VIRGINIA
Application for Certification of a Vital Record

Virginia statutes require a fee of $12.00 be charged for each certification of a vital record or for a search of the files when no certification is made. Please make check or money order payable to **State Health Department**. There is a $50.00 service charge for returned checks.

Name of Requester: ______________________________ Daytime Phone Number (______) ______-______________
(person requesting the certificate)

Address: ______________________ City: ______________ State: __________ Zip: __________

What is your relationship to the person named on the certificate? (Check one)

◯ Self ◯ Mother ◯ Father ◯ Child ◯ Current Spouse ◯ Sister ◯ Brother ◯ Maternal Grandparent
◯ Paternal Grandparent ◯ Legal Guardian (submit custody order) ◯ Other (Specify) ______________________

What is your reason for requesting this certificate? ______________________________

I understand that making a **FALSE** application for a vital record is a **FELONY** under state and federal law.

Signature of Requester: ______________________________

IMPORTANT: The person requesting the vital record must submit an enlarged, legible (readable) clear photo copy of their identification. See list below.

BIRTH CARDS ARE NO LONGER AVAILABLE.

BIRTH
Number
of Copies
Paper: __________

Name at Birth: ______________________________
If name has changed since birth due to adoption, court order, or any reason other than marriage, please list changed name here:

____

Date of Birth: ______________ Race: __________ Sex: __________

Place of Birth: ______________ Hospital of Birth: ______________
(City/County in Virginia)

Full Maiden Name of Mother: ______________________________

Full Name of Father: ______________________________

◯ DEATH ◯ STILLBIRTH

Number
of Copies: __________

Name of Deceased: ______________________________

Date of Death: __________ Age at Death: __________ Race: ______ Sex: ______

Place of Death: ______________ Hospital Name: ______________
(City/County in Virginia)

Full Maiden name of Mother: ______________________________

Full Name of Father: ______________________________

MARRIAGE
Number
of Copies: __________

DIVORCE
Number
of Copies: __________

Full Name of Husband: ______________________________

Full Name of Wife: ______________________________

Marriage - Date: ______________ Place: ______________

Divorce - Date: ______________ Place: ______________
(City/County in Virginia)

If Marriage, place where license was issued: ______________________________

Please indicate the address you wish the certificate(s) mailed to in the box below. -- Please type or print clearly.

Name
Address
City/State/Zip

Send Completed Application To:

Division of Vital Records
P. O. Box 1000
Richmond, VA 23218-1000
(804) 662-6200
www.vdh.virginia.gov

GUIDELINES REGARDING THE ADOPTEE APPLICATION FOR DISCLOSURE

Attached is an Adoptee Application for Disclosure, which is used to initiate a search for your birth family member(s). Please complete the Application, have it notarized, and return it to the Permanency Unit, 801 East Main Street, Richmond, Virginia 23219-2901

Identifying information from closed adoption records cannot be released to you without good cause. Agreement from the birth family member(s) to the sharing of identifying information is considered good cause. Therefore, the purpose of the search is to determine whether the birth family member(s) on whom you wish to have information are willing to give consent to have information that would identify them released to you.

Once your Adoptee Application for Disclosure has been completed and submitted to the Permanency Unit, the agency that was initially involved in your adoption will be designated to conduct the search. The name and telephone number of that agency is listed below. The searching agency may charge a fee for attempting to locate the birth member(s) on whom you desire information. If the agency charges a fee, the fee must be paid to that agency before your application for disclosure is granted or denied. If you have questions about the fee, please contact the agency listed below before submitting your application to this office, as submission of the application authorizes the search.

The searching agency has ninety (90) days to conduct the search. Additional time can be granted to complete the search when there is good cause. Once the search is complete, the searching agency will send a report to the Permanency Unit with a recommendation about whether to grant or deny the Adoptee Application for Disclosure. Applications are usually denied when birth family members are not located, do not give consent, or are deceased.

If your application is denied, or if the Permanency Unit fails to designate an agency to conduct the search within thirty days of receipt of the Adoptee Application for Disclosure, you have the right to petition the court for disclosure. If you are a Virginia resident, you may petition the Circuit Court in the county or city where you reside. If you live out of state, you must petition the Richmond City Circuit Court.

Searching Agency: ____

Telephone Number: (Area Code) ______________ (Number)________________________

Adoptee Application for Disclosure

The applicant hereby applies to the Commissioner, Virginia Department of Social Services for Disclosure of Information PURSUANT TO THE VIRGINIA CODE SECTIONS 63.2-1246 AND 63.2-1247. ***Provide additional pertinent information on a separate page, if necessary.***

You may access additional information on your rights as an adoptee at:
http://www.dss.virginia.gov/files/division/dfs/ap/intro_page/guidance_procedures/records.pdf

(Type or Print Clearly)

Virginia Adoption Case Number ________________________

Applicant's Current Name ____________________

Applicant's Adoptive Name _____

---

1. I am over the age of eighteen having been born on _____ (complete date of birth)
2. My adoptive mother's name is _____
3. My adoptive father's name is _____
4. I wish to obtain non-identifying information [indicate by "X"]
   _____ Placement _____ Adoptive/Birth Family
5. I wish to obtain [indicate by "X's"] the identity of:

_____ Birth Mother _____ Birth Father _____ Adult Birth Sibling(s)

Residence Full Address	**Mailing Address (if different from residence address)**
Telephone Number:	Cell Number:
E-mail:	E-mail:

Signature of Applicant: ____
(Must be signed in front of a Notary Public)

STATE OF _______________ **County or City of** ______________________________ **Subscribed this date and sworn to before me on the** _____ **day of** _______________ **20**_____.

Notary Public: ____

My Commission Expires:__________________

032-02-0018-03-eng (08/13)

WASHINGTON

Send your requests to:

Washington State Department of Health
Center for Health Statistics
(Location: 101 Israel Road S.E., Turnwater, WA 98501)
P.O. Box 9709
Olympia, WA 98507-9709

Tel. (360) 236-4300
E-mail: ContactCHS@doh.wa.gov
www.doh.wa.gov/EHSPHL/CHS/cert.htm

The Center for Health Statistics has birth and death certificates from July 1, 1907, and marriage and divorce certificates from January 1, 1968.

Cost for a certified Birth Certificate	$20.00
Cost for an Heirloom Birth Certificate	$40.00
Cost for a certified Marriage Certificate	$20.00
Cost for a certified Divorce Record	$20.00
Cost for a certified Death Certificate	$20.00

For birth records before July 1, 1907, in King, Pierce, Snohomish, and Spokane counties, contact the Washington State local health departments and districts (www.doh.wa.gov/AboutUs/PublicHealthSystem/LocalHealthJurisdictions.aspx).

For birth records before July 1, 1907, for all other counties and for marriage certificates for the last two months and those before January 1, 1968, contact the county auditor in the county where the event took place.

For death records before July 1, 1907, contact the Research Office of the Washington State Archives (1120 Washington Street, P.O. Box 40238, Olympia, WA 98504; tel. 360-586-1492; www.sos.wa.gov/archives/).

For divorce certificates from the last two months and certificates before January 1, 1968, contact the county clerk in the county where the event was filed (see www.courts.wa.gov/court_dir/?fa=court_dir.countycityref for contact information).

For Genealogy Research:

The Washington State Archives (1129 Washington Street S.E., P.O. Box 40238, Olympia, WA 98504; tel. 360-586-1492; www.sos.wa.gov/archives/) has early birth and death registers on microfilm. A number of state and county vital records are searchable online at the Digital Archives (www.digitalarchives.wa.gov/).

The State Archives Regional Branches have multiple types of marriage records (marriage returns, marriage registers, applications, licenses, affidavits, and certificates) that were filed with county auditors and date from a county's formation to 1968. Additionally, the Regional Archives can provide assistance in locating divorce records from this period. Contact the State Archives local branch (www.sos.wa.gov/archives/archives.aspx) representing the county of interest.

For Adoption Record information, contact:

Washington State Department of Social & Health Services
Adoption Archives
P.O. Box 45713
Olympia, WA 98504

www1.dshs.wa.gov/ca/adopt/res_Records.asp

Washington State Department of Health
Birth / Death Certificate Mail Order Form

Instructions

- **Print clearly.**
- We issue certificates for births and deaths that occurred in **Washington State** only.
- For a birth or death before July 1, 1907, contact the local health department where the event occurred.
- We only accept checks or money orders for mail orders. **Do not send cash or credit card information.**
- **$20.00 per certificate.**
- If adopted, provide your adoptive name and adoptive parents' information.
- Visit www.doh.wa.gov for more information and ordering options or call 360-236-4300, Monday through Friday between 8:00 a.m. and 5:00 p.m. Pacific Time.

Contact Information

Name of person ordering certificate(s):

Company name (if applicable):

Address sending certificate(s) to:
(Street address required for FedEx orders)

City:	State:	ZIP Code:

Daytime Phone: (______) ____________________	Email Address:

Complete ALL fields below with exact and complete information.

☐ **Paternity Verification Letter** (Copy of Parent ID required). Court activities such as custody, parenting plan or child support may require a paternity verification letter AND a birth certificate.

Birth Certificate Request

Number of Certificates Ordering_____

Full Name on Certificate: (First) (Full Middle Name) (Last)

Date of Birth (Month/Day/Year): (7/1/1907 – present)	City or County of Birth:

Father/Parent Birth Name: (First) (Full Middle Name) (Birth Last Name) ☐ Not Listed

Mother/Parent Birth Name: (First) (Full Middle Name) (Birth Last Name)

Death Certificate Request

Number of Certificates Ordering______

Name on Certificate: (First) (Middle) (Last)

Approximate Date of Death or 10 year search range (7/1/1907 – present):	Date of Birth, if known:
City or County of Death:	Spouse, if known:

Complete payment and mailing information below:

Total number of certified certificates:	______	x $20.00 =	$
Total number of Heirloom+ birth certificates:	______	x $40.00 =	$
Fee for filing a Paternity Acknowledgment OR an Adoption	☐	$15.00 =	$
Paternity Verification Letter (copy of parent ID required)	☐	$15.00 =	$
Paternity Verification Letter ($15) + certified birth certificate ($20)	☐	$35.00 =	$
First Class Mail (allow 2-3 weeks for delivery)	☐	No additional charge	
*USPS Express Mail Delivery (street address or PO Box)	☐	$18.30 =	$
*Fed Ex to continental US (no PO Box)	☐	$15.00 =	$
*Fed Ex to AK/HI/Canada/Mexico (no PO Box)	☐	$25.00 =	$
TOTAL AMOUNT DUE			$

Make checks or money orders payable to DOH.

MAIL ORDERS TO:
Department of Health
PO Box 9709
Olympia WA
98507-9709

*Additional charges for express delivery are per order, not per certificate.
*Signature is required at time of delivery for USPS Express Mail and Federal Express orders.
+Go to our website at www.doh.wa.gov for information on Heirloom Birth Certificates.

DOH 422-044 May 2013

Washington State Department of Health
Marriage / Divorce Certificate Mail Order Form

Instructions

- **Print clearly.**
- We issue certificates for marriages and divorces that took place in **Washington State** only.
- For marriages and divorces before 1968, contact the local County Auditor for marriage or County Clerk for divorce.
- We only accept checks or money orders for mail orders. **Do not send cash or credit card information.**
- **$20.00 per certificate.**
- Visit www.doh.wa.gov for more information and ordering options, or call 360-236-4300, Monday through Friday, between 8:00 a.m. and 5:00 p.m. Pacific Time.

Contact Information

Name of person ordering certificate(s):		
Company Name (if applicable):		
Address sending certificate(s) to: (Street address required for FedEx Orders)		
City:	State:	ZIP Code:
Daytime Phone: (______) ____________________	Email Address:	

Complete Person A and Person B information below, to the best of your knowledge. Exact date or county information not required.

Marriage Certificate Request	**Number of Certificates Ordering________**	
Person A	Legal Name *Before* Marriage: (First) (Middle) (Last)	
	Birth Last Name (if different):	Circle one: Bride, Groom, Spouse
Person B	Legal Name *Before* Marriage: (First) (Middle) (Last)	
	Birth Last Name (if different):	Circle one: Bride, Groom, Spouse
Approximate Date of Marriage or 10-year Search Range (after January 1, 1968):		Licensing County, if known:

Divorce Certificate Request	**Number of Certificates Ordering________**	
Spouse A	Name Listed on Divorce Decree: (First) (Middle) (Last)	
	Birth Last Name (if different):	Circle one: Wife, Husband, Spouse
Spouse B	Name Listed on Divorce Decree: (First) (Middle) (Last)	
	Birth Last Name (if different):	Circle one: Wife, Husband, Spouse
Approximate Date of Divorce or 10-year Search Range (after January 1, 1968):		Filing County, if known:

Make checks or money orders payable to DOH.

MAIL ORDERS TO:
Department of Health
PO Box 9709
Olympia WA
98507-9709

Complete payment and mailing information below:

Total number of certified certificates: ______ x $20.00 = $ ________

First Class Mail (allow 2-3 weeks for delivery)	☐	no additional charge
*USPS Express Mail Delivery (street address or PO Box)	☐	$18.30 = $ ________
*Fed Ex to continental US (no PO Box)	☐	$15.00 = $ ________
*Fed Ex to AK/HI/Canada/Mexico (no PO Box)	☐	$25.00 = $ ________

TOTAL AMOUNT DUE $ ________

*Signature is required at time of delivery for USPS Express Mail and Federal Express Orders.
*Additional charges for express delivery are per order mailed, not per certificate.

DOH 422-104 May 2013

WEST VIRGINIA

Send your requests to:

Vital Registration
350 Capitol Street, Room 165
Charleston, WV 25301-3701

Tel. (304) 558-2931
Fax (304) 558-1051
www.wvdhhr.org/bph/hsc/vital/

The Vital Registration Office has birth and death records from January 1, 1917, with some delayed birth records starting around 1850; marriage records 1964–present and marriage indexes 1924–present; and divorce indexes 1967–present. Access to certified copies of birth certificates is restricted for 100 years and to death and marriage records for 50 years.

Cost for a certified Birth Certificate	$12.00
Cost for a certified Marriage Certificate	$12.00
Cost for a certified Death Certificate	$12.00

For Marriage Certificates prior to 1963 and earlier Birth and Death Records, contact:

County Clerk
County Court House
(County Seat), WV

For Divorce Records, contact:

Clerk of Circuit Court (in county where divorce was granted)
Chancery Side
(County Seat), WV

For Genealogy Research:

A good source of genealogy information is the West Virginia Division of Archives and History (The Cultural Center, 1900 Kanawha Boulevard East, Building 9, Charleston, WV 25305-0300; tel. 304-558-0230; www.wvculture.org/history/archivesindex.aspx). Archives and History has microfilm of birth, death, and marriage records kept at the county level, as well as microfilm of statewide birth records 1917–1930, statewide deaths 1917–1973, and indexes to some more recent delayed births, deaths, and marriages. Some of these records can be searched online at www.wvculture.org/vrr/va_select.aspx.

For Adoption Record information, contact:

West Virginia Department of Health and Human Services
Office of Social Services
Mutual Consent Voluntary Adoption Registry
350 Capitol Street, Room 691
Charleston, WV 25301

Tel. (304) 558-2891
E-mail: adoptwvchild@wvdhhr.org

There is no cost for registration with the Voluntary Adoption Registry.

Application for Certified Copy of West Virginia Birth Certificate

Please complete on-line, print, sign, and mail as instructed below or print except where signature is required.

The following pertains to information that would be found on the certificate being requested.

Name of person on the certificate

First Middle Last

Date of Birth

Month/Day/Year

Mother's Maiden Name

First Middle Last

Sex:

☐ Male ☐ Female

Father's Name

First Middle Last

Place of Birth

City ______ County ______ State ______

Hospital ______

Requestor's Relationship:

Parent/Grandparent ☐ Guardian or agent ☐ Child/Grandchild ☐

Certificate of my own birth ☐ Spouse ☐ Brother/Sister ☐

Making false statements and misuse of vital records will result in criminal and civil penalties pursuant to WV Code §16-5-38.

Signature (Required)

Printed Name (Required)

Requesting _____ copies at $12.00 per copy and enclosing $______________.

Please send check or money order. Please do not send cash.
Make checks payable to: Vital Registration

Send copies to: Print your address below.

City State Zip

( )
Area Code Your daytime telephone number:

E-Mail address

Submit form with check or money order to:

Vital Registration
Room 165
350 Capitol Street
Charleston, WV 25301-3701

Telephone: (304) 558-2931

Last Revised 1/9/09

Application for Certified Marriage Certificate

For Office Use Only	
WHEN STAMPED PAID THIS IS YOUR RECEIPT	
CASH	
CHECK	
MONEY ORDER	
NO. COPIES	
AMOUNT	

Note: A $12.00 nonrefundable search fee must accompany this application. This fee includes one copy, if found. Each additional copy is $12 . Cashis sent at sender's risk. Make check or money order payable to "VITAL REGISTRATION"

Vital Registration Office
Room 165
350 Capitol Street
Charleston WV, 25301-3701
(304) 558-2931
www.wvdhhr.org

GROOM'S NAME
(FIRST-MIDDLE-LAST)

DATE OF MARRIAGE

BRIDE'S MAIDEN NAME
(FIRST-MIDDLE-LAST)

MONTH/DAY/YEAR

PLACE OF APPLICATION

CITY **COUNTY** **STATE** WV

Mail Certificate to

Mailing Address

Suite or Apartment Number

City, State, Zip

What is Your Relationship to the Bride or the Groom ?

____

I understand that intentionally making a false statement on this application or obtaining, possessing, or using a vital record other than is allowed by law or using the vital record of another with an intent to deceive is a *FELONY* under the law of the State of West Virginia (WV Code §16-5-38).

____

Signature Required

Application for Copy of West Virginia Death Certificate

Please print except where signature is required.

The following pertains to information that would be found on the certificate being requested.

Name of person on the certificate **Date of Death**

First Middle Last Month/Day/Year

City County State **Sex:** ☐ Male ☐ Female

The information below pertains to the person requesting the certificate.

Requestor's Relationship: Parent ☐ Guardian or agent ☐ Grandparent ☐

Child of decedent ☐ Spouse ☐

Other ☐ (Describe)

Making false statements and misuse of vital records will result in criminal and civil penalties pursuant to WV Code §16-5-38.

Signature (Required) Printed Name (Required)

Reason for request:

Enclosed is $__________ for ______ copies at $12.00 per copy.

Please send check or money order. Please do not send cash.
Make checks payable to: Vital Registration

Send copies to: **Print** **your address below.**

( ) Area Code Your daytime telephone number:

City State Zip E-Mail address

Submit form with check or money order to:

Vital Registration
Room 165
350 Capitol Street
Charleston, WV 25301-3701

Telephone: (304) 558-2931

Last Revised 01/06/09

WISCONSIN

Send your requests to:

Wisconsin Department of Health and Family Services
Vital Records Office
(Location: 1 West Wilson Street)
P.O. Box 309
Madison, WI 53701-0309

Tel. (608) 266-1373;
recording (608) 266-1371
Fax (608) 255-2035
E-mail: DHSVitalRecords@wisconsin.gov
www.dhs.wisconsin.gov/vitalrecords/

Birth, marriage, and death records are incomplete prior to October 1907; you can check the table of earliest registered events at www.dhs.wisconsin.gov/vitalrecords/genereq.htm#G4 to see what earlier records may be available. There are no divorce records before October 1907. For mail orders, include a self-addressed, stamped, business-size envelope. Fax applications are charged an expedited service fee.

Certified and uncertified copies of birth, death, and marriage certificates are also available at the Register of Deeds office in the county in which the event occurred; see www.wisconsinhistory.org/genealogy/vitalrecords/courthouse_address.asp for addresses.

Cost for a certified Birth Certificate	$20.00
Cost for a certified Marriage Certificate	$20.00
Cost for a certified Declaration of Domestic Partnership Record	$20.00
Cost for a certified Divorce or Termination of Domestic Partnership Record	$20.00
Cost for a certified Death Certificate	$20.00
Cost for a duplicate copy, when ordered at the same time	$3.00

For Genealogy Research:

The Vital Records Office will provide an uncertified copy of a birth, death, or marriage certificate to anyone who applies; this copy will contain the same information as a certified copy but will not be acceptable for legal purposes. With an advance appointment, in-person searchers at the Vital Records Office can get supervised access to most Wisconsin birth, death, marriage, and divorce records; see the Vital Records website for more information.

The Wisconsin Historical Society (816 State Street, Madison, WI 53706-1417; tel. 608-264-6535; www.wisconsinhistory.org/) holds microfilm copies of the births, marriages, and deaths recorded in Wisconsin at the state level before October 1, 1907. The Society's website features the Wisconsin Genealogy Index (http://www.wisconsinhistory.org/vitalrecords/), where you can search more than 150,000 Wisconsin obituaries and biographical sketches published before 1999, as well as 1,000,000 births, 400,000 deaths, and 1,000,000 marriages registered before September 1907.

For Adoption Record information, contact:

Adoption Records Search Program
Wisconsin Department of Children and Families
P.O. Box 8916
Madison, WI 53708-8916

Tel. (608) 266-7163
E-mail: dcfadoptionsearch@wisconsin.gov
http://dcf.wisconsin.gov/children/adoption/adoption_search/default.htm

WISCONSIN BIRTH CERTIFICATE APPLICATION

(for Mail or In-Person Requests)

TYPE or PRINT.

PENALTIES: Any person who wilfully and knowingly makes a false application for a birth certificate is guilty of a Class I felony [a fine of not more than $10,000 or imprisonment of not more than 3 years and 6 months, or both, per s. 69.24(1)]. Any person who wilfully and knowingly obtains a birth certificate for fraudulent purposes is guilty of a Class I felony [a fine of not more than $10,000 or imprisonment of not more than 3 years and 6 months, or both, per s. 69.24(1), Wis. Stats.].

I. APPLICANT INFORMATION

The information in Section I is about the person completing this application.

YOUR **CURRENT** NAME - First	Middle	Last	YOUR DAYTIME TELEPHONE NUMBER ( )

YOUR **STREET** ADDRESS *(**CANNOT** be a P.O. Box address)*	Apt. No	**MAIL TO** ADDRESS *(if different)*	Apt. No

City, Village, or Township	State	ZIP Code	City	State	ZIP Code

TYPE OF CURRENT VALID PHOTO ID *(See item 4 on page 2.)*	**PHOTO** ID NUMBER	STATE OF ISSUANCE	EXPIRATION DATE

II. APPLICANT'S RELATIONSHIP TO PERSON NAMED ON THE CERTIFICATE

According to Wisconsin Statute, a CERTIFIED copy of a birth certificate is only available to those with a "direct and tangible interest" ***(categories A – E below.)*** **You may select to receive an uncertified copy if you just need a copy for informational purposes OR if you do not meet the criteria for categories A – E. In that case, you may check category F below.** *(See item 1 on page 2 for more details.)*

Check one box which indicates YOUR RELATIONSHIP to the PERSON NAMED on the birth certificate.

☐ A. I **am** the PERSON NAMED on the birth certificate.

☐ B. I am a **member of the immediate family** of the PERSON NAMED on the birth certificate. *(Only those listed below qualify as immediate family.)*
NOTE: Grandchildren, step-parents, step-children and step-brothers/step-sisters may only obtain certified copies as section II, categories C – E.)

CHECK ONE. ☐ Parent (whose name is on the birth certificate and whose parental rights have not been terminated)
☐ Current Spouse ☐ Brother / Sister ☐ Grandparent ☐ Child ☐ Current Domestic Partner (registered in the WIs. Vital Records System)

☐ C. I am the **legal custodian or guardian** of the PERSON NAMED on the birth certificate. *(Legal proof is required. See item 1 on page 2.)*

☐ D. I am a **representative authorized**, in writing, by any of the aforementioned (categories A - C). *(The written and **notarized** authorization must accompany this application. See item 1 on page 2.)*
Specify whom you represent. ______

☐ E. I can demonstrate that the information from the birth certificate is necessary for the **determination or protection of a personal or property right** for myself/my client/my agency. *(Proof is required.)*
Specify your interest. ______

☐ F. Uncertified copy (information purposes only; not valid for legal purposes) – Persons not in categories A – E above OR who do not need a copy for legal purposes. *(See item 1 on page 2.)*

PURPOSE FOR WHICH CERTIFICATE IS REQUESTED *(Specify. This information will assist us in processing your request.)*

III. FEES

FEE IS NOT REFUNDABLE IF NO RECORD IS FOUND. CANCELLATION REQUESTS ARE NOT ACCEPTED.

☒ Search Fee **(includes one copy, if found)** .... $ 20.00 20.00

☐ Each additional copy of the same record, issued at the same time as the first copy ______ (Number of additional copies) X $ 3.00 ______

Note: If you cannot provide a specific year of birth (at least within a 5-year period), additional search fees will be charged for locating the record

TOTAL ______

Make check or money order payable to:
STATE OF WIS. VITAL RECORDS

Be sure to include (1) completed form, (2) acceptable identification, (3) any additional proof or authorization required, (4) self-addressed, stamped, business-size envelope, and (5) check or money order.
Mail your application materials and fee to: STATE VITAL RECORDS OFFICE / PO BOX 309 / MADISON, WI 53701-0309

IV. BIRTH RECORD INFORMATION

BIRTH NAME - First	**Middle**	**Last Name** ***as it appears on the birth certificate***

SEX ☐**Male** ☐**Female**	**BIRTHDATE (Month / Day / Year)**	**PLACE OF BIRTH - County**	**PLACE OF BIRTH – City, Village, or Township**

Mother's First Name	Mother's Middle Name	Mother's Last Name ("Maiden Name") *as it appears on the birth certificate*
Father's First Name	Father's Middle Name	Father's Last Name *as it appears on the birth certificate*

I hereby attest that the information provided on this application is correct to the best of my knowledge and belief and that I am entitled to copies of the requested birth certificate in accordance to the categories listed above.

SIGNATURE - Applicant (person named in section I who is completing this application) ➢	Date Signed (Month / Day / Year)

Important: If you do not sign and date this form above ↑, your request cannot be processed.

Vital Records Staff Use: File Date ______ **Mother's County of Residence** ______ **Certificate Number** ______

1. What is the difference between a "certified" and an "uncertified" copy of a birth certificate?

A **certified** copy of a birth certificate issued by the State Vital Records Office will have a raised seal, will show the signature of the State Registrar, and will be printed on security paper. A certified copy may be required to obtain a state-issued driver's license or identification, for travel to foreign countries, to obtain a passport, or for benefit purposes.

State law restricts who may obtain a **certified** copy of a birth certificate. A **certified** copy can only be issued to those people with a "direct and tangible interest" (section II, categories A – E) which means the following people:

- The person named on the birth certificate (section II, category A).
- An immediate family member, defined as current spouse, current domestic partner (Declaration of Domestic Partnership registered in the Wis. Vital Records System under Chapter 770, Wis. Stats.), child, or parent (whose name is on the birth certificate and whose parental rights have not been terminated), brother/sister, or grandparent of the subject of the record (section II, category B).
- NOTE: Grandchildren, step-parents, and step-children can only obtain certified copies as in section II, categories C – E.
- The legal custodian or guardian of the person named on the birth certificate. Legal proof, *e.g.*, a court order of custody or guardianship, is required (section II, category C).
- A person authorized in writing by one of the above. A written and notarized authorization must accompany the application and the authorization must clearly state the relationship of the authorizing party to the subject of the record (section II, category D).
- A person who can demonstrate that the birth certificate is required to determine or to protect a personal or property right (section II, category E). Proof is required.

If you do not meet one of the above criteria, you cannot receive a **certified** copy of a birth certificate.
An **uncertified** copy will contain the same information as a certified copy but it is **not** acceptable for legal purposes, such as proof of identity (section II, category F).

2. Limitations on access to certain birth certificates

An **uncertified copy** will contain the same information as a certified copy but it is **not** acceptable for legal purposes, such as proof of identity.

According to Chapter 69, Wis. Stats., **uncertified copies** of the following types of birth certificates may not be obtained by anyone:

- A child born to unmarried parents and paternity has not been established.
- A child born to unmarried parents and paternity was established by court order.

Only persons with a "direct and tangible interest" (categories A – E) may obtain **certified copies** of those types of birth certificates listed directly above.

3. How long will it take to process my request?

Copies of birth certificates are available from the State Vital Records Office no less than 3 weeks from the date of the birth.

- Applying in Person
  - In-person requests for **certified** copies of birth certificates are usually completed within 2 business hours of application, if the birth certificate is on file.
  - In-person requests for **uncertified** copies of birth certificates are not completed on the same schedule as requests for certified copies. In-person requests for uncertified copies may take up to 1 month to complete.
- Applying by Mail
  - Requests for **certified** copies of birth certificates may take up to 2 weeks plus mail time to complete.
  - Requests for **uncertified** copies of birth certificates are not completed on the same schedule as certified copies. Mail requests for uncertified copies may take up to 1 month plus mail time.

4. What identification is required when applying for a certified or uncertified copy of a birth certificate?

A photocopy of the applicant's current ID as listed below must be submitted with **all** mail applications. A current ID as listed below is required when applying in-person.

At least one form of ID must show your current name and current address. Expired cards or documents will not be accepted.

The acceptable forms of identification are:

One of these:

- Wisconsin driver's license
- Wisconsin photo ID
- Out-of-state driver's license or photo ID card

OR

Two of these:

- Government-issued employee ID card or badge with photo
- US Passport
- Check or bank book
- Major Credit Card
- Health Insurance Card
- Recent dated, signed lease
- Recent utility bill or traffic ticket

If you have questions regarding this form, please call 608-266-1373
or visit our website at http://www.dhs.wisconsin.gov/vitalrecords

DEPARTMENT OF HEALTH SERVICES
Division of Public. Health
F-05292 (Rev. 06/13)

STATE OF WISCONSIN
Chapter 69.21(1a), (2b), Wis. Stats

FAX APPLICATION FOR A WISCONSIN BIRTH CERTIFICATE

Personally identifying information requested on this form, including credit card information and your signature, will be used to process your application and payment for the requested copies. Failure to supply this information may result in denial of your request for copies of any Wisconsin Birth Certificate.

Your credit card number and expiration date are required. The credit card number and expiration date will only be used to process payment for the fees specified in SECTION III – FEES below on this FAX Application for a Wisconsin Birth Certificate.

PENALTIES: Any person who willfully and knowingly makes a false application for a birth certificate is guilty of a Class I felony [a fine of not more than $10,000 or imprisonment of not more than 3 years and 6 months, or both, per s. 69.24(1)]. Any person who willfully and knowingly obtains a birth certificate for fraudulent purposes is guilty of a Class I felony [a fine of not more than $10,000 or imprisonment of not more than 3 years and 6 months, or both, per s. 69.24(1), Wis. Stats.].

INSTRUCTIONS: Please complete this form and **FAX to 608-255-2035**. ***All FAX applications are charged an expedited service fee.***
See Page 2 of this form for valid photo ID requirements for processing this application.

SECTION I - SHIP TO INFORMATION (Print or type.) (You must complete this section for application to be processed.)

1. FULL NAME (First, Middle, Last)	2. DAYTIME TELEPHONE NUMBER ( )

3. STREET ADDRESS or P.O. BOX **(You must provide a street address if you are requesting shipping by UPS.)**	APT. NUMBER

4. CITY	5. STATE	6. ZIP CODE

SECTION II - APPLICANT'S RELATIONSHIP TO THE PERSON NAMED ON THE BIRTH CERTIFICATE (CHECK ONE)

☐ A. This is **my** birth certificate.

☐ B. I am a **member of the immediate family** of the person named on the birth certificate. *(Only those listed below qualify as immediate family.)*
NOTE: Grandchildren, step-parents, step-children and step-brothers/step-sisters may only obtain certified copies as section II. categories C – E.

CHECK ONE. ☐ Parent (whose name is on the birth certificate and whose parental rights have not been terminated)
☐ Current Spouse ☐ Brother / Sister ☐ Grandparent ☐ Child ☐ Current Domestic Partner (registered in the Wis. Vital Records System)

☐ C. I am the **legal custodian or guardian** of the person named on the birth certificate. *(Legal proof is required. See item 1 on page 2.)*

☐ D. I am a **representative, authorized** in writing, by any of the above checkboxes (categories A - C). *(The written and notarized authorization must be attached to this application. See item 1 on page 2.)*
Specify the person you represent: ______________________________

☐ E. I can demonstrate that the information from the birth certificate is necessary for the **determination or protection of a personal or property right** for myself/my client/my agency. *(Proof is required.)*
Specify your interest: ______________________________

☐ F. None of the above. I am requesting an uncertified copy. Copy will not be valid for legal identity or benefit purposes. See Item 1 and 2 on page 2.

I hereby attest that the information provided on this application is correct to the best of my knowledge and belief and that I am entitled to a copy of the requested birth certificate in accordance with the categories listed above.

SIGNATURE – Applicant (person named in section I, who is completing this application) ➢	Date Signed (Month / Day / Year)

SECTION III - FEES FEES ARE NOT REFUNDABLE IF NO RECORD IS FOUND. CANCELLATIONS ARE NOT ACCEPTED.
Mandatory fees are already filled in. Fill in additional fees for extra copies or UPS delivery, if applicable.

1.	Search Fee (includes one copy if found)	$ 20.00	20.00
2.	Additional copies of the same certificate issued at the same time as the first copy ______ (Number of Additional Copies) X	$ 3.00	$0.00
3.	Expedited Service Fee	$ 20.00	20.00
4.	Credit Card Processing Fee	$ 6.00	6.00
5.	Shipping ☐ Regular Mail - No additional cost; mailed within five business days	$ 0.00	
	☐ UPS Next Day - $19.00 in the continental U.S.A.; shipped within two business days **UPS packages require a signature for delivery.**	$ 19.00	______
	NOTE: If no shipping box is checked, the copy will be sent by regular mail.	**TOTAL**	$46.00

SECTION IV - CREDIT CARD INFORMATION We accept Visa, MasterCard, American Express, or Discover.

CREDIT CARD NUMBER ______________________________ EXPIRATION DATE ______________

➢ **SIGNATURE** - Credit Card Holder ______________________________ DATE SIGNED ______________

SECTION V - BIRTH CERTIFICATE INFORMATION

BIRTH NAME (First, Middle, Last Name as it appears on the birth certificate)		SEX ☐ Male ☐ Female
DATE OF BIRTH (Month / Day / Year)	PLACE OF BIRTH - City, Village, or Township	PLACE OF BIRTH - County
Mother's First Name	Mother's Middle Name	Mother's (Maiden) Last Name (as it appears on the birth certificate)
Father's First Name	Father's Middle Name	Father's (Birth) Last Name (as it appears on the birth certificate)

VITAL RECORDS OFFICE USE ONLY **Certificate No.** ______________ **File Date** ______________ **Mother's Res. Co.** ______________

1. What is the difference between a "certified" and an "uncertified" copy of a birth certificate?

A **certified** copy of a birth certificate issued by the State Vital Records Office will have a raised seal, will show the signature of the State Registrar, and will be printed on security paper. A certified copy may be required to obtain a state-issued driver's license or identification, for travel to foreign countries, to obtain a passport, or for benefit purposes.

State law restricts who may obtain a **certified** copy of a birth certificate. A **certified** copy can only be issued to those people with a "direct and tangible interest" (section II, categories A – E) which means the following people:

- The person named on the birth certificate (section II, category A).
- An immediate family member defined as a parent (whose name is on the birth certificate and whose parental rights have not been terminated), current spouse, brother, sister, grandparent, child, or current domestic partner (Declaration of Domestic Partnership registered in the Wis. Vital Records System under Chapter 770, Wis. Stats.) of the subject of the record (section II, category B).
- NOTE: Grandchildren, step-parents, step-children, step-brothers and step-sisters can only obtain certified copies as section II, categories C-E.
- The legal custodian or guardian of the person named on the birth certificate. Legal proof, *e.g.*, a court order of custody or guardianship, is required (section II, category C).
- A person authorized in writing by one of the above. A written and notarized authorization must be attached to this application and the authorization must clearly state the relationship of the authorizing party to the subject of the record (section II, category D).
- A person who can demonstrate that the birth certificate is required to determine or to protect a personal or property right (section II, category E). roof is required.

If you do not meet one of the above criteria, you cannot receive a **certified** copy of a birth certificate.

An **uncertified** copy will contain the same information as a certified copy but it is **not** acceptable for legal purposes, such as proof of identity (section II, category F).

2. Limitations on access to certain birth certificates

According to Chapter 69, Wis. Stats., **uncertified copies** of the following types of birth certificates may not be obtained by anyone:

- A child born to unmarried parents and paternity has not been established.
- A child born to unmarried parents and paternity was established by court order.

Only persons with a "direct and tangible interest" (categories A – E) may obtain **certified copies** of those types of birth certificates listed directly above.

3. How long will it take to process my request?

Copies of birth certificates are available from the State Vital Records Office no less than 3 weeks from the date of the birth.

- **Applying by Fax requesting Regular Mail Shipping**

  Requests for copies of birth certificates may take up to 5 business days plus mail time to complete.

- **Applying by Fax requesting UPS Shipping**

Requests for copies of birth certificates are usually completed and shipped within two business days.

4. What identification is required when applying for a certified or uncertified copy of a birth certificate?

A photocopy of the applicant's current ID as listed below must be submitted with all fax applications.

At least one form of ID must show your current name and current address. Expired cards or documents will not be accepted.

The acceptable forms of identification are:

One of these:

- Wisconsin driver's license
- Wisconsin photo ID
- Out-of-state driver's license or photo ID card

OR

Two of these:

- Government-issued employee ID card or badge with photo
- US Passport
- Check or bank book
- Major Credit Card
- Health Insurance Card
- Recent dated, signed lease
- Recent utility bill or traffic ticket

If you have questions regarding this form, please call 608-266-1373
or visit our website at http://www.dhs.wisconsin.gov/vitalrecords

DEPARTMENT OF HEALTH SERVICES
Division of Public Health
F-05281 (Rev. 03/12)

STATE OF WISCONSIN
Chapter 69.21 Wis.Stats.

WISCONSIN MARRIAGE CERTIFICATE APPLICATION

(for Mail or In-Person Requests)

TYPE or PRINT.

PENALTIES: Any person who willfully and knowingly makes a false application for a marriage certificate shall be fined not more than $1,000 or imprisoned not more than 90 days, or both, per s. 69.24(2), Wis. Stats. Any person who willfully and knowingly obtains a marriage certificate for fraudulent purposes is guilty of a Class I felony [a fine of not more than $10,000 or imprisonment of not more than 3 years and 6 months, or both, per s. 69.24(1), Wis. Stats.].

I. APPLICANT INFORMATION

The information in Section I is about the person completing this application.

YOUR **CURRENT** NAME - First	Middle	Last	YOUR DAYTIME TELEPHONE NUMBER ( )
YOUR **STREET** ADDRESS (***CANNOT*** *be a P.O. Box address*) Apt. No.		**MAIL TO** ADDRESS *(if different)* Apt. No.	
City, Village, or Township	State / ZIP Code	City	State / ZIP Code
TYPE OF CURRENT VALID PHOTO ID *(See item 3 on page 2.)*	PHOTO ID NUMBER	STATE OF ISSUANCE	EXPIRATION DATE

II. APPLICANT'S RELATIONSHIP TO PERSON(S) NAMED ON THE CERTIFICATE

According to Wisconsin Statute, a CERTIFIED copy of a marriage certificate is only available to those with a "direct and tangible interest" ***(categories A – E below.)*** **You may select to receive an uncertified copy if you just need a copy for informational purposes OR if you do not meet the criteria for categories A–E. In that case, you may check category F below.** *(See item 1 on page 2 for more details.)*

Check one box which indicates YOUR RELATIONSHIP to one of the PERSONS NAMED on the marriage certificate.

☐ A. I am **one of the persons named** on the marriage certificate.

☐ B. I am a **member of the immediate family** of one of the persons named on the marriage certificate. *(Only those listed below qualify as immediate family.)* *NOTE: Grandchildren, step-parents, step-children, step-brothers/ step-sisters may only obtain certified copies as section II, categories C – E.*

CHECK ONE. ☐ Parent (whose name is on the bride or groom's birth certificate and whose parental rights have not been terminated)
☐ Brother / Sister ☐ Grandparent ☐ Child

☐ C. I am the **legal custodian or guardian** of one of the persons named on the marriage certificate. *(Legal proof is required. See items 1 and 2 on page 2.)*

☐ D. I am a **representative, authorized** in writing, by any of the above checkboxes (categories A - C). *(The written and notarized authorization must be attached to this application. See item 1 on page 2.)*
Specify the person you represent: ____________________

☐ E. I can demonstrate that the information from the marriage certificate is necessary for the **determination or protection of a personal or property right** for myself / my client/my agency. *(Proof is required.)*
Specify your interest ____________________

☐ F. None of the above. I am requesting an uncertified copy. Copy will not be valid for legal identity or benefit purposes. See Items 1 and 2 on page 2.

PURPOSE FOR WHICH CERTIFICATE IS REQUESTED (*Specify. This information will assist us in processing your request.)*

III. FEES

FEE IS NOT REFUNDABLE IF NO RECORD IS FOUND. CANCELLATIONS ARE NOT ACCEPTED.

☒ Search Fee **(includes one copy, if found)** .... $ 20.00 20.00

☐ Additional copies of the same certificate issued at the same time as the first copy ... ______ (Number of Additional Copies) X $ 3.00 ______

TOTAL ______

Make check or money order payable to:
STATE OF WIS. VITAL RECORDS

Be sure to include (1) completed form, (2) acceptable identification, (3) any additional proof or authorization required, (4) self-addressed, stamped business-size envelope, and (5) check or money order.

Mail your application materials and fee to: **STATE VITAL RECORDS OFFICE / PO BOX 309 / MADISON, WI 53701-0309**

IV. MARRIAGE INFORMATION

GROOM'S BIRTH NAME - First	Middle	BIRTH Last Name
BRIDE'S BIRTH NAME - First	Middle	BIRTH Last Name
LOCATION OF MARRIAGE – City, Village, or Township	LOCATION OF MARRIAGE - County	DATE OF MARRIAGE (Month/Day/Year)

I hereby attest that the information provided on this application is correct to the best of my knowledge and belief and that I am entitled to copies of the requested marriage certificate in accordance with the categories listed above.

SIGNATURE Applicant (person named in section I, who is completing this application)	Date Signed (Month / Day / Year)

Important: If you do not sign and date this form above ↑, your request cannot be processed.

VITAL RECORDS OFFICE USE ONLY	**Certificate Number**

1. **What is the difference between a "certified" and an "uncertified" copy of a marriage certificate?**

A **certified** copy of a marriage certificate issued by the State Vital Records Office will have a raised seal, will show the signature of the State Registrar, and will be printed on security paper. A certified copy may be required to change your last name or to obtain benefits.

State law restricts who may obtain a **certified** copy of a marriage certificate. A **certified** copy can only be issued to those people with a "direct and tangible interest" (section II, categories A – E) which means the following people:

- The bride or groom named on the marriage certificate (section II, category A).
- An immediate family member defined as a parent (whose name is on the bride or groom's birth certificate and whose parental rights have not been terminated), brother, sister, grandparent, or child of the subject of the record (section II, category B).
- NOTE: Grandchildren, step-parents, step-children, step-brothers and step-sisters can only obtain certified copies as section II, categories C – E.
- The legal custodian or guardian of the bride or groom named on the marriage certificate. Legal proof, *e.g.*, a court order of custody or guardianship, is required (section II, category C).
- A person authorized in writing by one of the above. A written and notarized authorization must be attached to this application and the authorization must clearly state the relationship of the authorizing party to the subject of the record (section II, category D).
- A person who can demonstrate that the marriage certificate is required to determine or to protect a personal or property right (section II, category E). Proof is required.

If you do not meet one of the above criteria, you cannot receive a **certified** copy of a marriage certificate.

An **uncertified** copy will contain the same information as a certified copy but it is **not** acceptable for legal purposes, such as claiming insurance benefits (section II, category F).

2. **How long will it take to process my request?**

Copies of marriage certificates are available from the State Vital Records Office no less than 3 weeks from the date of the marriage.

- **Applying in Person**
  - Requests for **certified** copies of marriage certificates are usually completed within 2 business hours of application, if the marriage certificate is on file.
  - Requests for **uncertified** copies of marriage certificates are not completed on the same schedule as requests for certified copies. In- person requests for uncertified copies may take up to 1 month to complete.
- **Applying by Mail**
  - Requests for **certified** copies of marriage certificates may take up to 2 weeks plus mail time to complete.
  - Requests for **uncertified** copies of marriage certificates are not completed on the same schedule as certified copies. Mail requests for uncertified copies may take up to 1 month plus mail time.

3. **What identification is required when applying for a certified or uncertified copy of a marriage certificate?**

A photocopy of the applicant's current ID as listed below must be submitted with **all** mail applications. A current ID as listed below is required when applying in-person.

At least one form of ID must show your current name and current address. Expired cards or documents will not be accepted.

The acceptable forms of identification are:

One of these:

- Wisconsin driver's license
- Wisconsin photo ID
- Out-of-state driver's license or photo ID card

OR

Two of these:

- Government-issued employee ID card or badge with photo
- US Passport
- Check or bank book
- Major Credit Card
- Health Insurance Card
- Recent dated, signed lease
- Recent utility bill or traffic ticket

If you have questions regarding this form, please call 608-266-1373 or visit our website at http://www.dhs.wisconsin.gov/vitalrecords

FAX APPLICATION FOR A WISCONSIN MARRIAGE CERTIFICATE

Personally identifying information requested on this form, including credit card information and your signature, will be used to process your application and payment for the requested copies. Failure to supply this information may result in denial of your request for copies of any Wisconsin Marriage Certificate.

Your credit card number and expiration date are required. The credit card number and expiration date will only be used to process payment for the fees specified in SECTION III – FEES below on this FAX Application for a Wisconsin Marriage Certificate.

PENALTIES: Any person who willfully and knowingly makes a false application for a marriage certificate shall be fined not more than $1,000 or imprisoned not more than 90 days, or both, per s.69.24(2) Wis. Stats. Any person who willfully and knowingly obtains a marriage certificate for fraudulent purposes is guilty of a Class I felony [a fine of not more than $10,000 or imprisonment of not more than 3 years and 6 months, or both, per s. 69.24(1) Wis. Stats.]

INSTRUCTIONS: Please complete this form and **FAX to 608-255-2035**. ***All FAX applications are charged an expedited service fee.***
See Page 2 of this form for valid photo ID requirements for processing this application.

SECTION I - SHIP TO INFORMATION (Print or type.) (You must complete this section for application to be processed.)

1. FULL NAME (First , Middle , Last)		2. DAYTIME TELEPHONE NUMBER ( )
3. STREET ADDRESS OR P.O. BOX **(You must provide a street address if you are requesting shipping by UPS.)**		APT. NUMBER
4. CITY	5. STATE	6. ZIP CODE

SECTION II - APPLICANT'S RELATIONSHIP TO ONE OF THE PERSONS NAMED ON THE MARRIAGE CERTIFICATE (CHECK ONE)

☐ A. I am **one of the persons named** on the marriage certificate.

☐ B. I am a **member of the immediate family** of one of the persons named on the marriage certificate. *(Only those listed below qualify as immediate family.)*
NOTE: Grandchildren, step-parents, step-children and step-brothers/step-sisters may only obtain certified copies as section II, categories C – E.

CHECK ONE. ☐ Parent (whose name is on the bride or groom's birth certificate and whose parental rights have not been terminated)
☐ Brother / Sister ☐ Grandparent ☐ Child

☐ C. I am the **legal custodian or guardian** of one of the persons named on the marriage certificate. *(Legal proof is required. See item 1 on page 2.)*

☐ D. I am a **representative, authorized** in writing, by any of the above checkboxes (categories A – C). *(The written and notarized authorization must be attached to this application. See item 1 on page 2.)*
Specify the person you represent: ____________________

☐ E. I can demonstrate that the information from the marriage certificate is necessary for the **determination or protection of a personal or property right** for myself/my client/my agency. *(Proof is required.)*
Specify your interest: ____________________

☐ F. None of the above. I am requesting an uncertified copy. Copy will not be valid for legal identity or benefit purposes. See Item 1 and 2 on page 2.

I hereby attest that the information provided on this application is correct to the best of my knowledge and belief and that I am entitled to copies of the requested marriage certificate in accordance with the categories listed above.

SIGNATURE – Applicant (person named in section I, who is completing this application) ➢	Date Signed (Month / Day / Year)

SECTION III - FEES FEES ARE NOT REFUNDABLE IF NO RECORD IS FOUND. CANCELLATIONS ARE NOT ACCEPTED.
Mandatory fees are already filled in. Please fill in additional fees for extra copies or UPS delivery, if applicable.

1. Search Fee (includes one copy if found) .... $ 20.00 — 20.00
2. Additional copies of the same certificate issued at the same time as the first copy ______ (Number of Additional Copies) X $ 3.00 — ______
3. Expedited Service Fee .... $ 20.00 — 20.00
4. Credit Card Processing Fee .... $ 6.00 — 6.00
5. Shipping ☐ Regular Mail - No additional cost; mailed within five business days .... $ 0.00
   ☐ UPS Next Day - $19.00 in the continental U.S.A.; shipped within two business days .... $ 19.00 — ______
   UPS packages require a signature for delivery.

NOTE: If no shipping box is checked, the copy will be sent by regular mail. **TOTAL** $46.00

SECTION IV - CREDIT CARD INFORMATION We accept Visa, MasterCard, American Express, or Discover.

CREDIT CARD NUMBER ____________________ EXPIRATION DATE __________

➢ **SIGNATURE** - Credit Card Holder ____________________ DATE SIGNED __________

SECTION V - MARRIAGE CERTIFICATE INFORMATION

GROOM'S NAME (First , Middle , Last Name)	BRIDE'S (Maiden) NAME (First , Middle , Last Name)	
PLACE OF MARRIAGE - City, Village, or Township	PLACE OF MARRIAGE - County	DATE OF MARRIAGE (Month / Day / Year)

VITAL RECORDS OFFICE USE ONLY	**Certificate Number**

1. What is the difference between a "certified" and an "uncertified" copy of a marriage certificate?

A **certified** copy of a marriage certificate issued by the State Vital Records Office will have a raised seal, will show the signature of the State Registrar, and will be printed on security paper. A certified copy may be required to change your last name or to obtain benefits.

State law restricts who may obtain a **certified** copy of a marriage certificate. A **certified** copy can only be issued to those people with a "direct and tangible interest" (section II, categories A – E) which means the following people:

- The bride or groom named on the marriage certificate (section II, category A).
- An immediate family member defined as a parent (whose name is on the bride or groom's birth certificate and whose parental rights have not been terminated), brother, sister, grandparent, or child of the subject of the record (section II, category B).
- NOTE: Grandchildren, step-parents, step-children, step-brothers and step-sisters can only obtain certified copies as section II, categories C-E.
- The legal custodian or guardian of the bride or groom named on the marriage certificate. Legal proof, *e.g.*, a court order of custody or guardianship, is required (section II, category C).
- A person authorized in writing by one of the above. A written and notarized authorization must be attached to this application and the authorization must clearly state the relationship of the authorizing party to the subject of the record (section II, category D).
- A person who can demonstrate that the marriage certificate is required to determine or to protect a personal or property right (section II, category E). Proof is required.

If you do not meet one of the above criteria, you cannot receive a **certified** copy of a marriage certificate.

An **uncertified** copy will contain the same information as a certified copy but it is **not** acceptable for legal purposes, such as claiming insurance benefits (section II, category F).

2. How long will it take to process my request?

Copies of marriage certificates are available from the State Vital Records Office no less than 3 weeks from the date of the marriage.

- **Applying by Fax requesting Regular Mail Shipping**

  Requests for copies of marriage certificates may take up to 5 business days plus mail time to complete.

- **Applying by Fax requesting UPS Shipping**

  Requests for copies of marriage certificates are usually completed and shipped within two business days.

3. What identification is required when applying for a certified or uncertified copy of a marriage certificate?

A photocopy of the applicant's current ID as listed below must be submitted with **all** fax applications

At least one form of ID must show your current name and current address. Expired cards or documents will not be accepted.

The acceptable forms of identification are:

One of these:

- Wisconsin driver's license
- Wisconsin photo ID
- Out-of-state driver's license or photo ID card

OR

Two of these:

- Government-issued employee ID card or badge with photo
- US Passport
- Check or bank book
- Major Credit Card
- Health Insurance Card
- Recent dated, signed lease
- Recent utility bill or traffic ticket

If you have questions regarding this form, please call 608-266-1373 or visit our website at http://www.dhs.wisconsin.gov/vitalrecords

DEPARTMENT OF HEALTH SERVICES
Division of Public Health
F-00123 (Rev. 03/12)

STATE OF WISCONSIN
Chapter 69.21 Wis.Stats.

WISCONSIN DECLARATION OF DOMESTIC PARTNERSHIP APPLICATION
(for Mail or In-Person Requests)

TYPE or PRINT.

PENALTIES: Any person who willfully and knowingly makes a false application for a domestic partnership shall be fined not more than $1,000 or imprisoned not more than 90 days, or both, per s. 69.24(2), Wis. Stats. Any person who willfully and knowingly obtains a declaration of domestic partnership for fraudulent purposes is guilty of a Class I felony [a fine of not more than $10,000 or imprisonment of not more than 3 years and 6 months, or both, per s. 69.24(1), Wis. Stats.].

I. APPLICANT INFORMATION

The information in Section I is about the person completing this application.

YOUR **CURRENT** NAME - First	Middle	Last	YOUR DAYTIME TELEPHONE NUMBER ( )

YOUR **STREET** ADDRESS (***CANNOT** be a P.O. Box address*)	Apt. No.	**MAIL TO** ADDRESS (*if different than street address*)	Apt. No.

City, Village, or Township	State	ZIP Code	City	State	ZIP Code

TYPE OF CURRENT VALID PHOTO ID (*See item 3 on page 2.*)	PHOTO ID NUMBER	STATE OF ISSUANCE	EXPIRATION DATE

II. APPLICANT'S RELATIONSHIP TO PERSON(S) NAMED ON THE RECORD

According to Wisconsin Statute, a CERTIFIED copy of a declaration of domestic partnership is only available to those with a "direct and tangible interest" *(categories A – E below.)* You may select to receive an uncertified copy if you just need a copy for informational purposes OR if you do not meet the criteria for categories A – E. In that case, you may check category F below. *(See item 1 on page 2 for more details.)*

Check one box which indicates YOUR RELATIONSHIP to one of the PERSONS NAMED on declaration of domestic partnership.

☐ A. I am **one of the persons named** on the declaration of domestic partnership.

☐ B. I am a **member of the immediate family** of one of the partners named on the declaration. *(Only those listed below qualify as immediate family.)*
NOTE: Grandchildren, step-parents, step-children, step-brothers/step-sisters may only obtain certified copies as section II, categories C – E.
CHECK ONE. ☐ Parent (whose name is on one of the partners' birth certificates and whose parental rights have not been terminated)
☐ Brother / Sister ☐ Grandparent ☐ Child

☐ C. I am the **legal guardian** of one of the partners named on the declaration. *(Legal proof is required. See item 1 on page 2)*

☐ D. I am a **representative, authorized** in writing, by any of the above checkboxes (categories A - C). *(The written and notarized authorization must be attached to this application. See item 1 on page 2)*
Specify the person you represent: ____________________

☐ E. I can demonstrate that the information from the declaration is necessary for the **determination or protection of a personal or property right** for myself/my client/my agency. *(Proof is required.)*
Specify your interest: ____________________

☐ F. None of the above. I am requesting an uncertified copy. Copy will not be valid for legal identity or benefit purposes. See Item 1 and 2 on page 2.

PURPOSE FOR WHICH DOCUMENT IS REQUESTED *(Specify. This information will assist us in processing your request.)*

III. FEES

FEE IS NOT REFUNDABLE IF NO RECORD IS FOUND. CANCELLATIONS ARE NOT ACCEPTED.

☒ Search Fee **(includes one copy, if found)**		$ 20.00	20.00
☐ Additional copies of the same certificate issued at the same time as the first copy	______ Number of Additional Copies	X $ 3.00	______
		TOTAL	______

Make check or money order payable to: **STATE OF WIS. VITAL RECORDS**

Be sure to include: (1) completed form; (2) acceptable identification; (3) any additional proof or authorization required; 4) self-addressed, stamped, business-size envelope, and; (5) check or money order.
Mail your application materials and fee to: **STATE VITAL RECORDS OFFICE / PO BOX 309 / MADISON, WI 53701-0309**

IV. DECLARATION F DOMESTIC PARTNERSHIP

PARTNER "A" BIRTH NAME- First	Middle	Last Name

PARTNER "B" BIRTH NAME First	Middle	Last Name

COUNTY (where the declaration of domestic partnership was filed)	DATE OF THE OFFICIAL DECLARATION (Month/Day/Year)

I hereby attest that the information provided on this application is correct to the best of my knowledge and belief and that I am entitled to copies of the requested declaration of domestic partnership in accordance with the categories listed above.

SIGNATURE - Applicant (person named in Part I who is completing this application) ➤	Date Signed (Month / Day / Year)

Important: If you do not sign and date this form above ↑, your request cannot be processed

VITAL RECORDS OFFICE USE ONLY	**Document Number**

1. **What is difference between a "certified" and an "uncertified" copy of a declaration of domestic partnership?**
A **certified** copy of a declaration of domestic partnership issued by the State Vital Records Office will have a raised seal, will show the signature of the State Registrar, and will be printed on security paper. A certified copy may be required to assert legal rights that apply to domestic partners.
State law restricts who may obtain a **certified** copy of a declaration of domestic partnership. A **certified** copy can only be issued to those people with a "direct and tangible interest" (section II, categories A – E) which means the following people:

   - One of the partners named on the declaration of domestic partnership (section II, category A).
   - An immediate family member defined as a parent (whose name is on one of the partner's birth certificate and whose parental rights have not been terminated), brother, sister, grandparent, or child of the subject of the record (section II, category B).
   - NOTE: Grandchildren, step-parents, step-children, step-brothers and step-sisters can only obtain certified copies as section II, categories C – E.
   - The legal guardian of a partner named on the declaration of domestic partnership. Legal proof, *e.g.*, a court order of guardianship, is required (section II, category C).
   - A person authorized in writing by one of the above. A written and notarized authorization must be attached to this application and the authorization must clearly state the relationship of the authorizing party to the subject of the record (section II, category D).
   - A person who can demonstrate that the declaration of domestic partnership is required to determine or to protect a personal or property right (section II, category E). Proof is required.

   If you do not meet one of the above criteria, you cannot receive a **certified** copy of a declaration of domestic partnership.

   An **uncertified** copy will contain the same information as a certified copy but it is **not** acceptable for legal purposes. (section II, category F)

2. **How long will it take to process my request?**
Copies of declarations of domestic partnerships are available from the State Vital Records Office no less than 3 weeks from the date of the event.
   - **Applying in Person**
     - Requests for **certified** copies of declaration of domestic partnerships are usually completed within 2 business hours of application, if the declaration of domestic partnership is on file.
     - Requests for **uncertified** copies of declaration of domestic partnerships are not completed on the same schedule as requests for certified copies. In-person requests for uncertified copies may take up to 1 month to complete.
   - **Applying by Mail**
     - Requests for **certified** copies of declarations of domestic partnerships may take up to 2 weeks plus mail time to complete.
     - Requests for **uncertified** copies of declarations of domestic partnerships are not completed on the same schedule as certified copies. Mail requests for uncertified copies may take up to 1 month plus mail time.

3. **What identification is required when applying for a certified or uncertified copy of a declaration of domestic partnership?**
A photocopy of the applicant's current ID as listed below must be submitted with **all** mail applications. A current ID as listed below is required when applying in-person.

At least one form of ID must show your current name and current address. Expired cards or documents will not be accepted.

The acceptable forms of identification are:

One of these:
- Wisconsin driver's license
- Wisconsin photo ID
- Out-of-state driver's license or photo ID card

OR

Two of these:
- Government-issued employee ID card or badge with photo
- US Passport
- Check or bank book
- Major Credit Card
- Health Insurance Card
- Recent dated, signed lease
- Recent utility bill or traffic ticket

FAX APPLICATION FOR A WISCONSIN DECLARATION OF DOMESTIC PARTNERSHIP

Personally identifying information requested on this form, including credit card information and your signature, will be used to process your application and payment for the requested copies. Failure to supply this information may result in denial of your request for copies of any Wisconsin Declaration of Domestic Partnership.

Your credit card number and expiration date are required. The credit card number and expiration date will only be used to process payment for the fees specified in SECTION III – FEES below on this FAX Application for a Wisconsin Declaration of Domestic Partnership.

PENALTIES: Any person who willfully and knowingly makes a false application for a domestic partnership shall be fined not more than $1,000 or imprisoned not more than 90 days, or both, per s. 69.24(2), Wis. Stats. Any person who willfully and knowingly obtains a declaration of domestic partnership for fraudulent purposes is guilty of a Class I felony [a fine of not more than $10,000 or imprisonment of not more than 3 years and 6 months, or both, per s. 69.24(1), Wis. Stats.].

INSTRUCTIONS: Please complete this form and **FAX to 608-255-2035**. ***All FAX applications are charged an expedited service fee.***
See Page 2 of this form for valid photo ID requirements for processing this application.

SECTION I - SHIP TO INFORMATION (Print or type.) (You must complete this section for application to be processed.)

1. FULL NAME (First , Middle , Last)		2. DAYTIME TELEPHONE NUMBER ( )
3. STREET ADDRESS OR P.O. BOX (**You must provide a street address if you are requesting shipping by UPS.**)		APT. NUMBER
4. CITY	5. STATE	6. ZIP CODE

SECTION II - APPLICANT'S RELATIONSHIP TO ONE OF THE PERSONS NAMED ON THE DECLARATION OF DOMESTIC PARTNERSHIP (CHECK ONE)

☐ A. I am **one of the persons named** on the declaration of domestic partnership.

☐ B. I am a **member of the immediate family** of one of the persons named on the declaration. *(Only those listed below qualify as immediate family.)*
NOTE: Grandchildren, step-parents, step-children and step-brothers/step-sisters may only obtain certified copies as section II, category C – E .

CHECK ONE. ☐ Parent (whose name is on one of the partner's birth certificate and whose parental rights have not been terminated)
☐ Brother / Sister ☐ Grandparent ☐ Child

☐ C. I am the **legal custodian or guardian** of one of the persons named on the declaration. *(Legal proof is required. See item 1 on page 2.)*

☐ D. I am a **representative, authorized** in writing, by any of the above checkboxes (categories A - C). *(The written and notarized authorization must be attached to this application. See item 1 on page 2.)*
Specify the person you represent: ______

☐ E. I can demonstrate that the information from the birth certificate is necessary for the **determination or protection of a personal or property right** for myself/my client/my agency. *(Proof is required.)*
Specify your interest: ______

☐ F. None of the above. I am requesting an uncertified copy. Copy will not be valid for legal identity or benefit purposes. See Item 1 on page 2.

I hereby attest that the information provided on this application is correct to the best of my knowledge and belief and that I am entitled to copies of the requested declaration of domestic partnership in accordance with the categories listed above.

SIGNATURE – Applicant (person named in section I, who is completing this application) ➢	Date Signed (Month / Day / Year)

SECTION III - FEES FEES ARE NOT REFUNDABLE IF NO RECORD IS FOUND. CANCELLATIONS ARE NOT ACCEPTED.
Mandatory fees are already filled in. Please fill in additional fees for extra copies or UPS delivery, if applicable.

1. Search Fee (includes one copy, if found)		$ 20.00	20.00
2. Additional copies of the declaration issued at the same time as the first copy	______ (Number of Additional Copies) X	$ 3.00	$0.00
3. Expedited Service Fee		$ 20.00	20.00
4. Credit Card Processing Fee		$ 6.00	6.00
5. Shipping ☐ Regular Mail - No additional cost; mailed within five business days		$ 0.00	
☐ UPS Next Day - $19.00 in the continental U.S.A.; shipped within two business days **UPS packages require a signature for delivery.**		$ 19.00	
NOTE: If no shipping box is checked, the copy will be sent by regular mail.		**TOTAL**	$46.00

SECTION IV - CREDIT CARD INFORMATION We accept Visa, MasterCard, American Express, or Discover.

CREDIT CARD NUMBER ______ EXPIRATION DATE ______

➢ **SIGNATURE** - Credit Card Holder ______ DATE SIGNED ______

SECTION V - DECLARATION OF DOMESTIC PARTNERSHIP INFORMATION

PARTNER "A" BIRTH NAME (First , Middle , Last)	PARTNER "B" BIRTH NAME (First , Middle , Last)
COUNTY (where the declaration of domestic partnership was filed)	DATE OF DECLARATION (Month/Day/Year)

VITAL RECORDS OFFICE USE ONLY	**Record Number**

1. What is the difference between a "certified" and an "uncertified" copy of a declaration of domestic partnership?

A **certified** copy of a declaration of domestic partnership issued by the State Vital Records Office will have a raised seal, will show the signature of the State Registrar, and will be printed on security paper. A certified copy may be required to assert legal rights that apply to domestic partners.

State law restricts who may obtain a **certified** copy of a declaration of domestic partnership. A **certified** copy can only be issued to those people with a "direct and tangible interest" (section II, categories A – E) which means the following people:

- One of the partners named on the declaration of domestic partnership (section II, category A).
- An immediate family member defined as a parent (whose name is on one of the partner's birth certificate and whose parental rights have not been terminated), brother, sister, grandparent, or child of the subject of the record (section II, category B).
- NOTE: Grandchildren, step-parents, step-children, step-brothers and step-sisters can only obtain certified copies as section II, categories C-E.
- The legal guardian of a partner named on the declaration of domestic partnership. Legal proof, *e.g.*, a court order of guardianship, is required (section II, category C).
- A person authorized in writing by one of the above. A written and notarized authorization must be attached to this application and the authorization must clearly state the relationship of the authorizing party to the subject of the record (section II, category D).
- A person who can demonstrate that the declaration of domestic partnership is required to determine or to protect a personal or property right (section II, category E). Proof is required.

If you do not meet one of the above criteria, you cannot receive a **certified** copy of a declaration of domestic partnership.

An **uncertified** copy will contain the same information as a certified copy but it is **not** acceptable for legal purposes, such as claiming insurance benefits (section II, category F).

2. How long will it take to process my request?

Copies of declarations of domestic partnership are available from the State Vital Records Office no less than 3 weeks from the date of the action.

- **Applying by Fax requesting Regular Mail Shipping**

  Requests for copies of declarations of domestic partnership may take up to 5 business days plus mail time to complete.

- **Applying by Fax requesting UPS Shipping**

  Requests for copies of declarations of domestic partnership are usually completed and shipped within two business days.

3. What identification is required when applying for a certified or uncertified copy of a declaration of domestic partnership?

A photocopy of the applicant's current ID as listed below must be submitted with all fax applications.

At least one form of ID must show your current name and current address. Expired cards or documents will not be accepted.

The acceptable forms of identification are:

One of these:

- Wisconsin driver's license
- Wisconsin photo ID
- Out-of-state driver's license or photo ID card
- Government-issued employee ID card or badge with photo
- US Passport
- Check or bank book

OR

Two of these:

- Major Credit Card
- Health Insurance Card
- Recent dated, signed lease
- Recent utility bill or traffic ticket

If you have questions regarding this form, please call 608-266-1373 or visit our website at http://www.dhs.wisconsin.gov/vitalrecords

DEPARTMENT OF HEALTH SERVICES
Division of Public Health
F-05282 (Rev.03/12)

STATE OF WISCONSIN
Chapter 69.21 Wis.Stats

WISCONSIN DIVORCE CERTIFICATE APPLICATION
(for Mail or In-Person Requests)

TYPE or PRINT.

PENALTIES: Any person who willfully and knowingly makes a false application for a divorce certificate shall be fined not more than $1,000 or imprisoned not more than 90 days, or both, per s. 69.24(2), Wis. Stats. Any person who willfully and knowingly obtains a divorce certificate for fraudulent purposes is guilty of a Class I felony [a fine of not more than $10,000 or imprisonment of not more than 3 years and 6 months, or both, per s. 69.24(1), Wis. Stats.].

I. APPLICANT INFORMATION

The information in Section I is about the person completing this application.

YOUR **CURRENT** NAME - First	Middle	Last	YOUR DAYTIME TELEPHONE NUMBER
			( )

YOUR **STREET** ADDRESS (***CANNOT*** *be a P.O. Box address*)	Apt. No.	**MAIL TO** ADDRESS (*if different tban street address*)	Apt. No.

City, Village, or Township	State	ZIP Code	City	State	ZIP Code

TYPE OF CURRENT VALID PHOTO ID (*See item 3 on page 2.*)	PHOTO ID NUMBER	STATE OF ISSUANCE	EXPIRATION DATE

II. APPLICANT'S RELATIONSHIP TO PERSON(S) NAMED ON THE CERTIFICATE

According to Wisconsin Statute, a CERTIFIED copy of a divorce certificate is only available to those with a "direct and tangible interest" ***(categories A – E below.)*** **You may select to receive an uncertified copy if you just need a copy for informational purposes OR if you do not meet the criteria for categories A-E. In that case, you may check category F below.** *(See item 1 on page 2 for more details.)*

Check one box which indicates YOUR RELATIONSHIP to one of the PERSONS NAMED on the divorce certificate.

☐ A. I am **one of the persons named** on the divorce certificate.

☐ B. I am a **member of the immediate family** of one of the persons named on the divorce certificate. *(Only those listed below qualify as immediate family.) NOTE: Grandchildren, step-parents, step-children, step-brothers/step-sisters may only obtain certified copies as section II, categories C – E.*

CHECK ONE. ☐ Parent (whose name is on the husband or wife's birth certificate and whose parental rights have not been terminated)
☐ Brother / Sister ☐ Grandparent ☐ Child

☐ C. I am the **legal custodian or guardian** of one of the person named on the divorce certificate. *(Legal proof is required. See item 1 on page 2.)*

☐ D. I am a **representative, authorized** in writing, by any of the above checkboxes (categories A - C). *(The written and notarized authorization must be attached to this application. See item 1 on page 2.)*
Specify the person you represent: ____________________

☐ E. I can demonstrate that the information from the divorce certificate is necessary for the **determination or protection of a personal or property right** for myself/my client/my agency. *(Proof is required.)*
Specify your interest: ____________________

☐ F. None of the above. I am requesting an uncertified copy. Copy will not be valid for legal identity or benefit purposes. See Item 1 and 2 on page 2.

PURPOSE FOR WHICH CERTIFICATE IS REQUESTED *(Specify. This information will assist us in processing your request.)*

III. FEES

FEE IS NOT REFUNDABLE IF NO RECORD IS FOUND. CANCELLATIONS NOT ACCEPTED.

☒ Search Fee **(includes one copy, if found)** .... $ 20.00 20.00

☐ Additional copies of the same certificate issued at the same time as the first copy ________ X $ 3.00 ________
Number of Additional Copies

TOTAL ________

Make check or money order payable to:
STATE OF WIS. VITAL RECORDS

Be sure to include (1) completed form, (2) acceptable identification, (3) any additional proof or authorization required, (4) self-addressed, stamped business-size envelope, and (5) check or money order.
Mail your application materials and fee to: **STATE VITAL RECORDS OFFICE / PO BOX 309 / MADISON, WI 53701-0309**

IV. DIVORCE INFORMATION

HUSBAND'S BIRTH NAME - First	Middle	BIRTH Last Name
WIFE'S BIRTH NAME - First	**Middle**	**BIRTH Last Name**

LOCATION OF DIVORCE - County	DATE OF DIVORCE (Month/Day/Year)

I hereby attest that the information provided on this application is correct to the best of my knowledge and belief and that I am entitled to copies of the requested divorce certificate in accordance with the categories listed above.

SIGNATURE - Applicant (person named in section I, who is completing this application)	Date Signed (Month / Day / Year)
➢	

Important: If you do not sign and date this form above ↑, your request cannot be processed.

VITAL RECORDS OFFICE USE ONLY	Certificate Number

1. **What is the difference between a "certified" and an "uncertified" copy of a divorce certificate?**
A **certified** copy of a divorce certificate issued by the State Vital Records Office will have a raised seal, will show the signature of the State Registrar, and will be printed on security paper. A certified copy may be required to change your last name or to marry.
State law restricts who may obtain a **certified** copy of a divorce certificate. A **certified** copy can only be issued to those people with a "direct and tangible interest" (section II, categories A – E) which means the following people:

- The husband or wife named on the divorce certificate (section II, category A).
- An immediate family member defined as a parent (whose name is on the husband or wife's birth certificate and whose parental rights have not been terminated), brother, sister, grandparent, or child of the subject of the record (section II, category B).
- NOTE: Grandchildren, step-parents, step-children, step-brothers and step-sisters can only obtain certified copies as section II, categories C – E.
- The legal custodian or guardian of the husband or wife named on the divorce certificate. Legal proof, *e.g.*, a court order of custody or guardianship, is required (section II, category C).
- A person authorized in writing by one of the above. A written and notarized authorization must be attached to this application and the authorization must clearly state the relationship of the authorizing party to the subject of the record (section II, category D).
- A person who can demonstrate that the divorce certificate is required to determine or to protect a personal or property right (section II, category E). Proof is required.

If you do not meet one of the above criteria, you cannot receive a **certified** copy of a divorce certificate.

An **uncertified** copy will contain the same information as a certified copy but it is **not** acceptable for legal purposes, such as remarriage. (section II, category F)

2. **How long will it take to process my request?**

Copies of divorce certificates are available from the State Vital Records Office no less than 3 weeks from the date of the divorce.

- **Applying in Person**
  - Requests for **certified** copies of divorce certificates are usually completed within 2 business hours of application, if the divorce certificate is on file.
  - Requests for **uncertified** copies of divorce certificates are not completed on the same schedule as requests for certified copies. In-person requests for uncertified copies may take up to 1 month to complete.
- **Applying by Mail**
  - Requests for **certified** copies of divorce certificates may take up to 2 weeks plus mail time to complete.
  - Requests for **uncertified** copies of divorce certificates are not completed on the same schedule as certified copies. Mail requests for uncertified copies may take up to 1 month plus mail time.

3. **What identification is required when applying for a certified or uncertified copy of a divorce certificate?**

A photocopy of the applicant's current ID as listed below must be submitted with all mail applications. A current ID as listed below is required when applying in-person.

At least one form of ID must show your current name and current address. Expired cards or documents will not be accepted.

The acceptable forms of identification are:

One of these:

- Wisconsin driver's license
- Wisconsin photo ID
- Out-of-state driver's license or photo ID card
- Government-issued employee ID card or badge with photo
- US Passport
- Check or bank book

OR

Two of these:

- Major Credit Card
- Health Insurance Card
- Recent dated, signed lease
- Recent utility bill or traffic ticket

If you have questions regarding this form, please call 608-266-1373
or visit our website at http://www.dhs.wisconsin.gov/vitalrecords

FAX APPLICATION FOR A WISCONSIN DIVORCE CERTIFICATE

Personally identifying information requested on this form, including credit card information and your signature, will be used to process your application and payment for the requested copies. Failure to supply this information may result in denial of your request for copies of any Wisconsin Divorce Certificate.
Your credit card number and expiration date are required. The credit card number and expiration date will only be used to process payment for the fees specified in SECTION III – FEES below on this FAX Application for a Wisconsin Divorce Certificate.
PENALTIES: Any person who willfully and knowingly makes a false application for a divorce certificate shall be fined not more than $1,000 or imprisoned not more than 90 days, or both, per s. 69.24(2), Wis. Stats. Any person who willfully and knowingly obtains a divorce certificate for fraudulent purposes is guilty of a Class I felony [a fine of not more than $10,000 or imprisonment of not more than 3 years and 6 months, or both, per s. 69.24(1), Wis. Stats.].

INSTRUCTIONS: Please complete this form and **FAX to 608-255-2035**. ***All FAX applications are charged an expedited service fee.***
See Page 2 of this form for valid photo ID requirements for processing the application.

SECTION I - SHIP TO INFORMATION (Print or type.) (You must complete this section for the application to be processed.)

1. FULL NAME (First , Middle , Last)	2. DAYTIME TELEPHONE NUMBER ( )
3. STREET ADDRESS OR P.O. BOX **(You must provide a street address if you are requesting shipping by UPS.)**	APT. NUMBER

4. CITY	5. STATE	6. ZIP CODE

SECTION II - APPLICANT'S RELATIONSHIP TO ONE OF THE PERSONS NAMED ON THE DIVORCE CERTIFICATE (CHECK ONE)

☐ A. I am **one of the persons named** on the divorce certificate.
☐ B. I am a **member of the immediate family** of one of the persons named on the divorce certificate. *(Only those listed below qualify as immediate family.)*
NOTE: Grandchildren, step-parents, step-children and step-brothers/step-sisters may only obtain certified copies as section II, categories C – E.

CHECK ONE. ☐ Parent (whose name is on the husband or wife's birth certificate and whose parental rights have not been terminated)
☐ Brother / Sister ☐ Grandparent ☐ Child

☐ C. I am the **legal custodian or guardian** of one of the persons named on the divorce certificate. *(Legal proof is required. See item 1 on page 2.)*
☐ D. I am a **representative, authorized** in writing, by any of the above checkboxes (categories A - C). *(The written and notarized authorization must be attached to this application. See item 1 on page 2.)*
Specify the person you represent: ____________________
☐ E. I can demonstrate that the information from the divorce certificate is necessary for the **determination or protection of a personal or property right** for myself/my client/my agency. *(Proof is required.)*
Specify your interest: ____________________
☐ F. None of the above. I am requesting an uncertified copy. Copy will not be valid for legal identity or benefit purposes. See Item 1 on page 2.

I hereby attest that the information provided on this application is correct to the best of my knowledge and belief and that I am entitled to copies of the requested divorce certificate in accordance with the categories listed above.

SIGNATURE – Applicant (person named in section I, completing this application) ➢	Date Signed (Month / Day / Year)

SECTION III - FEES FEES ARE NOT REFUNDABLE IF NO RECORD IS FOUND. CANCELLATIONS ARE NOT ACCEPTED.
Mandatory fees are already filled in. Please fill in additional fees for extra copies or UPS delivery, if applicable.

1. Search Fee (includes one copy of the divorce certificate, if found) .... $ 20.00 20.00
2. Additional copies of the same certificate issued at the same time as the first copy ________ X $ 3.00 ________
   Number of Additional Copies
3. Expedited Service Fee .... $ 20.00 20.00
4. Credit Card Processing Fee .... $ 6.00 6.00
5. Shipping ☐ Regular Mail - No additional cost; mailed within five business days .... $ 0.00
   ☐ UPS Next Day - $19.00 in the continental U.S.A.; shipped within two business days .... $ 19.00 ________
   UPS packages require a signature for delivery.
   NOTE: If no shipping box is checked, the copy will be sent by regular mail. **TOTAL** ________

SECTION IV - CREDIT CARD INFORMATION We accept Visa, MasterCard, American Express, or Discover.

CREDIT CARD NUMBER ____________________ EXPIRATION DATE ________

➢ **SIGNATURE** - Credit Card Holder ____________________ DATE SIGNED ________

SECTION V - DIVORCE CERTIFICATE INFORMATION

HUSBAND'S BIRTH LAST NAME (First , Middle , Last Name)	COUNTY OF DIVORCE
WIFE'S (Maiden) NAME (First , Middle , Last Name)	DATE OF DIVORCE (Month / Day / Year)

VITAL RECORDS OFFICE USE ONLY	**Certificate Number**

1. **What is the difference between a "certified" and an "uncertified" copy of a divorce certificate?**

   A **certified** copy of a divorce certificate issued by the State Vital Records Office will have a raised seal, will show the signature of the State Registrar, and will be printed on security paper. A certified copy may be required to change your last name or to marry.

   State law restricts who may obtain a **certified** copy of a divorce certificate. A **certified** copy can only be issued to those people with a "direct and tangible interest" (section II, categories A – E) which means the following people:

   - The husband or wife named on the divorce certificate (section II, category A).
   - An immediate family member defined as a parent (whose name is on the husband or wife's birth certificate and whose parental rights have not been terminated), brother, sister, grandparent, or child of the subject of the record (section II, category B).
   - NOTE: Grandchildren, step-parents, step-children, step-brothers and step-sisters can only obtain certified copies as section II, categories C – E.
   - The legal custodian or guardian of the husband or wife named on the divorce certificate. Legal proof, *e.g.*, a court order of custody or guardianship, is required (section II, category C).
   - A person authorized in writing by one of the above. A written and notarized authorization must be attached to this application and the authorization must clearly state the relationship of the authorizing party to the subject of the record (section II, category D).
   - A person who can demonstrate that the divorce certificate is required to determine or to protect a personal or property right (section II, category E). Proof is required.

   If you do not meet one of the above criteria, you cannot receive a **certified** copy of a divorce certificate.

   An **uncertified** copy will contain the same information as a certified copy but it is **not** acceptable for legal purposes, such as remarriage. (section II, category F)

2. **How long will it take to process my request?**

   Copies of divorce certificates are available from the State Vital Records Office no less than 3 weeks from the date of the divorce.

   - **Applying by Fax requesting Regular Mail Shipping**

     Requests for copies of divorce certificates may take up to 5 business days plus mail time to complete.

   - **Applying by Fax requesting UPS Shipping**

     Requests for copies of divorce certificates are usually completed and shipped within two business days.

3. **What identification is required when applying for a certified or uncertified copy of a divorce certificate?**
   A photocopy of the applicant's current ID as listed below must be submitted with **all** fax applications.

   At least one form of ID must show your current name and current address. Expired cards or documents will not be accepted.

   The acceptable forms of identification are:

One of these:

- Wisconsin driver's license
- Wisconsin photo ID
- Out-of-state driver's license or photo ID card

OR

Two of these:

- Government-issued employee ID card or badge with photo
- US Passport
- Check or bank book
- Major Credit Card
- Health Insurance Card
- Recent dated, signed lease
- Recent utility bill or traffic ticket

**If you have questions regarding this form, please call 608-266-1373
or visit our website at http://www.dhs.wisconsin.gov/vitalrecords**

DEPARTMENT OF HEALTH SERVICES
Division of Public Health
F-05280 (Rev. 03/12)

STATE OF WISCONSIN
Chapter 69.21 Wis.Stats.

WISCONSIN DEATH CERTIFICATE APPLICATION
(for Mail or In-Person Requests)

TYPE or PRINT.

PENALTIES: Any person who willfully and knowingly makes a false application for a death certificate is guilty of a Class I felony [a fine of not more than $10,000 or imprisonment of not more than 3 years and 6 months, or both, per s. 69.24(1)]. Any person who willfully and knowingly obtains a death certificate for fraudulent purposes is guilty of a Class I felony [a fine of not more than $10,000 or imprisonment of not more than 3 years and 6 months, or both, per s. 69.24(1). Wis. Stats.].

I. APPLICANT INFORMATION

The information in Section I is about the person completing this application.

YOUR **CURRENT** NAME - First	Middle	Last	YOUR DAYTIME TELEPHONE NO. ( )

YOUR **STREET** ADDRESS (***CANNOT*** *be a P.O. Box address*)	Apt. No.	**MAIL TO** ADDRESS (*if different than street address*)	Apt. No.

City, Village, or Township	State	ZIP Code	City	State	ZIP Code

TYPE OF CURRENT VALID PHOTO ID (*See item 3, on page 2.*)	**PHOTO** ID NUMBER	STATE OF ISSUANCE	EXPIRATION DATE

II. APPLICANT'S RELATIONSHIP TO PERSON NAMED ON THE CERTIFICATE

According to Wisconsin Statute, a CERTIFIED copy of a death certificate is only available to those with a "direct and tangible interest" ***(categories A – D below.)*** **You may select to receive an uncertified copy if you just need a copy for informational purposes OR if you do not meet the criteria for categories A-D. In that case, you may check category E below.** *(See item 1 on page 2 for more details.)*

Check one box which indicates YOUR RELATIONSHIP to the PERSON NAMED on the death certificate.

☐ A. I am a **member of the immediate family** of the person named on the death certificate. *(Only those listed below qualify as immediate family.)*
NOTE: Grandchildren, step-parents, step-children, step-brothers/step-sisters may only obtain certified copies as section II, categories B – D.

CHECK ONE. ☐ Parent (whose name is on the death certificate and whose parental rights have not been terminated)

☐ Current Spouse ☐ Brother / Sister ☐ Grandparent ☐ Child ☐ Current Domestic Partner (registered in the Wis. Vital Records System)

☐ B. I am the **legal custodian or guardian** of the person named on the death certificate. *(Legal proof is required. See item 1 on page 2.)*

☐ C. I am a **representative, authorized** in writing, by any of the above check boxes (categories A and B). *(The written and notarized authorization must be attached to this application. See item 1 on page 2.)*

Specify the person you represent: ______________________________

☐ D. I can demonstrate that the information from the death certificate is necessary for the **determination or protection of a personal or property right** for myself/my client/my agency. *(Proof is required.)*

Specify your interest. ______________________________

☐ E. None of the above. I am requesting an uncertified copy. Copy will not be valid for legal purposes. See Item 1 and 2 on page 2.

PURPOSE FOR WHICH CERTIFICATE IS REQUESTED *(Specify. This information will assist us in processing your request.)*

III. FEES

FEE IS NOT REFUNDABLE IF NO RECORD IS FOUND. CANCELLATION REQUESTS ARE NOT ACCEPTED.

SEARCH FEE (Includes one copy, if found.) .... $ 20.00 $20.00

☐ Fact of Death (without cause of death) (sufficient for most financial transactions)

OR ☐ Extended Fact of Death (with cause of death) (for insurance benefit claims) *

EACH ADDITIONAL COPY (issued at the same time as the first copy)

☐ Fact of Death .... ________ (Number of Additional Copies) X $ 3.00 ________

☐ Extended Fact of Death .... ________ (Number of Additional Copies) X $ 3.00 ________

* For deaths that occurred before 2003, the applicant will automatically receive extended fact of death unless specified otherwise.

TOTAL ________

Make check or money order payable to:
STATE OF WIS. VITAL RECORDS

Be sure to include: (1) completed form; (2) acceptable identification; (3) any additional proof or authorization required; (4) self-addressed, stamped, business-size envelope, and; (5) check or money order.
Mail your application materials and fee to: **STATE VITAL RECORDS OFFICE / PO BOX 309 / MADISON, WI 53701-0309**

DEATH RECORD INFORMATION

FULL NAME OF DECEDENT (First / Middle / Last)	DATE OF DEATH (Month / Day / Year)

PLACE OF DEATH – City, Village, or Township *	PLACE OF DEATH - County	DECEDENT'S SOCIAL SECURITY NUMBER *

DECEDENT'S AGE / BIRTHDATE *	DECEDENT'S OCCUPATION *	NAME OF DECEDENT'S SPOUSE *

NAME OF DECEDENT'S MOTHER * (First / Middle / BIRTH Last Name)	NAME OF DECEDENT'S FATHER * (First / Middle / BIRTH Last Name)

I hereby attest that the information provided on this application is correct to the best of my knowledge and belief and that I am entitled to copies of the requested death certificate in accordance with the categories listed above.

SIGNATURE - Applicant (person named in section I, who is completing this application) ➢	Date Signed (Month / Day / Year)

Important: If you do not sign and date this form above ↑, your request cannot be processed.

*The fields marked with an asterisk (*) do not have to be completed. The information is helpful but not required.	**OFFICE USE ONLY**	**Certificate Number**

1. What is the difference between a "certified" and an "uncertified" copy of a death certificate?

A **certified** copy of a death certificate issued by the State Vital Records Office will have a raised seal, will show the signature of the State Registrar, and will be printed on security paper. A certified copy may be required to settle an estate or to claim insurance benefits.

State law restricts who may obtain a **certified** copy of a death certificate. A **certified** copy can only be issued to those people with a "direct and tangible interest" (section II, categories A – D) which means the following people:

- An immediate family member defined as a parent (whose name is on the death certificate and whose parental rights have not been terminated), current spouse, brother, sister, grandparent, child, or current domestic partner (Declaration of Domestic Partnership registered in the Wis. Vital Records System under Chapter 770, Wis. Stats.) of the subject of the record (section II, category A).
- NOTE: Grandchildren, step-parents, step-children, step-brothers and step-sisters can only obtain certified copies as section II, categories B – D. The legal custodian or guardian of the person named on the death certificate. Legal proof, *e.g.*, a court order of custody or guardianship, is required (section II, category B).
- A person authorized in writing by one of the above. A written and notarized authorization must be attached to this application and the authorization must clearly state the relationship of the authorizing party to the subject of the record (section II, category C).
- A person who can demonstrate that the death certificate is required to determine or to protect a personal or property right (section II, category D). Proof is required.

If you do not meet one of the above criteria, you cannot receive a **certified** copy of a death certificate.

An **uncertified** copy will contain the same information as a certified copy but it is **not** acceptable for legal purposes, such as claiming insurance benefits (section II, category E).

- For pre-2003 death certificates, an **uncertified** copy of a death certificate will contain the same information as a certified copy.
- For death certificates 2003 to the present, only persons named in categories A – D on the previous page may have access to information which includes cause of death.

	PRE-2003 DEATH CERTIFICATES	**2003 TO PRESENT DEATH CERTIFICATES**
CERTIFIED COPY A certified copy has a raised seal, will show the signature of the State Registrar, and will be printed on security paper. It can be used for legal purposes, such as settling an estate or claiming insurance benefits.	TYPE OF CERTIFICATE AVAILABLE Extended Fact of Death * TYPE OF RECIPIENT Must have a "direct and tangible interest"	TYPE OF CERTIFICATE AVAILABLE Fact of Death ** Extended Fact of Death * TYPE OF RECIPIENT Must have a "direct and tangible interest"
UNCERTIFIED COPY (An uncertified copy is for informational purposes only; It CANNOT be used for legal purposes.)	TYPE OF CERTIFICATE AVAILABLE Extended Fact of Death * TYPE OF RECIPIENT Anyone	TYPE OF CERTIFICATE AVAILABLE Fact of Death ** TYPE OF RECIPIENT Anyone

* **Extended Fact of Death Certificate.** Cause of death included; can be used for insurance benefit claims.
** **Fact of Death Certificate.** No cause of death included; can be used for banking and most other financial transactions.

2. How long will it take to process my request?

Copies of death certificates are available from the State Vital Records Office no less than 3 weeks from the date of the death.

- Applying in Person
  - Requests for **certified** copies of death certificates are usually completed within 2 business hours of application, if the death certificate is on file.
  - Requests for **uncertified** copies of death certificates are not completed on the same schedule as requests for certified copies. In-person requests for uncertified copies may take up to 1 month to complete.
- Applying by Mail
  - Requests for **certified** copies of death certificates may take up to 2 weeks plus mail time to complete.
  - Requests for **uncertified** copies of death certificates are not completed on the same schedule as certified copies. Mail requests for uncertified copies may take up to 1 month plus mail time.

3. What identification is required when applying for a certified or uncertified copy of a death certificate?

A photocopy of the applicant's current ID as listed below must be submitted with all mail applications. A current ID as listed below is required when applying in-person.**At least one form of ID must show your current name and current address. Expired cards or documents will not be accepted.**

The acceptable forms of identification are:

One of these:
- Wisconsin driver's license
- Wisconsin photo ID
- Out-of-state driver's license or photo ID card

OR

Two of these:
- Government-issued employee
- ID card or badge with photo
- US Passport
- Check or bank book
- Major Credit Card
- Health Insurance Card
- Recent dated, signed lease
- Recent utility bill or traffic ticket

If you have questions regarding this form, please call 608-266-1373 or visit our website at http://www.dhs.wisconsin.gov/vitalrecords

DEPARTMENT OF HEALTH SERVICES
Division of Public Health
F-05297 (Rev. 06/13)

STATE OF WISCONSIN
Chapter 69.21(1a), (2b), Wis. Stats.

FAX APPLICATION FOR A WISCONSIN DEATH CERTIFICATE

Personally identifying information requested on this form, including credit card information and your signature, will be used to process your application and payment for the requested copies. Failure to supply this information may result in denial of your request for copies of any Wisconsin Death Certificate.

Your credit card number and expiration date are required. The credit card number and expiration date will only be used to process payment for the fees specified in SECTION III – FEES below on this FAX Application for a Wisconsin Death Certificate.

PENALTIES: Any person who willfully and knowingly makes a false application for a death certificate is guilty of a Class I felony [a fine of not more than $10,000 or imprisonment of not more than 3 years and 6 months, or both, per s. 69.24(1)]. Any person who willfully and knowingly obtains a death certificate for fraudulent purposes is guilty of a Class I felony [a fine of not more than $10,000 or imprisonment of not more than 3 years and 6 months, or both, per s. 69.24(1), Wis. Stats.].

INSTRUCTIONS: Please complete this form and **FAX to 608-255-2035.** ***All FAX applications are charged an expedited service fee.***
See Page 2 of this form for valid photo ID requirements for processing this application.

SECTION I - SHIP TO INFORMATION (Print or type.) (You must complete this section for application to be processed.)

1. FULL NAME (First , Middle, Last)		DAYTIME TELEPHONE NUMBER ( )
3. STREET ADDRESS or P.O. BOX **(You must provide a street address if you are requesting shipping by UPS.)**		APT. NUMBER
4. CITY	5. STATE	6. ZIP CODE

SECTION II - APPLICANT'S RELATIONSHIP TO THE PERSON NAMED ON THE DEATH CERTIFICATE (Decedent) (CHECK ONE)

☐ A. I am a **member of the immediate family** of the person named on the death certificate. *(Only those listed below qualify as immediate family.)*
NOTE: Grandchildren, step-parents, step-children and step-brothers/step-sisters may only obtain certified copies as section II, categories C – E.

CHECK ONE. ☐ Parent (whose name is on the death certificate and whose parental rights have not been terminated)
☐ Current Spouse ☐ Brother / Sister ☐ Grandparent ☐ Child ☐ Current Domestic Partner (registered in the Wis. Vital Records System)

☐ B. I am the **legal custodian or guardian** of the person named on the death certificate. *(Legal proof is required. See item 1 on page 2.)*

☐ C. I am a **representative, authorized** in writing, by any of the above checkboxes (categories A and B). *(The written and notarized authorization must be attached to this application. See item 1 on page 2.)*

Specify the person you represent: ______________________________

☐ D. I can demonstrate that the information from the death certificate is necessary for the **determination or protection of a personal or property right** for myself/my client/my agency. *(Proof is required.)*

Specify your interest: ______________________________

☐ E. None of the above. I am requesting an uncertified copy. Copy will not be valid for legal identity or benefit purposes. See Item 1 and 2 on page 2.

I hereby attest that the information provided on this application is correct to the best of my knowledge and belief and that I am entitled to copies of the requested death certificate in accordance with the categories listed above.

SIGNATURE – Applicant (person named in section I, who is completing this application) ➢	Date Signed (Month / Day / Year)

SECTION III - FEES READ INSTRUCTIONS ON PAGE 2 OF THIS FORM BEFORE COMPLETING THIS SECTION.
Mandatory fees are already filled in. Fill in additional fees for extra copies or for UPS delivery, if applicable.
FEES ARE NOT REFUNDABLE IF NO RECORD IS FOUND. CANCELLATIONS ARE NOT ACCEPTED.

1. Search Fee (includes one copy if found) .... $ 20.00 — 20.00
   ☐ Fact of Death (without cause of death) **or** ☐ Extended Fact of Death (with cause of death)
2. Additional copies of the same certificate issued at the same time as the first copy
   ☐ Fact of Death Certificate (without cause of death) .... ________ (number of additional copies) X $ 3.00 — $0.00
   ☐ Extended Fact of Death Certificate (with cause of death) .... ________ (number of additional copies) X $ 3.00 — $0.00
3. Expedited Service Fee .... $ 20.00 — 20.00
4. Credit Card Processing Fee .... $ 6.00 — 6.00
5. Shipping ☐ Regular Mail - No additional cost; mailed within five business days .... $ 0.00
   ☐ UPS Next Day - $19.00 in the continental U.S.A.; shipped within two business days .... $ 19.00 ______
   UPS packages require a signature for delivery.

NOTE: If no shipping box is checked, the copy will be sent by regular mail. **TOTAL** $46.00

SECTION IV - CREDIT CARD INFORMATION We accept Visa, MasterCard, American Express, or Discover.

CREDIT CARD NUMBER ______________________ EXPIRATION DATE ______________

➢ **SIGNATURE -** Credit Card Holder ______________________ DATE SIGNED ______________

SECTION V - DEATH CERTIFICATE INFORMATION

FULL NAME OF DECEDENT (First, Middle, Last)		DATE OF DEATH (Month / Day / Year)
PLACE OF DEATH - City, Village, or Township *	PLACE OF DEATH - County	AGE or DATE OF BIRTH*
NAME OF SPOUSE * (First, Middle , Last)		DECEDENT'S SOCIAL SECURITY NUMBER *

* The fields marked with an asterisk (*) do not have to be completed. The information is helpful but not required.	**VITAL RECORDS OFFICE USE ONLY**	**Certificate Number**

1. **What is the difference between a "certified" and an "uncertified" copy of a death certificate?**

A **certified** copy of a death certificate issued by the State Vital Records Office will have a raised seal, will show the signature of the State Registrar, and will be printed on security paper. A certified copy may be required to settle an estate or to claim insurance benefits.

State law restricts who may obtain a **certified** copy of a death certificate. A **certified** copy can only be issued to those people with a "direct and tangible interest" (section II, categories A – D) which means the following people:

- An immediate family member defined as a parent (whose name is on the death certificate and whose parental rights have not been terminated), current spouse, brother, sister, grandparent, child, or current domestic partner (Declaration of Domestic Partnership registered in the Wis. Vital Records System under Chapter 770, Wis. Stats.) of the subject of the record (section II, category A).
- NOTE: Grandchildren, step-parents, step-children, step-brothers and step-sisters can only obtain certified copies as section II, categories B - D.
- The legal custodian or guardian of the person named on the death certificate. Legal proof, *e.g.*, a court order of custody or guardianship, is required (section II, category B).
- A person authorized in writing by one of the above. A written and notarized authorization must be attached to this application and the authorization must clearly state the relationship of the authorizing party to the subject of the record (section II, category C).
- A person who can demonstrate that the birth certificate is required to determine or to protect a personal or property right (section II, category D) Proof is required.

If you do not meet one of the above criteria, you cannot receive a **certified** copy of a death certificate.

An **uncertified** copy will contain the same information as a certified copy but it is **not** acceptable for legal purposes, such as claiming insurance benefits (section II, category E).

- For pre-2003 death certificates, an **uncertified** copy of a death certificate will contain the same information as a certified copy.
- For death certificates 2003 to the present, only persons named in categories A – D on the previous page may have access to information that includes cause of death.

	PRE-2003 DEATH CERTIFICATES	**2003 TO PRESENT DEATH CERTIFICATES**
CERTIFIED COPY A certified copy has a raised seal, will show the signature of the state Registrar, and will be printed on security paper. It can be used for legal purposes, such as settling an estate or claiming insurance benefits.	TYPE OF CERTIFICATE AVAILABLE Extended Fact of Death * TYPE OF RECIPIENT Must have a "direct and tangible interest"	TYPE OF CERTIFICATE AVAILABLE Fact of Death ** Extended Fact of Death * TYPE OF RECIPIENT Must have a "direct and tangible interest"
UNCERTIFIED COPY An uncertified copy can NOT be used for legal purposes.	TYPE OF CERTIFICATE AVAILABLE Extended Fact of Death * TYPE OF RECIPIENT Anyone	TYPE OF CERTIFICATE AVAILABLE Fact of Death ** TYPE OF RECIPIENT Anyone

* **Extended Fact of Death Certificate.** Cause of death included; can be used for insurance benefit claims
** **Fact of Death Certificate.** No cause of death included; can be used for banking and most other financial transactions

2. **How long will it take to process my request?**

Copies of death certificates are available from the State Vital Records Office no less than 3 weeks from the date of the death.

- **Applying by Fax requesting Regular Mail Shipping:**

  Requests for copies of death certificates may take up to 5 business days plus mail time to complete.

- **Applying by Fax requesting UPS Shipping:**

  Requests for copies of death certificates are usually completed and shipped within two business days.

3. **What identification is required when applying for a certified or uncertified copy of a death certificate?**

A photocopy of the applicant's current ID as listed below must be submitted with **all** fax applications.

At least one form of ID must show your current name and current address. Expired cards or documents will not be accepted.

The acceptable forms of identification are:

One of these:
- Wisconsin driver's license
- Wisconsin photo ID
- Out-of-state driver's license or photo ID card

OR

Two of these:
- Government-issued employee ID card or badge with photo
- US Passport
- Check or bank book
- Major Credit Card
- Health Insurance Card
- Recent dated, signed lease
- Recent utility bill or traffic ticket

If you have questions regarding this form, please call 608-266-1373 or visit our website at http://www.dhs.wisconsin.gov/vitalrecords

DEPARTMENT OF CHILDREN AND FAMILIES
Division of Safety and Permanence

Adoption Records Search Program
P.O. Box 8916
Madison, WI 53708-8916
(608) 266-7163

For Office Use Only	
AF No.	______________
CMT No.	______________
Search No.	______________

Adoption Search Application

Use of form: Completion of this application is required to request adoption information from the Adoption Records Search Program. Personal information you provide may be used for secondary purposes [Privacy Law, s. 15.04(1)(m), Wisconsin Statutes]. Provision of your social security number (SSN) is voluntary; not providing it could result in an information processing delay.

Instructions: Complete and return the signed and notarized application with the $40.00 application fee and the appropriate attachments to the address above.

Applicant Information

Current name: ______________________________________
(First, Middle, Last)

Address – Street: ______________________________________

City: ____________________ State: ________ Zip Code: ______________

Telephone numbers: ______________ (Home) ______________ (Work) ______________ (Cell)

Email address: ______________________________________

Social Security Number: ______________

Best method and time to contact you during the day: ______________________________

Access to confidential adoption information is restricted to the following requesters age 18 or older. Check the box that applies.

I am:

- ☐ An adult adoptee (adopted in Wisconsin).
  Complete Part A
- ☐ A person whose birth parents(s) rights were terminated in Wisconsin but was never adopted.
  Complete Part A
- ☐ An adoptive parent of person adopted in Wisconsin.
  Complete Part B
- ☐ A guardian or legal custodian of a person adopted in Wisconsin or whose birth parent(s) rights were terminated in Wisconsin. **Attach proof of guardianship.**
  Complete Part B
- ☐ An offspring (child) of a person adopted in Wisconsin. (Provide proof of relationship to adopted person.)
  Complete Part B
- ☐ An agency or social worker assigned to provide services to a person adopted in Wisconsin or whose birth parent(s) right's were terminated.
  Complete Part B

Confirmation of Identity

Instructions:
1. **Complete the following information and sign before a notary public. (Bank or attorney's office.)**
2. **Attach a copy of a current state issued photo ID.**
3. **Include proof of name change (not necessary for marriages).**

I, ______________________________________ whose date of birth is ________________
(Name – Applicant) (mm/dd/yyyy)

certify that I have submitted a request to the Wisconsin Department of Children and Families for adoption search services.

I certify that the attached identification card contains my actual photograph and signature and that the information provided on this application is true.

____
SIGNATURE – Applicant

Subscribed and Sworn to before me

this _____ day of __________________, 20 _____,

____

Notary Public, State of ________________________

My commission expires ________________________

(SEAL)

As provided under Wisconsin Statute section 946.32(1)(a), making a statement under oath or affirmation that you believe to be false for purposes of confirming your identity to obtain information from the Adoption Records Search Program is a Class H felony, punishable by a fine of up to $10,000, or imprisonment up to 6 years, or both.

PART A

Adoptee Application

Instructions: Complete this page if you are an adult adoptee (18 years or older and adopted in Wisconsin) or a person whose birth parent(s) terminated parental rights in Wisconsin but was never adopted.

1. Information to help us locate your adoption or commitment record.

Adoptive name: ______________________________
(First, Middle, Last)

Birthdate: ______________ Birth place: ______________________________
(mm/dd/yyyy) (City, State)

Name(s) of adoptive parent(s) at time of placement: Mother: ______________________________
(First, Middle, Last)

Father: ______________________________
(First, Middle, Last)

Name – Adoption agency (if known): ______________________________

County of adoption (if known): ______________

☐ Yes ☐ No Was this a step-parent or relative adoption?
☐ Yes ☐ No Were you adopted more than once?

Birth name (if known): ______________________________
(First, Middle, Last)

Names of birth parents (if known): Mother: ______________________________
(First, Middle, Last)

Father: ______________________________
(First, Middle, Last)

2. Information requested – Check each type of information you are requesting.

Non-identifying information – All information leading to the identity of the birth parent(s) will be removed.

☐ Copy of adoption record – Includes all information concerning circumstances of adoption, and birth parent(s) family medical and social history information collected at the time of placement.

☐ Updated family health history. A search for birth parent(s) will be conducted in order to obtain requested information. **Attach physician's letter with the application.**

☐ Information regarding eligibility for tribal enrollment. If eligible, we will assist with the enrollment application process. **Attach a photocopy of your social security card.**

Identifying information – Can only be released with the written consent of the birth parent(s). A search for birth parent(s) will be conducted if consent is not currently on file with DCF.

☐ Current names and addresses of birth parent(s). Birth fathers can only be contacted if paternity was legally established.

☐ Impounded birth certificate.

PART B

Application Request for Adoptive Parents, Guardians / Legal Custodians and Offspring of Wisconsin Adoptees

Instructions: Complete this page if you are requesting information on behalf of a Wisconsin adoptee.

1. **Your relationship to adoptee:** ______________________________
   Provide proof of relationship if this is an offspring request.

2. **Information to help us locate the adoption record.**

   Current name of adopted person: ______________________________
   (First, Middle, Last)

   Adoptive name: ______________________________
   (First, Middle, Last)

   Birthdate: ______________ (mm/dd/yyyy) Birth place: ______________________ (City, State)

   Name(s) of adoptive parent(s) at time of placement: Mother: ______________________ (First, Middle, Last)

   Father: ______________________ (First, Middle, Last)

   Name – Adoption agency (if known): ______________________________

   County of adoption (if known): ______________

   ☐ Yes ☐ No Was this a step-parent or relative adoption?
   ☐ Yes ☐ No Is adoptee deceased?
   If "Yes", provide date, city and state: ______________________
   ☐ Yes ☐ No Was this person adopted more than once?

   Birth name (if known): ______________________________
   (First, Middle, Last)

   Names of birth parent(s) (if known): Mother: ______________________ (First, Middle, Last)

   Father: ______________________ (First, Middle, Last)

3. **Information requested –** Check each type of information you are requesting.

   Non-identifying information – All information leading to the identity of the birth parent(s) will be removed.

   ☐ Copy of adoption record – Includes all information concerning circumstances of adoption, and birth parent(s) family medical and social history information collected at the time of placement.

   ☐ Updated family health history. A search for birth parent(s) will be conducted in order to obtain requested information. **Attach physician's letter with the application.**

   ☐ Information regarding eligibility for tribal enrollment. If eligible, we will assist with the enrollment application process. **Attach a photocopy of the adoptee's social security card.**

Adoption Records Search Program Fees

$40.00 Application Fee

A non-refundable application fee of $40.00 in the form of a check or money order made payable to the "**Department of Children and Families**" (DCF) must be submitted with the application for all requests. This fee covers the search of Vital Records and the Central Birth Registry which is necessary to confirm your identity, locate the adoption record and search for updated birth family information that may be on file with the Department of Children and Families.

Fee for Non-Identifying Copy of Adoption Record

There is an hourly charge for copying, deleting identifying information, proofreading and recopying the adoption record. The department's charge is $75.00 / hour. The average adoption record takes about one hour to prepare. **The fee for this service will not exceed $150.00.**

Fee for Birth Parent Search and Outreach

There is an hourly charge for the time it takes to locate birth parent(s) when a search for identifying information or updated medical / genetic information is requested and affidavits of consent are not already on file with DCF. The department's charge is $75.00 / hour. Your fees will not exceed $100.00 per birth parent. A typical search for a birth parent takes approximately one hour.

Tribal Enrollment

There is no fee for determining eligibility for tribal enrollment or for DCF assistance with the enrollment process, however, the $40 application fee is required. If you are eligible for enrollment and wish to apply, a Vital Records fee will be requested from you at a later date in order to obtain certified documents required by the tribe.

Fee Reductions – Fee reductions are based on the Uniform Fee Schedule, s.46.03(18), Wisconsin Statutes. Complete page 7 if you wish to apply for a fee reduction.

I agree to pay the adoption search fees for my request as stated above.

____ ____________________

SIGNATURE – Applicant Date Signed

Application for Fee Reduction

Instructions: Complete this page if you wish to apply for a fee reduction. If eligible your maximum fee will be a one hour charge.

Name – Applicant: ____
(First, Middle, Last)

Income Allowances for Families of Different Sizes

Family Size	1	2	3	4	5	6	7	8	9	10
Annual Allowance	$18,672	$30,180	$35,916	$41,700	$47,436	$52,104	$55,716	$58,212	$60,732	$63,252

Above Allowances Based on Uniform Fee System Standard Schedule, 2011

Charge Based on Income

1. Enter family size.	
2. Enter total annual family income.	$
3. Enter allowance for family size: If amount of line 2 is less than amount of line 3, **STOP**! Your maximum fee is the one hour charge.	$
4. If the amount of line 2 is more than the amount of line 3, subtract line 3 from line 2.	$
5. Multiply line 4 by .05 (5%).	$
6. This is your maximum fee. a. For private agency cases, there is a minimum one hour charge.	
b. For DCF cases, the actual charge is based on the amount on line 5 or $75.00, whichever is greater, except when less than one hour is needed.	

All fee reductions are based on current family size. If you can be claimed as a dependent on someone else's tax return, you must provide a copy of their tax return for verification.

A signed and dated copy of my federal income tax return or W-2's from last year are attached. If you had no family income last year, we must have a statement that explains why, proof of no income, or confirmation of assistance. If you are receiving disability benefits, you must provide documentation.

☐ I am applying for a fee reduction.

______________________________ ______________________
SIGNATURE – Applicant Date Signed

Office Use: Fee Reduction ☐ Eligible
☐ Not eligible

DID YOU REMEMBER TO . . .

- ☐ Enclose the non-refundable application fee of $40.00. Make the check payable to the "**Department of Children and Families.**"
- ☐ Notarize your Confirmation of Identity form (page 2).
- ☐ Attach a copy of a current state issued photo ID.
- ☐ Attach proof of guardianship if you are the guardian of an adoptee or an individual / person whose birth parent(s) terminated their rights.
- ☐ Include a letter from your physician if you are requesting updated medical / genetic information.
- ☐ Attach a photocopy of the adoptee's social security card if you have requested tribal enrollment.
- ☐ Provide proof of relationship to adopted person if you are the offspring of an adoptee.
- ☐ Sign and date page 6 if you are **not** applying for a fee reduction.
- ☐ Complete, sign and date page 7 if you are applying for a fee reduction. Include a signed copy of last year's federal income tax return or W-2's.

Mail your application materials to:

Adoption Records Search Program
P.O. Box 8916
Madison, WI 53708-8916

Questions?

Call us at (608) 266-7163, Monday – Friday, 8:00 – 4:30 P.M.

OR

Visit our website at http://dcf.wisconsin.gov/children

WYOMING

Send your requests to:

Wyoming Department of Health
Vital Records Services
Hathaway Building
2300 Capitol Avenue
Cheyenne, WY 82002

Tel. (307) 777-7591
Fax (307) 635-4103
www.health.wyo.gov/rfhd/vital_records/index.html

Vital Records has birth and death records from July 1909, and marriage and divorce records from May 1941. Birth records in Wyoming are restricted for 100 years; death, marriage, and divorce records are restricted for 50 years. Earlier marriage records are available from the county clerk (http://soswy.state.wy.us/Elections/CountyClerks.aspx), and earlier divorce records from the clerk of the District Court in the county where the event occurred.

Records from Wyoming State Vital Records Services:

Cost for a certified Birth Certificate	$13.00
Cost for a certified Marriage Certificate	$13.00
Cost for a certified Divorce Record	$13.00
Cost for a certified Death Certificate	$10.00

For Genealogy Research:

Vital records that are open to the public (death, marriage, and divorce records more than 50 years old and birth records more than 100 years old) are available at the Wyoming State Archives (Barrett Building, 2301 Central Avenue, Cheyenne, WY 82002; tel. 307-777-7826; http://wyoarchives.state.wy.us/). The Archives has a variety of genealogy sources, including copies of county marriage record books and indexes up to the 1960s, though dates vary by county; some delayed birth certificates for people born in Wyoming prior to 1909; and a few birth and death records filed with county physicians. These include Albany County (births and deaths beginning in 1899), Fremont County (Shoshone Indian Reservation, 1884 births), Laramie County (births from February to April 1896 and deaths from 1896 to 1900), and Niobrara County (births dating from 1892).

A work in progress is the online Death Certificate Database 1909–1939, available at http://wyoarchives.state.wy.us/DCD/Index.aspx.

For Adoption Record information, contact:

Confidential Adoption Intermediary Services
Wyoming Department of Family Services
Hathaway Building, 3rd floor
2300 Capitol Avenue
Cheyenne, WY 82002

Tel. (307) 777-3570
https://sites.google.com/a/wyo.gov/dfsweb/social-services/adoption

CERTIFIED BIRTH APPLICATION FOR THE STATE OF WYOMING

A fee of $13.00 per copy must accompany this request. A money order or personalized check from the person making the request should be made payable to VITAL RECORDS SERVICES

If you do not have a birth record on file, you will be sent instructions for filing a Delayed Birth Certificate, and your $13.00 fee will be retained as a searching fee.

Enclosed is $________ for _____certified copy/copies

PLEASE ENCLOSE A SELF-ADDRESSED STAMPED ENVELOPE WITH YOUR APPLICATION

WARNING: **Wyoming Statute 35-1-431 states that it is a criminal violation to, willfully and knowingly, use or attempt to use a birth certificate for any purpose of deception.**

Requests must include a current photocopy of the driver's license, state issued ID card, or passport of the person requesting the certificate. We will also accept a notarized signature of the person making the request.

TAPE A

CURRENT PHOTOCOPY OF IDENTIFICATION HERE

Written signature must be permanent part of ID

PLEASE MAKE CERTAIN YOUR SIGNATURE AND THE EXPIRATION DATE ARE CLEARLY VISIBLE

Name as it appears on birth certificate
First Name ______________________________
Middle Name ______________________________
Last Name ______________________________

If this record could be recorded under any other name, list that name here

____

Date of Birth ____/____/____

Sex ☐ Male ☐ Female

Place of Birth

__________________, WY

Mother's Full Maiden Name (First, Middle, Last)

Full Name of Father (First, Middle, Last)

Signature of Person Whose Certificate is Being Requested or Parent Named on Certificate. If under 18 years of age, signature of parent or legal guardian required. Legal guardian must submit a copy of guardianship papers.

X______________________________

Address to Which Copy is to be Mailed

____

____

____

Mail your request to:

Vital Records Services
Hathaway Building
Cheyenne, WY 82002

STATE OF WYOMING

APPLICATION FOR CERTIFIED COPY OF MARRIAGE OR DIVORCE CERTIFICATE

A request for a certified copy of a marriage or divorce certificate should be submitted on this form along with the fee of $13.00 per copy. A money order or a personalized check from the person making the request should be made payable to VITAL RECORDS SERVICES. If a record is not located, your fee will be retained as a searching fee.

Please enclose a self-addressed, stamped envelope with the application.

Type of record requested

(check one): Marriage____ Divorce____

Enclosed is $_______for______certified copy/copies.

The fee listed above includes a surcharge for the Wyoming Children's Trust Fund used to establish programs for the prevention of child abuse and neglect. Wyoming Statute 35-1-428 requires Vital Records Services to collect this surcharge on all certified copies and search of the files.

Name of Husband

First Name ______________________

Middle Name ______________________

Last Name ______________________

Name of Wife

First Name ______________________

Middle Name ______________________

Last Name ______________________

Maiden Name ______________________

Date of Occurrence _____/_____/_____

Place of Occurrence

City________________ or County________________

Address to Which Copy Should be Mailed

____

____

____

Signature of Husband or Wife Named on Certificate

X______________________________

PHOTOCOPY OF IDENTIFICATION

Written signature must be a permanent Part of ID

Mail your request to:

Vital Records Services
Hathaway Building
Cheyenne, WY 82002

STATE OF WYOMING

APPLICATION FOR CERTIFIED COPY OF DEATH CERTIFICATE

A request for a certified copy of a death certificate should be submitted on this form along with the fee of $10.00 per copy. If the date of death is unknown, a searching fee of $13.00 for every five years searched is charged, which includes either a certified copy or verification of the record if one is found. A money order or a personalized check from the person making the request should be made payable to VITAL RECORDS SERVICES.

If a death record is not located, your fee will be retained as a searching fee.

Enclosed is $_______for______certified copy/copies.

The fee listed above includes a surcharge for the Wyoming Children's Trust Fund used to establish programs for the prevention of child abuse and neglect. Wyoming Statute 35-1-428 requires Vital Records Services to collect this surcharge on all certified copies and search of the files.

Full Name of Deceased

First Name ______________________________

Middle Name ______________________________

Last Name ______________________________

Date of Death ______/______/______

Place of Death

City________________ or County________________

Name of Surviving Spouse

Relationship to Deceased (If funeral director or attorney, state the relationship of the person for whom you are obtaining the copies. (i.e. Attorney for spouse.)

Purpose for Which Copy is needed

Signature of Person Requesting Certificate

X______________________________

Address of Applicant

____

____

____

PHOTOCOPY OF IDENTIFICATION

Written signature must be a permanent Part of ID

If certificates are to be mailed to a different address, a Self Addressed Stamped Envelope must be enclosed.

Mail your request to:

Vital Records Services
Hathaway Building
Cheyenne, WY 82002

2. U.S. Trust Territories & Commonwealths

AMERICAN SAMOA

Send your requests to:

American Samoa Government
Department of Homeland Security
Office of Vital Statistics
P.O. Box 6894
Pago Pago, AS 96799

Tel. (684) 633-1406
http://americansamoa.gov/

The Vital Statistics Section has birth, marriage, and death records from 1900.

Cost for a certified Birth Certificate	$7.00
Cost for a certified Marriage Certificate	$5.00
Cost for a certified Death Certificate	$7.00

For Divorce Records, contact:

High Court of American Samoa
American Samoa Government
Pago Pago, AS 96799

Cost for a certified Divorce Record	$5.00

GUAM

Send your requests to:

Office of Vital Statistics
Department of Public Health and Social Services
P.O. Box 2816
Agana, Guam 96910

Tel. (671) 735-7292
www.dphss.guam.gov/content/office-vital-statistics

The Office of Vital Statistics has birth, marriage, and death records from October 1901.

Cost for a certified Birth Certificate	$5.00
Cost for a certified Marriage Certificate	$10.00
Cost for a certified Death Certificate	$5.00

Send your requests for Divorce Records to:

Clerk of the Superior Court of Guam
Guam Judicial Center
120 West O'Brien Drive
Hagatna, Guam 96910

NORTHERN MARIANA ISLANDS

Send your requests for Birth and Death Records to:

Vital Statistics Office
Division of Public Health
P.O. Box 500409
Saipan, Northern Mariana Islands 96950

Tel. (670) 236-8717
Fax (670) 236-8700

The Vital Statistics Office has birth and death records since 1946, though the records from 1946 to 1950 are incomplete. Marriage records from 1954 and divorce records from 1960 are available from the Superior Court (Vital Records Section, P.O. Boxes 307, Saipan, Northern Mariana Islands; tel. 670-236-9830).

Cost for a certified Birth Certificate	$20.00
Cost for a certified Marriage Certificate	$10.00
Cost for a certified Divorce Decree	$2.50 plus $.50/page
Cost for a certified Death Certificate	$25.00

For additional assistance, contact:

Director of Health Services
Trust Territory of the Pacific Islands
Saipan, Northern Mariana Islands 96950

PANAMA CANAL ZONE

Send your requests to:

U.S. Department of State
Passport Services
Vital Records Section
1111 19th Street NW, Room 510
Washington, DC 20036

Tel. (202) 955-0307
www.travel.state.gov/passport/faq/faq_5055.html

Since December 1, 1999, vital records formerly issued by the Panama Canal Commission have been issued by the Department of State in Washington, DC. Vital records for births and deaths in the former Panama Canal Zone are available for the period between February 26, 1904, and September 30, 1979.

Cost for a certified Birth Certificate	$50.00
Cost for a certified Death Certificate	$50.00

The National Archives (NARA) in College Park has marriage records 1904–1979. You may submit a request for a copy to Civilian Records (NWCTC), Textual Archives Services Division, 8601 Adelphi Road, College Park, MD 20704-6001. If the marriage record you request is located, NARA will let you know the fee.

Court records of divorces and adoptions that took place in the Canal Zone during American jurisdiction are held in the National Archives (700 Pennsylvania Avenue, NW, Washington, DC 20408-0001; www.archives.gov/) in the Records of District Courts of the United States (Record Group 21).

PUERTO RICO

Send your requests to:

Puerto Rico Department of Health
Demographic Registry
P.O. Box 11854, Fernández Juncos Station
San Juan, Puerto Rico 00910

Tel. (787) 767-9120, ext. 2405 and 2412
www.salud.gov.pr

Birth, death, and marriage records after June 1, 1931, are available at the Department of Health. Copies of earlier records may be obtained by writing to the local registrar (Registrador Demográfico) in the municipality where the event occurred.

Cost for a certified Birth Certificate	$5.00
Cost for a certified Marriage Certificate	$5.00
Cost for a certified Death Certificate	$5.00
Cost for a duplicate copy, when ordered at the same time	$4.00

RD-225
MOD 12/08

COMMONWEALTH OF PUERTO RICO
DEPARTMENT OF HEALTH
DEMOGRAPHIC REGISTRY

BIRTH CERTIFICATE APPLICATION BY MAIL

PART I: REGISTRANT'S INFORMATION

1. Name at birth: ______ Father's Last Name ______ Mother's Last Name ______ First Name ______ Middle Name	
2. Date of birth: (month/date/year)	3. Place of birth: (town and hospital)
4.Father's Name:	5. Mother's Name:
6. The certificate will be used for:	7. Number of copies:

Part II: APPLICANT'S INFORMATION*

1.Applicant's Name: Father's Last Name Mother's Last Name First Name Middle Name	2. Relationship:**
3. Applicant's address:	4. Address where you want the certificate to be sent:
5. Applicant's identification included: __Other ___Driver's Lic. ___State ID. ___Passport. ___Public Assistance. ___ Other	6. Applicant's signature and date:

IMPORTANT: FIRST COPY $5.00 EACH / ADDITIONAL COPY $4.00 OF SAME PERSON

1. Applicants living out of Puerto Rico send the application to the following address: Demographic Registry PO Box 11854. San Juan Puerto Rico 00910
2. If the applicant lives in Puerto Rico can visit any Local Registry near his/her house to complete an application.
3. Applicant must send a photocopy of a recent valid photo-identification card.
4. Applicant in Puerto Rico: Please send $5:00 internal Revenue Stamp for the first copy requested and $4.00 for each additional copy for the same person.
5. Applicant out of Puerto Rico: Please send $5.00 Money Order payable to Secretary of the Treasury.
6. Please send a self-addressed-stamped-envelope to mail in your certificate.
7. For rush mail as Fedex. Exp. Mail. Registered. UPS. etc. our address is: 171 Quisqueya Street. Hato Rey. PR 00917

WRITE CLEARLY YOUR NAME AND ADDRESS

*Applicant - means registrant, their children over 18 years of age, legal representative.
**Relationship - relation between the applicant and the registrant. This blank will be filled out if applicant and Registrant is not the same person.

Please send with your request an envelope with your mailing address and a $1.50 postal stamp, so we can send your Certificate as requested

(Other methods to receive your Certificate might be applying for it on www.pr.gov or www.VitalCheck.com)

VIRGIN ISLANDS—St. Croix

Send your requests to:

Virgin Islands Department of Health — Tel. (340) 773-1311, ext. 3086
St. Croix District
Office of Vital Records and Statistics
3500 Estate Richmond
Christiansted, St. Croix, Virgin Islands 00820

The Office of Vital Records has birth and death records since 1840. Current registration is considered to be complete.

Cost for a certified Birth Certificate	$15.00
Cost for a Birth Verification	$6.00
Cost for a certified Death Certificate	$15.00
Cost for a Death Verification	$6.00
Cost for Birth and Death Certificates in Person	$12.00

Send your requests for Marriage Certificates and Divorce Records to:

Superior Court of the Virgin Islands — Tel. (340) 778-9750
P.O. Box 929
Christiansted, St. Croix, Virgin Islands 00821

VIRGIN ISLANDS—St. Thomas and St. John

Send your requests to:

Virgin Islands Department of Health — Tel. (340) 774-6680
St. Thomas/St. John District
Office of Vital Records and Statistics
1303 Hospital Ground, Suite 10
St. Thomas, Virgin Islands 00802

The Office of Vital Records has birth records from July 1, 1906, and death records from January 1, 1906. Current registration is considered to be complete. Certificates can be ordered in person from the above address as well as from the Department of Health office at the Morris F. De Castro Clinic, B and C Strand Street, Cruz Bay, St. John, VI.

Cost for a certified Birth Certificate	$15.00
Cost for Birth Verification	$6.00
Cost for a certified Death Certificate	$15.00
Cost for Death Verification	$6.00

Send your requests for Marriage Certificates and Divorce Records to:

Superior Court of the Virgin Islands
(Location: 5400 Veteran's Drive)
P.O. Box 70
St. Thomas, Virgin Islands 00804

THE VIRGIN ISLANDS OF THE UNITED STATES
DEPARTMENT OF HEALTH
OFFICE OF VITAL RECORDS AND STATISTICS

APPLICATION FOR CERTIFIED COPY OF BIRTH RECORD

Do Not Complete This Application Before Reading The Instructions And Information On The Back Of This Form

PART A. TYPE OF CERTIFIED COPY REQUESTED:

CHECK ONE: Birth Verification Fee $6.00
A verification is an abstract from the birth record that gives the name and date of birth.

Birth Certificate Fee $15.00
A certificate is an abstract from the birth record that gives the name. date of birth. gender. place of birth and parents' names.

PART B. ELIGIBILITY:

CHECK ONE: I am the person listed on the record and am at least 18 years.
I am a parent or legal guardian of the minor person listed on the record.
I am a party entitled to receive the record as a result of a court order or power of attorney.
I am an attorney representing the person listed on the record.

PART C. DISTRICT APPLYING TO: CHECK ONE - St. Croix District St. Thomas/St. John District

PART D. BIRTH RECORD INFORMATION:

First Name On Record		Middle Name On Record	Last Name On Record	
Date Of Birth – mm/dd/yy	Place Of Birth (City And Island)			Gender (Check One) Male Female
Father's Name			Father's Place Of Birth	
Father's Physical Address (At Time Of Birth Of Person Whose Record Is Requested)			Father's Age At Birth (Of Person Whose Record Is Requested)	
Mother's Name			Mother's Place Of Birth	
Mother's Physical Address (At Time Of Birth Of Person Whose Record Is Requested)			Mother's Age At Birth (Of Person Whose Record Is Requested)	

PART E. APPLICANT INFORMATION:

Applicant's First Name	Applicant's Middle Name	Applicant's Last Name		
Applicant's Mailing Address		State	City	Zip Code
Type Of Photo Id	Photo Id#	Relationship To Person on Record		
Purpose For Which Record Is Requested		Amount Enclosed	Money Order ID #	

PART F. MAIL COPY OF RECORD TO: (ONLY COMPLETE THIS SECTION IF FORWARDING ADDRESS IS DIFFERENT FROM APPLICANT'S MAILING ADDRESS)

First Name	Middle Name	Last Name		
Mailing Address		State	City	Zip Code

Signature Of Applicant Physical Address Date Telephone # ( )

Do Not Complete Below Unless In The Presence Of A Notary Public

Sworn To And Subscribed Before Me This ________ Day Of ________________ _______. WITNESS My Hand And Official Seal.
Day Month Year

____
(Notary Public's Signature)

INSTRUCTIONS

Please submit the following:

1. Completed, notarized application ***TO THE DISTRICT WHERE THE BIRTH OCCURRED.***

   Virgin Islands Department of Health
   St. Thomas/St. John District
   Office of Vital Records and Statistics
   1303 Hospital Ground, Suite 10
   St. Thomas, VI 00802.

   or

   Virgin Islands Department of Health
   St. Croix District
   Office of Vital Records and Statistics
   3500 Estate Richmond
   St. Croix, VI 00820.

2. Photocopy of your valid, picture identification document such as your driver's license, passport, military identification card, permanent resident card, state issued identification card, employee identification card, or school identification card.

3. Certified copy of court/appointment document if applying as legal representative or legal guardian.

4. United States Postal Money Order in the amount of $15.00, made payable to the Virgin Islands Department of Health. (NO PERSONAL CHECKS WILL BE ACCEPTED)

5. Stamped envelope in the amount of $5.60 for return by certified mail or $18.30 for return by express mail.

INFORMATION

- Submittal of an incomplete application will delay processing.
- If a record is not found, a certified "No record found" letter will be issued.
- Walk-in Service is available between 8:30 A.M. and 3:00 P.M. at the following locations:

  Virgin Islands Department of Health
  John Moorehead Complex, Hospital Ground
  (located directly behind Lionel Roberts Stadium)
  St. Thomas, VI Tel#: (340) 774-9000 ext. 4685.

  Virgin Islands Department of Health
  Charles Harwood Memorial Complex
  3500 Estate Richmond, Christiansted
  St. Croix, VI Tel#: (340) 773-1311 ext. 3086.

  Virgin Islands Department of Health
  Morris F. De Castro Clinic
  B and C Strand Street, Cruz Bay
  St. John, VI Tel#: (340) 776-6400 ext. 6014.

VIRGIN ISLANDS OF THE UNITED STATES
LICENSE AND CERTIFICATE OF MARRIAGE

Please Type

FOR INSTRUCTIONS SEE HANDBOOK

LICENSE NUMBER

STATE FILE NUMBER

GROOM

1. GROOM'S NAME *(First, Middle, Last)*
2. AGE LAST BIRTHDAY

3a. RESIDENCE-CITY, TOWN, OR LOCATION
3b. COUNTY OR ISLAND

3c. STATE
4a. BIRTHPLACE *(State or Foreign Country)*
4b. DATE OF BIRTH *(Mo., Day, Yr.)*
5. SOC. SEC. NO.

6a. FATHER'S NAME *(First, Middle, Last)*
6b. BIRTHPLACE *(State or Foreign Country)*
7a. MOTHER'S NAME *(First, Middle, Maiden Surname)*
7b. BIRTHPLACE *(State or Foreign Country)*

BRIDE

Ea. BRIDE'S NAME *(First, Middle, Last)*
8b. MAIDEN SURNAME *(if different)*
9. AGE LAST L.RTHDAY

10a. RESIDENCE-CITY, TOWN, OR LOCATION
1 Ob. COUNTY OR ISLAND

10c. STATE
11 a. BIRTHPLACE *(State or Foreign Country)*
1 1 b. DATE OF BI RTH(Mo., Day, Yr.)
12. SOC. SEC. NO.

13a. FATHER'S NAME *(First, Middle Last)*
13b. BIRTHPLACE *(State or Foreign Country)*
14a. MOTHER'S NAME *(First, Middle Maiden Surname)*
14b. BIRTHPLACE *(State or Foreign Country)*

SIGNATURES

WE HEREBY CERTIFY THAT THE INFORMATION PROVIDED IS CORRECT TO THE BEST OF OUR KNOWLEDGE AND BELIEF AND THAT WE ARE FREE TO MARRY UNDER THE LAWS OF THIS STATE.

15. GROOM'S SIGNATURE ▶
16. BRIDE'S SIGNATURE ▶

LICENSE TO MARRY

This License Authorizes the Marriage in This State of the Parties Named Above by any Person Duly Authorized to Perform a Marriage Ceremony under the Laws of the State of ______________________

17. EXPIRATION DATE *(Month, Day, Year)*

18. SUBSCRIBED TO AND SWORN TO BEFORE ME ON: *(Month, Day, Year)*
19. SIGNATURE OF ISSUING OFFICIAL ▶
20. TITLE OF ISSUING OFFICIAL

CEREMONY

21. I CERTIFY THAT THE ABOVE NAMED PERSONS WERE MARRIED ON: *(Month, Day, Year)*
22a. WHERE MARRIED-CITY, TOWN, OR LOCATION
22b. ISLAND

23a. SIGNATURE OF PERSON PERFORMING CEREMONY ▶
23b. NAME *(Type/Print)*
23c. TITLE

23d. ADDRESS OF PERSON PERFORMING CEREMONY *(Street and Number or Rural Route Number, City or Town, State, Zip Code)*

24a. SIGNATURE OF WITNESS TO CEREMONY ▶
24b. SIGNATURE OF WITNESS TO CEREMONY ▶

LOCAL OFFICIAL

25. SIGNATURE OF COURT REGISTRATION OFFICIAL ▶
26. DATE FILED BY COURT *(Month, Day, Year)*

CONFIDENTIAL INFORMATION. THE INFORMATION BELOW WILL NOT APPEAR ON CERTIFIED COPIES OF THE RECORD.

	27. NUMBER OF THIS MARRIAGE - *First, Second, etc. (Specify below)*	28. IF PREVIOUSLY MARRIED, LAST MARRIAGE ENDED		29. RACE-American Indian, Black, White, etc. *(Specify below)*	30. EDUCATION *Specify only highest grade completed)*	
		By Death, Divorce, Dissolution, or Annulment *(Specify below)*	*Date (Month, Day, Year)*		Elementary / Secondary (0-12)	College (1-4 or 5 +)
GROOM	27a.	28a.	28b.	29a.	30a.	
BRIDE	27b.	28c.	28d.	29b.	30b.	

VIRGIN ISLANDS OF THE UNITED STATES
CERTIFICATE OF DIVORCE, DISSOLUTION OF MARRIAGE, OR ANNULMENT

TYPE
SEE HANDBOOK FOR INSTRUCTIONS

COURT FILE NUMBER

STATE FILE NUMBER

HUSBAND

1. HUSBAND'S NAME (*First Middle Last*)

2a. RESIDENCE-CITY, TOWN OR LOCATION | 2b. COUNTY OR ISLAND

2c. STATE | 3a. BIRTHPLACE (*State or Foreign Country*) | 3b. DATE OF BIRTH (*Month Day Year*) | 4. SOC. SEC. NO.

WIFE

5a. WIFE'S NAME (*First Middle Last*) | 5b. MAIDEN SURNAME

6a. RESIDENCE-CITY, TOWN OR LOCATION | 6b. COUNTY OR ISLAND

6c. STATE | 7a. BIRTHPLACE (*State or Foreign Country*) | 7b. DATE OF BIRTH (*Month Day Year*) | 8. SOC. SEC. NO.

MARRIAGE

9a. PLACE OF THIS MARRIAGE-CITY, TOWN OR LOCATION | 9b. COUNTY OR ISLAND | 9b. STATE OR FOREIGN COUNTRY | 10. DATE OF THIS MARRIAGE (*Month, Day, Yr*)

11. DATE COUPLE LAST RESIDED IN SAME HOUSEHOLD (*Month Day Year*)

12. NUMBER OF CHILDREN UNDER 18 IN THIS HOUSEHOLD AS OF THE DATE IN ITEM 11
Number ☐ None

13. PETITIONER
☐ HUSBAND ☐ WIFE ☐ BOTH
☐ Other (*Specify*) ______

ATTORNEY

14a. NAME OF PETITIONER'S ATTORNEY (*Type/Print*)

14b. ADDRESS (*Street and Number or Rural Route Number, City or Town, State, Zip Code*)

DECREE

15. I CERTIFY THAT THE MARRIAGE OF THE ABOVE NAMED PERSONS WAS DISSOLVED ON (*Month Day Year*)

16. TYPE OF DECREE-Divorce, Dissolution, or Annulment (*Specify*)

17. DATE RECORDED (*Month Day Year*)

18. NUMBER OF CHILDREN UNDER 18 WHOSE PHYSICAL CUSTODY WAS AWARDED TO:
Husband Wife
Joint (Husband/Wife) Other
☐ No Children

19. ISLAND OF DECREE

20. TITLE OF COURT

21. SIGNATURE OF CERTIFYING OFFICIAL

22. TITLE OF CERTIFYING OFFICIAL

23. DATE SIGNED (*Month Day Year*)

CONFIDENTIAL INFORMATION. THE INFORMATION BELOW WILL NOT APPEAR ON CERTIFIED COPIES OF THE RECORD.

	24. NUMBER OF THIS MARRIAGE (First, Second, etc. (Specify below))	25. IF PREVIOUSLY MARRIED, LAST MARRIAGE ENDED: By Death, Divorce, Dissolution or Annulment (Specify below)	25. Date (Month, Day, Year)	26. RACE-American Indian, Black, White, etc. (*Specify below*)	27. EDUCATION (Specify only highest grade completed): Elementary/Secondary (0-12)	27. College (1-4 or 5+)
HUSBAND	24a.	25a.	25b.	26a.	27a.	
WIFE	24b.	25c.	25d.	26b.	27b.	

THE VIRGIN ISLANDS OF THE UNITED STATES
DEPARTMENT OF HEALTH
OFFICE OF VITAL RECORDS AND STATISTICS

APPLICATION FOR CERTIFIED COPY OF DEATH RECORD

Do Not Complete This Application Before Reading The Instructions And Information On The Back Of This Form

PART A. TYPE OF CERTIFIED COPY REQUESTED:

CHECK ONE: Death Verification Fee $6.00
A verification is an abstract from the death record that gives the name and date of death..

Death Certificate Fee $15.00
A certificate is an abstract from the death record that gives the name, date of death, gender, place of death and cause of death.

PART B. ELIGIBILITY:

DEATH VERIFICATION → Anyone may apply for a death verification.

DEATH CERTIFICATE → CHECK ONE: I am a parent, legal guardian or sibling of the person listed on the record.
I am a party entitled to receive the record as a result of a court order.
I am an attorney representing the estate of the person listed on the record.
I can establish that the record is needed for settlement of estate, entitled benefits, or other proper purpose.

PART C. DISTRICT APPLYING TO: CHECK ONE - St. Croix District St. Thomas/St. John District

PART D. DEATH RECORD INFORMATION:

First Name On Record	Middle Name On Record	Last Name On Record
Date Of Death – mm/dd/yy	Place Of Death (City And Island)	
Father's Name	Mother's Name	

PART E. APPLICANT INFORMATION:

Applicant's First Name	Applicant's Middle Name	Applicant's Last Name		
Applicant's Mailing Address		State	City	Zip Code
Type Of Photo Id	Photo Id#	Relationship To Person on Record		
Purpose For Which Record Is Requested	Number Of Copies	Amount Enclosed	Money Order ID #	

PART F. MAIL COPY OF RECORD TO: (ONLY COMPLETE THIS SECTION IF FORWARDING ADDRESS IS DIFFERENT FROM APPLICANT'S MAILING ADDRESS)

First Name	Middle Name	Last Name		
Mailing Address		State	City	Zip Code

Signature Of Applicant ____ Physical Address ____ Date ____ Telephone # (   )

Do Not Complete Below Unless In The Presence Of A Notary Public

Sworn To And Subscribed Before Me This ________ Day Of ________________ ______. WITNESS My Hand And Official Seal.
Day Month Year

____
(Notary Public's Signature)

INSTRUCTIONS

Please submit the following:

1. Completed, notarized application ***TO THE DISTRICT WHERE THE DEATH OCCURRED.***

   Virgin Islands Department of Health
   St. Thomas/St. John District
   Office of Vital Records and Statistics
   1303 Hospital Ground, Suite 10
   St. Thomas, VI 00802.

   or

   Virgin Islands Department of Health
   St. Croix District
   Office of Vital Records and Statistics
   3500 Estate Richmond
   St. Croix, VI 00820.

2. Photocopy of your valid, picture identification document such as your driver's license, passport, military identification card, permanent resident card, state issued identification card, employee identification card, or school identification card.

3. Certified copy of court/appointment document if applying as legal representative or legal guardian.

4. United States Postal Money Order in the amount of $15.00, made payable to the Virgin Islands Department of Health. (NO PERSONAL CHECKS WILL BE ACCEPTED)

5. Stamped envelope in the amount of $5.60 for return by certified mail or $18.30 for return by express mail.

INFORMATION

- Submittal of an incomplete application will delay processing.
- If a record is not found, a certified "No record found" letter will be issued.
- Walk-in Service is available between 8:30 A.M. and 3:00 P.M. at the following locations:

Virgin Islands Department of Health
John Moorehead Complex, Hospital Ground
(located directly behind Lionel Roberts Stadium)
St. Thomas, VI Tel#: (340) 774-9000 ext. 4685.

Virgin Islands Department of Health
Charles Harwood Memorial Complex
3500 Estate Richmond, Christiansted
St. Croix, VI Tel#: (340) 773-1311 ext. 3086.

Virgin Islands Department of Health
Morris F. De Castro Clinic
B and C Strand Street, Cruz Bay
St. John, VI Tel#: (340) 776-6400 ext. 6014.

3. International

AFGHANISTAN

Send your requests to:

The Embassy of Afghanistan—Consular Office
2233 Wisconsin Avenue, NW
Suite #216
Washington, DC 20007

Tel. (202) 298-9125
www.embassyofafghanistan.org

The Consulate Services Department (CSD) issues marriage certificates, birth certificates, identification certificates, and verifications of National Identification (Tazkera) documents.

If you are applying by mail, include a prepaid, self-addressed return envelope and use certified or registered U.S. mail, or a Federal Express or UPS shipping envelope.

Cost for Birth and Marriage Certificate	$50.00

دافغانستان لوی سفارت - واشنگتن دی سی  سفارت کبرای افغانستان - واشنگتن دی سی

Embassy of Afghanistan

Washington, D.C.

APPLICATION FOR BIRTH CERTIFICATE

Form EOA-BC

First Name (First, middle & last) لطفاً خپل نوم په پشتو یا دری ولیکی.

Father's Name | Mother's Name

Date of Birth

Place of Birth

Please attach any documents (American or Afghan that bear your name and your date of birth; a copy of your Afghan passport, tazkera, or a copy of an American passport, or alien registration card (green card

Present Address (Street or Rural Route)

(City or Post Office) (State) (Zip Code)

Telephone (Home) (Work)

Embassy of Afghanistan
Consulate Section
2233 Wisconsin Ave., N.W.
Suite 216
Washington, D.C. 20007

Tel: (202) 298-9125
Fax: (202) 298-9126

Signature ______ Date / / /

دافغانستان لوی سفارت - واشنگټن دی سی

سفارت کبرای افغانستان - واشنگتن دی سی

Embassy of Afghanistan

APPLICATION FOR MARRIAGE CERTIFICATE

Form EOA-MC

Groom's Name (First, middle & last)

لطفاً خپل نوم په پشتو یا دری ولیکی.

Father's Name ولد	Mother's Name
Date of Birth	Place of Birth

Bride's Name (First, middle & last)

Father's Name ولد	Mother's Name
Date of Birth	Place of Birth

Marriage Date (Month) (Date) (Year)

Present Address (Street or Rural Route)

(City or Post Office) (State) (Zip Code)

Telephone (Home) (Work)

Embassy of Afghanistan
Consulate Section
2233 Wisconsin Ave., N.W.
Suite 216
Washington, D.C. 20007

Tel: (202) 298-9125
Fax: (202) 298-9126

Signature (Groom) امضا تاریخ Date / / /

Signature (Bride) امضا تاریخ Date / / /

Witness امضا شاهد تاریخ Date / / /

ALBANIA

Send your requests to:

Central State Archives
Rruga "Jordan Misja"
Tirana, Albania

Tel/Fax. (011) (355) 4 4200004
E-mail: dpa@albarchive.gov.al

There was no civil registration until 1929. Existing civil registration is likely kept in local municipality and community offices. Older civil registration records are likely held by the Central State Archives of Albania in Tirana. For current civil registration records, contact the local municipality.

For additional assistance, contact:

The Embassy of Albania
1312 18th Street, NW, 4th Floor
Washington, DC 20036

Tel. (202) 223-4942

ALGERIA

Send your requests to:

Consulate General of Algeria
866 UN Plaza, Suite 580
New York, NY 10017

Tel: (212) 486-6930
E-mail: info@algeria-cgny.org

Vital registration began in Algeria in 1882 and included principally Muslims in the North. By 1905 coverage also included Muslims in the South. Today the registration of vital records is not considered to be comprehensive. Certificates may be obtained from the city hall (Baladia) in the town where the event took place.

The Archives nationals d'outre-mer (the National Archives of the Overseas Territories), which is located in the south of France, has digitized the civil and parish records for all French in Algeria from 1830 to 1904. The records can now be viewed online at www.archivesnationales.culture.gouv.fr/anom/fr/.

ANDORRA

Civil Registry (Registro Civil)
c/ Dr. Vilanova, 11, 4t
AD500 Andorra la Vella

For additional assistance, contact:

Embassy of the Principality of Andorra
Two United Nations Plaza, 27th Floor
New York, NY 10017

Tel. (212) 750-8064
E-mail: contact@andorraun.org

The Embassy can help with any documents for the Civil Registry.

ANGOLA

Send your requests to:

Primeira Conservatória de Luanda
Largo Kinaxixe 3 Ave Lenine
Luanda, Angola

Birth, marriage, and death certificates are issued by the Conservatory of Records (Conservatória dos Registos) where the applicant lived or was registered while in Angola. There are seven Conservatórias in Luanda. Each of the eighteen provinces of Angola also has at least one Conservatória. The oldest and largest Conservatória in Luanda is located at the above address. During the long period of civil war, not all Conservatórias were able to maintain civil records and many records storage areas were destroyed. Thus, not all records are available. Recently, the government established the Integrated Services for Citizen Assistance (SIAC) to centralize government departments, including the Conservatory of Records.

An index of the births and deaths in Angola from 1858 through 1908 is available at www.familysearch.org.

For additional assistance, contact:

Embassy of Angola, Consular Section — Tel. (202) 785-1156
2100-2108 16th Street, NW
Washington, DC 20009

ANTIGUA and BARBUDA

Send your requests to:

Registrar of Births, Marriages, and Deaths — Tel. (268) 462-0609
High Court
High Street
Parliament Drive
St. John's, Antigua, West Indies

Antigua was discovered by Columbus in 1493 and became independent in 1967. The Registrar has records from August 1, 1856. The local churches also have their own records. St. John's birth records stretching back to 1905 have now been compiled into a searchable database.

For additional assistance, contact:

Embassy of Antigua and Barbuda — Tel. (202) 362-5122
3216 New Mexico Avenue, NW
Washington, DC 20016

ARGENTINA

Send your requests to:

Dirección del Registro Civil
Oficina de Inscripciones y Rectificaciones
(City), (Province), Argentina

Civil registration records are kept at the local municipal district civil registration office (Dirección del Registro Civil). Civil authorities began registering births, marriages, and deaths in 1886. For records before 1886, you should consult church records. Provincial and tribunal archives maintain duplicates of vital records sent to them by the municipal districts. You may write to these archives and request searches of the records.

The 1895 and 1869 national censuses for Argentina are available at www.familysearch.org.

For additional assistance, contact:

Embassy of the Argentine Republic — Tel. (202) 238-6400
1600 New Hampshire Avenue, NW
Washington, DC 20009

ARMENIA

Send your requests to:

Civil Status Registration Department
Ministry of Justice
(Town), Armenia

Certificates are issued by the Ministry of Justice's Civic Status Registration Department (also known as ZAGS) having jurisdiction over the locality where the individual resides or lived. There is one exception—in Yerevan, death certificates may be obtained at the Civic Status Registration Department at the "Public Special Service" CJSC (also known as the funeral bureau) of the Municipality of Yerevan, located at 18 Arshakunyats Avenue, Yerevan, Armenia.

For additional assistance, contact:

Embassy of Armenia — Tel. (202) 319-1976
2225 R Street, NW
Washington, DC 20008

AUSTRALIA—AUSTRALIAN CAPITAL TERRITORY

Send your requests to:

Registrar-General's Office
(Location: 255 Canberra Avenue, Fyshwick ACT 2609)
G.P.O. Box 158
Canberra City ACT 2601, Australia

Tel. (011) (61) (2) 6207 3000
www.ors.act.gov.au

The Registrar General holds records from January 1, 1930.

Cost for a certified or commemorative Birth, Death, or Marriage Certificate over the counter	Au$41.00
Cost for a certified or commemorative Certificate by post within Australia	Au$49.00
Cost for a certified or commemorative Certificate by international post	Au$59.00

For additional assistance, contact:

Embassy of Australia
1601 Massachusetts Avenue, NW
Washington, DC 20036

Tel. (202) 797-3000

BIRTHS, DEATHS AND MARRIAGES
OFFICE OF REGULATORY SERVICES
Justice and Community Safety Directorate

APPLICATION FOR CERTIFICATE

Form 208 - APP

Civil Partnerships Act 2008
Births, Deaths and Marriages Registration Act 1997
Births, Deaths and Marriages Registration Regulation 1998

IMPORTANT INFORMATION

This form can be used to apply for a birth, death, marriage, civil partnership, or change of name certificate for events that have occurred and are registered in the Australian Capital Territory only. Single status and parentage searches can also be applied for by using this form. If you are unable to comply with the stated requirements, you will need to contact this office for further assistance.

If you are not applying in person at our office, the certificate will be sent to you by registered person-to-person post. As a result, you will need to produce appropriate identification at the post office in order to collect the certificate. Without that identification, Australia Post will not allow you to collect the certificate.

For applications received through the post, we commit to fulfilling your request for a certificate within three working days of receiving your application providing we have enough information and evidence to establish your entitlement to the certificate. If your application does not meet our proof of identity requirements, we may need you to reapply and provide additional identification and/or more information either by post or by attending our office.

PRIVACY INFORMATION

The *Births, Deaths and Marriages registration Act 1997* authorises the Registrar-General to collect the information required by this form. The Registrar-General prevents any unreasonable intrusion into a person's privacy in accordance with the *Privacy Act 1988* (C'wlth). The Registrar-General may provide identifiable information to law enforcement organisations and authorised organisations that have legal authority to request information under prescribed circumstances. Documents provided as proof of identity may have their authenticity verified through Certificate Validation System (CVS) and the National Document Verification System (DVS). Documents issued by this office may also be verified by external agencies using CVS and/or DVS.

Once a person attains 18 years of age, the person's parents are unable to access the register without the persons consent. Further information and a copy of our access policy can be found on our website: www.ors.act.gov.au.

CONTACT INFORMATION

Send completed forms to the Office of Regulatory Services:	**GPO Box 158, Canberra ACT 2601**
Lodge in person at the Office of Regulatory Services:	**255 Canberra Avenue, Fyshwick ACT 2609**
Office Hours:	**9:00am to 4:30pm Monday to Friday**
General enquiries telephone number:	**(02) 6207 3000**
Website address:	**www.ors.act.gov.au**

INSTRUCTIONS FOR COMPLETION

- If completing this form by hand please use black pen only.
- This office will not accept lodgement of this form if it is not completed in full.
- Any alteration to information provided on this form must be struck through with black pen and substitute information must be clear and all parties must sign in the margin. Do not use white out.

FEES CURRENT TO 30 JUNE 2014

The fee for a standard certificate is $41.00. The commemorative package fee (which includes a standard certificate and a commemorative certificate) is $56.00. If delivered by mail, the certificate will attract a $8.00 registered person-to-person postage fee. If the certificate is to be sent overseas, an $18.00 international express post fee will apply.

Payment can be made by cash, credit card, EFTPOS, money order or cheque. All cheques should be made payable to the Office of Regulatory Services. Applications paid by personal cheque will be held for 7-10 working days for the cheque to clear.

If you require further information or need advice, a language assistance service is available by phoning the Translating and Interpreting Service (TIS) on 13 14 50.

PROOF OF IDENTITY REQUIREMENTS

All photocopies of identification must be certified as true copies of the originals by a Solicitor, Police Officer, or Justice of the Peace. If you are applying for a birth, death, marriage, change of name certificate, civil partnership certificate, single status or parentage search, there are particular identification requirements necessary for you to either apply for own certificate or the certificate of another person.	
☐ Your own certificate	You will require 3 forms of identification as described in table A. (see below)
☐ A certificate for your child who is under 18	You will require 3 forms of identification as described in table A. (see below)
☐ A certificate for your child who is over 18	The Privacy Commissioner has advised that a parent does not have an automatic right of access to their child's birth certificate, once the child has turned 18. As a result, the Registrar-General will only provide access where the child consents in writing. You will require 3 forms of identification as described in table A. (below) for you as the applicant, 3 forms of identification as described in table A. (below) for the child whose behalf you are requesting the certificate, and a letter from the child giving consent that you may apply for the certificate on their behalf.
☐ A certificate for another person	You will require 3 forms of identification as described in table A. (below) for you as the applicant, 3 forms of identification as described in table A. (below) for the person named on the certificate, and a signed letter from the person named on the certificate giving you consent that you may apply for the certificate on their behalf.
☐ A certificate for another person where there is a legal need – solicitor, under power of attorney, welfare group, legal guardian.	You will require 3 forms of identification as described in table A. (see below) for you as the applicant and evidence of your authority to obtain the certificate which may include the following; Registered Power of Attorney, Court Order or Guardianship Order. For further information, please contact the office on (02) 6207 0460.

TABLE A – IDENTIFICATION REQUIRED TO BE PROVIDED UPON APPLICATION

Three forms of current identification must be provided upon application. At least one form must be Primary Proof of identity and at least two forms of Secondary Identity . In cases where a person is unable to provide enough forms of identification please contact this office.

Primary Proof of Identity	**Secondary Proof of Identity**
Photographic Drivers Licence issued in Australia (current or expired up to 2 years	Current Medicare Card
	Current Credit Card or Account Card
Australian Birth Certificate (not a commemorative or an extract)	Current Centrelink or Department of Veteran Affairs Concession Card
Australian or Overseas Passport (current or expired up to 2 years)	ACT Services Access Card issued by ACT Government (Asylum seekers)
Australian Citizenship Certificate or Naturalisation Certificate	Australian-issued Security Guard/Crowd Controller Licence (with photo)
Dept of Immigration and Citizenship travel documentation (valid up to 5 year after issue)	Australian Issued Firearm Licence (with photo)
Dept of Immigration and Citizenship Certificate of Evidence of Resident Status	Current Student Identity Document (with photo)
Australian Proof of Age Card	Current State, Territory or Federal Government employee photo-identity card
Police Officer Photo Identity (ACT only)	

BIRTHS, DEATHS AND MARRIAGES
OFFICE OF REGULATORY SERVICES
Justice and Community Safety Directorate

APPLICATION FOR CERTIFICATE

Form 208 - APP

Civil Partnerships Act 2008
Births, Deaths and Marriages Registration Act 1997
Births, Deaths and Marriages Registration Regulation 1998

Processing Officer (Office use only)		**Application Number** (Office use only)	

DETAILS OF APPLICANT (Person completing form)

Surname	**Given Name(s)**

Current Residential Address

Daytime Contact Number	**E-mail Address**	**Signature of Applicant**
Reason Certificate is Required	**Relationship to Person Named on Certificate**	

POSTAGE DETAILS (All Certificates forwarded by mail attract a $8.00 registered person to person postage fee)

Postal Address (If different from residential address)

BIRTH CERTIFICATE APPLICATION

☐ Standard Birth certificate ☐ Commemorative certificate (unable to be used for legal purposes) ☐ Commemorative Birth package

☐ Canberra ☐ Capital ☐ Bluebell ☐ Year 2000 ☐ Clowns ☐ Blue Bunny ☐ Pink Bunny ☐ Bears ☐ Duck

Surname at Time of Birth	**Given Name(s) at Time of Birth**

Date of Birth	**Place of Birth**
/ /	

Mothers Full Former Name (If any)	**Father/Parents Full Name**

DEATH CERTIFICATE APPLICATION

Surname of Deceased	**Given Name(s)**

Date of Death	**Place of Death in the ACT**
/ /	

Mothers Full Former Name (If any)	**Father/Parents Full Name**

Approved form AF2013-55 approved by Josh Rynehart, Deputy Registrar-General on 01/07/2013 under section 69 of the *Births, Deaths and Marriages Registration Act 1997* (approved forms) This form revokes AF2012-148

☐ **MARRIAGE CERTIFICATE** (commemorative certificate available) ☐ **CIVIL PARTNERSHIP CERTIFICATE**

☐ Standard Marriage certificate ☐ Commemorative Marriage certificate ☐ Commemorative Marriage package

(Commemorative certificates are currently not available for civil partnerships).

Surname of Groom/Partner 1	Given Name(s) of Groom/Partner 1	Date of Birth
		/ /
Surname of Bride/Partner 2	**Given Name(s) of Bride/Partner 2**	**Date of Birth**
		/ /

Date of Marriage/Endorsement	Place of Marriage/Endorsement
/ /	

☐ **CHANGE OF NAME CERTIFICATE** ☐ **PARENTAGE SEARCH CERTIFICATE** ☐ **SINGLE STATUS SEARCH**

Surname at Time of Birth	Given Name(s) at Time of Birth
Current Surname (If different)	**Current Given Name(s)** (If different)

Date of Birth	Place of Birth
/ /	

PAYMENT DETAILS (COMPLETE DETAILS FOR POSTAL APPLICATIONS ONLY)

☐ Visa ☐ Mastercard		Expiry Date	/	Amount	$
Cardholder Name		**Cardholder Signature**			
Card Number					

PLEASE NOTE: Payments may be made by cheque, money order or credit card if lodged by post, or also by cash or EFTPOS if lodged in person. Applications paid by personal cheque will be held for 7-10 working days for the cheque to clear.

AUSTRALIA—NEW SOUTH WALES

Send your requests to:

Registry of Births, Deaths & Marriages
(Location: 35 Regent Street, Chippendale NSW 2008)
G.P.O. Box 30
Sydney, New South Wales 2001, Australia

E-mail: bdm-webmail@agd.nsw.gov.au
www.bdm.nsw.gov.au/

The Registry has birth, marriage, and death records from March 1, 1856. It also has early church records of baptisms, marriages, and burials from 1788 to 1855. Birth records are restricted for 100 years, death records for 30 years, and marriage records for 50 years—they are normally only available to the person named on the certificate, and identification is always required. Older records, referred to as Family History Records, are available to anyone, with no identification required. The Registry provides free access to unrestricted birth, death, and marriage family history indexes. For a fee, you can purchase a full birth, death, or marriage Family History Certificate online.

The Registry does not handle matters relating to divorce. The Family Law Court can assist you with your divorce inquiries; go to www.familycourt.gov.au for more information. For inquiries relating to adoptions, contact the Department of Human Services, Community Services; Adoption Information Unit; 4-6 Cavill Avenue, Locked Bag 4028; Ashfield NSW 2131.

Cost for a certified Birth Certificate	Au$51.00
Cost for a commemorative Birth or Death Certificate package	Au$74.00
Cost for a certified Marriage Certificate	Au$51.00
Cost for a certified Death Certificate	Au$51.00

For additional assistance, contact:

Embassy of Australia
1601 Massachusetts Avenue, NW
Washington, DC 20036

Tel. (202) 797-3000

Application for a Birth Certificate

NSW Registry of Births Deaths & Marriages ABN 30 854 211 521 GPO Box 30 Sydney NSW 2001 Tel: 1300 655 236

☐ **Commemorative Certificate Package** (Includes a standard certificate - specify design e.g. Fauna: 2) ☐ Urgent ☐ Non-urgent

☐ Fauna: (Qty) ______ ☐ Be Blessed (Qty) ______ ☐ Spirit Baby (Qty) ______

☐ Handprint: ☐ Blue (Qty) ______ ☐ Pink (Qty) ______ ☐ Feet: ☐ with parents details (Qty) ______ ☐ no parents details (Qty) ______

☐ **Standard Certificate** (Qty) ________ ☐ Urgent ☐ Non-urgent ☐ International Express Post

Your certificate will be mailed to you if your application was received by post and is charged a postage and handling fee. See separate "Fees for Products and Services" Flyer.

Please PRINT clearly in BLACK pen. Start at the left. Write one letter in each box. Leave one box between words. Please complete all details.

APPLICANT'S DETAILS (details of person completing this form). Please provide copies of 3 forms of current identification with your application.

Family Name

Given Names

Street Address

Suburb State Postcode

Postal Address (if different from street address)

Suburb State Postcode

I certify that I understand the provisions overpage on "Identification, Privacy & Disclosure" and that the information I have provided is true and correct.

Signature of Applicant

Your Relationship to the Person Registered (e.g. self, daughter)

Reason Certificate is Required (e.g. passport, school)

Daytime Phone Number ( )

Email

DETAILS OF BIRTH REQUIRED

Family Name at Birth

Given Names

Date of Birth* / /

Present Age

* If Date Unknown, Period to be Searched - From To

(Note, each extra 10 year search or part thereof incurs a cost)

Place of Birth (Town/City)

State

Father's Full Name

Mother's Full Name (Before Marriage)

PAYMENT DETAILS (complete this section for mail applications only). For schedule of fees, see Fees for Product and Services flyer.

Enclosed is a Cheque*/ Money Order for $.

OR Please Debit my: AMEX ☐ MasterCard ☐ Visa ☐ $.

Card Number

Name of Cardholder

Expiry Date /

Signature of Cardholder

Cheques payable to the 'NSW Registry of Births Deaths & Marriages'

*Personal/company cheques are not accepted for urgent applications.

NSW GOVERNMENT | Registry of Births Deaths & Marriages | Attorney General & Justice

OFFICE USE ONLY Identification Date Issued

07/13

Certificate entitlement

This application form can only be used if the birth occurred in NSW.

If you are the person to be named on the certificate, or a parent of the person to be named on the certificate, the birth certificate can be issued to you.

If you DO meet the above criteria, you must provide:

1 Three (3) copies of your own identification (see below).

If you DO NOT meet the above criteria, you must provide:

1 A letter giving permission from the person named on the certificate or their parent. Please include their address, daytime telephone number and signature.
2 Three (3) copies of identification from the person giving permission (see below).
3 Three (3) copies of your own identification (see below).

Identification

Please provide at least three (3) forms of identification, one of each from Categories 1, 2 and 3. If you are unable to provide identification from Categories 1 and 2, you must still provide at least three (3) forms of identification. At least two (2) of these must be from Category 3.

All documents except foreign passports must be current.

Category 1	Category 3
If born in Australia: An Australian Birth Certificate **Record of immigration status:** Citizenship Certificate New Zealand Citizenship Certificate together with passport New Zealand Birth Certificate	• Medicare Card • Credit or Debit Card • Centrelink or Department of Veterans Affairs Card • Security Guard/Crowd Control Licence • Tertiary Education Institution ID Card
Category 2	**Category 4**
Australian Driver's Licence Australian Passport Firearms Licence Foreign Passport Proof of Age Card	• Recent utility account with current residential address

Disclosure of Information

When you complete this application form, understand that you have consented to the release of information provided, to those agencies who may be able to validate the information in support of your application. More information: www.bdm.nsw.gov.au

Privacy

To protect your privacy, the Registry requires proof of your identity. In line with the *NSW Births, Deaths and Marriages Registration Act 1995* and the *Privacy and Personal Information Protection Act 1998*, the Registry collects information to determine your eligibility to obtain a certificate and to prevent fraud. Information may be used for statistical purposes and by law enforcement agencies, and other uses by law. For more information on privacy please visit our website.

Commemorative certificates

Capture the joy and excitement of a new birth or celebrate a birth from many years ago with a special Commemorative Birth Certificate.

With each order for a Commemorative Birth Certificate package, you will receive a Standard Birth Certificate that you can use for official purposes. Commemorative Birth Certificates do not contain security features and organisations may not accept them as a proof of identity document. See separate 'Fees for Products and Services' flyer.

Fauna

Be Blessed

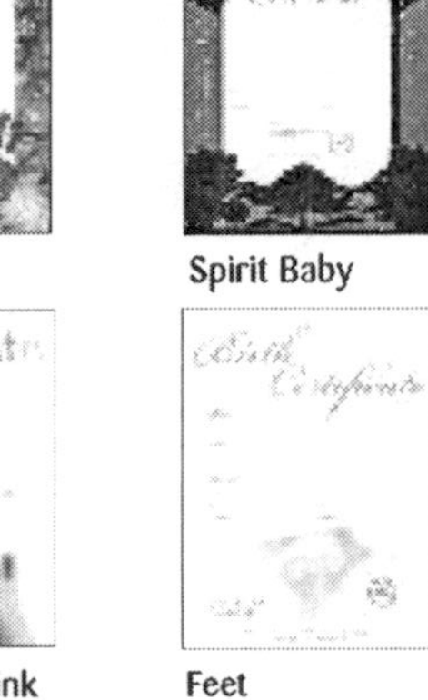

Spirit Baby

Handprint Blue

Handprint Pink

Feet

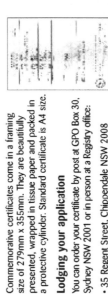

Commemorative certificates come in a framing size of 279mm x 355mm. They are beautifully presented, wrapped in tissue paper and packed in a protective cylinder. Standard certificate is A4 size.

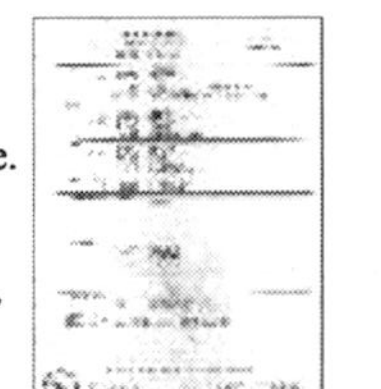

Standard Certificate

Lodging your application

You can order your certificate by post at GPO Box 30, Sydney NSW 2001 or in person at a Registry office:

- 35 Regent Street, Chippendale NSW 2008
- 95 Tudor Street, Hamilton NSW 2303
- 2/74 Kembla Street, Wollongong NSW 2500
- 160 Marsden Street, Parramatta NSW 2150

Office hours are Monday to Friday – 8.00am to 4.30pm

Tel: 1300 655 236 TTY: 9354 1371

www.bdm.nsw.gov.au

Application for a Birth Certificate

Registry of Births
Deaths & Marriages
Attorney General & Justice

Application for a Marriage Certificate

NSW Registry of Births Deaths & Marriages ABN 30 854 211 521 GPO Box 30 Sydney NSW 2001 Tel: 1300 655 236

☐ **Commemorative Certificate Package** (Includes a standard certificate. Specify design e.g Diamond Rings: 2) ☐ Urgent ☐ Non-urgent

☐ Cut the Cake (Qty) ____ ☐ Diamond Rings (Qty) ____ ☐ Holding hands: (Qty) ____

☐ Marriage Rings (Qty) ____ ☐ Rose (Qty) ____ ☐ Waratah (Qty) ____

☐ **Standard Certificate** (Qty) ____ ☐ Urgent ☐ Non-urgent ☐ International Express Post

Your certificate will be mailed to you if your application was received by post and is charged a postage and handling fee. See separate "Fees for Products and Services" Flyer.

Please PRINT clearly in BLACK pen. Start at the left. Write one letter in each box. Leave one box between words. Please complete all details.

APPLICANT'S DETAILS (details of person completing this form). Please provide copies of 3 forms of current identification with your application.

Family Name

Given Names

Street Address

Suburb State Postcode

Postal Address (if different from street address)

Suburb State Postcode

I certify that I understand the provisions overpage on "Identification, Privacy & Disclosure" and that the information I have provided is true and correct.

Your Relationship to the Person Registered (e.g. self)

Reason Certificate is Required (e.g. passport)

Signature of Applicant

Daytime Phone Number ( )

Email

DETAILS OF MARRIAGE REQUIRED

Family Name of Groom

Given Names

Family Name of Bride (Before Marriage)

Given Names

Date of Marriage* / /

* If Date Unknown, Period to be Searched – From To

(Note, each extra 10 year search or part thereof incurs a cost)

Place of Marriage (Town/City)

State

PAYMENT DETAILS (complete this section for mail applications only). For schedule of fees, see Fees for Product and Services flyer.

Enclosed is a Cheque*/ Money Order for $.

OR Please Debit my: AMEX ☐ MasterCard ☐ Visa ☐ $.

Card Number

Name of Cardholder

Expiry Date /

Signature of Cardholder

Cheques payable to the 'NSW Registry of Births Deaths & Marriages'

*Personal/company cheques are not accepted for urgent applications.

NSW GOVERNMENT | Registry of Births Deaths & Marriages | Attorney General & Justice

OFFICE USE ONLY Identification Date Issued

03/13

Certificate entitlement

This application can only be used if the marriage occurred in NSW.

If you are the bride or groom, your marriage certificate can be issued to you. If you are a child of the bride or groom, the certificate can be issued to you if the bride and groom are deceased. If you are not a child of the bride or groom, but need to establish your legal right or entitlement, e.g. under a Will, your application will be considered.

If you DO meet the above criteria, you must provide:

1. Three (3) copies of your own identification (see below).

If you DO NOT meet the above criteria, you must provide:

1. A letter giving permission from the person named on the certificate or if deceased, their next of kin. Please include their address, daytime telephone number and signature.
2. Three (3) copies of identification from the person giving permission or their next of kin (see below).
3. Three (3) copies of your own identification (see below).

Identification

Please provide at least three (3) forms of identification, one of each from Categories 1, 2 and 3. If you are unable to provide identification from Categories 1 and 2, you must still provide at least three (3) forms of identification. At least two (2) of these must be from Category 3.

All documents except foreign passports must be current.

Category 1	Category 3
If born in Australia: - An Australian Birth Certificate **Record of immigration status:** - Citizenship Certificate - New Zealand Citizenship Certificate together with passport - New Zealand Birth Certificate	• Medicare Card • Credit or Debit Card • Centrelink or Department of Veterans Affairs Card • Security Guard/Crowd Control Licence • Tertiary Education Institution ID Card
Category 2	**Category 4**
• Australian Driver's Licence • Australian Passport • Firearms Licence • Foreign Passport • Proof of Age Card	• Recent utility account with current residential address

Disclosure of Information

When you complete this application form, understand that you have consented to the release of information provided, to those agencies who may be able to validate the information in support of your application. More information: www.bdm.nsw.gov.au

Privacy

To protect your privacy, the Registry requires proof of your identity. In line with the *NSW Births, Deaths and Marriages Registration Act 1995* and the *Privacy and Personal Information Protection Act 1998*, the Registry collects information to determine your eligibility to obtain a certificate and to prevent fraud. Information may be used for statistical purposes and by law enforcement agencies, and other uses by law. For more information on privacy please visit our website.

Commemorative certificates

Capture the joy and excitement of a new marriage or celebrate a marriage from many years ago with a special Commemorative Marriage Certificate.

With each order for a Commemorative Marriage Certificate package, you will receive a Standard Marriage Certificate. Commemorative Marriage Certificates do not contain security features and organisations may not accept them as a proof of identity document. See separate 'Fees for Products and Services' flyer.

Cut the Cake

Diamond Rings

Holding Hands

Marriage Rings

Rose

Waratah

Commemorative certificates come in a framing size of 210mm x 297mm (A4). They are beautifully presented, wrapped in tissue paper and packed in a protective cylinder.

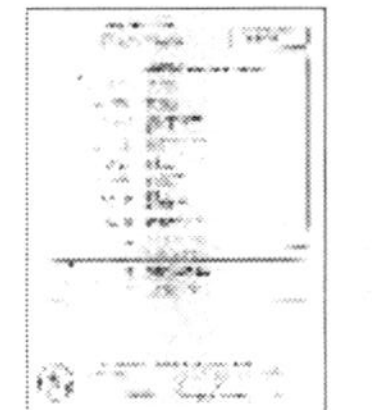

Standard

Lodging your application

You can order your certificate by post at GPO Box 30, Sydney NSW 2001 or in person at a Registry office:

- 35 Regent Street, Chippendale NSW 2008
- 95 Tudor Street, Hamilton NSW 2303
- 2/74 Kembla Street, Wollongong NSW 2500
- 160 Marsden Street, Parramatta NSW 2150

Office hours are Monday to Friday – 8.00am to 4.30pm

Tel: 1300 655 236   TTY: 9354 1371

www.bdm.nsw.gov.au

Application for a Marriage Certificate

NSW GOVERNMENT | Registry of Births Deaths & Marriages
Attorney General & Justice

Application for a Death Certificate

NSW Registry of Births Deaths & Marriages ABN 30 854 211 521 GPO Box 30 Sydney NSW 2001 Tel: 1300 655 236

☐ **Standard Certificate** (Qty) ____ ☐ Urgent ☐ Non-urgent

If your application was received by post, your certificate will be mailed to you: ☐ Secure Post ☐ International Express Post ☐ To be Collected

Please PRINT clearly in BLACK pen. Start at the left. Write one letter in each box. Leave one box between words. Please complete all details.

APPLICANT'S DETAILS (details of person completing this form). Please provide copies of 3 forms of current identification with your application.

Family Name

Given Names

Street Address

Suburb State Postcode

Postal Address (if different from street address)

Suburb State Postcode

I certify that I understand the provisions overpage on "Identification, Privacy & Disclosure" and that the information I have provided is true and correct.

Your Relationship to Deceased (e.g. son, mother, executor)

Reason Certificate is Required (e.g. probate, executor)

Signature of Applicant

Daytime Phone Number ( )

Email

DETAILS OF DEATH REQUIRED

Family Name of Deceased

Given Names

Date of Death* / / Age at Death Registration Number (if known) /

* If Date Unknown, Period to be Searched – From To (Note, each extra 10 year search or part thereof incurs a cost)

Place of Death (Town/City) State

Name of Spouse

Father's Full Name

Mother's Full Name (Before Marriage)

PAYMENT DETAILS (complete this section for mail applications only). For schedule of fees, see Fees for Product and Services flyer.

Enclosed is a Cheque*/ Money Order for $. OR Please Debit my: AMEX ☐ MasterCard ☐ Visa ☐ $.

Card Number

Name of Cardholder Expiry Date /

Signature of Cardholder

Cheques payable to the 'NSW Registry of Births Deaths & Marriages'
*Personal/company cheques are not accepted for urgent applications.

NSW Government | Registry of Births Deaths & Marriages | Attorney General & Justice

OFFICE USE ONLY Identification Date Issued

03/13

Certificate entitlement

This application form can only be used if the death occurred in NSW.

If you are a next of kin named on the death certificate, i.e. spouse (married/defacto/same sex defacto), parent or child of the deceased, the death certificate can be issued to you. If you are a relative not listed on the certificate, the certificate can be issued to you if the deceased had no living spouse, children or parents.

If you DO meet the above criteria, you must provide:

1. Three (3) copies of your own identification (see below).

If you DO NOT meet the above criteria, you must provide:

1. A letter giving permission from the next of kin. Please include their address, daytime telephone number and signature.
2. Three (3) copies of identification from the next of kin (see below).
3. Three (3) copies of your own identification (see below).

Identification

Please provide at least three (3) forms of identification, one of each from Categories 1, 2 and 3. If you are unable to provide identification from Categories 1 and 2, you must still provide at least three (3) forms of identification. At least two (2) of these must be from Category 3.

All documents except foreign passports must be current.

Category 1	Category 3
If born in Australia: • An Australian Birth Certificate **Record of immigration status:** • Citizenship Certificate • New Zealand Citizenship Certificate together with passport • New Zealand Birth Certificate	• Medicare Card • Credit or Debit Card • Centrelink or Department of Veterans Affairs Card • Security Guard/Crowd Control Licence • Tertiary Education Institution ID Card

Category 2	Category 4
• Australian Driver's Licence • Australian Passport • Firearms Licence • Foreign Passport • Proof of Age Card	• Recent utility account with current residential address

Privacy

To protect your privacy, the Registry requires proof of your identity. In line with the *NSW Births, Deaths and Marriages Registration Act 1995* and the *Privacy and Personal Information Protection Act 1998*, the Registry collects information to determine your eligibility to obtain a certificate and to prevent fraud. Information may be used for statistical purposes and by law enforcement agencies, and other uses by law. For more information on privacy please visit our website.

Disclosure of Information

When you complete this application form, understand that you have consented to the release of information provided by you, to those agencies who may be able to validate that information in support of your application.

This information may be provided to agencies including (but not limited to) other Registries of Births, Deaths & Marriages, Law Enforcement agencies, Department of Foreign Affairs and Trade (DFaT), Department of Immigration and Citizenship (DIAC), and motor vehicle or driver licencing authorities. Usually these referrals will be to simply verify the documents or other evidence that you have provided us in making your application for a certificate. If there are discrepancies, we may require you to correct any errors with the issuing agency, before being able to process your application. It is extremely important that all your identity documents are accurate and reflect your correct identity information.

Documents provided as proof of identity may have their authenticity verified through the online Certificate Validation Service (CertValid) and the National Document Verification Service (DVS). Documents issued by this office may also be verified by other organisations using CertValid and/or DVS.

Lodging your application

You can order your certificate by post at
GPO Box 30, Sydney NSW 2001 or in person at a Registry office:

- 35 Regent Street, Chippendale NSW 2008
- 95 Tudor Street, Hamilton NSW 2303
- 2/74 Kembla Street, Wollongong NSW 2500
- 160 Marsden Street, Parramatta NSW 2150

Office hours are Monday to Friday – 8.00am to 4.30pm

Tel: 1300 655 236 TTY: 9354 1371

www.bdm.nsw.gov.au

Application for a Death Certificate

NSW Government | Registry of Births Deaths & Marriages | Attorney General & Justice

AUSTRALIA—NORTHERN TERRITORY

Send your requests to:

Registry of Births, Deaths & Marriages
G.P.O. Box 3021
Darwin, Northern Territory 0801, Australia

Tel. (011) (61) (8) 8999-6119
E-mail: RegistrarGeneral.DOJ@nt.gov.au
www.nt.gov.au/justice/bdm/

The Registry has birth records from August 24, 1870, marriage records from 1871, and death records from 1872. Certificates can also be ordered online using the link on the website. In addition to the office in Darwin, there is also one in Alice Springs (P.O. Box 8043, Alice Springs, NT 0871). For divorces, contact the Family Law Court (NT), G.P.O. Box 9991, Darwin NT 0801.

Cost for a certified Birth Certificate	Au$41.00
Cost for a certified Marriage Certificate	Au$41.00
Cost for a certified Death Certificate	Au$41.00

For additional assistance, contact:

Embassy of Australia
1601 Massachusetts Avenue, NW
Washington, DC 20036

Tel. (202) 797-3000

DEPARTMENT OF
THE ATTORNEY-GENERAL AND JUSTICE www.nt.gov.au

NORTHERN TERRITORY OFFICE OF THE REGISTRAR OF BIRTHS, DEATHS AND MARRIAGES

APPLICATION FOR BIRTH, DEATH OR MARRIAGE CERTIFICATE

Certificate Required to be: Certified Copy ▼ ☐ Extract ▼ ☐ *(specify if more than one)*
(gives details of child, mother, father etc) *(gives only child's name, date and place of birth)*

APPLICANT DETAILS (Please use BLOCK LETTERS) **$41.00 PER CERTIFICATE – POSTAGE SEE BELOW**

Name of Person filling in form / Applicants Name	SIGN HERE (Person filling in form) Date / /	
Postal Address	Postcode	Daytime telephone No.
Reason document is required	Relationship of Person filling form to person named in certificate (eg. self; mother; father; authorised agent)	
Certificate is to be: COLLECTED ☐	POSTED $12.30 ☐	LAMINATING SERVICE $3.30 ☐

PLEASE COMPLETE IF YOU REQUIRE A BIRTH CERTIFICATE (Identification must accompany all applications- see over)

SURNAME	
GIVEN NAMES	
DATE OF BIRTH	
PLACE OF BIRTH	STATE:
MOTHER'S GIVEN NAMES	
MOTHER'S MAIDEN SURNAME	
FATHER'S GIVEN NAMES	
FATHER'S SURNAME	

PLEASE COMPLETE IF YOU REQUIRE A DEATH CERTIFICATE –INDICATE IF YOU REQUIRE THE CAUSE OF DEATH ☐

SURNAME OF DECEASED	
GIVEN NAMES OF DECEASED	
DATE OF DEATH	
PLACE OF DEATH	STATE:

PLEASE COMPLETE IF YOU REQUIRE A MARRIAGE CERTIFICATE

SURNAME OF GROOM	
GIVEN NAMES OF GROOM	
MAIDEN SURNAME OF BRIDE	
GIVEN NAMES OF BRIDE	
DATE OF MARRIAGE	
PLACE OF MARRIAGE	STATE:

OFFICE USE ONLY
REG NO
REG NO
REG NO
APPLICATION NO

DATE RECEIVED
RECEIVER (SIGNATURE)
ID:

Visa ◯ MasterCard ◯ Cheque / Money Order ◯

Card No _ _ _ _ _ _ _ _ _ _ _ _ _ _ _ _ Expiry Date _____ / _____

Card Holder Name (print) ____________ Signature ____________ Amount $ ______

*American Express / Bank Card **NOT ACCEPTED***

The Registrar
Births, Deaths & Marriages
GPO Box 3021, Darwin NT 0801
Ph: (08) 8999 6119
Fx: (08) 8999 6324

Nichols Place
cnr Cavenagh & Bennett St
Darwin NT 0800
Palmerston Community Care Centre
Palmerston Health Precinct on Gurd Street
Fridays 8.00am to 12.00pm

The Registrar
Births, Deaths & Marriages
PO Box 8043
Alice Springs NT 0871
Ph: (08) 8951 5339
Fx: (08) 8951 5340

Centre Point Building
Gregory Terrace
Alice Springs NT 0870

DEPARTMENT OF
THE ATTORNEY-GENERAL AND JUSTICE www.nt.gov.au

I.D. NOTICE FOR NORTHERN TERRITORY

It is now a requirement that all applications are supported by sufficient means of identification, therefore every person applying for either a birth, death, marriage or change of name certificate must produce I.D.

Evidence confirming identity may be in the following form:

Primary Source Acceptable By Themselves

* Current Drivers Licence
* Defence Force ID
* NT Ochre Card
* Current Passport
* Police Service ID
* Evidence of age cards

Secondary Source Can Be Any TWO Of The Following

* Medicare Card
* Overseas Passport
* Citizenship / Immigration papers
* Student Photo ID
* Interstate Driver's Licence
* NT Security ID
* ID Letter from Aboriginal Community
* Larrakia Nation ID Card
* Taxation Assessment Notice
* Pensioner Card / Health Care Card
* Credit Card / Key Card / Passbook
* Bank Statement
* Phone Bill / Electricity Bill / Rates
* Student ID Card or Letter of Enrolment
* Expired Driver's Licence - Last 2 Years
* Other evidence deemed by the Deputy Registrar to be sufficient

Please note that access to Births, Deaths & Marriages records may be denied if a person is unable to or refuses to produce some sort of I.D.

PLEASE NOTE: If posting or faxing an application, the identification must be certified as a true copy by a Justice of the Peace, Commissioner for Oaths or other qualified person.

AUTHORISED AGENT

If you wish someone else to apply for a certificate on your behalf you will need to give them written authority to do so.

Identification will be required from **both you as applicant, and your authorised agent.**

I, ______________________________
(Insert full name of person giving authority)

Of ______________________________
(Insert address of person giving authority)

Hereby authorise ______________________________
(Insert name of person who you are allowing to apply for the certificate)

To apply for a ______________________ **certificate**
(birth / death / marriage / change of name / no record)

For my ______________________________
(Insert your relationship to the person named on the certificate - e.g. self / son / daughter / parent)

Signed: ______________________ **Dated:** ____________
(signature of person giving authority)

AUSTRALIA—QUEENSLAND

Send your requests to:

Registry of Births, Deaths and Marriages
(Location: 110 George Street, Brisbane)
P.O. Box 15188
City East, Queensland 4002, Australia

Tel. (011) (61) (7) 3404 3343
E-mail: bdm-mail@justice.qld.gov.au
www.justice.qld.gov.au/

The Queensland Registry of Births, Deaths and Marriages (BDM) holds records of births, deaths, and marriages in Queensland since 1829. Birth records are restricted for 100 years, marriage records for 75 years, and death records for 30 years. You can search Queensland's historical births, deaths, and marriages indexes online (www.justice.qld.gov.au/829.htm) and can buy historical life event certificates without providing proof of identity.

There's also an index to Queensland divorces online at http:// www.archives.qld.gov.au/Researchers/Indexes/Courts/Pages/Divorces.aspx.

For information about Adoption, contact the Queensland Department of Communities, Child Safety and Disability Services (www.communities.qld.gov.au/childsafety/adoption/past-adoptions/).

Cost for a certified Birth Certificate	Au$40.50
Cost for a commemorative Certificate	Au$54.00
Cost for a certified Marriage Certificate	Au$40.50
Cost for a certified Death Certificate	Au$40.50
Cost for a Historical Certificate	Au$28.00
Cost for an Online Historical Image	Au$20.00

For additional assistance, contact:

Embassy of Australia
1601 Massachusetts Avenue, NW
Washington, DC 20036

Tel. (202) 797-3000

Office use only	
Court/QGAP:	Date:
Court/QGAP Receipt No.:	
Payment Amount:	
BDM POS Receipt No.:	
BDM CORRES Receipt No.:	

(Version 7)

Birth certificate/extract application

Effective as of 1 June 2010

Births, Deaths and Marriages Registration Act 2003
Surrogacy Act 2010

Proof of identity is required with submission of this form. Please print clearly and do not use correction fluid.

1. Priority (Only available if birth is already registered)

Priority service	☐ (attracts additional fee–visit www.justice.qld.gov.au/bdm to view fees)

2. Type of record (*To view fees and commemorative designs visit www.justice.qld.gov.au/bdm)

Certified copy or	☐ (indicate quantity) ______		
*Commemorative package (additional fee) includes certified copy	☐ (indicate quantity) ______	Specify design	

3. Applicant's details (*To determine applicant eligibility visit www.justice.qld.gov.au/bdm for certificate access policy)

Your relationship to the person named on the certificate (tick option)	☐ Yourself ☐ Parent ☐ *Other (please specify) ______		
Reason certificate is required			
First names		Signature of applicant	
Surname			
Current residential address (street, suburb, state and country)		Postcode	
Telephone number		Mobile number	
Date of application	DD / MM / YYYY	Email	

The personal information on this form is collected by the Registry of Births, Deaths and Marriages for the purpose of providing services and undertaking related activities. Only authorised persons will have access to this information. Your details will not be disclosed to a third party without your consent unless the disclosure is authorised by law.

4. Postal details (Non standard mail services will incur additional fees—visit www.justice.qld.gov.au/bdm to view fees)

First names Mr/Mrs/Dr/Ms/Miss		Surname	
Postal address (include country only if not Australia)		Postcode	

5. Birth details

First names		Surname	
Date of birth	DD / MM / YYYY	Present age	
If date unknown, period to be searched (search fees may apply)	from DD / MM / YYYY	to	DD / MM / YYYY
Place of birth (must be born or adopted in Queensland)			
Father's/parent's name			
Mother's/parent's name and maiden name			

6. Payment details (*Your credit card will be charged according to current fees and your selections above)

a) I have enclosed a **cheque** or **money order** payable to the Registry of Births, Deaths and Marriages for			$
b) Debit my **credit card***	$	☐ MasterCard ☐ Visa	Expiry date MM / YY
Card number	____ / ____ / ____ / ____		
Name on card		Signature of cardholder	

JAG 12/4395

www.justice.qld.gov.au

7. Submission options

Post to	Registry of Births, Deaths and Marriages, PO Box 15188, City East Queensland 4002
Lodge at	110 George Street, Brisbane or your local Queensland Magistrates Court or Queensland Government Agent Program (QGAP).

Proof of identity requirements

Before a certificate, information or source document is released, an applicant's entitlement to the document must be established and proof of identity produced in accordance with the Certificate Access Policy, Part 4 Proof of Identity Principles.

Applicants are required to provide:

- One form of identification from each list (at least one containing a signature); or
- If unable to provide identification from List 1, two forms of identification from List 2 and one form of identification from List 3 must be provided (at least one containing a signature).

Table 1: Proof of identity document

List 1	List 2	List 3
☐ Current Australian photo driver's licence, front and back	☐ Current Medicare card	☐ Recent utility account (gas, electricity, home phone, etc) with current residential address
☐ Current Australian passport	☐ Current financial institution debit or credit card with your signature and full name or passbook	☐ Recent financial Institution statement with current residential address
☐ Current overseas passport	☐ Current entitlement card issued by the Commonwealth or State Government	☐ Rent/lease agreement with current residential address
☐ Current Australian Firearms licence	☐ Educational institution student identity document (must include photo and/or signature) or statement of enrolment	☐ Rates notice with current residential address
☐ Current Defence Force or Police Service photo ID card	☐ School or other educational report, less than twelve months old	☐ A renewal notice for vehicle registration showing current residential address, or a renewal notice for driver licence showing current residential address
☐ Adult Proof of Age Card.	☐ Current document of identity issued by the Passport Office	☐ Recent official correspondence from Government Service Providers (not from this agency) with current residential address.
	☐ Naturalisation, citizenship or immigration papers issued by the Department of Immigration and Multicultural and Indigenous Affairs	
	☐ Full birth certificate	
	☐ Security guard/crowd control licence.	

Proof of Identity documents are to be in the English language otherwise these must be translated by an accredited translator. The official translation document is to accompany the certified copy of original documents.

The Registrar-General's discretion in deciding acceptable proof of identity documents is not exhausted by the above lists. Decisions may be made by the Registrar-General on any unusual case that may fall outside the requirements of the above table.

As part of establishing Proof of Identity, copies of documents submitted to the Registry in support of an application must be certified as a true and correct copy by a qualified witness.

The following persons are considered to be qualified witnesses and are able to certify photocopies of documents as being "a correct copy of the document":

- **Justice of the Peace**
- **Commissioner for Declarations**
- **Barrister/Solicitor**
- **Notary Public**

Where applications are received at the Brisbane Registry, Magistrates Courts or Queensland Government Agent Program (QGAP) Offices, client service officers are able to sight original proof of identity documents submitted in support of an application.

Privacy statement

All items marked with an asterisk (*) are for statistical, administrative and community planning purposes and will not appear in the Registers.

The collection of information on this form is authorised by the *Births, Deaths and Marriages Registration Act 2003*. It is used for the purposes of the Act which include registering births in Queensland and issuing birth certificates.

The information on this form may be provided to law enforcement agencies and to government and non-government agencies for verification of data. Access to this information or to a certificate may be granted to any person who has adequate reason to obtain it, or who meets the requirements of the access policy. To obtain details about the access policy and rights of access to this information contact the registry on 1300 366 430. For general information about the registry visit **www.justice.qld.gov.au**

Office use only	
Court/QGAP:	Date:
Court/QGAP Receipt No.:	
Payment Amount:	
BDM POS Receipt No.:	
BDM CORRES Receipt No.:	

(Version 7)

Marriage certificate/extract application

Effective as of 1 June 2010

Births, Deaths and Marriages Registration Act 2003

Proof of identity is required with submission of this form. Please print clearly and **do not** use correction fluid.

1. Priority (Only available if marriage is already registered)

Priority service	☐ (attracts additional fee–visit www.justice.qld.gov.au/bdm to view fees)

2. Type of record (*To view fees and commemorative designs visit www.justice.qld.gov.au/bdm)

Certified copy or	☐ (indicate quantity) ______		
Short extract and/or	☐		
*Commemorative package (additional fee) includes certified copy	☐ (indicate quantity) ______	Specify design	

3. Applicant's details (*To determine applicant eligibility visit www.justice.qld.gov.au/bdm for certificate access policy)

Your relationship to the person named on the certificate (tick option)	☐ Husband/Wife ☐ *Other (please specify) ______		
Reason certificate is required			
First names		Signature of applicant	
Surname			
Current residential address (street, suburb, state and country)		Postcode	
Telephone number		Mobile number	
Date of application	DD / MM / YYYY	Email	

The personal information on this form is collected by the Registry of Births, Deaths and Marriages for the purpose of providing services and undertaking related activities. Only authorised persons will have access to this information. Your details will not be disclosed to a third party without your consent unless the disclosure is authorised by law.

4. Postal details (Non standard mail services will incur additional fees – visit www.justice.qld.gov.au/bdm to view fees)

First names Mr/Mrs/Dr/Ms/Miss		Surname	
Postal address (include country only if not Australia)		Postcode	

5. Marriage details

Groom's first names			Groom's surname	
Bride's first names			Bride's maiden name	
Date of marriage If date unknown, period to be searched (search fees may apply)	DD / MM / YYYY			
	from	DD / MM / YYYY	to	DD / MM / YYYY
Place of marriage (must be registered in Queensland)				

6. Payment details (*Your credit card will be charged according to current fees and your selections above)

a) I have enclosed a **cheque** or **money order** payable to the Registry of Births, Deaths and Marriages for				$
b) Debit my credit card*	$	☐ MasterCard ☐ Visa	Expiry date	/
Card number	____ / ____ / ____ / ____			
Name on card		Signature of cardholder		

Queensland Government

7. Submission options

Post to	Registry of Births, Deaths and Marriages, PO Box 15188, City East Queensland 4002
Lodge at	110 George Street, Brisbane or your local Queensland Magistrates Court or Queensland Government Agent Program (QGAP).

Proof of identity requirements

Before a certificate, information or source document is released, an applicant's entitlement to the document must be established and proof of identity produced in accordance with the Certificate Access Policy, Part 4 Proof of Identity Principles.

Applicants are required to provide:

- One form of identification from each list (at least one containing a signature); or
- If unable to provide identification from List 1, two forms of identification from List 2 and one form of identification from List 3 must be provided (at least one containing a signature).

Table 1: Proof of identity document

List 1	List 2	List 3
☐ Current Australian photo driver's licence	☐ Current Medicare card	☐ Recent utility account (gas, electricity, home phone, etc) with current residential address
☐ Current Australian passport	☐ Current financial institution debit or credit card with your signature and full name or passbook	☐ Recent financial Institution statement with current residential address
☐ Current overseas passport	☐ Current entitlement card issued by the Commonwealth or State Government	☐ Rent/lease agreement with current residential address
☐ Current Australian Firearms licence	☐ Educational institution student identity document (must include photo and/or signature) or statement of enrolment	☐ Rates notice with current residential address
☐ Current Defence Force or Police Service photo ID card	☐ School or other educational report, less than twelve months old	☐ A renewal notice for vehicle registration or driver licence for coming period with current residential address
☐ Over 18's ID card.	☐ Current document of identity issued by the Passport Office	☐ Recent official correspondence from Government Service Providers (not from this agency).
	☐ Naturalisation, citizenship or immigration papers issued by the Department of Immigration and Multicultural and Indigenous Affairs	
	☐ Full birth certificate	
	☐ Security guard/crowd control licence	

Proof of Identity documents are to be in the English language otherwise these must be translated by an accredited translator. The official translation document is to accompany the certified copy of original documents.

The Registrar-General's discretion in deciding acceptable proof of identity documents is not exhausted by the above lists. Decisions may be made by the Registrar-General on any unusual case that may fall outside the requirements of the above table.

As part of establishing Proof of Identity, copies of documents submitted to the Registry in support of an application must be certified as a true and correct copy by a qualified witness.

The following persons are considered to be qualified witnesses and are able to certify photocopies of documents as being "a correct copy of the document":

- **Justice of the Peace**
- **Commissioner for Declarations**
- **Barrister/Solicitor**
- **Notary Public**

Where applications are received at the Brisbane Registry, Magistrates Courts or Queensland Government Agent Program (QGAP) Offices, client service officers are able to sight original proof of identity documents submitted in support of an application.

Privacy statement

All items marked with an asterisk (*) are for statistical, administrative and community planning purposes and will not appear in the Registers.

The collection of information on this form is authorised by the *Births, Deaths and Marriages Registration Act 2003*. It is used for the purposes of the Act which include registering births in Queensland and issuing birth certificates.

The information on this form may be provided to law enforcement agencies and to government and non-government agencies for verification of data. Access to this information or to a certificate may be granted to any person who has adequate reason to obtain it, or who meets the requirements of the access policy. To obtain details about the access policy and rights of access to this information contact the registry on **1300 366 430**. For general information about the registry visit **www.justice.qld.gov.au**.

Office use only	
Court/QGAP:	Date:
Court/QGAP Receipt No.:	
Payment Amount:	
BDM POS Receipt No.:	
BDM CORRES Receipt No.:	

(Version 8)

Death certificate/extract application

Effective as of 1 June 2010

Births, Deaths and Marriages Registration Act 2003
Surrogacy Act 2010

Proof of identity is required with submission of this form. Please print clearly and do not use correction fluid.

1. Priority (Only available if death is already registered)

Priority service	☐ (attracts additional fee–visit www.justice.qld.gov.au/bdm to view fees)

2. Type of record (To view fees visit www.justice.qld.gov.au/bdm)

Certified copy or	☐ (indicate quantity) ______
Short extract	☐

3. Applicant's details (*To determine applicant eligibility visit www.justice.qld.gov.au/bdm for certificate access policy)

Your relationship to the person named on the certificate (tick option)	☐ Parent ☐ Son/Daughter ☐ Husband/Wife ☐ *Other (please specify)		
Reason certificate is required			
First names		Signature of applicant	
Surname			
Current residential address (street, suburb, state and country)		Postcode	
Telephone number		Mobile number	
Date of application	/ /	Email	

The personal information on this form is collected by the Registry of Births, Deaths and Marriages for the purpose of providing services and undertaking related activities. Only authorised persons will have access to this information. Your details will not be disclosed to a third party without your consent unless the disclosure is authorised by law.

4. Postal details (Non standard mail services will incur additional fees – visit www.justice.qld.gov.au/bdm to view fees)

First names Mr/Mrs/Dr/Ms/Miss		Surname	
Postal address (include country only if not Australia)		Postcode	

5. Deceased person's details

Surname (at time of death)		First names	
Date of death If date unknown, period to be searched (search fees may apply)	/ / from / /	to / /	
Place of death (must be registered in Queensland)			
Father's/parent's name			
Mother's/parent's name and maiden name			

6. Payment details (*Your credit card will be charged according to current fees and your selections above)

a) I have enclosed a **cheque** or **money order** payable to the Registry of Births, Deaths and Marriages for			$
b) Debit my **credit card***	$	☐ MasterCard ☐ Visa	Expiry date /
Card number	____ / ____ / ____ / ____		
Name on card		Signature of cardholder	

7. Submission options

Post to	Registry of Births, Deaths and Marriages, PO Box 15188, City East Queensland 4002
Lodge at	110 George Street, Brisbane or your local Queensland Magistrates Court or Queensland Government Agent Program (QGAP).

Proof of identity requirements

Before a certificate, information or source document is released, an applicant's entitlement to the document must be established and proof of identity produced in accordance with the Certificate Access Policy, Part 4 Proof of Identity Principles.

Applicants are required to provide:

- One form of identification from each list (at least one containing a signature); or
- If unable to provide identification from List 1, two forms of identification from List 2 and one form of identification from List 3 must be provided (at least one containing a signature).

Table 1: Proof of identity document

List 1	List 2	List 3
☐ Current Australian photo driver's licence	☐ Current Medicare card	☐ Recent utility account (gas, electricity, home phone, etc) with current residential address
☐ Current Australian passport	☐ Current financial institution debit or credit card with your signature and full name or passbook	☐ Recent financial Institution statement with current residential address
☐ Current overseas passport	☐ Current entitlement card issued by the Commonwealth or State Government	☐ Rent/lease agreement with current residential address
☐ Current Australian Firearms licence	☐ Educational institution student identity document (must include photo and/or signature) or statement of enrolment	☐ Rates notice with current residential address
☐ Current Defence Force or Police Service photo ID card	☐ School or other educational report, less than twelve months old	☐ A renewal notice for vehicle registration or driver licence for coming period with current residential address
☐ Over 18's ID card.	☐ Current document of identity issued by the Passport Office	☐ Recent official correspondence from Government Service Providers (not from this agency).
	☐ Naturalisation, citizenship or immigration papers issued by the Department of Immigration and Multicultural and Indigenous Affairs	
	☐ Full birth certificate	
	☐ Security guard/crowd control licence.	

Proof of Identity documents are to be in the English language otherwise these must be translated by an accredited translator. The official translation document is to accompany the certified copy of original documents.

The Registrar-General's discretion in deciding acceptable proof of identity documents is not exhausted by the above lists. Decisions may be made by the Registrar-General on any unusual case that may fall outside the requirements of the above table.

As part of establishing Proof of Identity, copies of documents submitted to the Registry in support of an application must be certified as a true and correct copy by a qualified witness.

The following persons are considered to be qualified witnesses and are able to certify photocopies of documents as being "a correct copy of the document":

- **Justice of the Peace**
- **Commissioner for Declarations**
- **Barrister/Solicitor**
- **Notary Public**

Where applications are received at the Brisbane Registry, Magistrates Courts or Queensland Government Agent Program (QGAP) Offices, client service officers are able to sight original proof of identity documents submitted in support of an application.

Privacy statement

All items marked with an asterisk (*) are for statistical, administrative and community planning purposes and will not appear in the Registers.

The collection of information on this form is authorised by the *Births, Deaths and Marriages Registration Act 2003*. It is used for the purposes of the Act which include registering births in Queensland and issuing birth certificates.

The information on this form may be provided to law enforcement agencies and to government and non-government agencies for verification of data. Access to this information or to a certificate may be granted to any person who has adequate reason to obtain it, or who meets the requirements of the access policy. To obtain details about the access policy and rights of access to this information contact the registry on 1300 366 430. For general information about the registry visit **www.justice.qld.gov.au.**

AUSTRALIA—SOUTH AUSTRALIA

Send your requests to:

Births, Deaths & Marriages Registration Office
Consumer and Business Services
(Location: Chesser House 91-97
Grenfell Street, Adelaide, SA 5000)
G.P.O. Box 1351
Adelaide, South Australia 5001, Australia

Tel. (011) (61) (8) 131 882
E-mail: applications.bdm@agd.sa.gov.au
www.ocba.sa.gov.au/bdm/

Birth records are restricted for 75 years, death records for 25 years, and marriage records for 60 years. The Registrar has records from July 1, 1842. You can also apply for certificates online using a credit card at www.cbs.sa.gov.au/bdm/applyonline.html.

Cost for a certified Birth Certificate	Au$44.75
Cost for a commemorative Birth or Marriage Certificate	Au$63.00
Cost for a certified Marriage Certificate	Au$44.75
Cost for a certified Death Certificate	Au$44.75

For Adoption Record information write to:

Adoption and Family Information Service
G.P.O. Box 292
Adelaide, South Australia 5001

E-mail: adoptions@dfc.sa.gov.au
www.families.sa.gov.au/pages/adoption/

Adoption records and original birth certificates are open upon request.

For additional assistance, contact:

Embassy of Australia
1601 Massachusetts Avenue, NW
Washington, DC 20036

Tel. (202) 797-3000

Who Can Apply

Birth Certificates

Are only available to the registered person, parents, children, non-parental legal custodians/guardians (documentary evidence required) or their current marital spouse.

Existing Change of Name/Deed Poll Certificates

Are only available to the registered person or their parents/legal custodians/guardians (documentary evidence required) if the child is less than 18 years. To register a Change of Name, please contact the Births, Deaths and Marriages registration office.

Death Certificates

Are only available to the current spouse, parents, children and non-parental legal custodians/guardians (documentary evidence required).

Marriage Certificates

Are only available to the registered persons or children of the marriage.

Family History

If a birth registration is over 75 years, a death registration over 25 years, or a marriage registration over 60 years, any person may apply.

Persons other than those mentioned above may apply for a certificate if they have written authorisation from an eligible party and upon production of identification from that person as well as themselves.

Fees

Current fees are on our website at www.cbs.sa.gov.au, displayed at the Post Office or can be obtained from Births, Deaths and Marriages.

The fee covers a search of a ten-year period (or part thereof). Please provide as much information as possible with your application, as incorrect or insufficient information may result in a 'No Record' finding, with a further fee payable to search again with added details.

How to Apply

This form may be used to apply for interstate certificates, however please note that fees and identification requirements are different for each State/Territory.

Contact information for interstate Registries can be obtained from our website www.cbs.sa.gov.au, Births, Deaths and Marriages, Service SA or the Post Office.

You may apply for a certificate:

Online at
www.cbs.sa.gov.au
Payment only by credit card.

By Post
By completing this form and sending it with a copy of your identification and a cheque or money order (payable to Births, Deaths and Marriages) or your credit card details to the: **Births, Deaths and Marriages Registration Office, GPO Box 1351, Adelaide SA 5001.**

Phone 131 882

Paying in Person
Payment can be made in person at:

Consumer and Business Services
Consumer Services Centre
91 Grenfell Street
Adelaide SA 5000

Service SA customer service centres in:

Berri	Naracoorte
Gawler	Port Augusta
Kadina	Port Lincoln
Mount Gambier	Port Pirie
Murray Bridge	Whyalla

www.cbs.sa.gov.au

Consumer and Business Services

Application Form

Birth, Death, Marriage or Change of Name Certificate

Application for an existing certificate
Births, Deaths and Marriages Registration Office
South Australia

Your Checklist

Check the following to avoid delays:

- ☐ **Can you apply?** – you as an **applicant** should read 'who can apply' to determine if you can obtain a certificate of the **registered** person
- ☐ **Applicant's details** – complete in full
- ☐ **Current ID** – ensure you provide correct type of ID
- ☐ **Fees** – ensure payment details are completed correctly and in full

Government of South Australia
Attorney-General's Department

Applicant's Identification
For South Australian applications, attach a copy of the following to your application:

ONE of the following (showing photo and current name, address and signature):
- Current Australian Driver's licence
- Proof of age card.

OR TWO of the following (one must show current name and address and one must show signature):
- Passport
- Current Australian Firearms licence
- Centrelink or health care card
- Pension/seniors card
- Credit/direct debit **OR** bank statement
- Department of Veterans' Affairs card
- Business and Occupational Services licence
- Defence force/Police service ID card
- Electricity/gas/other utilities account
- Telephone/mobile account.

Please contact the Births, Deaths and Marriages Registration Office for additional identification examples if you have none of the above.
Please DO NOT send originals of documents of identification.

Service and Delivery

☐ **Normal service** (processed within 5 working days)
☐ **Priority service** ***Priority available for registered events only***
(priority fee payable – processed within 1/2 hour if lodged at BDM counter, 91-97 Grenfell St, or express posted within 1 day for all other applications

☐ I will **collect** the certificate available only at BDM (91-97 Grenfell St, Adelaide)
☐ Please **post** certificate

Applicant's Details

Surname | **Given Names**
Residential Address | Postcode
Postal Address | Postcode
Reason for Certificate (e.g. passport) | **Signature**
Relationship to Registered Person (e.g. self, mother) | **Telephone Number**

If you knowingly make a false or misleading representation on this application form, you may be guilty of an offence under section 51 of the *Births, Deaths and Marriages Registration Act 1996.*

☐ Birth Certificate or an ☐ Existing Change of Name Certificate (not available at Service SA) QTY.

Surname at Birth | **Surname at Present**
Given Names | **Place of Birth** (town) | State
Date of Birth / / If date unknown, 10 year period search: (from) / / (to) / / **Present Age**
Father's/Co-parent's Full Name | **Mother's Full Name** (at birth)

☐ Death Certificate QTY.

Surname | **Given Names**
Date of Death / / If date unknown, 10 year period search: (from) / / (to) / / **Age at Death**
Place of Death (town) | State | **Funeral Director's Name** (if death within 6 months)

☐ Marriage Certificate QTY.

Groom's Surname | **Given Names**
Bride's Surname (Before Marriage) | **Given Names**
Date of Marriage / / If date unknown, 10 year period to search: (from) / / (to) / /
Place of Marriage (town) | State

Payment Details
Enclosed is a cheque/money order payable to Births, Deaths and Marriages Registration Office, for amount **$** **OR**

Name of Cardholder | **Please Debit**
Signature of Cardholder
From My ☐ Visa ☐ MasterCard ☐ Other________ **Expiry Date** ☐☐/☐☐
Card Number ☐☐☐☐ ☐☐☐☐ ☐☐☐☐ ☐☐☐☐ **CVV Number** ☐☐☐☐

Application and Order form for Birth Certificate (for South Australian births only)

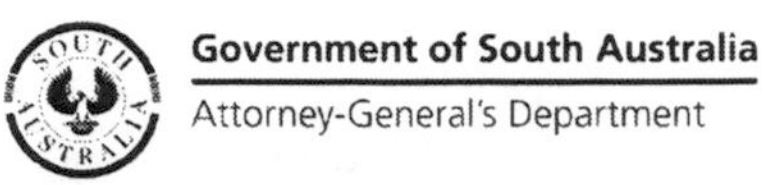

Applicant's details

Full name (mother/father/self)

Daytime contact phone number

Residential address

Postcode

Postal address

Postcode

Relationship to child

Signature

Applicant's identification (for South Australian applications) Please DO NOT send original identification documents

If this application form is **NOT** accompanied by the Birth Registration Statement, attach a copy of the following:

ONE of the following (showing photo and current name, address and signature):

- Current Australian driver's licence
- Proof of age card

OR

TWO of the following (one must show current name and address and one must show signature):

- Passport
- Current Australian Firearms licence
- Centrelink or health care card
- Pension/seniors card
- Credit/direct debit card **OR** bank statement
- Department of Veterans' Affairs card
- Business and Occupational Services licence
- Defence force/police service ID card
- Electricity/gas/other utilities account
- Telephone/mobile account

Please contact the Births, Deaths and Marriages Registration Office for additional identification examples if you have none of the above.

Order details

Birth certificates are not issued automatically or free of charge.
You may order a Standard Certificate (only) OR
Choose from designs over the page (see reverse side)

Standard Certificate $43.50
OR
Commemorative Certificate $61.00
(including standard certificate)

For (child's name)	Code (see over)	Date of birth	Qty	Price $	Amount
		/ /			$
					$
					$
					$
				Total $	$

Please complete payment details below and post your order to **Consumer and Business Services, Births, Deaths and Marriages, GPO Box 1351, Adelaide SA 5001.**

For further information please telephone 131 882 or visit our website at **www.cbs.sa.gov.au**

Payment details

I enclose a cheque/money order, payable to Births, Deaths and Marriages Registration Office, for **Amount** $ OR

Name of cardholder

Amount
$

Signature

Date
/ /

Debit my ☐ Mastercard ☐ Visa ☐ Other (please specify) __________

Card number

Expiry date /

CVV

Commemorative Certificate(s)
You can order a Standard Certificate (below)

OR

You can order a Commemorative Certificate package
(which includes a standard certificate)

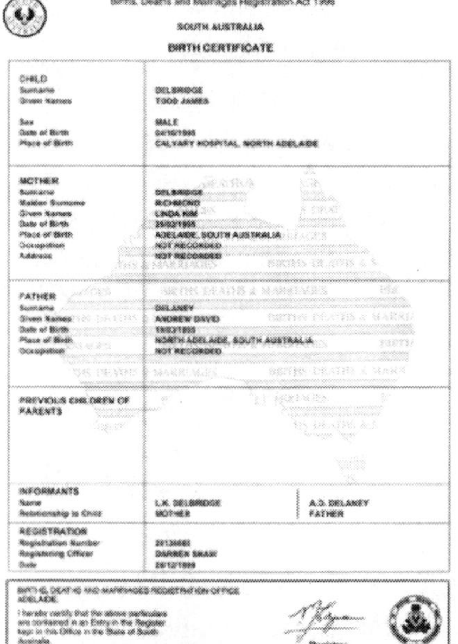

Births, Deaths and Marriages Registration Act 1996

SOUTH AUSTRALIA

BIRTH CERTIFICATE

CHILD Surname Given Names Sex Date of Birth Place of Birth	 DELBRIDGE TODD JAMES MALE 04/10/1995 CALVARY HOSPITAL, NORTH ADELAIDE
MOTHER Surname Maiden Surname Given Names Date of Birth Place of Birth Occupation Address	 DELBRIDGE RICHMOND LINDA KIM 25/02/1955 ADELAIDE, SOUTH AUSTRALIA NOT RECORDED NOT RECORDED
FATHER Surname Given Names Date of Birth Place of Birth Occupation	 DELANEY ANDREW DAVID 19/03/1955 NORTH ADELAIDE, SOUTH AUSTRALIA NOT RECORDED
PREVIOUS CHILDREN OF PARENTS	
INFORMANTS Name Relationship to Child	 L.K. DELBRIDGE A.D. DELANEY MOTHER FATHER
REGISTRATION Registration Number Registering Officer Date	 20134660 DARREN SHAW 28/12/1999

BIRTHS, DEATHS AND MARRIAGES REGISTRATION OFFICE
ADELAIDE

I hereby certify that the above particulars are contained in an Entry in the Register kept in this Office in the State of South Australia.
Given under my hand and seal this 21st day of FEBRUARY, 2000

Registrar

Code **Standard**

Code **Pandas**

Code **Teddy Bears**

Code **Duck**

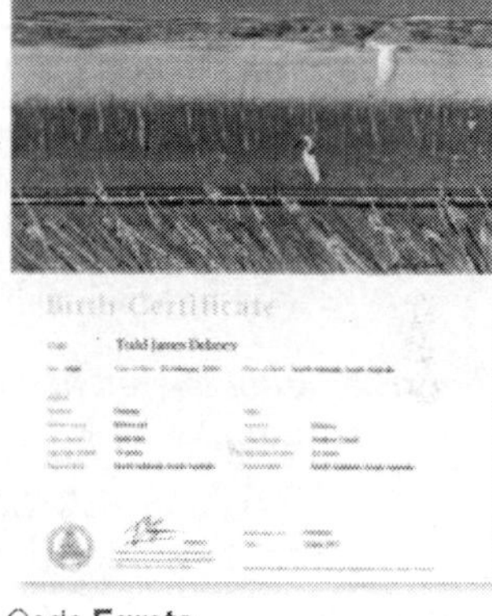

Code **Egrets**

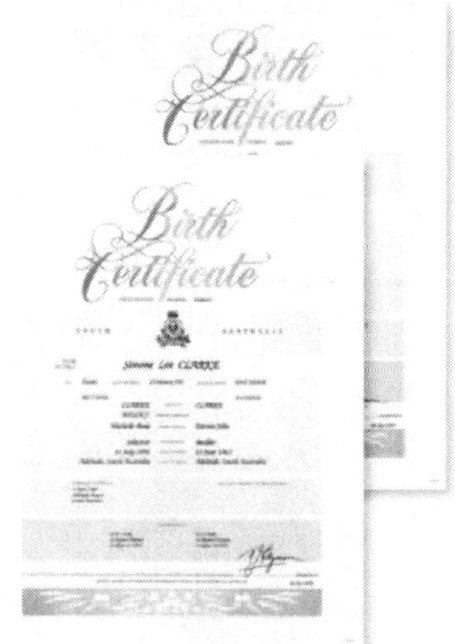

Code **Australian Pink** **Australian Blue**

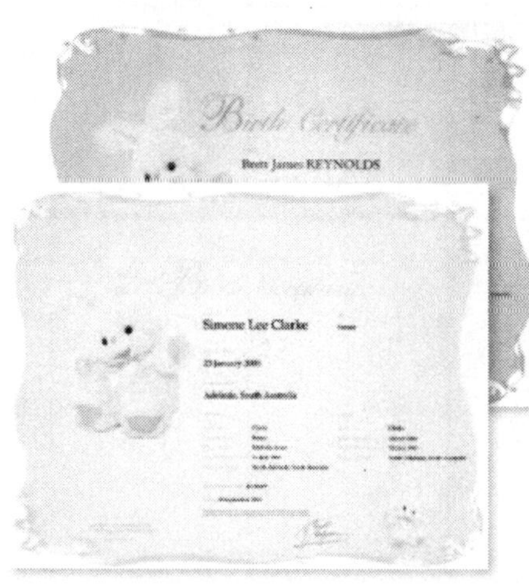

Code **Bunny Pink** Code **Bunny Blue**

Code **Wings**

Code **Fauna**

Code **Birds**

Code **Flowers**

AUSTRALIA—TASMANIA

Send your requests to:

Registry of Births, Deaths and Marriages
G.P.O. Box 198
Hobart, Tasmania 7001, Australia

Tel. (011) (61) (3) 6233 3793
E-mail: BDM@justice.tas.gov.au
www.justice.tas.gov.au/bdm/

The Registry has church records from 1803 to 1839 and birth, death, and marriage registrations from 1839 to date. Birth records are restricted for 100 years, marriage records for 75 years, and death records for 25 years. Two types of certificates are offered—a standard certificate and an extract, which contains name, sex, and date and place of the event but is not suitable for most identification purposes. Decorative birth certificates are also available. In addition, an extended search is available for an extra fee.

Cost for a certified Birth Certificate	Au$45.26
Cost for a decorative Birth Certificate Package	Au$70.08
Cost for a certified Marriage Certificate	Au$45.26
Cost for a certified Death Certificate	Au$45.26
Cost for Birth, Death, and Marriage Extracts	Au$45.26

For Adoption Record information write to:

Adoption and Permanency Services
Department of Health and Human Services
G.P.O. 538
Hobart, Tasmania 7001, Australia

E-mail: adoption.service@dhhs.tas.gov.au
www.justice.tas.gov.au/bdm/adoptions

For additional assistance contact:

Embassy of Australia
1601 Massachusetts Avenue, NW
Washington, DC 20036

Tel. (202) 797-3000

Births Deaths and Marriages
Phone (03) 6233 3793
Email BDM@justice.tas.gov.au
Web www.justice.tas.gov.au/BDM

Application for Search
Birth Tasmania

STARS Product Code BSC / BSE / BSP
EPOST - Express Post
RPOST - Registered Post
OFFICE USE ONLY

Receipt no ______________

Folio no ______________

CERTIFICATE DETAILS

Certificate Types - Please refer to the **BDM website** for information on the types of certificate and the associated fees.

Extended Search - An extended search is mainly used for family history applications, when the specific date of an event is not known. If you opt for an extended search you will need to specify the years to be searched. If the search is for more than a 5 year period, extended fees apply - refer **Extended Search fees**.

Please select the type of certificate you are applying for:

☐ Standard Certificate ☐ Extract (not suitable for ID purposes) ☐ Decorative

☐ Extended Search ☐ Decorative and Standard

Please select the type of Decorative Certficate. ______

DETAILS OF BIRTH

If you were born outside of Tasmania you will need to apply in the State or Territory where you were born.

Surname at Birth ______

Given Name/s ______

Place of Birth in Tasmania: *(City or Town)* ______

Date of Birth ______ Current age ______

If you do not know the above details please enter the years to be searched: From ______ To ______

This office searches a five year period for the standard fee. For searches of six years or more, extended fees are payable. Click here to check the current fees.

DETAILS OF PARENTS

Please select if you are providing details of natural parents or adopted parents. ☐ Natural ☐ Adopted

Father's Name ______

Mother's Name ______

Mother's Maiden Name ______

PURPOSE FOR WHICH CERTIFICATE IS REQUIRED

______

APPLICANT DETAILS

Applicant Name ______

Relationship to person registered ______

If you are not the registered person Births, Deaths and Marriages may contact you requesting further evidence of relationship documentation.

Contact Name ______

Postal Address ______

Suburb ______ State ______ Pcode ______

Country [ ] Email [ ]

Work [ ] Home [ ] Mobile [ ]

Signature ______________ Date signed [ ]

Your certificate will be sent by standard mail. If you wish to pay for postage please indicate below:

- [ ] Registered Post
- [ ] Express Post

APPLICANT'S IDENTIFICATION

Please note that any document you provide must not be expired. It must also be issued in the name you are currently using.

Select any ONE of the following:

- [ ] Australian Photo Driver Licence
- [ ] Australian Passport
- [ ] Document of identity issued by Passport Office
- [ ] Defence Force or Police Service Photo ID card

OR Select any TWO of the following:

- [ ] Overseas Passport, with current entry permit
- [ ] School or educational report, less than 12 mths old
- [ ] Medicare card
- [ ] Credit card, account card, passbook account statement
- [ ] Naturalisation/citizenship/immigration papers by the Department of Immigration
- [ ] Student identity card or statement of enrolment
- [ ] Entitlement card issued by the Commonwealth Government

Other forms of identification may be accepted at the discretion of Births, Deaths and Marriages or Service Tasmania staff.

PAYMENT DETAILS

Please include with your application a cheque or money order made payable to Births, Deaths and Marriages. Alternatively, please complete the credit card authorisation below.

- [ ] **Priority - If you require the certificate as a priority please tick here. Additional fees will apply.**

Credit Card Type [ ] Visa [ ] Mastercard

Card Number [ ] Expiry date [ ] / [ ]

Cardholder Name [ ] Amount ($): [ ]

Signature ______________ Date signed [ ]

HOW TO APPLY FOR A BIRTH SEARCH

You must complete all relevant parts of this form and **lodge with the required identification.**

By Post:
Send the form with your cheque, money order or credit card details to:
Births, Deaths and Marriages,
GPO Box 198, Hobart, Tasmania, 7001.
Overseas applicants must pay by credit card or bank draft in Australian dollars.

In Person:
You may apply and pay for your certificate at any Service Tasmania shop. Click here for a list of Service Tasmania shops.

Enquiries
For processing times and details about who can apply for a certificate please see our website - www.justice.tas.gov.au/BDM or email BDM@justice.tas.gov.au.

PERSONAL INFORMATION PROTECTION STATEMENT

In line with the *Personal Information Protection Act* 2004, the Registry of Births, Deaths and Marriages is collecting this information so that it can determine your eligibility to obtain the requested certificate and to prevent fraud. If you do not provide all of the information requested, particularly that relating to the reason the document is required and your relationship to the registered person, then you may not be provided with a copy of the certificate. Your personal information may be disclosed to law enforcement agencies, courts and other organisations authorised to collect it.

Births Deaths and Marriages
Phone (03) 6233 3793
Email BDM@justice.tas.gov.au
Web www.justice.tas.gov.au/BDM

Application for Search
Marriage - Tasmania

STARS Product Code MSC / MSP
EPOST - Express Post
RPOST - Registered Post

OFFICE USE ONLY

Receipt no ______________

Folio no ______________

CERTIFICATE DETAILS

Please refer to the BDM website - www.justice.tas.gov.au/BDM for information on the types of certificate and the associated fees.

An extended search is mainly used for family history applications, when the specific date of an event is not known. If you opt for an extended search you will need to specify the years to be searched. If the search is for more than a 5 year period, extended fees apply - refer Extended Search fees.

Please select the type of certificate you are applying for:

- ☐ Standard Certificate
- ☐ Extract (not suitable for ID purposes)
- ☐ Extended Search

BRIDEGROOM DETAILS

Surname

Given Name(s) Date of Birth

BRIDE DETAILS *(Name prior to marriage)*

Surname

Given Name(s) Date of Birth

DETAILS OF MARRIAGE

Place of Marriage in Tasmania *(city or town)*

Date of Marriage

If you do not know the above details please enter the years to be searched:

From: To:

This office searches a five year period for the standard fee. For searches of six years or more, extended fees are payable. Click here to check the current fees.

PURPOSE FOR WHICH CERTIFICATE IS REQUIRED

APPLICANT DETAILS

Applicant Name

Relationship to person registered

If you are not the registered person Births, Deaths and Marriages may contact you requesting further evidence of relationship documentation.

Postal Address

Suburb State Pcode

Country

Email

Work [ ] Home [ ] Mobile [ ]

Signature ______________________ Date signed [ ]

Your certificate will be sent by standard mail. If you wish to pay for postage please indicate below:

☐ Registered Post ☐ Express Post

APPLICANT'S IDENTIFICATION

Please note that any document you provide must not be expired. It must also be issued in the name you are currently using.

Select any ONE of the following:

- ☐ Australian Photo Driver Licence
- ☐ Australian Passport
- ☐ Document of identity issued by Passport Office
- ☐ Defence Force or Police Service Photo ID card

OR Select any TWO of the following:

- ☐ Overseas Passport, with current entry permit
- ☐ School or educational report, less than 12 mths old
- ☐ Medicare card
- ☐ Credit card, account card, passbook account statement
- ☐ Naturalisation/citizenship/immigration papers by the Department of Immigration
- ☐ Student identity card or statement of enrolment
- ☐ Entitlement card issued by the Commonwealth Government

Other forms of identification may be accepted at the discretion of Births, Deaths and Marriages or Service Tasmania staff.

PAYMENT DETAILS

Please include with your application a cheque or money order made payable to Births, Deaths and Marriages. Alternatively, please complete the credit card authorisation below.

☐ **Priority - If you require the certificate as a priority please tick here. Additional fees will apply.**

Credit Card Type ☐ Visa ☐ Mastercard

Card Number [ ] Expiry date [ ] / [ ]

Cardholder Name [ ] Amount ($): [ ]

Signature ______________________ Date signed [ ]

HOW TO APPLY FOR A MARRIAGE SEARCH

You must complete all relevant parts of this form and **lodge with the required identification.**

By Post:
Send the form with your cheque, money order or credit card details to:
Births, Deaths and Marriages,
GPO Box 198, Hobart, Tasmania, 7001.
Overseas applicants must pay by credit card or bank draft in Australian dollars.

In Person:
You may apply and pay for your certificate at any Service Tasmania shop. Click here for a list of Service Tasmania shops.

Enquiries
For processing times and details about who can apply for a certificate please see our website or email Births, Deaths and Marriages.

PERSONAL INFORMATION PROTECTION STATEMENT

In line with the *Personal Information Protection Act* 2004, the Registry of Births, Deaths and Marriages is collecting this information so that it can determine your eligibility to obtain the requested certificate and to prevent fraud. If you do not provide all of the information requested, particularly that relating to the reason the document is required and your relationship to the registered person, then you may not be provided with a copy of the certificate. Your personal information may be disclosed to law enforcement agencies, courts and other organisations authorised to collect it.

Births Deaths and Marriages
Phone (03) 6233 3793
Email BDM@justice.tas.gov.au
Web www.justice.tas.gov.au/BDM

Application for Search

Death - Tasmania

STARS Product Code DSC / DSP
EPOST - Express Post
RPOST - Registered Post

OFFICE USE ONLY

Receipt no ______

Folio no ______

CERTIFICATE DETAILS

Please refer to the BDM website for information on the types of certificate and the associated fees.

An extended search is mainly used for family history applications, when the specific date of an event is not known. If you opt for an extended search you will need to specify the years to be searched. If the search is for more than a 5 year period, extended fees apply - refer Extended Search fees.

Please select the type of certificate you are applying for:

☐ Standard Certificate

☐ Extract (not suitable for ID purposes)

☐ Extended Search

DETAILS OF DECEASED

Surname at Death ______

Given Name/s ______

Place of Death in Tasmania ______

Date of Death ______ Date of Birth ______

If you do not know the above details please enter the years to be searched:

From ______ To ______

This office searches a five year period for the standard fee. For searches of six years or more, extended fees are payable. Click here to check the current fees.

Other identifying information *(eg Occupation)* ______

Name of spouse *(if married)* ______

Name of parents *(if single)* ______

PURPOSE FOR WHICH CERTIFICATE IS REQUIRED

______

APPLICANT DETAILS

Applicant Name ______

Relationship to person registered ______

Births, Deaths and Marriages may contact you requesting further evidence of relationship documentation.

Postal Address ______

Suburb ______ State ______ Pcode ______

Country ______

Email ______

Work ______ Home ______ Mobile ______

Signature ______ Date signed ______

Your certificate will be sent by standard mail. If you wish to pay for postage please indicate below:

☐ Registered Post ☐ Express Post

APPLICANT'S IDENTIFICATION

Please note that any document you provide must not be expired. It must also be issued in the name you are currently using.

Select any ONE of the following:

☐ Australian Photo Driver Licence

☐ Australian Passport

☐ Document of identity issued by Passport Office

☐ Defence Force or Police Service Photo ID card

OR Select any TWO of the following:

☐ Overseas Passport, with current entry permit

☐ School or educational report, less than 12 mths old

☐ Medicare card

☐ Credit card, account card, passbook account statement

☐ Naturalisation/citizenship/immigration papers by the Department of Immigration

☐ Student identity card or statement of enrolment

☐ Entitlement card issued by the Commonwealth Government

Other forms of identification may be accepted at the discretion of Births, Deaths and Marriages or Service Tasmania staff.

PAYMENT DETAILS

Please include with your application a cheque or money order made payable to Births, Deaths and Marriages. Alternatively, please complete the credit card authorisation below.

☐ **Priority - If you require the certificate as a priority please tick here. Additional fees will apply.**

Credit Card Type ☐ Visa ☐ Mastercard

Card Number ☐☐☐☐ ☐☐☐☐ ☐☐☐☐ ☐☐☐☐ Expiry date ☐☐ / ☐☐

Cardholder Name ______________________ Amount ($): ________

Signature ______________________ Date signed ________

HOW TO APPLY FOR A DEATH SEARCH

You must complete all relevant parts of this form and **lodge with the required identification.**

By Post:

Send the form with your cheque, money order or credit card details to:
Births, Deaths and Marriages,
GPO Box 198, Hobart, Tasmania, 7001.
Overseas applicants must pay by credit card or bank draft in Australian dollars.

In Person:

You may apply and pay for your certificate at any Service Tasmania shop. Click here for a list of Service Tasmania shops.

Enquiries

For processing times and details about who can apply for a certificate please see our website - www.justice.tas.gov.au/bdm or email BDM@justice.tas.gov.au.

PERSONAL INFORMATION PROTECTION STATEMENT

In line with the *Personal Information Protection Act* 2004, the Registry of Births, Deaths and Marriages is collecting this information so that it can determine your eligibility to obtain the requested certificate and to prevent fraud. If you do not provide all of the information requested, particularly that relating to the reason the document is required and your relationship to the registered person, then you may not be provided with a copy of the certificate. Your personal information may be disclosed to law enforcement agencies, courts and other organisations authorised to collect it.

AUSTRALIA—VICTORIA

Send your certificate applications to:

Victorian Registry of Births, Deaths & Marriages
(Location: 595 Collins Street, Melbourne)
G.P.O. Box 5220
Melbourne, Victoria 3001, Australia

Tel. (011) (61) (3) 9613 5111
www.bdm.vic.gov.au/

Send general mail and all other applications to:

Births, Deaths & Marriages
G.P.O. Box 4332
Melbourne, Victoria 3001, Australia

The Registry holds records of births from 1837, deaths from 1836, marriages from 1837, and changes of name from 1904. Birth records are restricted for 100 years, marriages for 60 years, and deaths for 10 years. Online indexes to births, deaths, and marriages going back to 1853, as well as church baptism, marriage, and burial records dating back to 1836, are searchable online at https://online.justice.vic.gov.au/bdm/home#search. From that website, you can order a certificate or purchase and download an image to your computer.

Cost for a certified Birth Certificate	Au$29.20
Cost for a commemorative Birth Certificate	Au$49.50
Cost for a certified Marriage Certificate	Au$29.20
Cost for a certified Death Certificate	Au$29.20

For Adoption Record information, write to:

Family Information Network and Discovery
Level 20
570 Bourke Street
Melbourne, VIC 3000

Tel: (011) (61) (3) 8608 5700; local call: 1300 769 926
www.bdm.vic.gov.au/home/births/adoptions/

For additional assistance, contact:

Embassy of Australia
1601 Massachusetts Avenue, NW
Washington, DC 20036

Tel. (202) 797-3000

Victorian Registry of Births, Deaths and Marriages
Births, Deaths and Marriages Registration Act 1996

Application for a Victorian Birth Certificate

Instructions. Please use **blue** or **black** ink and **BLOCK** letters.

Office use only

$

CC	MO	CQ	NF	EX	RM
C	NC	IP	NP	DP	FH

PART ONE – Your details

1. Which certificate do you require?

- ☐ Standard Birth Certificate
- ☐ Replacement Change of Name Certificate
- ☐ Historical Certificate
- ☐ Abridged Birth Certificate
- ☐ Uncertified (historical) image
- ☐ Deed Poll Certificate

2. Surname (family name)

3. Given name(s)

4. Residential address
a) Street no. and name

b) Suburb/Town

c) State

d) Postcode

5. Postal address (if different to above)
a) Street no. and name

b) Suburb/Town

c) State

d) Postcode

6. Daytime telephone number

7. Email address

8. Whose certificate are you applying for?

☐ My own ☐ Someone else's – please specify
(e.g. husband, daughter, son)

9. Reason certificate is required
(e.g. passport, driver licence, school enrolment)

PART TWO – Details of person on certificate

10. Surname (family name at birth)

11. Given name(s)

Birth details

12. Date of birth DD/MM/YYYY

Or if unsure, please estimate date of birth

From DD/MM/YYYY To DD/MM/YYYY

13. Place of birth
a) Suburb/Town

b) State

c) Postcode

14. Registration number (if known)

Parent's details

15. Mother's maiden name (surname at birth)

16. Mother's given name(s)

17. Father's/Parent's surname (family name)

18. Father's/Parent's given name(s)

PART THREE – Proof of identity

Note

- You must provide proof of your identity if the birth or change of name occurred within the last 100 years or the person is still living.
- If applying for a historical certificate or uncertified historical image (i.e. the birth occurred over 100 years ago), you do not have to prove proof of identity.
- For further information about access to records refer to the Registry's Access Policy at www.bdm.vic.gov.au

19. Whose certificate are you applying for?

19.1 My own certificate or the birth certificate of my child who is under 18 years of age

☐ You must submit three identity documents of your own, one from each list on page 3.

19.2 The certificate of someone else who is 18 years of age or over

☐ **You must submit:**

a) three identity documents of your own, one from each list on page 3; and
b) a letter from the person named on the certificate (or their next of kin if the person is deceased) which authorises you to access their record. The letter must include the person's address, daytime telephone number and signature; or a letter which establishes your power of attorney; and
c) three identity documents of the person named on the certificate (unless you have power of attorney), one from each list on page 3.

If you are applying for the certificate of someone who is under 18 and not your child, please contact the Registry for proof of identity requirements.

PART FOUR – Certificate payment

20. I wish to order the following:

	Price*	Subtotal
Proof of identity required		
Standard Birth Certificate	$29.20	$.
Replaced Change of Name Certificate	$29.20	$.
Abridged Birth Certificate	$29.20	$.
Deed Poll Certificate	$29.20	$.
Proof of identity NOT required		
Historical Certificate	$29.20	$.
Uncertified (historical) image – *you must provide a registration number at Q.14 or the fee for a standard birth certificate applies.#*	$20.00	$.
Delivery/Collection method (NOTE: you must select ONE only)		
In person**	$0.00	$.
OR		
Standard post	$0.00	$.
Registered Post (within Australia)	$6.00	$.
OR		
Express Post (within Australia)	$6.50	$.
	Total	$.

* All prices on this form are subject to change. Current fees may be confirmed at www.bdm.vic.gov.au
\# You can search the historical indexes for a registration number at www.bdm.vic.gov.au
** Certificates can only be collected in person from our Melbourne Customer Service Centre. All online and mail applications will be delivered using Standard Post if you do not specify your postal delivery method above.

21. How do you wish to pay?

- Cash payments will only be accepted if you apply in person.
- Make cheques and money orders payable to Registry of Births, Deaths and Marriages.
- If paying by credit card, please complete the Credit Card Payment Slip on page 3.

☐ Cash (in person only) ☐ Credit Card ☐ EFTPOS card ☐ Cheque ☐ Money Order

PART FIVE – Declaration

22. I certify that I have read and understood the declaration below:

I declare that all statements made in this application are true and correct. I understand that this application remains the property of the State of Victoria and that some or all of the information provided, including documents submitted as proof of identity, may be disclosed to and/or verified with other persons or bodies with adequate entitlement to the information under the *Births, Deaths and Marriages Registration Act 1996* or the Registry's Access Policy. I understand that it is an offence to knowingly make a false or misleading representation in this application or its supporting documents and that penalties may apply.

Signature ____________________ **Date** DD / MM / YYYY

Go to Page 4 for lodgement instructions.

Three documents are required, one from each list below

LIST 1 Evidence of link between photo and signature

- Australian driver licence (or learner permit)
- Australian passport
- Australian firearm licence
- Overseas passport

LIST 2 Evidence of operating in the community

- Medicare card
- Credit card or ATM card
- Australian security guard or crowd controller licence
- Marriage Certificate issued by the Victorian Registry
- Student or tertiary identity card
- Australian Citizenship Certificate
- Standard Birth Certificate issued in Australia
- Department of Veterans' Affairs card
- Working with Children Check card

LIST 3 Evidence of current residential address

- Utility account (including gas, water, electricity, mobile or home phone)
- Rates notice
- Centrelink concession card (Pension Concession Card, Health Care Card or Commonwealth Seniors Health Card)
- Bank statement (including passbook, credit, savings or cheque accounts)
- Current lease or tenancy agreement
- Superannuation fund statement

All applicants please note:

- All documents must be current
- If you cannot provide an identity document from List 1 you must provide two from List 2 and one from List 3
- Your List 3 document must show your current residential address
- A List 1 document can also be used as a List 3 document if it shows your current residential address
- Bank statements, utility accounts, rates notices or superannuation fund statements must have been issued within the last 12 months
- If you submit printed online bank, superannuation or utility statements they must contain an official company letterhead or be stamped and approved by the bank, superannuation fund or utility company.

Under 18 years?
If you are unable to submit all three identity documents, a List 2 document can be a:

- Medicare card showing your name
- Current school report card or exam certificate.

Certifying and submitting your documents

How to certify your identity documents

1. Make a photocopy of each identity document. Make sure the document from List 3 shows the current residential address.
2. Take your original documents and the photocopies to a police station and ask either a sworn member of police or a Justice of the Peace located in the station to certify them.

Submitting in person?
You must bring your original identity documents or certified photocopies with your application and submit at our Melbourne Customer Service Centre or at selected Justice Service Centres (JSC). To find your nearest JSC, visit www.bdm.vic.gov.au/jsc

Submitting by mail?
You must mail certified photocopies of each identity document.

Note

- Do not send original identity documents by mail. These can only be used if you submit your identity documents in person.
- The Registry does not accept identity documents sent via fax or email.
- The Registry does not accept photocopties of identity documents that are expired, uncertified or certified incorrectly.
- Failure to correctly submit your proof of identity documents will delay your application.

Applying from outside Victoria?
If you are applying from other Australian states or territories you may have photocopies of your identity documents certified by a sworn member of police or a Justice of the Peace.

Applying from outside Australia?
If you live outside Australia, you can provide overseas equivalents to Australian identity documents, such as a foreign driver licence.

You may have photocopies of your identity documents certified by an Australian consulate or embassy official, a Notary Public or a local member of police.

If any identity documents are not written in English, you must also provide a certified translation. The Registry will only accept translations by an accredited translator.

If you are unable to meet these requirements please contact the Registry via www.bdm.vic.gov.au or on 1300 369 367.

Credit Card Payment Slip

Card type ☐ Visa ☐ MasterCard ☐ Amex **Total $** ____ . ____

Name on card ____________________

Card number ____________________ **Expiry date** /

Signature of cardholder ____________________

If applying by mail, attach proof of identity, supporting documents and payment here.

PART SIX – Lodgement

Submit your form, payment, proof of identity (if required) and any supporting documents:

By mail
Victorian Registry of Births, Deaths and Marriages
GPO Box 5220, Melbourne VIC 3001

In person
Victorian Registry of Births, Deaths and Marriages Customer Service Centre
Ground floor, 595 Collins St, Melbourne
(8.30am – 4.30pm, Monday to Friday, except public holidays)

or

Selected Justice Service Centres (JSCs).
To find your nearest JSC go to www.bdm.vic.gov.au/jsc

Checklist

I have stated the reason I require the certificate at Q.9.

I have supplied all three identity documents at Part 3 (unless applying for a historical certificate or uncertified image).

I have signed the declaration at Part 5.

If applying by mail:

I have had photocopies of my proof of identity documents certified at a Justice Service Centre or by a sworn member of police.

I have included payment or completed the Credit Card Payment Slip.

If applying for a certificate of someone else (other than your child who is under 18 years of age):

I have supplied the required three proof of identity documents both for myself and the person whose certificate I am applying for as specified in Q.19.1 or Q.19.2.

I have supplied the required authority and documents as specified in Q.19.1 or Q.19.2.

FAQs

Can I use this form to change my name?
No. You must complete an Application to Register a Change of Name form, available at the Registry or at www.bdm.vic.gov.au

Can I use this form to register the birth of my child?
No. You must complete a Birth Registration Statement which is available from the Registry.

Which certificate will I need when applying for a driver licence or passport?
You will generally be required to produce a standard birth certificate. A standard marriage certificate issued by the Registry may also be required.

I was married in Victoria and now use my spouse's surname. Do I need a Change of Name certificate to prove this?
No. You need a standard marriage certificate issued by the Registry. Please note, the certificate issued on your wedding day is not a commonly accepted identification document.

What is a Deed Poll certificate?
A Deed Poll certificate was used up to October 1986 as proof of a name change. If you have changed your name by Deed Poll and need proof, you may need to register a name change.

Note. It is best to check with the authority requesting your identification documents before you order a certificate.

Privacy

In line with the *Information Privacy Act 2000*, the Registry is collecting information in this form to determine your eligibility to obtain the requested certificate and to prevent fraud. A copy of the Registry's Privacy Policy is available at www.bdm.vic.gov.au

If you do not provide all of the information requested, particularly that relating to the reason the document is required and your relationship to the registered person, then you may not be provided with a certified copy of the certificate.

If you require access to a translation or interpreter service, please contact the Translating and Interpreting Service (TIS) on 13 14 50 and ask them to contact the Victorian Registry of Births, Deaths and Marriages.

Victorian Registry of Births, Deaths and Marriages
General enquiries 1300 369 367
(8.30am – 4.30pm, Monday-Friday, except public holidays)
Website www.bdm.vic.gov.au

THIS FORM IS PRINTED ON ENVIRONMENTALLY FRIENDLY PAPER USING VEGETABLE INKS

Victorian Registry of Births, Deaths and Marriages

Office Use Only

APPLICATION FOR COMMEMORATIVE BIRTH CERTIFICATE

BY MAIL: GPO Box 4332, Melbourne, Victoria, 3001, Australia

IN PERSON: Ground floor, 595 Collins Street, Melbourne
8.30am - 4.30pm Monday to Friday (excluding public holidays)

Certificate style	Quantity	Price*	Subtotal
Classic		$49.50	$.
Australian Blue		$49.50	$.
Australian Pink		$49.50	$.
Victorian Bird		$49.50	$.
Victorian Flora		$49.50	$.
Victorian Fauna		$49.50	$.
Victorian Aboriginal		$49.50	$.
Victorian Footprints		$49.50	$.
Total price (not subject to GST)			$.

Commemorative birth certificates are not recognised proof of identity documents. If you require a certificate for identity purposes, most organisations require a standard certificate.

*All prices listed on this form are subject to change. Current fees may be confirmed at www.bdm.vic.gov.au

YOU MUST PROVIDE PROOF OF YOUR IDENTITY WITH THIS APPLICATION - SEE PAGE 2

COMMEMORATIVE BIRTH CERTIFICATE DETAILS:

If this application relates to a person other than yourself, written authority and identification from that person may also be required. Please read the Registry's Access Policy for further details.

Registration No. (if known)		Place of birth *Town and State*	
Date of birth	Day / Month / Year	Or years to be searched	From .... to ....
Family name (at birth)		Given names	
Other family name used		Present age	
Father's name	Family name	Given names	
Mother's name	Maiden name (surname at birth)	Given names	

PLEASE USE BLOCK LETTERS

APPLICANT'S DETAILS See page 2 for Proof of Identity requirements

I declare that the statements made in this application are true and correct. I understand that this application will remain the property of the State of Victoria and that some or all of the information provided on this form, and some or all of the documents submitted as Proof of Identity, may be disclosed to and/or verified with Commonwealth agencies responsible for immigration, passports and citizenship, with State Registrars responsible for births and electoral registration, with driver licensing authorities, credit authorities and law enforcement agencies.

Applicant's name		Signature of applicant	
Applicant's address	Postcode	Daytime telephone no.	
Postal address if different to above	Postcode	Fax number	
Reason certificate is required		Relationship of applicant	

PAYMENT DETAILS

Enclosed is a Cheque/Money Order for $ ....

or debit my ☐ Visa ☐ MasterCard ☐ Amex for: $........................

Card number		Expiry date	/
Name on card		Signature of cardholder	

CBC2013

IDENTIFICATION REQUIREMENTS

You MUST provide proof of your identity when you apply for a birth certificate if:

- the birth occurred within the last 100 years, or
- the birth occurred more than 100 years ago and the person is still living.

If this certificate relates to an adult person other than yourself, you **must also** provide:

- Written consent or authority from that person or from a person authorised under the Access Policy.
- Three identity documents from that person, one from each list below.

Three documents are required, one from each list below.

LIST 1 – Evidence of link between photo and signature	**LIST 2** – Evidence of operating in the community	**LIST 3** – Evidence of current residential address
• Australian driver licence (or learner permit) • Australian passport • Australian firearm licence • Overseas passport	• Medicare card • Credit card or ATM card • Australian security guard or crowd controller licence • Marriage Certificate issued by the Victorian Registry • Student or tertiary identity card • Australian Citizenship Certificate • Standard Birth Certificate issued in Australia • Department of Veterans' Affairs card • Working with Children Check card	• Utility account (including gas, water, electricity, mobile or home phone) • Rates notice • Centrelink concession card (Pension Concession Card, Health Care Card or Commonwealth Seniors Health Card) • Bank statement (including passbook, credit, savings or cheque accounts) • Current lease or tenancy agreement • Superannuation fund statement

All applicants note:

- All documents must be current
- If you cannot provide an identity document from List 1 you must provide two from List 2 and one from List 3
- Your List 3 document must show your current residential address
- A List 1 document can also be used as a List 3 document if it shows your current residential address
- Bank statements, utility accounts, rates notices and superannuation fund statements must have been issued within the last 12 months
- If you submit printed online bank, superannuation or utility statements they must contain an official company letterhead or be stamped and approved by the bank, superannuation fund or utility company.

Under 18 years?

If you are unable to provide all three identity documents, a List 2 document can be a:

- Medicare card showing your name
- Current school report card or exam certificate

Certifying and submitting your documents

How to certify your identity documents

1. Make a photocopy of each identity document. Make sure the document from List 3 shows the current residential address.
2. Take your original documents and the photocopies to a police station and ask either a sworn member of police or a Justice of the Peace located in the police station to certify them.

Submitting in person?

You must bring your original identity documents or certified photocopies with your application and submit at our Melbourne Customer Service Centre or at a selected Justice Service Centre (JSC). To find your nearest JSC, visit www.bdm.vic.gov.au/jsc

Submitting by mail?

You must mail certified photocopies of each identity document.

Note:

- Do not send original identity documents by mail, these can only be used if you submit your identity documents in person
- The Registry does not accept identity documents sent via fax or email
- The Registry does not accept photocopies of identity documents that are expired, uncertified or certified incorrectly.
- Failure to correctly submit your proof of identity documents will delay your application.

Applying from outside Victoria?

If you are applying from other Australian states or territories you may have photocopies of your identity documents certified by a sworn member of police or a Justice of the Peace.

Continued over page.

Applying from outside Australia?

If you live outside Australia, you can provide overseas equivalents to Australian identity documents, such as a foreign driver licence.

You may have photocopies of your identity documents certified by an Australian consulate or embassy official, a Notary Public or a local member of police.

If any identity documents are not written in English, you must also provide a certified translation. The Registry will only accept translations by an accredited translator.

If you are unable to meet these requirements please contact the Registry via www.bdm.vic.gov.au or on 1300 369 367.

PRIVACY STATEMENT

In line with the *Information Privacy Act 2000*, the Registry is collecting this information so that it can determine your eligibility to obtain the requested certificate and to prevent fraud.

A copy of the Registry's Privacy Policy is available at www.bdm.vic.gov.au or by contacting 1300 369 367.

If you do not provide all of the information requested, particularly that relating to the reason the document is required and your relationship to the registered person, then you may not be provided with the certificate.

Further, if you knowingly make a false or misleading representation on the application form, you may be guilty of an offence under section 53 of the *Births, Deaths and Marriages Registration Act 1996*. Penalties apply.

Access to a copy of this application form may be obtained from the Registry, or under the provisions of the *Freedom of Information Act 1983*.

Victorian Registry of Births, Deaths and Marriages
Births, Deaths and Marriages Registration Act 1996

Application for a Victorian Marriage Certificate

Office use only

$

CC MO CQ NF EX RM

C NC IP NP DP FH

Instructions. Please use **blue** or **black** ink and **BLOCK** letters.

PART ONE – Your details

1. Which certificate do you require?

☐ Standard Marriage Certificate

☐ Historical Certificate

☐ Uncertified (historical) image

2. Surname (family name)

3. Given name(s)

4. Residential address
a) Street no. and name

b) Suburb/Town

c) State   d) Postcode

5. Postal address (if different to above)
a) Street no. and name

b) Suburb/Town

c) State   d) Postcode

6. Daytime telephone number

7. Email address

8. Whose certificate are you applying for?

My own   Someone else's – please specify
(e.g. mother, father, daughter)

9. Reason certificate is required
(e.g. passport, driver licence)

PART TWO – Marriage details

10. Bride's surname (family name) at time of marriage

11. Bride's given name(s)

12. Groom's surname (family name)

13. Groom's given name(s)

14. Place of marriage
a) Suburb/Town

b) State   c) Postcode

15. Date of marriage / /

Or if unsure, please estimate date of marriage

From / /   To / /

16. Registration number (if known)

Celebrant's details (if known)

17. Celebrant's surname (family name)

18. Celebrant's given name

PART THREE – Proof of identity

Note

- You must provide proof of your identity if the marriage occurred within the last 60 years or either person is still living.
- If applying for a historical certificate or uncertified image, you do not have to provide proof of identity.
- For further information about access to records refer to the Registry's Access Policy at www.bdm.vic.gov.au

19. Whose certificate are you applying for?

19.1 My own marriage certificate

☐ You must submit three identity documents of your own, one from each list on page 3.

19.2 Someone else's marriage certificate

☐ **You must submit:**

a) three identity documents of your own, one from each list on page 3; and

b) a letter from one of the parties to the marriage which authorises you to access the marriage record. The letter must include the authorising person's address, daytime telephone number and signature; and

c) three identity documents of the person giving you authority to access the marriage record, one from each list on page 3.

PART FOUR – Certificate payment

20. I wish to order the following:

	Price*	Subtotal
Proof of identity required		
Standard Marriage Certificate	$29.20	$.
Proof of identity NOT required		
Historical Certificate	$29.20	$.
Uncertified (historical) image – *you must provide a registration number at Q.16 or the fee for a standard marriage certificate applies.#*	$20.00	$.
Delivery/Collection method (NOTE: you must select ONE only)		
In person**	$0.00	$.
OR		
Standard post	$0.00	$.
Registered Post (within Australia)	$6.00	$.
OR		
Express Post (within Australia)	$6.50	$.
	Total	**$** .

* All prices on this form are subject to change. Current fees may be confirmed at www.bdm.vic.gov.au

\# You can search the historical indexes for a registration number at www.bdm.vic.gov.au

** Certificates can only be collected in person from our Melbourne Customer Service Centre. All online and mail applications will be delivered using Standard Post if you do not specify your postal delivery method above.

21. How do you wish to pay?

- Cash payments will only be accepted if you apply in person.
- Make cheques and money orders payable to Registry of Births, Deaths and Marriages.
- If paying by credit card, please complete the Credit Card Payment Slip on page 3.

☐ Cash (in person only) ☐ Credit Card ☐ EFTPOS card ☐ Cheque ☐ Money Order

PART FIVE – Declaration

22. I certify that I have read and understood the declaration below:

I declare that all statements made in this application are true and correct. I understand that this application remains the property of the State of Victoria and that some or all of the information provided, including documents submitted as proof of identity, may be disclosed to and/or verified with other persons or bodies with adequate entitlement to the information under the *Births, Deaths and Marriages Registration Act 1996* or the Registry's Access Policy. I understand that it is an offence to knowingly make a false or misleading representation in this application or its supporting documents and that penalties may apply.

Signature ____________________ **Date**   /   /

Go to Page 4 for lodgement instructions.

Three documents are required, one from each list below

LIST 1 Evidence of link between photo and signature

- Australian driver licence (or learner permit)
- Australian passport
- Australian firearm licence
- Overseas passport

LIST 2 Evidence of operating in the community

- Medicare card
- Credit card or ATM card
- Australian security guard or crowd controller licence
- Marriage Certificate issued by the Victorian Registry
- Student or tertiary identity card
- Australian Citizenship Certificate
- Standard Birth Certificate issued in Australia
- Department of Veterans' Affairs card
- Working with Children Check card

LIST 3 Evidence of current residential address

- Utility account (including gas, water, electricity, mobile or home phone)
- Rates notice
- Centrelink concession card (Pension Concession Card, Health Care Card or Commonwealth Seniors Health Card)
- Bank statement (including passbook, credit, savings or cheque accounts)
- Current lease or tenancy agreement
- Superannuation fund statement

All applicants please note:

- All documents must be current
- If you cannot provide an identity document from List 1 you must provide two from List 2 and one from List 3
- Your List 3 document must show your current residential address
- A List 1 document can also be used as a List 3 document if it shows your current residential address
- Bank statements, utility accounts, rates notices or superannuation fund statements must have been issued within the last 12 months
- If you submit printed online bank, superannuation or utility statements they must contain an official company letterhead or be stamped and approved by the bank, superannuation fund or utility company.

Under 18 years?

If you are unable to submit all three identity documents, a List 2 document can be a:

- Medicare card showing your name
- Current school report card or exam certificate.

Certifying and submitting your documents

How to certify your identity documents

1. Make a photocopy of each identity document. Make sure the document from List 3 shows the current residential address.
2. Take your original documents and the photocopies to a police station and ask either a sworn member of police or a Justice of the Peace located in the station to certify them.

Submitting in person?

You must bring your original identity documents or certified photocopies with your application and submit at our Melbourne Customer Service Centre or at selected Justice Service Centres (JSC). To find your nearest JSC, visit www.bdm.vic.gov.au/jsc

Submitting by mail?

You must mail certified photocopies of each identity document.

Note

- Do not send original identity documents by mail. These can only be used if you submit your identity documents in person.
- The Registry does not accept identity documents sent via fax or email.
- The Registry does not accept photocopties of identity documents that are expired, uncertified or certified incorrectly.
- Failure to correctly submit your proof of identity documents will delay your application.

Applying from outside Victoria?

If you are applying from other Australian states or territories you may have photocopies of your identity documents certified by a sworn member of police or a Justice of the Peace.

Applying from outside Australia?

If you live outside Australia, you can provide overseas equivalents to Australian identity documents, such as a foreign driver licence.

You may have photocopies of your identity documents certified by an Australian consulate or embassy official, a Notary Public or a local member of police.

If any identity documents are not written in English, you must also provide a certified translation. The Registry will only accept translations by an accredited translator.

If you are unable to meet these requirements please contact the Registry via www.bdm.vic.gov.au or on 1300 369 367.

Credit Card Payment Slip

Card type ☐ Visa ☐ MasterCard ☐ Amex **Total $** ____ . ____

Name on card ____________________

Card number ____________________ **Expiry date** /

Signature of cardholder ____________________

If applying by mail, attach proof of identity, supporting documents and payment here.

PART SIX – Lodgement

Submit your form, payment, proof of identity (if required) and any supporting documents:

By mail
Victorian Registry of Births, Deaths and Marriages
GPO Box 5220, Melbourne VIC 3001

In person
Victorian Registry of Births, Deaths and Marriages Customer Service Centre
Ground floor, 595 Collins St, Melbourne
(8.30am – 4.30pm, Monday to Friday, except public holidays)

or

Selected Justice Service Centres (JSCs).
To find your nearest JSC go to www.bdm.vic.gov.au/jsc

Checklist

I have stated the reason I require the certificate at Q.9.

I have supplied all three identity documents at Part 3 (unless applying for a historical certificate or uncertified image).

I have signed the declaration at Part 5.

If applying by mail:

I have had photocopies of my proof of identity documents certified at a Justice Service Centre or by a sworn member of police.

I have included payment or completed the Credit Card Payment Slip.

If applying for a certificate of someone else other than my own:

I have supplied the required three proof of identity documents both for myself and the person whose certificate I am applying for as specified in Q.19.2.

I have supplied the required authority and documents as specified in Q.19.2.

FAQs

I was married in Victoria. Can I use the certificate we received on our wedding day as proof of my new surname to update my passport or driver licence?
No. You will usually need a standard marriage certificate issued by the Registry as proof of marriage and your new surname.

I was married overseas. Can I use my marriage certificate as proof of my new surname?
To prove you have a new surname you may need to apply to register a name change with the Victorian Registry of Births, Deaths and Marriages.

I was married outside of Victoria. Which certificate do I need as proof of my new surname to update my passport or driver licence?
You will usually need a standard marriage certificate issued by the registry of the state or territory you were married in.

Note. It is best to check the requirements of the authority requesting your identification documents before you order a certificate.

Privacy

In line with the *Information Privacy Act 2000*, the Registry is collecting information in this form to determine your eligibility to obtain the requested certificate and to prevent fraud. A copy of the Registry's Privacy Policy is available at www.bdm.vic.gov.au

If you do not provide all of the information requested, particularly that relating to the reason the document is required and your relationship to the registered person, then you may not be provided with a certified copy of the certificate.

If you require access to a translation or interpreter service,
please contact the Translating and Interpreting Service (TIS) on 13 14 50
and ask them to contact the Victorian Registry of Births, Deaths and Marriages.

Victorian Registry of Births, Deaths and Marriages
General enquiries 1300 369 367
(8.30am – 4.30pm, Monday-Friday, except public holidays)
Website www.bdm.vic.gov.au

Department of Justice

Victorian Registry of Births, Deaths and Marriages
Births, Deaths and Marriages Registration Act 1996

Application for a Victorian Death Certificate

Instructions. Please use **blue** or **black** ink and **BLOCK** letters.

Office use only

$

CC	MO	CQ	NF	EX	RM
C	NC	IP	NP	DP	FH

PART ONE – Your details

1. **Which certificate do you require?**
- ☐ Standard Death Certificate
- ☐ Abridged Death Certificate
- ☐ Historical Certificate
- ☐ Uncertified (historical) image

2. **Surname (family name)**

3. **Given name(s)**

4. **Residential address**
a) Street no. and name

b) Suburb/Town

c) State d) Postcode

5. **Postal address (if different to above)**
a) Street no. and name or P.O. Box Number

b) Suburb/Town

c) State d) Postcode

6. **Daytime telephone number**

7. **Email address**

8. **What is the relationship to the person on the certificate?**
(e.g. husband, wife, son)

9. **Reason certificate is required**
(e.g. estate, genealogy)

July 2013

PART TWO – Details of the deceased

10. **Surname (family name) at time of death**

11. **Given name(s)**

12. **Place of death**
a) Suburb/Town

b) State c) Post code

13. **Age at death** years

14. **Date of death** D D / M M / Y Y Y Y

Or if unsure, please estimate date of death

From D D / M M / Y Y Y Y To D D / M M / Y Y Y Y

15. **Registration number (if known)**

16. **Mother's maiden name (surname at birth)**

17. **Mother's given name(s)**

18. **Father's surname (family name)**

19. **Father's given name(s)**

20. **Spouse's surname (family name)**

21. **Spouse's given name(s)**

22. **Other information (e.g. place of birth, children, date of birth)**

PART THREE – Proof of identity

Note

- You must provide proof of your identity if the death occurred within the last ten years.
- If the death occurred more than ten years ago, go to Q.24.
- For further information about access to records, refer to the Registry's Access Policy at www.bdm.vic.gov.au

23. What is your relationship to the deceased?

23.1 I am the deceased's next of kin

☐ You must submit three identity documents of your own, one from each list on page 3.

23.2 I am not the deceased's next of kin

☐ **You must submit:**

a) three identity documents of your own, one from each on page 3; and

b) a letter from the deceased's next of kin which authorises you to access the death record.
The letter must include the authorising person's address, daytime telephone number and signature; and

c) three identity documents of the person giving you authority to access the record, one from each list on page 3.

PART FOUR – Certificate payment

24. I wish to order the following:

Proof of identity required	Price*	Subtotal
Standard Death Certificate	$29.20	$.
Abridged Death Certificate – *May not be accepted for official purposes*	$29.20	$.
Proof of identity NOT required		
Historical Certificate – *for Historical purposes*	$29.20	$.
Uncertified (historical) image – *You must provide a registration number at Q.15 or the fee for a standard death certificate applies.#*	$20.00	$.
Deliver/Collection Method (Note; You must select ONE only)		
In Person** OR		
Standard Post (within Australia) OR	$0.00	
Registered Post (within Australia) OR	$6.00	$.
Express Post (within Australia)	$6.50	$.
	Total	$.

* All prices on this form are subject to change. Current fees may be confirmed at www.bdm.vic.gov.au
** Certificates can only be collected in person from our Melbourne Customer Service Centre.
All online and mail applications will be delivered using Standard Post if you do not specify your postal delivery method above.
\# You can search the historical indexes for a registration number at www.bdm.vic.gov.au

25. How do you wish to pay?

- Cash payments will only be accepted if you apply in person.
- Make cheques and money orders payable to Registry of Births, Deaths and Marriages.
- If paying by credit card, please complete the Credit Card Payment Slip on page 3.

☐ Cash (in person only) ☐ Credit card ☐ EFTPOS card ☐ Cheque ☐ Money order

PART FIVE – Declaration

26. I certify that I have read and understood the declaration below:

I declare that all statements made in this application are true and correct. I understand that this application remains the property of the State of Victoria and that some or all of the information provided, including documents submitted as proof of identity, may be disclosed to and/or verified with other persons or bodies with adequate entitlement to the information under the *Births, Deaths and Marriages Registration Act 1996* or the Registry's Access Policy. I understand that it is an offence to knowingly make a false or misleading representation in this application or its supporting documents and that penalties may apply.

Signature ______________________ **Date** D D / M M / Y Y Y Y

Go to Page 4 for lodgement instructions.

Three documents are required, one from each list below

LIST 1 Evidence of link between photo and signature

- Australian driver licence (or learner permit)
- Australian passport
- Australian firearm licence
- Overseas passport

LIST 2 Evidence of operating in the community

- Medicare card
- Credit card or ATM card
- Australian security guard or crowd controller licence
- Marriage Certificate issued by the Victorian Registry
- Student or tertiary identity card
- Australian Citizenship Certificate
- Standard Birth Certificate issued in Australia
- Department of Veterans' Affairs card
- Working with Children Check card

LIST 3 Evidence of current residential address

- Utility account (including gas, water, electricity, mobile or home phone)
- Rates notice
- Centrelink concession card (Pension Concession Card, Health Care Card or Commonwealth Seniors Health Card)
- Bank statement (including passbook, credit, savings or cheque accounts)
- Current lease or tenancy agreement
- Superannuation fund statement

All applicants please note:

- All documents must be current
- If you cannot provide an identity document from List 1 you must provide two from List 2 and one from List 3
- Your List 3 document must show your current residential address
- A List 1 document can also be used as a List 3 document if it shows your current residential address
- Bank statements, utility accounts, rates notices or superannuation fund statements must have been issued within the last 12 months
- If you submit printed online bank, superannuation or utility statements they must contain an official company letterhead or be stamped and approved by the bank, superannuation fund or utility company.

Under 18 years?

If you are unable to submit all three identity documents, a List 2 document can be a:

- Medicare card showing your name
- Current school report card or exam certificate.

Certifying and submitting your documents

How to certify your identity documents

1. Make a photocopy of each identity document. Make sure the document from List 3 shows the current residential address.
2. Take your original documents and the photocopies to a police station and ask either a sworn member of police or a Justice of the Peace located in the station to certify them.

Submitting in person?

You must bring your original identity documents or certified photocopies with your application and submit at our Melbourne Customer Service Centre or at selected Justice Service Centres (JSC). To find your nearest JSC, visit www.bdm.vic.gov.au/jsc

Submitting by mail?

You must mail certified photocopies of each identity document.

Note

- Do not send original identity documents by mail. These can only be used if you submit your identity documents in person.
- The Registry does not accept identity documents sent via fax or email.
- The Registry does not accept photocopties of identity documents that are expired, uncertified or certified incorrectly.
- Failure to correctly submit your proof of identity documents will delay your application.

Applying from outside Victoria?

If you are applying from other Australian states or territories you may have photocopies of your identity documents certified by a sworn member of police or a Justice of the Peace.

Applying from outside Australia?

If you live outside Australia, you can provide overseas equivalents to Australian identity documents, such as a foreign driver licence.

You may have photocopies of your identity documents certified by an Australian consulate or embassy official, a Notary Public or a local member of police.

If any identity documents are not written in English, you must also provide a certified translation. The Registry will only accept translations by an accredited translator.

If you are unable to meet these requirements please contact the Registry via www.bdm.vic.gov.au or on 1300 369 367.

Credit Card Payment Slip

Card type ☐ Visa ☐ MasterCard ☐ Amex **Total $** ____ . ____

Name on card ____________________

Card number ____________________ **Expiry date** MM / YY

Signature of cardholder ____________________

If applying by mail, attach proof of identity, supporting documents and payment here.

PART SIX – Lodgement

Submit your form, payment, proof of identity (if required) and any supporting documents:

By mail
Victorian Registry of Births, Deaths and Marriages
GPO Box 5220, Melbourne VIC 3001

In person
Victorian Registry of Births, Deaths and Marriages Customer Service Centre
Ground floor, 595 Collins St, Melbourne
(8.30am – 4.30pm, Monday to Friday, except public holidays)

or

Selected Justice Service Centres (JSCs).
To find your nearest JSC go to www.bdm.vic.gov.au/jsc

Checklist

I have supplied all three proof of identity documents (unless applying for a historical certificate or an uncertified image).

I have stated the reason I require the certificate at Q.9.

I have signed the declaration at Part Five.

If applying by mail:

I have had photocopies of my proof of identity documents certified at a Justice Service Centre or by a sworn member of police.

I have included payment or completed the Credit Card Payment Slip.

If the deceased is not my next of kin:

I have supplied the required three proof of identity documents both for myself and the person who authorised me to apply for the certificate, as specified in Q.23.2.

I have attached the required authority and documents as specified in Q.23.2.

Privacy

In line with the *Information Privacy Act 2000*, the Registry is collecting information in this form to determine your eligibility to obtain the requested certificate and to prevent fraud. A copy of the Registry's Privacy Policy is available at www.bdm.vic.gov.au

If you do not provide all of the information requested, particularly that relating to the reason the document is required and your relationship to the registered person, then you may not be provided with a certified copy of the certificate.

If you require access to a translation or interpreter service, please contact the Translating and Interpreting Service (TIS) on 13 14 50 and ask them to contact the Victorian Registry of Births, Deaths and Marriages.

Victorian Registry of Births, Deaths and Marriages
General enquiries 1300 369 367
(8.30am – 4.30pm, Monday-Friday, except public holidays)
Website www.bdm.vic.gov.au

THIS FORM IS PRINTED ON ENVIRONMENTALLY FRIENDLY PAPER USING VEGETABLE INKS

AUSTRALIA—WESTERN AUSTRALIA

Send your requests to:

Registry of Births, Deaths & Marriages
(Location: Level 10, 141 St. Georges Terrace)
P.O. Box 7720
Cloisters Square
Perth, Western Australia 6850, Australia

Tel.: 1300 305 021 (calls from within Australia only); overseas calls only: (011) (61) (8) 9264 1555
E-mail: rgoperth@justice.wa.gov.au
www.bdm.dotag.wa.gov.au/

Civil registration of births, deaths, and marriages has been compulsory in Western Australia since September 1841. Birth records less than 75 years old, death records less than 25 years old, and marriage records less than 60 years old are restricted. The Registry maintains a free online historic index of births, deaths, and marriages from 1841 at www.bdm.dotag.wa.gov.au/_apps/pioneersindex/default.aspx. The J S Battye Library in Perth, which is part of the State Library of Western Australia, has some church records prior to 1841.

Cost for a certified Birth Certificate	Au$44.00
Cost for a commemorative Birth Certificate	Au$54.00
Cost for a certified Marriage Certificate	Au$44.00
Cost for a certified Death Certificate	Au$44.00

For Adoption Information, contact:

Post Adoption Services
P.O. Box 641
Belmont, Western Australia 6104

Email: adoptions@dcp.wa.gov.au
www.childprotection.wa.gov.au

For additional assistance, contact:

Embassy of Australia
1601 Massachusetts Avenue, NW
Washington, DC 20036

Tel. (202) 797-3000

BDM1

Registry of Births, Deaths and Marriages, Western Australia
141 St Georges Terrace, Perth WA TEL: 1300 305 021

(Western Australia ONLY)

BIRTH CERTIFICATE APPLICATION FORM

Payment details over the page – you MUST return pages 1 and 2 if applying via mail

Fees including standard postal delivery effective 1 July 2009 – Subject to change without further notice — No GST is payable on these certificates

☐ **BIRTH CERTIFICATE**	**$44.00**	
☐ **BIRTH CERTIFICATE** (Reduced Fee)	**$31.00**	Only applies where the **full registration number** is supplied by you and the birth is more than 75 years old. Otherwise full fee applies.
☐ **URGENT FEE**	**$34.00**	In addition to any other fee. **Does not** include Express Post.

Urgent fee not payable for computerised certificates if applied in person at the Perth Registry Office or certain Regional Courthouses. See **Locations & Links** webpage. For eligibility see the **Birth certificate access policy** on the **Births** webpage.

Identification and Certificate Access Requirements

See page 2 or visit www.bdm.dotag.wa.gov.au

Processing Times for Mailed Certificate Applications

Standard - Please allow up to 2 working days plus postal delivery time
Urgent - Processed within 24 hours of receipt plus postal delivery time

BIRTH DETAILS REQUIRED

Please PRINT clearly ABN: 70 598 519 443

Surname (at birth)					
Given name(s)					
Date of birth	Day / Month / Year	**Present age**		**Male** ☐	**Female** ☐
Place of birth in Western Australia	Suburb / Town				
Father's name	Surname	Given name(s)			
Mother's name	Maiden surname	Given name(s)			

APPLICANT'S DETAILS (please see next page for access conditions and identification requirements)

Full name			
Postal address	Suburb	State	Postcode
Your **Relationship** to the person whose certificate you are requesting	e.g. self, mother	**Daytime phone number**	
Email address			
Reason required	Passport ☐ Driver's licence ☐ Centrelink ☐ Bank requirements ☐ Legal ☐ Marriage ☐ Lost ☐ Family history ☐ Other		

Declaration: I declare that the information I have provided is true and correct. I understand that the WA Registry of Births, Deaths and Marriages may make enquiries with any organisation or individual to verify the information provided with this application.

SIGNATURE OF APPLICANT — Signature must be completed

OFFICE USE ONLY

LIST 1 *(with photo)*: Driver's Licence ☐ Passport ☐ Proof of Age ☐ Firearm's Licence ☐ Defence/police ☐ DIAC Certificate ☐ Learner's permit card ☐
ID Ref: ....

LIST 2: Birth Cert(Aust) ☐ Citizenship ☐ Cr/Debit Card ☐ Health ☐ Medicare ☐ Centrelink ☐ Student card ☐ Travel Doc ☐
ID Ref: ....

LIST 3 *(current address)*: Bank Statement ☐ Rates notice ☐ Educational report ☐ Motor Vehicle Rego ☐ Utility account ☐ Rental agreement ☐
ID Ref: .... *If ID provided from Lists 2 and 3, one ID must contain a signature*

Other ☐ .... Initial ID sighted........

BIRTH CERTIFICATE APPLICATION INSTRUCTIONS

HOW TO APPLY

POST the completed form (pages 1 & 2) to:

Registry of Births, Deaths & Marriages
PO Box 7720 Cloisters Square
PERTH WA 6850 **OR**

BRING the completed form (pages 1 & 2) to:

Registry of Births, Deaths & Marriages
Level 10, 141 St Georges Terrace Perth
between 8.30 am - 4.30 pm, Monday to Friday

Note: Faxed applications will not be accepted

WHO CAN APPLY FOR A CERTIFICATE

Birth certificates are available to the registered person (16 years of age or over) or a parent named in the birth certificate.

If the certificate relates to a person other than yourself and you do not qualify under the Registry's Certificate Access Policy, you must provide the written consent or authority from a person entitled to the certificate and you must also provide identification for yourself **and** the person for whom you are acting.

Information regarding the Registry's Certificate Access policy is located on our website at www.bdm.dotag.wa.gov.au, or telephone the Registry on **1300 305 021**.

Privacy Considerations and Personal Records

Certificates held by the Registry contain sensitive and personal information. However the Registry allows unrestricted access for birth certificates which occurred more than 100 years ago.

IDENTIFICATION REQUIREMENTS

When applying for a Western Australian certificate, evidence of your identity must be provided.

- You **MUST** provide at least **three** forms of identification:
  - One document from each List (1, 2 **and** 3). At least one containing a photograph; **or**
  - One from List 1 and two from List 2. At least one containing a photograph, **or**
  - Two from List 2 and one from List 3. At least one containing a signature.
- All forms of identification **MUST** be **current**.
- Documents from List 3 **MUST** show your **current residential address**.
- Bank statements, utility accounts or rates notices **MUST** have been **issued within the last six months**.

CERTIFICATION REQUIREMENTS

Applying in person - original documents must be provided.

Applying by post - please send clear **certified** photocopies of your identification documents with your application.

Photocopies of identification will only be accepted if they are **certified by a qualified witness** as being "true copies" of the original documents. See page 3 for *Certifying documents*.

√ Tick the forms of identification that are supporting your application

LIST 1 - Evidence of link between photo & signature

- ☐ **Australian driver's licence** (with photo)
- ☐ **Australian passport** (with photo)
- ☐ **Australian firearm's licence** (with photo)
- ☐ **Defence Force/Police ID card** (with photo)
- ☐ **Department of Immigration and Citizenship (DIAC) certificate** with evidence of residence status (with photo)
- ☐ **Over 18 or Proof of Age Identity card** (with photo)
- ☐ **Australian learner driver's permit card** (with photo)

LIST 2 - Evidence of operating in the community

- ☐ **Debit or Credit card** (one or the other, not both) issued by a financial institution
- ☐ **Document of identity** issued by the Passport Office
- ☐ **Entitlement card** issued by the Commonwealth or State Government (Centrelink, Health Care card, Veterans Affairs card etc)
- ☐ **Full Birth certificate** issued in Australia (birth extracts not accepted)
- ☐ **Medicare card**
- ☐ **Naturalisation, citizenship or immigration papers** issued by DIAC
- ☐ **Overseas passport** with current Australian Entry Permit
- ☐ **Security guard or crowd control licence** (Australian)
- ☐ **Student identity document or statement of enrolment** issued by an educational institution, including Tertiary(should include photo and/or signature)
- ☐ **Working with children card**

LIST 3 – Evidence of current residential address

- ☐ **Driver's licence renewal notice**
- ☐ **Financial institution statement** less than six months old
- ☐ **Motor vehicle registration**
- ☐ **Property lease or tenancy agreement**
- ☐ **Shire/water rates notice**
- ☐ **School or other educational report or certificate** less than twelve months old
- ☐ **Utility account** less than six months old (gas, electricity, home phone, etc)

FURTHER INFORMATION

For further information, please visit our website at www.bdm.dotag.wa.gov.au or call 1300 305 021 between 8.30 am and 4.30 pm, Monday to Friday.

PAYMENT DETAILS *If applying for more than one certificate only complete payment details on one form*

Applicant's Full Name

Enclosed is a cheque/money order* for $ **OR** Debit my MasterCard ☐ or Visa ☐ for $

* Your cheque or money order should be made payable to the *"Registry of Births, Deaths and Marriages"*

Card No	☐☐☐☐ ☐☐☐☐ ☐☐☐☐ ☐☐☐☐	Expiry Date	☐☐ / ☐☐
Name of Cardholder		Signature of cardholder	

BDM20

Registry of Births, Deaths & Marriages, Western Australia
141 St Georges Tce, Perth Tel: 1300 305 021

COMMEMORATIVE BIRTH CERTIFICATE APPLICATION FORM

(Western Australia ONLY)

Payment details over the page – you MUST return pages 1 and 2 if applying via mail

Birth details required

Please PRINT clearly

ABN: 70 598 519 443

Surname		
Given name(s)		
Date of birth	/ /	
Place of birth in **WA**		
Mother's name	Maiden surname	Given name(s)
Father's name	Surname	Given name(s)

Applicant's details (please see page 2 for access conditions and identification requirements)

Full name			
Postal address			
			Postcode
Your **Relationship** to the person whose certificate you are requesting	e.g. self, mother	**Daytime phone number**	
Email address			

Order Form

CERTIFICATE TYPE	QUANTITY	PRICE	AMOUNT
1. Standard Birth Certificate	Free when you order a commemorative birth certificate		
2. Our Golden Past		$ 54	$
3. Floral		$ 54	$
4. Wildlife		$ 54	$
5. Landscapes		$ 54	$
6. Hands		$ 54	$
7. Bears		$ 54	$
8. Baby Prints		$ 54	$
No GST is payable on these certificates		**TOTAL**	$

Prices current as at 1 July 2009 and are subject to change without further notice

Processing time - Please allow 14 days for delivery

Declaration: I declare that the information I have provided is true and correct. I understand that the WA Registry of Births, Deaths and Marriages may make enquiries with any organisation or individual to verify the information provided with this application.

SIGNATURE OF APPLICANT — Signature must be completed

OFFICE USE ONLY

LIST 1 *(with photo)*: Driver's Licence ☐ Passport ☐ Proof of Age ☐ Firearm's Licence ☐ Defence/police ☐ DIAC Certificate ☐ Learner's permit card ☐
ID Ref: ....

LIST 2: Birth Cert(Aust) ☐ Citizenship ☐ Cr/Debit Card ☐ Health ☐ Medicare ☐ Centrelink ☐ Student card ☐ Travel Doc ☐
ID Ref: ....

LIST 3 *(current address)*: Bank Statement ☐ Rates notice ☐ Educational report ☐ Motor Vehicle Rego ☐ Utility account ☐ Rental agreement ☐
ID Ref: .... *If ID provided from Lists 2 and 3, one ID must contain a signature*

Other ☐ .... Initial ID sighted

COMMEMORATIVE BIRTH CERTIFICATE APPLICATION INSTRUCTIONS

HOW TO APPLY

POST the completed form (pages 1 & 2) to:

Registry of Births, Deaths & Marriages
PO Box 7720 Cloisters Square
PERTH WA 6850 **OR**

BRING the completed form (pages 1 & 2) to:

Registry of Births, Deaths & Marriages
Level 10, 141 St Georges Terrace Perth
between 8.30 am - 4.30 pm, Monday to Friday

Note: Faxed applications will not be accepted

WHO CAN APPLY FOR A CERTIFICATE

Commemorative birth certificates are available to the registered person or a parent named in the birth certificate.

If the certificate relates to a person other than yourself and you do not qualify under the Registry's Certificate Access Policy, you must provide the written consent or authority from a person entitled to the certificate and you must also provide identification for yourself **and** the person for whom you are acting.
Information regarding the Registry's Certificate Access policy is located on our website at www.bdm.dotag.wa.gov.au, or telephone the Registry on **1300 305 021**.

Privacy Considerations and Personal Records

Certificates held by the Registry contain sensitive and personal information. However the Registry allows unrestricted access for birth certificates which occurred more than 100 years ago.

IDENTIFICATION REQUIREMENTS

When applying for a Western Australian certificate, evidence of your identity must be provided.

- You **MUST** provide at least **three** forms of identification:
  - One document from each List (1, 2 **and** 3). At least one containing a photograph; **or**
  - Two from List 2 and one from List 3. At least one containing a signature.
- All forms of identification produced from Lists 1 to 3 **MUST** be **current**.
- Documents from List 3 **MUST** show your **current residential address.**
- Bank statements, utility accounts or rates notices **MUST** have been **issued within the last six months**.

CERTIFICATION REQUIREMENTS

Applying in person - original documents must be provided.

Applying by post - please send clear **certified** photocopies of your identification documents with your application.

Photocopies of identification will only be accepted if they are **certified by a qualified witness** as being "true copies" of the original documents. See attached for *Certification Requirements*.

√ Tick the forms of identification that are supporting your application

LIST 1 - Evidence of link between photo & signature

- ☐ **Australian driver's licence** (with photo)
- ☐ **Australian passport** (with photo)
- ☐ **Australian firearm's licence** (with photo)
- ☐ **Defence Force/Police ID card** (with photo)
- ☐ **Department of Immigration and Citizenship (DIAC) certificate** with evidence of residence status (with photo)
- ☐ **Over 18 or Proof of Age Identity card** (with photo)
- ☐ **Australian learner driver's permit card** (with photo)

LIST 2 - Evidence of operating in the community

- ☐ **Debit or Credit card** (one or the other, not both) issued by a financial institution
- ☐ **Document of identity** issued by the Passport Office
- ☐ **Entitlement card** issued by the Commonwealth or State Government (Centrelink, Health Care card, Veterans Affairs card etc)
- ☐ **Full Birth certificate** issued in Australia (birth extracts not accepted)
- ☐ **Medicare card**
- ☐ **Naturalisation, citizenship or immigration papers** issued by DIAC
- ☐ **Overseas passport** with current Australian Entry Permit
- ☐ **Security guard or crowd control licence** (Australian)
- ☐ **Student identity document or statement of enrolment** issued by an educational institution, including Tertiary (should include photo and/or signature)
- ☐ **Working with children card**

LIST 3 – Evidence of current residential address

- ☐ **Driver's licence renewal notice**
- ☐ **Financial institution statement** less than six months old
- ☐ **Motor vehicle registration**
- ☐ **Property lease or tenancy agreement**
- ☐ **Shire/water rates notice**
- ☐ **School or other educational report or certificate** less than twelve months old
- ☐ **Utility account** less than six months old (gas, electricity, home phone, etc)

FURTHER INFORMATION

For further information visit our website at www.bdm.dotag.wa.gov.au or call 1300 305 021 between 8.30 am and 4.30 pm, Monday to Friday.

PAYMENT DETAILS *If applying for more than one certificate only complete payment details on <u>one</u> form*

Applicant's Full Name

Enclosed is a cheque/money order* for $ **OR** Debit my MasterCard ☐ or Visa ☐ for $

* Your cheque or money order should be made payable to the *"Registry of Births, Deaths and Marriages"*

Card No ☐☐☐☐ ☐☐☐☐ ☐☐☐☐ ☐☐☐☐ Expiry Date ☐☐ / ☐☐

Name of Cardholder		Signature of cardholder	

BDM3

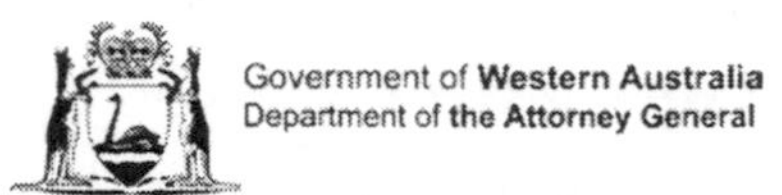

Government of **Western Australia**
Department of **the Attorney General**

Registry of Births, Deaths and Marriages, Western Australia
141 St Georges Terrace, Perth WA TEL: 1300 305 021

(Western Australia ONLY)

MARRIAGE CERTIFICATE APPLICATION FORM

Payment details over the page - you MUST return pages 1 and 2 if applying via mail

Fees including standard postal delivery effective 1 July 2009 – Subject to change without further notice		No GST is payable on these certificates
☐ **MARRIAGE CERTIFICATE**	**$44.00**	
☐ **MARRIAGE CERTIFICATE** (Reduced Fee)	**$31.00**	Only applies where the **full registration number** is supplied by you and the marriage is more than 75 years old. Otherwise full fee applies.
☐ **URGENT FEE**	**$34.00**	In addition to any other fee. **Does not** include Express Post.

Urgent fee not payable for computerised certificates if applied in person at the Perth Registry Office or certain Regional Courthouses. See **Locations & Links** webpage. For eligibility see the **Marriage certificate access policy** on the **Marriages** webpage.

Identification and Certificate Access Requirements

See page 2 or visit www.bdm.dotag.wa.gov.au

Processing Times for Mailed Certificate Applications

Standard - Please allow up to 2 working days plus postal delivery time
Urgent - Processed within 24 hours of receipt plus postal delivery time

MARRIAGE DETAILS REQUIRED

Please PRINT clearly ABN: 70 598 519 443

Date of marriage	Day / Month / Year		
Place of marriage in Western Australia	Suburb / Town		
Groom's surname			
Groom's given name(s)			
Bride's surname (at time of marriage)		**Maiden surname** if different	
Bride's given name(s)			

APPLICANT'S DETAILS (please see next page for access conditions and identification requirements)

Full name			
Postal address	Suburb	State	Postcode
Your **Relationship** to the person whose certificate you are requesting	e.g. self, spouse	**Daytime phone number**	
Email address			
Reason required	Passport ☐ Legal ☐ Family history ☐ Lost ☐	Divorce ☐ Estate ☐	Bank requirements ☐ Property settlement ☐
	Other		

Declaration: I declare that the information I have provided is true and correct. I understand that the WA Registry of Births, Deaths and Marriages may make enquiries with any organisation or individual to verify the information provided with this application.

SIGNATURE OF APPLICANT — Signature must be completed

OFFICE USE ONLY

LIST 1 *(with photo)*: Driver's Licence ☐ Passport ☐ Proof of Age ☐ Firearm's Licence ☐ Defence/police ☐ DIAC Certificate ☐ Learner's permit card ☐
ID Ref: ....

LIST 2: Birth Cert(Aust) ☐ Citizenship ☐ Cr/Debit Card ☐ Health ☐ Medicare ☐ Centrelink ☐ Student card ☐ Travel Doc ☐
ID Ref: ....

LIST 3 *(current address)*: Bank Statement ☐ Rates notice ☐ Educational report ☐ Motor Vehicle Rego ☐ Utility account ☐ Rental agreement ☐
ID Ref: .... *If ID provided from Lists 2 and 3, one ID must contain a signature*

Other ☐ .... **Initial ID sighted** ....

MARRIAGE CERTIFICATE APPLICATION INSTRUCTIONS

HOW TO APPLY

POST the completed form (pages 1 & 2) to:
Registry of Births, Deaths & Marriages
PO Box 7720 Cloisters Square
PERTH WA 6850 **OR**

BRING the completed form (pages 1 & 2) to:
Registry of Births, Deaths & Marriages
Level 10, 141 St Georges Terrace Perth
between 8.30 am - 4.30 pm, Monday to Friday

Note: Faxed applications will not be accepted

WHO CAN APPLY FOR A CERTIFICATE

Marriage certificates are available to the bride and groom.

If the certificate relates to a person other than yourself and you do not qualify under the Registry's Certificate Access Policy, you must provide the written consent or authority from a person entitled to the certificate and you must also provide identification for yourself **and** the person for whom you are acting.

Information regarding the Registry's Certificate Access policy is located on our website at www.bdm.dotag.wa.gov.au, or telephone the Registry on **1300 305 021**.

Privacy Considerations and Personal Records

Certificates held by the Registry contain sensitive and personal information. However the Registry allows unrestricted access for marriage certificates which occurred more than 75 years ago.

IDENTIFICATION REQUIREMENTS

When applying for a Western Australian certificate, evidence of your identity must be provided.

- You **MUST** provide at least **three** forms of identification:
  - One document from each List (1, 2 **and** 3). At least one containing a photograph; **or**
  - One from List 1 and two from List 2. At least one containing a photograph, **or**
  - Two from List 2 and one from List 3. At least one containing a signature.
- All forms of identification **MUST** be **current**.
- Documents from List 3 **MUST** show your **current residential address**.
- Bank statements, utility accounts or rates notices **MUST** have been **issued within the last six months**.

CERTIFICATION REQUIREMENTS

Applying in person - original documents must be provided.

Applying by post - please send clear **certified** photocopies of your identification documents with your application.

Photocopies of identification will only be accepted if they are **certified by a qualified witness** as being "true copies" of the original documents. See page 3 for *Certifying documents*.

√ Tick the forms of identification that are supporting your application

LIST 1 - Evidence of link between photo & signature

- ☐ **Australian driver's licence** (with photo)
- ☐ **Australian passport** (with photo)
- ☐ **Australian firearm's licence** (with photo)
- ☐ **Defence Force/Police ID card** (with photo)
- ☐ **Department of Immigration and Citizenship (DIAC) certificate** with evidence of residence status (with photo)
- ☐ **Over 18 or Proof of Age Identity card** (with photo)
- ☐ **Australian learner driver's permit card** (with photo)

LIST 2 - Evidence of operating in the community

- ☐ **Debit or Credit card** (one or the other, not both) issued by a financial institution
- ☐ **Document of identity** issued by the Passport Office
- ☐ **Entitlement card** issued by the Commonwealth or State Government (Centrelink, Health Care card, Veterans Affairs card etc)
- ☐ **Full Birth certificate** issued in Australia (birth extracts not accepted)
- ☐ **Medicare card**
- ☐ **Naturalisation, citizenship or immigration papers** issued by DIAC
- ☐ **Overseas passport** with current Australian Entry Permit
- ☐ **Security guard or crowd control licence** (Australian)
- ☐ **Student identity document or statement of enrolment** issued by an educational institution, including Tertiary(should include photo and/or signature)
- ☐ **Working with children card**

LIST 3 – Evidence of current residential address

- ☐ **Driver's licence renewal notice**
- ☐ **Financial institution statement** less than six months old
- ☐ **Motor vehicle registration**
- ☐ **Property lease or tenancy agreement**
- ☐ **Shire/water rates notice**
- ☐ **School or other educational report or certificate** less than twelve months old
- ☐ **Utility account** less than six months old (gas, electricity, home phone, etc)

FURTHER INFORMATION

For further information, please visit our website at www.bdm.dotag.wa.gov.au or call 1300 305 021 between 8.30 am and 4.30 pm, Monday to Friday.

PAYMENT DETAILS *If applying for more than one certificate only complete payment details on one form*

Applicant's Full Name

Enclosed is a cheque/money order* for $ **OR** Debit my MasterCard ☐ or Visa ☐ for $ * Your cheque or money order should be made payable to the *"Registry of Births, Deaths and Marriages"*			
Card No ☐☐☐☐ ☐☐☐☐ ☐☐☐☐ ☐☐☐☐		Expiry Date ☐☐ / ☐☐	
Name of Cardholder		Signature of cardholder	

BDM2

Registry of Births, Deaths and Marriages, Western Australia
141 St Georges Terrace, Perth WA TEL: 1300 305 021

(Western Australia ONLY)

DEATH CERTIFICATE APPLICATION FORM

Payment details over the page – you MUST return pages 1 and 2 if applying via mail

Fees including standard postal delivery effective 1 July 2009 – Subject to change without further notice — No GST is payable on these certificates

☐ **DEATH CERTIFICATE**	**$44.00**	
☐ **DEATH CERTIFICATE** (Reduced Fee)	**$31.00**	Only applies where the **full registration number** is supplied by you and the death is more than 75 years old. Otherwise full fee applies.
☐ **URGENT FEE**	**$34.00**	In addition to any other fee. **Does not** include Express Post.

Urgent fee not payable for computerised certificates if applied in person at the Perth Registry Office or certain Regional Courthouses see **Locations & Links** webpage. For eligibility see the **Death certificate access policy** on the **Deaths** webpage.

Identification and Certificate Access Requirements

See page 2 or visit www.bdm.dotag.wa.gov.au

Processing Times for Mailed Certificate Applications

Standard - Please allow up to 2 working days plus postal delivery time
Urgent - Processed within 24 hours of receipt plus postal delivery time

DEATH DETAILS REQUIRED

Please PRINT clearly

ABN: 70 598 519 443

Surname					
Given name(s)					
Date of death	Day / Month / Year	**Age at death**		**Male** ☐	**Female** ☐
Place of death in Western Australia	Suburb / Town				
Father's name	Surname	Given name(s)			
Mother's name	Maiden surname	Given name(s)			

APPLICANT'S DETAILS (please see next page for access conditions and identification requirements)

Full name			
Postal address	Suburb	State	Postcode
Your **Relationship** to the person whose certificate you are requesting	e.g. spouse, daughter	**Daytime phone number**	
Email address			
Reason required	Estate ☐ Insurance ☐ Bank Requirements ☐ Superannuation ☐ Family History ☐ Passport ☐ Property Settlement ☐ Legal ☐ Other		

Declaration: I declare that the information I have provided is true and correct. I understand that the WA Registry of Births, Deaths and Marriages may make enquiries with any organisation or individual to verify the information provided with this application.

SIGNATURE OF APPLICANT — Signature must be completed

OFFICE USE ONLY

LIST 1 *(with photo)*: Driver's Licence ☐ Passport ☐ Proof of Age ☐ Firearm's Licence ☐ Defence/police ☐ DIAC Certificate ☐ Learner's permit card ☐
ID Ref: ....

LIST 2: Birth Cert(Aust) ☐ Citizenship ☐ Cr/Debit Card ☐ Health ☐ Medicare ☐ Centrelink ☐ Student card ☐ Travel Doc ☐
ID Ref: ....

LIST 3 *(current address)*: Bank Statement ☐ Rates notice ☐ Educational report ☐ Motor Vehicle Rego ☐ Utility account ☐ Rental agreement ☐
ID Ref: .... *If ID provided from Lists 2 and 3, one ID must contain a signature*

Other ☐ .... Initial ID sighted....................

DEATH CERTIFICATE APPLICATION INSTRUCTIONS

HOW TO APPLY

POST the completed form (pages 1 & 2) to:
Registry of Births, Deaths & Marriages
PO Box 7720 Cloisters Square
PERTH WA 6850 **OR**

BRING the completed form (pages 1 & 2) to:
Registry of Births, Deaths & Marriages
Level 10, 141 St Georges Terrace Perth
between 8.30 am - 4.30 pm, Monday to Friday

Note: Faxed applications will not be accepted

WHO CAN APPLY FOR A CERTIFICATE

Death certificates are available to the spouse (including defacto partner), parents or children. (Evidence of relationship is required in all cases).

If you do not qualify under the Registry's Certificate Access Policy, you must provide the written consent or authority from a person entitled to the certificate and you must also provide identification for yourself **and** the person for whom you are acting.
Information regarding the Registry's Certificate Access policy is located on our website at www.bdm.dotag.wa.gov.au, or telephone the Registry on **1300 305 021**.

Privacy Considerations and Personal Records

Certificates held by the Registry contain sensitive and personal information. However the Registry allows unrestricted access for death certificates which occurred more than 30 years ago.

IDENTIFICATION REQUIREMENTS

When applying for a Western Australian certificate, evidence of your identity must be provided.

- You **MUST** provide at least **three** forms of identification:
  - One document from each List (1, 2 **and** 3). At least one containing a photograph; **or**
  - One from List 1 and two from List 2. At least one containing a photograph, **or**
  - Two from List 2 and one from List 3. At least one containing a signature.
- All forms of identification **MUST** be **current**.
- Documents from List 3 **MUST** show your **current residential address**.
- Bank statements, utility accounts or rates notices **MUST** have been **issued within the last six months**.

CERTIFICATION REQUIREMENTS

Applying in person - original documents must be provided.

Applying by post - please send clear **certified** photocopies of your identification documents with your application.

Photocopies of identification will only be accepted if they are **certified by a qualified witness** as being "true copies" of the original documents. See page 3 for *Certifying documents*.

√ Tick the forms of identification that are supporting your application

LIST 1 - Evidence of link between photo & signature

- ☐ **Australian driver's licence** (with photo)
- ☐ **Australian passport** (with photo)
- ☐ **Australian firearm's licence** (with photo)
- ☐ **Defence Force/Police ID card** (with photo)
- ☐ **Department of Immigration and Citizenship (DIAC) certificate** with evidence of residence status (with photo)
- ☐ **Over 18 or Proof of Age Identity card** (with photo)
- ☐ **Australian learner driver's permit card** (with photo)

LIST 2 - Evidence of operating in the community

- ☐ **Debit or Credit card** (one or the other, not both) issued by a financial institution
- ☐ **Document of identity** issued by the Passport Office
- ☐ **Entitlement card** issued by the Commonwealth or State Government (Centrelink, Health Care card, Veterans Affairs card etc)
- ☐ **Full Birth certificate** issued in Australia (birth extracts not accepted)
- ☐ **Medicare card**
- ☐ **Naturalisation, citizenship or immigration papers** issued by DIAC
- ☐ **Overseas passport** with current Australian Entry Permit
- ☐ **Security guard or crowd control licence** (Australian)
- ☐ **Student identity document or statement of enrolment** issued by an educational institution, including Tertiary(should include photo and/or signature)
- ☐ **Working with children card**

LIST 3 – Evidence of current residential address

- ☐ **Driver's licence renewal notice**
- ☐ **Financial institution statement** less than six months old
- ☐ **Motor vehicle registration**
- ☐ **Property lease or tenancy agreement**
- ☐ **Shire/water rates notice**
- ☐ **School or other educational report or certificate** less than twelve months old
- ☐ **Utility account** less than six months old (gas, electricity, home phone, etc)

FURTHER INFORMATION

For further information, please visit our website at www.bdm.dotag.wa.gov.au or call 1300 305 021 between 8.30 am and 4.30 pm, Monday to Friday.

PAYMENT DETAILS *If applying for more than one certificate only complete payment details on one form*

Applicant's Full Name

Enclosed is a cheque/money order* for $ **OR** Debit my MasterCard ☐ or Visa ☐ for $
* Your cheque or money order should be made payable to the *"Registry of Births, Deaths and Marriages"*

Card No	☐☐☐☐ ☐☐☐☐ ☐☐☐☐ ☐☐☐☐	Expiry Date	☐☐ / ☐☐
Name of Cardholder		Signature of cardholder	

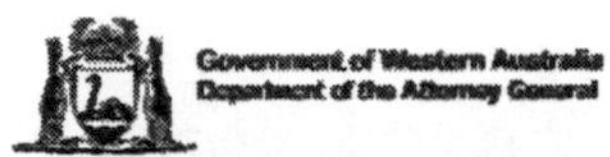

WHO CAN CERTIFY DOCUMENTS?

This page is NOT to be forwarded to the Registry of Births, Deaths and Marriages

Certifying documents (photocopies of identification)

Before certifying a document, ensure that the copy to be certified is an identical copy of the original. Suggested wording for the certification is as follows:

I certify that this appears to be a true copy of the document produced to me on < date >
Signature
Name
Qualification (eg JP, Pharmacist)

List of persons who can Certify Documents:

Academic (post-secondary institution)	Loss adjuster
Accountant	Marriage Celebrant
Architect	Member of Parliament (State or Commonwealth)
Australian Consular Officer	Minister of religion
Australian Diplomatic Officer	Nurse
Bailiff	Optometrist
Bank Manager	Patent Attorney
Chartered secretary	Physiotherapist
Chemist	Podiatrist
Chiropractor	Police officer
Company auditor or liquidator	Post Office manager
Court officer (Judge, master, magistrate, registrar or clerk)	Psychologist
Defence Force officer (Commissioned, Warrant or NCO with 5 years continuous service)	Public Servant (State or Commonwealth)
Dentist	Public Notary
Doctor	Real Estate agent
Engineer	Settlement agent
Industrial organisation secretary	Sheriff or deputy Sheriff
Insurance broker	Surveyor
Justice of the Peace	Teacher
Lawyer	Tribunal Officer
Local government CEO or deputy CEO	Veterinary surgeon
Local government councillor	

AUSTRIA

Send your requests to:

Standesamt
(Town), Austria

There is no central office for vital records in Austria. Records of birth, marriage, and death are generally kept at the Austrian vital records office (Standesamt) where the event occurred. The addresses and phone numbers of all vital records registries in Austria are listed at www.help.gv.at. When you order a certificate, ask for it to be issued in the "international" version to avoid any translation hassles later on.

Until 1938 (in Burgenland until 1895), births, marriages, and deaths were registered by the local churches and religious communities. From 1870 to 1938 vital records of individuals without a religious affiliation were issued by the county government.

Austrian church registers are in the process of being digitized and made available online at http://matricula-online.eu/.

For additional assistance, contact:

Embassy of Austria
3524 International Court, NW
Washington, DC 20008
Tel. (202) 895-6700

AZERBAIJAN

Send your requests to:

Bureau of Acts of Civil Status
(Town), Azerbaijan

Authenticated and certified copies of vital records may be obtained by Azerbaijani citizens by applying to the Bureau of Acts of Civil Status (ZAGS) of the locality having custody of the record. In the United States, documents can be requested through the Embassy of Azerbaijan in Washington, D.C. The process, however, often takes several months.

For additional assistance, contact:

Embassy of Azerbaijan
2741 34th Street, NW
Washington, DC 20008
Tel. (202) 337-3500

BAHAMAS

Send your requests to:

Registrar General's Department
(Location: #50 Shirley Street)
P.O. Box N-532
Nassau, NP, Bahamas

Tel. (242) 323-0594/5
Fax (242) 322-5553
www.bahamas.gov.bs/rgd

Birth and death records are available from January 1850 to the present. Marriage records are available from January 1799 to the present.

For additional assistance, contact:

Embassy of the Commonwealth of the Bahamas
2220 Massachusetts Avenue, NW
Washington, DC 20008

Tel. (202) 319-2660

THE REGISTRAR GENERAL'S DEPARTMENT
P.O.BOX N-532
NASSAU, BAHAMAS

TELEPHONE: (242) 323-0594/5 or 356-6704
FAX: (242) 322-5553

APPLICATION FOR BIRTH CERTIFICATE

I desire to have a search made for * ______________________ copy/copies supplied off the Register of Birth of

____
(Enter All Names)

A.
Born at (Institution) ____________________________

On the island of ____________________________

Date of Birth ____________________________

Father's full name ____________________________

Mother's Full name ____________________________

Mother's maiden name ____________________________

Signature of applicant ____________________________

Email of applicant ____________________________

*Insert number of copies required

PAYMENT

CERTIFIED COPIES @ U.S. $10.00 PER COPY: International Postal Money Order or Bank Draft or Cashier's Check payable to "THE REGISTRAR GENERAL'S DEPARTMENT."

APOSTILLE FEE @U.S. $10.00: Cashier's Check or Bank Draft payable to the "PUBLIC TREASURY."

PLEASE DO NOT SUBMIT PERSONAL CHEQUES OR CASH PAYMENTS.

OFFICIAL USE ONLY

B.
Period searched ____________________________ By ______________
Period checked ____________________________ By ______________
Certified copies made____________________________ By ______________
Examined by ____________________________ By ______________
Copies received by ____________________________
Registration found in year ____________________________ At Page ____________

C.
___(a) No record of birth can be found on file
___(b) Birth record shows information given about to be correct.
___(c) Birth of male/female child recorded without name
___(d) Father's name not recorded
Indicate with (√)Where appropriate at (a), (b), (c) or (d).

BAHRAIN

Send your requests to:

Birth and Death Records Office
Public Health Department
P.O. Box 12
Manama, State of Bahrain

Birth certificates are available for all persons whose births occurred in a hospital. The certificate is in both Arabic and English. Requirements are an application form (acquired from the above address), copies of parents' passports, name of child, and date and place of birth. There may be a fee for this service.

Marriages between Muslims are performed by local religious leaders according to Islamic law and custom. Marriage certificates are kept on file with the appropriate Sharia Court. Requests for copies of these certificates should be addressed either to the Sunni or Shi'a Sharia Court, Ministry of Justice, P.O. Box 450, Manama, State of Bahrain. Each request should state the date of the marriage. These certificates are available only in Arabic. Marriages between two Christians can only be performed in four designated Christian churches, each maintaining its own records. Requests for these records should be directed to the church where the marriage took place. Between 1930 and 1971 all Christian marriages were recorded by the British Political Agent. Information from these records can be obtained from the British Embassy, P.O. Box 114, Manama, State of Bahrain. Divorce certificates are available from the Chief Justice of the Sharia Court, Bahrain Ministry of Justice, P.O. Box 450, Manama, State of Bahrain.

For additional assistance, contact:

Embassy of the State of Bahrain — Tel. (202) 342-1111
3502 International Drive, NW
Washington, DC 20008

BANGLADESH

Send your requests to:

Registrar
(Town), Bangladesh

Local registrar offices throughout Bangladesh issue copies of birth and death certificates. Applicants should contact the designated office in the locality where the event occurred. According to Bangladeshi civil law, all marriages in Bangladesh require registration with the appropriate marriage registrar. For Muslim marriages the applicant should contact the Kazi office or the registrar who solemnized the marriage to obtain the marriage certificate and the Nikah Nama (Bengali and English version).

For additional assistance, contact:

Embassy of the People's Republic of Bangladesh — Tel. (202) 244-0183
3510 International Drive, NW
Washington, DC 20008

BARBADOS

Send your requests to:

The Registrar of the Supreme Court
Registration Department
Coleridge Street
Bridgetown, St. Michael, Barbados

Tel. (246) 426-3461

The Registrar has birth records from January 1, 1890; marriage records from 1637; and death records from January 1, 1925. The Registrar also holds baptismal records before 1890 and burial records before 1925. These may be requested by using the appropriate birth and death certificate application forms. Vital registration is considered to be comprehensive.

The Barbados Department of Archives (Black Rock, St. James BB24001; tel. 246-425-5150) holds the following records: Baptisms 1637–1930, Marriages 1643–present, Burials 1643–present.

For additional assistance, contact:

Embassy of Barbados
2144 Wyoming Avenue, NW
Washington, DC 20008

Tel. (202) 939-9200

A64:128

GOVERNMENT OF BARBADOS

REGISTRATION DEPARTMENT
RECORDS BRANCH

APPLICATION FOR BIRTH CERTIFICATE

Please read notes overleaf before completing this form in BLOCK LETTERS

SECTION 1. APPLICANT'S NAME AND ADDRESS	
Name	
Address	
National Registration No.	
Applicant's Signature	

SECTION 2. RELATIONSHIP TO PERSON NAMED IN THE CERTIFICATE

Applying for own Birth certificate? *Please tick appropriate box* ☐ *Yes* ☐ *No*

If answer is No state your relationship to the person to whom the Birth certificate relates:

....

Reason for requesting the certificate: ....

....

Is the person to whom the certificate relates deceased? ☐ *Yes* ☐ *No*

If the answer is *Yes* state date of Death ....

Number of certificates required: .... copies

SECTION 3. DETAILS OF BIRTH CERTIFICATE REQUIRED

Surname	Christian Names		
Date of Birth	Day	Month	Year
National Registration No.:			
Place of Birth:			
Place of Baptism:			

PARENTS' NAMES

	Surname	Christian Names
Father		
Mother		

FOR OFFICE USE ONLY	
Cost of Certificate(s)	Receipt No.:

Filling in this application form

This office holds records of Births in Barbados from 1890. This application is for applying for **Birth** certificates only. Please complete the application form in **BLOCK LETTERS**.

Section 1.

Fill in your name, full address and National Registration No.

Section 2.

- Tick the Yes box if you are applying for your own Birth certificate.
- Tick the No box if you are applying for another person's Birth certificate.
- If you are applying for another person's Birth certificate you must
    1. State your relationship to the person to whom the certificate relates.
    2. Your reason for applying for the Birth certificate.
- Tick the Yes box if the person to whom the certificate relates is deceased and **supply the date of death.**
- Tick the No box if the person to whom the certificate relates is not deceased.
- Indicate the number of certificates required. The cost is as follows:
    1. Certificates for persons **60 years and over $1.00 each.**
    2. Certificates for persons **less than 60 years $5.00 each.**

Section 3.

The more details of the Birth certificate you supply the better the chance we will have of locating the correct record.

- A search will be conducted two years either side of the date quoted.
- If you do not know the full date of birth, please state a two-year search you require us to undertake (e.g. 1990-1991).
- **If insufficient details are provided to conduct a search your application will be returned to you.**

For purposes of the detection and prevention of crime, information relating to this application may be passed to other Government Departments or law enforcement agencies.

A64·130

GOVERNMENT OF BARBADOS

REGISTRATION DEPARTMENT
Records Branch

Application for Marriage Certificate

Please read notes overleaf before completing this form in BLOCK LETTERS

Section 1. Applicant's Name and Address	
Name	
Address	
National Registration No.	
Applicant's Signature	

Section 2. Relationship to Person Named on the Certificate

Are you applying for own Marriage Certificate? *Please tick appropriate box* ☐ *Yes* ☐ *No*

If answer is No state your relationship to the person to whom the certificate relates:

....

Reason for requesting the certificate: ....

Number of Certificates required: .... copies

Section 3. Details of Marriage Certificate Required

	Surname	Christian Names		
Husband				
Wife *(Maiden)*				
Date of Marriage		Day	Month	Year
Place of Marriage				
National Registration No. – Husband				
National Registration No. – Wife				

FOR OFFICE USE ONLY	
Cost of Certificate(s)	**Receipt No.:**
Due Date:	**Officer Assigned:**

Filling in this application form

This office holds records of Marriages registered in Barbados from 1884. This application is for applying for **Marriage** certificates only. Please complete the application form in **BLOCK LETTERS.**

Section 1.

Fill in your name, full address and National Registration No.

Section 2.

- Tick the **Yes** box if you are applying for **your own Marriage certificate.**
- Tick the **No** box if you are applying for **another person's Marriage certificate.**
- If you are applying for another person's Marriage certificate you must
  1. State your relationship to the person to whom the certificate relates.
  2. Your reason for applying for the certificate.
- Indicate the number of certificates required. The cost is as follows:
  1. Marriage certificates for Nationals – **$10.00 each.**
  2. Marriage certificates for Non-Nationals – **$20.00 each.**

Section 3.

The more details of the Marriage certificate you supply the better the chance we will have of locating the correct record.

- A search will be conducted two years either side of the date quoted.
- If you do not know the full date of Marriage, please state a **two-year** search you require us to undertake (e.g. 1990-1991).
- **If insufficient details are provided to conduct a search your application will be returned to you.**

For purposes of the detection and prevention of crime, information relating to this application may be passed to other Government Departments or law enforcement agencies.

A64/129

GOVERNMENT OF BARBADOS

REGISTRATION DEPARTMENT

RECORDS BRANCH

APPLICATION FOR DEATH CERTIFICATE

Please read notes overleaf before completing this form in BLOCK LETTERS

SECTION 1. APPLICANT'S NAME AND ADDRESS	
Name	
Address	
National Registration No.	
Applicant's Signature	

SECTION 2. RELATIONSHIP TO THE PERSON NAMED ON THE CERTIFICATE
State your relationship to the Deceased: ....
Reason for requesting the certificate: ....
Number of certificates required: .... copies   Cause of Death: ....

SECTION 3. DETAILS OF DEATH CERTIFICATE REQUIRED			
Deceased Surname	Deceased Christian Names		
Date of Death	Day	Month	Year
Deceased National Registration No.:			
Place of Death:			

FOR OFFICE USE ONLY	
Cost of Certificate(s)	Receipt No.:
Due Date:	Officer Assigned:

Filling in this application form

This office holds records of deaths registered in Barbados from 1925. This application is for applying for **Death** certificates only. Please complete the application form in **BLOCK LETTERS.**

Section 1.

Fill in your name, full address and National Registration No.

Section 2.

- State your relationship to the deceased.
- Give your reason for applying for the Death certificate.
- Indicate the number of certificates required. The Office issues **two** types of Death certificates. The cost is as follows:

  1. Death Certificate – **$5.00 each.**
  2. Cause of Death Certificate – **$10.00 each.**

Section 3.

The more details of the Death certificate you supply the better the chance we will have of locating the correct record.

- A search will be conducted two years either side of the date quoted.
- If you do not know the full date of Death, please state a two-year search you require us to undertake (e.g. 1990-1991).
- **If insufficient details are provided to conduct a search your application will be returned to you.**

For purposes of the detection and prevention of crime, information relating to this application may be passed to other Government Departments or law enforcement agencies.

BELARUS

Send your requests to:

State Archive for Registration of Vital Statistics
(Town), Republic of Belarus

For periods roughly after 1920, vital records can be found at regional and local state archives and also in the state archives of registry offices (ZAGS). Earlier records from the former Minsk, Mogilev, and Vitebsk provinces of the Russian Empire and a part of the Grodno Province are kept at the National Historical Archives of Belarus in Minsk (ul. Kropotkina, 55, Minsk, 220002). The National Historical Archives of Belarus in Grodno (pl. Tizengauza, 2, Grodno, 230023) has records from the former Grodno and Vilno provinces. In the U.S., Belarusian documents can be requested through the Belarusian Embassy in Washington, D.C. (see below for address) or the Consulate General in New York (708 Third Avenue, 20th Floor, New York, NY 10017). Some civil records were destroyed during World War II and may not be available.

The JewishGen Belarus Database (www.jewishgen.org/databases/belarus/) contains more than 600,000 entries from Belarus, including births, marriages, and deaths. The Routes to Roots Foundation (www.rtrfoundation.org) hosts an online database that includes documents for towns within the current borders of Belarus and towns that were formerly in Poland, but are now within the borders of Belarus.

For additional assistance, contact:

Embassy of the Republic of Belarus — Tel. (202) 986-1604
1619 New Hampshire Avenue, NW
Washington, DC 20009

BELGIUM

Send your requests to:

Officier de l'État Civil/Burgerlijke Stand
(Town), Belgium

There is no central office for vital records in Belgium. To obtain copies of birth, marriage, and death certificates, write to the town where the event occurred. For divorce decrees contact the Clerk of the Lower Court (Greffe du Tribunal de lere Instance/Griffie van de Rechtbank van Eerste Aanleg) in the commune in which the judgment was rendered. Vital records are on file from 1796, and the current registration is considered to be comprehensive.

For additional assistance, contact:

Embassy of Belgium — Tel. (202) 333-6900
3330 Garfield Street, NW
Washington, DC 20008

BELIZE

Send your requests to:

Registrar General Department
Vital Statistics Unit
Supreme Court Building
Belize City, Belize

Tel. (011) (501) 223-5625
E-mail: vitalstatsbz@yahoo.com

Formerly British Honduras, Belize became independent in 1964. The Vital Statistics Unit has birth and death records from 1885, and marriage records from 1881. The Unit also will provide adoption certificates. Original adoption orders are kept by the Supreme Court of Belize, Supreme Court Building, Belize City, Belize.

For additional assistance, contact:

Embassy of Belize
2535 Massachusetts Avenue, NW
Washington, DC 20008

Tel. (202) 332-9636

BENIN

Send your requests to:

Mayor's Office or Prefecture
(Town), Benin

Certificates are issued by the mayor's office or prefecture where the event took place. Vital registration began in Benin, formerly known as Dahomey, in 1933 and included mostly French citizens and foreigners. By 1950 registration included most residents within 15 miles of a registration center. Benin became independent on August 1, 1960.

For additional assistance, contact:

Embassy of the Republic of Benin
2124 Kalorama Road, NW
Washington, DC 20008

Tel. (202) 232-6656

BERMUDA

Send your requests to:

Registry General
1st Floor
Government Administration Building
30 Parliament Street
Hamilton, HM12, Bermuda

Tel. (441) 297-7693
www.registrygeneral.gov.bm/

The Registry has birth and marriage records from 1866, and death records from 1865. The registration is considered to be comprehensive. The current fees for certified copies of records are listed on the Registry's website. Divorce certificates can be obtained from the Registrar's Chambers, Supreme Court of Bermuda, Hamilton 5-24, Bermuda.

BHUTAN

Send your requests to:

Bhutan Mission to the United Nations (Consulate General)
343 East 43rd Street
New York, NY 10017

Tel. (212) 682-2268
www.un.int/wcm/content/site/bhutan

Birth and death certificates are generally unavailable in Bhutan, since births are not registered and death certificates are not issued, though village records do exist. Copies of marriage records may be obtained from the local civil office that registered the marriage.

BOLIVIA

Send your requests to:

Dirección Nacional de Registro Civil
Ministerio del Interior, Migración, y Justicia
Av. Arce No. 2409
La Paz, Bolivia

While some records exist from 1898, modern vital registration in Bolivia didn't begin until July 1940. Certificates are also available from the Registro Civil where the event took place. The Bolivian Consulate in the U.S. can provide civil registry services (see contact information below).

For additional assistance, contact:

Consulate General of Bolivia
1825 Connecticut Ave, NW, Suite 200c
Washington, DC 20009

Tel. (202) 232-4827/28
www.bolivia-usa.org/

BOSNIA and HERZEGOVINA

Send your requests to:

Civil Registration Office
(Town), Bosnia and Herzegovina

This country has no central office for vital records. Birth (Izvod iz maticne knjige rodenih), marriage (Izvod iz maticne knjige vjencanih) and death (Izvod iz maticne knjige umrlih) certificates are available from the civil registrar (maticar) having jurisdiction over the locality where the event occurred. Vital records are on file from 1946. Records before that were kept by the local churches. The practice in Bosnia-Herzegovina has been that changes in civil status, such as divorce or name change, are entered onto birth certificates.

For additional assistance, contact:

Embassy of Bosnia and Herzegovina
2109 E Street, NW
Washington, DC 20037

Tel. (202) 337-1500

BOTSWANA

Send your requests to:

Registry of Births, Deaths and Marriages
Ministry of Home Affairs
Private Bag 002
Gaborone, Botswana

The Registry has birth records from 1915, marriage records from 1895, and death records from 1904. Botswana became independent in 1966 and vital registration became compulsory in 1969.

Birth, death, and marriage certificate requests can be made in writing and faxed to (202) 244 4164 or mailed to the Consular Section of the Botswana embassy at the below address. Requests must include contact phone numbers.

For additional assistance, contact:

Embassy of the Republic of Botswana
Consular Section
1531-1533 New Hampshire Avenue, NW
Washington, DC 20036

www.botswanaembassy.org/

BRAZIL

Send your requests to:

Registro Civil
(Town, State), Brazil

Registration of births and deaths has been required by law since 1850, but until 1870 the Catholic Church kept these records. Because the Church continued to keep birth, marriage, and death records after civil registration began in 1870, there may be two types of vital records available. Civil registration records are kept by all the states on a municipal level. There are over 3,700 municipalities (municípios) in Brazil, with offices of civil registration. The Family History Library has microfilmed the civil registration records of many of these municipalities.

An adoption certificate (decreto de adocao) may be obtained by an applicant or his or her agent at the Civil Registry where the adoption was registered.

For additional assistance, contact:

Embassy of Brazil
3006 Massachusetts Avenue, NW
Washington, DC 20008

Tel. (202) 238-2700

BRUNEI

Send your requests to:

Registrar of Births and Deaths
Medical and Health Department
Ministry of Health
Bandar Seri Begawan 2062
Brunei Darussalam

Birth and death records are available from 1948 and for British subjects from 1926. Certificates are also available from the Superintendent of Births and Deaths for the registration area in which the birth or death was registered. Marriage certificates are available from the Registrar of Marriages (Attorney General's Chambers, Bandar Seri Begawan) or from the Registrar of Marriages for the area in which the marriage was solemnized and/or registered.

For additional assistance, contact:

Embassy of Brunei Darussalam — Tel. (202) 237-1838
3520 International Court, NW
Washington, DC 20008

BULGARIA

Send your requests to:

Registrar
(Town), Bulgaria

Civil registration began in 1893, though there are many gaps in the records. Church registers are available before that time. The records are located at the district archives in each of the 28 districts of Bulgaria.

The Family History Library has microfilms of civil registration for the districts of Sofia and Plovdiv, and these records usually cover the 1893–1912 time period.

For additional assistance, contact:

Embassy of the Republic of Bulgaria — Tel. (202) 387-0174
1621 22nd Street, NW
Washington, DC 20008

BURKINA FASO

Send your requests to:

City Hall
Office of Vital Statistics (Service d'État Civil)
(Town), Burkina Faso

Certificates are available from the Office of Vital Statistics in the town where the event took place. Vital registration in Burkina Faso, formerly known as Upper Volta, began in 1933 for French citizens and expanded in 1950 to include all residents living within 15 miles of registration centers.

For additional assistance, contact:

Embassy of Burkina Faso — Tel. (202) 332-5577
2340 Massachusetts Avenue, NW
Washington, DC 20008

BURUNDI

Send your requests to:

Officer of Vital Statistics (Officier de l'État Civil)
Mairie de Bujumbura
B.P. l790
Bujumbura, Burundi

Vital registration for the entire nation began in 1922. Even though efforts have been made to include all areas, the registration is not considered to be comprehensive.

For additional assistance, contact:

Embassy of Burundi — Tel. (202) 342-2574
2233 Wisconsin Avenue, NW, Suite 212
Washington, DC 20007

CAMBODIA

For assistance contact:

Royal Embassy of Cambodia — Tel. (202) 726-7742
4500 16th Street, NW
Washington, DC 20011

Records are available for some births, marriages, and deaths since 1980, and for all births, marriages, and deaths since 1992. Because all archives were destroyed during the regime of 1975–1979, and because Cambodia has had some difficulty reestablishing its civic institutions, contemporary and retrospective civil documents are now issued by local authorities for a fee using information provided by the requester.

CAMEROON

Send your requests to:

Office of Mayor (la Mairie)
(Town), Cameroon

Vital registration began for Western Cameroon in 1917. By 1935 registration also included Eastern Cameroon.

For additional assistance, contact:

Embassy of the Republic of Cameroon — Tel. (202) 286-0984
3400 International Drive, NW
Washington, DC 20008

CANADA—ALBERTA

Send your requests to:

Service Alberta — Tel. (780) 427-7013
Vital Statistics — E-mail: vs@gov.ab.ca
Box 2023 — www.servicealberta.gov.ab.ca/VitalStatistics.cfm
Edmonton, Alberta, Canada T5J 4W7

Non-Alberta residents send your requests to:

Registry Connect — Tel. (780) 415-2225
Authorized Agent for the Government of Alberta, Vital Statistics — E-mail: registry.connect@aara.ca
Suite 202, 1003 Ellwood Road, SW
Ellwood Office Park South
Edmonton, Alberta, Canada T6X 0B3

Vital Statistics has Alberta birth records dating from approximately 1850 to the present and Alberta marriage and death records dating from approximately 1890 to the present. Birth records are restricted for 120 years, marriage records for 75 years, and death records for 50 years.

To apply for a certified copy of a vital record, an applicant who is a resident of Alberta must apply through a registry agent (for a list of agents, go to www.health.alberta.ca/documents/AHCIP-Registry-Agent-poster.pdf). There is a fee for the registry agent in addition to the fee for the certificate. Non-Alberta residents should apply through Registry Connect (see contact information above).

The Provincial Archives of Alberta (8555 Roper Road, Edmonton, Alberta T6E 5W1; http://culture.alberta.ca/paa/) holds birth, marriage, and death records for Alberta from about 1870 to the 1980s for some communities. There is an index available for the records created up to 1905. It also houses divorce records ca. 1918 to ca. 1975.

Cost for a certified Birth Certificate (Alberta residents)	Can$20.00
Cost for a certified Birth Certificate (Alberta non-residents)	Can$39.64
Cost for a certified Marriage Certificate (Alberta residents)	Can$20.00
Cost for a certified Marriage Certificate (Alberta non-residents)	Can$39.64
Cost for a certified Death Certificate (Alberta residents)	Can$20.00
Cost for a certified Death Certificate (Alberta non-residents)	Can$39.64

For additional assistance, contact:

Embassy of Canada — Tel. (202) 682-1740
501 Pennsylvania Avenue, NW
Washington, DC 20001

Ordering Birth, Stillbirth and Marriage Documents

Vital Statistics

What kinds of documents are available to order?

Alberta Vital Statistics maintains a registration record of births, marriages, deaths, legal changes of name and stillbirths (events) that **occur in Alberta.**
NOTE: To order documents for events that occurred outside Alberta, contact the province / territory / country where the event took place

CERTIFICATE

Certificates contain the following information:

BIRTH
Personal Information Only - Child's last and given name(s), date of birth, place of birth, sex, registration number, registration date, date issued.

Personal Information and Parentage - Same as personal information only plus mother's last and given name(s), mother's place of birth (province / country), father's last and given name(s), father's place of birth (province / country).

MARRIAGE
Small - Name(s) of both parties to the marriage, date of marriage, place of marriage, registration number, date issued, registration date.

Large - Same as small, plus the birthplace of both parties to the marriage (province/country only).

PHOTOCOPY OF REGISTRATION

A photocopy of the original *Registration of Birth, Marriage* or *Stillbirth.*

NOTE: Photocopies are rarely needed. They are not recommended for use as identification.

SEARCH LETTER

A search letter does not provide actual detailed information. The Vital Statistics office will notify the client whether or not the event is registered, nothing more.

What is acceptable proof of identity and why is it needed?

When ordering Vital Statistics certificates / documents, the applicant must present an acceptable proof of identity document. This document must be issued by a provincial or federal government. It must contain a recognizable photograph, full name, and a distinctive identification number. If the document has an expiry date, the document must currently be valid. If the document has no expiry date, then it must have been issued within the last 5 years. If the document is in a language other then English, then the applicant must provide a notarized English translation and an affidavit from the translator stating that the translation is accurate.

How do I submit an application?

Alberta residents applying for an Alberta Vital Statistics document must apply in person at a registry agent office - an authorized representative of the Alberta Government. For registry agent information, please contact:

Edmonton	780-427-7013
Alberta rite-line (toll free Alberta only)	310-0000 then dial 427-7013
SUPERPAGES™	under Licensing and Registry Services
Website	www.servicealberta.gov.ab.ca

What if I don't have acceptable proof of identity or am unable to apply in person at a registry agent office?

Consent may be provided to another person to act as the applicant's designated agent. The designated agent must have known the applicant for at least 1 year, must complete the statutory declaration on page 3, and must present acceptable proof of identity. Not all applicants may provide their consent to a designated agent - see eligibility restrictions on the next page.
NOTE: You will still be the applicant. You will need to sign the application form and enter your personal information and relationship to the person listed on the certificate.

How much do certificates/documents cost?

For certificates or photocopies, the government fee is $20.00 per certificate / document, plus a registry agent fee. For search letters, the fee is $20.00 for each three-year period searched or portion thereof, plus a registry agent fee.

How long does it take to process an application?

Under normal circumstances when the application has been completed correctly and there are no further requirements, certificates / documents are usually mailed within 3 business days.

How will the certificate / document be delivered to me?

Certificates / documents are mailed to the applicant, unless other arrangements have been made with a registry agent office.

Who can apply for Vital Statistics' documents?

The areas below show who is eligible and what proofs of eligibility are required.

Certificates and / or Photocopies of a Registration

Birth

a) The **person** whose birth is registered.

b) The **parent** of the person whose birth is registered as established by the Registration of Birth or by court order. A copy of the applicable court order must be attached to this application.

c) A **person adopting** a child. Proof of a pending adoption must be attached to this application, e.g., petition for adoption.

d) A **guardian, trustee** or person with **power of attorney** for a person described in a) or b). A copy of the legal document must be attached to this application.

e) A person who is designated by a **personal directive** as an agent of the person described in a). Acceptable legal document as proof must be attached to this application.

f) A person who is a **designated agent** for a person described in a) to e). Consent and statutory declaration must be completed. See bottom of application form.

g) A person with an **order from the court**. A copy of the order must be attached to this application.

h) A **lawyer** for a person described in a) to e) or g). A copy of a valid Law Society card must be attached to this application.

i) A person who requires it to comply with **another legislation**. A copy of the legislation must be attached to this application.

When the person whose birth is registered is a minor:

j) If the minor is younger than 12 years of age, the application must be made on behalf of the child by a parent or guardian of the minor.

k) Between the ages of 12 and 14 the minor may make the application with the written consent of the minor's parent or guardian.

l) Over the age of 14, the minor may make the application on his or her own behalf.

When the person whose birth is registered is deceased:

m) An **adult next-of-kin*** of the person whose birth is registered, including a minor parent. Death certificate and either proof of relationship or an Affidavit of Relationship** must be attached to this application.

n) The **executor** of the deceased person's estate. Death certificate and a copy of the will identifying the executor must be attached to this application.

o) An **adult relative** of the deceased person when there are no eligible applicants. Death certificate and either proof of relationship or an Affidavit of Relationship** must be attached to this application.

Anyone may apply for a Birth document when:

p) The birth record is 120 years old or older; or

q) 50 years has passed since the death of the person whose birth is registered.

Marriage

a) A **party to the marriage** (bride/groom).

b) A **guardian, trustee** or person with **power of attorney** for a person described in a). A copy of the legal document must be attached to this application.

c) A person who is a **designated agent** for a person described in a) or b). Consent and statutory declaration must be completed. See bottom of application form.

d) A person who is designated by a **personal directive** as an agent of the person described in a). A copy of the legal document must be attached to this application.

e) A person with an **order from the court**. A copy of the order must be attached to this application.

f) A **lawyer** for a person described in a), b), d), or e). A copy of a valid Law Society card must be attached to this application.

When the person who was a party to the marriage is deceased:

g) An **adult next-of-kin*** of a person who was a party to the marriage. Death certificate and either proof of relationship or an Affidavit of Relationship** must be attached to this application.

h) The **executor** of an estate of a party to the marriage. Death certificate and a copy of the will identifying the executor must be attached to this application.

i) An **adult relative** of a deceased party to the marriage when there are no eligible applicants. Death certificate and either proof of relationship or an Affidavit of Relationship** must be attached to this application.

Anyone may apply for a Marriage document when:

j) The marriage record is 75 years old or older.

Stillbirth

a) An **adult next-of-kin*** of the stillborn child, including a minor who is a parent of the child. Proof of relationship or an Affidavit of Relationship** must be attached to this application.

b) An **adult relative** of the stillborn child when there are no living persons described in a). Proof of relationship or an Affidavit of Relationship** must be attached to this application.

c) A person who is a **designated agent** for a person described in a) or b). Consent and statutory declaration must be completed. See bottom of application form.

d) A person with an **order from the court**. A copy of the order must be attached to this application.

e) A **funeral home representative** who is making disposition arrangements for the stillborn child. Proof of occupation must be attached to this application.

f) A **lawyer** for a person described in a), c), or d). A copy of a valid Law Society card must be attached to this application.

Anyone may apply for a Stillbirth document when:

g) The stillbirth record is 75 years old or older.

Medical Certificates of Stillbirth

a) Adult **next-of-kin*** of the stillborn child, including a minor parent. Proof of relationship must be attached to this application.

b) A person who is a **designated agent** for a person described in a). Consent and statutory declaration must be completed. See bottom of application form.

c) Any person with an **order from the court**. A copy of the order must be attached to this application

d) The **lawyer** for a person described in a) or c). A copy of a valid Law Society card must be attached to this application.

* **Next-of-Kin:** Mother, father, brother, sister, children, spouse or adult interdependent partner. This does not include in-laws, grand children, step relatives, aunts, uncles, nieces or nephews. Persons who have been adopted or who have placed their child for adoption are not "next-of-kin" to biological relations.

** Affidavit of Relationship available from a registry agent.

 Government

Application for Birth, Stillbirth and Marriage Documents

This information is collected in accordance with the Vital Statistics Act and Regulations. It is required to determine your eligibility to apply for products and services, search Vital Statistics registration records and process your request. Collection is authorized under s. 33(a) and (c) of the Freedom of Information and Protection of Privacy Act. Questions about the collection can be directed to Vital Statistics' staff @ Box 2023, Edmonton, AB T5J 4W7 or (780) 427-7013 (toll free 310-0000 within Alberta).

IMPORTANT INFORMATION TO AVOID DELAYS

- This application **must** be returned to a registry agent in person.
- The applicant **must** provide acceptable proof of identity. *(see the front page for what to do if you do not have acceptable proof of identity)*
- Read all instructions carefully before filling in this form.
- Make sure you are eligible to apply and have the necessary supporting documents - see the opposite page.
- Information must be as complete as possible. Attach a written explanation if you cannot provide the information required in the applicable section(s).
- If a record or event cannot be found, a search for a three-year period is carried out automatically and the applicant will be notified.

PRINT CLEARLY - This information will be used to mail your documents. All areas of this section must be completed.

Full Name of Applicant		Phone No. *(during the day)*
Mailing Address *Street*		*Apartment No.*
City / Town / Village	*Province / Country*	*Postal / Zip Code*
If Company, Attention of		Your Reference No. *(if applicable)*
Reason Certificate Required		
State Your Relationship to Person Named on Certificate		
Signature of Applicant X		Date Signed *(month by name, day, year)*

The Quantity column must be completed. →

BIRTH or STILLBIRTH

Last Name *(give **MAIDEN** name if certificate is for a married person)*		Given Names		☐ Male ☐ Female
Date of Birth	Place of Birth *(city, town or village)*	Name of Hospital *(if known)*	Type of Birth ☐ Live Birth ☐ Stillbirth	
Last Name of Father / Parent	Known by any Other Last Name	Given Names	Birthplace of Father / Parent	
Maiden Name of Mother / Parent	Known by any Other Last Name	Given Names	Birthplace of Mother / Parent	

Type	Quantity
Birth Certificate with Personal Information Only	
Birth Certificate with Personal Information and Parentage	
Photocopy of Registration	
Search Letter	
Photocopy of Medical Certificate of Stillbirth	

MARRIAGE

Last Name of Bride / Spouse 1 *(prior to this marriage)*	Given Names	Birthplace	☐ Male ☐ Female
Last Name of Groom / Spouse 2 *(prior to this marriage)*	Given Names	Birthplace	☐ Male ☐ Female
Date of Marriage	Place of Marriage *(city, town or village)*		

Type	Quantity
Small Certificate	
Large Certificate	
Photocopy of Registration	
Search Letter	

Only complete the section below if you are providing consent to a designated agent to apply on your behalf.

APPLICANT'S CONSENT TO DESIGNATED AGENT

I, ______________________________
Full name of Applicant

of ______________________________
Street Address *City/Town/Village*

____
Province/Country *Postal/Zip Code* *Phone Number*

give my consent to ______________________________
Full Name of the Designated Agent

of ______________________________
Street Address *City/Town/Village*

____
Province/Country *Postal/Zip Code* *Phone Number*

whom I have known for ________ year(s) to make this application on my behalf.
Number

X ______________________________
Signature of Applicant

DESIGNATED AGENT'S STATUTORY DECLARATION

I, ______________________________
Full name of Designated Agent

of ______________________________
Street Address *City/Town/Village*

____
Province/Country *Postal/Zip Code* *Phone Number*

do solemnly declare that I have known ______________________________
Full Name of the Applicant

for ________ year(s). X ______________________________
Number *Signature of Designated Agent*

Declared before me at ______________________________ Alberta

dated ______________________________

X ______________________________
Signature of Commissioner for Oaths in and for the Province of Alberta / Notary Public

DVS3522 (2012/05)

RETURN THIS APPLICATION TO YOUR NEAREST REGISTRY AGENT

Alberta Government

Registry Connect
Authorized Agent for the Government of Alberta
Suite 202, 1003 Ellwood Road, SW
Edmonton, Alberta, Canada T6X 0B3
Telephone: 780-415-2225 / Fax: 780-415-2226
E-mail: registry.connect@aara.ca

BEFORE YOU BEGIN, HERE IS SOME INFORMATION DESIGNED TO HELP YOU COMPLETE YOUR APPLICATION

Are you eligible to apply for the certificate you would like to order?

Please see the eligibility page which lists the types of certificates that are available and who is able to order them.

Did the birth, marriage, death, or change of name happen in the Province of Alberta?

We are only able to produce certificates where the event happened in Alberta.

Do you have acceptable proof of identity?

A Statutory Declaration is required stating that the person who is applying for the certificate possesses acceptable identification. This Statutory Declaration must be executed by a Notary Public or a Commissioner for Oaths.

Are you in a hurry or looking to obtain your important document without delay?

We offer a selection of service options to accommodate your needs. One of our most popular service options for people who are in a hurry, or simply want to avoid any potential delays of regular processing, is the Silver Service Option.

Silver Service Option:
- Priority processing of your application (your application will be worked on first).
- You will receive a phone call and/or e-mail if there are any problems or concerns with your application.
- Your certificate will be sent out by regular mail (Canada Post).

Are you in an extreme hurry (RUSH) or looking for the most secure way to receive your important document?

For those people who are in an extreme rush to receive their certificate or who want the most secure and traceable method of delivery, we offer the Gold Service Option (urgent/rush service).

Gold Service Option:
- This is the fastest service option we offer.
- Rush processing of your application.
- You will receive a phone call and/or e-mail if there are any problems or concerns with your application.
- Your certificate will be sent out by courier.
- This is the most secure delivery option available.
- This option enables you to track your package using the waybill number.
- Your signature will be required at the time your certificate is delivered.

Please see the following pages for more information regarding the certificates and how to apply.

Registry Connect
Authorized Agent for the Government of Alberta
Suite 202, 1003 Ellwood Road, SW
Edmonton, Alberta, Canada T6X 0B3
Telephone: 780-415-2225 / Fax: 780-415-2226
E-mail: registry.connect@aara.ca

Alberta Government

Application for Vital Statistics Documents by Mail through Registry Connect

Before completing this application, check below to see if you are eligible to apply for Vital Statistics' documents, as there are restrictions and proof requirements.

Certificates and/or Photocopies of a Registration

Birth

a) The **person** whose birth is registered.

b) The **parent** of the person whose birth is registered as established by the Registration of Birth or by court order. A copy of the applicable court order must be attached to this application.

c) A **person adopting** a child. Proof of a pending adoption must be attached to this application, e.g., petition of adoption.

d) A **guardian, trustee** or person with **power of attorney** for a person described in a) or b). A copy of the legal document must be attached to this application.

e) A person who is designated by a **personal directive** as an agent of the person described in a). Acceptable legal document as proof must be attached to this application.

f) A person who is a **designated agent** for a person described in a) to e). Consent and statutory declaration must be completed. See bottom of application form.

g) A person with an **order from the court**. A copy of the order must be attached to this application.

h) A **lawyer** for a person described in a) to e) or g). A copy of a valid Law Society card must be attached to this application.

i) A person who requires it to comply with **another legislation**. A copy of the legislation must be attached to this application.

When the person whose birth is registered is a minor:

- j) If the minor is younger than 12 years of age, the application must be made on behalf of the child by a parent or guardian of the minor.
- k) Between the ages of 12 and 14 the minor may make the application with the written consent of the minor's parent or guardian.
- l) Over the age of 14, the minor may make the application on his or her own behalf.

When the person whose birth is registered is deceased:

- m) An **adult next-of-kin*** of the person whose birth is registered, including a minor parent. Death certificate and either proof of relationship or an Affidavit of Relationship must be attached to this application.
- n) The **executor** of the deceased person's estate. Death certificate and a copy of the will identifying the executor must be attached to this application.
- o) An **adult relative** of the deceased person when there are no eligible applicants. Death certificate and either proof of relationship or an Affidavit of Relationship must be attached to this application.

Anyone may apply for a Birth document when:

- p) The birth record is 120 years old or older; or
- q) 50 years has passed since the death of the person whose birth is registered.

Marriage

a) A **party to the marriage** (bride/groom).

b) A **guardian, trustee** or person with **power of attorney** for a person described in a). A copy of the legal document must be attached to this application.

c) A person who is a **designated agent** for a person described in a) or b). Consent and statutory declaration must be completed. See bottom of application form.

d) A person who is designated by a **personal directive** as an agent of the person described in a). A copy of the legal document must be attached to this application.

e) A person with an **order from the court**. A copy of the order must be attached to this application.

f) A **lawyer** for a person described in a), b), d), or e). A copy of a valid Law Society card must be attached to this application.

When the person who was a party to the marriage is deceased:

- g) An **adult next-of-kin*** of a person who was a party to the marriage. Death certificate and either proof of relationship or an Affidavit of Relationship must be attached to this application
- h) The **executor** of an estate of a party to the marriage. Death certificate and a copy of the will identifying the executor must be attached to this application
- i) An **adult relative** of a deceased party to the marriage when there are no eligible applicants. Death certificate and either proof of relationship or an Affidavit of Relationship must be attached to this application

Anyone may apply for a Marriage document when:

- j) The marriage record is 75 years old or older.

Legal Change of Name

a) The **person** whose name was changed.

b) The person who **applied** for the change of name.

c) A **guardian** or **trustee** of a person whose name was changed. A copy of the guardianship or trusteeship document must be attached to this application.

d) A person who is a **designated agent** for a person described in a), b), c), g) or h). Consent and statutory declaration must be completed. See bottom of application form.

e) A person who holds a **power of attorney** to act on behalf of the person described in a). A copy of the legal document must be attached to this application.

f) A person with an **order from the court**. A copy of the order must be attached to this application.

When the person whose name was changed is a minor:

g) The **parent** of the person whose name was changed as established by a Registration of Birth or court order. A copy of the applicable court order must be attached to this application.

h) A **guardian, trustee** or **person with power of attorney**, for a parent of the person whose name was changed. A copy of the legal document must be attached to this application.

When the person whose name was changed is deceased:

i) The **executor** of a person's estate. Death certificate and a copy of the will identifying the executor must be attached to this application.

Anyone may apply for a Legal Change of Name search letter.

Stillbirth

a) An **adult next-of-kin*** of the stillborn child, including a minor who is a parent of the child. Proof of relationship or an Affidavit of Relationship must be attached to this application

b) An **adult relative** of the stillborn child when there are no living persons described in a). Proof of relationship or an Affidavit of Relationship must be attached to this application

c) A person who is a **designated agent** for a person described in a) or b). Consent and statutory declaration must be completed. See bottom of application form.

d) A person with an **order from the court**. A copy of the order must be attached to this application.

e) A **funeral home representative** who is making disposition arrangements for the stillborn child. Proof of occupation must be attached to this application.

f) A **lawyer** for a person described in a), c), or d). A copy of a valid Law Society card must be attached to this application.

Anyone may apply for a Stillbirth document when:

g) The stillbirth record is 75 years old or older.

Death

a) The **executor** of the deceased person's estate. A copy of the will identifying the executor must be attached to this application.

b) An **adult next-of-kin*** of the deceased person including a minor parent, spouse or partner. Proof of relationship or Affidavit of Relationship must be attached to this application.

c) A **guardian** or **trustee**, for the deceased person immediately before death as established by court documents. A copy of the legal document must be attached to this application.

d) A person with an **order from the court**. A copy of the order must be attached to this application.

e) A **joint tenant** with the deceased immediately before the deceased's death. Certified copy of the title to property showing joint tenancy must be attached to this application.

f) A person who is a **designated agent** for a person described in a) to c). Consent and statutory declaration must be completed. See bottom of application form.

g) An **adult relative** of the deceased person when there is no person eligible to apply as described in a) to d). Proof of relationship or an Affidavit of Relationship must be attached to this application.

h) A **funeral home representative** who is making arrangements for the deceased person. Proof of occupation must be attached to this application.

i) A **lawyer** for the person described in a) to e), g). A copy of a valid Law Society card must be attached to this application.

Anyone may apply for a Death document when:

j) The death record is 50 years old or older.

Medical Certificates of Death or Stillbirth

a) Adult **next-of-kin*** of the deceased person or stillborn child, including a minor parent. Proof of relationship must be attached to this application - when a birth certificate is supplied, it must show parentage.

b) A person who is a **designated agent** for a person described in a). Consent and statutory declaration must be completed.

c) Any person with an **order from the court**. A copy of the order must be attached to this application.

d) A **lawyer** for a person described in a) or c). A copy of a valid Law Society card must be attached to this application.

* **Next-of-Kin:** Mother, father, brother, sister, children, spouse or adult interdependent partner. This does not include in-laws, grand children, step relatives, aunts, uncles, nieces or nephews. Persons who have been adopted or who have placed their child for adoption are not "next-of-kin" to biological relations.

Registry Connect
Authorized Agent for the Government of Alberta
Suite 202, 1003 Ellwood Road, SW
Edmonton, Alberta, Canada T6X 0B3
Telephone: 780-415-2225 / Fax: 780-415-2226
E-mail: registry.connect@aara.ca

IMPORTANT INFORMATION

Processing time of application

Under normal circumstances, and if the application has been completed correctly, certificates/documents are usually sent out within five business days of receipt. Unless other arrangements have been made, certificates/documents are sent out to the applicant's address.

For RUSH service, please see our Gold and Silver Service options on the payment page.

Documents available to order

Alberta Vital Statistics maintains a registration record of all births, marriages, deaths and stillbirths (events) that occur in Alberta. If a record or event cannot be found, a search for a three-year period is carried out automatically and the applicant will be notified.

Certified Certificates - containing the following information:

Birth	Marriage	Death
Personal Information Only	**Small**	**Large**
Full name of individual, date of birth, place of birth, sex, registration number and registration date **Size:** 12.5cm (4.9") x 17.6cm (6.9")	Name of spouse/partner 1/groom, name of spouse/ partner 2/bride, date or marriage, place of marriage, registration number and registration date **Size:** 9.5 x 6.4cm (3 3/4 x 2 1/2")	Name of deceased, age of deceased at the time of death, date of death, usual residence of the deceased (province/country only), sex, marital status, registration number and registration date **Size:** 21.6 x 17.8cm (8 1/2 x 7")
Personal Information and Parentage	**Large**	
Same as above, plus the names of parents and birthplaces of parent (province/country only) **Size:** 12.5cm (4.9") x 17.6cm (6.9")	Same as small, plus the birthplace of spouse/ partner 1/groom and spouse/partner 2/bride (province/country only) **Size:** 21.6 x 17.8cm (8 1/2 x 7")	

Please Note: the wallet size birth certificate is no longer available. If the type and quantity columns are left blank on the application, the applicant will be receiving the Personal Information and Parentage Certificate.

Photocopy

A photocopy contains all the information appearing on the original *Registration of Birth, Marriage, Death and Stillbirth*. For **Death** and **Stillbirth** a photocopy of the original *Medical Certificate of Death or Stillbirth* is available. See the previous page to find out if you are eligible to request this as there are restrictions.

Note: Photocopies are rarely needed. They are not recommended for use for identification purposes.

Search Letters

A Birth, Marriage or Death search letter only states that according to the Alberta Vital Statistics office an event is **or** is not recorded. No actual information is provided or confirmed. Each Birth, Marriage or Death search is a three-year period or portion thereof.

A Legal Change of Name search letter includes the new and previous names as well as the date of registration.

Cost of Certificates

The cost for **each** certificate/photocopy of registration/search letter or genealogical search is **$39.64 Canadian Dollars** which includes GST and the certificate(s) being returned by **regular** mail. Please note that the postal regulations do not allow cash to be sent through the mail.

* **In the event that a record is not found, all processing fees are still applicable.**

How to submit an application

All applications must be sent to Registry Connect and addressed as follows (we cannot accept any applications by e-mail or fax):

Send applications to:

Registry Connect
Suite 202, 1003 Ellwood Road, SW
Ellwood Office Park South
Edmonton, Alberta, Canada T6X 0B3

Note: You must be a minimum age of 12 to apply. Children under the age of 12 must have a parent or guardian apply on their behalf. Children between the ages of 12 and 14 need written authorization from a parent or guardian.

Please do not send in applications more than one time. Each application received will be processed and all fees will apply. If you are concerned that your application did not arrive, please call or e-mail Registry Connect.

What Identification is to be submitted with each application?

The Statutory Declaration for Proof of identity (page 7 of this application booklet) must be signed by you, or your Designated Agent, and executed by a Notary Public or a Commissioner for Oaths. This Statutory Declaration will serve as your proof of ID. DO NOT MAIL ORIGINALS OR COPIES OF YOUR ID.

How to apply if you cannot produce acceptable identification?

If you are unable to produce an identification document that satisfies all requirements of the Statutory Declaration for Proof of Identity, you can grant consent to another individual, who must produce acceptable ID and who has known you for at least one year, to act as your Designated Agent. You will need to sign the Consent to the Designated Agent, and the Designated Agent will need to sign the Statutory Declaration for Proof of Identity and have it executed.

NOTE: You will still be the applicant. You will need to sign the application form and enter your personal information and relationship to the person listed on the certificate.

Registry Connect
Authorized Agent for the Government of Alberta
Suite 202, 1003 Ellwood Road, SW
Edmonton, Alberta, Canada T6X 0B3
Telephone: 780-415-2225 / Fax: 780-415-2226
E-mail: registry.connect@aara.ca

This information is collected in accordance with the Vital Statistics Act and Regulations. It is required to determine your eligibility to apply for products and services, search Vital Statistics registration records and process your request. Collection is authorized under s. 33(a) and (c) of the Freedom of Information and Protection of Privacy Act. Questions about the collection can be directed to Vital Statistics' staff @ Box 2023, Edmonton, AB T5J 4W7 or (780) 427-7013 (toll free 310-0000 within Alberta).

Application for Certificate/Documents
Vital Statistics

PRINT CLEARLY
The information below will be used to mail your documents.
All areas of this section MUST be completed OR the application will be returned.

Full Name of Applicant			Telephone Number	
Mailing Address (*Apartment Number, Street Address*)	City / Town / Village		Province / Country	Postal Code
If Company, Attention of			Your Reference Number (*if applicable*)	
Reason Certificate Required			State Your Relationship to Person Named on Certificate	
Signature of Applicant X	Date Signed (*yyyy-mm-dd*)			

Complete the appropriate section(s) below for the type of certificate you require. All fields within that section must be completed. If you cannot provide this information, attach a written explanation OR the application will be returned.

The Quantity column must be completed. ↓

BIRTH or STILLBIRTH

Last Name (*give MAIDEN name if certificate is for a married person*)		Given Names	☐ Male ☐ Female	Type	Quantity
				Birth Certificate with Personal Information Only	
Date of Birth (*yyyy-mm-dd*)	Place of Birth (*city / town / village*)	Name of Hospital (*if known*)	Type of Birth ☐ Live Birth ☐ Stillbirth	Birth Certificate with Personal Information and Parentage	
Last Name of Father / Parent	Known by any Other Last Name	Given Names	Birthplace of Father / Parent	Photocopy of Registration	
				Search Letter	
Maiden Name of Mother / Parent	Known by any Other Last Name	Given Names	Birthplace of Mother / Parent	Photocopy of Medical Certificate of Stillbirth	

MARRIAGE

Last Name of Bride / Spouse 1 (*prior to this marriage*)	Given Names	Birthplace	☐ Male ☐ Female	Small Certificate	
Last Name of Groom / Spouse 2 (*prior to this marriage*)	Given Names	Birthplace	☐ Male ☐ Female	Large Certificate	
Date of Marriage (*yyyy-mm-dd*)	Place of Marriage (*city / town / village*)			Photocopy of Registration	
				Search Letter	

DEATH

Last Name of Deceased	Last Name Used Immediately Prior to Death (if different)	Given Names		Certificate	
Age ☐ Male ☐ Female	Date of Death (*yyyy-mm-dd*)	Place of Death (*city / town / village*)	Marital Status ☐ Never Married ☐ Married ☐ Widowed ☐ Divorced	Photocopy of Registration	
Usual Residence of Deceased Prior to Death (*province / country*)		Date of Birth (*yyyy-mm-dd*)		Medical Certificate	
				Search Letter	

NAME CHANGE

Last Name before Name Change		Given Names before Name Change		Certificate	
New Last Name after Name Change		New Given Names after Name Change		Search Letter	
Date of Birth (*yyyy-mm-dd*)	Place of Birth (*city / town / village*)	☐ Male ☐ Female	Date of Name Change (*yyyy-mm-dd*) (*only for name changes that occurred in Alberta*)		

 Government

Statutory Declaration for Proof of Identity

This information is collected in accordance with the Vital Statistics Act and Regulations. It is required to determine your eligibility to apply for products and services, search Vital Statistics registration records and process your request. Collection is authorized under s. 33(a) and (c) of the Freedom of Information and Protection of Privacy Act. Questions about the collection can be directed to Vital Statistics' staff @ Box 2023, Edmonton, AB T5J 4W7 or 780-427-7013 (toll free 310-0000 within Alberta).

In the matter of this Statutory Declaration being used as Proof of Identity to make application for Alberta Vital Statistics documentation/service

I, ______________________________
Full Name of Applicant or Designated Agent

of ______________________________
Street Address

______________ ______________ ______________ ______________
City / Town / Village | Province | Country | Postal Code

Do solemnly declare that all the following statements are true:

1. I have an acceptable and original Proof of Identity document that is required to make application for Alberta Vital Statistics documentation/services.
2. My Proof of Identity document is: ______________________________
   Name of Proof of Identity document (e.g., drivers licence)
3. My Proof of Identity document was issued by: ______________________________
   Name of provincial, state or federal government
4. My name as shown on my Proof of Identity document is: ______________________________
   Applicant's full name as shown on Proof of Identity document
5. The identification number on my Proof of Identity document is: ______________________________
6. My Proof of Identity document contains a photograph of me.
7. My Proof of Identity document (check one):
   - ☐ Does not expire and was issued within the last five years. The date of issuance was: ______________ Date *(yyyy-mm-dd)*
   - ☐ Does expire, but is currently valid. The expiration date is: ______________ Date *(yyyy-mm-dd)*

And I make this solemn declaration conscientiously believing it to be true and knowing that it is of the same force and effect as if made under oath.

Declared before me at ______________

in the Province/State of ______________

dated ______________

X ______________
Signature of Applicant

X ______________ ______________ ______________
Commissioner for Oaths / Notary Public | Print Name of Commissioner for Oaths / Notary Public | Expiry Date

Note to Commissioner for Oaths/Notary Public: If there are any interlineations, alterations or erasures on a statutory declaration (including the jurat), you should place a check mark at the beginning and end of each of the changes and then write your initials beside each change. Unless changes are authenticated by your initials, the statutory declaration may not be accepted in court proceedings.

Important Information

As the applicant is not able to appear in person at a registry agent office and provide his/her original Proof of Identity document, the identification requirement may be provided in the form of this Statutory Declaration.

Proof of Identity must be acceptable.
- The applicant must have the original Proof of Identity document in his/her possession (it cannot be a copy, fax, etc).
- The Proof of Identity document must be issued by a provincial, federal or state government.
- The Proof of Identity document must contain the person's full name.
- The Proof of Identity document must contain the person's photograph.
- The Proof of Identity document must contain a distinct identification number.
- When the Proof of Identity document is one that expires, the document must be valid at the time it is presented to a Commissioner for Oaths or Notary Public.
- When the Proof of Identity document is one that does not expire, the document must have been issued not more than 5 years ago.

If the Proof of Identity document does not meet all the above criteria, it cannot be used as Proof of Identity in this Statutory Declaration.

Examples of possible acceptable documents include:
- Drivers licence, provincial identification card, treaty status card, citizenship card, permanent residency card, etc.

Examples of non-acceptable documents include:
- Bank card, Alberta Health Care card, Social Insurance card, charge card, library card, student identification card, etc.

Take your original Proof of Identity document with you to the Commissioner for Oaths or Notary Public who is signing your Statutory Declaration.
This Statutory Declaration cannot be faxed or e-mailed as Vital Statistics requires the original executed Statutory Declaration to process the application.

 Government

Applicant's Consent to Designated Agent

This information is collected in accordance with the Vital Statistics Act and Regulations. It is required to determine your eligibility to apply for products and services, search Vital Statistics registration records and process your request. Collection is authorized under s. 33(a) and (c) of the Freedom of Information and Protection of Privacy Act. Questions about the collection can be directed to Vital Statistics' staff @ Box 2023, Edmonton, AB T5J 4W7 or 780-427-7013 (toll free 310-0000 within Alberta).

Only complete this page if you are providing consent to a designated agent to apply for a document on your behalf.

How to apply if you cannot produce acceptable identification

If you are unable to produce an identification document that satisfies all requirements of the Statutory Declaration for Proof of Identity (page 6) you can grant consent to another individual, who must produce acceptable ID and who has known you for at least one year, to act as your Designated Agent.

You will need to sign this form *(Applicant's Consent to Designated Agent)*, and the Designated Agent will need to provide acceptable ID and sign the *Statutory Declaration for Proof of Identity* (page 6) and have it executed by a Commissioner for Oaths or Notary Public.

Note: You will still be the applicant on the application (page 5). You will need to sign the application form and enter your personal information and relationship to the person listed on the certificate.

I ______________________________
Full name of the Applicant

of ______________________________ ______________________________
Street Address City / Town / Village

______________________________ ______________________________ ______________________________
Province / Country Postal Code Phone Number

give my consent to ______________________________
Full name of the Designated Agent

of ______________________________ ______________________________
Street Address City / Town / Village

______________________________ ______________________________
Province / Country Postal Code

whom I have known for _______ year(s) to make this application on my behalf.
Number

X ______________________________
Signature of Applicant

This page must be completed and sent with the application.

Cost of Certificates: **Each certificate/document costs $39.64 Canadian Dollars.**

Choose one of the following service options:
Please do not send in your own pre-paid or pre-addressed envelopes of any kind.

☐ **GOLD SERVICE OPTION**

- **Cost - $39.64 per document fee, plus $25 rush processing service fee, plus delivery fee of the courier.** (Delivery cost varies according to destination. Registry Connect will add the courier cost to the sub total and charge your credit card accordingly).
- **Rush processing of application (contact by phone if there are problems with your application).**
- **Document sent out by Rush courier (fastest delivery option).**

* If your documents are being delivered to a company, the company name, full street address, postal code, phone number and contact name must be provided. If the contact person is not you, please provide an explanation.

* Courier packages cannot be delivered to a PO Box or left in a mailbox. For delivery by courier, provide a daytime address where the package can be delivered to in person and signed for. Any additional courier costs for an undeliverable, redirected, or returned package will be charged directly to the client.

* **For Gold (Courier) Service, payment must be made by credit card only.** The total amount charged to your credit card will include:

- the cost for the certificate(s) - each certificate is $39.64, **plus**
- the rush processing service fee of $25, **plus**
- the delivery fee of the courier *(delivery costs vary according to the destination)*

☐ **SILVER SERVICE OPTION**

- **Cost - $39.64 per document fee, plus $25 priority processing service fee.**
- **Priority processing of application (contact by phone if there are problems with your application).**
- **Document sent out by regular mail.**

☐ **BRONZE SERVICE OPTION**

- **Cost - $39.64 per document fee only (no other fees will apply).**
- **Regular processing of application.**
- **Contact by letter if there are problems with your application.**
- **Document sent out by regular mail.**

For all Service Options:
If applicable, provide e-mail address:

____

Payment Options: **PAYMENT IS NON-REFUNDABLE**

A $30.00 service fee is charge for all NSF or returned payments. It is considered fraudulent to obtain a government issued document without payment. All fraudulent payments will be investigated.

Cheque or Money Order ***(for Canadian or American residents only)***

☐ Cheque or Money Order payable to Registry Connect Number of Certificates: ________ Amount Enclosed: $ ________

Credit Card Number of Certificates: ________

☐ **GOLD SERVICE - $39.64 per document fee only, plus $25 rush processing fee, plus delivery fee of courier**
☐ **SILVER SERVICE - $39.64 per document fee, plus $25 priority processing service fee**
☐ **BRONZE SERVICE - $39.64 per document fee (no other fees will apply)**

☐ VISA ☐ MASTERCARD Expiry Date (month/year): ________ 3 Digit Security Code (on back of card) ☐☐☐

Credit Card Number ☐☐☐☐ ☐☐☐☐ ☐☐☐☐ ☐☐☐☐

I authorize Registry Connect to charge my credit card according to the service option and number of certificates I have chosen.

Name of Cardholder and Relationship to the Applicant	Signature of Cardholder	Telephone Number of Cardholder (include area code)

Please PRINT your e-mail address clearly: ______________________________

DVS3317 (2013/05)

Ordering Death and Legal Change of Name Documents
Vital Statistics

What kinds of documents are available to order?
Alberta Vital Statistics maintains a registration record of births, marriages, deaths, legal changes of name and stillbirths (events) that **occur in Alberta.**
NOTE: To order documents for events that occurred outside Alberta, contact the province / territory / country where the event took place.

CERTIFICATE

Certificates contain the following information:

DEATH

Name of deceased, age at the time of death, date and place of death, usual residence of the deceased (province/country only), sex, marital status, registration number, registration date, date of issue.

LEGAL CHANGE OF NAME

Old name(s), new name(s), registration number, certificate number, registration date, date of issue.

PHOTOCOPY OF REGISTRATION

A photocopy of the original *Registration of Death*.

A photocopy of the original *Medical Certificate of Death* is available.

NOTE: Photocopies are rarely needed. They are not recommended for use as identification.

SEARCH LETTER

A Death search letter does not provide actual detailed information. The Vital Statistics office will notify the client whether or not the event is registered, nothing more.

A Legal Change of Name search letter includes the new and previous names as well as the date of registration.

What is acceptable proof of identity and why is it needed?
When ordering Vital Statistics certificates / documents, the applicant must present an acceptable proof of identity document. This document must be issued by a provincial or federal government. It must contain a recognizable photograph, full name, and a distinctive identification number. If the document has an expiry date, the document must currently be valid. If the document has no expiry date, then it must have been issued within the last 5 years. If the document is in a language other then English, then the applicant must provide a notarized English translation and an affidavit from the translator stating that the translation is accurate.

How do I submit an application?
Alberta residents applying for an Alberta Vital Statistics document must apply in person at a registry agent office - an authorized representative of the Alberta Government. For registry agent information, please contact:

Edmonton	780-427-7013
Alberta rite-line (toll free Alberta only)	310-0000 then dial 427-7013
SUPERPAGES™	under Licensing and Registry Services
Website	www.servicealberta.gov.ab.ca

What if I don't have acceptable proof of identity or am unable to apply in person at a registry agent office?
Consent may be provided to another person to act as the applicant's designated agent. The designated agent must have known the applicant for at least 1 year, must complete the statutory declaration on page 3, and must present acceptable proof of identity. Not all applicants may provide their consent to a designated agent - see eligibility restrictions on the next page.
NOTE: You will still be the applicant. You will need to sign the application form and enter your personal information and relationship to the person listed on the certificate.

How much do certificates/documents cost?
For certificates or photocopies, the government fee is $20.00 per certificate / document, plus a registry agent fee. For Legal Change of Name search letters, the fee is $20.00, plus a registry agent fee. For Death search letters, the fee is $20.00 for each three-year period searched or portion thereof, plus a registry agent fee.

How long does it take to process an application?
Under normal circumstances when the application has been completed correctly and there are no further requirements, certificates / documents are usually mailed within 3 business days.

How will the certificate / document be delivered to me?
Certificates / documents are mailed to the applicant, unless other arrangements have been made with a registry agent office.

 Government

Application for Death and Legal Change of Name Documents

This information is collected in accordance with the Vital Statistics Act and Regulations. It is required to determine your eligibility to apply for products and services, search Vital Statistics registration records and process your request. Collection is authorized under s. 33(a) and (c) of the Freedom of Information and Protection of Privacy Act. Questions about the collection can be directed to Vital Statistics' staff @ Box 2023, Edmonton, AB T5J 4W7 or (780) 427-7013 (toll free 310-0000 within Alberta).

IMPORTANT INFORMATION TO AVOID DELAYS

- This application **must** be returned to a registry agent in person.
- The applicant **must** provide acceptable proof of identity. *(see the front page for what to do if you do not have acceptable proof of identity)*
- Read all instructions carefully before filling in this form.
- Make sure you are eligible to apply and have the necessary supporting documents - see the opposite page.
- Information must be as complete as possible. Attach a written explanation if you cannot provide the information required in the applicable section(s).
- If a record or event cannot be found, a search is carried out automatically and the applicant will be notified. For Death documents the search is limited to a three-year period.

PRINT CLEARLY - This information will be used to mail your documents. All areas of this section must be completed.

Full Name of Applicant	Phone No *(during the day)*
Mailing Address *Street*	*Apartment No.*
City / Town / Village *Province / Country*	*Postal / Zip Code*
If Company, Attention of	Your Reference No. *(if applicable)*
Reason Certificate Required	
State Your Relationship to Person Named on Certificate	
Signature of Applicant X	Date Signed *(month by name, day, year)*

The Quantity column must be completed. ⟶

DEATH				Type	Quantity
Last Name of Deceased	Given Names	Age	☐ Male ☐ Female	Certificate	
Date of Death	Place of Death *(city, town or village)*	Marital Status ☐ Never Married ☐ Married ☐ Common Law ☐ Widowed ☐ Divorced		Photocopy of Registration	
Usual Residence of Deceased Prior to Death *(province / country)*	Date of Birth			Medical Certificate	
				Search Letter	

NAME CHANGE			Type	Quantity
Last Name before Name Change	Given Names before Name Change		Certificate	
New Last Name after Name Change	New Given Names after Name Change		Search Letter	
Date of Birth	Place of Birth *(city, town or village)*	Date of Name Change *(only for name changes that occurred in Alberta)*		

Only complete the section below if you are providing consent to a designated agent to apply on your behalf.

APPLICANT'S CONSENT TO DESIGNATED AGENT

I, ______________________
Full name of Applicant

of ______________________
Street Address City/Town/Village

____
Province/Country Postal/Zip Code Phone Number

give my consent to ______________________
Full Name of the Designated Agent

of ______________________
Street Address City/Town/Village

____
Province/Country Postal/Zip Code Phone Number

whom I have known for ________ year(s) to make this application on my behalf.
Number

X ______________________
Signature of Applicant

DESIGNATED AGENT'S STATUTORY DECLARATION

I, ______________________
Full name of Designated Agent

of ______________________
Street Address City/Town/Village

____
Province/Country Postal/Zip Code Phone Number

do solemnly declare that I have known ______________________
Full Name of the Applicant

for ________ year(s). X ______________________
Number Signature of Designated Agent

Declared before me at ______________________ Alberta

dated ______________________

X ______________________
Signature of Commissioner for Oaths in and for the Province of Alberta / Notary Public

DVS3523 (2012/05)

RETURN THIS APPLICATION TO YOUR NEAREST REGISTRY AGENT

Who can apply for Vital Statistics' documents?

The areas below show who is eligible and what proofs of eligibility are required.

Certificates and / or Photocopies of a Registration

Death	Legal Change of Name
a) The **executor** of the deceased person's estate. A copy of the will identifying the executor must be attached to this application. b) An **adult next-of-kin*** of the deceased person including a minor parent, spouse or partner. Proof of relationship or Affidavit of Relationship** must be attached to this application. c) A **guardian** or **trustee**, for the deceased person immediately before death as established by court documents. A copy of the legal document must be attached to this application. d) A person with an **order from the court**. A copy of the order must be attached to this application. e) A **joint tenant** with the deceased immediately before the deceased's death. Certified copy of the title to property showing joint tenancy must be attached to this application. f) A person who is a **designated agent** for a person described in a) to c). Consent and statutory declaration must be completed. See bottom of application form. g) An **adult relative** of the deceased person when there is no person eligible to apply as described in a) to d). A proof of relationship or an Affidavit of Relationship must be attached to this application. h) A **funeral home representative** who is making arrangements for the deceased person. Proof of occupation must be attached to this application. i) A **lawyer** for the person described in a) to e), g). A copy of a valid Law Society card must be attached to this application. Anyone may apply for a Death document when: j) The death record is 50 years old or older.	a) The **person** whose name was changed. b) The person who **applied** for the change of name. c) A **guardian** or **trustee** of a person whose name was changed. A copy of the guardianship or trusteeship document must be attached to this application. d) A person who is a **designated agent** for a person described in a), b), c), g) or h). Consent and statutory declaration must be completed. See bottom of application form. e) A person who holds a **power of attorney** to act on behalf of the person described in a). A copy of the legal document must be attached to this application. f) A person with an **order from the court**. A copy of the order must be attached to this application. When the person whose name was changed is a minor: g) The **parent** of the person whose name was changed as established by a Registration of Birth or court order. A copy of the applicable court order must be attached to this application. h) A **guardian**, **trustee** or **person with power of attorney**, for a parent of the person whose name was changed. A copy of the legal document must be attached to this application. When the person whose name was changed is deceased: i) The **executor** of a person's estate. Death certificate and a copy of the will identifying the executor must be attached to this application. Anyone may apply for a Legal Change of Name search letter.

Medical Certificates of Death

a) Adult **next-of-kin*** of the deceased person including a minor parent, spouse or partner. Proof of relationship must be attached to this application - e.g., if a birth certificate is supplied, it must show parentage.

b) A person who is a **designated agent** for a person described in a). Consent and statutory declaration must be completed. See bottom of application form.

c) Any person with an **order from the court**. A copy of the order must be attached to this application.

d) A **lawyer** for a person described in a) or c). A copy of a valid Law Society card must be attached to this application.

* **Next-of-Kin:** Mother, father, brother, sister, children, spouse or adult interdependent partner. This does not include in-laws, grand children, step relatives, aunts, uncles, nieces or nephews. Persons who have been adopted or who have placed their child for adoption are not "next-of-kin" to biological relations.

**Affidavit of Relationship available from a registry agent.

CANADA—BRITISH COLUMBIA

Send your requests to:

British Columbia Vital Statistics Agency
P.O. Box 9657 STN PROV GOVT
Victoria, British Columbia, Canada V8W 9P3

Tel. (250) 952-2681
www.vs.gov.bc.ca/

The British Columbia Vital Statistics Agency has records of birth, marriage, and death occurring in British Columbia since 1872, though some of the early records are incomplete. Certificates can be ordered in person, by mail, or online at https://ecos.vs.gov.bc.ca/. An electronic index to births (1854–1903), marriages (1872–1937), deaths (1872–1992), colonial marriages (1859–1872), and baptisms (1836–1888) is available online at http://search-collections.royalbcmuseum.bc.ca/Genealogy/basicSearch.

For genealogical research purposes, the Agency issues unique registration copies, which include all the information recorded on the original event record. To learn more about genealogy services, visit www.vs.gov.bc.ca/genealogy.

Cost for a certified Birth Certificate	Can$27.00
Cost for a commemorative Birth or Marriage Certificate	Can$50.00
Cost for a genealogy verification abstract of Birth Certificate	Can$50.00
Cost for a certified Marriage Certificate	Can$27.00
Cost for a genealogy verification abstract of Marriage Certificate	Can$50.00
Cost for a certified Death Certificate	Can$27.00
Cost for a genealogy verification abstract of Death Certificate	Can$50.00
Cost for an Adoption Record	Can$50.00

For additional assistance, contact:

Embassy of Canada
501 Pennsylvania Avenue, NW
Washington, DC 20001

Tel. (202) 682-1740

APPLICATION FOR BIRTH CERTIFICATE OR REGISTRATION PHOTOCOPY

Did you know that you can save yourself time and effort by ordering your certificate using our on-line electronic ordering system? This service is secure and easy to use and does not cost anything additional. ***Click here*** *or type* ***https://www.vs.gov.bc.ca/ecos/*** *into your Internet Browser.*

MAILING ADDRESS INFORMATION

NOTE: Please PRINT your name, address and identifying information clearly. This portion will be used when mailing your service or correspondence.

FOR OFFICE USE ONLY: AFS#

SURNAME		GIVEN NAMES
MAILING ADDRESS		
CITY, PROVINCE/STATE, COUNTRY		POSTAL CODE
HOME PHONE (INCLUDING AREA CODE)	WORK PHONE (INCLUDING AREA CODE)	IF COMPANY, ATTENTION:

BIRTH DETAILS

SURNAME					***NOTE:*** *If application is for the birth certificate of a married person, the surname at birth/adoption or following a legal change of name, must be provided; not the surname from marriage*
GIVEN NAMES & SEX	First			Middle Names	☐ MALE ☐ FEMALE
DATE & PLACE OF BIRTH	Month (ex: Feb)	Day	Year	City	Province **BRITISH COLUMBIA**

FATHER / PARENT DETAILS

SURNAME			
GIVEN NAMES	First	Middle Names	
BIRTH PLACE	City	Province/State	Country

MOTHER DETAILS

SURNAME*			*** NOTE:*** *Mother's Maiden Surname (Surname before marriage)*
GIVEN NAMES	First	Middle Names	
BIRTH PLACE	City	Province/State	Country

NUMBER OF SERVICES REQUIRED ***(see reverse for fee information and limits on number of certificates)***

The Birth Certificate is available in 2 versions. One contains personal information only, the other includes parental information. Both are the same size and are mailed separately.

☐ Certificate (Individual Information only)
☐ Certificate (Includes Parental Information)
} regular service - $27.00 per certificate *(average 2 to 5 business days processing time)*

☐ Certificate (Individual Information only)
☐ Certificate (Includes Parental Information)
} Courier Service* - $60.00 per event

☐ Registration Photocopy, Regular Service - $50.00 per photocopy *(average 20 business days processing time)*

☐ Registration Photocopy, Courier Service* - $60.00 per photocopy

***NOTE: All services, other than courier services, will be mailed. Courier service requests are produced the next business day. Delivery time is dependent on shipping destination. Fee includes the cost of the search of our records. A certificate will be generated upon confirmation of a record held. If no record of the event is found, the fee will be applied to the search process. Courier Service will <u>not</u> be attempted at the following residence types: post office box, apartment complex, homes that utilize Super Box mailboxes and Basement suites. Instead, a delivery notice with instructions will be left at those residences and the package delivered to the nearest postal outlet. ID and signature will be required upon pick up.**

YOUR RELATIONSHIP TO BIRTH

☐ Self ☐ *Mother ☐ *Father/Parent ☐ *Other ______________

(*if child is under 19 or incapable) (*requires written authorization from an eligible applicant)

Reason Certificate Required ______________

NOTE: If the above particulars are not completed in full, or if the correct payment per service requested is not enclosed, your request will be returned by mail.

YOUR SIGNATURE (written):

Payment Methods

☐ Cheque * ☐ Money Order ☐ Visa ☐ MasterCard ☐ American Express

*** Postdated cheques are not accepted**

AMOUNT ENCLOSED $ ______

Interac/Cash payment may be made in person at one of our three offices. If paying by cheque or money order, make payable to the Minister of Finance.

____
Card holder signature

____
PRINT Card holder name as shown on Credit Card

Credit Card # ______________ Expiry date ______

VSA 430B 2013/06/10

IMPORTANT INFORMATION

TO AVOID DELAY

* Complete all sections in full. *(All requests with incomplete information must be accompanied by a written explanation for the omission and include two pieces of identification, including one picture ID, and written verification of identity on official letterhead from a Physician, Lawyer, Notary Public, or Religious Representative who has known you for at least two years.)*

* Please note who qualifies to apply for a certificate (see Section 3 below).

* It is against postal regulations to send cash through the mail. Payment in **Canadian funds** should be forwarded by cheque **(postdated cheques are not accepted),** bank draft or money order made **payable to the Minister of Finance**. Credit Card payments are accepted. Please complete the Credit Card portion on the front of this form.

* Be sure your address and telephone number are correct and clear.

* A service charge of $30.00 will be levied on all cheques not honoured by the payees' financial institution.

1) FEES AND LIMITS ON NUMBER OF CERTIFICATES

Fees as noted for each requested copy on the front of this form.
**Fees effective January 2, 1996. All fees subject to change. If ordering after April 1, 2012, contact our office for current fees.*
For security purposes the maximum number of each version of the birth certificate which may be ordered is **TWO (2)** of each version.

2) INFORMATION PROVIDED

Certificates contain the following information and are in upper case.
Birth (Individual Information only) - name, date, place, sex, registration date and number
Birth (Includes Parental Information) - name, date, place, sex, registration date and number, parents' names and birthplace
NOTE: *If you are applying for a birth certificate to support the application of other identification such as a Passport, Driver's Licence, BC ID, Social Insurance Number, etc. please check with the organization to ensure you obtain the correct version of birth certificate.*

Photocopies

a) Registration Photocopies are rarely needed by citizens and by law are for restricted use only.
b) A Photocopy of a Registration of Birth, contains all the information which appears on the original Birth Registration.
c) Should you believe that you require a certified photocopy of a birth event registration, please visit our web site at www.vs.gov.bc.ca or contact our customer enquiry line at 250 952-2681 (Victoria & Outside BC) or toll free at 1-888-876-1633 (within BC) for eligibility information. ***NOTE***: Registration Photocopies are generally only required for court purposes. **They are not for use as identification.**

3) WHO QUALIFIES TO APPLY FOR A BIRTH CERTIFICATE

Birth certificates may be released to:
a) The person who is the subject of the certificate;
b) A parent of the person who is subject to the certificate, if that person is less than 19 years of age or incapable;
c) A custodial guardian if no parent under paragraph (b) is capable; (see note below)
d) A person who has written authorization from a person described in paragraph a), b) or c) to be issued the certificate;
e) An officer of any provincial government or the government of Canada who requires the certificate for use in the discharge of official duties;
f) Any other person who satisfies the Chief Executive Officer concerning the good faith of the person's cause for requiring the certificate.
***NOTE*: Custodial guardians must provide a copy of guardianship papers.**

OTHER SERVICES - For Records held in British Columbia only
Certified Genealogy Copy and/or Commemorative Birth Certificates
To obtain an application for either of these services, please visit our web site or contact one of our offices by telelphone or in person.

MAILING ADDRESS
Vital Statistics Agency
PO Box 9657 STN PROV GOVT
Victoria BC V8W 9P3

ENQUIRIES & CREDIT CARD ORDERS
Telephone: **250 952-2681** (Victoria & Outside BC)
Toll free: **1 888 876-1633** (within BC)

OR VISIT ONE OF OUR OFFICES

VICTORIA:	VANCOUVER:	KELOWNA:
818 Fort Street	250 - 605 Robson Street	305 - 478 Bernard Ave
Victoria BC	Vancouver BC	Kelowna BC

Check our Web Site at: http://www.vs.gov.bc.ca

The information on this form is collected under the authority of the ***Vital Statistics Act*** (RSBC 1996, c.479, Sec. 37 & 38). The information provided will be used to fulfill the requirements of the ***Vital Statistics Act*** for the release of birth information. If you have any questions about the collection or use of this information, please contact a Vital Statistics Client Service Representative at 250 952-2681, or write to the mailing address given below.

APPLICATION FOR BIRTH/DECEASED CERTIFICATE

MAILING ADDRESS INFORMATION

NOTE: Please PRINT your name, address and identifying information clearly. This portion will be used when mailing your service or correspondence.

FOR OFFICE USE ONLY: AFS#

SURNAME		GIVEN NAMES
MAILING ADDRESS		
CITY, PROVINCE/STATE, COUNTRY		POSTAL CODE
HOME PHONE (INCLUDING AREA CODE)	WORK PHONE (INCLUDING AREA CODE)	IF COMPANY, ATTENTION:

BIRTH DETAILS

SURNAME					***NOTE:*** *If application is for the birth/death certificate of a married person, the surname at birth/adoption or following a legal change of name, must be provided; not the surname from marriage*
GIVEN NAMES & SEX	First		Middle Names		☐ MALE ☐ FEMALE
DATE & PLACE OF BIRTH	Month (ex: Feb)	Day	Year	City	Province **BRITISH COLUMBIA**

FATHER/ PARENT DETAILS

SURNAME			
GIVEN NAMES	First	Middle Names	
BIRTH PLACE	City	Province/State	Country

MOTHER DETAILS

SURNAME*			**** NOTE:*** *Mother's Maiden Surname (Surname before marriage)*
GIVEN NAMES	First	Middle Names	
BIRTH PLACE	City	Province/State	Country

NUMBER OF SERVICES REQUIRED

The Birth/Deceased Certificate contains parental information and is only available in one size.

☐ Birth/Deceased Certificate (includes Parental information) } Regular service - $27.00 per certificate *(average 2 to 5 days processing time)*

☐ Birth/Deceased Certificate (includes Parental information) } Courier service - $60.00 per event*

***NOTE: All services, other than courier services, will be mailed. Courier service requests are produced the next business day. Delivery time is dependent on shipping destination. Fee includes the cost of the search of our records. A certificate will be generated upon confirmation of a record held. If no record of the event is found, the fee will be applied to the search process. Courier service will not be attempted at the following residence types: post office box, apartment complex, homes that use Super Box mailboxes and basement suites. Instead, a delivery notice with instructions will be left at those residences and the package delivered to the nearest postal outlet. ID and signature will be required upon pick up.**

NOTE - if the death occurred:

Within BC:
You must submit an original or a photocopy of a death certificate for the deceased individual.

Outside BC:
You must submit an original death certificate or a certified* photocopy of a death certificate for the deceased individual.

**** A certified copy is a photocopy of a document, authenticated by an authorized official (Lawyer, Notary Public or Commissioner for Taking Affidavits), as a true photocopy of the original document.***

YOUR RELATIONSHIP TO BIRTH

☐ Executor/ Executrix ☐ Relative [**Relative is defined as: Mother, Father, Son, Daughter, Sister, Brother, Spouse, Grandparent, Grandchild. Proof of relationship is required. See reverse for acceptable documentation.**] ☐ Other* ____________ (*requires written authorization from an eligible applicant)

Reason Certificate Required ____________

NOTE: *If the above particulars are not completed in full, or if the correct payment per service requested is not enclosed, your request will be returned by mail.*

YOUR SIGNATURE (written): ____________

Payment Methods

☐ Cheque * ☐ Money Order ☐ Visa ☐ MasterCard ☐ American Express

*** Postdated cheques are not accepted**

AMOUNT ENCLOSED $ ________

Interac/Cash payment may be made in person at one of our three offices. If paying by cheque or money order, make payable to the Minister of Finance.

____
Card holder signature

____
PRINT Card holder name as shown on Credit Card

Credit Card # ____________ Expiry date ________

VSA 413 2013/06/05

IMPORTANT INFORMATION

TO AVOID DELAY

* Please note who qualifies to apply for a certificate (see Section 3 below).
* It is against postal regulations to send cash through the mail. Payment in **Canadian funds** should be forwarded by cheque **(Postdated cheques are not accepted),** bank draft or money order made **payable to the Minister of Finance**. Credit Card payments are accepted. Please complete the Credit Card portion on the front of this form.
* Be sure your address and telephone number are correct and clear.
* A service charge of $30.00 will be levied on all cheques not honoured by the payees' financial institution.
* Please attach a photocopy of the death certificate to this application form and state your relationship to the deceased. **Read note on the front of this form for further details.**

1) FEES

Fees as noted for each requested copy on the front of this form.
**All fees subject to change. If ordering after April 1, 2012, contact our office for current fees.*

2) INFORMATION PROVIDED

Certificates contain the following information and are in upper case.
Birth/Deceased Certificates (Includes name, date, place, sex, registration date and number, parents' names and birthplace).

3) WHO QUALIFIES TO APPLY FOR A BIRTH/DECEASED CERTIFICATE

Birth/Deceased certificates may be released to:

a) The Executor or Executrix of the estate (a photocopy of a will or court order is required to support the application);
b) A relative with proof of relationship;
c) A person who has written authorization from a person described in line a) and b);
d) An officer of any provincial government or the government of Canada who requires the certificate for use in the discharge of official duties;
e) Any other person who satisfies the Chief Executive Officer concerning the good faith of the person's cause for requiring the certificate.

Note: A relative is defined as: Mother, Father, Son, Daughter, Sister, Brother, Spouse, Grandparent, Grandchild.

Acceptable documentation to establish proof of relationship for a relative includes:

- photocopy of a certified birth registration;
- photocopy of a parental certificate and if required;
- associated marriage certificates.

MAILING ADDRESS
Vital Statistics Agency
PO Box 9657 STN PROV GOVT
Victoria BC V8W 9P3

ENQUIRIES & CREDIT CARD ORDERS
Telephone: **250 952-2681** (Victoria & Outside BC)
Toll free: **1 888 876-1633** (within BC)

OR VISIT ONE OF OUR OFFICES

VICTORIA:	**VANCOUVER:**	**KELOWNA:**
818 Fort St	250 - 605 Robson St	305 - 478 Bernard Ave
Victoria BC	Vancouver BC	Kelowna BC

Check our Web Site at: http://www.vs.gov.bc.ca

APPLICATION FOR MARRIAGE CERTIFICATE OR REGISTRATION PHOTOCOPY

Did you know that you can save yourself time and effort by ordering your certificate using our on-line electronic ordering system? This service is secure and easy to use and does not cost anything additional. ***Click here*** *or type* ***https://www.vs.gov.bc.ca/ecos/*** *into your Internet Browser.*

APPLICANT AND MAILING ADDRESS INFORMATION

NOTE: Please PRINT your name, address and identifying information clearly. This portion will be used when mailing your service or correspondence. ***Rush courier packages need to be signed for.***

FOR OFFICE USE ONLY: AFS#

SURNAME	GIVEN NAMES	
MAILING ADDRESS		
CITY, PROVINCE/STATE, COUNTRY		POSTAL CODE
HOME TELEPHONE NUMBER (INCLUDE AREA CODE)	WORK TELEPHONE NUMBER (INCLUDE AREA CODE)	IF COMPANY, ATTENTION
E-MAIL ADDRESS FOR CORRESPONDENCE **(PLEASE PRINT CLEARLY)**		

DATE AND PLACE OF MARRIAGE

MONTH (ex: Feb)	DAY	YEAR	CITY	PROVINCE
				BRITISH COLUMBIA

PARTY 1 DETAILS

SURNAME (BEFORE MARRIAGE)	GIVEN NAME(S)
BIRTHPLACE (CITY, PROV/STATE, COUNTRY)	

PARTY 2 DETAILS

SURNAME (BEFORE MARRIAGE)	GIVEN NAME(S)
BIRTHPLACE (CITY, PROV/STATE, COUNTRY)	

NUMBER OF SERVICES REQUIRED ***(see reverse for fee information and limits on number of certificates)***

Large and small certificates are mailed separately

- ☐ Certificate (Small) } regular service - $27.00 per certificate
- ☐ Certificate (Large) } *(average 2 to 5 business days processing time)*
- ☐ Certificate (Small) } Courier Service* $60.00 per event.
- ☐ Certificate (Large) }
- ☐ Registration Photocopy, regular service - $50.00 per photocopy *(average 20 business days processing time)*
- ☐ Registration Photocopy, Courier Service* - $60.00 per event.

***NOTE: All services, other than courier services, will be mailed. Courier service requests are produced the next business day. Delivery time is dependent on shipping destination. Fee includes the cost of the search of our records. A certificate will be generated upon confirmation of a record held. If no record of the event is found, the fee will be applied to the search process. Courier Service will not be attempted at the following residence types: post office box, apartment complex, homes that utilize Super Box mailboxes and Basement suites. Instead, a delivery notice with instructions will be left at those residences and the package delivered to the nearest postal outlet. ID and signature will be required upon pick up.**

YOUR RELATIONSHIP TO MARRIAGE: ☐ Self ☐ *Other ______________________

(*requires written authorization from an eligible applicant)

Reason Certificate Required: ______________________

YOUR SIGNATURE (written) : ______________________

PAYMENT METHODS

☐ Cheque * ☐ Money Order ☐ Visa ☐ MasterCard ☐ American Express

*** Postdated cheques not accepted**

AMOUNT ENCLOSED $ __________

Interac/Cash payment may be made in person at one of our three offices. Cheque or money order made payable to the Minister of Finance.

____
Card holder signature

____
PRINT Card holder name as shown on Credit Card

Credit Card # ______________________ Expiry Date __________

VSA 430m 2013/03/12

PLEASE READ NOTES ON REVERSE OF THIS FORM

IMPORTANT INFORMATION

TO AVOID DELAY

* Complete all sections in full (All requests with incomplete information must be accompanied by a signed, written explanation for the omission and include two pieces of identification, including one picture ID, and written verification of identity on official letterhead from a Physician, Lawyer, Notary Public, or Religious Representative who has known you for at least two years.)
* Be sure you are authorized to make the request (see Section 3 below).
* It is against postal regulations to send cash through the mail. Payment in **Canadian funds** should be forwarded by cheque, bank draft or money order made **payable to the Minister of Finance**. Postdated cheques not accepted. Credit card payments are accepted, please complete the Credit Card portion on the front of this form.
* Be sure your address and telephone number are correct and clear.
* A service charge of $30.00 will be levied on all cheques not honoured by the payees financial institution.

1) FEES

Fees as noted for each requested copy on the front of this form. The following conditions apply: where a certificate or registration photocopy cannot be issued because no record exists or the applicant has not supplied sufficient or correct information, a $27.00 search fee will be assessed. **All fees subject to change. If ordering after April 1, 2012, contact our office for current fees.*

2) INFORMATION PROVIDED

Certificates contain the following information:

Marriage Small - name of each party, date, place, registration date, and registration number
Marriage Large - same as small plus birthdates and places of birth of each party

Photocopies

a) Registration photocopies are rarely needed by citizens, are not required for court purposes, and are not suitable for identification purposes.
b) Registration photocopies contain all the information about the event as recorded at the time, and are rarely needed for reasons other than personal records.
c) Should you believe that you require a certified photocopy of a marriage event registration, please visit our web site at: **www.vs.gov.bc.ca** or contact our customer enquiry line at **250 952-2681** (Victoria & Outside BC) or toll free at **1-888-876-1633** (within BC) for eligibility information.

3) WHO QUALIFIES TO APPLY FOR A MARRIAGE CERTIFICATE

Marriage certificates may be released to:

a) Either party of the marriage
b) A person who has written authorization of either party to the marriage

OTHER SERVICE - For Records held in British Columbia only

Genealogy Registration Photocopy

To obtain an application for this service, please visit our web site or contact one of our offices by telephone or in person.

MAILING ADDRESS
Vital Statistics Agency
PO Box 9657 STN PROV GOVT
Victoria BC V8W 9P3

ENQUIRIES & CREDIT CARD ORDERS
Telephone: **250 952-2681** (Victoria & Outside BC)
Toll free: **1 888 876-1633** (within BC)

OR VISIT ONE OF OUR OFFICES

VICTORIA:	VANCOUVER:	KELOWNA:
818 Fort Street Victoria BC	250 - 605 Robson Street Vancouver BC	305 - 478 Bernard Avenue Kelowna BC

Check our Web Site at: http://www.vs.gov.bc.ca

The information on this form is collected under the authority of the ***Vital Statistics Act*** (RSBC 1996, c.479, Sec. 37). The information provided will be used to fulfill the requirements of the ***Vital Statistics Act*** for the release of marriage information. If you have any questions about the collection or use of this information, please contact a Vital Statistics Client Service Representative at 250-952-2681, or write to the mailing address given above.

APPLICATION FOR DEATH CERTIFICATE OR REGISTRATION PHOTOCOPY

Did you know that you can save yourself time and effort by ordering your certificate using our on-line electronic ordering system? This service is secure and easy to use and does not cost anything additional. ***Click here*** *or type* ***https://www.vs.gov.bc.ca/ecos/*** *into your Internet Browser.*

APPLICANT AND MAILING ADDRESS INFORMATION

NOTE: *Please PRINT your name, address and identifying information clearly. This portion will be used when mailing your service or correspondence.* ***Rush courier packages need to be signed for.***

FOR OFFICE USE ONLY: AFS#

SURNAME	GIVEN NAME(S)
MAILING ADDRESS	
CITY, PROVINCE/STATE, COUNTRY	POSTAL CODE
HOME TELEPHONE NUMBER (Include Area Code)	WORK TELEPHONE NUMBER (Include Area Code)
E-MAIL ADDRESS FOR CORRESPONDENCE **(PLEASE PRINT CLEARLY)**	IF COMPANY, ATTENTION:

DEATH DETAILS

SURNAME		
GIVEN NAME(S)	AGE	☐ MALE ☐ FEMALE
DATE OF DEATH: MONTH (ex: Feb) / DAY / YEAR	PLACE OF DEATH (City)	PROVINCE **BRITISH COLUMBIA**
PERMANENT RESIDENCE BEFORE DEATH (City, Province/State, Country)	PLACE OF BIRTH (City, Province/State, Country)	

NUMBER OF SERVICES REQUIRED *(see reverse for fee information)*

☐ Certificate (Large) Regular service - $27.00 per certificate *(average 2 - 5 business days processing time*

☐ Certificate (Large) Courier Service* - $60.00 per event

☐ Registration Photocopy, Regular service - $50.00 per photocopy *(average 20 business days processing time)*

☐ Registration Photocopy, Courier Service* - $60.00 per event.

***NOTE: All services, other than courier services, will be mailed. Courier service requests are produced the next business day. Delivery time is dependent on shipping destination. Fee includes the cost of the search of our records. A certificate will be generated upon confirmation of a record held. If no record of the event is found, the fee will be applied to the search process. Courier Service will not be attempted at the following residence types: post office box, apartment complex, homes that utilize Super Box mailboxes and Basement suites. Instead, a delivery notice with instructions will be left at those residences and the package delivered to the nearest postal outlet. ID and signature will be required upon pick up.**

YOUR RELATIONSHIP TO EVENT: ______________________________
(requires written authorization from an eligible applicant)

Reason Certificate Required: ______________________________

YOUR SIGNATURE (written): ______________________________

PAYMENT METHODS

☐ Cheque * ☐ Money Order ☐ Visa ☐ MasterCard ☐ American Express

*** Postdated cheques not accepted**

AMOUNT ENCLOSED $ __________

Interac/Cash payment may be made in person at one of our three offices. Cheque or money order made payable to the Minister of Finance.

____
Card holder signature

____
PRINT Card holder name as shown on Credit Card

Credit Card # ______________________ Expiry Date __________

VSA 430d 2013/03/12

PLEASE READ NOTES ON REVERSE OF THIS FORM

IMPORTANT INFORMATION

TO AVOID DELAY

* Complete all sections in full (All requests with incomplete information must be accompanied by a signed, written explanation for the omission and include two pieces of identification, including one picture ID, and written verification of identity on official letterhead from a Physician, Lawyer, Notary Public, or Religious Representative who has known you for at least two years.)

* Be sure you are authorized to make the request (see Section 3 below).

* It is against postal regulations to send cash through the mail. Payment in **Canadian funds** should be forwarded by cheque, bank draft or money order made **payable to the Minister of Finance**. Postdated cheques not accepted. Credit card payments are accepted, please complete the Credit Card portion on the front of this form.

* Be sure your address and telephone number are correct and clear.

* A service charge of $30.00 will be levied on all cheques not honoured by the payees financial institution.

1) FEES

Fees as noted for each requested copy on the front of this form. The following conditions apply: where a certificate or registration photocopy cannot be issued because no record exists or the applicant has not supplied sufficient or correct information, a $27.00 search fee will be assessed. **All fees subject to change. If ordering after April 1, 2012, contact our office for current fees.*

2) INFORMATION PROVIDED

Certificates contain the following information:

Death Large only - name, date of death, age, sex, place of death, birthplace, residence, registration number, certificate issuance date

Photocopies

a) Registration photocopies are rarely needed by citizens and are not required for court purposes.

b) Registration photocopies contain all the information about the event as recorded at the time, and are rarely needed for reasons other than personal records.

3) WHO QUALIFIES TO APPLY FOR A DEATH EVENT DOCUMENT

a) Death certificates may be released to any person who has a valid reason.

b) Should you believe that you require a certified photocopy of a death event registration, please visit our web site at: **www.vs.gov.bc.ca** or contact our customer enquiry line at **250 952-2681** (Victoria & Outside BC) or toll free at **1-888-876-1633** (within BC) for eligibility information.

OTHER SERVICES - For Records held in British Columbia only

Genealogy Verification Extract

To obtain an application for this service, please visit our web site or contact one of our offices by telephone or in person.

MAILING ADDRESS
Vital Statistics Agency
PO Box 9657 STN PROV GOVT
Victoria BC V8W 9P3

ENQUIRIES & CREDIT CARD ORDERS
Telephone: **250 952-2681** (Victoria & Outside BC)
Toll free: **1 888 876-1633** (within BC)

OR VISIT ONE OF OUR OFFICES

VICTORIA:
818 Fort Street
Victoria BC

VANCOUVER:
250 - 605 Robson Street
Vancouver BC

KELOWNA:
305 - 478 Bernard Ave
Kelowna BC

Check our Web Site at: www.vs.gov.bc.ca

The information on this form is collected under the authority of the ***Vital Statistics Act*** (RSBC 1996, c.479, Sec. 38). The information provided will be used to fulfill the requirements of the ***Vital Statistics Act*** for the release of death information. If you have any questions about the collection or use of this information, please contact a Vital Statistics Client Service Representative at 250-952-2681, or write to the mailing address given above.

APPLICATION FOR GENEALOGY CERTIFICATE

MAILING ADDRESS INFORMATION

FOR OFFICE USE ONLY: AFS#

SURNAME	GIVEN NAME(S)
MAILING ADDRESS	
CITY, PROVINCE/STATE, COUNTRY	POSTAL CODE
HOME TELEPHONE NUMBER (Include Area Code)	WORK TELEPHONE NUMBER (Include Area Code)
E-MAIL ADDRESS FOR CORRESPONDENCE **(PLEASE PRINT CLEARLY)**	IF COMPANY, ATTENTION:

BIRTH

SURNAME (FOR MARRIED WOMAN: SURNAME AT BIRTH OR ADOPTION OR AFTER LEGAL NAME CHANGE)	GIVEN NAMES	SEX	**Please indicate type and number of certificates required**
DATE OF BIRTH MONTH DAY YEAR	PLACE OF BIRTH (CITY, TOWN OR VILLAGE)	**BRITISH COLUMBIA**	☐ Genealogy - Registration copy **OR** ☐ Commemorative Certificates
SURNAME OF FATHER	GIVEN NAMES	BIRTHPLACE OF FATHER (CITY, PROV/STATE, COUNTRY)	Click on link below to see certificate options and their item numbers. Enter your selection in the box (below).
MAIDEN/BIRTH SURNAME OF MOTHER	GIVEN NAMES	BIRTHPLACE OF MOTHER (CITY, PROV/STATE, COUNTRY)	www.vs.gov.bc.ca/commemorate/index.html Item #

MARRIAGE

DATE OF MARRIAGE MONTH DAY YEAR	PLACE OF MARRIAGE (CITY, TOWN OR VILLAGE)	**BRITISH COLUMBIA**	**Please indicate number of certificates required**
SURNAME OF PARTY 1	GIVEN NAMES	BIRTHPLACE OF PARTY 1 (CITY, PROV/STATE, COUNTRY)	☐ Genealogy - Registration copy
SURNAME OF PARTY 2	GIVEN NAMES	BIRTHPLACE OF PARTY 2 (CITY, PROV/STATE, COUNTRY)	

DEATH

SURNAME OF DECEASED	GIVEN NAMES	DATE OF DEATH MONTH DAY YEAR	SEX	AGE	**Please indicate number of certificates required**
PLACE OF DEATH (CITY, TOWN OR VILLAGE)	**BRITISH COLUMBIA**	PLACE OF BIRTH (CITY, PROV/STATE, COUNTRY)			☐ Genealogy - Registration copy
PERMANENT RESIDENCE AT TIME OF DEATH (STREET AND CITY IF KNOWN)					

YOUR RELATIONSHIP TO EVENT: ☐ Self ☐ Mother ☐ Father ☐ Spouse ☐ Other: ____________

REASON CERTIFICATE REQUIRED: ____________

YOUR SIGNATURE (written): ____________

PAYMENT METHODS

☐ Cheque* ☐ Money Order ☐ Visa ☐ MasterCard ☐ American Express

*** Postdated cheques not accepted**

AMOUNT ENCLOSED $ ____________

Interac/Cash payment may be made in person at one of our three offices. Cheque or money order made payable to the Minister of Finance.

____
Card holder signature

____
PRINT Card holder name as shown on Credit Card

Credit Card # ____________ Expiry Date ____________

VSA 013_fill 2013/03/12

PLEASE READ NOTES ON REVERSE OF THIS FORM

COMPLETING THE APPLICATION FORM

WHO QUALIFIES TO APPLY

* **Commemorative Birth Certificates** may be released to
  a) you, if the record pertains to your own birth
  b) parents of a child
  c) guardian; copy of guardianship papers must be attached
  d) a person on the written consent of "a" or "b" above

* **Birth Genealogy** (Certified Registration Copy for Genealogical Research) may be released to
  a) you, if the record pertains to your own birth
  b) parents of a child
  c) custodial guardian; copy of guardianship papers must be attached
  d) anyone, as long as the person has been dead for 20 years, and proof of death is provided
  e) anyone, if the record has been in existence for 120 years
  f) a relative of the person named, on production of proof of death and relationship ***
  g) a person on the written consent of the eligible person

* **Marriage Genealogy** (Certified Registration copy for Genealogical Research) may be released to
  a) you, if the record pertains to your own marriage
  b) a relative of the person named, on production of proof of death and relationship***
  c) anyone, as long as the parties to the marriage have both been dead for 20 years, and proof of death is provided
  d) anyone, if the record has been in existence for 75 years
  e) a person on the written consent of an eligible person

* **Death Genealogy** (Certified Registration Copy for Genealogical Research) may be released to
  a) a relative of the deceased, on production of proof of relationship***
  b) anyone if the event occurred more than 20 years ago
  c) a person on the written consent of an eligible person

*** *Note: Eligible applicants are as follows, and proof of relationship must be provided*
Mother Father Son Daughter Sister Brother Spouse Grandparent Grandchild

Acceptable proof of relationship for a relative includes photocopy of a certified birth registration, a parental certificate and/or associated marriage certificates.

FEES

* For each certificate $50.00. Fee is for a search of records and a positive search will result in service. Where a service cannot be provided because no record exists, a $50.00 search fee will be assessed.
* Payment to be made in Canadian funds by credit card, cheque or money order payable to the Minister of Finance. Prices are current as of January 1, 2009 and are subject to change without notice. If ordering after April 1, 2012, contact our office for current fees.

TO AVOID DELAY

* Complete the appropriate section in full *(All requests with incomplete information must be accompanied by a signed, written explanation for the omission. If any portion of the relevant event information is left blank the application will be returned by mail for completion).*
* Be sure you are authorized to make the request.
* Enclose the correct fee by cheque, money order or credit card (Canadian Funds).
* Be sure your address and telephone number are correct and clear.
* A service charge of $30.00 will be levied on all cheques not honoured by the payees financial institution.

MAILING ADDRESS
Vital Statistics Agency
PO Box 9657 STN PROV GOVT
Victoria BC V8W 9P3

ENQUIRIES & CREDIT CARD ORDERS
Telephone: **250 952-2681** (Victoria & Outside BC)
Toll free: **1 888 876-1633** (within BC)

OR VISIT ONE OF OUR OFFICES

VICTORIA:
818 Fort St
Victoria BC

VANCOUVER:
250 - 605 Robson St
Vancouver BC

KELOWNA:
305 - 478 Bernard Ave
Kelowna BC

Check our Web Site at: www.vs.gov.bc.ca

The information on this form is collected under the authority of the ***Vital Statistics Act*** (RSBC 1996, c.479, Sec. 36, 37, 38 & 39). The information provided will be used to fulfill the requirements of the ***Vital Statistics Act*** for the release of information. The release of this information is in compliance with the ***Vital Statistics Act*** and the ***Freedom of Information and Protection of Privacy Act***. If you have any questions about the collection or use of this information, please contact a Vital Statistics Representative at 250-952-2681.

GENEALOGICAL SERVICES

The Vital Statistics Agency (Agency) provides a number of services and certificates for genealogical purposes. Listed below are the services which we provide.

Genealogy

Copies of original vital event records are an important resource for the family historian. Records of birth, marriage, and death occurring in the province of British Columbia since 1872, if registered with the Agency, are available to qualified applicants.

For genealogical research purposes the Agency issues unique registration copies, which make available all the information recorded on the original event record.

Births prior to 1951 may not include the weight or time of birth. This information will be provided separately along with the registration copy when available. This information is often of general interest and particularly useful to persons interested in numerology and astrology.

To learn more about genealogy services visit our web site at **www.vs.gov.bc.ca/genealogy**.

The Vital Statistics Agency and British Columbia Archives now provide an electronic index to British Columbia's historical birth, death, and marriage records from as early as 1872. Access to this electronic index is through **www.bcarchives.gov.bc.ca** or you can link to this site through our web page at the address noted in the previous paragraph.

Adoption Services

Over the last few decades, social attitudes towards adoption have changed, and as such, many people involved in adoptions want greater openness and access to information.

To ease the access to adoption information, the *Adoption Act* allows an adopted person 19 years of age or older to obtain a copy of their birth registration and adoption order, if the events occurred in British Columbia. The act also allows the birth parents access to the adopted person's birth registration and adoption order, once the adopted person reaches his/her 19th birthday.

To learn more about Adoption Services, visit our web site at **www.vs.gov.bc.ca**, or contact a Vital Statistics Representative at 250 952-2681.

Commemorative Certificates

The Agency offers a decorative series of commemorative birth certificates suitable for framing. There are 42 styles in this series.

- The Newborn style features playful toys as well as a place to display a newborn's photograph. This is now available in 5 background colours.
- The Classic style features the Flag and Coat of Arms of British Columbia.
- The BC Series has 36 stylized scenes portraying various regions of the province. See our website at: **www.vs.gov.bc.ca/commemorate/index.html** to view the complete collection.

Important Note

Commemorative certificates are not identification documents and cannot be used to obtain benefits or services (example: passport).

Genealogical Resources for British Columbians

After acquiring a genealogy certificate or using the Vital Events Indexes, many individuals inquire to the Vital Statistics Agency about additional sources of genealogical information. To help individuals begin their genealogical research, the Vital Statistics Agency published the guide, *Genealogical Resources for British Columbians*. This resource guide contains descriptions of various institutions' genealogical holdings and provides contact information. Readers will find information on genealogical societies, vital statistics offices, libraries, churches, internet sites, and many other sources of genealogical information.

The guide can be downloaded and printed from our website at: **www.vs.gov.bc.ca/forms/vsa006.pdf**.

Vital Statistics Agency Web Site

The Agency web site, located at **www.vs.gov.bc.ca,** is an excellent source of information about BC Vital Statistics services and products. Users starting at the Agency's home page can access a wide variety of informative pages, download forms, read electronic versions of some Agency publications, access the Vital Events Index and view samples of some certificates.

APPLICATION FOR GENEALOGICAL SEARCH OF MARITAL RECORDS

MAILING ADDRESS INFORMATION			
NOTE: Please PRINT your name, address and identifying information clearly. This portion will be used when mailing your service or correspondence.			FOR OFFICE USE ONLY: AFS#
SURNAME	GIVEN NAMES		FOR OFFICE USE ONLY
MAILING ADDRESS			
CITY, PROVINCE/STATE, COUNTRY		POSTAL CODE	
HOME NUMBER (INCLUDING AREA CODE)	WORK NUMBER (INCLUDING AREA CODE)	IF COMPANY, ATTENTION	

Upon acceptance of your application, a search of all British Columbia marriage records created after your 15th birthday will be undertaken. The results of this search will be provided to you in certificate form.

It is important that you understand that the Vital Statistics Agency only maintains records of events that take place in British Columbia. Each province of Canada maintains its own records.

Complete the following information in full:

BIRTH – Birth Details				
SURNAME & SEX				☐ MALE ☐ FEMALE
GIVEN NAMES	FIRST		MIDDLE NAMES	
BIRTH PLACE	CITY		PROVINCE/STATE	COUNTRY
BIRTH DATE	MONTH (ABBREVIATED)	DAY	YEAR	

If previously married in British Columbia, please provide the following details:

YOUR NAME AT TIME OF MARRIAGE	SURNAME			GIVEN NAMES
DATE AND PLACE OF MARRIAGE	MONTH (ABBREVIATED)	DAY	YEAR	CITY
YOUR NAME AT TIME OF MARRIAGE	SURNAME			GIVEN NAMES
DATE AND PLACE OF MARRIAGE	MONTH (ABBREVIATED)	DAY	YEAR	CITY

☐ SEARCH OF BRITISH COLUMBIA MARRIAGE RECORDS - $50.00 (Processing time is approximately 2 - 5 business days.)

Eligibility: Only the individual themselves, or an individual to whom they have provided written consent to apply on their behalf, may make application for a search of marriage records in their name.

YOUR SIGNATURE (written): ______________________ DATE SIGNED: ____________

PAYMENT METHODS

☐ Cheque * ☐ Money Order ☐ Visa ☐ MasterCard ☐ American Express

*** Postdated cheques not accepted**

Interac/Cash payment may be made in person at one of our three offices. Cheque or money order made payable to the Minister of Finance.

AMOUNT ENCLOSED $ ____________

____
Card holder signature

____
PRINT Card holder name as shown on Credit Card

Credit Card # ______________________ Expiry Date ____________

VSA430G 2013/03/12

GENEALOGICAL SEARCH OF MARRIAGE RECORDS, Also Known As AFFIDAVIT OF ELIGIBILITY/FREEDOM TO MARRY/MARITAL STATUS

Marriages performed abroad are done so in accordance with the laws of that country. Some foreign countries require nonresidents wishing to marry in their country to provide some form of documentation to confirm that they are in fact eligible to marry. The requested documentation may be in the form of an affidavit or certificate issued from the province/state where the individual resides, confirming that the individual is not currently married.

While we cannot confirm one's marital status, our agency provides a service wherein BC marriage records from the individuals reported 15th birthday to the date of application are researched to determine if a record is held. The result of our search of records is provided in certificate form and appears to satisfy such requirements. However, it is the applicant's responsibility to ensure that this service is what they require; once completed there is no ability to refund the service fee.

To view a sample of the information provided, visit our web page at:
http://www.vs.gov.bc.ca/genealogy/geneal_serch_marit_recrd.html

IMPORTANT INFORMATION

TO AVOID DELAY

- Complete all sections in full.
- It is against postal regulations to send cash through the mail. Payment in Canadian funds should be forwarded by cheque (**Postdated cheques not accepted**), bank draft or money order made **payable to the Minister of Finance**. Credit Card payments are accepted, please complete the Credit Card portion on the front of this form.
- Be sure your address and telephone number are correct and clear.
- A service charge of $30.00 will be levied on all cheques not honoured by the payees financial institution.

FEES

Fees as noted for each requested search on the front.

All fees subject to change. If ordering after April 1, 2012, contact our office for current fees.

MAILING ADDRESS
Vital Statistics Agency
PO Box 9657 STN PROV GOVT
Victoria BC V8W 9P3

ENQUIRIES & CREDIT CARD ORDERS
Telephone: **250 952-2681** (Victoria & Outside BC)
Toll free: **1 888 876-1633** (within BC)

OR VISIT ONE OF OUR OFFICES

VICTORIA:
818 Fort St
Victoria BC

VANCOUVER:
250 - 605 Robson St
Vancouver BC

KELOWNA:
305 - 478 Bernard Ave
Kelowna BC

Check our Web Site at: http://www.vs.gov.bc.ca

The information on this form is collected under the authority of the ***Vital Statistics Act*** (RSBC 1996, c.479, Sec. 37 & 38). The information provided will be used to fulfill the requirements of the ***Vital Statistics Act*** for the release of marriage information. If you have any questions about the collection or use of this information, please contact a Vital Statistics Client Service Representative at 250 952-2681, or write to the mailing address provided above. This information is protected for unauthorized use and disclosure in accordance with the ***Freedom of Information and Protection of Privacy Act*** and may be disclosed only in accordance with that Act.

CANADA—MANITOBA

Send your requests to:

Vital Statistics Agency
254 Portage Avenue
Winnipeg, Manitoba, Canada R3C 0B6

Tel. (204) 945-3701; (866) 949-9296 toll free
Fax (204) 948-3128
E-mail: vitalstats@gov.mb.ca
http://vitalstats.gov.mb.ca/

The Vital Statistics Agency has records from 1872. Birth records are restricted for 100 years, death records for 70 years, and marriage records for 80 years. For genealogical research purposes, the Agency issues a certified photocopy of the registration of the event, which is stamped "Genealogical Purposes Only." Genealogy searches of unrestricted records can be made online at http://vitalstats.gov.mb.ca/Query.php.

Cost for a certified Birth Certificate	Can$30.00
Cost for a commemorative Birth or Marriage Certificate	Can$30.00
Cost for a certified Marriage Certificate	Can$30.00
Cost for a certified Death Certificate	Can$30.00
Cost for a Genealogical Photocopy	Can$30.00

For additional assistance, contact:

Embassy of Canada
501 Pennsylvania Avenue, NW
Washington, DC 20001

Tel. (202) 682-1740

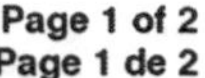

Application for a Manitoba Birth Document
Demande d'attestation de naissance au Manitoba

Please PRINT clearly to complete the front and back of this application. Incomplete applications or those with insufficient payment will be returned.
Veuillez écrire lisiblement EN LETTRES MOULÉES en remplissant les deux côtés du formulaire. Les demandes incomplètes ou accompagnées d'un paiement insuffisant seront retournées.

Section 1 - Mailing address / Adresse postale

Name / Nom ______________________

Daytime phone number(s) / Numéro(s) de téléphone (jour)
( ) ______ - ______
( ) ______ - ______

Address / Adresse ______________________

City / Ville ______ Province ______ Postal Code / Code postal ______

Email address / Adresse de courriel ______________________

Section 2 - Type of document requested / Type de document demandé

	Quantity / Quantité
☐ Birth Certificate with parents' names / Certificat de naissance comportant le nom des parents	_____
☐ Birth Certificate without parents' names / Certificat de naissance ne comportant pas le nom des parents	_____
☐ Copy of registration (this is not a birth certificate) / Copie du bulletin d'enregistrement (pas un certificat de naissance)	_____

Reason for application / Raison de la demande : ______________________

DOCUMENT ISSUED IN / LANGUE DEMANDÉE : ☐ English / Anglais **OR / OU** ☐ French / Français

Section 3 - Manitoba birth / Naissance au Manitoba

Last name on birth record / Nom de famille inscrit sur le certificat | First name / Prénom | Middle name(s) / Deuxième(s) prénom(s)

Date of birth / Date de naissance
Month / Mois ____ Day / Jour ____ Year / Année ____

Sex / Sexe ☐ Male / Masculin ☐ Female / Féminin

Place of birth (town/city) / Lieu de naissance (ville ou village) ______________________ MANITOBA

Father or other parent / Père ou autre parent
Last name / Nom de famille | First name / Prénom | Middle name(s) / Deuxième(s) prénom(s)

Place of birth / Lieu de naissance (province if born in Canada - country if born outside of Canada / province si né[e] au Canada et pays si né[e] à l'extérieur du Canada)

Mother or other parent / Mère ou autre parent
Maiden name / Nom de jeune fille | First name / Prénom | Middle name(s) / Deuxième(s) prénom(s)

Place of birth / Lieu de naissance (province if born in Canada - country if born outside of Canada / province si né[e] au Canada et pays si né[e] à l'extérieur du Canada)

OFFICE USE ONLY / RÉSERVÉ À L'ADMINISTRATION

Checked: __________

Entered: __________

Reg. # __________
____

Edited: __________

Issued: __________

Revised 08/12

Continue on back / Suite au verso →

Section 4 - Birth document may be released to: / La personne suivante peut recevoir l'attestation de naissance :

Check one box that applies to you and sign below / Cochez la case qui s'applique à vous et signez ci-dessous :

☐ You, if the application is for your own certificate / Vous-même, si la demande concerne votre propre certificat

☐ Either parent named on the record of the child / Un des parents inscrits sur le certificat d'un enfant

☐ Legal guardian (submit a complete copy of guardianship papers) / Tuteur légal (présenter une copie de tous les documents relatifs à la tutelle)

☐ Representative with written authorization from person entitled, parent, or guardian / Représentant disposant d'une autorisation écrite de personne autorisée, du parent ou du tuteur

☐ Next-of-kin, if application is for a birth certificate for a deceased person / Personne faisant partie des plus proches parents, dans le cas d'une demande pour un certificat de naissance touchant une personne décédée.

Familial relationship to deceased / Lien familial avec la personne décédée :______________________

Date & place of death / Date et lieu du décès :______________________

Signature of eligible person / Signature de la personne admissible : ______________________

Print name of eligible person / Nom de la personne admissible (en lettres moulées) : ______________________

Section 5 - Type of service / Type de service

☐ **REGULAR SERVICE / SERVICE ORDINAIRE**

(Processing time may vary / Le délai de traitement peut varier)

- Delivered by Canada Post / Livraison par Postes Canada
- Fee / Coût : **$30** per document / **30 $** par document

☐ **RUSH SERVICE / SERVICE RAPIDE**

(Processed within 24 hours, if birth is registered. Courier time is additional. / Une fois la naissance enregistrée, le certificat est produit dans les 24 heures sans compter le temps de livraison)

- Delivered by Courier / Livraison par messager
- Fee / Coût :

	Fee / Coût	
Canadian destination / Livraison au Canada	**$65 / 65 $**	Includes one document. Cheques for rush service must be certified / Comprend un document. Pour le service rapide, les chèques non certifiés ne seront pas acceptés
US destination / Livraison aux États-Unis	**$75 / 75 $**	
International destination / Livraison internationale	**$105 / 105 $**	

Courier address (if different than mailing address) / Adresse du messager (si elle diffère de l'adresse postale)

signature required upon delivery / signature requise au moment de la livraison

Name / Nom			Company name (if applicable) / Nom de l'entreprise (s'il y a lieu)		
Street No. / N° de rue	Street Name / Nom de rue		Apt. no. / N° d'app.	Buzzer No. / N° de sonnerie	PO Box / C. P.
Postal Code/ Code postal	City / Ville		Province		Country / Pays
Fees subject to change without notice, please check our website for current fee schedule Les montants peuvent être modifiés sans préavis, veuillez voir notre site Web pour le barème des droits courants.				Telephone number / N° de tél.	

Section 6 - Method of payment / Mode de paiement

☐ Cash / Argent comptant
☐ Debit card / Carte de débit
} In person only / en personne seulement

☐ MasterCard / Visa

☐ Cheque / Chèque
☐ Money Order / Mandat
☐ Certified Cheque / Chèque certifié
} Payable to the Minister of Finance / À l'ordre du ministre des Finances

I authorize the Vital Statistics Agency to charge to my card:
J'autorise le Bureau de l'état civil à débiter de ma carte la somme de : $______________

Credit Card number / Numéro de carte de crédit

Expiry date / Date d'expiration

Cardholder's name / Nom du titulaire de la carte

Cardholder's signature / Signature du titulaire de la carte

- No post dated cheques will be accepted / Aucun chèque postdaté ne sera accepté.
- A $20 service fee will be charged on returned cheques / Des frais administratifs de 20 $ seront imposés pour les chèques retournés.

A $30 ADMINISTRATION FEE WILL BE RETAINED WHEN CUSTOMERS DO NOT RESPOND TO REQUESTS FOR ADDITIONAL INFORMATION REQUIRED TO COMPLETE THE SERVICE.

NOTICE UNDER THE FREEDOM OF INFORMATION AND PROTECTION OF PRIVACY ACT

The information requested on this form is collected pursuant to *The Vital Statistics Act* to fulfill the requirements for the release of birth information. If you have any questions regarding the collection or use of this information, please contact Vital Statistics Agency.

Available in other formats upon request.

DES FRAIS ADMINISTRATIFS DE 30 $ SERONT RETENUS SI LE CLIENT NE FOURNIT PAS LES RENSEIGNEMENTS SUPPLÉMENTAIRES NÉCESSAIRES POUR FOURNIR LE SERVICE REQUIS.

AVIS EN VERTU DE LA LOI SUR L'ACCÈS À L'INFORMATION ET LA PROTECTION DE LA VIE PRIVÉE

Les renseignements demandés sur le formulaire sont recueillis conformément à la *Loi sur les statistiques de l'état civil* afin de satisfaire aux exigences relatives à la délivrance de documents d'attestation de naissance. Si vous avez des questions au sujet de la collecte ou de l'utilisation de ces renseignements, veuillez communiquer avec le Bureau de l'état civil.

Disponible en autres formats sur demande

Inquiries

Telephone:	(204) 945-3701
Toll-Free (within Canada)	1-866-949-9296
Fax:	(204) 948-3128
E-Mail:	vitalstats@gov.mb.ca
Web-Site:	http://vitalstats.gov.mb.ca
Address:	Vital Statistics Agency 254 Portage Ave Wpg MB R3C 0B6

Renseignements

Téléphone :	204 945-3701
Numéro sans frais (au Canada) :	1 866 949-9296
Télécopieur :	204 948-3128
Courriel :	vitalstats@gov.mb.ca
Site Web :	http://vitalstats.gov.mb.ca
Adresse :	Bureau de l'état civil 254, avenue Portage, Wpg MB R3C 0B6

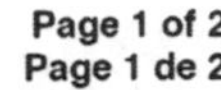

Application for a Manitoba Marriage Document
Demande d'attestation de mariage au Manitoba

Please PRINT clearly to complete the front and back of this application. Incomplete applications or those with insufficient payment will be returned.
Veuillez écrire lisiblement EN LETTRES MOULÉES en remplissant les deux côtés du formulaire. Les demandes incomplètes ou accompagnées d'un paiement insuffisant seront retournées.

Section 1 - Mailing address / Adresse postale

Name / Nom

Address / Adresse

City / Ville   Province   Postal Code / Code postal

Daytime phone number(s) / Numéro(s) de téléphone (jour)

( ) -

( ) -

Email address / Adresse de courriel

Section 2 - Type of document requested / Type de document demandé

Quantity / Quantité

☐ Marriage Certificate / Certificat de mariage

☐ Copy of registration (this is not a marriage certificate) / Copie du bulletin d'enregistrement (pas un certificat de mariage)

Reason for application / Raison de la demande :

DOCUMENT ISSUED IN / LANGUE DEMANDÉE : ☐ English / Anglais **OR / OU** ☐ French / Français

Section 3 - Manitoba Marriage / Mariage au Manitoba

First party / Première partie

Last name prior to this marriage / Nom de famille avant ce mariage   Given name(s) / Prénom(s)   Middle name(s) / Deuxième(s) prénom(s)

Place of birth / Lieu de naissance (province if born in Canada - country if born outside of Canada / province si né[e] au Canada et pays si né[e] à l'extérieur du Canada)

Second party / Deuxième partie

Last name prior to this marriage / Nom de famille avant ce mariage   Given name(s) / Prénom(s)   Middle name(s) / Deuxième(s) prénom(s)

Place of birth / Lieu de naissance (province if born in Canada - country if born outside of Canada / province si né[e] au Canada et pays si né[e] à l'extérieur du Canada)

Date of marriage / Date du mariage

Month / Mois   Day / Jour   Year / Année

Place of marriage / Lieu du mariage

M A N I T O B A

OFFICE USE ONLY / RÉSERVÉ À L'ADMINISTRATION

Checked:

Entered:

Reg. #

Edited:

Issued:

Revised 08/2012

Continue on back / Suite au verso →

Section 4 - Marriage document may be released to: / La personne suivante peut recevoir l'attestation de marriage :

Check one box that applies to you and sign below / Cochez la case qui s'applique à vous et signez ci-dessous :

☐ A) First party or second party as above / La première partie ou la deuxième partie (voir la section précédente)

☐ B) A child or parent if both parties are deceased / Enfant ou parent si les deux parties sont décédées
Date & place of death / Date et lieu du décès : ______________________
Date & place of death / Date et lieu du décès : ______________________

☐ C) A person with written authorization from either A or B above / Personne ayant une autorisation écrite provenant des personnes décrites dans les catégories A et B ci-dessus

Signature of eligible person / Signature de la personne admissible : ______________________

Print name of eligible person / Nom de la personne admissible (en lettres moulées) : ______________________

Section 5 - Type of service / Type de service

☐ **REGULAR SERVICE / SERVICE ORDINAIRE**
(Processing time may vary / Le délai de traitement peut varier)
- Delivered by Canada Post / Livraison par Postes Canada
- Fee / Coût : **$30** per document / **30 $** par document

☐ **RUSH SERVICE / SERVICE RAPIDE**
(Processed within 24 hours, if marriage is registered. Courier time is additional. / Une fois le mariage enregistré, le certificat est produit dans les 24 heures sans compter le temps de livraison)
- Delivered by Courier / Livraison par messager
- Fee / Coût :

	Fee / Coût	
Canadian destination / Livraison au Canada	**$65 / 65 $**	Includes one document. Cheques for rush service must be certified / Comprend un document. Pour le service rapide, les chèques non certifiés ne seront pas acceptés
US destination / Livraison aux États-Unis	**$75 / 75 $**	
International destination / Livraison internationale	**$105 / 105 $**	

Courier address (if different than mailing address) / Adresse du messager (si elle diffère de l'adresse postale)
signature required upon delivery / signature requise au moment de la livraison

Name / Nom		Company name (if applicable) / Nom de l'entreprise (s'il y a lieu)		
Street No. / N° de rue	Street Name / Nom de rue	Apt. no. / N° d'app.	Buzzer No. / N° de sonnerie	PO Box / C. P.
Postal Code/ Code postal	City / Ville	Province		Country / Pays
Fees subject to change without notice, please check our website for current fee schedule Les montants peuvent être modifiés sans préavis, veuillez voir notre site Web pour le barème des droits courants.			Telephone number / N° de tél.	

Section 6 - Method of payment / Mode de paiement

☐ Visa
☐ MasterCard
☐ Cheque / Chèque
☐ Money Order / Mandat
☐ Certified Cheque / Chèque certifié

(Cheque, Money Order, Certified Cheque) Payable to the Minister of Finance / À l'ordre du ministre des Finances

I authorize the Vital Statistics Agency to charge to my card:
J'autorise le Bureau de l'état civil à débiter de ma carte la somme de : $______________

Credit Card number / Numéro de carte de crédit ______________ Expiry date / Date d'expiration ______

Cardholder's name / Nom du titulaire de la carte ______________

Cardholder's signature / Signature du titulaire de la carte ______________

- No post dated cheques will be accepted / Aucun chèque postdaté ne sera accepté.
- A $20 service fee will be charged on returned cheques / Des frais administratifs de 20 $ seront imposés pour les chèques retournés.

A $30 ADMINISTRATION FEE WILL BE RETAINED WHEN CUSTOMERS DO NOT RESPOND TO REQUESTS FOR ADDITIONAL INFORMATION REQUIRED TO COMPLETE THE SERVICE.

NOTICE UNDER THE FREEDOM OF INFORMATION AND PROTECTION OF PRIVACY ACT

The information requested on this form is collected pursuant to *The Vital Statistics Act* to fulfill the requirements for the release of marriage information. If you have any questions regarding the collection or use of this information, please contact Vital Statistics Agency.

Available in other formats upon request.

DES FRAIS ADMINISTRATIFS DE 30 $ SERONT RETENUS SI LE CLIENT NE FOURNIT PAS LES RENSEIGNEMENTS SUPPLÉMENTAIRES NÉCESSAIRES POUR FOURNIR LE SERVICE REQUIS.

AVIS EN VERTU DE LA LOI SUR L'ACCÈS À L'INFORMATION ET LA PROTECTION DE LA VIE PRIVÉE

Les renseignements demandés sur le formulaire sont recueillis conformément à la *Loi sur les statistiques de l'état civil* afin de satisfaire aux exigences relatives à la délivrance de documents d'attestation de mariage. Si vous avez des questions au sujet de la collecte ou de l'utilisation de ces renseignements, veuillez communiquer avec le Bureau de l'état civil.

Disponible en autres formats sur demande

Inquiries

Telephone:	(204) 945-3701
Toll-Free (within Canada)	1-866-949-9296
Fax:	(204) 948-3128
E-Mail:	vitalstats@gov.mb.ca
Web-Site:	http://vitalstats.gov.mb.ca
Address:	Vital Statistics Agency 254 Portage Ave Wpg MB R3C 0B6

Renseignements

Téléphone :	204 945-3701
Numéro sans frais (au Canada) :	1 866 949-9296
Télécopieur :	204 948-3128
Courriel :	vitalstats@gov.mb.ca
Site Web :	http://vitalstats.gov.mb.ca
Adresse :	Bureau de l'état civil 254, avenue Portage, Wpg MB R3C 0B6

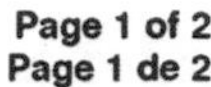

Application for a Manitoba Death Document
Demande d'attestation de décès au Manitoba

Please PRINT clearly to complete the front and back of this application. Incomplete applications or those with insufficient payment will be returned.
Veuillez écrire lisiblement EN LETTRES MOULÉES en remplissant les deux côtés du formulaire. Les demandes incomplètes ou accompagnées d'un paiement insuffisant seront retournées.

Section 1 - Mailing address / Adresse postale

Name / Nom

Daytime phone number(s) / Numéro(s) de téléphone (jour)

( ) -

( ) -

Address / Adresse

City / Ville   Province   Postal Code / Code postal

Email address / Adresse de courriel

Section 2 - Type of document requested / Type de document demandé

Quantity / Quantité

☐ Death Certificate / Certificat de décès ____

☐ Copy of registration (this is not a death certificate) / Copie du bulletin d'enregistrement (pas un certificat de décès) ____

Reason for application / Raison de la demande : ____

DOCUMENT ISSUED IN / LANGUE DEMANDÉE : ☐ English / Anglais **OR / OU** ☐ French / Français

Section 3 - Manitoba Death / Décès au Manitoba

Last name of deceased / Nom de famille de la personne décédée

Given name(s) / Prénom(s)   Middle name(s) / Deuxième(s) prénom(s)

Date of death / Date du décès   Age / Âge   Sex / Sexe ☐ Male / Masculin ☐ Female / Féminin

Month / Mois   Day / Jour   Year / Année

Place of death (town/city) / Lieu du décès (ville ou village)

M A N I T O B A

A $30 ADMINISTRATION FEE WILL BE RETAINED WHEN CUSTOMERS DO NOT RESPOND TO REQUESTS FOR ADDITIONAL INFORMATION REQUIRED TO COMPLETE THE SERVICE.

NOTICE UNDER THE FREEDOM OF INFORMATION AND PROTECTION OF PRIVACY ACT

The information requested on this form is collected pursuant to *The Vital Statistics Act* to fulfill the requirements for the release of death information. If you have any questions regarding the collection or use of this information, please contact Vital Statistics Agency.

Available in other formats upon request.

DES FRAIS ADMINISTRATIFS DE 30$ SERONT RETENUS SI LE CLIENT NE FOURNIT PAS LES RENSEIGNEMENTS SUPPLÉMENTAIRES NÉCESSAIRES POUR FOURNIR LE SERVICE REQUIS.

AVIS EN VERTU DE LA LOI SUR L'ACCÈS À L'INFORMATION ET LA PROTECTION DE LA VIE PRIVÉE

Les renseignements demandés sur le formulaire sont recueillis conformément à la *Loi sur les statistiques de l'état civil* afin de satisfaire aux exigences relatives à la délivrance de documents d'attestation de décès. Si vous avez des questions au sujet de la collecte ou de l'utilisation de ces renseignements, veuillez communiquer avec le Bureau de l'état civil.

Disponible en autres formats sur demande

OFFICE USE ONLY / RÉSERVÉ À L'ADMINISTRATION

Checked: ____

Entered: ____

Reg. # ____

____

Edited: ____

Issued: ____

Revised 08/2012

Continue on back / Suite au verso →

Section 4 - Death document may be released to: / La personne suivante peut recevoir l'attestation de décès :

1) Any person may obtain a death certificate / Toute personne peut obtenir un certificat de décès
2) A copy of the registration may be released to the following persons / Les personnes suivantes peuvent recevoir une copie du bulletin d'enregistrement :
   - A spouse, child, parent, or sibling of the deceased / Conjoint, enfant, parent ou frère ou sœur de la personne décédée;
   - The executor or administrator of the estate of the deceased / Exécuteur ou administrateur nommé dans le testament de la personne décédée;
   - A person with written authorization from either A or B below / Personne ayant une autorisation écrite provenant des personnes décrites dans les catégories A et B ci-dessous.

Check one box that applies to you if a copy of the registration is requested and sign below / Cochez la case qui s'applique à vous si vous demandez une copie du bulletin d'enregistrement et signez ci-dessous.

☐ A) A spouse, child, parent, or sibling of the deceased / Conjoint, enfant, parent, frère ou sœur de la personne décédée

☐ B) The executor or administrator of the estate of the deceased (attach documentation) / Exécuteur ou administrateur nommé dans le testament de la personne décédée. (Veuillez joindre la documentation pertinente.)

☐ C) A person with written authorization from either A or B above (attach documentation) / Personne ayant une autorisation écrite provenant des personnes décrites dans les catégories A et B ci-dessus. (Veuillez joindre la documentation pertinente.)

Signature of eligible person / Signature de la personne admissible : ______________________

Print name of eligible person / Nom de la personne admissible (en lettres moulées) : ______________________

Section 5 - Type of service / Type de service

☐ **REGULAR SERVICE / SERVICE ORDINAIRE**

(Processing time may vary / Le délai de traitement peut varier)
- Delivered by Canada Post / Livraison par Postes Canada
- Fee / Coût : **$30** per document / **30 $** par document

☐ **RUSH SERVICE / SERVICE RAPIDE**

(Processed within 24 hours, if death is registered. Courier time is additional. / Une fois le décès enregistré, le certificat est produit dans les 24 heures sans compter le temps de livraison)
- Delivered by Courier / Livraison par messager
- Fee / Coût : Canadian destination / Livraison au Canada **$65 / 65 $**
  US destination / Livraison aux États-Unis **$75 / 75 $**
  International destination / Livraison internationale **$105 / 105 $**

} Includes one document. Cheques for rush service must be certified / Comprend un document. Pour le service rapide, les chèques non certifiés ne seront pas acceptés

Courier address (if different than mailing address) / Adresse du messager (si elle diffère de l'adresse postale)
signature required upon delivery / signature requise au moment de la livraison

Name / Nom		Company name (if applicable) / Nom de l'entreprise (s'il y a lieu)		
Street No. / N° de rue	Street Name / Nom de rue	Apt. no. / N° d'app.	Buzzer No. / N° de sonnerie	PO Box / C. P.
Postal Code / Code postal	City / Ville	Province		Country / Pays

Fees subject to change without notice, please check our website for current fee schedule.
Les montants peuvent être modifiés sans préavis, veuillez voir notre site Web pour le barème des droits courants.

Telephone number / N° de tél.

Section 6 - Method of payment / Mode de paiement

☐ Visa
☐ MasterCard
☐ Cheque / Chèque
☐ Money Order / Mandat
☐ Certified Cheque / Chèque certifié

} Payable to the Minister of Finance / À l'ordre du ministre des Finances

I authorize the Vital Statistics Agency to charge to my card:
J'autorise le Bureau de l'état civil à débiter de ma carte la somme de : $__________

Credit Card number / Numéro de carte de crédit

Expiry date / Date d'expiration

Cardholder's name / Nom du titulaire de la carte

Cardholder's signature / Signature du titulaire de la carte

- No post dated cheques will be accepted / Aucun chèque postdaté ne sera accepté.
- A $20 service fee will be charged on returned cheques / Des frais administratifs de 20 $ seront imposés pour les chèques retournés.

Inquiries

Telephone:	(204) 945-3701
Toll-Free (within Canada)	1-866-949-9296
Fax:	(204) 948-3128
E-Mail:	vitalstats@gov.mb.ca
Web-Site:	http://vitalstats.gov.mb.ca
Address:	Vital Statistics Agency 254 Portage Ave Wpg MB R3C 0B6

Renseignements

Téléphone :	204 945-3701
Numéro sans frais (au Canada) :	1 866 949-9296
Télécopieur :	204 948-3128
Courriel :	vitalstats@gov.mb.ca
Site Web :	http://vitalstats.gov.mb.ca
Adresse :	Bureau de l'état civil 254, avenue Portage, Wpg MB R3C 0B6

Application for an Unrestricted Manitoba Record / Demande d'un document du Manitoba ne faisant l'objet d'aucune restriction

Please PRINT clearly to complete the front and back of this application. Incomplete applications or those with insufficient payment will be returned.
Veuillez écrire lisiblement EN LETTRES MOULÉES en remplissant les deux côtés du formulaire. Les demandes incomplètes ou accompagnées d'un paiement insuffisant seront retournées.

VSA File Number:

Section 1 - Mailing address / Adresse postale

Name / Nom

Daytime phone number(s) / Numéro(s) de téléphone (jour)

(______) ______ - ______

Address / Adresse

(______) ______ - ______

City / Ville   Province   Postal Code / Code postal

Email address / Adresse de courriel

Section 2 - Type of document requested / Type de document demandé

NOTE: The fee for each search and document is $30.00 OR $12.00 if you provide the registration number. Search at http://vitalstats.gov.mb.ca /
REMARQUE : Les frais exigés pour chaque recherche et document sont de 30 $ OU de 12 $ si vous fournissez le numéro d'enregistrement que vous trouverez à http://vitalstats.gov.mb.ca/index.fr.html.

Quantity / Quantité

- ☐ Certified copy of a birth registration that is 100 years or older / Une copie certifiée d'un bulletin d'enregistrement de naissance datant de 100 ans ou plus ______
- ☐ Certified copy of a marriage registration that is 80 years or older / Une copie certifiée d'un bulletin d'enregistrement de mariage datant de 80 ans ou plus ______
- ☐ Certified copy of a death registration that is 70 years or older / Une copie certifiée d'un bulletin d'enregistrement de décès datant de 70 ans ou plus ______

The certified copies contain information exactly as recorded on the original registration. If the record you requested is not located you will receive a Search Receipt stating there is no record. The fees are not refundable. / Les copies certifiées contiennent les renseignements tels qu'ils sont inscrits sur le certificat original. Si le certificat demandé ne peut être trouvé, le Bureau de l'état civil émettra un reçu pour fins de recherche précisant qu'il n'existe pas de certificat.Les frais versés sont non remboursables.

Section 3 - Birth (over 100 years) / Naissance (datant de plus de 100 ans)

Last name on birth record / Nom de famille comme indiqué sur l'enregistrement   First name/ Prénom   Middle name(s) / Deuxième(s) prénom(s)

Date of birth / Date de naissance (Month / Mois | Day / Jour | Year/ Année)   Place of birth (town/city) / Lieu de naissance (ville ou village) , MANITOBA   Sex / Sexe ☐ Male / Masculin ☐ Female / Féminin

Father or other parent / Père ou autre parent
Last name / Nom de famille   First name/ Prénom   Middle name(s) / Deuxième(s) prénom(s)   Province & country of birth / Province et pays de naissance

Mother or other parent / Mère ou autre parent
Maiden name / Nom de jeune fille   First name/ Prénom   Middle name(s) / Deuxième(s) prénom(s)   Province & country of birth / Province et pays de naissance

If deceased/ En cas de décès: Date of death / Date du décès (Month / Mois | Day / Jour | Year/ Année)   Place of death (city/town)/ Lieu du décès (ville ou village)   registration number / numéro d'enregistrement

Section 4 - Marriage (over 80 years) / Mariage (datant de plus de 80 ans)

First party / Première partie
Last name prior to this marriage / Nom de famille avant ce mariage   First name/ Prénom   Middle name(s) / Deuxième(s) prénom(s)

Province & country of birth / Province et pays de naissance

Second party / Deuxième partie
Last name prior to this marriage / Nom de famille avant ce mariage   First name/ Prénom   Middle name(s) / Deuxième(s) prénom(s)

Province & country of birth / Province et pays de naissance

Date of marriage / Date de mariage (Month / Mois | Day / Jour | Year/ Année)   Place of marriage (town/city) / Lieu de mariage (ville ou village) , MANITOBA   registration number / numéro d'enregistrement

Section 5 - Manitoba Death (over 70 years) / Décès au Manitoba (datant de plus de 70 ans)

Last name of deceased / Nom de famille de la personne décédée   First name/ Prénom   Middle name(s) / Deuxième(s) prénom(s)

Date of death / Date du décès (Month / Mois | Day / Jour | Year/ Année)   Place of death (city/town)/ Lieu du décès (ville ou village) , MANITOBA

Sex / Sexe ☐ Male / Masculin ☐ Female / Féminin   Age / Âge   Date of birth / Date de naissance (Month / Mois | Day / Jour | Year/ Année)

Spouse's name / Nom du conjoint   registration number / numéro d'enregistrement

Continue on back / Suite au verso →

Section 6 - Other Information / Autres renseignements

If you have any additional information that would assist us in our search please indicate below:
Si vous avez des renseignements supplémentaires qui pourraient nous aider dans notre recherche, veuillez indiquer ci-dessous :

Section 7 - Method of payment / Mode de paiement

Fee for each search and document is $30.00 OR $12.00 if you provide the registration number. Search at http://vitalstats.gov.mb.ca / Les frais exigés pour chaque recherche et document sont de 30 $ OU de 12 $ si vous fournissez le numéro d'enregistrement que vous trouverez à http://vitalstats.gov.mb.ca/index.fr.html

☐ Visa
☐ MasterCard
☐ Cheque / Chèque
☐ Money Order / Mandat
☐ Certified Cheque / Chèque certifié

Payable to the Minister of Finance / À l'ordre du ministre des Finances

I authorize the Vital Statistics Agency to charge to my card:
J'autorise le Bureau de l'état civil à débiter de ma carte la somme de: $__________

Credit Card number / Numéro de carte de crédit

Expiry date / Date d'expiration

Cardholder's name / Nom du titulaire de la carte

Cardholder's signature / Signature du titulaire de la carte

- No post dated cheques will be accepted / Aucun chèque postdaté ne sera accepté.
- A $20 service fee will be charged on returned cheques / Des frais administratifs de 20 $ seront imposés pour les chèques retournés.
- A $30 administration fee will be retained when customers do not respond to requests for additional information required to complete the service / Des frais administratifs de 30 $ seront retenus si le client ne fournit pas les renseignements supplément aires nécessaires pour fournir le service requis.

NOTICE UNDER THE FREEDOM OF INFORMATION AND PROTECTION OF PRIVACY ACT

The information requested on this form is collected under *The Vital Statistics Act* to process your application for birth, marriage, and death information. If you have any questions regarding the collection or use of this information, please contact the Vital Statistics Agency.

Available in other formats upon request.

AVIS EN VERTU DE LA *LOI SUR L'ACCÈS À L'INFORMATION ET LA PROTECTION DE LA VIE PRIVÉE*

Les renseignements exigés sur ce formulaire sont recueillis en vertu de la *Loi sur les statistiques de l'état civil* pour traiter les demandes de renseignements concernant une naissance, un mariage ou un décès. Si vous avez des questions sur la collecte et l'utilisation de ces renseignements, veuillez communiquer avec le Bureau de l'état civil.

Disponibles dans d'autres formats sur demande.

Inquiries

Telephone:	(204) 945-3701
Toll-Free (within Canada)	1-866-949-9296
Fax:	(204) 948-3128
E-Mail:	vitalstats@gov.mb.ca
Web-Site:	http://vitalstats.gov.mb.ca
Address:	Vital Statistics Agency 254 Portage Ave Wpg MB R3C 0B6

Renseignements

Téléphone :	204 945-3701
Sans frais (au Canada) :	1 866 949-9296
Télécopieur :	204 948-3128
Courriel :	vitalstats@gov.mb.ca
Site Web :	http://vitalstats.gov.mb.ca
Adresse :	Bureau de l'état civil 254, av. Portage, Winnipeg (Manitoba) R3C OB6

OFFICE USE ONLY / RÉSERVÉ À L'ADMINISTRATION

Checked: ________

Entered: ________

Edited: ________

Issued: ________

CANADA—NEW BRUNSWICK

Send your requests to:

Service New Brunswick Vital Statistics
P.O. Box 1998
Fredericton, New Brunswick, Canada
E3B 5G4

Tel. (506) 453-2385
Fax (506) 444-4139
www.snb.ca/e/0001e.asp

The Vital Statistics Office has records from January 1888. If your request is for genealogical purposes, you may obtain a non-certified extract of the birth, marriage, or death record. Certificates can be ordered online using the link on the Service New Brunswick website.

Civil registration of vital events has taken place in New Brunswick since 1888. For a fee, Vital Statistics will search for birth records 1911–present, marriage records 1956–present, or death records 1956–present. Records of events before these dates may be accessed from microfilms, which can be borrowed through inter-library loans by contacting the Provincial Archives (P.O. Box 6000, Fredericton, NB E3B 5H1; tel. 506-453-2122) or searched online at http://archives.gnb.ca/APPS/GovRecs/VISSE/default.aspx?culture=en-CA.

Cost for a certified Birth Certificate	Can$30.00
Cost for a short-form Birth Certificate	Can$25.00
Cost for a certified Marriage Certificate	Can$30.00
Cost for a Photographic Print of Marriage Registration	Can$20.00
Cost for a certified Death Certificate	Can$30.00

For additional assistance, contact:

Embassy of Canada
501 Pennsylvania Avenue, NW
Washington, DC 20001

Tel. (202) 682-1740

APPLICATION FOR BIRTH CERTIFICATE
SERVICE NEW BRUNSWICK
VITAL STATISTICS
P.O. BOX 1998 FREDERICTON NB E3B 5G4
Telephone: (506) 453-2385
Fax: (506) 444-4139

PLEASE PRINT CLEARLY IN BLACK INK

Part 1: Applicant Information

"Applicant" is the person who is completing this request. An **"Applicant"** must enter their contact information so they can be contacted if problems arise with this request.

Your Last Name	Your First Name	Your Mailing Address	
City	Province	Postal Code	Country
Day Telephone (___) ____-______	Alternate Telephone (___) ____-______	Your relationship to the person named on certificate ☐ Self ☐ Mother ☐ Father ☐ Other: __________ (specify)	

Signature of Applicant : X____________________ Date:________________
(Person applying for certificate)

Part 2: Birth Details

Enter the birth information of the person in whose name the certificate will be issued including the names of both parents and their respective places of birth. If father's information is not applicable, please put "N/A" in corresponding fields.

Last Name		Given Name(s)	
Date of Birth ☐☐ Day ☐☐ Month ☐☐☐☐ Year	Sex ☐ M ☐ F	Place of Birth (City, Town or Village)	County
Father's Surname		Father's Given Name(s)	Father's Birthplace
Mother's Maiden Surname		Mother's Given Name(s)	Mother's Birthplace

Part 3 : Certificate Details

Step 1: Select the type, quantity of each certificate and the language you are requesting (details on what each certificate includes are outlined on the first page).

Short form certificate **$25.00** x _______ (**Quantity**) **Long form** certificate **$30.00** x _______ (**Quantity**)

Language ☐ **English** or ☐ **French**

Step 2: Choose the appropriate reason for why the certificate is being requested (Not providing a reason will delay processing time)

☐ Health Card	☐ Native Status	☐ Social Insurance Number
☐ ID Card	☐ Passport	☐ Other (specify):
☐ Land Deed	☐ Pension	________________
☐ Lost/Stolen	☐ School	________________

Step 3: Choose the type of service and delivery for the certificate

Service Options:

☐ **Regular Service** **OR** ☐ **Expedited Service - $50.00 fee (does not include certificate or courier fees)**

Delivery Options:
- ☐ **REGULAR MAIL** **(no delivery charges apply)**
- ☐ **COURIER** within NB, NS or PE **$10.00 (plus applicable taxes)**
- ☐ **COURIER** to other Canadian destinations **$25.00 (plus applicable taxes)**
- ☐ **COURIER** to the United States **$40.00 (no tax outside Canada)**
- ☐ **COURIER** outside Canada & US **Applicant must contact the Vital Statistics office at (506) 453-2385 to make payment arrangements**

NOTE: Selecting courier as the delivery option does not expedite processing time. You must choose expedited service ($50.00) to rush your application.

Payment Options :
- Credit Card (Visa, MasterCard or American Express)
- Cheque or money order payable to SNB

Credit Card # ________________ Expiry Date: ____
Signature: ________________

PART 4 – CONSENT

If you are not the person named on the birth certificate requested or if you are a parent applying for your adult child's birth certificate (child 19 years of age or older), written consent is required. Please make sure that this section is signed by the person named on the birth certificate **OR** that a signed letter of consent is provided with your application.

I ____________________ authorize that my birth certificate be issued to ____________________.
(Person named on birth certificate) (Name of Applicant)

Signature: X ____________________ Date: ________________
(Person named on birth certificate)

VITAL STATISTICS OFFICE USE ONLY

Registration Number	gBiz Reference Number	Date Issued	Issued By

35-5246e (08/12)

APPLICATION FOR BIRTH CERTIFICATE

Applying For A Birth Certificate:

1. Certificates can only be issued for births which occurred in New Brunswick.
2. Requests for birth certificates are usually processed by the Vital Statistics office within 10 business days.
3. Service New Brunswick is committed to protecting the personal information of its customers. The information collected on this application form will be used solely by SNB Vital Statistics to fulfill your application request. By completing this application form you are agreeing to provide information for this purpose.

Who Is Entitled To Apply For A Birth Certificate?

- You, if you are the person named of the birth certificate.
- The parent(s) of a child under 19 years of age. Parent(s) must be listed on the birth record or provide court documents proving parentage.
- The parent(s) of a child over 19 years of age who is physically or mentally incapable - proof is required.
- A person who has been granted guardianship from one of the above – proof is required.
- A person with a court order – proof is required.
- A person who requires it to comply with a specific Act or Regulation – proof is required.
- For a deceased individual, proof of death is required.

Information Contained On Birth Certificates:

a) Short form certificates include the following information: Surname and given names of individual, date of birth, place of birth, sex, registration date, registration number and date issued.
b) Long form certificates include all of the above information plus the names of the parents and the Province or Country of the parents' birth. **Note:** The long form birth certificate is recommended when applying for the certificate of a minor child.
c) For married women, birth certificates are issued in the maiden name.

Processing Times:

Regular Service - If an application is complete, the information given in the application agrees with our records, and the event is registered, "Regular" requests will be processed within 10 business days. This does not include postal or courier delivery time.

Expedited Service - If an application is complete, the information given in the application agrees with our records, and the event is registered, "Expedited" requests will be processed within 24 business hours for pick up at 435 King Street, Suite 203 (Monday through Friday) or sent by courier the next business day.

Fees: (subject to change)

a) Long form certificate	$30.00
b) Short form certificate	$25.00
c) Expedited Service Fee	$50.00 (**does not include cost of certificate <u>or</u> shipping**)

Payment Options:

- Cheque or money order payable to Service New Brunswick
- Debit card or cash (In person at any Service New Brunswick service centre)
- Visa, MasterCard or American Express

Delivery Options: (subject to change)

Birth certificates are shipped via mail, free of charge. You may choose to have your birth certificate couriered to you for an extra fee:

Courier service within NB, NS or PE	$10.00 (plus applicable taxes)
Courier service to other Canadian destinations	$25.00 (plus applicable taxes)
Courier service to the United States	$40.00 (no tax outside Canada)
Courier service outside Canada & US	(Please contact the Vital Statistics office at (506) 453-2385 to make payment arrangements.)

35-2262b (08/12)

Application for / Demande de
MARRIAGE OR DEATH CERTIFICATE / CERTIFICAT DE MARIAGE OU DE DÉCÈS

- Please print clearly in blue or black ink. / Prière d'écrire clairement en letters moulées à l'encre noire ou bleue.
- See back of form for additional information. / Voir au verso pour des renseignements additionnels.
- Please submit payment with this application. / Veuillez inclure votre paiement avec cette demande.

Name of Applicant / Nom du demandeur		
Mailing Address / Adresse postale		
City / Ville	Province	Postal Code / Code postal
Telephone / Téléphone Home / Résidence Work / Travail	X ______ **Signature of Applicant / Signature du demandeur**	

MARRIAGE CERTIFICATE / CERTIFICAT DE MARIAGE

Surname (prior to this marriage) / Nom de famille (avant ce mariage)	Given Name(s) / Prénom(s)			Place of Birth / Lieu de naissance
Surname (prior to this marriage) / Nom de famille (avant ce mariage)	Given Name(s) / Prénom(s)			Place of Birth / Lieu de naissance
Date of Marriage / Date du mariage Yr./Année Month/Mois Day/Jour	Place of Marriage / Lieu du mariage			
Reason why certificate is required / La raison de la demande de certificat	Type of Certificate / Le genre de certificat	Long Form / Format détaillé ☐	Photographic Print / Épreuve Photographique ☐	In English / en anglais ☐ In French / en français ☐

STATE YOUR RELATIONSHIP TO THE INDIVIDUAL NAMED ON THE MARRIAGE CERTIFICATE /
INDIQUEZ VOTRE LIEN DE PARENTÉ AVEC LA PERSONNE INSCRITE SUR LE CERTIFICAT DE MARIAGE

☐ Self / Moi-même ☐ Other / Autre ______________
(State your relationship / Indiquez votre lien de parenté)

CONSENT

If you are not one of the individuals named on the marriage certificate, please make sure that this section is signed by either individual **OR** that a signed letter of consent from either individual is provided with your application.

I ______________ authorize that my
(Name of person married)

marriage certificate be issued to the applicant stated above.

Signature :
X______________

Date :
____

CONSENTEMENT

Si vous n'êtes pas une des personne nommée sur le certificat de mariage, assurez-vous que cette section est signée par l'un ou l'autre des personnes nommées **OU** qu'une lettre de consentement signée par l'une ou l'autre des personnes nommées est incluse avec votre demande.

Je ______________, autorise que mon
(Nom de la personne mariée)

certificat de mariage soit délivré au demandeur indiqué ci-dessus.

Signature :
X______________

Date :
____

DEATH CERTIFICATE / CERTIFICAT DE DÉCÈS

Surname of Deceased / Nom de famille du défunt	Given Name(s) / Prénom(s)			Sex / Sexe M ☐ F ☐
Date of Death / Date du décès Yr. / Année Month / Mois Day / Jour	Place of Death / Lieu du décès	Date of Birth / Date de naissance Yr. / Année Month / Mois Day / Jour		
If deceased was married, give name of spouse / Si le défunt était marié, indiquez le nom du conjoint	Reason why certificate is required / Raison de la demande de certificat	Number of Certificates required / Le nombre de certificats requis	#	In English / En anglais ☐ In French / En français ☐
Name of Funeral Home (if known) Nom de la maison funéraire (si connu)	State your relationship to the individual named on the Death Certificate / Indiquez votre lien de parenté avec la personne inscrite sur le certificat de décès	______ State your relationship / Indiquez votre lien de parenté		

VITAL STATISTICS OFFICE USE ONLY / À L'USAGE DU BUREAU DES STATISTIQUES DE L'ÉTAT CIVIL SEULEMENT

Registration Number / Numéro d'enregistrement	Date Issued / Date de délivrance	Issued By / Délivré par

SERVICE NEW BRUNSWICK
VITAL STATISTICS
P.O. BOX 1998,
FREDERICTON, NB E3B 5G4
Telephone: (506) 453-2385
Fax: (506) 444-4139

SERVICES NOUVEAU-BRUNSWICK
STATISTIQUES DE L'ÉTAT CIVIL
C.P. 1998
FREDERICTON (N.-B.) E3B 5G4
Téléphone : (506) 453-2385
Télécopieur : (506) 444-4139

NOTES

1. Certificates can only be issued for marriages and deaths which occurred in New Brunswick.

2. Written consent is required for marriage certificates where applicant is not named on record. Proof of death is required if they are deceased.

Information contained on marriage certificates :

a) A long form marriage certificate includes the following information: Name, sex, province or country of birth of both parties, date of marriage, place of marriage, registration number, registration date and date issued.
b) A restricted photographic print of a marriage registration is available upon written consent of the parties.

Information contained on death certificates :

A long form death certificate includes the following information: Name of deceased, sex, date of death, place of death, date of birth, province or country of birth, registration date, registration number and date issued.

Fees : (subject to change)

(a) Long form certificates $25.00
(b) Photographic print (marriage) $25.00

Delivery Options :

- REGULAR MAIL
  (no delivery charges apply)
- COURIER within NB, NS or PE
  $10.00 (plus applicable taxes)
- COURIER other Canadian destinations
  $25.00 (plus applicable taxes)
- COURIER within US
  $40.00 (no taxes outside Canada)
- COURIER outside Canada & US
  Applicant must contact the Vital Statistics office at (506)453-2385 to make payment arrangements.

NOTE: Requesting courier as the delivery option does not expedite processing time.

PAYMENT OPTIONS

Payment must accompany the applications; please complete and check appropriate section below. (Note: A fee of $25.00 will be charged for any dishonored cheques)

Amount of payment $__________

☐ Cheque or Money order payable to Service New Brunswick enclosed

☐ Visa or ☐ MasterCard
(You must pay by credit card if you are faxing your application – Fax Number (506) 444-4139)

\# __________________ Expiry Date ____ / ____

Signature ________________________

Mail applications (and payment) to :

Vital Statistics
Service New Brunswick
P. O. Box 1998
Fredericton, NB
E3B 5G4

REMARQUES

1. Les certificats ne peuvent être émis que pour les mariages ou décès qui ont eu lieu au Nouveau-Brunswick.

2. Le consentement écrit doit accompagner toute demande de certificat de mariage où le demandeur n'est par reconnu sur le registre. Preuve de décès est requise s'il s'agît d'une personne décédée.

Les renseignements indiqués sur les certificats de mariage :

a) Un certificat de mariage inclut les renseignements suivants : nom, sexe, province ou pays de naissance des mariés, date du mariage, lieu du mariage, numéro et date d'enregistrement et date de délivrance.
b) Une épreuve photographique limitée d'un enregistrement de mariage ne peut être émise sans le consentement écrit de l'une des deux parties.

Les renseignements indiqués sur les certificats de décès :

Un certificat de décès inclut les renseignements suivants : nom du défunt(te), sexe, date du décès, lieu du décès, date de naissance, province ou pays de naissance, date et numéro d'enregistrement et date d'émission.

Montant à débourser : (sous réserve des changements)

(a) Certificat format détaillé 25$
(b) Épreuve photographique d'un enregistrement (mariage) 25$

Options de livraison:

- POSTE REGULIER
  (aucune dépense de livraison ne s'applique)
- MESSAGERIE au N.-B., N.-E. ou Î.-P.-E.
  10,00 $ (plus taxe applicable)
- MESSAGERIE autres destinations canadienne
  25,00 $ (plus taxe applicable)
- MESSAGERIE au États-Unis
  40,00 $ (aucune taxe en dehors du Canada)
- MESSAGERIE en dehors du Canada et États-Unis
  Le demandeur doit contacter le bureau des Statistiques de l'état civil au (506)453-2385 afin de faire les arrangements de paiment.

REMARQUE : Demander l'option de livraison par messagerie n'expédiera pas le temps de traitement.

MODE DE PAIEMENT

Le paiement doit accompagner la demande, cochez / remplissez la section appropriée. (Remarque : Un montant de 25,00 $ sera facturé pour tout chèque impayé.

Montant du paiement $ __________

☐ Chèque ou Mandat (ci-joint) fait à l'ordre de Services Nouveau-Brunswick.

☐ Visa ou ☐ MasterCard
(Vous devez payer par carte de crédit si vous faites votre demande par télécopieur – numéro du télécopieur (506) 444-4139)

\# __________________ Date d'expiration ____ / ____

Signature ________________________

Faire parvenir vos demandes (et votre paiement) à :

Statistiques de l'état civil
Services Nouveau-Brunswick
C. P. 1998
Fredericton (N.-B.)
E3B 5G4

CANADA—NEWFOUNDLAND

Send your requests to:

Vital Statistics Division
Service NL
(Location: 5 Mews Place)
P.O. Box 8700
St. John's, Newfoundland, Canada A1B 4J6

Tel. (709) 729-3308
Fax (709) 729-0946
E-mail: vstats@nl.gov.ca
www.servicenl.gov.nl.ca/birth/

The Newfoundland Vital Statistics Division has birth, marriage, and death records from 1892. For records prior to 1892, contact The Rooms Provincial Archives (9 Bonaventure Avenue, P.O. Box 1800, Station C, St. John's, NL, Canada A1C 5P9; tel. 709-757-8088; www.therooms.ca/archives/).

Cost for a certified Birth Certificate	Can$20.00
Cost for a certified Marriage Certificate	Can$20.00
Cost for a certified Death Certificate	Can$20.00

For additional assistance, contact:

Embassy of Canada
501 Pennsylvania Avenue, NW
Washington, DC 20001

Tel. (202) 682-1740

Service NL

Application for Birth Certificate

Please read important instructions before completing this application
Each section must be FULLY completed

1 **APPLICANT INFORMATION**

Name

Mailing Address

Address (con't) | City & Province | Postal Code

Home Telephone | Bus. Telephone | Fax No. (if Applicable)

State your relationship to the subject named on the birth certificate you are requesting

Self (you must be at least 16 years of age) ☐
Mother (if child is under 19 years of age) ☐
Father or Other Parent (if child is under 19 years of age) ☐
Other (please specify) ☐ ____________

FOR OFFICE USE ONLY

Signature of Applicant | Reason certificate is required

Please check only one of the following
I will pick up the certificate. ☐ or Send certificate by mail ☐

2 **CONSENT**

If you are not the subject named on the birth certificate requested (or if you are a parent applying for your adult child's birth certificate - child 19 years of age or over), written consent is required. Please ensure that this section is signed by the subject named on the birth certificate or that a signed and dated letter of consent is provided with your application.

I, ______________________ , authorize that my birth certificate be issued to the applicant stated above.
Subject named on birth certificate

______________________ Signature of subject of birth certificate

______________________ Date

3 **BIRTH INFORMATION**

Surname at birth | All given names | Female ☐ Male ☐

Date of birth: Month Day Year | Place of Birth (city or town) **NL**

Surname of father/other parent | (Given names)

Birth surname of mother/other parent | (Given names)

Certificate required: Long form ☐ Short form ☐
***Note: short form will be issued if neither is specified. Short form does not contain parent's names**

Is this person deceased? Yes - proof of death must be attached ☐ No ☐

4 **FOR OFFICE USE ONLY**

	Initials	Date
Search		
Second Search		
Issued		

Acceptable ID presented? Yes ☐ No ☐
Entitled? Yes ☐ No ☐

Record no.
Date of registration
Certificate no.
File no.
Receipt no.
Amount received
Refund

5 **METHOD OF PAYMENT**

CASH ☐ CHEQUE ☐ MONEY ORDER ☐ VISA ☐ MASTERCARD ☐ EXPIRY DATE ____________

CREDIT CARD NUMBER ____________ SIGNATURE ____________

02 03 008d 2011 11

PRIVACY NOTICE
Personal information contained on this form is collected under the authority of the *Vital Statistics Act, 2009*. The Information provided will be used to fulfill the requirements of the *Vital Statistics Act, 2009* for the release of birth Information. If you have any questions about the collection or use of this information, please contact a Vital Statistics Client representative at your nearest Government Service Centre.

Who is entitled to apply for a Birth Certificate?

- You, if you are the subject of the birth certificate. You must be at least sixteen years of age.
- A parent of a child (as established by registration documents or by court documents) until the child reaches the age of 19 years or if the child is incapable because of mental incapacity.
- A custodial guardian(if no parent is capable). Proof of guardianship is required.
- A person with written authorization from one of the above.
- A person with a court order.
- A person who requires it to comply with a specific Act or Regulation - proof is required.
- When the individual is deceased (proof of death is required):
  - the following person; a spouse, cohabitating partner, adult child, parent or adult sibling of the deceased.
  - the executor, trustee or administrator of the estate; or
  - a person with written authorization from one of the above.

Short form birth certificates include the following information:
FULL NAME of the INDIVIDUAL, DATE OF BIRTH, PLACE OF BIRTH, SEX, REGISTRATION NUMBER, REGISTRATION DATE, and DATE ISSUED.

A long form birth certificate contains all information on the short form certificate and also contains the parents' names.

Certificates contain information extracted from the original registration filed in our office.

Identification

Any person applying for a certificate is required to present acceptable identification - one piece of photo ID or two pieces of other ID, at least one of which contains their signature or address. A person who has written authorization to apply for or pick up someone else's certificate is required to present their own ID. Persons applying by mail or fax are required to submit photocopies of their ID documents.

To avoid delay

Complete the appropriate sections in full. **(All requests with incomplete information must be accompanied by a written explanation for the omission.)**

Payment must be enclosed with the application and can be either by cheque or money order (Canadian Funds) payable to the Newfoundland Exchequer Account.

Be sure your address and telephone number are correct and are clearly printed.

Please indicate whether you wish to receive your certificate by mail or will pick it up.

Service is available at the following Government Service Centre locations:

Government Service Centres

ST. JOHN'S OFFICE
5 Mews Place
P. O. Box 8700
St. John's, NL A1B 4J6
Telephone: (709) 729-3308
Facsimile: (709) 729-0946

HARBOUR GRACE OFFICE
P. O. Box 512
7-9 Roddick Crescent
Harbour Grace, NL A0A 2M0
Telephone: (709) 945-3106/3107
Facsimile: (709) 945-3114

CLARENVILLE OFFICE
8 Myer's Avenue, Suite 201
Clarenville, NL A5A 1T5
Telephone: (709) 466-4061/4068
Facsimile: (709) 466-4070

GANDER OFFICE
Fraser Mall, 230 Airport Blvd.
P. O. Box 2222
Gander, NL A1V 2N9
Telephone: (709) 256-1420
Facsimile: (709) 256-1438

GRAND FALLS-WINDSOR OFFICE
3 Cromer Avenue
Grand Falls-Windsor, NL A2A 1W9
Telephone: (709) 292-4348/4206
Facsimile: (709) 292-4528

CORNER BROOK OFFICE
Sir Richard Squires Bldg.
Corner Brook, NL A2H 6J8
Telephone: (709) 637-2387/2389/2490
Facsimile: (709) 637-2905

HAPPY VALLEY-GOOSE BAY OFFICE
2 Tenth Street
P. O. Box 3014, Stn. "B"
Happy Valley-Goose Bay, NL A0P 1E0
Telephone: (709) 896-5428/5430
Facsimile: (709) 896-4340

MARYSTOWN OFFICE
1 Harris Drive
P. O. Box 698
Marystown, NL A0E 2M0
Telephone: (709) 279-0837
Facsimile: (709) 279-8031

STEPHENVILLE OFFICE
35 Alabama Drive
Stephenville, NL A2N 3K9
Telephone: (709) 643-8650/8635
Facsimile: (709) 643-8654

ST. ANTHONY OFFICE
6 - 8 North Street
P. O. Box 28
St. Anthony, NL A0K 4S0
Telephone: (709) 454-8833
Facsimile: (709) 454-3206

LABRADOR CITY OFFICE
118 Humphrey Road
Labrador City, NL A2V 2J8
Telephone: (709) 944-5859
Facsimile: (709) 944-5630

website: http://www.servicenl.gov.nl.ca/department/bmd_contact.html
e-mail: vstats@gov.nl.ca

Government Services

Application for Marriage or Death Certificate

Each section must be FULLY completed

Applicant Information

(Please see important information on reverse regarding who is entitled to apply for a marriage certificate and acceptable ID)

1

Name			
Mailing Address			**FOR OFFICE USE ONLY**
City & Province		Postal Code	
Home Telephone	Bus. Telephone	Fax No. (if applicable)	
Signature of Applicant	**Please check only one of the following:** I will pick up the certificate, or ☐ Send certificate by mail ☐		

If MARRIAGE Certificate(s) required complete this section (please print)

2

Surname Before Marriage	All Given Names	Female ☐ Male ☐	Birthplace
Surname Before Marriage	All Given Names	Female ☐ Male ☐	Birthplace
Date Of Marriage Month Day Year	Place of Marriage (City or Town) NL		
State your relationship to the parties to the marriage	Self ☐ Other ☐ Specify ______ Requires Written Authorization From Eligible Applicant (see Reverse For Details)		

ID REQUIRED TO OBTAIN MARRIAGE CERTIFICATE

CONSENT Please see important information on reverse regarding who is entitled to apply for a Marriage Certificate

3 If you are not one of the individuals named on the marriage certificate requested, written consent is required. Please ensure that this section is signed by either of the parties to the marriage or that a signed and dated letter of consent is provided with your application.

I, ______________________ , authorize that my marriage certificate be issued to the applicant stated above.
Person named on marriage certificate

______________________ ______________________
Signature of person named on marriage certificate Date

If DEATH Certificate(s) required complete this section (please print)

4

Surname of Deceased	All Given Names		Female ☐ Male ☐
Date of Death Month Day Year	Place of Death (City or Town) NL	Place of Birth	
Permanent Residence of Deceased Prior To Death		Date of Birth Month Day Year	
State your Relationship to the Deceased			

For Office Use Only

5

	Initials	**Date**	Record No.
Search			Date Of Registration
Second Search			Certificate No.
			File No.
Issued			Receipt No.
			Amount Received
Acceptable ID Presented? Yes ☐ No ☐	Entitled? Yes ☐ No ☐		Refund

Method of Payment

6 Cash ☐ Cheque ☐ Money Order ☐ Visa ☐ Mastercard ☐ Expiry Date: ______

Credit Card Number ______ Signature ______

02 03 015b_2010 02

PRIVACY NOTICE

Personal information contained on this form is collected under the authority of the *Vital Statistics Act, 2009*. The Information provided will be used to fulfill the requirements of the *Vital Statistics Act, 2009* for the release of marriage and death Information. If you have any questions about the collection or use of this information, please contact a Vital Statistics Client representative at your nearest Government Service Centre.

Who is entitled to apply for a marriage certificate?

- Either party to the marriage.
- A person with written authorization from a party to the marriage.
- A person with an order from the Court.
- When both parties to the marriage are deceased (proof of death is required):
  - the children or parents of the deceased party;
  - the executor, trustee or administrator of the estate; or
  - a person with written authorization from one of the above.

Who is entitled to apply for a death certificate?

- Any person may apply for a death certificate.

Identification required

Any person applying for a certificate is required to present acceptable identification - one piece of photo ID or two pieces of other ID, at least one of which contains their signature or address. A person who has written authorization to apply for or pick up someone else's certificate is required to present their own ID. Persons applying by mail or fax are required to submit photocopies of their ID documents.

To avoid delay

Complete the appropriate section in full (All requests with incomplete information must be accompanied by a written explanation for the omission.)

Payment must be enclosed with the application and can be either by cheque or money order (Canadian Funds) payable to the Newfoundland Exchequer Account.
Be sure your address and telephone number are correct and are clearly printed.

Please indicate whether you wish to receive your certificate by mail or will pick it up.

Marriage Certificates

Long form only is available and contains the name of each party to the marriage, date of marriage, place of marriage, registration number, registration date, and date issued.

Death Certificates

Long form only is available and contains the name, date of death, place of death, age, sex, registration number, registration date, marital status and date issued.

Certificates contain information extracted from the original registration filed in our office.

Service is available at the following locations:

Government Service Centres

ST. JOHN'S OFFICE
5 Mews Place
P. O. Box 8700
St. John's, NL A1B 4J6
Telephone: (709) 729-3308
Facsimile: (709) 729-0946

HARBOUR GRACE OFFICE
P. O. Box 512
7-9 Roddick Crescent
Harbour Grace, NL A0A 2M0
Telephone: (709) 945-3106/3107
Facsimile: (709) 945-3114

CLARENVILLE OFFICE
2 Masonic Terrace
Clarenville, NL A5A 1N2
Telephone: (709) 466-4061/4068
Facsimile: (709) 466-4070

GANDER OFFICE
Fraser Mall, 230 Airport Blvd.
P. O. Box 2222
Gander, NL A1V 2N9
Telephone: (709) 256-1420
Facsimile: (709) 256-1438

GRAND FALLS-WINDSOR OFFICE
3 Cromer Avenue
Grand Falls-Windsor, NL A2A 1W9
Telephone: (709) 292-4348/4206
Facsimile: (709) 292-4528

CORNER BROOK OFFICE
133 Riverside Drive, Noton Bldg.
P. O. Box 2006
Corner Brook, NL A2H 6J8
Telephone: (709) 637-2387/2389/2490
Facsimile: (709) 637-2905

HAPPY VALLEY-GOOSE BAY OFFICE
2 Tenth Street
P. O. Box 3014, Stn. "B"
Happy Valley-Goose Bay, NL A0P 1E0
Telephone: (709) 896-5428/5430
Facsimile: (709) 896-4340

MARYSTOWN OFFICE
1 Harris Drive
P. O. Box 698
Marystown, NL A0E 2M0
Telephone: (709) 279-0837
Facsimile: (709) 279-8031

STEPHENVILLE OFFICE
35 Alabama Drive
Stephenville, NL A2N 3K9
Telephone: (709) 643-8650/8635
Facsimile: (709) 643-8654

ST. ANTHONY OFFICE
Viking Mall
P. O. Box 28
St. Anthony, NL A0K 4S0
Telephone: (709) 454-8833
Facsimile: (709) 454-3206

LABRADOR CITY OFFICE
118 Humphrey Road
Labrador City, NL A2V 2J8
Telephone: (709) 944-5859
Facsimile: (709) 944-5630

Government Services

Application For Service

Pertaining to an Adopted Person or Birth Parent
Please Read Information on Reverse of this Form

The information on this form is collected under the authority of the Adoption Act. The information provided will be used to fulfill the requirements of the Adoption Act for the release of adoption information. The release of this information is in compliance with the Adoption Act.

Information about the Person Applying (Please print)

APPLICANT'S DATE OF BIRTH (MONTH / DAY / YEAR)	APPLICANT BORN IN NEWFOUNDLAND AND LABRADOR ☐ YES ☐ NO	**SHADED AREA FOR OFFICE USE ONLY APPLICATION FOR SERVICE NUMBER**
SURNAME	GIVEN NAMES	
MAILING ADDRESS		
CITY/PROVINCE/STATE/COUNTRY	POSTAL CODE	
HOME PHONE NUMBER ( )	WORK PHONE NUMBER ( )	
COPY OF BIRTH CERTIFICATE ATTACHED ☐ YES ☐ NO (If no, please explain)		

I am ☐ AN ADOPTED PERSON (18 years or older) COMPLETE SECTION A ☐ A BIRTH PARENT COMPLETE SECTION B

SECTION A: To be completed by **adopted person - as applicant** (PLEASE PRINT)

NAME ON BIRTH CERTIFICATE AFTER ADOPTION: SURNAME / GIVEN NAMES	☐ MALE ☐ FEMALE	DATE OF BIRTH (MONTH / DAY / YEAR)
BIRTHPLACE (CITY/PROVINCE/STATE/COUNTRY)	PLACE OF ADOPTION (CITY/PROVINCE/STATE/COUNTRY)	
MAIDEN SURNAME OF ADOPTED MOTHER / GIVEN NAMES	BIRTHPLACE OF ADOPTIVE MOTHER (CITY/PROVINCE/STATE/COUNTRY)	
SURNAME OF ADOPTED FATHER / GIVEN NAMES	BIRTHPLACE OF ADOPTIVE FATHER (CITY/PROVINCE/STATE/COUNTRY)	
BIRTH NAME (IF KNOWN) / GIVEN NAMES	BIRTH REGISTRATION NUMBER (FROM BIRTH CERTIFICATE)	

SECTION B: To be completed by **birth parent - as applicant** (PLEASE PRINT)

PARTICULARS OF BIRTH PARENTS (AT TIME OF ADOPTED PERSON'S BIRTH)

MAIDEN NAME OF MOTHER / GIVEN NAMES	SURNAME OF FATHER / GIVEN NAMES
DATE OF BIRTH (MONTH / DAY / YEAR) — BIRTHPLACE (CITY/PROVINCE/STATE/COUNTRY)	DATE OF BIRTH (MONTH / DAY / YEAR) — BIRTHPLACE (CITY/PROVINCE/STATE/COUNTRY)

PARTICULARS OF ADOPTED PERSON PRIOR TO ADOPTION

SURNAME / GIVEN NAMES ☐ MALE ☐ FEMALE	DATE OF BIRTH (MONTH / DAY / YEAR) — BIRTHPLACE (CITY/PROVINCE/STATE/COUNTRY)
NAME OF ADOPTED PERSON FOLLOWING ADOPTION (IF KNOWN	

VS-007/05-06-28

SIGNATURE OF APPLICANT: X ____________________
WRITTEN SIGNATURE OF APPLICANT (DO NOT PRINT)

IMPORTANT INFORMATION

TO AVOID DELAY

- Complete the appropriate section in full and attach a photocopy of your legal birth certificate. **A baptismal certificate is not acceptable.** (All requests with incomplete information must be accompanied by a written explanation for the omission. If any portion of the relevant event information is left blank the application will be returned for completion.)
- Be sure you are authorized to make the request (see front section)
- Enclose the correct fee by cheque or money order (Canadian funds)
- Be sure your address and telephone number are correct and clear

FEES

- The fee for each search of records and copy of birth registration and adoption order is $50.00
- Payment to be made in Canadian funds by cheque or money order payable to the Newfoundland Exchequer Account

Fees are subject to change. Please contact a Government Service Centre for current fees.

MAKING A FALSE STATEMENT

Under the Adoption Act, it is an offence to make a statement that the person knows to be false or misleading in an application, or in connection with an application, for a copy of a birth registration or other record from the Vital Statistics Division, or for filing a disclosure veto or a no-contact declaration.

A person who makes a false statement commits an offence and is liable on conviction to a maximum fine of up to $10,000 and/or a term of imprisonment.

MAILING ADDRESS:

Confidential Services
Vital Statistics Division
Department of Government Services
P. O. Box 8700, 5 Mews Place
St. John's, NL A1B 4J6
Phone # (709) 729-3308
Fax # (709) 729-0946
Website: www.gs.gov.nl.ca/vs

Adoption Brochures and forms are available from Government Service Centres/Departmental Office listed below or may be downloaded from the government website: www.gs.gov.nl.ca/vs

GOVERNMENT SERVICE CENTRES/DEPARTMENTAL OFFICE

ST. JOHN'S OFFICE
5 Mews Place
P. O. Box 8700
St. John's, NL A1B 4J6
Telephone: (709) 729-3308
Facsimile: (709) 729-0946

HARBOUR GRACE OFFICE
P. O. Box 512
7-9 Roddick Crescent
Harbour Grace, NL A0A 2M0
Telephone: (709) 945-3106/3107
Facsimile: (709) 945-3114

CLARENVILLE OFFICE
8 Myers Avenue
Clarenville, NL A5A 1T5
Telephone: (709) 466-4061/4068
Facsimile: (709) 466-4070

GANDER OFFICE
Fraser Mall, 230 Airport Blvd.
P. O. Box 2222
Gander, NL A1V 2N9
Telephone: (709) 256-1420
Facsimile: (709) 256-1438

GRAND FALLS-WINDSOR OFFICE
3 Cromer Avenue
Grand Falls-Windsor, NL A2A 1W9
Telephone: (709) 292-4348/4206
Facsimile: (709) 292-4528

CORNER BROOK OFFICE
133 Riverside Drive, Noton Bldg.
P. O. Box 2006
Corner Brook, NL A2H 6J8
Telephone: (709) 637-2387/2389/2490
Facsimile: (709) 637-2905

HAPPY VALLEY-GOOSE BAY OFFICE
2 Tenth Street
P. O. Box 3014, Stn. "B"
Happy Valley-Goose Bay, NL A0P 1E0
Telephone: (709) 896-5428/5430
Facsimile: (709) 896-4340

MARYSTOWN OFFICE
1 Harris Drive
P. O. Box 698
Marystown, NL A0E 2M0
Telephone: (709) 279-0837
Facsimile: (709) 279-8031

STEPHENVILLE OFFICE
35 Alabama Drive
Stephenville, NL A2N 3K9
Telephone: (709) 643-8650/8635
Facsimile: (709) 643-8654

ST. ANTHONY OFFICE
Viking Mall
P. O. Box 28
St. Anthony, NL A0K 4S0
Telephone: (709) 454-8833
Facsimile: (709) 454-3206

LABRADOR CITY OFFICE
118 Humphrey Road
Labrador City, NL A2V 2J8
Telephone: (709) 944-5859
Facsimile: (709) 944-5630

website: http://www.gs.gov.nl.ca/gs/vs/
e-mail: vstats@gov.nl.ca

Government Services

Accessing Records From Newfoundland & Labrador Vital Statistics
Under the Adoption Act: Filing An Application For Service

ACCESS TO VITAL STATISTICS RECORDS UNDER THE ADOPTION ACT

This explains the release of records under the Adoption Act and how to file the enclosed Application for Service Pertaining to an Adopted Person or Birth Parent Form. Additional forms may be obtained from any Government Service Centre listed on the back of this guide.

ACCESS TO ADOPTION INFORMATION

Over the last few decades societal attitudes toward adoption have changed. Increasingly, people involved in adoptions want greater openness and access to information.

The Adoption Act provides for greater openness in adoption. Adopted persons and birth parents may apply to the Vital statistics Division to obtain copies of birth registrations and adoption orders.

ELIGIBILITY UNDER THE ADOPTION ACT

The option of filing an application for service is available to adopted persons 19 years of age or older and to birth parents when the adopted person has reached 19 years of age.

WHAT RECORDS ARE AVAILABLE TO ELIGIBLE APPLICANTS?

Persons who were born and adopted in Newfoundland and Labrador will receive a copy of their original birth registration in their birth name (including the name of any birth parent on record) and a copy of their adoption order provided a disclosure veto has not been filed. This relates to adoptions finalized prior to April 30, 2003.

Birth parents of persons born and adopted in Newfoundland and Labrador will receive a copy of the adopted person's original birth registration; the adopted person's birth registration following adoption (including any changes of name consequent to the adoption); and a copy of the adoption order.

Persons who were not born in Newfoundland and Labrador but were adopted in the province will receive a copy of the adoption order and any identification particulars of the adopted person. Similarly, birth parents of persons adopted in Newfoundland and Labrador but not born in the province will receive a copy of the adoption order and any identification particulars of the adopted person following the adoption.

Before an adoption order is released to a birth parent, all identifying information pertaining to adoptive parents is deleted to protect their right to privacy.

CANADA—NORTHWEST TERRITORIES

Send your requests to:

Vital Statistics
Department of Health & Social Services
Bag #9
107 MacKenzie Road
Inuvik, NT, Canada X0E 0T0

Tel. (867) 777-7400; (800) 661-0830 toll free
Fax (867) 777-3197
E-mail: hsa@gov.nt.ca
www.hss.gov.nt.ca/vital-statistics

The Northwest Territories Registrar General has records from 1925.

Cost for a certified Birth Certificate	Can$20.00
Cost for a certified Marriage Certificate	Can$20.00
Cost for a certified Death Certificate	Can$20.00

For additional assistance, contact:

Embassy of Canada
501 Pennsylvania Avenue, NW
Washington, DC 20001

Tel. (202) 682-1740

APPLICATION FOR CERTIFICATE OF:

❑ BIRTH ❑ MARRIAGE ❑ DEATH

ONCE COMPLETE, RETURN THIS FORM WITH PAYMENT TO THE ADDRESS ON PAGE 2

This personal information is being collected under the authority of the *Vital Statistics Act* and will be used to issue certificates for births, deaths and marriages. This information is protected by the privacy provisions of the *Access to Information and Protection of Privacy Act*. If you have any questions about the collection of this information, contact the Department of Health and Social Services (see contact information provided on this form).

MAILING ADDRESS (PLEASE PRINT)

Name Certificate is Being Mailed To		Mailing Address	
Home Phone No.	Work Phone No.		
E-mail		City/Town/Village	Postal Code

IF BIRTH CERTIFICATE(S) REQUIRED, COMPLETE THIS SECTION (PLEASE PRINT)

Surname at Birth	Given Name(s)	Birth Date-Y/M/D	Gender ❑ M ❑ F
Place of Birth (City/Town/Village)		NORTHWEST TERRITORIES	
Surname of Father or Other Parent	Given Name(s)	Birthplace of Father or Other Parent	
Surname of Mother at Birth	Given Name(s)	Birthplace of Mother	
Type of Certificate Required (specify quantity) ____ Wallet ____ Paper (Long Form) ____ Restricted Photocopy		OFFICE USE ONLY	Registration Number

IF MARRIAGE CERTIFICATE(S) REQUIRED, COMPLETE THIS SECTION (PLEASE PRINT)

Surname of First Party	Given Name(s)	Birthplace of First Party	
Surname of Second Party	Given Name(s)	Birthplace of Second Party	
Date of Marriage - Y/M/D	Place of Marriage (City/Town/Village)	NORTHWEST TERRITORIES	
Type of Certificate Required (specify quantity) ____ Wallet ____ Paper (Long Form) ____ Restricted Photocopy		OFFICE USE ONLY	Registration Number

IF DEATH CERTIFICATE(S) REQUIRED, COMPLETE THIS SECTION (PLEASE PRINT)

Surname of Deceased	Given Name(s)	Age	Date of Death-Y/M/D	Gender ❑ M ❑ F
Place of Death (City/Town/Village)			NORTHWEST TERRITORIES	
Permanent Residence of Deceased, prior to death		Marital Status		
Mother's Name	Father/Other Parent's Name	Spouse's Name		
Type of Certificate Required (specify quantity) ____ Paper		OFFICE USE ONLY	Registration Number	

PLEASE INDICATE REASON FOR REQUEST

Signature of Applicant X	Date - Y/M/D	State Relationship to Person Named	Fee Enclosed $

OFFICE USE ONLY

Amount Received	Refund/Return	Notes
Receipt No.		

NWT8627/1112

WOULD YOU LIKE US TO CALL YOU FOR CREDIT CARD INFORMATION? ❑ Yes ❑ No

Formulaire disponible en français sur demande. Translation into other NWT official languages will be provided upon reasonable request.

INFORMATION

Certificates can only be issued for births, marriages and deaths if they occurred in the **Northwest Territories.**

ALL sections **must be completed** for the certificate that you are requesting; otherwise your application will not be processed and will be returned to you to provide the missing information.

Certificates contain information exactly as recorded on the original registration filed in our office.

Where names exceed the capacity to print on requested certificate, restricted photocopies will be issued.

A *restricted photocopy* is a copy of the original registration and is usually required for legal purposes. A restricted photocopy can only be issued if authorized by the Registrar General of Vital Statistics or on the order of a court. If no reason is provided, your application will not be processed and will be returned to you.

FEE SCHEDULE:

a) *Wallet and paper (long form) size* certificates are $20.00 for **each** certificate.
b) *Restricted Photocopy* certificates are $30.00 for **each** certificate.

BIRTH CERTIFICATES:

a) A *wallet size* birth certificate contains the following information:
  - Full name of the individual, date of birth, place of birth, gender, registration number and registration date.
  - **Names longer than 40 characters** (last name and given names included) will be issued a framing (paper) size copy as the names are too long to fit on a wallet certificate.

b) A *paper (long form) size* birth certificate contains the above information along with the following information:
  - Names and birthplaces of parents. (Generally used for children's Canadian Passports)

c) Birth certificates for married women are issued only in their surname at birth.

MARRIAGE CERTIFICATES:

a) A *wallet size* marriage certificate contains the following information:
  - Name of First Party, name of Second Party, date of marriage, place of marriage, registration number and registration date.
  - **Names longer than 40 characters** (last name and given names included) will be issued a framing (paper) size copy as the names are too long to fit on a wallet certificate.

b) A *paper (long form) size* marriage certificate contains the above information along with the following information:
  - Birthplaces of the First and Second Parties.

c) The ages of the parties do not appear, and surname prior to marriage appears.

DEATH CERTIFICATES:

a) A *paper size* death certificate contains the above information along with the following information:
  - Full name of the deceased, date of death, place of death, gender, age, marital status, name of spouse, registration number and registration date.

SEND PAYMENT AND APPLICATION FORM TO:

Registrar General of Vital Statistics
Department of Health and Social Services
Government of the NWT
Bag #9 (107 MacKenzie Road / IDC Building, 2nd Floor)
Inuvik, NT X0E 0T0

If paying by Cheque or Money Order
please make payable to
Government of NWT
(It is against postal regulations to send cash through the mail)

Courier service is available for an additional fee. Please call us for an accepted list of couriers.

FOR *FASTER* SERVICE YOU CAN FAX YOUR REQUEST *ONLY IF* PAYING BY CREDIT CARD:

Please fill out the following:

☐ Visa ☐ MasterCard Amount: ____________

Card No: |____|____|____|____| Exp. Date: |__|__| **Security Code:** |_____| (on back of card)

Name of Cardholder: ______________________ Contact Number: ____________

Signature of Cardholder: ✗ ______________________

Fax: (867) 777-3197
USE ONLY IF PAYING BY CREDIT CARD

E-mail: hsa@gov.nt.ca
Phone: (867) 777-7400
Toll Free: 1-800-661-0830

CANADA—NOVA SCOTIA

Send your requests to:

Vital Statistics
(Location: 300 Horseshoe Lake Drive)
P.O. Box 157
Halifax, Nova Scotia, Canada B3J 2M9

Tel. (902) 424-4381; (877) 848-2578 toll free
Fax (902) 450-7313
E-mail: vstat@gov.ns.ca
www.gov.ns.ca/snsmr/vstat/

Civil birth and death registrations were recorded in Nova Scotia between 1864 and 1876. Some delayed registrations of birth were filed between 1876 and 1908, but province-wide recording of births didn't begin again until January 1, 1909; province-wide recording of deaths began again on October 1, 1908. Birth records filed after January 1, 1911, and death records from 1961 to the present are held at Vital Statistics. Birth, marriage, and death certificates can be ordered online—see the Vital Statistics website for more information.

Early birth, death, and marriage records are held by the Nova Scotia Archives (6016 University Avenue, Halifax, Nova Scotia B3H 1W4; www.gov.ns.ca/nsarm/). These records are searchable online at https://www.novascotiagenealogy.com/.

Birth certificates of deceased persons born less than 100 years ago or married less than 75 years ago are restricted. Death certificates can be released if the death occurred more than 20 years ago and the deceased would be 75 years of age or more.

Cost for a certified long-form Birth Certificate	Can$38.75
Cost for a short-form Birth Certificate	Can$32.05
Cost for a certified long-form Marriage or Domestic Partnership Certificate	Can$38.75
Cost for a short-form Marriage or Domestic Partnership Certificate	Can$32.05
Cost for a certified long-form Death Certificate	Can$38.75
Cost for a short-form Death Certificate	Can$32.05

For additional assistance, contact:

Embassy of Canada
501 Pennsylvania Avenue, NW
Washington, DC 20001

Tel. (202) 682-1740

Service Nova Scotia
and Municipal Relations
Vital Statistics

Birth Certificate Application

Office Use Only - Our File #

MAILING ADDRESS INFORMATION - Please Print

Surname	Given Names		
Mailing Address			
City	Province/State	Country	Postal Code
Civic Address (If different than above)			
City	Province/State	Country	Postal Code
Home Number	Work Number	Fax Number	E-mail address

BIRTH DETAILS - Use maiden name if married - include french symbols if applicable

Surname					
First Name				Middle Name(s)	☐ Male ☐ Female
Date of Birth	Month	Day	Year	Place of Birth (City, Town, or Village)	Province *Nova Scotia*

FATHER'S/OTHER PARENT'S DETAILS - If stated on Birth Record

Surname		
First Name	Middle Name(s)	
Birth Place - City, Town, or Village	Province/State	Country

MOTHER'S DETAILS - Use Mother's maiden surname (surname before marriage)

Surname		
First Name	Middle Name(s)	
Birth Place - City, Town, or Village	Province/State	Country

SERVICES REQUESTED - Please indicate if more than one copy is required

☐ Short Form: $32.05 per certificate
☐ Long Form: $38.75 per certificate
☐ Certified copy: $38.75 per document
☐ Courier Service: $20.00

Payment Type	**Submitted by**	**Credit Card**	**Submitted by**
☐ Cheque	☐ Mail	☐ Visa ☐ American Express	☐ Mail ☐ In person
☐ Money Order	☐ In person	☐ MasterCard	☐ Fax ____________

☐ Credit Card - Complete credit card section on right

☐ Interac/Cash payment may only be made in person at the counter

Your Signature ________________________________

Credit Card Number ________________________________

Name as shown on credit card ________________________________

Expiry Date ________________________________

Cardholder Signature ________________________________

YOUR RELATIONSHIP TO BIRTH EVENT

☐ Self	☐ Mother	☐ Father/Other Parent	☐ Other - Please indicate relationship
Reason Certificate required			
Note: If above particulars are not completed in full, or if the correct payment per service requested is not enclosed, your request cannot be processed.			

Rev. 03/13

Important information on reverse

IMPORTANT INFORMATION

To Avoid Delay

- Complete all sections **in full**. (All requests with incomplete information must be accompanied by a written explanation for the omission. If any portion of the relevant event information is left blank, the application will be returned for completion.
- Be sure you are authorized to make the request (see Section 3 below)
- It is against postal regulations to send cash through the mail. Payment in Canadian funds should be forwarded by cheque, bank draft or money order made payable to the Minister of Finance.
- If you are paying by credit card, include the card number, expiry date, and the actual name of the cardholder that appears on the card. NOTE: Only Visa, MasterCard and American Express are accepted.
- Be sure your address and telephone number are correct and clear.

1) Fees - As noted for each requested copy on the front of this form.

2) Information provided

Certificates contain the following information:

a) Short Form: Full name, sex, date of birth, place of birth, registration date, registration number, and date issued.

b) Long Form: Full name, sex, date of birth, place of birth, registration date, registration number, date issued, names of parents, and birthplaces of parents.

c) Certified Copy: All the information which appears on the original registration, including full name, sex, date of birth, place of birth, registration date, registration number, date issued, names of parents, birthplaces of parents, plus other information, for example, the name of the person who assisted at the birth, birth weight, etc.

NOTE: Certified copies are generally only required for court purposes. They are not for use as identification.

3) Who qualifies to apply for a Birth Certificate

Birth certificates may be released to:

a) You, if the record pertains to your own birth

b) Parents of a child

c) A lawyer who specifically indicates they are working on behalf of "a" or "b" above, or a person on the written authorization of "a" or "b" above

d) The executor/executrix or trustee of an estate.

e) Guardian (copy of guardianship papers must be attached to this application)

Other Services

Death and marriage certificates, legal change of name, domestic partnership registrations, and genealogy searches. To obtain an application for any of these services, please visit one of our offices, or contact us by telephone at 1-877-848-2578 or on the internet at: http://www.gov.ns.ca/snsmr/vstat

The information on this form is collected under the authority of the Vital Statistics Act (Revised Statutes of Nova Scotia 1989, chapter 494). The information provided will be used to fulfill the requirements of the Vital Statistics Act for the release of birth information. If you have any questions about the collection or use of this information, please contact Vital Statistics at 1-877-848-2578.

Mailing Address:

Vital Statistics
P.O. Box 157
Halifax, Nova Scotia
B3J 2M9 Canada

Enquiries:

Local: (902) 424-4381
Toll Free: 1-877-848-2578 (Nova Scotia only)
Fax: (902) 450-7313
E-mail: vstat@gov.ns.ca

Or Visit Our Office:

300 Horseshoe Lake Drive
Bayer's Lake Business Park
Halifax, Nova Scotia
B3S 0B7 Canada

Hours: 8:30 a.m. to 4:30 p.m. Monday to Friday, except holidays.

Website and ordering online: http://www.gov.ns.ca/snsmr/vstat

Service Nova Scotia
and Municipal Relations
Vital Statistics

Marriage or Death Certificate Application

Office Use Only - Our File #

MAILING ADDRESS INFORMATION - Please Print

Surname	Given Names		
Mailing Address			
City	Province/State	Country	Postal Code
Civic Address (If different than above)			
City	Province/State	Country	Postal Code
Home Number	Work Number	Fax Number	E-mail address

MARRIAGE CERTIFICATE DETAILS - INCLUDE FRENCH SYMBOLS IF APPLICABLE

Date of Marriage	Month	Day	Year	Place of Marriage (City, Town, or Village)	Province Nova Scotia
Surname Before Marriage					
First Name				Middle Name(s)	☐ Male ☐ Female
Birth Place - City, Town, or Village				Province/State	Country
Surname Before Marriage					
First Name				Middle Name(s)	☐ Male ☐ Female
Birth Place - City, Town, or Village				Province/State	Country

DEATH CERTIFICATE DETAILS - INCLUDE FRENCH SYMBOLS IF APPLICABLE

Surname						
First Name				Middle Name(s)	Age	☐ Male ☐ Female
Date of Death	Month	Day	Year	Place of Death (City, Town, or Village)	Province Nova Scotia	
Residence Before Death	City, Town, or Village			Province/State	Country	

SERVICES REQUESTED - Please indicate if more than one copy is required

☐ Short Form: $32.05 per certificate ☐ Certified Copy: $38.75 per document

☐ Long Form: $38.75 per certificate - Death Certificate only ☐ Courier Service $20.00

Payment Type	Submitted by	Credit Card		Submitted by	
☐ Cheque	☐ Mail	☐ Visa	☐ American Express	☐ Mail	☐ In person
☐ Money Order	☐ In person	☐ MasterCard		☐ Fax ______	

☐ Credit Card - Complete credit card section on right

☐ Interac/Cash payment may only be made in person at the counter

Your Signature ____________________

Credit Card Number ____________________

Name as shown on credit card ____________________

Expiry Date ____________________

Cardholder Signature ____________________

YOUR RELATIONSHIP TO EVENT (MARRIAGE OR DEATH)

☐ Self	☐ Mother	☐ Father/Other Parent	☐ Spouse	☐ Other - Please indicate relationship
Reason Certificate required				
Note: If above particulars are not completed in full, or if the correct payment per service requested is not enclosed, your request cannot be processed.				

Rev. 03/13

Important information on reverse

IMPORTANT INFORMATION

To Avoid Delay

- Complete all sections **in full**. (All requests with incomplete information must be accompanied by a written explanation for the omission. If any portion of the relevant event information is left blank, the application will be returned for completion.
- Be sure you are authorized to make the request (see Section 3 below)
- It is against postal regulations to send cash through the mail. Payment in Canadian funds should be forwarded by cheque, bank draft or money order made payable to the Minister of Finance.
- If you are paying by credit card, include the card number, expiry date, and the actual name of the cardholder that appears on the card. NOTE: Only Visa, MasterCard and American Express are accepted.
- Be sure your address and telephone number are correct and clear.

1) Fees - As noted for each requested copy on the front of this form.

2) Information provided on Marriage Certificate

a) *Short Form Certificate:* Names of parties to the marriage, date of marriage, place of marriage, registration number, registration date and date issued.

b) *Long Form Certificate:* (see certified copy below)

c) *Certified Copy:* The certified photographic copy of the original marriage registration contains all of the information on a short form certificate and may contain the following information of both parties to the marriage: marital status, age, religious denomination, residence, place of birth, full name of parents, birthplace of parents, marriage officiant.

Information provided on Death Certificate

a) *Short Form Certificate:* Given and surname, sex, date of death, age, place of death, registration number, registration date, date issued.

b) *Long Form Certificate:* The Long Form Death Certificate contains all the above information and the following, **if** recorded on death record; date of birth, place of birth, residence, occupation, marital status, name of spouse, names of parents, attending physician, funeral director, disposition, place of disposition, name of informant, address, relationship.

c) *Certified Copy:* The certified photographic copy of the original death registration contains all of the information on a long form certificate as well as medical cause of death.

3) Who qualifies to apply for a Marriage Certificate

Short form marriage certificates may be released to any person who has a valid reason for requiring the document.

Certified copies may be released to:

a) either party to the marriage

b) a lawyer representing one of the parties to the marriage in a divorce action

c) to a third party upon the written consent of one of the parties.

Who qualifies to apply for a Death Certificate

Short form death certificates may be released to any person who has a valid reason for requiring the document.

Long form death certificates may be released to:

a) next-of-kin of the deceased

b) trustee or executor of an estate

Certified copies of death registrations containing cause of death are released only to next-of-kin or an executor of an estate in selected circumstances and with authorization of the Minister or a court order.

Other Services

Birth certificates, legal change of name, domestic partnership registrations, and genealogy searches. To obtain an application for any of these services, please visit one of our offices, or contact us by telephone at 1-877-848-2578 or on the internet at: http://www.gov.ns.ca/snsmr/vstat

The information on this form is collected under the authority of the Vital Statistics Act (Revised Statutes of Nova Scotia 1989, chapter 494). The information provided will be used to fulfill the requirements of the Vital Statistics Act for the release of marriage or death information. If you have any questions about the collection or use of this information, please contact Vital Statistics at 1-877-848-2578.

Mailing Address:

Vital Statistics
P.O. Box 157
Halifax, Nova Scotia
B3J 2M9 Canada

Enquiries:

Local: (902) 424-4381
Toll Free: 1-877-848-2578 (Nova Scotia only)
Fax: (902) 450-7313
E-mail: vstat@gov.ns.ca

Or Visit Our Office:

300 Horseshoe Lake Drive
Bayer's Lake Business Park
Halifax, Nova Scotia
B3S 0B7 Canada

Hours: 8:30 a.m. to 4:30 p.m. Monday to Friday, except holidays.

Website and ordering online: http://www.gov.ns.ca/snsmr/vstat

CANADA—ONTARIO

Send your requests to:

Office of the Registrar General
(Location: 189 Red River Road)
P.O. Box 4600
Thunder Bay, Ontario, Canada P7B 6L8

Tel. (416) 325-8305; (800) 461-2156 toll free
Fax (807) 343-7459
www.serviceontario.ca

The Office of the Registrar General has birth records for the past 95 years, marriage records for the past 80 years, and death records for the past 70 years. Birth and marriage records are restricted; however, anyone may request a letter confirming that the birth, marriage, or death record is on file. Requests for certificates may be submitted in person at the Office of the Registrar General or at the Land Registry Offices throughout Ontario. They can also be ordered online at www.serviceontario.ca.

Earlier records are at the Archives of Ontario (134 Ian Macdonald Boulevard, Toronto, Ontario M7A 2C5; www.archives.gov.on.ca/en/index.aspx).

Cost for a certified long-form Birth Certificate	Can$35.00
Cost for a short-form Birth Certificate	Can$25.00
Cost for a certified long-form Marriage Certificate	Can$22.00
Cost for a short-form Marriage Certificate	Can$15.00
Cost for a certified Death Certificate	Can$22.00

For additional assistance, contact:

Embassy of Canada
501 Pennsylvania Avenue, NW
Washington, DC 20001

Tel. (202) 682-1740

Ministry of Government Services | Office of the Registrar General

Request for Birth Certificate

(For births which took place in Ontario only)

If you have any questions, please contact the
Office of the Registrar General
189 Red River Road, PO Box 4600
Thunder Bay ON P7B 6L8
Outside Toronto 1 800 461-2156 or in Toronto 416 325-8305 or
Fax 807 343-7459

(THIS SPACE RESERVED FOR OFFICE USE ONLY)

Please PRINT clearly in blue or black ink.
In the context of this form, the word "Applicant" refers to the person completing this Request.
This may or may not be the 'Person Named on the Birth Certificate'.

Applicant's Name

First Name | Last Name

Mailing Address

Organization / Firm (if applicable)

Street No. | Street Name | Apt. No. | Buzzer No. | PO Box

City | Province

Country | Postal Code | Telephone Number (including area code) | Ext.

What Information are you Requesting and How much will it Cost?

☐ **Birth Certificate** (Short form) *Not issued for deceased persons*
This includes basic information, such as name, date and place of birth

First birth certificate..........$25.00 $

Replacement birth certificate..........$35.00 $

☐ **Certified Copy of Birth Registration** (Long form)
This contains all registered information, including parent's information and signatures.
It is provided in the form of a certified copy.

First certified copy of Birth Registration..........$35.00 $

Replacement certified copy of Birth Registration..........$45.00 $

☐ **Search Letter**
This is a letter saying the record is or is not on file. If you don't know the exact date of the birth event, choose a year based on information you may have obtained for this purpose, and write it in the space provided for the date. We will search that whole year plus two years before and after, for a total of five years.

Search Letter..........$15.00 for each 5 year period to be searched $

Information

If you're sending your payment from anywhere other than Canada, you must pay with an international money order in Canadian funds drawn on a Canadian clearing house, or by VISA, MasterCard or American Express.

We will not accept post-dated cheques. We will charge $35.00 if your cheque is rejected because of insufficient funds.

There is a limit on the number of documents issued.
(See #7 on pg. 4).

Please note that fees are subject to change without notice. If you send your request by mail, you can pay by cheque or money order, made payable to Minister of Finance, or by VISA, MasterCard or American Express.
At our public counter, you can also pay by cash or debit card.

Your Payment Options

Cheque or Money Order. Please make payable to: "Minister of Finance" ☐

Credit card payment: You must pay by credit card if you are faxing your request to us.
Our fax number is: **807 343-7459.**

☐ Visa ☐ MasterCard ☐ American Express

Card Number | Expiry Date *(Month / Year)*

Name of Cardholder | Signature of Cardholder

Who is the Person Named on the Birth Certificate (each box must be filled in)

Last Name (at time of Birth) | First Name | Middle Name(s)

☐ Male ☐ Female | Date of Birth: Year / Month / Day | Place of Birth (City) | Weight at Birth | No. of older brothers / sisters born before this child

Where did the birth take place ☐ Hospital (name) ☐ Other (specify) ☐ Home ☐ Birthing Centre

You must check one box ☐ Physician ☐ Midwife ☐ Other ☐ Undetermined

Name of Doctor or Attendant (at birth) | Address of Doctor or Attendant

Parent(s) Information (at time of this child's birth)

Mother's Maiden Name (see #1 on pg. 4) | First Name | Middle Name(s)

Mother's Address (at the time of this child's birth) | City | Province | Country

Mother's Marital Status (at the time of this child's birth)

☐ Single ☐ Married ☐ Divorced ☐ Widowed ☐ Common law

Any Other Last Name(s) Used by Mother

Mother's Age (at time of this birth) | Mother's Date of Birth: Year / Month / Day | Mother's Place of Birth (City and Province / Country)

Father / Other Parent Last Name | First Name | Middle Name(s)

Father / Other Parent Age (at time of this birth) | Father / Other Parent Date of Birth: Year / Month / Day | Father / Other Parent Place of Birth (City and Province / Country)

Has a Birth Certificate (Short Form) been previously issued for this birth?** ☐ Yes ☐ No

Has a Certified Copy of the Birth Registration been previously issued for this birth?** ☐ Yes ☐ No

Has the person named on the Birth Registration ever had a legal name change? If 'yes', provide previous name(s) below: ☐ Yes ☐ No

Last Name | First Name | Middle Name(s)

Last Name | First Name | Middle Name(s)

**All previously issued documents will be cancelled.

Who can Obtain this Information?

Where the person named on the certificate is alive
(Check one or more boxes)

☐ The person named on the Birth Certificate is the 'Applicant'. (You must be at least 13 years of age)

A parent of the person named on the Birth Certificate is the 'Applicant'. (Your name must appear on the Birth Registration)

☐ Mother ☐ Father / Other Parent

☐ A person who has legal custody of the person named on the Birth Certificate is the 'Applicant'. (Proof of Custody is required)

☐ Proof of Custody attached.

Where the person named on the certificate is deceased, only a Certified Copy of the Birth Registration will be issued.
(Check one or more boxes)

☐ The Next of Kin is the 'Applicant'. (see #2 on pg. 4)

Specify relationship to deceased ____________

☐ Proof of Death attached. (see #3 on pg. 4)

☐ Estate Trustee is the "Applicant". (see #4 on pg. 4)
(Certificate of Appointment or similar proof required)

☐ Certificate of Appointment or similar proof attached. (see #5 on pg. 4)

Why are you requesting this information?

Please specify: ____________

You MUST check one of the following boxes:

☐ First time applying for Birth Certificate/Certified Copy of Birth Registration

☐ Lost Birth Certificate / *Certified Copy* of Birth Registration (see #6 on pg. 4)

☐ Stolen Birth Certificate/ Certified Copy of Birth Registration (see #6 on pg. 4)

☐ Damaged/destroyed Certificate / Certified Copy of Birth Registration (see #6 on pg. 4)

I authorize the Office of the Registrar General to issue the requested document/information, and consent to the Ministry of Government Services collecting information about myself and the person named on the Birth Certificate (if other than myself) from the guarantor and such other sources as may be necessary to verify the information on this form and my entitlement to the service required and to the disclosure of such information to the Ministry of Government Services. I am aware that it is an offence to wilfully make a false statement on this form.

Signature of Applicant | Daytime Telephone Number (including area code) Ext. | Date Signed: Year / Month / Day

This Page MUST be completed in Full if the Person Named on the Certificate is 9 years of Age or Older

To the Applicant

Please select one of the following persons to act as your Guarantor. When contacted, the Guarantor will be asked to verify that:

- the statements made in this application are true;
- as the Guarantor, he or she is a Canadian citizen belonging to one of the listed categories; and
- he or she has known you (the applicant) for at least two years.

No person shall charge a fee for acting as a guarantor (Section 45.1(2) of the *Vital Statistics Act*).

The Applicant certifies that the individual named below has consented to act as Guarantor.

The Guarantor

The persons described in this section are prescribed as **guarantors** for the purposes of section 45.1 of the *Vital Statistics Act:*

1. Canadian citizens who have known the applicant for at least two years and who are ***currently serving*** as one of the following:
   - i. Judge, justice of the peace, municipal police officer, provincial police officer or officer of the Royal Canadian Mounted Police, First Nations police officers and constables.
   - ii. Mayor.
   - iii. Member of the Legislative Assembly of Ontario.
   - iv. Minister of religion authorized under provincial law to perform marriages.
   - v. Municipal clerk or treasurer who is a member of the Association of Municipal Managers, Clerks and Treasurers of Ontario.
   - vi. Notary public.
   - vii. Principal or vice-principal of a primary or secondary school.
   - viii. Senior administrator or professor in a university or a senior administrator in a community college or in a CEGEP in Quebec.
   - ix. Signing officer of a bank, caisse d'économie, caisse populaire, credit union or trust company.
   - x. Chief of a band recognized under the *Indian Act (Canada).*

Canadian citizens who have known the applicant for at least two years and ***who are practicing members in good standing*** of a provincial regulatory body established by law to govern one of the following professions:

- i. Chiropractor, dentist, midwife, nurse, optometrist, pharmacist, physician or surgeon, psychologist or veterinarian.
- ii. Lawyer.
- iii. Professional accountant.
- iv. Professional engineer.
- v. Social worker or social service worker.
- vi. Teacher in a primary or secondary school.

The list above is not an endorsement by the Office of the Registrar General of professional status or recognition of superior qualifications.

Name of Applicant *(must be completed)*

Last Name	First Name

Guarantor Information

Guarantor's Last Name	First Name

Organization / Firm (if applicable)	Occupation	Registration No. (if applicable)

Work Telephone No. (including area code) / Ext.	Fax No. (optional) (including area code)

Work address

Street No.	Street Name	City/Town	Province	Postal Code

Personal information contained on this form is collected under the authority of the *Vital Statistics Act,* R.S.O. 1990, c.V.4 and will be used to provide certified copies, extracts, certificates, or search notices and to verify the information provided and your entitlement to the service requested and for law enforcement and security purposes. It is an offence to wilfully make a false statement on this form. Questions about this collection should be directed to: Deputy Registrar General, Office of the Registrar General 189 Red River Road, PO Box 4600 Thunder Bay ON P7B 6L8. Telephone Outside Toronto 1 800 461-2156 or in Toronto 416 325-8305.

Instructions

Instruction #1

Mother's Maiden Name

Mother's maiden name is the mother's last name at the time of her own birth, unless the mother was adopted. If the mother was adopted, record the adoptive name.

Instruction #2

Next of Kin includes:

*Spouse, **Common Law Partner, Mother, Father / Other Parent, Daughter, Son, Sister, Brother.
If none of the above are available, the closest surviving Next of Kin *(Grandmother, Grandfather, Aunt, Uncle, First Cousin, Niece, Nephew or Grandchild) may apply but must provide, along with the prescribed fees and a complete and signed application, an affidavit swearing that they are the closest surviving Next of Kin.*

*Spouse means either party to a marriage.
**Common Law Partner means two people living together continuously in a conjugal relationship outside of marriage for a period of no less than 3 years or two people who have lived together in a relationship of some permanence if they are the parents of a child.

Instruction #3

Proof of Death

i.e., Death Certificate, Funeral Director's Statement, Certificate of Appointment of Estate Trustee or, an order under the *Declarations of Death Act, 2002.*

Instruction #4

Estate Trustee includes an Executor or an Administrator.

Instruction #5

Acceptable proof includes a Certificate of Appointment of Estate Trustee, letters probate, letters of administration or a will.

Instruction #6

Lost, Stolen, Damaged / Destroyed Birth Certificates

Birth Certificates or certified copies of Birth Registration that are lost, stolen, or damaged/destroyed must be reported to the Office of the Registrar General immediately. Found birth certificates or certified copies of Birth Registration must be returned to the Office of the Registrar General immediately or delivered to a police or lost and found service.

Instruction #7

Not more than one Birth Certificate and one Certified Copy of a Birth Registration may be issued.

Instruction #8

Application for Reconsideration

If your application for a Birth Certificate or Certified Copy of Birth Registration is refused, you may apply in writing to the Deputy Registrar General for your application to be reconsidered. You must provide your full name, mailing address, phone number, name of the person whose Birth Certificate or Certified Copy of Birth Registration is being applied for, file number of the application and reasons why your application should be reconsidered.

Instruction #9

Safeguarding your Certificates

Please remember that it is important to keep your Birth Certificate in a secure location such as a safety deposit box and not in your wallet. By keeping it in a safe place, you are doing your part to protect your identity.

Instruction #10

Father / Other Parent

The father's or other parent's information must be included on this application if the information appears on the child's original birth registration. An "other parent" refers to a non-biological parent of a child, where the biological father is unknown and where the child was born from assisted conception.

What records does the Office of the Registrar General have?

The Office of the Registrar General holds records for births that happened in Ontario during the past 95 years.

To obtain older records, contact:
Archives of Ontario
134 Ian Macdonald Boulevard
Toronto ON M7A 2C5
800 668-9933
416 327-1600

Mail the Completed Request to:
The Office of the Registrar General
189 Red River Road
PO Box 4600
Thunder Bay ON P7B 6L8
Fax 807 343-7459

If you require faster service than 6-8 weeks, please apply online at www.serviceontario.ca

Ministry of Government Services

Office of the Registrar General

REQUEST FOR MARRIAGE CERTIFICATE

(For marriages which took place in Ontario only)

If you have any questions, please contact the Office of the Registrar General
189 Red River Road, PO Box 4600
Thunder Bay ON P7B 6L8
Outside Toronto 1 800 461-2156 or in Toronto 416 325-8305
or Fax: 807 343-7459

(THIS SPACE RESERVED FOR OFFICE USE ONLY)

Please PRINT clearly in blue or black ink.
In the context of this form, the word "Applicant" refers to the person completing this Request.

Applicant Name

First Name	Last Name

Mailing Address

Organization / Firm (if applicable)

Street No.	Street Name	Apt. No.	Buzzer No.	PO Box

City	Province

Country	Postal Code	Telephone Number (including area code)	Ext.

1. What information are you requesting and how much will it cost?

☐ **Marriage Certificate (File Size)** ***NOTE: Section 4a must be completed***
This contains basic information, such as names, date and place of marriage.
$15.00 each — Quantity ☐ $ ______

☐ **Certified Copy of Statement of Marriage (Long form)** ***NOTE: Section 4b must be completed***
This contains all information registered on the statement of marriage including signatures.
$22.00 each — Quantity ☐ $ ______

☐ **Search**
A search results in a letter that either confirms the marriage registration exists or that there is no registration (see Instruction #4). If you don't know the exact date of the marriage event, choose a year based on information you may have obtained for this purpose, and write it in the space provided for the date. We will search that whole year plus two years before and after, for a total of five years. You may also request a search of additional years, in increments of five years.

Range of years searched ________ to ________ Each 5 years searched...............$15.00 $ ______

Information

If you're sending your payment from anywhere other than Canada, you must pay with an international money order in Canadian funds drawn on a Canadian clearing house, or by VISA, MasterCard or American Express. We will not accept post-dated cheques. We will charge $35.00 if your cheque is rejected because of insufficient funds. Please note that fees are subject to change without notice. If you send your request by mail, you can pay by cheque or money order, made payable to Minister of Finance, or by VISA, MasterCard or American Express. At our public counter, you can also pay by cash or debit card.

The Office of the Registrar General holds records for marriages that happened in Ontario during the past 80 years.
To obtain older records, contact:
Archives of Ontario
134 Ian Macdonald Boulevard
Toronto ON M7A 2C5
800 668-9933
416 327-1600

Your Payment Options

Cheque or Money Order. Please make payable to: "Minister of Finance" ☐

Credit card payment: You must pay by credit card if you are faxing your request to us. Our fax number is: **807 343-7459.**

☐ Visa ☐ MasterCard ☐ American Express

Card Number

Expiry Date *(Month / Year)*

Name of Cardholder

Signature of Cardholder

Ministry of Government Services

Office of the Registrar General

REQUEST FOR DEATH CERTIFICATE

(For deaths which took place in Ontario only)

(THIS SPACE RESERVED FOR OFFICE USE ONLY)

If you have any questions, please contact the
Office of the Registrar General
189 Red River Road
PO Box 4600
Thunder Bay ON P7B 6L8
Outside Toronto: 1 800 461-2156 or in Toronto: 416 325-8305 or
Fax: 807 343-7459

Please PRINT clearly in blue or black ink.
In the context of this form, the word 'Applicant' refers to the person completing this Request.

Applicant Name

First Name	Last Name

Mailing Address

Organization / Firm (if applicable)

Street No.	Street Name	Apt. No.	Buzzer No.	PO Box

City/Town	Province	Country	Postal Code

Telephone Number (including area code)	Ext.

What Information are you Requesting and How much will it Cost?

☐ **Death Certificate (File Size)**
This contains basic information, such as name, date and place of death.

$15.00 each Quantity ☐ $ ☐

☐ **Certified Copy of Statement of Death (Long Form)**
This contains all information registered on the Statement of Death including signatures.

$22.00 each Quantity ☐ $ ☐

☐ **Certified Copy of Statement of Death and Medical Certificate of Death (Extended Long Form)**
This contains all information registered on both the Statement of Death and Medical Certificate of Death including signatures and cause of death information.

$22.00 each Quantity ☐ $ ☐

☐ **Search**
A search results in a letter that either confirms a death registration exists or that there is no registration. If you don't know the exact date of death, choose a year based on information you may have obtained for this purpose, and write it in the space provided for the date. We will search that whole year plus two years before and after, for a total of five years. You may also request a search of additional years, in increments of five years.

Range of years searched _______ to _______

Each 5 years searched ....$15.00 $ ☐

Information

If you're sending your payment from anywhere other than Canada, you must pay with an international money order in Canadian funds drawn on a Canadian clearing house, or by VISA, MasterCard or American Express. We will not accept post-dated cheques. We will charge $35.00 if your cheque is rejected because of insufficient funds. Please note that fees are subject to change without notice. If you send your request by mail, you can pay by cheque or money order, made payable to Minister of Finance, or by VISA, MasterCard or American Express. At our public counter, you can also pay by cash or debit card.

The Office of the Registrar General holds records for deaths that happened in Ontario during the past 70 years.
To obtain older records, contact:
The Archives of Ontario
134 Ian Macdonald Boulevard
Toronto ON M7A 2C5
800 668-9933
416 327-1600

Your Payment Options

Cheque or Money Order. Please make payable to: "Minister of Finance" ☐

Credit card payment: You must pay by credit card if you are faxing your request to us. Our fax number is: **807 343-7459.**

☐ Visa ☐ MasterCard ☐ American Express

Card Number	Expiry Date *(Month / Year)*
Name of Cardholder	Signature of Cardholder

Details of Deceased Person

Last Name of Deceased				First Name		Middle Name(s)
Date of Death Year	Month	Day	Sex	Age (at time of death)	Marital Status (at time of death)	Place of Death (City, Town, Village)

If the person was married or in a common-law relationship at the time of death, name of spouse or partner

(Last name before marriage)	First Name	Middle Name(s)
Mother's Maiden Name (Last Name before marriage)	First Name	Middle Name(s)
Father/Other Parent's Name (Last Name)	First Name	Middle Name(s)

Details of Applicant (If you are only applying for a death certificate, please skip this section.)

If you are applying for a Certified Copy of a Statement of Death and/or a Medical Certificate of Death (Long Form or Extended Long Form), please indicate to which category of entitled individuals (see Instruction #1) you belong:

Next of Kin

☐ Parent ☐ Spouse/Common Law Partner ☐ Child ☐ Sibling

If all of the above Next of Kin are deceased, and you are the Extended Next of Kin (see instruction #1), please indicate you relationship to the deceased person ______________________

When you request a Certified Copy of Statement of Death, the Office of the Registrar General requires you to certify that you are the Next of Kin or if all the Next of Kin are deceased, you are the Extended Next of Kin.

I, ____________________, am the ____________________ of ____________________. I certify that I am the Next of Kin, or all of the Next of Kin are deceased, and I am the Extended Next of Kin.

Authorized Representative

☐ Authorized Representative of any entitled individual (see Instruction # 2).
Proof of authorization is required and must be attached to the application (see Instruction #3).

Why are You Requesting this Information? (Select One)

☐ pension benefits ☐ insurance

☐ immigration ☐ estate settlement ☐ other *(describe)* ______________________

I authorize the Office of the Registrar General to issue the requested document/information, and consent to the Ministry of Government Services collecting information about myself and the person(s) named on the Record from such other sources as may be necessary to verify the information on this form and my entitlement to the service required, and to the disclosure of such information to the Ministry of Government Services. I am aware that it is an offence to wilfully make a false statement on this form.

Signature of Applicant	Daytime Telephone Number (including area code)	Ext.	Date Signed Year	Month	Day

Personal information contained on this form is collected under the authority of the *Vital Statistics Act*, R.S.O. 1990, c.V.4 and will be used to provide certified copies, extracts, certificates, or search notices and to verify the information provided and your entitlement to the service requested and for security and law enforcement purposes. It is an offence to wilfully make a false statement on this form. Questions about this collection should be directed to: The Deputy Registrar General, Office of the Registrar General, 189 Red River Road, PO Box 4600 Thunder Bay ON P7B 6L8.
Telephone Outside Toronto: 1 800 461-2156 or in Toronto: 416 325-8305 or Fax: 807 343-7459.

Instruction #1

Next of Kin are entitled to apply for a Certified Copy of a Statement of Death and/or a Medical Certificate of Death. Next of Kin include: *Spouse, **Common Law Partner, Mother, Father / Other Parent, Daughter, Son, Sister, and Brother.
If all of the above individuals are deceased, the Extended Next of Kin may apply. Extended Next of Kin include: Grandmother, Grandfather, Aunt, Uncle, First Cousin, Niece, Nephew or Grandchild.

*Spouse means either party to a marriage.
**Common Law Partner means two people living together continuously in a conjugal relationship outside of marriage for a period of no less than 3 years or two people who have lived together in a relationship of some permanence if they are the parents of a child.

Instruction #2

Authorized Representatives include an estate trustee, an executor or administrator, a person with power of attorney or a person with legal guardianship acting on behalf of the deceased or an entitled individual.

Instruction #3

Proof of Authorization includes a certificate of appointment of estate trustee, letters of administration, a will, proof of power of attorney and proof of legal guardianship.

Mail the Completed Request to:
The Office of the Registrar General
189 Red River Road
PO Box 4600
Thunder Bay ON P7B 6L8
Fax: 807 343-7459

If you require faster service than 6-8 weeks, please apply online at www.serviceontario.ca

CANADA—PRINCE EDWARD ISLAND

Send your requests to:

P.E.I. Vital Statistics
Department of Health
(Location: 126 Douses Road)
P.O. Box 3000
Montague, Prince Edward Island,
Canada C0A 1R0

Tel. (902) 838-0880; (877) 320-1253
Fax (902) 838-0883
www.gov.pe.ca/health/VitalStatistics

The Vital Statistics Division has birth records dating back to 1840; marriage records back to 1886, and extracts from baptismal records from 1886 to 1919. There are no death records before 1906. Birth and marriage records are restricted.

The Public Archives and Records Office (Hon. George Coles Building, 4th floor, 175 Richmond Street, Charlottetown, PE; 902-368-4290; www.gov.pe.ca/archives/) has a large collection of early vital records, including a searchable database of baptismal records 1777–1923, taken from existing church records from across the Island.

Cost for a certified standard Birth Certificate	Can$25.00
Cost for a long-form Birth Certificate	Can$35.00
Cost for a long-form Marriage Certificate	Can$35.00
Cost for a certified Death Certificate	Can$30.00

For additional assistance, contact:

Embassy of Canada
501 Pennsylvania Avenue, NW
Washington, DC 20001

Tel. (202) 682-1740

P.E.I. Vital Statistics, Dept. of Health
P.O.Box 3000, Montague, PEI C0A 1R0
Telephone:(902)838-0880 Fax:(902)838-0883

APPLICATION FOR SERVICE
(Section 32 of the Act)

Name of Applicant:______________________

Mailing Address:______________________

City/Province:__________ Postal/Zip code________

Method of payment: (must accompany application):
Money Order ☐ Visa ☐ Mastercard ☐
Card #

Exp. Date ________Signature __________

Phone.: (H) ________ (W)__________ Relationship to person named on certificate:______________

Specific reason certificate is required:______________________

If birth certificate required, complete this section (PLEASE PRINT)

Last name at Birth:____________ 1st Given Name: ____________ 2nd Given Name:____________

Other Given Names:______________ Male ☐ Female ☐ Date of birth:__________/____/____
Month (written out) day year

Place of birth (city, town or village)______________, PRINCE EDWARD ISLAND

Surname of Mother(At Her Birth):__________ Given name(s):__________ Birthplace:__________

Surname of 2nd Parent (at Birth):__________ Given name(s):__________ Birthplace:__________

Type: Standard ☐ Detailed ☐ / Regular Service ☐ Rush Service ☐

If marriage certificate required, complete this section (PLEASE PRINT)

Last name of spouse__________ Given name(s):__________ Birthplace:__________

Last name of spouse__________ Given name(s):__________ Birthplace:__________

Date of marriage:__________/____/____ Place of marriage (city/town/village):__________, PEI
Month (written out) Day Year

Type: Detailed ☐ / Regular Service ☐

If death certificate(s) required, complete this section (PLEASE PRINT)

Surname of deceased:______________ Given name(s):______________

Date of death:__________/____/____ Male ☐ Female ☐ Age: _____ Date of birth:__________/____/____
Month(written out) Day Year Month(written out) Day Year

Place of death:__________, PEI Usual Residence prior to death:______________

Marital Status: Single ☐ Married ☐ Widow ☐ Divorced ☐

Type: Certificate of Death ☐ / Regular Service ☐

X ______________________ ______________________
Signature of applicant Date of application

FOR OFFICE USE ONLY
Receipt No.________ Invoice No.________ Certificate typed by: ________ Date Issued ________
Registration Date:________ Registration No.________ Certificate No.________ Fee Chg'd ________

2. Details of Brides/Grooms

Name of Bride/Groom	Last name before marriage	First Name	Middle Name
Any other last name used		Place of Birth (Province/Country)	
Name of Bride/Groom	Last name before marriage	First Name	Middle Name
Any other last name used		Place of Birth (Province/Country)	

3. Details of Event

Date of Marriage Year / Month / Day	OR, If date unknown, range of years to search TO	Place of Marriage (City, Town or Village)

Is either bride/groom deceased? ☐ YES ☐ NO

4. Details of the Applicant (Please indicate to which category of entitled individuals the applicant belongs)

4a. Applicants for a Marriage Certificate (File Size):

I am: ☐ bride/groom ☐ parent of either bride/groom ☐ child of the marriage

Only the individuals above are entitled to apply for a Marriage Certificate (File Size). If either or both bride(s)/groom(s) are deceased, the following additional Next of Kin (see Instruction #1) are entitled to apply for a Marriage Certificate (File Size):
My relationship is:

☐ sibling of either bride/groom

☐ If either bride(s)/groom(s) is deceased, and the Next of Kin are also deceased, the Extended Next of Kin (see Instruction #1) may apply. Please indicate the applicant's relationship to either bride/groom

In the case that the applicant is the Next of Kin or the Extended Next of Kin, please complete the following certification:

I, ______ (name, please print), am the ______ of ______. I certify that I am the Next of Kin, or the Next of Kin are deceased, and I am the Extended Next of Kin.

☐ Authorized Representative of any entitled individual (see Instruction #2). Proof of authorization is required and must be attached to this application (see Instruction #3)

4b. Applicants for a Certified Statement of Marriage (Long Form):

I am: ☐ bride/groom. Only bride(s)/groom(s) are entitled to apply

If either or both bride(s)/groom(s) are deceased, the Next of Kin are entitled to apply (see Instruction #1). My relationship is:

☐ parent of either bride/groom

☐ child of the marriage

☐ sibling of either bride/groom

☐ If either or both the bride(s)/groom(s) is deceased, and the Next of Kin are also deceased, the Extended Next of Kin (see Instruction #1) may apply. Please indicate the applicant's relationship to the bride/groom

In the case that the applicant is the Next of Kin or the Extended Next of Kin, please complete the following certification:

I, ______ (name, please print), am the ______ of ______. I certify that I am the Next of Kin, or all the Next of Kin are deceased, and I am the Extended Next of Kin.

☐ Authorized Representative of any entitled individual (see Instruction #2). Proof of authorization is required and must be attached to this application (see Instruction #3)

5. Why are You Requesting this Information? (Select One)

☐ pension benefits ☐ insurance ☐ divorce

☐ estate settlement ☐ immigration ☐ other *(specify)* ____________

I authorize the Office of the Registrar General to issue the requested document/information, and consent to the Ministry of Government Services collecting information about myself and the person(s) named on the record (if other than myself) from such other sources as may be necessary to verify the information on this form and my entitlement to the service required, and the disclosure of such information to the Ministry of Government Services. I am aware that it is an offence to wilfully make a false statement on this form.

Signature of Applicant	Daytime Telephone Number (including area code) Ext.	Date Signed Year Month Day

Instructions

Instruction #1

For the purposes of entitlement to a Marriage Certificate (File Size), Next of Kin to the Bride/Groom include: Parents of either the Bride/Groom and Children of the marriage. If either (or both) of the Bride/Groom is deceased, Sibling(s) are entitled. Extended Next of Kin (closest surviving relative) to the Bride/Groom include: Grandmother, Grandfather, Aunt, Uncle, First Cousin, Niece, Nephew, or Grandchild.

For the purpose of entitlement to a Certified Copy of Statement of Marriage (Long Form), Next of Kin to the Bride/Groom include: Parents of either the Bride/Groom, Children of the marriage, Sibling(s) of the Bride/Groom . Extended Next of Kin (closest surviving relative) to the Bride/Groom include: Grandmother, Grandfather, Aunt, Uncle, First Cousin, Niece, Nephew, or Grandchild.

Instruction #2

Authorized Representative includes an estate trustee, an executor or administrator, a person with power of attorney or a person with legal guardianship acting on behalf of the deceased or an entitled individual.

Instruction #3

Proof of Authorization includes a certificate of appointment of estate trustee, letters of administration, an order under the *Declarations of Death Act, 2002*, a will, proof of power of attorney and proof of legal guardianship.

Instruction #4

A search may be requested by an individual getting married in another jurisdiction to demonstrate that he/she has not been married in Ontario (sometimes referred to as a letter of non-impediment).

Mail the Completed Request to:
The Office of the Registrar General
189 Red River Road
PO Box 4600
Thunder Bay ON P7B 6L8
Fax 807 343-7459

If you require faster service than 6-8 weeks, please apply online at www.serviceontario.ca

Personal information contained on this form is collected under the authority of the *Vital Statistics Act*, R.S.O. 1990, c.V.4 and will be used to provide certified copies, extracts, certificates, or search notices and to verify the information provided and your entitlement to the service requested and for security and law enforcement purposes. It is an offence to wilfully make a false statement on this form. Questions about this collection should be directed to: The Deputy Registrar General, Office of the Registrar General, 189 Red River Road, PO Box 4600, Thunder Bay ON P7B 6L8. Telephone Outside Toronto 1 800 461-2156 or in Toronto 416 325-8305 or Fax: 807 343-7459.

IMPORTANT INFORMATION

Certificates can only be issued for births, marriages, and deaths which occurred in P.E.I.

WHO CAN APPLY FOR CERTIFICATES:

◆ **BIRTH CERTIFICATES:**

- Person named on the certificate
- A parent whose name appears on the registration from which the certificate is to be issued
- A person authorized in writing by the person named on the certificate, or the parents of the person named on the certificate
- A court order
- A lawyer authorized in writing to act for the person, parents or spouse named on the certificate
- Long form birth certificates can only be issued to the person named on the certificate or to the parents of that person (Long form birth certificates contain parent(s) name(s) on document)

◆ **MARRIAGE CERTIFICATES:**

- Person named in the certificate
- A spouse whose name appears on the registration from which the certificate is to be issued
- A person on the authorization in writing of the person named on the certificate or spouse of the person named on the certificate
- A lawyer (authorized in writing) acting for the person(s) named on the certificate
- A court order

◆ **DEATH CERTIFICATES:**

The following may apply for a death certificate:

- Any person furnishing information satisfactory to the Director, may obtain a certificate in the prescribed form in respect of the registration of death.

TO AVOID DELAY:

- Complete the appropriate section in full (PLEASE PRINT)
- Ensure that you are authorized to make the request
- Enclose the correct fee by cheque, money order, visa or mastercard (Canadian Funds)
- Ensure that your phone number and address are correct and clear
- Ensure **All** given names of parents are included (initials are not acceptable)
- If required immediately, **48** hour **Rush Service for Printing** is available (Does Not Include Delivery Time)
- Certificate **can be couriered at Applicant's expense**

IDENTIFICATION:

Any person applying for a certificate is required to present Government issued Photo ID. A person who has written authorization to apply for or pick up someone else's certificate is required to present their own ID. Persons applying by mail or fax are required to submit photocopies of their ID documents.

FEES:

Birth - Standard size	- $25.00	Marriage - Long Form	- $35.00
Birth - Long Form	- $35.00	Death Certificate	- $30.00

Searches: $10.00 for every three years of search

Rush Service: $7.50 (Island Residents)
$25.00 (Non-residents)
Both rush fees do not include Courier

Mailing Address: Vital Statistics PO Box 3000, Montague, PE C0A 1R0
Telephone: (902)838-0880 Fax: (902) 838-0883
Toll Free within the province: (877) 320-1253
Email address: vsmontague@gov.pe.ca

Make cheque/money order payable to Vital Statistics P.E.I.

CANADA—QUEBEC

Send your requests to:

Le Directeur de l'état civil
2535, boulevard Laurier
Québec, Québec, Canada G1V 5C6

Tel. (418) 643-3900
E-mail: etatcivil@dec.gouv.qc.ca
www.etatcivil.gouv.qc.ca/

Records are available from 1900. Certificates can be ordered in person, by mail, or online (see the website for information on online ordering). Earlier records can be found at the Archives nationales du Québec (Campus de l'Université Laval, Pavillon Louis-Jacques-Casault, 1055, avenue du Séminaire, Case postale 10450, succursale Sainte-Foy, Québec G1V 4N1; www.banq.qc.ca/).

Cost for a certified Birth, Marriage, Civil Union, or Death Certificate at service counter	Can$49.00
Cost for a certified Certificate by mail	Can$44.00
Cost for a certified Certificate online	Can$31.00
Cost for a copy of an Act of Birth, Marriage, Civil Union, or Death at service counter	Can$55.00
Cost for a copy of an Act by mail	Can$51.00

For additional assistance, contact:

Embassy of Canada
501 Pennsylvania Avenue, NW
Washington, DC 20001

Tel. (202) 682-1740

Directeur de l'état civil
Québec

BIRTH
Application for a Certificate or Copy of an Act

Version
2013-2014
In effect until
March 31, 2014

N FO-1113-A 20130401

TO THE APPLICANT

- Read the general information and instructions.
- Complete **all sections** of the form.
- Write in block letters in **black** or **blue** ink.
- Include a **photocopy** of your valid photo ID.
- Include a **photocopy** of your valid proof of home address.
- **Sign** and **date** your application.
- Include your **payment**.
- **If your application is incomplete, it will be returned to you.**

ⓘ The "Information" pictogram appears in certain boxes to denote information that will help you to complete the form. Click on the pictogram to access the information.

Before starting | Print the form | Delete data entered

Section 1: Information on the applicant

1. Applicant's surname ⓘ
2. Applicant's given name
3. Home address (number, street) ⓘ — Apartment
4. City, town, village or municipality
5. Province
6. Postal code
7. Country
8. Area code — Phone number (home)
9. Area code — Phone number (other) — Extension ⓘ
10. If your application concerns someone other than yourself or your child, please explain why you are submitting it and attach an official document supporting your reason. ⓘ
11. Does the application concern someone who is deceased? ⓘ ☐ Yes ☐ No

Section 2: Information on the birth of the person concerned (This section must be completed for your application to be processed.)

12. Surname ⓘ
13. Usual given name ⓘ
14. Other given names (separated by commas)
15. Sex ☐ Male ☐ Female
16. Date of birth ⓘ Year Month Day
17. Place of birth (city, town, village or municipality, province or country, if abroad)
18. Place of registration of birth if birth occurred before 1994 (parish, place of worship,city, town, village or municipality) ⓘ

Parents
19. Surname and given name of parent
20. Quality of parent ☐ Father ☐ Mother
21. Surname and given name of parent
22. Quality of parent ☐ Father ☐ Mother

Section 3: Documents requested – The following fees are in effect until March 31, 2014.

You can mail your application or submit it at a service counter. The cost varies accordingly. **The documents you order will be sent to you by mail.** ⓘ

Normal processing – Enter the number of documents requested.

23. Birth certificate (short-form) ⓘ	24. Birth certificate (long-form) ⓘ	25. Copy of an act of birth ⓘ	26. Subtotal (boxes 23 to 25)
____ x $44 (by mail) ____ x $49 (at a counter) $____ ⊕	____ x $44 (by mail) ____ x $49 (at a counter) $____ ⊕	____ x $51 (by mail) ____ x $55 (at a counter) $____ ⊜	$

Accelerated processing – Enter the number of documents requested.

27. Birth certificate (short-form) ⓘ	28. Birth certificate (long-form) ⓘ	29. Copy of an act of birth ⓘ	30. Subtotal (boxes 27 to 29)
____ x $65 (by mail) ____ x $70 (at a counter) $____ ⊕	____ x $65 (by mail) ____ x $70 (at a counter) $____ ⊕	____ x $65 (by mail) ____ x $70 (at a counter) $____ ⊜	$

Add the amounts in boxes 26 and 30 to determine the amount payable. 31. **Total:** $ ⓘ

Section 4: Applicant's declaration

32. I solemnly declare that, to the best of my knowledge, the information provided is accurate and that I have the right to obtain the documents requested.

X ______________________ ⓘ
Applicant's signature (**mandatory**)

33. Date Year Month Day

Section 5: Methods of payment

34.
☐ Cash (at a service counter)
☐ Debit card (at a service counter)
☐ Postal or bank money order } Payable to Services Québec
☐ Cheque* ⓘ
* A $35 surcharge applies to cheques returned for insufficient funds

35. Credit card
☐ VISA
☐ MasterCard
ⓘ Expiry date Month Year

I authorize Services Québec to charge the amount entered in Box 31 to my credit card.

X ______________________ ⓘ
Cardholder's signature (**mandatory**)

Detach here.

General Information and Instructions
for an Application for a Certificate or Copy of an Act

Do not return this document with your application.

What should you know?

Certificates and copies of an act are documents issued by the Directeur de l'état civil to prove events that generally occurred in Québec.

Certificates and copies of an act contain information in the original act, spelled as therein, not the information provided on the application form. Furthermore, the language in which certificates and copies of an act are issued is the language in which the event was registered.

Application for a certificate or copy of an act of birth, marriage, civil union or death

- Certificates and copies of an act for each of these events are obtained by using the corresponding form.
- Be sure you have a version of the form that is in effect, in order to avoid any delay in processing your application. The version of the form is indicated in the upper right–hand corner, next to the title of the form.
- These forms are available on our website, at our service counters and at Services Québec offices, or by contacting us.
- You can submit your application over the Internet using one of our online services at **www.etatcivil.gouv.qc.ca**. Your documents will cost less and you eliminate delivery time to our office.

Who can be the applicant?

The **applicant** is the person who requests the certificate or copy of an act of birth.

The Directeur de l'état civil requires the **applicant** to provide valid photo ID and proof of home address to verify his or her identity. For the mandatory documents to be attached to your application, see page 3.

To protect the identity of the persons entered in the Québec civil status register, a birth certificate or copy of an act of birth can only be issued to persons mentioned in the act requested or those who justify their interest.

If your name does not appear on the act concerned by the application, you must explain in Box 10 of the form why you wish to obtain a certificate or a copy of an act pertaining to someone else and attach an official document supporting the reason given. The Directeur de l'état civil will evaluate the reason. However, if the document applied for concerns someone who is deceased and you are that person's spouse, child, brother or sister, you do not have to provide an official document supporting your application.

If you are applying for documents for a minor

Since the applicant must provide documents for his or her own application and the child is not necessarily able to provide them, it is recommended that one of the parents act as the applicant for the child.

A parent mentioned in his or her child's act of birth can obtain the child's birth certificate or copy of the child's act of birth regardless of the child's age.

Checklist

✓ **To ensure that my application is processed:**

- ☐ I have completed **all of the sections** of the form.
- ☐ I have completed the form in block letters in **black** or **blue** ink.
- ☐ I have attached a legible **photocopy** of a valid photo ID.
- ☐ I have attached a legible **photocopy** of a valid proof of home address.
- ☐ I have **signed** and **dated** my application.
- ☐ I have made sure that the documents requested correspond to the documents I require.
- ☐ I have included the **payment** corresponding to the type of processing selected.

Protection of personal information

The information gathered on this form is used solely to process your application. Failure to provide this information may result in delay or refusal of your application. Only our authorized personnel can access this information. You can consult your personal information and correct it. This personal information is shared with other organizations only where permitted by law.

Website and online services

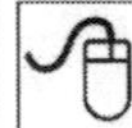

Please visit our website, at **www.etatcivil.gouv.qc.ca**, for information about our services or to download our forms.

Accessible and safe!

Thanks to DE*Clic!* and DE*Clic!* Express (certain conditions apply) services, you can apply for a certificate or copy of an act online. Try them!

Which document to request: a birth certificate or a copy of an act of birth?

Before applying, find out the type of document and the format required by the organization requesting the document.

When submitting an application concerning the birth of a **minor**, the Directeur de l'état civil recommends requesting the **long-form birth certificate**, as it includes the parents' names. Some organizations require this type of certificate in the case of minors.

Type and format	Information contained in the document*
Birth certificate Long-form 21.5 cm x 18.5 cm	▪ Surname, given names, sex, date, hour and place of birth, registration number and date of issue ▪ Father's and mother's surnames and given names
Birth certificate Short-form 8.7 cm x 5.5 cm	▪ Surname, given names, sex, date, hour and place of birth, registration number and date of issue
Copy of an act of birth 21.5 cm x 26.7 cm	▪ Integral reproduction of the civil status information contained in the act.

* Information may be missing if the event occurred before 1994.

If the format of the document requested is not indicated in the application, the long-form of the birth certificate will be issued.

Type of processing and fees

The Directeur de l'état civil offers **normal** and **accelerated** processing. Cost, processing time and method of delivery vary according to the type of processing and the mode of transmission you choose.

Processing type and time	Mode of transmission of your application	Cost per document*		Delivery of documents requested
NORMAL** In **12** business days***	By Internet By mail At a service counter	$31 per certificate $44 per certificate $49 per certificate	$37 per copy of an act $51 per copy of an act $55 per copy of an act	Regular mail
ACCELERATED** In **3** business days***	By Internet By mail At a service counter	$60 per certificate $65 per certificate $70 per certificate	$60 per copy of an act $65 per copy of an act $70 per copy of an act	Xpresspost within Canada Regular mail outside Canada

* These amounts are in Canadian dollars.
** Costs include processing, the printed document and shipping fees.
*** The number of days excludes delivery time.

Additional processing time may be required, particularly if the event occurred recently and is not yet entered in the Québec register of civil status. See our website for more information about processing time.

Fee changes

The above fees are in effect until March 31, 2014.

Apply for a certificate or a copy of an act over the Internet using one of our online services and pay less for your documents.

What payment methods are accepted?

At a service counter

Cash, debit card (Interac), credit card, cheque, postal money order, bank money order

By mail

Credit card, cheque, postal money order, bank money order

Credit cards accepted: ***VISA*** Visa  MasterCard

Cheque

- Cheque payable to **Services Québec**.
- No post-dated cheques accepted.
- A $35 surcharge applies to cheques returned for insufficient funds.

Postal or bank money order

- Money order payable to **Services Québec**.

Separate payment

If you are submitting more than one application form at a time, send a separate payment with each form to speed processing.

How to submit the application?

At a service counter

Québec
Ground floor
2535, boulevard Laurier

Montréal
Ground floor (RC.01)
2050, rue De Bleury

You can also submit your application at certain Services Québec offices that provide our services. See our website for the list of offices or contact us.

By mail

Directeur de l'état civil
2535, boulevard Laurier
Québec (Québec) G1V 5C6

What documents enable us to establish the applicant's identity?

The Directeur de l'état civil applies security measures to ensure that the person applying for a civil status document is authorized to obtain it. To allow us to establish the identity of **applicants**, we require them to attach **two different documents issued by two separate entities**:

- **a valid photo ID**
- **a valid proof of home address**

If you submit your application **by mail**, you must attach **photocopies** and not original documents. If you submit your application at **one of our service counters**, it is preferable to present **original documents** and not photocopies.

A valid photo ID

Only the identity documents listed below are accepted. **If you cannot provide one of these documents, contact us** to determine the solution best suited to your situation or fill out the *Declaration du répondant* form and attach it to your application. This form is available on our website.

- Québec or Ontario health insurance card bearing a photograph
- Driver's licence issued by Québec, another Canadian province or a US state

A driver's licence is accepted as an ID **only if it is not submitted as proof of home address.**

- Canadian or foreign passport
- Canadian Citizenship Card (issued since 2002)
- Canadian Permanent Resident Card
- US Permanent Resident Card (green card)
- Federal immigration documents (IMM 1442, for one of the situations covered by this document)
- Official IDs for members of the military, police officers or diplomats posted in Canada
- Certificate of Indian Status
- ID card issued by a Canadian province

A valid proof of home address

The civil status document will be sent to the address shown on the proof of your current home address. Only the proofs of home address listed below are accepted. **If you cannot provide one of these documents, please contact us**.

- Driver's licence issued by Québec, another Canadian province or a US state

A driver's licence is accepted as a proof of home address **only if it is not submitted as a photo ID.**

- Municipal or school tax bill (no more than one year old)
- Government postal correspondence (no more than one year old)
- Recent bill from an energy, telephone service or cable provider (no more than three months old)
- Construction competency certificate (apprentice or journeyperson)
- Hospital card accompanied by health insurance card bearing a photograph
- Record of employment or pay slip (no more than three months old)
- Home or car insurance certificate or statement (no more than one year old)
- School transcript (no more than one year old)
- Bank statement (no more than three months old)
- Canada Post change of address receipt (no more than three months old)

The document's validity is determined according to the date the Directeur de l'état civil receives the application.

Document validity
All documents submitted must be in effect or comply with the validity period specified.

Front and back document
Remember to include the photocopy of the back of a document when required, particularly if it shows a change of address.

Language of documents
If the required documents are written in a language other than French or English, attach a French translation done or certified true by a member of the Ordre des traducteurs, terminologues et interprètes agréés du Québec.

Quality of photocopies
All photocopied documents must be legible.

Separate photocopies
If you are submitting more than one application form at a time, attach separate photocopies to each form to speed processing.

Instructions

This section is a reference tool. The "Information" pictogram ⓘ appears in certain boxes on the form. It indicates that particular information is provided to help you complete the form correctly.

Section 1: Information on the applicant

Box 1 – **Applicant's surname**

Enter your family name. This name must correspond to the family name indicated on the photo ID and proof of home address submitted.

Box 3 – **Home address (number, street, apartment)**

The address must correspond to the address indicated on the proof of home address submitted. The documents requested will be sent to this address.

Box 9 – **Phone number (other)**

Indicate a phone number where we can reach you **during the day** or where we can leave a message, if necessary.

Boxes 10 and 11 – **If the application concerns someone other than yourself or your child, or if it concerns a deceased person, explain why you are submitting the application and attach an official document supporting the reason given.**

If you are not mentioned in the act, you must justify why you wish to obtain a certificate or copy of an act concerning another person and **provide a photocopy of one or more supporting documents**. An extra sheet may be used if more space is required. However, if the document applied for concerns someone who is deceased and you are that person's spouse, child, brother or sister, you do not have to provide an official document supporting your application.

Section 2: Information on the birth of the person concerned

Box 12 – **Surname**

Use the family name as indicated on the act used to enter the birth in the register. In cases involving adoption or a name change, enter the family name used after the adoption or the name change.

Box 13 – **Usual given name**

The usual given name is a name that, in addition to being mentioned in the act, is used on a daily basis to identify the person and confirm his or her identity.

Box 18 – **Place of registration of birth if the birth occurred before 1994 (parish, place of worship, city, town, village or municipality)**

Complete this box only if the person was born **before 1994**. Enter the name of the place of worship or parish and municipality (city, town or village) where the religious registration took place, or the name of the municipality in the case of a civil registration.

Section 4: Applicant's declaration

Box 32 – **Applicant's signature**

The signature of the applicant (the person named in Section 1 of the form) is mandatory. If the declaration is not signed, your application will be refused.

Section 5: Methods of payment

Box 35 – **Credit card**

The credit cardholder's signature is mandatory even if he or she also signed as the applicant. Without the cardholder's signature in the appropriate place, the application will be refused.

To reach us

By phone

Québec: 418 644-4545
Montréal: 514 644-4545
Elsewhere in Québec: 1 877 644-4545
Teleprinter (TTY): 1 800 361-9596

By mail

Directeur de l'état civil
2535, boulevard Laurier
Québec (Québec) G1V 5C6

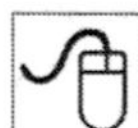

By e-mail
etatcivil@dec.gouv.qc.ca

Website
www.etatcivil.gouv.qc.ca

Only you, as the applicant, can obtain information on the status of your application. You must contact us by phone or go to one of our service counters.

Directeur
de l'état civil
Québec

MARRIAGE or CIVIL UNION

Application for a Certificate or Copy of an Act

Version **2013-2014**
In effect until March 31, 2014

M FO-1119-A 20130401

TO THE APPLICANT

- Read the general information and instructions.
- Complete **all sections** of the form.
- Write in block letters in **black** or **blue** ink.
- Include a **photocopy** of your valid photo ID.
- Include a **photocopy** of your valid proof of home address.
- **Sign** and **date** your application.
- Include your **payment**.
- **If your application is incomplete, it will be returned to you.**

(i) The "Information" pictogram appears in certain boxes to denote information that will help you to complete the form. Click on the pictogram to access the information.

Before starting | Print the form | Delete data entered

Section 1: Information on the applicant

1. Applicant's surname (i)
2. Applicant's given name
3. Home address (number, street) (i) Apartment
4. City, town, village or municipality
5. Province
6. Postal code
7. Country
8. Area code Phone number (home)
9. Area code Phone number (other) Extension (i)
10. If your application concerns someone other than yourself, please explain why you are submitting it and attach an official document supporting your reason. (i)
11. Is one of the spouses deceased? (i) ☐ Yes ☐ No

Section 2: Information on the marriage or civil union of the persons concerned

12. Type of union ☐ Marriage ☐ Civil union (i)
13. Place of registration of marriage or civil union (city, town, village or municipality, place of worship, province or country, if abroad) (i)
14. Date of marriage or civil union (i) Year Month Day

Section 3: Information on the two spouses concerned by the application

A	B
15. Surname (i)	25. Surname (i)
16. Given names (begin with the usual given name; separate the given names with a comma (i)	26. Given names (begin with the usual given name; separate the given names with a comma (i)
17. Sex ☐ Male ☐ Female / 18. Date of birth (i) Year Month Day	27. Sex ☐ Male ☐ Female / 28. Date of birth (i) Year Month Day
19. Place of birth (city, town, village or municipality, province or country, if abroad)	29. Place of birth (city, town, village or municipality, province or country, if abroad)
20. Place of registration of birth (parish, place of worship, city, town, village or municipality) (i)	30. Place of registration of birth (parish, place of worship, city, town, village or municipality) (i)
21. Surname and given name of parent / 22. Quality of parent ☐ Father ☐ Mother	31. Surname and given name of parent / 32. Quality of parent ☐ Father ☐ Mother
23. Surname and given name of parent / 24. Quality of parent ☐ Father ☐ Mother	33. Surname and given name of parent / 34. Quality of parent ☐ Father ☐ Mother

Detach here.

Section 4: Documents requested – The following fees are in effect until March 31, 2014.

You can mail your application or submit it at a service counter. The cost varies accordingly. **The documents you order will be sent to you by mail.** (i)

Normal processing – Enter the number of documents requested.

35. Marriage or civil union certificate (i)
_____ x $44 (by mail)
_____ x $49 (at a service counter) = $ _____ (+)

36. Copy of an act of marriage or civil union (i)
_____ x $51 (by mail)
_____ x $55 (at a service counter) = $ _____ (=)

37. Subtotal (boxes 35 and 36) $

Accelerated processing – Enter the number of documents requested.

38. Marriage or civil union certificate (i)
_____ x $65 (by mail)
_____ x $70 (at a service counter) = $ _____ (+)

39. Copy of an act of marriage or civil union (i)
_____ x $65 (by mail)
_____ x $70 (at a service counter) = $ _____ (=)

40. Subtotal (boxes 38 and 39) $

Add the amounts in boxes 37 and 40 to determine the amount payable. 41. **Total:** $ (i)

Section 5: Applicant's declaration

42. I solemnly declare that, to the best of my knowledge, the information provided is accurate and that I have the right to obtain the documents requested.

X ______________________ (i)
Applicant's signature (**mandatory**)

43. Date Year Month Day

Section 6: Methods of payment

44.
☐ Cash (at a service counter)
☐ Debit card (at a service counter)
☐ Postal or bank money order } Payable to Services Québec
☐ Cheque* (i)

* A $35 surcharge applies to cheques returned for insufficient funds

45. Credit card (i) Expiry date Month Year
☐ VISA
☐ MasterCard
I authorize Services Québec to charge the amount entered in Box 41 to my credit card.
X ______________________ (i)
Cardholder's signature (**mandatory**)

Directeur
de l'état civil
Québec

General Information and Instructions

for an Application for a Certificate or Copy of an Act

Do not return this document with your application.

What should you know?

Certificates and copies of an act are documents issued by the Directeur de l'état civil to prove events that generally occurred in Québec.

Certificates and copies of an act contain the information in the original act, spelled as therein, not the information provided on the application form. Futhermore, the language in which certificates and copies of an act are issued is the language in which the event was registered.

Application for a certificate or copy of an act of birth, marriage, civil union or death

- Certificates and copies of an act for each of these events are obtained by using the corresponding form.
- Be sure you have a version of the form that is in effect, in order to avoid any delay in processing your application. The version of the form is indicated in the upper right-hand corner, next to the title of the form.
- These forms are available on our website, at our service counters and at Services Québec offices, or by contacting us.
- You can submit your application over the Internet using one of our online services at **www.etatcivil.gouv.qc.ca**. Your documents will cost less and you eliminate delivery time to our office.

Who can be the applicant?

The **applicant** is the person who requests the certificate or copy of an act of marriage or civil union.

The Directeur de l'état civil requires the **applicant** to provide valid photo ID and proof of home address to verify his or her identity. For the mandatory documents to be attached to your application, see page 3.

To protect the identity of the persons entered in the Québec civil status register, a certificate of marriage or civil union or a copy of an act of marriage or civil union can only be issued to persons mentioned in the act requested or those who justify their interest.

If your name does not appear on the act concerned by the application, you must explain in Box 10 of the form why you wish to obtain a certificate or a copy of an act pertaining to someone else and attach an official document supporting the reason given. The Directeur de l'état civil will evaluate the reason. However, if the document applied for concerns someone who is deceased and you are that person's child, brother or sister, you do not have to provide an official document supporting your application.

Checklist

✓ **To ensure that my application is processed:**

- ☐ I have completed **all of the sections** of the form.
- ☐ I have completed the form in block letters in **black** or **blue** ink.
- ☐ I have attached a legible **photocopy** of a valid photo ID.
- ☐ I have attached a legible **photocopy** of a valid proof of home address.
- ☐ I have **signed** and **dated** my application.
- ☐ I have made sure that the documents requested correspond to the documents I require.
- ☐ I have included the **payment** corresponding to the type of processing selected.

Protection of personal information

The information gathered on this form is used solely to process your application. Failure to provide this information may result in delay or refusal of your application. Only our authorized personnel can access this information. You can consult your personal information and correct it. This personal information is shared with other organizations only where permitted by law.

Website and online services

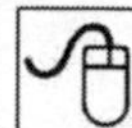

Please visit our website, at **www.etatcivil.gouv.qc.ca**, for information about our services or to download our forms.

Accessible and safe!

Thanks to DE*Clic!* and DE*Clic!* Express (certain conditions apply) services, you can apply for a certificate or copy of an act online. Try them!

Which document to request: a certificate or a copy of an act of marriage or civil union?

Before applying, find out the type of document required by the organization requesting the document.

Type of document	Information contained in the document*
Marriage certificate 21.5 cm x 18.5 cm	▪ Spouses' surnames and given names, spouses' sex, date and place of marriage, registration number and date of issue
Civil union certificate 21.5 cm x 18.5 cm	▪ Spouses' surnames and given names, spouses' sex, date and place of civil union, registration number and date of issue
Copy of an act of marriage 21.5 cm x 26.7 cm	▪ Integral reproduction of the information contained in the act
Copy of an act of civil union 21.5 cm x 26.7 cm	▪ Integral reproduction of the information contained in the act

* Information may be missing if the event occurred before 1994.

Type of processing and fees

The Directeur de l'état civil offers **normal** and **accelerated** processing. Cost, processing time and method of delivery vary according to the type of processing and the mode of transmission you choose.

Processing type and time	Mode of transmission of your application	Cost per document*		Delivery of documents requested
NORMAL** In **12** business days***	By Internet By mail At a service counter	$31 per certificate $44 per certificate $49 per certificate	$37 per copy of an act $51 per copy of an act $55 per copy of an act	Regular mail
ACCELERATED** In **3** business days***	By Internet By mail At a service counter	$60 per certificate $65 per certificate $70 per certificate	$60 per copy of an act $65 per copy of an act $70 per copy of an act	Xpresspost within Canada Regular mail outside Canada

* These amounts are in Canadian dollars.
** Costs include processing, the printed document and shipping fees.
*** The number of days excludes delivery time.

Additional processing time may be required, particularly if the event occurred recently and is not yet entered in the Québec register of civil status. See our website for more information about processing time.

Fee changes
The above fees are in effect until March 31, 2014.

Apply for a certificate or a copy of an act over the Internet using one of our online services and pay less for your documents.

What payment methods are accepted?

At a service counter
Cash, debit card (Interac), credit card, cheque, postal money order, bank money order

By mail
Credit card, cheque, postal money order, bank money order

Credit cards accepted: **VISA** Visa  MasterCard

Cheque
- Cheque payable to **Services Québec**.
- No post-dated cheques accepted.
- A $35 surcharge applies to cheques returned for insufficient funds.

Postal or bank money order
- Money order payable to **Services Québec**.

Separate payment
If you are submitting more than one application form at a time, send a separate payment with each form to speed processing.

How to submit the application?

At a service counter

Québec
Ground floor
2535, boulevard Laurier

Montréal
Ground floor (RC.01)
2050, rue De Bleury

You can also submit your application at certain Services Québec offices that provide our services. See our website for the list of offices or contact us.

By mail

Directeur de l'état civil
2535, boulevard Laurier
Québec (Québec) G1V 5C6

What documents enable us to establish the applicant's identity?

The Directeur de l'état civil applies security measures to ensure that the person applying for a civil status document is authorized to obtain it. To allow us to establish the identity of **applicants**, we require them to attach **two different documents issued by two separate entities**:

- **a valid photo ID**
- **a valid proof of home address**

If you submit your application **by mail**, you must attach **photocopies** and not original documents. If you submit your application at **one of our service counters**, it is preferable to present **original documents** and not photocopies.

A valid photo ID

Only the identity documents listed below are accepted. **If you cannot provide one of these documents, contact us** to determine the solution best suited to your situation or fill out the *Declaration du répondant* form and attach it to your application. This form is available on our website.

- Québec or Ontario health insurance card bearing a photograph
- Driver's licence issued by Québec, another Canadian province or a US state

  A driver's licence is accepted as an ID **only if it is not submitted as proof of home address.**

- Canadian or foreign passport
- Canadian Citizenship Card (issued since 2002)
- Canadian Permanent Resident Card
- US Permanent Resident Card (green card)
- Federal immigration documents (IMM 1442, for one of the situations covered by this document)
- Official IDs for members of the military, police officers or diplomats posted in Canada
- Certificate of Indian Status
- ID card issued by a Canadian province

A valid proof of home address

The civil status document will be sent to the address shown on the proof of your current home address. Only the proofs of home address listed below are accepted. **If you cannot provide one of these documents, please contact us**.

- Driver's licence issued by Québec, another Canadian province or a US state

  A driver's licence is accepted as a proof of home address **only if it is not submitted as a photo ID.**

- Municipal or school tax bill (no more than one year old)
- Government postal correspondence (no more than one year old)
- Recent bill from an energy, telephone service or cable provider (no more than three months old)
- Construction competency certificate (apprentice or journeyperson)
- Hospital card accompanied by health insurance card bearing a photograph
- Record of employment or pay slip (no more than three months old)
- Home or car insurance certificate or statement (no more than one year old)
- School transcript (no more than one year old)
- Bank statement (no more than three months old)
- Canada Post change of address receipt (no more than three months old)

The document's validity is determined according to the date the Directeur de l'état civil receives the application.

Document validity

All documents submitted must be in effect or comply with the validity period specified.

Front and back document

Remember to include the photocopy of the back of a document when required, particularly if it shows a change of address.

Language of documents

If the required documents are written in a language other than French or English, attach a French translation done or certified true by a member of the Ordre des traducteurs, terminologues et interprètes agréés du Québec.

Quality of photocopies

All photocopied documents must be legible.

Separate photocopies

If you are submitting more than one application form at a time, attach separate photocopies to each form to speed processing.

Instructions

This section is a reference tool. The "Information" pictogram ⓘ appears in certain boxes on the form. It indicates that particular information is provided to help you fill out the form correctly.

Section 1: Information on the applicant

Box 1 – **Applicant's surname**

Enter your family name. This name must correspond to the family name indicated on the photo ID and proof of home address submitted.

Box 3 – **Home address (number, street, apartment)**

The address must correspond to the address indicated on the proof of home address submitted. The documents requested will be sent to this address.

Box 9 – **Phone number (other)**

Indicate a phone number where we can reach you **during the day** or where we can leave a message, if necessary.

Boxes 10 and 11 – **If the application concerns someone other than yourself or a deceased person, explain why you are submitting the application and attach an official document supporting the reason given.**

If you are not mentioned in the act, you must justify why you wish to obtain a certificate or copy of an act concerning another person and **provide a photocopy of one or more supporting documents**. An extra sheet may be used if more space is required. However, if the document applied for concerns someone who is deceased and you are mentioned in the act, or you are that person's child, brother or sister, you do not have to provide an official document supporting your application.

Section 2: Information on the marriage or civil union of the persons concerned

Box 12 – **Type of union**

In June 2002, the National Assembly of Québec passed the *Act instituting civil unions and establishing new rules of filiation*. It created a new institution, namely, civil union, that allows same-sex or opposite-sex couples to make a public commitment to live together and comply with the resulting rights and obligations. (Source: Ministère de la Justice)

Box 13 – **Place of registration of marriage or civil union (city, town, village or municipality, place of worship, province or country, if abroad)**

For a religious marriage, enter the name of the place of worship or parish, or municipality (city, town or village). For a civil marriage or civil union, enter the name of the municipality (city, town or village). Do not enter the place where the reception was held following the marriage or civil union.

Section 3: Information on the two spouses concerned by the application

Boxes 15 and 25 – **Surname**

Use the family name as indicated on the act used to register the birth in the register. In the case of adoption or a name change, enter the family name used after the adoption or name change.

Boxes 16 and 26 – **Given names (begin with the usual given name; separate given names with a comma)**

The usual given name is the name that, in addition to being mentioned in the act, is used on a daily basis to identify the person and confirm his or her identity.

Boxes 20 and 30 – **Place of registration of birth (parish, place of worship, city, town, village or municipality)**

Complete this box only if the person was born before **1994**. Enter the name of the place of worship or parish and municipality (city, town or village) where the religious registration took place, or the name of the municipality in the case of a civil registration.

Section 5: Applicant's declaration

Box 42 – **Applicant's signature**

The signature of the applicant (the person named in Section 1 of the form) is mandatory. If the declaration is not signed, your application will be refused.

Section 6: Methods of payment

Box 45 – **Credit card**

The credit cardholder's signature is mandatory even if he or she also signed as the applicant. Without the cardholder's signature in the appropriate place, the application will be refused.

To reach us

By phone

Québec:	418 644-4545
Montréal:	514 644-4545
Elsewhere in Québec:	1 877 644-4545
Teleprinter (TTY):	1 800 361-9596

By mail

Directeur de l'état civil
2535, boulevard Laurier
Québec (Québec) G1V 5C6

By e-mail

etatcivil@dec.gouv.qc.ca

Website

www.etatcivil.gouv.qc.ca

Only you, as the applicant, can obtain information on the status of your application. You must contact us by phone or go to one of our service counters.

Directeur de l'état civil
Québec

DEATH

Application for a Certificate or Copy of an Act

Version **2013-2014**
In effect until March 31, 2014

D FO-1120-A 20130401

TO THE APPLICANT

- Read the general information and instructions.
- Complete **all sections** of the form.
- Write in block letters in **black** or **blue** ink.
- Include a **photocopy** of your valid photo ID.
- Include a **photocopy** of your valid proof of home address.
- **Sign** and **date** your application.
- Include your **payment**.
- **If your application is incomplete, it will be returned to you.**

The "Information" pictogram appears in certain boxes to denote information that will help you to complete the form. Click on the pictogram to access the information.

Before starting | Print the form | Delete data entered

Section 1: Information on the applicant

1. Applicant's surname
2. Applicant's given name
3. Home address (number, street) — Apartment
4. City, town, village or municipality
5. Province
6. Postal code
7. Country
8. Area code — Phone number (home)
9. Area code — Phone number (other) — Extension
10. In what capacity are you filing out this application?
☐ Declarant of the death ☐ Other. Specify: ______
11. Give the reason for your application if you checked "Other" in Box 10, and attach an official document supporting the reason.

Section 2: Information on the deceased

12. Place of death (city, town, village or municipality, province or country, if abroad)
13. Date of death — Year — Month — Day
14. Surname
15. Given names (begin with the usual given name; separate each given name with a comma)
16. Sex ☐ Male ☐ Female
17. Date of birth — Year — Month — Day
18. Marital status at the time of death ☐ Single ☐ Married ☐ Widow or widower ☐ Divorced ☐ United in civil union ☐ Former spouse under a civil union
19. Place of birth (city, town, village or municipality, province or country, if abroad)
20. Place of registration of birth if birth occured before 1994 (parish, place of worship, city, town, village or municipality)
21. Surname and given name of parent
22. Quality of parent ☐ Father ☐ Mother
23. Surname and given name of parent
24. Quality of parent ☐ Father ☐ Mother

Information on the spouse if the deceased was married or united in a civil union

25. Place of registration of marriage or civil union (city, town, village or municipality, place of worship, province or country, if abroad)
26. Date of marriage or civil union — Year — Month — Day
27. Surname
28. Given names (begin with the usual given name; separate each given name with a comma)
29. Sex ☐ Male ☐ Female
30. Date of birth — Year — Month — Day
31. Place of birth (city, town, village or municipality, province or country, if abroad)
32. Place of registration of birth
33. Surname and given name of parent
34. Quality of parent ☐ Father ☐ Mother
35. Surname and given name of parent
36. Quality of parent ☐ Father ☐ Mother

Section 3: Documents requested – The following fees are in effect until March 31, 2014

You can mail your application or submit it at a service counter. The cost varies accordingly. **The documents you order will be sent to you by mail.**

Normal processing – Enter the number of documents requested.

37. Death certificate
____ x $44 (by mail)
____ x $49 (at a service counter) = $ ____ +
38. Copy of an act of death
____ x $51 (by mail)
____ x $55 (at a service counter) = $ ____ =
39. Subtotal (boxes 37 and 38) $

Accelerated processing Enter the number of documents requested.

40. Death certificate
____ x $65 (by mail)
____ x $70 (at a service counter) = $ ____ +
41. Copy of an act of death
____ x $65 (by mail)
____ x $70 (at a service counter) = $ ____ =
42. Subtotal (boxes 40 and 41) $

Add the amounts in boxes 39 and 42 to determine the amount payable. 43. **Total:** $

Section 4: Applicant's declaration

44. I solemnly declare that, to the best of my knowledge, the information provided is accurate and that I have the right to obtain the documents requested.
X ______
Applicant's signature (**mandatory**)
45. Date — Year — Month — Day

Section 5: Methods of payment

46.
☐ Cash (at a service counter)
☐ Debit card (at a service counter)
☐ Postal or bank money order } Payable to Services Québec
☐ Cheque* } Payable to Services Québec
* A $35 surcharge applies to cheques returned for insufficient funds

47. Credit card
☐ VISA
☐ MasterCard
Expiry date — Month — Year
I authorize Services Québec to charge the amount entered in Box 43 to my credit card.
X ______
Cardholder's signature (**mandatory**)

Detach here.

Directeur de l'état civil
Québec

General Information and Instructions
for an Application for a Certificate or Copy of an Act

Do not return this document with your application.

What should you know?

Certificates and copies of an act are documents issued by the Directeur de l'état civil to prove events that generally occurred in Québec.

Certificates and copies of an act contain the information in the original act, spelled as therein, not the information provided on the application form. Futhermore, the language in which certificates and copies of an act are issued is the language in which the event was registered.

Application for a certificate or copy of an act of birth, marriage, civil union or death

- Certificates and copies of an act for each of these events are obtained by using the corresponding form.
- Be sure you have a version of the form that is in effect, in order to avoid any delay in processing your application. The version of the form is indicated in the upper right–hand corner, next to the title of the form.
- These forms are available on our website, at our service counters and at Services Québec offices, or by contacting us.
- You can submit your application over the Internet using our DE*Clic!* online service at **www.etatcivil.gouv.qc.ca**. Your documents will cost less and you eliminate delivery time to our office.

Who can be the applicant?

The **applicant** is the person who requests a death certificate or copy of an act of death.

The Directeur de l´état civil requires the **applicant** to provide valid photo ID and proof of home address to verify his or her identity. For the mandatory documents to be attached to your application, see page 3.

To protect the identity of the persons entered in the Québec civil status register, a death certificate or copy of an act of death can only be issued to persons mentioned in the act requested or those who justify their interest.

If your name does not appear on the act concerned by the application, you must explain in Box 11 of the form why you wish to obtain a certificate or a copy of an act pertaining to someone else and attach an official document supporting the reason given. The Directeur de l'état civil will evaluate the reason. However, if you are that person's child, brother or sister, you do not have to provide an official document supporting your application.

Checklist

✓ **To ensure that my application is processed:**

- ☐ I have completed **all of the sections** of the form.
- ☐ I have completed the form in block letters in **black** or **blue** ink.
- ☐ I have attached a legible **photocopy** of a valid photo ID.
- ☐ I have attached a legible **photocopy** of a valid proof of home address.
- ☐ I have **signed** and **dated** my application.
- ☐ I have made sure that the documents requested correspond to the documents I require.
- ☐ I have included the **payment** corresponding to the type of processing selected.

Protection of personal information

The information gathered on this form is used solely to process your application. Failure to provide this information may result in delay or refusal of your application. Only our authorized personnel can access this information. You can consult your personal information and correct it. This personal information is shared with other organizations only where permitted by law.

Website and online service

Please visit our website, at **www.etatcivil.gouv.qc.ca**, for information about our services or to download our forms.

Accessible and safe!

Thanks to DE*Clic!* service, you can apply for a certificate or copy of an act online. Try it!

Which document to request: a death certificate or a copy of an act of death?

Before applying, find out the type of document required by the organization requesting the document.

Type of document	Information contained in the document*
Death certificate 21.5 cm x 18.5 cm	▪ Surname, given names, sex, date, hour and place of death, date of birth, registration number and date of issue
Copy of an act of death 21.5 cm x 26.7 cm	▪ Integral reproduction of the information contained in the act

* Information may be missing if the event occurred before 1994.

Type of processing and fees

The Directeur de l'état civil offers **normal** and **accelerated** processing. Cost, processing time and method of delivery vary according to the type of processing and the mode of transmission you choose.

Processing type and time	Mode of transmission of your application	Cost per document*		Delivery of documents requested
NORMAL** In **12** business days***	By Internet By mail At a service counter	$31 per certificate $44 per certificate $49 per certificate	$37 per copy of an act $51 per copy of an act $55 per copy of an act	Regular mail
ACCELERATED** In **3** business days***	By Internet By mail At a service counter	$60 per certificate $65 per certificate $70 per certificate	$60 per copy of an act $65 per copy of an act $70 per copy of an act	Xpresspost within Canada Regular mail outside Canada

* These amounts are in Canadian dollars.
** Costs include processing, the printed document and shipping fees.
*** The number of days excludes delivery time.

Additional processing time may be required, particularly if the event occurred recently and is not yet entered in the Québec register of civil status. See our website for more information about processing time.

Fee changes

The above fees are in effect until March 31, 2014.

Apply for a certificate or a copy of an act over the Internet using our DE*Clic!* online service and pay less for your documents.

What payment methods are accepted?

At a service counter

Cash, debit card (Interac), credit card, cheque, postal money order, bank money order

By mail

Credit card, cheque, postal money order, bank money order

Credit cards accepted: ***VISA*** Visa  MasterCard

Cheque

- Cheque payable to **Services Québec**.
- No post-dated cheques accepted.
- A $35 surcharge applies to cheques returned for insufficient funds.

Postal or bank money order

- Money order payable to **Services Québec**.

Separate payment

If you are submitting more than one application form at a time, send a separate payment with each form to speed processing.

How to submit the application?

At a service counter

Québec
Ground floor
2535, boulevard Laurier

Montréal
Ground floor (RC.01)
2050, rue De Bleury

You can also submit your application at certain Services Québec offices that provide our services. See our website for the list of offices or contact us.

By mail

Directeur de l'état civil
2535, boulevard Laurier
Québec (Québec) G1V 5C6

What documents enable us to establish the applicant's identity?

The Directeur de l'état civil applies security measures to ensure that the person applying for a civil status document is authorized to obtain it. To allow us to establish the identity of **applicants**, we require them to attach **two different documents issued by two separate entities**:

- **a valid photo ID**
- **a valid proof of home address**

If you submit your application **by mail**, you must attach **photocopies** and not original documents. If you submit your application at **one of our service counters**, it is preferable to present **original documents** and not photocopies.

A valid photo ID

Only the identity documents listed below are accepted. **If you cannot provide one of these documents, contact us** to determine the solution best suited to your situation or fill out the *Declaration du répondant* form and attach it to your application. This form is available on our website.

- Québec or Ontario health insurance card bearing a photograph
- Driver's licence issued by Québec, another Canadian province or a US state

A driver's licence is accepted as an ID **only if it is not submitted as proof of home address.**

- Canadian or foreign passport
- Canadian Citizenship Card (issued since 2002)
- Canadian Permanent Resident Card
- US Permanent Resident Card (green card)
- Federal immigration documents (IMM 1442, for one of the situations covered by this document)
- Official IDs for members of the military, police officers or diplomats posted in Canada
- Certificate of Indian Status
- ID card issued by a Canadian province

A valid proof of home address

The civil status document will be sent to the address shown on the proof of your current home address. Only the proofs of home address listed below are accepted. **If you cannot provide one of these documents, please contact us**.

- Driver's licence issued by Québec, another Canadian province or a US state

A driver's licence is accepted as a proof of home address **only if it is not submitted as a photo ID.**

- Municipal or school tax bill (no more than one year old)
- Government postal correspondence (no more than one year old)
- Recent bill from an energy, telephone service or cable provider (no more than three months old)
- Construction competency certificate (apprentice or journeyperson)
- Hospital card accompanied by health insurance card bearing a photograph
- Record of employment or pay slip (no more than three months old)
- Home or car insurance certificate or statement (no more than one year old)
- School transcript (no more than one year old)
- Bank statement (no more than three months old)
- Canada Post change of address receipt (no more than three months old)

The document's validity is determined according to the date the Directeur de l'état civil receives the application.

Document validity
All documents submitted must be in effect or comply with the validity period specified.

Front and back document
Remember to include the photocopy of the back of a document when required, particularly if it shows a change of address.

Language of documents
If the required documents are written in a language other than French or English, attach a French translation done or certified true by a member of the Ordre des traducteurs, terminologues et interprètes agréés du Québec.

Quality of photocopies
All photocopied documents must be legible.

Separate photocopies
If you are submitting more than one application form at a time, attach separate photocopies to each form to speed processing.

Instructions

This section is a reference tool. The "Information" pictogram ⓘ appears in certain boxes on the form. It indicates that particular information is provided to help you fill out the form correctly.

Section 1: Information on the applicant

Box 1 – **Applicant's surname**

Enter your family name. This name must correspond to the family name indicated on the photo ID and proof of home address submitted.

Box 3 – **Home address (number, street, apartment)**

The address must correspond to the address indicated on the proof of home address submitted. The documents requested will be sent to this address.

Box 9 – **Phone number (other)**

Indicate a phone number where we can reach you **during the day** or where we can leave a message, if necessary.

Box 11 – **Give the reason for your application if you checked "Other" in Box 10 and attach an official document supporting the reason.**

If you are not mentioned in the act, you must justify why you wish to obtain a certificate or copy of an act concerning another person and **provide a photocopy of one or more supporting documents**. An extra sheet may be used if more space is required. However, if you are mentioned in the act or if you are that person's child, brother or sister, you do not have to provide an official document supporting your application.

Section 2: Information on the deceased

Box 14 – **Surname**

Use the family name indicated on the act used to enter the birth in the register. In cases involving adoption or a name change, enter the family name used after the adoption or name change.

Box 15 – **Given names (begin with the usual given name; separate each given name with a comma)**

The usual given name is a name that, in addition to being mentioned in the act, is used on a daily basis to identify the person and confirm his or her identity.

Box 20 – **Place of registration of birth if the birth occurred before 1994 (parish, place of worship, city, town, village or municipality)**

Complete this box only if the person was born **before 1994**. Enter the name of the place of worship or parish and municipality (city, town or village) where the religious registration took place, or the name of the municipality in the case of a civil registration.

Information on the spouse if the deceased was married or united in a civil union

You do not have to complete this section if the deceased was single, living in a de facto union, a widow or widower, divorced or the former spouse under a civil union.

Box 25 – **Place of registration of marriage or civil union (city, town, village or municipality, place of worship, province or country, if abroad)**

For a religious marriage, enter the name of the place of worship and the municipality (city, town or village). For a civil marriage or civil union, enter the name of the municipality (city, town or village). Do not enter the place where the reception was held following the marriage or civil union.

Box 27 – **Surname**

Use the family name indicated on the act used to enter the birth in the register. In cases involving adoption or a name change, enter the family name used after the adoption or name change.

Box 28 – **Given names (begin with the usual given name; separate each given name with a comma)**

The usual given name is a name that, in addition to being mentioned in the act, is used on a daily basis to identify the person and confirm his or her identity.

Section 4: Applicant's declaration

Box 44 – **Applicant's signature**

The signature of the applicant (the person named in Section 1 of the form) is mandatory. If the declaration is not signed, your application will be refused.

Section 5: Methods of payment

Box 47 – **Credit card**

The credit cardholder's signature is mandatory even if he or she also signed as the applicant. Without the cardholder's signature in the appropriate place, the application will be refused.

To reach us

By phone

Québec:	418 644–4545
Montréal:	514 644–4545
Elsewhere in Québec:	1 877 644–4545
Teleprinter (TTY):	1 800 361–9596

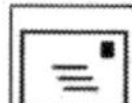

By mail

Directeur de l'état civil
2535, boulevard Laurier
Québec (Québec) G1V 5C6

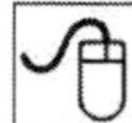

By e-mail

etatcivil@dec.gouv.qc.ca

Website

www.etatcivil.gouv.qc.ca

Only you, as the applicant, can obtain information on the status of your application. You must contact us by phone or go to one of our service counters.

CANADA—SASKATCHEWAN

Send your requests to:

eHealth Saskatchewan
Vital Statistics Registry
101–1445 Park Street
Regina, Saskatchewan, Canada S4N 4C5

Tel. (855) 347-5465
Fax (306) 787-2288
E-mail: VitalStatistics@eHealthsask.ca
www.ehealthsask.ca/vitalstats/Pages/default.aspx

Certificates can be ordered quickly and easily online or by mail, fax, or in person at the Customer Service Centre (1445 Park Street, Regina).

You can search their records for free to find births registered more than 100 years ago or deaths registered more than 70 years ago. Records are available from 1878. Birth records are restricted for 100 years, death records for 70 years, and marriage records for 75 years. You can, however, apply for a genealogical photocopy of a restricted record, which contains all the information that appears on the original registration and is stamped "For Genealogy Only." You can search births more than 100 years old and deaths more than 70 years old online at http://genealogy.ehealthsask.ca/vsgs_srch.aspx (marriages more than 75 years old will be available soon).

Cost for a certified Birth Certificate	Can$25.00
Cost for a certified Marriage Certificate	Can$25.00
Cost for a certified Death Certificate	Can$25.00
Cost for a certified Photocopy	Can$50.00
Cost for a Genealogical Photocopy	Can$50.00

For additional assistance, contact:

Embassy of Canada
501 Pennsylvania Avenue, NW
Washington, DC 20001

Tel. (202) 682-1740

Vital Statistics
Payment Information Form

Payment Method

Total Amount Enclosed / Authorized $ ____________________

☐ Visa ☐ MasterCard Card Number ____________________ Expiry Date ______/______

Name on Card ____________________ Cardholder Signature ____________________

Payment

- **Do not send cash.** It is against postal regulations to send cash through the mail.
- Persons living outside of Canada should obtain a Canadian money order.
- Payments by Cheque or Money Order should be made payable to eHealth Saskatchewan.

Priority Service – Fee $30.00

- Delivery time for Priority Service is posted on our website.
  - *For existing registered events*, the posted time represents the expected number of days it will take to issue the product(s) after receiving the application(s).
  - *For unregistered events*, product(s) will be issued within the number of days posted following completion of the registration.
- The products will be sent by courier to the applicant. eHealth is not responsible for delays in shipping.
- Products are also available for pick-up during regular business hours in Regina only.
- The Priority Service fee is charged on a per order basis in addition to the cost of requested products.
- Priority Service may not be available or may be charged more than once, particularly for large orders and those with multiple delivery destinations.

Certificates – Fee $25.00

- The certificate contains information extracted from the original registration.

Certified Photocopies of Registration – Fee $50.00

- A certified photocopy of a registration is a duplicate of the original registration.

Genealogical Photocopies of Registration – Fee $50.00

- A genealogical photocopy of a Registration is a duplicate of the original registration and is stamped "For Genealogy Only".

Registration Search – Fee $25.00 for each search period of 3 or less consecutive years

- The fee will be charged if a search of the registry is requested and no product is issued.

Vital Statistics Registry
101 - 1445 Park Street, Regina, Saskatchewan, S4N 4C5
Toll Free: 1-855-347-5465 Fax: 306-787-2288

APPLICATION FOR BIRTH CERTIFICATE

Please read instructions carefully and print clearly. Incomplete applications WILL NOT be processed.
If boxes marked with an "*" are not filled in, your application is incomplete.

ORDER DETAILS

1 **PRODUCT DETAILS**

Type of Product Requested	**Quantity*	*Type of Product Requested*	**Quantity*
Short Form Birth Certificate ($25.00)		Certified Photocopy of Registration of Live Birth ($50.00)	
Long Form Birth Certificate ($25.00) *(Needed for Passport if 16 and under)*		Genealogical Photocopy of Registration of Live Birth ($50.00)	

BIRTH DETAILS

2 ***DETAILS OF PERSON NAMED ON CERTIFICATE ["Subject"]***

3 ***Subject's Last Name at Birth***	4 ***Subject's First Given Name***	5 Subject's Second Given Name(s)
6 Subject's Current Last Name	7 ***Subject's Sex*** ☐ Female ☐ Male	8 ***Subject's Date of Birth*** - Month/Day/Year

9 ***Subject's Place of Birth*** - City/Town/Village/Other , Saskatchewan	10 Birth Registration Number	11 Sibling Order

MOTHER'S DETAILS

12 ***Mother's Last Name at Birth***	13 ***Mother's First Given Name***	14 Mother's Second Given Name(s)
15 Mother's Current Last Name	16 Mother's Date of Birth Month/Day/Year	17 ***Mother's Place of Birth*** - City/Town/Village/Other AND Province/State AND Country

FATHER'S DETAILS

18 Father's Last Name at Birth (If on Birth Registration)	19 Father's First Given Name	20 Father's Second Given Name(s)
21 Father's Current Last Name	22 Father's Date of Birth Month/Day/Year	23 Father's Place of Birth - City/Town/Village/Other AND Province/State AND Country

OTHER PARENTS' DETAILS

24 Other Parent's Last Name at Birth (If on Birth Registration)	25 Other Parent's First Given Name	26 Other Parent's Second Given Name(s)
27 Other Parent's Current Last Name	28 Other Parent's Date of Birth Month/Day/Year	29 Other Parent's Place of Birth - City/Town/Village/Other AND Province/State AND Country
30 Other Parent's Last Name at Birth (If on Birth Registration)	31 Other Parent's First Given Name	32 Other Parent's Second Given Name(s)
33 Other Parent's Current Last Name	34 Other Parent's Date of Birth Month/Day/Year	35 Other Parent's Place of Birth - City/Town/Village/Other AND Province/State AND Country

APPLICANT DETAILS MAILING ADDRESS DETAILS

36 ***THE FOLLOWING MUST BE COMPLETED BY THE PERSON APPLYING FOR THE BIRTH CERTIFICATE ["Applicant"]***
*A readable photocopy of the Applicant's identification MUST be attached to this Application for Birth Certificate.

37 ***Applicant's First Given Name***	38 Applicant's Second Given Name(s)	39 ***Applicant's Current Last Name***

40 ***Mailing Address*** - Apartment #- Street # - Street Name - P.O. Box	41 If Mailing Address is to a Business, Attention:

42 ***City/Town/Village/Other***	43 ***Province/State***	44 ***Country***	45 Postal / Zip Code

46 Telephone - Home	47 Telephone - ☐ Work ☐ Cell	48 Email

49 ***Reason Why Certificate is Requested***	50 ***Applicant's Relationship to Person Named on Certificate*** ☐ Myself ☐ Mother ☐ Father ☐ Other Parent ☐ Other: ____

51 ***Method of Delivery Requested*** ☐ Mailed ☐ Picked Up ☐ Priority Service: *Additional $30.00*	52 ***Payment Method: CANADIAN FUNDS ONLY*** ☐ Debit or ☐ Cash - In Person Only ☐ Cheque or ☐ Money Order - Payable to eHealth Saskatchewan <u>*IF*</u> ☐ Visa , ☐ MasterCard *(Complete Payment Information Form and attach to Application)*	53 ***Payment Amount***

54 ***Signature of Applicant***	55 ***Date Applicant Signed Application*** - Month/Day/Year

56 Reg Date: **FOR OFFICE USE ONLY** Reg #:
Date Received: Date of Pick-Up:

Vital Statistics Registry
101 - 1445 Park Street, Regina, Saskatchewan, S4N 4C5
Toll Free: 1-855-347-5465 Fax: 306-787-2288

APPLICATION FOR MARRIAGE CERTIFICATE

Please read instructions carefully and print clearly. Incomplete applications WILL NOT be processed.
If boxes marked with an "" are not filled in, your application is incomplete.*

ORDER DETAILS

1 **PRODUCT DETAILS**

Type of Product Requested	****Quantity***	***Type of Product Requested***	****Quantity***
Small Size Marriage Certificate ($25.00)		Certified Photocopy of Registration of Marriage ($50.00)	
Framing Size Marriage Certificate ($25.00)		Genealogical Photocopy of Registration of Marriage ($50.00)	

MARRIAGE DETAILS

2 ***DETAILS OF PERSON NAMED ON CERTIFICATE ["Subject"]***

3 ****Subject's Last Name Prior to this Marriage***
4 ****Subject's First Given Name***
5 Subject's Second Given Name(s)
6 Subject's Last Name at Birth
7 Subject's Sex ☐ Female ☐ Male
8 ****Subject's Date of Marriage*** - Month/Day/Year
9 ****Subject's Place of Marriage*** - City/Town/Village/Other
, Saskatchewan
10 Marriage Registration Number
11 Subject's Date of Birth - Month/Day/Year
12 Subject's Place of Birth - City/Town/Village/Other AND Province/State AND Country

SPOUSE DETAILS

13 ****Spouse's Last Name Prior to this Marriage***
14 ****Spouse's First Given Name***
15 Spouse's Second Given Name(s)
16 Spouse's Last Name at Birth
17 Spouse's Sex ☐ Female ☐ Male
18 Spouse's Date of Birth - Month/Day/Year
19 Spouse's Place of Birth – City/Town/Village/Other AND Province/State AND Country

APPLICANT DETAILS MAILING ADDRESS DETAILS

20 ***THE FOLLOWING MUST BE COMPLETED BY THE PERSON APPLYING FOR THE MARRIAGE CERTIFICATE ["Applicant"]***
*A readable photocopy of the Applicant's identification MUST be attached to this Application for Marriage Certificate.

21 ****Applicant's First Given Name***
22 Applicant's Second Given Name(s)
23 ****Applicant's Current Last Name***
24 ****Mailing Address*** - Apartment #- Street # - Street Name - P.O. Box
25 If Mailing Address is to a Business, Attention:
26 ****City/Town/Village/Other***
27 ****Province/State***
28 ****Country***
29 Postal / Zip Code
30 Telephone - Home
31 Telephone - ☐ Work ☐ Cell
32 Email
33 ****Reason Why Certificate is Requested***
34 ****Applicant's Relationship to Person Named on Certificate***
☐ Myself ☐ Daughter ☐ Son
☐ Other: ______________________
35 ****Method of Delivery Requested***
☐ Mailed ☐ Picked Up
☐ Priority Service: *Additional $30.00*
36 ****Payment Method: CANADIAN FUNDS ONLY***
☐ Debit or ☐ Cash - In Person Only ☐ Cheque or ☐ Money Order - Payable to eHealth Saskatchewan
IF ☐ Visa, ☐ MasterCard ***(Complete Payment Information Form and attach to Application)***
37 ****Payment Amount***
38 ****Signature of Applicant***
39 ****Date Applicant Signed Application*** - Month/Day/Year

40 **FOR OFFICE USE ONLY**

Reg Date:
Reg #:
Date Received:
Date of Pick-Up:

Vital Statistics Registry
101 - 1445 Park Street, Regina, Saskatchewan, S4N 4C5
Toll Free: 1-855-347-5465 Fax: 306-787-2288

APPLICATION FOR DEATH CERTIFICATE

Please read instructions carefully and print clearly. Incomplete applications WILL NOT be processed.
If boxes marked with an "*" are not filled in, your application is incomplete.

ORDER DETAILS

1 **PRODUCT DETAILS**			
Type of Product Requested	**Quantity*	*Type of Product Requested*	**Quantity*
Framing Size Certificate ($25.00)		Certified Photocopy of Registration of Death ($50.00)	
		Genealogical Photocopy of Registration of Death ($50.00)	

DEATH DETAILS

2 ***DETAILS OF PERSON NAMED ON CERTIFICATE ["Subject"]***

3 ***Subject's Last Name at Death***	4 ***Subject's First Given Name***	5 Subject's Second Given Name(s)
6 Subject's Last Name at Birth	7 ***Subject's Sex*** ☐ Female ☐ Male	8 ***Subject's Date of Death** - Month/Day/Year*
9 ***Subject's Place of Death** - City/Town/Village/Other*, Saskatchewan		10 Death Registration Number
11 Subject's Date of Birth - Month/Day/Year	12 Subject's Place of Birth - City/Town/Village/Other AND Province/State AND Country	13 ***Subject's Age at Death***
14 Subject's Address Prior to Death – Street Address AND City/town/Village/Other AND Province/State AND Country		15 ***Subject's Marital Status*** ☐ Never Married ☐ Married ☐ Widowed ☐ Divorced ☐ Common Law

SPOUSE'S DETAILS

16 Subject's Spouse's Last Name at Birth	17 Spouse's First Given Name	18 Spouse's Second Given Name(s)	19 Spouse's Current Last Name
20 Common Law Spouse's Last Name at Birth	21 Common Law Spouse's First Given Name	22 Common Law Spouse's Second Given Name(s)	23 Common Law Spouse's Current Last Name

MOTHER'S DETAILS

24 Subject's Mother's Last Name at Birth	25 Mother's First Given Name	26 Mother's Second Given Name(s)	27 Mother's Current Last Name
28 Mother's Place of Birth – City/Town/Village/Other AND Province/State AND Country			

FATHER'S DETAILS

29 Subject's Father's Last Name At Birth	30 Father's First Given Name	31 Father's Second Given Name(s)	32 Father's Current Last Name
33 Father's Place of Birth – City/Town/Village/Other AND Province/State AND Country			

APPLICANT DETAILS MAILING ADDRESS DETAILS

34 ***THE FOLLOWING MUST BE COMPLETED BY THE PERSON APPLYING FOR THE DEATH CERTIFICATE ["Applicant"]***
*A readable photocopy of the Applicant's identification MUST be attached to this Application for Death Certificate.

35 ***Applicant's First Given Name***	36 Applicant's Second Given Name(s)		37 ***Applicant's Current Last Name***
38 ***Mailing Address** -* Apartment # - Street # - Street Name - P.O. Box			39 If Mailing Address is to a Business, Attention:
40 ***City/Town/Village/Other***	41 ***Province/State***	42 ***Country***	43 Postal / Zip Code
44 Telephone - Home	45 Telephone - ☐ Work ☐ Cell	46 Email	
47 ***Reason Why Certificate is Requested***		48 ***Applicant's Relationship to Person Named on Certificate*** ☐ Spouse ☐ Mother ☐ Father ☐ Other Parent ☐ Daughter ☐ Son ☐ Other: ______	
49 ***Method of Delivery Requested*** ☐ Mailed ☐ Picked Up ☐ Priority Service: *Additional $30.00*	50 ***Payment Method: CANADIAN FUNDS ONLY*** ☐ Debit or ☐ Cash - In Person Only ☐ Cheque or ☐ Money Order - Payable to eHealth Saskatchewan; IF ☐ Visa, ☐ MasterCard *(Complete Payment Information Form and attach to Application)*		51 ***Payment Amount***
52 ***Signature of Applicant***		53 ***Date Applicant Signed Application** - Month/Day/Year*	

54 **FOR OFFICE USE ONLY**
Reg Date: Reg #:
Date Received: Date of Pick-Up:

CANADA—YUKON

Send your requests to:

Yukon Health and Human Resources
Division of Vital Statistics
(Location: 4th Floor, 204 Lambert Street)
P.O. Box 2703
Whitehorse, Yukon, Canada Y1A 2C6

Tel. (867) 667-5207
Fax (867) 393-6486
E-mail: Vital.Statistics@gov.yk.ca
www.hss.gov.yk.ca/programs/vitalstats/

The Vital Statistics Agency has records of birth, marriage, and death occurring in Yukon since 1896 (some events occurring during that time were not registered). Birth and marriage certificates are issued in a wallet size and framing size. The framing size is a more complete document. A photocopy of the original birth or marriage certificate is also available, but it is a restricted document.

Cost for a certified Birth Certificate	Can$10.00
Cost for a wallet-size Birth Certificate	Can$10.00
Cost for a certified Marriage Certificate	Can$10.00
Cost for a wallet-size Marriage Certificate	Can$10.00
Cost for a certified Death Certificate	Can$10.00

For additional assistance, contact:

Embassy of Canada
501 Pennsylvania Avenue, NW
Washington, DC 20001

Tel. (202) 682-1740

Health and Social Services
Vital Statistics
Santé et Affaires sociales
Statistiques de l'état civil

APPLICATION FOR CERTIFICATE OR SEARCH

Box 2703, Whitehorse, Yukon Y1A 2C6
(867) 667-5207, toll free 1-800-661-0408

Note: Certificates may only be issued for births, marriages and deaths which have occurred in the Yukon. The fee for each certificate is $10.

*PLEASE READ NOTES ON REVERSE OF THIS FORM.

DEMANDE DE CERTIFICAT OU DE RECHERCHE

C.P. 2703, Whitehorse (Yukon) Y1A 2C6
867-667-5207, sans frais 1-800-661-0408

Remarque : On ne peut délivrer de certificat que pour les naissances, les mariages et les décès survenus au Yukon. Le droit pour chaque certificat est de 10 $.

**VOIR AU VERSO.*

Incomplete applications may cause delay.
Des renseignements incomplets peuvent retarder le traitement de la demande.

Please indicate type and number of certificates required
Veuillez indiquer le type et le nombre de certificats demandés

BIRTH • *NAISSANCE*

If birth certificate(s) required, complete this section (please print).
Pour un certificat de naissance, remplir cette partie (en lettres détachées).

Surname (if married, give surname at birth) • *Nom (dans le cas d'une personne mariée, nom à la naissance)* | Given names • *Prénom(s)* | M • *H* | F • *F*

Year • *Année* | Month • *Mois* by name • *(en lettres)* | Day • *Jour* | Place of birth (city, town, village) • *Lieu de naissance (ville/village)* | Territory/province • *Territoire/province*

Birth surname of parent • *Nom du parent à la naissance* | Given names • *Prénom(s)* | Birthplace of parent • *Lieu de naissance du parent*

Birth surname of parent • *Nom du parent à la naissance* | Given names • *Prénom(s)* | Birthplace of parent • *Lieu de naissance du parent*

Individual Information *Certificat abrégé* ______
Includes Parental Information *Certificat détaillé* ______
Restricted photocopy *Photocopie à usage restreint* ______

No. of older siblings born to this mother *Nombre de frères et sœurs plus âgés nés de la même mère* ______

MARRIAGE • *MARIAGE*

If marriage certificate(s) required, complete this section (please print).
Pour un certificat de mariage, remplir cette partie (en lettres détachées).

Surname • *Nom* | Given names • *Prénom(s)* | Birthplace • *Lieu de naissance* | M • *H* ☐ | F • *F* ☐

Surname • *Nom* | Given names • *Prénom(s)* | Birthplace • *Lieu de naissance* | M • *H* ☐ | F • *F* ☐

Year • *Année* | Month • *Mois* by name • *(en lettres)* | Day • *Jour* | Place of marriage (city, town, village) • *Lieu du mariage (ville/village)* | Territory/province • *Territoire/province*

Wallet *Portefeuille* ______
Framing *Encadrement* ______
Restricted photocopy *Photocopie à usage restreint* ______

DEATH • *DÉCÈS*

If death certificate(s) required, complete this section (please print).
Pour un certificat de décès, remplir cette partie (en lettres détachées).

Surname of deceased • *Nom de la personne décédée* | Given names • *Prénom(s)* | Age • *Âge* | M • *H* ☐ | F • *F* ☐

Year • *Année* | Month • *Mois* by name • *(en lettres)* | Day • *Jour* | Place of death (city, town, village) • *Lieu du décès (ville/village)* | Territory/province • *Territoire/province*

Permanent residence of deceased prior to death • *Résidence permanente de la personne décédée avant son décès* | Marital status • *État civil*

Framing *Encadrement* ______

Please indicate the reason for application • *Veuillez indiquer le motif de la demande*

Telephone • *Téléphone*
Daytime • *Jour* (   ) Evening • *Soir* (   )

Language preferred French__________ English__________ • *Langue de correspondance Français__________ Anglais__________*

State relationship to person named • *Indiquez votre lien de parenté avec la personne susmentionnée*

Remarks • *Remarques*

Signature of applicant • *Signature du demandeur* [1]

X

Year • *Année* | Month • *Mois* | Day • *Jour* | *Fee enclosed with this application **Droits joints à la présente demande* $

Credit Card No. • *Numéro de carte de crédit*

Expiry Date • *Date d'expiration* | 3-4 Digit Security No. (CVD#) • *Code de validation*

☐ Visa ☐ Master Card ☐ American Express

MAILING ADDRESS *ADRESSE POSTALE*

Name • *Nom*

Address • *Adresse*

City • *Ville/village* | Territory, province • *Territoire/province* | Postal code • *Code postal*

Signature • *Signature*

[1] *Dans le présent document, les expressions désignant les personnes visent à la fois les hommes et les femmes.*

*Please read notes on reverse of this form • **Veuillez lire les remarques au verso*

YG(3385Q)F2 Rev. 10/2010

IMPORTANT

It is against postal regulations to send cash. Please make your **cheque** or **money order** payable to **Government of the Yukon** and send to:

Government of the Yukon
Vital Statistics
Box 2703
Whitehorse, Yukon Y1A 2C6

Certificates may also be ordered by fax or phone. Payment by Visa, MC, American Express.

(867) 667-5207
1-800-661-0408 EXT. 5207 (YUKON ONLY)
Fax: (867) 393-6486
email: Vital.Statistics@gov.yk.ca
Internet Address: www.hss.gov.yk.ca

Notes

1. Certificates can only be issued for births, marriages, and deaths if they **occurred in the Yukon**.
2. **Birth certificates**
   - Individual Information birth certificates include the following information: full name of the individual, date of birth, place of birth, sex, registration number and registration date.
   - Includes Parental Information birth certificate contains the following additional information: names and birthplaces of parent(s).
   - Birth certificates for married persons are issued only in their surname at birth.
3. **Marriage certificates**
   - Wallet-size certificates contain the following information: names of the parties married, date of marriage, place of marriage, registration number and registration date.
   - Framing-size certificates contain the following additional information: birth places of parties.
   - The ages of the parties do not appear and the married surname of either party does not appear.
4. A **restricted photocopy** contains all the information appearing on the original registration. They are by law for restricted use only. If you believe you need such a certificate, please state your reason.
5. In the Yukon, Vital Statistics can be reached toll free through the Yukon government inquiry centre during weekday office hours. The number is 1-800-661-0408. (Note: This number is not applicable outside of the Yukon.) Outside Yukon - (867) 667-5207
6. **Fee schedule**
   - The fee for each certificate is $10. The fee for a search is $1 per year to a maximum of $20. This applies only where information is not known.
7. **For urgent requests,** contact Vital Statistics for delivery options.

IMPORTANT

Le règlement sur les postes interdit l'envoi d'espèces. Veuillez faire votre ***chèque*** *ou votre* ***mandat poste*** *payable au* ***Gouvernement du Yukon*** *et l'envoyer à l'adresse suivante :*

Gouvernement du Yukon
Statistiques de l'état civil
C.P. 2703
Whitehorse, Yukon Y1A 2C6

On peut aussi commander des certificats par télécopieur ou par téléphone en payant avec Visa, MC ou American Express.

867-667-5207
1-800-661-0408, poste 5207 (au Yukon seulement)
Télécopieur : 867-393-6486
Courriel : Vital.statistics@gov.yk.ca
Internet : www.hss.gov.yk.ca

Remarques

1. *On ne peut délivrer de certificat que pour les naissances, les mariages et les décès qui sont* ***survenus au Yukon****.*
2. ***Certificat de naissance***
   - *Le certificat abrégé contient les renseignements suivants : nom au complet de la personne, date de naissance, lieu de naissance, sexe, numéro d'enregistrement et date d'enregistrement.*
   - *Le certificat détaillé contient les renseignements supplémentaires suivants : nom et lieu de naissance des parents.*
   - *Le certificat de naissance d'une personne mariée n'est délivré qu'en son nom de famille à la naissance.*
3. ***Certificat de mariage***
   - *Le certificat de mariage de dimensions portefeuille contient les renseignements suivants : noms des parties, date du mariage, lieu du mariage, numéro d'enregistrement et date d'enregistrement.*
   - *Le certificat de mariage à encadrer contient les renseignements supplémentaires suivants : lieux de naissance des parties.*
   - *L'âge des parties et le nom de famille adopté par l'une ou l'autre partie à la suite du mariage n'y figurent pas.*
4. ***Une photocopie à usage restreint*** *contient tous les renseignements figurant sur l'enregistrement original. La loi en restreint l'usage. Si vous croyez avoir besoin d'un tel certificat, veuillez en indiquer le motif.*
5. *Au Yukon, on peut communiquer avec les Statistiques de l'état civil en appelant sans frais le service de renseignements du gouvernement du Yukon pendant les heures de bureau. Le numéro à composer est le 1-800-661-0408. (Remarque : Ce numéro ne s'applique pas à l'extérieur du Yukon.) À l'extérieur du Yukon - 867-667-5207*
6. ***Tarif***
   - *Le droit à acquitter pour chaque certificat est de 10 $. Le droit à acquitter pour une recherche est d'un dollar par année jusqu'à concurrence de 20 $. Ces frais de recherche s'appliquent seulement si on ne connaît pas les renseignements.*
7. ***Pour les demandes urgentes, communiquez avec les Statistiques de l'état civil.***

			$
Number of certificates requested *Nombre de certificats demandés*	________	x 10.00 =	________
Request for special delivery *Demande d'envoi par exprès*	________	x 15.00 =	________
Transfer this amount to the front of this form under "Fee enclosed with this application." *Reporter ce montant au recto, à la case « Droits joints à la présente demande ».*	▶	**Total** ***Total***	________

Personal information is being collected under the authority of the *Vital Statistics Act* for the release of Birth, Dealth and Marriage information. For further information, contact the Deputy Registrar, Vital Statistics, at (867)667-5207 or toll free at 1-800-661-0408, or write to Vital Statistics, Box 2703, Whitehorse, Yukon Y1A 2C6.

Certificates contain information exactly as recorded on the original registration filed in our office.

Les renseignements personnels fournis dans les présentes sont recueillis en application de la Loi sur les statistiques de l'état civil *aux fins de publication de données concernant les naissances, les décès et les mariages. Pour obtenir de plus amples renseignements sur le sujet, communiquez avec le registraire adjoint, Statistiques de l'état civil, par téléphone au 867-667-5207 ou, sans frais, au 1-800-661-0408, ou par écrit à l'adresse C.P. 2703, Whitehorse (Yukon) Y1A 2C6.*

Le certificat contient les renseignements tels qu'ils figurent dans l'enregistrement original conservé à notre bureau.

CAPE VERDE

Send your requests to:

Direccao Geral dos Registos e Notariado
Ministerio de Justiça
C.P. 204
Praia, Cape Verde

Birth and marriage records are available through 1910 for family members. All death records are available. Certificates are available from the Conservatória dos Registos of the island where the event occurred. Older records are held by the Arquivo Historico Nacional (C.P. 321, Praia, Santiago, Republica de Cabo Verde).

For additional assistance, contact:

Embassy of the Republic of Cape Verde — Tel. (202) 965-6820
3415 Massachusetts Ave., NW
Washington, D.C. 20007

CAYMAN ISLANDS

Send your requests to:

Registrar General — Tel. (345) 244-3404
Tower Building
George Town, Grand Cayman
Cayman Islands, BWI

Vital registration in the Cayman Islands is considered to be comprehensive. No forms are required to apply for copies of vital records.

CENTRAL AFRICAN REPUBLIC

Send your requests to:

Service de l'État Civil et du Recensement Demographique
B.P. 689
Bangui, Central African Republic

Vital registration began in 1940 in the Central African Republic for French citizens and foreigners. By 1966 registration expanded to the entire population. Certificates may be available from the Mairie of the municipality or the Sous-Prefecture of the rural area where the event took place. Certificates of birth, death, marriage, and divorce for French nationals who were born, married, etc., in the Central African Republic may be obtained from the Consular General de France, B.P. 784, Bangui, within one year of the event, or from the Ministère des Affaires étrangères, État Civil, Falles Brancos, Nantes, France, if more than one year after the event.

For additional assistance, contact:

Embassy of the Central African Republic — Tel. (202) 483-7800
1618 22nd Street, NW
Washington, DC 20008

CHAD

Send your requests to:

Registrar
Direction de la Statistique, des Études Économiques et Demographiques
B.P. 453
N'Djamena, Chad

Vital records in Chad are generally unavailable, since all records are presumed destroyed as a result of civil strife that occurred in Chad between February and December 1980.

For additional assistance, contact:

Embassy of the Republic of Chad — Tel. (202) 462-4009
2002 R Street, NW
Washington, DC 20009

CHILE

Send your requests to:

Servicio de Registro Civil e Identificación — www.registrocivil.cl/
Ministerio de Justicia
Huérfanos 1560
Santiago, Chile

Church registers date from the 1500s, while vital registration began January 1, 1885. Certificates can be ordered online from the Servicio de Registro Civil website.

For additional assistance, contact:

Embassy of Chile — Tel. (202) 785-1746
1732 Massachusetts Avenue, NW
Washington, DC 20036

CHINA

Send your requests to:

Population Registration
Ministry of Public Security
(City), China

or

Section Chief
Administrative Division for Population Registration
Third Bureau
Ministry of Public Security
14 Dong Chang An Jie
Beijing, China

China uses a household registration system to record and identify each person in China. China has kept family registers for the past 4,000 years. Most vital records can be obtained from one of China's notarial offices (Gong Zheng Chu). All Chinese documentation to be used abroad is processed through the notary offices and issued in the form of notarial certificates. Notarial offices are located in all major Chinese cities and in rural county seats.

For direct assistance with Chinese genealogical research, contact:

Genealogical Research Center
Shanghai Library
1555 Huaihaizhong Road
Shanghai 200031, China

www.library.sh.cn/english/

Shanghai Library has more than 110,000 volumes of Chinese genealogy and close to 50,000 genealogies extending back 1,000 years.

For additional assistance, contact:

Embassy of the People's Republic of China
2300 Connecticut Avenue, NW
Washington, DC 20008

Tel. (202) 328-2500

CHINA—HONG KONG

Send your requests to:

The Births and Deaths General Register Office
3/F, Low Block
Queensway Government Offices
66 Queensway
Hong Kong (HKSAR), China

Tel. (011) (852) 2867-2785;
(011) (852) 2824-6111
www.info.gov.hk/immd/

Church registers date from the colonial period, while vital registration in Hong Kong began in 1872. Requests for certificates are a two-step process. For births and adoptions, use form BDR 40 to search for a record and form BDR 87 to request a copy of the located record. For deaths use search form BDR 41 and copy request form BDR 62. Requests for searches and copies of marriage records require only one form, MR 10. Birth and death certificates are available for any person who was born or who died in Hong Kong since 1872, except during the Japanese occupation of Hong Kong (1941–1945). Marriage records are available from 1945; pre-war records of the Registrar of Marriages are not normally available but in certain cases may be obtained from the church where the ceremony was performed.

Personal identification cards have been issued since 1949. On July 1, 1987, special "Hong Kong Permanent Identity Cards" were issued as a guarantee of the "right of abode in Hong Kong." Each person receives an identity card at age 11. Currently the aged, blind, infirm, and Vietnamese refugees are excluded from receiving an identity card.

For direct assistance with Chinese genealogical research, contact:

Genealogical Research Center
Shanghai Library
1555 Huaihaizhong Road
Shanghai 200031, China

www.library.sh.cn/english/

Shanghai Library has more than 110,000 volumes of Chinese genealogy and close to 50,000 genealogies extending back 1,000 years.

For additional assistance, contact:

Embassy of the People's Republic of China
2300 Connecticut Avenue, NW
Washington, DC 20008

Tel. (202) 328-2500

CHINA—MACAU

Send your requests to:

Conservatória do Registo Civil de Macau
Secretario-Adjunto para a Administracao
Rua do Campo, No. 162
Edificio Administração Pública, 15°
Andar, Macau, China

Church registers date from the colonial period, while vital registration in Macau began in 1887. The Conservatória has birth records from 1890 and marriage, death, and church records from 1900 to the present. In May 1987 two separate departments were created: the Birth & Death Registry, and the Marriage Registry.

For direct assistance with Chinese genealogical research, contact:

Genealogical Research Center
Shanghai Library
1555 Huaihaizhong Road
Shanghai 200031, China

www.library.sh.cn/english/

Shanghai Library has more than 110,000 volumes of Chinese genealogy and close to 50,000 genealogies extending back 1,000 years.

For additional assistance, contact:

Embassy of the People's Republic of China
2300 Connecticut Avenue, NW
Washington, DC 20008

Tel. (202) 328-2500

CHINA—TAIWAN

Send your requests to:

Department of Civil Affairs
9F, No.1, Shifu Rd., Xinyi District
Taipei City 110, Taiwan
Republic of China

China uses a household registration system to record and identify each person in China. China has kept family registers for the past 4,000 years. Currently this is handled by the local registration office and is considered to be comprehensive.

For direct assistance with Chinese genealogical research, contact:

Genealogical Research Center
Shanghai Library
1555 Huaihaizhong Road
Shanghai 200031, China

www.library.sh.cn/english/

Shanghai Library has more than 110,000 volumes of Chinese genealogy and close to 50,000 genealogies extending back 1,000 years.

For additional assistance, contact:

Embassy of the People's Republic of China
2300 Connecticut Avenue, NW
Washington, DC 20008

Tel. (202) 328-2500

COLOMBIA

Send your requests to:

Registraduria Nacional del Estado Civil
AC 26 #51-50 - CAN
Bogota, Colombia

www.registraduria.gov.co

Copies of vital records are available from the notary who registered the event. Church registers date from the 1500s, vital records from June 3, 1852.

For additional assistance, contact:

Embassy of Colombia
2118 Leroy Place, NW
Washington, DC 20008

Tel. (202) 387-8338

COMOROS

Send your requests to:

Registrar General
Moroni, Comoros

Previously under French control, Comoros became independent in 1975. Its official language is Arabic. Vital registration in Comoros is not considered to be comprehensive.

For additional assistance, contact:

Embassy of the Federal and Islamic Republic of the Comoros
420 E. 50th Street
New York, NY 10022

Tel. (212) 750-1637

REPUBLIC OF CONGO

Send your requests to:

Mayor (la Mairie)
(Town), Republic of Congo

Birth, death, marriage, and divorce certificates are obtainable from the office of the mayor (la Mairie) where the event took place. Vital registration began in 1922 for all residents of the Congo. Certificates of birth, marriage, death, and divorce for French persons who were born in the Congo before independence (August 15, 1960) should write to Ministère des Affaires Étrangères, État-Civil, Falles Branxos, Nannies, France. French people born in the Congo after independence should write to the Consulat de France at Brazzaville or Pointe-Noire, depending on the consular district in which the act took place.

For additional assistance, contact:

Embassy of the Republic of Congo
4891 Colorado Avenue, NW
Washington, DC 20011

Tel. (202) 726-5500

DEMOCRATIC REPUBLIC OF CONGO (former Zaire)

Send your requests to:

Registrar (Officier de l'État Civil)
(District), Democratic Republic of Congo

Birth certificates (Actes de Naissance or Extraits d'Actes de Naissance), together with records of marriage, death, and divorce, are maintained by the Registrar (Officier de l'État Civil) in the district where the event took place. The first birth registers were inaugurated on January 7, 1886. They do not include natives of the Democratic Republic of the Congo still living in tribal conditions.

For additional assistance, contact:

Embassy of the Democratic Republic of Congo — Tel. (202) 234-7690
1726 M Street, NW
Washington, DC 20036

COSTA RICA

Send your requests to:

Dirección de Registro Civil y Notariado — www.tse.go.cr/
Tribunal Supremo de Elecciones
AP 10218-1000
San José, Costa Rica

The Civil Registry of San Jose (Registro Civil) issues certificates of all births in Costa Rica subsequent to January 1, 1888, the date the registry was established. Births prior to that date may be evidenced by a baptismal certificate (Fe de Bautismo) issued by an ecclesiastical authority of the Roman Catholic Church. The Civil Registry also issues marriage, death, divorce, and adoption certificates. Church registers date from 1594, while modern vital registration began in the 1880s and is currently considered to be comprehensive.

For additional assistance, contact:

Embassy of Costa Rica — Tel. (202) 234-2945
2114 S Street, NW
Washington, DC 20008

CÔTE D'IVOIRE

Send your requests to:

Monsieur le Maire
(Town), Côte d'Ivoire

Vital registration began in 1933 for French citizens, was expanded in 1950 to include residents within 15 miles of registration centers, and was extended in 1964 to the entire nation. Birth, death, and marriage certificates can be obtained from Monsieur le Maire, or Monsieur le sous-Préfet, or the Préfet of the locality where the event took place. Copies of divorce records (Jugement de Divorce) may be obtained from the Greffe du Tribunal Civil where the judgment was pronounced. All civil documents originating from the northern half of the country (above the UN Forces-monitored Zone of Confidence) should be treated as suspect: Due to loss, theft, and destruction of many civil records registries in the North during the period of rebel control, many of these documents are unverifiable.

For additional assistance, contact:

Embassy of the Republic of Cote d'Ivoire
2424 Massachusetts Avenue, NW
Washington, DC 20008

Tel. (202) 797-0300

CROATIA

Send your requests to:

Civil Registration Office
(Town), Croatia

This country has no central office for vital records. To obtain copies of birth, marriage, and death certificates, write to the Civil Registration District Office in the town where the event occurred. Vital records are on file from 1946. Records before that were kept by the local churches.

For additional assistance, contact:

Embassy of the Republic of Croatia
2343 Massachusetts Avenue, NW
Washington, DC 20008

Tel. (202) 588-5899

CUBA

Send your requests to:

Director Registros y Notarias
Registro Civil
Ministerio de Justicia
13 Calle: O No. 216
3/23 y 25, Vedado
Havana, Cuba

While church registers date from the 1500s, modern vital registration in Cuba didn't begin until 1885. Vital registration currently is compulsory and is considered to be comprehensive. However, it is very difficult to get a vital record from the Registro Civil if you are a U.S. citizen. You might have better luck going through the parish priest, if you know the parish where the event occurred. There are some organizations in the U.S. that will help locate Cuban vital records for you, and you can contact the Cuban Interests Section (see below) for more information.

For additional assistance, contact:

Cuba Interests Section — Tel. (202) 797-8518
2630 16th Street, NW
Washington, DC 20009

CYPRUS

Send your requests to:

Registrar
District Office
(Town), Cyprus

Since July 1974 civil records for the districts of Kyrenia and Famagusta have been under Turkish-Cypriot control. The government of Cyprus cannot issue birth, death, civil marriage, or divorce certificates for these districts unless a new registration is made in the Republic of Cyprus-controlled area of the island. Certificates are available from the district where the event occurred. Civil registration began in Cyprus in 1895 for births and deaths, and in 1923 for marriages.

For additional assistance, contact:

Embassy of Cyprus — Tel. (202) 462-5772
2211 R Street, NW
Washington, DC 20008

CZECH REPUBLIC

Send your requests to:

Town Hall
(Town), Czech Republic

The certificates of birth, marriage, and death are issued by the local town hall in the place where the event occurred. Many early vital records—including those of Bohemia and Moravia, as well as the Catholic parish duplicates—are in the Czech State Archives in Prague (Milady Horakove 133, 166 21 Praha 6, Czech Republic). The State Archives will conduct basic genealogical research for a fee.

For additional assistance, contact:

Embassy of the Czech Republic
3900 Spring of Freedom Street, NW
Washington, DC 20008

Tel. (202) 274-9100

DENMARK

Send your requests to:

Lutheran Pastor
(Town), Denmark

The Lutheran church was the primary recording authority for vital information such as births, marriages, and deaths. You can obtain copies of birth, marriage, and death certificates by writing to the local Lutheran pastor. Church registers are on file from the 1600s. Divorce records are kept in the county archives (Amtsarkiver). Vital records more than 30 years old are kept at the respective provincial archives. All Danish parish registers older than 1892 are digitized and available online at www.arkivalieronline.dk/English/default.aspx.

The Danish government created the system of local municipal registers in 1924 and required the local Lutheran pastors to file copies of vital records with the registrars. In 1968, with the passage of the National Registration Act, each person in Denmark received a personal identification number and identity card. The system is now completely computerized and can be searched by the local registrars. Information is kept on all persons who have lived in Denmark since 1968, citizens, permanent resident aliens, and Danish citizens who are living outside of Denmark. Genealogists should note that each registration includes the names of the individual's parents, thus extending the reach of the register back 100 years. All births, adoptions, marriages, divorces, changes of name, and deaths are centralized in the national register. There are currently 8 million entries in the system.

For additional assistance, contact:

Royal Danish Embassy
3200 Whitehaven Street, NW
Washington, DC 20008

Tel. (202) 234-4300

DJIBOUTI

Send your requests to:

Police Nationale
Service de la Population
Section État Civile
B.P. 37
Djibouti, Djibouti

Formerly known as French Somalia and later as the French Territory of the Affars and the Issas, Djibouti became independent in 1977. Vital registration in Djibouti is not considered to be comprehensive.

For additional assistance, contact:

Embassy of Djibouti — Tel. (202) 331-0270
1156 15th Street, NW, Suite 515
Washington, DC 20005

DOMINICA

Send your requests to:

Registrar General — Tel. (767) 448-2401
High Court
Bay Front
P.O. Box 304
Rouseau, Commonwealth of Dominica
West Indies

This former British colony became independent in 1978. The Registrar General has records from April 2, 1861. The local churches also have their own records. The Registry was burned by a fire in June 1979, resulting in the destruction of many records. The current vital registration is considered to be comprehensive.

For additional assistance, contact:

Embassy of the Commonwealth of Dominica — Tel. (202) 364-6781
3216 New Mexico Avenue, NW
Washington, DC 20016

DOMINICAN REPUBLIC

Send your requests to:

Dirección General de las Oficialías del Estado Civil de la República
Calle Paul Harris esq. Horacio Vicioso
Santo Domingo, Dominican Republic

Certified copies of birth, marriage, adoption, divorce, and death certificates may be obtained by visiting the Civil Registry Office (Oficialía del Estado Civil) having jurisdiction over the area in which the event took place. Alternatively, such certificates may be obtained by writing directly to the General Directorate of Civil Registry Offices of the Republic (Dirección General de las Oficialías del Estado Civil de la República) in Santo Domingo. Church registers date from the 1500s, and vital registration began January 1, 1828. For earlier vital records, contact the Archivo General de la Nación (Cesar Nicolas Penson 91, Plaza de la Cultura, Santo Domingo, Dominican Republic).

For additional assistance, contact:

Embassy of the Dominican Republic — Tel. (202) 332-6280
1715 22nd Street, NW
Washington, DC 20008

ECUADOR

Send your requests to:

Dirección General de Registro Civil, Identificación y Cedulación
Ministerio de Gobierno
Av. Amazonas 743 y Veintimilla
Ed. Espinosa, 3er Piso
Quito, Ecuador

While church registers date from the 1500s, modern vital registration in Ecuador didn't begin until January 1, 1901. Certificates are issued by the Civil Registry Offices of each canton and parroquia for events recorded in that canton or parroquia, and also by the Dirección General de Registro Civil in Quito, which maintains records for the whole country.

Some records are available at the Archivo Municipal (National Museum Building, Quito, Ecuador).

For additional assistance, contact:

Embassy of Ecuador — Tel. (202) 234-7200
Consular Section
2535 15th Street, NW
Washington, DC 20009

EGYPT

Send your requests to:

Civil Registration Department
Ministry of Interior
Abassia, Cairo, Egypt

While Egypt had the world's first vital records registration program, dating from the period of Ramses II in 1250 BC, modern civil registration didn't begin until 1839. Only births and deaths are registered. Marriage records are kept by the denomination that performed the wedding, and divorce records are kept by the court issuing the decree. To request certificates from the Egyptian civil authorities, one must know the exact date and the specific district within Cairo, Alexandria, etc., where the event occurred.

For additional assistance, contact:

Embassy of the Arab Republic of Egypt — Tel. (202) 895-5400
3521 International Court, NW
Washington, DC 20008

EL SALVADOR

Send your requests to:

Alcadia Municipal de Registro Civil
(Town), El Salvador

Birth certificates are available for all persons born in El Salvador with the possible exception of some persons born in outlying villages or rural areas. The certificates are issued by the Civil Registry (Registro Civil) of the city or village where the birth took place. The applicant should submit his/her full name, date of birth, and names of parents to the appropriate Civil Registry. Church registers date from the 1500s, while vital registration began January 1, 1879.

For additional assistance, contact:

Embassy of El Salvador — Tel. (202) 265-9671
2308 California Street NW
Washington, DC 20008

EQUATORIAL GUINEA

Send your requests to:

Ministerio de Justicia
Malabo, Equatorial Guinea

Equatorial Guinea does not have an established system of recording vital statistics. Furthermore, most Equatoguineans do not register births, marriages, divorces, and deaths when they occur. In response to the growing demand for civil documents by Equatoguineans, civil registry offices of the Ministry of Justice around the country have recently begun to issue civil documents in standardized formats. Before civil registries began to establish birth certificates, some births were declared and maintained by the church authorities, especially the Roman Catholic Church. Equatorial Guinea, the only Spanish-speaking nation in Africa, became independent in 1968.

For additional assistance, contact:

Embassy of Equatorial Guinea — Tel. (202) 518-5700
2020 16th Street, NW
Washington, DC 20009

ERITREA

Send your requests to:

Office of Civil Status
Asmara, Eritrea

Requests for copies of birth, death, and marriage certificates should be addressed to the Office of Civil Status, Municipality of Asmara, or to the equivalent office of any other municipality in which the event was registered.

For additional assistance, contact:

Embassy of Eritrea — Tel. (202) 319-1991
1708 New Hampshire Avenue, NW
Washington, DC 20009

ESTONIA

Send your requests to:

Director General
State Office of Vital Records (Perekonnaseisuamet)
Lossi Plats
Rnu Mnt 67
EE0100 Tallinn, Estonia

Copies of birth, death, marriage, and divorce certificates can be obtained by writing to the Office of Vital Records. Adoption requests should be submitted to the Ministry of Social Welfare (Room 217, Gonsiori 29, EE0104 Tallinn, Eesti).

For additional assistance, contact:

The Estonian Historical Archives — www.eha.ee/english/english.htm
J. Liivi 4
50409 Tartu, Estonia

Embassy of Estonia — Tel. (202) 588-0101
2131 Massachusetts Avenue, NW
Washington, DC 20008

ETHIOPIA

Send your requests to:

Office of Region 14 Administration
Vital Statistics Service
Municipality of Addis Ababa
P.O. Box 356
Addis Ababa, Ethiopia

Certificates are available only to those who are physically present in Ethiopia. Requests for copies should be addressed to the Office of Region 14 Administration, Vital Statistics Service, or to the equivalent office of the municipality in which the event was registered.

For additional assistance, contact:

Ethiopian National Archives and Library
P. O. Box 717
Addis Ababa, Ethiopia

Embassy of Ethiopia — Tel. (202) 364-1200
3506 International Drive, NW
Washington, DC 20008

FIJI

Send your requests to:

Registrar General
Office of the Attorney General
Crown Law Office
P.O. Box 2213
Suva, Fiji

Tel. (011) (679) 211-598

Vital registration began in Fiji in 1874. A full register with names of siblings is available.

For additional assistance, contact:

National Archives of Fiji
P.O. Box 2125
Government Buildings
Suva, Fiji

Embassy of Fiji
2233 Wisconsin Avenue, NW
Washington, DC 20008

Tel. (202) 337-8320

FINLAND

Send your requests to:

Pastor
Lutheran Church
(Town), Finland

or

Registrar
District Registry Office (Maistraatti)
(Town), Finland

Birth, death, marriage, and divorce records in English can be obtained by mail or in person from the local civil registry office. Records before September 30, 1999, are also available from local Lutheran or Orthodox Church officials (kirkkoherranvirasto). Over 90 percent of Finland's vital records are registered by the Lutheran Church. Church registers date back to 1686. Non-Lutherans were allowed to register with their respective churches or the government after 1917. These records are forwarded to the Population Register Center and are not open to public inspection.

For additional assistance, contact:

Embassy of Finland
3301 Massachusetts Avenue, NW
Washington, DC 20008

Tel. (202) 298-5800

FRANCE

Send your requests to:

Le Mairie
(Town), France

There is no central office for vital records in France. Vital records are on file from the late 1700s. Current registration is considered to be comprehensive.

For additional assistance, contact:

Embassy of France
4101 Reservoir Road, NW
Washington, DC 20007

Tel. (202) 944-6000

GABON

Send your requests to:

Bureau de l'État Civil
(Town), Gabon

Certificates can be obtained from the Civil Registry Office (Bureau de l'État Civil) in the office of the mayor (Mairie) of the town where the event took place, or in the town of residence. For small towns and interior regions, the request may be addressed to the nearest Préfecture.

Vital registration in Gabon, formerly French Equatorial Africa, began in 1940 for French citizens and in 1972 for the entire population. Gabon became independent in 1960.

For additional assistance, contact:

Embassy of Gabon
2034 20th Street, NW, Suite 200
Washington, DC 20009

Tel. (202) 797-1000

THE GAMBIA

Send your requests to:

Director of Medical Services
Statistics Section
Medical and Health Department
Ministry of Health, Labour and Social Welfare
The Quadrangle
Banjul, Gambia

Tel. (011) (220) 227-872

The Gambia, formerly under British control, became independent in 1970. Birth and death records are available from the Director of Medical Services in Banjul. Certified copies of marriage certificates are obtainable from the Registrar General, Ministry of Justice, Banjul. Certified copies of Mohammedan marriage certificates are obtainable from the Khadi's Court, Independence Drive, Banjul.

For additional assistance, contact:

Embassy of The Gambia
1155 15th Street, NW, Suite 1000
Washington, DC 20005

Tel. (202) 785-1399

GEORGIA

Send your requests to:

Civil Registry Agency
Ministry of Justice
4 Vani Str.
0154 Tbilisi, Georgia

www.cra.gov.ge/

Some civil records were destroyed during World War II or during the internal conflict in Abkhazia and may not be available. Unauthenticated and uncertified copies of records may be obtained from a local ZAGS (Bureau of Acts of Civil Status) office.

For additional assistance, contact:

Embassy of Georgia
2209 Massachusetts Avenue, NW
Washington, DC 20008

Tel. (202) 387-2390

GERMANY

Send your requests to:

Standesamt
(Town), Germany

Vital records are on file from as early as 1809 but usually from 1875. There is no central office for vital records in Germany. To obtain copies of birth, marriage, and death certificates, write to the local registrar's office or the parish church in the town where the event occurred. For the former East Germany, this applies only to those civil status cases that occurred after October 2, 1990. For events occurring prior to this date in this part of Germany, documents are issued by the district office where the event occurred.

For additional assistance, contact:

Embassy of the Federal Republic of Germany
4645 Reservoir Road, NW
Washington, DC 20007

Tel. (202) 298-4000

GHANA

Send your requests to:

Registrar of Births and Deaths
Central Registry Office
Ministry of Local Government
P.O. Box M270
Accra, Ghana

While a system for vital records registration dates from 1888 in Accra and Christianborg, and was expanded to other principal towns in 1912, registration for the entire nation was not begun until 1965. The Registrar has birth records from 1912 and death records from 1888. Certificates for marriages entered under civil law are available from the Principal Registrar of Marriages, c/o Registrar General's Office, P.O. Box 118, Accra, Ghana.

For additional assistance, contact:

National Archives of Ghana
P.O. Box 3056
Accra, Ghana

Embassy of Ghana — Tel. (202) 686-4520
3512 International Drive, NW
Washington, DC 20008

GIBRALTAR

Send your requests to:

Registrar General
Registry of Births, Deaths and Marriages
Supreme Court
277 Main Street
Gibraltar

The Registrar General has birth records from October 3, 1848; stillbirth records from November 24, 1951; marriage records from April 10, 1862; and death records from September 1, 1859. Registration was not compulsory for births until January 20, 1887; marriages until July 17, 1902; and deaths until January 1, 1869. The Supreme Court has divorce records on file from November 6, 1890.

For additional assistance, contact:

Government Statistician
Statistics Office
Treasury Building
John Mackintosh Square
Gilbraltar

GREECE

Send your requests to:

Registrar
Civil Registry Office
(Town), Greece

or

Department of Civil Registry
Ministry of Internal Affairs
Stadiou 27 & Dragatsaniou 2
Klafthmonos Square
101 83 Athens, Greece

A birth or death certificate is obtainable from the local city hall (Dimarhio) or from the local president of the community (Kinotita). A marriage, birth, or death registration is also available from the Registrar's Office (Lixiarhio).

Vital registration started in 1924. Current registration is considered to be comprehensive. Before contacting the Department of Civil Registry, you should consult the local church registers. The National Library's address is Odos El Venizelu 32; 106 79 Athens, Greece.

For additional assistance, contact:

Embassy of Greece — Tel. (202) 939-1300
2221 Massachusetts Avenue, NW
Washington, DC 20008

GRENADA

Send your requests to:

Registrar General's Office — Tel. (473) 440-2030
Ministry of Health
Church Street
St. George's, Grenada
West Indies

The Registrar General has records from January 1, 1866. Current vital registration is considered to be comprehensive. The local churches also have their own records.

For additional assistance, contact:

Public Library/National Archives — Tel. (473) 440-2506
2 Carenage
St. George's, Grenada

Embassy of Grenada — Tel. (202) 265-2561
1701 New Hampshire Avenue, NW
Washington, DC 20009

GUATEMALA

Send your requests to:

Director
Registro Civil
Municipalidad de Guatemala
21 Calle 6-77 Zona 1
Guatemala City, Guatemala

Records are relatively complete in Guatemala City, but less so in some outlying towns, especially in the areas affected by the civil war. Requests should be sent to the Registro Civil (Civil Registry) in the place where the event took place or town nearest to it. While church registers date from the 1500s, vital registration in Guatemala didn't begin until 1877. Current vital registration is considered to be comprehensive.

For additional assistance, contact:

Embassy of Guatemala
Consular Section
2220 R Street, NW
Washington, DC 20008

Tel. (202) 745-4952

GUINEA

Send your requests to:

Chef de la Division
Recensement et Statistiques de la Population
Ministère de l'Intérieur et de la Sécurité
B.P. 3495
Conakry, Guinea

Individuals not physically present in the Republic of Guinea may be able to obtain certificates only if they have a family member or associate in Guinea who is willing to pursue the applications and follow up on their behalf. Records are available from the governor of the appropriate administrative region or, in the Administrative Region of Conakry, from the chief of the appropriate arrondissement. Registration began in 1979 and is not comprehensive.

For additional assistance, contact:

Archives nationales de Guinée
B.P. 1005
Conakry, Guinea

Embassy of Guinea
Consular Section
2212 Leroy Place, NW
Washington, DC 20008

Tel. (202) 986-4300

GUINEA–BISSAU

Send your requests for Birth and Death records to:

Conservatória de Registo Civil
Ministerio de Justica
Caixa Postal
Bissau, Guinea-Bissau

Send your requests for Divorce records to:

Vara Civil
Ministerio de Justica
Caixa Postal 17
Bissau, Guinea-Bissau

Vital registration began in 1976 and is not comprehensive.

For additional assistance, contact:

Institut national d'études et de recherches (INER)
Archives historiques
B.P. 112, Bairro Cobornel
Complexo Escolar 14 de Novembro
Bissau, Guinea-Bissau

GUYANA

Send your requests to:

Registrar-General
General Register Office
Ministry of Home Affairs
G.P.O. Building
Robb Street
Georgetown, Guyana

Send your requests for Divorce records to:

Supreme Court Registrar
Avenue of the Republic
Georgetown, Guyana

Church registers date from the 1500s, while vital registration in Guyana began in 1880. Current vital registration is not comprehensive.

For additional assistance, contact:

Embassy of Guyana — Tel. (202) 265-6900
Consular Section
2490 Tracy Place, NW
Washington, DC 20008

HAITI

Send your requests to:

Archives Nationales
Rue Borgella
Port-au-Prince, Haiti

www.anhhaiti.org/

At the time of registration, a hand-written certificate on official, stamped paper is issued by the registrar of the section in which registration takes place. The record is also entered into an official register, which is transferred to the National Archives in Port-au-Prince, usually after one year. Once this transfer occurs, a transcript of the record, known as an extrait, can be obtained from the National Archives. The National Archives has an online searchable database of civil records held by the Archives (www.agh.qc.ca/indexen.html), with more than 500,000 names, starting in 1793. The database is updated daily.

For additional assistance, contact:

Embassy of Haiti
2311 Massachusetts Avenue, NW
Washington, DC 20008

Tel. (202) 332-4090

HONDURAS

Send your requests to:

Registro Nacional de las Personas
(Town), Honduras

or

Archivo Nacional de Honduras
6a Avenida 408
Tegucigalpa, Honduras

Church registers date from the 1500s, while vital registration in Honduras began January 1, 1881. There is no centralized system of civil records in Honduras except for police records. Civil documents are recorded in the Registro Nacional de las Personas where the event occurred. Records from 1906 to the present are kept at the Honduras National Archives.

For additional assistance, contact:

Embassy of Honduras
3007 Tilden Street, NW
Washington, DC 20008

Tel. (202) 966-7702

HUNGARY

Send your requests to:

Civil Registration Office
(Town), Hungary

There is no central office for vital records in Hungary. To obtain copies of birth, marriage, and death certificates, write to the Civil Registration District Office or the city Vital Statistics Records Office having jurisdiction over the locality where the event in question occurred. Vital records are on file from 1895. Current vital registration in Hungary is considered to be comprehensive. Early records are available from the local parish church or county archives (Megyei Levéltár). The National Office of Personal Registration (H-Budapest PF 81, 1450 Hungary) also maintains files on residents of Hungary as part of the national identity card system. Divorces are approved by the local District Court. Adoptions are approved by the Children Care and Welfare Institute (GYIVI) and finalized by the local County Public Administration Office.

For additional assistance, contact:

Embassy of the Republic of Hungary — Tel. (202) 362-6730
3910 Shoemaker Street, NW
Washington, DC 20008

ICELAND

Send your requests to:

Registers Iceland (Þjóðskrá Íslands) — Tel. (011) (354) 569-2900
Borgartún 21 — E-mail: skra@skra.is
150 Reykjavík, Iceland — www.skra.is

Records are available from 1953 for all residents of Iceland. Prior to this time records were kept by the local—usually Lutheran—church. These church registers go back to 1785. The current vital registration is considered to be comprehensive.

For additional assistance, contact:

National Archives of Iceland
P.O. Box R5-5390
Laugavegur 162
105 Reykjavik, Iceland

Embassy of Iceland — Tel. (202) 265-6653
1156 15th Street, NW
Washington, DC 20005

INDIA

Send your requests for Birth, Death, and Hindu Marriage and Adoption certificates to:

Chief Registrar of Births, Deaths & Marriages
(Capital City; State, Union or Territory), India

Send your requests for records of British Nationals in pre-Independent India to:

Oriental and India Office Collections
British Library
96 Euston Road
London NW1 2DB, England

The Bengal Births and Deaths Registration Act was passed in 1873, and in 1886 the Births, Deaths and Marriages Registration Act went into effect in British India. Compliance has been uneven outside of the major cities and states. The Indian Christian Marriage Act first took effect in 1872. Registration of non-Hindu marriages is not compulsory. For marriage records you should also contact the denomination where the wedding occurred. Registration of marriages and divorces is required in only a few states.

The India Office Records at the British Library are the documentary archives of the administration in London of the pre-1947 government of India. They include the archives of the East India Company (1600–1858), the Board of Control or Board of Commissioners for the Affairs of India (1784–1858), the India Office (1858–1947), the Burma Office (1937–1948), and a number of related British agencies overseas. The India Office Family History Search online database (http://indiafamily.bl.uk/UI/) contains around 300,000 births, baptisms, marriages, deaths, and burials for British and European people in India between 1600 and 1949.

For additional assistance, contact:

Embassy of India — Tel. (202) 939-7000
2107 Massachusetts Avenue, NW
Washington, DC 20008

INDONESIA

Send your requests to:

Civil Registration Office
(Town), Indonesia

It was in 1815, during the British period, that population registers were introduced. The Dutch began vital registration of all Indonesians in Jakarta in 1929. Marriage and divorce records can be found in the records of the denomination, recorded at the vital registration office, and in the Indonesian Department of Religious Affairs. Under the direction of the Minister of Internal Affairs, all births and deaths must also be registered in each town on individual forms called triplikats. Both registrations should be consulted.

For additional assistance, contact:

Embassy of Indonesia — Tel. (202) 775-5200
2020 Massachusetts Avenue, NW
Washington, DC 20036

IRAN

Send your requests to:

Deputy, Ministry of the Interior and Head of Civil Registration
Civil Registration Organization
Eman Khomaini Street
Central Building No. 184
Tehran, Iran 11374

Identification cards have been required for Iranian men since 1918. Currently, each Iranian is registered and receives an ID card. Marriage and divorce records are also kept by the Notarial Office and Court of Justice where the event occurred. In 1994 the Registration Organization computerized its records for 80 million Iranians who have lived in Iran over the past 100 years.

For additional assistance, contact:

Interests Section of the Islamic Republic of Iran — Tel. (202) 965-4990
2209 Wisconsin Avenue, NW
Washington, DC 20007

IRAQ

Send your requests to:

Department of Civil Status
(Town), Iraq

Vital records registration of births and deaths has been compulsory in Iraq since 1947. The nation also requires an identity card for each individual, which is issued by the Director General of the Office of Civil Status. Marriages are recorded by the denomination that performed the wedding, and divorces are kept by the court that issued the decree.

For additional assistance, contact:

Embassy of the Republic of Iraq — Tel. (202) 483-7500
Consular Section
1801 P Street, NW
Washington, DC 20036

IRELAND

Send your requests to:

General Register Office (GRO)
Government Offices
Convent Road
Roscommon
Co. Roscommon, Ireland

Tel. (011) (353) 90 6632900
Fax (011) (353) 90 6632999
www.groireland.ie/

The GRO's records of births, deaths, and Roman Catholic marriages date back to January 1, 1864. Records of marriages other than Roman Catholic marriages date back to April 1, 1845. Vital registration is considered to be comprehensive. Birth, death, and marriage certificates are also available in person or by mail from any Superintendent Registrar's Office (SRO), and online at www.hse.ie/eng/services/list/1/bdm/Certificates/. These local offices usually have a much faster response time than the GRO, as they generally receive a smaller amount of applications. For the period before 1864, parish registers provide the only source of information relating to births, marriages, and deaths.

The GRO maintains a genealogical/family history research facility at the Irish Life Centre (Lower Abbey Street, Dublin 1).

Cost for a certified Birth Certificate	€20.00
Cost for a certified Marriage Certificate	€20.00
Cost for a certified Civil Partnership Certificate	€20.00
Cost for a certified Death Certificate	€20.00
Cost for an uncertified Photocopy	€4.00

Send your requests for Adoption Records to:

The Adoption Authority of Ireland
Shelbourne House
Shelbourne Road
Dublin 4, Ireland

E-mail: adoptioninfo@aai.gov.ie
http://www.aai.gov.ie/

For additional assistance, contact:

The Irish Family History Foundation

www.irish-roots.ie/

The Irish Family History Foundation is the coordinating body for a network of county-based genealogical research centers. These centers have computerized millions of Irish genealogical records, including church records, census returns, and gravestone inscriptions. Centers are now making their records available via an online research system (ORS), which will allow you to search an index of records and pay to view a record. Go to www.irish-roots.ie/ for more information.

Embassy of Ireland
2234 Massachusetts Avenue, NW
Washington, DC 20008

Tel. (202) 462-3939

Application for Birth Certificate

How Do I Apply?

In Person: Complete details below and present at public counter.

By Post: Complete details below and send to *Civil Registration Office,*
Office of the Registrar General,
Government Offices,
Convent Road,
Roscommon,
Co. Roscommon,
Ireland.

By Fax: Complete details below and fax to +353 906632999.

Types and Costs of Certificates

Type	Description	Cost €
Birth Certificate	This is a full copy of the registered entry and can be used for legal and administrative purposes.	€20.00
Specified Services Certificate	This is a full copy of the registered entry. Proof that the certificate is needed for such purpose will be required from the relevant office/agency.	€1.00
Authenticated	This is required in certain circumstances (in addition to the copy of the registered entry) and is available on request from the Civil Registration Office, Convent Road, Roscommon, Ireland.	€10.00

Note Photocopies of entries in the registers are also available at a cost of €4.00. These contain exactly the same information as a Certificate but are only of use for research purposes.

How Do I Pay?

Cash: Personal applications only please. **Only Euro Cash will be accepted**.

Cheque: Please note that cheques should be made payable to '**Civil Registration Service**'. **Only Euro cheques drawn on a branch of a bank located in the Republic of Ireland will be accepted.**

Credit Card: MasterCard and Visa credit cards are accepted. The name of the applicant and the name on the credit card must be the same.

Debit Card: Laser Card and Visa debit cards are accepted. The name of the applicant and the name on the debit card must be the same.

Application for Birth Certificate

- **PLEASE COMPLETE USING BLOCK CAPITALS.**
- **ITEMS MARKED WITH * MUST BE COMPLETED.**
- **INCOMPLETE FORMS MAY BE RETURNED.**

SECTION 1: Details of person applying for the certificate

*Applicant's Forename: .... *Applicant's Surname: ....

*Full Postal Address: ....

Telephone: .... E-mail Address: ....

SECTION 2: Details of person whose birth certificate is required

Birth Surname: .... Date of Birth (dd/mm/yyyy): ....

*Forename(s) in full: ....

PPS Number (if known): ....

*Address of Place of Birth (Hospital/Home): ....

Town: .... County: .... Sex: ....

*Mother's Birth Surname: .... Mother's Forename: ....

Father's Surname: .... Father's Forename: ....

Father's Occupation: .... Mother's Occupation: ....

*Has the person for whom the certificate is required been legally adopted? Yes ☐ No ☐

SECTION 3: Further Details

PLEASE ENTER NUMBER AND TYPE OF CERTIFICATES REQUIRED IN THE RELEVANT BOXES. DETAILS OF CERTIFICATE TYPES AND COSTS ARE SHOWN ABOVE.

ALL APPLICATIONS FOR SPECIFIED SERVICES CERTIFICATES MUST BE ACCOMPANIED BY A LETTER FROM THE RELEVANT OFFICE/AGENCY.

Full (Long Form) ☐ Specified Services ☐ Authenticated ☐ Photocopy ☐

Method of Payment:

Cash ☐ Cheque ☐ Credit Card ☐ Laser/Visa Debit Card ☐

If paying by credit card, please indicate whether: MasterCard ☐ Visa ☐

If paying by Credit Card/Debit Card all of the following details <u>must</u> be furnished:

Name of Card Holder **(Block Capitals)** ....

Credit Card Billing Address..

Signature of Card Holder: .... Expiry Date(mm/yyyy): ....

Card Number: ☐☐☐☐--☐☐☐☐--☐☐☐☐--☐☐☐☐

3 Security digits (located on the back of card) -------☐☐☐

Official Use DATE STAMP

Application for Marriage/Civil Partnership Certificate

How Do I Apply?

In Person: Complete details below and present at public counter.

By Post: Complete details below and send to *Civil Registration Office,*
Office of the Registrar General,
Government Offices,
Convent Road,
Roscommon,
Co. Roscommon,
Ireland.

By Fax: Complete details below and fax to +353 906632999.

Types and Costs of Certificates

Type	**Description**	**Cost €**
Certificate	This is a full copy of the registered entry and can be used for legal and administrative purposes.	€20.00
Specified Services Certificates	This is a full copy of the registered entry. Proof that the certificate is needed for such purpose will be required from the relevant office/agency.	€1.00
Authenticated	This is required in certain circumstances (in addition to the copy of the registered entry) and is available on request from the Civil Registration Office, Convent Road, Roscommon, Ireland.	€10.00

Note Photocopies of entries in the registers are also available at a cost of €4.00. These contain exactly the same information as a Certificate but are only of use for research purposes.

How Do I Pay?

Cash: Personal applications only please. **Only Euro Cash will be accepted**.

Cheque: Please note that cheques should be made payable to "**Civil Registration Service**". **Only Euro cheques drawn on a branch of a bank located in the Republic of Ireland will be accepted.**

Credit Card: MasterCard and Visa credit cards are accepted. The name of the applicant and the name on the credit card must be the same.

Debit Card: Laser Card and Visa debit cards are accepted. The name of the applicant and the name on the debit card must be the same.

Application for Marriage/Civil Partnership Certificate

- **PLEASE COMPLETE USING BLOCK CAPITALS.**
- **ITEMS MARKED WITH * MUST BE COMPLETED.**
- **INCOMPLETE FORMS MAY BE RETURNED.**

SECTION 1: Details of person applying for the certificate

*Applicant's Forename: .... *Applicant's Surname: ....

*Full Postal Address: ....

Telephone: .... E-mail address: ....

SECTION 2: Details of person whose marriage/civil partnership certificate is requested

1st Party	**2nd Party**
*Surname:	Surname: ....
*Forename:	Forename: ....
PPS Number (if known):	PPS Number (if known): ....

*Date of Marriage/Civil Partnership (dd/mm/yyyy): ....

Place of Marriage/Civil Partnership and denomination (if any): ....

SECTION 3: Further Details

PLEASE ENTER NUMBER AND TYPE OF CERTIFICATES REQUIRED IN THE RELEVANT BOXES. DETAILS OF CERTIFICATE TYPES AND COSTS ARE SHOWN ABOVE.

ALL APPLICATIONS FOR SPECIFIED SERVICES CERTIFICATES MUST BE ACCOMPANIED BY A LETTER FROM THE RELEVANT OFFICE/AGENCY

Full (Long Form) ☐ Specified Services ☐ Authenticated ☐ Photocopy ☐

Method of Payment:

Cash ☐ Cheque ☐ Credit Card ☐ Laser/Visa Debit Card ☐

If paying by credit card, please indicate whether: MasterCard ☐ Visa ☐

If paying by Credit Card/Debit Card all of the following details <u>must</u> be furnished:

Name of Card Holder (Block Capitals) ....

Credit Card Billing Address ....

Signature of Card Holder: .... Expiry Date (mm/yyyy): ....

Card Number ☐☐☐☐--☐☐☐☐--☐☐☐☐--☐☐☐☐

3 Security Digits (located on back of card) --☐☐☐

Official Use DATE STAMP

Application for Death Certificate

How Do I Apply?

In Person: Complete details below and present at public counter.

By Post: Complete details below and send to *Civil Registration Office,*
Office of the Registrar General,
Government Offices,
Convent Road,
Roscommon,
Co. Roscommon,
Ireland.

By Fax: Complete details below and fax to +353 906632999.

Types and Costs of Certificates

Type	Description	Cost €
Death Certificate	This is a full copy of the registered entry and can be used for legal and administrative purposes.	€20.00
Specified Services Certificate	This is a full copy of the registered entry. Proof that the certificate is needed for such purpose will be required from the relevant office/agency.	€1.00
Authenticated	This is required in certain circumstances (in addition to the copy of the registered entry) and is available on request from the Civil Registration Office, Convent Road, Roscommon, Ireland.	€10.00

Note Photocopies of entries in the registers are also available at a cost of €4.00. These contain exactly the same information as a Certificate but are only of use for research purposes.

How Do I Pay?

Cash: Personal applications only please. **Only Euro Cash will be accepted**.

Cheque: Please note that cheques should be made payable to **'Civil Registration Service'**. **Only Euro cheques drawn on a branch of a bank located in the Republic of Ireland will be accepted.**

CreditCard: MasterCard and Visa credit cards are accepted. The name of the applicant and the name on the credit card must be the same.

Debit Card: Laser and Visa Debit cards are accepted. The name of the applicant and the name on the debit card must be the same.

Application for Death Certificate

- **PLEASE COMPLETE USING BLOCK CAPITALS.**
- **ITEMS MARKED WITH * MUST BE COMPLETED.**
- **INCOMPLETE FORMS MAY BE RETURNED.**

SECTION 1: Details of person who is requesting the certificate

*Applicants Forename: .... *Applicant's Surname: ....

*Address: ....

Telephone: .... E-mail Address: ....

SECTION 2: Details of Person whose Death Certificate is Required

*Surname: ....

*Forename(s) in full: ....

*Date of Death (dd/mm/yy): .. .. *Date of Birth (dd/mm/yyyy) or Approx Age: ....

PPS Number (if known): ....

*Place of Death : ....

*Sex: ....

Occupation: ....

*Civil Status: ....

SECTION 3: Further Details

PLEASE ENTER NUMBER AND TYPE OF CERTIFICATES REQUIRED IN THE RELEVANT BOXES. DETAILS OF CERTIFICATE TYPES AND COSTS ARE SHOWN ABOVE.

ALL APPLICATIONS FOR SPECIFIED SERVICES CERTIFICATES MUST BE ACCOMPANIED BY A LETTER FROM THE RELEVANT OFFICE/AGENCY.

Full (Long Form) ☐ Specified Services ☐ Authenticated ☐ Photocopy ☐

Method of Payment:
Cash ☐ Cheque ☐ Credit Card ☐ Laser/Visa debit ☐
If paying by credit card, please indicate whether MasterCard ☐ Visa ☐

If paying by Credit Card/Debit Card all of the following details <u>must</u> be furnished:

Name of Card Holder **(Block Capitals)** ....

Credit Card Billing Address ....

Signature of Card Holder: .... Expiry Date (mm/yy): ....

Card Number: ☐☐☐☐--☐☐☐☐--☐☐☐☐--☐☐☐☐

3 Security Digits (located at back of card) --☐☐☐

Official Use DATE STAMP

ISRAEL

Send your requests to:

Registrar
Immigration Services and Population Registration
Ministry of the Interior
P.O. Box 2420
Jerusalem, Israel

Civil documents for Israel are generally available, though some records were destroyed. Certificates for Palestinian residents of the West Bank and Gaza must be submitted to the Palestinian Authority Ministry of Interior office located nearest the applicant's place of residence. Requests for marriage certificates should be sent to the appropriate religious community. Adoption records are finalized by the local District Court and supervised by the Ministry of Social Welfare.

For additional assistance, contact:

Yad Vashem — Tel. (011) (972) (2) 6443400
P.O. Box 3477
Jerusalem, 91034, Israel

Embassy of Israel — Tel. (202) 364-5500
3514 International Drive, NW
Washington, DC 20008

ITALY

Send your requests to:

Ufficio dello Stato Civile
(Town), Italy

There is no central office for vital records in Italy. To obtain copies of birth, marriage, and death certificates, write to the town where the event occurred. Vital records are on file for most areas from the early 1800s but are more generally available from 1870 to the present. Older records are often on deposit at the State Archives. Current vital registration is considered to be comprehensive.

For additional assistance, contact:

Embassy of Italy — Tel. (202) 612-4400
3000 Whitehaven Street, NW
Washington, DC 20008

JAMAICA

Send your requests for Births, Marriages, and Deaths to:

Registrar General's Office
Twickenham Park
Spanish Town, St. Catherine
Jamaica, West Indies

Tel. (876) 984-5869
E-mail: information@rgd.gov.jm
www.rgd.gov.jm/

Send your requests for Divorce Records to:

Registrar of the Supreme Court
Public Building E
134 Tower Street
Kingston, Jamaica

Forms for certified copies of birth, death, and marriage certificates should be submitted online from the Registrar General's website. Modern vital registration began January 1, 1878, in Jamaica, though church registers were kept from colonial times. Current vital registration is considered to be comprehensive.

For additional assistance, contact:

Embassy of Jamaica
1520 New Hampshire Avenue, NW
Washington, DC 20036

Tel. (202) 452-0660

JAPAN

Send your requests to:

Municipal Office
(Town), Japan

Japan instituted its current system of Koseki or Family Registers in March 1868. These registers began as early as 451 AD. The system has its roots in the Chinese tradition of keeping family registers for the past 4,000 years. The Japanese extract of the family register, available from the Municipal Office, generally contains all current information that would be found in separate birth, adoption, marriage, divorce, or death records. Each resident is required to have a national identification card. All civil records for the Okinawa prefecture were destroyed during World War II, except those records maintained on the islands of Miyako and Yaeyama. The destroyed records were recreated, based on the testimony of the persons involved. Buddhist temples and Shinto shrines/temples may also maintain some family records.

For additional assistance, contact:

The Embassy of Japan
2520 Massachusetts Avenue, NW
Washington, DC 20008

Tel. (202) 238-6700

JORDAN

Send your requests to:

Department of Civil Status and Passport
Ministry of the Interior
(Location: Jebal Amman, Yafa Street, Building No. 9)
P.O. Box 3102
Amman, Jordan

Tel. (011) (962) (6) 4636370
E-mail: cspd@cspd.gov.jo
www.cspd.gov.jo

Jordan has a long history of civil registration although a more reliable system only started fairly recently. The Department of Civil Status and Passport (CSP) (under the Ministry of Interior) is responsible for the civil registration in the country. Marriage certificates are obtainable from the Sharia Courts for Muslims and the churches for Christians. No civil marriage is performed in Jordan.

For additional assistance, contact:

Embassy of the Hashemite Kingdom of Jordan
3504 International Drive, NW
Washington, DC 20008

Tel. (202) 966-2664

KAZAKHSTAN

Send your requests to:

Office of Registration of Civil Events (ZAGS)
287 Baizakov Street
Almaty, Republic of Kazakhstan

Some civil records were destroyed during World War II and may not be available. In the U.S., Kazakhstani documents can be requested through the Embassy of Kazakhstan (see below).

For additional assistance, contact:

Embassy of the Republic of Kazakhstan
1401 16th Street, NW
Washington, DC 20036

Tel. (202) 232-5488

KENYA

Send your requests for Birth Records to:

Department of Civil Registration
Office of the President
P.O. Box 49179
Nairobi, Kenya

Send your requests for Death and Marriage Records to:

Department of the Registrar General
State Law Office, Harambee Avenue
P.O. Box 30031
Nairobi, Kenya

Send your requests for Divorce Records to:

Registrar
The Law Courts
P.O. Box 30041
Nairobi, Kenya

Although church registers were kept from colonial times, modern vital registration for Europeans didn't begin until 1904. Registration was expanded to include Asians in 1906 and the entire population by 1971.

For additional assistance, contact:

Embassy of Kenya
2249 R Street, NW
Washington, DC 20008
Tel. (202) 387-6101

KIRIBATI

Send your requests to:

Registrar General of Births, Deaths and Marriages
Civil Registration Office
P.O. Box 75
Bairiki, Tarawa, Republic of Kiribati

Civil registration began in the 19th century and is not comprehensive. All records through 1989 have been microfilmed.

For additional assistance, contact:

National Archives and Library
P.O. Box 6
Bairiki, Tarawa, Kiribati
Tel. (011) (686) 21-337

DEMOCRATIC PEOPLE'S REPUBLIC OF KOREA (NORTH KOREA)

Family household registers are maintained by:

Police Department
(Town), North Korea

There is no information on availability of documents for residents/nationals of North Korea. The U.S. and North Korea have no diplomatic relations.

THE REPUBLIC OF KOREA (SOUTH KOREA)

Send your requests for copies of Household Registrations to:

Ward Office
(Town), Korea

Since January 1, 2008, new forms of family register certificates have been issued by government offices, ward offices, city halls, Myun offices, Eup offices, and Dong offices throughout the country. The Family Relation Register certificate of family relation shows names of spouse, parents (including adoptive parents), and children (including adopted children). The Identification Certificate shows only the individual's date of birth, place of birth, changed names, and death. The Marriage Relation Certificate provides information on the individual's marital status only.

The former Family Census Register (FCR) is still available as an archived Family Relation Register (Jejeok Deung-Bon). The former FCR contains information reported before January 1, 2008, concerning birth, marriage, divorce, adoption, death, and other history for the head of family and other family members.

For additional assistance, contact:

Embassy of the Republic of Korea
2450 Massachusetts Avenue, NW
Washington, DC 20008

Tel. (202) 939-5600

KOSOVO

Send your requests to:

Civil Registrar
(Locality), Kosovo

Birth, marriage, and death certificates are available from the civil registrar with jurisdiction over the locality where the event occurred. Citizen records for adults (18 and over) are indexed by the unique registry number assigned each citizen, similar to the U.S. Social Security number. Identity cards, containing the person's photograph and date and place of birth, are issued by the Ministry of Internal Affairs through the municipality of residence. Copies of divorce judgments are available from the District Court that decided the case.

For additional assistance, contact:

Embassy of the Republic of Kosovo
1101 30th Street, NW, Suite 330
Washington, DC, 20007

Tel. (202) 380-3581
E-mail: embassy.usa@rks-gov.net

KUWAIT

Send your requests to:

Central Record for Birth and Death Department — Tel. (011) (965) 2562-2716
Ministry of Health
(Location: Jamal Abdulnasser Street, Al Solaibeykhat Area)
P.O. Box 5
Kuwait City, Safat 13001, Kuwait

Birth and death records must be applied for in person by either the applicant or his/her agent (consult the Kuwait embassy at the below address for information about appointing an agent).

For additional assistance, contact:

Embassy of the State of Kuwait — Tel. (202) 966-0702
2940 Tilden Street, NW
Washington, DC 20008

KYRGYZSTAN

Send your requests to:

Chief
Registry Office
Ministry of Justice
140 Kalina Street
Bishkek, Kyrgyzstan

The person to whom the record pertains can obtain a certified copy of a vital record at a local notary office, then must authenticate the notary's seal and signature at the Ministry of Justice, and authenticate the Ministry of Justice official's signature and seal at the Ministry of Foreign Affairs. In the U.S., Kyrgyz documents can be requested through the Embassy of Kyrgyzstan in Washington, DC. The process often takes several months. Some civil records were destroyed during World War II and may not be available. Unauthenticated and uncertified copies of vital records may be obtained by Kyrgyz citizens for a nominal fee upon direct application to the Bureau of Acts of Civil Status (ZAGS) of the locality having custody of the records.

For additional assistance, contact:

Embassy of the Kyrgyz Republic — Tel. (202) 449-9822
2360 Massachusetts Avenue, NW
Washington, DC 20008

LAO PEOPLE'S DEMOCRATIC REPUBLIC (LAOS)

Send your requests to:

District Administrator
(Town), Lao

There are no central registries of vital records in Lao (the word "Laos" has no meaning; it was used by mistake by the French during colonial times). There are no standard forms for any civil record other than the Household Registry Book and National Identification Card. Documents can be obtained only by those applying in person and resident in Lao, and occasionally by family members applying in person. The Japanese Army destroyed virtually all extant French colonial records when it invaded Lao in World War II. When the Pathet Lao came to power in 1975, they destroyed most extant records of the former royal government.

For additional assistance, contact:

Bibliothèque nationale
B.P. 122
Vientiane, Lao People's Democratic Republic

Embassy of the Lao People's Democratic Republic — Tel. (202) 332-6416
2222 S Street, NW
Washington, DC 20008

LATVIA

Send your requests to:

Archive of the Civil Registration Department
38a A.Caka Street
Riga 1011, Latvia

The consular section of the Embassy of Latvia (see contact information below) can assist you in requesting a birth, marriage, or divorce certificate.

Civil records up to 1910 are available from the State History Archive, 16 Slokas St., Riga, LV-1048, tel. (011) (371) 676 13118 or (011) (371) 676 12406. References and duplicates of civil records prepared in Riga City from May 1, 1921, to the present should be requested from the Riga City Civil Registry Office, 86 Brivibas St., Riga, LV-1010, tel. (011) (371) 673 12 114.

References or duplicates of all other civil records are available through local district or city civil registration offices (their location may be specified at the Civil Registration Department of the Ministry of Justice) or the Archive of the Civil Registration Department, 38a A.Caka St., Riga, LV-1011, tel. (011) (371) 678 30677, (011) (371) 678 30682. Until 1921 only churches registered the birth of a child; therefore a person must know the name of the church when requesting data.

The Latvian State Historical Archives website (www.lvva-raduraksti.lv/en.html) provides online access to the church books of congregations of various denominations, as well as to many vital records (birth, baptism, marriage, and death registers).

For additional assistance, contact:

Embassy of Latvia — Tel. (202) 328-2881
Consular Section — E-mail: consulate.usa@mfa.gov.lv
2306 Massachusetts Avenue, NW
Washington, DC 20008

LEBANON

Send your requests to:

Vital Statistics Bureau
(District), Lebanon

Birth, marriage, divorce, and death certificates may be obtained from the district office of the Vital Statistics Bureau in the district where the event was registered. There is no fee for a death certificate. Alternate civil documentation of birth (for Lebanese nationals whose place of birth is Lebanon) can be the individual or family civil registration sheet issued by the Vital Statistics Bureau, which records all members of a family. Lebanese identity cards also contain biographic information.

For additional assistance, contact:

Embassy of Lebanon — Tel. (202) 939-6300
2560 28th Street, NW
Washington, DC 20008

LESOTHO

Send your requests to:

Senior District Administrator
P.O. Box MS 174
Maseru, Lesotho

Vital registration began in 1880.

For additional assistance, contact:

Embassy of the Kingdom of Lesotho — Tel. (202) 797-5533
2511 Massachusetts Avenue, NW
Washington, DC 20008

LIBERIA

Send your requests to:

Bureau of Health and Vital Statistics
Ministry of Health and Social Welfare
P.O. Bag 3762
Monrovia, Liberia

Liberia gained its independence in 1847. Some genealogical records from the 1800s are available in the Liberian Collections Project at Indiana University (www.onliberia.org/).

For additional assistance, contact:

Embassy of Liberia — Tel. (202) 723-0437
5201 16th Street, NW
Washington, DC 20011

LIBYA

Send your requests to:

Municipal Registration Office
(Town), Libya

To obtain a Libyan birth certificate, non-national applicants must send all pertinent information (including name, date and place of birth, and full names of parents) to their respective embassy in Tripoli. The embassy will then make a formal request to the Ministry of Foreign Affairs to obtain the certificate from the appropriate municipality. Libyan applicants, or a friend or relative of the applicant, must appear in person at the appropriate municipality office.

In Libya there are no records of vital registration for the period of Turkish rule. Vital registration began in urban areas during the period of Italian rule. Modern vital registration began in 1968. Marriage and divorce records are kept by both the religious law courts and the Municipal Registration Office.

LIECHTENSTEIN

Send your requests to:

Amtsvorstand/Zivilstandsamt des Furstentums Liechtenstein
St. Florinsgasse 3
9490 Vaduz, Liechtenstein

Vital records in Liechtenstein are available from 1878. Current vital registration is considered to be comprehensive. Church records date back to the 1600s.

For additional assistance, contact:

Liechtenstein National Archives
Liechtensteinisches Landesarchiv
Städtle 51
9490 Vaduz, Liechtenstein

Embassy of Liechtenstein — Tel. (202) 331-0590
2900 K Street, NW
Suite 602B
Washington, DC 20007

LITHUANIA

Send your requests to:

Civil Registrar's Office
K. Kalinausko 21
Lt 2600
Vilnius, Lithuania

Tel. (011) (370) 233-53-54

Birth, marriage, divorce, and death certificates from 1975 may be obtained from the local civil registration bureau, commonly called the "Marriage Palace," in the city where the applicant is registered. Civil documents from 1915 to 1975 are located in the Vilnius "Marriage Palace" at Kalinausko Street 21. There is no standard procedure or form for requesting these documents.

A database containing Jewish birth, marriage, divorce, and death records from Lithuania is available online at www.jewishgen.org/databases/lithuania/vitalrecs.htm.

The Lithuanian State Historical Archives (Gerosios Vilties 10, LT-03134 Vilnius, Lithuania) has vital records books (birth, marriage, and death) up to 1940 for the different religious communities and churches of Lithuania, and civil registration records up to 2008.

For additional assistance, contact:

Embassy of Lithuania
2622 16th Street, NW
Washington, DC 20009

Tel. (202) 234-5860

LUXEMBOURG

Send your requests to:

Registrar of the Civil Status
(Town), Luxembourg

or

Luxembourg State Archives
Plateau du Saint-Esprit
B.P. 6
2010 Luxembourg, Luxembourg

Tel. (011) (352) 2478 66 60
E-mail: archives.nationales@an.etat.lu
http://anlux.lu/

Birth certificates (Geburtsschein, Geburtsurkunde, or Acte de naissance) and marriage certificates can be obtained from the Standesamt or État Civil. The records are complete for more than the past 100 years. Death certificates are issued by the Mayor's office in the community where the death took place.

Birth, death, and marriage records from 1795 to 1923, as well as parish records before 1795, are housed at the Luxembourg State Archives (see contact information above).

The following free online databases are available at www.familysearch.org: Luxembourg Births and Baptisms, 1662–1840; Luxembourg Marriages, 1700–1810; Luxembourg Deaths and Burials, 1702–1798; and Luxembourg Civil Registration, 1793–1923.

For additional assistance, contact:

Embassy of Luxembourg
2200 Massachusetts Avenue, NW
Washington, DC 20008

Tel. (202) 265-4171

MACEDONIA

Send your requests to:

Civil Registration Office
(Town), Macedonia

Birth (Izvod od Maticna Kniga na Rodeni), marriage (Izvod of Maticna Kniga na Vencani), and death certificates (Izvod od Maticna Kniga na Umreni) are available from the civil registrar (maticar) having jurisdiction over the locality where the event occurred. Vital records are on file from 1946. Prior to May 10, 1946, records were maintained by Orthodox Church authorities. Since that date, only civil marriages have been legal. The Orthodox Church continues to issue birth and marriage certificates, but these are not legal until the event is recorded with the appropriate registrar's office. Copies of divorce judgments are available from the municipal court that decided the case.

For additional assistance, contact:

Embassy of the Republic of Macedonia
2129 Wyoming Avenue, NW
Washington, DC 20008

Tel. (202) 667-0501

MADAGASCAR

Send your requests to:

Mairie (Mayor's Office)
(Town), Madagascar

Vital registration began for the entire nation in July 1878. Birth, death, and marriage certificates are available from the mayor's office in the town where the event took place. You can also apply for copies of certificates through the Consular Affairs department of the Madagascar Embassy (see contact information below).

For additional assistance, contact:

Embassy of Madagascar
2374 Massachusetts Avenue, NW
Washington, DC 20008

Tel. (202) 265-5525
www.madagascar-embassy.org/embassy/consular.html#etat-civil

MALAWI

Send your requests to:

Registrar General
Ministry of Justice
P.O. Box 100
Blantyre, Malawi

The Registrar General has birth and death records from 1886, marriage records from 1903, and divorce records from 1905. These early records are mostly from Europeans living in Malawi.

For additional assistance, contact:

Embassy of the Republic of Malawi
2408 Massachusetts Avenue, NW
Washington, DC 20008

Tel. (202) 721-0270

MALAYSIA

Send your requests to:

Registrar-General of Births and Deaths
National Registration Department
No 20, Persiaran Perdana
Presint 2
62551 Federal Territory of Putrajaya, Malaysia

E-mail: pro@jpn.gov.my
www.jpn.gov.my/en

Malaysia, as a Commonwealth nation, has had vital registration laws from the late 1800s. The National Registration Department was organized in 1948 and requires all individuals 12 and older to carry a national identity card. This system was computerized in 1990. Birth and death certificates (certified extracts from the register of births and deaths) are also available from the Superintendent of Registrar of Births and Deaths for the registration area in which the birth and death were registered (Petaling Jaya for West Malaysia, Kuching for Sarawak, and Kota Kinabalu for Sabah).

Civil marriage certificates (certified copies of entries in a marriage register) may be obtained from the Malaysian Registrar-General of Marriages, National Registration Department, Headquarters at Petaling Jaya, Selangor, Malaysia. Certified copies of civil marriages for those marriages contracted in the state of Sabah and Sarawak may be obtained from the Superintendent Registrar of Marriages in Kota Kinabalu, Sabah and Kuching, Sarawak, respectively. Certified copies of Islamic marriage certificates may be obtained from the Mahkamah Syariah Court Headquarters at Kuala Lumpur, Malaysia.

For additional assistance, contact:

Embassy of Malaysia
3516 International Court, NW
Washington, DC 20008

Tel. (202) 572-9700

MALDIVES

Send your requests to:

Ministry of Health
Ameenee Magu
Male' 20379, Republic of Maldives

www.health.gov.mv/

Send your requests for Marriage and Divorce Records to:

Registrar
Ministry of Justice
Justice Building
Orchid Magu
Male' 20212, Republic of Maldives

http://justice.gov.mv/

While vital registration began in the 1500s, the modern system did not begin until the 1950s. Birth and death records are kept by the Ministry of Health; marriage and divorce certificates are available from the Ministry of Justice. Foreign nationals may obtain birth, death, marriage, and divorce certificates from the Department of External Affairs.

MALI

Send your requests to:

Direction Nationale de l'Administration Territoriale
Ministère d'État Charge de l'Administration
Territoriale et de la Sécurité Intérieur
B.P. 78
Bamako, Mali

Vital registration began in 1938. Malian birth certificates are issued only to those Malians born in maternity centers or to those whose birth is declared within three months after birth. Many Malians simply have court declarations of approximate place and date of birth. Copies of these declarations or birth certificates are obtained from the headquarters of the Cercle (administrative unit) in which the applicant was born or obtained the declaration. French nationals born before January 1, 1960, may obtain birth certificate copies from the Direction des Archives de France (Outre-Mer, 27 rue Oudinot, Paris). French nationals born after that date in Mali whose births were registered with the Consulate General in Bamako may obtain copies from Le Service de l'État Civil du Ministère des Affaires Étrangères (7 Allees Brancas, Nantes [Loire Atlantique], France).

Before 1962, marriage by a civil official was not required so many Malians have only *jugements de mariage* given by justices of the peace or tribunals. Records of marriages after 1962 may be obtained from the mayors of the towns in which the marriage took place. Divorce certificates are obtainable from the court that issued the divorce decree.

For additional assistance, contact:

Embassy of Mali — Tel. (202) 332-2249
2130 R Street, NW
Washington, DC 20008

MALTA

Send your requests to:

Director
Public Registry
Ministry of Justice and Parliamentary Affairs
197 Merchants Street
Valletta, Malta

The Public Registry has records beginning in 1863. Certificates for persons born in Malta are obtainable from the Director of the Public Registry in Valletta; certificates for persons born in Gozo may be obtained from the Acting Director of the Public Registry, Victoria, Gozo. Current vital registration is considered to be comprehensive. No separate divorce records are kept. Divorce information is annotated onto the marriage certificate.

For additional assistance, contact:

Embassy of Malta — Tel. (202) 462-3611
2017 Connecticut Avenue, NW
Washington, DC 20008

MARSHALL ISLANDS

Send your requests to:

Registrar's Office
P.O. Box 546
Majuro, Marshall Islands 96960

The Registrar's Office holds records beginning November 12, 1952. The National Archives (see below) also has birth and death certificates in its collection.

For additional assistance, contact:

Alele Museum of the Marshall Islands
Library & National Archives
P.O. Box 629
Majuro, Marshall Islands 98960
Tel. (011) (692) 625-3372
http://alelemuseum.tripod.com/Archives.html

Embassy of Marshall Islands
2433 Massachusetts Avenue, NW
Washington, DC 20008
Tel. (202) 234-5414

MAURITANIA

Send your requests to:

Administrateur
Secretariat d'État Charge de l'État Civil
B.P. 195
Nouakchott, Mauritania

Because Mauritania is a young country and some of its population is still nomadic, occasionally no records exist with regard to a particular applicant. In such a case, the cadi or local court (tribunal) can issue an *extrait de jugement d'acte de* (birth, marriage, death, etc.). This document may replace a birth certificate, death certificate, marriage certificate, or divorce certificate. A birth or death certificate may be obtained from the mayor of the commune in which the applicant was born, if he was born within a commune. Otherwise, the document may be obtained from the cadi (Islamic judge) of the place where he was born, or if there is no cadi, from the Commandant du Cercle of the administrative district where he was born. The mayor will charge the commune tax applicable in that particular commune; otherwise the service is free. A marriage certificate attesting the marriage of nationals may be obtained from the cadi of the place where the marriage occurred. A marriage certificate attesting the marriage of non-nationals (non-Muslim ceremonies) may be obtained from the Commandant du Cercle of the administrative district where the marriage took place.

For additional assistance, contact:

Embassy of Mauritania
2129 Leroy Place, NW
Washington, DC 20008
Tel. (202) 232-5700

MAURITIUS

Send your requests to:

Civil Status Office
Emmanuel Anquetil Building, 7th Floor
Port Louis, Mauritius

Tel. (011) (230) 201-3118
E-mail: civstat@mail.gov.mu
http://csd.pmo.gov.mu/English/Pages/Services.aspx

Extracts of civil status certificates may be applied for either at the central Civil Status Office in Port Louis or at the Civil Status Office where the event was registered. The Civil Status Office has birth and death records from 1539, marriage records from 1579, and divorce records from 1793. Mauritius is one of the few countries in Sub-Saharan Africa where the modern registration of births and deaths is considered to be comprehensive.

For additional assistance, contact:

Embassy of Mauritius
1709 N Street, NW
Washington, DC 20036

Tel. (202) 244-1491
E-mail: mauritius.embassy@verizon.net

MEXICO

Send your requests to:

Registro Civil
(Town, State), Mexico

Birth Certificates (acta de nacimiento) are generally available since 1870, although in many municipalities the records prior to 1915 have been partially or totally destroyed. A letter may be obtained certifying that no record is available, except in the Federal District where civil registry officials decline to issue such negative statements to individuals. Birth, death, marriage, and divorce certificates are issued by the appropriate Official del Registro Civil (official of the Civil Registry), and, in the Federal District by the Jefe de la Oficina del Registro Civil del Distrito Federal (Chief of the Office of the Federal District) in whose archives are consolidated the records of subordinate civil registries of the Federal District.

A number of historical collections containing church and civil registration records for Mexico are available at www.familysearch.org.

For additional assistance, contact:

Embassy of Mexico
1911 Pennsylvania Avenue, NW
Washington, DC 20006

Tel. (202) 728-1600

MICRONESIA—Federated States of Micronesia

Send your requests to:

Kosrae:
Clerk of Courts
Kosrae State Supreme Court
P.O. Box 27
Lelu, Kosrae, FSM 96944

Pohnpei:
Clerk of Courts
Pohnpei State Supreme Court
P.O. Box 1449
Kolonia, Pohnpei, FSM 96941

Chuuk (Truk):
Clerk of Courts
Chuuk State Supreme Court
P.O. Box 187
Moen, Chuuk, FSM 96942

Yap:
Clerk of Courts
Yap State Supreme Court
P.O. Box 308
Colonia, Yap, FSM 96943

The Court has records from November 12, 1952. Birth certificate request forms are available on the Micronesia Embassy's website (see below).

For additional assistance, contact:

Embassy of the Federated States of Micronesia
1725 N Street, NW
Washington, DC 20036

Tel. (202) 223-4383
E-mail: admin@fsmembassydc.org
www.fsmembassydc.org/

CHUUK STATE SUPREME COURT
P.O. Box 187
Weno, Chuuk, FSM 96942

OFF-ISLAND REQUEST FOR BIRTH CERTIFICATE

This document must be filled out in its entirety and signed and notarized in the presence of an officer of the court in whatever jurisdiction in which you are currently residing. This form will be the only acceptable format to request Certified Birth Certificates from Chuuk State. The off island processing fee of $5.00 (pursuant to Chuuk State Supreme Court General Court Order No. 01-2007) must be submitted with this form and must be in the form of a cashier's check or a money order (no personal checks will be accepted). Make payment out to the *"Chuuk State Supreme Court"* and mail to the address above.

A Police Clearance from the jurisdiction in which you reside must be submitted with this form or it will not be processed. The Clearance may be in any format, but shall include fingerprints and state that you have no outstanding warrants or fines presently due.

This Form will not be accepted without a copy of identification attached.

NAME: ____
Last First Middle

GENDER: ☐Male ☐Female

Date of Birth: ____

Mothers Maiden Name ____
Last First Middle

Fathers Full Name ____
Last First Middle

Address: ____
(The address you wish Birth Certificate be mailed to.)

I swear under penalty of perjury that the above statements are true.

____

Sworn to and subscribed before me this ________ day of ________________ 20___.
Picture Identification presented: ____.

____
Court Official's Name and Title

Seal

____
Notary Public: Name & Date of Seal Expiration

Kosrae State Birth Certificate Request Form

Kosrae Branch Statistics Office
Division of Statistics
FSM Department of Economic Affairs
P.O. Box 878
Tofol, Kosrae FM 96944

Dear Sir or Madam:

The purpose of this letter is to authorize and request your office to issue and forward the original certified copy of my birth certificate to the following address:

My address:

____
____
____

Name:____________________________________

Date of Birth:______________________________

Place of Birth:_____________________________

Municipality:______________________________

Father's Name:____________________________

Mother's Name:____________________________

I am enclosing a US Postal Money Order in the amount of $3.00, payable to <u>Kosrae Branch Statistics Office,</u> for processing fee. I would appreciate greatly your assistance in processing this request as early as possible.

Thank you for your assistance.

Sincerely,

______________________________ ______________________________
Requestor's Name Date

POHNPEI STATE BIRTH CERTIFICATE REQUEST FORM

T.H. Benjamin F. Rodriguez
Chief Justice
Pohnpei State Supreme Court
Kolonia, Pohnpei FM 96941

Dear Chief Justice Rodriguez:

The purpose of this letter is to authorize and request your good office to issue a certified copy of my Birth Certificate to be mailed to current residential address below:

Current Residential Address:

____
____
____
____
____

Contact Phone Number: ____
Email Address: ____

Full Name (First Middle Last) :___________________________________
Date of Birth (Month/Day/Year) :___________________________________
Place of Birth:____
Home Municipality:____
Father's Full Name:____
Mother's Full Name:____

I am enclosing a Money Order in the amount of $2.00, payable to Pohnpei State Supreme Court, as payment for the processing fee. I would greatly appreciate your assistance in processing my request as soon as possible.

Thank you for your kind assistance.

Sincerely,

____
Requestor's Name (Print Full Name)

____ __________________________
Requestor's Signature Date

Pohnpei State Supreme Court Contact:
Chief Clerk: Mr. Leon Felix
Tel: 011-691-320-2355/5667
Fax: 011-691-320-5126

MOLDOVA

For information, contact:

Moldovan Ministry of Foreign Affairs, Consular Affairs Department
80, str. Alexei Mateevici
Chisinau MD 2009
Republica Moldova

Tel. (011) (373) 22 20 10 46
E-mail: consdep@mfa.md

Most civil documents from areas outside the Transnister region in Eastern Moldova are available from the National Archives in Chisinau (Arhiva Nationala a Republicii Moldovei, str. Gheorghe Asachi, Nr. 67-B, Chisinau 277028) and are generally reliable. Certified copies can be obtained through the Moldovan Ministry of Foreign Affairs Consular Directorate.

For additional assistance, contact:

Embassy of the Republic of Moldova
2101 S Street, NW
Washington, DC 20008

Tel. (202) 667-1130
E-mail: washington@mfa.md

MONACO

Send your requests to:

Mairie de Monaco
Bureau de l'État-Civil
Monte Carlo, Monaco

Records of birth have been kept since November 24, 1796. Current vital registration is considered to be comprehensive.

For additional assistance, contact:

Embassy of Monaco
3400 International Drive, NW
Suite 2K-100
Washington, DC 20008-3006

Tel. (202) 234-1530
E-mail: info@monacodc.org

MONGOLIA

Send your requests to:

Civil Registration Office
(Country or Municipality), Mongolia

Mongolian civil documents are unavailable to non-Mongolians and to Mongolians abroad who are not in possession of valid, unexpired Mongolian travel documents. Birth and death certificates can be applied for from the Civil Registration Office in the country (Sum) or municipality (Hot) of birth or death. Since birth records before 1961 are incomplete, the Peoples Passport, a standard identity card, is acceptable in place of a birth certificate for all citizens born before 1961. Marriage and divorce certificates can be obtained from the Marriage Registration Office where the original action was registered.

For further assistance contact:

Embassy of Mongolia
2833 M Street, NW
Washington, DC 20007

Tel. (202) 333-7117

MONTENEGRO

Send your requests to:

Civil Registration Office
(Town), Montenegro

Birth (Izvod iz Maticne Knjige Rodjenih) and death certificates (Izvod iz Maticne Knjige Umrlih) are consolidated into a national database and are available from the civil registrars throughout Montenegro. Marriage certificates (Izvod iz Maticne Vencanih) are currently only available at the civil registry where the event occurred. Copies of divorce judgments are available from the District Court (okruzni sud) that decided the case. Many records, particularly in Montenegro, were destroyed during the Second World War and reconstructed afterward.

For further assistance contact:

Embassy of Montenegro — Tel. (202) 234-6105
1610 New Hampshire Avenue, NW
Washington, DC 20009

MONTSERRAT

Send your requests to:

Registrar General's Office — Tel. (664) 491-2129
High Court Registry
Government Headquarters
Brades, Montserrat

The Registrar General's Office has records from February 12, 1862. The local churches also have their own records.

For further assistance contact:

Montserrat Public Library — Tel. (664) 491-4706
BBC Building
Brades, Montserrat

MOROCCO

Send your requests to:

Bureau d'État Civil
(Jurisdiction), Morocco

Upon presentation of a *Livret de Famille,* Muslims and Moroccan Jews may obtain birth certificates from the Bureau d'État Civil having jurisdiction over their place of birth. Should the applicant's birth not be recorded with the civil authorities, an *Acte de Notoriete* (affidavit by witnesses) may be substituted. Only residents of Morocco can procure such documentation. Muslims should apply to the Cadi Court (Koranic Court) having jurisdiction over their place of birth. Moroccan Jews should apply to the Rabbinical Court having jurisdiction over their place of birth. The accuracy of these documents is often doubtful.

Non-Moroccans may obtain birth certificates if the birth occurred after 1960 in the former International Zone of Tangier, or if the birth occurred after 1956 in the former French or Spanish Protectorate Zones. Applicants should apply to the Municipal Registry (Bureau d'État Civil) having jurisdiction over the place of birth. Non-Moroccans whose birth was not recorded with the Bureau d'État Civil, or whose birth occurred prior to the dates indicated above, should contact their embassy or consulate for assistance.

Moroccan Muslims may obtain a copy of their marriage certificate by applying to the Cadi Court (Koranic Court) that presided over their marriage. Divorce certificates are obtained from the court rendering the decree. Mail applications for both marriage and divorce certificates are best handled through an attorney or a third party in the country. Moroccan Jews married or divorced prior to September 30, 1965, should apply for marriage or divorce certificates to the Rabbinical Court that presided over the marriage or rendered the divorce decree. Moroccan Jews married after September 30, 1965, should apply to the Bureau d'État Civil having authority over their place of marriage. Moroccan Jews divorced after September 30, 1965, should apply to the Tribunal de lere Instance that rendered the divorce decree. Non-Moroccans who were married in the former French Protectorate Zone during the period from 1912 to 1956 may obtain a marriage certificate from the Bureau d'État Civil having jurisdiction over the place where the marriage was celebrated. Non-Moroccans who were married in the former Spanish Protectorate Zone during the period from 1912 to 1956 may obtain a marriage certificate by applying to the church where the marriage was celebrated. Non-Moroccans married in the former Tangier International Zone during the period from 1912 to 1960 should write to their consulate or embassy for assistance.

For additional assistance, contact:

Embassy of Morocco
1601 21st Street, NW
Washington, DC 20009

Tel. (202) 462-7979

MOZAMBIQUE

Send your requests to:

Conservatória dos Registos
(Town), Mozambique

Birth, marriage, and death certificates are issued by the Conservatória dos Registos of the city where the event took place. The Civil Registry issues divorce certificates in cases of mutual consent, and the court (Tribunal Judicial) issues certificates in cases of contested divorce.

For additional assistance, contact:

Arquivo Histórico de Moçambique
Travessa do Varietá No. 58
C.P. 2033
Maputo, Moçambique

www.ahm.uem.mz/

Embassy of the Republic of Mozambique
1525 New Hampshire Avenue, NW
Washington, DC 20036

Tel. (202) 293-7146
E-mail: embamoc@aol.com

MYANMAR (BURMA)

Send your requests to:

Office of the Divisional Health Director
Yangon Health Division
No. 520, West Race Course Road
Yangon (Rangoon), Myanmar

During the years 1942–1945, Burma was devastated by nearly continuous fighting. Almost every part of the country suffered heavy damage, often repeatedly. As a result, almost no civil records predate 1945, although, in rare instances, families may have preserved their own copies of birth certificates and family registers. Applicants from Rangoon Division may request birth or death certificates from the above address. Those born outside Rangoon Division must apply to the Township Medical Officer of the township of their birth or death. Marriage certificates are available from the church where the wedding took place, but only for marriages between two Christians, or a Christian and a non-Christian. However, few such church records earlier than 1945 are available. Marriages between persons of other faiths are not officially registered.

For additional assistance, contact:

Embassy of Myanmar
2300 S Street, NW
Washington, DC 20008

Tel. (202) 332-3344

NAMIBIA

Send your requests to:

Subdivision of Births, Deaths and Marriages
Ministry of Home Affairs
Cohen Building
Kasino Street
Private Bag 13200
Windhoek, Namibia

Birth, marriage, and death records are available from the Ministry of Home Affairs in Windhoek, while divorce records are available from the Office of the Registrar (Room 34, High Court of Namibia, Windhoek). Namibia became independent in 1990. Vital registration follows the model of South Africa.

For additional assistance, contact:

Embassy of the Republic of Namibia — Tel. (202) 986-0540
1605 New Hampshire Avenue, NW
Washington, DC 20009

NAURU

Send your requests to:

Registrar General
Republic of Nauru
Nauru Island

Nauru's current vital registration is considered to be comprehensive. The currency in Nauru is the Australian dollar.

NEPAL

Send your requests to:

Village Development Committee (VDC) or Registrar's Office
(Town), Nepal

Although the birth and death registration bill was passed in 1974, it was implemented in some parts of Nepal only since 1980 or 1982. Certificates for events before 1974, if they exist, are issued by the Village Development Committee (VDC) or municipality where the event took place. People born after 1974 can obtain certificates from the local Registrar's Office.

For additional assistance, contact:

Embassy of Nepal — Tel. (202) 667-4550
2131 Leroy Place, NW
Washington, DC 20008

THE NETHERLANDS

Send your requests to:

Burgerlijke Stand
(Town)
The Netherlands

There is no central office for vital records in the Netherlands. Birth, death, marriage, and divorce certificates are available from the Civil Registry Office in the city/town where the event was registered. Vital records are on file from 1811. Current vital registration is considered to be comprehensive.

A large database of extracted civil registration records from all over the Netherlands can be found at https://www.wiewaswie.nl/.

For additional assistance, contact:

Centraal Bureau voor Genealogie
Postbus (PO Box) 11755
NL-2502 AT Den Haag (The Hague)
The Netherlands
Tel. (011) (31) 70-3150570
www.cbg.nl/

Royal Netherlands Embassy
4200 Linnean Avenue, NW
Washington, DC 20008
Tel. (877) 388-2443

NEW ZEALAND

Send your requests to:

The Department of Internal Affairs
Births, Deaths and Marriages
(Location: Level 3, 109 Featherston Street)
P.O. Box 10526
Wellington 6143, New Zealand
Tel. (011) (64) (4) 463 9362
E-mail: bmd.nz@dia.govt.nz
www.dia.govt.nz/Births-Deaths-and-Marriages

Registration in New Zealand was first required in 1848 for births and deaths, and in 1854 for marriages. The registration of Maori births and deaths did not become compulsory until 1913, although some earlier Maori births and deaths were registered in the general system. Genealogists may order a printout (which usually contains more information than a certificate).

You can view online indexes to historical vital records and order certificates at https://bdmhistoricalrecords.dia.govt.nz/Home/.

Cost for a certified Birth Certificate	NZ$26.50
Cost for a certified Marriage Certificate	NZ$26.50
Cost for a certified Civil Union Certificate	NZ$26.50
Cost for a certified Death Certificate	NZ$26.50
Cost for a Genealogy Printout for events 1848–1874	NZ$26.50
Cost for a Genealogy Printout for events after 1874	NZ$20.50

For additional assistance, contact:

National Archives of New Zealand
(Location: 10 Mulgrave Street)
P.O. Box 12-050
Wellington, New Zealand
Tel. (011) (64) (4) 499-5595
http://archives.govt.nz/

Embassy of New Zealand
37 Observatory Circle, NW
Washington, DC 20008
Tel. (202) 328-4800

BDM93B

Request for New Zealand Birth Certificate or Printout

You may be able to order your certificate and/or printout by phoning us

☎ Freephone 0800 22 77 77 (+64 4 463 9362 if outside New Zealand)

Step 1

The birth certificate/printout I want (Fields with * must be completed)

Surname*

First names*

Place of birth* (town or city)

Date of birth*

Parent 1 full name

Parent 2 full name

Parent 1 full name at birth, if different from above

Parent 2 full name at birth, if different from above

Other information (e.g. folio number)

Step 2

Delivery Address

If ordering certificates and printouts the certificate will be posted to you and the printout will be emailed

Delivery name

Flat number (if applicable) | Street number | Street

Suburb or rural locality

City, town or district

Postcode

Country (if not New Zealand)

If a standard certificate is ordered, it will be folded and the delivery name and address will appear on the back

Your daytime phone number ☎

Your email address (If ordering a Printout we will email it to you)

Definitions:

A certificate is an official document containing registered information.

A printout is a copy of the information from the registration and is not a legal document. Printouts are usually used for genealogical information purposes. A printout is either typed or a copy of the handwritten entry. Whether a typed or copy of the handwritten entry is issued depends on the record - *this is not an option*.

Step 3

How many certificates/printouts and Payment details

DO NOT POST CASH

Certificates

A certificate is an official document containing registered information

Standard & Forest	Standard & Beach	Standard	Forest	Beach
$39.80 per set	$39.80 per set	$26.50 each	$26.50 each	$26.50 each
Quantity	Quantity	Quantity	Quantity	Quantity

Printouts

A printout is either typed or a copy of the handwritten entry

1874 and before $26.50 each

1875 and after $20.40 each

Quantity

Courier fee (optional): ◯ To a New Zealand address add $5.00

Total amount to pay $

◯ I enclose a New Zealand cheque, New Zealand money order or International bankdraft in New Zealand dollars made out to: The Department of Internal Affairs

◯ Charge my credit/debit card:

◯ VISA ◯ Mastercard ◯ Amex ◯ Prezzy Card

Card number

Expiry date

Cardholder's name

Cardholder's signature

- If paying in person at our Auckland, Manukau, Wellington or Christchurch office we also accept EFTPOS and cash payments
- If the record cannot be found we will contact you and search fees will apply

Continued from Page 1 ☎ Freephone 0800 22 77 77
Phone +64 4 463 9362 (if outside New Zealand)

Warning It is an offence, punishable by imprisonment and/or a fine of up to $10,000, to make a false statement to obtain a certificate, printout or a source document, or to provide any means of identification knowing that it is false or is suspected to be forged or falsified

Steps 4 and 5 must be completed unless you are requesting a certificate/printout of a birth that occurred more than 100 years ago, or of a still-birth (this means the baby was not alive at birth) that occurred more than 50 years ago

Step 4

My declaration (the person ordering the certificate/printout must complete)

My Details

Surname | First names

Surname at birth (if different from above) | First names at birth (if different from above)

Place of birth (town or city) including country if not New Zealand | Date of birth

I declare that the information about me that is entered on this form is true and correct

Signature | Date signed

If ordering on behalf of a company state their name below and include an original signed request on letterhead

Your details or the company name will be entered in the Access Register. For information about the Access Register visit www.bdm.govt.nz

Step 5

Referee's declaration (any other person 16 years of age or older must complete)

I am 16 years of age or older and have known the orderer for at least 6 months or have seen a government issued photo identification of the orderer and I am satisfied the information about the orderer's identity stated in this form is true and correct

Signature of referee | Date signed

Full name of referee | Phone number of referee ☎

Contact address of referee

Step 6

Before posting make sure Step 5 is completed by any other person 16 years of age or older (even if you are ordering your own or a family members certifcate)

Post with fee to:
Certificate Team
Births, Deaths and Marriages
PO Box 10526
Wellington 6143
New Zealand

Privacy Statement The information on this form is collected under the Births, Deaths, Marriages, and Relationships Registration Act 1995. As part of processing your request, your identification details will be checked against other records held by Births, Deaths and Marriages or other government agencies, as authorised by law

Last updated 27 July 2013

Office Use Only B D

BDM93M

Request for New Zealand Marriage Certificate or Printout

You may be able to order your certificate and/or printout by phoning us
☎ Freephone 0800 22 77 77 (+64 4 463 9362 if outside New Zealand)

Definitions:
A certificate is an official document containing registered information.
A printout is a copy of the information from the registration and is not a legal document. Printouts are usually used for genealogical information purposes. A printout is either typed or a copy of the handwritten entry. Whether a typed or copy of the handwritten entry is issued depends on the record - *this is not an option.*

Part A The marriage certificate/printout I want (Fields with * must be completed)

Brides details

Bride's surname* (State the name married under, not that assumed on marriage) | Brides first names*

Groom's details

Groom's surname* (State the name married under, not that assumed on marriage) | Groom's first names*

Place of marriage* (town or city) including country if not New Zealand | Date of marriage*

Other information (e.g. folio number)

Part B Delivery Address

If ordering certificates and printouts: the certificate will be posted to you and the printout will be emailed

Delivery name

Flat number (if applicable) | Street number | Street

Suburb or rural locality

City, town or district | Postcode

Country (if not New Zealand)

If a certificate is ordered, the delivery name and address will appear on the back

Your daytime phone number ☎ | Your email address (If ordering a Printout we will email it to you)

Part C How many certificates/printouts and Payment details

DO NOT POST CASH

Certificates

A certificate is an official document containing registered information

$26.50 each — Quantity

Printouts

A printout is either typed or a copy of the handwritten entry

1874 and before $26.50 each — Quantity
1875 and after $20.40 each

◯ **Courier fee (optional)** add $5.00 if to a New Zealand address
If you wish to courier to an overseas address contact us for details

Total amount to pay $

◯ I enclose a New Zealand cheque, New Zealand money order or International bankdraft in New Zealand dollars made out to: The Department of Internal Affairs

◯ Charge my credit/debit card:

◯ VISA ◯ Mastercard ◯ Amex ◯ Prezzy Card

Card number

Expiry date

Cardholder's name

Cardholder's signature

- If paying in person at our Auckland, Manukau, Wellington or Christchurch office we also accept EFTPOS and cash payments
- If the record cannot be found we will contact you and search fees will apply

Continued from Page 1

☎ Freephone 0800 22 77 77
Phone +64 4 463 9362 (if outside New Zealand)

Declaration 1. and 2. must be completed unless you are requesting a certificate and/or printout of a marriage that occurred more than 80 years ago

Part D Declarations

Warning It is an offence, punishable by imprisonment and/or a fine of up to $10,000, to make a false statement to obtain a certificate, printout or a source document, or to provide any means of identification knowing that it is false or is suspected to be forged or falsified.

1. My declaration (the person ordering the certificate/printout must complete)

My Details

Surname

First names

Surname at birth (if different from above)

First names at birth (if different from above)

Place of birth (town or city) including country if not New Zealand

Date of birth

I declare that the information about me that is entered on this form is true and correct

Signature

Date signed

If ordering on behalf of a company state their name below and include an original signed request on letterhead

Your details or the company name will be entered in the Access Register. For information about the Access Register visit www.bdm.govt.nz

2. Referee's declaration (any other person 16 years of age or older must complete)

I am 16 years of age or older and have known the orderer for at least 6 months or have seen a government issued photo identification of the orderer and I am satisfied the information about the orderer's identity stated in this form is true and correct

Signature of referee

Date signed

Full name of referee

Phone number of referee ☎

Contact address of referee

Declarations - Make sure that both 1. and 2. are completed and signed

Post with fee to:
Certificate Team
Births, Deaths and Marriages
PO Box 10526
Wellington 6143
New Zealand

Privacy Statement The information on this form is collected under the Births, Deaths, Marriages, and Relationships Registration Act 1995. As part of processing your request your identification details will be checked against other records held by Births, Deaths and Marriages or other government agencies, as authorised by law.

Office Use Only

B D

Version 5 April 2012

BDM93C

Request for New Zealand Civil Union Certificate or Printout

You may be able to order your certificate and/or printout by phoning us
☎ Freephone 0800 22 77 77 (+64 4 463 9362 if outside New Zealand)

Definitions:
A certificate is an official document containing registered information.
A printout is a copy of the information from the registration and is not a legal document. Printouts are usually used for genealogical information purposes. A printout is either typed or a copy of the handwritten entry. Whether a typed or copy of the handwritten entry is issued depends on the record - *this is not an option.*

Part A The civil union certificate/printout I want (Fields with * must be completed)

Partner 1 details

Surname* (State the name entered into the civil union under) | First names*

Partner 2 details

Surname* (State the name entered into the civil union under) | First names*

Place of civil union* (town or city) | Date of civil union*

Other information

Part B Delivery Address

If ordering certificates and printouts: the certificate will be posted to you and the printout will be emailed

Delivery name (if different from above)

Flat number (if applicable) | Street number | Street

Suburb or rural locality

City, town or district | Postcode

Country (if not New Zealand)

If a standard certificate is ordered, the delivery name and address will appear on the back

Your daytime phone number (daytime) ☎ | **Your email address (If ordering a Printout we will email it to you)

Part C How many certificates/printouts and Payment details DO NOT POST CASH

Certificates

A certificate is an official document containing registered information

$26.50 each Quantity

Printouts

A civil union printout is a typed copy of the entry

$20.40 each Quantity

Total amount to pay $

○ I enclose a New Zealand cheque, New Zealand money order or International bankdraft in New Zealand dollars made out to: The Department of Internal Affairs

○ Charge my credit/debit card:

○ VISA ○ Mastercard ○ Amex ○ Prezzy Card

Card number

Expiry date

Cardholder's name

Cardholder's signature

○ **Courier fee (optional)** add $5.00 if to a New Zealand address
If you wish to courier to an overseas address contact us for details

- If paying in person at our Auckland, Manukau, Wellington or Christchurch office we also accept EFTPOS and cash payments
- If the record cannot be found we will contact you and search fees will apply

Continued from Page 1 ☎ Freephone 0800 22 77 77
Phone +64 4 463 9362 (if outside New Zealand)

The following two Declarations must be completed

Part D Declarations

Warning It is an offence, punishable by imprisonment and/or a fine of up to $10,000, to make a false statement to obtain a certificate, printout or a source document, or to provide any means of identification knowing that it is false or is suspected to be forged or falsified.

1. My declaration (the person ordering the certificate/printout must complete)

My Details

Surname

First names

Surname at birth (if different from above)

First names at birth (if different from above)

Place of birth (town or city) including country if not New Zealand

Date of birth

I declare that the information about me that is entered on this form is true and correct

Signature

Date signed

If ordering on behalf of a company state their name below and include an original signed request on letterhead

Your details or the company name will be entered in the Access Register. For information about the Access Register visit www.bdm.govt.nz

2. Referee's declaration (any other person 16 years of age or older must complete)

I am 16 years of age or older and have known the orderer for at least 6 months or have seen a government issued photo identification of the orderer and I am satisfied the information about the orderer's identity stated in this form is true and correct

Signature of referee

Date signed

Full name of referee

Phone number of referee ☎

Contact address of referee

Declarations - Make sure that both 1. and 2. are completed and signed

Post with fee to:
Certificate Team
Births, Deaths and Marriages
PO Box 10526
Wellington 6143
New Zealand

Privacy Statement The information on this form is collected under the Births, Deaths, Marriages, and Relationships Registration Act 1995. As part of processing your request, your identification details will be checked against other records held by Births, Deaths and Marriages or other government agencies, as authorised by law

Office Use Only

B D

BDM93D

Request for New Zealand Death Certificate or Printout

You may be able to order your certificate and/or printout by phoning us
☎ Freephone 0800 22 77 77 (+64 4 463 9362 if outside New Zealand)

Definitions:
A certificate is an official document containing registered information.
A printout is a copy of the information from the registration and is not a legal document. A printout is either typed or a copy of the handwritten entry. Whether a typed or copy of the handwritten entry is issued depends on the record - *this is not an option.*

Part A The death certificate/printout I want (Fields with * must be completed)

Deceased's surname* | Deceased's first names*

Place of death* (town or city) including country if not New Zealand | Date of death*

Spouse/Partner's surname (if any) | Spouse/Partner's first names (if any)

Deceased's mother's surname | Deceased's mother's first names

Deceased's father's surname | Deceased's father's first names

Other information (e.g. folio number)

Part B Delivery Address

If ordering certificates and printouts, the certificate will be posted to you and the printout will be emailed

Delivery name

Flat number (if applicable) | Street number | Street

Suburb or rural locality

City, town or district | Postcode

Country (if not New Zealand)

If a certificate is ordered, the delivery name and address will appear on the back

Your daytime phone number (daytime) ☎ | **Your email address (If ordering a Printout we will email it to you)

Part C How many certificates/printouts and Payment details

DO NOT POST CASH

Certificates

A certificate is an official document containing registered information

$26.50 each | Quantity

Printouts

A printout is either typed or a copy of the handwritten entry

1874 and before $26.50 each | Quantity
1875 and after $20.40 each

○ **Courier fee if within New Zealand (optional)** add $5.00
If you wish to courier to an overseas address contact us for details

Total amount to pay $

○ I enclose a New Zealand cheque, New Zealand money order or International bank draft in New Zealand dollars made out to: The Department of Internal Affairs

○ Charge my credit/debit card:

○ VISA ○ Mastercard ○ Amex ○ Prezzy Card

Card number

Expiry date

Cardholder's name

Cardholder's signature

- If paying in person at our Auckland, Manukau, Wellington or Christchurch office we also accept EFTPOS and cash payments
- If the record cannot be found we will contact you and search fees will apply

☎ Freephone 0800 22 77 77
Phone +64 4 463 9362 (if outside New Zealand)

The following two Declarations must be completed unless you are requesting a certificate/printout

- of a death that occurred more than 50 years ago, or
- the deceased's date of birth is more than 80 years ago

Part D Declarations

Warning It is an offence, punishable by imprisonment and/or a fine of up to $10,000, to make a false statement to obtain a certificate, printout or a source document, or to provide any means of identification knowing that it is false or is suspected to be forged or falsified.

1. My declaration (the person ordering the certificate/printout must complete)

My Details

Surname

First names

Surname at birth (if different from above)

First names at birth (if different from above)

Place of birth (town or city) including country if not New Zealand

Date of birth

I declare that the information about me that is entered on this form is true and correct

Signature

Date signed

If ordering on behalf of a company state their name below and include an original signed request on letterhead

Your details or the company name will be entered in the Access Register. For information about the Access Register visit www.bdm.govt.nz

2. Referee's declaration (any other person 16 years of age or older must complete)

I am 16 years of age or older and have known the orderer for at least 6 months or have seen a government issued photo identification of the orderer and I am satisfied the information about the orderer's identity stated in this form is true and correct

Signature of referee

Date signed

Full name of referee

Phone number of referee ☎

Contact address of referee

Declarations - Make sure that both 1. and 2. are completed and signed

Post with fee to:
Certificate Team
Births, Deaths and Marriages
PO Box 10526
Wellington 6143
New Zealand

Privacy Statement The information on this form is collected under the Births, Deaths, Marriages, and Relationships Registration Act 1995. As part of processing your request, your identification details will be checked against other records held by Births, Deaths and Marriages or other government agencies, as authorised by law.

Office Use Only B D

NICARAGUA

Send your requests to:

Registrador del Estado Civil
Central Registry Office
Managua, Nicaragua

Birth, death, marriage, and divorce certificates must be obtained from the Central Registry in Managua. Records in the Central Registry are maintained for the entire country and are stored on microfilm. These microfilm records were fortunately not destroyed during the 1972 earthquake or the civil strife in 1979. While church registers date from the 1500s, vital registration in Nicaragua didn't begin until 1867.

For additional assistance, contact:

Embassy of Nicaragua — Tel. (202) 939-6570
1627 New Hampshire Avenue, NW
Washington, DC 20009

NIGER

Send your requests to:

Mairie
Service d'État Civil
(Town), Niger

Certificates for events recorded in the cities of Niamey, Maradi, Tahoua, and Zinder are issued by the Mairie (Office of the Mayor), Service d'État Civil (Office of Vital Statistics) of the city. Other requests should be sent to the Sous-préfecture where the event was recorded. Formal vital registration began in 1933 for French citizens. It was expanded to include residents within fifteen miles of the registration centers in 1950.

For additional assistance, contact:

Embassy of Niger — Tel. (202) 483-4224
2204 R Street, NW
Washington, DC 20008

NIGERIA

Send your requests for Birth and Death Records to:

State Ministry of Health
Old Secretariat
Ikeja, Lagos, Nigeria

Send your requests for Marriage Records to:

Marriage Registry
19 Kingsway Road
Ikoyi, Lagos, Nigeria

Certified copies of Lagos birth and death records before 1979 can be obtained at the State Ministry of Health; for records after 1979, contact the local government that issued the original certificate. The Marriage Registry in Lagos has marriage records dating back to 1802. The records are filed by year and place of marriage and can be obtained by writing to the Marriage Registry, 19 Kingsway Road, Ikoyi, Lagos. For vital records outside of Lagos, contact the local government.

For additional assistance, contact:

Embassy of the Federal Republic of Nigeria — Tel. (202) 986-8400
3519 International Court, NW
Washington, DC 20008

NORWAY

Send your requests to:

Folkeregister
Local Population Register
(Town), Norway

or

Parish Church
(Town), Norway

A birth certificate (fødselsattest) is available for those born after January 1, 1916. Copies can be obtained from the parish where the parents resided at the time of birth (if born between 1916 and 1946) or from the Public Census Office, Folkeregisteret, in the city or town of birth if born after 1946.

If the marriage occurred before October 1, 2004, the marriage certificate (vielsesattest or vigselsattest) can be obtained from the church or civil authority where the marriage was solemnized. If the marriage took place after October 1, 2004, the marriage certificate can be obtained from the Public Census Office, Folkeregisteret. Divorce decree certificates (skillsmissesattest) rendered prior to 1954 can be obtained from the State Archives (Statesarkivet). The County Governor (Fylkesmann) furnishes certificates for divorces obtained after 1954.

A death certificate (dødsattest) can be obtained from the parish where the death occurred, from the sheriff (Lensmann), the police, or the probate court (Skifterett). Death certificates from the probate court are preferred.

For additional assistance, contact:

The National Archives of Norway
(Location: Folke Bernadottes vei 21)
Postboks 4013 Ullevål Stadion
0806 Oslo

Tel. (011) (47) 22 02 26 00
E-mail: riksarkivet@arkivverket.no
www.arkivverket.no/eng

The Norwegian Emigration Center
Strandkaien 31
4005 Stavanger
Norway

Tel. (011) (47) 51 53 88 60
E-mail: post@emigrationcenter.com
www.emigrationcenter.com

Embassy of Norway
2720 34th Street, NW
Washington, DC 20008

Tel. (202) 333-6000

OMAN

Send your requests to:

Director General of Health Affairs
Ministry of Health
P.O. Box 803, PC 112
Muscat, Oman

Birth certificates are available after 1979 to all persons, and prior to that date to persons born in the American Mission Hospital at Matrah. Marriage certificates are only available to those married in the Catholic Church, in the Protestant Church, or by the British Consul. Death and divorce certificates are unavailable, although divorce attestations affirming that a divorce occurred may be obtained from the Shariah court. The registration is not considered to be comprehensive.

For additional assistance, contact:

Embassy of the Sultanate of Oman
2535 Belmont Road, NW
Washington, DC 20008

Tel. (202) 387-1980

PAKISTAN

Send your requests to:

Registrar of Births and Deaths
(Municipality), Pakistan

or

NADRA
Shahrah-i-Jamhuriat, G-5/2
Islamabad 44000, Pakistan

www.nadra.gov.pk/

Prior to 1961 in large cities, Municipal Corporations were registering births and deaths, but in 1961 the Muslim Family Law Ordinance (MFLO) was passed to formalize the marriages and divorces as well. Municipal Corporation records in big cities are still available but it is sometimes difficult to locate them, and the condition of these records is not good. After 1961 the government began regulating the provision of some documents, but different offices were responsible for different documents, and implementation of regulations was inconsistent. In 2000 the National Database and Registration Authority (NADRA) was created to develop a database for registering the citizens of Pakistan. NADRA-issued identity cards, birth and death certificates, and marriage and divorce certificates are now available. However, NADRA is only responsible for the computerized database used to register records; they are not responsible for the records themselves. Union Councils, Municipal Corporations, directors of Health Services, and other local organizations are responsible for the actual records.

Birth Certificates are available for a fee, which varies by location and depending on whether a NADRA or Union Council birth certificate is requested. In larger cities, such as Karachi, Lahore, and Rawalpindi, Municipal Corporations issued birth certificates prior to 2001. Birth certificates for older Pakistanis, particularly those born before partition in 1947, are often unavailable. These Pakistanis may present a "No Entry Certificate" issued by the Municipal Corporation or a late-registered birth certificate. Almost all records of vital statistics of the Karachi Municipality were burned in 1948.

Even today, birth records are not uniformly kept, particularly in rural areas. Where a record of birth exists, a certificate to that effect may be obtained from the Registrar of Births and Deaths, the Municipal Corporation, or the Union Council. Caution should be used, however, in accepting such certificates, since they frequently do not match the original ledgers.

Records of deaths are inconsistent because most people only request one when required for a specific reason, but where the death is recorded, a certificate can be obtained from the Registrar of Births and Deaths of the municipality or Union Council. Cantonment boards in urban areas are also authorized to issue death certificates.

The marriage certificate for Muslims, the Nikah Nama, is registered with a Nikah Registrar, who is appointed by the municipality, Panchayat committee, Cantonment Board, or Union Council. Marriage certificates for religious minorities (Christians, Hindus, Parsis) are issued by church or temple leaders and are not generally registered with local authorities. Divorce certificates are available from municipality or Union Council or (in Azad Kashmir) District Mufti. Pakistan issues identity cards to citizens at age 18.

For additional assistance, contact:

Embassy of the Islamic Republic of Pakistan
3517 International Court, NW
Washington, DC 20008

Tel. (202) 243-6500

PALAU (BELAU)

Send your requests to:

Clerk of Court
P.O. Box 2248
Koror, PW 96940

After three decades as part of the United Nations Trust Territory of the Pacific under U.S. administration, this westernmost cluster of the Caroline Islands opted for independence in 1978 rather than join the Federated States of Micronesia. A Compact of Free Association with the U.S. went into effect in 1994, when the islands gained independence. Under the Compact, most citizens of Palau (but not alien spouses or children who are not Palauan citizens) enjoy unique immigration privileges. They may enter, work, study and reside in the United States indefinitely without visas.

For additional assistance, contact:

Embassy of the Republic of Palau
1701 Pennsylvania Avenue, NW, Suite 300
Washington, DC 20036

Tel. (202) 452-6814

PANAMA

Send your requests to:

Dirección General del Registro Civil
Correspondencia del Exterior
Tribunal Electoral
Apartado 5281
Panama 5, Republic of Panama

Civil documents (birth, death, divorce and marriage certificates) may be obtained from the Registro Civil. You can also order documents through the Consular Services section of the Panama Embassy (see below for contact information).

Birth records are available for persons born since April 15, 1914. Incomplete records of births prior to that date are compiled from secondary sources. The Registro Civil provides a literal copy (copia integra), which is a legal-size document that includes the date of registration of the birth and name and relationship of registrant, as well as the names of the grandparents. Copia integra birth certificates are mandatory for cases in which the petition is based on a relationship by birth (parent-child, child-parent, or siblings).

Marriage certificates since April 15, 1914, are available. Only scattered records are available prior to that date.

For additional assistance, contact:

Embassy of the Republic of Panama
Consular Services
2862 McGill Terrace, NW
Washington, DC 20008

Tel. (202) 387-5601
E-mail: consular@embassyofpanama.org
www.embassyofpanama.org/cms/certificates3.php

PAPUA NEW GUINEA

Send your requests to:

Registrar General's Office
P.O. Box 470
Waigani, N.C.D. 131, Papua New Guinea

Tel. (011) (675) 327-1732

Vital registration began in British New Guinea in 1892; however, with a limited registration organization, there is a large under-registration of vital records. Birth, death, and marriage certificates are available from the Registrar General's Office. Most foreign nationals and residents of towns register births with this office. Births in rural areas are frequently not registered. A certified copy of a final divorce decree can be obtained from the Registrar of the National Court (P.O. Box 7018, Boroko, N.C.D.111, Papua New Guinea).

For additional assistance, contact:

Embassy of Papua New Guinea
1779 Massachusetts Avenue, NW, Suite 805
Washington, DC 20036

Tel. (202) 745-3680

PARAGUAY

Send your requests to:

Dirección del Registro Civil
Ind. Nacional Y Manuel Dominguez
Asunción, Paraguay

Birth, death, and marriage certificates are obtainable from the Civil Registry (Dirección del Registro Civil). A person who has been baptized in the Roman Catholic Church in Paraguay may have a certificate of baptism issued by Ecclesiastical Authorities. While church registers date from the 1500s, vital registration in Paraguay began September 26, 1880.

For additional assistance, contact:

Embassy of Paraguay
2400 Massachusetts Avenue, NW
Washington, DC 20008

Tel. (202) 483-6960

PERU

Send your requests to:

Registro Civil
Concejo Provincial (or Concejo Distrital)
(Town), Peru

Birth, marriage and death certificates are issued by the Provincial Council (Concejo Provincial) or the District Council (Concejo Distrital) of the district or province in which the event occurred and was registered. Registrations have been obligatory under the civil code since 1936. Certificates vary in form and can be transcriptions in long hand, typewritten on a template, or microfilm photocopies of the original record. All bear the seal of either the Provincial or District Council and are certified by the Chief of the Civil Registry.

Some historical Peruvian baptism, marriage, and death records are available from the Family History Library; see www.familysearch.org for more information.

For additional assistance, contact:

Embassy of Peru — Tel. (202) 337-6670
2141 Wisconsin Avenue, NW
Washington, DC 20007

PHILIPPINES

Send your requests to:

National Statistics Office (NSO)
Civil Registration Department
Vibal Building, EDSA, Quezon City, Philippines

or

Local Civil Registrar
Municipal Building
(Town) Philippines

The National Statistics Office (NSO) is the central repository for civil records. Vital registration began in 1898 but local civil records in many localities in the Philippines have been destroyed due to war and natural calamities. Church records are frequently unavailable for the same reasons. When a specific civil document is unavailable, it is advisable to obtain a certificate of non-availability from the National Statistics Office (NSO). Birth, death, and marriage certificates can be ordered online through the "e-Census" website (www.ecensus.com.ph). Certified copies of the divorce certificate can be obtained from the appropriate court. Divorce was recognized in the Philippines between March 11, 1917, and August 29, 1950; since the latter date, courts have been empowered to grant legal separation (annulment) but not divorce.

Certified copies of birth, death, and marriage certificates can also be obtained from the local civil registrar of the place where the event occurred. However, certificates issued by the NSO are preferred.

The National Archives of the Philippines (NLP Building, T.M. Kalaw Street, Ermita, 1000 Manila; www.nationalarchives.gov.ph/) has birth records 1921–1933, with some 1916–1920; death records 1921–1933 for the provinces and 1899–1969 for Manila; and marriage records 1921–1933, with some 1934–1935.

For additional assistance, contact:

Embassy of the Philippines — Tel. (202) 467-9300
1600 Massachusetts Avenue, NW
Washington, DC 20036

THIS FORM IS NOT FOR SALE

Republic of the Philippines
National Statistics Office
OFFICE OF THE CIVIL REGISTRAR GENERAL
APPLICATION FORM - BIRTH CERTIFICATE

IMPORTANT : PLEASE READ GENERAL INSTRUCTIONS BEFORE FILLING UP THE FORM

1. Please PRINT letters in the spaces provided. Please CHECK (✓) appropriate box(es).
2. A valid ID is required for both owner & requester of document.
3. An authorization is required from representative's upon filing of the application.

Request for : ☐ BIRTH CERTIFICATE ☐ AUTHENTICATION ☐ BIRTH CARD ☐ CDLI

Number of copies ? ☐ One ☐ Two Others (Specify) __________

Birth Reference No. BReN (if known) ☐☐☐☐☐ - ☐☐☐☐☐ - ☐☐☐ - ☐ Sex: Male ☐ Female ☐

OWNER'S PERSONAL INFORMATION (For married women, please use maiden name)

Last Name

First Name

Middle Name

Date of Birth MONTH DAY YEAR

Place of Birth City / Municipality

Province

Please specify country if born abroad only: Country

NAME OF FATHER

Last Name

First Name

Middle Name

MAIDEN NAME OF MOTHER

Last Name

First Name

Middle Name

REGISTERED LATE? Check (✓) appropriate box ☐ No ☐ Yes When: ____________________

Requester's Tax Identification No.(TIN) (if known) ☐☐☐ - ☐☐☐ - ☐☐☐

PLEASE TURN TO BACK PAGE ➡

FOR NSO USE ONLY
TRANSACTION NUMBER :

PURPOSE : Choose one and check (✓) appropriate box

☐ Claim Benefits / Loans ☐ Employment (Local) ☐ School Requirement

☐ Passport / Travel (Specify Country: ________) ☐ Others (Specify) : ____________

☐ Employment (abroad) (Specify Country: ____________)

REQUESTER'S INFORMATION

Last Name , First Name , M I

____

Mailing Address [ ] [ ]
House No. Street Name / Barangay

City / Municipality [ ]

Province [ ]

Tel. No. [ ]

NOTE : AUTHORIZATION and ID of the document owner together with requester's ID are required if the requester is NOT any of the following :

a. the owner of the document;
b. his/her parent;
c. his/her spouse;
d. his/her direct descendant;
e. his/her legal guardian/institution-in-charge, if minor;

I understand that as per PD 603 (Child & Youth Welfare Code),birth certificate documents,if available in this office cannot be released to me without proper authorization from the owner of the document, his/her parent (if minor), his/her spouse, his/her direct descendant, or his/her authorized guardian/institution-in-charge.

____
Signature of Applicant

FOR NSO USE ONLY

Converted ? ☐ Y ☐ N

	MONTH	DAY	YEAR
Date of Filing	[ ]	/ [ ]	/ 20[ ]
Date of Release	[ ]	/ [ ]	/ 20[ ]

Remarks :

For CDLI request only:
CDLI type : ____________
☐ Proper : ________ pages
☐ Attachment : ________ pages

Received by : ______________________ Date of receipt : ______________

THIS FORM IS NOT FOR SALE

RMAO Form 12
Revised 1998
PLEASE PRINT INFORMATION

NATIONAL ARCHIVES OF THE PHILIPPINES
MANILA
REQUEST FOR BIRTH RECORD

TR No. B - ____________

Date ____________

NAME (Full Name)	FATHER'S FULL NAME	MOTHER'S FULL MAIDEN NAME

PLACE OF BIRTH	DATE OF BIRTH

Born at Fabella Memorial Hospital? Yes ( ) No ( )

Indicate if Previous Request was already made Yes ( ) No ( )

Available ( ) Not available ( )

If not available, do you want to secure a Certification of Non-Availability?

Yes ( ) No ( )

PURPOSE	No. of Copies Requested

NAME OF REQUESTING PARTY	SIGNATURE	ADDRESS & TEL. NO.

FOR ARCHIVES PERSONNEL ONLY

Records Consulted	Record is : ( ) Available ( ) Not available ( ) Suspense	Schedule Date ____________ GDS / SDS ARCHIVIST

O.R. No.	Date Paid	Amount	RS Archivist	Typist / Archivist

THIS FORM IS NOT FOR SALE

Republic of the Philippines
National Statistics Office
OFFICE OF THE CIVIL REGISTRAR GENERAL

APPLICATION FORM - MARRIAGE CERTIFICATE

IMPORTANT : PLEASE READ GENERAL INSTRUCTION BEFORE FILLING UP THE FORM

Please PRINT letters in the spaces provided. Please CHECK (✓) appropriate box(es)

Request for : ☐ MARRIAGE CERTIFICATE ☐ AUTHENTICATION ☐ CDLI

Number of copies: ☐ One ☐ Two Others (Specify) : ________

Birth Reference No. of Husband
BReN (if known) ☐☐☐☐☐ - ☐☐☐☐☐ - ☐☐ - ☐

Birth Reference No. of Wife
BReN (if known) ☐☐☐☐☐ - ☐☐☐☐☐ - ☐☐ - ☐

NAME OF HUSBAND

Last Name

First Name

Middle Name

Husband's Tax Identification No.(TIN)
(if known) ☐☐☐ - ☐☐☐ - ☐☐☐

MAIDEN NAME OF WIFE

Last Name

First Name

Middle Name

Wife's Tax Identification No.(TIN)
(if known) ☐☐☐ - ☐☐☐ - ☐☐☐

DATE OF MARRIAGE

MONTH DAY YEAR

PLACE OF MARRIAGE

City / Municipality

Province

Please specify country if married abroad only:

Country

REGISTERED LATE? ☐ No ☐ Yes When: ____________
Check (✓) appropriate box

PLEASE TURN TO BACK PAGE ➡

FOR NSO USE ONLY
TRANSACTION NUMBER :

PURPOSE : Choose one and check (✓) appropriate box

☐ Claim Benefits / Loans ☐ Employment (Local) ☐ School Requirement

☐ Passport / Travel (Specify Country: ____________) ☐ Others (Specify) : ____________

☐ Employment (abroad) (Specify Country: ____________)

REQUESTER'S INFORMATION

Last Name , First Name , M I

____

Mailing Address ☐☐☐☐ ☐☐☐☐☐☐☐☐☐☐☐☐☐☐☐

House No. Street Name / Barangay

City / Municipality

Province

Tel. No.

FOR NSO USE ONLY

	MONTH	DAY	YEAR
Date of Filing	☐☐ /	☐☐ /	20☐☐
Date of Release	☐☐ /	☐☐ /	20☐☐

Remarks :

Converted ? ☐ Y ☐ N

For CDLI request only:

CDLI type : ____________

☐ Proper : ________ pages

☐ Attachment : ________ pages

Received by : ______________________ Date of receipt : ____________

THIS FORM IS NOT FOR SALE

NATIONAL ARCHIVES OF THE PHILIPPINES

PAMBANSANG SINUPAN

NAP Form No. 16
Rev. 2002

MANILA

REQUEST FOR MARRIAGE RECORD

TR No. M-____________
Date: ______________

PLEASE PRINT INFORMATION

Name of HUSBAND	WIFE's Maiden Name:
Place of Marriage:	Date of Marriage:
Purpose:	Copies of Requested:

Name of Requesting Party:	Signature:	Address & Tel. No.:

FOR ARCHIVES PERSONNEL ONLY

Records Consulted:	Record is: ( ) Available ( ) Not Available ( ) Suspense	Schedule Date: GD/SD Archivist:

O.R. No.:	Date Paid:	Amount:	RS Archivist:	Typist/Archivist:

THIS FORM IS NOT FOR SALE

Republic of the Philippines
National Statistics Office
OFFICE OF THE CIVIL REGISTRAR GENERAL

APPLICATION FORM - DEATH CERTIFICATE

IMPORTANT : PLEASE READ GENERAL INSTRUCTION BEFORE FILLING UP THE FORM

Please PRINT letters in the spaces provided. Please CHECK (✓) appropriate box(es)

Request for : ☐ DEATH CERTIFICATE ☐ AUTHENTICATION ☐ CDLI

Number of copies ? ☐ One ☐ Two Others (Specify) : ________

Birth Reference No. BReN (if known) ☐☐☐☐☐ - ☐☐☐☐☐ - ☐☐ - ☐ Sex: Male ☐ Female ☐

Last Name

First Name

Middle Name

Date of Death MONTH DAY YEAR

Place of Death City / Municipality

Province

Please specify country if died abroad only: Country

REGISTERED LATE? Check (✓) appropriate box ☐ No ☐ Yes When: ____________

Requester's Tax Identification No.(TIN) (if known) ☐☐☐ - ☐☐☐ - ☐☐☐

PURPOSE : Choose one and check (✓) appropriate box

☐ Claim Benefits / Loans ☐ Employment (Local) ☐ School Requirement

☐ Passport / Travel (Specify Country: ____________) ☐ Others (Specify) : ____________

☐ Employment (abroad) (Specify Country: ____________)

REQUESTER'S INFORMATION

Last Name , First Name , M I

Mailing Address House No. Street Name / Barangay

City / Municipality

Province

Tel. No.

FOR NSO USE ONLY
TRANSACTION NUMBER :

FOR NSO USE ONLY

	MONTH		DAY		YEAR
Date of Filing		/		/	20
Date of Release		/		/	20

Remarks :

Converted ? ☐ Y ☐ N

For CDLI request only:

CDLI type : ____________________

☐ Proper : ________ pages

☐ Attachment : ________ pages

Received by : ______________________________ Date of receipt : ____________________

THIS FORM IS NOT FOR SALE

NATIONAL ARCHIVES OF THE PHILIPPINES
MANILA

TR No. D - ____________

Date ____________

REQUEST FOR DEATH RECORD

PLEASE PRINT INFORMATION

NAME OF DECEASED	PLACE OF DEATH	DATE OF DEATH
PURPOSE		NO. OF COPIES REQUESTED
NAME OF REQUESTING PARTY	SIGNATURE	ADDRESS & TEL. NO.

FOR ARCHIVES PERSONNEL ONLY

Records Consulted	Record is : ☐ Available ☐ Not available ☐ Suspense	Schedule Date ____________ GDS / SDS ARCHIVIST

O.R. No.	Date Paid	Amount	RS Archivist	Typist / Archivist

POLAND

Send your requests to:

Urzad Stanu Cywilnego
(Civil Registry Office)
(Town), Poland

Birth, death, and marriage records are public records after 100 years; records prior to that period are confidential and restricted to authorized applicants. There is no central office for vital records in Poland. Copies of birth, death, and marriage records can be obtained from the Civil Registry Office (Urzad Stanu Cywilnego) of the appropriate locality. Vital records are on file from 1809, with many older vital records housed at the National Archives. Applicants residing outside Poland may apply for the documents at the nearest Polish consulate or directly from the Civil Registry Office. A copy of a divorce decree for all cases adjudicated after 1990 may be obtained from the District Court (Sad Okregowy) where the decree was rendered. Divorce cases before 1990 were handled by Regional Courts (Sady Rejonowe).

The Polish State Archives has digitized vital records online (www.szukajwarchiwach.pl/). In addition, there are a number of other online databases containing indexes and digitized images of Polish vital records, including the Poznań Project (http://poznan-project.psnc.pl); BASIA (www.basia.famula.pl/en/); PTG (www.ptg.gda.pl/); and Geneteka (www.geneteka.genealodzy.pl/).

For additional assistance, contact:

State Archives of Poland
ul. Rakowiecka 2D
02-517 Warsaw, Poland
E-mail: ndap@archiwa.gov.pl
www.archiwa.gov.pl/

Embassy of the Republic of Poland
Consular Division
2224 Wyoming Avenue, NW
Washington, DC 20008
Tel. (202) 499-1700
E-mail: washington.consular@msz.gov.pl

APPLICATION FOR COPY OF BIRTH CERTIFICATE

PLEASE PRINT OR TYPE ALL INFORMATION REQUIRED ON THIS FORM

FULL NAME ON CERTIFICATE (FIRST - LAST)	
FATHER'S NAME (FIRST - LAST)	
MOTHER'S MAIDEN NAME (FIRST - LAST)	
DATE OF BIRTH (DAY - MONTH - YEAR)	**RELIGION** (FOR BIRTHS BEFORE 1945)
PLACE OF BIRTH CITY COUNTY PROVINCE	

NOTE: **ALL NAMES OF LOCATIONS PROVIDED IN THIS FORM MUST BE IN POLISH**
If birth took place on the territory of the former Republic of Poland, you have to determine in what country (Poland, Ukraine, Belarus, Russia or Lithuania) the location of birth is now situated. It will be necessary to check an old map or atlas of the period for the name of the place. Names of many places were changed after both World Wars. Services provided through local library (geographical section), the Map Division of the Library of Congress, the National Geographic Society, etc. may be helpful to ascertain this type of information. Please also note that in Poland there are multiply locations with the same names. Make sure to state also county and the province of birth.

NAME	FIRST	MIDDLE	LAST
MAILING ADDRESS	STREET		
	CITY	STATE	ZIP CODE
TELEPHONE NUMBER		**APPLICANT'S SIGNATURE**	

A **41 USD** Non-refundable fee for each record requested must accompany this application. Make Money Order payable to "Embassy of Poland". Personal checks will not be accepted. If no record is found, a certificate stating that the record is unavailable will be issued. It may take up to 3 months to process the application. Please attach a notarized copy of your ID.

MAIL THIS FORM TO:

EMBASSY OF POLAND, CONSULAR DIVISION
2224 WYOMING AVE NW, WASHINGTON, DC 20008

APPLICATION FOR COPY OF MARRIAGE CERTIFICATE

PLEASE PRINT OR TYPE ALL INFORMATION REQUIRED ON THIS FORM

FULL NAME OF THE GROOM (FIRST - LAST)
NAME OF GROOM'S FATHER (FIRST - LAST)
FULL MAIDEN NAME OF THE BRIDE (FIRST - LAST)
NAME OF BRIDE'S FATHER (FIRST - LAST)
DATE OF MARRIAGE (DAY - MONTH - YEAR)
PLACE OF MARRIAGE CITY COUNTY PROVINCE

NOTE: **ALL NAMES OF LOCATIONS PROVIDED IN THIS FORM MUST BE IN POLISH**

If birth took place on the territory of the former Republic of Poland, you have to determine in what country (Poland, Ukraine, Belarus, Russia or Lithuania) the location of birth is now situated. It will be necessary to check an old map or atlas of the period for the name of the place. Names of many places were changed after both World Wars. Services provided through local library (geographical section), the Map Division of the Library of Congress, the National Geographic Society, etc. may be helpful to ascertain this type of information. Please also note that in Poland there are multiply locations with the same names. Make sure to state also county and the province of birth.

NAME	FIRST	MIDDLE	LAST
MAILING ADDRESS	STREET		
	CITY	STATE	ZIP CODE
TELEPHONE NUMBER		**APPLICANT'S SIGNATURE**	

A **41 USD** Non-refundable fee for each record requested must accompany this application. Make Money Order payable to "Embassy of Poland". Personal checks will not be accepted. If no record is found, a certificate stating that the record is unavailable will be issued. It may take up to 3 months to process the application. Please attach a notarized copy of your ID.

MAIL THIS FORM TO:
EMBASSY OF POLAND, CONSULAR DIVISION
2224 WYOMING AVE NW, WASHINGTON, DC 20008

APPLICATION FOR COPY OF DEATH CERTIFICATE

PLEASE PRINT OR TYPE ALL INFORMATION REQUIRED ON THIS FORM

FULL NAME ON CERTIFICATE (FIRST - LAST)	
FATHER'S NAME (FIRST - LAST)	
MOTHER'S MAIDEN NAME (FIRST - LAST)	
DATE OF BIRTH (DAY - MONTH - YEAR)	**RELIGION** (FOR BIRTHS BEFORE 1945)
PLACE OF BIRTH CITY COUNTY PROVINCE	

NOTE: **ALL NAMES OF LOCATIONS PROVIDED IN THIS FORM MUST BE IN POLISH**
If birth took place on the territory of the former Republic of Poland, you have to determine in what country (Poland, Ukraine, Belarus, Russia or Lithuania) the location of birth is now situated. It will be necessary to check an old map or atlas of the period for the name of the place. Names of many places were changed after both World Wars. Services provided through local library (geographical section), the Map Division of the Library of Congress, the National Geographic Society, etc. may be helpful to ascertain this type of information. Please also note that in Poland there are multiply locations with the same names. Make sure to state also county and the province of birth.

NAME	FIRST	MIDDLE	LAST
MAILING ADDRESS	STREET		
	CITY	STATE	ZIP CODE
TELEPHONE NUMBER	**APPLICANT'S SIGNATURE**		

A **41 USD** Non-refundable fee for each record requested must accompany this application. Make Money Order payable to "Embassy of Poland". Personal checks will not be accepted. If no record is found, a certificate stating that the record is unavailable will be issued. It may take up to 3 months to process the application. Please attach a notarized copy of your ID.

MAIL THIS FORM TO:

EMBASSY OF POLAND, CONSULAR DIVISION
2224 WYOMING AVE NW, WASHINGTON, DC 20008

PORTUGAL

Send your requests to:

Conservatória do Registo Civil
(Town), Portugal

Civil registration in Portugal began officially in 1878 but was used only by non-Catholics, since the Catholics had vital events recorded in their church registers. However, in 1911 civil registration was made compulsory. These records are in the local registrar offices—called Conservatórias do Registo Civil—in each municipality (a list of the registrar offices is available at www.portaldocidadao.pt). When records are 100 years old, they are transferred to the district archives with a copy sent to the National Archives in Lisbon (Alameda da Universidade, 1649-010 Lisboa, Portugal).

The Consular Section of the Portuguese Embassy in Washington (see contact information below) issues birth, marriage, and death certificates for Portuguese citizens, provided that these documents are in digitized form. For those older certificates that are not digitized, or those of deceased persons, you should contact the local registrar office directly.

For additional assistance, contact:

Embassy of Portugal
Consular Section
2012 Massachusetts Avenue, NW
Washington, DC 20036

Tel. (202) 332-3007
E-mail: mail@scwas.dgaccp.pt
www.embassyportugal-us.org/Embassy_of_Portugal/Consular_Affairs.html

QATAR

Send your requests to:

Ministry of Public Health
Doha, Qatar

Certificates are available for births and deaths occurring after 1969; prior to that date records are not complete. Applicants should apply at the Ministry of Public Health in Doha. Marriage and divorce certificates are available for Muslims after 1957 but are not available for Christians. Applicants should apply to the President of the Sharia Court (P.O. Box 232, Doha, Qatar).

For additional assistance, contact:

Embassy of the State of Qatar
2555 M Street, NW
Washington, DC 20037

Tel. (202) 274-1600

ROMANIA

Send your requests to:

Office of Vital Statistics (Oficiul Starii Civile)
(Town), Romania

There is no central office for vital records in Romania. Copies of birth, marriage, and death certificates are issued by the Office of Vital Statistics (Oficiul Starii Civile) in the local mayor's office, though records of marriages terminated by divorce are not available. Divorce records are available from the court that granted the divorce. Vital records are on file from 1865, and in many areas begin much earlier.

For additional assistance, contact:

Embassy of Romania — Tel. (202) 332-4848
1607 23rd Street, NW
Washington, DC 20008

RUSSIA

Send your requests to:

Bureau of Acts of Civil Status (ZAGS)
(Town), Russia

Certified copies of vital records may be obtained by applying to the Bureau of Acts of Civil Status (ZAGS) of the locality having custody of the records. In the United States, Russian documents can be requested through the Consular Division of the Russian Embassy in Washington, DC, or the Russian Consulates General in San Francisco, New York, or Seattle. Some civil records were destroyed during World War II.

For additional assistance, contact:

Embassy of the Russian Federation — Tel. (202) 939-8914
Consular Division
2641 Tunlaw Road, NW
Washington, DC 20007

RWANDA

Send your requests to:

Directeur de l'État Civil
Ministère de la Justice
Kigali, Rwanda

Vital registration began May, 4 1895. It is not comprehensive.

For additional assistance, contact:

Embassy of Rwanda — Tel. (202) 232-2882
1714 New Hampshire Avenue, NW
Washington, DC 20009

ST. KITTS and NEVIS

Send your requests to:

Registrar General's Office
Health Centre
P.O. Box 236
Basseterre, St. Kitts-Nevis

Tel. (869) 465-2521

The Registrar General's Office has records for St. Kitts from January 1, 1859, and for Nevis from August 1, 1869. Current vital registration is considered to be comprehensive. The Nevis Historical & Conservation Society Archives (P.O. Box 563, Charlestown, Nevis; tel. 869-469-0408) has Methodist and Anglican Church records, some dating back to 1825, as well as birth, marriage, and death records for St. James Parish and St. Pauls Parish.

For additional assistance, contact:

National Archives
Government Headquarters
Church Street
Basseterre, St.Kitts & Nevis, W.I.

www.nationalarchives.gov.kn

Embassy of St. Kitts and Nevis
3216 New Mexico Avenue, NW
Washington, DC 20016

Tel. (202) 686-2636
E-mail: stkittsnevis@embskn.com

ST. LUCIA

Send your requests to:

Registrar of Civil Status
Peynier Street
Castries, St. Lucia, West Indies

Tel. (758) 452-1257

The Registrar has records from January 1, 1869. Current registration is considered to be comprehensive. The local churches also have their own records.

For additional assistance, contact:

St. Lucia National Archives
P.O. Box 3060
La Clery
Castries, St. Lucia, West Indies

Tel. (758) 452-1654

Embassy of St. Lucia
3216 New Mexico Avenue, NW
Washington, DC 20016

Tel. (202) 364-6792

Registry of Civil Status

Application for a Vital Record

For official use only	
Amt: ______	Receipt#: _________
Collection date:	Signature:

1. Applicant Information

First Name: ______________________ Last Name: ______________________

Relationship to the subject: ☐ Mother ☐ Father ☐ Sister ☐ Brother ☐ Other:______________

Mailing address: ____

Telephone: ______________ Email Address: ______________________

NIS #: ______________ Other form of ID: ______________________

2. Subject Information

Last Name: | | | | | | | | | | | | | | | | | | | | | | |

First Name: | | | | | | | | | | | | | | | | | | | | | | |

Middle Name(s): ____

Date of birth (dd/mm/yyyy): ___/___/___ Place of birth: ______________ Sex(M/F): _____

Mother's name: ______________________ Maiden name: ______________

Mother's alias : ______________________

Father's name: ______________________ Father's alias: ______________

3. Type of Certificate

☐ Birth: enter number of copies______ ($8 per copy)

☐ Baptism: enter number of copies______ ($8 per copy)

☐ Death: enter number of copies______ enter date of death (dd/mm/yyyy): ______________ ($5 per copy)

☐ Burial: enter number of copies______ enter date of burial (dd/mm/yyyy): ______________ ($6 per copy)

☐ Adoption: enter number of copies______ enter date of adoption (dd/mm/yyyy): ____________ ($8 per copy)

enter names of adoptive parents: ______________________________________

Signature: ______________________ **Date:** ______________________

Explanation Notes

You must be at least 18 years of age to apply. Personal information collected on this form will be used to provide certified copies of civil registry records, to verify the information provided, and for security purposes. It is an offense to willfully make a false statement on this form. Questions may be directed to: The Assistant Registrar, Registry of Civil Status, Castries, St. Lucia.

1. Applicant Information

This is information about yourself (the person completing the application form), and must be the same person who is submitting the form to the Registry of Civil Status.

First Name, Last Name - Enter your full first and last names

Relationship to the subject - Select the relationship between yourself and the person named on certificate. If other relationship, then enter the type of relationship for example Guardian.

Mailing address - Enter the mailing address, or the nearest local post office to where you live.

Telephone - Full telephone number (include area code if phone is listed outside of St. Lucia)

Email Address - Optional.

NIS #, Other form of ID - Enter your NIS number. If you do not have an NIS card, then enter another form of ID such as Passport and the passport number, or Driver's License and Driver's License number if available. Your photo id must be shown when submitting this application

2. Subject Information

This is information about the person who is named on the certificate.

First Name, Last Name - Enter the full first and last names of the subject. If the person is (or was) married, enter the maiden name as the last name.

Middle Name(s) - Enter all known middle names of the subject

Date of birth - Enter the subject's date of birth in the form shown. For example if the person was born on the 22nd of October 1979, then enter 22/10/1979

Place of birth - Enter the place of birth if known. For example Victoria Hospital, St. Jude's Hospital.

Mother's name - Enter the full legal name of the mother of the subject

Maiden name - If the mother is married, enter her maiden name

Mother's alias - Enter any known aliases of the mother, that is any other names that the mother may be known as

Father's name - Enter the full name of the father as listed on the certificate if known

Father's alias - Enter any known aliases of the father

3. Type of Certificate

In this section select the type(s) of certificates you are applying for, as well as the number of copies of each type of certificate. If ordering a death, burial, or adoption certificate, also enter the additional information indicated. Note the following:

- The maximum number of copies of a certificate that can be applied for at any one time is TWO
- Certificate costs are as listed. However an additional amount will be charged if a detailed search for the record is required or if application is made for an emergency certificate.

Signature, Date: By signing the form you authorize the Registry of Civil Status to issue the requested information, and consent to the Government of St. Lucia verifying the collected information from any other sources that may be necessary. You also indicate that you are aware that it is an offence to willfully make a false statement on this form.

Registry of Civil Status

Application for a Vital Record

For official use only
Amt: ______ Receipt#: __________
Collection date: ________ Signature: __________

1. Applicant Information

First Name: ____________ Last Name: ____________

Mailing address: ____________

Telephone: ____________ Email Address: ____________

NIS #: ____________ Other form of ID: ____________

Are you the: ☐ Bride ☐ Groom ☐ Other: ____________

2. Wedding Information

Date of wedding (dd/mm/yyyy): ____________ Parish: ____________

Church/Denomination/Other: ____________

3. Bride's Information

First Name:

Maiden Name:

Middle Name: ____________ Date of birth (dd/mm/yyyy): / /

4. Groom's Information

First Name:

Last Name:

Middle Name: ____________ Date of birth (dd/mm/yyyy): / /

5. Certificate Information

Number of copies______ ($8 per standard copy)

Signature: ____________ **Date:** ____________

Explanation Notes

You must be at least 18 years of age to apply. Personal information collected on this form will be used to provide certified copies of civil registry records, to verify the information provided, and for security purposes. It is an offence to willfully make a false statement on this form. Questions may be directed to: The Registrar, Registry of Civil Status, Castries, St. Lucia.

1. Applicant Information

This is information about yourself (the person completing the application form), and must be the same person who is submitting the form to the Registry of Civil Status.

First Name, Last Name - Enter your full first and last names

Mailing address - Enter the mailing address, or the nearest local post office to where you live.

Telephone - Full telephone number (include area code if phone is listed outside of St. Lucia)

Email Address - Optional.

NIS #, Other form of ID - Enter your NIS number. If you do not have an NIS card, then enter another form of ID such as Passport and the passport number, or Driver's License and Driver's License number. Your photo id must be shown when submitting this application.

Relationship to the bride or groom - If you are not the bride or the groom, then select 'Other' and enter the relationship for example 'Mother of bride' or 'Minister of religion'

2. Wedding Information

Date of wedding - Enter the date of the wedding in the format indicated

Parish of wedding - Indicate parish where the wedding was held for example Castries, Gros Islet, etc

Denomination/Church/ Other - Indicate the Church where the wedding took place; if not at a church, then indicate the location for example 'Pigeon Island Park' or the full name of the hotel

3. Bride's Information

First name - Enter the full first name of the bride

Maiden name - The last name which appears on the birth certificate of the bride

Middle name - At least one middle name of the bride

Date of birth - Full date of birth in the format indicated

4. Groom's Information

First name, Last name, Middle name - Enter the complete name of the groom as would appear on his birth certificate

Date of birth - Full date of birth in the format indicated

5. Certificate Information

Enter the number of copies required. Note that the maximum number of certificates issued at any one time is TWO (2)

- Certificate costs are as listed. However an additional amount will be charged if a detailed search for the record is required or if application is made for an emergency certificate.

Signature, Date: By signing the form you authorize the Registry of Civil Status to issue the requested information, and consent to the Government of St. Lucia verifying the collected information from any other sources that may be necessary. You also indicate that you are aware that it is an offence to willfully make a false statement on this form.

ST. VINCENT and the GRENADINES

Send your requests to:

Registrar General's Office — Tel. (784) 457-1424
Government Buildings
Kingstown, St. Vincent and the Grenadines

Birth and death records are complete since 1864, and marriage records are complete since 1868. Current registration is considered to be comprehensive. The local churches also have their own records. Divorce certificates are available from the Registrar of the Supreme Court, Kingstown, and are complete since 1915.

For additional assistance, contact:

National Archives — Tel. (784) 457-1424
Department of Libraries, Archives and Documentation Services
Lower Middle Street
Kingstown, St. Vincent and the Grenadines

Embassy of St. Vincent and the Grenadines — Tel. (202) 364-6730
3216 New Mexico Avenue, NW
Washington, DC 20016

SAMOA (FORMERLY WESTERN SAMOA)

Send your requests to:

Registrar General of Births, Deaths, Marriages and Adoptions
Department of Justice
P.O. Box 49
Apia, Samoa

The Independent State of Samoa was known as Western Samoa from 1914–1997. Vital registration began in the mid-1800s and is now centrally administered by the Registrar General. The Registrar of the Supreme Court is required to send copies of all divorces to the Registrar General.

For additional assistance, contact:

Embassy of the Independent State of Samoa — Tel. (212) 599-6196
800 Second Avenue, Suite 400D
New York, NY 10017

SAN MARINO

Send your requests to:

Office of Vital Statistics (Ufficio de Stato Civile)
(Town), San Marino

or

Parish Priest
(Parish), San Marino

Certificates are obtainable from the office of Vital Statistics (Ufficio de Stato Civile) of the town (comune) where the event took place. Prior to 1985 divorce was not granted. Presently a divorce decree or a certificate showing that a person is divorced can be obtained from the Office of Vital Statistics. Vital records are also available from the Roman Catholic parish churches in San Marino. Current vital registration is considered to be comprehensive.

For additional assistance, contact:

Archivio di Stato della Repubblica di San Marino (State Archives)
Contrada Omerelli 13
47890 San Marino
E-mail: archivo@pa.sm

Embassy of the Republic of San Marino
1711 N Street, NW, 2nd Floor
Washington, DC 20036
Tel. (202) 223-2418

SÃO TOMÉ and PRÍNCIPE

Send your requests to:

Conservatória do Registo Civil
Ministry of Interior
São Tomé, São Tomé and Príncipe

São Tomé and Príncipe were under Portuguese control until independence in 1975. Vital registration here is considered to be comprehensive.

For additional assistance, contact:

Arquivo Historico (National Archives)
C.P. 87
São Tomé, São Tomé and Príncipe
Tel. (011) (239) 222 23 06
E-mail: arquivo@ahstp.org

Permanent Mission of São Tomé and Príncipe
122 E. 42nd Street
New York, NY 10168
Tel. (212) 557-2043

SAUDI ARABIA

Send your requests to:

Agency of Civil Affairs
The Ministry of Interior
P.O. Box 11134
Riyadh, Kingdom of Saudi Arabia

For persons born prior to 1968 in the western (Jeddah) and eastern (Dhahran) provinces and 1980 in the central (Riyadh) province, birth certificates are not available. In lieu of birth certificates, the nationality card (Tabiya) should be used. Marriages and divorces are conducted in accordance with Sharia (Islamic) law. Sharia courts issue marriage and divorce certificates.

For additional assistance, contact:

Royal Embassy of Saudi Arabia — Tel. (202) 944-3126
Consular Section
601 New Hampshire Avenue, NW
Washington, DC 20037

SENEGAL

Send your requests to:

Office of the Mayor (La Mairie)
(Town), Senegal

Certificates can be obtained from the Mayor's Office in the town where the event took place. Church registers date from the colonial period, and vital registration began in 1916 for most French citizens. Modern vital registration began in 1961 and is not comprehensive.

For additional assistance, contact:

Embassy of Senegal — Tel. (202) 234-0540
2031 Florida Avenue, NW
Washington, DC 20009

SERBIA

Send your requests to:

Civil Registration Office
(Town), Serbia

Birth (Izvod iz Maticne Knjige Rodjenih), marriage (Izvod iz Maticne Knjige Vencanih), and death certificates (Izvod iz Maticne Knjige Umrlih) are available from the civil registrar having jurisdiction over the locality where the event occurred. Prior to May 10, 1946, records were maintained by church authorities, except in Vojvodina where civil records were kept. Records before that were kept by the local churches. Divorce records are available from the District Court that decided the case.

For additional assistance, contact:

Embassy of the Republic of Serbia — Tel. (202) 332-0333
2134 Kalorama Road, NW
Washington, DC 20008

SEYCHELLES

Send your requests for records after 1902 to:

Chief Civil Status Officer
Victoria
Mahe, Seychelles

Send your requests for earlier records to:

Seychelles National Archives
(Location: 5th June Avenue)
P.O. Box 720
Victoria
Mahe, Seychelles

Tel. (011) (248) 432-1333
E-mail: archives@seychelles.net
www.sna.gov.sc/

Birth, marriage, and death certificates are available from the Chief Civil Status Officer, Victoria, Mahe. Divorce certificates are available from the Registrar of the Supreme Court, Victoria, Mahe. Vital registration began in Seychelles for the entire population in 1893. It is one of the few countries in Sub-Saharan Africa where the registration of births and deaths is considered to be comprehensive.

For additional assistance, contact:

Embassy of the Republic of Seychelles
800 Second Avenue, Suite 400
New York, NY 10017

Tel. (212) 972-1785

SIERRA LEONE

Send your requests to:

Office of the Registrar of Births and Deaths
3 Wilberforce Street
Freetown, Sierra Leone

Vital registration of births and deaths began in Sierra Leone as early as 1801 in Freetown and Granville. A certified copy of an entry in the register of births or deaths may be obtained from the Office of the Registrar of Births and Deaths. Local registrars record births and deaths outside of Freetown. When registry volumes are full, usually after a period of several years, they are forwarded to the central archives of the Freetown Registrar. Records of recent births and deaths outside Freetown are available only at the local registries.

All civil and Christian marriages are required to be registered. Certified copies of certificates of registered marriages are available from the Office of the Registrar General, Walpole Street, Freetown. Certificates of Muslim marriages are also available from the mosque where they were performed; a certificate of a native marriage may also be obtained from the local authority that sanctioned the marriage. Certified copies of registered divorce decrees are available from the Master and Registrar, High Court, Freetown. A certificate of Muslim divorce may be obtained from the mosque that sanctioned the divorce, and a certificate of native divorce may be obtained from the local authority that sanctioned the divorce.

The Sierra Leone Public Archives, located at Fourah Bay College in Freetown, holds many old documents, including 1858–1894 birth and death registers.

For additional assistance, contact:

Embassy of Sierra Leone
1701 19th Street, NW
Washington, DC 20009

Tel. (202) 939-9261

SINGAPORE

Send your requests for Birth and Death Records to:

Registry of Births and Deaths
10 Kallang Road, ICA Building
Singapore 208718

Tel. (011) (65) 6391-6100
www.ica.gov.sg

Send your requests for Marriage Records to:

Registrar, Registry of Marriage
7 Canning Rise
Singapore 179869

Tel. (011) (65) 6338-9987
www.romm.gov.sg

The Registrar of Births and Deaths has records from 1872; certified copies of certificates can be ordered online at www.ica.gov.sg. Marriage certificates dated January 1984 and after can be ordered online at www.romm.gov.sg. The Supreme Court has divorce records from 1937.

For additional assistance, contact:

National Archives of Singapore
1 Canning Rise
Singapore 179868

E-mail: nas@nlb.gov.sg
www.nas.gov.sg/

Embassy of Singapore
3501 International Place, NW
Washington, DC 20008

Tel. (202) 537-3100

THE SLOVAK REPUBLIC (SLOVAKIA)

Send your requests to:

Registrar's Office
Town Hall
(Town), Slovak Republic

Post-1895 certificates of birth, marriage, or death are held by the local town hall in the place where the event occurred. Records prior to 1895 were transferred to the Slovak Republic State Archives, which also holds some later records. Persons not physically present in Slovakia may apply for the required documents through Slovakian diplomatic or consular representatives abroad.

For additional assistance, contact:

Embassy of the Slovak Republic
3523 International Court, NW
Washington, DC 20008

Tel. (202) 237-1054

SLOVENIA

Send your requests to:

Civil Registration District Office
(Town), Slovenia

Birth (Izpisek iz maticnega registra o rojstvu), marriage (Izpisek iz maticnega registra o sklenjeni zakonski zvezi), and death certificates (Izpisek iz maticnega registra o smrti) are available from the civil registrar (maticar) at any of Administrative Unit (Upravna Enota) office in the country. The first certificate of birth, marriage, or death is free, but subsequent copies require payment of a small fee. Individuals may also request the international version of the certificate, which is issued in Slovene, English, and six other languages. Applicants and their authorized representatives may apply for all certificates in person or by mail, or online at http://e-uprava.gov.si if no fee is required. Copies of divorce judgments are available from the Family Law Division of the District Court (Družinski oddelek okrožnega sodišca) that decided the case.

Birth, marriage, and death certificates can be ordered from the Consular Section of the Slovenian embassy (see contact information below).

For additional assistance, contact:

Embassy of the Republic of Slovenia
Consular Section
2410 California Street, NW
Washington, DC 20008

Tel. (202) 386-6614

SOLOMON ISLANDS

Send your requests for Birth and Death Records to:

Registrar General
P.O. Box 404
Honiara, Solomon Islands

Central Hospital in Honiara (P.O. Box 349, Honiara, Solomon Islands) can issue a Certificate of Live Birth for births occurring there. Births in rural areas are rarely reported. If a child has at least one non-national parent, a birth certificate can be obtained from the Registrar General in Honiara. This service is not available for children whose parents are both Solomon Island nationals.

Certificates are available for civil marriages from the Provincial Magistrate of the district where the marriage occurred, and for religious marriages from the church. Death certificates are generally not available. If an expatriate dies in Honiara, the death may be registered with the Registrar General's Office in Honiara.

For additional assistance, contact:

Embassy Solomon Islands
800 2nd Avenue, Suite 400L
New York, NY 10017

Tel. (212) 559-6192

SOMALIA

The Government of Somalia ceased to exist in December of 1990. Since that time the country has undergone a destructive and brutal civil war, in the course of which most records were destroyed. Those few records not destroyed are in the hands of private individuals or are otherwise not retrievable.

SOUTH AFRICA

Send your requests to:

Department of Home Affairs
Private Bag X114
Pretoria 0001, South Africa

www.home-affairs.gov.za/index.php

Submit applications for birth to the nearest office of the Department of Home Affairs if you are in South Africa, or to the nearest South African embassy, mission, or consulate if you are overseas. Divorce certificates should be requested from the Registrar of the Supreme Court located in the magisterial district where the divorce was obtained. A number of South African records are available online at www.familysearch.org, including civil death and marriage records and parish registers.

For additional assistance, contact:

The National Archives & Records Service of South Africa
(Location: 24 Hamilton Street, Arcadia, Pretoria)
Private Bag X236
Pretoria, South Africa 0001

www.national.archives.gov.za/

Embassy of South Africa
3051 Massachusetts Avenue, NW
Washington, DC 20008

Tel. (202) 232-4400

G.P.-S. 017-0174

BI-154

DEPARTMENT: HOME AFFAIRS
REPUBLIC OF SOUTH AFRICA

APPLICATION FOR BIRTH CERTIFICATE

This form must be handed in at a Regional or District office together with the prescribed fee. The receipt of fees paid must accompany the form.

THE REASON FOR THE APPLICATION MUST BE SUBMITTED [in terms of section 29 (2) (b)]

....

....

For use in the Republic of South Africa a computer printed certificate of birth particulars is normally issued. Such a certificate complies with the requirements for which a birth certificate is required. An unabridged certificate is available and is issued mainly for overseas purposes. Indicate with an X which certificate is required.

Unabridged certificate ☐ **Computer printed abridged certificate** ☐

Certified copy of birth register ☐ **(Vault copy)** **Handwritten abridged certificate** ☐

PARTICULARS OF PERSON CONCERNED

Identity Number

Surname

Maiden name if a married woman

Forenames in full

Date of birth Y M D Birth entry number

Town/City and Province of birth

PARTICULARS OF FATHER

Surname

Forenames in full

PARTICULARS OF MOTHER

Maiden name

Forenames in full

PARTICULARS OF APPLICANT

Surname

Forenames in full

Postal address

Postal code

Telephone number (Work) Telephone code

Telephone number (Home) Telephone code

G.P.-S. 017-0172

BI-130

REPUBLIC OF SOUTH AFRICA
DEPARTMENT OF HOME AFFAIRS

APPLICATION FOR MARRIAGE CERTIFICATE

(Complete in block letters please)

Indicate in the appropriate square whether an abridged or an unabridged full certificate is required.

N.B.: **(1) An abridged certificate generally answers to the purpose for which a marriage certificate is required in the Republic of South Africa. An unabridged certificate is mainly issued for *overseas* purposes.**

(2) A vault copy is a certified copy of the original register.

If an unabridged certificate is required, state fully the purpose for which it is required:

....

....

....

☐ **Abridged certificate** ☐ **Unabridged certificate** ☐ **Vault copy**

Full names and surname of husband ....

....

Identity number of husband ☐☐☐☐☐☐ ☐☐☐☐ ☐☐ ☐

Date of birth of husband ....

Full names and maiden name of wife ....

....

Identity number of wife ☐☐☐☐☐☐ ☐☐☐☐ ☐☐ ☐

Date of birth of wife ....

Date of marriage ....

Name of church or magistrate's office ....

Place where marriage took place ....

Name of marriage officer (if married in church) ....

Name of applicant ....

Address of applicant ....

....

....

Postal code.. Tel. No.: Work ....

Home ....

....

Signature

G.P.-S. 017-0064

BI 132

REPUBLIC OF SOUTH AFRICA

DEPARTMENT OF HOME AFFAIRS

APPLICATION FOR DEATH CERTIFICATE

This form must be handed in at a Regional or District office of the Department of Home Affairs together with the prescribed fee.

THE REASON WHY THE CERTIFICATE IS REQUIRED MUST BE SUBMITTED [In terms of section 29 of the Births and Deaths Registration Act, 1992 (Act No. 51 of 1992)]

....

....

For use in the Republic of South Africa a computer printed certificate of death particulars is normally issued. Such a certificate complies with the requirements for which a death certificate is required. An unabridged certificate is available and is issued mainly for overseas use. Indicate with an X which document is required.

Unabridged certificate [ ] Computer printed certificate [ ] Certified copy of register [ ]

A. PARTICULARS OF DECEASED

1. Identity Number ______ 2. Date of birth (Y M D) ______
3. Surname ______
4. Maiden name if married woman ______ 5. Place of birth ______
6. Forenames in full ______
7. Date of death (Y M D) ______ 8. Death entry number (Must be completed by regional or district office) ______
9. Town/City of death ______ 10. Province ______
11. Name of undertaker ______

B. PARTICULARS OF APPLICANT

1. Surname ______
2. Initials ______ 3. Identity number ______
4. Residential address ______
5. Postal address ______ 6. Postal address code ______

Telephone number (Work) ______ Telephone code ______

Telephone number (Home) ______ Telephone code ______

....

Signature ***Date***

SPAIN

Send your requests to:

Registro Civil Central
Calle Montera, 18
28013 Madrid, Spain

www.mjusticia.es

or

Municipal Court (Juzgado Municipal)
(Town), Spain

Birth, death, and marriage certificates can be obtained from the Registro Civil Central in Madrid in person, by mail, or online, or from the Juzgado Municipal of the district where the event took place. Spanish civil registration records began in 1871, though some municipalities may have civil registration records beginning as early as 1837. Some Spanish vital records have been digitized and are available online at www.familysearch.org.

For additional assistance, contact:

Embassy of Spain
2375 Pennsylvania Avenue, NW
Washington, DC 20037

Tel. (202) 452-0100

SRI LANKA

Send your requests to:

Registrar General of Marriages, Births and Deaths
Ministry of Home Affairs
340, R.A. De Mel Mawatha
Colombo 3, Sri Lanka

Sri Lanka, originally known as Lanka and more recently as Ceylon, has had vital registration since the Dutch period (1640–1796). The British improved coverage with laws passed from 1815 on. By 1867 registration included the entire population. Divorce certificates may be obtained from the Registrar of the District Court where the decree was granted.

For more assistance, contact:

Department of National Archives of Sri Lanka
P.O. Box 1414
Philip Gunawardena Mawatha
Colombo 7, Sri Lanka

E-mail: narchive@slt.lk
www.archives.gov.lk/

Embassy Sri Lanka
2148 Wyoming Avenue, NW
Washington, DC 20008

Tel. (202) 483-4025

SUDAN

Send your requests to:

Department of Statistics
Ministry of Social Affairs
Khartoum, Sudan

Vital registration only began in Sudan in recent times and is not uniform throughout the country. Marriages in Sudan are conducted by religious authorities, and those certificates may be authenticated by the Ministry of Foreign Affairs for submission to foreign government authorities. Certificates of divorce may be obtained from the court that granted the divorce. There has been ongoing conflict in the states of Southern Kordofan and Blue Nile. Civilians in rebel-controlled areas of these states do not receive or have access to government services. Accordingly, birth, marriage, divorce, and military records may not be available to certain residents in these states.

For additional assistance, contact:

The National Records Office
Jumhuria Avenue
P.O. Box 1914
Khartoum, Sudan

Embassy of Sudan — Tel. (202) 338-8565
Consular Section
2210 Massachusetts Avenue, NW
Washington, DC 20008

SURINAME

Send your requests to:

Centraal Bureau voor Burgerzaken (CBB) — Tel. (011) (597) 490340
Coppename straat 170
Paramaribo, Suriname

Applicants for vital records may apply through the Embassy of Suriname (see contact information below), directly to the Centraal Bureau voor Burgerzaken, or at their local district office (Burgerlijke Stand).

For additional assistance, contact:

Embassy of the Republic of Suriname — Tel. (202) 244-7488
Consular Services
4301 Connecticut Avenue, NW, Suite 460
Washington, DC 20008

SWAZILAND

Send your requests to:

Register General's Office
P.O. Box 460
Mbabane, Swaziland

Birth, marriage, and death certificates are issued by the Registrar General's Office in Mbabane. If the applicant provides the exact date of the requested document, there is no search fee. Records are available from 1927 to present. Divorce certificates are available from the District Court in which the divorce decree was issued: Hhohho District, P.O. Box 542, Mbabane; Piggs Peak District, P.O. Box 98, Piggs Peak; Manzini District, P.O. Box 13, Manzini; and Nhlangano District, P.O. Box 99, Nhlangano.

For additional assistance, contact:

Swaziland National Archives
P. O. Box 946
Mbabane, Swaziland

Embassy of Swaziland — Tel. (202) 234-5002
1712 New Hampshire Avenue, NW
Washington, DC 20009

SWEDEN

Send your requests for records before July 1, 1991, to:

Lutheran Church Parish Office (Pastorsämbetet)
(Town), Sweden

Send your requests for records after July 1, 1991, to:

Lokala Skattemyndigheten
(Local Tax Office)
(Town), Sweden

The local Lutheran pastors have kept Sweden's records since the 1600s, when the Church Law of 1686 went into effect. Since July 1, 1991, the local tax officers have had the responsibility of keeping vital records. Current vital registration is considered to be comprehensive.

Birth, marriage, and death records for persons born after July 1, 1991, are issued by the local office of the Swedish Tax Agency (Skatteverket) covering the applicant's place of residence at the time of the event. Records for persons born before July 1, 1991, can be obtained both from the parish office (Pastorsämbetet) in the parish of the applicant's birth or from the Swedish Tax Agency (Skatteverket). A divorce decree (Skilsmassoprotokoll) is issued by the City Court (Tingsratten).

Birth, death, and marriage indexes can be searched online at www.svar.ra.se/. A DVD containing the Swedish Death Index 1901–2009 and CDs containing the 1880, 1890, and 1900 Swedish censuses can be purchased from the Swedish National Archives (SVAR, P.O. Box 160, 880, 40 Ramsele, Sweden). There is also information on the National Archives website (www.svar.ra.se) about the holdings of all Sweden's archives and a link to the National Archival Database.

For additional assistance, contact:

Embassy of Sweden — Tel. (202) 467-2600
2900 K Street, NW
Washington, DC 20007

SWITZERLAND

Send your requests to:

Zivilstandsandsbeamter
(Town), Switzerland

To obtain copies of birth, marriage, and death certificates, write to the Civil Registration Officer (Zivilstandsbeamter for German-speaking areas, Officier de l'État Civil for French-speaking areas, and Ufficiale dello Stato Civile for Italian-speaking areas) in the town where the person was born. These records date from January 1, 1876, though some earlier ones exist in some cantons. Previous to 1876, records were kept by church authorities and are available for all living persons. Current vital registration is considered to be comprehensive. Divorce certificates are issued by the courthouse where the divorce took place.

For additional assistance, contact:

Embassy of Switzerland
2900 Cathedral Avenue, NW
Washington, DC 20008

Tel. (202) 745-7900

SYRIA

Send your requests to:

Civil Affairs Office
(Town), Syria

The Civil Affairs Offices in Syria maintain records of birth, marriage, divorce, and death for most Syrians. As of July 2011 Syrian citizens can register new civil events and obtain civil documents from any Civil Affairs Office in Syria without going back to the original secretariat of their civil records. Civil documents are reasonably reliable for events occurring after 1924 but are usually unavailable for earlier dates. Church records are generally the only source of information for documents pertaining to events prior to 1924.

The JewishGen website (www.jewishgen.org) has databases containing marriage, death, and circumcision records from Aleppo, Syria.

For additional assistance, contact:

Embassy of Syria
2215 Wyoming Avenue, NW
Washington, DC 20008

Tel. (202) 232-6316

TAJIKISTAN

Send your requests to:

Office for Registration of Civil Status (ZAGS)
(District), Tajikistan

Copies of these documents can be obtained by Tajik citizens for a nominal fee upon direct written application to the ZAGS archives at the district, city, or regional level, depending on where the civil act was registered. Some civil records were destroyed during World War II and may not be available.

Documents can be requested through the Embassy of Tajikistan in Washington (see contact information below) by submitting an application requesting the document. This process can take several months to complete.

For additional assistance, contact:

Embassy of Tajikistan — Tel. (202) 223-6090
1005 New Hampshire Avenue, NW
Washington, DC 20037

TANZANIA

Send your requests to:

Register General of Births and Deaths
P.O. Box 9183
Dar es Salaam, Tanzania

Certificates of birth since April 1921 can be obtained from the Register General of Births and Deaths. Marriage certificates can be obtained for all civil and other marriages after May 1971. Certificates are issued by the Registrar of Marriages (P.O. Box 9183, Dar es Salaam). Marriage certificates prior to May 1971 are available from a church or religious institution. Certified copies of divorce decrees can be obtained from the Registrar, High Court (P.O. Box 9004, Dar es Salaam). For divorces prior to May 1971 and those that took place outside the courts under customary procedures, certificates may be available from churches or communal organizations.

For additional assistance, contact:

Embassy of the United Republic of Tanzania — Tel. (202) 884-1080
1232 22nd Street, NW
Washington, DC 20037

THAILAND

Send your requests to:

Nai Amphur
(District of registration), Thailand

Vital records must be requested from the district office that recorded the original certificate. The issuance of birth certificates in Thailand began in Bangkok in 1917. Records of birth are often lacking for people born in Bangkok before World War II and for those born in other areas of the country up until the 1970s. In 1956 family registration became required, and in 1982 the nation instituted a computerized national identification card system to centralize data on all individuals.

For additional assistance, contact:

Royal Thai Embassy
1024 Wisconsin Avenue, NW
Washington, DC 20007

Tel. (202) 944-3600

TOGO

Send your requests to:

État Civil Central
Commune de Lomé, Togo

In Lomé records are available at the État Civil Central. Neighboring districts of Lomé have stored their own archives since 1988. Prior to that, the records were stored at the État Civil Central. The suburbs of Lomé (Baguida, Agoe Nyive, Afloa Sagbado, Amoutivé, Togblekope, Legbassito, Sangera) transfer their records to the general archives of the État Civil Central at the end of each year; no records are kept on-site.

For additional assistance, contact:

Embassy of Togo
2208 Massachusetts Avenue, NW
Washington, DC 20008

Tel. (202) 234-4212

TONGA

Send your requests to:

Registrar of the Supreme Court
Justice Department
P.O. Box 11
Nuku'alofa, Tonga

Tel. (011) (676) 23 599

The Registrar General has complete birth and death records dating back to 1867, marriage records dating back to 1892, and divorce records dating back to 1905. Certificates are available only to Tongan subjects, with the exception of marriage certificates, which have been available to non-Tongans since 1952.

For additional assistance, contact:

Tonga Consulate General
360 Post Street, Suite 604
San Francisco, CA 94108

Tel. (415) 781-0365
E-mail: consulategeneraloftonga@gmail.com

TRINIDAD and TOBAGO

Send your requests to:

Registrar General's Office
Ministry of Legal Affairs
Registration House
72-74 South Quay
Port of Spain, Trinidad and Tobago

Tel. (868) 623-7163
www.legalaffairs.gov.tt/registrar/

The Registrar General's Office has records for Trinidad from January 1, 1848, and for Tobago from January 30, 1868. Trinidad and Tobago were united in 1889. Current registration is considered to be comprehensive. Certificates can also be ordered from the following Civil Registry Offices: 9 Leotaud Street, San Fernando; Pennywise Building, 7 Devenish Street, Arima; and Caroline Building No. 2, # 11 Hamilton Street, Scarborough, Tobago. The local churches also have their own records.

For additional assistance, contact:

Embassy of the Republic of Trinidad and Tobago
1708 Massachusetts Avenue, NW
Washington, DC 20036

Tel. (202) 467-6490

REPUBLIC OF TRINIDAD AND TOBAGO

APPLICATION FOR COMPUTERIZED BIRTH CERTIFICATE

A person is entitled to only one (1) free Birth Certificate.

Notice: For Mail in applicants the free birth certificate will be delivered free of charge to a Trinidad and Tobago postal address only. The person receiving the Certificate is required to produce their valid Trinidad and Tobago government issued ID.

ALL INFORMATION MUST BE WRITTEN IN CAPITAL LETTERS

PART I - APPLICANT INFORMATION (TO BE COMPLETED BY THE PERSON REQUESTING THE BIRTH CERTIFICATE)

Type of Service: ☐ MAIL IN ☐ WALK IN	State the purpose for which the Certificate is required
First Name	Surname
ADDRESS Mail In (home or office) Walk In (home)	
Telephone Number Between 8:00 am to 4:00 pm	Type of Identification: ID ☐ DP ☐ PP ☐ Number

Are you applying for your own Birth Certificate? If not, please state your relationship to the person who owns the Birth Certificate.

Yes ☐ No ☐ Relationship:

Please Note :

- If you are applying for a Birth Certificate which is NOT yours nor your child's you must submit a letter of authorization from the owner of the Birth Certificate together with a copy of their valid government issued ID.
- All Mail in applications must include a photocopy of a valid government issued ID. Mail In applications are for the first free Birth Certificate only.

PART II - BIRTH CERTIFICATE INFORMATION AS REGISTERED AT THE TIME OF BIRTH

First Name	Middle Names
Date of Birth Day Month Year	Sex ☐ Male ☐ Female
Place of Birth - Full address or Name of Hospital	
Mother's First Name	
Mother's Current Surname	Mother's Maiden Name
Father's First Name	Father's Surname

TO AVOID DELAY:
Complete all sections clearly
Be sure you are authorized to make the request
Be sure your address and telephone number are correct
We may be unable to issue the birth certificate if the information provided is incomplete or inaccurate

.... Date of Application

.... Signature of Person applying for Birth Certificate (by signing this application you are certifying that you are legally entitled to, or are authorized to apply for the Certificate)

FOR OFFICIAL USE ONLY			
Registration No.	Certificate No.	Comments	Processed By
Date Posted (DD/MM/YY)			

INSTRUCTIONS OVERLEAF

INSTRUCTIONS

WALK IN APPLICANTS

• Persons applying for their own Birth Certificate or their child's must provide:	▶ Their valid government issued ID (Driver's Permit, ID or Passport)
• Persons applying for a Birth Certificate that does not belong to them must provide:	▶ Their valid government issued ID; and A letter of authorization from the owner of the Birth Certificate; and A copy of the owner's valid government issued ID

MAIL IN APPLICANTS

All applicants should provide a photocopy of their handwritten birth certificate
Applications must include a photocopy of the applicant's valid government issued ID; and must be placed in a sealed envelope addressed to Registrar General's Department, Ministry of Legal Affairs, and sent in one of the following ways:

A) Posted To: Registration House
72-74 South Quay
Port of Spain
Tel. 624-1660 ext. 3017

B) Deposited in drop-boxes located at Registrar General's Department Head Office in Port of Spain or its sub-offices in Tobago, San Fernando and Arima

Sub Offices		
	Arima	#32 Pro Queen Street, Arima
	San Fernando	#10 Leotaud Street, San Fernando
	Tobago	Jerningham Street, Scarborough, Tobago

C) Given to a TTPost agent at any one of the 22 selected TTPost outlets listed below.

Selected TTPost Agents

Trinidad North	St. Ann's	Carl Charles, Evergreen Green Grocers #13 St. Ann's Avenue
	Maraval	Richard Dass, Ross Budget Drugs, Royal Palm Plaza, Maraval
	Port-of-Spain	TTPOST, 177 Tragarete Road, Port of Spain
South	San Fernando	Merle Marshall, Carlton Centre, San Fernando
	Marabella	Trinpad Ltd., #225 Southern Main Road, Marabella
	Point Fortin	Grace Sieunarine, c/o GGR Insurance Services, #29 Adventure Road, Point Fortin
	Princes Town	Mohammed's Bookstore #22 High Street, Princes Town
	Rio Claro	Avind Moonan, Moonan's Stationery Supplies, High Street, Rio Claro
Central	Chaguanas	Patricia Xavier, #9 St. Yves Street, Chaguanas
	Couva	Feroz Khan Quality Cash & Carry, Railway Road, Couva
	Caroni	Leo Seebaran, 146 Southern Main Road, Caroni
East	Arima	Vere Bhaggan's Drug Store, #48 Broadway, Arima
	San Juan	Ramesh & Leela Supermarket, 48-50 Eastern Main Road, San Juan
	Sangre Grande	Sanjive Ramlogan, Auto Masters, LP# 914 Eastern Main Road, Sangre Grande
	Toco	Anthony Mc Pherson, Crystal's One Stop Shop, LP #51, Cor. Pasea & Galera Raods, Toco
	Valsayn	Tru Valu Supermarket, Valpark Shopping Plaza, Valsayn
	Trincity	Sylvia Mayer-Charles, Trincity Mall, Trincity
West	Diego Martin	Prescott Singh, Payless Hardware, Diego Martin Main Road, Diego Martin
Tobago	Scarborough	Lillis Jordon, Port Mall, Scarborough, Tobago
	Charlotteville	Desery Moore, Bayview Shopping Mart, Spring Street, Charlotteville, Tobago
	Plymouth	Courtney Phillip's Grocery, Shelbourne Street, Plymouth, Tobago
	Roxborough	Hollis Toppin, Ecomart, 198 Main Road, Roxborough, Tobago

- **ONLY THE FREE BIRTH CERTIFICATE WILL BE DELIVERED TO YOUR POSTAL ADDRESS FREE OF CHARGE. THE PERSON RECEIVING THE CERTIFICATE MUST PRESENT A VALID FORM OF GOVERNMENT ISSUED ID.**

APPLICATION FORM FOR DEATH CERTIFICATE

TO: Consul General, New York

FROM:

DATED:

Kindly obtain on my behalf a copy of a Death Certificate from the Registrar General's Office, Port of Spain, Trinidad and Tobago.

THE DETAILS ARE:-

NAME (AT THE TIME OF DEATH)____________________________________

DATE OF DEATH:____

MAIDEN NAME (IF APPLICABLE):____________________________________

DATE OF DEATH: _______________ _______________ _______________
Day Month Year

PLACE OF BIRTH:____
(Local District/Hospital)

____
(Country)

MY ADDRESS IN THE UNITED STATES OF AMERICA IS:

____
____
____

FEE: US$6.00 (Money Order Only)
RECEIPT NO:_______________
DATE ____________________

TELEPHONE NO: (Home):_________________
(Daytime): _________________

TUNISIA

Send your requests to:

Registrar
Bureau de l'État-Civil
(Town), Tunisia

Compulsory registration of births of Tunisian Muslims and Jews began on December 30, 1908. This measure was extended on August 1, 1957, to include all births, regardless of faith, nationality, or race. Persons of European descent born in Tunisia before August 1, 1957, whose births were not recorded with the appropriate Office of the Registrar may have their births recorded in their respective consulates in Tunis. The French Consulate in Tunis appears to have records of all French citizens beginning January 1, 1920. The Italian Consulate in Tunis maintains records of birth from 1873, provided the birth was reported. The Prelature of Tunis maintains records of all persons of the Catholic faith baptized in Tunisia.

For additional assistance, contact:

Embassy of the Republic of Tunisia — Tel. (202) 862-1850
1515 Massachusetts Avenue, NW
Washington, DC 20005

TURKEY

Send your requests to:

Nufus Mudurlugu
(Town), Turkey

The birth and death records of Turkish citizens are maintained by the Nufus Mudurlugu (Registration Office). An extract of the records (Nufus Kayit Ornegi/Extract of Vital Record) is available by applying to any Nufus Mudurlugu office in Turkey. Birth certificates for non-Turkish persons are not available.

Since October 4, 1926, only the civil marriages performed by marriage officers have been considered valid in Turkey. Religious marriages/ceremonies, while still performed, have no legal standing. Records are kept and certificates are obtainable from the marriage officers. If one/both parties are Turkish citizens, the marriage is also recorded in their Nufus registration. Certified copies of divorce decrees are available from the court granting the divorce.

For additional assistance, contact:

Embassy of Turkey — Tel. (202) 612-6700
2525 Massachusetts Avenue, NW
Washington, DC 20008

TURKMENISTAN

Send your requests to:

Bureau of Registration of Acts of Civil Status (ZAGS)
(Town), Turkmenistan

Unauthenticated and uncertified copies of these documents may be obtained by Turkmen citizens for a nominal fee upon direct application to the Bureau of Registration of Acts of Civil Status (ZAGS) of the locality having custody of the records. Some civil records were destroyed during World War II and may not be available.

For additional assistance, contact:

Embassy of Turkmenistan — Tel. (202) 588-1500
2207 Massachusetts Avenue, NW
Washington, DC 20008

TURKS and CAICOS ISLANDS

Send your requests to:

Registry of Births, Deaths & Marriages — Tel. (649) 946-2800
Front Street, Turks & Caicos Islands
British West Indies

Records are available from January 2, 1863. A large number of birth, death, and marriage records are available from at least two churches on the island, St. Mary's Anglican Church on Grand Turk and St. Thomas Church (denomination unknown), both of which are located within the Turks & Caicos National Museum (see contact information below). The St. Mary's records cover marriages, baptisms, and deaths from several parishes on Grand Turk and Salt Cay, dating from the 1790s to the 1920s.

For additional assistance, contact:

Turks & Caicos National Museum — Tel. (649) 946-2160
Guinep House — E-mail: info@tcmuseum.org
Front Street
Grand Turk, Turks & Caicos Island
British West Indies

TUVALU

Send your requests to:

Office of Chief Minister
Vaiaku, Funafuti, Tuvalu

Tuvalu, consisting of nine islands in the Pacific, became independent in 1978. Current vital registration in Tuvalu is considered to be comprehensive. The Family History Library has civil registrations of birth, marriage, and death records on microfilm for the years 1866–1979.

For additional assistance, contact:

National Library and Archives
Funafuti, Tuvalu

Consulate of Tuvalu — Tel. (212) 490-0534
800 Second Avenue, #400 B
New York, NY 10017

UGANDA

Send your requests to:

Registrar of Births and Deaths
Ministry of Justice and Constitutional Affairs
P.O. Box 7183
Kampala, Uganda

Vital registration of births and deaths began in Uganda as early as 1905 for Europeans and was expanded in 1915 to include Asians. Registration for the entire population did not begin until 1973. Birth and death records are available from the Registrar of Births and Deaths. Copies of marriage records are obtainable from the District Commissioner of the District in which the marriage took place or from the Government Agent, Kampala, and copies of divorce decrees may be obtained from the Registrar, The High Court, Kampala. These do not apply to the majority of marriages and divorces between Ugandans, which are performed according to customary tribal law and for which no records exist.

For additional assistance, contact:

Embassy of Uganda
5911 16th Street, NW
Washington, DC 20011
Tel. (202) 726-7100

UKRAINE

Send your requests to:

Department of State Registration of Acts of Civil Status (DRATsS)
(Town), Ukraine

Civil documents are generally available in Ukraine through local or oblast (district or regional) Departments of State Registration of Acts of Civil Status (DRATsS). The list of these offices can be found at www.drsu.gov.ua/show/6110. Diplomatic missions and consular sections of Ukraine abroad, as well as the Ministry of Foreign Affairs of Ukraine (2, Velyka Zhytomyrska St., Kyiv, 01018), can also accept requests for civil documents. Some civil records were destroyed in World War II. In other cases, records of persons in what used to be Ukraine were transferred to neighboring countries when borders shifted. A town-by-town inventory of archival documents is available in a searchable database (at no cost to the inquirer) on the Routes to Roots website at www.rtrfoundation.org.

For additional assistance, contact:

State Archives of Ukraine
24 Solomianska Str.
03110 Kyiv, Ukraine
E-mail: mail@archives.gov.ua
www.archives.gov.ua

Embassy of Ukraine
Consular Services
3350 M Street, NW
Washington, DC 20007
Tel. (202) 349-3376

UNITED ARAB EMIRATES

Send your requests to:

Birth or Death Certificates Section
Preventive Medicine Centre
P.O. Box 1583
Dubai, United Arab Emirates

or

Birth or Death Certificates Section
Preventive Medicine Centre
P.O. Box 344
Abu Dhabi, United Arab Emirates

The United Arab Emirates, formerly called the Trucial States, is a federation of seven states: Abu Dhabi; Dubai; Ash Sharigah (Sharjah); Adjam; Umm Al-Qaiwain; Ras Al-Khaimah; and Fujairah. Dubai is the administrative center for the Northern Emirates and maintains records for all the Emirates outside of Abu Dhabi. Certificates can be ordered online at www.abudhabi.ae, and birth certificates are also available online at www.haad.ae. For marriage and divorce certificates, write to the Marriage/Divorce Archives Section of the Sharia Court in the locale where the event took place.

For additional assistance, contact:

Embassy of the United Arab Emirates
3522 International Court, NW, Suite 400
Washington, DC 20008

Tel. (202) 243-2400

UNITED KINGDOM—ENGLAND and WALES

Send your requests to:

Certificate Services Section
General Register Office
P.O. Box 2
Southport, Merseyside
United Kingdom PR8 2JD

Tel. (011) (44) 28 9151 3101
E-mail: certificate.services@ips.gsi.gov.uk
www.gro.gov.uk

The General Register Office (GRO) is part of Her Majesty's Passport Office and oversees civil registration in England and Wales. It maintains the national archive of all births, marriages, and deaths dating back to 1837. Applications for events registered within the last six months (for marriages this period is extended to eighteen months) should be made to the Register Office in the district where the birth, death, or marriage took place. Certificates can be ordered from the GRO online at www.gro.gov.uk/gro/content/certificates/default.asp.

Microfiche copies of birth, marriage, and death indexes from 1837 onward are available at many local libraries, record offices (including the National Archives at Kew), and other facilities. FreeBMD (www.freebmd.org.uk/) is an ongoing project, the aim of which is to transcribe the Civil Registration index of births, marriages, and deaths for England and Wales and to provide free online access to the transcribed records. It is a part of the FreeUKGEN family, which also includes online census data (www.freecen.org.uk/) and parish registers (www.freereg.org.uk/). Some local register offices have made their own indexes available online at www.ukbmd.org.uk/.

For certificates from Jersey, apply to the Superintendent Register, States Office, Royal Square, St. Helier, Jersey. For Guernsey, Sark, and Alderney certificates, apply to the Registrar General's Office, Greffe, Guernsey; and for those from the Isle of Man, apply to the Registrar General, General Registry Building, Douglas, Isle of Man.

Divorce records for England and Wales (including the Scilly Isles and Isle of Wight) may be obtained from the Principal Register, Divorce Registry, Room G45, Somerset House, Royal Courts of Justice, Strand, London WC2A 2LL.

Cost for a full Birth Certificate	£9.25
Cost for a full Marriage Certificate	£9.25
Cost for a full Death Certificate	£9.25
Priority Fee	£23.40

Send your request for Adoption Certificates to:

Adoptions Section
Room C202
General Register Office
Trafalgar Road
Southport
PR8 2HH, England, UK

For additional information, contact:

The National Archives of the United Kingdom
Kew, Richmond, Surrey, TW9 4DU
United Kingdom

Tel. (011) (44) 20 8876 3444
www.nationalarchives.gov.uk/

Embassy of the United Kingdom and Northern Ireland
3100 Massachusetts Avenue, NW
Washington, DC 20008

Tel. (202) 588-6500

GRO Birth Certificate Application Form

Please read the guidance notes before completing this form in **CAPITALS** and **BLACK INK**

The General Register Office holds records of births registered in England and Wales from the 1st July 1837.

Section 1 - Customer Details

1.1 GRO Customer Account Number

1.2 Title | Forename

Surname

Company Name

Address

Town

County

Country | Postcode

1.3 Email *(please use capital letters)*

@

Telephone

Section 2 - Details of Birth

Please refer to Guidance Notes for required information

2.1 Forenames at Birth

Surname at Birth

2.2 Date of Birth d d - m m - y y y y | Male | Female

Place of Birth

2.3 Mother's Forenames

Surname *(at time of birth)*

Maiden Surname

Father's / *Parent's Forenames

Surname

2.4 Applying for your own certificate? | Adopted and applying for your original certificate?

Section 3 - GRO Index Reference

3.1 District Name *(or number)*

3.2 Year　　Quarter　　3.3 Volume　　Page

3.4 Register Number　　Entry Number　　3.5 Date of Registration

Section 4 - Other Information

4.1 Your Reference

4.2 Priority Despatch　　4.3 Number of Certificates　　Full　　Short

Section 5 - Payment Information

5.1 Total Value of Application

5.2 Payment by Cheque　　Payment by Postal Order

Cheque / Postal Order Number

5.3 Payment by Debit/Credit Card　　Visa　　MasterCard　　Maestro/Visa Debit

Card Number　　Security Number

Expiry Date　　Start Date　　Issue Number *(if applicable)*

Name of Cardholder *(as it appears on the card)*

WorldPay ID *(for official use only)*

Please note that the application fee includes a return postal charge, therefore customers are NOT required to send a SAE with their application form

Please return to the following address by post.

General Register Office, PO Box 2
Southport, Merseyside
United Kingdom, PR8 2JD

For the purpose of detecting and preventing crime, information relating to an application may be passed to other Government departments or law enforcement agencies.

GRO Marriage Certificate Application Form

Please read the guidance notes before completing this form in **CAPITALS** and **BLACK INK**

The General Register Office holds records of marriages registered in England and Wales from the 1st July 1837.

Section 1 - Customer Details

1.1 GRO Customer Account Number

1.2 Title

Forename

Surname

Company Name

Address

Town

County

Country

Postcode

1.3 Email *(please use capital letters)*

@

Telephone

Section 2 - Details of Marriage

Please refer to Guidance Notes for required information

2.1 Groom's Forenames

Surname

Bride's Forenames

Surname

2.2 Date of Marriage d d m m y y y y

Applying for your own certificate?

2.3 Place of Marriage

2.4 Groom's Father's Forenames

Surname

Bride's Father's Forenames

Surname

Section 3 - GRO Index Reference

3.1 District Name *(or number)*

3.2 Year | Quarter | *3.3* Volume | Page

3.4 Register Number | Entry Number | *3.5* Date of Registration m m / y y y y

---

Section 4 - Other Information

4.1 Your Reference

4.2 Priority Despatch | *4.3* Number of Certificates

Section 5 - Payment Information

5.1 Total Value of Application £

5.2 Payment by Cheque | Payment by Postal Order

Cheque / Postal Order Number

5.3 Payment by Debit/Credit Card | Visa | MasterCard | Maestro/Visa Debit

Card Number | Security Number

Expiry Date m m / y y y y | Start Date m m / y y y y | Issue Number *(if applicable)*

Name of Cardholder *(as it appears on the card)*

WorldPay ID *(for official use only)*

Please note that the application fee includes a return postal charge, therefore customers are NOT required to send a SAE with their application form

Please return to the following address by post.

General Register Office, PO Box 2
Southport, Merseyside
United Kingdom, PR8 2JD

For the purpose of detecting and preventing crime, information relating to an application may be passed to other Government departments or law enforcement agencies.

GRO Death Certificate Application Form

Please read the guidance notes before completing this form in **CAPITALS** and **BLACK INK**

The General Register Office holds records of deaths registered in England and Wales from the 1st July 1837.

Section 1 - Customer Details

1.1 GRO Customer Account Number

1.2 Title   Forename

Surname

Company Name

Address

Town

County

Country   Postcode

1.3 Email *(please use capital letters)* @

Telephone

Section 2 - Details of Death

Please refer to Guidance Notes for required information

2.1 Forenames at Death

Surname

2.2 Date of Death d d m m y y y y   Age at Death

2.3 Mother's Forenames

Surname

Father's / *Parent's Forenames

Surname

2.4 Place of Death

Occupation *(at time of death)*

Marital Status *(if deceased is female)*   Male   Female

Section 3 - GRO Index Reference

3.1 District Name *(or number)*

3.2 Year Quarter 3.3 Volume Page

3.4 Register Number Entry Number 3.5 Date of Registration

Section 4 - Other Information

4.1 Your Reference

4.2 Priority Despatch 4.3 Number of Certificates

Section 5 - Payment Information

5.1 Total Value of Application

5.2 Payment by Cheque Payment by Postal Order

Cheque / Postal Order Number

5.3 Payment by Debit/Credit Card Visa MasterCard Maestro/Visa Debit

Card Number Security Number

Expiry Date Start Date Issue Number *(if applicable)*

Name of Cardholder *(as it appears on the card)*

WorldPay ID *(for official use only)*

Please note that the application fee includes a return postal charge, therefore customers are NOT required to send a SAE with their application form

Please return to the following address by post.
General Register Office, PO Box 2
Southport, Merseyside
United Kingdom, PR8 2JD
For the purpose of detecting and preventing crime, information relating to an application may be passed to other Government departments or law enforcement agencies

UNITED KINGDOM—NORTHERN IRELAND

Send your requests to:

General Register Office
Oxford House
49-55 Chichester Street
Belfast BT1 4HL, Northern Ireland

Tel. (011) (44) 28 9151 3101
E-mail: gro.nisra@dfpni.gov.uk
www.nidirect.gov.uk/general-register-office-for-northern-ireland

The General Register Office (GRO) has birth and death records from 1864 to the present. Marriage certificates are available from 1845 for registered non-Roman Catholic marriages and from 1864 for all registered marriages. The GRO also holds records of persons adopted by court order in Northern Ireland on or after January 1, 1931. You can order birth, death, marriage, and adoption certificates online; see the GRO website for more information. Some certificates are also available from local district registration offices.

Cost for a certified Birth Certificate	£15.00
Cost for a short-form Birth Certificate	£15.00
Cost for a Statutory Purpose Birth Certificate	£8.00
Cost for a certified Marriage or Civil Partnership Certificate	£15.00
Cost for a certified Death Certificate	£15.00
Cost for an Adoption Certificate	£15.00
Cost for a duplicate copy, when ordered at the same time	£8.00

For additional assistance:

Public Record Office of Northern Ireland (PRONI)
2 Titanic Boulevard
Belfast BT3 8HQ, Northern Ireland

E-mail: proni@dcalni.gov.uk
www.proni.gov.uk/

PRONI holds literally millions of documents that relate chiefly, but by no means exclusively, to Northern Ireland. These records cover a period from c.1600 (with a few dating back as far as the early 13th century) to the present day. Some of PRONI's records have been digitized and indexed and are available on the PRONI website.

The Irish Family History Foundation
www.irish-roots.ie/

This website contains a unique set of Irish family history records, including birth, death, marriage, and gravestone records—the majority of which are only available online on this website and cannot be found online elsewhere.

Embassy of the United Kingdom and Northern Ireland
3100 Massachusetts Avenue, NW
Washington, DC 20008

Tel. (202) 588-6500

PLEASE READ THE FOLLOWING NOTES TO HELP YOU COMPLETE THE APPLICATION FORM

THE ATTACHED APPLICATION FORM SHOULD BE COMPLETED IN CAPITAL LETTERS. THE INFORMATION PROVIDED SHOULD BE AS ACCURATE AS POSSIBLE. ALL SECTIONS OF THE APPLICATION FORM SHOULD BE FULLY COMPLETED.

INCOMPLETE APPLICATIONS WILL BE RETURNED

Section 1 ***Applicant (Person Applying)***

(Box a) Insert the full name of the person applying for the certificate and the address to which the certificate is to be forwarded. A daytime telephone number should be included, where you can be contacted if necessary.

(Box b) State if you are applying for your own certificate, if not, please go to Box c.

(Box c) State your relationship to the person to whom the certificate relates.

(Box d) Give the reasons the certificate is required ie passport, driving licence etc.

Section 2 ***Details of Person whose Certificate is Required***
Failure to provide full information may prevent GRO from being able to issue information/certificate you have requested.

(Box a) Give details of the person whose certificate is required. This information is mandatory and should be filled in, if not, it could result in the return of the application form.

(Box b) Give details of the person's parents.

(Box c) State if the person is adopted. If you require a certificate, please fill in a birth certificate application form for an adopted child.

Section 3 ***Number and Type of Certificate(s) Required***

State the number of full, short or statutory birth certificates required.

Full Birth Certificate: This shows all details related to the birth including place of birth, mother's and father's names, mother's maiden name and the residence at the time of birth.

Short Birth Certificate: This shows only the surname, name, date of birth and (in most cases) the district of birth. Such a certificate is generally accepted for purposes for which evidence of age only is required.

Additional Copies: Where two or more certified copies of the same entry are applied for at the same time, the first copy will be charged at the full rate and any additional copies at a reduced fee.

Statutory Certificate: A letter issued by the Social Security Agency/Education and Library Board is required. **NB. These certificates may only be used for the purposes provided.**

Search Only: A search of the registers will be carried out within the **5 year period stated in this application - No Certificate will be produced.** However, you will receive a letter stating the outcome of the search.

Section 4 ***Signature***

Please sign and date the form whether or not you are paying by credit card.

Section 5 ***Payment***

(Box a) Indicate your method of payment - cash (if applying in person) cheque, postal order. Cheques or postal orders should be made payable to 'The Registrar General'. For postal applications please ensure the correct fee is enclosed as refunds cannot be made. **PLEASE DO NOT SEND CASH BY POST.**

(Box b) Complete this section if you are paying by credit card.

IF YOU HAVE FURTHER QUESTIONS OR REQUIRE HELP WITH THIS APPLICATION FORM. PLEASE CONTACT THE GENERAL REGISTER OFFICE ON THE TELEPHONE NUMBER LISTED OVERLEAF, OR EMAIL gro.nisra@dfpni.gov.uk

CP No.

Birth Certificate Application (Northern Ireland)

- **ALL SECTIONS OF THE FORM SHOULD BE FULLY COMPLETED. INCOMPLETE APPLICATIONS WILL BE RETURNED.**
- This form should only be completed for persons born in Northern Ireland.
- **For the certificate of an adopted child, please complete an Adopted Child Application form.**
- Please complete Sections 1, 2, 3 in CAPITAL letters and sign at Part 4.

Office Use
Date / /
Tie Up Nos.
Reference no.

Section 1 Applicant (Person Applying)

(a) Full name
Full postal address
Postcode
Daytime telephone no.
email address

For purposes of detection and prevention of crime, information relating to this application may be passed on to other Government or Law Enforcement Agencies.

(b) Are you applying for your own certificate? Yes ☐ No ☐
(c) If No, please state your relationship to the person whom the certificate relates
(d) Please give reasons for wanting a certificate: ie passport, driving license etc.

Section 2 Details of the person whose Certificate is required

	Surname at Birth	Forename(s)	Date of Birth	Place of Birth (Hospital Name or Address of Place of Birth)
(a) Details of person				

Apart from a married name, have you ever had a different surname, if so, please state

	Surname	Forename(s)	Maiden Surname	Mother's Address (at time of child's birth)
(b) Father				
Mother				

(c) Is the person named in section 2(a) Adopted? Yes ☐ No ☐

Section 3 Number and Type of Certificate(s) required

FULL ☐ (additional copies of the same entry will be charged at the reduced fee) SHORT ☐ STATUTORY ☐ (Proof from SSA/Education & Library Board required) Search Only letter (5 year period) ☐

Section 4 Signature (Must be completed)

Your signature Date

Section 5 Payment

(a) I enclose cash (if applying in person), cheque / postal order for ☐ made payable to REGISTRAR GENERAL. (For postal applications please enclose the correct fee as refunds cannot be made.)
(b) or debit my
Maestro ☐
Visa ☐ by £ card no. Issue Number (Maestro only)
Mastercard ☐
(Please tick appropriate box) Cardholders name (CAPITAL letters) expiry date

Please return to: **The Registrar General, Oxford House, 49/55 Chichester Street, Belfast BT1 4HL.**

Name:
Address:
Postcode:

PLEASE FILL IN YOUR NAME AND FULL POSTAL ADDRESS ON THE STICKER, TO ASSIST US IN SENDING OUT YOUR CERTIFICATE PROMPTLY.

CUSTOMER SERVICE EXCELLENCE CSE

PLEASE READ THE FOLLOWING NOTES TO HELP YOU COMPLETE THE APPLICATION FORM

THE ATTACHED APPLICATION FORM SHOULD BE COMPLETED IN CAPITAL LETTERS. THE INFORMATION PROVIDED SHOULD BE AS ACCURATE AS POSSIBLE. ALL SECTIONS OF THE APPLICATION FORM SHOULD BE FULLY COMPLETED.

INCOMPLETE APPLICATIONS WILL BE RETURNED

Section 1 — ***Applicant (Person Applying)***

(Box a) Insert the full name of the person applying for the certificate and the address to which the certificate is to be forwarded. A daytime telephone number should be included, where you can be contacted if necessary.

(Box b) State if you are applying for your own certificate, if not, please go to Box c.

(Box c) State your relationship to the person to whom the certificate relates.

(Box d) Give the reasons the certificate is required ie passport, driving licence etc.

Section 2 — ***Details of Adopted Person whose Certificate is Required***
Failure to provide full information may prevent GRO from being able to issue information/certificate you have requested.

(Box a) Give details of the adopted person whose certificate is required.

(Box b) Give details of the person's adopted parents.

(Box c) Give the name of the Court which made the order and the date it was made if known.

Section 3 — ***Number and Type of Certificate(s) Required***

State the number of full, short or statutory birth certificates required.

Full Birth Certificate: This shows adoptive name and surname, country of birth, adoptive parent's names, address and occupation, date of adoption order and description of court by which the order was made.

Short Birth Certificate: This shows only the adoptive surname, name, date of birth and the district/place of birth. Such a certificate is generally accepted for purposes for which evidence of age only is required.

Additional Copies: Where two or more certified copies of the same entry are applied for at the same time, the first copy will be charged at the full fee and any additional copies at a reduced fee.

Statutory Certificate: A letter issued by the Social Security Agency/Education and Library Board is required. **NB. These certificates may only be used for the purposes provided.**

Section 4 — ***Signature***

Please sign and date the form whether or not you are paying by credit card.

Section 5 — ***Payment***

(Box a) Indicate your method of payment - cash (if applying in person) cheque, postal order. Cheques or postal orders should be made payable to 'The Registrar General'. For postal applications please ensure the correct fee is enclosed as refunds cannot be made. **PLEASE DO NOT SEND CASH BY POST.**

(Box b) Complete this section if you are paying by credit card.

IF YOU HAVE ANY FURTHER QUESTIONS OR REQUIRE HELP WITH THIS APPLICATION FORM. PLEASE CONTACT THE GENERAL REGISTER OFFICE ON THE TELEPHONE NUMBER LISTED OVERLEAF, OR EMAIL gro.nisra@dfpni.gov.uk

GRO 40A

CP No.

Birth Certificate Application of Adopted Children (N.I.)

- **ALL SECTIONS OF THE FORM SHOULD BE FULLY COMPLETED. INCOMPLETE APPLICATIONS WILL BE RETURNED.**
- Please complete Sections 1, 2, 3 in CAPITAL letters and sign at Part 4.
- This form should only be completed for persons whose adoption was registered in N.I.

Office Use
Date / /
Tie Up Nos.
Reference no.

Section 1 Applicant (Person Applying)

(a) Full name
Full postal address
Postcode
Daytime telephone no.
email address

(b) Are you applying for your own certificate? Yes ☐ No ☐
(c) If No, please state your relationship to the person whom the certificate relates
(d) Please give reasons for wanting a certificate: ie. passport, driving license etc.

For purposes of detection and prevention of crime, information relating to this application may be passed on to other Government or Law Enforcement Agencies.

Section 2 Certificates / Search from Adopted Children Register (from 1 January 1931 only)

(a) Adopted person — Surname — Forename(s) — Date of Birth

(b) Name of Adopters — Surname — Forename(s)
Father
Mother

(c) Adoption Order — Name of Court which made the order — Date of order

Section 3 Number and Type of Certificate(s) required

FULL (additional copies of the same entry will be charged at the reduced fee.) — SHORT — STATUTORY (Proof from SSA/Education & Library Board required)

Section 4 Signature (Must be completed)

Your signature — Date

Section 5 Payment

(a) I enclose cash (if applying in person), cheque / postal order for — made payable to REGISTRAR GENERAL. (For postal applications please enclose the correct fee as refunds cannot be made.)

(b) or debit my
Maestro
Visa
Mastercard
(Please tick appropriate box)
by £ — card no. — Issue Number (Maestro only)
Cardholders name (CAPITAL letters) — expiry date

Please return to: The Registrar General, Oxford House, 49/55 Chichester Street, Belfast BT1 4HL.

CUSTOMER SERVICE EXCELLENCE — CSE

Name:
Address:
Postcode:

PLEASE FILL IN YOUR NAME AND FULL POSTAL ADDRESS ON THE STICKER, TO ASSIST US IN SENDING OUT YOUR CERTIFICATE PROMPTLY.

GRO 40A

PLEASE READ THE FOLLOWING NOTES TO HELP YOU COMPLETE THE APPLICATION FORM

THE ATTACHED APPLICATION FORM SHOULD BE COMPLETED IN CAPITAL LETTERS. THE INFORMATION PROVIDED SHOULD BE AS ACCURATE AS POSSIBLE. ALL SECTIONS OF THE APPLICATION FORM SHOULD BE FULLY COMPLETED.

INCOMPLETE APPLICATIONS WILL BE RETURNED

Section 1 ***Applicant (Person Applying)***

(Box a) Insert the full name of the person applying for the certificate and the address to which the certificate is to be forwarded. A daytime telephone number should be included, where you can be contacted if necessary.

(Box b) Give the reasons the certificate is required ie passport, driving licence etc.

Section 2 ***Details of Parties whose Certificate is Required***
Failure to provide full information may prevent GRO from being able to issue information/certificate you have requested.

(Box a) State the forename(s) and surname of the man.

(Box b) State the forename(s) and maiden surname of the woman.

(Box c) State any other surname the woman may have had before the marriage.

(Box d) State the place of marriage ie name of church, Registrar's Office etc. along with the full postal address of the place of marriage.

(Box e) Insert the date of marriage.

Section 3 ***Number and Type of Certificate(s) Required***

State the number of certificates required. Additional copies of the same entry will be charged at the reduced fee. Please see fee leaflet GRO 384 for details.

Statutory Certificate: A letter issued SSA/Education and Library Board or polling card is required. **NB. These Certificates may only be used for the purposes provided.**

Search Only: A search of the registers will be carried out within the **5 year period stated in this application - No certificate will be produced**: However, you will receive a letter stating the outcome of the search.

Section 4 ***Signature***

Please sign and date the form whether or not you are paying by credit card.

Section 5 ***Payment***

(Box a) Indicate your method of payment - cash (if applying in person) cheque, postal order. Cheques or postal orders should be made payable to the Registrar General. For postal applications please ensure the correct fee is enclosed as refunds cannot be made. **PLEASE DO NOT SEND CASH BY POST.**

(Box b) Complete this section if you are paying by credit card.

IF YOU HAVE ANY FURTHER QUESTIONS OR REQUIRE HELP WITH THIS APPLICATION FORM. PLEASE CONTACT THE GENERAL REGISTER OFFICE ON THE TELEPHONE NUMBER LISTED OVERLEAF, OR EMAIL gro.nisra@dfpni.gov.uk

CP No. ______

Marriage Certificate Application (Northern Ireland)

Office Use
Date / /
Tie Up Nos.
Reference No.

* **ALL SECTIONS OF THE FORM SHOULD BE FULLY COMPLETED. INCOMPLETE APPLICATIONS WILL BE RETURNED.**
* Please complete Sections 1, 2, 3 in CAPITAL letters and sign at Part 4.
* This form should only be completed for persons married in Northern Ireland.

Section 1 Applicant (Person Applying)

(a) **Full name** ______
Full postal address ______
Postcode ______
Daytime telephone no. ______
email address ______

(b) **Please give reasons for wanting a certificate: ie passport, driving licence etc.** ______

For purposes of detection and prevention of crime, information relating to this application may be passed on to other Government or Law Enforcement Agencies

Section 2 Details of the Parties Involved

MAN
(a) **Forename(s)** ______
Surname ______

WOMAN
(b) **Forename(s)** ______
Maiden Surname ______

(c) **Any other surname before this marriage** ______

(d) **Place of marriage** ______
Full postal address ______

(e) **Date of marriage** ______

Please note that marriages before 1922 cannot be traced unless the CHURCH and DISTRICT are known.

Section 3 Number Type of Certificate(s) required

***STANDARD** ☐ **STATUTORY** (Proof from SSA/Education & Library Board required) ☐ **SEARCH ONLY** ☐

*additional copies of the same entry will be charged at the reduced fee

Section 4 Signature (Must be completed)

Your signature ______ **Date** ______

Section 5 Payment

(a) **I enclose cash (if applying in person), cheque / postal order for** ______ **made payable to REGISTRAR GENERAL.** (For postal applications please enclose the correct fee as refunds cannot be made.)

(b) **or debit my**
Maestro ☐
Visa ☐
Mastercard ☐
(Please tick appropriate box)

by £ ______ **card no.** ______ **Issue Number (Maestro only)** ______
Cardholders name (CAPITAL letters) ______ **expiry date** ______

Please return to: **The Registrar General, Oxford House, 49/55 Chichester Street, Belfast BT1 4HL.**

Name:
Address:
Postcode:

PLEASE FILL IN YOUR NAME AND FULL POSTAL ADDRESS ON THE STICKER, TO ASSIST US IN SENDING OUT YOUR CERTIFICATE PROMPTLY.

CUSTOMER SERVICE EXCELLENCE CSE

PLEASE READ THE FOLLOWING NOTES TO HELP YOU COMPLETE THE APPLICATION FORM

THE ATTACHED APPLICATION FORM SHOULD BE COMPLETED IN CAPITAL LETTERS. THE INFORMATION PROVIDED SHOULD BE AS ACCURATE AS POSSIBLE. ALL SECTIONS OF THE APPLICATION FORM SHOULD BE FULLY COMPLETED.

INCOMPLETE APPLICATIONS WILL BE RETURNED

Section 1 ***Applicant (Person Applying)***

(Box a) Insert the full name of the person applying for the certificate and the address to which the certificate is to be forwarded. A daytime telephone number should be included, where you can be contacted if necessary.

(Box b) Give the reasons for requiring the certificate ie insurance purposes, family tree etc.

(Box c) Please state your relationship to the deceased.

Section 2 ***Details of Certificate Required***
Failure to provide full information may prevent GRO from being able to issue information/certificate you have requested.

(Box a) State the surname and forename(s) of the deceased.

(Box b) State the deceased's usual address.

(Box c) State the date of death.

(Box d) State the place of death. Please note deaths before 1922 are difficult to trace if the place of death is not known.

(Box e) State the deceased's date of birth or age at the time of death.

(Box f) Enter the name of the deceased's spouse if he/she was married or widowed at the time of death.

(Box g) Please state deceased's occupation if known.

(Box h) If the death occured within the last three years was the coroner notified? (please tick Yes or No.)
Please note: If the death has not been registered we will be unable to provide a certificate.

(Box i) If deceased is aged 16 or under please enter parent's names.

Section 3 ***Number and Type of Certificate(s) Required***

State the number of certificates required.

Death Certificate Where two or more certified copies of the same entry are applied for at the same time, the first copy will be charged at the full fee and any additional copies at a reduced fee.

Statutory Certificate: A letter issued by the Social Security Agency/Education and Library Board is required **NB. These certificates may only be used for the purposes provided.**

Search Only Letter: A search of the registers will be carried out within the **5 year period stated in this application - No certificate will be produced.** However, you will receive a letter stating the outcome of the search.

Section 4 ***Signature***

Please sign and date the form whether or not you are paying by credit card.

Section 5 ***Payment***

(Box a) Indicate your method of payment - cash (if applying in person) cheque, postal order. Cheques or postal orders should be made payable to the Registrar General. For postal applications please ensure the correct fee is enclosed as refunds cannot be made. **PLEASE DO NOT SEND CASH BY POST.**

(Box b) Complete this section if you are paying by credit card.

IF YOU HAVE ANY FURTHER QUESTIONS OR REQUIRE HELP WITH THIS APPLICATION FORM. PLEASE CONTACT THE GENERAL REGISTER OFFICE ON THE TELEPHONE NUMBER LISTED OVERLEAF, OR EMAIL gro.nisra@dfpni.gov.uk

CP No. ____

Death Certificate Application (Northern Ireland)

*** ALL SECTIONS OF THE FORM SHOULD BE FULLY COMPLETED. INCOMPLETE APPLICATIONS WILL BE RETURNED.**

* Please complete Sections 1, 2, 3 in CAPITAL letters and sign at Part 4.

* This form should only be completed for persons who died in Northern Ireland.

Office Use
Date / /
Tie Up Nos.
Reference no.

Section 1 Applicant (Person Applying)

(a) Applicant's Full name
Full postal address
Postcode
Daytime telephone no.
email address

(b) Please give reasons for wanting a certificate: ie insurance and benefit purposes etc.

(c) Please state your relationship to the deceased.

For purposes of detection and prevention of crime, information relating to this application may be passed on to other Government or Law Enforcement Agencies.

Section 2 Details of Certificate required

(a) Surname
Forename(s)

Please note that deaths before 1922 are difficult to trace if the place of death is not known.

(b) Usual Address
Postcode

(c) DATE OF DEATH **(d) Place of death**

(e) Date of birth or age at death **years**

(f) If the person was married or widowed at death, please give the name of spouse.

(g) Occupation (if known)

(h) If death occurred within the last 3 years was the Coroner notified? Yes ❑ No ❑ **If so, has the death been registered?**

(i) If the deceased is aged 16 or under please supply the following information Father's Name / Mother's Name

Section 3 Number and Type of Certificate(s) required

Death Certificate (additional copies of the same entry will be charged at the reduced fee) **STATUTORY CERTIFICATE** (Proof from SSA/Education & Library Board required) **Search Only Letter (5 year period)**

Section 4 Signature (Must be completed)

Your signature **Date**

Section 5 Payment

(a) I enclose cash (if applying in person), cheque / postal order for ____ **made payable to REGISTRAR GENERAL.** (For postal applications please enclose the correct fee as refunds cannot be made.)

(b) or debit my
Maestro
Visa **by** £ **card no.** **Issue Number (Maestro only)**
Mastercard **Cardholders name (CAPITAL letters)** **expiry date**
(Please tick appropriate box)

Please return to: **The Registrar General, Oxford House, 49/55 Chichester Street, Belfast BT1 4HL.**

Name:
Address:
Postcode:

PLEASE FILL IN YOUR NAME AND FULL POSTAL ADDRESS ON THE STICKER, TO ASSIST US IN SENDING OUT YOUR CERTIFICATE PROMPTLY.

CUSTOMER SERVICE EXCELLENCE CSE

UNITED KINGDOM—SCOTLAND

Send your requests to:

National Records of Scotland
New Register House
3 West Register Street
Edinburgh
EH1 3YT Scotland

Tel. (011) (44) 131 535 1314 (General Register House)
(011) (44) 131 334 0380 (New Register House, Ladywell House & Cairnsmore House)
(011) (44) 131 314 4411 (to order post-1855 certificates)
www.nrscotland.gov.uk/

On April 1, 2011, the General Register Office for Scotland merged with the National Archives of Scotland to become the National Records of Scotland (NRS). NRS is responsible for the registration of births, marriages, civil partnerships, deaths, divorces, and adoptions.

Certificates can be ordered in person at New Register House (3 West Register Street, Edinburgh) or the ScotlandsPeople Centre (see contact information below), or by telephone using NRS's Extract Ordering Service for post-1855 births, deaths, and marriages. You can also search and order certificates on the ScotlandsPeople website (www.scotlandspeople.gov.uk/), a fully searchable pay-per-view website that gives access to birth, marriage, and death records; old parish records; wills and testaments; and more.

Official extracts from the Scottish records may also be obtained from local registrars of births, marriages, and deaths.

Cost for certified certificates when ordered by mail, fax, or phone	£15.00
Cost for certified certificates when ordered in person at New Register House	£15.00
Cost for certified certificates when ordered in person at ScotlandsPeople Centre	£10.00
Cost for Priority Service	£30.00
Cost for Open Census Record when ordered in person at ScotlandsPeople Centre	£10.00
Cost for Open Census Record when ordered by mail, fax, or phone	£15.00

For more assistance, contact:

ScotlandsPeople Centre
HM General Register House
2 Princes Street
Edinburgh
EH1 3YY Scotland

Tel: (011) (44) 131 314 4300
www.scotlandspeoplehub.gov.uk

The ScotlandsPeople Centre is a family history center where visitors can access key Scottish resources such as birth, marriage, and death records, wills, census records, and coats of arms, going back almost 500 years. Everything has been digitized so all the records are available on computer screens in the search rooms.

Embassy of the United Kingdom and Northern Ireland
3100 Massachusetts Avenue, NW
Washington, DC 20008

Tel. (202) 588-6500

New Register House Edinburgh EH1 3YT

Switchboard	0131 334 0380 (+44 131 334 0380)
Extract Ordering Service	0131 314 4411 (+44 131 314 4411)
Fax	0131 314 4400 (+44 131 314 4400)
E-mail	records@gro-scotland.gsi.gov.uk
Web	http://www.nrscotland.gov.uk

Application for Certificate(s)

Searching undertaken by NRS staff for a particular event ('Particular Search'). For details see Leaflet S2.

Please complete this application overleaf and return it to the address above along with the appropriate fee. Details of charges are given in Leaflet S2 including the PRIORITY SERVICE for urgent orders. Please indicate in the appropriate box(es) below how many of each certificate you want

1. ☐ Extract of entry from a register of births. ('Full Certificate')
2. ☐ Abbreviated certificate of birth or death. This shows only the person's name, surname, sex, date and place of birth or death. Not applicable to records before 1855
3. ☐ Extract of entry from a register of adopted children. This shows the person's adopted name, not the name in the register of births which may be different. It is however a legal "birth certificate" which may be used for all purposes
4. ☐ Extract of entry from a register of marriages or civil partnerships (see note)
5. ☐ Extract of entry from a register of divorces (see note)/dissolutions
6. ☐ Extract of entry from a register of deaths
7. ☐ Additional priority fee (applicable to birth, death, marriage extracts from 1855 to date; divorce extracts from 1 May 1984 to date; adoption extracts from 1930 to date and civil partnership extracts). For further details, see leaflet S2

Note: recording of marriages ending in divorce
When a **decree of divorce** was granted by the Court of Session, it was formerly the practice to annotate the marriage entry to reflect that a divorce had taken place. This was discontinued on 1 May 1984. Where a divorce was notified to the Registrar General on or after that date, there will be no corresponding annotation on the marriage entry or on any extract of the entry. A separate Register of Divorces was set up from 1 May 1984, from where extracts are available. An extract of divorce granted in Scotland *prior* to 1 May 1984 is obtainable from the Court of Session, Parliament House, 1 Parliament Square, Edinburgh EH1 1RF. Tel: 0131 225 2595

Applicant Information			
Mr/Mrs/Miss/Ms		Existing Customer YES/NO	
Full postal address		Telephone number	
		Email:	
		Date:	

If you order an extract(s) by post, you may pay by cheque in British pounds Sterling, crossed and made payable to 'The Registrar General'. **PLEASE DO NOT SEND CASH.** You can also pay by **Maestro**, **Visa** or **Mastercard** by completing the appropriate sections below.

Cardholder's Name: .... Signature: ....
(as it appears on card)

Cardholder's Address ....
(if different from applicant)

Card Number: ☐☐☐☐ ☐☐☐☐ ☐☐☐☐ ☐☐☐☐

Security Code: ☐☐☐ Start Date: ..../....... Expiry Date: ..../.......

MAESTRO TRANSACTIONS ONLY

Issue number on card: ☐ Last 3 numbers if Maestro 19-digit card: ☐☐☐

Application for a birth, adoption, Marriage, Civil Partnership, Divorce, Death or Old Parish Register Certificate

Searching undertaken by GRO(S) staff for a particular event ('Particular Search'). For details see Leaflet S2. Tick as appropriate (see notes overleaf on birth or divorce certificates)

Birth ☐ / Adoption ☐	Marriage ☐ / Divorce ☐ — Civil Partnership ☐ / Dissolution ☐	Death ☐
Surname at Birth/Adoption*	Surname	Surname
Forename(s)	Forename(s)	Forename(s)
Male/Female*	Surname	Age at Death
Place (town or parish) in which Birth occurred	Forename(s)	Place (town or parish) in which Death occurred
Date of adoption *(if known)*	Place (town or parish) in which Marriage/Civil Partnership occurred	
Parents/Adoptive Parents*		**Parents**
Father's surname	Widow or Divorcee – Please state former married name	Father's surname
Father's forename(s)		Father's forename(s)
Mother's maiden surname		Mother's maiden surname
Mother's forename(s)	**Date of Marriage/Civil Partnership**	Mother's forename(s)
	Day / Month / Year	
Date of Birth	**Date of Divorce/Dissolution** *(if applicable)*	**Date of Death**
Day / Month / Year	Day / Month / Year	Day / Month / Year

For Office Use Only

RD No	Year	Entry No	RD No	Year	Entry No	RD No	Year	Entry No
RCE			RCE			RCE		

* Delete as applicable

Form SU3 (April 2012)

New Register House Edinburgh EH1 3YT

Switchboard 0131 334 0380 (+44 131 334 0380)
Extract Ordering Service 0131 314 4411 (+44 131 314 4411)
Fax 0131 314 4400 (+44 131 314 4400)
E-mail records@gro-scotland.gsi.gov.uk
Web http://www.nrscotland.gov.uk

Application for Certificate(S) /No Trace Divorce Letters

Searching undertaken by NRS staff for a particular event ('Particular Search'). For details see Leaflet S2.

Please complete this application overleaf and return it to the address above along with the appropriate fee.

1. ☐ Extract of marriage entry

2. ☐ Letter stating no trace of divorce in the Register of Divorces

Note: recording of marriages ending in divorce

When a **decree of divorce** was granted by the Court of Session, it was formerly the practice to annotate the marriage entry to reflect that a divorce had taken place. This was discontinued on 1 May 1984. Where a divorce was notified to the Registrar General on or after that date there will be no corresponding annotation on the marriage entry or on any extract of the entry. A separate Register of Divorces was set up from 1 May 1984 from where extracts are available. An extract of divorce granted in Scotland *prior* to 1 May 1984 is obtainable from the Court of Session, Parliament House, 1 Parliament Square, Edinburgh EH1 1RF. Tel: 0131 225 2595

Applicant Information			
Mr/Mrs/Miss/Ms		Existing Customer YES/NO	
Full postal address		Telephone number	
		Email	
		Date	

If you order an extract(s) by post, you may pay by cheque in British pounds Sterling, crossed and made payable to 'The Registrar General'. **PLEASE DO NOT SEND CASH.** You can also pay by **Maestro, Visa** or **Mastercard** by completing the appropriate sections below.

Cardholder's Name: .... Cardholder's Signature: ....
(as it appears on card)

Cardholder's Address: ....
(if different from applicant)

Card Number: ☐☐☐☐ ☐☐☐☐ ☐☐☐☐ ☐☐☐☐

Security Code: ☐☐☐ Start Date ....../...... Expiry Date ....../......

MAESTRO TRANSACTIONS ONLY

Issue number on card: ☐ Last 3 numbers if Maestro 19-digit card: ☐☐☐

Marriage Details

Groom's surname
Forenames
Bride's surname
Forenames
Place (town or parish) in which Marriage occurred
Widow or Divorcee please state former married name

Date of Marriage		
Day	Month	Year

Date of application: ....

Signature: ....

For Office Use		
RD No	Year	Entry No

New Register House Edinburgh EH1 3YT

Switchboard 0131 334 0380 (+44 131 334 0380)
Extract Ordering Service 0131 314 4411 (+44 131 314 4411)
Fax 0131 314 4400 (+44 131 314 4400)
E-mail records@gro-scotland.gsi.gov.uk
Web http://www.nrscotland.gov.uk

Application for census certificate(s)

Searching undertaken by NRS staff for a particular event ('Particular Search'). For details see Leaflet S2.

1. Census Year 1841 ☐ 1851 ☐ 1861 ☐ 1871 ☐ 1881 ☐ 1891 ☐ 1901 ☐ 1911 ☐
2. Full name of person sought ....
3. Approximate age in Census ....
4. His/Her occupation at that time ....
5. His/Her full address at that time ....
   House number and name of street ....
   Name of house .... Town/Parish ....
6. Householder's name .... Wife's name ....
   His/Her occupation ....
7. Relationship of person named at 2 to the householder State whether boarder. ....

Applicant Information			
Mr/Mrs/Miss/Ms		Existing Customer YES/NO	
Full postal address		Telephone number:	
		Email :	
		Date:	

If you order an extract(s) by post, you may pay by cheque in British pounds Sterling, crossed and made payable to 'The Registrar General'. **PLEASE DO NOT SEND CASH.** You can also pay by **Maestro, Visa** or **Mastercard** by completing the appropriate sections below.

Cardholder's Name .... Cardholder's Signature ....
(as it appears on card)

Cardholder's Address ....
(if different from applicant)

Card Number: ☐☐☐☐ ☐☐☐☐ ☐☐☐☐ ☐☐☐☐

Security Code ☐☐☐ Start Date ....../...... Expiry Date ....../......

MAESTRO TRANSACTIONS ONLY

Issue number on card: ☐ Last 3 numbers if Maestro 19-digit card ☐☐☐

URUGUAY

Send your requests to:

Dirección General del Registro de Estado Civil
Uruguay 933
Montevideo, Uruguay

Tel. (011) (598) 2900 50 85

Certificates can be ordered online at www.uruguay.gub.uy/dgrec/usuario/FormasDePago.asp. Certificates are also available from city halls (Intendencias Municipales) in the town where the registration of the event took place. Divorce decrees (Sentencia de Divorcio) may appear as a footnote to the marriage certificates issued by the Dirección General del Registro de Estado Civil or as a document issued by the Justice of the Peace Office (Juzgado de Paz) of the district where the divorce took place.

For additional assistance, contact:

Embassy of Uruguay
1913 I Street, NW
Washington, DC 20006

Tel. (202) 331-1313

UZBEKISTAN

Send your requests to:

Office for Registry of Civil Status (ZAGS)
(Town), Uzbekistan

Civil documents from Uzbekistan are generally made available to the person to whom the record pertains. He or she must submit a request through the appropriate Office for Registry of Civil Status (ZAGS) at the district, city, or regional level, depending on where the civil act was registered, or through an embassy or consulate of Uzbekistan. Documents can be requested through the Embassy of Uzbekistan in Washington or the Consulate General of Uzbekistan in New York City by submitting an application requesting the document.

For additional assistance, contact:

Embassy of the Republic of Uzbekistan
1746 Massachusetts Avenue, NW
Washington, DC 20036

Tel. (202) 530-7291

VANUATU

Send your requests to:

Civil Status Department
Port Vila Municipality
P.O. Box 99
Port Vila, Vanuatu

Tel. (011) (678) 22113

Extracts of birth, marriage, and death records are generally available except for residents of the outer islands.

For additional assistance, contact:

Vanuatu Mission to the U.N.
800 Second Avenue, Suite 400B
New York, NY 10017

Tel. (212) 661-4303

VENEZUELA

Send your requests to:

Jefe Civil (Chief Civil Authority)
(District and Town), Venezuela

You can order birth, death, and marriage certificates online from the Embassy of Venezuela (http://venezuela-us.org/registro-civil/). In addition, some Catholic Church records and birth, marriage, and death records created by civil registration offices in Venezuela are searchable online at www.familysearch.org. A copy of the decree of divorce may be obtained from the civil tribunal of the Court of First Instance (Juzgado de la Primera Instancia en lo Civil) where the divorce was obtained.

For additional assistance, contact:

Embassy of the Bolivarian Republic of Venezuela
Consular Section
1099 30th Street, NW
Washington, DC 20007

Tel. (202) 627-1444

VIETNAM

Send your requests to:

Registrar
(Town), Vietnam

Vietnam has no centralized national system for vital records. Many records have been lost through war and inconsistent record keeping, but larger cities may have old documents on file, and records from the north are generally available. Registrars will sometimes certify that certain documents were lost or destroyed. Records for Ho Chi Minh City (Saigon)-Cholon since 1953 are kept at the Central Registrar's Office of the Ministry of the Interior (Phong Ho Tich So Tu Phap) in Ho Chi Minh City (HCMC). Some pre-1954 records from Haiphong, former North Vietnam, are now at the Central Court of Records in HCMC and are available for extracting. Fraudulent civil documents are common in Vietnam, and it has been relatively easy to establish false identities both before and after 1975.

Requests for extracts of previously issued certificates are made at the Registrar's Office where they were issued and should include the document registration number, date, and place of registration. Without this information, fees may be higher and it is less likely the document will be found. Only relatives resident in Vietnam may request extracts of documents for their overseas relatives. Documents cannot be requested through a Vietnamese diplomatic mission, nor can a request be sent to a local office from overseas.

For additional assistance, contact:

Embassy of the Socialist Republic of Vietnam — Tel. (202) 861-0737
1233 20th Street, NW, Suite 400
Washington, DC 20036

YEMEN

Send your requests to:

Civil Registry Office
(Town), Yemen

Yemen does not yet have an established system of recording vital statistics. Furthermore, most Yemenis do not register births, marriages, divorces, and deaths when they occur. To satisfy the need for civil documents for immigration and other purposes, Yemenis generally prepare "court judgments." These can be issued at any time by any District Court within the country. Information in these documents is normally based on the testimony of an informant or his proxy and witnesses who may or may not have direct knowledge of the events about which they are testifying. Dates in these documents are always suspect.

Recently, Civil Registry Offices around the country have begun to issue birth and death certificates in standardized formats, normally on orange or green cards approximately 5 x 8 inches in size. These certificates are issued at any time after the event on the basis of information provided to the Civil Registry Office by the person requesting the document and, therefore, cannot be considered reliable.

Parts of the former People's Democratic Republic of Yemen (South Yemen) had an established Civil Registry System based on the British system, and documents were issued in a format similar to that used in the U.K. and some of its former colonies.

For additional assistance, contact:

Embassy of Yemen — Tel. (202) 965-4760
2319 Wyoming Avenue, NW
Washington, DC 20008

ZAMBIA

Send your requests to:

Registrar General of Births, Deaths and Marriages
P.O. Box 32311
10101 Lusaka, Zambia

Tel. (011) (260) 211 236427

Birth certificates are available to any applicant born on or after January 1, 1973, and can be obtained by applying to the Registrar General of Births, Deaths and Marriages. Marriages can either be contracted under civil law or under customary law. For marriages contracted under civil law, certificates are issued by the Registrar General of Births, Deaths and Marriages. Divorce records are obtainable from one of the following addresses, depending on the section of Zambia in which the divorce took place: Registrar of High Court, P.O. Box 50067, Lusaka, Zambia; Registrar of High Court, P.O. Box 70004, Ndola, Zambia; Registrar of High Court, P.O. Box 60110, Livingstone, Zambia.

For additional assistance, contact:

Embassy of Zambia
2419 Massachusetts Avenue, NW
Washington, DC 20008

Tel. (202) 265-9717

ZIMBABWE

Send your requests to:

Registrar General of Zimbabwe
Central Registry for Passports, Citizenship, Births, Deaths and Marriages
P. Bag 7734
Causeway, Harare, Zimbabwe

Birth, death, and marriage certificates are available from the Central Registry for Passports, Citizenship, Births, Deaths and Marriages. Certified copies of divorce decrees are obtainable from the Register of the High Court (P.O. Box 8050, Causeway, Harare) for Harare divorces, and from the Assistant Registrar of the High Court (P.O. Box 579, Bulawayo) for Bulawayuo divorces.

For additional assistance, contact:

Embassy of Zimbabwe
1608 New Hampshire Avenue, NW
Washington, DC 20009

Tel. (202) 332-7100

CPSIA information can be obtained at www.ICGtesting.com
Printed in the USA
LVOW09s0855271113

362983LV00014B/156/P